A Citizen's Chronological History of World War II

Written daily from December 7, 1941 until August 14, 1945

by Shelton Kenneth Peterson

Poetic Matrix Press/PM Library
www.poeticmatrix.com

A Citizen's Chronological History of World War II

Preface
and Memories by Owen Kent Peterson

The original manuscript of Dad's journal history of World War II lay undiscovered in a bank safety lock-box for many years. We all worried that it may have been lost during Mom's move from San Mateo to Bella Vista, California in 1995. It wasn't until after Mom's passing that the lock-box was discovered and opened, revealing the old type-written manuscript. Ruth arranged to have it scanned onto a computer and copies were made on CD as a precaution. Eventually the original manuscript, along with a CD copy, was given to me with the expectation that I would find a way to prepare it to be printed in book form. John and I decided to make this a team effort, with me preparing a cleaned-up Word document to be prepared and printed in hard-back book format by John's press (Poetic Matrix Press). My initial idea was to use OCR (Optical Character Recognition) software to convert the computer scanned pages to computer text. This proved to be less than optimal to the point that I decided it would be quicker to retype from scratch the entire manuscript. I began the project in 2011 and completed it in 2013. It was a slow but ultimately enjoyable exercise as I had the opportunity to not only carefully read the manuscript but in the process to truly hear my father's voice.

During the process of typing what now represents over 900 pages of journal history, I was taken back to those long-ago days when I, as a very young boy, lay in bed observing my seldom seen father across the hallway typing away on the old vintage typewriter late at night, night after night. This book is a testament to the fact that he never missed a day, for 1345 days, sitting at that typewriter, no matter the hour, and regardless of how tired or sick he might have felt.

An examination of this history reveals many things about the author and the times he lived through. It was a time when

America was re-emerging from the great depression. And yet there is no sense that Dad was still feeling the effects of those difficult times. He projects a very positive, up-beat attitude about the country, its strength, its goodness, and its ability to weather the initial blows from the enemy and to ultimately triumph. His patriotism is unquestioned, but he is also riding the popular emotion of a nation fired with righteous indignation over the treachery of this little understood, far-eastern Asian nation. There were already stereotypes about who and what the Japanese people represented, stereotypes that were magnified by a propaganda campaign that sought to stir up strong resentment and a do-or-die mentality that would endure whatever sacrifices might be necessary to right this great wrong.

It is, of course, true that the Germans were also the enemy, but in this case most of the public outrage was directed at Hitler and his henchmen, and not so much towards the German people. Hence, the derogatory reference to the Germans as "Huns", which was common during WWI, only occurs three times in this entire history. On the other hand, the Japanese are referred to as "Japs" hundreds of times. Although we considered altering such references to be more politically correct and also to remove any accusation that Dad was racist, we decided to let that and any other derogatory references to the Japanese people stay as written with the understanding that trying to soften the sentiments of a nation at war would be disingenuous—and those were the sentiments of the nation of which Dad was very much a part.

Even though we have long ago stopped seeing people of different races in such pejorative ways, the fact is that at that time the Japanese had become, along with Hitler and his ilk, the very symbol of evil. While it is now a national disgrace that some 93,000 Japanese-Americans were removed from their homes and placed in internment camps for the duration of the war, nevertheless, the actual enemy we were fighting in the Pacific was inspired by a very different set of moral imperatives. Based on the code of Bushido, the Japanese warrior was taught to view war as purifying and death a duty. As a result few Japanese prisoners were ever taken while on the other hand, surrender by Allied troops was viewed by the Japanese as dishonorable, leading to gross mistreatment of Allied prisoners, including many cases of executions. In addition, stories of atrocities by Japanese forces in China, such as the Nanking Massacre of 1937, also known as the Rape of Nanking, added to the view that the Japanese were barbarians. Dad was no more a racist than 90% of Americans, and yet during such a time, the Japanese were the bad guys and this war became a no-holds-barred, all-out fight to the finish. We today cannot judge those who lived through the greatest war ever waged in a world gone crazy and which would ultimately witness the deaths of from 50 million to more than 80 million men, women and children. Dad was fortunate that he did not have to actually face the enemy on the field of battle. But through his keen eyes, and homey writing style, we are able to glimpse the world in which he lived and in which some of us were raised. He was a great man and an astute observer and recorder of what some have referred to as "the greatest generation."

Biography of Shelton Kenneth (Ken) Peterson and Memories by Joyce Eileen Peterson Clark

Dad was born on 1 February 1911 to Minnie Lee Harkin and Charles Mauritz Peterson in Salt Lake City Utah. He had two brothers, M. Wayne, Charles Wendall and two sisters, Ruth Maurine, who died when she was 7 years old and Beverly Baine.

Dad's family lived in Provo, Utah where he attended the Brigham Young Academy for elementary learning. Later they lived in Salt Lake City at 2007 Douglas Street. Both of his parents were school teachers and that is how they met. After they were married in 1907 his mother no longer taught school but his father continued and eventually became a Principal. His mother passed away on September 10, 1932 of complications from rheumatic fever. His father passed away on April 18, 1950.

Because Dad's father was a teacher he had the summers off and so his father would work as a ticket taker at Great Saltair, a resort near the Great Salt Lake. Dad often talked about the wonderful summers spent out there.

Dad said his school years were enjoyable and in high school he excelled in his studies as well as in the ROTC program. In ROTC he became a captain and received a medal for marksmanship. He graduated from high school at 17 years old and took a job with the Federal Reserve Bank in Salt Lake City. He began as a messenger boy and when he passed away in 1970 was a Department Head of Bonds and Redemption. He worked at the bank for 42 years.

He was always an active member of the Church of Jesus Christ of Latter-day Saints.

His brothers enjoyed camping and hunting. One time they took a trip in an old Ford coupe. In the process of their travels they lost the gas tank and had to tie it back on with rope in order to get back home.

Dad enjoyed playing golf and that is where he first saw the girl he would marry. He finally had the nerve to call on her for a date and after a few months of dating Mary Geneva (Eva) Stahr, they were married in the LDS Temple in Salt Lake City on May 31, 1935. Early in 1941 he received a promotion at the bank that required a move to San Francisco, California. On December 7, 1941 the Japanese attacked Pearl Harbor in Hawaii and that is when he decided to chronicle the war.

Ken and Eva are the parents of 6 children, 3 boys and 3 girls. Joyce Eileen, Ruth Irene, Sylvia Kathleen and Owen Kent, John Charles and Craig Stahr. There are 26 grand children and many many great grandchildren and great great grandchildren.

There were many hardships, one of which was the illness of Eva for two years, however after that, life settled down and the children grew and thrived.

In March of 1965 Dad entered the hospital for tests on his heart. It resulted in cardiac arrest and in trying to revive him he suffered a cracked collar bone, injured larynx and esophagus and damaged spleen. Also during the test he received a pin point puncture of an artery and later discovered blood was draining into his chest cavity. This resulted in his health fading and no one realized the problem until a physician explained what was going on. The missionaries of the Church arrived to visit and realized he was seriously ill. On Friday Elder Robert Collins and his companion said they would fast for him until Monday and then return. Meanwhile all of the family was also asked to fast for their Dad and grandfather. The Lord heard the prayers and blessings of the missionaries and his family for he felt health return. Eva said she could see a light and recognition return to his eyes.

He spent the next five years resuming his job at the bank and activities in his life, until July 18, 1970 when he peacefully passed away at home.

Journal of Mary Geneva Stahr Peterson
Beginning December 7, 1941

It was fall and then December rolled around. It was Sunday morning December 7, 1941. Kent took Owen for a walk to downtown San Bruno. While he was gone I dressed the two girls, Joyce and Ruth, then turned on the radio. Suddenly there was an interruption in the music program and the announcer said; "This morning Pearl Harbor was attacked and bombed by Japan's air fighters. Great devastation and loss of life."

In the meantime, while at the store Kent heard the announcement. He picked up Owen and ran all the way home. As he burst in the front door he said, "Pearl Harbor was attacked and bombed by Japanese planes this morning." I said, "Yes, I heard it on the radio." Kent then said, " Boy is this going to make a big change. The bank will be on a war time basis and I'll be classified IA because of my ROTC training. You and the children better be prepared for a move."

Monday evening Kent informed me the bank (The Federal Reserve Bank) would be handling War Bonds and things were moving swiftly.

There was an immediate announcement of War Time preparation. Blackout restrictions and preparations for a possible West Coast attack by the Japanese. We were totally unprepared. There were mock guns set up on the coast and people were called to man telegraph coast units to track possible planes and submarines off the coast.

The shipyards began twenty-four hour shifts. Men and women came to the call. The country united all the way. It was a shock to realize America was at war. San Francisco became a port of embarkation of troops and war equipment. Trains rolled by loaded with tanks, trucks and endless war paraphernalia. California was a scene of action I had never known. My brother

Gene enlisted in the Air Force. My brother Howard's company was called for special equipment as was my brother Theodore's. Wendall, Kent's brother, was called up by the Army and went into training.

Kent received his IA classification and was getting ready to go when the bank asked for his deferment as a vital worker in the War Bond program. He began handling thousands upon thousands of letters requesting bonds and was responsible for large amounts of money sent in to purchase them. He set up a program to efficiently handle the large volume of requests for Bonds. The Bank officials were amazed at his efficiency with regard to this program. As a result he did much good and had a great part in helping in the war years.

The children and I spent many hours alone for eventually Kent was working a seventy hour week. He left at 6 AM and seldom was home before 1 AM in the morning, Sundays included.

There were frequent black-outs. One time submarines were sighted outside the Golden Gate and the warning sounded for black-out. I had put the children to bed about seven o'clock and was sitting up listening to the radio, waiting for Kent. The siren came about eleven o'clock and I immediately took the crib mattress into the small hallway, between the two bedrooms, bathroom and living room. Closed all the doors, hung a blanket between the hall and living room and put the youngsters on the mattress. Turned out all lights, got the flashlight and radio and settled down for a long night, and I do mean a long night. This happened many times and Kent would have to remain at the bank.

The one great concern was of air attack. It was not known how well armed Japan was or how many planes they had at their command. Rationing went into effect and because of five in the family I had plenty of stamps, but not much money; so we never did use up our ration stamp quota.

Concentration camps were set up and Japanese were sent to them immediately. One camp was opened at the Tanforan Race track one half block from our home. We could see them bringing in Japanese people and guards on patrol. I'm sure it was a sad time for those who were American citizens and patriots.

Memories of Ruth Irene Peterson Gamblin

I couldn't be happier that Dad's War Journal is now being published in book form. Thank you to Owen and John for their work and dedication.

I was only 3, 4 and 5 years old during the war. Mostly I remember that Dad was not around much during those years. He worked for the Federal Reserve Bank in San Francisco. When every man at that time, under 35 years old, was being drafted, the bank needed him and he was given a deferment so he did not have to go to war. Instead he worked in the department at the bank that took care of War Bonds which were used to finance the war. I heard he was disappointed that he did not get to go to war as he had been in the ROTC in high school and liked that very much, especially the uniform. I wish I knew where that picture was because I have seen it.

I did not know about the book until sometime after the war when he was trying to get it published. He was told it was too big, but he did not want to shorten it.

The only part of the war that affected me was since we were close to San Francisco airport, airplanes would crash, sometimes close by. Also soldiers and sailors and sometimes tanks and trucks would go down our street to the race track at Tanforan. Tanforan was turned into a place where they kept the Japanese-American citizens at first.

I do remember some blackouts. Moma would drag a mattress into the hallway and we four kids (John was born in 1943) and Moma would stay there until the all clear sound came. Evidently Japanese submarines came close to our coast at times.

For a child as young as I was, the war did not affect me emotionally at all.

Memories of John Charles Peterson

I can't recall when I first learned of Dad's war time journal. I do remember something being said around the time of his passing in 1970. I had only been back from my time in the Vietnam War for about 3 years and was deeply involve and troubled in the confusions of that time. My Dad was proud of my service and gave me a big welcome home gathering. I was the first in his immediate family to serve; Owen had become an Air Force Officer in the Statigic Air Command. Our younger brother, Craig, had become a draft resister and had asked me to write a letter to the draft board in support of his request for Concientious Objector status shortly after I came back from Vietnam. That was a turning point for me as I wrote of my brother's act of conscience. I studied what lead us to that war and came to realize the wrong of it. Our Dad supported Craig in his legal problems to which I have been forever grateful. I'm sure it was difficult for him.

It was clear to me by 1970 that the war of my time was not like the war of his time. The Vietnam War was based on lies and deceit and those of us who came back from that war were not heros but harmed by our involvemnt. The country was in turmoil and the generations were in conflict. I do wish I had had more opportuities to discuss these conflicts with my Dad.

Some years later in an extraordinary conversation with our Mother I asked her if I could read his journal. She said no and ended the conversation. It was clear that that time period was hard and she had no desire to open it back up. I never broached the subject with her again. She is gone now as well and I hope that this is the time to open those pages with the care and love that we as their children can put forth. My love to you both.

Memories of Craig Stahr Peterson

When I turned 60 years of age the realization that I had lived longer than my father had lived hit me in ways I had not expected. I became very sad, even depressed. I missed him again and felt grateful for my life. A future was open for me. I'll be 70 in another year and life is still a miracle. Dad missed the advances in heart health and medical skills he needed by only a few years. What a shame.

Dad's writing and public speaking abilities were known at home and better known at work and Church.

Perhaps his writing skills developed during the war years. The determination to journal every night after work is to be admired and respected. He was a man who studied writing and had many books on the subject. A couple are still in my possession. Little was said to me about the War Years Journal until after Dad's death. I never read it or even saw it. I only knew that Mom kept it and much later that Ruth had it and was taking care of it.

Dad and I had a relationship when I was growing up that was loving and caring. My teen years were often frustrating and disappointing for him. I always knew he cared. Sadly we never fully developed an adult relationship.

Some Memories of him: The trombone he bought me in the 7th grade. His love of music and self-taught piano skills. Being his Golf Caddy on many outings. Our Ping Pong games that I lost 9 out of 10 times. Sunday drives he would take us on. Watching him water ski at Lake Shasta. His laughter and love of comedy shows. The pride and love he had for 'La Casa'. "What a view" he would often say. The fountain pens he carried to sign his name, and what a beautiful signature he had. I tried to develop a signature that would be as beautiful as his and never did.

Thank you Ruth, Owen and John for bringing Dad's Journal to a new level and a new life.

Memories of Sylvia Kathleen Peterson Leavitt

I am the author's youngest daughter. Although I was not even a twinkle in my parents eye during the time this manuscript was written, I remember as a child hearing about the late nights my father spent typing up the events of the day before retiring to bed only to get up 2 or 3 hours later to go to work, I felt as if I had been there. It fascinated me and I loved looking at the many typewritten pages that he had boxed away. My father would tell me that he would edit it and get it published one day when he retired.

For him that would not happen until now, 44 years after his passing. I am so grateful that his dream is coming true and I hope that not only our family can experience this, but others may have the opportunity to feel the true magnitude and effect that WWII had in the life of our family and I'm sure the lives of many families at that most significant time in history.

Dad and family during the war years.

Dad mowing the lawn in San Bruno, California
in 1941, just before the war broke out.

R to L Joyce, Dad, Mom, Owen and Ruth in the summer of 1942.
During the early war years.

Dad at the Federal Reserve Bank with collegues.

The family in September 1945 with John; Craig was due in November, Sylvia not until 10 years later in 1955. The war ended on August 14, 1945.

Craig, born in November 1945, at about 4 years old.

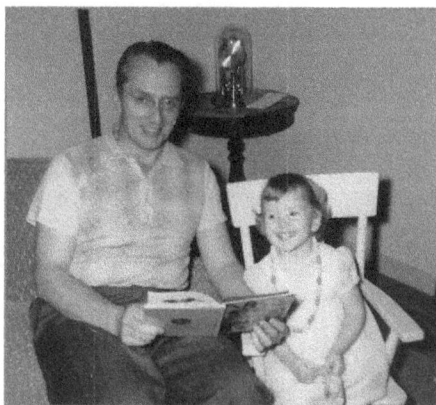

Dad and Mom's bonus, Sylvia, at 2 years old.

The entire family shortly after Sylvia was born in 1955.

Forward

The compilation of the historical record as it appears in the following pages was begun on December 7, 1941 and was finished three years, eight months, and seven days later on August 14, 1945.

As the bombs were falling on Pearl Harbor and as he (I) contemplated the dramatic impact of that "Day of Infamy" on the life of every human being, the author decided that it would be exceedingly interesting and perhaps valuable from an historical viewpoint, to record the course of the war as it unfolded chronologically in the life of one American citizen.

Accordingly, he (I) began compiling a daily record of the war as it was revealed through the mediums of newspapers, radio, and personal experiences; a daily record that was kept faithfully despite numerous obstacles ranging from eighty hours of grueling work each week during the early months of the war, to sickness and inertia. Many times the day's events were entered in the written record at two o'clock in the morning after a hectic day at the office or in bed when the "flu" laid him (me) low. Needless to say, the task seemed endless—the war would never be over—and then, as dramatically and suddenly as it began, came the atomic bomb and V-J Day.

As indicated in the opening article, the record contains many historical inaccuracies, but they are the inaccuracies that were part and parcel of the period involved. In other words, it is a picture of the war as it was currently presented to the people of the United States and as it was lived by one citizen of that nation. It is an historical record of a crucial period in the life of the Republic but it is not written in the dry, matter-of-fact manner of most histories. It is rather a living history, written in the present tense, in which you, as reader, can capture the atmosphere of the times. Through these pages you can re-live the war, day by day. In your mind you will hear once again the eerie wail of the air raid sirens and experience the helpless feeling of the blackout. You will know the dreadful waiting and feel the desperate suspense over the outcome of crucial battles. You will realize more vividly than ever how fearful was our plight during those first one hundred days when the "gallopin' Jap" was rampaging over the vast reaches of the south seas. You will sense our will to conquer and glory in the courageous stand of our fighting men during those bleak days. You will glow with pride as you watch our power grow through the efforts of millions of patriotic Americans and will hang your head in shame and anger at the antics of the fearful who would hamstring the war effort.

Before you will pass a complete and unabridged panorama of the war, both on the home front and the battle front, a panorama that will lead you through all the valleys of despair and heartbreak that lay before this nation on that fateful December day in 1941. And when, at last, you live again through that tumultuous orgy of wild celebration that marked the end of the war, you will not only thank God that the ultimate victory was ours, but you will also be moved to offer a silent prayer that humanity may never again be called upon to suffer in so monstrous a manner.

Shelton Kenneth Peterson

Content

A Citizen's Chronological History of World War II

Dedication

DEDICATED to the gallant fighting men and women of the Armed Forces of the United States and to their loyal comrades in the production army on the home front who unselfishly tried to do their bit to bring the fearful carnage to an end just one day sooner and thereby save a soldier's life.

December 7, 1941
San Francisco, California

Sunday, December 7, 1941: —WAR! WAR in the Pacific! Today, without warning, Japan struck at strategic American bases from the Philippines to Hawaii. News reports are confused, incoherent. Pearl Harbor attacked in great force. Wake Island captured. American transports sunk. Ships torpedoed only 700 miles at sea from San Francisco.

Thus, at 12:20 p.m. today, the news of the most treacherous attack in all American history broke the Sabbath quiet of the Nation. The complacent, strike-loving, peace seeking, yet unprepared American people were jolted with a sudden rush of anger to the realization that their hour had come. Now we shall see action! The President has called an emergency meeting of his cabinet and Congressional leaders; undoubtedly a declaration of war will follow in the morning. Censorship has been imposed. All military and naval leaves have been cancelled. Home guards are being mobilized. Civilians have been requested to enroll at their nearest fire department or police station. Mayor Rossi of San Francisco has issued a proclamation, declaring an emergency and demanding cessation of all strikes and disputes in order that a united front may face the uncertain future.

News bulletins flood in over the radio. Singapore is under attack. Thailand is invaded. Canada and the Dutch East Indies have declared war on Japan. Strangely enough Costa Rica has also jumped the gun with a declaration of war, evidently desiring to anticipate the United States' move. London seethes with excitement as the flame of WAR leaps with a great bound to encircle the earth. Washington boils with mounting anger and indignation at the treachery that brought the surprise attack while conversations for peace were still going on with Japan's special envoy, Kurusu. Hundreds are dying in Honolulu as orders are given throughout the Nation for production on a 24 hour basis.

1

The San Francisco Bay region should be the seething, bustling center of this tragic Pacific war. Its great harbor, its important naval establishments, its mighty bridges, its aircraft factories, its industrial and financial nerve centers all combine to make it a first class objective for enemy attack, as well as a natural area of strategic importance. Already steps are being taken to put the entire district on a total war footing. Soldiers guard the bridges, FBI agents are rounding up the numerous Japanese aliens, and citizens are being mobilized.

From this vantage point, therefore, because the cause is so great, the outcome so uncertain, I shall attempt to make a chronological record of events as they come to me, an ordinary citizen, through the mediums of the radio, newspapers, and personal experiences. For this reason the record will reflect all the propaganda, rumors, and inaccuracies which abound in those mediums. But it will show the picture as it is lived day by day in the midst of a terrible and fascinating moment in history. Thus it may prove interesting and of some historical value. So, until tomorrow, may God be with our beloved Country.

Monday, December 8, 1941: —Today has been momentous. Congress, with a mighty vote of unity, declared WAR ON JAPAN! The Senate vote was 82 to 0; the House vote was 388 to 1. The only dissenter was Miss Jeanette Rankin of Montana who voted the same way in 1917. A dubious distinction, hers.

Never in history has a single act so united a country. Japan's treachery, although it may gain her an initial advantage, has set in motion a single, united torrent of American will and American effort. That torrent will not be stopped until it has rolled over and forever destroyed the vicious military power of Japan. Our decision is clear, our objective certain. These sentiments have been expressed the length and breadth of the nation today.

There are tonight more nations at war than there were during the First World War In addition to the United States, other nations which have declared war up to now on Japan include England, Canada, China, who also declared war on Germany and Italy, the Netherlands, East Indies, Costa Rica, Nicaragua, and Australia. In all, 31 nations are now engaged in total war, as against 29 that fought in the first great catastrophe.

News from Hawaii and the Philippines is still muddled. The extent of Japanese success is not known. Grave fears are expressed that the losses may be heavier than expected. Japan claims great victories. The President hinted at disaster when he said, "No matter how long it takes us to overcome this premeditated invasion, the American people in their righteous might will win through to absolute victory." This after the overconfident pre-war belief that the U.S. Navy was greatly superior to Japan's. Apparently the Japs have delivered a staggering blow to the unsuspecting Pacific Fleet. At least one or two battleships have been sunk, several destroyers blown up and many warships damaged. Dozens of aircraft were destroyed on the ground. The death toll is heavy; first reports are well over 1,500. It is fierce, all-out war!

It can happen here. It has happened here! BLACKOUT! Tonight San Francisco had its first Air Raid Warning. Rumors flew as fast as the planes. What was believed to be merely a practice drill has turned out to be the real thing. At least two squadrons of hostile aircraft were sighted off the coast heading toward the Golden Gate. The attack, however, never developed as the planes veered off and disappeared into the Pacific. As the lights went out for the two hour period, the full realization of the meaning of War was brought home to the citizens of the Bay Area. There was no panic, no hysteria. The people were surprisingly calm and unafraid. Can we take it as have the British? God grant that we shall not have to. But if we must God give us that same fortitude and courage.

Tuesday, December 9, 1941: —The sudden shock and surprise of the Japanese attack has somewhat subsided today. People are quickly adapting themselves to think in war terms. At work the talk was mostly of the Blackout. Very few expressed any feeling of fear, but there were a few. Some thought the raid was a phony, but the authorities have very definitely stated that it was the real thing. Enemy planes in two large squadrons approached the Golden Gate and then turned back. They may have been on a reconnaissance flight only. However, we were lucky, for the first blackout was very spotty. More definite instructions are being issued for tonight. It is now 10:45 p.m. and no "alert" has been sounded as yet.

The big news of today is President Roosevelt's speech. His theme was our resolve to carry this war to a victorious conclusion and the unity and untiring effort that we shall display in this great endeavor. As to war news, the President said that the Government will not hide the truth from the people but will give out all news, good or bad, as soon as it is available and will not be of aid or comfort to the enemy.

The news so far has all been bad. Initial Jap success apparently is great. Wake, Guam, and Midway Islands have probably been lost. Thailand has capitulated to the enemy. British troops are engaged in Malay. But the most important news—how badly was the Navy damaged in Hawaii—has not yet been determined. It must be serious, however, for Congress has ordered an immediate investigation and intimates that court-martials of several navel officers are contemplated. Someone must have been caught napping. Let us hope it will not prove an irreparable mistake.

All radio stations are still on the air and a United Air Liner just roared overhead on its regular schedule, so it looks like tonight will be uneventful. Hope so!

I signed up for Civilian Defense at the local Fire Station tonight.

Wednesday, December 10, 1941: —More very bad news tonight. The Japs have sunk two of Great Britain's mightiest warships. The "unsinkable" battleship, Prince of Wales, and the battle cruiser Repulse were destroyed near Malay by Japanese planes. The enemy seems to be bombing with uncanny accuracy. Air power has won the greatest victory of the war over sea power. Prime Minister Churchill called it the worst individual disaster of the war—not excluding Dunkirk.

Accurate information as to the condition of the U.S. Navy is still scarce. News is muddled. Results of Sunday's initial attack are just beginning to seep through. It is reported that an American Admiral was killed in the first raid. Casualty lists appear in all the newspapers. The Mikado's grisly mill is grinding out its ghastly toll. What a senseless, horrible occupation for civilized men to follow. Blood-letting only leads to more blood-letting for the American people have sworn that this treacherous foe shall pay dearly for his perfidy.

Last night we had an air raid warning from about 2:30 a.m. until 4:00 a.m. We were awakened by the screaming wail of the sirens. We could hear them all up and down the Bay. Our local signal is two long blasts coming every minute for five. The "all clear" is one long blast. No need for us to blackout. We just lay in bed listening for awhile and then my wife said, "confound those Japs," and we went back to sleep. No bombs were dropped, however, although it is persistently claimed that enemy planes are near the coast. I don't like the sound of these rumors, they are too persistent.

Worked at the Bank tonight until 7:30. Sales of Defense Savings Bonds have jumped tremendously since Sunday. The slogan is "Bonds for shells, Stamps for bullets." That's a nice sentiment for the holiday season, isn't it? And Christmas only two weeks away.

Thursday, December 11, 1941: —Worked until 10:30 tonight. Sales of Defense Savings Bonds have doubled since Monday. Looks like it will be all work and very little play from now on.

The big news of today, although it seems anti-climactic now, is Hitler's and Mussolini's declaration of War against the United States. In speeches crammed with absurd charges they stated that they were taking their countries into the struggle to aid the Japanese in the fight that was forced on them. And that after Pearl Harbor on Sunday! Such guff is undoubtedly intended for home consumption. I wonder if it really fools the suffering people of Germany and Italy. How long are they going to follow such bloodthirsty egomaniacs?

Congress followed the Axis' declaration of war with our own declaration in less than 34 minutes. The vote was unanimous, with Jeanette Rankin of Montana declining to vote. In contrast to Sunday's attack the action of Germany and Italy surprised very few. Even former isolationist leaders took it as a matter of course.

The first American success is reported today. The Army Air Force in Manila sank a 29,000 ton Japanese Battleship, believed to be the Haruna. Marine pilots from Wake Island also sank a cruiser and destroyer to even the game up a bit. The Japs appear to be making some headway in their land attack on the Philippines, but the U.S. forces are resisting furiously.

There was no blackout last night and none so far tonight. The excitement seems to have died down although preparations are being pressed. Training of air raid wardens, fire fighters, and rescue squads is beginning. Seems strange and rather terrible for all this to be going on in this "civilized" world.

Friday, December 12, 1941: —It's after twelve midnight as I sit down to record the day's events. It has been eventful, too. Work has piled up at the Bank so bad that we were to work tonight. We were just getting into it when the alarm sounded. We immediately blacked out the whole building and moved everyone into the basement and vault area. Only a few of us were able to continue with any work—in the vault itself, which was still lighted.

The raid lasted over three hours and it is reported that the City was completely blacked out. Total darkness as compared with the first night's farce. The people appear to be learning rapidly. They don't like the nuisance, it's true, but they do a good job of it in the typical grumbling American way. There was no fear only disgust and anger at the Orientals who could disrupt our lives in such an abominable manner.

Some good news seeps out of the Far East. It looks as though our boys are giving a good account of themselves. Contrary to first fearful reports, the U.S. Marines are still hanging on to Wake Island in one of those magnificent stands for which they are famed. They have not budged under terrific air and naval assault.

It's hard to take this thing as seriously as it really is—after all the bomb-less blackouts and phony rumors—until you see the pictures in the papers of the first soldier heroes, boys, fine to look at, who have given their lives in defense of their country. Then the somber realization comes of the horrible crime that has been perpetrated against us and we quietly and sternly resolve to go "all out" in our effort to punish the bloody criminal.

Saturday, December 13, 1941: —News continues largely favorable today. American forces have decisively beaten off the main Japanese attack on the Island of Luzon in the Philippines. Native Filipino troops made a good showing. Many a Jap parachutist lost his head completely when attacked by native bolo wielders. The Netherlands East Indies Dutch reported that their submarines have sunk four large troop transports, drowning more than 4,000 Jap soldiers. The only adverse reports are that the Island of Guam has been definitely lost and the Tokyo statement that their forces have sunk another U.S. Battleship, the Arizona. This has not been confirmed by the U.S. and is probably untrue. No major naval engagements have taken place. The Japs are apparently trying a "whittling down" process. Their Navy won't stand up and fight—yet.

On the home front it's all work. All day today and back to work at 9 o'clock on Sunday morning. It's seven days a week and work until the job is finished. Some of the girls especially don't like it but that doesn't matter. For the most part, however, everyone is working with a will to conquer.

Sunday, December 14, 1941: —Sunday night and a full week of War has come and gone. Sunday night and the lives of Americans have changed tremendously since that eon of seven days ago when War was thrust upon us. Sunday night and gone, perhaps forever, is that old comfortable, secure existence of which we were so justly proud. Life now has become harder, more exacting, more dangerous. But the people don't complain; they are sure of their objective and sure of their collective ability to attain that objective. They are grimly determined to do the job, do it as quickly as possible, and get back to peace and the pursuit of happiness.

Our armed forces in the Philippines apparently have the same idea for in a terrific attack they have hurled the Jap invaders off the Island of Luzon. Three more Nippon transports were sunk, with cargo of troops, and their landing force annihilated. So for the present the Mikado's Philippines invasion has stubbed its toe.

Our British Allies in Malaya and Hong Kong do not appear to fare so well, however. The Japs have succeeded in landing a huge mechanized army in Malaya and are advancing in spite of stubborn jungle fighting. Tokyo claims that the fate of Hong Kong is sealed and they may be right from all news reports. They seem to have attained the all-essential air supremacy in their scrap with the British. We shall have to admit that the Japs are much better in the air than was formerly believed.

Monday, December 15, 1941: —REMEMBER PEARL HARBOR! This is our battle slogan in this war. Like "REMEMBER

THE MAINE" it will inspire and drive the Yanks to victory and revenge. Secretary of the Navy Knox today gave the American People their first accurate report of the Pearl Harbor attack. Three things stand out in his "first hand" report. (You will remember that Secretary Knox flew to Honolulu immediately upon receipt of the first news.) First: It is true that the Navy was completely surprised. An investigation is under way and some court-martials are to be expected. Second: After the initial surprise the army and navy pulled themselves together and met the situation efficiently and courageously. Third: For this reason the Japanese plan—to destroy the U.S. Fleet and Base—utterly failed. Staggering blows were struck and the Navy lost two battleships, the Arizona and Oklahoma, three destroyers and several auxiliary vessels. The harbor facilities, however, came through practically unscathed. The main fighting force of the Navy is still intact and seeking to come to grips with the enemy.

Epic tales of individual heroism were commonplace in Honolulu. Literally through fire and water the men of the fleet fought furiously and heroically. Their only thought was to reach their post and strike back. From the Captain who directed his ship from the bridge with his stomach literally laid wide open by shrapnel to the seaman who single handedly wielded a machine gun, bringing down the first enemy bomber, until he was blown overboard, the fighting men of our Hawaiian forces have made us proud of them. They have bravely upheld every glorious American tradition.

Tuesday, December 16, 1941: —This is really being written on Wednesday—at 1:00 o'clock in the morning. We worked at the Bank until 11:30 and caught the 12:15 train home. I'll be up again at 6:30 to go to work again. C'est L'Guerre!

Today's news tells of tiny two-man submarines used by the Japs in the attack on Pearly Harbor. One of them was captured by the American forces; two others were sunk. They are really suicide ships, being equipped, not only with torpedoes, but also with a heavy explosive charge so placed as to make the vessel itself a torpedo. They are apparently carried by larger warships and launched when near their objective.

Wake Island and Midway continue to hold out against the aggressor but Guam has definitely been captured, together with its small garrison. A Japanese Admiral, who seems to have planned all this, broadcast in Tokyo that not only Guam but Hawaii, the Philippines, and San Francisco will be occupied. He confidently looks forward to dictating peace to the United States from the White House in Washington. Ambitious, to say the least.

No air raid alarms have sounded since Friday. Eight brand new sirens have been received by the City of San Francisco, however, so I guess we can expect a test blackout anytime now.

Congress is debating revision of the draft law to make all men from 18 to 44 liable for military service. Looks like a huge citizen army is in the making, to be used anywhere in the world. Only God knows how much blood will spill before this thing is over.

Wednesday, December 17, 1941: —Congress is apparently getting more furious daily over what happened at Pearly Harbor on December 7. While the members are thrilled by the individual heroism and courageous comeback by the soldiers and sailors they are dismayed and angered at the apparent dereliction of some of the higher-ups. Their complacency and "it can't happen here" attitude caused them to be caught completely napping. It now appears that at least one admiral and probably two generals will lose their commands. France was lost by just such leadership. America may fare better only by the grace of God and geographical differences.

Row on row of fresh graves, draped with green banyan leaves and multi-colored flowers stretched across Hawaiian cemeteries today, marking only the beginning of the price we shall have to pay for our over confidence and carelessness. The price will be reasonable only if it arouses the people sufficiently so that such a thing shall not happen again.

While the fighting in Malaya seems to be going badly for the Allies, the picture in Europe and Africa is much better. The Russians are smashing ahead in their counter-offensive until the Nazis themselves admitted they are "astonished." It will be a long time before Hitler settles his Russian adventure which was to be all over in six weeks. The Fuehrer has retired to Berchtesgaden with a headache—and well he may.

In Libya the British are winning their first really decisive land victory over the German panzers. It is a good omen.

9

Thursday, December 18, 1941: —In general the war news today is favorable to the Allies. In Russia the German retreat is turning into a Nazi rout. The Red army is gaining momentum and is recapturing territory as fast as their foe had originally invested it. A strange and significant admission came out of Germany today. A Nazi army spokesman admitted that the Russians had been generally and grossly underrated and that the Red army was the equal and in some instances superior to the Reichwehr. In any event the Germans have got to stop the Russian advance soon or their goose may be cooked.

In Libya the British are mopping up. The German and Italian panzers are again trapped and this time will probably not escape. An evidence of their plight is disclosed by the fact that the British navy sank an Italian submarine in which twenty high Italian officers were attempting to escape from Libya. Some were captured, the rest drowned.

American submarines are operating successfully in Japanese waters. Tokyo itself admits the sinking of a troop transport and destroyer but claims, as usual, to have sunk three U.S. subs.

Only in Malaya and Hong Kong are the Allies faring poorly, although the Hong Kong garrison has rejected a Japanese ultimatum and continues to resist furiously. In Malaya, however, the Japs are advancing rapidly, using clever infiltration tactics. One observer likens the jungle warfare to "Indians fighting with Tommy guns."

Friday, December 19, 1941: —Right now, at 11:00 p.m., it seems so peaceful. Away from the terrific hustle and rush of the day's work, away from the yapping of the newsboys and the din of the city traffic, squatting comfortably in front of the radio which is softly playing a melodious tune of the "Wayne King" variety, it doesn't seem possible that over there, in the vastness of the "ocean of peace", little slant-eyed Orientals are trying to kill Americans. It's too peaceful, and yet, as it did to 2,700 sailor boys on Sunday in Hawaii, death and destruction may suddenly come winging its way out of the vast recesses of the Pacific. But come what may, we now have a country that's ready to fight, with a fighting slogan: "REMEMBER PEARL HARBOR!"

The latest news reports indicate that the Japs are putting all they have into their Malay drive. In spite of awful losses they are pounding their way inch by inch toward the vital base of Singapore. If they can take Singapore the whole strategic area will drop like a ripe apple into their laps. Much of Japan's raw material shortage would thus be solved and a long, bitter war of attrition would be required to break the "sons of heaven's" power of resistance. We can only hope fervently that the British and Australian troops can check the enemy drive before such a calamity comes about.

The Germans and Italians, meanwhile, are having to swallow some bitter pills in Russia and Libya. The Nazi hordes are reliving the terrible experience of Napoleon in his historic retreat from Moscow. Hitler's headache should be getting worse.

Saturday, December 20, 1941: —No record of this war would be complete without mentioning the name of the first great American hero. His name is Colin P. Kelly Jr. a captain in the air corps. Today he was awarded the Distinguished Service Cross for exemplary bravery and heroism far beyond any call of duty. His citation declared that Captain Kelly, in spite of terrible odds and in the face of heavy enemy gunfire, drove home his attack, scoring three direct hits on the battleship Haruna which then sank. Captain Kelly's plane was then attacked by three enemy pursuits whose fire set the American ship aflame. Kelly then ordered his crew to save themselves and in seeing that this was accomplished was trapped and killed in the flaming crash of his plane.[1]

In making the award posthumously, the Army stated that Captain Kelly's heroic conduct would continue to be an inspiration and example to his fellow officers and personnel of the Corps. By their deeds ye shall know them.

Great nations are made and upheld by men such as Colin P. Kelly Jr., but that fact does not lessen much of the grief and suffering of those loved ones who are left behind. Captain Kelly left a beautiful young wife and five year old son, Colin P. Kelly III. In grateful remembrance of the unselfish service rendered by his father to his country, President Roosevelt has addressed a letter to the President of the U.S. in 1956, asking that he appoint Colin P. Kelly III to the U.S. Military Academy at West Point in order that the son may be given the opportunity to carry on the glorious traditions for which the father so nobly died.[2]

Sunday, December 21, 1941: —Again we worked all day. It's a seven day, ten hour day week now. The only way to win a war, I guess, but hard on the nerves. Especially is it hard on the women. The men seem to be able and willing to take it, but the girls in many cases don't seem to be able to stand the pressure. This is very important because men are becoming scarcer and women are in great demand for clerical work. Consequently the choice is not good and it is difficult to obtain girls with the high type of ability and qualifications that has been customary heretofore. It's just a case of doing the best we can with what we have.

The biggest war news of the day is from Berlin. Hitler has fired his commanding General Von Brauchitsch. The alibi was heart trouble, but the truth is the Russian debacle. What started out to be a "six weeks" campaign has turned out to be a six month old full-scale war that is beginning to backfire with disastrous effect on the once invincible Nazi war machine. The trouble with General Brauchitsch is Russian frostbite. So now the "genius" Hitler has taken full command. We can expect this mad "Napoleon" to strike with all his fury at some other front in a desperate attempt to regain the initiative and reestablish his ailing prestige. But if this time he fails . . . !

Rumors and reports are being heard today that Jap submarines are attacking shipping off the coast of California. If so they are a long way from their bases. It's too bad that Congress delayed so long in authorizing the arming of merchant men.

Monday, December 22, 1941: —Another long day. Beginning to forget what my family looks like. Hoping, with fingers crossed, that we will not have to work Christmas Day. That's one day above all others that one likes to be home with the wife and children, with nothing but peace and happiness on one's mind. Sometimes, however, in a world at war, the things we like to do must be sacrificed. Many a soldier boy or sailor will have a mighty lonely Christmas. Would that God might aid in the speedy overthrow of those evil forces rampant in the world so that good men may once again resume the fascinating pursuit of happiness without fear of being stabbed in the back. That that day may not be too far distant, 130,000,000 Americans have rolled up their sleeves and buckled down to some good hard work.

The rumors about Jap subs off the Pacific Coast have been verified today. Huge ocean going submarines, capable of cruising 16,000 miles, have attacked several coastwise steamers. One was sunk with the loss of six lives; three others escaped by zigzagging and smoke screens. The Japanese shooting has been poor. Probably buck fever.

The Japs have launched another huge sea borne invasion attempt on the Philippines. Terrific fighting is raging on the Island of Luzon, where lies Manila. General MacArthur, commander of the U.S. Forces in the area reports that the "situation is well in hand" and that the American troops "are behaving well." Tanks and heavy coastal artillery are supporting the American counter attacks. Go get 'em, you doughboys!

Tuesday, December 23, 1941: —Stalled and beaten back in the bitter sub-zero weather of Russia, Adolf Hitler and his army of slaughterers are turning elsewhere, seeking a warmer and softer spot to strike. Unconfirmed, though usually reliable, reports have it that the Nazi hordes are pouring into Spain, probably to take a crack at Gibraltar and French Africa. If true, the Port of Dakar, vital to American defense is immediately threatened. It should now be a race to see who can occupy it first.

Meanwhile, subdued and beaten, France grovels restlessly under the heel of the conquerors. Fresh outbreaks of violence and sabotage have strained the relations between the fishy Vichy Government and Hitler almost to the breaking point. It is rumored that Petain, the former strong man of Verdun, and now the only man in the Vichy regime to oppose the will of the Fuehrer, is about to resign. Into full control will then come the Nazi collaborationist Admiral Darlan, who will probably turn over to the Germans not only the French fleet but also the French African bases. This would be a serious blow to the Allies and one they would not forget, especially around the peace table. Beware, France!

Sub warfare off the California coast is intensifying. Several more vessels have been attacked and one or two sunk. This brings the realities of war close, as many of the seamen are from the Bay area. The Japanese invasion of the Philippines is gaining momentum. At heavy cost they appear to have established bridgeheads for a pincer movement on Manila. Fear has already been expressed in Washington as to the outcome.

Wednesday, December 24, 1941: —Christmas Eve! The soft melodious strains of the "Sleighbell Serenade" floating out over the airways. The heart-warming glow from the multi-colored lights on the tinseled Christmas tree. The innumerable gifts, brightly wrapped, stacked high around the tree. The two beautiful little lady dolls peering, vixen like, from their miniature crib. That is the picture of Christmas Eve in an American home. Outside in the world a war rages. Why—?

Why? I guess there is no answer. It is beyond belief or reason why civilized human beings, with hearts that warm and souls that love, can struggle desperately and ferociously to maim and destroy each other. But it is so and we of America can only bend every effort to defeat those who have brought such a vicious thing to pass and see to it that such a tragedy is not again visited upon this planet. So help us God!

A full dress, all out invasion of the Philippines is the Christmas present of the Japs to those beleaguered Islands. It is estimated that the Orientals are using a force of more than 250,000 men in the attempt. General MacArthur's American and Filipino troops though outnumbered are still in command of the situation.

Down into the ranks of historic last stands, in the company of the Alamo, the Alcazars, and Custer, goes the gallant stand of the Marine garrison of Wake Island. Today the Navy considers the island lost as communications are severed. The fate of the doughty leathernecks is unknown. A great stand by a noble band.

Thursday, December 25, 1941: —Another Christmas has come and all but gone in this weary, sick old world of ours. The light of peace and goodwill that shone brightly over the little town of Bethlehem has been blacked out over most of the planet. In its stead has settled the gloom of despair—the shroud of death.

But here in America the light still shines, though gravely threatened. Here the hope of mankind lies, for from the flame still shining here will come the torch that will carry the light of hope back into countless darkened lives. By the united resolve of our mighty nation, with the help of God, the hated fetters that bind the world will be cast off and peace and happiness restored to all men of goodwill. The joyous sound of children's laughter in their carefree celebration of the birth of the Child of God will once more resound throughout all lands as it has throughout the land of America this day. The Star of Bethlehem has not fallen; it has merely been obscured by a cloud.

But the way will be hard. The aggressors are strong. Today it was reliably reported that Hong Kong, the British crown colony, has surrendered to the Japanese. The cutting off of their water supply was the decisive factor in the defenders' decision to cease resistance. The price tag for the Colony was high in Japanese blood and treasure and there was no markdown or discount.

Hitler's next move is still obscure. Apparently the rumor of his march on Spain fizzled out. But the Cobra will strike soon. Call out the Mongoose.

Friday, December 26, 1941: —The most important news to Americans, is the Battle of the Philippines. From all reports, it appears that the Japs are making some headway, having established and maintained several bridgeheads within striking distance of Manila. This has been done in spite of heavy losses and in the face of heroic resistance by crack American and Filipino troops. While General MacArthur's communiqués state that our troops are holding their own, the fate of the Islands is very much in doubt. Whether U.S. strategy contemplates holding the Philippines at any cost is doubtful. It may be that the plan is to exact the highest possible price for any temporary success which the enemy might gain in that area. Revenge and the recovery of the possessions would come later. Incidentally, the City of Manila was declared an open city today. This in order that the civilian population might be spared indiscriminate bombing.

Prime Minister Winston Churchill has been in Washington for two days now in conference with the President on war matters. Today he spoke to a joint session of Congress. It was the first time in history that the leader of Britain has addressed that Body. His words, while expressing supreme confidence in the eventual outcome, were realistic in that he expects a long, hard war. The next two years will be a period of vast preparation culminating in a huge Allied drive probably in 1943, a drive that will bring justice to the culprits that prey upon the world today.

No more air raid warnings, sub attacks, or sabotage of late. Nothing but work and more work.

Saturday, December 27, 1941: —Today the treacherous Japs struck viciously again. In a fire blitz of the 1940 London type, the Japs poured incendiaries and high explosives on defenseless Manila. In strict accordance with the terms of The Hague Convention of 1907, to which Japan was a signatory, General MacArthur had declared Manila an open city. All military personnel and equipment had been removed together with governmental offices. This was done in an attempt to spare the beautiful city and its civilian population from the horrors of bombardment. But today without warning and without opposition the Japanese air force in great numbers roared over the heart of the city and fired it with a wantonness that spoke eloquently of their total disregard of international law or common humanity. The bombing served no conceivable military objective and gained them nothing save perhaps an intensified hatred that will surely boomerang.

By their vicious action the Japs have thrown down the gauntlet for a "no-quarter" struggle. An even more terrible struggle will ensue, for the American people, without exception, are aroused and are determined to mete out suitable punishment, cost what it may.

While Axis armies in Russia and Libya struggle desperately to check Allied attempts to entrap them, the leaders of the democracies in Washington map out the Grand Strategy for the long-term conduct of the war. That victory will entail many more sacrifices of time and wealth from every citizen is only beginning to seep into the realization of many Americans. DO YOUR BIT is as appropriate in this war as in the last—and more.

Sunday, December 28, 1941: —I'm really weary tonight. Working every Sunday is no fun. You don't really realize how important Sunday is, how revitalizing it is to be able to rest that one precious day a week, until you can't do it anymore. It's just one more score to settle with those brown little Oriental murderers.

Speaking of murder, that's just what the Japs are doing to Manila. They're really making it an "open" city—by blasting it wide open. There are no rules in this war. It's a bitter struggle with the world itself at stake. Everything goes and sportsmanship is out—by the enemy's choice. Thank God, the country is at least united. If had to come it is a blessing that it came as it did. For the first time in our entire history there is no division of opinion. Every loyal person in the country has but one objective—the total defeat of the enemy. No other thing on earth could have solidified this nation as has this unprovoked attack.

The Japs broadcast today that San Francisco had been bombed and huge fires started. Nice propaganda. A fire couldn't have burned the city today if it wanted to. It rained so hard all day that you couldn't tell where the bay ended and the land began. The rainy season has really started. In a way it's a blessing as it lessens the possibility of an air raid. Tough on flyers, you know. Ceiling zero, visibility zero and all that sort of thing.

Monday, December 29, 1941: —Two more days of the year 1941 remain. A momentous year it has surely been. Historians will undoubtedly ponder at great length over the events of the year that reached their climax on December 7. On that day the war really became a World War, vastly eclipsing the scope attained by World War I. World War I, World War II, a fine state of affairs when we have started numbering our World Wars.

American attention is still centered on the tremendous battle being waged for Manila and the Philippines. U.S. submarines were reported to have sunk a Japanese destroyer, a transport, and several smaller vessels off the Luzon coast. Dutch submersibles and aircraft accounted for several more. The Dutch, by the way, are making a terrific fight of it. Their subs and air force, especially, are wreaking a terrible revenge on the enemy. General MacArthur's communiqué claimed today that American lines in all sectors are holding despite very heavy enemy pressure which is increasing. President Roosevelt yesterday hinted that help would be sent to the beleaguered Islands and apparently the U.S. forces are holding grimly until that help has had time to arrive. We may lose the Philippines but the Japs will know they've had a scrap.

Work at the Bank is very heavy and is beginning to tell on some of the women especially. Had a little council of war with the members of my department today. I really believe they were convinced that sacrifices of time and effort were absolutely essential and constituted our bit in the "all out" war effort. They really turned out the work today. I guess they realize that there's no 40 hour week for our boys in the front lines.

Tuesday, December 30, 1941: —The news from the Russian battle ground is really amazing. The Red Army seems to have seized the initiative on all fronts. Even in the Crimea, where it was thought the Germans would soon capture Sevastopol, the Russians are driving the Nazis back. The supposedly invincible Hitler war machine has definitely gone into reverse. It looks a bit as though reverse will not be enough and they will have to turn the machine around and put her into high if they would escape. And this is the "six weeks" campaign that the German warlords were going to take in their stride. Shades of Waterloo!

In the Far East the picture is not so good, however. The invasion of the Philippines is gaining momentum. The U.S. Forces have admittedly withdrawn to shorten and strengthen their lines. Jap pressure is being maintained in both the north and south.

Today a thrilling and significant event occurred on the Island of Luzon. Civilians, accustomed to scampering to cover at the sound of planes because the air has been dominated by the Japanese, were hovering in the scanty shelters warily watching the approach of a large force of bombers and fighters. Expecting momentarily to be showered with high explosives from planes bearing the rising sun on their wings, the natives were overjoyed to see, as the machines came closer, the white star insignia of the U.S. Army Air Force. Pouring into the streets, the cheers of the multitude drowned out even the roar of the motors. What more thrilling sight than those friendly wings and their omen of the power that has only now been aroused.

Wednesday, December 31, 1941: —Well, finally we come to the last day of another year. No one will deny that 1941 has made its mark in the history of the world. Tremendous changes have been wrought during those hectic 365 days. No one can say the times were dull.

It's hard to remember exactly what the conditions were a year ago. Certainly the world picture was far from reassuring. Hitler had just completed his amazing string of triumphs; practically the whole of Europe was prostrate at his feet. One of the world's greatest powers, France, had been brought to her knees. A complete and overwhelming victory for Hitler, with all its portents of evil for America, seemed almost inevitable. Seemingly, no power on earth was capable of halting the march of the world's most terrible war machine. Hitler himself, in a New Year's message to his people, confidently promised them that the year 1941 would see consummation of Germany's greatest victory. Wealth, power, glory, "Lebensraum", colonies, all this and more would drop like ripe plums into their laps. The "Master Race" would rule the earth.

Twelve months later, on the eve of a new year, this dream of conquest is fading, flickering like an elusive shadow before the tortured eyes of the German people. The wrath of the world is beginning to rise against all these international bandits. Arrayed against them, determined to bring them to justice, is the mightiest coalition of free men ever assembled. 1942 will see them gather, from all corners of the globe, the arms necessary to bring the criminals before the bar. Hitler, you mad genius; Hirohito, you blunders Oriental; Mussolini, you comic fop—your days are numbered.

[1] Captain Kelly and his crew aboard their B-17 Flying Fortress bombed the Japanese cruiser *Ashigara* (then mistakenly thought to be the battleship *Haruna*). On their return flight, Japanese Zeros attacked the B-17 badly damaging it. Kelly stayed at the controls so that his surviving crew could bail out. After the last crew member exited the plane, the B-17 exploded killing Kelly.

[2] Captain Kelly's son, Colin P. Kelly, III, graduated from West Point (Class of 1963). Kelly III would later become an Episcopal priest who served as the Assistant Chaplain at West Point.

1942

Thursday, January 1, 1942: —It has been a beautiful day, this first of the New Year. Not a cloud marred the blue of the sky, the rain of yesterday was just a lonely puddle here and there, and the sun glowed with a warmth more appropriate for a summer's day. It has been a good omen. Only the shortness of the daylight and the chill that came with the darkness reminded us that it is the first of January and winter.

While we feasted and rested, a rare treat, news reports brought home to us the fact that in the Philippines there was no time for celebration or merriment. There U.S. troops are fighting for their lives against terrible odds. It appears unlikely that our forces will be able to hold Manila. Whether that presages the total loss of the Philippines or not is guesswork. It is probable, however, that General MacArthur will withdraw part of his men to the Fortress of Corregidor in the harbor of Manila and there make a last stand. This fortress is reputedly very strong and should be able to withstand a long siege. The remainder of the defenders, principally Filipinos, may retire to the hills and resort to guerilla warfare. Nevertheless, we must be prepared for the complete loss of the Islands.

In happy contrast to the deadly fighting abroad was the annual Rose Bowl football game broadcast today. Due to the war, the game was transferred from Pasadena, California for the first time in its history, and was played at Durham, North Carolina, between Oregon State and Duke University. It was a thrilling battle, with fortunes changing constantly. Oregon State was the winner 20-16.

Friday, January 2, 1942: —MANILA FALLS! Red headlines shouted this news today. In three weeks the Japs have fought their way to Manila, the capital of the Philippines. General

MacArthur laconically announced the evacuation of the city, necessitated by the need to consolidate his forces being threatened by a strong north and south pincer movement. In addition to the city, the important naval base of Cavite was abandoned to the enemy. All supplies were removed and properly destroyed before the U.S. troops left. MacArthur's army, nevertheless, is continuing the desperate struggle from stubbornly held lines north of the city and in the island fortress of Corregidor. The strategy seems to be to hold the enemy at bay as long as possible, forcing him to utilize important units of his forces which otherwise might be thrown into the more vital struggle for Singapore. It cannot be denied, however, that the Japs have done very well so far in their far eastern campaign. Some commentators lay the blame to our former lofty and shortsighted altruism that culminated in the disarmament agreement of 1922. This agreement prevented us from even beginning to fortify the Philippines until far too late. Naturally the U.S. was the only nation that even pretended to live up to the terms of the agreement. But that's all water over the spillway. The thing to do now is to chalk it up as unfinished business; someday we'll restore the Islands with a vengeance that Japs yet unborn will tremble to remember.

Somewhat compensating for the loss of Manila was the capture of Bardia in Libya by the British. Total disaster for the Axis looms in the African desert.

Saturday, January 3, 1942: —We had a forty minute blackout tonight. The alert sounded at 6:52 p.m. First alarm in a long time. The army claimed it was called because unidentified planes were heard off the coast. No attack developed. It was fortunate too because there wasn't much use blacking out. The moon was full and with a clear sky it was almost as light as day. From the sixth floor of the Bank building we could see the whole bay area, shimmering in the lush moonlight.

The fortress of Corregidor in Manila Bay continues to hold out in spite of heavy bombing attacks by the Japs. Fighting in the Philippines is far from ended.

We overlooked mentioning yesterday that President Roosevelt and Prime Minister Churchill, who is in Washington, announced the signing of a "fight to the finish" pact by 26 anti-axis nations headed by the U.S., Britain and Russia. This imposing array vows never to conclude a separate peace with the enemy. Having sown the wind the Nazi, Fascist, Yellow Peril, will soon reap the whirlwind.

General Archibald Wavell, brilliant British General who knocked the Italians around in the first Libyan offensive, has been named commander-in-chief of all the allied forces in the Far East. His task will be to unify all available forces of the allies in the Far East and prepare the groundwork for the grand offensive that is to come. The General is 58 and is considered the first really great British officer to come out of this war. Upon his shoulders has been placed a terrific responsibility.

Sunday, January 4, 1942: —It's hard to remember that this is Sunday, the day of worship and rest. In war time it seems there is no rest. We worked eleven hours today. Sales of Defense Savings Bonds have increased by leaps and bounds. Since Pearl Harbor our output has more than doubled and will have to increase much more if we are to catch up. And this in spite of the fact that no drives such as were made during Liberty Loan days have yet been started. The Treasury Department is contemplating one, however, to commence about January 10. It is only the beginning.

News reports today tell of brutal treatment of whites in Manila. The Japs are apparently venting their wrath not only upon captured Americans but upon all members of the white race, including Germans, Italians, and Spaniards. That old bogey man known as the "Yellow Peril" has really come to life. The struggle may yet develop into primarily a racial war. The Japs are attempting to lure the Filipinos away from the Americans on racial issues, but so far, without success. The record of the Filipino defenders has been one of loyalty and bravery. No doubt they realize their fate and independence are safer under the U.S. than they would ever be under Japanese domination.

The Russians are continuing their mighty offensive with the Germans apparently unable to check the drive. Already the Red Army is vowing to clear Russian soil of all Nazis and carry the war to where it will hurt the worst—to Germany itself.

Monday, January 5, 1942: —American Army four motored bombers today succeeded in dropping a few reminders on the

Japanese Navy, reminders that we have not forgotten Pearl Harbor. Preliminary reports state that one enemy destroyer was sunk, a battleship damaged with three direct hits. Many auxiliary vessels were also damaged. The raid was off Davao in the southern Philippines where a large portion of the Jap fleet has been based. Our planes returned unscathed.

The fortress of Corregidor in the harbor of Manila still holds firm. Many vicious aerial attacks have been beaten off with 15 or 20 of the enemy bombers being shot down. Corregidor will be an expensive nut to crack. Meanwhile, General MacArthur's forces, digging in on the jutting tongue of Manila Bay, today beat off a frontal attack by superior numbers of Japs while inflicting heavy casualties. Apparently the American and Filipino forces have decided on a last ditch fight to the finish. Their delaying action is a vital link in the over-all strategy of the Allies.

Today in San Francisco the Examiner and other agencies instigated a "Buy a Bomber for Uncle Sam" campaign. Contributions, large or small, will be gladly accepted until the $300,000.00 necessary to purchase a flying fortress is accumulated. San Francisco's bomber can then carry our answer to Japan's treachery. REMEMBER PEARL HARBOR!

Tuesday, January 6, 1942: —Today President Roosevelt presented his plan for an "all out" victory effort. A tremendous program it is. He calls for the production of 60,000 planes this year, 125,000 next; 45,000 tanks this year, 75,000 next; 20,000 anti-aircraft guns now, next year 35,000; eight million tons of shipping in 1942, up to 10 million in 1943. It is such a program that if achieved it will leave the Axis nations hopelessly behind. Several U.S. Senators whistled incredulously at the President's figures but generally the Congress and the people accepted it as a goal at which to aim and to attain if superhumanly possible.

In addition to his production forecast, the President also hinted at a huge AEF (American Expeditionary Force) to be used anywhere in the world. This is the tragedy of the whole business. All of Europe and Asia combined is not worth the blood of any one of our boys who must lay down his life on foreign soil. But the attack has been made on us. We must defend ourselves and strike the enemy wherever he may be, preferably on his own soil. We must bring home to him the seriousness of the crime he has perpetrated.

An interesting sidelight on the war occurred today. Jack Dempsey, the greatest heavy weight champion of all times, today enlisted in the army as a buck private. If he is accepted—he's in his late forties—he hopes to meet up with Max Schmeling when he gets to Berlin. Jack also says he's got the proper answer to some of those Japanese Jiu Jitsu tricks too.

Wednesday, January 7, 1942: —Tonight's newspaper had the figure $77,000,000,000.00 spread across the front page in big black type. Now, undoubtedly that's a lot of money. How much I don't know, nor does anyone else because it's beyond the conception of the human mind. But according to President Roosevelt that is the amount that the U.S. is going to spend in the next 18 months. A billion dollars a week for war. A billion a week for destruction. What this vast expenditure will mean to our way of life, our standard of living can only be imagined. That it will mean the end to a lot of comforts and conveniences to which we have become accustomed is inevitable. Food and clothing will be scarcer and more expensive. Automobiles, tires, batteries and gasoline will almost disappear. Rationing and heavy taxes will add their burden to the pile accumulating on the shoulders of the common man.

All this adds up to the incontestable fact that the old and comfortable American way of life is going, perhaps never to return. It will leave a nostalgic memory in the hearts of the people who were fortunate enough to live during the most pleasant era of American history: An era that catered as never before to the comforts and convenience of humanity. An era that put to use all of man's productive genius to improve and brighten the everyday lives of the people—a genius which will now go to destructive purposes. A period when leisure time was important, when men were valued for their ability to invent constructive gadgets, not murderous weapons. A time when sports and human enjoyments were encouraged and the pursuit of happiness was man's principal vocation. To that era—Adios!

Thursday, January 8, 1942: —Nothing startling in the war news today. All the major battles now in progress seem to have settled into endurance contests. The battle for Singapore appears to be the most crucial. It looks as though the Japs are putting everything they have into this drive. After all, Singapore is really the key to the whole southeastern Pacific area. Once the Nipponese have captured this stronghold they will be doubly hard to dislodge. For this reason, leaders in the British Parliament today demanded in no uncertain terms that reinforcement be immediately dispatched to the Malay Peninsula.

More details were revealed today about the heroic stand of the U.S. Marines at Wake Island. Seven Japanese warships and numerous enemy planes were destroyed by the Marines before the sheer weight of the foe's numbers settled the issue. Citations for high courage and brilliant fighting ability were made. The stand of the Marines on this tiny Island is fully entitled to stand side by side with other historic last stands.

British and American-made planes today raided Bangkok, the capital of Thailand in what was described as a successful attack on enemy installations.

Civilian Defense is the most talked of issue in the legislative halls of the nation today. Some dissatisfaction is shown in the progress of Mayor La Guardia's organization to date. The Mayor should realize that the task is much more than a part time job. In their opinion he should devote himself to one or the other—not both.

Friday, January 9, 1942: —The war seems to have settled down into a regular routine at last. The preliminaries are just about over and the contestants are warming up for the main event. That the preliminaries went to the Japanese is beyond doubt. But it's the main event that pays off.

Speaking of main events, Joe Louis, the heavyweight champion of the world, and Buddy Baer, 250 pounds of punching bag, met tonight in what was to have been a fight. Louis' proceeds were to go to the Navy Relief Fund and apparently the Brown Bomber didn't want to overwork for nothing. In just 2 minutes and 56 seconds of the first round he bombed the big Baer into a worse wreck than Rotterdam. It was all over before the heavy paying spectators had settled back into their seats. It was just no contest. The Navy and Louis were the only ones that were happy about it, the Navy because of the $125,000.00 they got and Louis because he was tired and wanted to go back to sleep. He hates to have his rest disturbed by such trifling and boring details.

It's too much to hope that the War's main event will prove to be such an easy task as was Louis'. We will have to train and prepare a lot longer. Even then the fight will doubtless be a long, hard one. The treacherous foe has sneaked in a few crippling body blows ahead of the bell and it will take a little while to recover. But we have only just begun to fight. Our turn will come and when it does . . .!

Saturday, January 10, 1942: —Singapore, the gateway to the East Indies is in dire peril. The British just don't seem to be able to stop the Jap drive. The little Orientals are adept at jungle warfare. Their tactics are superb. In small bands or even singly they infiltrate the British lines and wreak havoc with communications and supplies. They hide in the tops of trees and pick off unwary troops. Utilizing their knowledge that Orientals all look alike to most whites, they disguise themselves as Malayans and stab their incautious enemies in the back. Feeding the natives inborn distrust of their white masters with tasty bits of propaganda they are making it exceedingly difficult for the British authorities to win cooperation from the native population. Their guerilla tactics are more dangerous and maddening than the steaming jungle, its snakes and vicious insects, and the tropical diseases, put together. Besides, the British are sorely under-manned, under-gunned, and under-planed. They haven't the equipment or the men simply because right up until it happened the Brass Hats were supremely confident that it would never happen. The Japs would back down.

The Philippine situation is not much better. Corregidor is still holding as are MacArthur's lines on the Bataan peninsula. Today was spent in heavy artillery duels preparatory to the final all out assault which the Nipponese are readying. Will MacArthur's army survive or will they too be annihilated? Will reinforcements arrive in time? Where and what is the U.S. Navy doing? The future holds the answers.

Sunday, January 11, 1942: —Worked again this Sunday. Makes it hard to keep track of the days. Sunday seems just like any other day. We are averaging better than seventy hours a week working time. This is one of the penalties of war but a necessary requisite for victory.

As though not satisfied to see any portion of this weary old world still at peace, the Japanese today launched their all out invasion of the Netherlands East Indies. Not content to concentrate on the Philippines or on the key point, Singapore, the Japs are further extending themselves in this third sea-borne invasion attempt. Their real strategy behind all these simultaneous moves is not readily discernible, unless they believe that they can, by these actions, prevent any concentration of Allied power to counter their attack. It would seem, however, that they may be laying themselves open to successful counter-attack by thus dispersing their strength before attaining any one of the three crucial objectives. If it were possible to cut their communications at any of the three points and isolate their invading force at that point, a major Allied victory might result. However, it may be that the Japanese feel that they are able to maintain complete control of the sea and air in the Southeastern Pacific area, especially since Pearl Harbor. So far they are right.

Reports are being received that the Chinese, from whom we have heard very little since December 7, are doing their bit by soundly beating a Jap army in a battle at Changsha. Chinee very much a contender yet.

Monday, January 12. 1942: —The Japanese invasion of the East Indies appears to be making some headway in spite of fierce resistance by the Dutch. The Dutch have been the toughest opponents the Japs have thus far encountered since the war began. The Dutch air force and submarines especially have done heroic service.

Singapore is still hanging in the balance. The yellow men have forced their way to within almost 100 miles of the Base. Allied air reinforcements are just beginning to be felt, however, and it is believed a determined effort will be made to save Singapore. The loss of this crucial bastion would surely lengthen the war by months or years. It must be saved!

It is reported today that an American transport has been set afire off the coast of Alaska. The ship and cargo have been lost but the personnel are safe. Whether this loss was caused by enemy action is not disclosed. The presence of the transport in Alaskan waters gives an inkling of what is going on. The U.S. forces are undoubtedly strengthening the fortifications and reinforcing the garrisons at Alaskan, Hawaiian, and Panama bases.

In this connection, one might have observed from the Peninsula commuter trains this morning, long lines of navy barges on a siding near San Bruno, stretching all the way to South San Francisco. There must have been several hundred barges, each loaded with gun carriages and boxed materiel. All are closely guarded by armed troops, and to follow them to their destination would answer many questions the layman is pondering. Are we to strike back soon—and where?

Tuesday, January 13, 1942: —Headlines tonight proclaim an important American victory. In a terrific artillery duel between General MacArthur's Philippine Army and the Nipponese forces, the Americans established definite superiority. Their well placed barrages shattered enemy tank and infantry concentrations and forced the retirement of the Jap big guns to safer and more distant positions. The first round has thus been won by our boys, but there are many more rounds to go—winner takes all. In truth, MacArthur's army is really in a very desperate position, its back to the sea with little hope of reinforcement and no hope of escape if things go bad. There'll be no Dunkirk from the Philippines. All we can do is hope that a miracle will turn the tide. The only alternative to a miracle is to accept the inevitable and strive for vengeance at some later date.

Yielding to a growing demand for one-man authority, President Roosevelt today appointed Donald Nelson, former Sears Roebuck executive, as the new production boss. Lack of efficient leadership with adequate authority and power has been the principal bottleneck in the Defense Program. Nelson will have approximately the same job as Bernard Baruch had in the last World War.

Just for the record it should be mentioned that the Nazis are going to great lengths to spread the report of much restlessness and dissatisfaction in Germany. It's an old and transparent trick to make an opponent overconfident and lax in their war efforts. But it won't work this time.

Wednesday, January 14, 1942: —Submarine activity has been observed off the east coast of the United States today. One freighter was sinking and others were attacked. This is the work of German U-Boats and only emphasizes the fact that we are faced with what we hoped would never happen, a war on both oceans at once.

For the first time news reports tell of U.S. planes and pilots aiding the Dutch in fending off the attack against the East Indies. In one sortie the Americans destroyed two enemy fighters and broke up one landing attempt. It is not clear, however, how successful the Japs have been so far in their thrust at this fabulously wealthy area. That they have sea control and are landing many troops with slight resistance is apparent. However, they are not getting much booty because the Dutch have adopted the "scorched earth" policy of the Chinese and Russians. It seems contrary to all human concepts to deliberately destroy wealth and property, but the only alternative is to have them fall into the enemy's possession and be turned against us.

The Russians are still driving on, seizing upon the hope that the invader may yet be completely ousted from the country before spring. That is a trifle over-optimistic. The Russians have done well indeed but the Germans are far from beaten. Spring will find them ready to go on the offensive again. It is then that the Red Army will meet its supreme test.

Thursday, January 15, 1942: —Today an American submarine was credited with sinking a 17,000 ton Japanese liner, one of the most luxurious and fastest of the Yawata class. Our subs are giving the Dutch considerable competition in slugging the Japs.

The army today announced plans to double the present size of the armed forces. They figure on having 3,600,000 troops in the field this year. This is in addition to a million men in both the Air Force and the Navy. These figures are just starters, like the defense budget of a year ago. An army of this size means that all registered men will have to be reclassified to get at a lot of those who were originally deferred because of minor defects. For example, they will probably draft my younger brother now. Originally he was placed in Class 1-B due to faulty teeth. Also those fellows who have married since the start of the draft may expect to receive their calls. Before long they may even get to men like me who are within the age limit but are married with several dependents. In my individual case, however, my work may be considered essential to defense. Nevertheless, I shall welcome a call and will do anything or go anywhere that will be of the most value in beating the Nation's enemies. That is for the record and nothing further need be said. My only desire is to do my bit.

A hint of what may be coming is contained in a Tokyo dispatch that claims that Nipponese troops captured supplies of poison gas from the American forces in Manila. This falsehood is probably the opening excuse for the Japs to launch this horrible form of warfare.

Friday, January 16, 1942: —The sinking of five more Jap vessels is claimed in the U.S. Navy's communiqué today. Part of this damage was done by surface vessels showing that the much-wondered-about Pacific Fleet is actively engaged in tracking the enemy down and destroying him.

More encouraging news comes from Luzon. General MacArthur's gallant defenders of the Bataan peninsula have thrown the Japs back time after time. Already the Jap schedule for the capture of the Philippines is a week behind and it appears that our forces can hold out either on the peninsula or on Corregidor Island indefinitely. Give 'em hell, boys!

The Singapore situation is still obscure but apparently desperate. Fresh Australian troops have been thrown into the struggle in an attempt to save the day. Man for man, gun for gun, the Anzacs are twice as good as the vicious little Orientals. The only danger is that there will be more than twice as many invaders as defenders. The Aussies have sworn not to retreat and they usually do exactly what they say. Their reputation as fighters is second to none. A high American army officer once said, on visiting Australia, that he liked to visit that country because the people look like Americans and fight like Americans. They're our kind of warriors. Let's hope that they more than live up to their reputation.

The spotlight of the world is on this bitter fight for Singapore. Upon the outcome of that struggle hinges the possible fate of the entire Far East.

Saturday, January 17, 1942: —Huge red headlines today announced that Carole Lombard, the famous actress and wife of the great screen lover, Clark Gable, together with 20 other persons, was killed in the crash of an airliner last night. This is really war news because the actress was engaged in a defense bond drive at the time of the tragedy. Clark Gable had chartered the plane to take Carole and her party over the country to help sell bonds for war financing. Included in the party were fifteen army officers. Apparently the ship flew head-on into the rugged sides of Spring Mountain in Nevada. The plane exploded upon impact and everyone was burned beyond recognition. It was a terrible blow to filmdom and to everyone, as she was one of the most popular actresses on the silver screen. Just one more score to settle with the Japs.

Helping to settle with the Japs today was an American submarine which sank three more enemy merchantmen. In a daring raid into the most closely guarded waters of the Japanese empire, the very, very private waters of Tokyo Bay, the U.S. sub chalked up 27, 28, 29 on the list of enemy ships sunk by the U.S. Navy since December 7.

This record would not be complete without mentioning the historic conference of foreign ministers of the North and South American republics meeting in Rio de Janeiro. It is expected that all nations will give evidence of their solidarity with the U.S. by jointly severing diplomatic relations with the Axis powers. Only Argentina, as usual, is bucking the resolution at all. It is expected that she will come through, however, but not without assurances and special concessions from the United States.

Sunday, January 18, 1942: —Another Sunday has rolled around but it was just another day of work for me. We haven't had any time off since the New Year began. It has been almost eighty hours of hard work per week recently and the pace is beginning to tell—I just don't seem to be able to get enough rest. I hope the damn Japs are satisfied.

War news is rather scarce tonight. The most important battlefront is still Singapore, where the Australians have taken over in an attempt to stabilize the situation. Submarines, undoubtedly German, are making it miserable and dangerous for shipping all along the eastern seaboard.

Visible from one of the windows at the Bank is the superstructure of a U.S. battleship, said to be the Pennsylvania, which is tied up in dry dock for repairs. The vessel was damaged in the Pearl Harbor attack. Apparently she was struck by several bombs as repair crews are mending rents torn in her

31

superstructure. The Pennsylvania is a huge ship, one of the biggest and most powerful of the U.S. Navy. The Japs probably struck a heavier blow on December 7th than has ever been divulged. Someday the full truth may be known. What we may be certain of now is that the Navy will somehow, someway get its revenge. They have not, they will never, forget Pearl Harbor.

For the first time in over a month, my wife and I went to a movie tonight. It was Bob Hope in *Nothing but the Truth,* and afforded us some much needed amusement and a lot of good belly-laughs.

Monday, January 19, 1942: —Latest news flashes don't sound so good. It looks like Singapore's fate is sealed. Many experts are already conceding its fall. It seems to be one of those all-too-frequent occasions of "too little, too late." Lack of foresight and realization of the danger which confronted them have been the main weakness of the Allied leaders. From all reports the defenders of Singapore, like all the rest, just wouldn't believe that "it could happen here."

Sub warfare off the Atlantic coast has reached serious proportions. Twenty three members of the crew of an American tanker were lost today when their oil-laded vessel was torpedoed without warning. The ship burst into flames and many of the crew were burned to death. That sort of thing is terrible on land, but at sea it must be a doubly horrible experience to go through. Some survivors have been rescued.

The Red Army in Russia and the British Imperials in Libya provide the only cheerful aspect to the war from the Allied point of view. The Russians are still driving ahead and there are signs that the Nazis are becoming desperate. The Russians are drunk with victory and cannot be stopped, at least not for the winter. It'll be a long road back for the Germans in the spring. Maybe so long they'll never make it—we hope.

Tuesday, January 20, 1942: —The Yanks are striking back according to the news reports of today. In one of these daring, hit and run attacks that catch the imagination, a U.S. torpedo boat slipped into Subic Bay under heavy gunfire and blasted a 5,000 ton Jap vessel out of the water. The torpedo boat escaped without casualties. In the southern Philippines, Army bombers successfully attacked an enemy cruiser, sinking her and setting a tanker afire. American Flying Fortresses have joined in the defense of Singapore, having attacked, with much success, two large enemy bases in Malaya.

Reports are received of another force of U.S. "forgotten men" still holding out against the Japs on the Island of Mindanao in the southern part of the Philippines. The soldiers had long since been given up as lost or captured but it is now revealed that they are still fighting a desperate last stand, with no hope of rescue. This war so far has been a succession of last stands by hopelessly outnumbered but heroic bands of Americans. Many fascinating and thrilling tales could probably be told if the facts were known. Dramatic stories of heroism, sacrifice, courage, and yes, even of cowardice and fear, will someday be revealed.

The principal villain, Adolf Hitler, today ends his first month as commander-in-chief of the invincible German Army. In that month he has not only failed to cover himself with glory but now finds his glorious army in headlong retreat, losing heavily in both men and equipment. May his future be even worse than his first month. If Hitler wants more territory, let's give him Hell!

Wednesday, January 21, 1942: —Probably the most important news today is the signing by the 21 Pan American Nations of the declaration of intent to break diplomatic relations with the Axis prepared at the Conference in Rio de Janeiro. This is the first time in history when absolute unity has been attained in Pan American relations. Even Chile and Argentina indicated their fundamental solidarity with the rest by signing the accord in spite of their reluctance to be drawn into actual belligerency. This action of our southern neighbors is undoubtedly the most staggering long range blow yet dealt the world's aggressors. It is a vindication of the "good neighbor" policy and evidence of excellent American statesmanship at the present conference.

General MacArthur's lines are still holding in the Philippines. Several frontal attacks by the Japs have been beaten off with considerable loss to the enemy. The Japanese pressure is constantly increasing, however, showing they are becoming increasingly anxious to conclude the Philippine conquest in order to throw their entire strength into the Singapore drive. For this reason, every day that MacArthur holds out on the Bataan peninsula is invaluable. Singapore's fate may well depend on the brilliant defense by the Americans in the Philippines.

Australia is becoming exceedingly fearful of an invasion attempt. The Japs have been raiding nearby islands and bases in force and the Australians have been warned to expect the worst.

Thursday, January 22, 1942: —Tremendous activity of the U.S. armed forces is hinted at in today's news. The transfer of over a half million troops to the west coast, destination a secret, was reported in Washington. We'll be hearing of a big offensive one of these days. Then the Japs will get an opportunity to see how Americans can really roll once they get started. Wait until those ex-football players begin carrying the ball and throwing a few blocks. The Japs will need more than their Jiu Jitsu tricks from now on.

But even at this moment General MacArthur's heroic troops in the Philippines are playing a pretty rough preliminary game. In his daily communiqué the American General states that the enemy is using his entire 14th Army, about 200,000 to 300,000 men, in a terrific effort to smash the U.S. defense lines on the Bataan peninsula. Until now they have not been successful. Eventually their weight of numbers alone, about 10 to 1, must tell. But every day's delay is extremely important to the Allied cause.

The amazing Russian drive in the bitter cold of the eastern front has not yet been stopped by the desperate Germans. Fighting effectively in cold as low as 50 degrees below zero, the Red Army is giving the mighty Reichwehr a terrible shellacking. Reports of growing discontent and rebellion in the Nazi ranks is encouraging but should probably be discounted.

We haven't had a blackout or "alert" for some time. It looks as though this war is settling down into a long war of work and endurance.

Friday, January 23, 1942: —When you stop to think about it, this war is really a terrific mess. There's no other way to express it. A mess—a confused, uncertain and spectacular mess! Just to take a glance at the daily papers will leave no doubt as to the accuracy of this statement. From London to Sidney, from Hong Kong to Washington; from Benghazi to Moscow to Berlin, the world has gone mad. No quarter of the globe has been spared. How can it—how will it all end?

This war is indeed the war men wrote and argued about constantly since the first Great War. This is the next Great World War that would probably mean the end to modern civilization. Sober, sensible men feared this catastrophe with a dread born of the knowledge of man's genius in producing engines of destruction. If this genius could but once be turned to solving the problems of peace with the same effort put forth in solving the stratagems of war, then there would be no more war and no more economic problems which culminate in war. Then would mankind be free, free to continue the pursuit of happiness for which he was created. Man is that he might have joy. Those are scriptural words. We can only hope with humble hearts that out of this mess will come a new civilization wherein men and women of good will may live together in happiness unmarred by the dangers of treacherous attacks by those who would rule the world by force and terror. Upon the heads of those criminals will be heaped the wrath of God until the earth is forever purged of their ilk and their kind will never again dare to encroach upon the rights and freedoms of those who, loving peace, are yet ready to die to obtain it.

Saturday, January 24, 1942: —President Roosevelt's Commission appointed to investigate the Pearl Harbor attack and to fix the responsibility for the Japanese success today submitted its report to the Government. Admiral Husband E. Kimmel, Commander-in-Chief of the fleet and General Walter C. Short, commanding General of the Hawaiian Department were accused of "dereliction of duty." All blame for the lack of alertness which permitted the Japanese to completely surprise the U.S. Armed Forces in the Pacific area was laid on the shoulders of these two senior officers.

The report prepared by Justice Owen J. Roberts, W.H. Standley, J.M. Reeves, Frank R. McCoy, and Joseph T. McNarney, set forth in detail the events that preceded and led up to December 7. In it the War and Navy Departments, the Secretary of State, Secretaries of War and Navy, the Chiefs of Staff and Navel Operations all had fulfilled their obligations well and had repeatedly warned and exhorted the responsible commanders in the Pacific. As late as November 27, 1941 these officers had been warned that negotiations with Japan were all but ended and a belligerent move by the Nipponese was expected at any moment.

In spite of this the commanding officers failed to confer or plan concerted action and allowed themselves to be lulled into a state of false security and unpreparedness.

Whether Admiral Kimmel and General Short will be court-martialed and further punished is not yet known. Both were relieved of their commands on December 22nd. They held the fate of the nation in their hands and failed. Navy and army traditions alone will mete out sufficient punishment in the unique way only military men can understand.

Sunday, January 25, 1942: —At last, a day of rest! Today we did not work. It is the first day off since New Years' day. Twenty-five straight days, averaging eleven hours per day. The bank officials felt that that was a long enough stretch and they are right. I didn't realize how tired a person could be until I really relaxed today. I slept until ten o'clock this morning and have loafed the rest of the day. I could hardly force myself to write this article.

Today another country declared war—not an unusual occurrence these days. This time it was Thailand, ancient land of the Siamese twins. Enraged by what they claimed was an unprovoked air attack on Bangkok by the British, this little country, which is already merely a puppet of Japan, formally declared war on Great Britain and the United States. At the same time they stepped up their attack on Burma which they had already invaded in conjunction with the Japanese. It was this same Burma attack that was the motive for the British raid on Bangkok.

The Singapore and Philippine situations have shown little change in the last two days. MacArthur is still entertaining a huge Jap army on the Bataan peninsula, thus upsetting the little yellow men's time table. Australian troops in Malaya have stalled the Jap push in that region also. Both positions are precarious however.

Rationing of sugar is to commence early in February, it was announced today. We can expect similar rationing of many foodstuffs. The pinch is only beginning.

Monday, January 26, 1942: —The U.S. Navy tonight claims the greatest naval victory since Admiral Dewey smashed the Spanish fleet in Manila Bay. In a terrific battle with a Japanese invading fleet in the Makassar Strait on the water approach to Java, our Navy sank eleven enemy vessels and battered 23 others. It is believed that an American torpedo crashed into a Jap aircraft carrier which later sank. The enemy invaders were completely smashed and with little loss to ourselves. It was the first major engagement for our Asiatic Fleet under Admiral Hart. The battle of Makassar Straits will go down in history as a great U.S. naval victory. The battle has been in progress since Friday and mopping up operations are still going on. [1]

Today is General Douglas MacArthur's 62nd birthday. The whole country is lavish in its praise of the General for his magnificent stand in the Philippines. President Roosevelt cabled him that the Nation is watching him with pride and gratitude. There is no doubt but that General MacArthur has done a brilliant piece of campaigning since the war started. Outnumbered 10 to 1 since the beginning he has outwitted and outgeneraled the Japs who have been forced to concentrate a huge army on the Philippines and have not yet been able to crush the small American force. Bataan peninsula and Corregidor still are firmly in U.S. hands.

Today, as a quarter of a century ago, an A E F (American Expeditionary Force) landed in the British Isles. Cheering Britons greeted the first thousands of doughboys who are "over there." Their crossing was safe and uneventful and a perfect secret until their arrival. The Yanks are coming—once again.

Tuesday, January 27, 1942: —The Battle of Makassar Straits continues on through today. The extent of the battle grows daily. It appears now that the Japs attempted to convoy an invading force of over 100 vessels through the narrow straits. The Dutch and American forces, both aerial and naval, pounced on them and wreaked havoc. More than 31 enemy warship and troop transports have been either sunk or crippled already. Thousands of Japanese soldiers have perished by shell fire or drowning. Included in the number of Jap warships either sunk or hopelessly wrecked were a battleship and an aircraft carrier. It looks as though the battle will turn out to be the most impressive Allied sea victory of the war, at least to date.[2]

Australia still has the jitters. They figure that they are next on the Japanese schedule if Singapore falls. They are probably right. Making concession to Australian demands for additional voice in the conduct of the war, Great Britain through Prime Minister Churchill announced that Australia would be represented on the War Cabinet from now on. The Anzacs, however, seem to be looking more than ever to the United States for help.

President Roosevelt today signed the first price control bill of the war. Emasculated by heavy opposition on its way through the Congress, the bill only makes a stab at effective measures for the control of inflation. Without control of wages, mere ceilings on prices of goods are not very effective. However, it is a beginning in the right direction.

Wednesday, January 28, 1942: —The climactic battle for Singapore approaches. The relentless drive of the Japs has carried them very close to the great naval base, in some places only 25 to 40 miles distant. The British, Indian, Australian defenders are digging in the last all important battle. The outcome of this battle may either shorten or lengthen the war by years. If the Japanese win and consolidate themselves in this area, it will take some powerful and very costly fighting to dislodge them. In fact it could probably only be accomplished by waiting until the vast armament program of the U.S. has borne fruit and overwhelming naval and air superiority has been attained.

Things look a little better elsewhere. U.S. Flying Fortresses are still carrying the attack to the enemy in Makassar Straits and continue to pick off the enemy transports, one by one.

Across the world, the Russians are maintaining their momentum against the tired, discouraged, and frozen Nazis on the eastern front. The Russians are becoming so bold and confident that they are beginning to sass the Japs as well and hint that they might decide to take them on too. If they can do this, it might take a lot of the pressure off Singapore and the Philippines. But Hitler is Russia's principal opponent at the moment and the Red Army will probably want to make dead certain of their success against the Germans before involving themselves in another major conflict. One fact stands out regarding Russia. They have proved that they were the most grossly underrated country in the world. History may consider Hitler's misjudgment of the Red Army his one great blunder—his Waterloo.

Thursday, January 29, 1942: —The headline news today is the overwhelming vote of confidence which Prime Minister Churchill received from Parliament. The vote was 464 to 1. Obviously the rotund, cigar mouthing Prime Minister is extremely popular with the British in spite of the serious reverses which England and her Empire have recently suffered. It is undoubtedly true that Churchill and Churchill alone injected that spark of fire and courage to the British people in their terrible hour of need that has carried them now to the point where it is possible to see a chance of victory ahead. He is truly a great leader.

Tonight, on two fronts, the armies of Churchill's Government are in serious straits. In Libya the Germans have rallied and recaptured Bengasi. The Nazi General Rommel appears to be very capable. In recognition of his prowess, Hitler today advanced him to the rank of Colonel General. In the Singapore battle things look very bad. The Japs are within 25 miles of the city and are inexorably advancing despite sanguinary losses.

Speaking of serious straits, the Japs have run into one themselves—the Makassar Straits. That battle is running into its sixth day and the Allies claim a bag of over 38 vessels out of the 100 ship convoy. Most of these have been accounted for by Americans and the Dutch. The British state that it is a victory to be compared with that of Jutland in the First World War.

A tale of horror comes out of the Atlantic tonight. A Nazi submarine torpedoed the Canadian liner Lady Hawkins and 250 passengers, including many women and children, burned and drowned to death.

Friday, January 30, 1942: —Blood, sweat, and tears. That is Winston Churchill's formula for victory. Very little of the old fashioned "Glory of War" theme in that promise. But for a nation that is attacked by aggressors there is no choice but to fight. Men die by fighting but nations die only by yielding. By this concept Rumania, Bulgaria, and their ilk will perish but the people of Greece, Holland, Norway, Yugoslavia and all the other peoples who rose to defend their homes and country will one day see their freedom restored and the conqueror driven from their lands. That this day will not be far off, countless brave men of the overrun nations of Europe have escaped and organized armies to continue the battle against Hitlerism. Their contribution to ultimate Allied victory will probably be very great.

The "sweat" part of the formula has already reached into American lives, at least into mine and the rest of the men at the Bank. Things have settled down enough so that we have arranged an eight hour day, six day week for the women employees. The rest of us are still averaging eleven or twelve hours per day. The work seems endless, but mine, at least, is interesting. The expansion has been huge. For example, in one division alone under my supervision, there were approximately 20 people prior to December 7th, now there are 79. And this is only the beginning.

The food pinch is beginning also. Today my wife tried to buy some table sugar. No luck. Apparently the warning that rationing is coming started a hoarding spree, causing an entirely unnecessary shortage.

Saturday, January 31, 1942: —The siege of Singapore is on! Will it prove to be another Verdun? Or will it collapse and fall after a brief siege as did Hong Kong. Knifing their way down the Malayan peninsula with the highly successful infiltration tactics they have employed since the beginning, the Japanese have completed the conquest of the peninsula in less than eight weeks of fighting. Outnumbered and tired, the defending British, Indian, and Australian troops suddenly decided on a similar maneuver that MacArthur so perfectly executed in the Philippines. The defenders suddenly abandoned their line about eighteen miles from the Singapore fortress and withdrew their forces intact into the strongly fortified island itself. Then the causeway connecting the island from the mainland a mile away was destroyed and the defenders settled down to meet the siege. Taken completely by surprise by the quick withdrawal, the Japs were unable to attain their objective of dividing and annihilating the defending army. This same strategy had enabled MacArthur to save his entire army with small losses and establish them strongly in a naturally well fortified area—the Bataan peninsula and Corregidor. Here they have successfully repulsed every effort by 200,000 Jap troops to dislodge them. Let's hope that the Singapore garrison will do as well.

An amazing sideline is the attitude the Nazi press has taken on the practice of the English and Americans of calling the

Japanese just plain "Japs." Insulting, say the Nazis. In retribution they have started to call the British "Brits." American and English editors are toying with the almost too perfect come-back. Call the Germans—"Germs."

[1] This was actually the **Battle of Balikpapan**, sometime confused with the Battle of Makassar Strait which occurred on February 4, 1942.

While a Japanese invasion force was landing at Balikpapan, on the early morning of 24 January, at around 02:45, the 59th US Navy Destroyer Division under Rear Admiral William A. Glassford and Commander Paul H. Talbot attacked the Japanese navy escort led by Rear Admiral Shoji Nishimura for about four hours. The U.S. Destroyer Division composed of Paul Jones, Parrott, Pope and John D. Ford attacked the 12 transport ships and three patrol boats escorting them. The Japanese destroyer escorts were undertaking a search for a Dutch submarine which had been sighted earlier. At least three transport ships, the *Kuretake Maru*, *Sumanoura Maru* and *Tatsukami Maru* and patrol boat *P-37* were sunk in torpedo attacks.

The battle was the first surface engagement, in southeast Asia, the United States Navy participated in since the Battle of Manila Bay in 1898. However, most of the torpedoes launched by the Allied destroyer missed the targets or did not explode. Because the landing had taken place around 21:30, the raid was too late to stop the capture of Balikpapan.

[2] Such incorrect and exaggerated reporting of events in the theater of war seem to have been the result of either deliberate misinformation being communicated by the military for propaganda purposes or the fog of war in the early days of the conflict was so thick that minor engagements were easily blown completely out of proportion by eager correspondents.

February

Sunday, February 1, 1942: —The U.S. Navy today struck back viciously at the enemy, feeding him a little of his own medicine. A strong attack force including two battleships, cruisers, and many aircraft surprised and heavily pounded two Jap bases in the Pacific. If I heard them right over the radio, the names of the bases are Marshall and Gilbert islands, two tiny but highly strategic stepping stones across the wide ocean. Severe damage was inflicted to shore establishments and many auxiliary naval vessels were sunk in the harbors. Two American warships were damaged and eleven aircraft failed to return. The significant feature of the attack is that the Navy is beginning to take the offensive in force. A really decisive naval battle could change the outcome of the war overnight. The war could be won or lost in an afternoon if the two main fleets could meet in a finish fight.

General MacArthur and his gallant army is still "giving them h—ll" in the Philippines. They have contemptuously refused two Japanese demands for a truce. The Americans feel they can hold out indefinitely and only hope for air reinforcement to attain the ultimate victory. One day's output of planes would turn the tide, they believe. The big problem is getting them there before it's too late.

On the home front the talk of coming shortages and sacrifices are more prevalent than are the actual scarcities. Shortages will undoubtedly come but it's this hording that causes unnecessary want that angers me. Such hoarding is only human, I guess, but it surely aggravates an otherwise mild situation—mild at least at present.

Monday, February 2, 1942: —Today's good news comes out of the Philippines. General MacArthur and his gallant army are making history on the Bataan peninsula. Today they decisively beat off two major frontal attacks by the best of the Jap troops. Two enemy divisions were practically wiped out. The Japs are continuing the attacks, however, with no thought for the terrible cost. Eventually the weight of numbers alone will probably wear the American and Filipino defenders to the point of collapse.

Allied prospects are gloomier in the other theaters of war. At Singapore an ominous silence reigns across the narrow strait of Johore where the huge Jap army is setting itself for the attack on the mighty fortress. American Flying Fortresses are aiding in the Singapore defense by bombing airfields and bases of the enemy far up the Malayan peninsula.

In Libya, the German counter-offensive is continuing to roll, pushing the British back another 100 miles. Large Nazi reinforcement plus the withdrawal of Australians to defend their homeland have contributed to the success of the counter attack.

In Russia the Red Army is losing ground in the Crimea but advancing rapidly in all other sectors.

On the home front the F.B.I. has announced that all important defense areas will be banned to enemy aliens effective almost immediately. This will hurt many innocent Italians and Germans who have lived here for many years, but through carelessness and oversight have failed to obtain citizenship. Now, many of them will be evicted from their waterfront homes and sent to do the best they can in unrestricted districts. Most of them are loyal to the government but must now pay the penalty for being careless about such an important thing as U.S. citizenship.

Tuesday, February 3, 1942: —News today centers around the gallant defenders of Luzon. Two more heavy assaults, these by night, were repulsed with great loss of men and equipment by the Japs. The accuracy of the American artillerymen is commanding a healthy respect from the enemy. The boys are shooting the big 155's with the accuracy of rifles. The Jap artillery is no match at all. In fact the Yanks are shooting up their gun emplacements as fast as they are established.

In another daring hit and run attack, a U.S. torpedo boat weathered terrific fire in the glare of spotlights and planted two torpedoes into the side of a Jap warship in the harbor of Manila. The U.S. boat escaped without damage.

The U.S. naval tanker Neches did not fare so well, however. The Navy announced her sinking from enemy action with a probable loss of 56 men. 126 survivors were rescued.

Singapore is being pounded by Jap planes in an evident attempt to soften it up for the frontal attack. Almost incessant raids have burned most of the island and caused many casualties.

The Dutch are getting their share too. The important naval base in Java, called Soerabaja I believe, was heavily pounded by Jap bombers and very considerable damage inflicted according to the Dutch communiqué.

Wednesday, February 4, 1942: —General Wavell, supreme commander of the Allied Nations in the Far East, today ordered the defenders of Singapore to hold at all costs. Formidable help is rapidly being organized and dispatched to their aid. He likened the Singapore garrison to the original British expeditionary force which stopped the Germans and saved Europe in the first battle of Ypres. "We must be worthy successors of such men", he said. The tide of battle will turn in the Far East as it has in Russia and as it did in the air war over England.

The German counter offensive in Libya is gaining momentum. Either the Nazis have received great reinforcements or the British have withdrawn too many of their crack troops for the far eastern battle. In any event the British are now taking the shellacking in Africa. This theater of war has certainly been a see-saw affair. Now it is the Germans who are rolling. They have recaptured Bengasi and Derna and are again nearing Tobruck, where the British forces made such a brilliant stand last year. Your guess is as good as anyone's as to how this African melee is going to turn out.

Yesterday the Office of Price Administration announced that sugar rationing cards would soon be issued. These cards will permit each individual to purchase 12 ounces of sugar per week. Retail concerns will be permitted to order only 80% of their normal purchases for 1941. This country is beginning to sound just like Europe did two years ago. I hope we've learned enough lessons so we won't end up in the same fix as did that unhappy continent.

Thursday, February 5, 1942: —F.B.I. agents today cracked an extensive spy and saboteur ring in Vallejo, California near the important Mare Island Navy Yard. Sixteen suspects were taken into custody. In their possession were U.S. Navy signal flags, illegal guns and radios and many cameras.

California, as you know, has a very large Japanese population. These, together with the thousands of Germans and

44

Italians living here, would make California a fertile field for such spies and saboteurs. However, I believe it would be a very dangerous condition, were it not that almost all of these people are really loyal Americans. But there are enough enemies among them to cause plenty of trouble in the event of a Japanese attack.

Singapore and Luzon both have settled down into that ominous lull that comes before the worst of the storm. Nothing but artillery duels are reported today. It is the Dutch who are getting the pounding today. The Japs are bombing the East Indies with all they've got, probably to prevent the forming of substantial help to relieve Singapore.

The Nazis in Libya are within 60 miles of Tobruck at the latest reports. They may turn the tables entirely on the British and even threaten Egypt again if something isn't done.

The Russians are still on the offensive, though not so successfully as heretofore from the drift of the reports. Either they are tiring or the Nazis are bracing.

Friday, February 6, 1942: —Rain made the headlines today. Northern California is a quagmire from almost incessant rains for the past two weeks. Four people were killed and great property damage caused by landslides. Several houses in San Francisco itself were torn from their foundations when a hillside grave way. A woman was buried alive in a mountain of mud. Her body has not been recovered. It's not only a war with men but with the elements as well. Life is really an eternal struggle against obstacles of all kinds.

More horror stories come out of the Atlantic and Pacific sea lanes every day. The present one tells of the torpedoing of the American tanker India Arrow off the Atlantic coast. Twelve survivors relate how the torpedo ripped the ship apart without warning, plunging dozens of men into a sea covered with flaming oil. Twenty six men died horrible deaths. The survivors battled for two days against the sea before being rescued. Death is certainly having a field day on this old planet of ours.

News out of Germany today indicates that there is considerable dissatisfaction among the people. Propaganda Minister Goebbels attributed it to the fact that the people are "over-worked and irritable." A more individualistic race of people than the Germans would not have put up with one half of what the Germans have gone through since Hitler came into power. But these people seem to like the iron rule of dictatorship. They like to be told what to do and when to do it. Bismark once said that "he was sick and tired of ruling a nation of slaves." Hitler is now slaughtering these "slaves" by the thousands with but few complaints.

Saturday, February 7, 1942: —Tragedy follows upon tragedy in these troublesome times it seems. Today a Navy submarine was rammed and sunk by another U.S. vessel near Panama. The commander of the sub and two men with him on the bridge of the undersea boat were thrown clear by the collision and were rescued. The rest of the sub's crew went down with their ship. Some were trapped alive in the hull and succeeded in getting a message to the surface by signal gun but there was no chance of rescuing them. A slow death from asphyxiation was their lot.

The assault on Singapore has not yet begun. The Japanese are gathering their forces across the mile wide Johore strait and we can expect some real fireworks from there pretty soon. It is believed that the Singapore garrison has been heavily reinforced and perhaps the Japs will get a warmer reception than anticipated. Let's hope so at any rate.

Admiral Kimmel and General Short, the scapegoats of the Pearl Harbor debacle today asked for retirement. Kimmel is 60 and Short is 61. Both have splendid records of service prior to the surprise attack of December 7th. It's a pity such careers should be so tarnished at their end. These officers were no more asleep than the majority of Americans. But upon their shoulders had rested the responsibility of guarding their nation's safety from just such treachery. Their failure will undoubtedly result in the loss of countless precious lives and inestimable wealth. They fell down on the cardinal law of every military force, even the Boy Scouts. ALWAYS BE PREPARED!

Sunday, February 8, 1942: —It has been such a peaceful, beautiful day today. The sun was warm and bright all day without a cloud in the sky. The neighbors spent the day cutting lawns and puttering around their gardens. It seemed more like a day in June than the 8th of February. It seemed so good to loaf around and bask in the sunlight. The cares of the world were gone like the rain of the previous week, all dried up and evaporated in the exhilarating warmth of the sun. It's hard to be angry at anyone, even the Japs, on a day like this. It's more a day for peace, for communion with God and your family—or maybe a round of golf. Certainly not a day for war and destruction.

But far across the Pacific, the little yellow men of Japan have other ideas. The attack on Singapore has opened. The first feint of the frontal assault across the strait of Johore was beaten off by the defenders. But the Japs are just feeling them out, looking for a soft spot. When they really come they'll come in droves, heedless of losses. They'll come stealthily at night, in disguise, by parachute, by transport, by glider, by every diabolical method that Jap or Nazi can devise; there'll be no let up until the decision has been reached. The world hangs breathless on the outcome of this crucial battle.

President Roosevelt today announced that the U.S. Air Force would be immediately expanded to 2,000,000 officers and men. An astronomical figure a few months ago, now it caused barely a ripple of comment. Big figures are a dime a dozen these days. The question is: How much is just talk? How much action?

Monday, February 9, 1942: —Today the Nation went on Daylight Savings time, to be known as War Time from now on. At two A.M. the clocks of the country were set one hour ahead. This morning it was still dark as I left for work. The clock said 7:30 but the sun just ignored the law. Independent cuss, I guess. All in all, I think it is a good idea. About ninety percent of the people seem to like it, especially in the summer time. Some folks, for example, the theater owners, fight the idea because it presumably injures their business. But the purpose is to get the most out of the daylight hours, both in work and in power conservation.

The Battle of Singapore doesn't look so good today. Already the Japs have forced a landing at one spot on the Island. The Australian and British defenders are fighting desperately but appear to lack that all essential element of air support. The Japs still have that vital superiority in the air without which victory is impossible in the modern version of war.

The great French liner Normandie, which the U.S. Government took over recently for army service and renamed the

Lafayette, was burning today, set afire by accident by sparks from a welder's torch. A $60,000,000.00 luxury liner in pre-war days, the great ship was being reconditioned either as a troop transport or an aircraft carrier.

The Russians are still winning in Russia, the Germans are winning in Africa, the Japs are winning in Singapore, and the Americans - - well, let's wait and see.

Tuesday, February 10, 1942: —With an ignominious splash the great liner, Normandie (now the Lafayette) capsized today. Waterlogged and topheavy with ice, the former luxury liner toppled onto its side at its Brooklyn pier. All efforts to prevent the calamity failed in the 20 degree temperature which almost immediately solidified the tons of water poured on the vessel by the firemen. Engineers claim the great ship can be righted and repaired but it looks like a big job.

The crucial Battle of Singapore appears to be nearing its climax today. It's the same old story. The British were not prepared. The Japs, with their tremendous superiority in the air are landing troops at several beachheads on the island almost at will. Courageous but ineffective resistance is being made by the defenders. Not only are the British outnumbered in the air but are outgunned in heavy artillery, and outmaneuvered in general tactics. It looks as though the fate of the vital bastion is sealed. It will be a tragic defeat for the Allied Nations and will make the road back doubly difficult.

The only bright spot in the far eastern situation is still with the Americans on Luzon Island in the Philippines. General MacArthur and his men are still taking on all comers and winning every round. Constant and ever increasing pressure by great numbers of fresh Jap troops is the real danger. Someday the gallant American boys and their Filipino comrades are going to collapse from sheer exhaustion. But no matter what the eventual outcome, their stand is an epic without a peer.

Wednesday, February 11, 1942: —The news from Singapore grows worse hour by hour. It's hard to believe that the great base, considered impregnable only a little while ago is being invested by the enemy with so little apparent difficulty. The lack of preparation is appalling. The story is that the big guns of the island are worthless in this fight, being able to fire only in one direction, that is, towards the sea.

It is said that the British spent over $400,000,000.00 on the defenses of the great Naval Base during the last few years, yet no real defenses were ever prepared against the possibility of a land attack from the rear. Dependence was placed entirely on the steaming Malayan jungles which proved to be duck soup for the Japs.

Today has been a black day indeed for the cause of the Allied Nations. Everywhere, even in Russia, the vicious Axis hordes seem to be successful. In Russia, the Nazi lines are stiffening and the evidence is that the Red Army's offensive is nearing an end. Spring is not far away. Beware!

The disaster at Singapore indicates that a long, hard war may be expected. The gallant Dutch are really in a precarious situation. It is hard to see how they can expect to hold the East Indies with all its fabulous wealth once the Japs have consolidated themselves at Singapore. The time has come for positive, aggressive action by someone other than the Axis. How long is it going to be before the great potential power of the Allied Nations can be mobilized sufficiently to seize the initiative from the Japs. A great shakeup of Allied leadership will probably result from this defeat. The time has come for younger, more aggressive men to take over.

Thursday, February 12, 1942: —Lincoln's birthday today but work just the same. Today is a black one in this war, but I guess Abraham Lincoln saw many days that were far gloomier. Through all the terrible trials of civil war, amid more appalling inefficiencies and bungling than even that of today, the great President persevered and led his country safely through the storm.

At dawn today, as I walked to the depot to board the train for work, I saw a thrilling sight. With a rush and roar of high powered motors, the dawn patrol of P-38s, the Army's new pursuit planes, took off from the airport just across the Bayshore Highway. They made a pretty sight and encouraging too. It will be more encouraging when there are hundreds of them taking off instead of just a few.

In a daring dash today, the German battle cruisers Scharnhorst and Gneisenau and the cruiser Prinz Eugen, which had been cooped up in the French harbor of Brest, braved the Straits of Dover and escaped towards Kiel. A terrific battle was fought in the straits and ended definitely in a German victory. The British lost 38 bombers and fighters, the Nazis only 15. Another case of surprise and flat footedness on the part of the Allies.

Singapore still hangs on but has been given up as lost in London. It is merely a mopping up operation for the Japs.

The only bright spot in the day's news is a belated recapitulation of the damage done by the U.S. Navy in the recent attack on the Gilbert and Marshall islands. A Japanese aircraft carrier and numerous war vessels and planes were reportedly destroyed.

Friday, February 13, 1942: —Friday the 13th today and it really lived up to its reputation. Everything seemed to go wrong. The alarm clock didn't ring and I missed my train, missed my breakfast, couldn't get the car started at first, and was almost late for work. Then, to top it all off, things got into such a jam at the Bank that we didn't finish until midnight. Ten minutes for lunch and fifteen for dinner. What a day! Talk about your war. Work itself is a civil war without the bloodshed.

To the amazement of everyone, Singapore is still hanging on. The Japs are paying heavily for every inch of ground. But that's all the consolation there is to it because it seems almost a certainty that the fortress will fall. The whole fate of the garrison appears to depend on the holding of two reservoirs from which the water supply must come. Lose those and the battle is over.

The surprising thing about the far eastern struggle is the tremendous amount of air power that the Japs have displayed. Where did they get it? In their struggle with China there was no indication that they could unleash such aerial strength. This strength has been the principal factor in the rapid conquest of the Malayan peninsula and Singapore. Clouds of fighters, screaming dive-bombers and effective level bombers have paved the way for the ground troops. To beat the Japs the Allies will have to muster huge air fleets that can more than match the enemy. This war has repeatedly demonstrated that without air support neither ground forces nor sea forces can hope to succeed. It looks like we will need those 185,000 planes the President requested.

Saturday, February 14, 1942: —The gallant Singapore defenders today even had enough strength to counter attack. Utilizing what few tanks were left to them they recaptured a number of strong points. But the Japs are swarming over the islands like flies—dying like flies too—and the position of the defenders grows more hopeless by the hour. Repercussions of the impending disaster are already being felt throughout the Allied Nations. London is boiling and Prime Minister Churchill is going to have to do a lot of explaining. It is already announced that he will talk to the people tomorrow.

Under the dark shadow of the Singapore defeat all other news seems unimportant. But the flame of war is flaring up here and there, now dying out, now breaking out with renewed violence and devastation. The Dutch pounced on a Japanese parachute invasion of Sumatra. The parachutists were "wiped out by the dozens." General MacArthur's sharp shooting artillerymen have driven the Japs to dig in on the defensive in Luzon. The Russians are still driving slowly yet steadily ahead around Smolensk, while the British have temporarily stopped the plunging tanks of General Rommel's Afrika Corps. The battle royal is really on, with the final outcome very much in doubt. There have been many knockdowns and drag outs, but the battle is only started. What a mess!

Today, tomorrow, and Monday the second registration of manpower will be made for selective service purposes. This registration covers all men from 20 to 45 years of age. Of course, those who previously registered in October of 1940 and members of the armed forces are exempt.

Sunday, February 15, 1942: —Well, it's all over! SINGAPORE HAS FALLEN! The first indication came when the Japs gleefully reported it over their Domei news broadcast. In a little over two months of fighting the Japanese have accomplished what the Allies thought impossible and for which the Japs themselves had allowed at least six months. The Japs' report told how the attempts of the British to pull another Dunkirk evacuation were smashed and the Commanding General finally asked to surrender unconditionally.

Confirmation of the worst came when Prime Minister Churchill, speaking somberly at one p.m. Pacific war time today, said that the mighty bastion was indeed lost; that the gallant defenders had been forced to capitulate to vastly superior Japanese units. In spite of this great and tragic defeat, Churchill still was defiant and pointed out that two all important events combine to make the outlook at present more optimistic by far than was the case even six months ago when he met with President Roosevelt on the ill-fated battleship Prince of Wales to draw up the Atlantic Charter. Then Russia was being beaten and the United States was only a benevolent neutral. Now the Red Army has turned the tables on the Nazi hordes and the overwhelming resources and power of the United States has been thrown wholeheartedly into the struggle on the side of the hard-pressed British Empire.

While the present looks bleak indeed, the Prime Minister promised that through blood and sweat the final victory would be on the side of freedom. Wait until the final campaigns of 1942 and 1943 have been written into the pages of history.

Monday, February 16, 1942: —The disastrous struggle for Singapore is today being unfolded in all its grim detail. The final capitulation ranks as one of the most bitter surrenders in all of British history. It is feared than over 60,000 of the finest Empire troops fell into the hands of the enemy. Japan today is celebrating probably the greatest victory in Japanese history.

The final days of the Singapore battle were described as a blazing hell, of screaming dive bombers and exploding shells. Hastily mobilized Chinese troops were sent out to help in the defense of the city, armed only with shotguns and knives with which to meet dive bombers and tanks.

The black news has swept over the British Empire like a cloud, giving rise to a growing anger that may even threaten the popularity of Winston Churchill. The English are getting awfully fed up with a steady diet of defeats. There is a great cry for new and more vigorous leadership. Churchill's cabinet at least will see a general overhauling.

The vivid drama of Singapore has somewhat dulled the news of the home front during the last hectic days. With the fall of the great stronghold the somber realization comes that now we are in greater danger than ever before. If the East Indies are now taken—and only a miracle can prevent it—we had better be prepared for the worst. Bombs over San Francisco seemed so remote not so long ago. Now take care!

Tuesday, February 17, 1942: —President Roosevelt today added his warning to the people that danger of enemy attack was very real and very threatening. Attacks from within are as likely and as dangerous as attack from without. The F.B.I. has swung into action and is rounding up enemy aliens in wholesale lots. Demands have been made that martial law be declared in California and that all Jap aliens and even American born Japanese citizens be removed to internment camps at once. All vital defense areas have been closed to aliens effective February 24th.

The Japanese campaign against the Dutch East Indies meanwhile is gaining momentum. The vital oilfields of Pelambang have been occupied. The Dutch however had set fire to the oil wells in accordance with their avowed scorched earth policy. The huge fires are visible for a hundred miles.

The next objectives of the rampaging Japs are Java, Sumatra, and then Australia. The Aussies have mobilized all available manpower in a frantic effort to prepare for the imminent invasion.

An interesting sidelight to the Pearl Harbor disaster was disclosed today. The destroyer Shaw that was reported blown up in the attack of December 7th today steamed into a west coast harbor under its own power. Both sides had admitted its destruction when bombs had found its magazines. The story today is that the vessel was in dry dock when the bombs fell. Its forward magazine exploded blowing off the entire bow. A wooden bow was subsequently fitted and the warship was brought to the mainland for complete repairs. She may yet get her revenge.

Wednesday, February 18, 1942: —The BayArea had another blackout tonight. The sirens wailed at exactly 9 o'clock p.m. and the "all clear" sounded 21 minutes later. We were caught at work and immediately blacked out according to standing instructions. The city seemed to be completely darkened from all that could be seen—or rather—could not be seen from the bank windows. There was no moon and, with a slight overcast to cover the stars, the town was as black as the far eastern situation. Only the occasional red gleam from the tail light of some parked car shown through the gloom.

Australia had its first bombing attack of the war today. Port Darwin on the northern coast was the victim. More of the same can be expected as the Japs are now based only 675 miles away on the Dutch island of Amboina.

Latest reports indicate that the Japs are about to launch their big push against General MacArthur's line on the Bataan peninsula. Accelerated bombing attacks and almost constant pounding by new batteries of heavy artillery are the lot of the heroic but exhausted American and Filipino defenders. Nevertheless, every report indicates that their morale is still very high and they command a healthy respect from the enemy.

The British, meanwhile, appear to be taking another beating in Burma. Rangoon is being evacuated by women and children and another last ditch fight is in prospect. Loss of the Burma road to China would be an extremely serious blow.

Thursday, February 19, 1942: —The Navy today released the first list of sailors, marines, and civilians being held by the Japanese as prisoners of war. About 2,200 were captured at Wake Island, Guam, Peiping, and Shanghai when the Japs overwhelmed those garrisons. Many San Francisco Bay Area men were included in the list.

The A.E.F. has landed in Java to aid in the defense of that last great stronghold in the Dutch East Indies. A small American air force is with them and has already joined battle with the enemy. Sixteen P-40 pursuit planes tackled over thirty Jap bombers and fighters, shooting down six to one.

The loss of Singapore resounded again in Britain today. Churchill formed a new seven-man war cabinet, eliminating Lord Beaverbrook, Minister of Production, Sir Howard Kingsley Wood, Chancellor of the Exchequer, and Arthur Greenwood, Minister without Portfolio. Sir Stafford Cripps, former ambassador to Russia was the outstanding replacement.

Sabotage and fifth-column dangers are giving the Government a headache. Plans are being rushed to evacuate, by force if necessary, all Japs, whether American born or not, from coastal areas. Curfew laws and "forbidden areas" laws go into effect February 24. Enemy aliens violating these laws will immediately be slapped into internment camps.

Port Darwin in Australia was bombed twice heavily today. Damage was reportedly considerable.

Friday, February 20, 1942: —The Army today was given a free hand to handle the alien situation. President Roosevelt ordered army rule over all strategic areas. All Japanese, even citizen Japs, may be removed from the Pacific coast. All this has come about because of startling evidence uncovered by the F.B.I. to the effect that an extensive network of spies and saboteurs is operating up and down the coast. In one raid alone the G-men picked up 2,500 rounds of ammunition, automatic rifles, signal guns, short wave radios, and cameras. It has been disclosed that several important aircraft plants and navy yards are completely surrounded by the residences of Japs and Italians. Nazi agents are very active also. In fact, Hitler once said that he could conquer America in six months from the inside.

The Japanese campaign against Java seems to be taking shape. The little island of Bali apparently has been invested by the Japs but Allied warships, aircraft, and fighting men were savagely trying to drive the invaders into the sea. U.S. forces are taking a more active part daily. An encouraging sign is the more frequent mention being made of the great Flying Fortresses in which category the United States is supreme. Enough of those mighty bombers and the tide of victory may well be reversed.

Sea warfare off both the Atlantic and Pacific coasts flared up again today. Submarines, in daring raids have torpedoed and sunk hundreds of thousands of tons of vital shipping right under our very noses since the outbreak of war. Lives, ships, and even more valuable cargoes have been sent crashing to the bottom within sight of our shores. What do the isolationists think of that?

Saturday, February 21, 1942: —I didn't realize one could get so tired. This week has been terrific. I have worked until after eleven p.m. every day except today. An enormous backlog of unfilled orders for savings bonds had piled up due to the inability of the Treasury Department to supply the necessary bond stock. The stock was finally received on Monday and we have spent the entire week in a frantic effort to catch up. By now we are up to date and the prospects are good that we may be able to stay that way. The first great rush for bonds has subsided and we should be able to eliminate the long hours from now on.

About the only good news from the Allied standpoint is the Russo-German situation. The Germans are still taking a beating from the Red Army. The way it's going, the amazing Russians may even upset the Nazi plans for a spring offensive. Some reports state that the Red Army has crossed the Latvian frontier. The Russians say that a good portion of their success is due to the war materials supplied by the Allies.

In spite of the terrific smashes by Allied warplanes and naval vessels, the Japs are moving ahead against Java. Notwithstanding all the courage displayed by the Dutch, Australians, English and Americans the Nipponese offensive appears to be moving according to schedule. You have to hand it to them, they have a well made plan and are carrying it out effectively. They must never again be underestimated. It's going to be a tough war.

Sunday, February 22, 1942: —Another birthday of that first great American, George Washington, has come. There are Americans today, in their fox holes on Bataan peninsula, who know what Americans under General Washington went through at Valley Forge. It was cold at Valley Forge; it is hot on Bataan, but the struggle is the same. Free men fought to remain free in those days, against heartbreaking odds. Today American men, with their stout hearted little Filipino friends, are proving themselves worthy of the heritage given them by the gallant men of Valley Forge. Out of a seemingly hopeless situation Washington's men emerged to glorious victory. A miracle may yet happen in the Philippines.

Enemy aliens by the hundreds are being rounded up on the Pacific coast since the army has taken over. Condemnation proceedings have been instigated against 1,500 Japanese and their properties near the vital Terminal Island ship building area in Los Angeles harbor. Dozens of dangerous Japs, some even with Imperial Army uniforms in their possession, have been lodged in jail in the Bay Area. Let's hope the situation is mastered before it is too late. At least the authorities seem awake to the danger. The principal contributing cause of the fall of France was the tardiness with which the Government took action against fifth-column activities.

President Roosevelt is to speak to the Nation and the world tomorrow evening. This will be his first report on the progress of the war since his statement on February 9th on the Pearl Harbor catastrophe.

Monday, February 23, 1942: —Tonight President Roosevelt made a fighting speech. "We'll win if we're tough!" he said. But we must expect more bitter reverses. But he is confident that the American people can take the worst with the best. The war will be first a production war. This we must first win. Then we will carry the fighting war to the enemy until he yells "uncle." Our objective must not be a "defensive" but an "offensive" war. The American eagle must be neither an ostrich nor a turtle, but a high flying, hard fighting bird worthy of its heritage.

Even as the President spoke the American coastline was undergoing its first actual attack of the war. The news flash came in that a large enemy submarine, presumably Japanese, had shelled an oil refining plant just north of Santa Barbara, California. About a dozen shells were lobbed into the plant causing only superficial damage. The most disquieting thing about it was the temerity and daring of the enemy, who leisurely conducted his "target practice" and then chugged away without even submerging. It is said that coast guard planes have taken up the chase, however.

Hitler, Hirohito, and their jackal Mussolini grinned with pleasure today as many defense plants closed to celebrate the holiday. At least that's the picture presented by most newspapers which were unanimous in condemning work stoppage on account of holidays. The trouble was, claimed both labor and employer, Washington's for not having settled the problem of double-time pay for holiday work. The employer wouldn't or couldn't pay it and the laborer wouldn't work for less—except in several notable instances where workers voted to work for double-time and to contribute it to the Red Cross.

Tuesday, February 24, 1942: —The British are still taking it on the chin in Burma. It looks as though Rangoon, its vital capital, is doomed. The British are already beginning to set the torch to everything of value which cannot be moved. If Rangoon is captured, the Japs will possibly be able to completely sever the famed Burma Road which carries vital supplies to China. What the effect of this loss would be on China and its war effort can only be conjectured. It could conceivably knock the Chinese out of the war.

On the eastern European front, however, the picture is more favorable to the Allies. The Russians are still driving ahead and today claimed a smashing victory near Leningrad. The 16th Nazi army of 45,000 men was shattered and at least 12,000 German dead littered the battlefield. Uncounted stores of war booty were captured by the victorious Red Army. I wonder how Hitler's headache is coming along.

The army and navy patrol bombers are still scouring the seas in an effort to apprehend the audacious raider who yesterday shelled the coast near Santa Barbara. This vicious attack has intensified the drive against aliens and fifth columnists as eye witnesses claim that signals were seen flashing between the submarine and some spot on the mainland.

Franz Von Papen, Nazi ambassador to Turkey, narrowly missed assassination today in Ankara. A bomb exploded within fifty feet of the Nazi and his wife but they escaped with minor scratches.

Wednesday, February 25, 1942: —Great excitement prevailed this morning in the Los Angeles area. At 2:25 a.m. the sirens wailed and the entire district was blacked out until 7:21 a.m. During the alarm actual planes, unidentified and presumably enemy, were sighted by spotters and hundreds of anti-aircraft batteries opened up with a noisy if not effective barrage. No bombs were dropped and no planes were shot down but some damage was caused by ack-ack shell fragments and several shells which failed to explode until they hit the ground. Five persons lost their lives during the alarm, either from accident or from heart failure caused by excitement.

The consensus of opinion among the people was that the raid was a false alarm, but the Army Defense Command stoutly maintains that it was a genuine alarm. Planes were indeed sighted by spotters and searchlight crews and did not identify themselves. Just another war mystery, I guess.

The Rangoon radio went off the air today, indicating that the Burmese capital either had been captured by the Japs or was being evacuated in great hurry by the British. Can no one stop these little yellow men?

The answer to this question is obvious. Yes, the gallant General MacArthur and his men are stopping them. A real stalemate has been reached on the Bataan peninsula, as the Japs seem to have given up the costly job of trying to oust the

Americans and Filipinos from their impregnable positions. They have decided now to sit down and wait for their ally—hunger, exhaustion, and lack of material reinforcements—to win the battle for them.

Thursday, February 26, 1942: —Many rumors have been spread regarding the "raid" on the Los Angeles area yesterday morning. The only facts that are incontrovertible are these: There was a five hour blackout; no bombs were dropped; no planes were shot down although anti-aircraft batteries fired 1,430 rounds of ammunition; no one can definitely prove that he saw planes; no fighter planes were sent up to meet the supposed invaders. It was serious business for both the army and the populace. The people did not get hysterical. Air raid wardens and police functioned very well. Secretary Knox of the Navy laughingly called the raid a "false alarm." Secretary of War Stimson, on the other hand, declared seriously that fifteen unidentified planes were known to have been over the area. They were thought to be commercial planes, probably operated by enemy aliens from hidden bases in the wilds of Nevada or Southern California. The purpose of the "raid" was probably to demoralize public morale and hinder defense work.

All in all, the consensus of opinion is that it is better to be over alert than not alert enough. The Army High Command has commended the actions of all defense units during the emergency.

The amazing MacArthur and his tiny Philippine Army today counter-attacked and gained several miles of the Bataan territory back from the Japs. The epic struggle of this little American band of heroes is astonishing military men the world over. Even the Japs themselves have tacitly admitted the superiority of the American force by abandoning their efforts to storm the U.S. lines even with vastly superior numbers. We could use a few more MacArthurs.

Friday, February 27, 1942: —Headlines tonight report that a great naval battle is raging off the coast of Java. It appears to be a major engagement between important naval forces of Japan and the Allied Nations. Upon the outcome of this one battle may hang the fate of the last great portion of the Netherlands East Indies—Java. Most of the wealth of this fabulously rich archipelago is located in Java. With its fall the Japs would have at their command enough raw materials and resources to supply them indefinitely with the sinews of war.

Vichy France made the news today. Much fear has been felt by Allied leaders that Vichy might go all the way in collaboration with the Nazis even to turning over the still considerable French fleet to the Germans. In line with this, Roosevelt warned the Vichy government on December 10th that any such collaboration in violation of the terms of the Armistice of 1940 would result in France being classified in the same category as the declared enemies of the American people. France has now assured Washington that she intends to maintain her neutrality to the letter.

A terrifying tale of Japanese espionage and fifth column work in California, especially in the Los Angeles area was disclosed by the Dies Congressional Committee on Un-American Activities. Complete maps of vital defense projects were uncovered as well as evidence of dangerous infiltration of Japanese aliens and American born Japs into defense areas such as Terminal Island and various aircraft factories. Let's hope effective action will be taken before its too late.

Saturday, February 28, 1942: —The great naval battle off the coast of Java appears to have resulted in total defeat of the Japanese invasion fleet.[1] Dutch and American sea and air forces inflicted terrible losses on the Japs, sinking several warships and many transports causing very heavy losses of men and material. The enemy fleet is in full retreat and nary a soldier has set foot on Java. Allied forces are pursuing relentlessly in an effort to completely smash this latest invasion threat. The extent of American losses have not been disclosed. From the size of the engagement they must have been heavy. I guess that is what we can expect in ever increasing ratios from now on. It will take some hard and bloody fighting to win this war. The tragedy of it is that human life means far more to us than it seems to mean to the Japanese.

Army and Navy authorities have far from finished with Pearl Harbor. Today they announced that General Short and Admiral Kimmel are to be court-martialed. The "goats" of that sad affair apparently are to be made to feel the full wrath of the military

Services. Their side of the story would undoubtedly make interesting reading. It is not known yet whether trial will be secret or public. In any event, the court will be composed of high ranking officers of the respective Services. Military law forbids the judging of a superior officer by his junior, unless absolutely unavoidable. The dates of the trials have not yet been set. They will be held whenever it is deemed that national safety will not be endangered or comfort to the enemy given.

[1] The **Battle of the Java Sea** was a decisive naval battle of the Pacific campaign of World War II, that sealed the fate of the Netherlands East Indies.

Allied navies suffered a disastrous defeat at the hand of the Imperial Japanese Navy, on 27 February 1942, and in secondary actions over successive days.

The main Allied naval force was almost totally destroyed: 10 ships and approximately 2,173 sailors had been lost. The Battle of the Java Sea ended significant Allied naval operations in South-East Asia in 1942, and Japanese land forces invaded Java on 28 February.

March

Sunday, March 1, 1942: —Today has been a glorious spring day. We basked, in shirtsleeves, in the warmth of a brilliant sun and contemplated once again the weaknesses of men that cause them to beat each other into bloody ribbons when there are such things as spring, and sun and warmth and beauty. It doesn't make sense, yet men haven't sense enough to sense the futility of such nonsense. Why kill and maim when there is so much joy and beauty to be found if one will but utilize the same effort he uses to make war in searching for the better things in life. But why muse. Man just doesn't do it. He prefers to suffer, I guess.

The reports of Allied victory in the Java war were, as usual, a bit premature. Although the Japs temporarily retreated, they came back and today succeeded in establishing several beachheads on the Java coast. Losses, however sanguine, apparently do not hinder this enemy. That's the successful way of waging war, I guess, whether we like it or not. Men are just so many "bullets" to be expended in accomplishing an objective.

The Japanese invasion of Burma also seems to be making headway. Although Rangoon is still in British hands, it has been evacuated and all military stores burned. Jap seizure of the vital port is momentarily expected. Aid for China will become increasingly difficult once the Burma Road is cut. The Japanese timetable seems to be still ahead of schedule. MacArthur alone has been able to upset to some extent the pattern of Japanese conquest. In this one little gallant band may rest the key to the eventual turning of the tide. God grant it may.

Monday, March 2, 1942: —Because of the critical state of affairs in Burma and India, General Sir Archibald Wavell has been relieved of his command as supreme Allied Commander in the Southwest Pacific and has been shifted to India to try and solve the difficulties there. The conditions in Burma especially are grave as it is reported that many native uprisings have made the British position almost untenable. It has not been decided who will be Wavell's successor as supreme Allied Commander but much agitation is being made to elevate General MacArthur to that position. It is more likely, however, since the Dutch have such a tremendous stake in the Southwest Pacific battle, that some Dutch officer will be given the job.

The Java battle is in that critical stage when the outcome is totally in doubt. Although the Allied forces are fighting stubbornly the long term defense of the vital island is very dubious. For some reason, the Allied Nations just don't seem to have what is needed, where it is needed, to stop the Jap plans. Those plans undoubtedly have been well laid and, so far, very well executed.

With a promise that the army and navy would soon be in a position to carry out offensive rather than defensive operations, President Roosevelt today announced the revamping of the whole organization of the U.S. Army to streamline it and eliminated cumbersome red tape and delay. Three unified major groups composed of the ground force, the air force, and the service of supply, are to function directly under the Chief of Staff. With all possible speed the war is going to be carried to the enemy.

Tuesday, March 3, 1942: —Well, the Javanese seem to be holding the Japanese, at least for today. Whether this is just the same old story that came out of Malaya and Singapore as well as the rest of the East Indies is conjectural. Time alone will tell. The Dutch have admitted that all of the major ships of their fleet have been sunk or otherwise put out of action. Thus deprived of most of their naval resistance, the Dutch can expect the Japs to augment their invasion army almost at will. The Tokyo radio claims already to have captured most of the island, including the important naval base of Surabaya, the last base big enough to handle capital ships in the Indies. The Japs are undoubtedly exaggerating but in the absence of very enthusiastic denials, may be coming pretty close to the truth. We shall see.

The U.S. Navy announced today that the Destroyer Jacob Jones was sent to his relative's locker by a Nazi submarine off the Atlantic coast. One hundred officers and men were lost; only eleven were rescued as two enemy hits detonated the destroyer's own depth charges, blowing the ship to bits.

Lieutenant General John L. DeWitt, commanding the Western Defense Command and the Fourth Army announced today that all Japanese aliens and Japanese-American born citizens will be evacuated from the entire Pacific Coast. Approximately 93,000 Japanese will be affected. Mid-west states will harbor them until the end of the war. Loyal Japanese are urged to evacuate voluntarily, thus saving a difficult, nasty job.

Plans for doubling taxes for the coming year were offered

by Secretary Morgenthau of the Treasury Department today. Taxes may well become confiscatory before the war is over.

Wednesday, March 4, 1942: —Like all the others, the battle for Java appeared to be entering its crucial stage today and it looks extremely bad for the Dutch. The Japs seemed to have won complete mastery of both the sea and air and were thus able to reinforce their attacking forces at will. Practically no hope is held that Java can survive. Australia will be next on the program. In fact, extensive bombing attacks have already begun on Australian towns and bases.

In a terrific aerial attack that out-blitzed even Coventry, the RAF today bombed the industrial area of Paris. Principal objective of the raid was the great Renault Motor Works which has been working 24 hours a day turning out planes, tanks, and other war material for the Germans. This plant was almost totally razed. In an effort to spare as many French lives as possible, the British had even broadcast to the French people that military plants in the Paris area were going to be bombed. In spite of this precaution and orders to pilots to bring back their bomb loads if they were unable to dump them on their objective, hundreds of French workers and civilians were killed. What effect this attack will have on the policies of the Vichy Government is to be seen. It may result in an open break with Vichy turning over the yet powerful French fleet to the Germans. Not much incentive has been given to attempt to placate the men of Vichy any longer and other munitions centers in France may expect bombs.

Additional groups of American troops are reported to have arrived in Ireland. These troops are not merely for show purposes. Some offensive is being planned which calls for the use of American troops in an effort to beat Hitler to the gun in his spring offensive.

Thursday, March 5, 1942: —"No use fooling ourselves," said Leon Henderson, National Price Administrator, today. "There'll be not one pound of rubber for private use soon." Thirty million passenger cars may be forced off the road from lack of tires before the war is over. The rubber shortage is so acute that tires of some private cars may be requisitioned for war purposes. The loss of the Dutch East Indies rubber supply is extremely serious.

Oh well, what with gasoline rationing not so far off, new car sales banned, and now no tires, we'll soon be back to the good old days of walking, bicycling, and riding the street cars. We'll get by.

General MacArthur's tiny air force today broke loose and sank more than 30,000 tons of Jap transports in the crowded waters of Subic Bay. Thousands of enemy troops were blown up or drowned in the surprise attack which apparently upset the Japanese plans for another big offensive on Bataan peninsula. The attack was a huge success and there were no American casualties.

MacArthur's stand, however, is the only bright spot in the Far Eastern situation. On Java the Allies are taking the usual beating. The Japs have won naval and air superiority and are blasting their way all over the island. Apparently Batavia has been captured and the island has been cut in two. The Dutch defenders are attempting to "pull a MacArthur" and set up some strong defensive positions in the mountains of central Java.

The Tokyo radio today admitted that Allied warplanes have raided Japanese held islands only 600 miles south of the Jap mainland.

Friday, March 6, 1942: —The situation in Java continues to be bad. Complete occupation by the Japs is probable. Allied bombers that have survived are being removed to Australia to bolster defense of that continent. It appears as though the Allied High Command has given up the Island of Java. It is said that American pilots of the big bombers were angered and disappointed that they had to withdraw because of the lack of adequate "fighter" support. Where are the planes to beat the Japs? Apparently they are still on the assembly lines.

In a noteworthy effort to speed up the production on that assembly line, workers at the great Bethlehem Steel shipbuilding yards today volunteered to donate a Sunday's work to Uncle Sam. Instead of the customary double time, they will work for nothing if the full benefit of their labor goes to the government. Their action shows that labor is willing to go all out in its effort to "beat the Japs." If management and labor will cooperate we shall have and unbeatable team.

One hundred fifty F.B.I. agents today swooped down on California's number one spy ring. More enemy supply "caches" were uncovered and several Japs, known as former members of the Japanese Imperial Army, were picked up. Plans to totally evacuate the Japanese, good and bad alike, from all coastal areas was given another impetus by the raid. No time should be lost. Obviously the Japs have laid extensive sabotage and fifth column plans for the "big day" of California invasion. When it comes let's hope we're ready. We don't want any more Pearl Harbors, Singapores, or Hong Kongs in this man's war.

Saturday, March 7, 1942: —With a note of sadness the official Java radio went off the air today. "We are shutting down now," the announcer said, "Good-bye 'til better times. Long live the Queen." Thus, apparently, has ended the short, epic drama of the East Indies struggle against the Japanese juggernaught. As all communications seem to be cut between Java and the rest of the anti-Axis world, it is presumed that the Japs have completely invested the island. It took only a week of furious fighting and again demonstrated that the Japs are tough customers. To beat them is going to be no picnic.

The next move by the Japs may well be Australia. The Australians expect it and are desperately preparing. In addition, it is reliably reported that thousands of American troops are already there and large convoys of soldiers, tanks, guns and planes are on the way. Australia must be held to be used later for a base from which to launch the inevitable offensive that will regain all the lost territory and drive the Japs back to Tokyo and Yokahoma.

The home front, meanwhile, has been comparatively quiet. Sales of defense bonds have leveled off somewhat resulting in more reasonable hours of work. Income tax time is here and probably accounts for the smaller amount of bond sales. "Pay your taxes and smash the Axis" is the slogan. More restrictions are being placed on ordinary peacetime goods. Civilian radio broadcasting is to be banned after April 22. No blackouts or other alarms have occurred for some time.

Sunday, March 8, 1942: —It has been another beautiful spring Sunday today. This is probably the most beautiful time of year in this locality. Everything is so green and fresh. The hills look like fairways, the valleys like green carpets. The sun is so warm and friendly, seems glad to be back up this way again.

Rather a startling announcement came from Berlin today.

For the first time since the beginning of the war, the Nazis admitted huge losses. In all the other campaigns they have claimed ridiculously small losses for themselves. Now they admit that more than one million, five hundred thousand men have been lost in the Russian war. If that is their admission, we may safely double it and come fairly close to the truth. That "six-week campaign" has certainly boomeranged. Even now the Russians are advancing steadily all along the front. Maybe the Germans won't even be able to get set for their expected spring offensive. The victory-scenting Russians are clamoring for the British and Americans to open up a new front, maybe through Norway where they could join in a common front with the Russians and perhaps finish off Hitler this year. Maybe it has possibilities. Once Hitler is out of the way, Hirohito wouldn't be such a tough job. The Allied Nations could really concentrate on the Japs then. Anyway, the Russians may have something there.

The "miracle" of Bataan continues. Enemy broadcasts hint that General MacArthur has a larger air force than anyone believes. They reported today to have raided and destroyed thirty or forty American planes on an airdrome behind the lines. We thought he had only two old hulks.

Monday, March 9, 1942: —Latest reports state that U.S. subs have been on the hunt again. Torpedoes inscribed with the slogan "Remember Pearl Harbor" crashed into five more Jap warships. A large destroyer and a tanker were definitely sunk and an aircraft carrier and three cruisers severely damaged. The Navy communiqué did not specify the locality in which the successful attacks took place but it is surmised that it was off the coast of Java.

Persistent reports from the Philippines state that the Japanese General Homma in charge of the invasion forces has committed hara-kiri over his inability to crush MacArthur's tiny army. He has been replaced by General Yamashita the conquering hero of Malaya and Singapore. This portends a terrific effort by the Japs to overwhelm the Bataan defenders and clean up resistance in the Philippines. Largely due to General MacArthur's magnificent stand, resistance by Moros and Filipinos all over the islands has intensified. The Japs, to their chagrin, have been obliged to maintain a disproportionately large force in the Philippines to handle the situation there. Let's hope our glorious heroes on Bataan will drive Yamashita and his entire ilk to commit their messy hara-kiri. Save us the trouble.

Now that the Japs have Singapore, Burma, Java and the rest of the Indies, the war has come to sort of an intermission period. The Japs apparently still have the initiative so it's a question as to where are they going to strike next. Will it be India? Australia? Alaska? Hawaiian Islands?

Tuesday, March 10, 1942: —A terrible, barbarous story of Japanese atrocities in the former British crown colony of Hong Kong was disclosed to the English Parliament by Foreign Secretary Anthony Eden today. It appears likely that the story is largely true as Eden stated that the Government was unwilling to publish any account of such atrocities until they were confirmed beyond the possibility of a doubt. "Unfortunately," he said, "there is no longer any room for doubt." He charged that 50 British officers and men were bound and used for bayonet practice. Women, both Asiatic and European, were raped and murdered and one entire Chinese district was declared a brothel regardless of the status of inhabitants. These atrocities were similar to the barbarities which aroused so much horror at the time of the Nanking massacre in 1937. So you see what we are up against in this war. This is no common enemy. He is a vicious, barbarous murderer with no consideration for any human rights but his.

The RAF has stepped up the tempo of their attacks on the industrial areas of both Germany and her slave France. Tons of bombs were dumped last night on the great Krupp arms factories at Essen. Paris radios went off the air indicating that the RAF was active in that area again. The power of Britain's bombing squadrons is slowly growing to the point where effective results may be had in their campaign to destroy Germany's industrial capacity and deal out to German cities a little of the medicine that was so "generously" given to English cities by the Nazis in 1940 and 1941. Revenge, though not a virtue, is sweet.

Wednesday, March 11, 1942: —Admiral Thomas C. Hart, retired commander of Allied naval forces in the Western Pacific (retired because of ill health), today reported in Washington that the Japs have won complete domination of the Western Pacific because of overwhelming superiority in the air. In every operation the enemy was able to dispose superior numbers of aircraft, thus winning the decision. But his victories have cost him dearly in shipping losses which may well cause him great concern in the future. Although the Admiral is in accord with the theory of "attack to win", he says that we must have more ships, more planes, and more men. In the meantime we will have to do the best we can with what we have.

The Japs are already pressing preliminary operations preparatory to invading the mainland of Australia. American and Australian flyers are pounding heavily at the spearheads of invasion, particularly at the Jap bridgeheads established on the island of New Guinea. Flying Fortresses were said to have either sunk or badly damaged at least seven enemy vessels without casualty.

In an effort to placate the teeming millions of India and possibly to enlist them whole heartedly into the war against Japan, Prime Minister Churchill today announced plans for the eventual granting of full dominion status to India. Sir Stafford Cripps, well known and trusted in India, is to go to that country to work out the plan. There is a source of untold manpower and wealth in India which if it can be tapped may well tip the scales in a hurry against Japan. Poorly used or antagonized, India, on the other hand, could sabotage and destroy the whole British war effort.

Thursday, March 12, 1942: —In a daring, lone-wolf raid deep into Japanese waters, a single U.S. submarine today was credited with sinking three big freighters and one passenger-cargo ship.

The stubborn, long-suffering Chinese army today took the offensive against the Japs in Burma. A spearhead of tough, seasoned Chinese regulars drove their way from Northern Burma into Thailand in the vicinity of Chiang Mai. The Chinese, apparently, do not stand in awe of the vaunted Japanese military might. Four years of bitter fighting with the little brown men from the Island Empire have taught the men of Chiang Kai-Shek that, given the material and equipment, they are more than their match. The British would do well to utilize the Chinese as much as possible in the defense of the balance of Burma and India.

Australian and American bombers are still pounding furiously at Japanese invasion fleets assembling off the coast of New Guinea. At least thirteen enemy troop transport ships have been sunk with heavy loss of enemy personnel. The Australian Prime Minister today transmitted an urgent appeal to President Roosevelt for increased reinforcements to repel the imminent Japanese invasion of the "down under" continent.

Angry mobs today rioted in Brazil in protest over Nazi torpedoing of Brazilian merchant ships in recent weeks. President Vargas of that powerful South American Republic indicated that a Declaration of War against the Axis nations may soon be made. All Brazilian ships have been ordered into safe ports until adequate convoys can be organized.

Friday, March 13, 1942: —The war in the Pacific is just a sparring match for the present. The Japs are feinting here and jabbing there. The latest stab is toward the Solomon Islands and the vital supply line from the United States to Australia and New Zealand. The jittery but unafraid Australians are desperately trying to complete their preparations for the expected invasion attempt. American and Australian heavy bombers continue to pound the Japs' advanced bases in New Guinea.

The lull continues in the Philippines. Reports state that Corregidor, the island fortress in the harbor of Manila, has stood up remarkably well under air attacks unparalleled in the war to date.

Here in San Francisco the F.B.I. has been making incessant raids on underground organizations of enemy aliens. Today, seventeen Germans, including at least one woman, were taken into custody. Well advanced plans for sabotage and other fifth column work were uncovered, involving such vital areas as Hamilton Field and the San Rafael Military Academy. The German-American Bund, which the country tolerated for so long, even to the point of defending its right to existence, appears to be at the bottom of all this Nazi underground work. Today's raids were the final ones before the mass evacuation of all enemy aliens from the Pacific Coast. The sooner we are rid of them the better—and safer. Undoubtedly some innocent and loyal aliens will suffer along with the guilty but we can afford to take no more chances with such vicious and unscrupulous enemies.

Saturday, March 14, 1942: —The Allied High Command and U.S. Navy today counted the toll that the United Nations' navies suffered in the bloody sea battle of Java. Thirteen warships of the United Nations were lost, including the U.S. heavy cruiser Houston and the U.S. destroyer Pope. Fighting for five days and nights against greatly superior enemy forces, that gallant ships and their crews went down in a blaze of gunfire. The Netherlands lost two heavy cruisers and two destroyers; Great Britain lost five destroyers and Australia lost one cruiser and a sloop. Enemy losses were uncertain. At least eight Jap warships were known to have been sunk but how many more were destroyed in the obscure and grim night fighting cannot be determined. Tokyo, of course, admits nothing; claims everything. But ships of both sides went out into the night and were never heard from again. Even the actual fate of the Houston is not known. With the Australian cruiser Perth, she contacted the enemy on the night of February 28. Neither ship has been heard from since. The next of kin of the crew have been notified. So ends another grand ship.

San Francisco was a quagmire today. When it rains here it isn't fooling. In spite of the weather, my wife and I carried out our plans today and did some very necessary shopping in the city. It's amazing how many soldiers and sailors are in the City; seems as though more than half of the people on the streets are in the military. Some of the boys, obviously from the interior, looked so forlorn and lonely here in the big city. Made you feel kind of blue when you think what is in store for many of them.

Sunday, March 15, 1942: —The master mind Hitler today announced revised plans for his crushing of Russian resistance. He complained bitterly that, although time and time again Russian armies were annihilated, they were replaced by new and fresh masses of soldiers. The Nazi dictator has postponed until summer his scheduled spring offensive to end once and for all the "Red Menace." This mad "genius" who has had to revise his promise to end the war victoriously from August of 1940 to September 1940 to sometime in 1941 to definitely in 1942, now admits that a long hard struggle is faced by the German Army. It's a different army now from the one that rampaged so victoriously over the fields of France in the spring of 1940—that great army has long since been buried, most of them in the cold, frozen earth of Russia. Even the leaders of the new army are different; the old

71

ones have resigned from "ill health", died of "heart trouble", or been otherwise purged. Somehow I don't believe this new Reichswehr has either the ability or "guts" of the original. Time, of course, will be the final judge. In the meantime, the Russian offensive is still battering, hammering and slugging its way ever westward. Wonder why Hitler had to postpone his schedule again?

Here at home, if we doubt there's a war going on, we just have to take a look at the spiraling climb of food prices to change our minds. Prices are 25 per cent higher than before the war. What this does to the average man's paycheck, which hasn't nearly increased in proportion, is most unpleasant. But in spite of all this and prospects of even worse to come, we still eat very well and are extremely thankful for the kind fate that made us Americans.

Monday, March 16, 1942: —More horror stories come out of Europe today. Neutral sources in Sweden report that the Nazis have started a systematic mass extermination of Jews in Western Russia and the Baltic countries. Included are many German Jews deported from the homeland. Heinrich Himmler, the Gestapo chief, is the perpetrator of the mass executions. According to reports, more than 86,000 Jews have been shot and their bodies buried in long ditches outside the towns. Everyone except those over 60 and those employed in German war factories are subject to extermination. Women and children are not excluded. Nice business.

Today marked the deadline for the payment of income taxes. Taxes to beat the Axis! That is the slogan. The biggest tax bill in history is being met willingly by the twenty odd millions of tax payers. Next year's bill, however, will make this one look like kiddies recreation. But if the money goes for guns to smash the Axis, tanks to crush the Axis, ships to sink the Axis, then the people won't complain.

Well, the Yank subs were on the prowl again. Two more Jap ships "bit the dust." A large tanker and a freighter were the victims. Flying Fortresses are still pounding the Jap bases in New Britain and New Guinea. Nine American P-40 pursuit planes encountered a large force of enemy bombers and fighters off the coast of Australia. Pouncing on them, the U.S. planes downed three with the loss of only one which rammed one of the Jap ships.

The astounding Russians today were stepping up their attack all along the front. The recapture of the great cities of Smolensk and Kharkov is near. The Red Army has the Nazi Army back on its heels and intends to keep it there.

Tuesday, March 17, 1942: —Probably the most stirring news since the start of the war was announced today. Mac Arthur is in Australia! General MacArthur, the hero of Bataan, was ordered by President Roosevelt to transfer his headquarters to Australia where he was commissioned to take over command of all the Allied land, sea, and air forces in the Southwest Pacific. This news gave a tremendous lift to everyone throughout the United Nations. To most it indicated the end of the defense and defeat and marked the beginning of offense and victory. A fighting General who has proved his mastery over the Jap, to lead Allied troops including a substantial A.E.F. in the defense of and attack from Australia. The famous General hated leaving his gallant little army in the Philippines and it took a Presidential order to effect the change. But it was emphasized that the Battle of Bataan was not considered lost. The continuance of that brilliant stand was left in the capable hands of Major General Wainwright.

The first wartime conscription lottery to happen in this war is taking place in Washington tonight. This lottery is to determine the order in which the men between the ages of 20 and 44 who registered on February 14-16 will be called into the service. Seven thousand numbers will be drawn from the big fish bowl and is an all day and night job.

The Russians are still shellacking the Nazi hordes with heavy losses being inflicted on both sides. Stalin, meanwhile, is keeping a weather eye cocked toward Japan as there are many indications that the Japs may attempt an attack on Vladivostok and eastern Siberia.

Wednesday, March 18, 1942: —As if in celebration of the arrival of General MacArthur in Australia, Yank and Aussie flyers made the most successful raid of the war against the Jap invasion bases in New Guinea. Twenty three enemy vessels including eleven warships were sunk and many others damaged. Evidence is growing that American air power in Australia is increasing rapidly. The point may soon be reached where it will be possible to take the offensive with a sufficient canopy of fighter planes and bombers to reasonably assure success. Once this allied offensive starts rolling it's going to roll clear to Tokyo.

The third conscription lottery was completed in thirteen hours yesterday. Seven thousand numbers were drawn, the first by Secretary of War Stimson and the last by Albert Carter, a bluejacket from Georgia. The list will decide the order in which 9,000,000 men may be drafted. The first number was 5,508; the last was 2,385.

Speaking of the draft, we learned tonight that my younger brother, Wendell, has just been inducted into the army. He is to leave March 30th and will join the tank corps, probably at Fort Knox, Kentucky. His letter states that it's pretty hard to take, leaving a good job, his girl, and home, to go and learn how to kill a man. That's the part he's uncertain about—killing. Just can't imagine doing it. He says that he, Dad, and my other brother were considering the part the three sons of the family were playing in this war drama. It's like this: I help to get the money to buy the bullets, my older brother, who works for Winchester, helps to make the bullets, and he, the youngest, will learn to use the bullets to kill the enemy. Truly all parts of that picture are essential. But I feel I'm doing nothing in the way of sacrifice compared to the boys in the armed forces. May God bless and protect all of them.

Thursday, March 19, 1942: —The gang scrap is really on for New Guinea. Having been blasted out of their bases on the northern coast of that island, the Japs have apparently decided that closer bases are necessary. To accomplish this they are striking straight across the island through the jungles to Port Moresby. From there the hop to Australia is a mere stone's throw.

Today, in broad daylight with no effort at secrecy, the great Queen Elizabeth, crammed with soldiers and equipment, and escorted by a bevy of warships, steamed out of the Golden Gate headed for the war zone. Just where they are headed is, of course, a military secret. The great ship carried probably an entire division of troops, about 15,000 men. It made a stirring sight. Let's hope they arrive safely at their destination. The Queen Mary, a sister ship to the Queen Elizabeth, was claimed to have been sunk by the Japs while she was carrying 10,000 troops. The truth of this claim is doubted but the actual fate of the huge liner is still shrouded in mystery—probably until she arrives safely in port somewhere.

In order to build the huge army planned, selective service authorities today announced relaxation of the former rigid requirements for induction into the armed forces. Now if you have enough teeth to chew and digest an army meal and can see enough to get around, they'll put you in and find something appropriate for you to do. Flat feet and adenoids won't keep you out of this man's war. You don't need 20-20 vision to do K.P. duty.

Friday, March 20, 1942: —The grim, determined Australians today gave General Douglas MacArthur a hero's welcome at Melbourne today. In a very brief statement typical of a fighting General, MacArthur said he had come at the behest of the President of the United States to organize an offensive against Japan. A primary objective of this offensive is the relief of the Philippines. It is plain to see that the General's heart is still with his gallant lads on Bataan peninsula. "I came through and I shall return," he said.

In yet another theater of war, an American General has taken over command. In Burma where the hard pressed British have been reinforced by a large force of Chinese, Generalissimo Chiang Kai-Shek has appointed Lieut. General Joseph W. Stilwell, U.S.A., as supreme commander. Stilwell is an old hand in China, talks the native tongue fluently and is highly regarded by the Chinese troops whom he regards as the equal of any soldiers on earth. The General promised he would carry the war to the Japs and like MacArthur, only asked to be supplied with the necessary tools.

It is reported that the Japanese in Burma are using thousands of elephants for transportation and supplies. The report comes from the pilots of the famous American Volunteer Group who stated that they had a field day in attacking the elephants. Stampeding pachyderms, frightened by the roaring, spitting, air birds, smashed and trampled many Jap troops. The elephant's thick hides were impervious to machine gun bullets but they were panicked by incendiary bombs.

Saturday, March 21, 1942: —The first day of spring today and a glorious spring day it was. Warm and clear, with the fragrance of countless green things in the air. Observing the revival and freshness of the new world renews one's faith that peace and happiness will likewise return. The bitterness of war is but a passing trial like a severe winter which will inevitably be succeeded by the beauty and warmth of spring.

President Roosevelt today ordered the government to take over the Toledo, Peoria and Western Railroad in the interests of the "successful prosecution of the war." Government control was necessitated because of an impasse between labor and management. The railroad was one of the very few struck outfits at which the strike continued after the outbreak of war.

The story of General MacArthur's journey through the Jap lines from the Philippines to Australia is said to be one of the most thrilling of the war, truly an epic. It was two nights of grueling racing over high seas in torpedo boats, hiding during the day in a jungle cove. A dangerous rendezvous with a great flying boat which brought the General and his staff safely through Jap infested skies to Australia. It was difficult military feat, successfully accomplished in absolute secrecy.

F.B.I. agents again raided Jap town in San Francisco this morning and seized several Japanese gamblers and gunmen, including a former murderer, who admitted their membership in the notorious and dangerous Black Dragon Society. Human bombs at the belly of America.

Sunday, March 22, 1942: —Sugar rationing is scheduled to begin May 4th. As a preliminary, all sugar sales will be suspended for one week beginning April 27, 1942. The amount that will be allowed each person thereafter has not been definitely decided. The limit may be as low as one half pound per week per person.

The greatest air battle of the Far Eastern war took place today. In an obvious attempt to wipe out the brilliant but small group of American Volunteer pilots in Burma, the Japs sent over more than 80 bombers and 30 fighter escorts to attack the American airport. The Yanks, gravely outnumbered, arose to meet them. The outcome of the battle is not yet known but it is feared that several U.S. planes were lost. The little U.S. force has won an enviable reputation in the Burma war and has consistently shellacked the invading Japs in the air. The boys are known to the Chinese as the "Flying Tigers" but have painted their ships to look like sharks. The Japs have learned to respect and fear them tremendously as witness their all out attempt to eliminate them.

General Wainwright reports that the Japs are readying their next big offensive on the Bataan front which is expected at any moment. Heavy artillery duels are in progress with the Nipponese using more and larger field pieces than ever before. All preliminary raids by enemy patrols have been easily repulsed. General Yamashita has generously suggested that the Americans surrender but the offer has been graciously refused!!!

Monday, March 23, 1942: —Two daring British submarines striking boldly to within sight of the Italian coast today were reported to have destroyed eleven Italian and German warships and troop transports en-route to reinforce the Axis forces in Africa. Hundreds of enemy troops and much materiel of war went to the bottom of "Mussolini's Sea."

It is also reported that the Japanese offensive toward Australia has been stalled and checkmated as at no other time in the Pacific war by the viciousness of the Allied air attack on Jap shipping and airbases on and around New Guinea.

In a scene reminiscent of Dust Bowl evacuations from Oklahoma and Texas a few years ago, the mass movement of Japanese aliens and American-born citizens from strategic areas on the coast began today. A caravan of 350 autos and trucks, both new and rattletrap, loaded down with household furnishings and children, headed east from the Pasadena Rose Bowl to the Army's reception center on the other side of the Sierra Nevada Mountains. At Manzanar, in Owens Valley, 230 miles north of Los Angeles, a colony is being constructed. Here, safe from the opportunity to sabotage and spy, the Japanese will be confined for the duration. Undoubtedly many innocent and loyal Japanese will suffer along with the dangerous fifth columnist, the treacherous saboteur and the murderous spy. But the whole country will be greatly relieved and much safer when all vital areas are cleared of these dangerous "borers from within."

No blackouts or other alarms have occurred in this district for a long time. Fingers are crossed.

77

Tuesday, March 24, 1942: —War fronts all over the world seem to be coming violently to life. A very crucial spring lies ahead of us. The war itself may be decided in the great offensives that are brewing in Europe and Africa and Asia. Where will they strike? Will the Axis strike first? Have the Allies accumulated sufficient striking power to hit back, through Norway, or France, or Holland, or Italy itself, the Achilles' heel of the foe? Will the Russian drive maintain its momentum and throw Hitler's plans out of kilter? Will Japan complicate the Red Army's task by striking at its rear in Siberia? Has MacArthur sufficient force to start a counter-drive yet or is this year to be another year of desperate defensive fighting until the weight of superior production begins to show? All these questions and many more face the world in this crucial spring of 1942. The tragedy of it all is that many thousands of human beings must die violently before the tale of this year is finally told.

A jittery Sweden is massing all the military force she possibly can in anticipation of a Nazi attack, ostensibly to secure Germany's northern flank from the danger of a British and American attack, but in reality to supply the German people with one of those quick, brilliant victories that have been lacking of late. A convenient, helpless victim is badly needed by the great Fuehrer. The Russian medicine has turned the Nazi stomach.

The Bataan front in the Philippines seems on the verge of exploding into the big Jap push to reach a decision before it becomes necessary for another Jap general to save his ugly face by the hara-kiri method.

Wednesday, March 25, 1942: —The ambitious Japs today extended themselves even further, this time in the direction of India, by occupying the Andaman Islands in the Bay of Bengal only 600 miles from Calcutta. This is the first Indian Territory to be invaded in the war and bodes ill for India unless she buries her differences with the British Crown and really makes an effort to defend herself. The small garrison of British troops on the Andaman Islands withdrew without opposing the Japanese landing force.

The Pacific war today spreads over a vast area of more than 22,000,000 square miles and is thus the greatest war ever fought. It makes Hitler's tiny war of 6,000,000 square miles seem like a war of "shut-ins." This tremendous meal the Japs are trying to digest may prove just a bit too rich for even their rapacious palates.

A fascinating sight has been occurring in the night skies throughout the Bay district during the last few nights. Like giant fingers, the beams from dozens of great searchlights along the ocean and bay coastlines have groped across the heavens in practice maneuvers. A high flying plane is picked up far down the peninsula by four great fingers of light and is "boxed in" and literally handed from battery to battery as the plane swoops in on San Francisco. The "raiding" plane is clearly silhouetted in the glare of at least four great searchlights all the way and would be a beautiful target for anti-aircraft batteries. Let's hope that these nightly maneuvers will never be the real thing, accompanied by the crash of high explosive bombs and the roar of defending guns. Then the beautiful sight would turn to horror.

Thursday, March 26, 1942: —Two young American pilots of the Volunteer Group in Burma went on a rampage the other day, it was revealed today. Ordered on a reconnaissance mission, they surprised the Japanese on the Moulmein airdrome and blasted at least fifteen enemy bombers and fighting planes on the ground. The enemy planes were lined up on the field "like a movie lineup for inspection" and it was "duck soup" for the two intrepid flyers to spray the entire group with incendiary bullets and light bombs. The raid was so sudden and unexpected that the Japs never had a chance to get into the air. Subsequent observation flights by other U.S. planes verified the great damage inflicted.

In another grim little war drama on the high seas, an unarmed freighter, attacked at night by a Nazi submarine which surfaced and fired a torpedo, suddenly wheeled on its course and rammed the submarine, sinking it in a rending crash of steel. The name of the freighter and the exact time of the action have been withheld by the Navy censors, but the actual deed has been officially verified.

Aerial warfare in the Mediterranean and European theaters has been stepped up in the last few days. Malta has been subjected to extremely heavy raids but all have been beaten off by the RAF. The heavy bombers of the British have been giving the industrial areas of the Reich a terrific pounding during the last few nights. Corregidor, the American fortress in Manila Bay, has also been subjected to the fury of incessant raids by large groups of Japanese heavy bombers. Some very nasty eggs are being laid.

Friday, March 27, 1942: —The RAF is pouring it on hot and heavy over Germany. The spring air offensive is on. Hundreds of British heavy bombers are blazing their thunderous way over Western Europe, unloading everything from fire bombs to massive two ton explosives on the industrial areas of the Nazi Reich. Every tank factory destroyed, every aircraft plant damaged, eases the pressure that the Nazi armies will be able to bring against the Russians in their anticipated spring offensive. The air offensive answers in part the Russian demand for the opening of a second front to divide the German efforts.

The gallant Chinese, meanwhile, have broken out of the trap set by the Japs at Toungoo in Burma. Fierce, bloody hand to hand fighting raged all day, but in the end the Chinese prevailed. But the entire Allied position in Central Burma remained very grave.

On the home front it has become necessary for the Office of Price Administration to crack down on rapidly rising food prices. The freezing of pork prices at those of mid-march was announced today. The OPA director flatly stated that meat sellers have an important obligation to the Nation's health to avoid further price rises that will make it impossible for many families to buy these products.

Soldier Joe Louis, heavyweight boxing champ, tonight again successfully defended his title, knocking out big Abe Simon in the sixth round at Madison Square Garden in New York. The fight was notable as Joe turned all his winnings over to the Army Relief Fund. Patriotic -yes!

Saturday, March 28, 1942: —Daring, mysterious British Commando troops, those black uniformed, sworn-to-conquer-or-die soldiers who strike in the night with blackened faces and blazing tommy-guns, last night carried out a spectacular assault against the big Nazi submarine base at the French west coast port of St. Nazaire. Supported by naval and air forces, the Commandos rammed an old destroyer loaded with tons of explosive into the locks and dry-docks of the base, seriously crippling that nest from whence the submarine "rattlesnakes" of the Atlantic come to lie in wait for the unsuspecting cargo ship.

The Nazis, of course, belittled the raid but evidenced their nerve-racking fear of these hard hitting foes who strike without warning and with such deadly effect. Nazi heads lie restless along the Channel coast these nights.

In what was described as the bloodiest battle of the Pacific war, the Japs pounded their way into the key town of Toungoo in Burma today. The Nips have thrown upwards of two full divisions, about 40,000 men, into this fray and the Chinese position is precarious. This battle is highly important for beyond Burma lies the wealth of India which the galloping Jap covets.

A further report of the American Volunteer Group's great victory in their air attack on a Jap airdrome in Burma last Wednesday, in which they destroyed forty enemy planes, is saddened by the disclosure of the death of John V. Newkirk, their heroic squadron leader, who was hit and crashed on the edge of the airfield he had just helped to smash. He was a great pilot with twenty five Jap planes officially credited to him, many more unofficially shot down. All Americans are forever indebted to hero Jack Newkirk, a fighting Yank.

Sunday, March 29, 1942: —Today has been another glorious spring day, warm and clear. Sunday, especially Sundays like today, have always been my favorite day. Vitamin D and health pour in upon us in generous measure from a friendly sun while beauty and cleanliness permeate the atmosphere—that is the picture. That is the picture that foolish man has seen fit to sully and spoil with his ugly and devastating squabbles. Ah me!

Probably the most important news today is the report that Sir Stafford Cripps, the British emissary to India, has announced an agreement with India whereby that country will acquire Dominion status after the war. This is what the Indians have been after for many years. The price of this political victory is all out participation in the war against the Axis, particularly Japan. If the immense wealth and endless manpower of India can be effectively put to use, the Allied cause will be immeasurably strengthened. The forces of retribution gather, Herr Hitler and you too, Hirohito. Your days are numbered.

Increased activity on the Bataan front is reported tonight. General Jonathan Wainwright's daily communiqué stated that heavy enemy attacks were repelled with heavy loss being inflicted. Jap bombers and heavy artillery continued to pound the Bataan rear and Corregidor but only inconsequential damage was caused. The island fortress big guns and anti-aircraft batteries had a few words of their own to speak and several enemy ships and one bomber were destroyed. Come on, Yamashita, when are you going to commit hara-kiri? Soon, I hope.

Monday, March 30, 1942: —Nothing much exciting in the news today. The Indians, naturally, are not yet satisfied with what Sir Stafford Cripps has offered them. Having howled for years for just what Britain now proffers they must of course demand more. They balk at the price they must pay—that of actual participation in the war. No nation ever prospered who was not willing to fight for its freedom. England would give them freedom but they must fight the Jap who would subjugate them.

The battle in Central Burma continues its bloody course, with the Chinese desperately holding their own. It is charged today that the Japs are even using poison gas in their effort to crack the Allied line. An idea of the vicious character of the fighting is given when it is reported that over thirty per cent of the casualties are a result of bayonet wounds.

In the Philippines the Japs are still cautiously feeling out the American positions by strong patrol action while their air force continues to pound Corregidor. Extremely accurate anti-aircraft fire has kept the Jap bombers at tremendous heights yet General Wainwright reports that one bomber was shot down from the unbelievable height of 27,000 feet. From this altitude the Jap bombing has been very ineffective, most of the bombs landing in the Bay.

German and British naval forces clashed in a blinding snowstorm in the frigid waters of the Arctic supply line to Murmansk. The British lost a cruiser, the Nazis a destroyer, but the convoy delivered the goods.

Tuesday, March 31, 1942: —Well, it's the end of another month but far from the end of the war. In fact it is more and more apparent that it is barely the beginning. Probably the major part of the period from December 7, 1941 to now will be known to history as "The One Hundred Days Head Start." It has been the period when the Gallopin' Jap jumped the gun, caught everyone napping at the post, and ran away with the field. This, we believe, is the high water mark of the Japanese conquest, when success beyond the Mikado's wildest dreams has crowned their perfidious efforts. From now on we will see the tide gradually recede, until the armies of retribution stride right up and over the gates of Tokyo and Yokahoma. Or is this wishful thinking?

The All-India Congress today put the crimp in Great Britain's efforts to enlist India wholeheartedly into the war against the Axis. Far from being satisfied with the promise of Dominion status after the war the Indians are demanding freedom now or never. At the time of Britain's sorest trial, the Indians are putting the screws on. They may find to their sorrow that Japanese rule is far worse medicine to swallow than government by the English.

The Japanese threat to India deepens in Central Burma where it is feared that a British army defending the Prome oilfields of Burma is trapped. U.S. General Stilwell's Chinese army meanwhile has hacked itself out of a similar trap at Toungoo, leaving 5,000 dead Japs on the field, most of them killed by bayonet.

Australian and American flyers have wrested local control of the air over New Guinea and Northern Australia. This is the most encouraging sign to date.

April

Wednesday, April 1, 1942: —It appears tonight as though the final big Jap smash at U.S. Filipino lines on Bataan peninsula is in progress. Successive waves of attackers surged at the center of General Wainwright's line and were only repulsed after fierce hand to hand fighting. At the same time the Japanese air force pounded Corregidor once again but the sharp shooting ack-ack artillerymen of the Fortress sent two of the heavy bombers crashing into Manila Bay. Outnumbered ten to one, the gallant orphans of Bataan have their job cut out for them.

The Navy today announced that two more Axis subs have been sunk by Navy flyers. Both were sent to the bottom of the Atlantic off the east coast of the United States where the deadly "sharks" of the sea have been sinking cargo ships faster than they can be replaced. One of the subs was sunk by the same Navy enlisted man named Donald Francis Mason who several weeks ago radioed the now famous report, "sighted sub, sank same."

Two nationally pesky fascists were arrested today in Los Angeles for sedition. The charge was based on published statements by the two men which libeled General MacArthur and characterized his departure from Bataan as cowardly and the whole defense of the Philippines as just plain foolishness. The right of free speech has its limitation also, especially in time of war.

General MacArthur, meanwhile, far from concerning himself with such trivialities today reported a new smash by Australian and American planes against Jap bases north of the continent. Success is claimed.

Thursday, April 2, 1942: —The eyes of the world are on Bataan. The brave and effective stand of the American and Filipino troops since the outbreak of the war has amazed and awed everyone throughout the world, including the enemy. Outnumbered as much as 10 to 1, the defenders have smashed every attempt by the Japs to liquidate resistance in the Philippines. A terrific toll has been exacted from the Nipponese, including the hara-kiri of one of their best generals. Now in desperation, the Japs, commanded by their most famous general, General Tamashita of Singapore fame, are throwing their full weight, regardless of losses, into an all-out attempt to smother the tiny defending army. How long the gallant "battlin' boys from Bataan" will be able to withstand the terrible pressure of overwhelming numbers is problematical. But to date, their lines remain unbroken, stanchly held by a long, thin line of sharp bayonets. No matter what the final outcome, their immortal place in history is secure. The American people's one hope is that somehow, someday they will be relieved. MacArthur left—but he will return! Until then, may God shed his strength and courage upon them. Amen.

Britain's negotiations with India appear to have reached an impasse, with the outcome very doubtful. And that with the Japanese only 75 miles from the soil of India. Talk about your fiddling around while Rome burns. This is a classic example.

The Russians, meanwhile, are giving everyone a lesson in not letting grass grow underfoot, by grimly hanging on to the initiative on the Eastern Front. Hitler, for all his big talk is going to have a difficult time regaining the offensive from the amazing Red Army—more power to them.

Friday, April 3, 1942: —The Navy announced in their communiqué tonight the sinking of three U.S. warships in Javanese waters late in February. This is the first inkling the public has had of these catastrophes. The former aircraft carrier, Langley, recently converted into an aircraft tender, the naval tanker Pecos and the destroyer Perry were destroyed by Japanese bombers with a loss of over 700 men. The next of kin of the dead are being notified by telegram. War's grisly mill is certainly working overtime—no forty hour week there.

Disheartening but inevitable tales of numerous draft dodgers, uncooperative labor unions, companies that had to be forced to cease trading with the Axis—all these gloom up the war news from time to time, making it harder than ever to reconcile the great sacrifice of those boys who went down with their ships while fighting the battles of all of us, including the slackers and backbiters.

The RAF and the Luftwaffe are trading haymakers in this round. In a raid reminiscent of 1940, the Germans plastered several towns in England while the English again smeared the French invasion ports and ranged inland to the industrial areas of occupied France and Germany.

85

In Bataan the boys are still holding fast but their long term outlook is very pessimistic. In Burma the British are pulling another retreat, this time from Prome. Stronger lines, they say, have been established between Prome and the vital oilfields of Yamanguang. Retreat, retreat, retreat! Is that all we are to hear? The calendar says today is Good Friday. But after examining the news I can't see that it's so good. There's not much to cheer about.

Saturday, April 4, 1942: —U.S. submarines have been busy again in the East Indies waters, the Navy communiqué stated today. A Jap cruiser was sunk by a direct torpedo hit. Another cruiser was probably sunk and six other smaller enemy vessels were either destroyed or put out of commission.

The heavy Jap attacks on the American lines on Bataan peninsula continue in a lesser degree. Apparently the Japs find that they bump their noses too hard when they try frontal attacks against the strong U.S. positions. They appear more likely to be content to wait until starvation and lack of ammunition accomplish what attack cannot do. How long that will be only General Wainwright and his men know. Meanwhile, the ack-ack men of Corregidor bagged two more enemy planes which attempted to attack the island fortress with a new type of incendiary bomb which explodes in mid-air, scattering flames over a wide area. Only slight damage was done by the bombs, however.

The Army today announced that they have acquired Tanforan race track as an assembly center for Japanese aliens who are being evacuated from vital coastal areas. I don't care much for the idea because Tanforan is here in San Bruno, just a stone's throw from our house. The idea of having 10,000 Japs that close isn't a very pleasant thought, especially when I am necessarily away until late at night sometimes. But it shouldn't be for long, however, as the assembly center is merely a concentration point where they may be fed and housed until the regular settlements are ready.

Sunday, April 5, 1942: —Easter Sunday! The day of renewed hope, when all Christians should contemplate the victory of life over death—the lesson that all is not lost in this bitter old world

86

of ours. Christ has risen and good must eventually triumph over the forces of evil.

In spite of this awakening of new hope, the world outside seemed rather gloomy all day. It rained as though the earth was shedding tears of anguish over the inhumanity of man. Only once or twice did the sun peek through the clouds, as though he was afraid of what he might see on this sordid planet, yet was insatiably curious and fascinated by the drama being enacted thereon.

There was to have been the first victory parade down Market Street today, giving the people for the first time, a chance to cheer the boys in uniform and a chance to work up that spirit and enthusiasm that brings a lump to your throat and a great desire to get in there and pitch in to help win the war. I don't know how the parade went because the rain drove us off. I hope it didn't spoil it entirely. The people need a little of that sort of thing to bring the war home to them and to create that competitive spirit that makes for a winning team.

Activity on the battlefronts seems to be confined to aerial warfare today. The Japs pounced on Ceylon for the first time with a large force of bombers and fighters but British Spitfires and Hurricanes trounced them decisively, knocking down more than 57 planes.

Monday, April 6, 1942: —The Jap tentacles reached out to India today as two cities on the Indian mainland felt the crash of bombs. This is the first instance of Jap bombing of India proper and perhaps marks the first phase of their threatened invasion of that country.

Extremely savage fighting is in progress in Bataan today, and General Wainwright's communiqué admits that the enemy has made some gains, though at heavy loss in men and equipment. This is the third day of almost continuous assaults. General Yamashita has apparently begun his all-out attempt to wear the little U.S. Filipino army down by sheer weight of superior numbers. How long our gallant lads can hang on before collapsing from total exhaustion is the big question on everyone's mind. The Jap General knows the peninsula can be his if he is willing to pay the price. But it's a pretty stiff price, Yamashita, for the hollow victory it will be.

The British sent one of the biggest air armadas of the war—more than 300 bombers—roaring over German industrial cities last night. Half of this number raided Cologne for the 105th time, dropping about 1,000 tons of high explosives and incendiaries among Nazi war factories. The Nazis are getting a taste of what they gave England in 1940. And more is coming.

Today is Army Day, celebrating the entry of this country into the First World War. This time it takes on a new meaning. We're proud of the army we're building this time and confident that it will be capable of handling the situation that confronts it. Our country and our lives are safe in their hands, along with the Navy and the Marines.

Tuesday, April 7, 1942: —The fourth month of the war with Japan has come to a close. Those four months seem like an eon of time. Vast changes have been wrought by the galloping Japs and even the most optimistic agree that the road back will be a long, bitter climb for the United Nations. Java, Sumatra, New Guinea, the Celebes, Singapore, Malaya, Burma, Thailand, French Indo-China, China itself, all must be regained—but at what cost? There is nothing pleasant in the prospect.

Soon the Philippines may be added to that long list of conquered places. The great and perhaps final offensive against the tiny U.S. and Filipino armies on Bataan is in progress. General Wainwright's daily communiqué indicates the gravity of the situation. The Jap pressure is steadily increasing, augmented by a constant stream of reinforcements. The attacks are supported by large numbers of tanks and dive bombers while countless heavy bombers blast away at supplies and communications in the rear. For the first time, the General admitted that U.S. losses are heavy and the enemy is making some progress. For the second time the Japs have bombed an American hospital causing many casualties. The hospital was plainly marked and the bombing was obviously intentional in spite of the Jap apology following the attack.

Two more Japanese merchant vessels were reported bagged by an American submarine in the China sea. Two of the huge, ocean-going subs capable of operating over such vast distances arrived in San Francisco Bay this afternoon. From the sixth floor window of the Bank building I had a ringside seat to view their run up the harbor.

Wednesday, April 8, 1942: —The Yanks on Bataan have been forced to retreat again in order to straighten out dents driven into the lines at various points by the Japs. The withdrawal was made in perfect order to a previously prepared defense position. The enemy attacks continue in unrelenting ferocity, with dozens of dive bombers and attack aircraft in continuous operation against our front line troops. Enemy losses are huge.

General George C. Marshall, U.S. Chief of Staff, arrived in London today for conferences with British military leaders. He hinted broadly that U.S. troops already in Ireland would very much like to "expand to Europe." It is possible that the U.S. and Britain may attempt some sort of an invasion of Europe this spring to aid the Russians and throw Hitler's offensive plans off schedule.

Hitler's offensive may already be getting under way as the African front springs into activity again. Approximately 135,000 German and Italian troops, mostly mechanized, have opened up an attack aimed at knocking out the British army and driving to cut the Suez Canal, thus eventually joining forces with the Japs in an invasion of India. The much fought over sands of Libya are due for another blood soaking. Accompanying they Libyan drive was a large scale attack on Malta. Nine Axis planes were destroyed.

The Russians are maintaining their offensive on the eastern front, today claiming to have driven the Nazis back to the province of White Russia, only 150 miles from the old Polish frontier. The Red Army is well on its way back.

Thursday, April 9, 1942: —BATAAN HAS FALLEN! With all the suddenness of December 7th, the news has come that the weary, exhausted, and terribly outnumbered heroes of Bataan have been overwhelmed. Terrific drives by constantly reinforced waves of Japs, supported by droves of dive bombers and tanks, finally turned the flank of the defenders' lines and enveloped them. The gallant Americans and their Filipino comrades either died in their tracks or were engulfed and captured. Very few were able to be evacuated to Corregidor and the other forts in Manila Bay. These forts are continuing the resistance. It is reported that 36,800 troops and 20,000 civilian refugees were left as casualties on the peninsula battleground. How many of that number were killed is not known. General Wainwright and his staff escaped to Corregidor.

A deep, angry gloom has settled over the Nation since the receipt of this news. The hearts of the people were on that tiny stretch of battlefield with those fighting doughboys. The story of their epic fight against such hopeless odds will live forever along with Wake Island, The Alamo, Valley Forge, and the Little Big Horn. We shall not forget! MacArthur will not forget! The Army, the Navy, the Marines will not forget! The men at the lathes and the drills will not forget! America is fighting mad. Pearl Harbor will be avenged! Wake Island will be avenged! BATAAN WILL BE AVENGED! One day American troops will march in triumph on the streets of Tokyo. The Filipinos will once again live in peace in the Philippines. All our energies, all our possessions, all our resources—even our lives if need be—are now, more firmly than ever, dedicated to that ultimate end.

Friday, April 10, 1942: —It has been hard to realize that American forces on Bataan have been overwhelmed. Before yesterday there was no inkling that the end was so close at hand. It was known, of course, that General Yamashita's great offensive had begun two weeks ago but the utter exhaustion of the U.S. and Filipino troops was not realized. Today we learn however, that 3,500 sailors and marines were successfully evacuated to Corregidor along with nurses and medical officers. Those left behind spent their last few hours in applying the torch to all supplies and the pitifully small store of munitions still remaining on the peninsula. Hundreds, anxious to continue the fight, then swam or rowed in anything they could find, to the island fortress. The Japs still have several hard nuts to crack in Manila Bay. General Wainwright is still directing the resistance from Corregidor.

Meanwhile a great naval battle is in progress in the Bay of Bengal. Possibly the fate of India itself may hang in the balance. The British admit the loss of the aircraft carrier Hermes and the cruisers Dorsetshire and Cornwall. Enemy losses are not known.

While this great battle rages in their front yard the Indian leaders are still arguing among themselves in the back yard. It looks as though all negotiations between Britain and India are collapsing. A very dangerous situation as thus developed.

Hitler is having serious internal troubles. A certain indication of this is his order issued today in Yugoslavia in which he threatened execution of more than 16,000 hostages, including women and children, if guerrilla warfare does not cease completely by Monday. Nice people, those Nazis.

Saturday, April 11, 1942: —The U.S. Navy announced today that the American submarine Perch has been overdue for more than a month and is presumed lost. The vessel was last known to be in Java waters during the fight for that island. Fifty officers and men are gone with their ship. This is the fourth U.S. sub to be lost in the war to date. In return more than fifty enemy warships and cargo vessels have been destroyed by American undersea boats since December 7th.

The triumphant Japs on Luzon are giving Corregidor a terrific pasting with everything they've got. Being only two miles away now they are in a position to bring heavy artillery into point blank range. Corregidor on the other hand is handicapped in returning the fire for fear of hitting American troops who are still somewhere on the peninsula probably as prisoners. The real horror that was Bataan during those last fifteen days of merciless attack is just beginning to trickle back from the mouths of survivors. Sleepless for days on end, subject to continuous aerial strafing and bombing, crushed by droves of heavy tanks and never-ending waves of fresh Japanese infantry, the weary men nevertheless stuck to their foxholes and exacted a tremendous toll from the enemy. But flesh has its limitations and even the supermen of Bataan could not last forever. No nation could ever ask for a finer display of courage and sheer fighting ability than was unstintingly shown by the "Battlin' Boys from Bataan." America is grateful. America will not break faith with ye who died that American principles might live! Ye may sleep peacefully knowing that your great sacrifice has not been made in vain.

Sunday, April 12, 1942: —Another Sabbath has rolled around and yet the world continues its cruel wickedness. From every front come tales of fresh horrors. Men's lives are being expended as freely as bullets; the earth's soil is steeped in human blood. What an evil sight this old planet must be in the eyes of the Lord. How long will he allow innocent as well as guilty to writhe and suffer under the brutal heel of the invaders? Time alone holds the answer.

Corregidor Fortress in Manila Bay is really taking a terrific pounding according to latest reports. From both sides of the bay the Japs are subjecting the stronghold to a cross-fire of heavy artillery while dozens of heavy bombers are keeping up a constant, round-the-clock bombardment of the tiny isle. Tokyo even claims that battleships of their fleet have joined in the siege put no confirmation of this has come from General Wainwright.

The Burma situation is almost as bad. Jap troops are steadily advancing against the British and are nearing the vital oilfields. Chinese troops under U.S. General Stilwell are barely holding their ground against greatly superior numbers. The only bright spot in this picture is the continued supremacy of the American Volunteer Group of pilots who in two battles last Thursday and Friday shot down eighteen of twenty-one enemy aircraft without the loss of a plane.

The only really heartening news comes from Australia where Allied airmen have won absolute control of the air over Northern Australia and the islands of New Guinea and New Britain. This air control has prevented the Japs from getting set for any offensive action.

Monday, April 13. 1942: —Corregidor continues to take it and is even dishing out a bit also. The big guns of the searched out and smashed two tank and truck columns on Bataan and sank a medium sized enemy vessel and damaged several others. The outlook for the Fortress, however, is gloomy as no prospects are in sight for any relief of any kind.

Harrowing tales of disaster at sea are commonplace nowadays. The latest tells of the torpedoing of a large British passenger vessel, from which 290 passengers and crew members were rescued. Many women and children were among the passengers. A lifeboat of another ship lost at sea was picked up after 58 days adrift. Out of 24 men aboard only one survived. His was an unbelievably tale of hardship that drove men mad before they died, of eating fish raw to survive, of a loneliness worse than Hell. I wonder how many other lifeboats full of dying men are drifting even now, victims of those "rattlesnakes of the sea", Axis submarines who strike without mercy and leave their victims to die in agony. It takes courageous men to sail the seas in these times.

Negotiations with India have broken down completely. Sir Stafford Cripps has gone home and India seems ripe for Japanese plucking. Another major set-back for the British.

Only two fronts seem to be going at all favorable to the Allied Nations and they are on opposite sides of the world. The American Australian air force in Australia and the Red Army in Russia are making it hot for the foe. The Russians in particular are maintaining their initiative against Hitler and even feel cocky enough to warn Japan to lay off Siberia. You've got to hand it to the Reds.

Tuesday, April 14, 1942: —Pierre Laval, the French Quisling who was nearly assassinated some time ago, has returned to power in the Vichy Government. Apparently done at the insistence of Hitler, this move bodes ill for relations between the French and the United States Government. Washington has studiously avoided trouble with Vichy because of the possibility that the still powerful French fleet might be turned over to the Nazis and that French bases in Africa might be used as submarine lairs. With Laval in power it looks as though all this might come to pass and there is some agitation in Washington to seize all French territory in the western hemisphere, by force if necessary. Some very interesting developments should result in the near future along this line.

A submarine attack on a U.S. merchantman was carried out so close to the Florida coastline yesterday that thousands of spectators along the shore watched the action. The Axis subs are becoming more and more daring and have intensified their attacks in both oceans. The submarine menace is one of the foremost problems to be conquered before the Allied Nations can hope to take the offensive.

Nothing exciting or of particular significance has happened on the home front for many days. Life has settled down into the regular routine of war work, doing without, salvage campaigns, first aid courses, rising food prices and countless civilian defense arguments that seem to get nowhere. These things and the ever increasing proportion of soldiers and sailors among the people on the streets constantly remind us of the war. Everything we do, or say, or hear, or see, seems bound up in that one great event— "THE WAR."

Wednesday, April 15, 1942: —The American Air Force made a down payment on the debt we owe the Japs for Pearl Harbor in a sensational 4,000 mile round trip bombing raid on enemy bases and airfields in the Philippines recently. General MacArthur proudly announced the successful completion of one of the longest bombing raids in the history of warfare. U.S. planes including Flying Fortresses flew 2,000 miles from their bases in Australia to pound Japanese military objectives in the Philippine Islands. One squadron even blasted an enemy airfield on the outskirts of Manila. Heavy damage was done and a total of eight Japanese ships were sunk. Only one American plane was lost but the crew of that one was rescued. Apparently the U.S. planes landed at some secret bases on the islands as a number of evacuees were brought back on the return trip. Brig. General Ralph Royce of Michigan, the commander of the bombing force, was awarded the Distinguished Service Cross upon his return.

The real importance of this raid is not in the damage wrought but the promise it brings of things to come. General Yamashita and his ilk can shake in their boots in anticipation of what the future holds in store for them when the Allied offensive really gets under way. Also, the sight of friendly wings must certainly have cheered the boys on Corregidor and the rest of the Islands who are still fighting grimly against terrific odds. General Wainwright himself was in communication with the raiding planes for several hours. The spirit of Bataan still lives in those wings with the white stars on them. Remember! Tokyo is not so far from Manila—not for the Flying Fortress!

Thursday, April 16, 1942: —San Francisco had its first daylight alert of 1942 today from 9:58 to 10:12 A.M. All radio stations went off the air and civilian defense officials stood by ready to go into action. Schools were closed immediately and students whose parents were at home were released. Nothing came of the "Alert", however, as the approaching planes turned out to be friendly. The authorities appeared to be well satisfied with the manner in which the alarm was handled.

Pierre Laval's ascendancy to power apparently has not pleased many Frenchmen because a wave of anti-Nazi terrorism greeted him upon his arrival in Paris to confer with Nazi overlords. A troop train loaded with German soldiers was derailed and about 40 soldiers killed and many injured.

Heavily reinforced Japanese columns in Burma are making things plenty tough for the hard pressed Chinese under General Stilwell and for the British defending the vital Burma oilfields. Air superiority is again the deciding factor in the Jap successes in this region.

The Japs are spreading their invasion of the Philippines by attacking the island of Panay in addition to their recent landing on Cebu. Fierce fighting is in progress on both of these islands and complete control of these strategic areas by the Japs is not yet conceded. Corregidor's big guns, meanwhile, were successful in silencing several big artillery emplacements on the mainland. An American minesweeper was sunk in the Corregidor harbor to even the score, however.

Friday, April 17, 1742: —As an expression of distrust of the motives and intentions of Pierre Laval and his pro-Nazi cabinet, the United States Government today recalled Admiral Leahy, the ambassador to France. This move did not constitute an outright severance of diplomatic relations with the Vichy regime but served merely as a warning to the French collaborationists under Laval. It is feared, however, that Laval will ignore the warning and plunge his unhappy country into full collaboration with Hitler in complete violation of the armistice provisions. Laval's course may even involve war with the Allied Nations. The French Quisling's complete determination to help Germany win the war no matter what the cost to the suffering French populace is plainly evident.

The RAF meanwhile, is continuing the longest sustained bombing offensive of the war against German war industries. The offensive started a week ago and is still in progress with increasing intensity. Communiqués state that American planes and pilots are joining in the raids which have taken hundreds of heavy bombers in both daylight and night time sweeps over occupied territories and vital German centers. Several cities in Germany have been "Coventryized" even worse than Coventry. Revenge is very sweet to those British pilots. Will the "Deutchers" be able to take it like "Tommy Atkins" did?

Corregidor's big guns are still barking and with considerable success, having knocked out a least two more enemy gun emplacements.

From Tokyo comes an interesting report, not yet confirmed by Allied sources, that Tokyo has been bombed. If true, Mr. Moto may well shiver. On the other hand, it may only be Mr. Moto's excuse to bomb, perhaps, San Francisco.

Saturday, April 18, 1942: —Apparently that flash we got last night that Tokyo had been bombed was correct. Although only the Japs have reported it so far they seem to be telling the truth on this one. Not only was Tokyo raided but also Yokohama, Kobe and Nagoya. Naturally the Japs emphasized that only hospitals, schools, and residential districts were damaged but they did admit that several large fires were started at Kobe. They also claimed that nine planes were shot down over Tokyo and that they were U.S. planes.

The bases from which the raiding planes came is not known but undoubtedly explains the silence on the part of the Allies. No report will be made by them until the planes and the carriers from which they originated have reached safety. Then we'll hear the U.S. version which will shed some real light on the damage that was caused.

In yet another field of action U.S. bombers went into action. Flying Fortresses based in India smashed at the Japs' jumping-off base at Rangoon. Docks and supplies were blasted, relieving some of the pressure on the British and Chinese troops who are attempting to stave off a many pronged Nipponese drive on the rich oil fields of central Burma.

The British RAF is also carrying the war to the enemy in their long nonstop aerial offensive against Germany. Despite heavy losses they raided as far as Augsburg, only 110 miles from Hitler's once-safe retreat at Berchtesgaden. A big diesel engine plant was destroyed in the target area.

Question to Hirohito, Hitler, et al: How does it feel to be catching instead of pitching?

Sunday, April 19, 1942: —The bombing of Japan proper by U.S. planes gave the long suffering people of many Allied Nations a tremendous lift. The Chinese people of Chungking who for so many bitter months have seen their homes flattened, their loved ones mangled and maimed in countless Jap bombing raids, danced in the streets today for joy upon hearing the great news. Chinese and British troops fighting desperately in Burma were mightily cheered, so much so that they stiffened to hold the Japs all along the front. The English who have suffered so much under the lash of enemy bombs called the news "a bit of all right", while the Australians rejoiced that it meant the beginning of the Allied offensive against the Nips. In this country one hundred and fifty million Americans accepted the news with grim satisfaction that the criminals who so brutally attacked Pearl Harbor, Manila, and Bataan were now getting a taste of their own bitter medicine. Never again, so long as this war lasts, can the people of Japan sleep feeling secure from their most dangerous foe, fire bombs. Once well started, their flimsy, paper and wood cities would burn like matchboxes.

As though the daring and spectacular raid on Japan acted as a tonic, Allied communiqués all over the world indicated new successes for the United Nations. The Russians are smashing ahead everywhere along the eastern front especially in the Leningrad area where the siege has been completely lifted and German-Finnish armies driven back with huge losses in men and equipment. Over France and Germany the RAF starts its second week of the nonstop aerial offensive.

In Australia the Allies are still smashing at Jap bases with superior air power. Corregidor, the pearl of great price in Manila Bay, is still taking everything they've got and dishing out a bit in return. But caution! The spring offensives are still to come.

Monday, April 20, 1942: —News reports tonight indicate that one result of the U.S. air raid on Japan is a complete shakeup by the Japs of their civilian defense setup. The jittery Japs admit by their confused broadcasts that the raid had pretty serious consequences, not the least of which was a crack in civilian morale. The official version of the raid has not yet been made by the Allied high command.

Pierre Laval, in a statement to the French people today, reiterated his determination to take France all the way into Hitler's "new order" for Europe. Russian sources say that Laval has already set in motion the procedure to turn over the French fleet to the Nazis. The only reaction shown by the French people to the "great collaborationist's" speech was an acceleration of sabotage and bomb throwing throughout Occupied France.

Reinforced Chinese forces under U.S. General Stilwell were rushed to the western Burma front and succeeded in relieving the hard-pressed British Imperials who had been encircled and threatened with annihilation. The Chinese also recaptured

Yenangyaung, the key to the Irrawaddy Valley oilfields. Their attack temporarily eased the serious situation that has existed in Burma for the last few days.

The Japs are throwing dive-bombers in addition to heavy artillery into the siege of Corregidor, but the accurate fire of the American gunners silenced at least four batteries on Bataan and broke up three troop and truck concentrations on the peninsula. Guerilla fighting by American-Filipino patrols is taking a heavy toll of the invaders all over the archipelago. The path of conquest is not easy, eh, Mr. Moto?

Tuesday, April 21, 1942: —The jittery Japs are still abuzz over the air raid of last Saturday. Court martials, recriminations, shakeups, to say nothing of almost constant air raid alarms, have plagued them ever since American bombers dropped the first Pearl Harbor reminder notices on Tokyo, Yokohoma, Kobe, etc. May their nights continue to be sleepless and their guilty consciences haunt them.

Lieutenant Edward O'Hare, the intrepid navy flyer who bagged six Jap bombers in one combat to break all records in the history of aerial warfare, today was personally presented the Congressional Medal of Honor by President Roosevelt. In addition, the flyer was elevated to the rank of Lieutenant Commander. The story of the hero's exploit is one of the most amazing tales of the war. During the raid by an American task force on the Gilbert and Marshall islands, the aircraft carrier to which Lieutenant O'Hare was assigned was attacked in succession by two flights of nine heavy enemy bombers. Out of the eighteen Jap bombers only two escaped. Pilot O'Hare personally accounted for six of them. At one time three enemy craft were falling simultaneously from the deadly blasts from O'Hare's six guns and cannon. The Lieutenant hedge-hopped his speedy pursuit ship up and down the enemy formation, knocking them out with uncanny accuracy. Only the fact that he ran out of ammunition permitted the two remaining Japs to escape. President Roosevelt characterized it as "probably the most daring single action in the history of combat aviation."

In another daring raid, the Navy announced today that an American PT torpedo boat had crashed thru a protective screen of four destroyers to torpedo and sink an enemy heavy cruiser.

Wednesday, April 22, 1942: —British Commandos, those mysterious, hard-hitting shock troops, who specialize in paralyzing hit and run attacks under cover of night, yesterday caught the Nazis completely off guard. The black faced Commandos struck terror in the hearts of the Germans as they penetrated the coastal defenses for several miles, killing enemy soldiers and demolishing fortifications and communications. As evidence of the completeness of the surprise, the Commandos reported that they returned without the loss of a man and with very few wounded.

While these raids by the Commandos are unimportant by themselves, the net result which they attain of keeping the Nazis jittery and causing them to expend much effort in fortifying the entire coastline of Europe is extremely valuable to the Allied cause. So jittery have the Germans become that they have withdrawn several of their best armored divisions from the Russian front to patrol the French coast in fear of an Allied invasion attempt. The tempo of Commando raids is steadily increasing in order to intensify this fear. Where will they strike next?

No new developments are reported in the Far Eastern theater of war where things seem to be in a state of preparation for a possible Allied counter offensive this summer. The Japs meanwhile are trying desperately to wrest complete control of the Philippines from the small U.S. and Filipino forces.

The main fighting of the war at the present time is in Russia where the Red Army is still advancing despite a sea of mud and a torrent of fresh Nazi reserves.

Thursday, April 23, 1942: —News from the home front made the headlines today. That bugaboo of every war, inflation, is raising its ugly head. The rapidly rising spiral of prices, profits, and wages threatens to upset the economic applecart unless drastic remedies are immediately applied. For this reason President Roosevelt is preparing a message to Congress to be delivered next Monday outlining an anti-inflation program which will probably include a price ceiling for almost everything, a 99% excess profits tax on war industries and some sort of limitation on individual incomes. All consumer goods may eventually be rationed and an intensive drive will be made to siphon off excess purchasing power by a high pressure sales campaign for War Bonds.

That reminds me that I did not mention that just a few days ago the Treasury Department announced that henceforth Defense Savings Bonds and Stamps will be known as War Savings Bonds and Stamps. This is in conformity with the new temper of the people who want to be done with Defense and to forthwith take the offensive which is more in line with the wartime tradition of Americans.

Admiral Emery S. Land of the Maritime Commission today charged that labor agitation and loafing on the job was hindering the attainment of the ship-building program. This is the second time he had made the charge of "loafing" and probably comes under the heading of "needling" the shipyard workers to put them on edge and thus up their productive capacity just a bit. This is an old and effective strategy on the part of "bosses."

Friday, April 24, 1942: —The Russians reported today that an American bomber, one of those who participated in the raid on Japan, landed in a remote part of Russia last Saturday. In accordance with international law, the crew of the plane were interned. The pilots stated that they had lost their way and were forced to land in Russia. They were all well and cheerful. The plane will now probably be "lend-lease" material.

The British RAF is really going to town. In what is claimed to be the biggest single aerial offensive of the war, they plastered the Heinkel airplane works in Rostock and attacked German occupied Flushing in the Netherlands. Fierce fires were started at both places and even the Germans admitted that serious damage had been caused. In retaliation the Nazis made a feeble raid on the south coast of England. No military damage was caused but sixteen civilians were killed.

On the Burma front the Japs are gaining some headway against the battle weary British and the outnumbered Chinese. The principal Allied difficulty in this battle as in others which have been lost is the lack of adequate air support. In addition to this the British troops have fought for three months without relief due to poor communications and lack of reinforcements. The British General Alexander and U.S. General Stilwell are still optimistic and determined to hold out until the approaching monsoon weather puts a stop to all fighting.

A spokesman for General MacArthur's headquarters in Australia announced today that the threat of a Japanese invasion of that continent had passed its peak. The trend from now on will be toward an Allied counter-offensive.

Saturday, April 25, 1942: —Today and tomorrow are "Registration Days" for the fourth time since the beginning of the emergency. This time it is the "old guard", men from 45 to 64 who must put their names on the dotted line for possible military service with Uncle Sam. It is estimated that more than 800,000 men in this age classification will sign up in California alone. Men who smelled gun powder during '98 and who so successfully "Remembered the Maine" together with their sons who carried Old Glory so proudly through dark days of the Meuse-Argonne, today and tomorrow with answer the call for additional manpower to aid their sons and grandsons who must fight this new and greater war. And although not as strong physically as in those other days, the old fighting spirit is still there as indicated from the eagerness with which they are flocking to registration stations.

The first report of the damage caused in last Saturday's raid on Tokyo has leaked out of Japan. The Japs admit that 114 people were killed in the surprise raid by American planes. No estimate was placed on property damage but admittedly several fires were started in Kobe which may have been more devastating than the Japs care to acknowledge. British broadcasts indicate that the raid on the Japs has been a great stimulant to morale in India— where a stimulant is sorely needed.

A late flash from Stockholm stated that Herr Hitler has suddenly returned from the debacle on the eastern front to Berlin where he is to make a speech before his rubber stamp Reichstag tomorrow. We shall be interested to hear what the great egomaniac has to brag about this time.

Sunday, April 26, 1942: —Another Sunday and it was with great pleasure that I took a full day off from work and war and trouble and once again was back on the green fairways in the warm sunshine and fresh air. Yes sir, I played golf again, the first time since Armistice day last November. What a joy. There isn't anything that will take your mind off your troubles like a good game of golf. It's a great tonic, a great revitalize. I'll bet those European and Asiatic troublemakers have never seen a golf course. You can't hate anybody or want to stab anybody in the back when you're swinging a driver or concentrating on that six foot putt. No sir, you just take a big lung full of sweet smelling air, stretch your arms and say, "Oh, boy!" It was sweet, especially after a week of rubbing your nose on the grindstone in the close confines of an office.

From all we can gather from late news reports, a very strange speech came out of Berlin today. The mighty Fuehrer didn't brag, he didn't claim more great victories, he didn't make any more rash promises about ending the war this summer. No, in the words of the Russian commentators, Hitler didn't take the offensive against any of his enemies, Hitler took the offensive against the German people themselves. He demanded more and greater sacrifices from the suffering masses, and demanded the power of life or death over them to enforce those sacrifices. Contrasted with the domineering, triumphant Hitler of 1939 and 1940, this Hitler is a frightened, sick, desperate man, feeling his house of cards begin to crumble about him. But he has some terrible convulsions left in him before his sickness becomes fatal, and his scourge is forever wiped from the face of the earth so freemen can once again live in peace.

Monday, April 27, 1942: —The rising spiral of prices and the high cost of living, with the attendant danger of runaway inflation, is demanding more and more attention by the leaders responsible for the conduct of the war effort. President Roosevelt today met this inflationary challenge by submitting a seven point program for combating the economic danger. Briefly his program included:

Taxes: All profits above what Congress considers a fair profit to be taken in heavy taxes. A $25,000 ceiling on personal net incomes after payment of taxes.

Farm Prices: The present 110% of parity imposed by law should be reduced to a flat 100%. Farm prices should then be set with a ceiling of parity.

Rationing: All essential commodities of which there is a shortage will have to rationed.

Wages: Stabilization of wages and elimination of double

time for overtime work must be included in the program.

Prices: Ceilings on prices of thousands of commodities together with rent ceilings must be considered.

Savings: People must buy so many War Savings Bonds that it will represent a real sacrifice on their part and draw off billions from dangerous purchasing power.

Credit: Credit and installment buying must be discouraged and the liquidation of debts, mortgages, and other obligations urged.

A glance at this program indicates what the public is in for in the way of restrictions, taxes, and corresponding lower standard of living. War is no fun.

Tuesday, April 28, 1942: —The President tonight, in one of his famous fireside chats, enlarged upon his seven point program of economic controls which was submitted yesterday to the Congress. He made a plea for all out effort by the entire nation to put his program into effect on a voluntary basis if possible. He pointed out that cooperation in this field was one way in which every man, woman, and child can help win the war. Not all of us can fight on the actual battlefront, but all of us help in this way on the home front.

The President also spoke briefly on other phases of the war situation. He warned Vichy France that the United States and her Allies would not permit French possessions to fall into the hands of Axis forces. He also promised China that aid would continue to reach that nations even though the Japs succeed in completely cutting off the Burma supply road. He concluded his speech by relating several tales of heroic conduct by men of our armed forces and stating that any price is not too high to pay to help these brave men win the fight and so preserve our freedom. If anyone thinks this price too high he should ask those people of the darkened continent of Europe who live in misery under the Dictators' tyranny.

The British have tasted some sweet revenge in the aerial war over Europe. The German Baltic port of Rostock has taken a more terrific pounding than did Coventry. British reconnaissance planes report that German civilians are fleeing enmasse from the city, totally ruined by four consecutive nights of huge RAF raids. Grimly pleased at the smoking embers of Rostock, the English flyers are now concentrating on the vital Ruhr industrial city of Cologne. Not so pleasant being on the receiving end, eh, Fritz?

Wednesday, April 29, 1942: —Not money, tears, nor threats could get you any sugar today. Retail sales of the sweet stopped last night until May 5th when rationing begins. This is the first of the many vital commodities that will eventually be doled out by ration card.

Persistent reports indicate that war weary Italy is stirring restlessly. The crisis is so severe due, it is claimed, to lack of discipline and shortage of food, that Mussolini's rule is threatened. Some reports have it that King Victor Emmanuel has decided to assert himself and oust Mussolini. Except for the omnipresent German soldiers that Italians would probably make a separate peace. It was a sad day for Italy when Il Duce decided to dash to the aid of the "victor" at the time France fell. Italy's prestige and power are doomed no matter which side triumphs in this struggle. And the Italian people know it. They are ripe for invasion. It wouldn't constitute much of a surprise if the Italian boot were the scene of opening of the much "talked of" second front. Beware, Benito, thou pitiful lackey of bloody Hitler.

The war news from Russia, Australia, Corregidor, Malta, Europe, all seem favorable to the Allies. The Russians are maintaining their initiative to prevent Hitler from getting set for his overdue spring offensive. Corregidor's magnificent artillerymen smashed two more enemy batteries on the Bataan peninsula. Aussie and American airmen again pounded Japanese bases in New Guinea, smashing enemy invasion concentrations.

In Burma only was the picture black. Weary British Imperials and outnumbered Chinese are slowly, bitterly being driven back, back towards Lashio, the key to China's lifeline.

Thursday, April 30, 1942: —Chalk up another victory for the gallopin' Jap. Today he smashed his way into the vital Burma town of Lashio. This victory completes the severance of the Burma Road lifeline to Chungking. Undismayed, the gallant Chinese announced that notwithstanding the seriousness of the loss, there would be no lessening of their resistance. The difficulties of supplying the Chinese with badly needed war supplies will now be almost insurmountable and may seriously affect their ability to successfully continue their fight. Some way must and will be found to get the help to China. Admittedly it is a grave problem.

The Jap victory renews the threat of invasion of India. In spite of the knowledge that their country is probably the next on the Nippon timetable, India's leaders apparently cannot be counted on to offer much assistance in their own defense. Leaders like Mahatma Gandhi openly favor only passive resistance. What a laugh to blitzkriegers like Yamashita and Hitler. The only language they understand is the hum of bullets.

General MacArthur today sadly announced that Brig. General H.H. George, the heroic commander of Bataan's tiny air force during the early days of the Philippine struggle, was killed in an airplane accident in Australia. Also killed in the same crash was Melville Jacoby, Time and Life correspondent.

As the crucial month of May arrives, all indications are that we are hanging precariously on the verge of mighty events. We shall soon see Hitler's final great lunge for victory. If it fails he is doomed—and he knows it. A mighty lunge it will be, therefore, and men must die!

May

Friday, May 1, 1942: —Another May day has rolled around and finds the world's laboring men at each other's throats. The weather in contrast to yesterday's drizzle has been dry, warm, and cloudless. This has always seemed right for May day, which has always seemed to really inaugurate spring. May of 1942 will in all probability be a fateful month. The snows of winter have melted and the rivers of mud are almost dried up. It's time for blitzkrieg.

The British spring offensive has been on for over two weeks already. The RAF is continuing its tireless pummeling of Germany and occupied Europe. Utilizing a tremendous force of over 4,000 bombers and fighters, the RAF air blitz has already caused the Nazis to yell "uncle" and has been credited with at least delaying Hitler's plans for a spring offensive. Several neutral sources have reported that unofficially the Nazis have attempted to call a truce with the British on the bombing of industrial cities, promising to call off all attacks on English cities if the RAF will let up. But the British will not so soon forget those terrible days of 1940. They have lived, dreamed, and sweated for the day of vengeance. Their day has arrived and they'll not soon relinquish it.

The Japs are going like a prairie fire in Burma, some units having infiltrated all the way to the fabled city of Mandalay. The outcome of the Burma disaster will hardly be a very tasty morsel to the Allied Nations. It's just another classic example of the dire results of a lack of adequate air power. Let's hope that Burma will be the last of these tragic cases.

Saturday, May 2, 1942: —The speed with which the Japs are smashing ahead in Burma is probably the headline news of today. The fabled city of Mandalay has fallen and the Nipponese are driving ahead with a two pronged attack aimed at separating the British Imperials from their Chinese allies and destroying each by itself. This they may do from present indications. The conquest of Burma completed the Japs may elect to attack China proper from the rear in an effort to knock out that oldest and now isolated foe. Or they may strike at India.

If the latter course is chosen the Japs may encounter

surprisingly little resistance. The most influential leaders of India, such as Mahatma Gandhi, are openly advocating no fighting, only passive non-cooperation. A lot of good such tactics would be in the face of one of the Mikado's tanks. However, British troops and some loyal Native troops together with a few American flyers and technicians are on hand as the welcoming committee. The only real hope for India is its very size, which may prove too large a mouthful even for the rapacious Japanese.

U.S. troops are now at battle stations all over the world it is indicated tonight as the announcement is made that American service troops are in North Africa to help the English in the defense of Libya and the Suez Canal.

Our closing thought is directed at these weak kneed mis-leaders of India who advocate non-resistance: As was so truthfully said of Yugoslavia and Greece at the time of their gallant fight against the overwhelming hordes of Hitler—Men may die from fighting but nations die only by yielding. Remember that, India!

Sunday, May 3, 1942: —The practical completion of Japan's conquest of Burma and the recent heavy reinforcements noted at Jap Bases in New Guinea have made the Australians slightly nervous. In addition, greatly increased numbers of Jap bombing and fighting planes have appeared over Port Moresby and Darwin and have wrested local control of the air. All this adds up to fears that the Nipponese may turn southward to invade Australia rather than proceed with any Chinese or Indian campaigns.

The British marathon aerial offensive against Germany and occupied Europe was finally broken up last night. The weather did it. Nasty flying conditions grounded the heavy artillery, big four motored bombers, and gave the Nazis a respite from the terrific pounding that has hurt more than they would have the world believe. Stockholm reports have frequently carried eye witness accounts of almost unbelievable damage at the Baltic port of Rostock. All civilian life has been disrupted and women and children evacuated. Whole sections of the city have been leveled like Rotterdam. Will the bitter medicine embitter the German people against their Fuehrer who has brought all this on them?

Neutral reports state that the Russians have offered the Finns peace with certain territorial gains. Gallant Finland, the heroic toast of the world two years ago, seems a rather pathetic partner to Germany in this war. I believe the whole democratic world would like to see them withdraw from the war and break up with their bloody partner. Besides, it would leave Russia and her allies free to concentrate on Hitler and his mob.

Shut Out, son of Equipoise, won the 68th running of the Kentucky Derby.

Monday, May 4, 1942: —Last night just after finishing my article at 11:o'clock the sirens wailed all up and down the Bay Area. We immediately blacked out, peeked-foolishly, I guess, out the window for a while, and then went to bed. The all clear sounded in about 30 minutes. The army reported the blackout was due to a "target" off the coast which was finally identified as friendly. Newspaper reports today said the blackout was pretty good, except for several glaring islands of lights, caused by people who claimed not to have heard the warning signals.

The big news today is that British troops have occupied the strategic island of Madagascar, off the coast of Africa. The island has been controlled by Vichy France and the move by the British was made to forestall any granting by Pierre Laval of bases in Madagascar to the Nazis. The United States' government announced that the occupation was made with its full knowledge and approval and warned Vichy against making any warlike move against the occupying forces. The only unfavorable repercussion possible from the move is to drive the Vichy collaborationists whole heartedly into the Nazi camp.

Corregidor, that mighty rock in the harbor of Manila, has really been taking a terrific pounding for the last two weeks. Air raids by heavy bombers and dive bombers average thirteen a day. One raid today sent the American gunboat Mindanao to the bottom of the Bay. Besides the bombers the Japs have been sending over a concentrated barrage of heavy artillery shells from shore batteries on both sides of the Bay. Ominous indications are that the defending U.S. guns are running short of ammunition. Buy bonds for shells.

Tuesday, May 5, 1942: —The British occupation of Madagascar has encountered some resistance. Pierre Laval's Vichy government not only spurned the British ultimatum to surrender the island but also rejected the American warning against offering armed resistance. The French collaborationist ordered the French garrison on the island to resist to the end. British Commandos and Paratroops attacking the great Diego Suarez naval base on the northern tip of the island met only light opposition from the white French and native troops. It is estimated that three fourths of the population of Madagascar are pro-Allies and anti-Axis. Successful defense of the island by the French is impossible. U.S. troops stand ready to aid the British if necessary.

The purpose of the Allied move on Madagascar is to prevent the eminent seizure of the vital island by Japanese and Nazi forces. Allied intelligence has hinted that such a move by the Axis forces was nearly at hand. The United States Government is likewise keeping a wary eye on other French possessions, especially the strategic island of Martinique.

The zero hour has apparently arrived for the gallant defenders of Corregidor. General Wainwright's communiqué stated that Japanese landing forces crossed the narrow two mile stretch of water between the fortress and Bataan peninsula at midnight last night and are storming the stronghold. Fierce fighting is in progress. Undoubtedly softened by continuous and devastating aerial and artillery barrages since March 24, the stout American fortress may go down. But the almost unbelievably heroic stand of the magnificent defenders of Corregidor will inspire all Americans to ultimate victory.

Wednesday, May 6, 1942: —CORREGIDOR HAS FALLEN! Almost five months to the day from the beginning of hostilities. Five months of hopeless, one-sided struggle against a ruthless enemy who was not afraid to utilize his tremendous superiority in numbers and pay the heavy cost of victory. But it was the heroic Filipino and American troops who have won their place in history along with the most gallant stands of all times. The value of their great fight, both on Bataan and then on Corregidor, cannot readily be measured. Some experts credit them with the saving of Australia. Their resistance has held immobile a huge Japanese army which might otherwise have made possible the even quicker conquest of Singapore, the Dutch East Indies and then Australia. Their delaying action has give the United States and its Allies time to recover from the first staggering blows. Australia has had time to recall its magnificent Egyptian Army.

The United States has had time to establish bases and lines of communications in vital areas and to transport an ever increasing Expeditionary Force to Australia. It will take history to truly evaluate the accomplishments of the "Battling Boys from Bataan", but their share in the attainment of ultimate victory will undoubtedly be large.

Approximately 7,000 Americans, including two or three thousand civilians, are presumed to have been captured at Corregidor. Included is Lieutenant General Jonathan M. Wainwright, the great commander who vowed to stay with his men and share their lot, whatever it may be. It is another bitter pill and another score to settle for the American people.

Bitter fighting continues for Madagascar, but the British assault forces appear to have the situation well in hand.

Thursday, May 7, 1942: —As if in thunderous reply to the Japs who smothered Corregidor, the Navy happily announced today that an outstanding victory has been won in a naval engagement off the Solomon Islands. Eleven enemy vessels were sunk, seven of them being warships, including a light cruiser and a 9,000 ton airplane tender. This highly successful action was accomplished with the loss of only three planes.

The British have all but completed their Madagascar coup. Prime Minister Churchill announced to a cheering parliament that the great naval base of Diego Suarez has surrendered and the British navy is about to make a triumphant entry into the harbor. Pierre Lava and his fishy Vichy government admitted that the 48 hour blitz of the British had succeeded but threatened reprisal action by the French fleet. Interesting developments should follow.

On the debit side of the ledger the British report that the heavy cruiser Edinburgh and three cargo ships were sunk out of a convoy bound for Russia. Apparently the 10,000 ton warship was struck simultaneously by two torpedoes. The rattlesnakes of the sea are more deadly than the rattlesnakes of the land. The ocean going breed strikes without the slightest warning.

Germany's big industrial center of Stuttgart is being given the Rostock treatment by the RAF. For the third straight night hundreds of heavy bombers have dumped their lethal loads on the doomed city, reducing its industrial plants to rubble. Heavy, heavy hangs over your poor head these nights, Herr Hitler.

Friday, May 8, 1942: —Glaring red headlines proclaim tonight that the naval engagement reported yesterday has developed into what will probably prove to be the greatest sea battle of the present war. It has even been likened to the Battle of Jutland in the First World War. Prime Minister Curtin of Australia, in announcing the first reports of American victory, cautioned the people that the battle was still in progress and the final outcome was very much in doubt. Upon the results will likely depend the whole course of Pacific strategy. If the Japs are beaten it may completely lift the threat of an invasion of Australia. If the fortunes of battle turn the other way some very somber days lie ahead.

According to General MacArthur's most recent communiqué, seventeen Japanese ships have been sunk or badly damaged. One Jap aircraft carrier and one heavy cruiser have been definitely sunk and one other of each category damaged. Two destroyers and four gunboats were also smashed to the bottom.

Tokyo claims, as must be expected, are just the contrary. They claim two American aircraft carriers, the Yorktown and Saratoga, destroyed, together with two battleships, one U.S. and one British, and a couple of heavy cruisers. For this they lost one shallow draft rowboat. Not bad, Mr. Moto. Did it all with a cap pistol too, I betcha.

All other news has been dwarfed today by the great sea battle. I might mention, however, that we bought our first sugar with the new ration books. One half pound of sugar per week per person. Seems like an ample supply. We have never used more than that at any time. But some of these people who use six lumps per cup of coffee may feel the pinch.

Saturday, May 9, 1942: —It seems almost certain that we can chalk the great naval battle of the Coral Straits[1] as an American victory. One hesitates to do this in the absence of complete details regarding the battle. General MacArthur's communiqué, however, flatly states that the enemy has been repulsed and that the initiative remains in Allied hands. It is far from conclusive and it appears that the pursuit continues in an effort to obtain a really decisive result. Tokyo seems a little less jubilant and even admits a little loss—the sinking of a small aircraft carrier and 31 planes. This in itself is a powerful indication that American forces were successful. It is at least clear that the lines of communication from the United States and Australia are still uncut. Further developments will undoubtedly prove very interesting.

On the Burma front, meanwhile, General Joseph Stilwell's hard fighting Chinese troops in a brilliant counter-attack threaten to recapture bomb wracked Mandalay which fell to the Japs over a week ago. Much as they would like to close the books on Burma, the Japs are finding that the Chinese under the American General cannot yet be counted out. General Stilwell wasn't far off when he called his Chinese regulars the "finest troopers in the world"!

A sinister word comes out of Russia today. The Russians claim that the Nazis are beginning to use poison gas. Many authorities have expressed the opinion that both the Nazis and the Japs would not hesitate to use the horrible weapon in a last desperate attempt to win the war. It is fervently hoped that the Allied Nations are ready for this gruesome and inhuman method of legalized slaughter—chemical warfare.

Sunday, May 10, 1942: —Another Sunday has rolled by. In another two hours it will be midnight and Monday, May 11, 1942 will be ready to take its bow in history. The days and weeks seem to flow past with almost incredible speed. But events are moving even faster. It was two years ago today that Hitler unleashed his terrible war machine on the Low Countries and France, beginning his fearful string of military victories that almost enslaved the entire world. But tonight, two long, bitter years later it is becoming increasingly clear that his dream of conquest has fallen short of its mark and by the narrowest of margins and the courage of the British and Russian people, the tide of Nazi success to beginning to ebb. Things are looking up for the United Nations.

Prime Minister Winston Churchill spoke today, on the second anniversary of his assumption of power in England. It was on that fateful day of May 10, 1940 that he grasped the reins of government from the faltering hands of Neville Chamberlain and began his herculean task of guiding Britain through the awful morass of defeat and despair until now the faint glimmer of a new dawn of victory and peace appears on the horizon. In his speech, the Prime Minister warned Hitler bluntly against the reported use, by the Nazis in the Crimean, of poison gas. He flatly stated that any use of the horrible weapon against the Russians will be treated as though it had been used direct against England. The Allies, with no intention of using the weapon first, were nevertheless fully prepared and equipped to employ gas in tremendous quantities in the ever increasing RAF offensive in the air. The only possible deterrent to enemy use of poison gas is the fear of reprisal.

Monday, May 11, 1942: —The United States Office of Civilian Defense today ordered what will be known as a "dim-out" all along the Pacific Coast. This means that all lights facing the ocean must be shaded or put out. The order was made at the request of the Navy in order to prevent what has already occurred several times off both coasts—the silhouetting of merchant and Navy ships with the result that they are perfect targets for lurking submarines. Several ship sinkings have already been attributed to this danger. So, for the duration, the brilliant lights of Seal Rock and Fleischacker's park and beach concessions will be doused. In addition, all street lights and private home windows that are visible from the ocean will be darkened. This war doesn't seem as far away as the last one— as indeed it isn't.

The amazing Chinese under U.S. General Stilwell are continuing their counter offensive in Burma that is taking the over confident Japs back over their recently won trail. Where a few days ago the Japs were invading China's own Yunnan province, the battle now rages in the outskirts of Mandalay with the Chinese threatening to encircle and annihilate the Japanese spearhead. The tables have very unexpectedly turned on the Burma front—most unexpectedly for the Japs. Even the British are pounding back from India. Things are looking up in Burma.

European commentators are still blowing off steam about the gas attack that Hitler is planning to throw against the Russians in a desperate effort to knock out the Red Army. This time it is supposed to be some new kind of nerve gas that is not poisonous but paralyzes the victim's power of intelligent action and decision making. Some fun, eh?

Tuesday, May 12, 1942: —Today at 11:20 A.M. there was an air raid alarm in San Francisco. But it was all a mistake—really a comedy of errors. The Interceptor Command ordered an "alert" which customarily precedes an actual alarm, but somebody at the Central Fire Alarm Station pressed the wrong button, setting the sirens to wailing. Some schools were closed and the children sent home, others merely waited in the schoolrooms, others didn't hear the sirens. The "all clear" sounded at 11:41 but again some did and others didn't hear it. All in all it was the most unsatisfactory alarm the city has experienced since the beginning. It's lucky the unidentified planes turned out to be friendly. Let's hope lots of improvements are made before the day of the "real raid."

Congress is currently working on the proposal to increase the base pay of army and navy enlisted men from $21 to $42 or $50 per month. The Senate has already passed the $42 rate but the House appears to favor the $50 scale. Anyway the boys are definitely going to get a substantial raise. It is also contemplated that dependents of married men drafted will be given an allowance, thus getting down to fellows like myself, for instance, who have a wife and children who must continue to eat and dress if and when we are drafted.

Late reports indicate that the Nazis' spring offensive may be getting under way in the direction of the Caucasian oilfields. About a million of Hitler's crack troops and more than two thousand planes are estimated to be surging forward on the Kerch peninsula. Russian reserves are being rushed up to meet this new and grave threat.

Wednesday, May 13, 1942: —The Nazis' great offensive in the Crimea seems to be making some headway. Even the Russians admit they have been pushed back in some sectors due to the terrific fire power the Germans have brought to bear. Both sides are undoubtedly suffering huge numbers of casualties. The Russians report that brand new three turret American tanks and speedy pursuit planes are doing yeoman service in helping to stem the fury of the Nazi attack. One thing is clear—a critical hour has arrived in Europe. Hitler is gambling everything this summer, and if he fails, he's lost.

The badly beaten Japanese fleet is massing again to attempt a comeback after the worst defeat in its history in the Battle of the Coral Sea last week. Many observers believe that that battle has finally opened the Japs' eyes to the magnitude of the task which faces them. For this reason it is expected that they will strike again very soon in an effort to obtain a decision before more American reinforcements can reach Australia. Like Hitler, the Japs are beginning to realize that their last hope lies in a quick victory this summer. After that the tremendous forces assembling under the banners of the United Nations will overwhelm them. A crucial six month period lies ahead.

San Francisco's "dim-out" for the first two nights has proved to be a brilliant failure. Apparently the trouble is in lack of official orders and proper enforcement. A great many people are trying to cooperate but it will take some expert fixing to really make the "dim-out" effective enough to serve its purpose.

Thursday, May 14, 1942: —Fighting in Russia is rapidly increasing in ferocity. The Germans are driving desperately on the Kerch peninsula and are undoubtedly making some headway against bitter Soviet resistance. But the big news today is that the Red Army itself is launching a brilliant counter offensive in the Kharkov area. A break through is already claimed by the Russians, which, if true, may threaten the whole flank of the Nazis driving south in the Crimean theater. I often wonder if we can even imagine the dimensions of these great battles between these two colossal giants. The extent of the slaughter involved when they speak of killings, is not in the hundreds, or thousands, but in the tens of thousands. The disregard for human life is appalling. How insignificant and helpless the individual soldier must feel. The thing that is amazing is that the people of Germany can stand the annihilation of their men-folk twice within twenty five years. The people of Russia are fighting for their homes, so the price they must pay is understandable, but what do the people of Germany believe they are throwing their lives away for?

A little known but highly effective thorn in the side of Hitler is the continued resistance of Serbian Guerrillas in the mountain strongholds of Yugoslavia. This resistance has attained such proportions that the Nazis have been forced to throw more than 24 divisions (about 350,000 men) into a "little" offensive in an attempt to wipe out this "second front" opposition. The men thus tied up might well turn the tide against the Nazis' on other battlefields, so a great deal of gratitude is due those gallant Serb patriots who wage a hopeless fight with the knowledge that a

115

firing squad awaits them if captured. They've got a special kind of courage.

Friday, May 15, 1942: —The most important war news at this time, of course, comes out of Russia where the two Goliaths are slugging it out. Both armies are advancing, the Nazis in the south around Kerch and the Soviets in the center of Kharkov. Which side has gained the edge cannot yet be determined. No doubt it is much too soon to tell. But the Russians claim that they bested the Nazis in a great tank battle on the outskirts of Kharkov and broke through to the German's second line of defense. On the other hand, the Germans claim and the Russians admit that Kerch is in dire peril and the fighting is extraordinarily fierce. Reserves and staying power will tell the tale.

German U-boats are becoming extremely daring. Two ships have actually been torpedoed in the St. Lawrence River and today it is reported that a large U.S. cargo ship was sunk by submarine action only a mile and a half from the mouth of the Mississippi river. It takes a hardy and courageous set of men to sail the merchant ships in the deadly waters of the seven seas where hidden death lies in wait and strikes without warning or mercy.

On the home front very little excitement has occurred recently. The big news is the huge drive that is beginning on the sale of War Savings Bonds and stamps. To us in the Bank it means just a big increase in headaches. The goal is 10% of everyone's payroll in bonds. The percentage at present is estimated to be about 3% so it can readily be seen how great our expansion must be. The problems are terrific and we fight our own little "bloodless" war every day. Sometimes we actually envy the boys with the guns.

Saturday, May 16, 1942: —The capitals or the world are tense tonight. Many observers are convinced that the war will be won or lost this summer on the plains of Russia. For this reason the whole world is hanging breathlessly on the outcome of the great battles now in progress in the Crimean and Ukraine. Nazi and Soviet claims are naturally at wide variance but a middle line between the two indicates that no conclusion has been reached in either theater of war. Both armies are still intact and the ferocious fighting continues.

Prime Minister Churchill, in a bristling speech, exuded complete confidence that the Red Army will be able to hold out and he cheerfully told the English people that although it would be premature to say that we were over the top, it is safe to say that the ridge is in plain sight and we should soon get over the hump. From there we'll go on to complete victory. Great trials still lie ahead but our ever increasing power will inevitably tip the scales in favor of the United Nations. He hinted that the governments of these nations are as anxious as the people to open up a second front in Europe to help relieve the Russians but he said that those responsible for this job must not fail the people either in daring or in wisdom.

Here at home we are constantly reminded of our particular enemies from the sizable little Tokyo that has been established just a stone's throw away at Tanforan. Seven or eight thousand Japs are more or less interned there pending completion of more distant settlement centers. It's really an American style concentration camp where the inmates live on the fat of the land even though a company of soldiers and blockhouses guard the fenced in enclosure.

Sunday, May 17, 1942: —The weeks dash by. Here it is another Sunday. The war seemed unusually far away today as we worked peacefully in the yard, removing weeds and cutting the lawn, while the warm spring sun poured its liberally quantity of Vitamin D upon us. But in distant lands the war raged on.

The Russo-German conflict continues its gargantuan see-saw in a river of blood. The whole mess is a melee, the outcome of which is extremely uncertain.

The Burma front has shifted back into China. Reinforced columns of Japs have succeeded in driving the British and Chinese almost completely out of Burma. The major fighting is now taking place in China's Yunnan Province. The story here is lack of men and equipment, mainly aircraft.

In Australia, MacArthur's offensive still is in the making, while his air fleet continues its pounding of Jap bases on New Guinea and Timor.

On the home front, the war against the high cost of living is slated to begin tomorrow. A ceiling on prices of thousands of commodities has been set by the Office of Price Administration.

This ceiling is to be the highest price paid for the commodity during the month of March of this year. The only exceptions to this ruling are the following food products: Butter and cheese, evaporated milk, poultry, eggs, fresh fruits and vegetables, flour, mutton and lamb, fresh fish, seafood and game, nuts, dried prunes and beans. Say that's quite a lineup at that. All essentials. But all other articles are covered and the plan should go a long way toward preventing the much feared run-away inflation.

Monday, May 18, 1942: —The big news of today is the arrival in North Ireland of the largest convoy of American troops yet to sail in this war. They brought their own weapons, tanks, artillery, trucks, and jeeps. After a brief "invasion" training they will be ready to "expand to the European Continent" as General Marshall promised. Hitler may well shake in his boots when he reads this news. The Yanks are coming, Adolf. Beware!

Another blow was struck by the RAF today as they caught the famous German cruiser Prinz Eugen off the southwest coast of Norway and sent two torpedoes crashing into her steel plates. German fighter planes drove off the British before they could witness the final results of their attack on the cruiser but, even though the vessel does not sink, it has at least been put out of action for two or three months. Damage to the Prinz Eugen and her sister ships is highly important at this time as they are a deadly peril to the Allied supply route to Russia by way of Murmansk.

Lieutenant John D. Buckeley, the intrepid skipper of the PT torpedo boats who wreaked so much havoc against the Japs in the Philippines, told a press conference in Washington D.C. where he is on furlough, that the speed boats caused terrific panic among the Nipponese. They even caused the Tokyo radio to announce that the Americans had developed a new, secret weapon—a monster with flapping wings which makes a lot of noise and fires torpedoes in all directions. The Nips will be glad to hear that the Lieutenant is very anxious to take another crack at them. Better duck quick, Mr. Moto.

Tuesday, May 19, 1942: —Another American hero was presented with the Nation's highest military award, the Congressional Medal of Honor. It was presented by President

Roosevelt himself in a White House ceremony. The hero was Brig. General James H. (Jimmy) Doolittle, a native of Alameda, California formerly a nationally known speed flyer. General Doolittle is the man who planned and led that daring attack by U.S. bombers on Tokyo just a month ago. The full story of the attack, except how they got there and where they went to was told today. The General stated that the raid was unbelievably successful. The Japs were completely taken by surprise as the heavy bombers streaked over just above the rooftops in broad daylight. Not a single American plane was shot down due to practically no fighter opposition and jittery anti-aircraft fire which succeeded only in shooting down some of their own barrage balloons. Previously picked targets were easily spotted and practically every U.S. bomb found its target. Navy yards, plane and tank factories as well as other industrial plants were the chief objectives and the results were "absolutely devastating."

Besides the General, seventy-nine other officers and men were decorated for their part in the brilliant raid. The whole nation tonight is joyfully repeating the saga of how "Yankee Doolittle went to town." And more is coming, Mr. Moto!

Canadian authorities today announced that one of Canada's most luxurious liners, the Empress of India, was sunk off Singapore in February while transporting troops to the Far East. Only the heroic efforts of an escorting warship averted great loss of life aboard the troop laden liner.

Wednesday, May 20, 1942: —Nazi and Soviet armies are locked in awful battles in the Kharkov area today. Masses of tanks and men are fighting furiously in confused melees all along the line. Above this infernal cauldron of destruction, thousands of fighting planes swirl and dive in deadly combat. American "Tomahawk" planes—called "Tomagauks" by the Russians—are performing superbly. From all indications the Red Army has the edge and is driving steadily ahead over the bloody graveyard of men and machines. The desperate Germans are pouring all their reserves, even boys, into the struggle in an effort to stem the Soviet onslaught.

At the Nazi rear the RAF is pounding industrial Germany with an ever increasing tempo. Three hundred bombers concentrated on Mannheim last night, dumping 40,000 incendiaries and tons of high explosives on the hapless town. Returning pilots described the damage as comparable to that recently inflicted on Rostock. The British optimistically look forward to sending more than 1,000 bombers over Germany every night in the near future. The German people have truly brought terrible retribution down upon them. How long will they be able to take it?

On the home front the war is much duller, thank goodness! It's just a case of work and sweat, and I mean sweat literally. Yesterday and today have been unseasonably hot in the Bay Area. A blistering sun shone brightly without the usual sea breeze or fog to temper its heat.

Gasoline shortages, rationing, wage arguments, rubber conservation, high cost of living, and Production and More PRODUCTION! Those are the topics of conversation.

Thursday, May 21, 1942: —San Francisco had an air raid alarm today. At 12:00 Noon the sirens shrieked. But it was all just a test warning. During all the real alarms up till now, many people have claimed they could not hear the sirens and today's test was to actually find out how effective the high priced equipment is. It isn't! Many "dead" spots were reported but today's practice will help to eliminate them. Maybe the next real night alarm will see the city really blacked out. Let's hope so.

News on the war fronts continues pretty much the same. Russians and Germans are slaughtering each other wholesale. The RAF is constantly on the prowl, evening up the score for 1940. The Australian front is quiet except for General MacArthur's air force which keeps pounding at the Japs' invasion bases in New Guinea and Timor. The hard pressed Chinese in Burma have received some assistance from heavy monsoon rains but are still compelled to retreat. Naval activity is confined to submarine action and Axis U-boats are continuing to exact a heavy toll of merchant shipping off the comparatively unprotected East Coast. Guns, tanks, munitions, and American troops are arriving in ever increasing numbers at various key points throughout the world—Australia, Ireland, India, Libya, Gibraltar, Alaska, and Hawaii. Throughout the entire world the United Nations are rapidly preparing to "give the Axis the axe."

Meanwhile, here at home, the American people are worrying

about how they are going to pay for all these guns, and tanks, and munitions. Bonds, yes; but taxes and more taxes. Today the Treasury Department recommended taxes by payroll deduction. Dig deep, America, the price of liberty is unmeasured!

Friday, May 22, 1942: —Several things are becoming scarce in this war. But the most serious shortage is in the vital substance—rubber! With over 90% of the rubber producing areas of the world in Axis hands, production chiefs are getting a real headache out of the problem of obtaining the necessary supply of the vital substance. Synthetic rubber will ultimately solve the problem but adequate production by this means cannot be expected before the end of 1943. Meanwhile drastic steps are in store for us in conserving the present stockpile. National gas rationing, to limit the use of private automobiles, is almost a certainty. Requisitioning of private passenger cars, both for government or army use and to solve transportation problems in war-boom communities, is entirely possible. A national speed limit of 40 miles per hour has been suggested to lengthen the mileage-life of tires. Many other schemes have been or will be proposed but few of our leaders fully realize how important the automobile really is to Americans. Restrictions on the use or elimination of the automobile from the everyday lives of American families will strike where it really hurts. Free and constant use of autos is an American habit. It won't be so easy to change.

On June 30th, the final registration of U.S. manpower will take place. On that date young men eighteen and nineteen years of age will sign up. This will add another two or three million of catalogued men to the Nation's pool of more than forty million.

President Roosevelt today warned the people to wipe that overly optimistic smile from their faces and get to work for there's "an awfully long war" ahead of us.

Saturday, May 23, 1942: —It looks as though the boys in the armed forces will get that pay raise after all. Senate and House conferees have agreed on the plan to raise the base pay for privates and apprentice seamen to $42.00 per month. This doubles the doughboys' present pay of $21.00 and makes American soldiers and sailors the second best paid fighting men in the world, topped only by the Australians. The bill which is sure to pass will make the new pay scale permanent. Previous bills had proposed the increase only for the duration.

The Russo-Nazi offensives seem to have reached a stalemate. The Soviets just don't appear to be able to crack the Germans' last ring of defenses around Kharkov. The Germans, on the other hand, have almost completely overrun the Kerch peninsula in the Crimea. Except for the great naval base of Sevastopol, all resistance in the Crimea has ceased. Only the narrow Kerch Straits now stand between the Nazi hordes and the rich oil lands of the Caucasus. But the Russian offensive at Kharkov has apparently upset the Nazis' hopes for a knockout blow against the Red Army for some time at least.

Our other main enemy, the Japs, are trying to do their own knocking out. This time they are trying to liquidate the China affair that has plagued them for five years. The Chinese are admittedly in dire straits. Their lifeline in Burma has been cut and the Japs are trying giant pincer movements from Burma on one side and Foochow on the other. It is believed that the Japs are desperate to conquer China from a great fear that China bases will soon be used by Allied planes to again bomb Japan proper. Mr. Moto probably has a sneaking hunch that President Roosevelt's "Shangri-La", from whence came "Yankee Doolittle" is in China.

Sunday, May 24, 1942: —Sunday again, and even the war seems to have taken a day of rest. News is extremely scarce. All attention appears to be centered on the titanic struggle on the plains of Russia around the vital city of Kharkov, known as the Pittsburg of Russia. The real truth of what is going on over there cannot yet be determined. Both sides are making claims of victory but the battle rages on.

In China the Japs are widening their bridgehead near Foochow, in Fukien province. The Chinese wiped out one landing force, killing 5,000 enemy soldiers, but the persistent Japs returned in even greater force and occupied the island of Chuan shih. All China's eastern seaboard is threatened by this new Japanese attack. On the other side of China, from the Burma theater of war we hear that U.S. General Stilwell who commanded the ill-fated Chinese Expeditionary force that tried to save Burma, has escaped to India. The General admits that the

British and Chinese took a bad beating in Burma but flatly states that somehow, someday Burma must be retaken because of its strategic importance. The General says he would like to have a few good old American doughboys with him when the day of revenge comes.

In Australia, General MacArthur's communiqué tells how those good old U.S. flyers are continually pounding the Japs' invasion bases in New Britain, New Guinea, and the Dutch East Indies. Like the British did to the Channel invasion bases in preventing the Nazis from getting an invasion set and under way, so the American flyers are doing to the Japs at their bases for invasion of the "Down-under" continent.

Monday, May 25, 1942: —I witnessed a terrible thing tonight, though at some distance. I had just alighted from the train at the San Bruno depot, and was walking with several other men along the sidewalk when our attention was attracted to a P-38 pursuit plane that had just taken off from Mills Field. The plane's engines were sputtering and coughing with puffs of black smoke, when suddenly the plane heeled over into a sharp dive straight for the ground. Just a second before it struck, the pilot in a desperate effort flattened the plane out of its dive but it smashed into a maze of high tension wires along the Bayshore Highway, zoomed up in a great arc, then crashed with awful force and burst into flames. Needless to say, the pilot, a Lieutenant Hampton, I think the radio announcement said, was instantly killed. Somehow you just stop and meditate in silence for a moment when you see such a thing happen. One second there is a sleek, powerful bird with a fine young man at the controls, the next second there is a jumbled mass of blazing wreckage and the fine, young man is gone!

Nasty charges were aired today in San Francisco at the opening session of Assemblyman Tenney's committee investigating un-American activities in Northern California. This section has a large Italian Colony, some members of which are in high positions. First witnesses accused Mayor Angelo Rossi and former Supervisor Sylvester Andriano of pro-fascist leanings and of giving the fascist salute on several public occasions. Both accused men denied the charges but a nasty scandal is likely to result. This is just another indication of the bitterness and hatred that is bred by war. Hatreds germinated by one war always grow and develop into future wars. 'Tis a vicious cycle.

123

Tuesday, May 26, 1942: —U.S. military experts, including top airmen, tank and infantry strategists, and others arrived in London today for extensive conferences, indicating that heavy Anglo-American blows will soon be launched against Hitler's Europe. It is believed that a mighty air armada of American bombers is already on hand to join the RAF in a terrific aerial offensive against Industrial Germany and occupied territories. In addition it is believed that preparations are being rushed towards the day when a full scale land offensive may be launched in Western Europe in a gigantic pincer movement with the Russians aimed at smashing once and for all the Nazi aggressors.

On the Russian front it is reported that the Red Army is ruthlessly slaughtering trapped Nazi forces in the Kharkov area while dissension reigns in the Germans' high command. Apparently top ranking Nazi Generals have demanded that Hitler, former World War I corporal, relinquish his self-assumed post as commander-in-chief of the Reichwehr. It is recalled that last fall Hitler ousted General Von Brauchitsch after the failure of the drive on Moscow and assumed full command. Hitler had seized all credit for the brilliant successes in Poland, France and the Netherlands and considered himself to be an even greater military genius than was Napoleon. Now, apparently, his Generals have advised the little Corporal to confine his activities to the political field and leave the prosecution of the war to those who know how. Hitler's present trip to the front is purportedly to show these recalcitrant Generals who is boss. Remember the "purge" boys!

The "Jackal" growls again. Italy is picking on poor Vichy France now, demanding immediate possession of Corsica and Nice and special privileges in Tunisia. The "fruits of victory", eh, Gauleiter Mussolini?

Wednesday, May 27, 1942: —The Libyan battlefield flared into renewed action today as General Erwin Rommel's armored Nazis opened what may well prove to be the long anticipated offensive against the Suez Canal. The Germans' first day dash carried them 75 miles across the desert no-man's land. British advance units are in contact with the enemy but details of the fighting are not yet available. Things are really starting to open up. Next will probably be a smash through Turkey into Iran and Iraq in conjunction with Rommel's offensive.

It is reported tonight that Reinhardt "The Hangman" Heydrich was seriously wounded in an assassination attempt. Heydrich is undoubtedly the most notorious and ruthless of the Nazi "protectors" of conquered countries. He has been administering Nazi justice and rule over the hapless Czechs and has earned the loving title of "The Hangman" for his gentle methods of squelching opposition. Severe reprisals will no doubt be visited upon the Czech populace because of this attack. Already 500 innocent hostages have been executed at the behest of Herr Heydrich. Many more will now follow. In addition a reward of 10 million kronas have been offered for the perpetrators of the attack.

Remember the $42.00 the soldier boys were going to get? Well, the House of Representatives are still insisting on the figure of $50.00 in spite of the Senate and House conferees. Senate opinion is that the House will win out. Looks like an even bigger raise, eh, boys!

Signs of the times (and good ones): Chinese kill 2,800 more Japs in Chekiang province. Russians advance over the bodies of countless Nazis at Kharkov. RAF and U.S. air forces promise 200 tons of bombs nightly over Germany. How's the headache, Hitler?

Thursday, May 28, 1942: —Mexico joined the ranks of the United Nations today by declaring war against the Axis. The formal declaration has not yet been made but awaits only the mechanics of assembly action. War was precipitated by continued attacks by Axis submarines on merchant ships flying the Mexican flag.

Brazil also, although not officially at war with the Axis, today announced a "shoot on sight" order similar to the one ordered by President Roosevelt prior to Pearl Harbor. Moreover, the Brazilian Government stated that Brazilian flyers have sunk an Axis sub off the South American coast. Brazil's action is also caused by unrestricted Axis submarine warfare that is becoming increasingly irritating and dangerous.

Meanwhile our own subs are getting in their licks against Japan's supply lines. The Navy announced that American subs recently sank two more large enemy cargo vessels and rammed home two torpedoes into a Japanese heavy cruiser leaving her in a badly damaged condition.

On the home front, Federal administrators have set in motion two plans to prevent the hi-jacking of labor by offering wage increases and the refusal of some persons to leave non-essential jobs for suitable employment in war industries. The first plan calls for the "freezing" of men on present jobs by requiring approval by the Nation Employment Agency before transfers may be made from one plant to a rival plant. The second calls for a virtual "work or fight" edict. Men refusing to accept a suitable job in a war plant will be subject to prompt induction into the armed forces. In order to win the fight for freedom we apparently must forego for the time being many of those freedoms for which we fight.

Friday, May 29, 1942: —As a measure designed to insure the physical fitness of military men and war workers, the Navy today demanded that all saloons and other liquor establishments be closed at midnight. Conditions inimical to the welfare of men in the service long prevalent in taverns and other bars and saloons have been the constant target of high ranking Army and Navy officers. They have even threatened to declare San Francisco "out of bounds" on several occasions unless conditions improved. It is believed, however, that things have been much cleaner and better in this war than was the case in World War I.

The long awaited supply of gas masks is beginning to arrive on the West Coast. San Francisco received 16,960 masks for distribution to air raid wardens and policemen. Oakland and the East Bay received approximately 15,000 masks and other cities along the coast were given similar numbers. Slow as preparations have been and complicated and hindered as they have been by inefficiency and bungling, it is encouraging to note that the West Coast is much better prepared to meet the "inevitable" bombing attack now than it was only a short while ago. Give us a few months more and we'll really be ready to take it if need be. But high Army Authorities don't think we'll get those few months. They believe that, since the devastating raid by General Doolittle and the boys on Japan, a face-saving attack on some part of the Pacific Coast by the Japs is as inevitable as dawn. And we must be prepared for it.

Latest reports are that the Nazi "Hangman" Heydrich, shot by Czech patriots last Wednesday is dead of his wounds. This information is not official but no tears will be shed if it is true.

Saturday, May 30, 1942: —Memorial Day. A day to pay tribute to men who have died in other wars that America might live. Men of Valley Forge, of Bunker Hill, of Gettysburg, and Chateau Thierry. Soldiers under General Pershing, and Grant and Andrew Jackson. Sailors under John Paul Jones, and Perry, and Farragut. Marines at Tripoli and doughboys at the Marne. Warriors of great traditions, men who have never yet tasted final defeat. We salute you—and you new men who are now being tested. Are you worthy to take up the colors where those heroes of old planted them? The gallant lads of Bataan, or Corregidor, and of Pearl Harbor have given us the answer. Yes, Americans can still fight with courage and skill for those things we love—our homes, our families, and our freedom. Memorial Day, yes, and a day of resolution, a day of belt tightening, a day of reverence and supplication for Divine Guidance in the grim struggle ahead. With God's help we shall not fail or falter. Disaster shall not swerve us nor fear un-nerve us. No sacrifice shall be too great, no task too hard. Some of us may die but the rest of us will advance—every advance. There will be no turning back, no hesitating, no slowing down, no contentions. America is on the offensive! On land, in the air, and on the sea, the might of America is on the march. And America will not cease its march until tyranny and oppression have been trampled into the dust and mankind is free once more. That, Hallowed Dead, is our Memorial Day promise to you. Rest in quiet contentment, my friends, until that distant Memorial Day when we shall meet again with you—in lasting Peace!

Sunday, May 31, 1942: —The RAF really smashed at Germany last night. It was probably the biggest air raid ever attempted. More than 1,250 planes took part in the attack which was directed against the industrial city of Cologne. Thousands of tons of high explosives and incendiaries left over half of the city in smoking ruins. Even the Germans admitted that damage was great, which means that the raid was really devastating when the Nazis will admit some damage. Talks of even larger raids to come were commonplace in London today. That the blows were having a telling effect was evident by "terror" raids by German planes in reprisal. Cultural and recreations centers such as Bath, having no conceivable military objectives, were heavily bombed. But the Jerries had their turn at dishing it out in 1940, now it's Tommy Atkins' turn—and does he love it.

The picture in China is not so cheerful, however. Every major line of supply and communication has been severed. China today is all alone, fighting with her back to the wall against a vastly better equipped enemy. She is in deadly danger of being completely knocked out of the war unless help arrives somehow from somewhere—and soon.

The gigantic battle for Kharkov that has raged for nineteen days has finally ended in a stalemate, but it is really a great Russian victory because it has thrown Hitler's timetable off schedule again. He was all set to start his spring offensive when Marshall Timoshenko beat him to the gun.

I forgot to mention that Mexico's senate yesterday unanimously approved the declaration of war on the Axis.

[1] The **Battle of the Coral Sea**, fought from 4-8 May 1942, was a major naval battle in the Pacific Theater of World War II between the Imperial Japanese Navy and Allied naval and air forces from the United States and Australia. The battle was the first fleet action in which aircraft carriers engaged each other.

On 3-4 May, Japanese forces successfully invaded and occupied Tulagi, although several of their supporting warships were surprised and sunk or damaged by aircraft from the U.S. fleet carrier *Yorktown. Now aware of the presence of U.S. carriers in the area, the Japanese fleet carriers entered the* Coral Sea with the intention of finding and destroying the Allied naval forces.

Beginning on 7 May, the carrier forces from the two sides exchanged airstrikes over two consecutive days. The first day, the U.S. sank the Japanese light carrier *Sho-ho, while the Japanese sank a U.S.* destroyer and heavily damaged a fleet oiler (which was later scuttled). The next day, the Japanese fleet carrier *Shokaku was heavily damaged, the U.S. fleet carrier Lexington was scuttled as a result of critical damage, and the Yorktown* was damaged.

Although a tactical victory for the Japanese in terms of ships sunk, the battle would prove to be a strategic victory for the Allies for several reasons. Japanese expansion, seemingly unstoppable until then, had been turned back for the first time. More importantly, the Japanese fleet carriers *Shokaku* and *Zuikaku — one damaged and the other with a depleted aircraft complement — were unable to participate in the* Battle of Midway, which took place the following month.

June

Monday, June 1, 1942: —British fighter planes zoomed in victory rolls over London today in celebration of the great raid on Cologne. It is now revealed that close to 1,500 bombers took part in the attack, making it the biggest and most devastating ever launched against any target. Reconnaissance planes reported that the German industrial   city is still burning with a huge pall of smoke visible for dozens of miles. Photographs of the damage inflicted are impossible at this time because of the smoke. The damage can be imagined when it is reported that 6,720,000 pounds of bombs were poured into the city which is about the size of Boston. It is terrible to contemplate the effect this man made earthquake must have had on the civilian population but as a British Minister today broadcast, Hitler introduced this total war with women and children equally as targets—and now he is reaping the harvest of his works. If the German people would escape the results of this total war they must "eliminate Hitler." Only then can they take their place alongside the decent, peace loving peoples of the world. Until they do this they can expect more and even greater attacks.

British sharpshooters shot down a reconnaissance plane yesterday over the Libyan desert and picked up quite a prize—none other than a General Ludwig Cruewell, second in command to General Rommel. In addition to this loss the Nazis were hard-pressed to extricate the bulk of their armored forces from a well executed British trap just short of Tobruk. The tide of war in Libya is definitely in favor of the English. But in no theater of war does the tide swing from side to side as rapidly as in the burning heat of Africa.

Tuesday, June 2, 1942: —The British are hanging on to the headlines today. Last night the RAF added the city of Essen, with its huge Krupp's arms factory, to the list of German cities to be blitzed. Over 1,000 planes took part in this latest raid and almost as many tons of explosives were loosed as were dumped on Cologne. The Hun will really get his stomach full of bombings before this summer is over. I hope he remembers Goering's boastful promise made in 1940 that if an enemy plane ever reached the skies over Berlin he would take off his coat and go to work. He's down to his undershirt by now.

President Roosevelt today asked Congress to recognize that a state of war exists between the United States and Bulgaria, Hungary, and Rumania. Those countries have declared war against the United States and while this government realizes that these declarations were contrary to the wishes of the peoples of the three Balkan nations and were made under duress by Hitler, they are aiding the Axis' war effort against the United Nations and we must treat them as enemies.

On the widely opposite theaters of war in Russia and Australia, things have settled down into periods of preparations for new offensives. Especially in Australia is the war confined to reconnaissance and bombing missions on enemy bases, while two of the tiny one man subs used by the Japs at Pearl Harbor were sunk in the harbor of Sydney. The sneak, suicide raid resulted in damage to only an old ferry boat.

President Manuel Avila Camacho of Mexico today completed the ceremony of declaring war on the Axis by signing the decree passed by Congress on May 30th.

Wednesday, June 3, 1942: —ALASKA WAS BOMBED TODAY! The flash came in early this afternoon over the radio. From first reports it appears that four large Jap bombers accompanied by about fifteen fighter planes raided Dutch Harbor, site of the United States' naval and air base in the Aleutian Islands. The Navy communiqué indicated that the raid was not a surprise and the station was fully prepared to meet it. The fate of the attacking planes is not yet known but the Navy claims that damage inflicted was very light and casualties few.

It is believed that this bold raid is Tokyo's long expected "answer" to General Doolittle's great raid on Japan proper during April. Knowing the Oriental mind it was to be expected that the Jap would soon try a reprisal attack for "face saving" purposes. A raid on San Francisco or other mainland cities would not even be a surprise in spite of the fact that such an attack would be in the nature of a suicide venture. Unlike the U.S. flyers in their attack on Japan, the Nipponese raiders would not have land bases on the opposite side of their target to which they could hie themselves. Their only chance would be to try to return to carriers lying off the coast. But the Japs specialize in suicide.

The British RAF again smashed at the Ruhr valley last night but in decreased numbers—only about four or five hundred bombers this time. Don't let anyone think these devastating raids aren't hurting the Nazis. Russia really has that second front she was pleading for—at least in the air. Hitler may have to abandon his hopes of smashing Russia this summer and try a desperate gamble at invading England to remove this terrible hornet's nest at his rear. Take care, Adolf!

Thursday, June 4, 1942: —Dutch Harbor received two more doses of bombing yesterday. Reports are very scarce as to the results. Either they're scarce or the Military is keeping the results secret, probably to avoid giving Japan just the information they would like to know—the success or failure of their attacks.

The Dutch Harbor attack may have been just a diversion to draw our attention from the real objective. This is indicated from the flash that has just come in that Midway Island, 1,300 miles northwest of Hawaii, was bombed today in what may develop into an all-out attempt to seize that Island. From there the next step would be Hawaii itself. This time we hope they won't be caught napping.

For the last two nights the entire Pacific Coast, from Panama to Alaska has been on the alert. All radio stations in the area have gone off the air at 9:o'clock. Leaves of all military men have been cancelled and it appears as though things are expected to really open up. I have bee listening tonight to a radio station in Phoenix, Arizona. They're pretty safe up that way, I guess.

A terrible thing happened at the Stockton Army Air Corps Advanced Flying School late last night. An explosion smashed one of the buildings and ten airmen were burned to death. Cause of the explosion has not yet been determined. Tragedy certainly stalks the earth nowadays.

The May 29th reports that the Nazi "Hangman" Heydrich had died were false. The Berlin radio, however, states that the "popular" Gestapo leader died today of the wounds receive eight days ago. He had time to think over his deeds.

Friday, June 5, 1942: —The Jap raid on Midway Island has developed into a full-fledged naval battle between a strong force of Japanese warships, including battleships and aircraft carriers, and an American naval force which intercepted the enemy. The battle is still raging and final results are of course unknown but early reports indicate that U.S. gunners haven't lost their touch yet. At least eleven Jap ships, including several aircraft carriers and one battleship, have been hit and severely damaged.

Inasmuch as the Japanese force includes several troop transports, the U.S. Navy believes the enemy's objective was an invasion of Hawaii. The alert American Navy, and thank God we can say "alert" this time, has nipped the plan in the bud. The outcome of the present engagement will determine the course of the Pacific war for some time to come.

Meanwhile, from other war fronts come the following reports:

Activity on the Russian front has simmered down to local skirmishes and patrols. Both sides are feverishly preparing for the new offensives to come.

In Libya ferocious fighting is in progress. General Rommel's famous Afrika Corps have been halted 28 miles short of Tobruk and the British have started a vicious counter-offensive. Blinding sand, stifling heat, insects, and thirst make the fighting in this theater of war particularly sanguine.

In Western Europe, the RAF is at it again. This time, in addition to smashing at Germany's Ruhr valley, the bombers gave Naples, Italy a taste of total war. How do you like it, Mussolini, my back-stabbing bucko?

Saturday, June 6, 1942: —It looks as though the U.S. Navy has won a great victory in the wide reaches of the Pacific off Midway Island. Although Admiral Nimitz, commander of the Pacific Fleet, would not yet claim the final victory, he announced that two and possibly three Japanese aircraft carriers have been sunk with all their planes amounting to more than one hundred. In addition, at least eleven or twelve other Japanese warships, including one or two additional carriers, three battleships, four cruisers and three transports were badly damaged, some probably sunk. The enemy fleet is in full retreat with U.S. forces in pursuit.

If the major portion of this Jap naval force is destroyed it may wrest complete control of the central Pacific area from the enemy and remove any serious threat against Hawaii and the west coast. It will also speed the day when the great Allied offensive can commence its march back over the wreckage of former defeats.

A story comes out of England showing how well the loyal agents of the British are keeping them posted on Nazi activities in occupied countries. It seems that Germans had very carefully prepared two important airbases. One of them, the real one, was beautifully camouflaged until it was invisible from the air; the other one was a dummy airport, complete with dummy hangars and wooden aircraft line up on the field. The day following the completion of the airports, two squadrons of British bombers come roaring over the channel. One headed for the dummy airdrome and dropped dozens of bombs—wooden ones. The other squadron blasted the real airdrome off the map.

Sunday, June 7, 1942: —It is six months to the day since the treacherous Japs stabbed an unsuspecting U.S. Navy in the back at Pearl Harbor, thus precipitating a war that has truly become global in its scope. Six months of disaster and defeat for the Allied Nations; six months of unbelievable victories and conquest by the back-stabbing little yellow men; six months of American unity, suddenly welded on December 7th into an unbreakable driveshaft of tremendous power, performing miracles of production and preparation—feats that will amaze the world when the full story can be told. A half year of unremitting toil that has transformed the most luxury loving, comfort seeking nation in the history of the world into a hardened, sacrificing, armed camp of determined men and women, about ready to take the offensive in the world's greatest crusade against the powers of evil and tyranny.

Appropriately enough, the half year anniversary of the war found the action centered near Pearl Harbor and the islands of Midway and Wake. But this time the Americans were not caught napping. A resounding triumph has been won by the hard-hitting Navy and its supporting cast of Army, Navy, and Marine airmen. The sorely hurt enemy is scattering for home, hotly pursued by avenging planes and surface craft. The extent of the damage inflicted on the enemy is greater than that of the Battle of the Coral Sea which up 'til now was the severest defeat the cocky Jap Navy had ever suffered.

In comparison, our Navy's losses were ridiculously light. One destroyer was sunk and an aircraft carrier damaged. Several bombers are missing and presumed lost.

Monday, June 8, 1942: —The spreading Pacific naval war is still raging in tumultuous seas off the Dutch Harbor, Alaska area. The action is shrouded in the obscurity of thick fog and heavy seas but continues unremittingly. Admiral King's communiqué admits that the situation up there is obscure because of the bad weather. "We have none too clear a picture of what is going on up there," he said, "but it is going on." It takes men of iron to fight a war in those waters. But America's Navy has those tough "hombres."

While the lads are out there battling for their lives and ours, the Congress is tossing the increased Service Pay Bill around like a medicine ball. The House, you remember, demanded a $50.00 base pay while the Senate wanted $42.00. The conferees agreed on a compromise of $46.00 but the House kicked it out. Now the Senate has revived it has decided to play ball and give the lads their $50.00 per. It looks like it will go through now and be retroactive to June 1st. They have also provided for dependents allowance for men of the four lowest grades. They'll get some of us married men now. I'm ready when they want me.

The Australians had a taste of that Santa Barbara, California experience yesterday when two large Jap submarines appeared and shelled the suburbs of Sydney and Newcastle. Damage light but threw the entire 1,200 mile coastline of the industrial New South Wales into blackout from fears of a repetition. Jap subs have become exceptionally bold in Australian waters of late and may presage an attempt to blockade Australia from American aid which has reached uncomfortable proportions—for the Japs.

Tuesday, June 9, 1942: —The excitement has tapered off on the war news today. The battle off the Aleutian Islands is completely obscured by the bad weather and the Navy has nothing to report from this sector. The Australians are rejoicing over the brilliant American victory at Midway and believe that this action will completely upset the Japanese timetable.

Across the sea to Europe we find that the Royal Air Force is pressing home its second front offensive in the skies over industrial Germany. Another thousand bombers dumped their lethal loads on the heavily punished Ruhr valley. The British have also warned the French civilians living along the Channel coast to evacuate their homes and move inland as large scale military operations are imminent in this area. The Germans on the other hand have forbidden this evacuation and are holding the French as virtual prisoners. Sabotage and uprisings are increasing daily in all the occupied countries of Europe, adding to the growing volcano under the uneasy feet of the Nazi conquerors.

Here in this Country, the war spotlight is turned on the desperate rubber situation. Some experts view this situation as the most serious aspect of the production schedule. President Roosevelt has taken cognizance of the seriousness of the situation to the extent of ordering a nation-wide salvage campaign to determine accurately just how much scrap rubber there is in the Country. If the war lasts very long we may find the vast majority of private passenger cars driven off the highways. Private tires may even be requisitioned for military use.

Wednesday, June 10, 1942: —Late radio reports state that a large taskforce of United States' warships, including at least one battleship, have arrived in English waters to help the British rid the North Sea of enemy surface raiders and submarines. This is just another evidence of the close cooperation which exists between the armed forces of the two nations.

The Nazis have launched another offensive against the Russians. This time their fury is directed against the last great citadel held by the Red Army in the Crimea, namely, Sevastopol. Totally disregarding huge piles of their dead, the Nazis are hurling hundreds of tanks, heavy artillery, and thousands of infantry against the stout bastion. The Russians admit that the situation is serious but every bit of ground won is costing the Germans very heavily.

In Libya, the Axis forces under General Rommel are increasing their pressure against Bir Hacheim, the vital desert crossroads 48 miles southwest of Tobruk. Bir Hacheim is being held valiantly by British and free French motorized troops. The fall of this vital salient might cause the whole collapse of the British defense of Libya. Both on this front and in the Crimea it is evident that the Germans are really opening up with their desperate summer offensives.

The Japs, meanwhile, after sourly admitting heavy losses in the Midway battle, which they attribute to lack of sufficient air support, were boasting that they have occupied several islands in the Aleutian group. U.S. Navy authorities deny any truth to this report, stating that "no inhabited islands under our control in this area have been occupied by any uninvited guests."

Thursday, June 11, 1942: —Washington and London today announced the results of the most important parley since the war began. The United States, Great Britain, and Russia, coincident with visits by Soviet Foreign Minister Molotov, formally agreed on the urgent need for establishing a second European front against the Axis this year rather than in 1943. Britain and Russia signed a 20-year Mutual Aid Pact and the three countries laid plans for the firm establishment of a more permanent peace at the end of the war. The agreement also provides that no separate peace will be made by any of the three powers.

Thrilling details of the brilliant American victory at Midway were told today by U.S. Army airmen who manned the great Flying Fortresses during the action. Several of these officers were in San Francisco today on their way to Washington D.C. on an undisclosed mission. They told of daring runs through thick anti-aircraft barrages to drop their heavy bombs "squarely on the nose" of important units of the Jap fleet. Indications are that the losses inflicted on the Japs will prove to be far greater than was at first believed. The invading fleet included more than 50 large warships of the Jap Navy and the entire fleet was either sunk or sent reeling back with untold damage. It is conservatively estimated that the enemy lost over 10,000 men in killed alone. The defeat is undoubtedly the greatest in Japan's history.

The only discouraging note is from Libya where the British and Free French withdrew from Bir Hacheim under terrific pressure.

Congress sent the bill giving doughboys $50.00 per month to the President for signature.

Friday, June 12, 1942: —Bad news today! The Navy has finally release the information that the great U.S. Aircraft Carrier, Lexington, was destroyed during the Battle of the Coral Sea. Japanese dive-bombers and torpedo planes scored several direct hits despite skillful handling of the great ship, and the efforts of anti-aircraft batteries and defending fighter planes. Fires raged for hours throughout the mighty floating airport until the situation become hopeless and the Captain ordered the crew to "abandon ship." Shortly thereafter the great vessel was ripped apart by terrific explosions of torpedoes and other munitions stored in the ship. The once proud queen of American aircraft carriers finally slid to her final resting place beneath the waves. Ninety two percent of her crew were rescued but the blow was a severe one. Chalk one up for the bloody Japs.

Another bit of unfavorable news, though not necessarily bad, is the confirmation today by Washington that the Japanese have actually made some landings on islands in the Aleutian archipelago. The islands invested were some very rocky and barren ones in the Rat Group, a very appropriate place for the Japs to go. It is doubted if the enemy has obtained much military advantage from the seizure but their landing parties are having the attention of the welcoming committee of the U.S. air force in Alaska. News of further developments must await reports coming piecemeal from this storm-ridden area.

Major General Clarence L. Tinker, commander of the Hawaiian air force has been reported missing in action during the Midway battle. It is feared the General is dead.

Saturday, June 13, 1942: —Late reports that another convoy, the biggest yet, of heavily armed American troops has arrived in Ireland. Tanks and all the other modern equipment of war was delivered with the soldiers. We must have a substantial A.E.F. over there by now. That invasion of the Continent may not be so far off. The Yanks are coming, Hitler. Beware! Remember those "Devil Dogs" of 1918. Well, they'll be even tougher this time.

Several U.S. bombers were forced down in Turkey today. The planes were returning from what is believed to have been a bombing attack on the Rumanian oilfields. They were forced off their course by defending Messerschmitts and ran out of fuel over Turkish territory. The flyers and planes were interned. This incident shows how the long arm of U.S. power is stretching out to smash at all enemies of the United Nations. It was a pointed reminder to the Rumanians, Bulgarians, and Hungarians that we haven't forgotten their unfriendly behavior and that we weren't fooling when we declared war on them eight days ago.

Marshall Erwin Rommel is shooting the works in an effort to take Tobruk from the British and thus split up their Libyan armies. The whole power of the Nazi's Afrika Corps is being thrown savagely into the terrific heat of the desert battle. The pendulum of battle is swinging back and forth rapidly. The vital outcome remains shrouded in uncertainty.

Reminiscent of 1940, the British Isles were attacked by two "waves" of bombers last night. The "waves" consisted of one plane each. How "reminiscent" of the fiery raids of June 1940, when hundreds upon hundreds of Nazi bombers smashed at London with ghastly regularity.

Sunday, June 14, 1942: —Another pleasant summer Sunday has come and almost gone. Pleasant in that the weather has been warm and balmy with nothing but peace and quiet in the air— unless, of course, you take a look at those flights of P-38's that roar past every half hour or that Navy blimp that floats by morning and night or notice those flatcars loaded with heavy army tanks that rumble by three or four times daily. Or you might take a look at those jeeps and peeps that dash by all the time with their smiling khaki clad boys aboard or walk over by Tanforan and see our 10,000 little slant-eyed guests. At night you might watch those giant searchlights that scan the skies. Except for these things it's hard to realize that the world is desperately at war, whole nations aiming to destroy other nations; men trying violently to remove other men from this existence. It can't be! It's too nice and comfortable to loll here in the warm sunshine. It can't be — but it is!

Tomorrow begins one of the most unique "drives" in history. At the request of the President of the United States, the people are going to gather all the scrap rubber they can find in garages, barns, bathrooms, etc., and deliver it to the nearest filling station. They will sell it at one cent a pound to the station which will in turn deliver it to the Government to help meet the serious rubber shortage.

Action in the Pacific war has again turned to Australia, where General MacArthur reports that the Japs bombed Port Darwin. Damage was light and four enemy planes were destroyed. Reconnaissance planes report that the Japs are massing for a probable invasion attempt against Northern Australia.

Monday, June 15, 1942: —Heavy-hitting American Army and Navy bombers are still smashing at the Nipponese Navy in the far reaches of the North Pacific. Six large Japanese naval units were claimed damaged and one Jap cruiser sunk in action off the Aleutian islands. The Nips, however, are still hanging on to their landing on the island of Attu. Unless they are ousted from all toeholds in the Aleutian chain, they remain a threat to Alaska and even the West Coast.

The Japs are making considerable progress against the Chinese armies. The Chinese admit that the situation is serious and they stand to lose the vital Chekiang-Kiangsi railroad. General Chiang-Kai-Shek's hard-pressed armies are badly in need of supplies and air support.

In Russia the fury of all-out Nazi offensives from Kharkov in the Ukraine to Leningrad in the North is daily mounting in intensity. The Nazis are throwing in their whole stack in a last desperate attempt to win the pot. But the stonewall defense of the Russians, such as that shown at Sevastopol, is exacting a terrific toll from the invaders. How long they can continue to pay such prices is problematical. Reports have even come through today from neutral Stockholm that bread riots have broken out in Germany's big seaport of Hamburg. It was here, you remember, that German sailors revolted in 1918 to start the Kaiser on his way down the skids.

Only in Libya do the Nazi arms appear to be meeting with any success at this time. Here the British admit that Marshall Rommel is bringing tremendous pressure to bear and has hacked his way to within fifteen miles of battle-scarred Tobruk. Losses have been huge on both sides.

Tuesday, June 16, 1942: —American planes and perhaps American warships put in their first appearance in the Mediterranean theater of war today. Big four motor Consolidated B-24 bombers helped to escort the biggest convoy of the war— more than 100 cargo vessels—through the gauntlet of enemy attack in the narrow Tunisian Straits. Italy's remaining battle fleet, in addition to Italian and Nazi aircraft, put to sea to intercept the convoy. There ensued what the Italians claimed was the biggest naval battle of the war thus far. Their claims, of course, were wildly exaggerated but Allied losses were undoubtedly heavy. The important thing, however, is that the convoy arrived at its destinations which were Tobruk and Malta. In addition, the British Navy and American planes inflicted serious damage to the attacking enemy forces. One Italian heavy cruiser was sunk and hits were made on at least one battleship. Several Italian destroyers were destroyed and others damaged. Dozens of enemy planes were shot down. The extent to which American warships participated was not revealed nor was the losses suffered by the convoy or defending escort vessels. This will not be done until the information will be of no tactical value to the foe.

In Australia, Port Darwin was heavily bombed for the fourth day in a row. Twenty seven Jap bombers, escorted by twenty five Zero planes attacked the town and lost six of their number to the defenders. In retaliation, U.S. and Aussie planes struck at Jap invasion bases in New Guinea.

First reports on the rubber salvage campaign are promising. Thousands of tons of the precious material are being rescued from garages, attics and bathrooms.

Wednesday, June 17, 1942: —More details of the great Mediterranean naval and air battle have seeped out today. Eye witnesses told how high flying U.S. bombers scored at least 35 direct hits on Italian battleships and cruisers. Following this attack up with torpedo planes, the British RAF succeeded in sending one heavy cruiser to the bottom and severely damaging two dreadnoughts. Green American pilots, fresh from training camps, conducted themselves like veterans.

The rest of the war news today hinges on the three other main theaters of war. Axis forces are on the offensive in all three sectors and are desperately throwing everything they've got into the struggle. In Russia, the Nazis are heaping their dead before the gates of Sevastopol, and have succeeded in overwhelming some local strong points. The Russians, however, are evidently carrying out their threat to defend the city to the last man.

On the other two fronts, Libya and China, the Axis forces are progressing more successfully. The tired British are battling desperately to save Tobruk from the steel-tipped prongs of Marshall Rommel's panzer troops. In China the Mikado's own panzers are driving relentlessly against the gallant Chinese. At the cost of 8,000 casualties, the Nips captured the important railroad junction of Shangjao in Chekiang province.

In this country, President Roosevelt today signed the bill into law, calling for a minimum pay of $50.00 per month for soldiers, sailors, and marines. That's the best news of the to date, eh, boys?!

Thursday, June 18, 1942: —The bad news of today comes from Libya where things are going badly for the British. The vital strongholds of El Adem and Sidi Rezegh have been abandoned in the face of terrific Nazi pressure. This leaves Tobruk virtually encircled and in a very precarious position. British authorities fear it may be necessary to evacuate Tobruk and retire to the Egyptian border, where a successful stand may be made. It appears that the Imperial Forces in Libya are in the worst position of the war to date. Egypt and the Suez Canal are definitely threatened.

In Russia, the courageous defenders of Sevastopol are grimly hanging onto their present lines, punishing the enemy with huge losses in men and equipment. The situation is admittedly grave but the defenders had sufficient strength left to sally forth today and retake several of the strongholds that were lost during the last few days fighting.

Information has been received that those U.S. bombers that were forced down in Turkey, as reported last Saturday, were part of a larger squadron that took off from Egypt and raided the important oilfields in Rumania. The raid caught the Rumanians and Nazis completely unawares and the oilfields were left in blazing ruin. No opposition was encountered and the target was so good that some of the American planes tarried a little too long and ran out of fuel on the way back to their base. We are beginning to forget our gentlemanly "Marquis of Queensbury" habits, which don't work in war, and are hitting the foe where he least expects it and when he isn't looking. It'll take more of the same to win this scrap.

Late flash is that Winston Churchill is in Washington D.C. for another confab. More on this tomorrow.

Friday, June 19, 1942: —The picture in Libya grows blacker. Late reports state that the British have retreated another 80 miles. Tobruk has been encircled and is under artillery fire. The balance of the Imperial Eighth Army has retired to the Egyptian frontier. It appears that the English have decided to try to hold Tobruk as they did for seven terrible months of last year. This time, however,

Rommel seems to have much heavier artillery at his disposal.

The complete reversal of the British in Libya has come as a bitter surprise. Just a few days ago it was believed that Rommel was in danger of being trapped and annihilated. But the brilliant Nazi General pulled the "hidden ball" play and has crossed the goal line standing up. Egypt and the Suez are their greatest danger since the war began. Their predicament may cause the Allied High Command to revise its whole strategy.

Emphasizing the seriousness of the situation, the United States Government today warned all American citizens to leave Egypt. This is merely a precautionary measure, in anticipation of transportation difficulties which will be encountered later as a result of the approaching battle for Cairo and Suez.

Reports have been received this evening that American bombers are again ranging over Rumania and the Black Sea area. It is apparent that U.S. leaders believe that any blow at Hitler's oil supply is an effective blow. The Nazis' desperate drive in the direction of the Caucasus is evidence of Hitler's growing need for more oil to supply his rapacious military machine.

Saturday, June 20, 1942: —The fate of the British in Libya is shrouded in conflicting reports. Some state that Bardia has fallen to the panzers; others claim that the English are hanging grimly on to the battle-scarred part. Tobruk is hourly expecting a frontal attack supported this time by heavy artillery and paratroops.

Some authorities in London and Washington discount the value of the German victory in Libya, claiming it has no decisive effect. But the majority of experts take a serious view of the situation, in only from the effect it has of upsetting Allied plans and returning the initiative to the enemy.

Another theater of war that is shrouded in mystery is the battle for the Aleutians. It's a weird, wild country up there, torn by terrific storms and hidden by interminable fog and rain squalls. The Japs apparently are hanging on to their precarious foothold on Attu but the Yanks are smashing them through every rift in the clouds. Some magnificent stories of courage and sacrifice, heroism and adventure will someday come out of those frozen wastes.

Mystery and secrecy seem to be the signs of the times

nowadays. The military talks between President Roosevelt and Prime Minister Churchill are of the highly private and confidential variety but the consensus of opinion is that far reaching decisions will come out of them dealing primarily with the opening of a second front in Europe to relieve some of the pressure from Russia. Where and when this front will be established is for us to conjecture and the Nazis to worry about. How's the headache nowadays, Herr Hitler?

Sunday, June 21, 1942: —The longest day of the year has arrived and with it the usual bad news of the Libyan war. Tobruk has fallen. Twenty five thousand British soldiers and heaven knows how much equipment have dropped like ripe plums into the paws of the Nazis. The conquest of Libya by Rommel's panzers is now complete and the Nile Valley and Cairo shiver nervously under the shadow of invasion. Apparently it was a tremendous and shattering attack that the Germans launched against the valiant Tobruk garrison for they didn't have a chance to repeat their brilliant defense of last year.

The west coast of the North American continent was attacked again today. For the first time in its history as a Dominion, Canada felt the impact of enemy shells on its territory. An enemy submarine, presumably Japanese, lobbed a dozen shells at a radio station on the west coast of the island of Vancouver, B.C. The extent of damage and casualties has not yet been disclosed. The attack is reminiscent of the shelling of an oil refinery by a Jap submarine off the coast of Santa Barbara, California. As a result of the latest attack, the entire coastline has been dimmed out for the duration.

From General MacArthur's headquarters in Australia comes the briefest communiqué of the war to date. The war in that theater has been reduced to "reconnaissance flights over all important enemy bases."

Four million identification tags for "The American Army of Occupation of Germany" have received A-1 priority rating. A hint of what's to come, eh?

Monday, June 22, 1942: —We're being attacked! That is, one puny Jap submarine is making a nuisance of itself along the West Coast of the North American Continent. Yesterday, you remember, it lobbed some shells onto Vancouver Island. Today, it moved down the coast and tried out its target practice on the Oregon coast near Astoria. The nine five inch shells that were fired were obviously aimed at nearby Fort Stevens but the aim was very bad and the shells, some of which were duds, landed harmlessly on the beach and swamp bordering the shoreline. The Tokyo radio claimed that the attacks threw the entire Coast into panic. Don't they wish that was true. The Jap crew that fired the shells will probably never arrive in Japan to tell the story as the U.S. Navy is hot on the scent of the sub.

The 16th day of the Nazi attack on the Russians entrenched in Sevastopol, fins the situation growing graver for the Red Army but ghastly losses in men and equipment have been inflicted on the advancing Germans. The Russians have apparently determined to fight to the last drop of blood and the capture of the city, if it occurs, will undoubtedly be a hollow victory for the Nazis. Can they continue to pay such terrible prices for minor victories?

Today marks the first anniversary of Hitler's "60 day campaign" against Soviet Russia and while the Sevastopol situation is bad, the Russians are satisfied that their general position is not nearly as forbidding as it was just one year ago when the "invincible, irresistible German juggernaut" rumbled across their border without warning. United and confident of the future, the Russian people bravely face their second year of "all-out, total war."

Tuesday, June 23, 1942: —The Battle for Egypt is developing. It is feared that the wily General Rommel will immediately press his advantage by launching a combined land and parachute invasion of Egypt. He is said to have perhaps 250,000 seasoned parachute troops available in Crete. The British on the other hand, are desperately reinforcing their Eighth Army and some American flyers have entered the fight. The famous B-24 Consolidated bombers with U.S. men aboard attacked Rommel's supply base at Benghasi.

In the far Pacific, U.S. submarines succeeded in smacking Japanese communications between Hong Kong and Shanghai, sinking four out of a seven ship enemy convoy of cargo vessels.

In London, the British are smoldering over the bitter defeat at Tobruk. Lack of aggressive spirit was blamed for the sudden reversal from imminent victory to black defeat. Marshall Rommel has also developed into a sort of "Bogey Man" to the British forces. Their tendency has been to wait and see rather than to go and attack. The most common fear among the Allied commanders was "where will Rommel hit next." This sort of thing has caused a great deal of dissatisfaction with the military leadership in Great Britain, so great that it may even affect Churchill's popularity.

Dreadful charges by the Chinese that the invading Japs have practiced wholesale murder of civilian men and rape of young and old women in their advance in Yunnan province, were hurled today. Such ghastly indictments should make the American people resolve mightily that no opportunity shall ever be afforded these yellow brutes to practice their particular kind of hell in this country.

Wednesday, June 24, 1942: —The cloud of war deepens and darkens over the plains of Russia and the deserts of Libya and Egypt. The gallant resistance of the Russian men and women in Sevastopol is showing signs of crumbling. Eighteen days of terrific pressure is beginning to take its toll of the endurance of the defenders. As was shown by the boys of Bataan, human powers of endurance have their limitations.

In Libya, the Nazi General Rommel is obviously preparing to take full advantage of his recent triumphs by driving immediately against Egypt. His powerful panzers were thrusting their steel tipped snouts across the Egyptian border, probing the British defense lines. The British, meanwhile, are desperately rushing up reinforcements and preparing to make a stand somewhere within the Egyptian frontier. The RAF and American Consolidated B-24 bombers are pounding at the Axis supply bases in an effort to disrupt the Nazi offensive. The general outlook is bleak.

Prime Minister Winston Churchill faces a storm of protest upon his return from conferences with President Roosevelt. Even conservative members of Parliament are losing confidence in the military leadership since the disaster at Tobruk. Churchill may risk everything on a vote of confidence.

Very little is heard from Australia nowadays. That front has quieted down as the Japs concentrate on their Chinese offensive.

We over here believe and hope that General MacArthur is quietly, quickly, and effectively preparing for his eventual counter-drive that will carry him back through Java, Singapore, Corregidor, Bataan, and Manila to Tokyo.

Thursday, June 25, 1942: —The Nazi offensive against Egypt is gaining momentum. Powerful Axis columns have smashed their way 100 miles into that country in two days. The British claim that their forces were withdrawn to better defense positions but this doesn't minimize the growing danger to Alexandria, Cairo, and the Suez Canal. Reports indicate that the Allied high command is rushing all available reinforcements into the fight including one U.S. armored division from Iraq. This last report, however, comes from enemy controlled sources.

On the Russian Kharkov front the Nazis are also making headway. The Soviets admit that the Germans have advanced in the Kharkov area, although at "enormous cost." In the Sevastopol theater, the Reds are hanging on bitterly, stopping every enemy drive at bayonet point. It is rumored that hundreds of Russian women are participating in the last ditch fight.

On this side of the oceans, Argentina and Chile, the only remaining South American countries which have stayed even partly friendly to the Axis nations, have been rudely jolted by recent Axis submarine sinkings of the merchant vessels. The most recent torpedoing has caused a wave of anti-axis agitation in Argentina that may end in a diplomatic break with America's enemies. If this could be accomplished it would result in a solid pan-American block against the Axis Nations.

The scrap rubber drive is going into its final stages with its total success very much in doubt. The last few days, however, may put it over the top. Let's hope so!

Friday, June 26, 1942: —The eyes of the world at the moment are on Egypt. The Axis armies are driving relentlessly onward although the decisive battle is yet to be fought. The British are striving desperately to regroup their battered Eighth Army while the RAF and American bombers try to slow up the enemy advance. Will the outcome be the same dismal picture as that of Hong Kong, Singapore, and Burma?

On the brighter side of the situation we find the Allied air fleets in Britain and Australia pounding heavily at the enemy. In Europe the RAF uncorked one of its super specials in a terrific raid on the vital port of Bremen. More than 1,300 planes participated in the affair which flattened Bremen in exactly 75 minutes. Fifty two planes were lost in the action for a less than 4% casualty rate which usually indicates a very successful operation. Reconnaissance planes which later flew over the target area reported the city is blazing furiously.

MacArthur's airmen from way down under blasted Jap bases on Timor Island and New Guinea in one of the biggest raids of the war in that area. Enemy shipping and supplies were severely damaged.

To end this report on a sour note which is the keynote of the news that last few days, it is necessary to point out that up to date we seem to be definitely losing the war in the Atlantic. In American waters only Axis submarines have destroyed 323 merchant vessels which is faster than they can be replaced. Unless a solution is forthcoming soon we face the prospect of seeing our swelling production of planes and tanks and guns rotting on the wharves for lack of shipping to take them to the fields of battle.

Saturday, June 27, 1942: —The battle for Egypt has not yet been joined. The British are consolidating their lines at Matruh, approximately 135 miles from the Libyan border. The Nazis have advanced to within about fifteen miles of the stronghold but have not yet started their main assault. Meanwhile the RAF and American bombers are pounding away at the invaders with some success.

The Germans haven't cracked the defenses of Sevastopol yet. The gallant garrison is holding out magnificently against furious attacks by Axis forces who surged forward over stacks of their dead. The Russians say that there has been more hand to hand fighting in the battle for Sevastopol than in all the rest of the war put together. The Nazis may find that it has taken them longer to take this one town than they expected it to take to conquer all of Russia. I wonder how their "six week campaign" seems to them now. The Red Army is really in a better relative position now than it was at the beginning of the struggle.

San Francisco is playing host to fifteen British and American war heroes today. This afternoon a parade honored them and they were leading it in "jeeps." As each hero was driven by with his name and rank emblazoned on his "jeep" he was warmly applauded by the multitude of spectators. Tonight at 7:30 they will speak to a throng at Civic Auditorium. They were all fine looking fellows, mostly quite young. The ranking officer of the lot is Squadron Leader John D. Nettleton, a British lad of 24. He has been decorated for bravery in leading his squadron on many daring raids deep into the heart of Germany. We should feel pretty secure with men like them fighting for us.

Sunday, June 28, 1942: —Today was the hottest day of the year in the Bay Area. No wind and the sun poured it on. It really felt good to get a real sun bath again. Vitality and strength seem to enter every pore as you lay exposed to the good old ultra-violet. Strength to start another week of struggle in a world at war. Over here, Sunday means relaxation and repair of worn-out nerves and tissues. But over there Sunday seems to mean just another day of strife and bloodshed. Let's see what the news says:

The Nazis are trying desperately to get their Russian offensive under way but the Red Army has a knack of upsetting their applecart before they can get started. In the Kharkov region, the Soviets smashed two great tank attacks and even threw the Nazis backwards by a slashing counter attack with their own tanks. In Sevastopol it is the same story except that the fighting is closer with frequent man to man clashes.

In this country the war has been brought home to residents of the Eastern seaboard by an acute gasoline shortage that has tied up countless automobiles and trucks. Eighty percent of the retail dealers had to hang out "sold out" signs. Many important function, such as war plants and physicians, were hampered by the transportation problem. This condition is the East is a bitter shame considering the vast supplies of gas and oil in other sections of the country, especially on the West Coast. But continued sinkings of tankers in the Atlantic and the lack of adequate pipeline facilities have brought about this "simply hellish" situation as one eastern oil leader called it.

Monday, June 29, 1942: —This evening we attended the beautiful Ice Follies Carnival in San Francisco. The smooth, flowing grace of the skaters provided a pleasant means of taking our minds off the grim subject of war. There is probably no more beautiful spectacle than this carnival on ice. Splendid skating adorned with gorgeous costuming and clever showmanship was the order of the evening.

Returning home, it is unusually difficult to take my mind off the enjoyable scene just witnessed to again contemplate the bitter course of the worldwide conflict. The course indeed continues to be quite bitter for our side as the powerful panzer corps of Nazi General Rommel surge over the desert sands of Egypt, brushing aside the defending British mobile units with disdain. The stronghold of Matruh where it was expected that the British would make their stand, fell to the Nazis in a wild, bloody battle which left the defenders in rapid flight toward El Daba, only eighty miles from the great naval base of Alexandria. The Egyptian picture is black indeed.

In the Pacific, however, American Army bombers reported a highly successful attack against the Japanese held base at Wake Island, where early in the war that small but heroic band of U.S. Marines made their famous stand. Favorable weather aided the attack and returning pilots reported their opinion that the base had been render at least temporarily useless.

The rubber drive that was scheduled to end tomorrow has been extended another ten days by the President. The move was necessary because of the relatively poor results obtained so far in the desperate drive for the vital commodity.

Tuesday, June 30, 1942: —News reports from Egypt continue to be disheartening. Apparently Nazi General Rommel's vicious drive toward Alexandria and Suez is very difficult to stop. The Germans have the British on the run and apparently intend to keep them that way. With no let up, the Axis forces have smashed 95 miles eastward from Matruh, on past El Daba, the gateway to the great English naval base of Alexandria. Loss of Alexandria would probably menace not only Suez, but also British control and communications throughout the entire Mediterranean area.

The anxious British, in a desperate effort to stem the drive, have relieved Lieut. General Neil M. Richie of his command of the

Eighth Army of Egypt, placing General Sir Claude Auchinleck, commander-in-chief in the Middle East, in personal command, and have rushed reinforcements, including American troops and equipment, to the battleground. American soldiers may thus get their first real taste of modern tank warfare.

The Nazis have also opened up on the Russian front and have increased the pressure on both the Sevastopol and Kharkov lines. The Russians claim the enemy was repulsed at both places, with may German tanks trapped and destroyed, but admit the loss of some territory and emphasize the gravity of the situation.

On the credit side of the ledger, chalk up another great raid by the RAF on the German port of Bremen. More 300 planes took part in this third big raid on the German town since the weekend.

July

Wednesday, July 1, 1942: —The Germans today claim the fall of Sevastopol. After 25 days of constant assault by a great army, the defenses collapsed and Nazi flags fly over the Crimean citadel—so says Hitler. No confirmation of this claim has come from the Russians but the fall of the beleaguered city has been expected for several days. If true, the capture of Sevastopol would complete the conquest of the Crimea by the Nazis and leave them separated from the rich oil lands of the Caucasus by only the narrow Kerch straits.

In Egypt the British claim their retreat has ended 62 miles west of Alexandria and the main battle of Egypt is about to begin. In an order of the day, the new commander of the Eighth Army, General Sir Claude Auchinleck, called upon his troops to "stick it out" in a supreme effort to save Egypt. The situation is very grave.

Let's take a look at our little yellow enemies on the other side of the earth. From all indications, the Japs are massing troops in Manchukuo for a probable back-stabbing attack on Siberia at the opportune moment when the Russians are fully occupied with Hitler on the European front. The threat is so obvious that it seems that it would be wise for the Russians to beat them to the punch by declaring war on Japan and turning over all available bases to the United States and our Allies for bombing attacks on Japan proper. Vladivostok, you remember, is only a bare 700 miles from the heart of Japan's industrial centers. General Doolittle's raid could be multiplied many times and with less preparation and risk. Are the Russians, too, going to wait until the enemy is ready and chooses his own sweet time to attack?

Thursday, July 2, 1942: —A slightly more cheerful note was sounded today in the Battle for Egypt. The British, heavily reinforced with Middle East troops, have counter-attacked and stopped the surging Nazis—at least for a time. More optimistic reports have even stated that General Rommel may have over extended himself and walked into a trap. His armored columns have raced over 400 miles since the start of the present drive.

In London, Prime Minister Churchill won a decisive vote of confidence in the House of Commons today. Assuming full governmental responsibility for the disasters in Libya and Egypt, the Prime Minister nevertheless declared his belief that "the general strength of the United Nations has greatly improved in 1942." Then he demanded a show down to either support the government or change the government. They supported the government by a vote of 475 to 25. In spite of some blunders and mistakes that Churchill may have made, he is really the only man in England fitted to inspire and lead the British Empire in its most critical hour. Down in their hearts the English know this—as does England's enemies.

Reading like a mystery magazine story, the United States Army and Navy Intelligence today announced the breaking up of an intricate espionage and sabotage ring of Axis agents in the Panama Canal Zone. A trap set by an adventurous young American Intelligence officer provided the top that led to wholesale arrests of leaders of the ring which included submarine supplying in its retinue.

War department figures on U.S. casualties so far in the ware are 12,939 Army Navy, and Marine Corps personnel killed, wounded, or missing. Of this number 10,917 are Navy casualties. These figures apparently do not cover prisoners.

Friday, July 3, 1942: —The Soviet High Command today confirmed the fall of Sevastopol. The exhausted defenders, worn out by eight months of siege and twenty-seven continuous days of terrific assault, were forced to evacuate the ruined city. The Nazis undoubtedly paid a tremendous price for this vital seaport but the Germans have all along evidenced their willingness to pay whatever is necessary to obtain their objectives. Apparently this is a required attitude in modern war. A sea of Nazi blood for a Russian sea port.

The German drive into Egypt has been definitely stopped. Vigorous counter-attacks by British armored forces and infantry put the Germans on the defensive in the El Alamein sector, sixty miles from Alexandria. Berlin reports state that United States' troops were encountered for the first time in the El Alamein battle but no confirmation of this has come from Allied quarters. Weariness from constant fighting and lack of adequate water supplies have contributed much to the stalling of the Nazi war machine. Germans captured have reported water rations as low as one pint per man per day, and that in heat up to 120 degrees during the day. The Allies have also maintained air superiority and have pounded enemy bases at Benghazi and Tobruk without cessation.

One of those daring "rattlesnakes" of the sea, a Nazi submarine, stole into Costa Rica harbor last night and torpedoed an American freighter, the San Pablo. There's no denying the audacity of the enemy sub crews but this raid has probably been a mistake. South American feelings towards the Axis nations has been none too good and these sub attacks against their sovereignty is driving every South American country to war against them—even Argentina.

Saturday, July 4, 1942: —Independence Day! One hundred and sixty sixth anniversary! Not a day for celebration this year. Rather a day for dedication. A day to dedicate ourselves to the rigors of the task before us. The Nation that was born one hundred and sixty six years ago—born of fire and disaster, is now faced with its greatest test of fire and steel. The test has barely begun but has already reached an intensity never before attained in the history of the Republic. We must dedicate ourselves, our all, to do everything demanded of us and many things not demanded of us to win our way through to a new dawn of peace and prosperity. We can do no less on this Fourth Day of July of the year of our Lord one thousand nine hundred and forty two!

Slashing in aerial-led counter-attacks, the British today continued to pound Nazi General Rommel's flanks in Egypt, putting him definitely on the defensive for the time being. Hope is even growing that Alexandria and the Nile Delta may yet be saved. Some of the heaviest fighting occurred about five miles south of El Alamein where Rommel's most determined efforts to effect a break-through had failed.

The U.S. Navy today announced that attacks are continuing against Japanese occupation forces in the Aleutian Islands. Army bombers severely damaged three Jap transports near Agattu Island, indicating that the enemy is trying to occupy that island in addition to Kiska and Attu which are now in their hands. Weather conditions up there still are hindering offensive action.

U.S. airmen, based in England celebrated the 4th today by making their first attack on occupied Holland and inflicted some telling damage on enemy installations.

Sunday, July 5, 1942: —News on this Sunday remains in the same general trend as reported yesterday. The tide in Egypt continues to turn slowly yet steadily in favor of the Allies. Crack New Zealand regiments slashed Rommel's flanks with vicious bayonet attacks that sent the Nazis and Italians squealing in reverse. That cold steel in the hands of the husky New Zealanders was a little too much for even Rommel's hardened desert fighters.

Far across the world in China, as tough a group of American fighters as the world has seen today issued a challenge to the Japanese air force. It came from the "Flying Tigers", that famous American Volunteer Group who have now been incorporated into the United States Army Air Corps as the 23rd Pursuit Group. Brigadier General Claire L. Chennault, former organizer and leader of the "Tigers" and now their commanding officer stated that for two months the Japs have been giving the American flyers a wide berth, fleeing on sight. Only twice in that time have the Americans brought the enemy to bay, each time annihilating him. The new American unit has issued an open challenge to the Japs to meet them in decisive combat.

Another brilliant feat of a U.S. airman was reported today. It happened in yesterday's attack by American flyers on enemy airdromes in Holland. A Douglas twin-motored light bomber, piloted by Captain Charles C. Kegelman, was badly shot up while attacking an airdrome at low level. With one propeller and starboard motor shot away and the wing in flames, the plane actually hit the ground but the intrepid pilot literally bounced the plane off the ground and attacked a gun tower on the field, knocking it out, and successfully nursed his crippled craft back over the Channel to safety.

Monday, July 6, 1942: —Action in the Aleutians made the headlines today. U.S. submarines joined in the fray and reported sinking three Japanese destroyers and leaving another enveloped in flames. In spite of this counter action, however, the situation in the Aleutians is fraught with danger, not only to Alaska and the West Coast, but also to our own plans for an offensive against Japan proper. Armchair strategists are criticizing the Navy for failing to oust the Jap invaders from the island chain before this. One can only believe that the military authorities are doing everything they can along this line.

Black news comes out of Russia today. The Germans' grand

offensive is really on. Following the fall of Sevastopol, the Nazis threw their war machine into high gear, smashing with terrific fury against the center of the southern front near Kursk. The Russians admitted large gains by the Nazis and made no effort to minimize the power of the German drive. Hitler is making his greatest bid for the wealth of the oil laden Caucasus. If he makes it he figures himself good to win the war. The Allies don't concede this but realize that successful penetration by the Nazis into the Middle East would undoubtedly add years to the war's length. Desperate efforts will be made by both sides, you can rest assured.

British Imperials continued to hold the initiative in Egypt today. Exhaustion of Axis troops and constant and effective pounding of Axis' bases by RAF and American bombers have been the principal causes of the reversal of form. Caution is still the watchword for predictions on the outcome of this crucial struggle.

Tuesday, July 7, 1942: —A mixture of good and bad dotted the war news picture today. Things look especially grave for the hard fighting Russians at this time. The Nazis are really putting the screws on. The German High Command claimed the capture of the important railhead of Voronezh on the highroad toward Rostov and the Caucasus. Marshall Semyon Timoshenko, however, was flinging his great fifty ton tanks into a counter blow but it is too early to determine its effectiveness. The Red Army is fighting desperately with its back to the wall and knows full well that the blue chips are on the table. That they will play their cards well we can be assured but it would be a wonderful thing if they only had an ace in the hole to flash at the crucial moment. Effective American and British aid could well be that "Ace in the hole." Let's hope it gets there in time.

In Egypt, the British are slowly edging Rommel back, retaining the initiative by superior air power and increased reinforcements, especially of bayonet wielding New Zealanders. Rumor has it that the Nazi General has either been killed or wounded in the recent fighting but Allied authorities give little credence to the report.

On the home front, the war is being fought mainly by the rationing boards and the "critical materials" shortage drives. The rubber outlook is dark, with the drive producing far less than expected and the President warned that all passenger car tires may have to be seized if the situation gets worse. Sugar, on the other hand, looks better. A "bonus" of a pound on the next ration card has been declared to absorb some of the excess supply that is stuffing the warehouses of the country. A grease and cooking fat campaign starts tomorrow.

Wednesday, June 8, 1942: —The Russian front commands first place in the news today. The Nazis have smashed a dangerous wedge into the Russian lines approximately eighty five miles southeast of Kursk and have captured Stary Oskol, another strategic railroad and river town. Their spearhead of tanks has also thrust west from Veronezh into the upper Don Valley. The Soviet High Command admits that the situation is extremely desperate and is calling frantically for increased aid from the Allies.

Balancing the scale somewhat is the Moscow report that Russian submarines have twice hit the great German battleship, Tirpitz, with torpedoes, inflicting serious damage. The Tirpitz is a sister ship to the ill-fated Bismarck which destroyed the great battle cruiser Hood last year and was in turn tracked down and sunk after a terrific battle. The Tirpitz, like her sister ship, was preying on Allied shipping lanes from England to Russia.

In Egypt, the battle has reached an impasse, with Nazi General Rommel digging in to defend his gains and to attempt to get his second wind before extending his conquest to Alexandria an Cairo. The British, however, with the American bombers, are making the crafty German General's task a difficult if not impossible one. The Axis forces may find themselves in a worse trap than the British walked into in Libya—we hope.

Another Jap destroyer has been reported sunk by U.S. submarines on the prowl in Aleutian waters. This raises to fifteen the number of enemy warships and transports sent to the bottom in this area since the Dutch Harbor attack.

Thursday, July 9, 1942: —I just about lost track of this day in history. I worked until eleven o'clock with hardly a breathing spell to find out what's going on. A huge drive is on to sell more and more Savings Bonds. July's quota is one billion dollars worth of the registered securities. Only in January was this total reached and then it was due to the tremendous surge of popular feeling which resulted from the Japs' treacherous sneak attack on Pearly Harbor. To attain the billion dollar goal in July, therefore, the Treasury Department is straining every nerve and utilizing every medium. Payroll Deduction Plans are growing in volume and account for a tremendous total of sales each month. Banks, Post Offices, Trust Companies, Building and Loan Associations, Federal Credit Unions have been designated in large numbers a issuing agents. To reach the July figure it is now decided to qualify responsible department stores and other large retail dealers as issuing agents for the sale of Bonds over the counter like any other merchandise.

It is proving to be a huge and expensive operation to attempt to finance a large part of the war cost by means of these small denomination, registered securities. In World War I Liberty Bonds of the coupon bearing, unregistered, negotiable type were sold but resulted in some damaging after effects. The Savings Bonds this time are not transferable and cannot be dumped on the market as were the Liberty Bonds. The registered variety will consequently be held by the original purchasers to be used after the war as an effective hedge against ruinous inflation and a stimulus to post war consumer buying. If it works out this way, the cost will be justified.

Friday, July 10, 1942: —The Navy Department today announced that Admiral Nimitz, Commander-in-chief of the Pacific Fleet, and hero of the Coral Sea and Midway battles, narrowly escaped serious injury or death when his plane crashed when landing at a West Coast airport. The co-pilot of the plane was killed. Admiral Nimitz was in this country to receive the Distinguished Service Medal and to confer on the Pacific naval situation.

The German Army's great offensive against the Russians is making some headway. The Nazis' monstrous tanks and charging infantry are churning through a river of their own and Russian blood, and crunching over the piled bodies of their dead. But they are moving forward nevertheless. The picture for Russia is the blackest since the latter part of last summer when it looked as if Moscow would fall momentarily. This time it is the entire Don Basin and the rich oil lands of the Caucasus that are in mortal danger. The Germans have forced a crossing of the Don

River and have pushed southward to cut the Moscow-Rostov railroad. The Red Army, however, seems to be trying the same strategy as last year when they slowly retired in face of the terrible pressure but maintained their armies intact and in good order. How well they will succeed this time remains to be seen.

The Egyptian front has flared anew today. Bitter fighting is in progress near the Mediterranean Coast in the region of El Alamein. The trend of the battle is not yet evident.

The national rubber drive comes to an end tonight. Fears are expressed that the total amount of scrap collected will fall far below expectations but actual figures will not be known for several days.

Saturday, July 11, 1942: —The British nipped a desperate attempt by Nazi General Rommel to reinforce his cornered army when the RAF intercepted a big group of huge Junkers-52 troop transport planes and destroyed more than a dozen of them, driving the rest back across the Mediterranean. Each of these great planes can carry from forty to sixty fully equipped soldiers and have been successfully utilized by the Nazis in both their invasion of Crete and their attack on Egypt. This time, however, the RAF and American air forces in Egypt have maintained superior air power for the first time and Rommel may find it extremely difficult to extricate his army by means of airborne reinforcements.

In Russia the German spearhead into the Don Valley is steadily edging forward, slipping and jabbing its way between the ribs of the Russian Army, feeling and probing for the vital spot to sink home the death blow. The Russians, however, are giving an excellent account of themselves, exacting a terrific price for every mile of Russian earth. Unless the Red Army's defenses suddenly crumble, the Nazis still have a long way and a lot of hard fighting to go yet before the rich oil of the Caucasus comes within their covetous reach.

The war with Japan seems to be just smoldering at the moment. Both sides are undoubtedly preparing feverishly for their next moves but until those moves erupt into action there is very little to report. In Australia, General MacArthur's activities are still confined to aerial sorties and reconnaissance. Some action flares daily and nightly in the skies over the advance Jap bases in New Guinea and Timor.

Sunday, July 12, 1942: —One interesting bit of war news that I overlooked mentioning on the day it happened was the capture by F.B.I. agents of eight German spies and saboteurs. These men were secretly landed in this country from Nazi submarines and brought with them a huge supply of explosives, incendiary material, and plans of numerous important defense factories and public utilities. It was their obvious intention, until the F.B.I. nabbed them, to spread death and destruction throughout the country.

All of the eight spies were former residents of this country, either as aliens or as naturalized citizens, who returned to Germany shortly before the outbreak of war to offer their services to Hitler. All spoke perfect idiomatic American, had plenty of U.S. money and connections throughout the country which would allay suspicion, and it was a magnificent piece of counter-espionage on the part of the F.B.I. to nab them before their career of destruction could begin. The Government men uncovered large caches of scientific and devilish mechanisms of sabotage.

In Germany captured spies would be executed immediately but in this country the processes of law must run their course even for enemy spies. The Government has appointed a military tribunal of seven Generals who will try the Nazis with the death penalty demanded by the prosecution. Attorney General Francis Biddle himself, will prosecute the case.

In addition to the spies the Government agents have today picked up fourteen relatives and assistants of the doomed men, thus completely breaking up one of the boldest Nazi schemes for spreading fear and panic among the people and damage among the vital industries. Nice going, F.B.I!

Monday, July 13, 1942: —With the strength born of desperation to win the war this summer, the Nazi hordes are driving slowly, steadily, and bloodily deeper into the vitals of Russia. Like the fingers of a gigantic hand grasping at the Russian throat, the Nazis are thrusting their steel-tipped Panzer claws forward in three great drives, near Veronezh in the Don Valley, Taganrog and Rostov near the Sea of Azov, and on the northern approaches to Moscow. The Russians are fighting fiercely and sacrificially but the situation is critical. Hitler is determined to smash the Red Army this summer no matter what the cost. He needs victory to feed his grumbling people; he needs oil to feed his rumbling war machine.

The British are still pounding Rommel's Afrika Corps in Egypt. The Royal Navy joined in the fracas today in a lightning bombardment of the Nazi base at Matruh. More than 700 high explosive shells were pumped into the town in fifteen minutes. Smoke and flames from the blasted harbor soared 6,000 feet into the air. On land, the tough, desert-tested Australians have returned to the battle. Almost all of the Aussies were withdrawn from the Egyptian front last winter when their homeland was threatened by the Japs. The swashbuckling men from "down under" were heavy contributors to the previous Allied victories in Libya, and their return to the fray should bolster the British outlook substantially.

In China, the much neglected Chinese are still battling the Japs to a standstill and have stalled the Nipponese drive towards the coast towns of Foochow and Wenchow. The important island of Futou near the mouth of the Min river was recaptured today by the fighting Chinese.

Tuesday, July 14, 1942: —One can almost feel the terrible pressure of the attack clear over here. The awful intensity of the fighting, the savage and brutal horror of the carnage, the stark reality of the danger to be faced. Russia is battling for here existence. Her fate is in grave doubt as the Nazi hordes pour on over mountains of German corpses, threatening to split the armies of Russia in twain. Rostov and the oil-rich lands of the Caucasus are threatened in the south while Moscow itself is endangered in the center. The Soviets are landing some telling blows of their own but as yet have not been able to slacken the power or pace of the German advance. Russia's main reliance this summer is to hang on until the Allies are able to open the promised second front in Europe to divert Hitler's legions, thus easing the terrific pressure being absorbed by the Red Army alone. That England and the United States will open this second front as soon as possible cannot be doubted but will it come soon enough? To attack in force before sufficient preparations have been made would be suicidal and only result in a repetition of Dunkirk. The Russians have their job cut out for them—they must hang on.

Meanwhile, in Egypt the British are continuing to pommel Rommel with everything they've got. The Nazis, however, are taking it and with the help of reinforcements are maintaining their positions. The battle for Egypt is still very much undecided, with both sides gathering strength for the decisive battle.

A U.S. Navy report today recapitulated the score of the great American victory at Midway. Twenty Jap warships were sunk or damaged, 275 enemy planes destroyed and 4,800 Jap officers and men lost. U.S. losses were light and victory was won by such men as the Marine pilot who deliberately flew his damaged plane right down the smokestack of a Jap carrier.

Wednesday, July 15, 1942: —Boastful claims a week ago by the Nazis that they had taken the vital city of Voronezh have proven to be false. More than 35,000 Germans have paid with their lives before the gates of this citadel but yet the Russians fight on. In other sectors of the front, however, the Nazi panzer troops are advancing with growing momentum. The Germans are less than 90 miles from Rostov, the key to the Caucasus. On the central front the invaders renewed the pressure on the Russian lines only 125 miles northwest of Moscow. The Red Army admits that the situation is the gravest since the start of the war nearly thirteen months ago.

In Egypt, the Nazis are again attacking but the British lines are apparently holding. The most bitter battle is raging on the Hill of Jesus, west of El Alamein. The main attack started just at dusk when the sun would be in the eyes of the British and see-sawed back and forth throughout the night. According to correspondents on the spot, it was a spectacular show with gleaming criss-crosses of tracer bullets, star shells and multi-colored flares that lent a fearsome aspect to the engagement. Heavy artillery flashes lit up the horizon like flashes of lightning and the explosions of the huge shells rocked the earth with flaming regularity. The final outcome of the battle is not yet clear but it is believed that the attack has bogged down.

On the home front, the ugly specter of inflation is causing the Government plenty of headaches. President Roosevelt indicated that he may have to take a hand in checking the dangerous trend. Strict wage controls may become necessary.

Thursday, July 16, 1942: —The eyes of the world are glued fascinated on the terrific battles for life being waged on the plains of Russia and the deserts of Egypt. The situation in Russia grows more critical hourly. The Nazi steamroller is pushing the Russians ever closer to Stalingrad, the Volga River, and the Caucasus. One lightning thrust by steel tipped panzers advanced more than seventy miles.

In Egypt the decisive battle appears to still be in progress. Hundreds of heavy tanks are involved in the sanguinary conflicts that may well decide the fate of the Nile valley. U.S. airmen are joining in the fight in increasing numbers and several U.S. bombers successfully raided the Nazi base at Benghazi. Vast German reinforcements said to be massing on the island of Crete may be thrown into the struggle by the sly German General Rommel. The British are also rushing up all available manpower for the show-down. Keep your fingers crossed!

The Chinese showed that they have some offensive power left in their weary armies today when they stormed and recaptured the important town of Tsingtien, northeast of Wenchow in Chekiang province. The gallant Chinese who have suffered longer and harder than any other people in the world are still full of confidence and fight. If anyone is entitled to taste the fruits of ultimate victory it is the long suffering Chinese.

The first group of "Waacies", women soldier auxiliaries were sworn in today. Monday morning they will report for duty at Fort Des Moines, IA, where they will join thousands of others from all over the country.

Friday, July 17, 1942: —It's the same story today. Interest centers around the two main theaters of action—Russia and Egypt. The fierceness of the fighting in Russia can only be half imagined. Both sides realize that this is it; this is the critical hour—the decisive hour for victory or defeat. The fate of two great nations, if not the world, hangs in the balance. Is it any wonder that the Nazis smash forward even over mountains of German corpses while the Russians resist every foot, jealously fighting for every inch of Russian soil, dying in the tracks rather than yield to the "fascist devils." Both Russia and Germany have shown their adeptness at waging "total war." Very little quarter is given and less asked. Death is having a field day on the plains of Russia.

In Egypt the decision has not yet been reached. It seems to

be a case of the irresistible meeting the immovable. Rommel is battering his head furiously against the stonewall defense of the British Imperials. But the tide can change swiftly in favor of one or the other of the contestants as it has so many times in the past. These desert battlefields are "a tactician's paradise but a quartermaster's headache" in the worlds of a captured Nazi General. The problems of supply and reinforcements will probably be the deciding factor.

The U.S. Navy today revealed that its forces in Alaska are taking determined steps to remove the Japanese threat that has developed in the Aleutians. American bombers and submarines have steadily pounded the enemy invasion forces on Kiska and Attu islands.

Saturday, July 18, 1942: —Not much to report today. The war picture from Russia is confusing. That terrific fighting is in progress is about all we can be certain of; all else is merely a case of claim and counter-claim. German communiqués would lead you to believe that their operations are merely mopping up tactics in pursuit of a "beaten enemy." The Russians claim that Nazi losses are so huge that the Reichwehr will not be able to recover and rebuild as it did last winter. The Soviets admit that they are retreating, but in perfect order and according to pre-arranged plans. They acknowledge the gravity of the situation but apparently are confident of eventual victory.

The picture in Egypt is clearer. Here the Nazis have succeeded in driving far into the land of the Pharaohs' but have fallen 60 miles short of their main primary objective of Alexandria, principally because of over-extended lines of communication and lack of air superiority. The British have rallied from their serious defeat and are apparently turning the tide once more against the foxy Nazi General Rommel. Superior air power, now augmented by the U.S. heavy bombers, have contributed much to the successful stemming of the Axis tide. Australian and New Zealand troops have also entered the fray once more and have proved once again their adeptness at this fiery desert warfare.

Very little excitement has occurred on the home front for a long time. The war has settled down here to work and prospects of more work, more taxes, more salvage campaigns, less gasoline, less traveling, less vacation, higher living costs and fewer luxuries—in short, Sherman was right![1]

Sunday, July 19, 1942: —Another Sunday has come and almost gone. Usually on Sunday we like to do something that takes our minds off the routine of work and trouble. Since the war we have not done much of this Sunday "gadding about" in line with rubber conservation and all. Today however, as we had two visitors from Salt Lake City, we piled in the car and spent most of the day in San Francisco at the magnificent Fleischacker Zoo, then a ride across the awe-inspiring Bay Bridge and down the east bay to San Leandro, then back. We won't be doing much more of this Sunday driving but a taste of it forcibly reminds us how "American" the habit is. Americans are the greatest Sunday drivers in the world and it hurts to have this pleasure curtailed. But it is just another reminder of how much we have to fight for in this "American way of life." No barbaric Nazi or treacherous Japs are going to destroy or curtail for long those "inalienable rights" of which we are so justly proud.

A sinister warning that the Japs may be up to some more treachery is reported in late dispatches which indicate that the Nipponese are massing additional troops in north China, menacing Russia's eastern Siberia. The Nips are only waiting for the psychological moment when it appears that the Russians are in serious straits in the west to pounce on the back in Siberia and administer the "coup de grace." As mentioned once before, Russia would be wise, in spite of the handful she has with Hitler, to beat Japan to the gun by opening Vladivostok and all her other bases to the Allies for bombing bases against Japan proper. Why wait for Japan's convenience?

Monday, July 20, 1942: —The Allied outlook in Egypt is improving somewhat. British lines have withstood all that Rommel has been able to muster in the way of an attack and are now showing signs of getting under way in a determined counter-attack. American heavy bombers in increased numbers are blasting at the Axis' supply bases in conjunction with the RAF. Especially was the enemy base of Tobruk raided with tremendous fires started among the harbor installations.

The all-out German drive in Russia is grinding on despite awful losses. Only in the Veronezh region were the Russians able to repulse the Nazis but farther south the Germans were nearing the key city of Rostov, the gateway to the Caucasus. Three dangerous panzer columns are threatening to pinch the city on three sides. A decisive battle is expected before the city actually falls—if it ever does—as Marshall Timoshenko is massing his reserves before the city for a major stand.

Meanwhile, the hard pressed Soviets are glancing nervously at Siberia, gravely menaced by the massed forces of the Rising Sun. The Nips are reported to have about 840,000 seasoned troops ready and raring to go at the first treacherous word from Tokyo. All that is holding them up is the possibility that the Russians may not be folding in the west and the Nazis will yet be stopped. But the Japs will not wait long if the Red Army shows real signs of slipping.

Final discouraging note: 415 U.S. merchant vessels have been torpedoed by Axis subs since December. That is a faster rate than we are building them. It can't go on!

Tuesday, July 21, 1942: —Good news comes from the Aleutians today. U.S. forces apparently are making a serious effort to dislodge the Japs from their isolated bases. American submarines operating in the dangerous waters have sent three more enemy destroyers to the bottom with torpedoes.

President Roosevelt today named Admiral William D. Leahy, recent ambassador to France and a hard-bitten old sailor-diplomat, as his Chief of Staff. The move is calculated to set up the long-needed unity of command between the various armed services. The Admiral will be accountable only to the President and is expected to eliminate much of the red-tape and delay previously resulting from a lack of a unified command.

The President also announced that results of the recent rubber drive. If I heard it right over the radio, 454,165 tons of scrap rubber were collected. While far short of the anticipated collection, this amount of the vital commodity will help considerably in relieving the dangerous shortage.

As the Egyptian front settles down, with the British holding at all points, talk is increasing in London regarding the possibility of a "second front" in Europe this summer to relieve the desperate Russians. Some authorities unofficially believe that the Allies may be forced to try a "second front" offensive this year even though not entirely ready. The risk of failure is great without adequate preparation but the risk from a Russian defeat is considered even greater. The full force of the Nazi war machine must be diverted—and soon!

There was a thirty-six minute "alert" tonight. No blackout. No bombs! The alert ended at 9:45 P.M.

Wednesday, July 22, 1942: —The war news tonight is a little more cheerful. While the Nazis'"big push" in Russia is still gaining ground, it is reported that Marshall Klimenti Voroshilov has amassed a great new army of freshly trained reserves on the line from Veronezh to Stalingrad, poised for a mighty blow against the Germans' flank. These new troops are recruits drawn from Russia's huge reservoir of manpower during last winter's campaign and trained behind the Ural mountains for just such an emergency as has now arisen.

In Egypt the British are starting to take the offensive, supported by increasingly superior air power. All remaining sectors in the important Hill of Jesus region were recaptured by Allied forces. The RAF reported it had complete freedom of action over the battle areas today, encountering practically no enemy fighter opposition.

In Europe the RAF resumed its aerial offensive against German industrial centers. More than fifty great 4,000 pound bombs, known as "block bombs" by the Germans—from their habit of leveling a whole block of buildings in one catastrophic explosion—were dumped on the manufacturing city of Duisburg. Favorable weather aided the flyers who stated that much of the enemy city was laid waste.

Hints, reminiscent of the propaganda used by Hitler during his attacks on France and the Low Countries, comes out of Washington, indicating that the United States may have a "secret weapon" of its own. Congress has included an item of $30,000,000.00 in the new budget to be used in developing the secret and lethal "weapon." Look out Hirohitler!

Thursday, July 23, 1942: —United States Bombers are putting in more frequent appearances all over the world lately. American-made Flying Fortresses are now aiding the Russians in their defense of the Don Valley and Rostov. Russian communiqués indicate that their Air Force has succeeded in slowing the Axis drive but that the position before Rostov may soon become untenable. At Veronezh, however, the Russians still have the edge, killing thousands of Nazis, destroying dozens of tanks, and seriously threatening the entire German flank.

In Egypt, American bombers are lashing the Afrika Corps, striking effective blows at the Nazis' supply bases and communication lines. The Allied position continues to improve in this area. Egypt, however will continue to remain in ghastly danger until Rommel and his legions are driven and smashed back across Libya.

In China, U.S. flyers caused heavy damage to the Japanese main base of Kiukiang, on the Yangtze.

Another great convoy of American troops arrived in Ireland today. It was the biggest yet and crossed the Atlantic without incident. Talk of opening a second front in Europe was revived but many experts believe that the Allies best bet to help Russia this year is an all-out, round-the-clock, daily air offensive against the industrial cities of Germany. Raids like those on Cologne and Emden, if maintained daily, would soon paralyze Germany's war effort and might win the war without a land invasion. The Allies could be ready for such an air offensive within three months.

Friday, July 24, 1942: —The Germans today claim the fall of Rostov. But we must remember that they also claimed the capture of Veronezh about a month ago and that town is still firmly in Russian hands. In the case of Rostov, however, the Nazi claim may be true for the Russians admitted yesterday that their position at Rostov was becoming untenable. No official confirmation of the loss of the city has come from Moscow, notwithstanding. Offsetting this probable defeat is the news from Veronezh where it is definitely the Red Army's battle. Still to be thrown into the battle are the vast reserves of Russian manpower, hoarded against the day when the German offensive clangs to a stop.

Like a thorn under the saddle of the Axis warhorse is the powerful guerrilla army of General Draja Mikhailovitch in Yugoslavia. Entrenched in impregnable positions in the hills this "army" has harassed and irritated Hitler and his Italian stooges no end. Several divisions of crack Axis troops have been diverted from the main Russian battleground to subdue these "outlaws." In rage at the tactics of the guerrillas, the Italians have resorted to Nazi Gestapo methods of wrecking numerous towns and ruthlessly killing countless civilians, including women and children. These pogroms only embitter the guerrillas even more.

The Allies are on the offensive in Egypt but Rommel is a hard nut to crack, especially with his deadly 88-millimeter anti-tank guns. This is the gun that recently put the British on the skids in Libya when they were tricked into a murderous "trap" in which 230 out of 300 British tanks were destroyed in one hour by these vicious guns.

Saturday, July 25, 1942: —Far ranging and daring United States submarines today were reported to have added five more Japanese ships to their long list of victims. The sinkings included a modern Japanese destroyer, a medium sized tanker and three cargo ships. These successes brought the toll of enemy vessels destroyed by Navy action alone to two hundred twenty three.

The sinking of the Jap destroyer brought to light a new development in submarine warfare. American subs are being equipped with periscope cameras with which they are able to verify their hits with pictures. The Jap destroyer was pictured in sinking condition.

The spotlight of the war remains in Russia where slaughter and carnage continues on a massive scale around the key city of Rostov. While the Nazis have bragged about taking this city, later communiqués from both sides indicate that this braggadocio is a little bit premature. The Russians admit the situation is extremely grave but state that the city is being defended "to the last drop of blood." Loss of territory does not mean so much to the Russians as long as they can preserve the principal part of the Red Army. This they apparently are doing.

Henry Kaiser, the American building genius, the man who is turning out ships three times as fast as anyone else and has been connected with almost every big construction job in the country, is plugging strongly for the idea of building a great fleet of huge cargo planes to whip the sub menace with one blow. Experts who say it can't be done—at least not quickly enough—are soon squelched by Kaiser. He says he can do it—and on a mass scale— in less than ten months.

Sunday, July 26, 1942: —Sunday again and another week of war has ended. Sunday, when men should be thinking of peace and brotherly love, is now spent in contemplation of new and more deadly means of destruction. Plans are laid for great thousand plane bombing raids nightly, to lay waste every important city in Germany. Well and good—they asked for it—but I can't help thinking of the poor innocents, the little children—not much different than our own—who must suffer the terror and death of it along with their parents. Such a ghastly business but apparently necessary. Unless Germany is pounded into submission, this terror and destruction may one day be visited upon American cities as it once was meted out with diabolical Nazi satisfaction upon English, Dutch, French, Belgian, Greek, Serbian and Polish towns. Sad and lamentable though it may be, it is either their lives or ours. And today is Sunday!

The news from the far flung battle fields is much the same as usual. The Russians are grimly hanging on to Rostov, filling the Don River and its approaches full of German bodies and Nazi machinery. A goodly harvest for the Grim Reaper. Perhaps the dead do not greatly envy the living—for them the war is over and all is peaceful once again. The living must face the morrow—with its terror and pain, its hunger and sorrow, and its hate. Dead soldier of Russia, your sleep should be more peaceful than that of your antagonist. At least you died in defense of your land, your home, your family. Your courage was strong, you did not surrender. Because you died, your country will yet live!

Monday, July 27, 1942: —Remember the thousand plane raids mention in this record yesterday? Well, the British didn't quite make a thousand last night but six hundred of their biggest bombers plastered the great German port of Hamburg with hundreds of tons of high explosives and thousands of incendiaries. Four thousand pound "block-buster" bombs were dropped with precision on shipyards, plane factories, submarine bases, and supply depots. Bitterly, the Nazis themselves admitted that the raid caused heavy damage, mostly to civilian targets—they said. U.S. made bombers and U.S. pilots with the RAF participated in the raid which was considered very successful. Only 29 planes were lost, amounting to less than 5% of the attacking force. Anything less than 10% is considered satisfactory.

Thousands of miles away, the United States Air Force did a little big scale bombing of its own. Four-motored Army bombers lashed at Tobruk in Libya in a highly effective operation. Catching an enemy convoy in the harbor, the American flyers destroyed several vessels and set a number of huge gasoline and oil fires.

Other activity on the Egyptian front was confined to artillery and patrol action.

In Russia it appears likely that the Germans have really conquered Rostov as the tide of battle seems to have swung twenty miles to the south down the Caucasian gateway to unlimited oil supplies. If Hitler is able to smash his way another 600 miles in this direction and hold it he will be fixed for oil for years to come. The next six weeks may tell the story of the next six, sixty of six hundred years.

Tuesday, July 28, 1942: —The German juggernaught crushes steadily on in Russia. The Red Army is resisting stubbornly but is forced to retreat in the face of superior enemy forces. The Russians admit the fall of Rostov and acknowledge that Nazi spearheads have thrust their way 32 miles eastward and 20 miles southward from the city. The Nazis are landing airborne whippet tanks behind the Russian lines to add to the confusion of retreat. The situation is extremely grave.

In the western European air war, the Germans tried a comparatively small reprisal raid on the English Midlands but were repulsed with heavy losses, inflicted by night fighter planes and new and secret anti-aircraft guns. About 50 or 75 Nazi bombers participated and at least eight were shot down.

Sharp fighting developed in Egypt today, as General Auchinleck's Imperials harassed the enemy in several offensive thrusts that resulted in some vicious hand-to-hand encounters and the taking of some Axis prisoners.

The Chinese and Australian theaters of war are comparatively quiet at this time. It is evident from Chinese reports that the Japs are still massing their troops near the Siberian border, to stab the Russian back at the crucial moment. It is said that General Yamashita, the conqueror of Singapore and the Philippines, is in command of these forces so it appears that offensive action against Siberia is not far off.

All is quiet on the home front.

Wednesday, July 29, 1942: —The two heavyweights continue to slug it out in southern Russia. Flaming battles, said to involve the masses of reserves that Marshal Timoshenko held as his ace-in-the-hole, are raging in the area just south of Rostov. The true picture is confused but persistent reports indicate that the

German war machine has finally been stalled, at least for the last twenty-four hours.

Meanwhile, in the sky over Germany, the British are doing what they can to create that second front so badly needed to relieve the pressure on the Soviets. For the second time in three nights, more than 600 big RAF bombers pounded the Nazi port of Hamburg. More "block-buster" bombs were dumped on the already smashed center lending credence to the belief that the RAF is making "hamburger out of Hamburg." Many experts believe that sustained mass bombing attacks of this nature are the surest way of knocking Germany out of the war this year. Others contend that no victory can be attained by bombing alone, but must be accompanied by an all-out land invasion by a great army of land troops. The consensus of opinion, however, is that until the land invasion is ready, the air invasion should continue in increased tempo. We certainly cannot lose the war by doing it and we might win it.

Land activity in Egypt is nil. The only activity today was by American bombers based in Egypt who successfully raided enemy installations in Suda Bay on the island of Crete.

On the home front, officials today were concerned with increased liquor consumption by service men with its attendant drunkenness, leading to loose, dangerous talk and disease. Total prohibition for service men is contemplated if less drastic measures fail. *John Barleycorn*[2] is on the loose again.

Thursday, July 30, 1942: —Retreat is finished! "Stand and fight to the death!" Those are the words of Josef Stalin to the officers and men of the Red Army. "Not one step back!" he said, "The execution of this task means the preservation of our country, the destruction of the hated enemy and a guarantee of victory." Those words indicate that the Russian armies are in desperate straits and must either snatch victory or suffer ignominious defeat. A very crucial hour has been reached in southern Russia. The Germans are pouring every last ounce of strength, every last reserve, into the struggle in a supreme effort to push the Red Army over the brink of disaster. The Reds are aware of their danger and are fighting magnificently, asking no quarter and giving none. It is a titanic moment in the history of the world. Anxiously and breathlessly, the people of all nations hang on the outcome.

The RAF alone is doing something to aid the Russians. In their third major raid in four nights, the British and American heavy bombers smashed the coal and industrial city of Saarbrucken, raining tons of explosives and incendiaries on coal pits, iron, steel and engineering works in the area. In a smaller raid by daylight Britain's hardworking bomber crews ripped the Calais-Boulogne district of the Nazi-held French coastline to shreds.

Pointing definitely to a more and more determined effort by Britain and America to strike a terrific blow against the Nazis in the west to relieve Russia is the arrival in England of an additional contingent of high officers of the United States Air Force. No doubt the urgency of the crisis in Russia is only too clear to Allied leaders.

Friday, July 31, 1942: —The largest scale fighting in history continues to rage in Russia. The battering ram panzer armies of the Nazis have been stopped fifty miles short of Stalingrad but are advancing steadily into the Caucasus south of Rostov. Losses of men and materiel on both sides have been staggering. The general situation remains extremely serious for Russia.

In this country interest centers around the military trial of the eight German saboteurs recently captured by the F.B.I. President Roosevelt had ordered the spies tired by a special military commission of seven generals. Counsel for the defendants attempted to save them by appealing for a writ of habeas corpus which would have taken them from the custody of the military and would have forced their trial to be held in civil court. The Supreme Court today denied the appeal and upheld the President's war time authority to try the men as any other enemy spies. The trial will continue tomorrow with the death penalty in prospect for the Nazis.

U.S. fighter pilots are pouring into England as prospects for an aerial "second front" in Europe increases. Some say that at the rate the flyers are coming over, they'll have to start a second front to find enough airdromes for the American ships. The American pilots are willing and eager to match their skill against the tough, experienced Nazi airmen.

The Navy today announced that about 10,000 Jap troops are established in the Aleutians. Steps are being taken to chase them out of allot them six feet of soil apiece as a permanent donation.

[1] I am tired and sick of war. Its glory is all moonshine. It is only those who have neither fired a shot nor heard the shrieks and groans of the wounded who cry aloud for blood, for vengeance, for desolation. War is hell. - William Tecumseh Sherman

[2] John Barleycorn - **a** personification of alcoholic drink, particularly beer and whisky.

August

Saturday, August 1, 1942: —The million Germans with their ten thousand tanks and three thousand airplanes have bumped their heads against a great wall of determined Russian soldiers who have obviously decided to die rather than yield much more of their land to the hated enemy. Perhaps they realize that the next six weeks will probably determine the fate of Russia for many years to come. At any rate the advance of the invader has been slowed almost to a halt, especially in the direction of Stalingrad. But south of Rostov, in the region near Bataisk, the Germans have claimed a new break through. If true this would send the Nazis pouring down the Caucasian Isthmus towards the great oilfields which are clearly Hitler's principal objective. But more than six hundred miles of mountainous battlegrounds lie between the Fuhrer's legions and the rich oil of Baku.

With the persistency and irritation of a thorn under Hitler's saddle, the RAF again pounced on an important center of Germany's war industry. The victim this time was Dusseldorf in the heart of the Rhenish-Westphalian area of the Rhineland. More than six hundred big bombers took part in the raid, dropping among other explosives and incendiaries, about 150 of the famous 4,000 pound "block-busters." It was a brilliant show, inflicting heavy damage, but thirty of the attacking planes did not return.

That's the part of war that gets me. The communiqué says, "Thirty planes did not return." But no mention is made of the boys who manned those planes. What happened to them? More than two hundred of them. Blown to bits by exploding shells? Crushed in flaming wreckage? Captured? Tortured? They're men—like me. What happened? The Russians have the answer, I guess. They say sentimentality—like fear—has no place in war.

Sunday, August 2, 1942: —Another Sunday and the world continues its mad whirl of war. Let's summarize:

In Russia it is reported that the Red Army has launched a strong counter-attack from Veronezh in the north to Stalingrad in the east. Enemy drives in those directions have been stopped and thrown back at many points. South of Rostov and Bataisk the Nazis still advance but are merely crawling. All is not yet lost.

In Egypt, Rommel is playing possum, probably waiting to see how the Russian drive will turn out, meanwhile resting his men and gaining reinforcements. The British, aided by American bombers, are blasting h-ll out of his communications and are desperately planning a counter-offensive of their own. All is comparatively quiet.

In Western Europe, the RAF holds the spotlight, as evidence of a second front, principally by air, continues to accumulate. Germany is due for some terrible punishment from the air. American planes and men will join in.

In Australia, General MacArthur is gnashing his teeth at the delays in obtaining men and equipment but is preparing as rapidly as possible for the day when he can start his offensive rolling back toward his beloved Philippines. Until the Jap consolidates his position both in this region and far north in the Aleutians.

In China, the battling Chinese are holding the Japs at bay, trading space for time. The Japanese apparently are readying themselves for a sneak attack on Siberia and Vladivostok when the crucial moment arrives which will be soon. All indications are that August, 1942 will be "bloody August" in the sordid history of this planet.

Monday, August 3, 1942: —It's still Russia that holds the spotlight. Marshal Timoshenko apparently has brought up many of his reserves and is counter-attacking all along the front from Veronezh to Stalingrad. It is evident from both German and Russian communiqués that the invaders have been stopped everywhere on this line but are still advancing south towards the important oil fields of Maikop. The picture is still confused and uncertain but extremely critical. It is even rumored that Winston Churchill has flown to Moscow to discuss the possibility of an immediate "second front" in Europe. A terrible decision may soon be required by the Allied Nations. It may well be a question of whether it shall be "too little or too late." This in view of the present unreadiness of Britain and the United States to launch an all-out land offensive in Western Europe.

The trial of the eight Nazi saboteurs and spies was concluded today and the findings and verdict were given in detail to President Roosevelt who may make the verdict public by tomorrow. It is believed that the death penalty has been asked for at least seven of the prisoners.

In the Australian theater, the Japs are sneaking up on the Allied advance base of Port Moresby on New Guinea. Their patrols seized the village of Kokoda and the airfield only 55 miles from the Allied base. The Japs make excellent sneaks—which is handy in this kind of war.

An interesting sidelight showing the vast scope of this conflict is the report that a lone Nazi bomber attacked American military installations in Iceland, causing little damage but serving to put the garrison on the alert.

Tuesday, August 4, 1942: —It's hard to tell just how the great struggle in Russia is going. It appears from tonight's bulletins that Red Army lines are cracking under terrific Nazi pressure. Moscow admits a fifty mile gain by the invaders down the Caucasian Isthmus. Berlin claims the advance was ninety five miles, giving them control of a large slice of northern Caucasia and bringing them dangerously near the minor but still substantial oilfields of Maikop. Only at the great elbow of the Don River do the Russians appear to be having much success in really stopping the Germans although every gain has cost the enemy dearly in men and equipment.

In spite of his apparent successes, Hitler's slumber is disturbed by the nightmare possibility of a second front invasion of Western Europe by the U.S. and Britain. The blow may strike unexpectedly at any point from the southern tip of France to the barren northern tip of Norway and Hitler, in spite of his bravado, is really worried. The English Parliament met in secret session today, with the second front presumably as its topic. Numerous conferences are in progress between high military and political figures of the Allied Nations. Something historic may definitely be in the wind.

President Roosevelt has not seen fit to reveal the findings of the military commission which tried the eight saboteurs. The records are voluminous and the President will require two or three days to complete his review.

Late reports state that Allied airmen in both Australia and China have been doing some good work. In China, 550 pound bombs found the headquarters of the Jap army in Kiangsi province. From Australia, Allied bombers completely wrecked the new Jap invasion base of New Guinea.

Wednesday, August 5, 1942: —Russian withdrawals appear to be general throughout the southern battle area today. A parade of crazy names of Russian cities, towns, and railroad junctions occupied by the invading Nazis tells the tragic story. Names like Tikhoretsk, Kletskaya, Tsimlyansk, Kushchevka mark spots on the great map of Russia newly groveling under the heels of Nazi boots. Those spots are precious to Russians, more precious because of the blood of sons and brothers shed in their defense. Their homes are gutted and burned, their wealth destroyed, but piles of German bodies and mountains of smashed tanks and guns have paid the price. And farther east and south the fight goes on. Someday the parade will be reversed and victorious Red Armies will march back through Kushchevka, and Tsimlyansk, and Kletskaya, and Tikhoretsk—and Rostov. Someday!

In India, meanwhile, a little, weaseled, diaper-wrapped opportunist name Mohandas K. Gandhi is putting the screws on Great Britain in her hour of dire need. He and his All-India Congress have practically issued an ultimatum to Britain, demanding that immediate independence be granted India or a "civil disobedience" revolution will begin. Civil disobedience is little different from actual revolution except that it *presumes* that there will be no bloodshed. If Britain refused to be coerced however, it would soon turn into actual fighting. The resultant confusion would offer Japan too good an opportunity for her to overlook. It would practically mean handing India with all her wealth and potentialities to Japan on a silver platter. Dear Mr. Gandhi is either a blundering fool or a Japanese collaborationist, an Indian quisling or both.

Thursday, August 6, 1942: —In the first conviction for treason by the Federal Government since the Pennsylvania Whiskey Rebellion in 1781, in which each convict was later pardoned, a Federal Court in Detroit today condemned Max Stephan, German-born citizen, to be hanged. The traitor was convicted of helping Oberlieutnant Hans Peter Krug after the latter's escape from a Canadian prison camp last April. The judge readily admitted the severity of the sentence but pointed out that it will serve as a warning to all disloyal Americans and aliens. He further stated that the life of this traitor is less valuable than the lives of our loyal sons which are being given to the cause of the United States.

Hopes of placating Gandhi and his violence-bound Congress were fading today. Britain has taken a firm stand and refuses to be coerced. Several compromise proposals have been offered but apparently have been rejected. The British have promised to do everything possible to maintain law and order but non-violent revolution with all its evil portents is expected shortly.

In Russia, powerful German columns moved steadily on towards the Maikop oilfields while other strong forces closed a formidable pincers on Stalingrad. Thousands of parachute troops, suicide squads of tommy-gunners, and hundreds of tiny whippet tanks have been dropped behind the Russian lines to add to the confusion of retreat.

Egyptian activities have been confined to artillery duels and bombing forays lately. Many observers believe that the British may delay too long before starting a counter-offensive and may allow Rommel to rally and drive on to Alexandria.

Friday, August 7, 1942: —General Claire L. Chennault and his brilliant band of former American Volunteer Group pilots—now U.S. Army flyers—surprised the Japs and successfully smashed many grounded planes and other installations on an enemy airdrome near Canton, it was reported today. The American flyers, considered by Chennault to be the worlds best, have inspired great fear and respect in the hearts of the Jap pilots. Their best Zero planes are no match for the American "Tigers." Since the American challenge for a "finish fight" the Japs have given the U.S. flyers wide berth when it comes to a showdown. All our boys need over there is more planes and pilots to fly them.

Mahatma Gandhi today addressed the All-India Congress, protesting his friendship to England and his desire not to "stab her in the back" but his ultimatum for independence was allowed to stand. The British moving to forestall the expected civil-disobedience campaign, forbade the closing of any shop or business dealing in necessities, on the penalty of the loss of the business and possible jail sentence.

Russia still fights with her back to the wall, or shall we say to the Caucasian mountains and the Volga. The Red Army has launched desperate counter-drives in the north in hopes of relieving the dangerous southern front but to little avail. The wall of Nazi armor and steel is crushing on towards all the vital points in the Caucasus.

An early radio report this morning stated that six of the Nazi saboteurs had been doomed to die in the electric chair within 24 hours but later reports from Washington changed the story. President Roosevelt has not yet finished studying the Commission's findings.

Saturday, August 8, 1942: —News is plentiful today. The report heard yesterday regarding the eight Nazi saboteurs was not far wrong as we learned today that six of the spies were electrocuted in the District of Columbia jail house beginning at noon. The other two had their sentences commuted for turning State's evidence. One was give life imprisonment at hard labor; the other thirty years at hard labor. This swift justice was meted out to the Berlin trained Nazis who would have wrecked, burned, and killed in this country had their foul plans not been upset by the alert Coast Guard and F.B.I.

The Pacific flared into action today as the United States Navy went into action in two theaters. An attack that may turn out to be a substantial offensive was launched against the Jap held Solomon Islands off the northeast coast of Australia. Naval and "other forces" were engaged, hinting that marine landing parties and aircraft participated. Perhaps General MacArthur is ready to hit the "high road" back towards his beloved Philippines or at least ready to make a diversion that might discourage Japan from stabbing Russia in the back.

Far north in the Aleutians, American warships moved to the attack on Japanese held Kiska Island. This is the first case of U.S. surface craft bombarding the enemy in this area, indicating that a determined effort is under way to dislodge the invaders from their footholds on the island chain.

In Russia things grow worse hourly. The German spearheads are now within thirty to sixty miles of the vital Maikop oil fields and Russian demolition squads are standing by to blast the wells and refineries sky high if it proves impossible to hold the Nazis. This is the hour of decision in Russia.

Sunday, August 9, 1942: —Violence flared in India today as the British Government took stern measures to control the situation. Mohandas k. Gandhi, his lieutenant Nehru and over a hundred of the All-India Congress members were placed under arrest by British police. This was the signal for violent demonstrations throughout India. Riots broke out in Bombay and New Delhi as well as in many other places. Police found it impossible to quell the riots with clubs and tear gas and were forced to fire upon the mobs. Several persons were killed and many wounded. Shops closed in spite of police warnings and Gandhi followers threw themselves across street car tracks and otherwise disrupted traffic. Excitement was rising and latest reports state that Gandhi's wife was also arrested as she attempted to address a crowd in her husband's stead. The situation is serious.

Indications are that the battle in the Solomon Islands off the coast of Australia is of considerable size and importance. Information on its progress is meager but Admiral Nimitz states in his brief communiqué that the action is continuing "favorably" to the Allied forces. Land based aircraft apparently are taking part in the attack as well as land and sea forces including carrier based aircraft. Evidently the Japs are resisting strongly and both sides are suffering heavy losses. We are fervently hoping for a victory that may set the Japanese plans awry. Another day or two will probably tell the story.

Henry Kaiser, the builder extra-ordinary, who recently proposed the construction of 5,000 super cargo planes has seen his plan approved by the Government. A letter of intent has been given him by the WPB authorizing 500 of the 70 ton flying boats of the Mars type and an experimental model of a super-super plane weighing 200 tons of revolutionary design.

Monday, August 10, 1942: —Big headlines announce the tradition-packed slogan that the "Marines have landed." This time it is on the Solomon Islands. It is not yet known whether they have "the situation will in hand" but late reports indicate that stiff resistance is being encountered. Losses on both sides have been severe and Admiral Ernest W. King admitted that our Navy has lost one cruiser sunk, another damaged and several destroyers and transports hit. But the Marines have apparently established a beach head in the Tulagi area which is the chief port on Florida Island.

The Japs, for their part, claim from Tokyo the destruction of a major part of the United States Fleet besides numerous Australian warships. According to Tokyo's claims, added up since the Coral Sea and Midway battles, the Japs have sunk both parts of our not-yet-built two-ocean Navy and another fleet which we were holding in reserve. Judging from the enemy's claims we would have been defending ourselves with rowboats long since. Jap reports must be taken with a whole shaker of salt.

Another large contingent of American troops has arrived in Great Britain and according to their commander they're not over there to "sit down." They hope to move soon to a new and more exciting rendezvous somewhere in France.

In Russia the Germans are smashing ahead. They claim the capture of the Maikop oilfields but this claim has not been confirmed by the Russians. Industrial Stalingrad is in dire peril as Nazi wedges have been driven into its defenses. The tone from Moscow is desperate.

Tuesday, August 11, 1942: —While the big-time slugging match goes on in Russia, interest at this time is centered on the United States' first attempt at offensive warfare in this conflict. In the far-off islands of the south Pacific, our Army and Navy, spearheaded by tough U.S. Marines, are endeavoring to wrest some of the Solomon Islands from Japanese control. On the hotly contested beaches at Tulagi on Florida Island, the Leathernecks are clashing hand-to-hand with the Japs and are apparently finding him a worthy foe. But our boys are proving their mettle and obtaining valuable combat experience. The landing of troops on enemy beaches that are well defended by a determined foe is acknowledged to be the most difficult and costly of all military operations. We must expect heavy losses and can only hope that the objectives will be achieved and held.

From Australia, General MacArthur's Air Force has been assisting the attack by vigorous and unrelenting bombing attacks on all enemy supply bases from Timor to Rabaul. In China, U.S. airmen pounded the enemy all along the front in a diversion attack to prevent the Japs from sending badly needed reinforcements to the South Pacific battleground. Docks, warehouses, and airdromes came in for vicious bombing.

Grave uncertainty clouds the picture in India tonight.

Howling mobs spent the day in roaming the streets of Bombay, Delhi, and other centers, shouting independence slogans and demanding that the British "get out of India." English as well as American nationals were the subjects of jeering throngs. It is believed that the demonstrations will peter out from lack of leadership as Gandhi and all his cohorts are being held incommunicado.

Wednesday, August 12, 1942: —United States Marines are apparently living up to their reputation as the best fighting men in the world. In the face of fierce resistance they have attained footholds on three of the Solomon Islands and are penetrating inland in several places. It is believed that the landing forces made effective use of parachutists which marks the first time American troops have used this new form of warfare in actual combat. Close-in fighting with bayonets and hand grenades has apparently occurred on all of the beaches. Official Navy communiqués have been cautiously optimistic and state that in spite of severe losses the attackers are approaching their objective which is the occupation of the three islands in the first step towards pushing the Japs back to Tokyo. More power to the "Devildogs."

An unconfirmed report tonight states that Allied planes, presumably American, have bombed the Jap island of Formosa. If true it would mark a renewal of the threat to Japan proper so forcibly brought home to the Japs by General Doolittle in April.

In Russia the situation in the northern Caucasus appears to be irretrievable. The only hope for Russia in this region lies in their scorched earth policy and steady retreat. The Maikop oilfields are definitely in Nazi hands but are said to be totally demolished and burning.

A heavy 300 plane raid on Mainz in the industrial Rhineland by the RAF and increased sabotage in France resulting in the killing of several Nazi pilots by daring French patriots are the only encouraging signs in Europe at this time.

Thursday, August 13, 1942: —American Marines are within sight of complete victory in the Solomon Islands offensive. They have apparently established firm bridgeheads on three and possibly four of the main islands and, with heavy reinforcements, are steadily pushing inland. Jap resistance is rapidly collapsing. The air and naval battle, however, appears to be increasing in intensity. Some reports indicate that the largest sea battle of the war is in progress, not excluding the Midway Battle. Whether intentional or not, the United States has opened a "second front" in the south Pacific. If successful, the diversion may prevent Japan from stabbing Russia in the back.

Very little additional news is available from the confused battlefields of Russia. Indications are that the Nazi offensive has slowed down considerably if from nothing more than exhaustion. Russian resistance in all areas except the northern Caucasus has stiffened but there the Germans are rolling towards the next big oil rich center of Grozny.

Another five hundred RAF bombers smashed at Mainz, Germany for the second night in a row and even the Nazis admitted heavy damage was done. No U.S. planes participated in the raid but indications are that the American Air Force in Britain is about ready to join in the aerial offensive. Then thousand plane raids will become commonplace.

Clark Gable, the he-man of the movies today began his real life he-man role. He was sworn in as a buck private in the Army Air Corps. Since his famous wife, Carole Lombard was tragically killed in a plane crash, the popular leading man has been anxious to get a crack at the Japs. The sooner he gets a gun, the happier he'll be, said the movie star.

Friday, August 14, 1942: —At last the final words to that famous Marine slogan can be added. To "The Marines have landed" we can add "and the situation is well in hand." It definitely appears that the first phase of the Solomon Battle has ended in signal American victories. The struggle is likely to continue for weeks, however. But in the first phase the Leathernecks have established themselves securely in the Tulagi-Florida-Guadalcanal chain of islands. Heavy reinforcements have been landed to aid in following up the first successes. Bitter hand-to-hand fighting continues in the interiors of the islands.

Japanese forces dispatched from their Rabaul base to reinforce the hard pressed Japs in the Solomons have been pounced upon by General MacArthur's far-flying bombers. Several direct hits were scored on warships and transports and the enemy force dispersed.

The British announced the results of a terrific convoy battle in the Mediterranean. The new cruiser Manchester and the aircraft carrier Eagle were destroyed. In spite of other serious losses, however, the big convoy was delivered safely to Malta with badly needed supplies and reinforcements, including fighter planes.

California draft boards announced today that the supply of eligible single men would be exhausted within sixty days and married men with and without dependents could expect induction at an increasing rate from then on. Only men in essential jobs could expect exemption.

The German's Caucasus drive has carried them to within 140 miles of the vital Grozny oilfields.

Saturday, August 15, 1942: —Striking silently, swiftly and with terrific effect, the British Mediterranean Fleet bombarded the Italian stronghold at Rhodes in the Dodecanese islands last Thursday. Reports of the surprise attack were delayed until today. The raid was a complete surprise and left the Italian base flaming like a "flash from Hell" as one correspondent put it. Tons and tons of armor piercing shells from the Navy's big guns ripped into barracks and harbor installations, smashing a big seaplane base and setting huge firs among oil and other supplies. No British warships was so much as scratched.

The tempo of the Nazis drive into Russia has slackened considerably during the last few days. While they have admittedly slashed far into the Caucasus and won important strongholds and rich lands they still haven't eliminated Russia by far. The Red Army is still intact and resisting furiously. For two weeks the Russians have stood firm on the lines before Stalingrad. Steady withdrawals before superior forces in the south have been successfully conducted by the Russians with minimum losses to themselves and exacting the heaviest possible toll from the enemy. Russia is still a factor to contend with, as Hitler has no doubt discovered.

Little additional news is available from the Solomon island battlefront. From all indications, the Marines are busily consolidating their hard-won toeholds on several of the island chain. They are using "heavy stuff" and mean to keep what they have won.

San Francisco and the entire coastal area is officially going to be "dimmed out" beginning August 20th.

Sunday, August 16, 1942: —For the first time since April I played a round of golf today. The Bank held a Tournament at the Berkeley Country Club. The day was beautiful, warm with just a kiss of cool wind from across the Bay. The green of the fairways was so soothing to the eyes and the whole atmosphere was refreshing after a stuffy week at the office. There's nothing like a good golf game to iron out the kinks in a man's mental muscles as well as give healthful exercise to his physical muscles. But golf like many other amusements is hard hit by the war. Golf balls are rare and expensive, the production of clubs and other equipment has been halted and club members are finding themselves too busy to adequately support the many courses. Golf's future for the duration is full of uncertainty.

But back to the war news. It appears tonight as though the India situation shows some sign of settlement. The British have acted with determination and toughness and Gandhi's leaderless Congress party appears ready to compromise. The Moslem minority likewise has shown that they will support Britain rather than the rebellious majority.

All is not yet lost in Russia. Stalingrad is proving to be another Sevastopol and German penetration into northern Caucasia has been slowed to a crawl. Russian communiqués do not appear hopeless and constantly emphasize the enormity of the enemy losses. The Russian bear still has power.

The U.S. Navy released some details of their successful raid on Kiska island in the Aleutians on August eighth and ninth. Over 3000 shells were poured into the enemy's shipping and shore installations. Huge fires were set and a destroyer and cargo ship sunk.

Monday, August 17, 1942: —A strange, mysterious thing happened yesterday. Drifting aimlessly in from the sea like a lost ghost ship, a U.S. Navy blimp, its gondola doors hanging open, its crew gone, bumped and scraped its way over the housetops in Daly City, finally coming to rest in a residential district, draping its tired shape across telephone wires and two parked automobiles. Naval authorities cannot explain its actions and the whereabouts of its two crew members is a mystery the sea may never reveal. No parachutes were missing from the craft nor was the rubber raft with which it was equipped. Consequently the men couldn't have bailed out. One of the two depth bombs carried was missing, the other one hung dangerously a few feet from the ground. War is full of strange, weird happenings.

London has revealed that Winston Churchill has just concluded a week's conference with Premier Josef Stalin in Moscow. High representatives of Russia, Britain, and the United States participated and it is assumed that great decisions regarding a second front and aid for Russia in the Caucasus were made. Most of the Allied war leaders in India and the Middle East were prominent in the parley, lending credence to the belief that Allied troops may move into the Caucasus to help stop the Germans.

In the "way down under" battle of the Solomon Islands, Japan grudgingly acknowledged that the U.S. Marines have occupied several positions in the area. The truth is that the Marines now hold "well established" positions on three of the main islands after overcoming vigorous resistance and the Navy has driven off a strong enemy rescue force. Jap prisoners have been taken and a definite victory has been chalked up.

Tuesday, August 18, 1942: —While Germany and Russia fall all over each other in claiming and counter-claiming huge losses in manpower for the other side—latest Moscow claim is that the Nazis have lost more than 1,250,000 men since May 1st while their own loss has been about 600,000—the United States is taking steps to build up a great army of American men to lay on the sacrificial alter of war. California draft boards announced today that their September quotas will be in many cases more than four times as large as their August quotas. This will necessitate calling men in 3-A classification, single men with dependents and married men without children.

As the first concrete aftermath of the historic Stalin-Churchill conference, the British today shook up and reshuffled their entire Middle Eastern command. General Sir Harold R.L.G. Alexander replaced General Auchinleck as commander-in-chief facing the wily desert fox Rommel. Generals all along the line were shifted in an apparent preparation for big doings in the Egyptian desert. General Alexander is the heroic retriever of

Dunkirk and Burma. Let's hope he can reverse his success in Egypt.

In Europe the growing American Air Force based in England made its first all U.S. raid on the Continent yesterday. Twelve giant Flying Fortresses supported by fighter planes made a high altitude precision attack on Rouen, in occupied France. The raid was led by Brig. General Ira C. Eaker himself and was hailed as a complete success as all bombers returned safely. Three enemy fighters were shot down and two American fighters were lost in the action.

Wednesday, August 19, 1942: —Sensational news today! In a tremendous Commando extravaganza, Yanks, Canadians, Free French and British joined in a large scale invasion dress rehearsal on the occupied French coast. More than 12,000 specially trained shock troops or Commandos, as they are known, supported by vast naval units and aircraft, hit the French coast in the Dieppe region. For more than nine hours the raiders smashed at the Nazi fortifications before they withdrew on schedule. Tanks and clouds of aircraft participated in the biggest military operation in Western Europe since Dunkirk. The British claimed the attack completely successful but admitted that casualties on both sides were heavy. Ammunition dumps, coast artillery and anti-aircraft batteries were wrecked and more than 100 enemy planes destroyed. Ninety five Allied planes were lost but many crew members were safe. A battalion of American "Rangers" joined in their first land attack against the Nazis. "Rangers" are the U.S. version of the Commandos. More of the same and worse is coming, Adolf!

A U.S. submarine bagged another Jap warship in the Aleutians, it was reported today, bringing to 23 the number of enemy warships sunk or severely damaged in that area.

The official dim-out goes into effect at midnight tonight on the Pacific Coast. All lights and reflections towards the ocean must be dimmed on penalty of severe fines or imprisonment. All neon lights and advertisements are gone for the duration. The city will seem more dingy at night than ever before without all the gay peacetime lights, but we're all in the war together and the rule is necessary for the protection of coastal shipping.

Thursday, August 20, 1942: —The papers are full of eye-witness tales of the great commando raid on Dieppe yesterday. Tired, begrimed survivors of the attack streamed into British ports with thrilling stories of terrific fighting. The sad, broken contingent of wounded men furnished proof enough of the vicious character of the struggle. Men with arms, legs, and faces shot away lay in silent, uncomplaining suffering in the hospital rooms. Grim faced surgeons moved about them, administering morphine, sulphanilimide, or first aid. Sixty miles back across the stormy channel the bodies of their comrades lay where they had fallen on the beaches and streets. But the survivors were back and in good spirits; they had only done what had to be done and the cost was to be expected. And they had done a good job. Across the Channel, the German armies would not sleep from now on. It would be a 24 hour daily alert for them and they would need reinforcements from the Russian front, reinforcements that would relieve some of the pressure from the hard-pressed Red Armies. And a hundred Nazi bombers would fly no more, hundreds of German soldiers would kill no more and gun batteries, radio stations, and munitions dumps were smashed beyond repair. Yes, the raid was a success.

Far across the world another Allied success was chalked up. The U.S. Navy announced finally that the Solomon Islands' adventure had resulted in complete victory for our troops. The Marines are now engaged in "mopping up" the remaining Japanese resistance on the islands occupied by American forces. The Marines are there to stay and have already put former enemy bases to our own use. It is the first successful step in the long trek back to the Philippines. Look out, Mr. Moto!

Friday, August 21, 1942: —Another great country joined the ranks of the United Nations today. It was Brazil, enraged over ruthless sinking of her ships by Nazi rattlesnakes of the Atlantic, who today declared war against Germany and Italy. This is the first nation south of Panama that has taken the final step against the common enemy. Brazil's action is expected to have great influence on the conduct of the rest of the South American nations, even the hesitant Chile and the cautious Argentina. Brazil is probably the most important South American country in this war because of her nearness to Africa and her vulnerability to Nazi infiltration. The large and well established nests of Nazis,

Japs, and Italians may now be weeded out before Hitler can take advantage of their many years of preparation.

Production Chief Donald Nelson today reported on the Nation's progress towards attaining the production goal set for this year. With the exception of combat planes, all phases of the schedule is about up to expectations in spite of serious difficulties such as shortages in several vital materials and some labor troubles. The combat plane situation is expected to be ironed out in the near future. Redoubled efforts on the part of every worker will be required to attain the final objectives.

The Russian situation is still the most critical for the United Nations. The Germans are said to have amassed over 800,000 men on a sixty mile front before Stalingrad in an effort to smash through quickly by sheer weight of numbers. The Russians are resisting furiously and appear to be holding for the time being but the outlook is very bleak.

Saturday, August 22, 1942:—Another great country joined the ranks of the United Nations today. It was Brazil, enraged over ruthless sinking's of her ships by Nazi rattlesnakes of the Atlantic, who today declared war against Germany and Italy. This is the first nation south of Panama that has taken the final step against the common enemy. Brazil's action is expected to have great influence on the conduct of the rest of the South American nations, even the hesitant Chile and the cautious Argentina. Brazil is probably the most important South American country in this war because of her nearness to Africa and her vulnerability to Nazi infiltration. The large and well established nests of Nazis, Japs, and Italians may now be weeded out before Hitler can take advantage of their many years of preparation.

Production Chief Donald Nelson today reported on the Nation's progress towards attaining the production goal set for this year. With the exception of combat planes, all phases of the schedule are about up to expectations in spite of serious difficulties such as shortages in several vital materials and some labor troubles. The combat plane situation is expected to be ironed out in the near future. Redoubled efforts on the part of every worker will be required to attain the final objectives.

The Russian situation is still the most critical for the United Nations. The Germans are said to have massed over

800,000 men on a sixty mile front before Stalingrad in an effort to smash through quickly by sheer weight of numbers. The Russians are resisting furiously and appear to be holding for the time being but the outlook is very black.

Sunday, August 23, 1942: —London reports reveal that another huge convoy of American troops and war supplies has arrived safely in England. The convoy was so big that it was necessary to disembark from several ports. American troops consisted principally of air force personnel and supporting services such as doctors and nurses. A very substantial A.E.F. is now in Britain, although actual figures are of course a military secret. Almost as important as the men was the large number of planes, guns, and other equipment with which the ships' holds were loaded.

No losses were suffered by the convoy on its journey across the submarine infested Atlantic. The troopships were escorted all the way by American men-of-war and were guarded half way to England by American bombers, the rest of the way by the RAF.

Brazil's declaration of war appears to have electrified South America. Several other nations apparently are toying with the idea of hopping on the United Nations' war bandwagon. Argentina even has called a special session to determine its attitude in view of Brazil's action. Nazi and Italian agents in Brazil are getting a taste of what Hitler has been dealing out so brutally in Europe. Desperate Nazis have fled in terror to neighboring Uruguay but the Uruguayan Government has granted Brazil non-belligerent status and is assisting in rounding up enemy aliens and returning them to Brazilian authorities for disposal. How does it feel to squirm on your own hook, you Nazi-Brazilian gauleiters?

From Australia, comes news of another Jap raid on Darwin. The score was two enemy bombers, nine Zero fighters to none. Pretty good batting average in any league.

Monday, August 24, 1942: —The war picture from Russia is bleak tonight. Powerful Nazi panzer columns are crunching ever nearer to Stalingrad and the Volga. Thousands of German tommy-gunners have swarmed over the Don river in spite of heroic do-or-die resistance of Russian Cossacks. Farther south also, the invaders are advancing closer to the important Grozny oilfields. Somehow, someway, the Russians have got to hold out for another eight weeks when winter will again descend upon the steppes of Russia and General Mud and General Cold will fling their reserves into the field against the intruders.

In Western Europe, American airmen and American planes are gaining momentum in their gathering offensive against the industrial life of Germany. Daylight attacks on Occupied France have been made several times by large numbers of Flying Fortresses without the loss of a bomber, proving beyond doubt the exceptional value of the American product.

In the Japanese raid on Port Darwin mentioned yesterday, new American P-40D interceptors employed what even General MacArthur stated was "brilliant tactical interception" in shooting down four bombers and at least nine Zero fighters out of a fleet of 57 enemy planes without the loss of a single man. The attacking Japs jettisoned their bombs before reaching their objectives and streaked for home.

On our home front, the picture was enlivened by a sharp debate on Congressional plans to hike income tax rates. It appears certain that allowances for dependents will be lowered from $400 to $300 which will raise approximately 220,000,000.00 from the poor family man.

Tuesday, August 25, 1942: —Today was California's Primary Election Day when candidates for various state offices from Governor on down were selected. The Governor race will no doubt be between the incumbent Olson and Earl Warren, the present Attorney General. Late reports indicate that the voting was light, the majority of people being interested in nothing but the war. As many experts see it, the principal issue in the Governor battle is whether the people of California will show by their votes that they are satisfied with the manner in which the present Governor has met the war emergency. Has he adequately provided for the State's defense and has his leadership been of the quality demanded of a wartime leader? The voters will decide.

Glaring headlines today tell of a determined attempt by the Japanese to oust the United States Marines from their Solomon Islands' foothold. A big air and naval battle is in progress off the islands but it is clear from the beginning that the Americans were ready and waiting. It'll be a long time before the Japs will find another sleepy Pearl Harbor to attack. In the present battle a substantial fleet of enemy warships with transports attempted to surprise the Marines at Tulagi but were intercepted by alert American airmen, some of whom were based on newly won fields on the Solomons. In the ensuing action two Japanese aircraft carriers, a battleship, several cruisers and a transport were hit. Flying Fortresses, based in Australia have joined in the fray and the battle continues, its outcome still in doubt.

Dined at "DiMaggio's" on Fisherman's Wharf tonight. The dim-out makes the whole town dingy, cold and uninviting, especially when you add a touch of fog.

Wednesday, August 26, 1942: —Further reports on the great battle that is developing in the Southwest Pacific area are encouraging to our side. It is still too early to predict victory but the Navy has announced that thirteen enemy ships have been heavily hit by bombs, thirty three enemy planes have been shot down so far, and at least one Jap force has withdrawn from the fracas. The scope of the engagement may widen into a showdown between the two main fleets which is probably just what the U.S. Navy wants. American fighters and dive bombers based on the newly-won airfield at Guadalcanal Island have done yeoman work so far in the battle. American losses to date are claimed to be of a "minor nature." The hopes and prayers of the whole nation are with our hard fighting boys in this crucial, history-making battle.

In Russia, it looks bad for Stalingrad. A great German force of 750,000 men and tanks is closing in on three sides of the city. Desperate efforts by the Russians seem to be of little avail against the terrific force of the Nazi drive.

Meanwhile, as a diversion attempt, the Soviets claim that they have taken the offensive above Moscow in the region of Kalinin and have achieved a "break-through." Forty thousand Germans have been slain and the Red Army has advanced twenty five or thirty miles. How sustained or successful this drive will be is problematical. We must be prepared for very bad news from Russia. We can only hope that the Russians can maintain their army and their will to fight for another six months at least. By then the Allies should be able to relieve the pressure. The results of a Russian collapse would be catastrophic.

Thursday, August 27, 1942: —Fighting spreads in the Southwest Pacific. The Japs, probably as a diversionary scheme to relieve their hard-pressed forces in the battle for the Solomons, have succeeded in landing an invasion party on the southern tip of New Guinea. From this point they could seriously threaten the Allied base at Port Moresby and even use it as a jumping off place for an attack on Australia proper. At the least they could badly hamper, if not cut, the Allied communication line between Australia and the newly-won Solomon Islands.

The landing was made under cover of some very nasty weather but only after surviving a ferocious bombing attack by General MacArthur's alert airmen. Skimming the waves to obtain visibility enough through the murk to see the enemy, the Allied flyers sank a troop transport, probably sank a heavy cruiser, damaged a destroyer, destroyed several landing barges and machine gunned enemy troops with considerable effect.

Despite this resistance, the Japs succeeded in landing the bulk of their forces. General MacArthur's headquarters announced that the Jap move had been anticipated and that counter action by Allied troops was already in progress.

On the Russian front Soviet resistance before Stalingrad appears to be stiffening although a terrific battle is continuing on three sides of the beleaguered city. The big Russian diversion offensive north of Moscow has rolled on to capture the German-held fortress city of Rzhev. Meanwhile Russian planes are reported to have bombed Berlin and other cities in eastern Prussia. The tempo of world conflict quickens as the fateful summer of 1942 slips rapidly into history.

Friday, August 28, 1942: —Late reports tonight indicate that a great, new battle is developing in the Pacific around the Solomon Islands. This is the third phase of the Solomon campaign. The first was the original surprise attack by U.S. Marines on the advance Japanese bases at Tulagi and Guadalcanal. The Marines succeeded in establishing themselves on the islands and the second round started when a Jap naval force counter-attacked and was thrown back after a ding-dong naval and air battle. The third phase thus opens today with a heavily reinforced counter-attack by the persistent Japs. The final outcome of the first offensive by the United States may well hang on the results of this latest engagement.

193

In Russia, the Red Army has braced before the gates of Stalingrad. Like a coiled spring that has been pushed back too far, the Soviet Army is lashing back with vicious counter-attacks all along the narrowing line. For twenty four hours the Nazis haven't advanced a foot and have even been put on the defensive at some points. Panzer spearheads have been lopped off and annihilated. The angered invaders have answered this increased resistance by air-blitzing the city itself. Hundreds of bombers are turning the home of 400,000 people into rubble. Russian interceptors are shooting down dozens of the bombers but more hundreds follow them up to dump their lethal loads indiscriminately on the hapless city.

Allied forces from Australia are moving to the attack on the newly landed Japs at Milne Bay in New Guinea through waste deep mud and storm lashed jungles.

Saturday, August 29, 1942: —Not much additional news about the Solomon battle. Apparently American planes from captured Jap bases in the Solomons are giving attacking enemy warships a warm reception. One group of four Jap destroyers was pounced on by Marine planes from Tulagi; one destroyer was sunk, another probably sunk, a third crippled and left burning, the fourth sent running.

Seasoned Australian troops, well versed in jungle fighting, along with a few United States Army troops have attacked invading Japanese forces at Milne Bay on New Guinea. The ground troops are being supported by U.S. medium bombers who have already succeeded in driving off the supporting Jap convoy, leaving the invading forces without naval assistance. Bitter fighting is in progress with no quarter being asked or given by either side.

The gallant Chinese deserve some mention at this time. For the last several weeks the Chinese have been on the offensive and have almost succeeded in driving the Japs from the two important provinces of Chekiang and Kiangsi, the winning of which had cost the Nipponese so dearly. The effectiveness of the Chinese army has increased considerably since the arrival of American aerial support, small though it has been as yet. Give the Chinese parity in the air and they will drive the invaders into the sea. The chief importance of the latest Chinese victories, however, is the recapturing of several vital airports within easy bombing range of Japan proper. Call Doolittle! A couple more "Shangri-La's" are waiting for you. Look out, Mr. Moto. We haven't forgotten those 2,400 little white crosses overlooking Pearl Harbor.

Sunday, August 30, 1942: —While we rest and enjoy a warm, quiet Sunday, across the world another people struggle desperately for their very existence. As we loll peacefully in the shade it seems hard to realize that unless we are vigilant we may someday be faced with the same terrible realities as are the Russians today. Before the gates of Stalingrad countless thousands of Russian men and women are meeting their fate and if it so comes to pass that we must meet the same test we can only hope that we will meet it with equal courage and unselfish devotion to country.

The general picture in Russia, though serious, is somewhat encouraging tonight. The Soviet armies are holding firm all along the 2,000 mile front. On the Rzhev front, 130 miles northwest of Moscow, the Red Army has seized the initiative in an offensive, which, if successful, may eventually threaten the whole German position in the south.

In a determined effort to aid the battered Russians, the RAF and U.S. Bomber Force in England have opened up a massive aerial blitz against Germany and occupied Europe that has already lasted more than sixty hours and is assuming a pattern similar to the all-out bombing assault on Britain by the Luftwaffe just two years ago. America Flying Fortresses are proving their worth in these raids, especially by their ability to return to their bases without losses even though some of them have had as many as 2,000 bullet and shrapnel holes in them. The Flying Fortresses can really take it.

Mohandas Gandhi's civil disobedience campaign in India seems to be gaining momentum by underground methods. Numerous riots and work stoppages have resulted.

Monday, August 31, 1942: —Though it has been but eight months since Pearl Harbor, today marks the end of the third year of World War II. Three years ago tomorrow morning Hitler sent his legions crashing into Poland, bringing onto the world its greatest catastrophe. Since then the amazing and fearful war machine of the Nazis has ground country after country under its treads, meeting its equal only in the air over England in 1940 and on the land in Russia during the winter of 1941. Joined, at France's fall in 1940, by the jackal Italy and at Pearl Harbor by the treacherous Japan, Germany and her Axis colleagues have continued their victorious march through Russia, Libya, Egypt, Burma, the Philippines, and the Dutch East Indies.

But facing the Axis coalition is the greatest aggregation of freedom-loving nations in the history of the world. These Allied Nations are headed by the "big four", Russia, Britain, China, and the United States, whose potential powers have barely been tapped. The strength of the Allied Nations is rapidly gathering all over the world—in the air over Europe, in Australia and the Solomon Islands, in Egypt and the Middle East and in Russia.

If World War II were to be compared with a prizefight it could be safely said that the first three rounds definitely belong to the contender in the Axis corner but it could also be said that his opponent in the Allied corner has weathered those rounds, absorbing every blow in the opponent's repertoire and has come back fighting. Now there are definite signs that the Axis fighter is becoming winded while the Allied contender is just getting warmed up. The next three rounds should see a "hellava scrap with the decision going to the Allied camp by way of the knockout route."

September

Tuesday, September 1, 1942: —The beginning of the fourth year of war is marked by a new Egyptian offensive opened today by Marshall Rommel. The Nazis made some progress in the south but were held in most places by the expectant British. RAF and American bombers are heavily engaged in attacking German troop and supply concentrations and it looks as though the final showdown is at hand in Egypt.

From Australia, General MacArthur reports that a substantial Allied victory has been won in the Milne Bay area of New Guinea. Aussie troops are rapidly mopping up the remnants of the Jap force that attempted to establish a base there. Severe fighting is in progress in the Kokoda region but the Allied victory at Milne Bay may foreshadow the retaking of the rest of New Guinea from the toe-stubbing Japs.

An interesting development has occurred in Japan that may give an inkling to future actions by Japanese warlords. Foreign Minister Shigenori Togo, the Jap who engineered the Russo-Japanese non-aggression pact and led his country into war last December has been ousted from the Japanese Cabinet and the blood-thirsty General Hideki Tojo, Premier, war minister, and home minister has taken the foreign portfolio also, making him virtual dictator of Japan. It is believed that General Tojo forced Togo's resignation because of the latter's unwillingness to countenance a "stab in the back" attack against Russian Siberia. We can now look for that treacherous attack at any time. Indications from China also point to this conclusion and may account for much of China's recent success as the Japs have withdrawn their men and gone into the defensive in the south in preparation for their attack on Russia.

Wednesday, September 2, 1942: —On three fronts it looks as though the Axis powers are preparing to pull their trick play out of the bag in a supreme effort to win the war before the snow flies. The trick play will be a "squeeze play" engineered by the Germans in Russia and Egypt and by the Japs in Siberia. The Russian and Egyptian prongs of the giant pincers have already begun to tighten and it is merely a matter of time until the Nipponese smash into Russia from the rear.

The situation at Stalingrad is desperate tonight with Nazi panzers having reached the Volga river only fifteen miles from the ruined city. Flying wedges of heavy German tanks supported by swarms of Stukas have overrun Soviet defense lines in many places and we must be ready to face the loss of the city with all its possible consequences to the Russian war effort. The Germans are making a supreme bid to knock the Red Army out of the war this month. If they succeed we can expect many more years of war.

In Egypt the course of the present battle is confused but it appears that, after the initial advance by the Germans, the British have fought them to a standstill. The Imperials are being aided some by American-made and American-manned tanks and many bombers and fighting planes operated by the American Air Force.

Only in the South Pacific is the Allied cause improving. After the rousing victory over the Japs at Milne Bay, the Australian and American forces have established contact with the enemy in the Kokoda region of New Guinea to smash their projected offensive against the Allied base at Port Moresby. Strong air attacks on enemy concentrations in that area were signally successful today.

Thursday, September 3, 1942: —The eyes of the world remain on Russia tonight although many other theaters of war are active. But it is in Russia where the most titanic battle is in progress, with the most at stake. The situation before Stalingrad is growing steadily worse, hour by hour. The battered city seems doomed, though the invaders are paying a tremendous price. Wave after wave of Nazi infantry have been mowed down until their bodies lay in piles but still the surviving hordes press on, heedless of losses. Even Moscow admits that the fall of the city is imminent.

Further south, the Nazis are driving deeper into the Caucasus. The steel-tipped prongs of Nazi panzer divisions are periling the Russian Black Sea port of Novorossiysk, with its important naval base. From there the Germans could by-pass the high ranges of the Caucasian mountains to strike at Baku and the Middle East.

Spain gained the headlines today and Hitler gained his first diplomatic defeat of the war when Generalissimo Francisco France ousted his Axis-loving, collaborationist Foreign Minister Ramon Serrano Suner. The shakeup indicates Franco's desire to avoid all-out entanglement with Hitler and to lean a little more toward the Allies. London considers the move as a substantial victory.

President Roosevelt today broadcast a message of hope to the youth of the world, promising them that their sacrifices in this world struggle will not be in vain. We have learned the lessons of the last war and from their hard-won victory in this one we shall strive mightily to build a world of freedom and justice, and decency—a world in which their sons, in another twenty years will not have to fight and die because of the mistakes we make today.

Friday, September 4, 1942: —The eyes of the Allied world are still fixed anxiously on the bloody steppes of Russia which lie before the gates of Stalingrad. Nazi panzers apparently have smashed gaping holes in the Russian defenses northwest and southwest of the city and are slowly crunching their way over stacks of their dead towards the heart of the doomed metropolis. But hundreds of thousands of battle-hardened Russian troops, aided by a great army of civilian volunteers are throwing themselves recklessly into the breach in an effort to stop the invaders. From Moscow has come the urgent plea to make a "Red Verdun" out of Stalingrad. Every hour, every day that the Germans are delayed brings winter that much closer with its great and overwhelming reinforcements—General Mud and General Cold. Russia can be saved if Stalingrad can hold out for just six weeks.

On three vital fronts, Allied planes were on the offensive today. In Australia, General MacArthur's growing Air Force attacked four Japanese air bases. Enemy bases in the northern Solomons were plastered in obvious preparation for further offensive action by the United States Marines. Other planes smashed at the remnants of the ill-fated Japanese expedition to Milne Bay on southern New Guinea.

In China, American planes were pounding Japanese concentrations and rail communications in an effort to oust the enemy from his last base in Kiangsi province.

In Egypt, Allied superiority in the air has completely stalled Marshal Rommel's recent offensive and has allowed the British to carry out a successful raid of their own against the Germans' southern flank. Many Italian and Nazi vehicles were destroyed and heavy casualties inflicted.

Saturday, September 5, 1942: —Well, the picture from Stalingrad looks a little brighter tonight. Russian reports speak no more of retreat and indicate that the dangerous drive by the Germans northwest of the city has been stopped in one of the bloodiest battles of the entire war. Thousands of Nazis were mowed down by Russian tommy-gunners and machine gunners. Dozens of Nazi tanks were smashed in the bitter struggle.

Even the Berlin press acknowledged the bitterness of the struggle and warned the German populace not to expect a quick, easy victory. "It's a case of annihilation or surrender and the Russians don't surrender," say the Germans. The city may fall all right but not before the foe has paid a tremendous, ruinous price. A million Russian soldiers and civilian volunteers have said, "They shall not pass."

The Allied position in the Egyptian desert also seems to be improving tonight. Persistent attacks by Rommel's forces have failed and the British Imperials have countered with several thrusts of their own which won a number of blockhouses in the center of the line and threaten the enemy on either flank. Nazi tank losses appear to be growing and may have forced Rommel to call off his forward drive prematurely.

At home the Federal Government is becoming increasingly anxious about the growing threat of inflation. The problem has come to the state where it has been dumped into the President's lap—too hot for anyone else to handle. Roosevelt has gone into a huddle with his closest advisor and is expected to outline his solution to Congress and the Nation in one of his famous "fireside chats" next Monday evening—Labor Day. More stringent sacrifices are in the offing.

Sunday, September 6, 1942: —The Russian city that was named for Josef Stalin, the man of steel, is living up to its name. A "steel" wall of Russian men and Russian machines is holding firm against the mightiest assaults that a half a million German "supermen" with their hordes of tanks and clouds of planes can muster. The Russians have really made Stalingrad a "Red Verdun." The battle is probably the bloodiest in all history. Moscow estimates its own casualties at more than seven thousand every twenty four hours and the attacking Germans must be losing at least fifteen to twenty thousand in the same space of time. The ratio of losses for the offensive as compared to the defensive is conservatively estimated to be at least three to one. The Russians believe that such terrible losses have forced the invaders to call up their final reserves in a desperate effort to win out. This is evidenced by the fact that the Russians have encountered wounded German soldiers who have been forced to fight in spite of their injuries. The back of the German drive may be broken if the Soviets can hold out for just a little while longer.

The German people will get their stomachs full of this war before it's over. As a further scourging, Allied bombers ranged far and wide over the Reich last night. The attack was featured by a simultaneous raid by Russian planes from the east and British and American planes from the west. The Soviet bombers ranged over Vienna, Budapest, Hungary, Konigsberg and Breslau while the RAF raked Bremen with two ton block-busters. American Flying Fortresses carried out highly successful raids against occupied France, particularly Bouen. You wanted all-out war, Herr Hitler—now take it!

Monday, September 7, 1942: —Nine months to the day since Pearl Harbor and the Nation is marking its first wartime Labor Day in twenty four years. The vast majority of the Nation's workers remained at their defense jobs today, turning out more weapons to smash the Axis.

The day's program was highlighted this evening by a "fireside chat" by President Roosevelt. The President's theme was a warning to Congress to take immediate and effective action against the rising danger of inflation or he would assume the responsibility himself. The spiraling cost of living must be stabilized and wages and prices, including farm prices must be controlled. The Congress has until October 1st to solve the problem or Roosevelt will take over. Inaction can mean economic chaos.

The Russians are hanging on at Stalingrad in the face of the greatest combined assault by land and air forces in the annals of warfare. Fifteen hundred German dive-bombers and fighter planes set the earth beneath them to quaking while herds of hundreds of tanks and hordes of hundreds of thousands of infantrymen smashed themselves against the defense lines. The carnage is tremendous but desperate and successful counter-attacks by Soviet defenders left the lines in approximately the same relative position at the end of the day as prevailed yesterday. No let-up is in sight.

The British in Egypt, aided by the RAF and American bombers, have wrested the initiative from the wily desert fox, Rommel. It is too early to claim a victory but at least the Nazis have been forced to withdraw to regroup. American operated tanks are seeing their first action in this theater.

Tuesday, September 8, 1942: —The Russians are still holding at Stalingrad although Moscow admits that tremendous pressure has forced Soviet troops to retreat on several sectors. Meanwhile, Russia and Japan appeared to be on the verge of war as the Soviet Government reportedly rejected Japanese demands for coveted bases in Siberia.

From London Prime Minister Churchill today made his periodical report on the state of the war to Parliament. He clearly indicated that the opening of a second front is having the first and foremost attention of all the military leaders of Britain and the United States. You may rest assured that a determined attempt to help and relieve the Russians will be made at the earliest possible moment, regardless of sacrifices and losses.

Details of the Nazis' recent setback in Egypt trickled out of Cairo today. America's roving representative, Wendell Willkie, the 1940 Republican presidential nominee, added his eyewitness account of the battle, saying that the Germans lost more than 100 first line tanks in the opening attack and as a result their whole offensive "has lost its punch." The British took a page from Rommel's own tactics and massed scores of artillery and anti-tank guns to meet the first enemy rush. The victory left the Nazi Afrika Corps in a bad hole that may change the entire complexion of the Middle Eastern campaign.

From Australia comes a report of a new Jap offensive against the important Allied base at Port Moresby on New Guinea. The Japs have tackled the terrific task of attacking over high mountain ranges and thick jungles but are apparently making some headway despite stiff resistance.

Wednesday, September 9, 1942: —About a week ago the Nazi mouthpiece, Goebbels, claimed the capture of Novorossiysk, the vital Russian naval base on the Black Sea. Today we learn that the claim was just some more Nazi propaganda and boasting. The Russians have held the Germans on the outskirts of Novorossiysk and heavy fighting is still in progress. The situation is admittedly bad but the invaders have not yet captured the city.

The same situation is found near Stalingrad, where the gallant Russian defenders have stopped the worst the enemy could offer and are still holding out in all direction. Terrific pressure is being made against the city from three direction, southwest, northwest, and in the center. The battle in the center has reached a crucial stage, with the Germans breaking through in several sectors.

Throughout Germany and Occupied Europe, radio stations went off the air tonight, indicating that Allied planes were raiding numerous centers throughout the continent. Apparently Russian bombers as well as RAF and American planes are in action, as radios went off the air in Hungary, Rumania, and eastern Germany.

Reports from Australia indicate that the Japs are making some progress in their offensive against the Allied base at Port Moresby in New Guinea. The Japs are employing their famous infiltration tactics so successful in the Singapore and Burma campaigns. Extremely difficult obstacles lay in their way in New Guinea as they must cross the high Owen Stanley mountains and dense jungles. In addition, crack Australian jungle fighters are offering stiff resistance.

Thursday, September 10, 1942; —We are vacationing this week and as contrasted with vacations of previous years when a long, extensive auto trip has been customary, we decided, in the interest of tire and gas conservation, to confine our traveling to a brief two day jaunt down the coast to Santa Cruz, 75 miles away. We left about one o'clock this afternoon and went by way of Half Moon Bay. The highway from there on down wound in dizzy figure eights along the coastline. The surf pounded with its interminable yet majestic roar against the jagged reefs and sheer cliffs, against sandy beaches from which we glimpsed here and there the camouflaged outlines of machine gun nests, guarding against saboteurs and invaders alike. The day was warm, with the heated shafts of sunlight vying for predominance with the cooling gusts of sea breezes. From Half Moon Bay where we watched the great Pacific swells climb up their blue green hills like countless Jack's and Jill's, only to stumble and fall head over heels with foaming crashes, to Pigeon Point where the tired breakers seem to slide by the lighthouse and come into the little azure bay to graze, it was a most enjoyable trip.

We arrived in Santa Cruz this afternoon about five o'clock after a leisurely ride, browsed about a bit, then located ourselves in a fine little Auto Court. We spent the evening on the famous boardwalk along the beach. Here the war is brought home to us with a jolt. A few years back during a previous trip, we marveled at the brilliant lights and joyful crowds. Tonight the boardwalk is dingy and dark, everything being dimmed out. We had to slide like furtive ghosts behind dim-out curtains and black boards to find what few amusements have survived. To bed—with the realization that war changes all things.

Friday, September 11, 1942: —Back tonight after a somewhat disappointing day on the beach at Santa Cruz, disappointing because the sun didn't shine—too much fog. We came back by way of Los Gatos through magnificent orchard country. Pears, plums, and other fruits are rotting under the trees by the bushel because of the lack of farm labor. It's a shame, because the fruit is so good. We sampled some of the pears— delicious! Governor Olson of California, despairing of getting any Mexican laborers in time, has begged the Army to let the soldiers help with the harvest. Let us hope something comes of it.

Getting back to the war news, we find that the special committee appointed August 6th by the President to review the dangerous rubber situation has made its report. The committee was headed by the grand old man of World War I, Bernard M. Baruch and was composed of some of the finest brains of the Nation. From the committee's report will come almost immediately, National gas rationing to conserve tires, a thirty five mile speed limit, periodic tire inspection, limitation of annual mileage to 5,000, a speed up of synthetic processes and other recommendations. The rubber situation is so serious that inaction or mismanagement could easily result in a military as well as a civilian collapse.

The Russians finally admit that Novorossiysk has fallen after bloody street fighting. Stalingrad still holds but the pressure of a million Nazis is growing rather than lessening. Our fingers are crossed for this vital city on Russia's Volga lifeline. Can the weary Soviet defenders hold out?

Reports state that Britain has lashed out from its recently won Madagascar base of Diego Suarez to capture the rest of the island thus preventing its use by enemy subs.

Saturday, September 12, 1942: —The battle for Stalingrad is still raging and has developed into what is probably the bloodiest battle of all time. Adolf Hitler has ordered his generals to take the city regardless of cost and the Nazi hordes are throwing themselves recklessly against the Russian defenses. Countless thousands are destroyed but are replaced instantly by thousands more. The ghastly mill of war is grinding the flower of Germany's manhood to bits and the fury of their attacks only evidences their desperation as the season grows late. The first winter snows are beginning to fall in the Caucasian mountains and Hitler can see the handwriting on the wall. Another terrible Russian winter is in store for those same men to whom Der Fuhrer promised victory in 1940—then 1941—then 1942. There will never be victory for you Fritz, or Karl, or Max, even though you survive the slaughter of the Russian battlefield—the wind your Leader sowed in 1939 has ripened into an awful whirlwind that will engulf all of you. There will be no victory—for you!

The British forces mopping up in Madagascar are moving ahead with only token resistance from the Vichy Frenchmen. Pierre Laval, the Vichy Quisling, has protested loud and vehemently against British and American "aggression" but his wails have been ignored by the Allies. The United States Government has voiced its complete approval of the British action.

Australian troops in New Guinea are engaged in a bitter struggle with the Japanese forces attacking Port Moresby. The Aussies are holding firm about forty miles from the vital Allied base.

Sunday, September 13, 1942: —Nothing much new in the news tonight. Principal interest centers around the terrific battle for Stalingrad. The Russians are holding magnificently, exacting a tremendous price for every foot of ground. But the Germans are really pouring it on and it doesn't seem humanly possible for the gallant defenders to prevent the eventual loss of the city. The most discouraging feature is the lack of Russian air power over the battle area. Hundreds of Stukas are ranging the air over

Stalingrad at will, blasting the defense positions with a terrible weight of high explosives. The manner in which the Russians are taking the air bombardment is really astounding. Their courage is writing an unforgettable epic in the history of mankind. Let us hope that their bravery will not be in vain.

The RAF let loose one of their big raids last night. More than six hundred heavy bombers smashed at the oft-hit city of Bremen. Fires that could be seen for a hundred miles were ravaging the heart of the city when the bombers left. We shall see the tempo of the air war in Western Europe increase daily with the approach of winter. When the Germans stabilize their Russian front for the winter they are sure to retaliate at Britain for the terrific pounding they have received all spring and summer.

The Russians are doing a bit of long range bombing themselves. For the last two weeks they have supplemented the scourging of the Reich in the west by the RAF by smashing at Hungary, Rumania and Eastern Germany, including Berlin itself. Late reports indicate that they are busy at it again tonight as Berlin and Budapest radios are off the air.

Monday, September 14, 1942: —The bone-crushing battle for Stalingrad continues. The Soviets are performing miracles of defense but apparently the Nazis are creeping closer and closer. Moscow admits that the Germans are "at the gates of the city" while Berlin states that street fighting is in progress in the suburbs. The ferocity of the struggle is unparalleled in the annals of warfare.

Action flared up on the Egyptian front today in the form of a Commando-like raid on the Axis base of Tobruk in Libya. The British landed from small naval vessels and succeeded in destroying much enemy equipment before retiring. The RAF aided in the attack.

President Roosevelt today reported on the progress of lend-lease aid to our allies and warned that our war effort was only about 50% effective up to now. Our civilian economy must be stripped to the bone if we are to turn out the war materiel in the quantities necessary to assure a victorious conclusion to the war. Approximately five billion, one hundred twenty nine million dollars in lend-lease material has been delivered to the Allies to date. About 35% has gone to Britain, 35% to Russia, and the balance to the Middle East, Australia and China.

Berlin has claimed victory in a great convoy battle in the North Atlantic in which they state that nineteen cargo vessels, two destroyers, and a corvette were sunk and the rest of the convoy dispersed. No confirmation of this report has come from any Allied source.

A dispatch from Pearl Harbor says that several hundred Jap prisoners from the Solomons battle have arrived in a mainland port.

Tuesday, September 15, 1942: —Urgently needed air reinforcements today saved the situation at Stalingrad. Red airmen drove off many of the hundreds of Nazi planes, giving the ground defenders welcome relief from the constant air bombardment. Nazi assaults on all sectors of the battle line were thrown back again and again as the Soviet troops fought with unequaled bravery. Heroic, desperate tales of defending Russians tying bundles of grenades on their bodies and throwing themselves in front of charging Nazi tanks give evidence of the desperate character of the fighting. By all the rules of ordinary warfare the Russians should have long since capitulated like the Poles, the Dutch, the Belgians, and the French did. But, like the British in 1940, the Russians do not know when they are beaten. For this reason they will never be beaten—and the Germans don't think they are playing fair. The Berlin papers complain that the Russians don't know when they've had enough—they only know how to die.

The United States proper apparently has been bombed from the air for the first time in history. Near the little seaside town of Brookings, Oregon a little unidentified seaplane, presumably Japanese, dropped some incendiary bombs that started a small forest fire that was quickly brought under control. It is believed that the plane was launched from a Jap sub. Fragments of the exploded bomb were recovered, bearing Japanese ideographs.

Over Suda Bay on the island of Crete as well as over Japanese occupied islands of the Aleutians American airmen struck some telling blows today. Axis shipping and supplies at Suda Bay were destroyed while cargo vessels and shore installations at Kiska Island were repeatedly hit by bombs.

Wednesday, September 16, 1942: —William M. Jeffers, President of the Union Pacific Railroad was appointed by Donald Nelson as Rubber Administrator to carry out the provisions and suggestions of the Baruch Committee. The new Administrator is to be absolute czar of the rubber situation and his assignment is a grave one—to prevent the dangerous shortage of the vital commodity from harming the war effort and to so conserve the present stockpile and develop the synthetic industry that not only the military needs but essential civilian functions may be maintained. His job is a big one and calls for full cooperation on the part of the public.

The Navy announced some more bad news today. The great aircraft carrier Yorktown was sunk as a result of the Battle of Midway. The ship was put out of action by enemy planes on June 4th and was being towed to safety when an enemy submarine sent two torpedoes crashing into her hull. The vessel heeled over and sank. Loss of life was light. Thus the Yorktown joined her sister ship the Lexington as victims of enemy action. The news of the loss was withheld by the Navy until today for military reasons.

The Japs have launched another determined attack on the Solomon Islands in an effort to retake those positions recently captured by the U.S. Marines. Heavy fighting is in progress and appears likely to develop into a major engagement.

The Stalingrad situation is worsening. The Germans have pounded into the suburbs of the city on the north and bitter street fighting is in progress. The worst feature of the battle is the fact that the Nazis seem to have complete air control.

Thursday, September 17, 1942: —The Stalingrad battle continues to hold the spotlight. The Germans were apparently expecting to claim the capture of the city today as they had broadcast that an important announcement would be made this morning but their hopes backfired as no announcement was forthcoming and very heavy fighting continued to rage all day on the outskirts of the city. The determined Russians have barricaded every street and every building and the Nazis are forced to blast their way forward foot by foot. The victory, if the invaders do gain it, may well prove to be a Pyrrhic victory.[1]

As September wears on, every day that the Soviets continue to fight at Stalingrad is a victory for the Allied Nations. Day by day, the prospects of winning the final decision in this war retreats step by step away from Hitler and his Axis satellites as the stubborn resistance of the Russians gives the other United Nations time to prepare for the final showdown which may well come in the spring. Meanwhile, all Hitler and his weary men have to look forward to is another bitter Russian winter.

The Australian front commands second place in the news today as Chinese reports state that the Japanese have dispatched a strong fleet, including at least four battleships, towards the Solomon Islands. A new and intensified attempt to recapture the Islands is in prospect. On New Guinea, the Japs have wriggled and infiltrated their way across the Owen Stanley Mountains to within 32 miles of Port Moresby. The situation there is precarious unless MacArthur is able to pull some of the strategy for which he is famous—and soon.

Friday, September 18, 1942: —The amazing Russians are still battling stubbornly in Stalingrad. The Nazis have pushed through to the Volga River in some places but reinforcements of Siberian troops have bolstered the Soviets. It will be remembered that the arrival of Siberian troops at the Moscow front at the crucial moment last year turned the tide and saved the capital. It is almost too much to hope for this year but time will tell.

The effect of Stalingrad's loss on Russia's ability to remain in the war has been the subject for discussion by many experts. Most believe that the Red Army will and can continue the fight even though most of its vital oil supplies will be cut off. Undoubtedly the Reds have laid up a considerable reserve and other routes and means will be found to obtain additional supplies. As long as their army and their will to fight are intact Russia can hang on until the growing might of Britain and the United States can come to the rescue. It is extremely vital that Russia does hang on.

On New Guinea the Japs are advancing closer and closer to Port Moresby in spite of everything the opposing Australians can do. Apparently the Allies have underestimated the Japs again, believing the rugged terrain rather than troops could stop the little yellow men. Is it to be Singapore all over again or can the Allied forces muddle their way out of this one? We shall soon see, for the decisive, pitched battle is expected momentarily.

On the home front nasty little things like outlaw strikes in war industries and bureaucratic, halfhearted administration of some vital war projects reflect a little of the complacency of a small section of the public which is hindering the all-out team work that will be necessary before this war is won.

Saturday, September 19, 1942: —It's still the Stalingrad battle that holds the limelight. The Russians are making a tremendous gallant stand. Their courage and determination are amazing. They are literally defending the city stone by stone. There is apparently no thought in their minds of capitulation. If the Germans win it will be because there are no more Russians to resist. The invaders are paying a terrible price for their gains. The front yards of Stalingrad's once neat homes seem planted with gray-green bodies while wrecked machines by the hundreds add to the clutter of fallen walls. The battle is one of movement; the surging back and forth of hundreds of tanks, armored cars, tommy-gunners and massed infantry while overhead roar countless dive bombers and fighters, their crashing bombs and screaming sirens adding to the hellish din. It's impossible to image being involved in such a holocaust—what must be the thoughts of an individual soldier as he faces the onrushing tank. Man, of all creatures, is cruelest to its own kind.

A Washington announcement stated today that there are now 4,000,000 men in the U.S. Army. This does not include the probable million in the Navy and the unknown number in the Marines and Coast Guard. This seems like a large figure until we remember that there have been more than this number of casualties already on the Russian front alone. It is expected that our army will expand to something like twice its present size before this war is much older. Let's hope we'll never run into casualties such as the Russians and Germans have suffered. It's unbelievable to me that the German people have been able to take such losses twice within a quarter of a century. No despots could ever lead the American people thus—once!

Sunday, September 20, 1942: —The amazing, unbelievable Russians are upsetting Hitler's timetable again. For twenty seven days they have fought fiercely for Stalingrad, the City of Steel, and the Russian flag still flies over the blood-soaked citadel. A fresh army of Siberian troops, backed up by a furious mass of overall garbed civilians and picturesque Volga boatmen have even seized the initiative and have driven the invaders from many of the city's streets. All along the line from Leningrad in the north, Veronezh in the center, and Novorossiysk in the south, Red Army troops have surged forward with renewed vigor as they catch the first glimmer of approaching winter and the first sign of Nazi desperation. How will Hitler explain another postponement of victory to his weary, bitter people as they look forward to another winter of privation and suffering? How's the headache now, Adolf?

Little news is available from the Solomon Island front. The Navy announced, however, that the Japanese naval task force that approached the Islands was driven off by land based Flying Fortresses on September 14th. It is believed that the enemy is regrouping his forces for the final all-out attempt to retake the Solomons. Our troops there have been reinforced, however, and are ready to meet any situation.

The RAF plastered Munich with bombs from about six hundred planes last night. The spawning ground of Nazism was flattened with fires left burning that were visible for a hundred miles. May those fires help burn out the evil cancer that started a decade ago in a little beer hall in Munich when Hitler and has henchmen began their evil careers that have cost the lives and fortunes of millions of human beings already.

Monday, September 21, 1942: —Back to work today after our brief vacation. Sales of War Savings Bonds continue at a fairly rapid clip. Many other types of Government securities, such as Treasury Bonds and Tax Savings Notes are helping to bring in the billions that are necessary to finance this greatest of all undertakings. The job facing the Treasury Department must be tremendous beyond belief. The financing of World War I was child's play compared with this one.

As usual for the last month, the war news tonight centers around the awe-inspiring battle for Stalingrad. Hopeful indications are that the Russians may make a real "Verdun" of this city and it will not fall after all. Typical of these signs are the complaints of the Berlin radio that bad weather has delayed their capture of the city. Such guff was Berlin's alibi last year for their failure at Moscow. At any rate, tonight's late radio newscasts state that a terrific artillery duel is in progress. The Nazis have brought up great siege guns and are pouring metal into the city at a terrific rate. The Russians are countering with their famous railroad artillery and armored trains. The Reds are giving every bit as good as they are taking. The tide may yet turn in favor of the defenders although it is admitted that the situation is still desperate.

From Australia comes information that the last of the ill-fated Japanese expedition to Milne Bay on the southern tip of New Guinea have been mopped up and MacArthur's whole attention may now be directed to the smashing of the Jap drive against Port Moresby. This front has been static for the last few days with the Japs held approximately 32 miles from the Allied Base.

Tuesday, September 22, 1942: —The almost incredible Russians are apparently driving the Nazis back from many points in the sanguinary battle for Stalingrad. Furious counter-attacks by crack detachments of Soviet Guards swept several Stalingrad streets clear of living invaders, leaving innumerable dead Germans as they drove forward. A large part of the fighting is at close quarters, with rifles, bayonets, hand grenades, and flaming benzene bottles as the principal weapons. The see-saw battle continues unabated as it goes into its 29th day with the final outcome still in doubt. Some experts feel that Stalingrad may well prove to be Hitler's Waterloo.

Several other developments in the global war have occurred which are favorable to the United Nations. First is the submarine situation off the Atlantic coast of the United States. For a time it appeared that there was no solution to the menace; sinkings were occurring at an alarming rate for beyond our capacity for replacement. The situation has now taken a definite turn in our favor with sinkings almost zero.

Representative Vinson, Chairman of the House Naval Affairs Committee states that Allied sea power is increasing rapidly to the point where an invincible offensive may soon be launched against our enemies.

Allied air power is also growing. U.S. and British air men are pounding Nazi Europe and Nazi Africa in ever increasing tempo and Major General Ira C. Eaker, U.S. Air Commander in Britain promises a crescendo of attacks that will rake Germany throughout the winter without respite. Hold your hat, Hitler— here comes trouble. I'll bet that headache's getting worse.

Wednesday, September 23, 1942: —While the Russians continue to successfully defend Stalingrad, talk increases regarding the possibility of a "second front" in Western Europe. The British in a radio broadcast to the people of France, warned them to evacuate all coastal areas in Occupied France as the offensive may come at any moment and the useless shedding of French blood was to be avoided if possible. Many other sources indicate that the real front will be in the air, with nightly raids by 1,000 planes or more to try for victory through air power alone. My guess—and just that—is that bombing raids on as large a scale as possible will continue throughout the winter, with a land invasion coming about March first. Let's see how far off I am.

The British smashed hard at Marshal Rommel's communications throughout Libya, it was revealed today. Large scale "commando" type raids were carried out against Bengasi and Barce, more than 500 miles behind the Egyptian front and severe damage was caused to enemy supplies and installations and many casualties were inflicted. Deep within Libya, about 135 miles southeast of Bengasi, English desert troops captured the oasis of Gialo which may further rupture Rommel's communications.

On the home front, an amazing feat of construction was recorded by Henry J. Kaiser's Oregon Shipbuilding Company of Portland, Oregon. A 10,500 ton Victory ship was launched just ten days after the keel was laid. This smashed all previous records by a mile. The ship will be completely outfitted and delivered by next Sunday. Compare this job with the best time recorded in World War I for a similar ship—212 days. Fourteen days from keel to cargo! Boy, that's some building.

Thursday, September 24, 1942: —Even the ferocious battle for Stalingrad is settling into a routine that seemingly goes on for endless days, with no end in sight to the slaughter. Even the Germans themselves are beginning to doubt whether the city will fall. The "Verdun" of the Volga has been pounded to rubble but it is still in Russian hands, bloody but unbowed.

From the Solomon Islands front comes some bad news. The Navy has announced the loss of a destroyer and a small troop transport, with the loss of about two hundred seventy two lives. The tragic tale of the full cost of the Solomon Islands offensive will sadden many an American home. And this is but the bare beginning. It is almost too terrible to contemplate the number of casualties that will occur when the Allied offensives really begin to roll both in Europe and in the Pacific.

The RAF gave Germany another nasty dose last night. The submarine yards at Flensburg near the Danish border was chosen as the target and tons of heavy bombs severely smashed that nest of "Atlantic rattlesnakes."

In Washington, Congress is trying to rush an anti-inflationary bill through to meet the President's deadline of October first. Farm bloc leaders however, are blocking the Administration bill by demanding a higher computation of parity on form prices which would include all farm labor costs and which, if accepted, would raise the cost of living by another five percent. Prospects of getting an acceptable bill through by the end of the month are slim and meanwhile prices continue to rise and the Nation slips steadily closer to the brink of unbridled inflation.

Friday, September 25, 1942: —For the last ten days the Germans have made very little progress in the Stalingrad battle and hope is growing that the city will be saved. The Red Army forces of General Timoshenko have launched a counter-offensive northwest of the beleaguered city and have gained enough momentum to smash through the Nazi lines for a considerable distance. Meanwhile, within the city the struggle continues with undiminished ferocity. Weary Russian faces are ashen with horror and lack of sleep but they stick to their posts through a rain of bombs and cannon fire until the enemy retreats or they die. They take countless Germans with them when they die and there is no time to bury the dead in this battle. The streets run red with the blood of friend and foe. No words can describe the magnitude of the catastrophe that has befallen the City of Steel on the Volga.

The British Admiralty today reported on the biggest convoy fight in the history of the war. A huge convoy of cargo vessels bound for Russia was attacked in the Arctic by large numbers of enemy planes and submarines. A destroyer, a minesweeper, and several cargo ships were sunk but enemy losses were also high, including more than 40 Nazi bombers and two submarines for sure, possibly six. The majority of the convoy arrived with their goods at the Russian port.

In this country, raw material shortages are having public attention. A great nation-wide scrap iron and steel campaign is under way to keep the blast furnaces going full tilt during the winter months. Steel shortages have kept shipbuilding and tank building schedules below par. An idea to collect a half million tons of high grade steel in the Nation's twenty eight million auto bumpers is in the mill at the present time. Seems like a good idea.

Saturday, September 26, 1942: —The Soviet counter-drive northwest of Stalingrad is rolling the Germans back. The success of this drive is forcing the Nazis to take some of the pressure off the stalwart defenders of the city. The dead are numbered in the thousands in each of these daily attacks which in themselves rival or exceed the fury of great battles of history. A hundred Waterloos have been fought on the approaches to Stalingrad while the magnificent defense of Verdun in the First World War has been dwarfed many times in this battle. While German dead averaged about 12,000 per month before the French bastion, it is conservatively estimated that the invaders lost more than 25,000 killed last week around Stalingrad. The defenders' losses have probably been just about as heavy.

The aircraft carrier Lexington sails again. But it is a new ship, launched at Quincy, MA a year ahead of schedule and name after the gallant vessel that went down in the Battle of the Coral Sea. Survivors of the lost ship were proud witnesses at the launching.

William S. Jeffers, the newly appointed Rubber Chief is expected to put nation-wide gas rationing into effect by November first. In the meantime he has urged the public to voluntarily reduce their speed and their use of automobiles. National gas rationing does not indicate a shortage of that commodity but is represented by the 28 million sets of auto tires in the country. Reduced speed is also essential as tires last many times longer at 35 miles per hour that at high speeds. A tire conserved is rubber saved for military purposes.

Sunday, September 27, 1942: —Another Sunday has come and almost gone as I sit down to write this record. The day has been so peaceful with warm sunshine and gentle breeze and everything so orderly and quiet. It seems almost impossible to conceive of a situation like that which is occurring in Stalingrad.

Reason tells you that human beings don't do such things. Men, especially of a Sunday, like a home and children, with a quiet stroll in the sunshine, the funny papers or perhaps a round of golf. Blood and murder and destruction are not for such men. It is difficult to realize that all men are not men of good will; that there are some men who glory in war, who would destroy, without mercy, those who do not bow before them; who would enslave those whom they consider their inferiors. Men such as these have, through the ages, brought misery and death to countless innocent men, women and children. It is men such as these with whom we are now engaged in so bitter a struggle, a struggle that will settle the fate of mankind for a thousand years. We must now highly resolve that when the victory, with God's help, is won we shall strive just as mightily to so win the peace, that an adequate international police force will be set up to forever prevent hoodlums of the Hitler, Mussolini, Tojo type from setting the world afire with their vicious schemes of deviltry. Only then will those gallant Russian lives and the lives of British and Americans to follow have been sacrificed for a worthy purpose.

As an appropriate overtone to the thoughts I am thinking as I close this record for the night is the roar, close above the house, of what sounds like a flight of deadly P-38's winging their way to patrol the darkened coastline, a roaring tribute to American industry and America's resolve to win the ultimate victory.

Monday, September 28, 1942: —Wendell Willkie, the 1940 Republican nominee for President and leader of the loyal opposition party in this country has been making a flying tour, as the President's special emissary, of the Middle Eastern, Russian, and Far Eastern battlefronts. Lately, Mr. Willkie has been in Russia, conferring with Soviet leaders and inspecting Russia's war effort with the objective in view of improving American-Soviet relations, cooled somewhat of late because of the delay in opening the badly needed second front. Willkie's observations are that great though Russia's losses have been—something like five million men—her will to fight is as strong as ever. Her one great need is more substantial assistance and he strongly advocates the opening of the second front at the first possible date on which the Allied military high command believes there is a chance of success. Next summer may well be too late. Russia has lost some of her most important territory and great quantities of materiel as well as manpower. Undue procrastination in creating the second front could possibly cause a collapse in the morale of her people, until now the most amazing and effective part of her resistance. We cannot afford to wait too long.

American airmen in the Aleutian Islands, in the Solomons, and in New Guinea have been steadily and successfully pounding Jap forces and installations. So effective have been their attacks, that the Jap offensive against Port Moresby has been thrown back on its heels, the enemy preparations for a counter-blow against the Solomons have been blasted and delayed, and Japanese garrisons and supplies in the Aleutians so mauled and softened up that no further expansion has been attempted by enemy forces in that region and the day may be near when a counter-drive by land forces may drive them out altogether.

Tuesday, September 29, 1942; —Today's war news is barren and repetitious. The Russian front, particularly at Stalingrad, continues to be a raging inferno of fire and explosives, with the issue very much in doubt. Whatever the final result, the Russians have produced an epic of courage at Stalingrad that has no peer in history. Their heroic defense, at the least, has thrown Hitler's timetable off schedule several months and has forced him to postpone the final decision until next year. The victory may well be beyond his reach by then.

The only other active theater of war today is New Guinea, where the Australians, strongly supported by General MacArthur's air force, have started an offensive of their own against the invading Jap forces driving towards Port Moresby. The Aussies are using the Japs' own infiltration tactics and successfully too. The attack is receiving additional support from newly arrived batteries of field artillery, a weapon that has been sadly lacking on our side up until now.

German authorities in Occupied France have started a campaign against American citizens in that country. More than 1,900 Americans have been rounded up and interned, being subjected to every calculated indignity that could be heaped upon them. For an example, a large group of Americans were confined to the monkey house at the Paris zoo while they were being checked.

San Francisco's scrap metal drive was accelerated today after a miserable start yesterday. Northern California's showing in scrap collecting is very poor for some reason, probably because of its cities' more metropolitan and congested character. At least that is the principal reason given by those who should know.

Wednesday, September 30, 1942: —Bad news from the Solomon Islands today. The Navy announced that two American transports were sunk in the Solomon offensive. One was the 8,378 ton naval transport George F. Elliot and the other the small 1,060 ton auxiliary transport Gregory. The announcement stated that the loss of life was small but no actual figures were given. The full toll in men and equipment for that victory will prove to be considerable, I am afraid. Such ventures are expensive.

Adolf Hitler let off some steam in Berlin today. In a customary bombastic speech he bragged of his great victories and minimized the dangers of the so-call second front. He, of course, predicted complete and final victory but it is significant that he didn't set his usual time limit. That one has back-fired on him so many times that he "dassn't pull it again." He promised dire retaliations for British bombings, however, and it is evident that those RAD raids are hurting—and plenty.

Russians and Australians, on the widely separated battlefronts, are pushing forward slowly but steadily on their counter-offensives against their respective enemies. The Russian drive north of Stalingrad threatens to outflank and encircle the Nazi forces within the city while the Aussies have forced the Japs back 10 miles towards the Owen Stanley Mountains. Savage and bitter fighting is in progress.

Pre-war headline news is the World Series baseball contest between the New York Yankees and the St. Louis Cardinals which started in the latter city today. In a thrilling game the Yankees started rolling towards their customary championship by beating the Cards by a 7 to 4 score. This may be the last World Series for the duration as it looks bad for baseball from now on.

[1] A **Pyrrhic** victory is a victory with devastating cost to the victor; it carries the implication that another such victory will ultimately cause defeat. *en.wikipedia.org/wiki/Pyrrhic_victory*

October

Thursday, October 1, 1942: —The big news of today is the report that has now been released regarding an extensive trip that President Roosevelt has just completed. His journey commenced on September 17th and took him 8,754 miles on a transcontinental tour of war plants and military training stations. Visits of inspection were made at great plants such as the Chrysler Tank factory and Henry Ford's Willow Run bomber factory in Detroit, Boeing, Douglas, and Consolidated Aircraft factories on the Pacific Coast, Henry Kaiser's ten-day shipbuilding yards in Oregon, and the Higgins Industries in New Orleans. His itinerary included inspections of Naval and air training stations throughout the country and American and captured Jap submarines were viewed at Mare Island in San Francisco Bay on September 24th. The entire trip was conducted with utmost wartime secrecy and no mention or report of the journey was made until the President was safely back in the White House.

The President stated on his return that he was well pleased with what he had seen; that the people were far ahead of Congress in war spirit. War preparations and precautions against attack on the West Coast also impressed him.

On the war fronts, things are pretty much in the same impasse at Stalingrad. The situation is admittedly critical for the Russians but they are still hanging on. In Egypt indications are that the British are almost ready to launch a real offensive against Rommel. A brief sortie today gained some positions which improved the Allied line somewhat. In Australia, the Aussies are still shoving the Japs back from their abortive thrust against Port Moresby. General MacArthur has the situation well in hand.

The St. Louis Cardinals evened matters today in the World Series by downing the Yanks 4-3.

Friday, October 2, 1942: —Home front news holds the spotlight today. Bay Area shipyards and unions have taken steps to stop labor pirating and migration by freezing all workers to their present jobs except for legitimate reasons. The labor situation all over the country is becoming acute. A grave manpower shortage is already beginning to be felt, with the

219

armed forces and war industries hungrily competing for the available supply of men. Women in greater and greater numbers are taking their places in the shipyards, the aircraft factories, and other vital industries. Five million more of them must be found to keep the production wheels turning next year. The thing is a necessity but one can't help but feel that a seed of tremendous postwar difficulty is being sowed here, for once women are firmly established throughout the economy of the Nation it will be extremely unlikely that they can or will be ousted to make way for the men returning to take up their old jobs after the fighting is over. However, those problems are secondary to the present need to successfully prosecute the war. Without victory there won't be a Nation to come back to let alone a job. So, more power to the army of women workers. Let's hope they turn out the ships to beat the Nips.

Congress, working faster than its usual gait, has turned out the anti-inflation legislation that the President demanded to curb the rapidly spiraling cost of living. The directive empowers the President to stabilize wages and salaries as well as fix ceilings for farm prices. The Chief Executive will undoubtedly act on this directive without delay.

Saturday, October 3, 1942: —President Roosevelt acted swiftly on the anti-inflation bill today. James F. Byrnes, Associate Justice of the Supreme Court was appointed as Director of Stabilization, with full control over the whole program. Byrnes resigned immediately from the Supreme Court position to accept his new responsibilities.

The President also ordered wages and salaries stabilized at September 15th levels and placed ceilings on all rents throughout the Nation. A top limit of $25,000 net was placed on individual salaries and all increases on salaries of $5,000 or more must be approved before becoming effective.

Price Administrator Henderson, under direction of the President, immediately announced that the prices of virtually all foods are to be frozen for a sixty day emergency period, or until a permanent program can be prepared.

Thus, with plenty of action and in dead earnest, the war on inflation really began today.

On the war fronts we find MacArthur's troops on New

Guinea pushing the Japs farther and farther away from Port Moresby. The situation there is much better.

Important and welcome news comes of American troops moving in on the Japanese bases in the Aleutian Islands. Our forces occupied in bad weather, without enemy opposition, the Andreanof Island group, only 125 miles east of the Jap base on Kiska Island. This new development indicates that the Army is determined to oust the Japs from the archipelago and makes it possible to provide a fighter escort to our big bombers in their daily attacks against the Jap bases. It also makes us that much nearer our ultimate objective—Tokyo.

Sunday, October 4, 1942: —Premier Josef Stalin of Russia today demanded in an open letter to the United States that the Allied Nations fulfill their obligation toward opening a second front and do it in time. The Russian leader's letter was written in reply to an American correspondent's plea for an interview but he gave specific answers to three pertinent questions propounded by the reporter. The questions were these: How effective has Allied aid been to Russia? What is needed to amplify and improve this aid? And how strong is Russia's capacity and will to continue resistance to the enemy? To these questions Stalin stated that compared with the help rendered the Allied Nations by Russia in taking upon herself the full weight of the Nazi attack, American and British aid is ineffective. The only way for the Allied Nations to amplify their aid is to fulfill their obligations to quickly open a second front. As far as Russia's will to fight on is concerned Stalin assured the world that Russia's capacity and confidence is as great, if not greater, than the ability of the Fascist invaders to attain domination of the world. In other words, he said, "We'll fight all right, but you'd better help us out— and quick."

The Stalingrad theater alone proves the Red Army's ability and will to fight. For forty one days that stubborn defenders have absorbed everything the mightiest army in the world could throw at them and still the city has not fallen. German dead are stacked high on all the approaches but the heart of the city is still denied to them. You've got to hand it to the Soviets. If any people ever deserved help it is certainly the fighting Russians.

221

Monday, October 5, 1942: —American airmen are pasting the Japs on widely scattered fronts today. It appears likely that a large scale offensive is getting under way in the Aleutians aiming at driving the Japs from their ill-gotten bases on Kiska and Attu islands. From the Andreanof Islands, only 125 miles from Kiska, U.S. bombers supported by fighters have been relentlessly pounding the Jap base with "continual fire." Five enemy seaplanes and shore installations were destroyed. Two ships in the harbor were beached following today's attack.

In the Solomons the Japs have succeeded in landing some reinforcements but the U.S. Marines are maintaining their positions firmly. American flyers have made it hot for the enemy forces, damaging four enemy destroyers and intercepting several Jap bombing formations, aiming at attacking Guadalcanal, shooting down at least four of the attacking aircraft. No American planes were lost.

The United States is taking its losses, however, as the Navy today announces the loss of the new submarine Grunion, with its crew of about sixty five men. The sub is long overdue and is believed to be sunk. There's very little of the glory of war in a submarine's life. They fight by stealth and die in solitude.

The Russians are still holding in Stalingrad and the Australians are still advancing in New Guinea, so all in all the war picture today presents a more cheerful aspect, even to the point that we can enjoy the surprising and thrilling finish to the World Series baseball that ended today with the brilliant St. Louis Cards knocking off their fourth victory in a row from the New York Yankees to win the series four games to one.

Tuesday, October 6, 1942: —The temp of fighting in the Solomons area is increasing today. The Navy's communiqué stated that U.S. dive bombers scored a direct hit on a heavy Jap cruiser and sent eleven Zero fighters crashing into the sea. One American plane was shot down but the crew escaped.

Across the Coral Sea to New Guinea we find MacArthur's crack Australian troops driving the Jap invaders almost all the way back over the Owen Stanley Mountains. Effective support by American planes has contributed much to the successful Allied counter-offensive.

To temper the good news, an unconfirmed claim is made by the Italian radio that their submarines have sunk an American battleship of the Mississippi class. Our Navy Department has declined to comment on the claim. Let's hope it's more Axis fabrication.

In Russia, the Red Army defenders in Stalingrad beat off nineteen ferocious attacks in one day, absorbing everything the Nazis could fling. Meanwhile, Marshal Timoshenko's counter-offensive northwest of the city has plowed forward to the Don River and is threatening the flank of the Stalingrad attackers. Continued success of this flanking attack could force the Germans to withdraw from before the city. This is the Russians' best hope of finally saving the embattled citadel.

On the home front it appears that gas rationing will soon be upon us. To supplement the rationing program a 35 mile speed limit has been imposed, with the loss of the gas ration book as a probable penalty for offenders. It was also decreed that a five-tire limit would be placed on private autos, with extra tires being confiscated by the Government—with compensation of course.

Wednesday, October 7, 1942: —Some cheerful news has been received today. Apparently the Japs found it too hot—or too cold—on the islands of Attu and Agattu in the Aleutian chain as our Navy reports that the enemy has withdrawn from these outposts, leaving themselves established only at Kiska where they are taking a terrific beating from American planes and submarines. It is entirely possible that our forces may be able to reduce the latter stronghold shortly and complete the reoccupation of the archipelago. Such a success would remove a serious threat to Alaska and our West Coast.

In New Guinea also, it looks as though a dangerous enemy threat has been removed at least for the time being. General MacArthur, once again, has shown that he is a master at handling the Japs as his Australian and American troops, with superior air support, have driven the little yellow men all the way back from their most advanced point, only 32 miles from Port Moresby, to the other side of the Owen Stanley Mountains. Thus the vital Allied citadel of Port Moresby is out of immediate danger.

The durable Russians are still holding the major part of the city of Stalingrad while their relief offensive, northwest of the city, is gaining momentum against the left flank of the Nazis. This developing drive by the Red Army is designed to rescue the embattled city by pinching off the invaders' line of communication. The Russians know a bit about "pincer movements" themselves.

President Roosevelt, looking forward to a successful conclusion of the war, today announced that the Allies are setting up a commission to gather evidence against the guilty "war criminals" of the Axis Nations, in order that adequate punishment may be meted out to the perpetrators of so many ghastly atrocities against civilization.

Thursday, October 8, 1942: —The Berlin radio today hinted that the Nazis may be giving up their attempt to capture all of Stalingrad. Their statement was that "they don't need Stalingrad" and that the rest of the city can easily be reduced by bombardment rather than direct assault. Not a very good alibi after their hundreds of desperate attacks during the last few weeks. What a terrible cost they must have paid for what little they have captured. Apparently even the hardened Nazis couldn't take it any longer.

An incredible story comes out of the Pacific warfront today. After the Battle of the Solomon Islands, a San Francisco boy— now known as "Indestructible Moore"—was officially reported as killed in action with the U.S. Marines. Today it is learned that he is very much alive, after having been in an American tank that was captured by sixty five Japs. The Japs smashed open the turret of the tank, threw a hand grenade inside and then set it afire. Having escaped the grenade explosion by a miracle, Moore and a comrade were forced out of the tank by the fumes and flames. Moore's comrade was immediately shot. The Japs grabbed Moore, knocked him down, kicked him, jabbed him with a pitchfork, knifed him and smashed him over the head. His apparently lifeless body was then tossed aside and he was later rescued by other Marines and nursed back to health by Navy doctors. Who says the Marines aren't tough?

Army leaders are pressing Congress for legislation to permit the drafting of 18 and 19 year old youths for military service. In

Britain, in Russia, and all over the world this war has proved to a young man's fight. The teen-agers make the best flyers and the most daring and durable soldiers.

Friday, October 9, 1942: —American heavy bombers and fighter planes in increasing numbers are joining the RAF in daylight raids on Occupied Europe. Today more than 100 Flying Fortresses and Liberators, flown by Americans and supported by American pursuit planes, made a successful sweep over Occupied France, striking particularly at the railroad center at Lille. Four of the bombers failed to return but the crew of one was reported safe. The tempo of air fighting over all of Western Europe is stepping up with the concentration of more and more American planes as a separate striking force to work in conjunction with Britain's own mighty RAF. I'd hate to be in Germany this winter.

In the Aleutians, the Army is hammering relentlessly at the Jap base at Kiska. Round-the-clock raids by heavy bombers have left the harbor strewn with burning ships and wreckage.

In the Solomons, the Navy announced that a Navy task force caught a Jap fleet napping off the Islands in a storm and damaged ten enemy vessels without a casualty to our men or ships.

In this country taxes and inflation hold the spotlight, especially in Washington D.C. The Senate today approved a proposed 5% Victory Tax that would be deducted from wages and salaries of persons earning $12.00 per week or more. This tax would bring in another three and one half billion in addition to the six and one half billion included in the regular income tax bill that recently became law. The Victory Tax money would be rebated to the taxpayer, at least in part, after the war. The idea is really a compulsory savings scheme which is bound to come in one way or another.

Saturday, October 10, 1942: —The Germans' offensive against Stalingrad apparently is petering out and it looks as though the Red Army is close to winning a clear-cut victory in defense of the vital Volga stronghold. Today's Nazi attacks in the region were small scale and gave the defenders a badly needed breathing spell. Hitler's recent promise that "Stalingrad will be taken, of that you can be sure" is about to boomerang on him.

Another Russian winter will soon be upon his battered and badly mauled army. The Russian "Verdun" may well prove to be the turning point in the war.

Not quite so good news comes from the Solomon Islands in the Southwest Pacific battleground. The U.S. Marines' position on Guadalcanal remains precarious as the Japs have succeeded frequently in landing reinforcements on the Island under cover of darkness. The important airfield on Guadalcanal is the prize sought by the Japs and in spite of heavy damage inflicted by American flyers on the enemy expeditions, the Marines have a difficult job cut out for them in holding our hard-won bases in the Island chain. That General MacArthur recognizes the danger is evident for his heavy bombers have smashed ceaselessly at Jap invasion bases and an especially vigorous attack was made today on the big Jap base of Rabaul, on New Britain Island. The greatest force of bombers yet used in any single operation in the Southwest Pacific shattered the base and left it a smoking ruin.

Here at home the Western Defense Command ordered eighteen prominent Italians and other enemy aliens ousted from the coastal area as a defense measure.

Sunday, October 11, 1942: —Enemy submarine activity along the West Coast has been resumed. The Navy announced that sinking several days ago of a tanker off the West Coast by enemy torpedoes. Six seamen lost their lives; the rest were rescued by another vessel that braved a similar attack to save the half-frozen survivors. This makes the fifth ship sunk and the eleventh attack off the coast since last December.

More details have been released of the large scale raid by American heavy bombers on Occupied France day before yesterday. The Flying Fortresses and their sister B-24's are proving to really be aerial dreadnoughts as they knocked down 48 enemy fighters for certain with 38 other probables against a loss of only four of the big bombers. The secret of this astonishing performance is their tight flying formations and their tremendous fire power—thirteen 50-caliber machine guns apiece. These mighty planes are making daylight attacks on the continent possible and effective.

Fighting in Russia has shifted away from Stalingrad. Marshal Timoshenko's relief offensive is still hammering at the Nazi flank

226

northwest of the city and with the aid of General Winter may force the Nazis to withdraw back to the line of the Don River, thus lifting the siege of the Volga city. Adolf Hitler has no doubt retired to Berlin with another splitting headache.

U.S. Marines in the Solomons are bracing themselves for an expected assault on Guadalcanal. The Nips are getting ready to do something drastic there in an effort to save their badly scarred faces.

Monday, October 12, 1942: —There's another score to settle with the Japs. Today, by rights, should have been a holiday but we worked just the same as though there never had been a Columbus or a year 1492. There'll be very few holidays from now on, I guess. There's too much work to be done.

Bad news again today. We're just beginning to hear the full story of the price we had to pay to capture the Japanese bases in the Solomon Islands. The Navy announced today that three heavy American cruisers were sunk in the first stages of the attack on the Solomons. The cruisers were the Quincy, Vincennes, and Astoria. There were many casualties. The warships were sent to the bottom in a furious, pointblank night engagement, illuminated by searchlights and star shells. The Navy admitted that the enemy fire was heavy and accurate. The announcement of such serious losses was delayed until the information could be of no use to the enemy. Apparently the full scope of the Solomons battle has not yet been revealed.

President Roosevelt made another of his famous fireside chats tonight. He reported to the Nation on his recent cross country trip of inspection. His impression is that the people's spirits are high and they are accomplishing miracles of production. The Army and Navy are receiving the finest training possible, he said. The President also advocated early drafting of 18 and 19 year old youths to swell our fighting forces and hasten an early victory. He further said that it was just too bad that Hitler, Mussolini, and Tojo couldn't have accompanied him on his trip to see what is in store for them. It's a sure thing that what they would have seen wouldn't have eased their headaches any.

Tuesday, October 13, 1942: —Disaster struck again off the West Coast. The Navy announced today that a second tanker has been torpedoed off the coast of Oregon. One seaman lost his life in the explosion. The vessel sank as it was being towed to port. A Japanese submarine was held responsible.

The Navy further announced additional naval action off the Solomon Islands in which our fleet gained a measure of revenge for the loss of our three cruisers by sinking one Jap cruiser and four destroyers. It was believed that a Jap transport was also sent to the bottom.

In Russia it looks definitely as though the Nazis have abandoned their attempt to crush Russian resistance this year as winter weather begins to set in all along the line from the Mozdok area of the eastern Caucasus to Leningrad and the far north. Fighting in Stalingrad has virtually ceased with the Soviets still in possession of most of the city. The Red Army counterattack northwest of the city is still gaining ground slowly but steadily. The Berlin radio confirms the belief that the Germans are adopting a defensive rather than offensive strategy for the coming months. Chalk a big one up for the Russians.

Very little has been said lately about conditions within Occupied Europe but now that the suffering peoples of those countries that are writhing under the Nazi yoke are facing the most terrible winter in the history of Europe, evidence has been piling up that there is increasing uneasiness throughout the Continent. Sabotage, riots, and underground movements appear to spread rapidly throughout the occupied zone. The Germans have made it clear that come what may the German people will eat though the rest of Europe starves and the oppressed peoples are not taking it lying down.

Wednesday, October 14, 1942: —Far ranging American submarines brought their score sheet up to date today. The "Silent Service" knocked off four medium sized Jap ships and one enemy heavy cruiser in two days. The attacks were carried out in enemy waters by the big ocean going subs that we see slipping through the Golden Gate almost every day. The submariner's life is a silent adventure. He seeks no glory and receives but little. Like a ghostly apparition he slips silently out to sea, shunned by friend and foe alike, and heads into the unknown. Suddenly and without warning he strikes his deadly blows for God and Country and disappears again into the veil of mystery that sometimes hides his fate forever. He asks no quarter and can give but little. To me, a landlubber, there is something austere and foreboding, yet terrifyingly heroic about the war-time life of the courageous underseamen.

A large scale battle seems to be developing down Guadalcanal way. The Nips apparently are determined to wrest control of the Solomons back from the American forces. Supported by strong naval units, the enemy has continued to successfully land reinforcements on the northern tip of the Island. A decisive battle may be shaping up near the American held Guadalcanal airbase. The desperate Japs are obviously willing to accept huge losses to save their yellow little buck-toothed faces down that-a-way. Give 'em hell, you Devildogs.

The Aeronautical Chamber of Commerce announced today that aircraft production is nearing 5000 planes per month, 60,000 planes per year, or 10,000 more than President Roosevelt's "impossible" 1940 goal of 50,000.

Thursday, October 15, 1942: —A crisis is developing in the Solomons battle. The Japanese are moving heavy units into the fracas, including several battleships. Navy flyers succeeded in landing one direct hit on a Jap battleship, doing severe damage. Both sides are pouring in reinforcements. For the first time, American Army units have joined the Marines in defense of the vital bases. U.S. Army ground troops may now have their first major crack at the Japs since Bataan. The Nips apparently are putting great store on the success of their counter-attack in the Solomons, probably fearful that failure here would mean the loss, once and for all, of their offensive initiative. They cannot afford to go on the defensive. A long defensive war is as unfavorable and dangerous to them as it is to Hitler.

Speaking of Hitler, the Nazis pulled the "hidden ball" trick on the Stalingrad front today. After a death-like lull of three days, they suddenly unleashed one of the most ferocious attacks of the entire campaign today and admittedly drove the Russians out of an important sector of the city. Berlin claims a major break-through was accomplished but this the Soviets stoutly deny. Time will tell.

In one of the most telling propaganda blows of the entire war, the United States has announced that the 600,000 Americans of Italian birth are no longer to be considered as enemy aliens. They have conclusively proved their absolute loyalty to this Government. It is believed this action will have considerable effect on Italy where a definite swing of public sentiment towards the United States has been discerned. Millions of good Italians have been duped into this war.

Friday, October 16, 1942: —United States positions on Guadalcanal are extremely precarious today as the Japs flung major forces into a desperate bid for possession of the vital base. In spite of heavy opposition from Allied forces, including for the first time in this theater, the famous motor torpedo boats, the enemy succeeded in landing additional reinforcements, including artillery. American positions are undergoing a vicious bombardment, both from the land and from the air. While high Army and Navy officials are confident of our ability to maintain our foothold in the Solomons, no effort is made to minimize the danger and the difficulties. "We face a tough, bitter, bloody battle with a determined enemy," emphasized the Secretary of the Navy, Frank Knox. The enemy is prepared to sacrifice 100,000 men if need be, to regain his prestige and the vital South Pacific base.

Meanwhile, here at home, interest centers around two measures that are receiving attention by Congress. One is the drafting of "teen-agers" into the armed forces. It is expected that a measure calling up all youths of eighteen and nineteen will reach the President's desk before the end of next week.

The other measure is the proposed five percent "Victory Tax" which will be deducted at the source from all salaries from $12.00 per week and up. A portion of this tax, up to about 48% would be returned to the taxpayer after the war. This measure, designed to bring in about $3,750,000,000.00 will probably become law within the next few days. There'll be a lot of belt-tightening before this ordeal is finished.

Saturday, October 17, 1942: —Flaming new battles in Stalingrad find that city facing its most dangerous crisis in the entire 54-day siege. The Germans have thrown vast new forces into the struggle and have driven the weary Russians out of several of their strongest positions. Hitler may yet win the city if the weather instead of the Russians holds out.

Another serious situation is developing in the Solomon Islands, where all reports indicate that a decisive battle is shaping up between heavy Japanese land and sea forces and defending U.S. Marines, now reinforced with regular Army units. Strong American naval forces are also in the vicinity and some observers believe that a battle even greater than those of the Coral Sea and Midway can be expected.

One of the hottest spots in the entire war picture has had but very little attention in the news reports. That spot is Malta, the most heavily bombed place in the world. Lately the tempo of enemy attacks on the stronghold has increased as the Axis Nations have desperately tried to eliminate this thorn in the side of their communications with Rommel's Afrika Corps. The British have succeeded in beating off countless attacks and have shot down more than 100 enemy planes so far this month to a loss of only 23 Spitfires. Malta has amazed the world in this war. It was expected to fall almost immediately after Italy entered the war but to everyone's surprise the fortified Island has proved to be impregnable. Its gallant defenders have beaten off literally thousands of attacks and have inflicted incalculable damage on the foe. Malta's story will be one of the greatest epics of this war.

Sunday, October 18, 1942: —Today has been one of the most beautiful days of the year. It seems that the San Francisco Bay Area, unable to really get a summer during the summer months, makes a specialty of Indian summers. The sun's rays seem to contain an unusually invigorating warmth and a gentle breeze always crops up just in time to brush them off when their warmth would become uncomfortable. Such days as these are ideal for flying and we really get an exhibition of Uncle Sam's fighting birds now. The results of our production efforts are showing in the skies overhead as increasing numbers of fighting craft roar high above on their training and patrolling maneuvers. Just a moment ago a squadron of eight P-38's streaked over the house, followed shortly thereafter by six long-nosed Airacobras. B-24's and other big multi-motored bombers rumble by so much slower that it seems they are loafing—but that's only the contrast to the incredible speed of the fighters. The real loafing comes when one of the big fat blimps floats by like a barrage balloon. There's something fascinating in all this sky activity.

Yesterday, the House of Representatives passed the new draft legislation lowering the minimum age to eighteen. This speedy action sent the measure to the Senate just a week after the President had asked for the law. It is anticipated that the Senate will soon add its approval to the measure to hasten the day when our boys of eighteen and nineteen will be in Khaki. There's no doubt that such youths make fine soldiers but it will wring many a mother's heart to see her boy sent to lay down his life in war that was not of his doing. Her only consolation can be that he is defending his country in a just cause and in a war that was not sought but was brought upon us by a treacherous enemy.

Monday, October 19, 1942: —Reports from the crucial Solomons area are encouraging today. Apparently the U.S. Navy is back on the job as late communiqués state that our war vessels heavily bombarded Jap concentrations on the northern tip of Guadalcanal and Navy dive bombers and other aircraft successfully raided enemy ship units. Forty enemy planes attacked our airfield on Guadalcanal and came a cropper [sic] as Marine flyers intercepted them and shot down eight bombers and eleven Zeros. Two American planes were lost. Not a bad average.

In spite of the good news, however, the Navy emphasized that the Japs are still gathering large forces for an all-out effort to recapture the American-held bases. A showdown battle may occur momentarily.

The Japs made a nasty threat today. They threatened to punish U.S. flyers captured while attacking Japanese occupied territory. The "punishment" doubtless would be death and would be in violation of every code of civilized warfare. The threat was made by the jittery Japs apparently in fear of renewed bombing attacks on Japan proper. Don't worry, Mr. Moto, your criminal threats won't stop us; they'll only serve to make us more determined than ever to rid the world of your kind.

A beautiful war time sight was in the darkened skies tonight. Powerful searchlight batteries on both sides of the Peninsula were practicing. Like a giant maypole in the sky, a cone of light fingers caught a dancing plane high in the heavens and followed it all the way down the Peninsula, handing it from one group of lights to another. It was just an inkling of the vast, secret preparations that have been made to defend this important area.

Tuesday, October 20, 1942: —News of the warfronts is exceptionally barren tonight. Nothing exciting has happened today and activity on all the major battlegrounds has dwindled to mere reconnaissance and artillery exchanges. The Japs in the Solomons area apparently are not yet ready to exert their full pressure and our forces appear to be holding all their gains. Too much optimism about the situation there must be avoided as every numerical advantage is still with the Nips.

In Russia, cold winds and rains have hampered operations and herald the coming of another bitter winter. I pity the poor soldier, friend or foe, who faces another campaign in the freezing blasts and icy death of a Russian winter. The torture of such a campaign must be even worse than the raging inferno of the Stalingrad siege.

The principal news is on the home front. Congress today passed the record tax bill, designed to raise approximately nine billions of dollars during next year. Exemptions were lowered, rates upped and a five per cent Victory Tax included and there remained only the President's signature to activate the law that will hit the citizen's pocketbook harder than ever before in history. War is indeed an expensive pastime.

Manpower trouble is beginning to beset the country. Between the armed forces and war industries, the demand for men exceeds the available supply and several steps will be necessary to solve the problem. Indications are that the production of luxury goods will be stopped completely and some consideration will probably be given to the furloughing of older men in the army into war industries, especially if the new measure drafting 18 and 19 year old youths is passed.

Wednesday, October 21, 1942: —The bitter Solomons battle has cost the United States two more destroyers, we learned tonight. The U.S.S. Meredith and the U.S.S. O'Brien were the vessels lost through enemy action during the last few days. The majority of the ship's crews were saved but bad tidings are due to be delivered into many American homes before this fight is over.

In Russia the main fighting is still in the Stalingrad area. The Russians are still holding tight and have even improved their positions with several successful counter-attacks. The failure of the Germans to crack the Stalingrad nut has undoubtedly been the most important event of the year and may well be considered by future historians as the final turning point of the European war. The turning point in the Pacific war probably has not yet been reached although some will claim that the battle of Midway turned the tables on the Japs.

Speaking again of the Japs, it is now apparent that their abortive drive against Port Moresby on New Guinea has really boomeranged. The Australians have driven the enemy all the way back over the Owen Stanley mountains and are now closing in on the Japanese base of Kokoda. "The engagement continues." That is the way the communiqué reads, but hidden in its cold terms is all the bitterness and suffering of the deadly jungle snakes and insects, the hunger and thirst and sweat, the crash of bombs, the flash of knife or bayonet, the sudden death—all these and more lie dormant in the simple words of the communiqué—"The engagement continues."

Thursday, October 22, 1942: —Tonight's news indicates that the struggle over Guadalcanal is still in its preparatory stage. The Japs are obviously finding it hard to get set in the face of steady and effective bombing attacks by U.S. airmen. The enemy tried a small-scale flank attack yesterday but it was easily repulsed by the American land forces. The brunt of the fighting, however, is still being borne by the Army, Navy and Marine Air Forces. Supremacy in the air will probably determine the trend and outcome of the entire operation.

Remember Japan's recent threat of severe punishment for any American flyers captured in attacks on Japanese territory? Well, it now develops that four participants in General Doolittle's April raid on Tokyo are missing and are probably in the hands of the Japs. The Jap radio has announced their names which agree with the War Department's admission. Previously, General Doolittle had stated that no airmen were lost in the attack but now agrees that the four missing men apparently had lost their way after leaving the Japanese mainland and later fell into enemy hands. The men's fate in the clutches of the treacherous Japs is extremely doubtful.

At home, Congressional attempts to hang a Prohibition rider on the proposed bill to draft youths of eighteen and nineteen was temporarily killed today. As in the last war, Prohibition forces in

234

the country are gaining strength because of the dangers to the countless young men in the armed forces from the too free flow of liquor, especially around army camps. Army leaders on the other hand are fighting the "dry" amendment, claiming its passage would be a serious blow to army morale. Both sides have cases; but the "dry's" should remember the sad failure of the previous "noble experiment."

Friday, October 23, 1942: —The principal news story tonight is the disappearance of Captain Eddie Rickenbacker on a routine flight in the Pacific from Oahu, Hawaii to an unidentified island. Captain Rickenbacker, you will remember, was America's foremost "Ace" in the first World War and has been a prominent figure in Aviation circles since that time. He was acting as a confidential advisor and inspector for the Secretary of War when his plane disappeared into the vastness of the Pacific. All available air and sea forces are conducting a search of the area in hopes of rescuing the popular flyer.

A second "feeler" attack by Jap land forces against American positions in the Solomons was repulsed today and Allied bombers plastered every enemy base in the Southwest Pacific with heavy bomb loads in numerous raids. The real showdown has not yet begun but a great tidal wave of action that will decide the issue one way or the other is nearing its crest and must soon smash against the bulwarks that have been set up to meet it. Either the wave will spend itself and recede or it will smash everything before it. Let us hope the bulwarks are strong.

Heavy rains have bogged General MacArthur's New Guinea drive but the hard fighting Aussies have driven to within ten miles of the Jap base at Kokoda. MacArthur still has the Jap's number.

In retaliation for the incessant Axis raids on Malta, the British last night sent a big fleet of heavy bombers over Italy, pounding Genoa and Turin. Comparatively few air raids have been made on Italy but the British have become angered over the vicious Italian raids on Malta—and with cause.

Saturday, October 24, 1942:—Great news today. The British Eighth Army, joined with many American tank units, and supported by an umbrella of American and RAF fighting planes, launched a gigantic offensive against the Axis lines in Egypt. The attack rolled against the entire front and is apparently a major attempt by the British to drive the Nazis back to Libya and if possible destroy, once and for all, the menace of the Afrika Corps.

In support of the ground forces, hundreds of British and American bombers and their fighter escorts smashed repeatedly at Axis bases and won complete supremacy in the skies over the battlefield. The offensive apparently found the foxy Marshal Rommel outfoxed for the first time. His own long expected offensive was no doubt nipped in the bud and completely thrown out of kilter.

Perfectly timed with the Egyptian attack was another heavy daylight raid by Allied bombers on northern Italy, especially on Genoa, the jumping off place for supplies to Africa. Huge fires, visible for many miles, were started among the docks and in the factories.

The U.S. Navy today announced a sweeping shakeup of its high command in the Pacific. Admiral Ghormley, who commanded the Naval forces in the Solomon's battle that cost one Australian and three American cruisers, five destroyers and other vessels, has been replaced by Admiral Halsey who gained fame by directing the highly successful raids on the Marshal and Gilbert Islands and the long range attack on the Jap island of Marcus. Admiral Halsey will soon get a real test of his ability as the Solomon situation approaches a showdown.

Sunday, October 25, 1942: —The Allied offensive in Egypt appears to be gaining some headway. It is intimated that the British and Americans are utilizing almost a million men and great numbers of tanks and planes. This looks like it. This apparently is to be an all-out attempt to clean up the North African situation. Many observers believe that the final turning point of the war may be found in the results of this struggle commencing on the shores of the Mediterranean. History has been made countless times before along the blood-soaked rim of this mighty island sea. Romans, Greeks, Persians, Egyptians, Mohammedans and Christians have struggled for supremacy and survival where now the British and Americans have locked themselves in mortal strife with the Germans and Italians. We are seeing a flaming page of history in the making.

The war in the Southwest Pacific seems to be building up to something big but what it is or will be is merely intimated rather than brought out by the news reports that we are receiving. It will not be until after the war that we will find out definitely how much of the news is being withheld from the public view. Sometimes belated reports of serious losses make us wonder just what the real situation is. The shakeup in the Navy high command in the Solomons also causes us to wonder just what is going on and how bad our losses have actually been. Our over-confidence regarding Japan is getting a severe shaking. There's a long, hard war awaiting us in the Pacific.

No sign of Captain Rickenbacker or the seven men who accompanied him have been found despite an intensive search. Hope for their rescue is waning.

Monday, October 26, 1942: —Glaring headlines gave us another jolt today. The Navy announced that the Aircraft Carrier Wasp was sunk by a Jap submarine on September 15th in the Solomons area. The news was withheld until this time to prevent the knowledge from assisting the enemy. Three torpedoes smashed into the mighty carrier's hull and she went down five hours later. Ninety percent of the ship's personnel were saved.

Meanwhile, two widely separated warfronts were flaming today. In Egypt Allied forces claimed a breakthrough on the Alamein front to a five mile depth and thousands of men and tanks are pouring through the gap. The major Nazi force has not yet been engaged, however.

On Guadalcanal it is evident that the Japs have launched their long expected all-out offensive against the American held positions around Henderson field. Late reports indicate that the Leathernecks and Doughboys are holding firm.

Probably the most interesting and perhaps important single event of the day was Wendell Willkie's radio report to the nation on his recent globe-circling trip. His speech, I believe, and I have not yet had time to hear the comments of the experts as it is only two hours since he finished, was the best and most constructive speech Willkie has ever made and one of the most fearless and forthright statements yet to come out of the war. With the utmost candor, he emphasized that the entire world expects great things of America and, in many ways, up to now we "have not done a good job." We have poked some sizeable holes in the great reservoir of goodwill borne us by the nations of the world and it is going to take a 100% mobilization rather than a 40% mobilization to plug up the dangerous gaps.

Tuesday, October 27, 1942: —Egypt and the Solomons vie for pre-eminence in the news tonight. On the gory beaches of Guadalcanal and on the turbulent seas surrounding it, a gigantic battle is raging. Both sides recognize the high stakes that are on the board and are flinging powerful forces into the fray. Losses on both sides are inevitably severe. It is a tough, hard battle of attrition against a ruthless and capable enemy with domination of the Southwest Pacific hanging in the balance. All reports indicate that our boys are making a game, heroic fight of it but the final outcome is still in doubt.

In Egypt, the Allied forces are grinding slowly forward in their great attack. Here again, the opposition is stubborn and hard to beat. The Germans have had a long time to erect their defenses in great depth and it has inevitably cost dearly in men and equipment to smash a hole through them. But with the aid of masses of artillery reminiscent of World War I, the British have succeeded in slugging ahead for five miles through the mazes of barbwire and mine fields. Overhead the British and American bombers and fighters have smashed relentlessly at Axis communications and supply bases. No easy victory can be expected.

Today is Navy Day and while previous Navy Days have gone by with just a passing thought, today we realize how much our independence and safety depend on the fighting men and ships of our Navy. We have a profound faith in the Navy's ability to win the ultimate triumph but in our hearts we utter a prayer that God's care and strength will be with them in this, their supreme test.

Wednesday, October 28, 1942: —It's still the Solomons and Egypt that hold the news spotlight. Thousands of Jap troops are being thrown against the American positions around Henderson field on Guadalcanal but so far the Marines and Doughboys have repulsed all attacks with huge losses to the enemy. Continued success in landing reinforcements, however have given the Japs a numerical advantage that may prove overwhelming. It is extremely vital that our own forces receive substantial assistance immediately if our hard-won gains are to be preserved. No doubt the American commanders are aware of the need and will do everything possible to retrieve the initiative.

Deeper wedges are being driven into Axis lines in the Egypt battle. Infantry and armored columns were filtering through gaps in Marshal Rommel's defenses and are attempting to bring the main enemy forces to bay. So far, however, the main body of Axis troops have avoided a showdown. The battle for air supremacy is raging furiously up and down the line with American planes and pilots playing important roles. The outcome on this as well as the Solomons front remains very much in doubt.

On the home front things are just barely beginning to get tough. Shortages of many products and rationing of many others are just beginning to be felt. Announcement has just been made that coffee will be rationed after November 28th limiting its use to one cup per day. There'll be some frayed nerves before the people get used to that.

Transportation problems throughout the Bay Area are terrific and promise to become far worse after gas rationing goes into effect. Staggered hours of work are imperative.

Thursday, October 29, 1942: —The battle for Guadalcanal has reached a critical stage. Heavy attacks by Japanese land forces have twice breached American lines around Henderson field but fierce counter-attacks by the U.S. troops succeeded in hurling the foe back and our original positions were regained. There is no let up in the enemy's attack despite severe losses in men and equipment. The Japs' offensive is supported by a numerically superior fleet making it difficult to deliver reinforcements to the Island. American fighting and bombing planes including Flying Fortresses dispatched from Australia by General MacArthur are exacting a heavy toll of enemy shipping but more troops and equipment, especially artillery is needed if the Island is to be held.

The Egyptian offensive is in the melee stage where it is hard to tell what is going on. The Allies are definitely on the move and are taking many prisoners indicating that they are advancing. There is no doubt, however, that the Nazis have erected strong defenses in depth that are stopping or slowing the Allied troops in many sectors. We can only wait and hope for success.

Not many new developments have occurred on the Russian front in the last few days. The Nazis are still beating their brains out against the Stalingrad defenses although they have admittedly gained some ground in that area. The most promising event is the onset of winter weather along the Russian front. Moscow tells of finding thinly clad bodies of frozen German soldiers huddled in their dugouts after one counter-attack on the Caucasian front near Grozny.

Friday, October 30, 1942: —There was just a bit of excitement on the home front today. We had a sixty five minute air raid alert this morning that lasted from 10:32 a.m. until 11:37 a.m. Traffic was stopped, school children were sent home in many cases, and all business houses were put on guard. Nothing came of the alarm, however, as the unidentified planes were finally found to be friendly. The evening papers report that San Francisco's civilian defense control system worked smoothly for the first time.

Meanwhile, over in the Solomons where the real trouble is, we find today that the American forces are holding their own. It appears that the major part of the enemy fleet has retired, either to regroup or to attack at some other point. Guadalcanal is still ours, and from the tone of the Navy's communiqué, our positions are as strong as ever. Supplies and reinforcements apparently are reaching the Island in considerable quantities. The first round is ours.

The Allies are rolling steadily on in Egypt today. Supported by heavy artillery and an umbrella of air power, the British Eighth Army is crushing its way forward over the wreckage of German tanks and guns. Allied air power has been particularly effective, with American planes and pilots doing yeoman service.

The play of mighty searchlights up and down the Peninsula can be seen almost every night now but we never tire watching the fascinating criss-cross of light fingers as they reach up into the sky and fasten a plane in their glare, a perfect target for the ack-ack guns that are no doubt there—and ready.

Saturday, October 31, 1942: —Late radio reports tonight stated that the Navy Department has announced the loss of another aircraft carrier. The name of the carrier was not revealed but it was said that the action occurred on October 26th. The vessel went down under the pounding of enemy aircraft and was the fourth U.S. carrier lost since Pearl Harbor. Only three of the seven with which we started the war are left. It is believe that several new carriers have joined the fleet since December but the Navy has not revealed their identities. It is known that some thirty carriers are in the process of being built and are in various stages of construction.

Apparently the loss of the carrier was not in vain as the Navy claims that the battle in which she was a casualty resulted in the retirement of the Jap fleet from the Solomons area, leaving our forces in command. Loss of life aboard the lost vessel was light.

The Nazi Luftwaffe struck back heavily at Britain today in the biggest daylight attack since the dark days of 1940. The cathedral town of Canterbury was the target and numerous casualties and considerable damage was caused. Mrs. Eleanor Roosevelt, the President's wife, who is visiting England missed being in the raid by only a few hours.

The Egyptian desert is probably the hottest spot in the world today not alone from the sun but from the fury of war as the British Imperials smash at Rommel's lines with terrific power in a determined effort to tip the scales against the Nazis. The attack was preceded by artillery barrages equaled only in France during 1914-1918.

November

Sunday, November 1, 1942: —Another Sunday and another month, almost the twelfth since the United States became involved in war. The global fire that was kindled that December day is still raging furiously with no sign that it will soon be extinguished. The opponents in this great struggle are too evenly matched to hope for any quick decision. It is a war of attrition, with the victory going eventually to the one who is able to produce the most planes, and guns, and tanks, and the ships to transport them to the scene of conflict. It is our kind of war, the kind of war in which we should excel. We have the factories; we have the resources, and the ability. If we settle down and play our cards well, there can be but one ultimate end—victory. But it will not be easy and we could lose—with complacency, with half-hearted effort, with red-tape and inefficiency. Many Americans have not yet come to this realization.

The War Department announced yesterday that more than 800,000 U.S. troops have been successfully transported overseas to date. Most of these have undoubtedly gone to England where intensive preparations are going on for the European offensive that must surely come next spring. Other troops are in all parts of the world: India, Egypt, the Middle East, Australia, and the islands of the Pacific. In fact, this vast dispersal of our forces is one of our chief disadvantages in fighting the war. As yet we have not been able to concentrate a force large enough to be effective on any of the principal war fronts. But 1942 has admittedly been a year of preparation. Watch us go in 1943.

Monday, November 2, 1942: —The war news is more cheerful tonight. Our forces have taken the offensive on Guadalcanal and have smashed two miles into the enemy's lines. Air power has been the vital factor again as our land based bombers and fighters have driven off the supporting Jap fleet and have paved the way for the infantry advance that may pin the Jap land forces back against the sea.

In New Guinea, also, late radio reports indicate that hard fighting Australians under General MacArthur have finally succeeded in crossing the Owen Stanley Mountains and capturing the Jap base at Kokoda. This is good news indeed as it definitely puts the Japs back on their heels in this area also. It looks like we might really be on the road back at last.

To add to the good news, the Navy released the latest reports from our far-ranging Pacific submarine fleet. Striking silently and with deadly effect right up to Tokyo's doorstep, the undersea raiders have destroyed nine more enemy ships of various tonnage. Unsung and unpraised, American submarines are silently making a very heavy contribution to the task of smashing Tojo's gang of cutthroats.

To keep today's report on its happy plane, we find that even the Egyptian drive is going our way. Here, also, the Australians are scoring as we learn that the Aussies have driven across the Alexandria-Matruh railroad line west of Alamein and have isolated a sizeable unit of the enemy. Indications are that the Axis African armies are in for a bad time. It will take all Rommel's fox-like strategy to squirm out of this predicament.

Tuesday, November 3, 1942: —The principal news tonight is, of course, the results of the first war time nationwide elections in twenty four years. Many states throughout the country have balloted today for governors and other state and local officers. Main interest has centered on the gubernatorial races in New York and California. Late returns indicate that both states have gone Republican. Thomas Dewey, the racket-busting former Attorney General, has been elected governor of New York State by an enormous plurality. In California, incomplete returns give Attorney General Earl Warren a clear cut victory over the incumbent, Culbert L. Olson. The main significance of the many Republican victories throughout the nation is the swing away from the New Deal and evident dissatisfaction with the present Administration's prosecution of the war. Even candidates endorsed by the President himself have received unmerciful trouncing. A substantial number of seats have also been won by the Republicans in both houses of Congress, although the Democrats will still have a majority.

Shifting from the war of ballots to the war of bullets, we find General MacArthur's Australian communiqué confirming the recapture of Kokoda and indicating that the Aussie troops are advancing far beyond that base toward the vital Jap base at Buna. The New Guinea battle is definitely going our way. MacArthur really has the Jap's number.

The Navy also reports that the Guadalcanal fight is progressing favorably but warns against too much optimism. Two Jap cruisers not previously reported were sent to the bottom on October 11-12 and the Marines are continuing their advance to the north on Guadalcanal.

Wednesday, November 4, 1942: —Latest results of yesterday's election indicate that the Republican victory is even more pronounced than was apparent last night. A minimum of 32 and possibly many more additional seats were won in the House while a gain of at least eight Senate seats were chalked up by the Republicans. This swing away from the Democrats may have a healthy reaction on the Administration who will now understand that the American people are not satisfied with their conduct of the war up to the present time. The people are way ahead of our leaders in their desire for "total effort" and the results of this election will serve as a gentle reminder that the people will tolerate no politics as usual or inaction as usual during this emergency. It may be just the prod needed. Time will tell.

The battle in Egypt is in just that stage where it is hard to tell how the tide is going to turn. We can be sure, however, that the British and Americans are hitting the enemy with everything they've got and it does appear that their superior air power and terrific striking force is beginning to tell as late bulletins indicate that Rommel is abandoning his Alamein line and is retreating to a new position. We can't forget, however, that the British once before were drawn into an anti-tank trap and were practically wiped out. So until things are clarified we dare not become too optimistic.

In New Guinea, MacArthur's troops are pressing on from Kokoda and closing in on the village of Oivi on the road to the main Jap base of Buna. Complete victory in New Guinea would certainly be another feather in General MacArthur's hat.

Thursday, November 5, 1942: —Tonight's news is the best in many months. Word has come from Egypt that a complete victory has been won by the British Imperials and their American Allies. Rommel's beaten army is fleeing desperately, pursued relentlessly by the exultant Allies. No respite is given the Nazis from the scourge of the Allied air fleet, who have won total command of the skies. At least ten thousand and probably many more prisoners have been taken and a majority of the enemy's armored equipment destroyed. In an order of the day, Lieutenant General Bernard L. Montgomery, the Commander of the British Eighth Army praised his troops and asked them to keep up the pressure until the Afrika Korps is totally destroyed.

London is jubilant. Spokesman there believe that the end of Axis resistance in North Africa is in sight. This time the Germans will not escape.

Berlin admits retreat but of course minimize the defeat. They are undoubtedly using reinforcements to Libya from the Russian front but this time they may be "too little and too late." At least we hope so.

In Rome, the Italians are scared. They admit heavy losses and retreat and even hint that they believe the Allies have taken their first step towards an invasion of Europe through Italy. They may be right.

Overshadowed by the great Egyptian victory but vitally important is the news from New Guinea and Guadalcanal indicating that American and Australian troops are advancing on both fronts. All in all, things are really looking better tonight. So it's off to bed but I've got two fingers tightly crossed.

Friday, November 6, 1942: —The British and Allied victory in Egypt continues to widen today. Triumphant Allied troops are pursuing the demoralized Axis forces. The famed Afrika Korps, Marshal Rommel's elite desert troops, have apparently abandoned the Italian army to its fate and are striving desperately to escape total rout. Whether they will be able to make a stand at the Libyan border remains to be seen. Many thousands of Axis troops have already been captured and literally hundreds of their tanks and other motorized equipment have been left smoldering on the battlefield. Two of the Nazis highest ranking generals have been captured, including General Ritter Von Thoma, chief of the Afrika Korps and second in command to Rommel. Another Nazi general was killed in action. The most decisive victory of the entire war so far appears to be in sight if the British play their cards properly.

Another most interesting development is the news that a large concentration of Allied warships, aircraft and transports have assembled at Gibraltar and have even commenced to move out across the Mediterranean. The warships include several battleships, with the British dreadnought Rodney leading the pack. Speculations are rife as to the use to which this force is to be put. But there are some jangled nerves in the Axis capitals as they express fears that an invasion attempt is to be made either against French Morocco, Dakar, or even against the Italian mainland itself. Our guess is that the expedition will be sent to block any attempt by Rommel to extricate his army from Africa or at least to prevent the delivery of reinforcements or supplies to his hard pressed troops. Or maybe they're heading for Benghazi or Tripoli.

Saturday, November 7, 1942: —Eleven full months of our war finds the military situation on all fronts considerably improved. The principal spotlight, of course, still focuses on Egypt and the rout of Marshal Rommel's "invincible" Afrika Korps. Latest reports state that already 20,000 prisoners and much equipment have been captured and 75,000 Italian troops have been cut off, surrounded and are about ready to surrender.

American planes and American tanks, many of them operated by American men are contributing their share to the great victory being won on the Egyptian desert. The new American tank, known as the General Sherman, has been particularly effective and is proving to the Axis troops that war is just what the General said it is. For the most part, however, the success of this latest Allied offensive belongs to the British. It is really their show and any credit for victory must go principally to them. General Montgomery, the British commander in this fight, is making Hitler eat his words when he said that British generals were "military idiots."

In the Southwest Pacific American and Australian forces are making headway against the Japs. In New Guinea, the Aussies have driven on from the captured base at Kokoda to Oivi, 50 miles from Buna on the northern coast. Late radio reports indicate that a column of American troops have also driven across the Owen Stanley Mountains in a pincer movement supporting the Australian advance and are seriously threatening Buna. Look out, Mr. Moto! We're coming after you.

Sunday, November 8, 1942: —THE WHOLE MEDITERRA-NEAN IS AFLAME! The Yanks are on the march! Big news broke today. A great American Expeditionary Force, the same one that was hinted about day before yesterday, today invaded North Africa on both the Mediterranean and the Atlantic side. Seems like all the big news breaks on Sunday. And this is really big. President Roosevelt, in a broadcast to the French people, informed them of the purpose of the expedition and stated that we were invading French possessions with no idea of gaining territory or to fight Frenchmen but only to fight the common enemy and to liberate not only the continent of Africa but also the whole of Europe from the tyrant's heel. The campaign is also aimed at forestalling an imminent Axis attempt to seize the French colonies, including the vital port of Kakar, and thus threaten not only all of the Mediterranean area but also the Americas themselves.

Perfectly timed with the British success in Egypt, division after division of well equipped American troops, supported by a great fleet of British and American warships and aircraft, established several beachheads at various points along the coast, including Casablanca and Algiers. Radio reports within the hour state that French authorities in Algiers have already capitulated to the American troops. The size of the invading force is not known but military circles in Washington agree that it is the biggest invasion attempt ever conducted by American forces. Hundreds of thousands of troops, equipped with the latest in modern blitz weapons, are participating in the operation that will fully vindicate Roosevelt and Churchill's promise to Russia of a second front in 1942. This is it!

Monday, November 9, 1942: —The African drive by American troops is rolling forward at a tremendous rate. Progress has been even greater than was expected. Resistance by the French has been confined mainly to naval and shore battery action but the entire situation for the Vichy regime in North Africa is rapidly deteriorating and complete victory for the Allied forces is in prospect. Free Frenchmen, aiding the Allied cause, have been joined by General Giraud, famous French general who fought the Germans to the bitter end in 1940, was then captured and subsequently made a daring escape from a German prison camp to the embarrassment of the entire German army. The General urged all real Frenchmen to rally to the cause of the Allied Nations and help in liberating France.

The speed of the American advance exceeds even the lightning invasion of Norway and the lowlands by the Germans in their great offensives. U.S. troops are approaching Tunisia, through which they aim to strike at Rommel as he flees from the victorious British Eighth Army. The complete ousting of the Axis from Africa is the objective of the entire campaign. So far, the operation is far ahead of schedule.

Other theaters of war, including the home front, took back seats in the war news but it was pleasing to note that American operations, both on Guadalcanal and New Guinea are progressing favorably. United States and Australian forces are closing in on the Buna-Gona area with prospects good that the vital base of Buna would soon fall. On Guadalcanal, American marines and doughboys continue to widen their holdings with little or no resistance by any strong group of the enemy. But here it is believed that Japs are preparing for further offensive action.

Tuesday, November 10, 1942: —Events are moving rapidly in North Africa today. After brief but bitter resistance, Oran, the last major Algerian city, surrendered to the American troops. The resistance was mainly naval and the French battleship, Jean Bart, was left burning in the harbor. Oran was the scene of the abortive Free French and British invasion attempt in 1941. The United States, however, did not send a boy to do a man's job. We sent an adequate force.

Admiral Darlan, the commander-in-chief of all Vichy forces was captured yesterday and there is some indication that he, as well as General Giraud, will come over to our side. Free French circles are jubilant.

The next important objective of the American blitz army is Tunisia and it appears that it will be a race between our troops and Axis forces being rushed by ship and plane from Sicily. Hitler, as well as his stooge, Mussolini, know that the loss of Tunisia will mean the end of Axis domination of any part of the African continent and he will undoubtedly do what he can to save the situation. But the odds seem heavily in favor of our General Eisenhower and his fast moving army, who apparently know how to swing a little "blitz" of their own.

Prime Minister Churchill today credited President Roosevelt with being the "author" of the North African offensive. The idea was his brain child and he was primarily responsible for bringing it to such a healthy maturity. No matter how important this offensive may be in bringing final victory over the Axis, it has given a tremendous "lift" to the Allied Nations who have grown so weary of "strategic retreats" and defensive measures.

Wednesday, November 11, 1942: —What a day this has been! Admiral Darlan, the Vichy commander-in-chief, chose this twenty fourth anniversary of the Armistice ending the first Great War, to call a halt to all French resistance to the American occupation of Algeria and Morocco. The command to cease firing, made in the name of Marshal Petain, ended all opposition to the Allied forces and tremendously simplified the job facing General Eisenhower. American troops are way ahead of schedule in their operations and are racing towards Tunisia to meet the growing Axis forces.

Adolf Hitler also chose this morning to scrap the Armistice that ended France's resistance in 1940, and sent his troops thundering into Unoccupied French. The situation there is very confused but late radio reports have confirmed that Marshal Petain and General Weygand have left Vichy by plane and it is believed that they intend to join the Allied forces in North Africa. Before leaving Vichy, Marshall Petain is said to have informed the French people that Hitler's action in direct violation of the 1940 Armistice releases them from any obligations and they are free to fight the Axis in any way they can. The possibilities are tremendous. All of France is believed to be a volcano of restlessness, ready to erupt into rebellion at the first chance.

What about the still considerable French fleet based at Toulon in Southern France? Rumor is chasing it all over the Mediterranean. Latest radio reports state that the fleet consisting of three battleships, a dozen cruisers, and more than fifty destroyers, has steamed from Toulon, to avoid falling into Hitler's hands, and is rendezvousing somewhere in the Mediterranean with the British and American fleets. We'll soon know.

Thursday, November 12, 1942: —Rumors are still flying thick and fast over the confused situation in France and North Africa. It is now evident that Marshal Petain is still in Vichy and as reversed his previous stand against German invasion of

249

Unoccupied France. Apparently he has been influenced by Pierre Laval and is now reconciled to the German action. Moreover, in spite of Admiral Darlan's plea to the French Navy at Toulon that they join the Allies at Gibraltar, the French warships are still anchored at their base and defy anyone, including the Nazis, to seize them.

In spite of these less favorable developments, the American offensive in North Africa is moving along in great style. All of French Morocco and Algeria have been occupied and a powerful striking force has reached Bone, only fifty miles from Tunisia. A strong force of British troops, including crack divisions of Dunkirk veterans, has joined the Americans in the race to beat the Axis to the vital and strategic French colony. Hitler, meanwhile, is desperately rushing troops and planes across the narrow Mediterranean in an effort to prevent a total defeat in Africa. The advantages this time are with the Allies and, for the first time, Hitler faces the terrible headache of trying to establish and sustain a sea and air borne army against a powerful enemy that can advance over the land. And this time it is the Allies who are manipulating the famous pincer movement from Egypt and Algeria against the Axis armies under Rommel. The tables have certainly changed, fortunately. Hitler can now retire to Berchtesgaden with a real headache.

Friday, November 13, 1942: —The first excitement has died down over the American offensive in North Africa. Our troops, aided by the British and Free French, have firmly established themselves all the way from Casablanca to Algiers and three heavily armored columns are driving into Tunisia, bent on reaching a showdown with Axis forces.

In Libya, meanwhile, the other jaw of the great Allied pincer movement is clamping down on Rommel's battered Afrika Korps. The Nazi General is retreating headlong across Libya and late reports indicate that Tobruk has already been recaptured by the advancing British. There is no evidence that Rommel intends to make a stand anywhere east of El Agheila on the Gulf of Sirte, east of Benghazi. Some observers believe Rommel is high-tailing it all the way back to Tripoli, where he may attempt to evacuate the remnants of his army to Sicily. American and British forces advancing in both directions may frustrate these plans.

Our attention tonight is returning to the Solomons area, where American land and naval forces have resumed offensive action. In a ten hour bombardment of enemy shore positions, the Navy announced today that the heavy cruiser San Francisco was damaged and thirty crew members killed. Thirty enemy planes were shot down in retribution.

In New Guinea, General MacArthur announced that American and Australian troops are closing in on Buna, with the entire Jap garrison facing annihilation. American Flying Fortresses are contributing much to the success of this drive.

President Roosevelt today signed the eighteen and nineteen year old draft bill and the youths will be called up rapidly, beginning around January first.

Saturday, November 14, 1942: —Joyful news received today. Captain Eddie Rickenbacker is safe! After twenty three days of drifting on a rubber raft the famous World War hero was found, alive and in good condition. Once again Rickenbacker has proved himself to the "indestructible man of aviation." Countless times in his spectacular career, he has brushed elbows with death and returned to tell the tale. This time looked like the last but he was too valuable a man to lose. The Army and Navy never relaxed their search and it was rewarded yesterday when the pilot of the missing ship was found floating alone on a raft. The hunt was intensified and today Rickenbacker and the remainder of the bomber's crew, save one, were rescued. One man succumbed to exposure and was buried at sea by the "Ace" and his companions. The story of their odyssey on the sea of missing men will undoubtedly make a thrilling tale.

On the war fronts interest still centers on the African situation. Fighting has begun in Tunisia but the picture is far from clear. Apparently the Nazis are rushing men and equipment to Bizerte and Tunis and the colonial French troops are resisting them. American and British ground forces have not yet encountered the enemy. It is believed that some American paratroopers may have landed at Tunis to help the fighting French.

Across Libya, the victorious British Eighth Army is chasing Rommel's unhappy Afrika Korps. Gazalla, 40 miles beyond Tobruk has been retaken by the British and General Montgomery is exhorting his men to "chase the Axis right out of North Africa." It looks as though they may do just that.

Sunday, November 15, 1942: —Today was a blustery, unsettled November Sunday. First it rained, then shined, then blew, then rained again. We played a round of golf through the squalls at El Camino while dozens of Army pursuit planes wheeled and dove in practice overhead. It seemed good to get out on the fairways again even in the blustery weather. Golf is a marvelous relaxation and clears all the cobwebs and war worries out of one's mind. Later on this afternoon we broke our customary Sunday rule and took the youngsters to see Walt Disney's beautiful little picture, "Bambi." It is a touching little piece, good for children, that would wring the heart of the hardened deer hunters of the world. It preaches a compassion for the helpless that is badly needed in this war-wracked world.

Our only contact with the news today was over the radio this evening. The latest flashes state that a big naval battle is raging off the Solomon Islands. It seems that such a battle is always raging in that area, which the Japs apparently have decided to recapture regardless of the price. There is no doubt but that this war with Japan is the greatest naval war in all history. Japan is very strong on the sea and her daring and brilliant strategy command respect. She will not easily be defeated and not without heavy losses.

On New Guinea the Americans and Australians have succeeded in joining forces and are drawing the noose tighter about Buna. Capture of this important Jap base would relieve Australia from fear of invasion and would give General MacArthur an additional stepping stone on his arduous trail back towards his beloved Philippines. Today is the seventh anniversary of the establishment of the Commonwealth of the Philippines and we are as determined as ever to drive the invaders from the islands.

Monday, November 16, 1942: —In a terrific, slam-bang, close range battle that began last Friday and ended Sunday night, the U.S. Navy won a smashing victory over a great armada of Japanese warships. It was the first real slugging match between heavy sea units and resulted in a conclusive triumph for Uncle

Sam's dreadnoughts. The Japanese lost a total of twenty three vessels sunk, including one battleship, three heavy cruisers, two light cruisers, five destroyers, eight heavily laden troop transports, and four cargo vessels. In addition, one battleship and six destroyers were badly damaged. Our Navy lost two light cruisers and six destroyers sunk.

The battle was said to be the biggest naval battle in American history and is rivaled only by the battle of Jutland in World War I. The Japanese were foiled in their all-out attempt to reinforce their Guadalcanal troops and regain control of the vital Solomon Islands.

Among the inevitable casualties of the engagement was Rear Admiral Daniel J. Callaghan, one of the Bay Area's outstanding naval officers, who was killed while directing the activities of his task force.

In North Africa, the developments are obscure but both sides are apparently rushing feverishly towards a showdown in Tunisia. Hitler obviously is going to make a desperate effort to prevent a total defeat which would oust him once and for all from the continent of Africa. The importance of Tunisia cannot be underestimated and the Nazis are prepared to gamble desperately for its control. But it looks like poor Adolf just missed the bus on this one.

Tuesday, November 17, 1942: —Admiral Chester W. Nimitz, the commander-in-chief of our Pacific fleet today enlarge upon the great American naval victory just concluded and stated that it means that we will now succeed in expelling all Japs from Guadalcanal Island. "We are going to clean them out," he said as he praised the men of his fleet for their daring and brilliant action during the battle.

Rear Admiral Norman Scott was the second Admiral to lose his life in the battle when he took his 10,000 ton cruiser to within 2,000 yards of an enemy dreadnought of 35,000 tons in a point-blank duel that cost him his life but severely damaged the Jap battlewagon. According to Secretary Knox, it was just such daring action as Admiral Scott's that brought victory to the American forces who drove a numerically superior enemy from the field with heavy losses. We must succeed when we have men like that manning our ships.

253

British and American paratroopers have joined in the headlong battle for control of the vital Bizerte area in Tunisia, it was learned tonight. Meanwhile, one American column is dashing across the center of Tunisia towards the Gulf of Gabes, in a move designed to split the Axis forces and trap them both in Tunis and Bizerte and prevent them from joining with Rommel who is retreating rapidly from Libya. From Gabes, it is only 190 miles to Tripoli where Rommel is expected to wind up shortly. The British Eighth Army is hot on his heels and is approaching Benghazi, which is a long, long way from El Alamein. It looks like curtains this time for the wily Desert Fox.

Wednesday, November 18, 1942: —While American and British troops race across Tunisia towards a showdown with the Axis forces and the U.S. Navy covers itself with glory in tremendous naval battles in the Solomons, let's take a look at the home front and see how the war is affecting everyday life.

Registration for nationwide gas rationing starts today, with thousands of car owners flocking to school buildings to sign up for the basic "A" books that will allow the average driver approximately four gallons of gasoline per week. The actual rationing of the gas is scheduled to begin on December 1st. The prime purpose of the restriction is to conserve the nation's rubber supply by making our present tires last longer and thus maintain our civilian economy at as nearly a normal level as possible.

Shortages in foodstuffs is beginning to be felt keenly, especially in certain commodities. In the Bay Area particularly during the last few weeks, meats of all kinds have been hard to get. During the last several days butcher shops and meat markets have been completely cleaned out. The situation has been further aggravated by a two day strike of several hundred members of the local butchers' union. The rationing of meat will undoubtedly be put into effect early next year.

President Roosevelt has ordered further registration of 'teen age youths while draft boards all over the country are calling up many 3A's to fill their quotas. The drafting of the eighteen and nineteen year oldsters will not get under way until the first of next year.

No alerts or other scares have been experienced here for considerable time. The Japs are plenty busy elsewhere no doubt.

Thursday, November 19, 1942: —Additional details have been released by the Navy regarding the smashing victory scored last weekend over the Japs. Dreadnoughts of either side met in their first real slugging match of the war and our faith in our own mighty, heavily armored battleships was fully justified. Latest reports indicate that two rather than just one of the enemy capital ships were sent to the bottom. Full results of such tremendous actions are never known until several days after the battle, if at all. But the Navy is confident that its claims are conservative and the Nips suffered losses even heavier than those reported. A significant fact to support this belief is Tokyo's own admission that they lost one battleship and two cruisers. That's really a breakdown by Tokyo.

The showdown has not yet arrived in Tunisia but it is expected that the coming weekend will be climactic. A three way Allied pincer drive is closing in on the Axis African forces. General Eisenhower's American and British Armies are rushing into Tunisia, General Montgomery's crack Eighth Army is pursuing the beaten Afrika Korps through the Libyan deserts and a third army of Free French troops is driving straight up through Libya from the Lake Chad region in French Equatorial Africa. All indications point to a rapid liquidation of Axis resistance on the Dark Continent.

In Russia, General Winter has taken command, slowing down all military operations but today's communiqué states that the Red Army has scored a signal victory in the Central Caucasus. Five thousand Germans were killed and considerable enemy equipment was captured.

Friday, November 20, 1942: —On three fronts American troops and their Allies are dishing out a bit of the medicine the Axis has been accustomed to administering during the last year or two. In New Guinea, General MacArthur's American Australian troops have pinned that Japs against the sea around their bases of Buna and Gona and are moving in for the kill. The desperate little yellow men are expected to make a determined effort to repel the attackers but this time things look pretty black for them.

In Tunisia, American troops clashed with German soldiers for the first time since 1917 and 1918. Our columns closing in on Bizerte and Tunis encountered sharp opposition from strong

A Citizen's Chronological History of World War II

Nazi formations including heavy tanks. The Americans were slowed down only temporarily and continued their advance after knocking out eight of the enemy tanks.

On the other side of the pincers, General Montgomery's victorious Eighth Army has rolled on to Benghazi, more than five hundred miles from El Alamein where only a few weeks ago the British were fighting desperately to defend Alexandria and the Suez Canal. Stiff opposition by Rommel's rear guard was brushed aside, with the Germans losing twenty eight more of their few remaining armored units.

As an indication of the sort of war this is, the Department of Commerce in its survey of current business, reported that the Nation's war expenditures are approaching six billion dollars a month and account for approximately one-half of the entire finished output of the country's economy.

Saturday, November 21, 1942: —General MacArthur's troops in New Guinea have the greatest land victory in the Pacific war within their grasp today. They have pinned the Japs against the sea in their Buna-Gona bases. Australian troops are within 500 yards of the Buna airdrome. The Japs, sensing impending disaster, are fighting furiously and have succeeded in obtaining some land and air reinforcements. Nevertheless, the Australians and Americans are closing inexorably, raking the defense positions with mortar and machine gun fire. Unless a Japanese miracle happens our forces will occupy both bases before another week is over.

The showdown in North Africa has not yet arrived but it is expected very soon as powerful columns of American and British troops, supported but French sympathizers, are nearing the Axis held ports of Bizerte and Tunis. Only skirmishes have occurred between the opposing forces to date with the Nazis being forced to retreat. Heavy Axis reinforcements have arrived by plane from Sicily and severe fighting can be expected before North Africa is cleansed and liberated.

Marshal Rommel's badly handled Afrika Korps has made some sort of a world's record for backtracking. In less than a month the Nazis have backpedaled more than 800 miles from El Alamein where they so seriously threatened all of Egypt and the Middle East. Now they have their backs to the wall at El Agheila, their last defense position short of Tripoli. Unless they make a

256

successful stand there they will find themselves caught in the fast closing nutcracker from Tunisia.

Sunday, November 22, 1942: —Developments on the Russian front lately indicate that the diversion created in North Africa has relieved some of the pressure on the Soviets. The Red Army is moving forward at many points along the fifteen hundred mile front and a particularly successful counter-attack at Stalingrad indicates that the Nazis may soon be forced to lift their siege of the "Verdun on the Volga." The Berlin radio admits that the Reichwehr is on the defensive and that the Russian winter offensive is in full swing.

The adding of Russia to the good news tonight completes the favorable picture for the Allied Nations since the beginning of the war. In Africa, in New Guinea, the Solomons, China and Russia, the initiative has gone over to the side of the Allies. Probably never again will the Axis Nations be able to choose the time and the place to strike. They are on the defensive, with their strategic position deteriorating daily. It looks as though the tide has turned. But there will be some desperate, costly writhing before the Axis beast dies.

On the home front the people face more shortages. Butter is the next commodity that has all but disappeared from the grocer's shelves. The Government has frozen sufficient butter stock to meet the requirements of the Armed Forces but we the people will probably find ourselves eating margarine and liking it.

Thousands of motorists failed to register for gas rationing last week and face a gasoline drought after December first unless agitation in Congress for a ninety day postponement is successful.

Monday, November 23, 1942: —More cheerful news comes out of Africa today. French West Africa, including the strategic base of Dakar, has broken its tie with the Vichy regime of Pierre Laval and has voluntarily aligned itself with the Allied forces in North Africa. This is an important development as Dakar is a vital base and potential jumping off place for any invasion of South America across the narrow of the Atlantic from Dakar to Brazil. The Nazis have long coveted Dakar and its loss is a serious blow to their long-term plans. In addition there is a considerable body of trained French troops and many powerful units of the French fleet at the base. Admiral Darlan, former heir apparent to Petain at Vichy and now commander of all anti-Axis French in North Africa, appears to have been instrumental in bringing French West Africa onto the Allied bandwagon.

All the other important Allied campaigns seem to be in that stage where things are rapidly nearing a showdown but the decisive battle has not yet been joined. In Tunisia it is evident that the Axis Generals have succeeded in landing powerful reinforcements and going to put up a desperate fight to hang on to their precarious footholds at Bizerte and Tunis. In Libya, the British Eighth Army is approaching the El Agheila bottleneck where Rommel may attempt a stand. In New Guinea, far away, Allied troops are drawing the noose tighter around the Jap bases of Buna and Gona. In Russia the Red Army is forging ahead in a major offensive northwest of Stalingrad that has sent 100,000 Germans reeling back fifty miles and threatens to cut off an army of 375,000 Nazis. The siege of Stalingrad may soon be lifted.

Tuesday, November 24, 1942: —The war news tonight is meager and unexciting. Operations on the four principal fronts are progressing towards the decisive stage but as yet are in a state of flux as both sides move their men and equipment with deadly efficiency in this gigantic game of chess. Neither side is a push-over in this struggle and victory can be won only at a terrific cost in blood and suffering.

Probably the most significant development of the last few days is the powerful offensive that has been launched by the Russians. Striking out in the classic pincer movement for which the Nazis themselves are so famous, the Red Army as pushed strong counter-offensives northwest and southwest of Stalingrad and are today threatening the Germans with complete encirclement of their Stalingrad assault army of upwards of 300,000 men. The success of these drives to date is due in a large degree to the preoccupation of the Nazis with the North African attack by the Americans and British and their diversion of many planes and men from Russia to the Tunisian battleground. To a certain very definite extent, therefore, the Allies have achieved that second front for which the Russians have begged so desperately.

Local news is topped by the Government decree banning the voluntary enlistment of shipyard and aircraft workers into the armed forces. From now on these defense workers may be drafted but may not enlist. This has been a major problem of the big shipyards and aircraft factories, especially since the manpower shortage has become acute. Further drastic steps can be expected before the manpower problem is solved.

Wednesday, November 25, 1942: —A bit of unusual war experience came to California this morning. Four German prisoners of war, captured while fighting with Marshal Rommel's Afrika Korps, leaped from a heavily guarded train in Alameda County and two of them were at large for more than seven hours. Two were picked up almost immediately but it was necessary to organize a posse of one hundred Civilian Defense Police and County Sheriff's officers to round up the other two who were headed for Mexico. Several citizens as well as the police had quite a bit of excitement.

The war fronts remain about the same today. Most activity is reported in Russia where the Red Army has the Nazis of the run. German casualties in less than a week were estimated at more than 160,000 men killed, wounded, or captured. Three hundred thousand more are in danger of being cut off in the Stalingrad area. The Red Army seems to have plenty of vigor and vitality left.

In New Guinea, American and Australian troops are now assaulting the prepared positions held by the Japs on the outskirts of Buna and Gona. Progress is inevitably slow against such strong positions but General MacArthur's communiqué indicates that the situation is developing favorably.

In Tunisia both sides are swinging into position for the final round. Today's news is the first that I have seen that refers to any considerable combat experience by our crack interceptor plane, the P-38. Today's reports state that the fighters destroyed fourteen enemy planes, some of them heavily loaded troop transports.

Thursday, November 26, 1942: —THANKSGIVING! Yes, we are a thankful people, even though this Thanksgiving Day finds us engrossed in a great war for survival. Though we face a grim, uncertain future, we are confident that, united as never before by the treacherous act of a despicable foe, we shall win the inevitable triumph, with the help of Almighty God.

We are facing hard, critical times. Not only on the battlefronts where our soldiers face death and suffering, but also on the home front where the entire populace faces an increasing amount of personal sacrifice if not actual hardship. We face shortages of many vital food commodities. Meat, butter, eggs, cream, coffee, and many other foodstuffs will be hard to get. There will be no new cars, new refrigerators, new radios or many other comforts and conveniences. Rationing of many other essentials is here or in the immediate offing. Prices are high and the cost of living almost prohibitive, especially for those salaried folks like us who haven't got in on the big defense work wages. Taxes, both direct and hidden, are increasing by leaps and bounds. Purchases of war Bonds to the limit of our ability is a duty and may soon be a required obligation. All real luxuries are out for the duration. Work is long and hard. There is little time for play and amusement. As a Nation we are becoming lean and hard. But above all other sacrifices is the one that takes our men and boys, the fathers, husbands, brothers and sons of this mighty land, to die and be maimed in its defense.

In spite of all this we are fervently thankful. Thankful that we are Americans; that, as Americans, we have known the highest degree of freedom and the highest standard of living ever experienced by mankind; that for this way of life we are willing to fight, sacrifice, and die if need be. We are privileged to live during this tremendous moment in history and to be an infinitesimal part of that unconquerable floodtide that is AMERICA ON THE MARCH.

Friday, November 27, 1942: —Sensational news today! Hitler's and Mussolini's hordes today cast aside the last vestige of respect for their armistice agreement with France and marched into the naval base of Toulon and attempted to seize the immobilized French fleet. After a brief, furious fight, the Nazis took the city but, according to latest reports, not before the French had succeeded in scuttling the vast majority of their fleet. Vichy reports placed the number of scuttled warships at sixty three. Inspired by the courageous action of the crew of the Strasbourg, 26,500 ton pride of the French battle fleet, who blew their vessel up and sent her to the bottom with many of her men going with her, the sailors of the French navy opened the seacocks or blew their ships apart to prevent their falling into the enemy's hands. How many ships actually were seized by the Nazis is not known for sure but apparently the principal part of the fleet was destroyed. At least two submarines succeeded in escaping to join the Allies.

Meanwhile, two Allied armies are closing in on Bizerte and Tunis. One armored column pushed to within ten miles of the Tunisian capital while others are drawing the ring tighter around Bizerte and its strongly entrenched Axis forces. The final decision in North Africa cannot be far away and Hitler's latest move against the French fleet will probably solidify anti-Axis French feeling in Africa.

In Russia and New Guinea our side is continuing to advance. The Americans and Australians in New Guinea are finding the going plenty tough as their offense bumps against strongly held and previously prepared positions protecting the Jap bases at Buna and Gona. In Russia the Red Army just keeps rolling along with tremendous offensive power.

Saturday, November 28, 1942: —Germany tightened its grip on the prostrate French Nation today by seizing all cities and military bases along the Mediterranean coast of France. Toulon is a smoking graveyard of French warships, gloriously and courageously scuttled by their crews rather than allow them to fall into the hands of the hated Hitlerites. Their brave act, done at the cost of many of their own lives, has purchased honor and glory for the Tri-color out of the degradation of complete Nazi conquest of their beloved homeland. Their act has also assured the Allies of continuing naval dominance of the Mediterranean. Hitler counted strongly on using the French battle fleet in the forthcoming showdown in that area. In addition the Toulon incident has proved to all remaining Frenchmen that Hitler's word as embodied in the 1940 Armistice agreement meant as little to him as did the Kaiser's some twenty eight years before. Indications are that all of the French African Army and the balance of France's sea power, anchored at Alexandria, Oran, Casablanca, and Algiers will now come wholeheartedly into the fight against the common enemy.

Meanwhile in Tunisia, powerful Allied columns are closing in ever closer to Tunis and Bizerte and the final dramatic climax to the North African campaign seems close at hand. American and British paratroopers are the loops of the noose being drawn about the necks of the Axis forces backed up against the sea in the ever narrowing corridor of Tunisia comprising the Tunis-Bizerte area.

At home as the first anniversary of December 7th, the "day that will live in infamy" nears, plans are being completed for a gigantic parade in memory of Pearl Harbor and all that has transpired since.

Sunday, November 29, 1942: —Prime Minister Winston Churchill made a notable speech tonight on the eve of his sixty eighth birthday. With pardonable satisfaction and pride he reviewed the manner in which the British people have fought through from the deepest chasm of despair and defeat to the present vista from whence they can glimpse the bright light of victory and peace. They have endured what few people have ever been called upon to face and have added a glorious page in the history of the British Empire.

The Prime Minister also pointed the finger of impending doom at Italy. He told the 40,000,000 Italian people that one man and his corrupt regime was responsible for putting their Nation into its present terrifying predicament. It is up to them to decide whether they shall continue to support the criminal Fascist gang that has sacrificed their empire and their honor or whether they will throw off the yoke of Mussolini and resume their customary and rightful place in the freedom-loving brotherhood of nations. Unless they throw off the yoke they face a terrible siege of bombing that will lay their cities in waste and destroy their factories and lives. If, as is confidently expected, the Allies drive the remnants of the Axis from North Africa, the tempo of bombings will greatly increase. It is up to the Italian people to decide whether they want this terrible thing to happen to them.

Fascist radios in Rome were quick to ridicule the British leader's warning, claiming that Italy will not be frightened by air attack but competent observers believe that the deadly warning will sink deep into the minds of the common man in Italy who will ponder deeply the growing calamity that has been brought upon him by his Fascist overlords.

Monday, November 30, 1942: —There are food shortages, heavy taxes, and coffee rationed to one cup per day beginning yesterday but tomorrow the American people will get hit with something that will strike a sensitive spot. Gas rationing beginning December 1st will put America back on its feet for the first time since the auto took the place of Old Dobbin. And Americans won't like it. Autos to them are like tea and pubs to the British. Take them away and you've irreparably altered their way of life. So thousands of motorists swamped the service stations today to fill-er-up for the last time until victory. Tomorrow, all but essential drivers, will get along on a paltry four gallons per week. No! there's no shortage of gasoline—the storage tanks are bulging with it—but that vital rubber on which the cars roll must be conserved. So we'll ride the streetcars, hike to the stores, and get along on the four gallons. But we won't forget that there's one more score to settle with the Japanazis.

Meanwhile, the Nazis part of the Japanazis are beginning to feel the full wrath of our revenge already. They are discovering how it feels to be blitzed. Allied columns are pounding forward on Bizerte and Tunis and one armored force has driven a wedge between the two cities, cutting them off from all railroad communication. Only one narrow coastal road remains to link the two Axis strongholds. A complete Allied cleanup in North Africa appears imminent.

Italian Fascist leaders too wrathfully attacked Winston Churchill's warning to the Italian people, thus evidencing a frantic effort to counteract its effect on the war weary Italians. But, knowing what is in store for them, they also ordered a nightly blackout of all Italy beginning at 5 p.m.

December

Tuesday, December 1, 1942: —The Tunisian campaign appears to be developing into a gigantic battle for aerial supremacy. Today's reports indicate that an air battle of an intensity unequaled since the Battle of Britain is raging in the skies over Tunis and Bizerte. General Eisenhower, the Allied commander-in-chief has thrown all his available air power into the fray. The twin-tailed P-38s that we have seen so much in the air around here are showing up well in their first real test. They are reputed to be the fastest plane yet developed and rival the famous Spitfire in armaments. Several enemy tanks were knocked out today by cannon fire from the P-38s.

In Russia the powerful forward surge of the rejuvenated Soviet Armies is slowly gaining momentum. Northwest and west of Stalingrad, the Red Army inched its way ahead, leaving the regained ground soaked with Nazi blood and burdened with Nazi bodies. This Russo-German war has undoubtedly been the most sanguinary in all history. Both sides have fought with terrible hatred and ferocity. The catastrophic impact of a battle such as raged for sixty days before the gates of Stalingrad can never be realized except by those who actually fought through it. Even to them it would probably be indescribable.

Today was the first day of nationwide gasoline rationing. Streetcar and bus companies reported about a ten percent increase in loads but the full effect will not be felt until the auto tanks are emptied of those gallons bought up before the deadline last midnight. After that staggered hours will be the only solution to the transportation problem.

Wednesday, December 2, 1942: —A sick and pathetic Mussolini today made a feeble effort to answer Winston Churchill's warning to the Italian people. His speech included some fantastic figures on Italian casualties and naval losses utterly irreconcilable with the terrific drubbing Italy has taken in Africa and the Mediterranean. In one sentence he said Italy was not afraid of bombings and in the next he called for total evacuation of the major Italian cities and industrial areas. He spoke of having been forced into the war by an arrogant England and a warmongering Roosevelt. He claimed the wholehearted support of his people when all reports and indications, especially from their soldiers whom the British have encountered in battle, show that the average Italian is anxious to surrender and has very little desire to die in support of Hitler's new order. All in all, the Mussolini of today is far from being the pompous, swaggering "Conqueror" of 1940. He is now a broken-down, whining puppet of Hitler.

Late reports from New Guinea are very favorable. Australian troops have succeeded in driving a wedge to the sea between the towns of Buna and Gona, thus splitting and isolating the two Jap garrisons. The final snap of the well prepared Allied "bear trap" can be expected momentarily, especially since the Army Flying Fortresses have turned back another attempt by the Nips to relieve and reinforce their New Guinea troops. This campaign has really boomeranged on the Nips. It was only a few months ago that they were threatening Port Moresby, far on the other side of the "impassable" Owen Stanley Mountains.

Thursday, December 3, 1942: —We had a bit of excitement in the Bay area today. This morning, frequent radio announcements stated that all shore leaves were cancelled and all naval personnel should report to their ships at once. Rumors flew thick and fast regarding the reason for this action. Some supposedly authentic reports were that Pearl Harbor had been attacked; others that an enemy fleet was approaching the West Coast. It was not until later that the truth was known. According to Admiral Greenslade, commanding the Western Sea Frontier, a Navy patrol stated that they had spotted a large number of unidentified surface vessels about 450 miles off the California coast and all precautions had been taken until the report could be checked. At about 11:00 a.m. the "Alert" was lifted as a thorough search had failed to confirm the presence of any unidentified vessels. It was just a false alarm that ruined many a sailor boy's leave.

The Navy Department announced that another big naval engagement was fought near Guadalcanal on the night of November 30-December 1st, resulting in the smashing of another desperate attempt by the Japs to reinforce their positions on Guadalcanal. Nine more Jap warships and transports were sent to the bottom with the loss of many soldiers, sailors, and equipment. We lost another cruiser and some smaller vessels.

The African campaign cost us at least five big transport ships it was learned today. They were all torpedoed by Axis submarines. Three of the big ships formerly plied commercial routes out of San Francisco. Their names were the Tasker H. Bliss, Hugh L. Scott, the Edward Rutledge, the Joseph Hewes, and the Leedstown. Tonnage aggregated 52,946.

Friday, December 4, 1942: —The easy victory expected in Tunisia is not panning out. The Axis forces are making a desperate stand and have achieved a definite air superiority over the battlefield due to the convenience of their well established bases in Sicily and Sardinia. Hitler has plenty of dive bombers left and he apparently has withdrawn hundreds of them from Russia to participate in the North African fight. Several local counter-attacks by the enemy have regained some ground but the Allied forces are consolidating their main positions before both Tunis and Bizerte. Eisenhower's strategy appears to be that of ignoring local and small-scale actions or temporary Axis successes and to build up his full, overwhelming strength before coming to final grips with the foe. Whether the Axis will be able to bring enough reinforcements through the Allied gauntlet to upset the American General's plans remains to be seen. In any event a terrific battle is expected.

On the home front innumerable problems are being faced. Gas rationing has added a tremendous burden to the already overtaxed transportation system. Shortages in meat, butter, eggs, and other dairy products have become acute in the Bay Area. Many retail butchers as well as some wholesalers are being forced out of business. Restaurants and other eating places are experiencing similar difficulties. Shipyard wages are luring many a small business owner who can't get goods to sell.

President Roosevelt today ordered the liquidation of the WPA. Thus comes to an end the Federal Relief Agency that cared for more than eight million people during the depression years. War work has eliminated the need for the Agency.

Saturday, December 5, 1942: —American planes for the first time have bombed Italy, it was announced today. Heavy Consolidated B-24s made the attack on Naples. According to the flyers, the Italians were caught flat-footed and offered only light, inaccurate anti-aircraft opposition. The Americans plastered the harbor and scored two direct bomb hits on a battleship. Rail lines into the city and many factories and warehouses were smashed with heavy caliber bombs and huge fires were started. The Rome radio admitted that severe damage was caused, with many casualties. Churchill's warning is already being borne out. Beware Benito! You're going to be an "ill Duce" before many more days have elapsed.

Everything indicates that the American, British, French Allies in Tunisia face a bitter, bloody fight before the Axis resistance in that French protectorate is overwhelmed. Hitler has obviously decided to risk many men and planes in a determined effort to maintain his foothold on the dark continent. He has apparently drawn heavily on his aircraft reserves in Russia and Western Europe to seize air supremacy in the African struggle. The final story of Tunisia has not yet been told and the Allies will need to exert every bit of their effort if complete victory is to be achieved.

FLASH! A late radio report states that the Navy Department has finally released the full story of the damage wrought by the Japanese in their dastardly attack on Pearl Harbor last December 7th. From what they say a fearful and tragic disaster occurred that terrible day, one that could well have meant our defeat if the Japs had known and had followed up their initial advantage. We'll report more on this tomorrow.

Sunday, December 6, 1942: —The big news today is, of course, the story of the Pearly Harbor disaster. The truth regarding our losses was withheld until yesterday for reasons of military security. Had the Japs known the full measure of their success they could almost certainly have captured the Hawaiian Islands and completely destroyed the Pacific Fleet. Yet one American Senator—Wheeler of Montana—dared to bitterly assail the administration for not revealing the truth immediately after the attack.

In the surprise raid, conducted by approximate 105 Jap torpedo planes, dive-bombers, and horizontal bombers, every American battleship in the Pacific area, eight in all, were put out of commission. Five of them were either sunk or so severely damaged as to be of no further use. The other three have since been repaired and returned to the battle line. The Arizona, Oklahoma, California, Nevada and West Virginia were the ones lost while the Pennsylvania, Maryland and Tennessee have been reconditioned.

Ten other important warships were destroyed or badly damaged, including the cruisers Helena, Honolulu and Raleigh, the destroyers Shaw, Cassin and Downes. One hundred and ninety five Army and Navy planes were destroyed, most of them on the ground.

The most excruciating loss was in trained personnel. In round figures, approximately 3,500 officers and men were killed and 1,300 wounded. Tales of heroism and devotion to duty were commonplace among these brave men and their loss was the most crippling blow to the Navy.

Japan, however, failed to follow up and has now lost her chance because our losses have been recouped, and a mighty nations is marching to avenge Pearl Harbor.

Monday, December 7, 1942: —Today marks the first anniversary of our entry into war. Behind us lies a year of tremendous events. For the most part it has been a year of bitter defeats and disappointing setbacks. Few years in all history have equaled it for breath-taking and epoch-making events that have so greatly changed the face of the earth. A kaleidoscopic chain of pictures flashes across one's memory when thinking of the year of war just closed. The peace and quiet of December 6, 1941. Then PEARL HARBOR! The unbelievable shock of bomb and torpedo on American ships and men. The President's speech. The declaration of war. The call to arms. BLACKOUTS! Work and more work. Manila! Bataan! Corregidor! Singapore! Burma! The Indies! Colin Kelly—and war bonds! Sugar rationing—and taxes, bigger taxes! The Coral Sea. Midway—and the Solomons! Meat, butter and eggs scarce—and gas rationing. Guadalcanal— the Marines—and work until midnight! Submarine sinkings— and thousand plane air raids—Cologne—and Stalingrad! The Russian winter—and death! The Egyptian desert—and death! A thousand other soul-stirring events and finally—North Africa, New Guinea—and the Allied Nations on the march—to Victory!

Yes, without a doubt, these are times that "try men's souls" but we have been privileged to see a great nation unite in a common cause and, in spite of almost insuperable obstacles and many human weaknesses, transform this peaceful country into a mighty arsenal of democracy and a powerful war machine. But it is only the beginning. We are only just flexing our muscles, feeling the first inkling of our potential strength. We alone are out producing all the Axis powers in every category. We can out work them, out sacrifice them and out fight them. Is this idle boasting? Le the year from December 7, 1942 to December 7, 1943 be the judge.

Tuesday, December 8, 1942: —We swing into the second year of war with the news from the battlegrounds somewhat more cheerful. The Americans and their French and British allies in Tunisia are maintaining their pressure on the Axis forces and are receiving some invaluable new air support. Our armored columns are edging the Nazis back in the strategic Tebourba area, 20 miles west of Tunis.

Meanwhile, the other claw of the Allied bear trap in Libya appears to be about ready to snap on Rommel's last ditch defense positions at El Agheila. The victorious British Eighth Army has had sufficient time to bring up its main force from Egypt and we can expect a double all-out offensive at El Agheila and in Tunisia, aimed at dealing the death blow to Axis domination in North Africa.

The truth about another important event has been disclosed today. Secretary of the Navy Knox told reporters today that the story of the scuttling of the French fleet based at Toulon was greatly exaggerated. Aerial reconnaissance reveals that at least fifteen French warships fell into the hands of the Nazis in a serviceable condition and some others, including the two biggest battleships, Dunkerque and Strasbourg, can be salvaged. Close to fifty other vessels were destroyed by the French crews.

General Francisco Franco, the dictator of Spain, made a speech today. It was a neat bit of fence walking, with the General hewing to his Fascist leanings but making a powerful bid for neutrality while leaving the gate open wide enough for him to slide gracefully over into the winning yard with very little embarrassment. That middle road is a tough one to follow, Franco! The way we look at it you're either for us or against us. Which shall it be?

Wednesday, December 9, 1942: —The Japanese made another desperate attempt to relieve and reinforce their beleaguered troops on Guadalcanal today. American airmen from Henderson Field, that unsinkable aircraft carrier, rose to meet the enemy force and saw their heavy bombs sink one Jap cruiser and hit three other warships. The Nips then retired, frustrated.

Meanwhile, in Europe, poor battered Italy is reaping the bitter fruits of her treachery in stabbing France and England in the back. RAF heavy bombers on several consecutive nights have alternated in blasting Milan and Turin. Swiss reports indicate that something like panic is spreading through northern Italy. The terrible crunch and smash of the huge 8,000 pound "triple block-busters" have sent tremors of fear through the population. Mass evacuation by women, children, and non-essential persons is proceeding with much disorder. The Mussolini government has issued strict orders and imposed severe penalties to prevent essential workers from leaving the danger areas. German troops and "tourists" are flocking into the country to prevent any uprising or revolt by the suffering masses. And these are only the first fruits of the "quick victory" that Il Duce expected when he leaped to the aid of victorious Germany in 1940.

In Russia, the Red Army is still on its winter offensive. Bitter fighting is in progress, especially in the Rzhev area, northwest of Moscow. The Nazis are hanging desperately to Rzhev, the loss of which Hitler once said would be as bad as losing a portion of Berlin. The German officers apparently believe this as Soviet dispatches state that Nazi commanders are shooting any soldier who attempts to leave his post.

Thursday, December 10, 1942: —Good news today. General MacArthur's headquarters today announced the glad tidings that American and Australian troops have captured Gona and are advancing toward the remaining Japanese forces in Buna. Thus half the battle is won and it is expected that Buna will fall in short order, putting the Allied forces into position to make their next step northward along the devious route back to Manila and Tokyo.

MacArthur's campaign in New Guinea has not received nearly the publicity and attention it deserves and has been overshadowed repeatedly by the vicious naval encounters off the

Solomon Islands but many experts believe that history will reveal its real importance and perhaps place it foremost in the victories that stopped the Japs and turned them back from Australia. Time will tell. Anyhow, General MacArthur now has the satisfaction of knowing that it is the Japs who are experiencing the unpleasantness of being trapped with their backs to the sea, with no hope of relief or reinforcement. This time it is he who is attacking, attacking, attacking—which is much to his liking.

On the home front, jobs and food hold the spotlight. Shortages that have developed in many commodities have drawn nationwide attention to the possibility that next year may see a serious food situation arise. The nearest thing to a famine may occur unless adequate measures are adopted. A victory garden in every backyard will probably be the answer. On the job side, War Manpower Commissioner McNutt ordered over 600,000 essential workers in Detroit frozen to their jobs and similar action in many other areas and industries is expected in the near future.

Friday, December 11, 1942: —Today has been a memorable day for the city beside the Golden Gate. The "Fightingest" ship in the U.S. Navy steamed slowly and proudly into the Bay this morning. It was the cruiser San Francisco, home for a rest and repairs after her epic and heroic battle in the Solomons. It was a mighty proud city that welcomed the battered but unbowed ship, the first naval vessel in this war to be decorated by the President for gallant service in defense of the Nation.

It was the San Francisco, you will remember, who led her task force of cruisers and destroyers down the slot between two mighty lines of Jap battleships, cruisers and destroyers and slugged out a tremendous victory over incalculable odds. The San Francisco matched her battery of eight inch guns against the formidable 14 inchers of a Jap battleship and that enemy ship now lies at the bottom of the Pacific. It was a feat worthy of John Paul Jones, Farragut or Dewey. It was in the finest tradition of the U.S. Navy. But there was a price to be paid. One fourteen inch shell tore into the cruiser's bridge and killed Admiral Daniel Callaghan and Captain Cassin Young, among many others. San Francisco and the whole nation owes a debt of gratitude and admiration that they can never repay to the brave men both living and dead, of a gallant cruiser. San Francisco is indeed proud of her namesake.

Probably the most important other news of the day is the terrific pasting that the RAF is giving Italy. The Italians apparently have made no real preparation for defense against air raids and the British are hurting them plenty at very little cost to themselves. Poor, unhappy Italy!

Saturday, December 12, 1942: —The Navy announced a tragic piece of news today. The President Coolidge, one of the biggest and finest liners in the world, has been sunk by a mine. The great ship was on a war mission as a troop transport and was loaded with 4,000 American troops when she struck a mine in the South Pacific and sank. Fortunately all but four of the troops were rescued by prompt and efficient action by escorting vessels. The mighty ship grossed 22,000 tons and before the war was the flagship of the American President Lines. It is a serious loss.

Late radio reports carry the Berlin claim that the British Eighth Army in Libya has started a new offensive against Marshal Rommel's positions at El Agheila. No confirmation of this report has come from any Allied source but we ardently hope it is true. Every day's delay before the Allied Armies move in Libya and Tunisia gives the enemy just that much more time to reinforce and strengthen his North African defenses. The sooner the pincers close the less the cost in valuable men and equipment. Apparently General Eisenhower's main trouble in Tunisia is lack of air superiority. The Germans have drawn heavily on their plane reserves and with the advantage of closer bases have wrested temporary control of the air over Tunisia. To solve this problem General Spaatz, the American air chief of the European theater, has arrived in North Africa from London. General Doolittle has done a magnificent job so far against heavy odds but the presence of General Spaatz emphasizes the importance of the operation. Once air control has been established the closing of the pincers will be greatly simplified.

Sunday, December 13, 1942: —Those reports from Berlin regarding new fighting in Libya were correct. Allied sources have confirmed that General Montgomery's crack Eighth Army is on the offensive again. This time they have smashed against Rommel's defense line at El Agheila and from all we can learn, the vaunted Nazi Afrika Korps is again in full flight, and is apparently relinquishing its strong defensive positions in the narrow bottleneck of El Agheila with only token resistance. Obviously the Germans have not yet recovered from their disastrous defeat at El Alamein and their bitter retreat over 700 miles of Egyptian and Libyan Desert. Rommel apparently is not yet capable of opposing the Eighth Army, even in the easily defended El Agheila sector which resembles the El Alamein area where the British were successful in stemming their own rout several months ago.

The quick breakthrough by the British at El Agheila is convincing evidence that the Axis' whole North African situation is desperate and it is possible, even probable, that Rommel may by-pass Tripoli and attempt to join his remnants with the Axis forces now in Tunisia. To further complicate the Nazis' problems, a great fleet of Allied fighters and bombers is pounding, without surcease, the Axis columns fleeing across Tripolitania. The Allied nutcracker is beginning to squeeze. And it's the Nazis who are on the receiving end for a change.

More good news also comes from New Guinea. American troops succeeded in entering the town of Buna yesterday and all that remains for a completely successful campaign is a mopping up job to clean out a few hotbeds of resistance and kill a few more Japs who won't be taken prisoner.

Monday, December 14, 1942: —The Axis retreat in Libya is continuing at an ever increasing speed. The Nazis are good runners, it seems. Allied airmen, however, are ripping their retreating columns with devastating effect while General Montgomery's exultant army is plowing forward over thickly planted minefields and booby traps. The retreating Nazis are experts at leaving innocent looking death-traps. Their sappers are no saps, as, neither are the British sappers who deactivate the enemy traps, or as the soldiers say, delouse the battlefield.

Meanwhile, air activity has also stepped up to an unprecedented scale in Tunisia, as Allied bombers smashed heavily at Bizerte and Tunis. Heavy rains have brought land action to almost a complete stop. Only routine patrol activity is possible in the quagmires caused by the violent downpour.

In New Guinea, sanguinary fighting continues in the Buna area. Although our forces have occupied the village, the Japs are still in possession of several strong-points, particularly the Buna mission area. The fighting is especially bitter as the Japs refuse to be taken alive and must be killed off one by one in a vicious mopping-up action. Like the "Injuns" of frontier days, "the only good Jap is a dead one." But it makes the whole mess a deadly and morbid affair.

Just a note on the home front:The OPA announced today that prices on 17 basic foodstuffs are slated to go up again immediately. Pretty tough on the regular salaried folks whose pay hasn't been much affected by the war and who can't afford the high cost of living the way the highly paid defense workers can. Just another inevitable sacrifice, I guess.

Tuesday, December 15, 1942: —Frontline dispatches lend credence to the belief that Marshal Rommel is preparing to forfeit the great Axis base of Tripoli without a struggle. Aerial reconnaissance indicates that the enemy is evacuating his forces from the vital base and will probably retire into Tunisia for a last stand. The magnitude of the British Eighth Army's victory is expanding daily and, together with the successful American expedition into the French colonies, will probably mean the complete expulsion of the Axis from Africa. But let's not count too many of our chickens—as the saying goes—for a grueling fight yet remains to be fought in Tunisia. The Allies have the advantage, however, and barring an adverse miracle, should treat the Nazis to their own private little Dunkirk—and see how they like it!

Tomorrow, San Francisco will turn out in mass to honor the crew of her namesake cruiser who brought so much honor and glory to this fair city. The sailors will be paraded up Market Street, each chauffeured by a soldier in his private little Jeep. After the parade there will be a mass meeting at the Civic Auditorium and entertainment for officers and men alike in the evening. It is well to heap honors upon those brave men who so gallantly offered their bodies as a bulwark in defense of those of us who remain at home in safety. Their courage has added new glory to Old Glory and we're mighty proud of them. And it is also well to remember with sadness and pride, the hundred odd men and boys, officers and seamen, of the gallant cruiser who did not come back. Their supreme sacrifice will not be forgotten.

Wednesday, December 16, 1942: —Thousands of San Franciscans today honored the heroic crew of the U.S.S. San Francisco. The crowd was unusually silent; there was very little loud cheering as the stalwart and handsome sailors, with their wounded comrades, paraded by. It seemed as if everyone was just a little sad, thinking of the equally fine lads who did not come back. War is no cheering matter to most people nowadays. It's just a nasty business that has been forced upon us and which we are determined to prosecute to final victory. But the men of the San Francisco richly deserve our thanks and applause for their courageous and brilliant action.

In Libya, the beaten Nazis are continuing their hasty retreat from El Agheila. The British Eighth Army has pushed more than fifty miles forward through thickly strewn minefields while Allied airmen allow the fleeing enemy no respite from bombing and strafing attack. There is no remaining doubt that Marshal Rommel's battered Afrika Korps has been badly mauled and is in desperate straits. The exultant British troops are aware of this fact and are pressing forward eagerly to the kill.

Ground action in Tunisia is still bogged down by heavy rainfall which has now ceased but has left the battlefields impassable. As soon as the ground is dry enough for tanks and other armored vehicles, we can expect a powerful Allied offensive, aimed at bringing the other jaw of the pincers down on the Axis forces in synchronization with the Eighth Army's offensive. All indications point to a smashing Allied victory, although a desperate and bitter fight can be expected.

Thursday, December 17, 1942: —Brilliant news today! All reports indicate that the Germans have suffered their worst defeat since 1918. General Montgomery has just completed one of the most successful flanking attacks of the war, slicing the Afrika Korps in two. After crushing his way through the narrow bottleneck at El Agheila, Montgomery sent part of his army on a wide end run around the Nazis' southern flank, followed by a beautiful cut-back to the sea a Wadi Matratin, leaving fully half of Rommel's Army trapped in a shallow pocket between El Agheila and Wadi Matratin. The cornered Axis forces are being rapidly hammered to pieces and face extermination or capture. Many observers believe it will be Rommel's last fight. We fervently hope so.

Nothing so spectacular has happened in Tunis today, although drying ground has permitted an increase in American and British tank action. A number of Italian prisoners were taken.

The important feature of the Tunisian picture is the heavily stepped up action by Allied air forces. The docks and other military installations at Tunis and Bizerte have taken eight tremendous poundings in the last 48 hours. If our forces can gain air dominance over this front as well as over the Libyan front, the Axis goose is cooked for good.

More sanguinary fighting is in progress in New Guinea, where MacArthur's men are slowly but surely mopping up in the Buna area. It is a case of Jap by Jap extermination, as the Nipponese soldiers have been ordered by Hirohito himself to resist to the last man. This attitude makes the sons of Heaven just plain sons of Hell to fight against.

Friday, December 18, 1942: —The most severe restriction yet meted out in this war was levied against citizens of seventeen eastern states today. All sales of gasoline was banned, except to holders of "T" coupons—truck, bus, and taxicabs—until further notice. President Roosevelt announced that the move was necessary because of a rush order for gasoline to supply our armies in North Africa. He expects that the restriction will last for only a few days but all pleasure traveling will be out for that time.

The actual battle picture on the North African front is quite confused today. A large part of Rommel's Afrika Korps apparently is trapped in a twenty mile pocket but British communiqués speak only of rear-guard action with the fleeing enemy. It will be a few days before the final answers will be known. Three hundred eighty five miles further west in Tunisia, activity is largely confined to air action and tank skirmishes. Both sides apparently are feverishly preparing for the showdown.

The Navy announced more victories for the silent service. Our far-ranging and unsung heroes of the undersea boats have sent seven more Japanese vessels to the half of the ocean that has been allotted to them—the bottom half. Some of the sinkings were right in Japan's front dooryard.

Another of the West Coast's worst subversive organizations was smashed today with the arrest of 16 members of Mankind United. The F.B.I. is doing a magnificent job of preventing sabotage and squelching seditious organizations.

Saturday, December 19, 1942: —The Allies are marching on another front today. British and Indian troops, supported by American aircraft, today crossed the India border and invaded Burma. Taken by surprise, the Japanese abandoned their fortified border defenses without a fight and retreated forty miles into Burma in the direction of Akyab.

Early reports of this new development are cautious. It is not certain that this is the beginning of the real Allied offensive, aimed at retaking Burma and reopening the famous supply route to China, or if it is merely a diversion attack, to upset Japanese plans for striking at India or driving through Hunnan province to knock China out of the war. But General Archibald Wavell, the British Commander in India had promised many months ago to launch an all-out offensive in Burma and this may be it. We will watch further developments with great interest.

Meanwhile, in Africa the British Eighth Army is giving the remnants of Marshal Rommel's Afrika Korps a severe mauling and the Axis retreat has brought the advance guard of General Montgomery's Army to a point 135 miles west of El Agheila while some Axis units are already streaming into Tripoli. Present indications are that even that strong enemy base will be abandoned without much of a fight in order that Rommel's force may be combined with the German General Nehring's army in Tunisia for a last ditch fight. Even Berlin is worried, if dispatches from neutral Sweden and Spain are true. One newspaper in neutral Turkey was so bold as to tell the Nazis bluntly that "the Allies are beating hell out of you both in Africa and in Russia."

Sunday, December 20, 1942: —As we sit here at 11:00 p.m. on a peaceful Sabbath night and contemplate the tragedy of a world at war, we cannot but contrast the present situation with that of a year ago. Then the little slant-eyed Orientals from Japan were well on their way to an amazing string of victorious conquests in southeastern Asia and the Indies. Their surprisingly effective jungle troops were snaking their way down the Malay Peninsula towards mighty Singapore. Manila was in the grip of powerful pincers moving down on her from north and south. The initiative and offensive power was all with the enemy and we had to content ourselves with solemn pride in the heroic Marines of Wake Island, in the unselfish sacrifice of the Colin Kelly's, and the gallantry of the men of Pearl Harbor. A ray of hope emanated from Russia where the Red Army fought magnificently in the bitter cold of a Russian winter but for the most part the picture was black and gloomy. A long, bitter uphill struggle lay before us with nothing but blood, sweat, and tears in prospect.

Now, in one short but epochal year, a new horizon has opened before us. Through colossal human effort and the magnificent courage of our fighting men, the initiative has been seized from the enemy. It is now the United Nations who are calling the turns. On every front throughout the world our armies are on the march. In Russia, three tremendous Soviet drives are sending the Nazis reeling back in disordered flight. In Africa, in New Guinea, in the Solomons, in Burma, and on the high seas our thrusts are continually probing the enemy armor, slipping through here and there to wound and bleed him, ever searching for the weakest link through which we can thrust the final war-winning blow. We are harrying, worrying and weakening him while all the while we grow immeasurably in strength. Yes, a mighty change has been wrought in one short year.

Monday, December 21, 1942: —Probably the most sensational war news of the day comes from Russia. On this the 63rd birthday of Josef Stalin, the Red Army is surging forward all along a fifteen hundred mile front. An especially strong attack has been launched in the vicinity of Milerovo, which is about 200 miles southwest of Stalingrad. This thrust is obviously aimed at making the whole Nazi position in the Caucasus untenable and the capture of Milerovo would come close to accomplishing this objective. Meanwhile, in the central Don front, the Soviets also succeeded in breaking the Nazi defense lines and offensive guns roared as far north as Leningrad. The Germans are taking a terrific beating in the savage fighting that rages in bitter cold that sometimes reaches fifty degrees below zero. One can only imagine the terrible suffering of troops fighting in such conditions but the Russians have proved many times that they are far more capable of taking it than their Nazi foe.

In Burma we hear that General Wavell's army is still advancing without opposition but the Japs have opened a counter-drive northward into China's Yunnan province and have twice bombed Calcutta, India within the last twenty four hours. Important developments can be expected soon.

In New Guinea, MacArthur's Allied troops are still mopping up around Buna and have finally succeeded in bringing up some light tanks to help finish the job. Already it appears that MacArthur is aiming a further offensive action against the remaining Jap bases in New Guinea, namely Lae and Salamaua.

By contrast, here at home our daily routine is work and more work; hunt for butter—no can find. Ham and eggs for breakfast without the ham—and no eggs. Canned salmon and like it.

Tuesday, December 22, 1942: —It's still Russia in the forefront of the news today. The Red Army's huge winter offensive is really unfolding. Particularly heavy fighting is in progress in the middle Don area, where Soviet troops succeeded in retaking eight large towns, capturing thousands of Axis troops and untold quantities of booty. This Russian drive is aimed at Rostov, the key to the Caucasus, around which so much heavy fighting occurred last spring. You will recall that the Germans took Rostov in the summer of 1941 only to lose it to the Russians in their first great winter campaign. The Nazis stream-rolled over the city again last spring and now the Red Army seems bent on duplicating its feat of last winter.

The RAF, about whom little has been reported lately, unleashed another tremendous raid against the Reich last night. This time it was Munich, the birthplace of the cancer that has afflicted the world. Several hundred planes participated and extremely heavy caliber bombs were dropped, including some of the triple block-busters of 8,000 pounds. It can only be hoped that Hitler was present in his favorite beer cellar at the time. Twelve British bombers failed to return, some because of the exceptionally poor weather conditions.

Grim justice and retribution is gathering over the heads of the Axis powers on the North African front. Like an avenging host, the British Eighth Army is looming up over the Tripolitanian desert within sight of Tripoli and the fleeing Axis army. Meanwhile the Allied forces in Tunisia are massing for the final showdown and the now prospective joining of Eisenhower and Montgomery should put the clincher on the victory.

Wednesday, December 23, 1942: —As evidence of growing Allied strength in the Pacific, we hear that a British aircraft carrier raided Jap positions off the northwest tip of Sumatra in the Dutch East Indies and scored many hits on vital Jap military installations. At the same time, American bombers were attacking Rangoon in Burma. The attack was made by a large force of heavy bombers and considerable damage was inflicted. In New Guinea, MacArthur's troops are completing their mopping-up operation on the Buna Mission area, with the Japanese position deteriorating rapidly. The American position on Guadalcanal, in the Solomons, is being further consolidated, with the Japs apparently convinced that further efforts, at least for the present, will be fruitless. All in all, the picture in the Pacific is definitely on the improve.

Meanwhile, the flames of war are licking higher and higher in Russia and North Africa. The Soviet counter-offensives, especially on the Middle Don sector, are smashing inexorably ahead, leaving thousands of German corpses and untold equipment wreckage strewn in their path. Every move of the Nazis indicates their growing desperation. Today's reports state that in some instances, the Nazi Luftwaffe is bombing its own troops in an effort to stem the headlong retreat.

In Africa, the victorious British are pressing closer to Tripoli through extensive mine fields laid by the retreating Afrika Korps. In Tunisia, Allied air power is gaining dominance and heavy bombing attacks are being conducted against Axis supply lines from Sicily. Torpedo and bomb attacks were claimed to have sunk six Axis supply ships today.

Thursday, December 24, 1942: —A sensational event that may have far-reaching consequences occurred this afternoon. Admiral Jean Francois Darlan, the former Vichy collaborationist and the man who turned on the Nazis when the Allies landed in North Africa, was assassinated shortly after twelve noon by a young assailant. The French leader was shot in the mouth and lungs as he stepped out of his office in Algiers. The assassin was overpowered by other French officers after a brief struggle in which one other officer was wounded.

Details regarding the shooting are lacking and the nationality and political affiliation of the murderer are not known as yet. Berlin and Rome, of course, are seizing upon the incident to sow suspicion and hatred among the French, British, and

Americans in North Africa. It was well known that Darlan was hated as a Hitlerite collaborationist by many free Frenchmen and his acceptance by the Allies as leader of the anti-Axis French in North Africa caused much resentment among de Gaullists and other free and fighting Frenchmen.

While the assassination of the man who handed a vast territory over to the Allies without a fight is deplorable, there is no doubt but that a lot of good as well as bad will result from the act. With one stroke, the principal cause of disunity and friction between the Allies and the French has been removed. Although Darlan had many followers it is believed that most of them will gladly follow some other and more acceptable leader such as General Giraud, who has temporarily assumed control.

Ah me! I hate to think of the work we have before us tonight. It's Christmas Eve, you know. Paging Santa!

Friday, December 25, 1942: —Our second wartime Christmas has come and almost gone as I sit down to compile this record. It has been a clear, crisp day, cold outside but warm within the hearts and homes of men and women of good will. As the President pointed out, this cannot be a Merry Christmas but it is a much Happier Christmas than last year's. Millions of homes have vacant chairs around their dinner tables and millions of American lads at their battle stations throughout the world are thinking of the good old Christmases at home. Perhaps next year will find most of them back again, back to the land, the families and friends they love. At least we can fervently pray that such may be the case.

Everything that could be done to make this a joyful Christmas for the boys in the service was done. Where ever possible, the traditional dinner of roast turkey with all the trimmings was served while the airways hummed with entertainments broadcast from various Army, Navy, and Marine camps, by the best entertainers in the business. Bob Hope, Bing Crosby, Betty Fields, Jerry Colona, Kay Kyser, and all the rest kept the boys rolling in the aisles all day long. It was one long round of command performances, with the boys really enjoying it.

Back on the war news, we hear that Admiral Darlan's assassin was a young Frenchman but his political connections, if known, were kept secret. A military tribunal has already sentenced the killer to death at sunrise tomorrow. Anxious observers in London and Washington are awaiting the repercussions that the shooting of the former French Vichy leader may have on the Allied position in Morocco, Algeria, and Tunisia.

Saturday, December 26, 1942: —Well, Christmas has come and gone and although Governor Olson of California had proclaimed Saturday an additional holiday, it was work as usual for us today. Ordinarily we all like an extra day's vacation at Yuletide, but the consensus of opinion at this time is that the Governor made a mistake in suggesting a stoppage of work today as well as yesterday. Doesn't he know there's a war!? There's no stoppage of fighting and dying in New Guinea or North Africa this weekend. There's no three day holiday for the weary marines on Guadalcanal. What does he think this is—a picnic? Most defense plants, including our Bank simply ignored the proclamation and worked as usual. Our outfit at least, has far too much to do to play around with weekend vacations during this man's war. After it's over and won, we'll take our rest.

Swift justice has overtaken the player of Admiral Darlan. He was executed before a firing squad this morning at sunrise while later in the day his victim was given a military funeral with high Allied dignitaries and military leaders in attendance. The purported confession of the assassin has been kept secret, however, and it is rumored that it will not be disclosed until after the war. This is undoubtedly in the interest of French unity in North Africa.

Allied offensive action is gaining momentum in New Guinea, Burma, and particularly in Russia, where by far the heaviest fighting is in progress. The Soviet forces are drawing a noose tighter and tighter around approximately 300,000 Nazi troops trapped before Stalingrad, where their grandiose attempt to take the city has turned into a desperate struggle for survival.

Sunday, December 27, 1942: —The French Imperial Council of Africa, meeting in Algiers, today unanimously elected General Henri Honore Giraud to succeed Admiral Darlan as French High Commissioner in North Africa. General Giraud, a grizzled old veteran of two world wars, an implacable foe of the Germans, and escape artist supreme, is very popular with all factions among the French people and it is believed that all of them, including General de Gaulle's Free French movement will rally behind the old General, who three times has engineered sensational and daring escapes from the Huns. It is to be hoped that the French will now back to the limit, the American and British forces that are fighting to oust the common enemy from the shores of Africa.

Meanwhile, the astonished eyes of the world are on the Russian battlefront, where a marvelously vigorous Soviet Army is staging a ferocious offensive against the cold and embittered Nazis. The Red Army's recuperative power is truly one of the greatest miracles of this war. The world's estimation of the fighting ability of the Russian soldier has risen to great heights never before reached by those people. Truly their staying powers, their determination and sacrificial bravery have amazed the world—especially Germany. If any men deserve victory it is the fighting Russians.

Some other equally good fighting men are a close grips in the steaming jungles of New Guinea. The stubborn Japs are clinging fanatically to their ever narrowing strip of beach at Buna Mission and the Doughboys and Diggers are blasting them out one by one in a bitter fight that calls for unbelievable courage and ingenuity. It's old fashioned Indian fighting with tommy guns and hand grenades.

Monday, December 28, 1942: —One of the most crucial and dynamite-packed problems of the war is food. The attention of the whole country in on this problem at the present time. Shortages of many vital commodities is becoming acute and the Federal Government has taken the bear by the tail—and a vicious and un-obliging bear it is. Last evening, radio talks were given on this subject by three of the Government leaders who are attempting to tackle this knotty problem. Elmer Davis, Chairman of the Office of War Information, outlined the situation and it relation and importance to the war effort, while Secretary of Agriculture Wickard and Price Administrator Leon Henderson discussed the ways and means by which the Government hopes to make the best use of food as a potent weapon of war.

Beginning as soon as possible after the first of the year, dozens of foodstuffs, including canned fruits and vegetables, butter, meat and other staples will be rationed by means of a point system similar to that now being used in England. Although unscrupulous citizens may seize upon this advance notice to hoard food, the Government is counting on the loyalty of the vast majority to prevent "runs" on foodstuff that will jeopardize the war effort. If calmness and reason prevail there will be enough of the essential foods to provide everyone with proper nutrition. But the main idea is to keep our Army the best fed Army in the world, to provide our Allies with sufficient food to keep them in good fighting condition, and finally to maintain the health and strength of American laborers and American women and children. It's a tremendous job that calls for the patriotic cooperation of every American. Food is a weapon. Food can win the war!

Tuesday, December 29, 1942: —Russia continues to hold the spotlight on the fighting fronts. Moscow's daily communiqué today announced one of the Red Army's greatest triumphs since the start of the winter offensive. Kotelnikovski, a key railroad town ninety miles southwest of Stalingrad has been captured by Soviet troops. Besides the enormous booty captured, including a whole trainload of new Nazi tanks plus seventeen undamaged fighter planes, the victory practically seals the doom of the 300,000 Nazi soldiers trapped before Stalingrad and very nearly closes the lid over the 1,000,000 Axis troops bogged down in the Caucasus. Bring out the Aspirin tablets, Herr Snicklegruber!

French unity in North Africa seems assured since the elevation of General Giraud to High Commissioner. Moreover, French Somaliland, the last Vichy stronghold in Africa, has broken its ties with the Axis dominated French Government and has joined the Allied camp under the leadership of the Fighting French and General de Gaulle.

While these political and behind-the-scene activities have held the spotlight in Africa, American and British forces in Tunisia have been building up their reserves. Active fighting on land has been scarce, due to torrential rains but air activity has increased tremendously in spite of unfavorable flying conditions. The weather Gods permitting, however, it is believed that the Allied ground forces are just about ready to roll forward in an overwhelming tidal wave against the remnants of Axis power on the dark continent. A simultaneous tidal wave can be expected to roll in from the Tripolitania desert in the guise of the British Eighth Army. Beware, Herrenvolk, beware!

Wednesday, December 30, 1942: —Yankee bombers on every war front were busy today. Our planes blasted Japanese bases in the Solomon Islands north of Guadalcanal, sinking two large cargo vessels and damaging several others. It is believed the enemy ships were loaded with supplies intended for the isolated and desperate Jap forces on Guadalcanal.

In Burma, heavy U.S. bombers again attacked Rangoon, scoring many direct hits on shipping in the harbor and setting several huge fires. A 6,000 ton freighter blew up after a direct hit. All of our planes returned to their base without casualty.

American Flying Fortresses based in England struck viciously at a Nazi rattlers' nest last night. It was the German submarine base at Lorient. The invincible Forts shot down nineteen enemy fighters who attempted to intercept them. Only two of the big bombers failed to return but their tons of bombs smashed into the docks and hideouts for the deadly undersea raiders.

In Tunisia, with the ground forces still bogged in the sticky mud, our bombers and P-38 Lightnings strafed and bombed enemy objectives in Sousse and Tunis. Across the way, General Montgomery's triumphant Eighth Army strode ever closer to Tripoli, while his air force constantly harassed the Axis columns fleeing from Tripoli towards Tunisia.

To complete the picture of universal retreat by the enemy at this time, we hear brilliant reports from Russia where the powerful Red Army that Hitler boasted had been destroyed a year ago are smashing forward in a torrent of vengeful destruction toward Rostov and the gate to the Caucasus.

Thursday, December 31, 1942: —Well, we come to the end of another year. As the strains of Auld Lang Syne announce the arrival of the unsuspecting youngster, 1943, we cannot but help glancing backwards at the amazing and epic year just ended. It was a year that started in the deep gloom of defeat and impending danger that seemed almost overwhelming. It ended with hope renewed and the enemy forces of evil in full retreat almost everywhere, a tribute to the most stupendous come-back in the history of the world. In one year, in the face of powerful enemy attack, America has transformed its great and complex peacetime economy into a mighty production machine of war. The full and uncensored story of that achievement will be the most amazing story of all time. As 1942 passes into the limbo of memories, a new horizon of victory is opened up before the people of the Allied Nations. The goal for 1943 is complete and final VICTORY. This is the year of VENGEANCE and JUSTICE to be meted out to the evil gangsters of the world. We shall see the fruits of free men's labors during 1943.

Back on the war news, we hear that a big naval engagement occurred early today between British warships and a German convoy in northern waters. The London communiqué did not disclose the exact location of the fight but indicated that it was the largest naval battle in which German and British ships were involved for over a year. One German cruiser and a destroyer were believed sunk.

The realities of war were brought home forcibly to fifty Bay Area homes today as the War and Navy Departments announced new casualty lists. Fifty local boys and men have been added to the growing roll of those who have made the supreme sacrifice of their lives. The grand total of dead, wounded, or missing now stands at 56,075.

1943

Friday, January 1, 1943: —HAPPY NEW YEAR! It has been a comparatively quiet and peaceful New Year's Day. The weather here has been overcast but warm, with a slight drizzle of rain this afternoon. I slept in this morning for a much needed rest after a safe and sane watching of the going of the old year. This afternoon we listened to America's favorite New Year's Day pastime, the Pasadena Rose Bowl football game. It was Georgia against U.C.L.A. and was an excellent game between two well-matched teams. The final score was Georgia 9, U.C.L.A. 0.

America owes a lot to her love of sports. It has been on the football gridiron, the baseball diamond, and the hockey field, that American boys have learned the team work and spirit that is proving so vital on the field of battle. From the playing fields of America to the battlefields of the world is merely the matter of the changing of a few rules to take the game out of the realm of sport and put it in the realm of "keeps." As American lads excelled in the Olympic Games so will they excel in the deadly game of war.

In grateful remembrance of, and vengeance for, the gallant band of U.S. Marines who battled the Japs to a standstill a year ago on Wake Island, our Army bombers paid that Jap held base a visit on Christmas Eve. The raid took the Japs completely by surprise and hunting was good. The bombers laid 75,000 pounds of "eggs" almost unopposed on the target area. Barracks, oil and gas dumps, and other buildings were left in ruins or on fire. Hundreds of Japs paid for their lack of alertness with their lives. Our planes returned to their base without loss.

Saturday, January 2, 1943: —In a bitter fight that was literally to the death, the Russians won their most important battle of the winter offensive today. For the first time in two winters the Red Army was able to capture one of Hitler's strong points in his winter defense line. The Nazis' whole system of defense has been based on a series of superbly fortified strong points, such as Velikie Luki, Rhev, Smolensk, Kharkov, and Rostov. The fall of any of these would threaten the whole Nazi position and the Soviet troops have finally broken through at Vlikie Luki. The Germans apparently resisted furiously and were annihilated almost to the last man before the flag of the Soviet Republic was raised in victory over the ruined town. Even the Russians admitted that the ferocity of the fighting has not been equaled anywhere, even in Stalingrad.

Every so often the Navy releases a dry communiqué, announcing the results of American submarine activity in enemy waters. Today we learned that our undersea boats have destroyed seven more Japanese cargo vessels and damaged a destroyer in forays that took them right into the enemy's front yard. None of the deadly danger encountered nor the unmatched courage demonstrated by the men who take their fragile craft into the heart of the enemy's territory is mentioned in the communiqué. Nothing but results is given but it does not take the imagination long to picture the countless days and nights of tense and watchful waiting, the wily maneuvering, the desperate and hairbreadth escapes that went into the making of those results. Of all the men in the Navy, none require a more unique and rare type of courage than those who go down to the sea in "pig boats."

Sunday, January 3, 1943: —More good news comes from New Guinea today. General MacArthur's headquarters announced triumphantly that the battle for Buna has ended in complete victory with all Jap troops cleaned out with the exception of a few snipers. The Government Station or Buna Mission area was the last to fall, with the exhausted Japs finally being driven from their strongly entrenched positions. With the liquidation of enemy resistance in the Buna area, there remains only the Jap bases of Lae and Salamaua between the Allied forces and complete occupation of all of New Guinea.

The State Department yesterday released for publication, a white book entitled "Peace and War" summarizing the political events of the decade from 1931 to 1941 that led to the present war. From first reports the book makes startling disclosures that this country had ample warning that the Japanese would open hostilities with the United States by secretly launching a treacherous attack upon Pearl Harbor. The document should make interesting reading.

The Secretary of the Treasury, Henry Morgenthau Jr., announced that the December Victory Bond drive netted an historic total of $12,906,000,000.00, more than 43% over the anticipated goal of nine billion. The success of the drive will obviate the necessity of conducting any more campaigns until April. The Secretary publicly thanked everyone who contributed to the notable achievement, including the banks of the country which cooperated wholeheartedly and efficiently in the tremendous financial task. The grand response of the people to the monetary needs of the Nation should help to quiet some of those who harp that the people must be compelled to save. Voluntary bond buying has done pretty well so far.

Monday, January 4, 1943: —The war news seems to be in one of those infrequent lulls today. Action on all fronts has died down for one reason or another. In Tunisia it's because of the inclement weather. In Libya, General Montgomery has paused momentarily to bring up supplies and reinforcements across the desert wastes from Benghazi. Rommel appears to be preparing a determined stand at Wadi Zem Zem, the last natural defensive position between the British and Tripoli. You can be sure that the pause on this front will be of short duration. The triumphant Eighth Army is not going to allow Rommel much time to recuperate.

In Russia the lull is purely a breather after the Russian victory at Velikie Luki. The Red Army is also reported to be massing on the southern front for another major attack against the trapped Nazis in Stalingrad and the Caucasus.

In New Guinea, all major resistance by the Japs has ceased in the Buna area and MacArthur's seasoned veterans, both Australian and American, are taking time out to mop up the few remaining Jap hideouts before setting out on the next phase of the New Guinea campaign.

On the home front another and equally as bitter a war is being waged against the unbridled forces of nature. Rampaging rivers in Ohio, Kentucky, and Oregon have inundated thousands of acres of land, driving many hundreds of families from their homes, causing untold damage and claiming several victims. It is the age old story of man against river as flood crests of seven to nine feet swept over the banks and levees of the Ohio and Willamette rivers, sweeping aside all the puny attempts of man to confine them to their allotted channels.

Tuesday, January 5, 1943: —Several items of home front news top the war picture tonight. Shortages of several food commodities have become acute. This is especially true of meat. Conditions in the meat industry have reached the stage where hundreds of butchers are giving up. Butcher shops by the dozens are closing up simply because there is no meat to sell and the employees are taking jobs in the shipyards. It is hard to believe that the supply of fresh meat has practically disappeared when it was so plentiful just a short time ago. It would be interesting to know the real reason behind it.

Off and on since the start of hostilities, labor disputes have cropped up in war industries that have defied solution until the President has been obliged to step in and order the men back on their jobs. In every case the President's command has been immediately obeyed. But at the present time a strike of a small group of CIO machinists in a vital Alameda shipyard has caused a serious interference with important war work since the first of the year. Unable to settle the dispute otherwise, the President issued a stern warning and order to the men and their union to return to their work but for the first time his order has apparently been defied. The machinists are still on strike and show no signs of complying with the directive from the President. It will be interesting to watch developments.

Another sore spot in the home news is the unfavorable report received today of results obtained at Japanese relocation centers. Rather than being ideal and self-sustaining communities, the centers in many cases have turned into a nightmare of confusion, loafing, waste of food, refusal to work and even threats against construction workers. Maybe the Japs are treated a little too well.

Wednesday, January 6, 1943: —The shipyard machinists finally yielded to the pressure being put on them and agreed to return to work tomorrow. Their action and others like it are doing the labor movement no good. The public as well as the Armed Forces and the Government is getting fed up with slow-downs, delays, and work stoppages caused by jurisdictional disputes between labor unions, prompted and directed by some labor leaders who would feather their own nests even at the expense of the National war effort. The people will not tolerate it for very long in times like these.

The 78th Congress of the United States convened today and President Roosevelt will make his annual State of the Nation address before a joint session tomorrow forenoon. The new Congress is facing tremendous problems that cry out for solution and indications are that the days of "rubber stamp" power to the President are over. Many new members are present, including a large number of Republicans, and it is expected that Congress will exercise a great deal more of its power to legislate than did the previous body.

The fighting in Russia is still going favorably for the Red Army. The German rout in the Don Valley and the Caucasus is steadily growing, with numerous inhabited localities and untold booty being captured by the hard-driving Soviet troops. The major objective of the Russians is the clamping of the lid down on the Nazi Caucasian army by retaking Rostov. If this can be accomplished, all of Hitler's bloody and expensive summer gains will have been practically wiped out.

Reports from the South Pacific indicate that the Japs are amassing another great armada at Rabaul for a smash at our Solomons positions. Admiral Halsey will be ready for them.

Thursday, January 7, 1943: —The biggest news of the day is of course President Roosevelt's annual message to Congress on the state of the Nation. The speech on the whole was cheerful and the President pointed with pride to the enormous accomplishments of our production lines during the past year. "The Arsenal of Democracy is making good," he said. We produced 48,000 military planes during 1942 and are now turning them out at the rate of 66,000 per year. That is more than all three Axis nations combined. A million and one half fighting men have been transported to fighting fronts throughout the world and are being supplied. Tank and armored car production is enormous and the production of guns and bullets he numbered in the thousands and millions. "Yes, the Nazis and the Fascists have asked for it—and they are going to get it," announced the President amid resounding cheers.

On the less optimistic side, the President warned of more necessity for civilian sacrifice and shortages and called for post-war planning and unity among the Allied Nations to solve the tremendous problems of peace. By dint of all-out effort on the part of every citizen, coupled with hard and costly fighting on the part of our armed forces, he foresees a definite possibility of complete victory in 1944. We have stopped the enemy and are now on the highroad to Tokyo, Berlin, and Rome.

On the war fronts, the Nazis, for the first time, acknowledged some of the seriousness of their Russian positions. They admit that their troops are in full retreat in the Caucasus, probably to avoid being bottled up should the Soviets succeed in retaking Rostov. A new shipment of aspirin has been sent posthaste to Berchtesgaden.

Friday, January 8, 1943: —General MacArthur released his longest communiqué of the war today in summarizing the results of his New Guinea campaign. The operation which can now be considered as successfully completed resulted in the total annihilation of a Japanese army of 15,000 veteran troops under Lieut. General Horii and the killing of an untold but large number of additional Japs in several unsuccessful attempts at landing reinforcements. 539 enemy planes were definitely destroyed, six cruisers, 13 destroyers, 1 destroyer tender, two sea-plane tenders, two gunboats, 83 merchant ships and 200 landing barges were destroyed or so badly damaged as to be of little further use. In addition, Port Moresby was saved and two valuable Japanese bases captured. This victory, accomplished under the most adverse conditions, is the worst defeat the Japs have yet suffered in this war. General MacArthur can now feel partially revenged for Bataan and Corregidor. But the General has only begun to fight.

Additional important fighting is developing in the South Pacific. A battle that may equal Midway in size and importance is shaping up as the Japs are amassing huge numbers of men and ships in obvious preparations for a large scale operation in some major theater. Allied bombers today hopped eagerly on a large enemy convoy sighted in the Huon Gulf between New Britain and New Guinea and sank a large transport loaded to the gunwales with Japanese troops. Another transport was left in flames.

The recent lull in fighting on all fronts appears to be over as ferocious new aerial blows were struck at Kiska, Tunisia, Libya, the Ruhr Valley, the North Atlantic Convoy lanes, and in Russia. Ground activity is picking up and is especially sanguinary in Russia. Death by wholesale rides the highways and skyways.

Saturday, January 9, 1943: —In continuing attacks on a Japanese convoy off Lae, New Guinea, General MacArthur's heavy bombers succeeded in sending a second and third enemy transport to the bottom with many Jap soldiers drowning. A fourth transport was damaged and 73 Jap planes were shot down in the three day battle.

American planes also attacked enemy bases on Bougainville Island and Rekata Bay on the Island of Santa Isabel in the Solomons. Our planes apparently came from Henderson field on Guadalcanal. Much damage was caused among enemy installations on the Islands attacked but two American planes were downed by extremely heavy anti-aircraft fire. In addition to the Solomons raid, Liberator heavy bombers from Alaska smashed at the Jap base at Kiska. Results were not observed.

Latest reports from the North African front also indicate that American air power is rapidly gaining dominance in that theater. Bizerte was raided three times in one day and resulted in the heaviest damage since the beginning of the campaign. Eight Nazi planes were shot down against the loss of five American craft. In Libya, Allied planes strafed fleeing enemy units to within 35 miles of the big Axis base of Tripoli. The Eighth Army planes then hopped over into Tunisia to join with the American forces in an attack on Tunis and Sfax. The increased tempo of Allied air activity is probably the result of Major General Carl Spaatz's appointment as commander-in-chief of all Allied air forces in North Africa. Clouds don't gather under the wings of General Spaatz's planes.

Sunday, January 10, 1943: —The Soviet armies are driving closer to the vital key city of Rostov. All of Hitler's bloodily earned gains of the summer campaign seem likely to be washed out if the Russians retake Rostov. The Germans are fully aware of this fact and even the Russians admit that they are fighting fiercely and desperately in a supreme effort to halt the Russian steamroller.

The aerial warfare rose to a violent pitch over this weekend. In Tunisia, Allied bombers and P-38 Lightnings subjected Bizerte and Tunis to their most devastating attacks while other American planes raided as far east as Tripoli where they joined with Britain's Eighth Army flyers in a bombing and strafing attack against Rommel's much-harried Afrika Korps.

In the South Pacific, the proportions of the American victory over a large Japanese convoy continued to mount. In addition to four heavily loaded transports sunk, the mighty Flying Fortresses and the "Lightning" escorts shot down a total of over 173 enemy planes. Once again the Flying Forts have proved that it is practically suicide to oppose them with their formidable armament of 50 caliber machine guns.

Signs of the times on the home front:

For the first time a landlord was convicted in Federal Court of violating OPA regulations on rents. The rent gouger, as he was called, was sentenced to six months in jail and $1,100.

Pleasure driving was recently banned. Yesterday, two young men were arrested for "parking" with their girlfriends. That comes under pleasure driving.

Monday, January 11, 1943: —President Roosevelt today submitted to the new Congress his war budget for the next fiscal year. The total was an astronomical $108,903,047,923.00, the largest ever contemplated in the history of the world. It was "maximum effort" budget, as the President called it and would call for harsh belt-tightening on the part of all the citizenry. "There is no easy, pleasant way to wage total war," he said. "Production of goods should be simplified and standardized; unnecessary costs and frills should be eliminated. Total war demands the simplification of American life." I guess we're really in for it. Our lot will be more and more regimentation, onerous though it may be, heavier and heavier taxes, less and less amusement, harder and harder work, longer and longer hours, and countless inconveniences. Not a pleasant prospect but the expected price of victory.

Speaking of inconveniences, the meat situation in the Bay Area has become critical. For several weeks now, housewives have found it almost impossible to obtain fresh meat. In our home, for example, we haven't had a Sunday roast for a month—and the last one was pickled pork. We can't remember what a roast of beef tastes like. Among the main reasons for the shortage is the vast increase of population in this area due to defense industries and the rationing of the meat supply on the basis of pre-war population figures. Some action toward relieving the situation is expected soon.

Some of the boys at work say that if things continue the way they are, they'll be joining the Army to get a square meal.

Tuesday, January 12, 1943: —More tragic news was announced by the Navy late last night. It was to be expected that eventually our inevitable losses in the terrific naval battles in the South Pacific during October and November would become known as soon as the information would be of no use to the enemy, but even so, the knowledge was still a shock. In fierce engagements that twice frustrated Japan's desperate effort to retake Guadalcanal, the American fleet lost the cruisers Atlanta, Juneau and Northampton, the aircraft carrier Hornet, and the destroyers Laffey, Cushing, Monssen, Barton, Preston, Walker, and Benham. Casualties were not announced but were undoubtedly heavy. The cruiser Juneau, for example, apparently blew up with all hands, including five brothers named Sullivan. What a blow that little telegram from the Navy Department must have been to the Sullivan home. Although the Japs lost heavily in ships and men, besides losing the battles, their whole fleet isn't worth the lives of those gallant men.

The Nazis and Russians are still doing their part to keep the grisly mill of war grinding out its mass of human wreckage. But it's going worse for the Germans than the Russians at the present time. Fresh Soviet reserves brought up from the Siberian training camps are battering the trapped German forces in the Caucasus. The Berlin radio acknowledged the seriousness of the situation and admits that the Red Army has broken through their main line on the southern front. Quite an admission for the boastful Goebbels.

In Tripolitania, Tunisia, New Guinea and Guadalcanal, Allied forces are scoring new gains against the enemy. Naples, Italy was bombed again last night, causing heavy damage.

Wednesday, January 13, 1943: —The slaughter continues on a grand scale today, especially in Russia, where the inexhaustible Red Army has launched a fifth major offensive in the vicinity of Veronezh, the Soviet stronghold in the upper Don Basin. The Germans themselves reported this new attack and admitted further Russian gains in the Caucasus. At the rate the Nazis are backtracking, another sixty days will see them thrown back to the point from which they launched their summer offensive. Hitler's chances of ever knocking the Russians out of the war have all gone a glimmering in the face of the magnificent Soviet resistance.

The reputation of the Boeing Flying Fortresses is growing by leaps and bounds wherever they have met the enemy, whether he be Jap or Nazi. Today, in a brilliant raid on Marshall Rommel's base at Tripoli, the big "Forts" accounted for at least 34 and possibly 44 Axis planes which were destroyed on the ground and in the air. The big ships are so well armored and have such tremendous fire power that they are capable of defending themselves under any kind of odds. The crews of the Fortresses love them because they get them to their targets and bring them home again, almost without fail.

The same story is true in the South Pacific. Tropical rains have bogged down the ground forces in New Guinea but the Flying Fortresses keep pouring it to them, rain or shine. Lae and Salamaua were the principal targets today. Much damage and large fires were started among supplies and shore installations and at least three Jap Zero planes were shot down by the accurate American gunners.

Thursday, January 14, 1943: —Except for Russia, the war today is largely in the air. British bombers have started anew their program of nightly bombing of German industrial regions. They have apparently changed their tactics from mighty 1,000 plane raids at long intervals to nightly attacks by smaller forces in order to maintain steady pressure against the frayed nerves of Germany's populace and to harass without surcease the strained home-front defenses of the Third Reich.

Allied forces in North Africa are also pounding steadily away at Axis positions in Tunisia. The main activity is by air craft and the French have organized a reversed version of the famous

Lafayette Escadrille. This time it is American planes being piloted by ambitious young French patriots.

In New Guinea, MacArthur's Air Force has achieved complete dominance of the skyways. B-17 Flying Fortresses, B-25 Mitchell bombers, and crack P-38 fighters have practically wiped out Japanese air power in that theater of action. Some attacks on Lae and Salamaua have been made without fighter opposition of any kind.

In the Solomons it was the famous PT torpedo boats that got in their lick today. The lightning fast and effective little boats pounced on an enemy flotilla of destroyers that was attempting to supply the isolated Jap garrison on Guadalcanal and routed them. Two and possibly three of the enemy vessels were hit with torpedoes. The PT boats came out of it unscathed.

Friday, January 15, 1943: —An unsavory morsel of home front news was revealed today as the F.B.I. cracked down on hundreds of draft law violators. It appears that among the citizenry there are a few who would avoid at all costs their patriotic obligation of fighting for their country if called. Upon these, including many single men without dependents, the wrath of the law is descending. Heavy penalties await them.

The Allied outlook in North Africa is considerably darkened by petty political sniping on the part of rival French factions, aided and abetted by a small but influential section of the British press. This section of the British public is favoring immediate installation of General Charles de Gaulle and his Fighting Frenchmen in power over North Africa, to the exclusion of General Giraud and his followers who have the support of our General Eisenhower and the American army of occupation. The attendant squabble is seriously distracting Eisenhower's attention and energies from his more important and difficult task of defeating the rapidly growing Axis armies in Tunisia. Unless Roosevelt and Churchill get together on a solution, the effect could be disastrous.

Local excitement here at home such as blackouts and invasion scares like those of a year ago has been absent for a long time. Apparently our victories in the Pacific at Midway and Guadalcanal have eliminated practically all possibility of an actual attack on our shores. The war is still a long way off except on the economic and financial fronts. We are plagued with annoying food shortages, high living costs that make us squirm even before we contemplate the tremendous taxes either here or on the way. The 5% Victory Tax went into effect, beginning with today's paycheck.

Saturday, January 16, 1943: —Things are still shaping up favorably for the Allies on all the major battlegrounds. The resilient Russian Army crashed through powerful German defenses in the Donets River area today. It was a bloody battle that swept the Soviet troops to within 90 miles of Rostov. Seven unpronounceable towns were recaptured. A thousand miles to the north Marshal Timoshenko made new gains in his drive to free Leningrad from its long and bitter siege.

American and British forces in Tunisia appear to be almost ready to launch their main attack against Nazi held Tunis and Bizerte. The American air force is rapidly gaining that all important air superiority over the battle field. Twenty-four Axis planes, including seven huge troop laden transports, were shot down today against the loss of eight American fighters. That's good hunting. Rumor also has it that at least one gunner in the lost Nazi planes was a woman. Old man Hitler must be getting pretty desperate.

On the other side of the earth, in the South Pacific, where our nasty little yellow enemy does his dirty work, we find that General MacArthur is still taking very good care of them. Just as at Gona and Buna, the General's troops are pinning the Japanese forces to the sea at Sanananda Point on the North New Guinea coast. Meanwhile our bombers are continuing their relentless aerial offensive against the big Jap bases of Lae and Rabaul. Only defensive action is being taken by the enemy, the initiative and offensive is ours. Contrast this with the situation of a year ago.

Sunday, January 17, 1943: —For the first time in thirteen months the British bombed Berlin last night. Apparently the Germans were caught flatfooted as only one Allied bomber was lost. It was either that or the Nazis have moved all their crack anti-aircraft gunners elsewhere due to manpower shortage and the fact that they believed Berlin safe from attack. In any event the British flyers reported extremely inaccurate "flak" as they subjected the city to the crunch and smash of two ton and four ton "block-busters." It was believed certain that heavy damage was inflicted.

Axis reports state that General Montgomery's British Eighth Army is attacking again. The enemy reports said that the attack was aimed at Rommel's positions at Wadi Zem-Zem, 180 miles from Tripoli. No confirmation has been heard from any Allied source as yet.

Late radio reports just heard stated that the German Luftwaffe has made a retaliatory raid of small dimensions on London. Four Nazi planes were downed in the much lighter raid than was expected by the British. Apparently the Germans are much too busy on other fronts.

Berlin may be getting it again tonight from all indications. All radios in Berlin and the rest of Germany were off the air indicating that Allied bombers were at their appointed tasks. It's your year to take it, Fritz!

Further indication of Germany's anxiety and uncertainty about the future comes in reports that the Nazis are feverishly building an "East Wall" in Poland to supplement their famous "West Wall" facing France. Poles and Jews are doing the work of course, with death as their reward.

Monday, January 18, 1943: —The RAF smashed at Berlin again last night, adding fuel to the fires that were set the night before. Returning pilots claim that large sections of the Nazi capital have been reduced to a condition comparable to that of Cologne and Essen. British plane losses were much heavier than the first night's raid when only one bomber was shot down. Last night twenty-two of the attacking planes failed to return, due in large part to bad weather and the lack of surprise such as was achieved the first time. Even so, the percentage of loss was not prohibitive in view of the large number of planes involved.

After sixteen months of grim siege in which no quarter was give or asked, the Russians have succeeded in freeing Leningrad from the bloody claws of the "fascist devils." Communications were finally established with Soviet forces southeast of the city through the recapture of the fortress city of Schlusselburg. More than 13,000 Germans were killed and incalculable quantities of booty were seized in the offensive that brought relief to the almost starved but courageous defenders of the second largest city in Russia.

The British Eighth Army is rolling ahead in Tripolitania. Apparently, Marshal Rommel has given up hope of making a successful stand short of Tripoli and has abandoned his strong lines at Wadi Zem-Zem. Allied superiority in the air is swinging the balance in our favor. It is also believed likely that the Eighth Army will achieve contact at any moment with the Fighting French Army coming up through the desert from the Lake Chad area. The old squeeze play is working.

Tuesday, January 19, 1943: —General MacArthur announced today in a special communiqué that his Australian and American troops have taken Sanananda Point, the last Jap stronghold in Papuan New Guinea. Fiercely fighting American and Australian infantrymen have thus succeeded in completing the annihilation of the once proud army of crack Japanese troops that several months ago started confidently out on an offensive aimed at Port Moresby and Australia proper. The extent of MacArthur's victory has not yet been fully appraised.

British troops in Tripolitania have driven to within thirty miles of the big Axis base of Tripoli and it is believed that only a miracle can save that vital enemy stronghold from the triumphant Eighth Army. It is rumored that Rommel has already abandoned the city with most of his units and is dashing headlong for Tunisia, were Axis forces are locked in a muddy stalemate with the British First Army and the American Fifth Army. The first ground action of any consequence occurred today when U.S. and French troops beat off a strong German attack in central Tunisia. Weather conditions, however, are abominable and make ground action almost impossible.

The weather here at home has also been inclement. Nights have been unusually cold for the Bay Area, while fog and rain have added to the discomfort. But discomforts such as weather are nothing compared to the inconveniences being encountered in food, transportation, taxation, regulations, and other every-day conditions caused by war. Many of these home-front problems will be equally as hard if not harder than those encountered on the field of battle. It's everybody's war.

Wednesday, January 20, 1943: —The most important news today comes from Tripolitania. British Eighth Army units are reported to have penetrated into the outskirts of Tripoli and are encountering only a feeble rear guard resistance from Marshal Rommel's defeated Afrika Korps. It is hinted that the Nazi General himself is already in Tunisia and has no intention of defending the vital Axis base at Tripoli. The majority of his troops are already in headlong flight westward from the base and are being unmercifully battered by avenging squadrons of Allied fighter and bombing planes. According to returning flyers the road from Tripoli to the Tunisian border is a "straffer's paradise" with hundreds of wrecked and burning vehicles blocking the highways and causing unimaginable confusion among the fleeing enemy.

These facts foretell what is almost certainly the beginning of the end for the Axis in Africa, and the Allies are giving them no respite from vicious air attacks aimed at preventing any possible attempt at evacuating the remnants of their forces in another "Dunkirk." Nothing short of total annihilation or capture will satisfy the Allies, especially the British who vividly remember their own bitter experience on the English Channel shore more than two years ago.

In Russia the powerful Red Army offensive in the Caucasus is gaining momentum. Several more inhabited localities with unpronounceable names were recaptured including a major rail junction leading from the Maikop oilfields. The Soviet armies are also threatening breakthroughs on the Veronezh and Kharkov sectors, with heavy losses in men and equipment being inflicted on the Fascists.

Thursday, January 21, 1943: —The elements gave the San Francisco Bay Area a bombardment last night and today in the form of heavy rains, swept in with terrific gales that uprooted trees, knocked over light poles, and lifted roofs off of many flimsy Housing Project homes. Hundreds of defense workers were made homeless and four persons lost their lives. One death was caused when a barrage balloon that was being "bedded" down against the wind, exploded, killing one member of the ground crew and seriously injuring nine others. Power lines throughout the area were knocked down, dousing all electrical power and thoroughly disrupting business and transportation facilities. It was a vicious attack by an enemy that gives no quarter and cannot successfully be opposed.

Chile, one of the two South American countries that balked at breaking with the Axis has finally seen the light and announced yesterday that she is severing diplomatic relations with Germany, Italy, and Japan effective immediately. This action leaves only Argentina maintaining relations with our enemies and preventing complete Pan-American solidarity in the present struggle. Argentina's position is becoming increasingly embarrassing and experts believe she cannot stay off the bandwagon much longer.

All major battles on all principal fronts are progressing favorably for the United Nations except the Battle of the Atlantic. Germany has apparently loosed a tremendous number of submarine wolf packs on Allied shipping lanes and sinking's are occurring at an alarming rate. Many valuable cargoes are going to the bottom and the situation is admittedly serious.

Friday, January 22, 1943: —Violent storms continued to lash the California coastline today and tonight as this record is written a heavy rain is being lashed about by wind of near gale proportions. Northern California Rivers are rising dangerously and at least one, the Bear River near Wheatland, has broken a levee, inundating thousands of acres and causing much damage. No immediate relief is forecast as the Weather Bureau warned that new storms were on the way.

Back from the war of nature to the war of men, we find that the British Eighth Army has succeeded in smashing the main defenses of Tripoli and its complete occupation by victorious British troops is only a matter of hours. British artillery commands the entire city from vantage points on surrounding heights. Captured Italians report that the Nazi Afrika Korps is beating a hasty retreat to the Tunisian border after assigning rear guard defense to the Italian Allies. Marshal Rommel is expected to attempt a stand along the Mareth line in Tunisia, also known as the little Maginot line, built by the French to protect their colonial frontier against Italian aggression.

Russia's winter offensive is growing in proportions even greater than last year's. Today the Moscow communiqué reported the capture of Salsk, key rail junction approximately 100 miles southeast of Rostov. The circle around 22 trapped Nazi divisions before Stalingrad is drawing smaller and tighter with the position of the Germans almost hopeless. Even the German high command acknowledged the seriousness of the situation, reporting Soviet break throughs in several sectors.

Saturday, January 23, 1943: —The last vestige of Benito Mussolini's hard won colonial empire vanished today as the triumphant British Eighth Army hoisted the Union Jack over Tripoli. This act was the climax of the remarkable offensive launched only three months ago by General Sir Bernard L. Montgomery that totally defeated the powerful Afrika Korps at Alamein in Egypt and pursued the beaten enemy across 1,400 miles of Libyan Desert. The capture of the "Jewel City" of the former Italian empire was a terrible blow to the suffering Italian people. It is expected that their waning morale will drop to a new low when they fully realize to what depths the treacherous acts of their Fascist leaders have led them. They will be ripe for invasion this spring.

War in the South Pacific has quieted down some. MacArthur's men are busy mopping up the remnants of the Japanese Papuan Army around Sanananda Point while his heavy bombers are staging daily attacks on enemy shipping at Lae, Salamaus, and Rabaul. On Guadalcanal, it's the Army now. Regular Army troops have replaced the Marines, whose job is finished, and have already shown their mettle by capturing an important Jap strong point on Mount Austen.

Here at home the storms that raged for two days have somewhat died down with the Army and Navy searching frantically for two huge transport planes missing since contact was last made with them by radio over the Bay Area as they groped blindly through the storm for a landing place. One carried nineteen passengers, the other six.

Sunday, January 24, 1943: —No trace has yet been found of the two transport planes reported lost in the storm yesterday. Weather conditions continued bad this morning but cleared off this evening. Storm damage throughout the area was large and the peril of floods from swollen rivers is mounting hourly.

War news today remained very cheerful. The British Eighth Army is still pursuing the Axis forces west of Tripoli while U.S. and British planes strafed and bombed the enemy's line of retreat, causing tremendous havoc and littering the trail with smashed men, equipment, and supplies. By Italian admission, the Battle of North Africa is coming to an end.

The mighty offensive of the Russian Red Army, stretching from the Baltic to the Caucasus, is sweeping the Germans westward all along the lines. The Russians are nearing the vital goals of Kharkov and Rostov in many pronged drives that leave but little doubt as to the final outcome. By German admission, their position is extremely critical.

The only unpleasant item in the war news tonight is the disclosure of an outrageous rent gouging scandal at Vallejo, the home of the Mare Island Navy Yard. Naval heroes, bringing their gallant ships in for repairs, have attempted to also bring their families in for a much deserved reunion, only to be gouged with unbelievably high rents by landlords who illegally charged as high as $150.00 per month for one dirty room. The OBA is finally stepping in.

Monday, January 25, 1943: —Home front problems hold the spotlight tonight. The food situation is particularly critical and Food Administrator Claude R. Wickard today warned that an additional 3,500,000 farm workers must be found somehow before summer if agriculture in general is to avoid a breakdown. Here on the west coast and especially in the San Francisco Bay Area the supply of fresh meat is practically exhausted with no signs of relief discernible in the near future. Tempers of the people are growing shorter over the scarcity of meat and in at least two instances, irate and hungry shipyard workers have beaten up butchers whose ice boxes and showcases were barren. Other defense workers are complaining vehemently that they must have their steaks and chops if they are to retain their strength. It will take direct action by the authorities in Washington D.C. if relief is to be had, but they apparently have no intention of taking a hand until point system rationing goes into effect this spring.

Other home front problems that are making this war real for civilians are the transportation and labor problems. The way they jam workers into the streetcars and busses makes sardines look like hermits. Furthermore, those overworked trains, busses, and streetcars are going to wear out all at once if this war lasts much longer. It's really a problem that calls for aspirin.

Labor disputes between the CIO, AFL, and the NLRB recently are threatening the whole west coast shipbuilding industry. AFL leaders are threatening to cancel their "No strike for the duration" promise unless the NLRB and the rival CIO quit picking on them.

Tuesday, January 26, 1943: —All morning and evening papers today carried the announcement that war news of transcendent importance would soon be released. The peoples' attention and curiosity were aroused to the breaking point and then the first big news came over the radios this evening. President Roosevelt and Winston Churchill, together with the combined high military staffs of the two great nations, have met for a ten day conference under the very noses of the Nazi foe— in North Africa near Casablanca. It was stunning news even to bigwigs in Washington D.C. most of who did not even know that the President was out of town. It was another famous precedent breaking episode by Mr. Roosevelt who flew to the rendezvous in North Africa by Clipper and four motor bomber with all the spirit and daring of a Marine lieutenant on Guadalcanal. It was the first time an american President had left the country during a war and the first time any such trip had been made by plane.

The purpose of the conference was to map out the offensive strategy to win the war with the least possible delay. Defense is over; from now on it is ATTACK, determined, unrelenting, smashing ATTACK! Roosevelt, in today's press conference, called the meeting the "Unconditional Surrender" meeting. He called it so because the United Nations have pledged themselves to regain peace but not until we have received the unconditional surrender of Germany, Italy, and Japan. No matter what the cost or how difficult the road, we will not stop until the Axis forces of enslavement are totally destroyed.

The sensational news sent a clarion note of hope ringing throughout the saddened and oppressed countries of Europe and Asia and sent a chill of alarm down the spines of guilty Axis oppressors.

Wednesday, January 27, 1943: —The papers today are, of course, filled with details of the epic making conference between President Roosevelt and Prime Minister Churchill. The meeting was held in Casablanca, which name itself means "White House."

The real accomplishments of the meeting were not divulged but will undoubtedly come to light in the form of violent action. Already the first hint of what is to come is shown by today's heavy raid by American planes on the great German naval base at Wilhelmshaven. It was the first raid on Germany proper by American pilots and planes—but it will not be the last.

Many rumors are spread of what went on in North Africa during the last ten days, even to reports that secret representatives of Finland and Italy were present, discussing plans to take their countries out of the war. This, of course, is not confirmed.

The only criticism and disappointment expressed in connection with the meeting was the fact that Stalin and Chiang Kai Shek did not see fit to attend or at least to send a top ranking representative. Russia in particular seems bent on conducting a private war of its own without collaborating fully with the other United Nations. This fact gives rise to worries over the future attitude of the Soviets, especially around a peace table. Stalin's excuse for not attending the meeting was that he is too busy conducting his great winter offensive—which may be very true—but does not explain the absence of a first-rate representative.

Thursday, January 28, 1943: —Important news today revealed that beginning February 1, draft boards will begin filling combined quotas for the Army, Navy, Marine Corps, and Coast Guard. Previously the Navy and Marines accepted only voluntary enlistments which was really part of their tradition. Manpower needs, however, made it imperative to obtain the necessary men in an orderly and controllable manner. Now all men from 18 to 38 who are called up will be assigned to the service for which they are best suited in the judgment of the draft boards and Army and Navy representatives. Preference may be indicated by the draftee and will be followed by the draft officials, if at all possible.

An incident that was overshadowed by North African news for the last few days was the large scale revolt of French citizens in Marseille against orders of the Nazis to evacuate their homes so that the Germans could prepare for an eventual Allied invasion attempt. Nazi guns were able to quell the uprising only after

306

hundreds of men, women, and children, were cut down. Unrest throughout Europe is mounting.

London reports state that Adolf Hitler has finally relinquished command of the German Army to his military leaders after having completely failed to conquer Russia by "intuition." The Nazi high command will now try to extricate the Reichwehr from the disastrous predicament in which their "Napoleon" has plunged it.

The Pacific war is in a temporary lull, the only activity being reported in the Aleutian Islands. The Army has also announced its intention of accepting loyal American citizens of Japanese ancestry for service in the army. A separate unit will be organized.

Friday, January 29, 1943:— In another move, President Roosevelt paid a visit to Brazil on his way home from North Africa, stopping off at Natal, Brazil for a conference with the Brazilian President Vargas. Although details of the conference are lacking, it is believed that Roosevelt's aim is to bring Brazil more actively into the war against the Axis, even to the sending of troops to Africa. The submarine menace in the Atlantic also was a subject for discussion, with the South American Republic being urged to assume full responsibility for the patrolling of South Atlantic waters. From all indications, President Vargas was most receptive, as were the Brazilian people who wildly cheered the two American Presidents.

U.S. bombers really plastered the Axis base at Sfax in Tunisia today. It was the largest single bombing raid of the campaign and practically devastated the base. More and even bigger raids were promised in what is undoubtedly and preliminary "artillery" pounding before the "big push."

Aerial activity in the South Pacific has stepped up recently with MacArthur's big bombers smashing at the big Jap base at Rabaul, New Britain in an effort to break up a growing concentration of Japanese warships and transports in what is obviously preparation for another major offensive move. Two enemy destroyers, two cargo vessels, one tanker, and ten planes were destroyed in the latest attack.

Saturday, January 30, 1943: —Corpulent Hermann Goering and the weasel Paul Joseph Goebbels, the assistant Fuehrers of

Nazi Germany, were scheduled to make magnificent radio speeches today in honor and celebration of the tenth anniversary of the mighty Hitler's rise to power. The speeches were to begin promptly at 11:O'clock. But it was not the ranting voices of the Nazi leaders that was heard, it was the crump and smash of British bombs. Yes, for the first time in the war, British bombers were over Berlin in daylight, timed perfectly to drop their potent calling cards in Goering's and Goebbels's laps. They were fast Mosquito bombers that lashed out of an overcast sky with such speed and surprise that their mission was successfully completed with the loss of only one plane. And the magnificent speeches were delayed a full hour—even the Fuehrer's message which was delivered by Master Goebbels as proxy for addled Adolf who was away somewhere "with his soldiers."

The vise is closing on Marshal Rommel and his tattered Afrika Korps. British patrols from the conquering Eighth Army have already crossed the Tunisian border thus completing the final destruction of Italy's colonial empire and driving the Axis forces into the uncertain protection of the Mareth line in Tunisia. These defensive positions, probably obsolete from lack of use, will be subjected to pressure from front and rear by both the British forces and the powerful American forces moving up from the west.

Sunday, January 31, 1943: —The Nation breathed a sigh of relief today as it learned that the globe-trotting President was safe in the White House again. He arrived with members of his staff in a private train from Miami, Florida where he had disembarked from the huge flying ship that brought him from Brazil by way of Trinidad where he inspected the big naval base.

The war news tonight is full of more Allied successes. In Russia, the Red Army has practically completed the annihilation of the Nazi army of 320,000 men trapped before Stalingrad. Another 18,000 troops were captured today, including a German Field Marshal and six other generals. Only one small pocket of resistance remains.

In Tunisia, Allied air power is asserting itself in heavy raids against Axis bases in Bizerte and Sfax, with American ground forces slowly closing in on the latter. General Montgomery's Eighth Army patrols have already crossed the Tunisian border, hot on the heels of the retreating Afrika Korps.

War Secretary Frank Knox has just arrived in Pearl Harbor after an inspection trip of our South Pacific positions and confidently predicts the complete ousting of Japanese forces from Guadalcanal within thirty days and warns Japan to prepare for more and bigger raids on Tokyo in the near future. "We are going to lick them," he says.

Late radio reports state that the big navy flying boat carrying nineteen persons that was lost over the San Francisco Bay Area during the recent storm has been located, smashed against a mountain peak in northern California. It was sighted from the air but no signs of life were observed.

February

Monday, February 1, 1943: —It was learned today that Prime Minister Churchill proceeded from the Casablanca meeting to Turkey where he conferred with the President of that country. Agreement was reached on plans for the strengthening and elaboration of details of the alliance now in existence between Britain and Turkey. The results of the conference put strategic Turkey more solidly in the Allied camp in exchange for continued and increased Allied aid, particularly in war supplies from the United States. Both President Roosevelt and Josef Stalin were personally informed of the results.

Heavy fighting is reported from North Africa tonight. American troops are involved in violent counter-attacks launched against powerful German infantry, artillery, and tank forces that yesterday cracked through the lightly held French line sixty miles west of Sfax in a drive aimed at widening the corridor through which the fleeing Afrika Korps might escape to join forces with other Axis units in Tunisia. Present indications are that the American attack is gaining ground against fierce resistance.

Events within Germany indicate growing dissatisfaction and unrest. Grand Admiral Erich Raeder has been dismissed as commander-in-chief of the German Navy and this together with news that Field Marshal Friedrich von Paulus and sixteen other Axis generals have been killed or captured on the Stalingrad front, further coupled with additional defeats in North Africa and more devastating raids by the RAF has sent a wave of discouragement over the Reich. Hitler's message, as well as that of the German newspapers, is starting the old whine about Versailles, Wilson's 14 points, and other excuses for causing this war.

Tuesday, February 2, 1943: —War manpower commissioner McNutt today warned all married men to get into war work or be drafted. He said that by 1944 ten out of every fourteen able-bodied men between the ages of 18 and 38 will be in the armed forces. Children or other dependents will not defer a man who is not already working in a defense industry.

An unusual draft case occurred at the Bank this week. One of our employees, a married man with a working wife, had previously been placed in class 4-F because of a very peculiar affliction. Since birth he had not been able to eat sugar of any kind whether in pure form or in fruits or vegetables. Medical science has no record of a parallel case but several doctors, including, I believe, Mayo Clinic doctors had verified the man's claim that sugar of any kind caused him violent sickness that could be fatal, His case had appeared in Ripley's Believe It or Not. Recently, despite all this evidence, this man was reclassified in 1-A and has now been inducted. Unless he can be placed in some army job where he can choose and pick his own food, he will likely prove to be a liability if not an actual charge of the Government. It's cases like this that substantiate the standing draft joke to the effect that "you're in—unless your seeing-eye dog has flat feet."

Not much has been heard from the South Pacific front lately. Today, however, Japanese reports state that a big naval battle is in progress, with the usual exaggerated claims of U.S. losses. No confirmation of the action has come from American sources but the possibility that action has transpired is likely in view of recent Jap preparations.

Wednesday, February 3, 1943: —The United States Navy today confirmed reports emanating from Tokyo that Japanese and American fleet units, both air and surface, are engaged in another pitched battle in the Solomons area. The battle was variously described by naval spokesmen as "a reconnaissance in force" to "a great battle of vital importance."

No figures on losses were released by the Navy because "the military situation does not permit publication of more details at this time." It was inevitable that some losses were suffered by our forces but their announcement will be held up until the battle is over so the information can be of no assistance to the enemy, and until a simultaneous report of enemy losses can be made.

The most favorable war news of the day comes from Soviet Russia. Twin Russian columns are closing in on Rostov in a gigantic pincer movement that threatens to entrap the remnants of the German Caucasian army, estimated at approximately 185,000 men. Complete mopping up of the Stalingrad front is now reported by Moscow and haggard civilian survivors of the siege are pouring out of their caves to commence the rebuilding of the City of Steel. The buildings are a shambles and thousands of frozen German bodies still litter the streets but Russian men and women are starting reconstruction, confident that the hated Fascists will never return.

On the home front, meanwhile, another blow was struck at the convenience and living habits of the American people. Millions of coffee drinkers, hard pressed to satisfy their wants on the present ration, were informed that the next pound of coffee must last six weeks rather than five.

Thursday, February 4, 1943: —Not much additional information is available on the progress of the air-naval engagements off the Solomon Islands but it is evident that the Japanese are making a strong effort to retrieve the situation and reinforce their beleaguered garrison on Guadalcanal. Violent serial action is occurring and losses have undoubtedly been heavy on both sides. We must be prepared to hear of many casualties, the inevitable price of war.

From Russia comes news that the powerful Red Army is within ten miles of Rostov and desperate Nazi units are already attempting a "Dunkirk" evacuation of the Caucasus across the Kerch Straits into the Crimea. Planes of the Russian Black Sea fleet are pouncing on them with a vengeance. The Germans themselves admit that Russian "Commandos" have landed and established a beachhead just north of the Black Sea base of Novorossiysk. This plus the pincer drive on Rostov will cut off any attempt by the Nazis to escape from the trap other than across the Kerch Straits.

Land fighting in Tunisia is of a minor nature with American troops, that succeeded in capturing a town called Sened on the road to Sfax, digging in to hold their gain and British troops likewise hanging grimly onto Djebel Mansour, an important height that they captured from the Germans yesterday. Allied airmen, mostly American, heavily pounded Axis supply lines running from southern Tunisia to the northeastern tip of Sicily.

Hamburg and northwestern Germany were subjected to a smashing assault by RAF and American bombers last night, with heavy damage being inflicted. Sixteen planes did not return.

Friday, February 5, 1943: —The "big battle" news from the South Pacific is apparently petering out a bit. The Navy only refers to the engagements as "sporadic clashes" now. Details are surrounded with secrecy as impenetrable as a North Atlantic fog bank. We have been warned to expect losses which may even be severe and from the reluctant manner in which the results of recent fighting are released by the Navy Department, it may even be that our Navy has suffered a setback. This is pure conjecture and is probably wrong but we can't expect to win every round. If it's bad news, the Navy should tell us about it. The American people can take it.

Amazing news continues to come from the bloody battlefields of Russia. The rejuvenated Soviet armies are surging at the gates of Bataisk, only ten miles from the vital city of Rostov. Other Russian tidal waves are sweeping towards Kharkov and Kursk, cities that figured prominently in the early news of Hitler's great offensive last summer. All the hard-won gains of that bloody drive are being wiped out rapidly by the resurgence of the Russian legions. These are the same legions that Hitler boasted of having "destroyed" on several occasions.

Allied ground forces in Tunisia don't seem to be able to start rolling. The obvious reasons are extremely bad weather and the superior defensive positions of the Axis forces. There may be some other and more secret reasons but the major activity is confined to the air. Led by the famous Flying Fortresses, Allied aircraft today destroyed a total of 52 enemy planes against the loss of 10 of their own.

Saturday, February 6, 1943: —Let's take a look at the situation on the home front. Nothing much in the way of excitement, such as air raids, submarine shellings or other acts of war violence, has happened for a long time. We can't remember the last time we had a blackout. In that way you might say that the war is a long way off, remote, unreal. But in other ways it is reaching into the lives and habits of each of us, bringing home to us the realities of war in an implacable and sometimes exasperating manner.

We are working harder and longer. In spite of the addition of the 5% Victory Tax and increased income taxes, the sale of War Savings Bonds flourishes. We put in an average of close to 48 hours a week and there will be no extra holidays this year with the exception of the Fourth of July and Christmas. This month, for example, we will work as usual on both Lincoln's and Washington's birthdays.

We don't eat as much meat as we used to and what we get is invariably pork. We haven't had a juicy roast of beef for months and we're getting a terrible craving for it. Butter and eggs are hard to get and expensive. It takes almost every cent we make for food and household expenses. Our present salary is 80 dollars more per month but is less in purchasing power than that of ten years ago. Gasoline is rationed and transportation problems are acute. Point system rationing of all food stuffs is coming soon but shortages of almost every item of consumer goods is making it tough to satisfy even moderate wants. Everything is short but the people's temper. They're taking it very well. C'est L'guerre!

Sunday, February 7, 1943: —The Red Army continues to roll towards Rostov. Late reports indicate that fighting is already taking place in the city's suburbs. The fall of Rostov would clamp the lid on ten divisions of Germans trapped in the Caucasus and would open the Donets Basin to further attack by the Soviets.

The German radio also admits that more Russian troops have landed at Novorossiysk and heavy fighting is in progress.

In two and one-half months the amazingly powerful offensive of the Russians has carried them forward from 150 to 350 miles and in many spots has regained all the territory lost in last summer's campaign. Not only do the Reds appear to be superior in equipment and fire power at the present time but their strategy and generalship have been better than the vaunted armies of Hitler.

In Tunisia the Germans have thrown a new tank into action. It is the Mark VI, an improved version of their famous Mark IVs, and is reported to have superior fire power to any Allied tank. This plus natural defensive positions foretells a bloody battle for control of the last Axis foothold in North Africa. Little doubt of the eventual outcome is expressed by Allied leaders but a stiff, sanguinary battle is in prospect.

Of diverting interest to the war news was the completion of the trial of popular movie hero, Errol Flynn, on charges of statutory rape of two teen-age Los Angeles girls. The verdict was not guilty on all counts and the famous actor found himself vindicated but broke. Those lawyers are plenty expensive, eh, Errol?

314

Monday, February 8, 1943: —Another important item was added to the rationed list today. It was shoes. No sales were permitted until midnight tonight. Tomorrow, each person is entitled to purchase one pair of shoes with coupon number 17 of ration book #1. This coupon is good any time between now and June 15.

In addition to the new restriction on shoes, the Government announced plans for the drafting of all women from 18-50 for war work. Bills now pending in Congress would make it obligatory for men from 18 to 65 and women from 18 to 50 to take any job assigned to them by the Government. The plan would work on Selective Service principles.

On the war fronts we hear more Russian success stories. The Soviets have captured Kursk, one of the main Nazi strongholds on the Kharkov line. The stepped up speed of the Russians lends credence to the belief that the Nazi retreat is becoming disordered. Soviet pressure is being maintained at all points and the extent of the German defeat is reaching the proportions of a major catastrophe for Hitler.

American and British airmen on both sides of the European continent gave the Axis another blasting last night. From North Africa, U.S. planes smashed at Naples, Sardinia, and Sicily, causing heavy damage, which even the Italians admitted. From Britain, the RAF lugged a few block-busters over the channel and dumped them on Lorient, the Nazi nest for submarines.

The Navy reported nothing but additional "sparring" from the Southwest Pacific. The big battle apparently has not yet been joined.

Tuesday, February 9, 1943: —President Roosevelt today stepped into the critical manpower situation by issuing an executive order establishing a 48-hour week in place of the present 40-hour schedule. The new ruling will apply immediately to thirty two areas where critical labor shortages prevail. In those designated sections of the country it will be mandatory for employers to establish 48-hour work week with overtime pay effective after the first 40 hours.

This step is only the first of many that will have to be taken by the Government if all the manpower needs of the Nation, including farms, war industries, and the armed forces, are to be met. The drafting of women and the deferment of farm workers are already contemplated moves.

The heroes of Bataan and Corregidor can rest a little easier tonight, feeling that they have been partially avenged. Tokyo admits and Washington agrees that the Japs have relinquished all hope of successful resistance on Guadalcanal and have evacuated as many of their beaten forces from the Island as possible, leaving only scattered, and starving remnants for our troops to mop up. Thus, after six months of fierce fighting under incredibly difficult conditions, our soldiers and Marines, ably supported by brilliant Navy action, have handed the Jap his second major defeat in land action. The first was in New Guinea and the combined operations have cost the enemy 90,000 in killed, 200 ships sunk or severely damaged and 2,000 planes destroyed. The way of the transgressor is hard, eh, Nippo?

Wednesday, February 10, 1943: —Russia again holds the spotlight in the war news tonight. Soviet armies are closing the pincers of a giant nutcracker on German forces defending the Nazi defense line from Kharkov to Rostov. Russian heavy artillery has already opened up on both positions. Vicious and increasingly desperate counter-attacks by the Nazis have failed to purchase them that badly needed breathing spell in which to prepare their permanent winter line. The Soviets have their hated foe on the run and have no intention of relaxing their pressure.

In Africa, the British commander-in-chief General Alexander claims that the last Axis fighting man has been driven out of Tripolitania, Libya, and Egypt. Eighth Army units are pouring over the Tunisian border for the anticipated union with the British and American forces already established there. Between this union lies the little matter of the Mareth line to which Marshal Rommel and his battered Afrika Korps have retired. With the expected improvement in weather conditions during the next few weeks, General Alexander confidently predicts that his victorious Eighth Army will easily turn the Mareth line and join with the rest of the Allied forces in the showdown battle. "All the dice are loaded in our favor," says General Alexander.

In a partial report on results of the sporadic naval clashes in the South Pacific during the last week, the Navy announced that two and probably five Jap destroyers were sunk in two abortive attempts to reinforce or evacuate their beaten Guadalcanal garrison.

Thursday, February 11, 1943: —Selective Service officials today warned the Nation that the drafting of married men with children is coming very soon. Induction into the services will be at the rate of 400,000 per month during the next four months and by May 1 the majority will be fathers because there will be no one else to induct. More weight will be given to what a man does than to the relationship he has with dependents.

Prime Minister Churchill reported the results of his recent conferences to Parliament today. He stated that a blueprint for victory had been made at the historic meeting in Casablanca. He revealed that the Allies have a well equipped army of 500,000 men in North Africa and possess a two to one superiority over the Axis forces in Tunisia. North Africa he asserted is the bridgehead to invasion of Europe which can be expected soon.

Dwight D. Eisenhower today formally assumed supreme command of Allied forces in the Mediterranean theater and was confirmed in Washington as a full four-star general. At the same time, Secretary of War Stimson warned the people to expect heavy fighting and heavy casualties in the near future, thus bearing out the belief that big military adventures are about to begin.

In the far Pacific, the war seems to have taken a new turn with the final defeat of the Japs on Guadalcanal. The turning point appears to have been reached. We have held the Japs and are now beginning to take the offensive. An increased tempo is noted in all phases of attack. Merciless bombing of Jap bases over a wide area from Kiska in the Aleutians to Munda in the Solomons was reported today.

Friday, February 12, 1943: —It was Lincoln's birthday today and normally is a holiday. This time, however, it was just another ten hour working day. But you can't help but recall that just about every ideal for which the great Emancipator fought are being challenged again today. The world now, even as the Nation then, cannot exist half slave and half free. We too, are fighting so that government of the people, by the people, and for the people shall not perish from the earth. The world, in honoring his birthday, could do well by contemplating his words of wisdom and heeding his sage counsel, especially when the day comes for world reconstruction.

American airmen in the Southwest Pacific, in the Aleutians, and in Burma are smashing the Japanese in some of the heaviest aerial attacks since the beginning of the Pacific war. Rangoon in Burma was twice pounded today and much damage was inflicted. Huge fires broke out in the harbor and railroad installations.

In New Guinea, General MacArthur's troops are nearing the Jap base of Salamaua and have decisively defeated a Japanese attempt to counter-attack against the Allied airdrome at Wau, 31 miles southwest of Salamaua.

Here at home, the Office of Price Administration has cracked down on some users of Class C ration books for gasoline, charging misuse of the privilege of buying increased quotas of motor fuel. Some books were revoked for drunken driving, others for using the gas for non-essential driving.

Saturday, February 13, 1943: —The center of fighting news is still in Russia tonight. Military observers believe that Germany's whole southern front in Russia is crumbling under the terrific sledge-hammer blows of the Red Army. Both Rostov and Kharkov are under direct attack and are expected to fall. The Nazis are said to be burning Rostov as a preliminary to withdrawal.

If the Russians succeed in capturing both Rostov and Kharkov which are main anchors of the German defense line in the south, they may entrap and seal the doom of a Nazi army of 500,000 men in the Donets Basin. Present indications are that a more disastrous defeat than Stalingrad is in store for the Germans.

President Roosevelt made a fighting speech last night. He reported to the Nation the results of the Casablanca conference and said that the decisions made at that historic meeting will be made known to our enemies in the form of action not words. 1943 will be a year of power and it is the intention of the United States and Great Britain to hit the Germans and Japanese so hard and from so many directions that they won't know which is their bow and which is their stern. He pledged increased aid to the gallant Chinese and promised them that great Allied offensives will be launched in the air over China and over Japan itself. We have no intention to inch our way back over the islands of the vast Pacific. "There are many roads that lead to Tokyo, we shall neglect none of them," he said.

Sunday, February 14, 1943: —It was a magnificent day today; no other word will suffice. There were only wisps of clouds in a blue sky from which a warm sun casts its life giving rays on to budding trees and bushes that smiled back gratefully in fresh green comfort. It was a day to plant things so I spent the morning in preparing my Victory garden. I succeeded in putting in two rows each of radishes, carrots, beets, and spinach. It's a right solid feeling to know that in nature's due course, nourishing food will come from the soil. There must be just a little farmer blood in my veins.

It still remains hard to realize on such a beautiful day, that across the world men are at each other's throats but radio reports flash the news of more bloody fighting on the Russian front. The Soviet steamroller apparently cannot be stopped in spite of fierce German resistance. Rostov and Kharkov have not fallen but fighting is now in their environs. Casualties on both sides are numbered in the tens of thousands.

Even in the midst of the present holocaust, the Russian High Command is said to be planning a great summer offensive that will dwarf anything that has gone before. Stalin has demanded that every Fascist soldier be driven from or buried in Russian soil by autumn and his generals are training a great new army in the Ural Mountains to carry out his demands. That is Russia's main strength—unlimited manpower. Millions die but other millions step up to take their places.

Monday, February 15, 1943: —The Russians are really rolling. Moscow today announced that Rostov has been taken. The city is a burned out shell, strewn with the wreckage of German men and machines. The bulk of the Nazi defenders escaped by the skin of their teeth but the Red Army is in hot pursuit.

Fierce fighting is also reported in the environs of Kharkov. If that stronghold is also captured it will leave Hitler's Army in serious straits. Their next defense line would be back on the

Dnieper line which would wipe out all the gains of a year and one half of bitter fighting. It is reported that Adolf "Napoleon" Hitler has relinquished the supreme command of the Reichwehr and has turned the running of the army back to the military leaders. This is the only bad news of the day from the Russian front.

Ground fighting in Tunisia is reaching considerable proportions. Rommel's retreating Afrika Korps has launched a surprise offensive against American lines in South Tunisia and early reports indicate that our troops have been driven back as much as 18 miles in some places. It is the first big all-American show and constitutes the baptism of fire for some of our armored units. Opposed to them are the veteran Panzer groups of Germany's elite Afrika Korps. The blue chips are down. Can the Yanks rally? Time alone will tell.

One other item of news that should be mentioned is the arrival in American ports of several important units of the French Navy, including the battleship Richelieu. The mighty ships are here for conditioning before joining the Allies in active warfare against the Axis.

Tuesday, February 16, 1943: —KHARKOV FALLS! The Russians today won their most important victory of the entire winter campaign. The hard-hitting Soviet troops smashed through the German hedge-hog defenses before Kharkov and occupied the city. A crack German Army Corps was routed in fierce fighting at close quarters. The battered remnants of the Nazi army are racing for their next prepared line of defense along the Dnieper River. The Moscow radio made a dramatic announcement of the victory and great was the rejoicing throughout Russia.

In Tunisia, American forces have temporarily rallied and have launched a counter-attack at one point. From the tenor of reports, however, things don't look too bright for our troops in southern Tunisia. Apparently Rommel has thrown his full weight against them, supported by clouds of deadly Stuka dive bombers. Our armored units still lack battle experience and are confronted by veteran panzer groups that know all the tricks. On the favorable side, however, is the fact that the powerful British Eighth Army is drawing ever closer to Rommel's rear and will eventually bring him to bay. Meanwhile, the green U.S. troops are taking the brunt of it.

The Navy Department announced that the heavy cruiser, Chicago, and a destroyer have been lost in the Solomons area. They took at least two Jap destroyers with them and damaged thirteen others.

American Flying Fortresses based in England made a sensational daylight attack on the Nazi submarine lair at St. Nazaire on the French coast today. Six of the big ships were knocked out of the sky by Goering's interceptors.

Wednesday, February 17, 1943: —More bad news from Tunisia today. American forces in a narrow sector of the South Tunisia front are apparently taking quite a licking. Rommel appears to have concentrated at least two armored divisions against an inferior U.S. force and has succeeded in driving a 35 mile wedge into the American lines. Our troops have abandoned three advanced airfields but are withdrawing in good order. Some equipment was lost and casualties were undoubtedly severe, particularly from the oldest "blitz" tactic of them all—the dive bomber. The green American troops are finding out what the Poles, Dutch, French and British had to face in the early months of the war. A mighty unpleasant experience no doubt.

Our far-ranging submarines added five more Japanese vessels to their Pacific score, the Navy Department announced today. Included among the enemy ships sunk was a Jap cruiser.

The city of San Francisco has just completed a fifteen-day bond selling drive, aimed at putting the gallant cruiser, San Francisco, back into the fight. The people really responded. In spite of the approaching income tax deadline, a total of $5,300,000 in war bonds was sold. That is enough to repair the "fightingest" cruiser and give a good start on the building of another. Quite encouraging!

Food shortages continue to be acute in the Bay Area. Ration books #2 will be distributed next week, during which time the sales of all canned foods will be frozen.

Thursday, February 18, 1943: —The Yanks in Tunisia are still retreating. The Germans have sent two powerful panzer columns smashing against thinly held American lines and have forced the defenders back to within 14 miles of the Algerian border in one place. Late reports indicate that our troops fought magnificently against superior enemy forces and inflicted severe casualties on the foe, sustaining heavy losses themselves. The Berlin reports state that they have attained their purpose in the Tunisian drive, evidently indicating that no further advance will be attempted. Allied sources believe this is the result of the rapidly growing threat of the British Eighth Army which is now closing in on the Mareth line and growling at the heels and flank of the panzer army that is attacking the American positions.

Reports from the Tunisian front state that the Nazis are using a new and deadly tank, known as the Mark VI, which has played an important part in their break-through of U.S. lines. Even our biggest anti-tank guns have difficulty stopping them. The success which the Germans may attain will be dependent upon how many of the deadly new monsters they have been able to transport to North Africa. Not many, we hope.

On the home front it's the draft situation that is having attention. The House of Representatives has voted to nullify war manpower commissioner McNutt's order to base deferment on occupational rather than dependent status. The House would require the draft boards to call men with children only if absolutely necessary and after all other classifications have been depleted.

Friday, February 19, 1943: —Ground fighting in Tunisia is increasing in intensity. The big guns of the British Eighth Army— the same big guns that blasted Rommel out of El Alamein—are thundering at the Axis held Mareth line and one southern outpost town of the line has already been occupied by British troops. American planes as well as British are blasting enemy communications and U.S. troops are regrouping in the hills west of the Axis occupied town of Feriana. Lieut. General Devers, chief of the American armored forces, reassured the Nation by stating that the present difficulty is not alarming in view of the thinness of the American line at the point attacked. He said that our troops are fighting superbly, their morale is high, and they will regain their present losses. All the cards are stacked against the Axis in North Africa and every man in the Allied armies is confident that their foe will be driven into the sea. Time will tell.

Madame Chiang Kai-Shek, first lady of China, is in Washington for a few days, pleading the cause of more aid for

China. The Madame is a brilliant and charming lady, speaks English fluently, having been educated in this country, and is adept at statecraft. If anything can be done to expedite the shipment of war materials to China it will be Madame Chiang. But I think everything humanly possible is now being done because China and its never-say-die people have won a special spot in the sympathies of the American Nation. Someday we'll help them retake all their land from the hated Japs.

Saturday, February 20, 1943: —The tide of battle in Tunisia is slowly turning our way again. The Axis offensive has been stopped and Americans dug in on the rocky ridges of central Tunisia have repelled two major attacks, inflicting considerable losses on the enemy. General Harold R.L.G. Alexander, the brilliant strategist, who planned the recent British Eighth Army drive against Rommel's Afrika Korps, arrived at Allied Headquarters to assume field command of all Allied forces in Tunisia as deputy to General Eisenhower. A squeeze play on the Axis by the Eighth Army on one side and American, British, and French forces on the other can be expected almost immediately. Most observers believe the Tunisian campaign will be concluded by the end of March, if not before.

Meanwhile, the German debacle in Russia continues to grow in size. A Stockholm report hints that Hitler has called Marshal Rommel out of Africa to head German armies on the Eastern front in an attempt to extricate them from the doom that is enveloping them. The report also intimates that Hitler has gone into seclusion at Berchtesgaden—probably with another splitting headache.

Here on the home front we bought our last unrationed canned goods today as all stocks were to be frozen at midnight tonight. Nothing will be sold for one week while everyone signs up for ration book #2. Advance notice of the deadline was responsible for a considerable run on the stores, some of which found themselves with pretty barren shelves this morning.

Sunday, February 21, 1943: —Another wartime Sunday has come and almost gone and all day the heavens seemed to be crying their eyes out because of man's cruelty to man. It started last night about midnight and drizzled or poured all day. No victory gardening was possible so we made it really a day of rest. I noticed this morning, however, that the radishes I planted last Sunday are already sprouting. Marvelous thing, Nature!

You can't think of the war right now without expressing amazement at Russia's brilliant stand. It looks as though the Red Army might defeat Germany almost singlehanded. This is a real possibility and a danger, I think, because, although no one can really estimate how much pressure was taken off the Russians by English and American action in the west and in Africa, it is really the Red Army that has taken everything the mighty German Reichwehr could give—twice—and has come back with a tremendous offensive that has rolled the enemy back almost to the Dnieper river at this writing. Even the Germans admit that they are in grave danger of total defeat on the eastern front and Moscow is more confident than at any time in the war. If Russia wins by herself she will expect to dictate the peace on her own terms which might conceivably menace the establishment of the kind of Europe we and the British would like. Russia, while a wonderful ally against Hitler, has never revealed her own secret plans or motives and a victory over Germany would make her top dog in Europe. Whether such a condition would be conducive to future peace on that sad continent is problematical.

Monday, February 22, 1943: —Washington's Birthday and ordinarily a holiday but this time it was just another working day. It was still raining so it didn't seem so bad to be inside at a desk all day.

The newspapers are full of death and destruction today so it's just as well to be busy—keeps you from pondering too much. The Navy announced the loss of two passenger-cargo ships in the North Atlantic, with more than 850 persons going down with the ships. Most of the victims were army, navy, and coast guard personnel. Both vessels were torpedoed at night and went down within thirty minutes, too fast for effective rescue work.

The Navy also reported the sinking of our largest submarine, the Argonaut, in a battle with a Japanese convoy off New Britain. The massive sub was believed to be the biggest in the world and her loss is a serious blow.

In Tunisia, the Yanks are coming back. In a ferocious counter-attack they threw the Nazi armored columns back more than ten miles. Thirteen enemy tanks were destroyed in the engagement. Apparently even the mighty Mark VIs are not proof against the sharpshooting Doughboys.

Here at home it's "freeze week." Schools and other registration centers will be crowded with people signing for their ration books #2. From the tables of point values on various foodstuffs published by the papers today, it is going to be a complicated headache for the housewife to intelligently buy groceries anymore. She'll have to be a mathematical genius with the patience a fisherman to do it right.

Tuesday, February 23, 1943: —Harassed grocers today delved into the complicated task of preparing their shelves for point system rationing which goes into effect March 1st. Meanwhile citizens filed into schools to get their #2 ration books and newspapers and radios went into great length to explain the workings of the new system. Heaven help the poor housewife.

According to latest newspaper and radio reports the Allied situation in Tunisia is improving although fierce fighting is in progress. American and British reinforcements have stopped the armored columns of Marshal Rommel in their tracks and have inflicted severe casualties on the obviously exhausted Axis forces. In the meantime, the British Eighth Army under General Montgomery appears to be probing for weak spots in the Mareth line defenses and is confining its activities to patrol and artillery duels. The showdown cannot be postponed much longer.

It is the same old story in Russia. The defeat of the Germans is increasing in scope and the Red Army today celebrated its 25th anniversary by capturing a major Nazi base at Sumy, northwest of Kharkov. Premier Stalin congratulated the Red Army today in a triumphant speech in which he declared that the Soviet army is bearing the complete brunt of the war and has seriously crippled but not yet conquered the German Army. He called for intensified efforts on the part of every Russian. Russian has, in fact, made probably the most remarkable fight for life in the history of the world. At almost unbelievable cost in blood and treasure the Russian people have really earned the right to victory and peace.

Wednesday, February 24, 1943: —Valiant American troops with their British Allies, and supported by clouds of fighting planes of all description, have completely turned the tables on Marshal Rommel and his vaunted Afrika Korps. After stopping the enemy's surprise offensive at the outskirts of Thales near the Algerian border, the thoroughly aroused and enraged American troops counter-attacked furiously and with the effective aid of the Allied air force completely overwhelmed the Nazi panzers and sent them reeling back through the narrow bottleneck of Kasserine Pass. Here American artillery and Allied aircraft pounded the retreating foe with tons of high explosive shells and bombs.

There is little doubt that the Tunisian Nazis have suffered a major defeat and our soldiers, who are now blooded veterans, have met their first big test in a most satisfactory manner. They have proved that they can suffer a reverse and come back fighting magnificently to snatch victory from defeat.

In Russia, Nazi resistance is admittedly stiffening although some additional gains were claimed by the Soviets. Obviously, the Red Army cannot keep up the pressure indefinitely without a breather and we can expect some slowdown. The psychological moment for the opening of a European second front is fast approaching and I think the Allies will be prepared for this one. It may be weeks or days, but it's almost sure to come. Look out! Hitler!

Thursday, February 25, 1943: —The Yanks in Tunisia are really handing the Nazis a smashing defeat. The enemy forces streaming back through Kasserine Pass were caught in that narrow bottleneck by swarms of Allied bombing and fighting planes and were given an unmerciful pounding. Secretary of War Stimson praised the conduct of our troops in their first real test and said that they were not demoralized by the initial enemy onslaught, rallied quickly and counter-attacked with great vigor. "All complacency has been dropped and they are thoroughly mad and ready to fight," he said.

The Russian offensive is still moving forward on the eastern front, though at a slower pace. Today's reports announce the capture of several more inhabited places south of Orel, west of Kharkov, and in the southwestern part of the Donets basin. The Red Army revealed that American tanks are leading the attack in many places.

The puzzling feature of the war in Russia is the German

claim that the Red Army has lost over eighteen million men since the start of the war. Though their losses have undoubtedly run into the millions, not even the Russians could continue in the war and mount a tremendous offensive such as the one now in progress, were the preposterous German claims even nearly true. As Hitler stated in Mein Kampf, when he tells a lie he believes in telling a whopper.

On the home front it's rationing, meat shortage, and taxes that occupy the people's minds these days. It is surely a time that tries men's souls.

Friday, February 26, 1943: —Our troops in Tunisia picked up another fifteen miles in their pursuit of the defeated Axis forces through Kasserine Pass. There is no indication that the Germans will attempt a stand very soon and it appears likely that they are racing for Sfax on the east Tunisian coast. The Allies have achieved complete mastery of the air which has contributed enormously to the sudden reversal of form after the initial success of the German offensive.

A tremendous air offensive is getting under way in Western Europe. A never ending stream of American and British bombers and fighters of every description are roaring up from the unsinkable aircraft carrier, England, to hammer at Nazi bases from Dunkirk to Berlin. The scale of the attack is indicated by the number of missing planes, numbered as high as sixty by latest reports. American planes participated in a huge daylight raid on the heavily defended Nazi base at Wilhelmshaven while RAF bombers plastered Nurnberg, Cologne and Naples in Italy. There was no indication of a let up in the air attack as a never-ending procession of planes shuttled back and forth across the channel in a round-the-clock offensive. Hitler is beginning to reap the whirlwind he so ruthlessly planted.

The Pacific war at this time is also confined mainly to the air as American planes again raided Kiska in the Aleutians and Munda in the Solomons. MacArthur's Flying Fortresses also gave Rabaul another plastering.

Saturday, February 27, 1943: —American troops are continuing their counter-offensive in central Tunisia but in the northern part of that colony the Nazis have mustered sufficient power to launch an attack against the British. Latest reports indicate that the British are holding but have had to throw in their heaviest tanks, the new "Churchills," in order to stem the advancing foe. Fierce fighting is in progress.

The Russian front is in a comparative lull today. The Red Army advance has stalled from pure exhaustion and on the southern Donets-Rostov sector they have even been forced to go on the defensive, due to fresh thousands of reserves and tanks that the Germans have thrown into the struggle. North of Kursk and west of Kharkov, however, the Soviets are still advancing despite furious resistance.

Back here on the home front many new headaches and sacrifices are taking place in the daily lives of the people. Point system rationing promises to be one of the biggest headaches but the women of England made it work over there so the women of America can do likewise over here. I believe I forgot to record a few days ago that the President had directed that all business in certain manpower shortage areas must go on a regular 48 hour week in place of the usual 40 hours. That doesn't worry yours truly much—we're on about a 60 hour schedule right now.

Labor disputes, especially in the aircraft industry, and particularly in the Boeing plants, are whitening the hair of many harassed business and government leaders.

Sunday, February 28, 1943: —Thank goodness for Sunday! The way we have been working recently would soon wear us out if it weren't for the chance to recuperate on Sunday. At the present time my duties are in connection with the redemption of Savings Bonds and the operation has mushroomed to great size due to the impending tax due date of March 15. Many people apparently are finding it necessary to redeem some of their bonds to meet the increased tax burden. It is too bad because it just amounts to the taking of funds out of one of Uncle Sam's pockets and the putting of the same funds back into another—but with an expensive operation in between. But apparently thousands of people must do it, which is another strong argument for some sort of pay-as-you-go tax plan. Congress has several such plans under consideration and the adoption of one of them can be expected before the year is over.

From the battlefront in Russia we learn that the mighty offensive of the Russians in the south has come to a halt and the

Germans have launched several strong counter-attacks, which have been repelled with heavy losses. The spring thaw, with its attendant flood and mud obviously has had much to do with the Soviet slowdown.

The situation in Tunisia, as far as can be gathered, is confused. The Nazis under Rommel in central Tunisia are badly battered and in retreat but Nazi forces in the north under Col. General Jurgen von Arnim are attacking British positions with great vigor. The British have been hard pressed to prevent a break-through.

March

Monday, March 1, 1943: —Point system rationing of canned goods and other essential foods went into effect today. The first day's experience was not bad. Housewives and grocers were very patient and cooperative in an effort to make successful use of the system. Each person is allotted 48 points per month and the housewife's problem is to make her family's coupons last throughout the month. So it will take at least 30 days to determine the probable success or failure of the plan.

The situation in Tunisia is shaping up more favorably for the Allied forces today. U.S. troops have reoccupied Feriana on the central front, retaking that important point that was lost in the initial German drive. Two strong counter-attacks by Marshal Rommel's panzers were beaten off with considerable loss to the enemy.

The great Allied air offensive across the English Channel has passed the 80 hour mark of continuous attack. Today's principal attack was against the Nazi submarine base at St. Nazaire. Many 1000 pound "block-busters" were seen to smash the docks and repair yards. Many raids have been launched lately against the lairs of German submarines due to the widespread belief that the battle of the Atlantic convoy lanes is going against us and that the best and surest way to combat the sub menace is to smash them in the factory and docks rather than to track them down in the vastness of the ocean.

Late reports indicate that the RAF is over central Germany in large force, maybe over Berlin itself.

Tuesday, March 2, 1943: —Good news from the South Pacific area today. Recent reports stated that the Japs were concentrating a large striking force in the New Britain area and General MacArthur warned that a large scale offensive by the Japs is in preparation, perhaps against Australia itself. Today however, our heavy bombers caught the Jap convoy as it moved from New Britain towards New Guinea and ripped it to pieces. One 10,000 ton transport, loaded with Jap troops, was hit with five 1,000 pounders and sunk. Another 8,000 tonner was hit amidship by a big one and broke in two, sinking immediately.

Direct hits were scored on two other transports and several escorting warships were either hit or damaged by near misses. The convoy was smashed and dispersed at the cost of only one of our big Fortresses.

On the home front another distasteful episode is occurring at a local shipyard where vital work is being done for the U.S. Navy. Because of a dispute over premium pay for Saturday and Sunday work, 260 machinists walked off the job today at the orders of their local union. Work was stopped despite a strongly worded plea from Admiral Greenslade of the 12th Naval District. The union's action is extremely serious and reprehensible in time of war and may result in some "work or fight" legislation by Congress. The public is getting more and more impatient with such work stoppages and will back the Government in any strong action it may take to prevent such cases. Jurisdictional disputes that result in slowdowns or work stoppages of any nature must be set aside for the duration. Dead men on Guadalcanal demand it.

Wednesday, March 3, 1943: —The machinists' strike that threatened to delay vital war work yesterday was short-lived. The men returned to their work today after one worker, who had been expelled from the union because of unauthorized Sunday work, resigned from his job in the interest of the war effort. This action averted what would probably have been a showdown between the union and the Government.

Another brilliant success was scored by the Russians today. After what appeared to be a lull in the fighting, the Soviets launched a furious assault that drove the hapless Germans from Rzhev, key stronghold about 130 miles northwest of Moscow. It was Rzhev, you will remember, that Hitler was talking about when he stated that its loss would be as serious as the loss of half of Berlin. The capture of the vital base, therefore, is evidence of the enormity of the Nazi defeat.

More cheerful news comes from General MacArthur's headquarters in the South Pacific. Apparently our flyers scored an even bigger victory over the Japanese convoy than was at first believed. Even yet, the full extent of the Jap disaster cannot be determined as the airmen are still stalking the remnants of the enemy force but it is already clear that the majority of the convoy was destroyed and many thousands of Jap sailors and troops drowned. It has been mighty good hunting and the boys are beginning to drop their eggs right down the smokestacks. From all reports, our bombardiers are aiming with greater accuracy every day—and with bigger bombs. They are certainly getting results, eh, Mr. Moto?

Thursday, March 4, 1943: —CRUSHING VICTORY! That is the only possible description of the final results of the big air-sea battle between American land-based bombers and fighters and a 22 ship Japanese convoy that was caught flat-footed in the narrow sea between New Britain and New Guinea and in the Bismarck Sea north of New Britain. The final reports are almost incredible as they state that not a single ship of the enemy convoy escaped. Ten Japanese warships, including cruisers and destroyers, and twelve transports carrying at least 15,000 men and quantities of equipment, were completely wiped out in the two day battle. Accurate bombing Fortresses and Liberators, with swift P-38 Lightnings as escort, literally filled the sea with Japanese debris. In addition to the surface vessels sunk, the sharpshooting Americans knocked 55 Jap planes out of the air as they attempted to protect the convoy. Allied military leaders in the area called the action the most decisive victory of the Pacific war and has undoubtedly thrown Japan's timetable completely off schedule. Nice going, men!

In Tunisia also, the Allied picture looks much better. American and British forces in the south and central have regained almost all the territory recently lost to Marshal Rommel in his abortive drive to Algeria. General Montgomery's veteran Eighth Army is the ace in the hole and is rapidly gathering its strength before the Axis held Mareth line. Something very sudden and very rough is going to happen to the enemy in North Africa before long. The Allied nutcracker is just about ready to crack down hard.

Friday, March 5, 1943: —Yesterday marked the end of a full decade of Franklin D. Roosevelt's administration. Such an event could not go by unmentioned. It is the first time an American President has held office for more than eight years. In many ways it has been the most momentous decade in the history of the Nation. It will be known as the Roosevelt Decade and whatever faults the man or his New Deal Party may have had, it was not inaction. Three things, I believe, will mark the political history of those ten years. Two are economic factors and the other is the war. The two economic factors are, first, the tremendous amount of experimentation, some good and much bad, with the economy of the Nation and, second, the total disregard for the "silly fool dollar sign" as Roosevelt himself has put it. In those ten years we have seen the most colossal spending spree in the history of the world, a spree that has sent the national debt soaring from a paltry fifteen billion to something around a stratospheric one hundred and twenty billion, and that is just the beginning.

But above all, it has been the war that has influenced the Roosevelt Administration and has assured Franklin Roosevelt the stature of greatness. The vast majority of the people are solidly behind his war policy and he has furnished the kind of popular leadership that appeals to Americans as well as the rest of the world. It might safely be said that if Roosevelt had to stand alone on his record of handling domestic economic problems during peacetime with his fiscal policies, there might be some grounds for suggestions of mediocrity, but his masterful war leadership will more than obscure all the economic bungling and tremendous waste and will secure for Franklin Roosevelt a place beside our greatest war Presidents. We're for him, God bless him. He'll make us or break us—and I do mean break!

Saturday, March 6, 1943: —Naval action flared again in the Solomons area today. An American task force bombarded the big Jap bases of Munda and Vila in the central Solomons. Two large enemy destroyers were sunk as they attempted to interfere with the attack. The raid was considered very successful.

U.S. airmen also were busy, carrying out sustained attacks against Lae and Salamaua, the remaining Japanese bases on New Guinea. Long range fighter planes also engaged the systematic extermination of the few remaining survivors of the recent convoy sinking. Lifeboats and rafts loaded with survivors were machine gunned and bombed until it is believed that few if any reached shore. The Japs themselves led the way in starting this type of warfare without quarter and are now reaping the bitter results. The shooting of helpless survivors is a Japanese trick that has backfired. We learned from sad experience that sportsmanship is out in the war with Japan. We must fight fire with fire, in the words of an old cliché.

American armored forces in Tunisia have also made a notable gain today. The important town of Pichon in central Tunisia was occupied by U.S. troops who have advanced to within fifty airline miles of the coast and are threatening the vital Axis port of Sousse. If our forces can drive through to that point they will have driven a wedge between the northern and southern Axis armies. Fierce fighting lies ahead, however.

Sunday, March 7, 1943: —I spent another Sunday on the job today. This time it was because of a tremendous rush of Savings Bonds redemption, due to the impending March 15th deadline for income taxes. Many people apparently are finding it necessary to redeem their bonds to pay their taxes. This is an unfortunate circumstance, because such action defeats both the purpose of the bonds as well as the taxes. It's taking it out with the right hand and putting it back with the left. What Uncle Sam needs is new money from both bonds and taxes. That is the principal reason for supporting some sort of a pay-as-you-go tax plan, to get the money before it's spent. But until some such plan is adopted, the poor short-sighted taxpayer must do what he can to dig up the money.

Apparently there's plenty of kick left in the Axis forces in Tunisia. Late reports indicate that Marshal Rommel's armored panzers have struck at the British Eighth Army with great strength, obviously in a strong effort to throw Montgomery's own offensive plans awry. The attack was launched at a point south of the Mareth line but well prepared British anti-tank units repulsed the first attack, destroying 21 enemy tanks. Fighting continues.

One of the biggest and most successful bombing missions of the European war was completed Friday night, the British and Canadian, freighted their "block-busters" and "triple block-busters" over Essex, the home of the great Krupp armament works. Returning pilots reported that one of the huge bombs must have hit a powder factory, causing the most colossal explosion of the war. A great sheet of flame shot a thousand feet into the air, lighting up the whole target area. Shades of Hades!

Monday, March 8, 1943: —This is really being written on Tuesday morning as I worked until 12:05 a.m. and caught the 12:30 train home, arriving about 1:00 a.m. It will be a good thing when the rush is over in about another week. Otherwise there would be some serious work casualties. People can't put in such long, hard hours indefinitely. The women especially are beginning to crack under the strain.

Well, the war news looks pretty favorable tonight. Marshal Rommel tried six times to smash through the Eighth Army's defenses but failed. Accurate shooting artillery and anti-tank units were largely responsible for the successful defense. Indications are now that Rommel has given up and has been forced to retreat toward the hills north and northwest of Medenine. Thirty three enemy tanks bit the dust.

Allied airmen also reported a highly successful attack on an Axis convoy off the Tunisian coast, evidently bringing supplies to Rommel. Two ships were sunk and four others were left in flames.

On the Russian front, the Soviet armies continue to hold the initiative and today's communiqués stated that the important town of Sychevka, on the Rzhev-Vyazma railroad, was captured in a ferocious battle in which 8,000 Nazis were slain and 310 tanks captured. According to the Germans the town was "evacuated according to plan."

The only home front news of any importance was a further announcement of the necessity of drafting large numbers of fathers during the next few months.

Tuesday, March 9, 1943: —The Russian and Tunisian battlefronts are still the most active. The Soviet armies launched a new offensive in the Orel sector today and late reports indicate that considerable success is crowning their efforts. Smolensk is the next major objective of the Russian drive and brings the name of that vital base back into the battlefront news almost for the first time since 1941.

A somewhat startling and possibly far-reaching statement was made yesterday by Admiral Wm. H. Standley, U.S. Ambassador to Russia. At a press conference in Moscow, the Ambassador complained publicly that the Russian Government was not informing the Russian people of the extent of American aid to

Russia. He said that Stalin and other leaders were leading the Soviet people to believe that Russia is bearing the entire brunt of the war with Germany. Lend-lease aid has been more than considerable and he believes the Russians should be told about it. The State Department at Washington was shocked at the statement and pointed out that it was made without the consent or approval of the American Government. Additional repercussions are expected.

The British Eighth Army apparently has Rommel's number. Once again they have handed the vaunted Afrika Korps a stunning defeat. The abortive attacks during the last two days left fifty Nazis tanks smashed and burning on the battlefield and the rest of the Axis forces in full retreat.

The latest pay-as-you-go income tax plan has been killed by the House Ways and Means Committee, while we and other Federal Reserve Banks are snowed under with redemptions of Savings Bonds.

Wednesday, March 10, 1943: —After killing a plan to "forgive" taxes on 1942 incomes, the House Ways and Means Committee today voted to inaugurate an at-the-source plan of collecting taxes by a 20% withholding tax on income, to apply on the last half of 1942's taxes and an opportunity to become current by paying both the regular installments and the payroll tax. There are many detail to be worked out.

The still powerful German Army today launched a savage counter-offensive against the Russians in the Kharkov area and succeeded in rolling the Red Army back—in some places as far as eighty miles. The attack is the first hint that the Nazis still have the strength left to launch a new and terrible offensive later this spring or early summer. It will be the last and most dangerous death flurry of the Nazi beast—and there is a conceivable possibility of its success. Let us hope that the Allies in the west may be able to beat Hitler to the draw this time.

Large scale fighting in Tunisia has died down today, as threatening weather finally made good its threat and drowned out activity by both sides. Bad weather has been the main reason for the unexpectedly long hold-out by the Tunisian Axis forces.

RAF bombers from the British Isles were over Germany again last night in great force. This time it was Munich, the birth place of Hitlerism, that felt the crunch of block-busters and the white-hot flames of incendiaries.

Thursday, March 11, 1943: —The British Air Ministry has summed up the results of last year's air fighting. Allied pilots have run up a score of three to one against their Axis enemies. The Germans alone have lost—excluding their losses against Russia—over 3,100 planes. One million Nazis have been made homeless by the devastating RAF raids and 2,000 industrial plants have been blasted. The Germans lost 1,477 planes in Libya and Egypt, against British losses of 345. In Tunisia the Germans lost 767 against American-British losses of only 392.

In France, widespread revolt has broken out against the Nazi move to draft an additional 400,000 Frenchmen for slave labor in Germany. Organized resistance in the form of a guerrilla army of 25,000 men is wreaking havoc among Nazi garrisons and against Nazi communications. The latest successful action was the blasting of a speeding troop train, with the killing of more than 250 Nazi troops and the maiming of hundreds of others. Terrible reprisals are bound to be exacted by the frightened and angered Germans.

In Tunisia it's the British Eighth Army that is engaging the enemy at present. So far the battle is going in favor of the British, with heavy casualties being inflicted on the retreating foe.

Only on one sector in Russia are the highly touted Nazis having any luck. That is in the Kharkov area where even the Russians admit that the situation is critical, with the city in danger of falling at any moment. At other points on the far-flung Russian front, particularly the center, the Soviet offensive continues to roll forward.

Friday, March 12, 1943: —Reinforced and revitalized German armies are striking the Russians heavily in the Kharkov area. Late German communiqués claim that the vital city has been recaptured but Soviet reports stoutly deny this, claiming their forces are resisting furiously. The most sanguinary battle since Stalingrad appears to be in progress.

On the central front, however, the Russians are still advancing and the Nazis admit the loss of Vyazma, on the road to Smolensk.

American and Allied airmen all over the world were smashing at enemy bases today. Two of the heaviest attacks of the war were levied against the Japanese island foothold on Kiska, in the Aleutians. Flying Fortresses staged a fierce raid on Rouen, France, where important railroad installations were smashed. Last night the RAF made a routine flight over Stuttgart, where they unloaded a cargo of block-busters. Across the world, in New Guinea, American P-38 Lightnings and P-40 Kittyhawks knocked out 14 Jap planes when 40 enemy bombers attempted to raid Allied positions.

On the home front, we learned today that rationing of meat, canned fish, butter, cheese, edible fats and oils will begin at midnight March 26. The red coupons in our new ration books No. 2 will be used for this purpose.

Only three days left in which to make the first installment of the heaviest income tax in our history and the last-minute rush is just beginning.

Saturday, March 13, 1943: —British Foreign Secretary Anthony Eden arrived yesterday in Washington for a conference with President Roosevelt and other high Government officials. It is believed his visit has to do with post-war planning and United Nations unity, particularly with respect to Anglo-American-Russian relations. Eden is one of the few Allied leaders who really have the confidence of the Soviet Government. As such, he can do much to iron out the all too evident crinkles in Russia's relations with the other Allied Nations. The dashing, typically English, Foreign Secretary, who has consistently called the international turn, warned that victory over Germany is far from achieved and can be won only after a hard, bitter fight.

A thrilling, dramatic story is told tonight of an old-fashioned gun duel between an American submarine and a small Japanese patrol vessel. The fight took place in mid-Pacific and was won by superior American marksmanship. It was one of those little engagements that lend spine-tingling color to an otherwise huge, impersonal, and remotely dreadful war. Our only casualty in the engagement was the death of one of the sub's gunners. There were no Jap survivors.

In Western Europe, the RAF staged another paralyzing raid on Essen, the home of the great Krupp munitions works. The

British Air Ministry held high hopes that the raid had finally wiped out the Krupp factories.

Supplementing the devastating night work of the RAF, American Flying Fortresses carried out daylight attacks on Nazi communications at Abbeville in Northern France.

Sunday, March 14, 1943: —General Henri Giraud, French commander-in-chief in North Africa, made a memorable bid for French unity today. He extended the hand of friendship and cooperation to General Charles de Gaulle, the leader of the Fighting French, and pledged himself and his North African government to the service of the French people. He promised to oust all Nazi sympathizers and declared that the will of the French people, as shown in free elections, will determine who shall rule them, once the invader has been driven from the sacred soil of continental France.

It is fervently hoped that the General's speech will serve to eliminate much of the bickering between and among the French in North Africa which has hindered and delayed the total Allied victory in Tunisia.

Here at home, San Francisco police have started a determined drive to combat the growing crime wave that is sweeping over the Bay Area. Such conditions are the inevitable aftermath of the tremendous influx of defense workers into the area, bringing with them the vagrants, the drunkards, and the criminals. Our police are determined that the situation shall not get out of hand.

I almost forgot it is Sunday today. I spent another long day at the office, redeeming bonds for people who lacked the foresight to prepare for their taxes out of income. Paying taxes with bonds defeats the purpose of both. Some cases are justified and necessary but many are not.

Monday, March 15, 1943: —The last day for the filing of income tax returns has come and almost gone, as I write this record. As expected, the Collector of Internal Revenue Office was packed all day with last minute taxpayers. Thousands of citizens who have never filed a return before are faced with the heaviest taxes in history. The volume of mail and over-the-counter business has completely swamped the facilities of the Collector's office.

The flood of mail that gets under the deadline of 12:o'clock midnight tonight will arrive on Tuesday and Wednesday. Shakespeare had it right when he said, "Beware the Ides of March!"

Reports from Berne, Switzerland indicate that a large scale revolt by organized guerrilla bands of determined Frenchmen is making life miserable for German authorities in eastern France. The rebellion is of such large proportions that the Germans and Italians, with Vichy aid, have been forced to send large military units, including artillery to handle the situation. The Swiss report states that on several occasions, supplies and ammunition have been dropped to the guerrillas from British planes. The seething kettle, on which Hitler is holding the lid, is about ready to explode with a world shaking roar. Frenchmen—at least most of them—will not be slaves.

On the Russian front the situation looks bad in the Kharkov area. Apparently Hitler is throwing in some entirely fresh divisions in an effort to capitalize on his recent success. Berlin claims that Kharkov has already fallen but no confirmation of this is available from the Russians.

Tuesday, March 16, 1943: —We had a brief air raid "alert" today about 1:30. It didn't amount to much, being only a yellow precautionary warning. No sirens sounded. In Los Angeles, however, a red "alert" was sounded and sirens blared. For the most part, people took it without raising an eyebrow. Reports from Los Angeles said that the people practically ignored the sirens and went about their business in the usual manner, disregarding all efforts of air raid wardens to herd them into shelters.

Submarine warfare made the headlines again today. Our hard-hitting subs reported the destruction of four more Jap ships, including one large transport and a destroyer.

In Washington, Ottawa, and London navy officials announced simultaneously the complete agreement of the American, Canadian, and British governments on methods to meet the growing threat of U-boat warfare on the high seas. Conquering of the submarine menace is a mandatory prelude to any full-scale invasion of the European Continent.

Greatly stepped-up aerial activity by the Allies in Tunisia

point to the proximity of the general Tunisian offensive which the Allies must launch soon if the Axis is to be driven from North Africa this spring.

The Moscow radio today admitted the evacuation of Kharkov in the face of overwhelming German attack but claimed their armies are advancing rapidly on the northern front near Staraya, Russia, on the road to Smolensk.

Wednesday, March 17, 1943: —War news is pretty barren tonight. From Russia comes evidence that the powerful Nazi counter-attack in the Kharkov area, that carried through to the capture of the city, has definitely been stopped by fiercely resisting Russians. The situation in this important sector, therefore, is under control for the first time in a week.

In the far north the Red Army has opened an arctic drive against Petsamo in Northern Finland and has advanced to within seven miles of the Finnish port. Poor, unhappy Finland. The only country which never missed a payment on her World War I debt, she has always had the sympathy and respect of the United States. This country would like to see her extricate herself from her unfortunate alliance with Nazi Germany and there is little doubt but that Finland would accept a separate peace if she could get reasonable terms from Russia. But Russia apparently is not going to be easy on the tiny republic.

Principal activity by American forces was confined to the air today. The Navy reported that six separate attacks were made against the Japanese held island of Kiska in the Aleutians. Results were not announced but it is said the raids were very heavy.

In Tunisia, British and American airmen pounded Axis positions so steadily and in such large force that observers believed the long-heralded final offensive has begun. The air attack takes the place of the tremendous World War I artillery barrages that preceded the "big push."

Thursday, March 18, 1943: —American armored forces struck out suddenly today in a lightning drive through central Tunisia. Meeting very little Axis resistance our troops succeeded in capturing the important enemy base at Gafsa, about 85 miles northwest of Gabes on the Mediterranean. After taking the town, the Americans continued the advance six miles beyond for a total gain for the day of 36 miles.

The armored forces spearheading the American attack are commanded by Lieut. General George S. Patton. The General is widely known by the nickname "Old Blood and Guts" from his very realistic viewpoint on the constituents of modern war. General Patton is considered our number one tank commander and is well fitted to match his wits with the wily desert fox, Nazi Field Marshal Erwin Rommel. Patton has the advantage in this struggle because Rommel must also face the powerful and experienced Eighth Army at his rear but it will be a ding dong battle nevertheless.

The resilient Russian armies have rebounded from their defeat at Kharkov and have launched strong counter-attacks in that sector, seizing two fortified strongholds and pushing the Nazis out of eighteen villages. The slaughter continues.

On the home front it is tax problems again that make the front page. Congress is about to debate the proposed withholding tax on all incomes. Arguments are bound to be bitter as to method, with most Republicans holding out for the Ruml "skip a year" plan, and the Administration adamant on the 20% plan with no forgiveness of debts.

Friday, March 19, 1943: —It appears from today's news that our hopes that the grand offensive had started in Tunisia were a bit premature. The only attack seems to be that of General Patton's forces in the south-central sector. Here the Americans have advanced another 14 miles and are now in a position to threaten the vital port of Gabes, on the gulf of the same name. Capture of Gabes would drive a wedge between Rommel's Afrika Korps and Colonel General Von Arnim's Axis armies of the north. This would practically seal the doom of Rommel and you may be sure that he will resist mightily to prevent such a breakthrough.

General Montgomery's Eighth Army apparently is not quite ready, besides being bogged down in rivers of mud from recent rains. It has undoubtedly been the inclement Tunisian weather that has long delayed the Allied "big push" and thus given the Axis forces time to muster considerable strength.

The Russo-German war on the eastern front continues unabated in fury. Today's communiqués indicate that the Germans are smashing wave after wave of fresh panzer troops against the Soviet lines in an effort to regain the initiative. In one spot southeast of Kharkov, the Nazis succeeded in driving a wedge into the Russian lines to a distance of 28 miles but fiercely resisting Russian soldiers are foiling every attempt by Hitler's men to widen the breach into a real breakthrough.

American Flying Fortresses today staged their most successful raid so far on Germany itself and smeared the Vegsack U-boats near Bremen. Keep 'em flyin' boys!

Saturday, March 20, 1943: —This has been a hectic and momentous day—for me and my family. My wife presented me with a baby boy at 4:58 p.m. this afternoon. I missed my first day's work since coming down here as I rushed my wife to Mills Memorial Hospital in San Mateo early this morning. Things were not so easy for her, however, and it wasn't over until this afternoon. He is a fine boy weighing 10 pounds 3½ ounces and standing 22½ inches in his stocking feet or something.

The above hasn't much to do with the war news except that it is further evidence of the tremendous war boom in babies. As happens in every war it seems, the stork is an exceptionally popular fellow and he brings an unusually large percentage of boys. This appears to be nature's way of compensating for the unholy slaughter of young men that is rampant in the world today.

There isn't much of note to report from the war front tonight. It appears that General Patton's drive in Tunisia has been slowed down by heavy rains that make armored movement practically impossible but the Americans are utilizing the lull to consolidate their recent gains around Gafsa. As soon as the weather permits they are expected to roll onward toward Gabes.

The picture in Russia is obscure. The Germans apparently have plenty of kick left in them and are throwing thousands of fresh reserves into the battle near Kharkov. Russians are fighting bitterly to hold their own. Farther north on the central and far north fronts the Red Army is making some forward progress but the whole 1,500 mile front is very fluid.

Sunday, March 21, 1943: —It is the first official day of spring today but the seasons are hard to distinguish here in California. Spring isn't much different from the other seasons except that the hills look like fairways and it rains a lot. You have to go to the Rocky Mountains to really appreciate the coming of spring. You have to experience the frozen cold of the winter with all green things hibernating, appearing as though dead. Then you see the spring sun's rays penetrate and liquidate the frozen mantle and warm the toes of all the trees and plants. They spring to life, invigorated and refreshed by their long rest, glowing with a fresh greenness unmatched anywhere. The flowers smile happily at them. Nature's children are reborn—and man's spirit with them. It is springtime in the Rockies.

But while nature is replenishing the earth, man himself is still pursuing his evil way of destruction and death. Late news reports from Tunisia indicate that General Patton's armored force is on the move again and has captured Sened. Supporting this thrust by the Americans, we learn that the British Eighth Army has finally opened up in what promises to be the decisive battle that will force either an attempted Stalingrad defense or a Dunkirk evacuation on the German North African armies.

Prime Minister Churchill made a stirring speech today. Among many other things, however, he warned against looking for a quick ending of the war. He calculates it will take about two more years to smash Hitler and then Japan. Not a very pleasant outlook but probably true.

Monday, March 22, 1943: —The "Big Push" is on in Tunisia. The British Eighth Army has begun an attack in force along a six mile front on the Mareth line and late reports indicate that early objectives were reached on schedule. Stern resistance was encountered. Northwest of the Eighth Army's positions, American forces under General Patton are racing towards Gabes, in a bid to outflank Rommel and cut off his escape line. So far the United States' advance has met little resistance and has captured Bou Hamran with 1,000 Italian prisoners being taken.

General Montgomery brought out his first team in all categories to prepare for the attack. Big Liberator and Halifax bombers softened up Axis positions with never-ending "shuttle bombing," while the famous Eighth Army artillery that blasted Rommel out of El Alamein not so many moons ago, crushed enemy fortifications to open the way for the infantry and tank attack. Meanwhile, Hitler, in an order of the day diametrically opposed to his former boasts of easy victory, called on his Tunisian forces to "fight to the finish, with the same valor as the

Sacred Sixth Army" which was killed or captured to the last man at Stalingrad. It's Adolf's turn to try and wriggle his way out of a disastrous situation. Has he the British valor and ability? Time will tell.

Naziland got another plastering from Flying Fortresses today. The mighty Flying Forts which have proved that daylight raiding over Germany proper can be made successfully without heavy loss, smashed the strongly defended naval base of Wilhelmshaven in one of the biggest raids of the war losing only three of the big ships.

Tuesday, March 23, 1943: —It looks like the beginning of the end in Tunisia. The Allied nutcracker is bearing down on Rommel and his trapped Afrika Korps. General Montgomery sent part of his veteran Eighth Army in a typically brilliant sweep around the end of the Mareth line and succeeded in flanking the whole Axis defense line in southern Tunisia. At the same time General "Old Blood and Guts" Patton's U.S. armored columns sliced forward another 25 miles to come within 31 miles of the sea and threaten to cut Tunisia in half, leaving Rommel with no avenue of retreat should he desire to join Colonel General Von Arnim for a last stand in the Tunis-Bizerte area. It looks like the desert fox has at last been treed.

Latest reports from the Southwest Pacific indicate that General MacArthur's victorious New Guinea army is strengthening its grip on the northern coast of that island. Our troops are slowly but surely advancing northward, wiping out several important bridgeheads and potential offensive springboards of the enemy as they progress. The capture of Salamaua and Lae and the complete ouster of the Japs from New Guinea is the objective and its realization may not be so far off.

The Russo-German struggle is a give and take affair. The Nazi offensive around Kharkov is still moving forward slowly but shows signs of subsiding while the Red Army drive on Smolensk has liberated 50 more inhabited places. The real extent of the success or failure of either side is obscure and it cannot be determined from the news reports how near to exhaustion the adversaries are at the present. Anything can happen in Russia and it wouldn't surprise me if it did.

345

Wednesday, March 24, 1943: —The Office of Price Administration today released the official list of points covering meats, fish, butter and fats to be rationed beginning next Monday, March 29th. Sixteen points per person, rich or poor, will be the quota per week. With these points each person must buy his share of meats and butter, salad oils and fish. Sixteen points will buy two pounds of steak and no butter or two pounds of butter and no steak. It's up to the individual to decide how he will utilize his share of points. For a family group rationing is more beneficial as the members of the family group can pool their coupons and thus buy larger quantities although the amount per person is equal. Single persons or couples without children will need to budget their coupons more carefully but at least everyone will be entitled to the same opportunity to share the limited supply of these vital commodities.

The fighting in Tunisia is rapidly increasing in ferocity. The British Eighth Army succeeded in driving a wide breach in the Mareth line by dint of some furious fighting, much of it hand to hand. Late reports, however, indicate that the Germans have retaken most of the lost territory with vicious counter-attacks. The issue is still in doubt. Meanwhile, in south-central Tunisia, American armored columns are knifing closer to the vital Gabes-Mareth coastal road down which Rommel would have to flee were he to escape annihilation. A long hard fight is expected before final victory is achieved. Rommel is playing for time. His armies are to be sacrificed in order that Hitler can prepare the European Continent for invasion.

Thursday, March 25, 1943: —San Francisco was honored today by a visit from Madame Chiang Kai Shek, the "Missimo" of Fighting China. The First Lady of the Orient is here to plead the cause of the gallant Chinese who have born the terrible brunt of war with Japan for more than five long years. She is not here to beg but to gain an understanding between the two great nations in order that they may help each other most effectively. A strong China is our most valuable ally in the far eastern war.

The Madame is the person most fitted of all China's millions to represent that nation in this country. She was educated here and speaks English with a fluency and command rarely attained by our own scholars. In addition she is charming and gracious of manner and capable of winning the hearts of all those who see and hear her. If anyone can secure more aid for China it will be the beautiful wife of Generalissimo Chiang Kai Shek, the strong man and lucky husband of China.

President Roosevelt today took a hand in the increasingly serious food situation by displacing Secy. of Agriculture Wickard as the national food administrator, naming Chester C. Davis as his successor. Considerable anxiety is felt throughout the country over food prospects for the future and Mr. Davis is to be given full power to act in an effort to solve the farm problem.

Fighting in Tunisia is raging full blast with no decision one way or the other having been reached as yet. The British are finding the Mareth line, manned by the veterans of the Afrika Korps, a hard nut to crack, and a protracted bloody battle is expected.

Friday, March 26, 1943: —Allied progress in the Battle of Tunisia is very slow due to determined resistance on the part of the enemy. Latest reports however, indicate that the British Eighth Army is developing its offensive against the Mareth line and is maintaining its salient in the line of fortifications despite fierce counter-attacks by Rommel's veterans. Much of the fighting is bitter, hand to hand combat. Meanwhile, General Patton's American "panzer" columns were hanging on to their advanced positions, having repelled several desperate attempts of the enemy to dislodge them. Today's activities were confined to patrols and it appears likely that both sides are awaiting the decision at the Mareth line before attempting further advances.

In Russia, the Red Army has not only stopped the German offensive near Kharkov but was able to seize the initiative in several sectors during the day. Fighting was on a smaller scale, however, as evidenced by the communiqués mention of companies and regiments rather than divisions and armies as heretofore.

The Pacific war at the present time is almost entirely confined to the air. General Douglas MacArthur's communiqué reports that our heavy bombers raked the Japanese base at Rabaul, New Britain for two hours today. It was the second large scale raid in three days against the big Jap base and the Flying Fortresses and Liberators left huge fires consuming Jap supplies and equipment in addition to heavy destruction of shipping and harbor installations.

Saturday, March 27, 1943: —General George S. Patton's American armored forces in south-central Tunisia lashed out in another surprise attack today, picking up on addition fifteen miles from their recently captured positions in the Maknassy and El Guetar sectors. Berlin reports admit the advance but claim heavy casualties were inflicted on the U.S. forces. No doubt that is true to some extent and is the sad, inevitable price to be paid for victory.

London's news reports state that the Eighth Army's sustained drive against the Mareth line is getting "satisfactory results" and is being supported by extremely effective aerial support. Allied planes are pounding the enemy's lines day and night without surcease and have won complete domination of the sky over the battlefront.

On the home front it is rationing and taxes that still hold the spotlight after the warfront news. In some places, despite public warnings, panic buying of meats, cheese, and other to-be rationed foods, cleaned out grocers' and butchers' shelves, leaving them little with which to start out on Monday morning when rationing of these commodities begins. Freezing of butter sales prevented a similar occurrence with respect to that commodity.

Congress is still debating the pay-as-you-go tax plan and appears hopelessly divided at the present time. The consensus of opinion is that a modified version of the Ruml Plan will eventually win passage.

Sunday, March 28, 1943: —Today was one of those rare spring days that serve to renew one's faith that God has not forsaken this suffering world. Although the bitter medicine of destruction and death is being meted out in fearful doses it is entirely of man's own doing and Heaven is displeased. Days of beauty, with warm sunshine and blue skies, days like today, are intended for man's happiness and God in his almighty power will destroy evil and make it possible for men of good will to once again enjoy the beauties of spring in peace and humble worship.

Meanwhile, the terrible ordeal that Hitler brought upon the German people is continuing with unabated fury. RAF planes, three hundred strong, winged their way deep into the heart of Germany to smash at Berlin in the heaviest raid of the war on that capital. 4,000 pound block-busters and thousands of incendiaries wrecked and burned the city until attacking pilots said it looked like a great open furnace beneath them. Conditions were ideal for the raid. Returning pilots said they were protected by a screen of clouds until just before they reached the target when the clouds opened up, exposing the entire city in perfect view below. Due to the favorable weather circumstances, only nine of the raiders were lost, despite the usual heavy anti-aircraft and fighter plane opposition. The British cannot but feel grim satisfaction at the results of the raid as they think of their own devastated cities of 1940 and 1941. Revenge is sweet.

Monday, March 29, 1943: —The Mareth line has crumbled! Rommel is in full retreat! The British Eighth Army has done it again! More than ten thousand prisoners and great quantities of booty have already fallen into the hands of the Allies. The fleeing Afrika Korps is being driven into the ever narrowing bottleneck of Gabes, where it is being assailed by land, sea, and air. The British have even sent part of their fleet to bombard Gabes with sixteen inch shells that hurtle and smash into the retreating enemy mass. From the other side, General George Patton's American troops are rushing to jam the stopper into the bottle and cut off the retreat of the Afrika Korps.

The break-through at the Mareth line came with great suddenness and was largely caused by the brilliant flanking movement by a part of General Montgomery's forces which swung around the south end of the line and suddenly burst upon Rommel's rear. This flanking movement will probably rank as one of the greatest forced marches in the history of warfare, across "impossible" wasteland—so impossible in fact that Rommel had not prepared defenses against it, believing it to be impassable.

Even in northern Tunisia, the Allied armies were on the offensive. The British First Army suddenly slashed forward, throwing Col. General Von Arnim off balance and forcing him to withdraw all along the line. All indications are that it is the beginning of the end in Tunisia. Only a miracle can prevent the Allies from driving the Axis armies into the sea—or into prison camps.

Tuesday, March 30, 1943: —Allied armies in Tunisia are smashing ahead. The British Eighth Army has seized the key port of Gabes and is pursuing Rommel's battered Afrika Korps on the road to Sfax, which late reports indicate is being burned by the retreating Nazis.

A juncture of the Eighth Army with General Patton's American forces is imminent. The only unsatisfactory feature to the situation is the apparent fact that Rommel was able to slip by before the jaws of the trap closed. Consequently, it appears that the remnants of his beaten army will join with Col. General Arnim's northern Tunisian forces for a final stand.

From all reports, complete domination of the air was a principal contributing factor in the crushing of Rommel and the Mareth line. General Carl Spaatz, the American air chief in North Africa obviously has done an excellent job. His next task will be to prevent the Nazis from staging a "Dunkirk" escape from Tunisia.

There are many indications in the South Pacific that big offensives are being prepared, to explode without warning in the faces of the Japs. General MacArthur's veteran air force is giving the enemy the worst and steadiest pounding since the war began. Things are definitely warming up in the Pacific.

Last night the RAF followed up its Saturday night raid on Berlin with an equally strong attack. This one did great damage but was not as successful as the first due to unfavorable weather and more effective opposition.

Wednesday, March 31, 1943: —The position of the Axis in North Africa is continuing to deteriorate. Marshal Rommel, the sly old desert fox, has temporarily elude the Allied bloodhounds and is pulling the remnants of his badly mauled Afrika Korps back through the bottleneck north of Gabes. But the end of the fox hunt is in sight and the Allied forces are surging forward for the kill. Diabolical "booby traps" and thickly sown minefields are slowing the Allied advance but there is a terrible inevitability about the fate that awaits the Axis in Tunisia.

In the South Pacific American airmen again intercepted a Japanese attempt to bolster their New Guinea forces. Flying through thick, soupy weather alert U.S. air patrols caught the Jap convoy, consisting mainly of destroyers, off the coast of New Ireland and scored one direct hit with a 500 pound bomb that ripped the stern off one large destroyer, sinking her, and putting the rest of the convoy to flight far short of their objective.

Evidencing the world-wide might of American air power, U.S. heavy bombers, based in England, staged an extremely effective raid on military objectives in Rotterdam today. Bombardiers in the big Flying Fortresses and Liberators saw their bombs burst with devastating effect on shipbuilding yards and other military installations. German fighter planes adopted new tactics in an effort to solve the "Forts" defenses, diving on a single plane six abreast, cannons roaring. American gunners claimed that it made their hunting just that much easier. Only one American plane failed to return.

April

Thursday, April 1, 1943: —While ground fighting in Tunisia has slowed down after the first phase, the Allies have unleashed an all-out aerial offensive, aimed at forestalling any attempt at a "Dunkirk" evacuation by the Axis forces. In the biggest raid ever staged by American Flying Fortresses, the huge bombers swept over southern Sardinia and smashed the Axis supply port of Cagliari, destroying five merchant ships. In addition, fourteen enemy interceptors that dared to oppose the American raiders were shot down. No U.S. planes were lost.

A reliable Madrid report stated today that Germany has commandeered the entire Italian fleet and all available French merchant ships in preparation for an attempt to rescue her imperiled African armies. It hardly seems possible, however, that the Nazis will be able to wrest sufficient control of the sea and air between Tunisia and Italy to duplicate the feat of the English at Dunkirk in 1940. Germany's task will be infinitely more difficult because of the greater distances involved and the strength of Allied sea power. There are powerful units of the British Navy based at Gibraltar and Alexandria that can be counted on to wreak havoc among any rescue fleet. But Hitler can hardly afford to sacrifice his entire African force which includes some of his finest and most experienced troops as well as large quantities of valuable equipment.

The meat situation here at home has improved considerably since rationing began. Already black market operations have died down and butchers shelves are no longer bare.

Friday, April 2, 1943: —The war spotlight is still on Tunisia, where American, British, and French troops are drawing a noose tighter around the trapped Axis forces. Marshal Rommel appears to have stopped his retreat thirty miles north of Gabes and is digging in for a stand along the wide, deep Wadi Akarit.

Meanwhile, massed Allied air forces smashed relentlessly against Axis supplies and fortifications at Sfax and Bizerte. Two-ton "block-busters" were carted by huge British and American bombers over Bizerte and plopped with devastating effect among shipping and harbor installations.

In Russia both invaders and defenders were "resting" after the tremendous efforts of the winter campaign and their commanders were feverishly preparing for the coming spring and summer drives. Russia's winter victories, though tremendous, still leave the Nazis in control of Kharkov and with a sharp claw still imbedded in the Caucasus. Red Army reconnaissance shows huge quantities of fresh German reserves of men and equipment moving to the eastern front in readiness for another desperate bid for Caucasian oil.

Here at home National Selective Service officials stated that the drafting of fathers with pre-Pearl Harbor children is soon to be unavoidable. Reclassification of all 3A, 3B, and 3C men will be accomplished in the near future.

Saturday, April 3, 1943: —General bad weather hindered the Tunisian campaign today but Allied air patrols gave the Axis armies and ports of supply no rest. American tanks and infantry also lashed at the main German positions near the Kebili Road junction southeast of El Quetar. Results are not yet known.

Moscow announced their triumphant winter campaign had liberated 185,328 square miles of territory and inflicted 1,193,525 casualties on the enemy. Of these casualties, the Red Army claims 850,000 were killed, the rest captured.

American heavy and medium bombers again pounded Japanese installations on Kiska in the Aleutians. Our aerial offensive against the Japs in the Aleutians has been stepped up to a daily routine since March 1st.

Meanwhile, from the southwest Pacific to Burma, other American bombers were sowing a path of destruction through Japanese supply lines. General MacArthur's fast flying airmen caught 13 Jap ships in the harbor of Kavieng, on the northern end of New Ireland above New Guinea and sent two of them up in smoke.

Two army officers seated near me today at a fountain in downtown San Francisco have decided that the civilians' lot is not so hot. They ordered coffee—no coffee. They ordered Cokes—no Cokes. Beef sandwich—no beef. How about pie ala mode? Pie, yes, but no ice cream. Buttered toast with Jelly? Toast, yes, but no butter and no jelly. They finally settled for a pot of tea and apple pie—without ice cream. Then they went joyfully back to camp—for a decent meal.

Sunday, April 4, 1943: —I forgot to mention that yesterday I talked by telephone with my brother, a staff sergeant stationed at Mather Field, near Sacramento. He has been in the army just one year—and we're mighty proud of him. Broke all records at Mather Field. Drafted as a buck private he became a staff sergeant in just seven and one half months. He is now a candidate for Officers' Training. My bet is that he'll end the war at least a Captain.

American forces attacking on the central Tunisian front found the going plenty tough. Rommel has sowed wide minefields through which our armored columns must pass. In one sector where our engineers had cleared a narrow path, the Germans launched a fierce counter-attack that forced our troops to withdraw temporarily. But General Eisenhower, inspecting the battlefront, said that every American has reason to be proud of the progress made by our troops and should share the pride of the British in the mighty achievements of the Eighth Army in driving Rommel from the "impregnable" Mareth line.

American Liberator bombers made a sweeping attack at treetop height on several Italian mainland objectives. Coming in at a height of only fifty feet the speedy craft were in and out before Italian defenses could go into operation. Railroad and ferry terminals were left in ruins. No American planes were lost and one lone German interceptor plane was shot down.

Monday, April 5, 1943: —The major portion of battlefront news is confined to the air tonight. Vast fleets of Allied bombers and fighter planes are pounding the enemy in every theater of war. In Tunisia, a mighty fleet of Flying Fortresses and Billy Mitchell bombers crossed the Mediterranean by daylight today to crush the Italian port of Naples with its heaviest raid of the war to date. Two hundred tons of bombs were dropped on the port in a fifteen minute attack that left numerous vessels wrecked in the harbor and countless fires raging on the quays and adjacent industrial areas. No fighter opposition was encountered by the raiders and only ineffectual anti-aircraft artillery fire. No planes were lost.

In the South Pacific, General MacArthur's bombing command apparently is concentrating on Jap bases on New Ireland. Flying Fortresses smashed at Kavieng Harbor on that island today and sank or badly damaged five cargo vessels.

In the European theater, more than 700 RAF bombers raided

the German naval base at Kiel and a large force of American planes smashed at the Nazi-operated Renault auto works near Paris. Another American raiding force attacked Nazi military installations in the Antwerp, Belgium area, encountering ferocious enemy resistance. More than 100 German fighters intercepted the big American bombers and threw everything in the book at them. Only three of the big planes failed to make the return trip but some of the surviving planes, including that of Brig. General Frank Armstrong, limped home after being riddled from nose to tail. The big ships can really take it.

Tuesday, April 6, 1943: —Ground activity in Tunisia flared up with new violence today. The invincible British Eighth Army was reported officially to have launched a powerful frontal attack against Marshal Rommel's positions at Wadi Akarit, 20 miles north of Gabes. At the same time, General George S. Patton's American armored forces slashed a new six mile salient into the flank of the Afrika Korps in the El Guetar sector.

Allied planes are contributing heavily to the success of the British and American drives in Tunisia. Today's report stated that they have broken all records by engaging in more than 1,000 sorties since the fighting began in North Africa. Axis supply lines and communications have been pasted night and day without surcease.

From Gibraltar comes the news that a big British battle fleet, including three battleships, three aircraft carriers, 35 destroyers, and other vessels, has departed from the base for an unknown destination. Big doings portend.

The Pacific war with Japan is confined mostly to the air at the present time. Burma popped back into the limelight with the report of a strong attack by U.S. bombers on the Japanese base at Mandalay where the dawn comes up like thunder according to Rudyard Kipling. The old pagodas felt the crunch of tons of high explosives that wrecked supply dumps, rail installations, and started many fires.

Wednesday, April 7, 1943: —Magnificent news comes out of Tunisia today. A special communiqué was released from Allied headquarters announcing that the United States Second Army Corps has smashed through the Axis lines and have made contact with the British Eighth Army advancing from Wadi Akarit.

The British have built up in their Eighth Army one of the most powerful striking forces in the history of the Empire. The successful juncture of the British and American armies today was due to a sensational frontal attack on the German defenses at Wadi Akarit by the Eighth Army. The attack, preceded by a terrific artillery barrage, was completely successful in breaching the strongly held Axis lines and the British streamed through. General Patton's American armored columns were instrumental in the victory by drawing off a substantial portion of Rommel's armored strength from the defense of Wadi Akarit. It must have been a momentous meeting when the two Allied armies met. I would have liked to have been in the first patrol to sight the British.

Army intelligence in London today reports that excitement over a probable invasion is sweeping Italy. Il Duce Mussolini is yelping for help from his boss, Hitler, and it is reported that the two dictators will meet in one of their famous Brenner Pass get-togethers to map out a plan for the defense of Italy after the anticipated fall of Tunisia. How different this meeting from those of two years ago when the two boastful and victorious conquerors whould meet to discuss the fate of other defenseless victims. Every dog has his day, Adolf, and you've certainly had yours.

Thursday, April 8, 1943: —From northern Tunisia where the British First Army under General Anderson drove forward for five miles today to the southern and central sectors where the combined British, American, and French forces smashed ahead for a total gain of fifteen miles, the Axis African Empire is rapidly crumbling into oblivion. A gigantic pincers is clamping down on the trapped enemy with escape extremely unlikely. The desert fox is cornered, his back pinned against the sea. How viciously will he fight before his ultimate defeat? Will the Germans show the courage of the British at Dunkirk and Tobruk, the Americans at Bataan, or the Russians at Stalingrad? We shall know the answer to this question before many weeks are over.

From the South Pacific comes news of a tremendous air battle off Guadalcanal. The Japs launched a 100 plane attack against an American convoy off the island. The raiders were intercepted by American Aircobra and Grumman Wildcat fighter planes and a terrific dogfight ensued. Thirty seven of the Japanese planes were knocked from the sky with a loss of seven U.S. planes. Our boys thus maintained their average of better than five to one against the little yellow enemy. The Navy did not announce the damage that was inflicted by the raiders on the convoy but we must be prepared for some bad news. A few of their bombs must have hit their targets. Nevertheless, the action was considered a notable victory for our air force.

On the home front the news is centered on the draft question, particularly with respect to the induction of fathers of dependent children. Present indications are that dependency will not be a basis for deferment much longer. Future deferment will be made only on occupational grounds.

Friday, April 9, 1943: —The Navy announced today that the 98 plane Japanese attack on a United States' convoy off Guadalcanal Island yesterday cost us four vessels, including a destroyer. The others were a tanker, a corvette, and a fuel boat.

Principal ground fighting at the present time is confined to Tunisia, where the Allies are drawing the noose tighter around the trapped Axis forces in the Tunis-Bizerte corner. The corridor of escape by Marshal Rommel after his disastrous defeat at the Mareth line has been growing shorter and narrower each day. Already at least fifteen thousand of his troops have been caught in the trap and captured by the fast moving British Eighth Army and General Patton's American and French columns. Complete victory in Tunisia is only a matter of time.

The grim specter of inflation raised its ugly head on the home front today. President Roosevelt took cognizance of the grave danger that prices and wages may get beyond control and announced a new anti-inflation program aimed at "holding the line" against the deadly peril of uncontrolled inflation. Principal features of his new program are specific retail price ceilings on almost all commodities, price controls of additional raw materials, banning of wage increases, prevention of workers transferring from one job to another for higher wages, new and heavier taxes, and control of transportation and utility rates. In short, we can expect to be regimented and controlled to a point never before attained in the history of the nation. The people must see to it that it is only for the duration.

Saturday, April 10, 1943: —Allied forces in Tunisia have finally attained a "blitz" speed in their drive against the Axis in North Africa.

357

The British Eighth Army especially was smashing forward at tremendous speed. The vanguard of the Eighth Army occupied Sfax at 8:15 a.m. today after covering the last 22 miles in 19 hours despite strong rearguard action by the Afrika Korps.

General Bernard L. Montgomery, commander of the Eighth Army, issued a triumphant personal message to his troops, praising them for their recent brilliant victories and urging them to relentlessly pursue the enemy. The battle cry is "On to Tunis! Drive the enemy into the sea!" "Let us make the enemy face up to, and endure a first class Dunkirk on the beaches of Tunis," he said. "If we collect prisoners at the present rate the enemy soon will have no infantry left to hold his positions."

With the crumbling of Axis defenses in North Africa, the invasion jitters are spreading over Italy. An unconfirmed report stated that Mussolini has already made plans for the moving of the Italian government from Rome to Florence or Bologna in case of emergency. The last named place would be most appropriate for Il Duce's regime.

In the South Pacific, General MacArthur's planes were busy again, smashing at the Japanese base of Madang in New Guinea. Bombs set fires that sent smoke billowing 3,000 feet into the air, several big explosions were observed among shipping in Madang Harbor. All planes returned.

Sunday, April 11, 1943: —It was a beautiful spring day today, without a cloud to mar the vast dome of blue sky above. It was a day to be outside and it was doubly enjoyable to us because we had occasion to drive across the San Francisco-Oakland Bay Bridge. That structure to me, is one of the most inspiring sights in the world. The first time across it literally takes your breath away by the incredible magnificence of its architecture. The very fact that man conceived and built it leaves one with a feeling of amazement and humility. It is the perfect example of the constructive power that man possesses if his energies are turned towards the pursuit of peace rather than war. What mighty edifices might have been erected for the benefit of mankind had the tremendous energies used in the prosecution of this war been channeled off into more peaceful streams.

But on with the war. In Tunisia the powerful British Eighth Army is really eating up the road north of captured Sfax. Marshal

Rommel's stricken Afrika Korps is hightailing it for Bizerte and Tunis, where General Montgomery is determined to make him endure "a first class Dunkirk." The fleeing Axis troops are being pounded relentlessly frm the air, with the Allied Air Force throwing everything in the book at them. American airmen, flying approximately 100 Flying Fortresses without fighter escorts, blitzed the Axis communication lines and caught two 10,000 ton Italian cruisers at anchor in a Sardinian port, smashing them with direct bomb hits that rendered them useless for any attempted evacuation sortie to Tunisia. All in all, the Allies, and particularly the British, are enjoying their first real opportunity to dish out the bitter medicine to the hated Nazis.

Monday, April 12, 1943: —Today marked the opening of the Treasury Department's Second War Loan Drive, aimed at borrowing the stupendous total of thirteen billion dollars during the next 30 days. It is the biggest undertaking of its kind ever conceived and the Treasury has organized a vast sales machine to conduct the campaign. The slogan of the drive comes from President Roosevelt who said, "They give their lives—you lend your money." In addition to the three series of Savings Bonds currently on sale, the Treasury is offering several new issues of 2½% Treasury Bonds and other shorter term Certificates of Indebtedness. A similar drive in December, aimed at bringing in nine billion dollars was way oversubscribed to better than thirteen billion, so it is likely that the present campaign will go "over the top."

The war news from Tunisia continues to be amazingly good. The Allied armies are really making up for the time lost because of bad weather during previous months and are bringing the contest to a rapid showdown. The British Eighth Army raced with overwhelming speed over the 100 miles from Sfax to Sousse and rolled in to capture that important base without permitting the fleeing enemy to organize any effective opposition. Marshal Rommel's battered Afrika Korps is streaming back into the Tunis-Bizerte pocket where the final battle will be fought. Thousands of stragglers, both German and Italian, are swelling the ranks of prisoners taken in the present drive to over 25,000.

Thundering flocks of Allied aircraft have practically wiped the German Luftwaffe from the Tunisian skies and are pounding the Axis front lines and communication lines with an unceasing rain of high explosives. The battle will soon reach the final climax.

Tuesday, April 13, 1943: —San Francisco had its own little war today as four hardened criminals from Alcatraz staged a suicidal escape attempt shortly before noon. The four men overpowered two guards and slipped from the "Rock" into the racing ebb tide of San Francisco Bay. The alarm was soon sounded and Alcatraz guards opened fire on the swimming men with rifles and tommy guns. Three of the desperate men were killed, the fourth captured.

Meanwhile other criminals, those of international repute, were being herded brusquely into the coffin corner of Tunisia. The Allied forces have finally joined together to weld a huge arc of steel around the trapped Axis armies in the Tunis-Bizerte area. The British Eighth Army forged ahead fourteen miles north of Sousse to join hands with the British First Army of the north under General Anderson. Together they advanced to contact the enemy who offered strong rearguard resistance.

Across the world, our little yellow enemies are evidently preparing some sort of a spring offensive north of Australia. Latest reports indicate that the Japs have concentrated 200,000 troops and a powerful air force in the area and are gambling daily for mastery of the air. Yesterday they sent a 100 plane raiding party over Port Moresby to bomb that port for the first time in many weeks. Intercepting American and Australian pilots gave their plans a severe jolt by knocking out 37 of the attacking planes and sending the others scurrying for cover. But the persistent Jap is far from through. He keeps coming back for more and does not count the price. He is a tough customer.

Wednesday, April 14, 1943: —General MacArthur today emphasized the growing threat of a Japanese spring offensive against Australia. He pointed out that the Nips are massing air, sea, and land powers on the outer rim of the Australian defense zone. They have increased the power and frequency of their bombing attacks against Allied bases and despite heavy losses have returned in even greater force. The only solution, according to MacArthur, is an immediate and rapid expansion of our air power in the South Pacific. In short, the General is warning in no uncertain terms, that a larger percentage of our combat plane production must go to the South Pacific theater if we would prevent an extremely dangerous situation from arising.

In Tunisia, the Allies made further gains, particularly north of Sousse, where the British Eighth Army has reached a point more than 27 miles north of the latter base and has encountered the first strong positions of the Axis in the Enfidaville zone. Unconfirmed reports from Morocco state that Enfidaville has been captured by the British but official communiqués do not mention this possibility. In any case, things are becoming plenty hot for the Axis in their Tunisian deathtrap. The American and British air forces are ranging constantly over their front lines and communication lines, unloosing a terrible hailstorm of explosives. I would not care to be in the boots of a Nazi or Fascist soldier in Tunisia during the next two weeks. They'll find out how right General Sherman was.

Thursday, April 15, 1943: —The Treasury Department announced today that the current War Bond Drive has netted over five billion in the first three days. Half of this total was purchased by banks, the balance by individuals and private companies.

As a further incentive to buy bonds, the newspapers today published the first interviews with wounded sailors and marines confined to the Oak Knoll Naval Hospital. These men were maimed in the fierce Pacific fighting on and about Guadalcanal. The title to the article is "The Wounded Don't Cry" and tells the tragic tale of men without arms and men without legs, men with broken backs and men with malaria. It brought the terrible meaning of war close to home. No sacrifice of material things could be too great if it helped to bring that sort of thing to an end any quicker.

Allied troops in Tunisia scored two small gains in today's fighting. The British Eighth Army, however, spent the day in massing for a gigantic frontal attack against Rommel's previously prepared positions on the outer fringe of the Tunisian coffin corner. This last big offensive, it is hoped, will administer the coup de grace and end the campaign.

Meanwhile, in the South Pacific, Allied spokesmen continued to warn against rising Japanese power, claiming that the Japs have concentrated a large naval task force at their big base of Truk and a heavy concentration of merchant shipping at Rabaul, on New Britain Island. Secretary of War Stimson, taking cognizance of these warnings, promised that ample reinforcements, particularly in aircraft, would be dispatched to that theater to meet any Japanese threat.

Friday, April 16, 1943: —General MacArthur's heavy bombers caught another Japanese convoy, consisting of six transports and escorting warships, approaching Wewak on New Guinea and sent three of the transports and supply ships to the bottom. The remainder of the convoy was dispersed, although MacArthur's communiqué stated that "we are continuing the attack."

The pending last-ditch battle in Tunisia is in the final stages of preparation. The British First Army, holding the northern flank, was engaged in a fierce attack and counter-attack today. The cornered Nazis, giving evidence of the ferocity with which they will resist final defeat, stormed up the key mountain height of Djebel Ang and drove the British from their strong positions on the crest. Later in the day, the Tommies counter-attacked and retook the hill in some of the fiercest fighting of the campaign to date.

Meanwhile, the Allied air force in North Africa was opening an all out offensive against Axis supply and communication lines. Heavy British and American bombers raided Sardinia, Sicily, and ranged as far as Naples on the Italian mainland. Block-busters wreaked havoc among supply depots, air fields, and naval installations at the many bases attacked. Allied superiority in the air over the Mediterranean war theater is growing daily.

The Navy stated today that the Japs on Kiska in the Aleutians are getting plenty of attention lately. Our flyers have raided the island more than eighty times in less than a month. And that is only the beginning.

Saturday, April 17, 1943:—Death and terrible destruction rode the skyways over Europe last night and today as the Allied campaign to destroy Hitler's war industries reached a new peak of fury. More than six hundred mighty RAF bombers, lugging their 4,000 and 8,000 pound "block-busters" made a 1,400 mile round trip to Pilsen, in Czechoslovakia, to attack the great Skoda armament works. Thirty-seven of the big bombers failed to return, paying the inevitable price of war, but the Air Ministry said that attack was considered very successful.

At the same time a large force of American Flying Fortresses and Liberators raided the Focke-Wulf Aircraft Factory at Bremen. Furious anti-aircraft and fighter plane opposition was encountered by the Americans and sixteen of the great ships were shot down. To more than offset this loss, fifty of the Nazi interceptors fell victims to the deadly firepower of the "Forts."

Kiska in the Aleutians, really took a pounding today. The Army and Navy announced that no less than thirteen separate raids were carried out by heavy, and medium bombers escorted by P-40 Warhawks and P-38 Lightnings. The only loss was one bomber shot down by enemy anti-aircraft fire. Heavy damage was inflicted on the enemy base. So many raids in one day on one target indicate that the High Command may be softening the base up for an attempt to oust the Japs completely. We'll see how good a guess that is.

President Roosevelt today announced a modified job-wage freeze order that will affect more than half of the nation's 52,000,000 workers.

Sunday, April 18, 1943: —Either a bad cold or an attack of the flu has laid me low today. I spent the day in bed, wracking my body with a terrible cough and feeling anything but comfortable. Between chills and fevers I had plenty of time to meditate on the unhappy state of this sick world of ours. It will take some fancy doctoring to bring this sad case through the crisis and build it back into a healthy, peaceful place in which to live. It will be an even harder job to win the peace than to win the victory. The after effects of the disease, the destroyed cities, the ruined homes and families, the maimed and crippled men, will bring problems greater than the war itself. It will take courage of another kind to face the peace and tackle the problems to come.

The Allies are slowly putting the screws on the Axis in the coffin corner of Tunisia. All along the line, Allied troops are gradually increasing the pressure against Axis positions. The British First Army in the north seized firm hold on the dominating height of Djebel Ang, north of Medjez-el-Bab while the American Second Army Corps and the French bore down on the flank of Marshal Rommel's Enfidaville line while the British Eighth Army felt out Axis positions for a frontal attack on that line.

In the air, the North African Allied Air Force scored heavily, shooting down twenty two enemy planes in the Sicilian Strait. Twelve of the destroyed planes were big German or Italian transport planes, probably laden with supplies or troops for the hard pressed ground forces under Generals Arnim and Rommel.

Monday, April 19, 1943: —Great news from Tunisia! Allied air forces in Tunisia scored the most decisive victory in the air since the Battle of Britain. The action occurred over the Sicilian Strait between Sicily and the Tunisian coffin corner. A strong force of American and British Warhawk and Spitfire fighting planes hovered high over the Strait and caught a great formation of 115 German and Italian transport planes, escorted by fighters, apparently evacuating technical troops and equipment from Tunisia. A gigantic dogfight ensued which ended in complete disaster for the Axis. Out of the 115 enemy planes, 85 were sent spinning into the Mediterranean. Something like 65 of them were the huge flying boxcars loaded with troops and equipment. Only eleven Allied planes were shot down in the most one-sided air battle since the sharpshooting pilots of the Spitfires saved England in the dark days of the Battle of Britain in the fall of 1940.

General Eisenhower's headquarters were jubilant over the great air victory and observers believed that Allied supremacy in the air over the North African theater was now absolute. The stage is set for the final assault.

Between violent coughs and the flu that has confined me to bed today let's take a brief look at the Russian front that has been overshadowed by the Tunisian battle for the last few weeks. Both great armies are deadlocked in the positions where they ended the winter offensive. The Nazis, though badly mauled in that test, still have a sharp claw fastened in the Caucasus where they still occupy Novorrosisk, the vital base on the Black Sea. Both armies are gathering reserves for the mighty summer drives ahead as the muddy ground dries and the stalled tanks roar to life and begin to move forward.

Tuesday, April 20, 1943: —President Roosevelt did the unusual and unpredictable again today. He made a secret visit to inspect army camps in the South and then slipped over the Mexican border to meet the President of the Republic of Mexico, Manuel Avila Camacho, at Monterrey, some 145 miles within the southern Republic. Both Presidents made impressive speeches in their own languages over the radio. It was a typical Roosevelt show, with all the drama and interest of a Casablanca conference. It was all a part of the President's Good Neighbor policy of getting better acquainted with all of our Pan-American sister republics. Vice-President Henry Wallace is also on a similar mission throughout South America at the present time and news reports indicate that he is very popular with the South Americans, particularly because of his ability to speak Spanish fluently.

Back to the war news we find it is still Tunisia that holds the spotlight. The magnificent British Eighth Army is doing it again. Following a tremendous artillery barrage, the veterans of El Alamain, El Agheila, and the Mareth Line, stormed to the attack along the Axis Enfidaville line and, by special communiqué, Radio Algiers announced that Enfidaville fell after a brilliantly executed flanking movement that forced Rommel to evacuate the town, which is a vital anchor on the Axis defense line. The Eighth still rolls on!

News tonight from other war theaters is pretty barren. Almost all the activity is confined to the air, with Allied air forces pounding enemy bases without surcease, both to prevent enemy concentrations and to soften them for our offensive that is sure to come sooner or later.

Wednesday, April 21, 1943: —The civilized world is horror stricken today. America is angered to a point only equaled by the infamy of Dec. 7, 1941. President Roosevelt announced today that it was with horror that he has to report the barbarous execution by the Japanese Government of some of the members of this country's armed forces. The wretched savages who have been treated heretofore as the civilized leaders of a civilized nation have condemned and executed several of the American aviators who participated in the Tokyo raid of a year ago. Two of the bombers were forced down in Japanese occupied parts of China and the crews were captured and brought back to the Jap mainland, tried, and condemned to death. The sentences of some were commuted but others suffered the penalty of death.

Words cannot express the anger of the American people at this savagery on the part of a supposedly civilized nation which had subscribed to all the rules of international law. We can only echo the President's vow to hold officially and personally responsible all the Japanese leaders who permitted and participated in this bestial outrage. "Attack and Revenge!" will be the slogan for all American fighting men. Far from intimidating us it will inspire us to greater effort to rid the world forever of such an inhuman and savage beast.

In Tunisia, the victorious British Eighth Army rolled on five miles beyond captured Enfidaville to threaten the Axis mountain fort of Takrouna while the First Army to the north increased its pressure in the Medjez-el-Bab sector, 35 miles west of Tunis.

Thursday, April 22, 1943: —The British Eighth Army continues to advance against desperate resistance. The magnificent Eighth, as General Montgomery's army will be known, captured the Axis mountain fort of Takrouna today after only one day's siege. The fighting was bitter, with the brown skinned, cocky, confident desert veterans of the Eighth hurling screaming enemy troops over sheer cliffs to their death. It was hand to hand fighting of the fiercest kind.

In the north the cornered Nazis attempted to relieve some of the pressure on Rommel by attacking the British First Army. This attack was stopped cold by superior Allied forces with 27 German tanks being destroyed and 500 prisoners taken. Here again the fighting was in close quarters with cold steel the predominating weapon.

The Pacific war took on a grimmer aspect since the announcement of the illegal and barbarous murder of American prisoners of war by the uncivilized Japs. Our armed forces have accepted the struggle as a fight to the finish with no quarter expected. As a partial answer to the Jap criminals, a large force of U.S. Army bombers delivered a devastating attack on Nauru Island, and important Nipponese base in the Gilbert Islands. Much damage was inflicted and all our planes returned.

Tokyo radio hurled further threats of similar action against future raiders and in reply were assured by our airmen that, far from being intimidated by such savage threats, they are looking forward to the not far distant day when they will hit Japan with more and bigger raids. Every bomb will be dropped in memory of our murdered comrades.

Friday, April 23, 1943: —Today was Good Friday and thousands of San Franciscans observed the day with religious services. But it is not a good world, occupied by good men worthy of the great sacrifice of the Savior. Men are savagely fighting each other, vying desperately for the opportunity to destroy rather than to save. Men are cruel, not merciful; revengeful, not forgiving. Human life is cheap and kindness and love are no longer virtues— at least so it seems when you contemplate the horrors that are being perpetrated throughout the world today. But despite all this, good will prevail in the end. We cannot lose faith in the power of the Lord. Peace will come and the earth will once again be governed by men of good will. We must not lose sight of this firm belief or all is indeed lost. Where there is faith there is hope.

Back on the war news we were informed by the Navy today that United States forces have occupied Funafuti, the largest of the Ellice Islands in the South Pacific that had been seized by the Japanese early in the war. The move was a total surprise to the Japs and the occupation was made without resistance. The captured island provides our forces with a base within easy striking distance of the Japanese held Gilbert Islands and is one more step back towards the Philippines and Tokyo.

The Tunisian battle is raging furiously with Allied troops gouging another three miles into Axis defenses west of Tunis. Our airmen shot down 38 enemy air craft today, including an entire formation of 20 huge transport planes loaded with troops and gasoline. It was mighty nice hunting.

Saturday, April 24, 1943: —General "Ike" Eisenhower, the Allied Commander in Chief in North Africa, reported in his communiqué today that the Allied offensive in Tunisia is really rolling now. The American Second Army Corps has come back into the news after a considerable absence and we find they have been transferred bag and baggage from the southern front where the British Eighth Army has taken over, to the northern front where they have reinforced the British First Army under General Anderson. The Americans were thrown into the battle today and lunged forward seven miles, holding their positions against all counter-attacks. The "big squeeze" is on, with the Allied air force engaging in unceasing sorties against enemy ground troops and communication lines. The Nazis and Fascists have really got themselves into a hot, tight corner and the United Nation forces are moving in eagerly for the kill.

The Pacific war continues to be waged almost exclusively in the air, with both sides attacking the other's bases in order to disrupt the preparation of offensive expeditions. Australian leaders are still warning of the deadly peril of a Japanese invasion of that Continent and emphasize that the Nips have more than 200,000 invasion troops poised and ready, with landing fields and facilities for 2,000 planes on an arc menacing Australia. Our forces, however, are not idle in the area, you may be assured.

John L. Lewis, the United Mine Worker Union boss, is crossing swords with President Roosevelt in a wage dispute that threatens a strike in the coal mining industry. My bet is that Roosevelt will win without much trouble.

Sunday, April 25, 1943: —It was a beautiful Easter Sunday today—clear, warm, and marred only by a stiff breeze that blew out of the northwest. It was a day of reverence, with countless church services honoring the resurrection of "The Prince of Peace." It was a day of spring and fresh hope—hope and prayer that the men who are fighting on many battlefronts for the freedom and dignity of mankind may soon overthrow the evil and criminal forces of the enemy and return once more to the ways of peace and freedom which they treasure.

Today in Arlington National Cemetery, a straight, erect figure of a grand old man of 82 years stepped forward to lay a wreath on the tomb of the Unknown Soldier. It was General John J. "Black Jack" Pershing, the beloved commander of the AEF during the First World War. He epitomizes the sturdiness and strength of American arms that will fight through to victory this time as they did in those days when he led them through the bloody struggle in Flanders Fields.

I overlooked mentioning a brilliant spectacle that occurred in the skies over the Bay Area yesterday. More than 150 heavy bombers of the Western Defense Command demonstrated their tactics over the city as an incentive in the Second War Loan Drive. It was thrilling.

The Los Angeles Area was blacked out tonight for 56 minutes. It was the first scare on the coast for some time. The alert was called because of unidentified targets off the southern California coast. They were finally identified as friendly.

Monday, April 26, 1943: —It's the Yanks again in Tunisia. The north end of the enemy's lines were bent close to the breaking point as the American troops lunged forward under cover of the most terrific aerial pounding of the entire Tunisian campaign. Flying Fortresses and A-20 attack bombers plastered front Axis positions at will, pulverizing pill boxes and trenches. The United States forces, however, are approaching some of the most formidable fortifications in the Axis defense perimeter protecting

368

Bizerte. German officers have boasted on previous occasions that the defenses are impregnable. It will take some fierce fighting and heavy artillery and air bombardment to blast the enemy out of their concrete and steel positions. Our losses will undoubtedly be severe.

United Nations unity was dealt a serious blow today. Soviet Russia announced that she was severing diplomatic relations with the Polish Government-in-exile. The dispute arose out of Polish charges, which Moscow claims were started and stirred up by German propaganda, that Russia had slain over ten thousand captured Polish troops in the Smolensk area. Moscow asserts that the prisoners were killed by the Germans when they marched into Smolensk during the first year of the war. Whatever the facts, the break is a distinct blow to British and American hopes for unity among the nations fighting the Axis. Berlin, of course, has gleefully seized upon the incident as a brilliant diplomatic victory for them and will undoubtedly do everything possible to widen the rift between the Polish Government now established in London and the Soviet Union. All is definitely not quiet on the diplomatic front.

Tuesday, April 27, 1943: —United States troops are doing the major offensive work on the Tunisian front for the time being. Today the Yanks stormed two strongly fortified hills defending the road to Mateur and Bizerte. The Doughboys succeeded in capturing the height of Djebel Azag after running into steel and concrete fortifications and flame throwing tanks. Allied bombers were called for another "softening up" of the position before the infantry takes another crack at storming the hill.

From England a mighty fleet of great four-engine Lancaster and Halifax bombers soared out last night to present the German river port and steel city of Duisburg with probably the most concentrated aerial attack of the war to date. Fifteen hundred tons of explosives, equal to the amount dumped on Cologne in the famous 1,000 plane raid, were poured on the ill-fated city. The huge 4,000 pound block-busters and the devastating 8,000 pound land mines packed by the big war planes left almost the entire city in smoking ruins. Seventeen attacking planes were lost in the raid that must have struck terror into the heart of every German. It is certainly a terrible retribution that has been brought upon them by the insane and near-sighted acts of the madman, Hitler.

Two interesting things occurred on the local home front today. California Selective Service leaders announced a surprise 12-

day moratorium on draft inductions in California. No more draftees will be called until May 10. San Franciscans today learned that Secretary of the Treasury Henry Morgenthau will arrive in the city tomorrow to spur the final effort in the Second War Loan Drive that ends April 30.

Wednesday, April 28, 1943: —Trouble flared anew on the labor front today. The bituminous coal situation has reached a critical stage. After failing to solve the bitter dispute between the United Mine Workers Union and the Mine Operators, largely through refusal by John L. Lewis, the Union boss, to appear or send a representative to appear at the hearings, the War Labor Board turned the case over to President Roosevelt for final action before the deadline of April 30 when the miners threaten to go on strike. What the President's action will be is unknown but it is expected that he will appeal direct to men before resorting to more forcible methods of preventing a disruption of vital coal production. Army occupation of the mines and Government operation are possible eventualities.

While the coal miners threaten to tie up steel, tank, and gun production unless they get another two dollars a day raise, American doughboys, at fifty per month, are storming up bloody Tunisian hills, into the mouths of roaring guns and in the face of searing blasts from flame-throwing tanks. They are laying down their lives in bitter hand to hand struggles with vicious foes with no thought of quitting or striking. An unnecessary stoppage of work on the home front at such a time is the closest thing to mutiny and treason—no matter what the provocation.

Secretary Morgenthau arrived in San Francisco today and praised the fighting war spirit he has encountered on the Pacific coast. After a slow start the Second War Loan Drive has surged ahead in this territory and indications are that our quota will be met 100%.

Thursday, April 29, 1943: —The coal mine situation is rapidly nearing its climax. President Roosevelt today dispatched a strongly worded telegram to John L. Lewis, the United Mine Workers boss, warning that if work is not resumed at the mines before 10:o'clock Saturday morning he will use his powers as Commander-in-Chief of the Army and Navy to prevent interference with prosecution of the war. The President appealed to the individual workers as a friend, urging them to forego strikes and work stoppages during the war and stated bluntly that any strike would not be a strike against the mine operators but a strike against the United States Government and as such could not be tolerated. The people will not stand for any retarding of the war effort and of our obligation to the men on the fighting fronts. The Government has ample machinery set up to settle labor disputes in a peaceful manner and will use the power vested in it by the people to prevent any hindrance to the prosecution of the war.

The progress of the American and British forces in Tunisia has slowed considerably as they have encountered the prepared and powerful defenses of the Tunis-Bizerte perimeter. American forces gained some important ground in northern Tunisia but indications are that the powerful British Eighth Army in the south is awaiting the massing of its artillery and storm troops before making the final smash into Tunis. Some desperate fighting is in prospect before "finis" is written to the North African campaign.

In Secretary Morgenthau's speech last night at the San Francisco War Memorial Opera House, he read a cablegram received from Generalissmo Chiang-Kai-Shek, stating that the Japs had massacred every man, woman, and child in several Chinese villages for aiding the escape of American Tokyo raiders.

Friday, April 30, 1943: —The coal situation still holds the news spotlight today. John L. Lewis, the union leader, replied to the President's ultimatum and renewed his demand that continued negotiations be made through collective bargaining. His principal bone of contention is with the National War Labor Board, which Lewis contends has prejudged the miner's case. He apparently is determined to go ahead with his work stoppage plans unless the case is put in other hands. It appears inevitable, therefore, that the Federal Government will take over the mines and call in the troops if necessary.

The fighting in Tunisia is taking on a grimmer, more bloody character as the Allies push their way into the core of Axis resistance around Tunis and Bizerte. French and American troops inched their way forward in the north, with our Doughboys storming entrenched hill positions 12 miles from Mateur, important rail junction outside Bizerte. Each advance is a costly business and too many American boys are finding their last resting place beneath the poppy fields of Tunisia. Yes, there are poppies there like those of Flanders where other American boys on another occasion made the supreme sacrifice. I wonder if man will be able to prevent another world war on some future date when other young men, not yet born, will be called upon to pour out their life's blood on some crimson field of poppies.

Here on the home front, American housewives have made the point rationing system a success. Meat rationing in particular has been beneficial. While our family, for example, went practically without meat for several months prior to rationing, we now can get just about enough to serve our needs.

May

Saturday, May 1, 1943: —Well, the Government stepped in on the coal mine situation today. President Roosevelt ordered Secretary of Interior Ickes to take over and operate the mines immediately, with the Army providing any protection necessary to maintain order. This action was taken by the President after the lapse of his 10:o'clock deadline this morning. "I now call upon all miners who may have abandoned their work to return immediately to the mines and work for their Government," the President said, "Their country needs their services as much as those of the members of the armed forces."

The reaction of the miners to the Government's action has not yet been observed but it is absolutely clear that the rest of the country is solidly behind any action Roosevelt may deem necessary to keep the mines operating without hindrance to the war effort. The President has stated that he will take the case to the people and the miners over the radio tomorrow. No one faction or union leadership should be permitted to obstruct the effort of all of us to win through to victory in this war for survival.

Action in Tunisia is slow and bloody, with the American Second Army Corps under General Patton succeeding in capturing Hill 609, dominating the road to Mateur, which long range American artillery is already shelling. The British First Army farther south was forced to make slight withdrawals in the Medjez-el-Bab area in the face of desperate Nazi counter-attacks. The British Eighth Army, our Ace-in-the-hole, is quiet, apparently massing for another of its famous Sunday punches.

Sunday, May 2, 1943: —The battle between the President of the United States and John L. Lewis, the leader of 500,000 coal miners reached an unusual climax today. President Roosevelt took his case directly to the people via the radio and made a notable address in his inimitable style that even his enemies agree is the most effective radio style in the world. He pleaded, he cajoled, but he left no doubt in the minds of his listeners but that we would have coal. No one man or faction in this country is powerful enough to prevent the mining of enough fuel to keep the war industries going at full blast. His speech was a masterpiece of sweet reasoning, forceful argument, and purposeful determination. Any coal miner who could listen to the President lay before them the urgent needs of our fighting men who are struggling day and night against a merciless and bloodthirsty foe and still choose to strike is very likely to have his patriotism sternly questioned.

On the other side, John L. Lewis, slyly hoping to take the sting out of the President's talk, announced only twenty minutes before the Chief Executive was to go on the air that he had concluded a fifteen day truce with Secretary of Interior Ickes. Under the truce, the men would go back to work on Tuesday and negotiations would continue. It was a clever ruse and postponed the final showdown. It left the question open as to whether the President or Mr. Lewis has won a victory. From the consensus of opinion expressed over the radio and in the newspapers, most people think Lewis should be required to spend a few days with the doughboys in Tunisia.

Monday, May 3, 1943: —United States forces fighting in Tunisia have scored their biggest land victory of the North African war. Hard-fighting American shock troops crashed through German defenses today and seized the key junction of Mateur. Sensational shooting by American artillery softened up the Nazi fortifications and enabled our infantry to pour through for a gain of fifteen miles. Both General Eisenhower and his British deputy, General Sir Harold R.L.G. Alexander expressed their pleasure over the brilliant advance of the American Second Army Corps. The successful offensive has made the first crack in the iron and concrete ring thrown up by the enemy to protect Bizerte and Tunis. This crack in the Axis armor may result in the complete crumbling of the enemy's North African defenses.

Meanwhile, across the world, the tempo of aerial activity has increased in the South Pacific. General MacArthur's communiqué reported a heavy Japanese bombing attack on Darwin in Australia. Twenty enemy bombers, escorted by 31 Zeros, raided the Port but caused only negligible damage to military objectives. For the first time, however losses by our fighter planes intercepting the raiders were heavy, although details were not announced. Obviously Australia is not yet out of danger of Japanese attack or even invasion.

In Russia, the Red Army has launched a powerful offensive in the northwest Caucasus, aimed at ousting the Nazis from their toehold in that area.

Tuesday, May 4, 1943: —United States forces today drove on past Mateur, bringing the big naval base of Bizerte within artillery range. Our troops also fanned out from the rail junction to threaten the right flank of the enemy's defenses before Tunis. Further south the British First Army also advanced, capturing two more hill positions. Meanwhile in the south, the powerful British Eighth Army opened up with heavy patrol action and artillery, indicating that Montgomery is just about ready to launch his final drive for Tunis and the sea.

The Navy Department reported more successes in our submarine campaign against Japan's lengthy communication lines in the Pacific. Our deadly "pig-boats" added two Nip destroyers and four auxiliary vessels to their long list of victims. In addition, a large Jap transport was listed as a "probable."

On the home front there were three outstanding news items. First was a nationwide draft crackdown in which several thousand draft evaders faced heavy punishment. The charges included failure to register, failure to notify boards of change of address, failure to answer questionnaires, submission of false information, refusal to report for physical examination and refusal to report for induction.

Second was the announcement by the national price administrator of price ceilings to be imposed on many grocery items beginning May 10. Such action is urgently needed to stop skyrocketing living costs and prevent inflation.

Third was the passing by the House of Representatives of a compromise pay-as-you-go tax bill, embodying the Ruml plan's forgiveness principle to a modified extent.

Wednesday, May 5, 1943: —The powerful United States Second Army Corps under General "Blood and Guts" Patton, aided by some French units, has smashed to within ten miles of the great naval base of Bizerte. The speed of the American advance threatens to cut the Axis armies in two and isolate the Bizerte garrison. Desperate counter-attacks by the Germans were turned back by our doughboys with heavy loss. Fierce fighting is still in progress although the enemy is showing signs of complete exhaustion.

From England last night, the RAF staged another of its colossal raids on industrial Germany. Between 700 and 800 huge four-motored bombers participated in the attack which was aimed at the coal and steel center of Dortmund. The raid was on a scale comparable to that loosed against Cologne a year ago. Nearly 1,500 tons of high explosives and incendiaries were dumped on the hapless city. It is almost impossible to imagine the destruction that such a weight of bombs must inflict on a city. Just think what a hundred, let alone a thousand, enemy bombers could do over San Francisco, for example. But 1,500 tons of fire and explosions! Why the city would be nothing but a pile of charred rubble. And Germany's cities are getting it every night and day. How long can they stand it?

Probably the most unsatisfactory situation in the Japanese Pacific war is the solid foothold the Nips have succeeded in establishing in the Aleutians. Both Kiska and Attu have become enemy fortresses. Our Army and Navy are aware of the danger and have launched countless aerial assaults against these bases. But despite the rain of explosives the Jap has continued to consolidate his position. Some more positive action is needed.

Thursday, May 6, 1943: —Axis defense lines in Tunisia are crumbling rapidly. Crack units of American armored forces smashed through to the southwest shore of Lake Bizerte and long-range American artillery pounded docks and military installations within the city itself.

Today's principal success was scored by the British First Army on the sector northeast of Medjez-el-Bab. British tanks and infantry captured two blood-soaked hills blocking their path and then broke through desperate Axis resistance to sweep onto the plains before Tunis. Massicault on the highway to the Tunisian capital fell before the onslaught of the victorious British. Supporting the Allied ground drive was the most concerted aerial offensive in history. American, British, and French planes engaged in more than 2,000 sorties during the day, pounding enemy front-line positions and communications with a never-ending rain of bombs. All evidence indicates that the pay-off in Tunisia is not many days away.

I overlooked reporting about a week ago that Lieut. General Frank M. Andrews, commander of U.S. forces in the European theater, was killed in the crash of an air transport plane in Iceland. Fourteen other high ranking officers and technical experts died in the same crash. Secretary of War Stimson today announced that Lieut. General Jacob L. Devers has been designated to succeed General Andrews. General Devers' post is one of extreme importance in the coming invasion of Europe and while he undoubtedly is very capable, the loss of General Andrews' experience and ability will be keenly felt.

Friday, May 7, 1943: —TUNIS AND BIZERTE HAVE FALLEN! Coming as a complete and most welcome surprise to the Allied world, was the news that victorious American shock troops smashed their way into the great Axis naval base of Bizerte at 4:15 p.m. this afternoon. The city was completely occupied by United States troops shortly thereafter with thousands of prisoners being taken and the remainder of the Axis defenders fleeing demoralized.

To the south, the triumphant British First Army crushed all enemy resistance on the plains before Tunis and occupied that city after fierce fighting at 4:20 p.m., almost to the minute when their American comrades were marching into Bizerte.

Almost all organized resistance in Tunisia collapsed with the fall of the two cities. Only isolated points of resistance were left for mopping up behind the Allied lines. It appears, however, that the bulk of the beaten German and Italian armies have fled into the Cap Bon peninsula where they may attempt either a last ditch stand in Bataan fashion or a Dunkirk evacuation. The only other alternative is surrender.

A large part of the credit for the sudden and far-ahead-of-schedule defeat of the Axis armies goes to the Allied Tunisian Air Force. In the 36 hours of the final all-out offensive, the Allied Air Force engaged in the greatest aerial onslaught in support of ground troops ever made. 2,500 separate sorties darkened the skies over the enemy positions and the ground troops were so gratified and thrilled over the tremendous show that on many occasions, they rose out of the fox holes to cheer lustily as literally hundreds of planes pulverized the enemy's positions. Remember 1940, Hitler?

Saturday, May 8, 1943: —The Allies are having a field day in Tunisia. Thousands of prisoners and great quantities of booty are being rounded up. Exactly how many enemy troops have been captured so far can only be estimated as there are too many for immediate count and more are coming in at the rate of about 1,000 per hour. American troops are in complete mastery of the Bizerte area and are rapidly mopping up isolated enemy groups that have chosen to resist.

From all reports, the conduct of the Second American Army Corps in this final offensive has been extremely gratifying. From a green, untried army that took a sound beating from Rommel's experienced Afrika Korps they have graduated into a first-rate fighting force. They have learned the art of war in the hard school of experience and have learned it rapidly and well. They have mastered the technique of using all branches of the service in perfect coordination and their brilliant drive through to Mateur was largely responsible for the final collapse of Von Arnim's defense that led to the capture of Bizerte and Tunis. The individual American soldier's courage and endurance was unexcelled throughout the campaign—through adversity and success. America has reason to be proud of the fighting Second.

World attention with respect to the Pacific war against Japan is centered tonight on the Aleutian Islands. Our Navy has revealed that American forces have occupied the island of Amchitka, only 15 minutes flying time from Kiska. This move was made in January and a formidable air base has been constructed on the island from which the almost incessant raids have been launched against Jap-held Kiska and Attu. It is hinted that our forces are about ready to make an attempt at wresting the latter two islands from Tojo's little yellow devils.

Sunday, May 9, 1943: —The mop-up continues in Tunisia. The Americans cleaned up the Bizerte sector and swept eighteen miles southeast of the city to cut the Axis escape road between Bizerte and Tunis. Meanwhile the victorious British First Army pressed the beaten remnants of the enemy back into the death trap of Cap Bon peninsula.

The only major resistance remained in the south where the enemy faces the formidable British Eighth Army. Even here, British patrols indicate that the Nazis' defenses are crumbling as they turn their ear to the disastrous roar in the north. Their only hope is to flee onto the Cap Bon peninsula where there is no hope. The relentless attack of countless Allied aircraft has already turned Cap Bon into a massacre. The waters between Cap Bon and Sicily will run red with Axis blood if they attempt any mass escape. Allied Headquarters indicate that they believe less than 50,000 of the enemy will be able to reach the peninsula and for these capture or death is certain.

Spurred by the Allied triumph in North Africa, the Russians launched a terrific offensive against the elaborate Nazi defenses before Novorossiysk, the great naval base on the black sea. A break-through was quickly achieved and Soviet troops poured through, threatening a Nazi debacle that would rival their Tunisian defeat. Berlin expressed its nervousness over the situation and stated that the Russian drive was gaining momentum and strength.

All in all, things look mighty glum for Herr Schnickelgruber, alias Herr Hitler. For which we're thankful.

Monday, May 10, 1943: —The extent of Allied victory and Axis defeat in Tunisia mounts with every passing hour. Latest reports state that more than 75,000 prisoners have been counted with many more thousands lining the roads and filling the fields waiting to be herded into prison camps. For the first time, German soldiers by the thousands are quitting and apparently are not sorry that for them the war is over. Six German generals are among the captives already taken, giving mute evidence of the complete inability of the Nazis to evacuate even high general officers and key men from the North African "coffin corner." Allied air power and naval power has thrown an iron ring around the Tunisian coast to crush any attempt by the remaining enemy forces to stage any "Dunkirk" evacuation.

What the effect of the Tunisian disaster will be on Hitler and the German people can only be conjectured. Aside from the loss of an army of more than 200,000 of his best trained and most experienced troops plus acres of irreplaceable materials and equipment, the blow to Hitler's prestige is the most serious result. Turkey, which has been a "mugwump" all along, waiting for the chance to rush to the aid of the victor, has been mightily impressed by the Allied success in Africa. An Allied invasion through the Balkans would now be assured of a sympathetic blessing from Turkey if not outright military assistance. In addition, Italy which has been quaking with fear ever since the first American set foot on North African soil, has now lost all confidence in their "supermen" Allies and is about ready to quit the war. All in all, the last few days may easily prove to have been the final turning point in the European war.

Tuesday, May 11, 1943: —The spotlight of the war swung momentarily away from the battlefields of Tunisia to center on Washington D.C. where it is learned that Prime Minister Winston Churchill, with high ranking members of the British High Command, has arrived for another momentous conference with President Roosevelt and American military leaders. No mention was made of the topic of discussion but it was generally assumed that further aggressive moves, possibly the immediate invasion of Europe, would be the conference topic.

This latest Churchill-Roosevelt meeting is another of those perfectly timed and dramatic sequences for which the two leaders are noted. The amazing feature is that although the meeting has synchronized so perfectly with the victorious end of the Tunisian campaign, it couldn't have been planned exactly that way because the collapse of Axis resistance came so suddenly and so far ahead of schedule. A conference of the scope reported for this one, including many high ranking officers from many war theaters, would obviously have required long planning and arranging. It is just another piece of Churchill-Roosevelt luck.

Back in Tunisia, the extent of the victory grows. More than 100,000 prisoners have been rounded up and practically all organized resistance has been crushed. British, French, and American tanks broke through last ditch enemy defenses on Cap Bon peninsula by daring flanking maneuvers that in one instance saw them send tanks roaring through the breakers on the coastline, leaving wakes like steamboats as they charged ashore to take the enemy from behind. As the San Francisco News put it: Hitler today got another kick in the panzers.

Wednesday, May 12, 1943: —Speculation is rife as to what the Roosevelt-Churchill conference will bring about in Washington. From the fact that many high ranking officers from the Pacific war theater are present, including Field Marshal Sir Archibald P. Wavell, commander-in-chief of British forces in India, Admiral Sir James Somerville, commander-in-chief of the far-Eastern fleet, and Air Marshal Sir Richard Peirse, commanding British air power in India, it is evident that the Japanese will receive their share of consideration. No doubt the entire global strategy will be reviewed in the light of the clean-up in North Africa.

The story of Tunisia is rapidly coming to a conclusion. Another 50,000 prisoners were added to the rolls today, bringing the number to well over 150,000 since the final push began. The German commander-in-chief, Col. General Von Arnim himself, has surrendered, leaving only scattered remnants to offer resistance. British veterans of Dunkirk have expressed amazement at the complete collapse of the Germans. Well equipped German soldiers have walked out of strong positions to give themselves up without a fight. The situation is a direct contrast to the Dunkirk affair when desperate British troops fought fiercely for every foot of ground in the face of terrific odds and no mercy. It is just another proof that the German is plenty good when he is on top and winning; get him down and he is far from being a superman.

One other item of news is the story of a terrific sub battle in the Atlantic in which 25 subs attacked a single convoy. Ten of the subs were destroyed in a terrible running battle in which a large number of merchantmen were lost.

Thursday, May 13, 1943: —Big events are in the making we learn tonight as the report is received that General Douglas MacArthur and Admiral William F. Halsey have met to plan and co-ordinate future offensive action against the Japs. All signs indicate that the two commanders have no intention of waiting until the European war is settled before launching their drive northward to Tokyo. They have full intention of using what men and equipment they have now or may get in a major effort against the Nipponese. Both men have the Japs' number. Both have taken everything the enemy has to offer and have come out on top. We can count on them. Our cause is in good hands in the South Pacific.

At the same time, Prime Minister Churchill and President Roosevelt were conferring in Washington with the High

Commands of Britain and the United States. It was believed that plans were being laid for several major offensives, both against the Nazi-held European fortress and the main Japanese forces in China. The first step in hitting the Japs in China will probably be the reopening of the Burma Road by a full scale offensive launched from India.

The German homeland is taking the most terrible beating ever administered, as the RAF and American air forces based in England carry out almost continuous raids over Europe. Last night, in celebration of the Tunisia triumph, the RAF smashed the German industrial city of Duisburg with the heaviest load of explosives ever packed in a single raid. Nearly 2,000 tons of bombs were dumped on the ill-fated city, compared with only 1,500 tons carried last year in the famous 1,000 plane Cologne raid and 450 tons carried by the Germans in their biggest attack on London during the "blitz" of 1940.

Friday, May 14, 1943: —Great news comes out of the Aleutians today. U.S. Army forces have attacked the Japanese base on the island of Attu. Landings were successfully made and the battle for possession is progressing "very satisfactorily" in the words of Secretary of the Navy, Frank Knox. No Marines are involved in the action. It is entirely an Army and Navy affair; the Navy took them there and the doughboys are doing the attacking.

News of this long-awaited offensive drive to oust the Japs from their bases nearest to the American mainland was received enthusiastically by residents of the Pacific Coast states. It was feared that the High Command might so concentrate on the European situation that the Japs would be given time to consolidate their positions in the Aleutians which have long been regarded as serious threats to Alaska and the Pacific Coast. Capture of Attu and Kiska would eliminate that threat and sharpen the dagger pointed at the heart of the Japanese mainland.

The American air force based in England appears to have finally reached its full stature as an offensive assistant to the RAF. Flying Fortresses by the hundreds have joined with the RAF to pound German targets with an unbelievable tonnage of explosives and incendiary bombs. And from the other side Russian bombers have joined in the scourge of the Third Reich. Berlin, Duisburg, Essen, Cologne, Kiel, Bochum, Wilhelmshaven—

all these and countless more are familiar "targets for tonight" to the men of the United States Air Force in Britain and their comrades of the RAF.

Saturday, May 15, 1943: —While official American sources were silent today about the battle for Attu, Berlin and Tokyo radio commentators obviously were preparing their listeners for the loss of the island. They reported that the United States invading force greatly outnumbered the defending Japanese but that they were resisting fiercely. Weather and climatic conditions in the Aleutians make fighting extremely difficult at the best and there is no doubt that the battle will be long and hard. The Japs are willing diers.

The serial scourge of Germany continued today as four hundred American heavy bombers smashed at the Nazi naval base of Emden. Fire bombs left the base in blazing ruins. Six of the big bombers failed to return but a large number of enemy planes were shot down in exchange. Meanwhile, Italy was getting her share. American and British air forces based in Africa have opened what they call a "ferry service" to Italy, carrying bombs with clock-like regularity over Sicily, Sardinia, Naples, and all of southern Italy. The roar of motors and the crash of bombs are playing a thunderous overture before the curtain raises on the biggest show on earth, "The Battle of Europe."

On the home front the most interesting news was the passage by the Senate last night of the Ruml plan for pay-as-you-go income taxes. The vote was 49 to 30. Approval by the House of Representatives and signature by the President will mean forgiveness of 1942's tax bill and the establishment of pay-as-you-go by means of a 20% withholding tax on salaries and wages effective July 1.

Sunday, May 16, 1943: —Spring in all its beauty and warmth is in full bloom here in the Bay Area. The rolling hills that have sported a shock of unbelievably green grass for so long are just beginning to show a little gray at the temples as the grass slowly dries out under the impact of almost daily sunshine. The rainy season is over, supplanted by the season of trade winds that sweep in from the northwest both morning and night. These constant winds prevent the temperature from ever getting too warm for comfort during the day and make a goodly covering of woolen blankets a necessity at night. This is a colorful time of year, with flowers of all description smiling in abundance from every front yard.

This year, however, something new has been added. Victory Gardens, countless Victory Gardens, are in evidence everywhere. Back yards, vacant lots, school grounds, parks and every imaginable place have yielded to the spade and hoe. Vegetables, not flowers, are the heroes, the pets, this year. Radishes, carrots, tomatoes, lettuce, corn, potatoes—these are the plants cared for by the back yard putterer these days. Schools have turned over their playgrounds, cities their parks for the cultivation of that mighty weapon of total war—food. Never before have so many people turned the soil, to the good earth, which after all is the one best friend of man, the one thing above all for which man is willing to fight and die if necessary. The Russians have fought so magnificently—not for Stalin, not for Communism, but for the soil of Mother Russia. The gallant Chinese have not suffered the agonies of six years of war Chiang-Kai-Shek or other war lords, but for the ground under their feet, the sacred soil of China. So it has been before and so it will be forever.

Monday, May 17, 1943: —The pre-invasion aerial barrage over Germany and Occupied Europe has reached an unprecedented intensity. Germany faces tonight probably the greatest disaster of the entire war as RAF bombers, in a daring and brilliant raid, smashed two of the biggest dams in the Reich. The big British Lancaster bombers carried huge land mines in a sensational sweep over the heavily defended Mohne dam which furnishes the chief water supply for the industrial Ruhr valley. The tremendous explosions of the mines ripped a great hole in the dam, sending hundreds of millions of tons of water roaring down through the valley, inundating whole cities and flooding thousands of acres of farm land.

At the same time other raiders smashed the great Eder dam, the Nazis biggest water reservoir, and sent another devastating flood pouring down the vital Weser valley. Late reconnaissance reports indicate that chaotic conditions exist in both valleys and that incalculable damage has been done. The Germans have declared a state of emergency in both areas. What a terrible fate the mad Fuehrer has brought to the German people.

Meanwhile, in the Aleutians, it appears that the battle for Attu is still progressing, with the final outcome in doubt. Bad weather is hampering our offensive operations, requiring much of the fighting to be done in fog of pea soup consistency. Secretary Knox hints that just one day of good weather might be enough to do the job but such days are rare in the Aleutians.

Tuesday, May 18, 1943: —The Navy Department today released some of the details of the fighting on Attu Island in the Aleutians. American forces have successfully landed at Holtz Bay and Massacre Bay and are pressing a two-pronged pincer attack against the Japs. Bad weather is hampering the operation and enemy resistance is determined but the occupation is progressing favorably and casualties have been much lighter than was expected. Naval bombardment and aerial attacks have supported the ground forces whenever the weather has permitted.

Another act of Japanese barbarity was perpetrated last Friday according to dispatches from Australia. The Australian hospital ship Centaur was sunk in flames off the New Guinea coast by a Japanese submarine. Approximately 299 lives were lost. The hospital ship was brightly lighted and plainly marked with the Red Cross so the sinking was a deliberate atrocity committed in violation of international agreement to which Japan was a signatory.

In Europe the aerial offensive continues unabated. Late reports indicate that the damage caused by the breaching of the two big dams in the Ruhr and Weser valleys has reached staggering proportions. Whole cities have been inundated, with thousands drowned and other thousands made homeless. The Nazis have proclaimed a state of siege in both areas in an attempt to bring order out of the chaos. The disaster has been a terrific blow to the German war effort.

At home it looks as though the Ruml income tax plan has failed for the third time in the House of Representatives. No acceptable alternate plan is in sight, leaving the tax situation in a hopeless muddle.

Wednesday, May 19, 1943: —Prime Minister Winston Churchill made one of his most brilliant speeches before a cheering Congress in Washington D.C. today. The British leader was at his oratorical best and thrilled his listeners with a classic analysis of the war's progress to date and intriguing hints of sensation developments to come. He promised that Britain will fight alongside the United States not only until Hitler is completely smashed but also until barbaric Japan is crushed into impotency. He could not predict when the war will end but he is confident of how it will end—in total victory for the United Nations.

From the bleak Aleutians comes further word that the American invasion of Jap-held Attu is nearing completion. The doughboys have forced the enemy to retreat in the face of a two-pronged attack that has already overrun the chief Japanese defense line along a rocky ridge between Holtz Bay and Chichagof Harbor toward which the defeated Japs are retreating.

In Europe Allied air fleets pounded Italian and Nazi bases in a continuation of the round-the-clock aerial offensive against the Axis. The Italian base of Pantelleria was razed with more than 200,000 pounds of high explosives. Flying Fortresses and P-38 Lightnings raided Sicily and wrecked ships, docks, and railroad yards at the Port of Trapani. From England other Fortresses struck by daylight at the German submarine pens at Kiel and Flensburg.

News reports from Russia hint that the final big test—the Nazis last and most desperate summer drive—may soon be at hand.

Thursday, May 20, 1943: —The American made trap for approximately 3,000 Japs on Attu Island has penned them in a fifteen mile square area around Chichagof Harbor where they, like the Nazis in Tunisia, have but two alternatives, death or capture. Most Japs seem to prefer death, which is all right with us—they're less bother that way.

Already the main part of Attu is in our possession, including a fully completed air field hewn out of the rocky island by the hard-working Japs. It's almost as though our Army did it intentionally—let the Japs complete the air field and other installations and then move in and take them over. Remember Henderson Field on Guadalcanal? The Marines pulled the same trick there. Not a bad idea at that.

Meanwhile the air war in Europe continues unabated. Fast

386

Mosquito bombers of the RAF blasted Berlin last night. It was the 65th raid of the war on the German capital. It was a comparatively light raid but highly successful as not a single attacking plane was lost. What bitter pills these raids on Berlin must be to fat Reichmarshal Hermann Goering, who once boasted that no enemy plane would ever be able to attack the Capital.

Here at home the big surprise in the news is the report that John L. Lewis, the belligerent leader of the United Mine Workers Union, has asked to return his Union to the American Federation of Labor. Lewis originally took the miners out of the Federation in 1936 to form the CIO, later withdrew from that organization also. The purpose behind his present move is obscure.

Friday, May 21, 1943: —More good news today. Admiral Isoroku Yamamoto, commander-in-chief of the Japanese Navy is dead. We just have to chuckle a bit as Yamamoto was the Jap braggart who boasted shortly after Pearl Harbor that he would dictate the peace from the White House in Washington D.C. Wonder how he can explain himself to his ancestors now.

The Tokyo announcement of the Admiral's death stated that he died while fighting the enemy in a combat plane. That sounds pretty phony and most American observers believe he either went down with one of the Jap battleships sunk in the big Solomons battles or else he was purged by the Jap High Command for his many failures in the South Pacific fighting.

The latest reports from the Aleutians indicate that Attu is ours. Secretary Knox of the Navy stated that only mopping up operations remained. To all intents and purposes the campaign can be considered over. The remnants of the Jap garrison are trapped in the Chichagof Harbor area with no hope of escape or relief. Our losses in taking Attu have been far less than expected.

In Europe American Flying Fortresses made one of their heaviest raids of the war against German U-boat and naval installations at Emden and Wilhelmshaven today and suffered their worst losses as twelve of the big bombers were shot down.

Berlin got another taste of RAF medicine last night as the speedy Mosquito bombers struck again and escaped without loss for the second consecutive night.

Saturday, May 22, 1943: —The most interesting item in the news today is the dissolution of the Red International by Russia. The Comintern, as it was called, long bred suspicion and fear of Russia in the other nations of the world as one of the International's basic principles had been the fomenting of revolution and the overthrow of capitalistic governments. Its dissolution by the Communists may substantially improve relations between the USSR and the United States.

The action of the Reds in dissolving their International organization was reportedly taken because of concern over strikes and work stoppages in American industry. The Red leaders urged all party members, wherever they may be, to cooperate fully in the common battle against the common foe—Hitlerism.

Los Angeles got a taste of aerial warfare last night as army pursuit planes fired their machine guns at a B-24 bomber to force its landing. An investigation disclosed that the bomber's radio went out of commission, preventing the crew from identifying themselves and caused the P-38 Lightnings to be sent up to intercept and identify the visitor. Some excitement was caused among the civilian population.

A final checkup of the Allied victory in North Africa shows that Axis troops captured has mounted to over 250,000 men with killed and missing running the enemy losses close to 300,000. In addition, thousands of vehicles, hundreds of guns and tanks, and vast stores of supplies and ammunition were taken intact. It was really a victory of major proportions.

Sunday, May 23, 1943: —Life under wartime conditions in the Bay Area presents many problems. Food scarcities have cropped up to plague the housewife's mealtime planning. Meats, butter, fats, and canned goods have been added to the commodities for which ration stamps are required. Although rationing is a nuisance and an inconvenience when shopping it is a necessary annoyance and has improved distribution of the limited supplies, particularly of meat. For several months before meat rationing it was almost impossible to get a steak or roast unless you knew the right party or had an inside track with a butcher. We lived entirely on canned Spam and an occasional piece of bacon. Now at least we can frequently get a lamb, pork or veal roast and last Sunday we had a luscious T-bone steak for dinner. But beef is still a delightful rarity.

Gasoline rationing has practically tied our car in the garage. We went only sixty miles in 30 days last month. It's not that our A ration book wouldn't allow more than that but we've just gotten out of the habit of taking our usual Sunday drive. We take a walk with the baby buggy instead.

Transportation to and from work is getting tougher every day. Trains are crowded every morning and I stand most of the way. Busses are packed at the depot and I've learned to sympathize with the lowly sardine.

Work is a hectic stretch that lasts anywhere from 40 to 80 hours a week. New problems are constantly arising in a business that is mushrooming at a terrific pace. Pleasures are few and far between. A theater now and then on Saturday night, a coke, or a night at home with the family. Even a candy bar is a thing to pounce on if you can find one. But we are lucky when all things are considered. Think of Europe and Russia.

Monday, May 24, 1943: —The War Manpower Commission today named the San Francisco Bay Area as an acute labor shortage region and ordered the entire area to go on a 48 hour work week as quickly as possible and not later than June 9 or June 24 depending on the classification of the various industries. The purpose for the order was to conserve the present supply of manpower and to force as many non-essential workers as possible into essential jobs. The only bad feature of the plan is the possible stimulus to inflation resulting from more overtime pay for more workers. Overtime must be paid on all time over 40 hours per week.

The battle for Attu Island in the Aleutians is not quite over. The Japs have launched an aerial offensive in an apparent effort to relieve their beleaguered garrison and to at least prolong the struggle. Twin motored Jap bombers have attacked our forces in several waves during the last 24 hours. The enemy planes are believed to have come either from the Jap held Kurile Islands or from one or more Jap aircraft carriers operating off the Aleutians. Five of the attacking planes were shot down by our P-38s.

History's greatest air raid was launched against the German industrial city of Dortmund last night. Between 700 and 800 huge RAF bombers carried and dropped the unbelievable total of 2,000 tons of high explosives over the hapless city. In sixty horrible minutes the entire city was reduced to rubble. Many important war plants, some of them moved from much bombed Essen, were wiped off the map. Thirty eight of the raiding planes were lost but the British Air Ministry considered that a small price to pay for the tremendous blow struck.

Tuesday, May 25, 1943: —The tempo of aerial warfare over the European Continent has increased to an unbelievable intensity. Hundreds of planes daily are leaving Allied bases and smashing at Axis war centers with a terrific weight of explosives and fire bombs. The Allied High Command is apparently putting into practice the experiment suggested by Winston Churchill in his recent speech to Congress. Mr. Churchill stated, at that time, that it was worth an experiment to determine if the Axis powers could be defeated by means of air attack alone. Can merciless air attack alone bring Germany and Italy to their knees? Apparently the Allied leaders are going to give it a try. Even should it fail, it will still be a necessary "softening up" prelude to invasion. We can gain much—what can we lose?

The mopping up operation on Attu in the Aleutians is still continuing but a final liquidation of the affair is being delayed and hampered by sleet, rain, and snow. Between squalls Japanese bombers again attacked in force but were intercepted by six P-38 Lightnings and dispersed, leaving seven wrecks behind. On land, the Army has the Japs "corralled" in the Chichagof Harbor area and is slowly putting the squeeze on. The enemy's position is hopeless and our troops are proceeding cautiously to keep casualties at a minimum. The Japs must soon capitulate or die and our commanders have no desire to waste the life of a single American soldier in any mad rush to hurry the inevitable. That is where our Army differs from the Nazis or the Japs; an American life is too valuable to waste. Our soldiers know that their officers believe this and they fight the better for it.

Wednesday, May 26, 1943: —Close to 1,000 planes a day are striking tremendous aerial blows against our Axis enemies in Europe and the Mediterranean. This is closely approaching the number which various experts have predicted will knock out the Axis powers within a reasonable time if maintained at a daily rate. It is impossible to conceive the terrible havoc that such raids must produce and almost incredible that anything like a total war effort can be maintained by Germany in the face of such destruction—at least for any great length of time. How can her war industries continue to produce the weapons and supplies of war while high explosive "block-busters" are leveling their factories nightly, killing and maiming their workers, and jamming up transportation facilities? How can efficiency be maintained in the midst of exploding bombs, raging fires, neurosis and panic caused by fear and sleepless nights? There must be a cracking point and the RAF aims to find it. They have not forgotten 1940 and 1941—the day of revenge and retribution is at hand.

Last night's major target was the city of Dusseldorf where more than 500 huge four-motored bombers loosed "block-busters" and land mines that totally razed great sections of the city. Mists and clouds over the target combined with the ghastly glow of countless fires to lend an aerie atmosphere to the attack, according to the reports of returning pilots.

Italy's punishment was meted out by more than 400 Allied planes, mostly American Liberators and Flying Fortresses. Sicily, Sardinia, and the Pantelleria Islands were the hardest hit. While these warning raids on Italy were in progress, Prime Minister Churchill was urging the Italian people by radio to oust their fascist rulers and throw themselves on the mercy and justice of the Allies.

Thursday, May 27, 1943: —For the first time in many months the spotlight of war news has shifted to China and that gallant nation's one-sided struggle against the Jap invader. Large scale ground fighting is in progress south of the Yangtze River where the Nipponese have launched a mighty offensive apparently aimed at the capture of Chungking and the "liquidating" of the so-called China incident. Since the loss of the Burma Road, China has been fighting virtually alone, aided only by General Claire Chennault's brilliant band of airmen, formerly known as the Flying Tigers, and it is recognized that the limit of China's resistance has almost been reached. The situation is fraught with danger that the United Nations may lose a valuable Ally if adequate aid is not forthcoming before it is too late.

The brave Chinese, however, are still in there fighting and have presented the new Jap offensive with a stone-wall resistance that seems to be holding for the present. We can only hope that General Chiang-Kai-Shek's armies will find that extra bit of stamina that will carry them through until the rapidly growing flood of Allied power can break through to aid them.

Several interesting events have occurred on the home front today. A Congressional compromise pay-as-you-go tax bill, embodying 75% forgiveness, appears headed for speedy enactment by both Houses. An ultimatum by President Roosevelt has sent 18,000 rubber company workers back on the job after a brief walk-out. A controversy is apparently raging over purported plans to return Japanese evacuees to their former California homes. We'll hear more of that later. J.W. Stevens, state fire marshal, predicted today that the continental United States is in for some bombing attacks. He predicts the Japs will bomb us on July 4th.

Friday, May 28, 1943: —President Roosevelt today established what is virtually a war cabinet. Former Supreme Court Justice James F. Byrnes was appointed to head a new Office of War Mobilization. His job will be practically that of a deputy president, with unlimited authority and control over all phases of the war effort except actual military operations. A five-man committee was also appointed to assist Mr. Byrnes.

This new move has long been needed according to many critics and observers. The President has tried to carry too much of the load and many phases of the war effort have suffered from lack of coordination and proper direction. There have been many cases of bungling, due to duplication and overlapping of authority, friction between departments, and failure or inability to make decisions with dispatch. The Office of War Mobilization has been designed to streamline the war effort and prevent future bungling. Mr. Byrnes has a tough job ahead of him but one of utmost importance.

The war news today is again confined principally to aerial activity. The RAF continued its death blow against Germany during the night by smashing the industrial city of Essen with the bomb loads of 500 planes. The attack inaugurated a new bombing technique by the RAF, known as "wave bombing." Ten waves of fifty bombers braved the most concentrated curtain of anti-aircraft fire yet thrown up by the Nazi to deluge the city with every known type of explosive and incendiary bombs. Each wave of bombers was part of a pattern aimed at obtaining the greatest devastation possible from the type of bomb load carried. The British said the experiment was highly successful although twenty-three bombers were lost.

Saturday, May 29, 1943: —Reports of heavy air fighting in the Caucasus indicate that the great summer campaigns in Russia are about to commence. The Berlin radio tells of vast movements of Russian troops, hinting that it may be the Soviets who will open the summer offensive rather that the Germans. There is little doubt but that the Red Army is desp0erately anxious to pry the Nazi claw out of the Caucasus by recapturing Novorossiysk on the Black Sea. This dangerous German claw keeps the door open to the vital Maikop oil fields and the wealth of the Middle East. Hitler's oil starved war machine can be counted on to make at least one more desperate effort to reach that promised land.

But Der Fuhrer's attention may soon be drawn to a new battle ground. From the furious intensity of the Allied aerial offensive against Sicily, Sardinia, Corsica, as well as Italy and Germany proper, it appears certain that the Allied High Command is about ready to strike. The second front is closer today than ever before. Where we will strike and when is the High Command's secret and Hitler's headache. It may by Sicily or Italy itself. It may be France, the Balkans, Norway or it may be several of them simultaneously. Only time will tell.

The Pacific war is in a comparative lull. The battle of Attu, while not yet entirely completed, is simply a bitter mopping up operation, performed in snow, sleet, and bitter cold. South Pacific activity is confined to the air, with General MacArthur's bombers striking heavily at the Jap base at Lae, New Guinea. New offensives on a major scale are expected to flare up in the Pacific at any moment. Be prepared!

Sunday, May 30, 1943: —The Attu affair has finally ended; all organized resistance has ceased, with even the mopping up operation completed. Only a few isolated snipers remain to be hunted down and eliminated. The first hint of our total victory in recapturing the first American soil sullied by the heel of the invader came from Tokyo itself. The Japanese radio admitted that their garrison of 3,000 men had been annihilated and complained that wicked Americans had attacked in overwhelming numbers— their figure was twenty to thirty thousand men. Imagine that! The Japs complaining that we got there too soon with too much. How different from a year ago when it was always "too little, too late." We didn't hear the little yellow men complaining then when their hordes were overrunning our gallant garrisons on Bataan and Corregidor or the unprepared British in Malaya and Singapore, or the stubborn Dutch in Java. You'll have plenty of reason to whine from now on, Mr. Moto.

From the Mediterranean comes evidence that the Italians have the invasion jitters. Their fears are undoubtedly well founded as the Allied Air Force in North Africa is pounding away at Italian bases in Sicily, Sardinia and Pantelleria without rest and thousands of invasion barges are concentrating in Tunisian, Algerian, and Moroccan ports. The Italian mainland also felt the wrath of Allied air power as more than 100 Flying Fortresses attacked the oil center of Leghorn, more than 200 miles north of Rome. Heavy damage was inflicted.

Monday, May 31, 1943: —Today is Memorial Day, a day of remembering those who have sacrificed their lives in the defense of their country. A day to remember those lads who fell in Belleau Woods and Chateau Thierry, or those lads who charged up to the cannon's mouth at Gettysburg. A day to remember the men who died at Valley Forge or swept with Teddy Roosevelt up San Juan Hill. And now a day to remember the brave dead of another war; the gallant Marines who bared their breasts against impossible odds at Wake Island, the men of Bataan and Corregidor and Pearl Harbor, the sailors of the Coral Sea, the men of Torpedo Squadron Eight at Midway, the five Callahan brothers and the Cruiser Juneau, the Marines of Guadalcanal and the Doughboys in Tunisia; our martyred flyers in Tokyo, the dead of Attu. There is so much for us to remember, so many sacrifices that we cannot repay, so much work to be done if we as a nation are to be worthy of such devotion. Abraham Lincoln's words are still a living pledge, "That we here highly resolve that these dead shall not have died in vain, that this Nation, under God, shall have a new birth of freedom and that Government of the people, for the people, and by the people shall not perish from the earth."

A brief summary of the war news tonight indicates that

destruction and death is being rained on the hapless Italians in ever increasing torrents. A great fleet of 100 Flying Fortresses blasted the Naples area, wrecking military installations and starting numerous fires. South Pacific action was confined to reconnaissance missions over a wide area. Home front news is centered about impending trouble in the still outstanding coal dispute and the new pay-as-you-go income tax legislation.

June

Tuesday, June 1, 1943: —The coal dispute has erupted into open defiance of governmental authority as John L. Lewis, the union dictator, has permitted his 530,000 coal miners to strike, halting production of the fuel so vitally needed to maintain our war industries. It is a strike against the Government itself and challenges the ability and authority of the Federal Government to prosecute the war. Since the Government seized the mines and has operated them as government property, the miners were in effect, government employees and this strike is the first instance in the long history of the nation when government employees have dared to strike against their employer—and that in war time. It will be very interesting to watch developments.

The rapidly growing concentration of Japanese ships on the bottom of the Pacific Ocean was augmented by seven more vessels during the last few weeks, sent there by our roving submarines. This latest bag brings the grand total of Jap ships sent to the bottom by our subs to 169. The "silent service" is doing a magnificent job.

From China comes word that the large scale offensive launched Thursday by the Japs has been stopped, with at least five divisions of the invaders being encircled and threatened with disaster. Heavy fighting is still in progress and it now appears as though Generalissimo Chiang-Kai-Shek's courageous troops may be able to snatch a victory out of what was a very dangerous situation.

Wednesday, June 2, 1943: —Final Congressional approval was given today to the long-debated Pay-as-you-go Tax Plan and the measure was sent to President Roosevelt for signature. The President is expected to quickly approve the bill that will put the nation's 44 million taxpayers on a current basis. From all accounts, the measure has many ramifications and is undoubtedly the most complicated piece of tax legislation ever concocted. Its operation will probably require an untold amount of paper work but the general principle of pay-as-you-go is sound and will no doubt prove beneficial in the long run.

The unprecedented coal strike is in its second day with no

sign of any solution. President Roosevelt has called a conference of War Labor Board officials and other government leaders to study the crisis and devise means of dealing with it. Strong governmental action is expected almost immediately.

The Chinese victory in stopping the Japanese offensive in Hupeh province is attaining larger proportions. The Chinese have succeeded in decimating five divisions of enemy troops, inflicting more than 30,000 casualties and forcing the main body of enemy troops to withdraw to their original positions. The latest and most serious threat to Chungking and the Chinese cause can be considered eliminated.

A final check-up of the Attu battle discloses that only four Jap prisoners were taken. This shows the bitterness of the fighting as more than 1,700 enemy dead have been counted, which does not include those bodies that were buried or cremated by the Japanese themselves or those destroyed by artillery or bomb explosions. It's a bitter fight, literally to the death, with our little yellow foe.

Thursday, June 3, 1943: —President Roosevelt minced no words today in calling the coal miners back to work. As President and Commander-in-chief he "ordered and directed the miners who are not now at work in the mines to return to their work on Monday, June 7, 1943." "I must remind the miners," he said, "that they are working for the Government on essential war work and it is their duty no less than that of their sons and brothers in the armed forces to fulfill their war duties."

By virtue of this directive the final showdown between John L. Lewis and the President of the United States was postponed until next week. Just what further steps would be taken by the President should the miners decide to back Lewis and defy the government is not known but there are several big sticks, such as reclassification in the draft and the use of Federal troops, if necessary, that he may employ.

The news from the war fronts is generally much better than the home front news. The Chinese are giving the Japs a good lacing in the Yangtze River valley, being ably assisted by the 14th United States Air Force. In Russia, it now appears, the big summer offensive may be launched by the Soviets rather than by the hard-pressed Nazis. The Red Army has stepped up its activities all along the front and has decisively defeated the German Luftwaffe, destroying 191 enemy aircraft in yesterday's air battles.

Further scarcities of meat, particularly beef, caused a hiking in ration point values today. Pretty slim pickings in meat eating these days.

Friday, June 4, 1943: —The United Mine Workers Union and John L. Lewis today bowed to the will of the Government as expressed by President Roosevelt and ordered the 530,000 members of the Union back to work on Monday next. The final result was a defeat for the bushy-browed Lewis, and many observers and friends of labor believe that his stubborn, selfish stand in this dispute has done irretrievable damage to the cause of organized labor. A great deal of anger was aroused throughout the country, and in the armed forces, at this attempt by one man to hinder and weaken the war effort. This public anger has taken form in a stringent anti-strike bill passed by the House today, providing stern penalties for those who "aid any operational interruption in war plants or mines seized by the Government." The bill further requires the registration of all labor unions and the filing of financial data. Organized labor itself has little to thank Lewis for in this case and he was denounced as a "traitor" today in a report submitted at the fifth biennial convention of the CIO International Longshoremen and Warehousemen's Union in San Francisco.

Argentina broke into the news today with a report of a successful military revolution in the South American republic that landed pro-Allied leaders in possession of the Government. President Ramon S. Castillo fled to a warship in the harbor, leaving the Presidential Palace in the hands of the military revolutionaries. The coup was brought about by widespread dissatisfaction by the majority of the Argentine people with the former government's pro-Axis policies. The new government will demand a break in diplomatic relations with the Axis powers and full American collaboration. It's just another defeat for Hitler's pals.

Saturday, June 5, 1943: —Not willing to establish permanent peace in the coal fields so that the country can get back to the more important job of concentrating on winning the war, John

L. Lewis today had to qualify his back-to-work order with a statement that it was only a truce and a new strike would be called on June 20 if a satisfactory agreement has not been worked out by then. Apparently he could not bring himself to admit defeat, even in the face of overwhelming public opinion, and hurled new threats of work stoppage if his demands are not met 100%. Obviously the only solution lies with Congress and maybe by June 20 the anti-strike legislation will have become law and they can put would-be strike leaders where they will be harmless—at least for the duration.

In condemning strikes and those who initiate them, we do not overlook the fact that coal miners and other workers at times may have just grievances. The whole point is that such grievances must be settled through the machinery of government set up by law to handle labor disputes—and there must not be a stoppage of any vital war work of any kind while such disputes are being settled. Our national duty to our fighting men forbids it.

The pro-Allied revolt in Argentina has ended in an almost bloodless victory for the military junta who overthrew the pro-Nazi administration in one day. General Arturo Rawson and General Pedro Ramirez have assumed control. It is believed that the Allied victory in Tunisia was the stimulus needed to bring about the defeat of Hitler's pals in the South American republic.

Sunday, June 6, 1943: —Our infant son, born March 20 was christened and blessed today. Looking at him, our hearts could not help but bleed for those parents who have been called upon to send their sons, once young and helpless as ours, to suffer and die upon foreign battlefields. May God grant that there may be an end to wars and their needless sacrifice of innocent young lives. It is hard to conceive of any good coming out of war and yet even that cloud may have a silver lining. One mother of a son in the service stood up in church today and told of her boy who found himself amidst the thunder of battle in North Africa. He had never been very religious before the war but he found his God in the mud and death of Tunisia. His letters to his mother affirms his great faith and he adds his belief to the thousands of other soldiers who have faced the enemy's guns that "there are no atheists in foxholes."

From all reports the Chinese victory in the Upper Yangtze River area has assumed the proportions of their greatest triumph

399

in the war to date. The great Japanese army that set out from Ichang last month to blast the Chinese from the war, have been driven in total defeat back to the outskirts of the main base itself. The exultant Chinese are already assaulting the city's outer defenses. Thirty thousand Japs were killed and another 60,000 trapped in the abortive offensive. It was a triumph of courage and bare flesh against the superior equipment of the Japanese invaders.

Monday, June 7, 1943: —Eighteen months of war finds the United States flexing muscles that are daily getting bigger and more powerful. With her Allies she has seized the initiative in both the European and Pacific theaters. After scoring the biggest victory of the war to date over the Germans in Tunisia, equaled only by the Russian defense of Stalingrad, the Allies find themselves poised and ready with a mighty military machine to be unleashed against the soft underbelly of Hitler's European fortress. Where and when they will strike is, of course, a military secret, but it is no secret that a great army of more than one million men, amply supported by ships and planes, are assembled on the southern coast of the Mediterranean awaiting the zero hour. It is anyone's guess where the first blow will come but the preliminary activity, principally in the air, indicates that the island stepping stones from Tunisia to the Italian mainland will be the first objectives. Sicily, Sardinia, and Pantelleria have taken a terrific aerial pounding for two weeks, obviously to soften them up for invasion. Italy is facing the most desperate moments in her history, her morale is bad, and a knockout blow aimed at her midsection would seem to be the logical move at the present time.

Aerial activity in the Solomons flared up again today after a considerable lull. American fighter pilots intercepted a flight of 50 Japanese bombers and Zeros near the Russell Islands and turned them back after downing nineteen enemy planes. Seven of our craft were shot down but three of the pilots were saved.

Tuesday, June 8, 1943: —Prime Minister Churchill made the headlines again today with a dramatic speech before Commons. His words fairly oozed with confidence and was in happy contrast to his famous "blood, sweat, and tears" promise made at the time he assumed the reins of government in the dark days of

1940. Today he asserted that the "mellow light of victory" was already playing on the Allied cause. He said plans have been completed for large scale offensive operations against the Axis and blasted any hope held by either Italy or Germany that a negotiated peace can save them. The Allied leaders are determined to use force in its "most intense and violent form" to wring an unconditional surrender from the gangster nations. Churchill was obviously happier and more confident than at any time in his career and he is one to understate rather than overstate a case.

Axis communiqués reported that British Commandos attacked the Italian island of Lampedusa but were repulsed with heavy losses. No confirmation has come from Allied sources. It is likely the action was merely a feeling out attack of minor importance.

Here at home things are far from quiet. Price and rationing complaints and labor problems keep things in a constant turmoil. The increasing complexities of life and sacrifices to be made are causing a noticeable amount of tenseness and irritations among the people. Squabbles of all kinds are cropping up to plague those charged with administering the war effort. Yet despite all the "crabbing" and apparent discontent you can feel all about you the mighty power that is rapidly taking shape and form as 130,000,000 Americans learn to wage total war.

Wednesday, June 9, 1943: —The Allied assault on Italy is rapidly taking shape and form. General Eisenhower's North African Headquarters announced that an ultimatum had been dispatched to the Italians, demanding the unconditional surrender of the battered island of Pantelleria. The full weight of Allied power, both naval and land, is poised to strike if no reply is received. The island stepping stone to Europe has been under constant air and sea bombardment since the fall of Tunisia and is about ripe to fall an easy prey to invasion. The Allied hope the Italian garrison will see the hopelessness of their situation and surrender without the necessity of a landing, thus sparing the civilian population of the island further suffering. Powerful units of the British Mediterranean fleet are standing by close offshore, ready to dump shells into Italian defenses should the ultimatum be rejected.

401

On the home front we find that Senate and House conferees have agreed on legislation outlawing strikes in Government operated war industries. Passage of the measure is likely to be accomplished before the June 20 deadline set by John L. Lewis and his United Mine Workers Union.

A nasty little semi-racial rumpus that may have international complications has flared up in Los Angeles. National attention has been called to widespread rioting between gangs of zoot-suited hoodlums, mostly Mexican, and service men. The fighting started when a sailor's girl friend was molested by one of the swarthy wearers of the fanciful costume. This and other attacks sent groups of sailors and soldiers roving in vengeful pursuit of the zoot-suited gangsters. Street fighting and knifings were common. Military and civilian police are not yet in control.

Thursday, June 10, 1943: —The principal item of news tonight remains the terrific serial pounding being administered to Italy's island fortress of Pantelleria. No reply has, as yet, been received to the ultimatum delivered to the Italian commander by General Eisenhower, demanding the unconditional surrender of the island to overwhelming Allied forces. The Italians have until tomorrow at noon, however, and they may see the handwriting on the wall by then. Meanwhile General Spaatz's and General Doolittle's boys are giving the Axis garrison no time to forget what lays in store for them should they choose to continue the fight. Wave after wave of heavy bombers heaped destruction all over the island saturating the coastal defenses with high explosives.

In addition to Pantelleria, our North African air force sent large numbers of bombers and fighters over Sicily, smashing unmercifully at Axis airdromes and knocking thirty six enemy planes out of the air. The ratio of Axis planes destroyed to Allied craft lost was maintained at more than 7 to 1 which is mighty good hunting in any man's war.

Here at home, President Roosevelt signed the Pay-as-you-go Tax Bill, embodying a payroll withholding tax to start July 1. Now begin the headaches involved in putting the new system into operation.

A further complication entered the coal mine dispute today as Administrator Harold Ickes declared a $1.00 per day fine will be levied against each miner who failed to work during the recent five day strike. John L. Lewis and his cohorts were quick to denounce the action and threaten further defiance.

Friday, June 11, 1943: —PANTELLERIA SURRENDERS! The Italian garrison on Mussolini's "Little Gibraltar" ran up the white flag at 11:40 a.m., just twenty minutes before the deadline. At noon Allied troops began landing on the island and at 12:22 p.m. the battered stronghold was in our possession. It was a notable victory and a milestone in the history of war. It is the first concrete proof of the efficacy of air power alone. An assault by landing forces had been planned but was rendered unnecessary by the efficiency with which the island's defenses were reduced to impotency by twenty days of the most intense and concentrated aerial bombardment in history. An examination of the island after the surrender indicated that hardly a square foot of any military objective escaped the devastating effect of block-busting bombs dropped with uncanny accuracy by our flyers. Between ten and fifteen thousand Italian troops who survived the attack by living underground were taken prisoners.

Allied Capitals hailed the good news and President Roosevelt seized the opportunity to call upon the Italian people to overthrow Mussolini and his traitorous Fascist regime and get out of the war. Once they have done so they will be free to choose a new government and seek to regain their rightful place among the law-abiding nations of the world.

Other interesting items in the news were the recognition by our government of the new regime in Argentina, the acceptance of the proposed no-strike bill by the House of Representatives, and the threat by John L. Lewis of further trouble in the tangled coal mine situation due to the fine recently levied against the miners by Admiral Ickes.

Saturday, June 12, 1943: —Resting only ninety minutes after the fall of Pantelleria, the Allied North Africa Air Force shifted its attention to the little Italian island of Lampedusa, showering its defenses with the famous block-busters and forcing its surrender only twenty four hours after the capitulation of the larger isle. General Eisenhower's Headquarters reported that our troops have already occupied the island outpost. It looks like Sicily and

Sardinia are next on the program. Remember Il Duce, or should I say "Ill" Duce, the mainland of Italy is only two miles from the tip of Sicily. What wrath have you brought down upon the heads of your unhappy people?

At the same time, Mussolini's boss, Adolf, was getting plenty of attention from the mighty Allied air forces based in England. The greatest number of planes (more than 1,400) ever launched in a single night, smashed vital military targets in the Reich last night. Dusseldorf and Munster were the principal objectives and were completely ruined by the explosive weight of more than 2,000 tons of bombs. During the daylight hours several hundred American heavy bombers plastered the German U-boat centers of Wilhelmshaven and Cuxhaven. Forty three planes were lost in the combined operations.

It appears likely in view of recent successes that air power will be given considerable time to prove whether or not it alone can force Germany's capitulation. It's worth a chance because of its comparative economy in Allied lives and equipment. In truth, it doesn't seem possible that the Germans can stand many more raids of last night's intensity.

Sunday, June 13, 1943: —Uncle Sam's nephews and nieces are faced with the second installment of Federal income taxes due next Tuesday and the rush to get funds through the redemption of Savings Bonds forced us to work all day today. It seems as though almost everyone waited until the last few days to pay his taxes, probably due to uncertainty regarding the effect of the pay-as-you-go tax law would have on this tax payment. The 20% withholding tax on salaries and wages goes into effect on July 1 but will not exempt anyone from paying the second installment due June 15 under the old system. This payment will be applied against 1943's taxes for the first six months. It appears likely, however, that much confusion and many headaches lie ahead of the Collector of Internal Revenue.

A bit of bad news was released by our Navy Department yesterday. Two of our gallant submarines, the Amberjack and the Grampus, have been lost while on patrols into enemy waters. This raises to eight the number of deadly American undersea boats that have been lost since the war began. It is sad to contemplate the fate of the sixty officers and men who normally constitute the complement of a sub. They are of the silent service and die in the lonely depths of the sea far from the shores of their beloved homeland.

From the far north comes word that American aerial attack on Kiska is increasing in intensity. Preparations may be under way to force the capitulation of that last foothold held by the Japs in the Western Hemisphere.

Monday, June 14, 1943: —The Navy Department announced another bag of Japanese ships destroyed by our far-ranging submarines. Twelve enemy vessels, including one destroyer and one huge transport, were sent to the bottom in one of the most successful expeditions of the war into far-eastern waters. The latest bag brought the grand total of Jap ships sunk by American subs, since Pearl Harbor, to 180.

Further details of the recent capture of Italy's Mediterranean islands disclose that the tiny island of Lamedusa was taken by a solitary English pilot whose plane was forced, through lack of fuel, to land on the Italian isle. The jittery garrison greeted him with a display of white flags. The pilot is now known to his buddies as "The King of Lampedusa."

From Pantelleria and Lampedusa, the Allied Air Force has transferred its undivided attention to the much larger island of Sicily. Heavy raids were concentrated on the island's airdromes, which almost always signify an approaching invasion. One hundred fifty eight German and Italian planes were destroyed on the ground during the day.

There is a lull in the Southwest Pacific war theater but it is anticipated that some very decisive offensive action will be launched in that area soon. Meanwhile General MacArthur's bombers are making their daily "milk runs" over Japanese bases.

The most interesting bit of home news today is a further announcement by Selective Service officials that the drafting of fathers cannot be avoided much longer.

Tuesday, June 15, 1943: —Allied invasion plans took on new mystery today as the British sealed the frontier between Syria and Turkey. The action was ostensibly taken to prevent Arabs from crossing into Turkey and disclosing important information to

German spies there. The move may also have been taken to cover up extensive troop movements. In any event it was another telling blow in the war of nerves against the jittery Axis. Hitler invented the "war of nerves" and is being repaid in kind.

Sicily caught it again today as Flying Fortresses attacked the port of Messina with block-busting bombs that smashed port facilities and railroad yards, starting huge fires. Italian anti-aircraft defenses were considerable but ineffective. No American planes were lost.

American flyers raiding Kiska in the Aleutians reported that the Japs have another enemy to worry about on that island. The Kiska volcano is threatening to erupt. Maybe the elements are going to lend us a hand in disposing of our vicious yellow foes.

For the fourth night in a row the RAF in England has sent a huge fleet of bombers over the Reich. Last night the arms center of Oberhausen was honored with a visit. Mustn't overlook anyone of any place, Adolf; don't want to show any partiality. Where will it be tonight, mein Herr?

On the home front, anxious eyes are being turned to the nation's food situation. The outlook is anything but pleasant and strong action is needed if a dangerous shortage is to be averted.

Wednesday, June 16, 1943: —There was plenty of excitement in our own neighborhood this afternoon. A P-40 fighting plane, taking off from Mills Field, crashed into a house just a block away from us. Apparently the plane's motor quit, burst into flames, and the pilot had to set her down in a hurry. He did a marvelous job—considering. He switched off the ignition and pancaked her in, skidding into the front of the house with a thunderous roar. Fortunately the house was empty, both occupants being at work. The whole corner of the house was sheared off, a brick fireplace come tumbling down, and the plane ended up in the parlor. The lucky pilot survived with nothing worse than a pair of broken legs. Gasoline was splashed all over the place but by a miracle did not ignite. What could have been a terrible disaster ended up as nothing more than a nice piece of demolition work.

Back on the war news, reliable British sources in Turkey reported that the Rumanian government has made several secret peace overtures toward the Allies. The Axis satellite government has indicated it would lay down its arms if favorable terms could be obtained. It is unlikely, however, that the Allies will make any concessions and will hold firmly to the "unconditional surrender" policy adopted at Casablanca.

Meanwhile, Mussolini's unhappy isle of Sicily was the recipient of another deluge of heavy bombs delivered by fleets of American bombers based in North Africa. Axis reports, reaching Spain and France, hinted that Il Duce is already evacuating equipment, records, and vital port installations from Sicily, Sardinia, and southern Italy to points in northern Italy.

Thursday, June 17, 1943: —Violent action flared anew in the Solomons today. The Japanese sent a fleet of more than 100 bombers and fighters against American shipping in the Guadalcanal area. A huge air battle ensued as Army, Navy and Marine fighters rose to meet them. Seventy seven of the raiders were sent plunging into the sea against the loss of only seven American planes. It was the most one-sided aerial victory of the war and took a big bite out of Japanese air power in the South Pacific. What damage the enemy bombers did before they were destroyed or driven away was not immediately revealed. Some shipping loss can be expected, however, as even the Japs can't miss with every bomb.

Of the 77 Jap planes destroyed, 32 were bombers and 45 were zeros.

Invasion jitters are shaking Italy to the roots. As if trying to justify their impending defeat, Rome radio commentators pointed out that the Allies have 5,000 planes and more than a million men poised in North Africa, ready to attack them. Reports seeping into Switzerland hint that peace demonstrations have already broken out in southern Italy in the face of heavy Allied aerial bombardment. Sicilian ports and military establishments were also subjected to terrific pounding during the day.

Germany received its nightly supply of high explosives, in gaseous form, by way of the RAF based in England last night. Much bombed Cologne was the target of this latest visitation. The goods were sent special delivery Air Mail, addressed to Hitler.

Friday, June 18, 1943: —As evidence of what is in store for them, the Axis should read the War Production Board's report of

American plane production for May. A record 7,200 aircraft of all descriptions were produced, a number far exceeding the combined production of all the Axis countries. Add to this the production of our Allies and you have an idea of the tremendous power that is gathering to smash through to final victory. Hitler's, Mussolini's, and Tojo's nightmares must be filled with American production figures.

Some of that air power right now is pounding hard at Italian objectives in Sicily, Sardinia, and the Italian mainland. Naples was the recipient of a merciless attack by heavy bombers, packing 4,000 pound block-busters. Naples is the jumping off spot for supplies to Sicily and Sardinia and Allied flyers are bent on smashing any attempt by the Germans or Italians to send reinforcements or supplies to the beleaguered Italian outposts. Your time is short, Benito!

Trouble is again brewing on the home front. We're not out of the woods yet in the coal mine dispute. The War Labor Board has refused to meet all the demands of John L. Lewis and further strike action is threatened at the end of the truce period Sunday night. The people are becoming impatient at this squabble and are demanding a final showdown.

The Bureau of Labor Statistics claimed today that living costs in San Francisco, the highest in the nation, have finally stopped their upward spiral—at least during the last thirty day period. That's encouraging news for the salaried man because prices, particularly on foodstuffs, are almost out of sight. The Bureau states that the cost of living index for the nation as a whole is up 24.1% over January 1941. San Francisco's increase was even greater.

Saturday, June 19, 1943: —General Jimmy Doolittle's African bomber force shot down 39 Axis fighter planes in fierce dogfights over Sicily and Sardinia today. It was the largest bog of enemy interceptors in one day since the invasion offensive began. Eight of our bombers were lost.

Meanwhile the jittery Italian High Command was feverishly preparing for the expected Allied landing. The entire southern province along a 700 mile front was placed under martial law and civilians were being evacuated from all key centers. It is a fearful spot to be in; maybe they will understand something of what England felt in 1940 when Mussolini plunged the dagger into the back of prostrate France and pounced on the cornered British.

News from Guadalcanal indicates that the recent aerial victory over the Japanese air force was even more decisive than first reported. In addition to the 77 zeros and bombers destroyed by American flyers, shore batteries and ship anti-aircraft gunners accounted for 17 more, bringing the grand total to 94 Jap planes eradicated. Not a bad day's work.

While all the good news comes from our gallant fighting men in foreign skies, all the bad news comes from dissention at home. The final showdown approaches in the coal deadlock, with war production slated to be the loser. Under Secretary of War Patterson reported today that war production, scheduled to increase by 3½% last month, rather decreased by 2%, a net loss of 5½%. This dangerous falling off must be stopped without delay or recent victories by our armed forces will have been in vain. Redoubled efforts and the kind of spirit displayed by our fighting men are needed on the home front.

Sunday, June 20, 1943: —There was a bit of excitement in the Bay Area last night but we slept right through it. With a terrific racket that apparently awakened everyone but us the air raid sirens sounded off at 1:07 a.m. last night. The blackout with all its attendant buzz and excitement lasted until 1:47 a.m. The all clear found this family blissfully asleep, unaware of the hubbub going on around us. Not a bad way to spend a blackout at that.

Nothing came of the alarm as all unidentified targets were found to be friendly. The alert did reveal many flaws in the Civilian Defense setup and left much to be desired in the management of the emergency. The great length of time between alarms and the consequent lack of practice is probably the main reason for lack of efficiency.

Persistent rumors coming out of London hint that high Italian officials, headed by Crown Prince Umberto, are on their way to Algiers to discuss peace terms with Allied leaders. These rumors are probably unfounded but the possibility that they may be true is strengthened by a realization of Italy's hopeless position in the face of tremendous Allied land, sea, and particularly air power. Mighty fleets of American and British bombers and fighters are sweeping daily from advanced bases in newly captured Pantelleria to crush the last vestige of defensive strength out of Sicily, Sardinia, and the sore toe of the Italian boot. The disillusioned Italians would do well to oust Il Duce and submit to unconditional surrender before many more of their cities are reduced to rubble.

Monday, June 21, 1943: —Allied air power continued to strike at the enemy all over the world today. Japanese bases in the Gilbert Islands took a particularly heavy pasting from long-range American bombers. Two separate flights struck simultaneously at Tarawa and Nauru, causing extensive damage among military installations. The raid called for a 1,500 mile round trip for the big planes, none of which were lost.

From England, mighty Lancaster bombers set out in large numbers to smash radio equipment factories at Friedrichshafen in southwestern Germany. Direct hits were observed on buildings of the important Luftschiffbau radio factory.

Italy's Sicilian and mainland cities shuddered under a deluge of bombs from squadrons of American and British planes based in North Africa and newly captured Pantelleria. Sixteen enemy fighter planes were shot down against the loss of five bombers.

While favorable reports continue to come from the battlefront, home front problems were not being met with equal success. The coal mine dispute that has resulted in a work stoppage for the third time today, will require some decisive action by the government if vital steel production is not to be hindered.

Confusion and difficulty in the meat packing industry is also becoming acute. Several large packing houses have closed their doors rather than operate at a loss under the Government's new "hold-the-line" and subsidy program.

Serious rioting has broken out in Detroit between Negroes and whites. The Governor of Michigan has ordered mobilization of state troops to meet the situation.

Tuesday, June 22, 1943: —Italy and Germany literally rocked under the weight of explosives rained upon them during the last 24 hours. The ruined city of Naples was a mass of flames after a block-busting raid by more than 100 Flying Fortresses. But the

Italian attack was a minor engagement compared with the terrific onslaught against the German Reich. Last night 700 great four motored RAF bombers smashed the war production center of Krefeld into what even the Nazis admitted was "smoldering ruins." Forty-four bombers were lost in this raid that saw 10,000 pounds of high explosives per minute rained on the vital industrial center.

The most sensational attack of the day was carried out in daylight by American heavy bombers. Bringing their precision bombing tactics into effective use the American force sought out a hidden synthetic rubber plant in the forest near Essen and completely obliterated it. Returning pilots said the entire area was left in a mass of red flames, obviously feeding furiously on some very flammable material. Twenty American planes failed to return to England.

Here at home, Federal troops finally managed to restore order to the Detroit Negro quarters where serious race riots have occurred, leaving 28 people dead and hundreds injured. The immediate cause of the riots was a fist fight between a white man and a Negro but the underlying cause is the unusually heavy influx of southern Negroes, attracted by highly paid war jobs, bringing with them serious racial problems.

Wednesday, June 23, 1943: —The final showdown in the coal dispute has been averted for the third time. John L. Lewis, the bushy-browed President of the United Mine Workers Union, called off the strike in the face of threatened action of a decisive nature by the Federal Government. He ordered the miners back on the job under the revised terms of the old contract until October 31 at which time we apparently will have to go through all this again.

An angered and aroused Congress may have something to say about that, however, as the Smith-Connelly anti-strike bill nears enactment into law. The bill provides stiff penalties for labor leaders or anyone else who instigates or coerces any worker in a war plant or mine to go on strike. Many other restrictions and provisions make the new bill the most drastic measure yet proposed to counter the abuse of union power. The War Labor Board will be furnished teeth with which to enforce compliance with its decisions. The Board may also subpoena anyone,

411

including Lewis himself, to appear before them.

It is possible that the anti-strike bill may fail from Presidential displeasure as those close to the Chief Executive indicate that he may veto it. He is reported to favor a substitute measure, raising the draft age limitation to 65 in order that striking miners may be inducted into the army. The obvious flaw in the latter method is the fact that it wouldn't touch the leaders of the unions, who, after all, are the ones responsible.

Thursday, June 24, 1943: —Coffee drinkers found the situation a bit more cheerful today as the O.P.A. promised them the largest ration since the beginning of the program. Beginning July 1st, the caffeine fanciers will be allowed one pound of their favorite brand—if they can find it—every three weeks. Pour out that extra cup, folks. Things are looking up.

As if to even the scale, however, beer drinkers saw their prospects for an adequate supply of the sparkling amber liquid darker, as the experts predicted a shortage of beer in the near future due to a lack of commercial corn. Better unlimber those shorter beer mugs, folks. Things don't look so good.

While we fuss about coffee and beer, the numbed, dazed residents of the bomb-shattered Ruhr are being evacuated by the German Government. More than 3,000,000 people are involved in what apparently is one of the major dislocations of a populace in the history of war. With the nerve-wracked citizenry out of the way, the German military are preparing for an all-out defense of the vital industrial region. More than 30,000 powerful anti-aircraft guns have been mounted along a 200 mile belt, 20-50 miles deep, supported by thousands of great searchlights. Down this corridor of death, where the long, bright fingers reach up to snatch them into oblivion with explosive fingertips, Allied planes and men by the thousands are pouring nightly, bringing with them their heavy loads of high explosive "eggs" to dump on the industrial heart of the desperate enemy below.

Friday, June 25, 1943: —Congress today displayed one of its rare moments of independence as it over-rode the President's veto of the Smith-Connelly Anti-strike Bill. It took the Senate only a few minutes after the reading of Mr. Roosevelt's veto message to garner the necessary two-thirds majority vote to upset the veto.

412

The House took a little more than two hours to accomplish the same end.

The action by Congress was interpreted as a sharp rebuke of the President for his indecisive and coddling actions in meeting the coal situation with its attendant drag on vital war production. Service men in the galleries of Congress roundly applauded the final passage of the new law.

The new measure is a big step forward in the control of unions and if many labor leaders don't like its drastic provisions, they can lay it all on John L. Lewis' doorstep. He alone is responsible for adverse public opinion in this case and his next strike attempt may end up with him in jail. Congress has spoken, Mr. Lewis; war production must not be hindered.

The fighting news is still confined to the air. American and British air fleets are pounding Axis cities and military installations with terrific power. American planes today ranged as far as Salonika, Greece to pound German air fields in that area. Three hundred Flying Forts smashed at Sardinia from North Africa while approximated 700 mighty RAF giants raided the industrial Ruhr again last night, dumping 1,500 tons of bombs on the already devastated city of Wuppertal.

Saturday, June 26, 1943: —The great Allied aerial experiment continued in full swing today. Can Germany be knocked out by air power alone? The Allies are going to give it a thorough tryout. 4,000 bombers have been sent in 14 gigantic raids in the last week. Last night's attack saw 700 huge RAF bombers smash at synthetic oil refineries, chemical works, and steel factories in the Bochum-Gelsenkirchen district. Thirty bombers were lost, bringing the total to 184 bombers lost in the week. Approximately 900 crew men were lost with the planes but these losses were considered light, in relation to vast amount of damage inflicted on the enemy.

Germany is beginning to cry out against the assault, for the first time admitting that the raids are hurting plenty. Berlin broadcasts have stated that the devastation is wide-spread, although insisting as usual, that the damage was confined to residential districts. British reconnaissance photographs give the lie to this claim.

Meanwhile, Italy was receiving her share. More than 100 Flying Fortresses ripped the Sicilian rail and ferry center of

413

Messina, across the straits from the Italian mainland. Swarms of enemy fighters were encountered in addition to heavy anti-aircraft fire but the big Forts broke through to plaster the enemy base with high explosive and incendiaries. Our plane losses were not announced.

Here at home, the Senate took the bit in its teeth again today and placed control of food subsidies in the hands of War Food Administrator Chester Davis rather than in the control of the Office of Price Administration as President Roosevelt desired.

Sunday, June 27, 1943: —It was a magnificent day today. Old Man Sunshine outdid himself in his generosity with the life-giving vitamin D. The warmth of the sun's rays made it exceedingly pleasant to stroll along the Bay Shore at Peninsula Beach and watch the antics of the outboard motorboats. A gentle breeze tempered the heat of midday and hundreds of bathers drank in the health giving sunshine with evident enjoyment.

But even as we were lolling on the beach the threat of war came close to home. The San Francisco Bay Area was thrown on guard by a "Blue Alert" that lasted for one hour beginning at 12:30. The alarm was sounded by the Army Air Defense Wing when unidentified targets were discovered approaching the coast. All radios were "off the air" and civilian defense groups were on the alert. What happened to the "targets" has not been announced. It was the 31st air raid alert in San Francisco since Pearl Harbor. It is well to be on guard as the Japs are almost certain to attempt a raid on this area before the war is over—if just for its propaganda value. To the Orient San Francisco represents America and it would be a fine feather in the Japanese hat if they could stage a successful raid on the famed City by the Golden Gate.

Reports coming from Stockholm hint that Nazi U-boat crews are rebelling, as they did in World War I, at going to sea on their dangerous missions. Allied warships and escort planes have taken a high toll of the undersea raiders lately and the Germans, in some cases at least, seem to have had enough.

Monday, June 28, 1943: —The cause of yesterday's air raid alarm is still a mystery today. The Army Air Defense Command that called the "alert" has given no clue as to the identity of the "targets" that were approaching the coast. Ordinarily they have announced shortly after the all-clear that the "unidentified targets" were finally identified as friendly. This time no further information has been furnished. The plot thickens, the mystery deepens.

Results of recent forays by American submarines were announced by the Navy today. Eight more Jap ships including a destroyer, have joined their relatives beneath the surface of the Pacific. The grand total of Jap ships definitely sunk by the "pig-boats" since Pearl Harbor climbed to 190. 29 others were probably sunk and fifty more were severely damaged. This is contrasted with the loss of only eight U.S. subs since the war began. Not bad hunting.

From Kiska in the far Aleutians to Naples in battered Italy, Allied air power continued to slash at enemy bases today. Kiska was peppered with seven attacks today, raising to sixteen the number of forays against the last Jap base in the Western Hemisphere in the last three days, giving rise to the speculation that a landing attempt to wrest control of the island is near at hand.

American Liberators again attacked Axis-held airdromes near Athens, Greece today, hinting that Greece and the Balkans are figuring prominently in Allied invasion plans.

London reports indicate that a powerful American fleet has joined the British in the Mediterranean, preparatory to the expected assault against the fortress of Europe.

Tuesday, June 29, 1943: —Newspapers are filled with dozens of stories that in peacetime would rate headlines and plenty of space. But the world at war is a reporter's paradise. Sensational news stories are so abundant that many of them gain only passing attention. The war is the number one subject and any news item not connected in some way with the war effort is practically ignored. Sports, the favorite peacetime subject, is dying of loneliness on the inside pages. Labor disputes, food shortages, rationing, shipbuilding and aircraft manufacturing, governmental policies, and service men's activities, consume the majority of news space available after the fighting front news has covered. A perusal of the daily papers will forcibly remind you of the tremendous transformation that has taken place in this country in the last year and a half. The changeover from ways of peace to ways of war seems like a journey from one planet to another where nothing is the same.

The battle of Europe continued in full blast last night as the mighty RAF shattered the battered city of Cologne with another 2,000 tons of bombs. The raid was carried out successfully in the face of greatly increased German defenses. Anti-aircraft fire was the heaviest yet encountered and swarms of night-fighter planes challenged the raiders. Only twenty-five bombers were lost despite this opposition which was an unusually small percentage of the large force involved.

The battle against the submarine in the North Atlantic is also going well. A naval authority in Canada reported that the situation is improving rapidly. Defense against the undersea raiders is increasingly effective and "we're having a U-boat every day for breakfast," he said.

Wednesday, June 30, 1943: —The Yanks are on the offensive again! This time it is in the South Pacific with the Japs on the receiving end. The Navy Department at Washington announced that combined U.S. forces have struck at enemy positions in the central Solomons. The immediate objective is the island of Rendova, where landings have already been made. Rendova is only five miles from the big Japanese base of Munda where many troublesome Jap expeditions have originated. Neutralization of this base would be a big step back along the road to Tokyo. Details of the new offensive are meager but from all indications the attack is proceeding according to schedule. Look out, Mr. Moto.

Prime Minister Churchill made another speech today, which is always good for the front page. He optimistically reported that German U-boats have taken a stunning defeat during the last two months. More than thirty of the undersea raiders were destroyed during May alone and June's Atlantic battles could be described as "a massacre of U-boats." The British leader also reiterated his promise that Britain would never cease the fight against Japan until that barbarous nation is brought to justice through unconditional surrender.

Today saw no let up in the terrific aerial blows being struck at Italy and Germany. U.S. bombers were particularly active on both fronts, striking heavily at French war plants producing arms for Hitler and pounding Sicilian and Italian ports with huge loads of high explosives and incendiaries. Messina, the ferry terminus in Sicily is earning the title of most bombed Italian city.

July

Thursday, July 1, 1943: —Furious fighting is raging in the vicinity of Japan's important base of Munda on New Georgia Island and American forces have captured Viru Harbor on the southeastern tip of that island, thirty miles from Munda. The landing on Rendova, nearby isle, is proceeding according to plan and its capture is virtually certain, according to latest Navy Department reports. The fighting has been particularly fierce in the air, with the Japs throwing in hundreds of planes in an effort to stem the offensive. Sixty five enemy planes were knocked out of the air by our aircraft and the guns of supporting warships. Seventeen of our planes are missing from all operations.

The present Solomons action, while not to be construed as a general offensive, is under the direct command of General Douglas MacArthur, assisted by Admiral Halsey. The importance of the new campaign is evident from this set up and is apparently the beginning of something really big. At the very least it is designed to upset any offensive notions of the Japs, again beating them to the gun.

Across the world other American flyers were continuing their softening up attack on the Italian isle of Sicily. The battered terminus of Messina was again devastated and it would appear that the big Italian island is about ready for plucking.

President Roosevelt today once again demonstrated the difference between a Democracy and a Fascist dictatorship by commuting the death sentence of Max Stephan, the convicted traitor who aided a Nazi flyer to escape, to life imprisonment. Imagine such mercy from Hitler or Hirohito.

Friday, July 2, 1943: —Singing their battle song, "Marching through New Georgia" American assault troops, strongly supported by bombing and fighter planes, smashed their way towards Munda, the big Jap base on New Georgia Island in the central Solomons. One prong of the pincers bearing down on Munda was landed at Viru Harbor, 35 miles down the coast from the enemy base. After capturing the harbor, the tough Americans commenced their jab through the jungles aimed at taking the Jap base from the rear. Meanwhile other American units completed their cleanup of Rendova Island and set up heavy artillery positions to shell Munda across the five mile strait.

The attack on Munda is only a small part of the offensive that is shaping up in the South Pacific. Allied troops on New Guinea opened up an attack on Jap bases at Lae and Salamaua on the northern coast. Australian troops from inland New Guinea drove against the Japs while American troops made a surprise landing at Nassau Bay, only 10 miles below Salamaua, to take the Nips from the rear. Fierce fighting is in progress.

While ground forces were thus occupied, General MacArthur's heavy bombers were pounding the Japanese main base at Rabaul, on New Britain. This strongpoint is undoubtedly the ultimate objective of the new offensive. Rabaul captured, the Allies will be set to launch the ultimate offensive against the Japanese homeland and to accomplish General MacArthur's plan to return the American flag to his beloved Philippines. May providence speed the day.

Saturday, July 3, 1943: —News from the South Pacific fighting is only fragmentary. Today's reports indicate that considerable naval action can be expected. A Japanese task force of seven warships was caught shelling American positions on Rendova last night and was dispersed "in short order" in the words of the Navy communiqué. Other large units of the Jap navy are known to be in the area and a major engagement may develop at any time.

From Gibraltar today comes news of a terrific battle between a 25 ship Allied convoy and a submarine wolf-pack. The final result was another victory for escorting warships and planes which destroyed five U-boats against the loss of only two small merchantmen. German sub crews haven't much to look forward to when they leave port-at least not much that's pleasant.

Italy's sorry plight continues to grow worse daily. The Allied North African Air Force is hitting Sicily, Sardinia, and the southern part of the Italian mainland without mercy. Nearly 100 American Liberators today smashed three important Italian airdromes in southeastern Italy with more than 200 tons of high explosives. Heavy damage was inflicted and only three of the raiders fell prey to anti-aircraft and fighter opposition.

As an interesting sidelight we learn tonight, that the colorful French General Henri Giraud has left North Africa to fly to Washington at the invitation of President Roosevelt. The 64 year old French leader, who was too slippery for the Nazis to hold prisoner, has great influence with all loyal and fighting Frenchmen throughout the world.

Sunday, July 4, 1943: —Another wartime Independence Day finds Americans still engaged in the struggle to preserve those ideals and principles propounded by the signers of the Declaration of Independence. The right of all men to Life, Liberty, and the Pursuit of Happiness is still worth fighting for, as thousands of American boys have proved from Bataan to North Africa. That nation that was launched upon the premise written by Thomas Jefferson and his fellow patriots is still producing men that are not afraid to die, if need be, to defend those principles. This nation, that Hitler scornfully derided as soft and degenerate, has thrown off its veneer of luxury and pleasure seeking and is rapidly developing into a race of tough fighting men who know how to wage war. Those boys who spent their spare time in the corner drugstore sipping sodas or knocking flies in the neighborhood sandlot are doing a magnificent job on the far-flung battlefields. As Major General Kenny, commanding our South Pacific Air Force, recently said, "I am proud of this generation of young men." The young American of today is an adaptable cuss. Taken from the corner drugstore and dumped on a tropical island he grins, pulls a gag, slaps the friendly native on the back, calls him "Bud" or "Fuzzy" and gets to work. And what a job he does. The impossible he does immediately, the miracle takes a little longer. He is the product of the American way. As General MacArthur once said long ago, "From the playing fields of America will come the heroes of the battlefields of tomorrow." The fate and future of America is safe in the hands of America's youth. God grant that but few of them must be sacrificed on the altar of war.

Monday, July 5, 1943: —Today for the first time since January we had a holiday, celebrating the Fourth of July. It was a chance, badly needed, to really catch up on my rest—and that I did. Countless other citizens of the Bay Area, however, took advantage of the double holiday to travel to vacation spots, despite the urging by the Office of Defense Transportation, that they stay at home. Trains and busses were packed and every auto that could rake up the necessary gasoline coupons was on the road. It's pretty hard to keep Americans away from the seashore or the mountains on beautiful summer days like these have been—even in wartime. Well, maybe it will help them to relax and forget their troubles and to return to work tomorrow with fresh vigor and enthusiasm. It's good for the morale.

From the battlefronts we hear news of a great new offensive drive launched by the Germans against the Russians in the 150 mile sector from Orel to Belgorod. First reports indicate that it is the long-heralded summer drive of the Nazis, aimed at eliminating Russia from the war. If so, the Nazis have already bumped their noses as Moscow reports that the first 24 hours of the offensive were disastrous for the invaders. 586 tanks, an incredible number, and 100 Nazis planes were destroyed by the Russians in addition to thousands of soldiers killed and wounded. The tone of Soviet communiqués is supremely confident.

From the Solomons in the South Pacific comes word of a major clash between Japanese and American naval forces in the narrow waters of Kula Gulf, between New Georgia and Kolombangara. The outcome has not been determined.

Tuesday, July 6, 1943: —The naval engagement in the narrow confines of Kula Gulf has ended in disaster for the Japanese. Nothing larger than light cruisers were involved in the clash which ended with the destruction of at least seven enemy warships. Our losses were not immediately announced although the Navy admitted the loss of the destroyer Strong in a previous encounter. All other phases of the Solomons offensive were progressing according to schedule.

Terrific fighting is again in progress in Russia where the Germans have launched what appears to be their long-heralded summer offensive. The resilient Red Armies, however, have stopped them cold, at least in the first phase. Moscow reports that in the first 48 hours of the drive, more than seven hundred Nazi tanks have been destroyed, 203 planes shot down and more than 10,000 Fascist soldiers killed. After absorbing the initial impact, the Russians counter-attacked powerfully to wipe out all salients driven into their lines by the attacking Nazis. The fury and savagery of the fighting continues unabated.

China today prepared to observe the sixth anniversary of her war with Japan. General Chiang Kai-Shek broadcast an optimistic message to his people, predicting the ultimate defeat of the common enemy but warned the United Nations against allowing Japan too much time to consolidate her ill-gotten gains, thus increasing the eventual cost in overcoming her.

From North Africa we learn that a San Francisco man, Staff Sergeant Benjamin F. Warmer, gunner in a Flying Fortress, established a record by shooting down 7 Nazi planes in a single encounter.

Wednesday, July 7, 1943: —The principal theater of fighting today is the Russian front where huge masses of German tanks, infantry, and planes battered furiously against the stonewall defenses of the Red Army. From Orel to Belgorod the titanic struggle rages, with the Nazis piercing the Russian lines at several points despite tremendous losses in men and equipment. Russian military observers claimed that German losses in the first three days of battle have mounted to 1,271 tanks, 314 planes and more than 13,000 men. In no place has the German breakthrough reached dangerous proportions and fierce counter-attacks by veteran Red Army units are rapidly reducing the salients. The critical point in the battle has not yet been reached.

Italy's tortured island of Sicily is taking further punishment in a round-the-clock aerial offensive by great numbers of Allied planes based in North Africa. Flight after flight of heavy RAF and American bombers pounded Axis airdromes and supply ports, overwhelming the diminishing number of enemy interceptors which arose to oppose them. The invasion jitters have seized upon the Italian populace.

Another glorious ship of the U.S. Navy has met her fate in the recent Battle of Kula Gulf, it was announced today. The cruiser Helens, damaged at Pearl Harbor and repaired to join the fleet in the South Pacific, was torpedoed during the furious battle in which nine enemy warships were definitely sunk and the rest dispersed. The gallant cruiser quickly sank but most of her crew was rescued.

Thursday, July 8, 1943: —A half-million Germans with thousands of tanks and planes are piling up against the dam of Soviet resistance along a 150 mile front in Russia. The great test, probably the last great test of the indomitable Red Army, has the dam's very foundation creeking under the strain. Several small leaks have been quickly plugged up with the bodies of Russian men, and unless something unforeseen gives way, the wall of flesh and blood, and steel, and courage so brilliantly built by the determined Soviet people, will stand and Hitler's last forlorn hope of world domination will fade as the legions of free men close in from the west to relieve their brave Russian ally.

Hitler well knows the penalty of failure in his last attempt to knock Russia out of the war and he is flinging everything he's got into this last mighty offensive. It seems doomed to failure, however, as the fiercely resisting Soviets apparently are destroying Nazi tanks at the rate of 500 a day and Nazi men at the rate of 10,000 per day. Even Hitler's desperate panzers cannot stand that rate of loss.

In the South Pacific we learn that American assault forces from captured Rendova Island have stormed across the five-mile Blanche channel between Rendova and New Georgia, to establish bridgeheads only six miles from the big Japanese base of Munda. Thus Munda is attacked from all sides, shelled from Rendova, and blasted from the air. Its capitulation is only a matter of time.

Friday, July 9, 1943: —The fury of the German offensive in Russia continues unabated. From all reports the greatest armored battle of all time is in progress. The giant German "Tiger" tanks, the 60 ton monster about which so many fearful stories have been told, is present by the hundreds. But the Russians sent a new war cry ringing over the battlefield. "We have tamed the terrible Tiger," they shouted defiantly as dozens of the terrible monsters burned and exploded under the attacks of the Russian "Tiger hunters." Heavy artillery, armor-busters, anti-tank gunners, and infantrymen flinging gasoline-filled pop bottles, all assisted in "taming the German Tiger." But despite the furious resistance of the Red Army, the Nazis were able to chalk up some advances by sheer weight of numbers. But the overall picture is favorable to the Russian cause.

The American advance on Munda in the central Solomons is

rapidly reaching a showdown. Yank patrols have clashed with Japanese outposts only two miles from the base. Heavy fighting is in store for our troops before the inevitable result is reached, however, for the Japs have strongly fortified the base and, as usual, will fight until the last man is dead.

For six days and nights now, the Allied air force in North Africa has pounded the defenses of Sicily in a non-stop aerial offensive that has laid waste most of the military installations of that great island. How long the defenders can take the merciless pounding or how long the Allies will wait before the high command believes the island has been "softened up" enough for actual invasion is conjectural.

Saturday, July 10, 1943: —INVASION! Great red headlines proclaimed the sensational news that the Allies have attacked the soft underbelly of the European continent. Under the leadership of General Dwight D. Eisenhower, mighty invasion forces of the United Nations stormed ashore on the island of Sicily, in the first of many blows to be struck toward the final liberation of Europe. American, British, and Canadian troops formed the spearheads of invasion as bridgeheads were established at several points simultaneously. The operation, undoubtedly the greatest amphibious venture in history, was supported by a great umbrella of air power and a covering force of battleships, cruisers, and destroyers comprising units of every member of the United Nations. Dutch, Polish, and Greek naval units joined with others to make this really a United Nations show.

The size of the undertaking can be imagined when it is estimated that the Allied invasion force comprises nearly a half-million men and their equipment and opposing them are more than 400,000 veteran German and Italian troops. The fight may be long and hard but all the odds favor victory for our side.

The tortured people of Europe seized eagerly upon the news as heralding their early rescue from Hitler's clutches but General Eisenhower broadcast a warning to Frenchmen and other subservient peoples to bide their time, that this was only the first step, that other landings directly on the continent may soon be made and that we would tell them when the time has come for them to rise against their oppressors.

424

Sunday, July 11, 1943: —All eyes are upon Sicily, that island lies like a football that has just been drop-kicked off the toe of the Italian boot. Thousands of landing barges line her beaches, disgorging thousands of eager American, British, and Canadian troops. According to General Eisenhower's headquarters, all operations are proceeding on schedule. Paratroopers, used effectively for the first time by the Allies, have already captured two Axis airdromes. Canadian and British troops landing at separate points on the southeastern tip of the island have succeeded in joining forces in a line that stretches across the peninsula with the Mediterranean on either flank. Resistance has been surprisingly weak at many points and almost all prisoners captured so far have been Italians, giving rise to the belief that the main Italian forces and all German units have withdrawn into the interior where great battles can be expected.

Russia received the news of the Allied invasion jubilantly, coming as it did at the height of their desperate battle against the Nazis on the Orel-Belgorod front. While not as satisfying to the Soviets as an actual attack against continental Europe, they are aware of the importance of the step and its diversionary effect upon the Germans. Many large units of the Nazi army and particularly the air force will have to be withdrawn from the eastern front to meet this new challenge in the Mediterranean.

Monday, July 12, 1943: —The Allied invasion of Sicily is gaining momentum. Ten important towns on the south and southeast coasts of the island were captured by American, British, and Canadian troops. Britons under Rommel's master, General Bernard L. Montgomery, captured the ancient city of Syracuse and gained an additional fifteen miles inland. Resistance from crack Italian troops and veteran German units was stiffening rapidly as the initial surprise wore off. The American forces were under Lieut. General George S. Patton and were battling north and eastward from Licata and Gela on the south coast. Paratroopers are playing a valuable part in the operation and captured some of the most important objectives in bloody street fighting. Our casualties so far have been comparatively light according to General Eisenhower's latest communiqué.

At the same time, the joint American-Australian offensive against the Japanese in the central Solomons is also making headway. Munda on New Georgia Island is isolated and cut off

425

from all supplies, while thousands of soldiers and marines closed in from all sides. The fall of the Jap base is expected within the week.

The gigantic battle of giants on the Russian front has developed into a seesaw struggle of mighty armored forces, with neither side able to gain a definite advantage. Despite tremendous losses the Germans are attacking furiously along the whole 165 mile front from Orel to Belgorod. The decision hangs in the balance.

Tuesday, July 13, 1943: —Further Allied advances were reported from Sicily today. New landings were made at Catania, only fifty miles south of the ferry terminus of Messina. These new forces, believed to be American and Canadian troops, were reported to have captured Augusta, important Italian naval base on the east coast. In other sectors, American, British, and Canadian troops, supported by planes and tanks, drove 25 miles inland, capturing many towns and approximately 7,000 Axis soldiers, mostly Italians. Eye witnesses revealed that many Sicilians are greeting our troops joyously, displaying the V for Victory sign and in many instances actively aiding our operations.

While the invasion of Sicily appears to be going very well, there is plenty of bitter fighting in store for the invading forces, as there were indications that the Axis is moving heavy reinforcements southward in Sicily, preparatory to launching a furious counter-attack. The Americans in particular have already encountered stiff resistance from crack Italian and German armored forces.

In support of the Sicily attack, the RAF based in England attacked northern Italy last night with a large force of four-motored bombers. The arsenal city of Turin was the principal target.

Another milestone in the conquest of the air was reported today. The Atlantic has been crossed by glider. The story of the 21 hour flight through sleet and ice, with the fog so thick at times that the tow-plane was lost from sight, is a thrilling tale of man's triumph over great odds. Squadron Leader R.G. Seys of the RAF piloted the glider Voo-doo on the historic flight.

Wednesday, July 14, 1943: —By all reports the Allied invasion of Sicily is progressing exceedingly well. Early gains have been greater than was expected and casualties much lighter. Opposition to the landings at some points was so meager that some of our troops asked the question, "Where is the war?" Allied air fleets patrolled the skies at will, drowning all opposition with overwhelming numbers.

Initial successes have not fooled the Allies into expecting a push-over campaign. The Axis has at least 400,000 crack troops on the island, including famous German units such as the Hermann Goering division. The main body of these forces has not yet been encountered and a decision reached. Our job is cut out for us.

More good news comes from Soviet Russia. The Red Army has totally smashed the German offensive and has launched a counter drive in the region of Kursk that shows promise of developing into a full-scale summer offensive of its own. Numerous reports coming from the battlefront indicate that Adolf Hitler has resumed command of German forces on the Russian front. As one London observer commented, "We fervently hope it's true."

To round out the cheerful picture we learn that the Allied offensive in the central Solomons is forging ahead. The big Japanese base of Munda on New Georgia is all but invaded by surrounding Australian and American shock troops. The fate of Munda is sealed.

Admiral Nimitz, American Pacific commander in chief, assured us today that the Jap base on Kiska in the Aleutians has been neutralized. It is almost ripe for plucking.

Thursday, July 15, 1943: —The Russian counter-drive against the German salient in the Orel sector has assumed the proportions of a major offensive. Berlin reports admitted that the Red Army is exerting tremendous pressure, equaling in intensity the two great winter drives by the Soviets that nullified most of the gains made by the Nazis in their summer offensives. Moscow stated that in the first day's fighting they destroyed 109 enemy tanks, 294 planes, and 46 field guns, besides capturing 40 tanks and 210 guns. Twelve thousand Nazi soldiers fell victim to Soviet firepower.

Furious counter-attacks by German and Italian armored forces on Sicily were of no avail today as American, British, and Canadian troops advanced steadily in all sectors of the invasion coastline. Heavy fighting occurred in the Augusta area where Nazi armored units broke through to the Harbor for a time but were finally pushed back by rallying British troops. A major battle for the vital town of Catania was expected. Eyewitness reports indicate that much of the glory and credit for the rapid Allied advance should go to the paratroopers who have performed heroic feats behind the enemy lines. In one instance two American paratroopers captured 40 Italian officers and men. Others reduced pillboxes and machine gun nests singlehanded of died in the attempt.

American and Australian jungle fighters scored against the Japanese today in New Guinea. They pinched off Mubo, the main Jap bastion just ten miles from the big base of Salamaua. More than 1,500 Jap troops were routed or slain before the stronghold fell.

Friday, July 16, 1943: —President Roosevelt and Prime Minister Churchill in a combined ultimatum to the Italian people today warned them to overthrow their false and dangerous Fascist leaders and surrender to the United Nations or suffer the devastation of war in their own front yard. Today Italy is faced with the combined armed forces of the United States and Great Britain, including the greatest array of sea power ever to appear in the Mediterranean. Their only hope is to seek peace and a restoration of their national dignity and honor by ousting Mussolini and his regime at once. The time has come for Italians to decide whether they shall die for Mussolini and Hitler—or live for Italy and civilization.

Lending force to the ultimatum that was drummed into Italian ears by radio and dumped on them from the air in the form of hundreds of thousands of pamphlets, were fast moving columns of Allied troops closing in on the east Sicilian port of Catania. Allied bombers in almost unopposed sorties ripped Messina to shred and pounded Naples on the mainland of Italy. Neutral sources reported signs of vast unrest throughout the unhappy nation. Mussolini, thin and worried, has left the capital for an unknown destination, perhaps to plead for more aid from his Nazi boss.

President Roosevelt acted on the home front also today. Taking heed of the bitter and public word battle between Vice-president Wallace and Secretary of Commerce Jones, the President issued a joint reprimand to both, relieving them of control over the disputed agencies, and ordered all appointive officials to cease bickering in public. This action was a much-needed step toward attaining unity in the national war effort on the home front.

Saturday, July 17, 1943: —Six miles was an important distance today. Six miles of flat Sicilian plain lay between advancing British forces and the vital east coast port of Catania, which lay pulverized and almost helpless from the weight of Allied shells and bombs pumped into it by great battleships from the sea and mighty bombers from the air. Between the British and the town stood but a few disheartened Italian troops and several divisions of desperate Germans. Slowly closing in on them were units of the crack British Eighth Army under brilliant General Bernard L. Montgomery, the desert fox hunter.

Six miles of churned up Russian soil, bloody with the gore of many frightful battles, lay between the powerful Red Army and the Nazi-held bastion of Orel on the central front. The Soviets, utilizing every weapon from bayonet to heavy artillery with consummate skill, ground their way into the elaborate German hedgehog defenses, exacting a terrific toll of Fascist flesh and equipment as they wrested the precious earth of Mother Russia from the invader foot by foot. The Germans were forced to abandon their own offensive on the Belgorod front and battled furiously to prevent a breakthrough at Orel. But the interminable legions of Russians only increased the pressure. Death is the only hope of rest for the weary German soldier.

Six miles of steaming, Jap infested jungle lay between American doughboys and the big New Guinea base at Salamaua. Monkey by monkey, pillbox by pillbox, the lads from main street and country lane, dug the little yellow enemy out and gradually closed in on the base from the west and north.

Sunday, July 18, 1943: —The barbaric Japs were served notice yesterday that an avenging flood of power is accumulating against them in the South Pacific. A great force of more than 200

United States torpedo bombers, dive bombers, heavy bombers, and fighter planes sallied forth to pulverize the main Japanese base in the northern Solomons, in one of the dazzling actions of the Pacific war so far. Caught in the harbor of Buin were fifteen Japanese warships, tankers, and supply ships, seven of which were sent to the bottom, including two destroyers and one cruiser. A never-ending stream of Japanese Zeros took to the skies to intercept the attackers and 49 of them were sent flaming brightly or streaming long plumes of smoke into the sea. The price paid for this sensational air victory was only six planes.

Meanwhile, on the other side of the world, other American troops were writing military history in the invasion of Sicily. Handling themselves with the calm efficiency of seasoned veterans, the American Seventh Army has advanced at least 25 miles inland from their invasion beachhead, driving all opposition before them and capturing Agrigento, key communication center for the Axis armies. No need to worry about American traditions with those lads, they have the situation very well in hand.

In the air war over Europe, the American Flying Fortress is again proving its worth. Its heavy protecting armor and its tremendous fire-power have combined to make it the nemesis of enemy fighter planes. One tight-flying formation yesterday accounted for fifty German planes in a deadly running fight that lasted only thirty minutes.

Monday, July 19, 1943: —For the first time in history the ancient city of Rome was attacked from the air today. Two hundred American heavy bombers escorted by fighter planes swept over the Italian capital in broad daylight to smash carefully selected targets of military importance. Encountering almost negligible opposition the big bombers were able to hit the selected targets with great precision. Extreme care was taken to avoid damaging any cultural or historical monuments and no bombs fell closer than four miles from Vatican City.

The bombing of Rome was made necessary because of its use by Mussolini and Hitler as a military center. Its railroad yards in particular are marshalling yards for military traffic from northern Italy and Germany to southern Italy and Sicily. Allied leaders have constantly warned that devastating raids could be avoided only by declaring Rome an open city and abandoning it as a military center. This Mussolini has refused to do. Consequently, as a war necessity, we must attack the city despite a strong desire to avoid any damage to church or historical property. Catholics throughout the world will understand where the blame lies for making such warfare necessary and will realize that the Allied flyers chose daylight, with its greater risks, to make the attack in order that they might aim their bombs with greater accuracy against military objectives only.

Axis defense forces all over Sicily appear to be cracking up except before the east coast port of Catania where a big battle is raging between the British Eighth Army and German defenders.

Tuesday, July 20, 1943: —The fierce battle between German and British troops before the gates of Catania in Sicily see-sawed back and forth savagely today without a decision being reached. In one main sector, however, the British edged forward to within 2½ miles from the shattered city.

Further south and west the American Seventh Army surged northward toward Enna, threatening to cut the island in two. Thousands of Italian prisoners have been taken by the Americans and in many cases it has been reported that Italian troops have mutinied against their German officers, in some instances shooting them when they opposed their surrendering.

From the North Pacific comes word that American bombers have raided the big Japanese naval base of Paramushiru, in the Kurile Islands. Paramushiru is Japan's Pearl Harbor and is situated on the Jap's home side of the North Pacific, protecting the string of islands pointing like a dagger at Tokyo. The raid was pronounced successful and much damage was caused. Participating planes were Consolidated Liberators.

Lest recent military successes on many battlefronts cause unwarranted complacency on the part of civilians, Secretary Knox announced that the Navy is making plans on the basis of having to fight in the Pacific until 1949. He declared that any successes achieved so far were only preliminary skirmishes compared with the battles that must yet be fought before final victory. Over optimism is dangerous to the war effort as it affects production figures. There must be no let-down on the home front as well as on the war front.

Wednesday, July 21, 1943: —American and Canadian troops have smashed their way to within 28 miles of the North Sicilian coast today and have seized the important communication center of Enna. General George S. Patton sent his U.S. Seventh Army spearhead roaring on to the northwest, driving all resistance before him in true "Blitz" fashion. The island stood in danger of being cut in two, with thousands of Axis troops being trapped in the western end of the island. Already more than 40,000 German and Italian prisoners have been taken, the majority falling to the rapidly advancing Americans.

Before Catania on the eastern coast, the British Eighth Army has been temporarily stopped by fiercely resisting German troops. A bitter battle is in progress with the British slowly gaining the upper hand. General Eisenhower reported that the Axis is moving reinforcements into northeastern Sicily and is expected to make a desperate stand opposite the toe of the Italian boot, on a line including Mt. Etna.

In the South Pacific American and Australian forces have tightened the ring around the Japanese base of Munda. The enemy garrison is completely isolated and his position is rapidly deteriorating. Capture of the base appears to be only a matter of time. The Japs attempted to reinforce and supply their base of Vila today but the attempt was frustrated by U.S. bombers which sank three and possibly four enemy warships, including one cruiser and three destroyers. Surviving vessels of the Jap convoy fled northward out of range.

Thursday, July 22, 1943: —The Navy today announced that a tragic airplane crash near Sitka, Alaska yesterday morning took the lives of Major General William P. Upshur, Marine commanding general of the Pacific Department, and his aide, Captain Charles Paddock, former Olympic track star. Paddock, though only a Captain, was by far the most famous of the two. Everyone remembers him as "the world's fastest human" when he was a member of the Southern California and Olympic track teams two decades ago. His flying feet and his famous "flying finish" carried him to many world sprint records. And now death, sudden and violent, has finally beaten him to the tape.

American shock troops are racing through central Sicily today, brushing aside crumbling Axis resistance and threatening to engulf Termini and Palermo on the north coast. On the east

432

coast, however, the British were still being successfully blocked by furiously resisting German troops on the outskirts of Catania. Nevertheless, the Battle for Sicily is progressing favorably, with the Allied timetable far ahead of the original schedule.

The U.S. Navy today reported the loss of the submarine Triton, the tenth American sub destroyed in the war so far. There is something particularly sad about the loss of a submarine. It is such a silent, lonely sort of death, thousands of miles from home, in the dark depths of the sea from whence no clue ever comes. Stand on the beach at midnight and look out over the vast Pacific, cold and endlessly rolling, if you would like to sense the meaning of the words "lost at sea."

Friday, July 23, 1943: —U.S. troops, displaying real "blitz" methods, cracked through Axis defenses to capture Palermo, the capital of Sicily and a city of 400,000 people. The American advance was so rapid and successful that the city was seized with practically no damage. Axis resistance crumbled before the advance and prisoners poured in by the thousands. Other thousands were trapped in western Sicily with no hope of escape. At least 70,000 enemy troops have been taken already and at least as many more are isolated in the west. Catania on the east coast remains the stumbling block to Allied advance in Sicily but already the Allied High Command is considering the Sicilian campaign practically over and is turning its attention to the Italian mainland.

While everything is under control on the war fronts, things are not so smooth on the home front. A Los Angeles strike of streetcar and bus operators has paralyzed service for nearly one million workers, most of them employed in vital defense industries. President Roosevelt is expected to act to end the strike immediately.

At the same time, the War Labor Board has voted against the general pay raise demanded by the Nation's shipyard workers. This action was taken yesterday and was justified as necessary to hold the line against inflation. Sky rocketing prices and failure of the OPA to roll back the high cost of living are the main reasons for labor's unrest but the working man should realize that run-away inflation would hurt him far worse than his present troubles.

Saturday, July 24, 1943: —The lightning American drive on Sicily has engulfed Marsala on the westernmost tip of the island. The number of prisoners taken was boosted to 60,000 as the U.S. forces smashed all opposition in one of the fastest movement of large bodies of troops in history. General Patton claimed that the American "blitz" even surpassed the German feat in overrunning the low-countries in May of 1940. Much of the drive was over rugged mountain terrain, along winding, easily defended roads. The General expressed great pride in his troop's achievement.

Hinting that the next Allied invasion may be into the Balkans, American and British bombers raided the island of Crete in large numbers today. Seventeen big bombers were lost in the attack that struck a German port, radio, and factory areas on the island. Late reports indicate that some Greek flyers participated in the raid that gave promise of an early liberation of their homeland.

For the first time since the Fascist invaders surged across the Russian frontier, the Red Army has smashed a German summer offensive without permitting it to gain any territory. Premier Josef Stalin today issued an order of the day, congratulating his troops and announcing that the abortive Nazi summer offensive has been "finally liquidated" without gain and the Red Army has launched a counter-offensive that already seriously threatens the vital German base at Orel.

Here at home, President Roosevelt was forced to take his attention away from the fighting of the war long enough to intervene in the Los Angeles streetcar strike. Upon his personal request the strike was called off pending mediation.

Sunday, July 25, 1943: —Today is a momentous day in the history of the war. Today the first of the criminal dictators fell in ignominious failure. It was a stunned world that heard in amazement the word from Rome that Mussolini, he of the pugnacious chin and the bellicose boasting, had been relieved of all power and had tendered his resignation as Commander-in-Chief, Prime Minister, and Secretary of State. In his place Victor Emmanuel III, the pint-sized King-Emperor, placed Marshal Pietro Badoglio, long-time Fascist hater and bitter enemy of Mussolini. The Marshal quickly ousted all Fascists from the Government, organized his own cabinet, and took stern measures to prevent an uprising on the part of Fascist supporters. Proclamations by the King and his new Prime Minister called upon the Italian people to support the new Government in this critical hour and promised ruthless punishment for any "who attempt to disturb the public order."

The whereabouts of Mussolini, who fell disgraced and friendless after almost 21 years as absolute ruler of Italy, was not known. It was probable that he was being held under arrest at his villa near Rome. Some reports, however, stated that he had fled or was in hiding. A trial and conviction awaits him as a "war criminal" if and when the Allies apprehend him.

The sensational coup in Rome presages an early withdrawal of Italy from the war. Although Badoglio is putting up a pretense of continuing the fight, his every move so far has indicated a desire to extricate his country from its terrible predicament as soon as the Germans can be ousted. Meanwhile, all over the civilized world the glorious word spreads that one third of the task has been accomplished, one third of the criminal dictators dethroned. It's one down and two to go!

Monday, July 26, 1943: —Martial law was in effect today throughout Italy as the King's new government under Marshal Badoglio moved to forestall an outbreak of civil war between ousted Fascists and supporters of the new regime. Proclamations were issued establishing a rigid curfew and banning all public meetings. Reports seeped into neutral countries indicating that Mussolini's old Fascist Headquarters and the offices of Il Duce's newspaper, Il Popolo d'Italia, have been sacked by angry mobs. Meanwhile the whereabouts of the deposed dictator remained shrouded in mystery.

The Germans in Berlin have made almost ludicrous efforts to cover up their anxiety over the Italian debacle. The Berlin radio said the change in government will not affect Axis relations and it was assumed that Mussolini's retirement was due to ill health. No doubt.

While the Italian mainland seethed with political upheaval, Axis resistance on Sicily was crumbling under sledge hammer blows by the American Seventh Army on the left, the Canadians in the center, and the British Eighth Army on the right. Rapid advances were scored in all sectors with the exception of the British right where crack German defenders remained adamant before Catania. Their doom is sealed, however, as the overwhelming Canadian and American forces closed in from the west.

On the home front the most interesting happening, from a purely personal viewpoint, was the beginning of my vacation. For two weeks I can forget work and relax. It has been a long stretch. Almost a year, averaging at least 60 hours per week. Even as a soldier, a war worker needs a furlough.

Tuesday, July 27, 1943: —Countless unconfirmed rumors and stories of confusion and disorder throughout the Italian nation were rife today. Clashes were reported between Italian and German troops in northern Italy and there were indications that the Nazi Gestapo was quitting the southern Axis partner and returning to Germany. Dissatisfied Italian troops were said to be rebelling in Jugoslavia and German troops were forced to occupy Albania's seaports to prevent the evacuation of Italian troops from that country.

Prime Minister Churchill made a 36 minute address today, reiterating the United Nations' determination to demand unconditional surrender from the Axis, including Italy under the Badoglio regime. He warned the Italians to surrender or be seared, scarred, and blackened by the rigors of war. Orders have already been given to all commanders to increase the pressure upon the hapless nation until such time as it throws itself upon the mercy and justice of the Allies.

The Italian picture has overshadowed other war fronts but tremendous blows are being struck by the RAF and the American Eighth Air Force based in England. For five straight nights heavy American and British bombers have ranged in force over Occupied Europe and Germany. The vital port of Hamburg has been plastered day and night, yesterday by the terrific weight of 2,300 tons of bombs. Reconnaissance photos reveal that vast sections of the city are in blackened ruins and a great pillar of smoke rising twenty thousand feet in the air over the dying city seems to signal the end that is in store for Hitler.

Wednesday, July 28, 1943: —Reports are seeping out of Italy, indicating that violent fighting has broken out between German and Italian troops in northern Italy. Nazi divisions are said to be pouring through Brenner Pass in an effort to set up a strong defense line along the Po River and at least keep northern Italy in the war. Italian troops are battling to prevent this German concentration.

At other points bloody fighting, bordering on outright revolution, is in progress between former Fascists and their liberated "slaves." Many a non-Fascist who writhed and was tortured under the heel of Mussolini and his gang now has his chance to get sweet revenge. Fascist heads will roll in Italy before peace and order are restored.

Meanwhile on Sicily, General George S. Patton's powerful American Seventh Army rolled on irresistibly on the northern coastal road. Six more important towns were captured bringing the Americans to within 60 miles of Messina, the final evacuation point for defeated Axis troops. The rapid U.S. advance is expected to outflank the German positions before Catania, where furious battles are still in progress between the Nazis and the British Eighth Army.

The terrific round-the-clock aerial offensive against the Reich established a new record last night and today. The tortured city of Hamburg was crushed with the record load of more than 2,300 tons of bombs carried by hundreds of mighty RAF bombers. By daylight, a large force of U.S. Flying Fortresses struck deeper than ever before into the heart of Germany to blast an airplane factory at Oschersleben, only 80 miles from Berlin.

Thursday, July 29, 1943: —Unfortunately I missed President Roosevelt's radio speech last night but I have just finished reading its text today. His opening words recalled his statement of a year ago that "The militarists in Berlin, Rome, and Tokyo started this war, but the massed, angered forces of common humanity will finish it." Those words are beginning to come true. The first crack in the Axis has come. Mussolini and his criminal gang have tried to escape by resigning but the President promises that they shall be brought to justice. "No criminal will be allowed to escape by the expedient of 'resignation,'" he said. He also reiterated as did Winston Churchill that our policy toward all the Axis is still "unconditional surrender." It should be certain, therefore, since the heads of the two great governments in Washington and London have put it so plainly, that no misconstruction can be placed upon the United Nations' policy toward the gangster nations. No turncoat Fascist should be able to whitewash himself and feather his own nest by pretending to renounce of disclaim his former ideology and negotiate terms with the Allies.

In line with the above stated policy we learn tonight that General Eisenhower has dispatched a formal offer of an "honorable peace" to the Italians if they will cease all aid to the Germans within their borders and surrender to the Allied armies. He promised that the Allies would then rid Italy of the Germans in short order and restore peace and security under a "mild and beneficent" occupation. The Italians are said to be giving the offer close attention.

Adding emphasis to Eisenhower's offer of peace or destruction are the rapidly advancing Allied armies in Sicily. That campaign has reached its final stage.

Friday, July 30, 1943: —Nothing definite has been announced yet but all indications are that negotiations are under way towards ending hostilities with Italy. The center of activity seems to be in London where the British Cabinet has been ordered to stand by over the week-end. Prime Minister Churchill called his official family into a secret meeting at midnight last night, presumably to discuss important war developments that could not wait for morning.

President Roosevelt pointedly warned neutral countries in his press conference today not to grant asylum to leaders of Axis nations or members of their gangs who may seek an easy avenue of escape after the fashion of Kaiser Wilhelm at the end of World War I. In diplomatic language the President asserted that neutrals who protected Axis war criminals would be considered "inconsistent with the principles for which the United Nations are fighting." Great Britain and Soviet Russia immediately approved the President's statement in a manner that should warn neutrals that this time we'll come and get them if necessary.

American heavy bombers based in England continued their all-out offensive against Germany today by stabbing deep into the heart of the Reich to deliver a smashing attack on Kassel, the home of the Fieseler Aircraft Factory which produces engines for the famous Messerschmitts and Focke Wulf fighters. Eleven of the great "Flying Forts" failed to return.

A word about the Pacific situation. American troops are still slashing at the Japanese defenses at Munda where advances are confined to yards. The Yanks are within 1,000 yards of the Munda air strip and digging the Japs out one by one.

Saturday, July 31, 1943: —The Allied High Command today warned the Italians that the new regime under Marshal Badoglio is stalling and unless immediate acceptance of unconditional surrender is forthcoming the Allies will be obliged to launch a crushing aerial offensive against the Italian mainland. Italian citizens were advised to keep away from military objectives where the bombs may fall and it was pointed out strongly that every drop of Italian blood that is spilled from now on can be laid at the doorstep of their leaders in Rome.

While disorders and riots increased throughout the mainland, Italian possession of Sicily was almost at an end. American, Canadian, and British troops are drawing the noose tighter around the remnants of Axis strength in the northeastern "coffin corner" of the island. At the same time Allied planes dominated the skies over the battlefield, blasting great gaps in the Axis defenses in their roles as aerial artillery.

While the land warfare in the European theater is larger in scale than the fighting going on in the South Pacific, it cannot equal the ferocity of the no-quarter struggle with the half-savage Japs. The tricky, treacherous yellow men have shown themselves to be deadly jungle fighters with a repertoire of dirty tricks that bear no resemblance to the code under which King Arthur's gallant knights once fought. Knives, grenades, and bayonets are wielded in close combat through the mud, gloom, and underbrush of the steaming jungle. It was reported tonight that our troops have utilized flame-throwers for the first time in their effort to oust the defending Japs from their countless pillboxes and dugouts before Munda on New Georgia Island.

August

Sunday, August 1, 1943: —The first week of my vacation has been almost unbelievably perfect as far as the weather is concerned. With but one morning's exception it has been clear and warm, with the customary breeze from the northwest to keep it from getting hot. The fog that frequently rolls in over San Francisco in the afternoons just misses San Bruno by about 1000 yards. A block away it is cool and damp, here it is dry and warm with a brilliant sun. It is as though a curtain is suddenly drawn aside as you drive out of the fog belt into the peninsula sunshine. From a frown to a smile in ten seconds.

It has been deliciously refreshing and vigor-restoring to loll around in the sun, or work in the yard, or perhaps to take in a round of golf. I already have acquired a satisfying coat of tan and feel like a new man. I have regular and wholesome meals, especially at breakfast, a rarity when I am working. After one more week of this I will really be rarin' to go. My efficiency should increase 100%. A vacation is a necessity, even in wartime— or should I say especially in wartime.

But back on the war news. From all reports, the main obstacle to an immediate surrender of Italy is the presence of large numbers of German troops in the country and their evident determination to keep Italy in the war as long as possible. Marshal Badoglio is squarely between German and Allied pressure and may not be able to survive. The Italian public is clamoring for peace while the Germans show no inclination to leave the country to its fate. The final result will probably find Italy the unhappy battlefield on which the Germans and the Allies will struggle to a decision.

Monday, August 2, 1943: —While Italian leaders stall and the Allies prepare to launch new and more devastating attacks against Italian cities, something akin to panic is seizing Germany. Reports reaching neutral Stockholm indicate that the effects of the terrible Hamburg disaster are being felt throughout the Reich. Hundreds of thousands of homeless and wounded residents of destroyed Hamburg are fleeing into other German cities, carrying with them some of the horror and panic created by the five days and nights of cataclysmic disaster that befell the Nazi port. Eye-witnesses state that the city has ceased to exist, its streets a litter of rubble and corpses, whole sections looking as though a giant plow had been at work. First estimates are that at least 14,000 people were killed and untold thousands wounded in the raids.

As evidence of the terrible fear that clutches the hearts of the German people, Dr. Paul Joseph Goebbels, gauleiter of Berlin, announced today that the city is to be immediately evacuated of all but essential war workers. In a leaflet mailed to all citizens, the Doctor stated that the mass exodus is to be made at the earliest possible moment. City by city the Reich will be scourged by the avenging Allied air fleets and Berlin may be next. Well might the Nazis quaver. An interesting feature of the evacuation order is the fact that it was not signed by Der Fuhrer.

The latest report that comes, strangely enough, from Vichy—and may well be false—is that U.S. troops have invaded Kiska in the Aleutians. No confirmation has been received from U.S. authorities but the fact remains that many softening-up raids have recently been made on the northern isle.

Tuesday, August 3, 1943: —The battle for Sicily is almost drawing to a close. All that remains to the Axis is a narrow triangular corner running from Catania on the east coast to San Stefano on the north coast. Bearing down on this triangle are three great Allied armies. On the north the amazing American Seventh Army that overran the entire western half of the island in a lightning "blitz" is crunching forward steadily against stiffening German and Italian resistance. In the center the doughty Canadians are forging ahead despite strong enemy resistance. On the left the mighty British Eighth Army is engaging the main German force and slowly driving it back. The "Magnificent Eighth" has encountered by far the stiffest resistance from crack German divisions, including the famous Hermann Goering division, and has gradually pinned the Germans back against their strong Mt. Etna defense line while the Americans and Canadians close in. All three armies are about ready to move in for the kill. No miracle can save the Axis garrison from annihilation or capture.

The grim battle of the Atlantic gained some attention today as a fierce fight was reported between a "wolf-pack" of some 25 or 30 Nazi submarines and a large east bound convoy. The Air

441

Ministry announced that the enemy subs were finally defeated by escorting British warships and long-range planes operating out of Iceland. Two of the attacking subs were definitely known to be destroyed and there were several other probables. The battle was a touch and go affair lasting for three days.

General MacArthur's jungle troops have finally cracked the Japanese defense line to reach the eastern edge of the Munda airport. The battle is far from over, however.

Wednesday, August 4, 1943: —Another major German defeat was evident today as 250,000 Nazi troops commenced to evacuate Orel on the central Russian front. The Germans were obviously withdrawing to prevent an encirclement such as befell General Paulus' Stalingrad army. Victorious Soviet troops are rapidly closing in on the vital city, close on the heels of the retreating Fascists. The Germans are employing strong rearguard action as well as laying vast minefields similar to those that hindered the Allies in the closing days of the Tunisian campaign. Russian sappers, however, are clearing the fields with great rapidity. The loss of Orel may cause the whole German defense line to crumble and force a general withdrawal by the invaders. The Russian bear's claws are still mighty sharp, eh, Adolf?

The Sicily trap is closing tighter around the doomed Axis legions in the northeast "coffin corner" of the island. General George S. Patton's American Seventh Army scored another six mile advance today on the north coast, capturing the town of Caronia and carried the United States flag to within 55 miles of Messina. American and British warships bombarded coastal roads on both sides of the island to further harry the harassed Axis forces. At the same time, Allied bombers subjected Naples, on the Italian mainland, to its third raid in 36 hours, lending emphasis to General Eisenhower's warning that further procrastination in surrendering will bring death and destruction raining from the skies over Italian cities.

The sanguinary battle for the New Georgian base of Munda has reached its final phase as U.S. troops close a death trap on the last Japanese defenses in that area. Flame-throwers and tanks have been utilized to oust the stubborn Japs.

Thursday, August 5, 1943: —Battlefront news continues to be almost incredibly good today. In all theaters, Allied armies are surging forward victoriously. The triumphant Red Army added a new victory to their first successful summer offensive. The City of Belgorod, mighty bastion on the central Russian front crumbled and fell today close upon the heels of the Orel which the Soviets occupied yesterday. This new defeat unhinged the entire German defense line on the central Russian front and forced a general withdrawal by the invaders. The Red Army is pursuing the enemy remorselessly.

In Sicily it was a red letter day for the Allies. The powerful British Eighth Army finally cracked the two week stalemate before the gates of Catania and occupied that vital city after sweeping across the Catania plains under cover of a tremendous artillery barrage. The citizens of the shattered city, second largest in Sicily, greeted the Tommies as deliverers from the hunger and terror of the siege. The momentum of the British attack carried them on through the town to capture the nearby junction of Paterno, driving the German and Italian defenders into the foothills of Mt. Etna.

From the South Pacific comes word that the Battle of Munda is in the mopping-up stage. U.S. and Australian troops have captured the airdrome and penned the remaining Japs on Kokengolo Hill, northwest of the base. Flame-throwers, tanks, and artillery finally solved the complicated system of fortified pillboxes made of tough coral and log construction. Thirty five days of bitter struggle were required to subdue the stubborn Japanese garrison who stuck grimly to their "no-surrender" policy.

Friday, August 6, 1943: —The great German defeat in Russia continues to grow in scope. The Red Army is exploiting its breakthrough at Orel and Belgorod with sharp pincer thrusts aimed at pinching off the two vital Nazi strongholds of Bryansk and Kharkov. The main weight of the massive Soviet drive is aimed at the latter city, capital of the Ukraine.

Moscow communiqués jubilantly proclaimed that the Red Army offensive since July 5 has successfully crushed the German summer campaign and has cost the enemy more than 120,000 and 12,000 captured. The momentum of the Red Army counter-offensive is steadily growing and indications are that at last the Russians have seized the initiative in a summer campaign rivaling in power and intensity the great winter drives that saved Russia in 1941 and 1942.

In Sicily, Allied troops are herding the Germans and Italians like a bunch of jackrabbits into an ever narrowing pen in the northeastern corner of the island. There they are inexorably doomed to be clubbed into death or submission as clouds of Allied planes guard the narrow straits of Messina to prevent any "Dunkirk" evacuation of the trapped enemy. Bitter fighting lies ahead, however, for the Germans are fighting with the desperation of mad men.

General Douglas MacArthur announced today that all organized Japanese resistance at Munda was ended. Attention can now be turned to the next phase in our northward drive that will eventually take us back to Manila, Yokahoma, and Tokyo.

Saturday, August 7, 1943: —The two main centers of war news tonight are still Sicily and the central Russian front. Bitter fighting is in progress in both places with the Germans getting the worst of it. The powerful American Seventh Army, spearheaded by its famous First Division smashed through Nazi defenses to capture Troina after a week-long siege that culminated in the fiercest battle of the Sicilian campaign so far. Loss of Troina, which lies atop a 3,600 foot peak, is a serious blow to the Germans and threatens to cut off their garrison at Adrano, nine miles to the south. Accurate American artillery, that has won an enviable reputation in Sicily and Tunisia, contributed much to the victory at Troina.

Fast moving columns of Russian tanks and motorized troops today were exploiting the breakthrough at Orel and Belgorod on the central front and smashed their way to within eighteen miles of Kharkov, capital of the Ukraine. Neutral observers predict the capture of that vital bastion is only a matter of days. Berlin reports themselves gloomily admit that the Russian drive is gaining great momentum. 250 miles to the north of Kharkov other Russian columns were surging through captured Orel towards Bryansk, seventy five miles to the west and the biggest Nazi stronghold on the central front. Gains up to 45 miles were reported.

The Pacific war has quieted down since the victory at Munda. But the lull will not be for long as Admiral Wm. F. Halsey commented today, "We shall push forward until the battle of the South Pacific becomes the Battle of Japan."

Nothing has come of last Monday's rumor that Kiska had been invaded by U.S. forces. Just another false one.

Sunday, August 8, 1943: —Rumors of unrest throughout Nazi-occupied Europe were rife today with hints that kaleidoscopic events of transcendent importance were occurring that would change the whole course of the war. Terror stricken Berliners by the thousands were said to be fleeing the German capital to avoid the expected "Hamburg treatment" from the Allied air forces. At the same time there were hints that Hitler himself has met the fate of Mussolini with a triumvirate of military leaders assuming Der Fuhrer's powers. Such a rumor is too good to be true and is probably false. We shall therefore discount it as wishful thinking until further news is available.

There were also reports that Italy's new premier, Marshal Badoglio will declare Rome an open city to avoid a repetition of the recent Allied bombing of the ancient capital. This and other evidence indicates that Badoglio intends to continue the war although his people are demanding peace in frequent and violent demonstrations. As a warning of the fate in store for them if Badoglio has his way, RAF heavy bombers last night pounded Milan, Turin, and other northern Italian cities.

From the far Pacific the confident voice of General Douglas MacArthur rang out today. Although the supply of men and equipment has come lamentably slow to that theater of war we have made decisive use of the forces we have. The Japs have definitely been stopped and are now completely on the defensive. Although the margin was very close, we can now say that the final victorious outcome of the Pacific war is no longer in doubt. How long it will take cannot be foretold but the decision will be ours.

The Navy added another clincher to the General's words by sinking a Jap cruiser and three destroyers today in Vella Gulf.

Monday, August 9, 1943: —I went back to work today following two very pleasant vacation weeks. The weather during the past fortnight has been ideal for which I am duly grateful. Ours was a typical wartime vacation, spent at home in rest and relaxation. The magnificent coat of tan I acquired came out of my own backyard and not from the beach at Santa Monica or the pool at Palm Springs. But that is a matter of patriotic pride rather than disappointment this year and if the urgent pleas of our harassed transportation leaders were heeded, a great many more civilians would take their vacations at home for the duration. Moreover, I have made the discovery, strange to most "tourist Americans," that a vacation at home can be very enjoyable and productive of far more rest and health recuperation than some of the bustling, gas-consuming, five thousand mile "tours" of previous years. Don't get the idea that I don't love that favorite American vacation pastime but for the duration at least, a nice, quiet vacation at home is not half bad. And don't forget it is the patriotic thing to do.

Back on the war news, we learn that General George S. Patton's fast stepping American Seventh Army has pulled a sensational end around play good for a twenty mile gain on the northern end of the ever-narrowing Allied line in Sicily. Amphibious units of the Seventh Army, supported by cruisers and destroyers landed on the north Sicily coast behind the German lines and threw the whole Nazi secondary defenses into pandemonium. The Yanks then cut back to join forces with other U.S. units driving on San Agata. The end of the day found General Patton's men smashing at German defenses only 30 miles from Messina, the end of the trail for the trapped enemy legions.

Tuesday, August 10, 1943: —It is Russia and Sicily which are again spotlighting the war news today. The mighty Red Army has driven its bear claws deep into the German defenses on the central front and have reached a point only eleven miles from the Ukrainian capital of Kharkov. There were indications that the Nazis already were evacuating the city as long range Soviet artillery brought prospective escape routes under fire. Farther north in the Bryansk sector, Russian columns recaptured 30 more towns and smashed to within 33 miles of the powerful Nazi stronghold.

In Sicily, the steel ring of Allied guns and bayonets tightened inexorably on the ever-narrowing corner of Axis resistance. Two magnificent armies, the American Seventh and the British Eighth, joined hands today at Randazzo, key town dominating the narrow defile between Mt. Etna and the Caronian range. The junction was believed to have cut off large bodies of German troops who will soon be added to the 125,000 prisoners already captured in the campaign. Gun to gun, the two great Allied armies plunged forward confidently toward the final Sicilian climax. All Italian soldiers apparently have been withdrawn from combat areas and discouraged German troops have begun demolition of roads and other communications in a desperate effort to stop the Allied advance. Whole mountains have been blasted onto roads by expert demolition crews but their best efforts are doomed to miserable failure. The fate of Sicily is already sealed.

It was announced today that Britain's Prime Minister, Winston Churchill, has arrived in Canada for important conferences with Canadian and American leaders.

Wednesday, August 11, 1943: —President Roosevelt today prepared to go to ancient Quebec in Canada for conferences with Prime Minister Churchill and Canadian war leaders. It was presumed that both Pacific and European strategy would be the subject for discussion, with Japan not being overlooked while plans are mapped for the final eradication of Nazism . It was likely that final plans will be drawn for the long-expected invasion of Europe through France and the lowlands, with Canadian troops scheduled to play a leading part.

While future military moves are in the making, the present campaigns are progressing far ahead of schedule. Sicily is almost ours, with British Eighth Army troops reported within sight of the Italian mainland today. As further evidence of Italy's prostrate condition, a strong force of British destroyers and cruisers steamed boldly into the Gulf of Naples and bombarded the Castellammare Di Stabi naval shipbuilding and repair yard only 20 miles southeast of Naples. After sending a stream of shells into the shore installations, the naval task force leisurely withdrew without opposition of any kind.

In Russia, victorious Soviet troops have smashed another four miles through "hedgehog" Nazi defenses to within seven miles of the Ukrainian fortress city of Kharkov. The fall of this vital stronghold was considered certain if not imminent.

In the central Solomons, American jungle troops that conquered Munda are closing in on the remnants of Japan's New Georgia garrison, pinned at Bairoko Harbor. The suicidal Japs are expected to die to the last man before yielding.

447

Thursday, August 12, 1943: —Japan got another taste of what is coming as American heavy bombers struck hard at Japanese positions in their Kurile Islands. The Liberators braved the perils of a 2,000 mile roundtrip journey from our Aleutian bases to carry a taste of actual warfare to the Japanese in their own bailiwick. Two of the attacking planes failed to return.

In Sicily, General George S. Patton again called the signals for the end around play that was so successful last Monday. Powerful amphibious forces of the Seventh Army landed on the northern coast of Sicily seven to ten miles ahead of the advancing Yank columns and were reported locked in a furious battle with surprised but counter-attacking German troops. The landing was made under cover of a tremendous artillery barrage throw down by Allied warships.

At the same time the Germans were tacitly admitting that all is lost in Sicily by frantically evacuating key personnel across the two mile wide Straits of Messina, under cover of the most concentrated anti-aircraft barrage ever encountered at one point. Approximately 500 powerful German guns were said to be massed on both sides of the narrow straits. Nevertheless, Allied flyers were pounding the evacuation point with heavy bombs, causing many casualties.

Here at home, San Francisco moved to help beleaguered farmers threatened with losing valuable fruit and vegetable crops by conducting a public "market" where farmers bartered truckloads of pears and apples which otherwise would have gone to waste. The "market" was set up in the center of the city and hundreds of urban customers cleaned up the stocks as fast as the farmers brought them in.

Friday, August 13, 1943: —Well it is Friday the 13th but apparently it has brought bad luck only to the tottering Axis. Allied aerial fleets took to the skies to plaster many Italian and German cities, including Rome and Berlin. The Eternal City was hit with more than 500 tons of high explosives, dropped with accurate precision by mighty U.S. bombers based in North Africa. As in the first raid on Rome, the bombs were aimed with great skill at the San Lorenzo and Littorio railroad yards and considerable damage was caused. Opposition, both by anti-aircraft batteries and fighter planes, was tougher, indicating that

Marshal Badoglio intends to continue resistance and defend his capital. I wonder what the weary Italian citizenry are thinking.

Milan and Turin also felt the wrath of Allied air power last night. Hundreds of huge RAF bombers based in England crossed the European continent to subject the Italian cities to their most severe pounding of the war. Reports from neutral sources indicated that panic stricken residents of Milan were frantically engaged in anti-war demonstrations.

Lightning-fast Mosquito bombers made of plywood struck at Berlin last night, streaking in to lay their eggs and disappear before effective German defenses could be thrown up.

To complete the picture of total Axis disaster, Allied armies in Sicily and Russian armies in the Ukraine are chasing defeated German troops. In Sicily, the Nazis are faced with a "Dunkirk" attempt at Messina or "Tunisian" surrender. In Russia, the Nazis face the imminent loss of their vital stronghold of Kharkov, with Soviet troops already in the suburbs.

Saturday, August 14, 1943: —Alarmed and frightened by a second Allied air attack on Rome, the Italian government of Marshal Badoglio and King Victor Emmanuel today declared that it would seek an "open city" status for the ancient capital. To secure Allied recognition of such status the Italians would have to remove the government and all military activities from the city and leave it undefended. Whether the city escapes further bombing is dependent upon Italian and German compliance with every condition necessary to reduce the capital to a totally non-military status.

It is a German "Dunkirk" on the beaches of Sicily tonight. Obviously giving up the battle for Sicily as lost, the surviving German troops are frantically shuttling dozens of ships and barges across the narrow Strait of Messina, endeavoring to save as many soldiers and as much equipment as possible for the impending Battle of Italy. The German evacuation is protected by thick minefields strewn in front of the advancing Allied armies and strong rearguard action which thus far has prevented the final closing of the trap.

Likewise, in Russia, German troops were in full flight from Kharkov as Soviet shock troops stormed in from the north, northeast, and east. The ever-narrowing escape corridor on the southwest was reported caught in a tremendous traffic jam as thousands of German vehicles tried to get through to safety. The Russian air force, holding mastery of the skies, had a field day.

Allied wrath did not overlook the Japanese today. General MacArthur's heavy bombers launched a record raid today against the Jap base at Salamaua, dropping over 150 tons of bombs.

Sunday, August 15, 1943: —President Roosevelt, Prime Minister Churchill, and other American and Canadian leaders engaged in preliminary talks today, preparatory to the important strategy conference scheduled this week in Quebec. The two allied leaders revealed that British and American efforts to combat the submarine menace in the Atlantic reached a new peak of success during the last three months. More than 90 undersea raiders were sent to the bottom during the three month period, for a better than one a day record.

President Roosevelt also reiterated his faith in the principles of the "Atlantic Charter" and declared that the Allies are determined to win "total victory" and would recognize as enemies not only Germany, Italy and Japan, but "all forces of oppression, intolerance, insecurity and injustice."

While their commanders-in-chief planned, the mighty American Seventh and British Eighth armies were rapidly writing the final chapter in the story of Sicily. With their center caved in by American capture of Randazzo, the remnants of the once elite German garrison were reeling under sledgehammer rights and lefts delivered by Doughboys and Tommies supported by overwhelming artillery, tanks, and aircraft. The vanguard of Allied troops drove to within 34 miles of Messina where frantic Nazis are striving desperately to emulate the British at Dunkirk.

Hitler's last hope somehow went glimmering last Friday when a powerful fleet of heavy American bombers raided the huge Messerschmitt aircraft factory at Wiener Neustadt, 27 miles south of Vienna, Austria. No longer can Herr Hitler believe that any part of his ill-gotten empire is safe from Allied bombs. The American planes traveled 2,500 miles roundtrip from the Middle East to administer this new dose of migraine to Der Fuhrer.

Monday, August 16, 1943: —Crack units of the American Seventh Army and British Eighth Army were racing "hell bent for election" toward Messina, the end of the road in Sicily. U.S. vanguards already are within artillery range of the battered city and have brought their "Long Toms," famous 155's, into action, shelling the already flaming evacuation point. All that remains of the Sicilian campaign is a mopping-up of Axis remnants and the slaughter of as many Nazi troops as can be caught in the bloody, two-mile wide strait between Sicily and the Italian mainland. As was frequently the case in North Africa, the Germans have deserted the Italian troops or left them to fight a delaying rearguard action while they took first priority in escaping.

Punishment for the Axis was equally strong in the air today. Milan was given another thorough drubbing last night by a large force of RAF bombers. American Flying Fortresses based in England struck heavily at Occupied France, including the famous Le Bourget airfield outside of Paris, shooting down 37 German fighters. Fast Mosquito bombers again raked Berlin in one of their damaging "nuisance" raids as the Germans call them.

Class will tell in the South Pacific also, we learned today from Allied Headquarters in that theater of war. Hard flying, straight shooting American flyers knocked 48 Jap Zeros and bombers out of the air in dogfights over the weekend. Our loss was five planes, running our average to nearly 10 to 1, which is mighty good hunting.

Tuesday, August 17, 1943: —THE BATTLE OF SICILY IS WON! After 38 days of slugging, tough veterans of the American Seventh Army stormed into bomb-crushed Messina today, ending the campaign. All Axis resistance ceased and thousands of Italian troops were rounded up and imprisoned. Few live Germans were left, the survivors having deserted their Italian allies and escaped across the narrow two-mile strait. German artillery stationed on the Italian mainland began throwing shells into the abandoned city while American heavy guns were rushed up to hurl back their challenge.

To many observers the fall of Sicily marks a turning point in the war not equaled even by the Russian victory at Stalingrad or by the Allied triumph in Tunisia. The present success puts American and British arms within immediate striking distance of the continent of Europe itself and presages an early smash against Hitler's fortress. Victory in Sicily put first class naval bases and more than twenty excellent air fields at the disposal of the Allies. It freed Mediterranean sea lanes from the threat of Axis air attack, thus shortening the route to Russia and the Middle East, releasing millions of tons of vital Allied shipping. It will undoubtedly convince neutrals such as Spain and Turkey of Germany's eventual defeat and will bring renewed faith and courage to the oppressed millions in Occupied Europe. It is in truth a magnificent victory and high praise is due General Eisenhower and his American and British lieutenants as well as the courageous Allied troops themselves. All America is proud of them.

Wednesday, August 18, 1943: —The eyes and ears of the whole world are upon Quebec, Canada today as the President of the United States, the Prime Minister of Great Britain, and their high ranking military and political advisors met in secret conferences to elaborate and perfect the master plan for the defeat of the Axis. The talks gained new importance in light of the Sicilian victory and speculation grew that final plans are being laid for the invasion of Europe to follow closely upon the capitulation of Sicily so as to allow the Axis no breathing spell to bolster his defenses. Great events are at hand.

Aerial reconnaissance patrols have revealed that the Germans have already begun evacuating the toe of the Italian boot, obviously conceding the impossibility of successfully defending that portion of the Italian mainland. Allied bombers ranged over southern Italy, pounding roads and other communications and disrupting the German troop movements. Pitiful Italy faces a bitter fate.

Meanwhile in the South Pacific American fighting men are equaling the performance of their comrades in the Mediterranean. General MacArthur's hard-flying airmen have scored one of the greatest victories of the war over the Japanese air force. Allied planes, for the first time numbered in the hundreds, caught the Japs flat-footed at Wewak on New Guinea and turned that base into a graveyard of enemy planes. Approximately 170 out of 225 Japanese planes were destroyed and an estimated 1500 Jap airmen and ground force personnel killed. General MacArthur said, "It was a crippling blow at an opportune moment."

Thursday, August 19, 1943: —The magnitude of the smashing aerial victory by American airmen in New Guinea was increased today as the final report on the battle came in. Out of the 225 Jap planes caught on the ground and engaged in the air, a grand total of 215 were destroyed in addition to the more than 1500 pilots and ground crew men killed. General MacArthur's headquarters spokesmen called it one of the major victories of the war against the Japanese. Today's action concluded the two day combat. Six American planes were lost.

In addition to the New Guinea air disaster, the Japs were handed another naval thrashing in a moonlight battle in Vella Gulf, between Vella Lavella Island and Kolombangara Island in the central Solomons. An American naval task force intercepted a Japanese convoy composed of destroyers and troop laden barges, escorted by 30 bombers, heading for Vella Lavella in an attempt to reinforce their beleaguered garrison on that island. The enemy destroyers were driven off and a majority of the barges sunk, along with hundreds of Jap soldiers. Only about 200 survivors of the attack were believed to have landed and escaped into the jungles.

While Allied armies were regrouping at Mediterranean bases, after the crushing victory in Sicily in preparation for the anticipated invasion of the continent, Allied warships and planes unleashed a furious sea and air bombardment of the Italian mainland. Heavy units of the American Navy boldly approached within range of the Italian coast and sent a torrent of shells screaming into the key railroad junctions of Palmi and Gioia Tauro.

Friday, August 20, 1943: —Units of the United States Navy have captured the Eolie Islands off the northern coast of Sicily. Little resistance was encountered on the Italian isles and no Germans were discovered although it was known that the Nazis had been using the islands. Obviously Hitler's men saw the handwriting on the wall after the Sicilian defeat and moved out just in time. The ridiculously easy occupation was just another humiliating defeat for Italian arms.

Rumors and speculation regarding the decisions being reached at the Quebec conference between President Roosevelt and Prime Minister Churchill are cascading in torrents from the tongues and pens of commentators and correspondents. The most persistent view expressed is the belief that the two leaders have decided against a European invasion this year in favor of giving air power its opportunity to crush Germany without an invasion. And, in any event, the all-out aerial offensive would soften up the Nazi fortress so that, should an invasion be necessary, the casualties would be much lighter. Only time will disclose the true answer.

While civilians speculate, the armed forces of the Allies are on the move in many theaters, obviously preparing for the zero hour. American and British warplanes are hammering at communications from the toe of the Italian boot to the northern coast of France. Warships of both nations have shelled the coast of Italy and the coast of France, near Boulogne. The war of nerves is on, with Hitler on the receiving end this time. Like a cornered rat he doesn't know which way to turn to meet the impending blow.

Saturday, August 21, 1943: —Big red headlines announced the most remarkable news of the Pacific war today. Kiska has been recaptured from the Japs without firing a shot. An amphibious force of American and Canadian troops invaded the island on August 15 to find the Japs gone. There was evidence of a hasty evacuation, presumably carried out under cover of the heavy fog that frequently blankets the area.

This amazing news is so remarkable because it marks the first time in this war that the Japs have relinquished a strong and vital position without a bitter fight. It is apparent to military observers that the capture of Attu and the merciless bombardment from air and sea since that time have combined to convince the Japs that their position on Kiska was untenable. Even so, the retreat from Kiska surprised Allied leaders as the Japs have made a practice in the past of dying like cornered rats rather than lose face by retreating. At any rate the retaking of the Aleutian isle clears the last vestige of Japanese menace from the western hemisphere and moves our own dagger that much closer to the heart of Japan. The Jap owned Kurile Islands are only 650 miles from Attu, Tokyo only 1800 miles from Kiska.

The Aleutian victory is particularly pleasant news to residents of the Pacific coast as many a wary and fearful eye had been turned toward the menacing claw of the oriental enemy as it dug itself into the quivering flesh of our exposed northern flank early in the war. Many a barb of criticism had been aimed at the military for its apparent delay in ousting the Jap invaders. At long last our citizens can rest easier, knowing that the enemy's Aleutian adventure has ended in a costly fiasco.

Sunday, August 22, 1943: —What is it like to live in the San Francisco Bay Area in wartime? San Francisco itself is a booming, lusty town that at times looks as though it had been taken over by the military. Market Street almost always is a sea of uniforms, with Navy blue predominating. I have seen sailors, four to six abreast, absolutely flooding lower Market Street on their way to the theaters and night spots. Intermingled with the Army khaki and the Navy blue are the nondescript "levis" and coveralls of the shipyard and defense workers. To me, the most incongruous spectacle of the wartime scene is the protruding buxomness of the coveralled and helmeted female shipyard worker who pours her "Mae West" figure into male attire and packs her lunchpail under her arm. One can readily picture Russian women doing it, or even English women—but American women! Well, at least it is a new concept.

The tremendous influx of military personnel and war workers has caused unbelievable transportation difficulties. During the peak hours I'll swear that some of the buses and trolleys actually bulge.

The cities and highways at night are dimmed out and gloomy. This condition is not conducive to law and order with the result that rapings and robberies have increased sharply. The increase in lawlessness is also due, of course, to the influx of drifters and gamblers always associated with "boom towns." There is some talk of reviving the "vigilantes" of frontier days to protect our women.

Monday, August 23, 1943: —Just a little more of the atmosphere of the Bay Area in time of war.

Skies at night are frequently coned with fingers of light from mighty searchlights groping in the heavens for "enemy" planes while the thunder of anti-aircraft and coastal batteries shakes the ground in practice. San Francisco Bay itself is almost invariably filled with ships of all kinds, mighty battleships in their blue and gray war paint, sleek destroyers and secretive submarines, countless freighters and transports, and occasionally a majestic aircraft carrier with flocks of war planes roosting on the wide deck.

Everything in the Area reminds you of the war. It is almost impossible to escape for a minute from the atmosphere of war. Army convoys are in constant movement on the highways. Troop trains and long freights carrying tanks, trucks and other war equipment rumble constantly over the rails not far from our home. Squadrons of P-38s, P-39s, Warhawks, Aircobras, Liberators, Mitchells, and Flying Fortresses continually roar overhead—two fighters have seen fit to crash almost within rock-throwing distance of the house so far. News hawkers are interminably blaring out the latest war news, emblazoned in great red headlines across the evening papers, while radio programs are full to overflowing with war news and its analysis by countless commentators and "experts." In short, the war is the topic of the day and the only news worth printing. The San Francisco Bay Area is a war area and its people are very war conscious. A great and vital job is being done here under very trying circumstances and the Bay Area's contribution to the war effort and final victory will be found worthy of commendation.

Tuesday, August 24, 1943: —Let's catch up on the war news. Yesterday found two significant and important events happening in Russia. Moscow jubilantly announced that the Red Army has finally stormed and captured Kharkov the capital of the Ukraine, a heavily fortified German bastion. Premier Stalin ordered 20 salvoes from 225 guns fired in celebration of the victory. Berlin ruefully admitted the loss and tried vainly to belittle the Red Army triumph.

The other Russian development did not cause quite so much pleasure in United Nations circles. The Moscow government last Sunday relieved Maxim Litvinoff, Russian ambassador to the United States, of his post and appointed Andrei A. Gromyko, former Embassy Counselor, to replace him. Many competent observers interpreted the move, coming as it did shortly after the transfer of Ivan Maisky from his post as ambassador to England, as evidence of official Russian displeasure with their American and British Allies, resulting from the delay in opening a full-scale second front on the continent of Europe. Litvinoff and Maisky had long been regarded as America's and Britain's best friends in Russia.

Berlin received the "Hamburg" treatment last night. Obviously chosen as the next objective for obliteration, the German capital was visited by over 700 RAF bombers and smashed with more than 1,700 tons of bombs and incendiaries. The record raid left the city a raging inferno, with towering flames visible for 250 miles. Fifty eight heavy bombers were lost in the attack as the Germans concentrated every available defense around the city in a vain effort to frustrate the assault.

Wednesday, August 25, 1943: —President Roosevelt broadcast a world-wide message today from Ottawa, Canada. Speaking before the Canadian Parliament and some 25,000 citizens of Ottawa, the President reiterated the Allies' determination to rid the world once and for all, of gangsterism among the community of nations. He warned Axis leaders that they would soon feel the result of the decisions reached at the Quebec conference and that unconditional surrender would pay them better now than later. The Chief Executive also told the world that post-war plans were discussed at Quebec, aimed at establishing a "real and lasting peace" that would justify the sacrifices being made in this war.

On the battlefronts we find the Russian juggernaut still crunching remorselessly ahead over the torn bodies and wrecked equipment of the once all-powerful German Wehrmacht. Sixty more Russian villages and towns were recaptured during the day by Soviet troops driving northwest of reoccupied Kharkov.

Neutral sources reported that near panic is reigning in Berlin after the devastating raid of Monday night. Thousands of fear-ridden Berliners are hastily evacuating the smoldering capital. The revengeful RAF, remembering the dark days of the Battle of Britain, is giving the Germans no respite. Fast Mosquito bombers attacked the tortured city with more bombs last night, causing little damage compared with the giant raid 24 hours earlier, but handing weary Berliners another sleepless and jittery night.

General MacArthur's air force saw to it that the Japs got their share of punishment last night. A large force of Liberators and Lightnings smashed the Wewak airdrome with 112 tons of explosives.

Thursday, August 26, 1943: —Mighty fleets of Allied bombers are giving southern Italy a furious pummeling in what appears to be a pre-invasion aerial barrage. Air bases and railroad yards at Foggia, 80 miles northeast of Naples, were the principal targets today, with the American Air Force throwing in their first-string Lightnings, Liberators, and Fortresses, in large numbers. Unusually strong enemy fighter opposition was stirred up by the raid but twenty six of the intercepting aircraft were shot down. The effectiveness of the raid was admitted by the Rome radio, which reported that heavy damage was done.

British Wellingtons and Halifaxes also were busy pounding the bruised Italian mainland. The naval base of Taranto, on the instep of the boot, and Crotone were severely damaged.

Berlin received the attention of British bombers for the third straight night last night. Fast Mosquito bombers streaked through smoke still pouring skyward from the great raid of Monday night, to dump more bombs and incendiaries on the hapless city. It is estimated that at least ten percent of Berlin has been laid in ruins since the first of the week, with greater raids to come.

The United States and Great Britain today formally announced "conditional" recognition of the French Committee of National Liberation but reserved the right to review the situation whenever necessary. The action did not recognize the Committee as a government of France's overseas territories until France itself can be liberated.

Friday, August 27, 1943: —Warfare, except on the blazing Russian front, was confined to the air today. More than 100 of General MacArthur's big bombers, escorted by Lightning fighter planes, raided Hansa Bay on the Japanese New Guinea supply line. It was one of the biggest and most successful aerial blows of the southwest Pacific war to date. Over 180 tons of explosives pulverized Jap installations in the area and left a five-mile-long mass of flames along the coast. All American planes returned safely and the pilots indicated that the Jap defenses were comparatively weak.

The Atlantic Anti-submarine Command today announced that specially equipped Army bombers, designed for long-range sea warfare with submarines, have sunk five U-boats and damaged another five in recent encounters not previously reported. The battles raged as far as 1,000 miles at sea and all ended with the destruction of the enemy or his rapid retreat. No planes were lost, although some were damaged and crewmen wounded.

The titanic struggle on the Russian front is still going favorably for the Soviets. The Red Army forged ahead three to five miles west of Kharkov and recaptured 20 more villages on the Bryansk front. The real extent of the slaughter going on all along that flaming battleground is hard to grasp from the bare communiqués released from Moscow and Berlin.

Mrs. Eleanor Roosevelt, the President's wife, has arrived in New Zealand for a tour of American hospitals and camps in the Pacific war theater. The First Lady really gets around, especially when you consider that only 12 days ago she was entertaining Prime Minister Churchill and his daughter Mary, at the President's estate at Hyde Park, N.J., more than 10,000 miles from New Zealand. 'Tis indeed a small world.'

Saturday, August 28, 1943: —King Boris III of Bulgaria, is dead today. His death was shrouded in mystery; Axis reports stating that the 49 year old monarch had died from illness, but neutral reports hint that the king was assassinated. Whatever the cause of his demise, severe repercussions are expected in the Balkans. The dead King had recently refused Hitler's request to send more troops to fight the Russians. Internal disorders and dissatisfaction with the war were common before the King's death and may now explode into real trouble. The King's six-year old son succeeded to the throne as King Simeon II, while pro-German Premier Bogdan Philov retained temporary control of the government. Further developments will be watched with interest, as it was Bulgaria which was the first to collapse and throw Balkan doors open to the Allies in the First World War.

Trouble is brewing in Nazi-dominated Denmark also. The unhappy Danes apparently are fed up with their German over-lords and are openly rebelling. Always freedom loving, the Danes have frequently regretted the "no-fight" capitulation to the Nazis in 1940 and have wished that they had retained their honor and self-respect like the gallant Dutch and Norwegians. They also have learned that "men may die from fighting but nations die only by surrendering."

The RAF chose Nurnberg, industrial and railroad center deep in the heart of Germany, for destruction last night. For two hours, great fleets of four-motored bombers blasted vast sections of the city despite furious opposition by large numbers of German night fighters. Thirty three bombers were lost but the raid was believed to be one of the biggest of all time.

Sunday, August 29, 1943: —Late reports indicate that the disturbances in Denmark have flared into large-scale revolt against the Nazis. The London radio broadcast a report that the Danish cabinet has resigned and the Germans are moving in ruthlessly to stamp out the rebellion. Danish Army and Navy officers and reservists are being rounded up by the Gestapo along with leaders of the Jewish community. Violent street fighting is raging at many points while heroic members of the Danish Navy succeeded in scuttling 30 warships and slipping ten others safely through the Nazi blockade to neutral Sweden.

The debacle in Denmark has demonstrated once and for all the total failure of Hitler's New Order. Denmark was to have been Der Fuhrer's model state, designed to show the world how wonderful life could be if people would only submit peacefully and attain the full advantages of collaboration with the "super race" in its New Order. But the peaceful Danes have found the domineering arrogance of their Nazi overlords too humiliating to endure, even though resistance might mean total destruction. Better to share the fate of their Dutch and Norwegian neighbors than to "prosper" under the degrading heel of despotism. Welcome, Denmark, into the ranks of United Nations.

While German attention was being diverted by the rebellion in Denmark, their great antagonist in the east, Russia, was rolling ahead with ever-increasing momentum. Fifty more villages that have long felt the weight of the invaders' boots have been re-occupied by victorious Soviet troops.

Monday, August 30, 1943: —The center of war news is still in Soviet Russia tonight. The surging Red Army has cracked the southern end of the German line and captured the vital city of Taganrog on the Sea of Azov. The Nazis admitted the loss of the stronghold but claimed that they voluntarily relinquished it to shorten their lines. Moscow jubilantly painted a different picture, stating that the new break-through, won after a series of furious battles, might enable them to roll the invaders clear out of the Donets basin. Remnants of the German Taganrog garrison have been encircled and are being systematically annihilated. Vast quantities of booty fell with the city.

The situation in Denmark has steadily worsened. King Christian X, popular Danish monarch, is reported a prisoner of the Germans. The King was taken only after a brisk fight on the palace grounds between Danish guards and overwhelming numbers of grenade wielding Nazi troopers. Many Danish patriots succeeded in escaping to Sweden despite vigilant air and sea patrols by the Nazis.

Italy felt the fury of American bombers again today. Flying Fortresses, escorted by the sleek, powerful P-38 Lightnings, successfully attacked and wrecked the Orte railroad junction 40 miles north of Rome. Big bombs, dropped with precision accuracy, tangled and knotted rails and reduced freight cars and locomotives to piles of smoking rubble.

In the southwest Pacific, American troops are slowly closing in on Kolombangara Island in the central Solomons, site of Vila, the last major Japanese base in the area.

Tuesday, August 31, 1943: —The mighty Russian offensive has chewed two more great gaps in German lines on a 200 mile front, stretching from the Smolensk area southward to the Ukraine. The sensational breakthroughs were triumphantly announced in two unprecedented orders of the day by Marshal Stalin. Smolensk itself, the key to the whole Nazi defense system, was imminently threatened by Soviet columns that burst through the outer fringes of the famous "hedgehog" defenses of the Fascists to surge like a tidal wave of vengeance against the ramparts of the main enemy bastion. Yelnya, key position in the Germans' right wing, was engulfed along with 170 other inhabited points. Meanwhile, in the language of the Russian communiqué, "Soviet troops are completing the liquidation of the surrounded enemy in the area of Taganrog, on the Sea of Azov." All this amazing news rounded out what appears to be Russia's best day in the war so far.

Prime Minister Winston Churchill broadcast his twice postponed speech from the historic citadel in Quebec where the recent war conference was held. The prime theme of his address was a bid for unity among the Allies, with specific emphasis on Anglo-American-Russian relations. He reiterated his fervent wish for a tri-partite meeting with Stalin and attributed the Russian's absence from the Quebec conference to the fact that Russia is not at war with Japan (which was the main subject for discussion) and the fact that the Marshal is preoccupied with the great battles now being fought on the central front. "To judge from the latest news from Russia, Stalin is certainly not wasting his time," the Prime Minister drily pointed out.

September

Wednesday, September 1, 1943: —Today is an anniversary. The fourth anniversary of disaster. Four years ago today, the lid was blown off the boiling pot of man-made hell and the horrors of war were once again loosed upon mankind. Four years ago today, Hitler's legions inaugurated their 38 day "blitz" in Poland, grinding that unprepared but heroic little nation into oblivion in the first demonstration of modern "lightning" warfare. What a long, bitter trail the world has been led through during those four "eons" of time. And, in Winston Churchill's words, "We have only come to the end of the beginning."

From Russia comes news that the Russian bear has clawed and chewed the ill-fated remnants of the Nazi garrison at Taganrog into total annihilation. More than 35,000 German soldiers were killed and only 5,100 captured in the bloody liquidation. At the same time, Moscow reported new gains of from four to eighteen miles all along the 600 mile front from Smolensk to the Sea of Azov. At some points the German defeat has reached the proportion of a rout with enemy tanks and guns being abandoned intact.

In the Pacific an American naval task force was today reported engaged in a daring raid against the Japanese-held Marcus Island, only 1,100 miles from Tokyo. Naval guns and planes blasted the island in a furious bombardment that had repercussions in the frantic Tokyo radio.

Berlin was again honored with a visit from hundreds of huge four-motored RAF bombers last night. The raid was comparable to the August 23 attack which laid 1/10 of the German capital in ruins. Forty seven British bombers were lost.

Thursday, September 2, 1943: —German resistance is rapidly crumbling in Russia's Donets Basin, with the invaders obviously choosing headlong retreat to avoid the threat of envelopment by Russian forces far ahead of them in the northwest beyond Kharkov. Farther north the Red Army drive against Smolensk is developing rapidly, with the Soviet troops reoccupying more than 100 villages and towns. General advances were reported all along the flaming 600 mile front.

There was a dearth of exciting war news from other battlefronts today. British and American planes based in England made routine sorties over occupied Europe, with the RAF striking one telling blow in Holland by destroying the three-lock gates at the south end of the important Hansweert Canal connecting the east and west estuaries of the Schelde River. In Italy, Allied bombers pounded railroads and other communications at will, encountering comparatively little opposition.

From the Southwest Pacific we are informed that American troops are making slow but steady progress in their campaign against the Japanese base of Salamaua in New Guinea. The rugged nature of the terrain favors the defending Japs and renders any advance extremely slow and tedious.

On the home front preparations are under way for the Third War Loan Drive which must rope in fifteen billions of dollars from non-banking sources. Even in these days of astronomical budgets, it is going to be a tremendous financial venture.

Newspapers tonight indicated that an improvement can be expected in the meat supply for civilians. Ration points were reduced on many meat items. Butter, however, was slated to go up from ten to twelve points per pound.

Friday, September 3, 1943: —ITALY IS INVADED! Troops of the famous British Eighth Army swarmed across the Straits of Messina this morning and established a beachhead at Reggio Calabria from whence they are smashing inland on the toe of the Italian boot. General Sir Bernard L. Montgomery's orders to his veteran troops were "to knock Italy out of the war." Early reports indicate that the invading forces are already well established and making considerable headway. German forces were said to be hurriedly evacuating southern Italy in fear of being cut off by other Allied landings farther up the peninsula.

The absence of American troops from the early Italian landings caused considerable speculation regarding the whereabouts of the American Seventh Army. There was little doubt in anyone's mind but that a powerful blow will soon be struck by that formidable U.S. force.

Opposition to the British landing was confined almost entirely to land forces, principally Italian security troops, with the skies being completely dominated by Allied air power. This fact seemed to assure a speedy victory.

While the Battle of Italy got underway, the Russians continued their unbroken string of victories in the Donets valley. The Germans were pressed back a distance of twelve miles on a wide front, releasing another 400 towns and villages from the yoke of the invader. The Germans themselves were gloomy regarding the Russian situation and hinted that further withdrawals would be necessary. Hitler's headache is definitely a migraine.

Saturday, September 4, 1943: —Several more successful landings by British and Canadian invasion troops have strengthened the Allied toehold on Italy. The first day of fighting saw General Montgomery's men establish themselves solidly on a fifteen mile bridgehead and fan out inland against ineffective opposition. The Eighth Army's progress was far greater than was expected and it was apparent that the Germans were abandoning the Italians to their fate in southern Italy, evidently in fear of being cut off by other Allied invasion attempts further north. The bulk of heavy fighting can be expected from Naples up to and including the fortified Po River line in northern Italy.

Violent peace demonstrations spread throughout Italy as the panicky citizenry learned of the Allied landings in Calabria. Only the presence of so many Germans seemed to prevent the fed-up Italians from throwing themselves on the mercy of the Allies. Even that reason appeared unlikely to prevail much longer in the face of an imminent and complete political collapse. An emergency meeting of the Badoglio cabinet has been called to deal with the situation. Rumors say King Victor Emmanuel may abdicate.

Berlin felt the awful vengeance of RAF bombers again last night. Another 1,000 tons of fire and explosives ripped the city apart in the third major raid in the last 12 nights. Great sections of the German capital have taken on the appearance of a seared and blackened battlefield. The tortured and maimed ghosts that hover over the ruins of Rotterdam and Warsaw, and Coventry can rest easier tonight.

Sunday, September 5, 1943: —The British and Canadian invasion of Italy is moving along with little exciting news to report. Absolute mastery of the air has enabled the British to advance well ahead of schedule and with a minimum of casualties. The towns of Reggio, San Giovanni and Gallic were easily captured, along with Reggio's important airfield. Italian troops put up only a show of resistance and seemed more than willing to surrender. German troops have either evacuated the peninsula or, in the case of some units, have retired to the mountains to engage in delaying actions.

No news has come of any American action in the Mediterranean, but two powerful U.S. forces are known to be poised and ready. General Patton's sensational Seventh Army that proved its worth in the Sicilian campaign and General Mark Clark's veteran Fifth Army, famous for its work in Tunisia, are all keyed up and rarin' to go, as some of the doughboys themselves would say. The movements of both forces are shrouded in mystery—to us as well as to the Axis.

From the South Pacific comes news of another Japanese withdrawal, similar to that which released Kiska to us without a fight. This time it is the once important enemy sea plane base at Rekata Bay on Santa Isabel Island, 145 miles northwest of Guadalcanal. It is not yet known whether the retreating Japs have abandoned the entire island but it is interesting to again note that the little yellow enemy does give up when his position becomes untenable.

Here at home we are in the middle of the Labor Day weekend. For most defense workers tomorrow will be just another work day but there are some "patriots" who will clutter up the nation's transportation system for vacation jaunts.

Monday, September 6, 1943: —Today is Labor Day and for most people it was literally that. About 95% of the nation's defense industries were hard at it today turning out more of the vital war materials needed by the fighting men in Italy, Russia, and New Guinea. Bankers could be spared for a day so we were off, catching our second wind, so to speak, before we embark on the Third War Loan Drive that officially gets under way on the ninth of the month. We have no doubt but that we will pay for our holiday with many a long night's work before this drive is over. But like the troops in Italy, we have our objective to attain— fifteen billion dollars from non-banking sources—before our victory is achieved.

Speaking of objectives, General MacArthur's ground forces struck the Japs a surprise blow by affecting a landing between the besieged Japanese garrison at Salamaua and the important enemy base at Lae, New Guinea. The new move took the Japs completely by surprise and was made with powerful amphibious forces. The landing force struck swiftly from its beachhead 22 miles east of Lae and drove to within 9 miles of that objective. Both Salamaua and Lae appear to be doomed by this new attack.

More sensational news is expected momentarily from the Mediterranean theater as persistent but as yet unconfirmed rumors indicate that the American Seventh Army has embarked for an unknown destination. The German and Italian radios are frantically trying to guess where the Yanks will strike and their speculation includes Crete, Greece, and France, as well as many points in central and southern Italy.

Tuesday, September 7, 1943: —General Douglas MacArthur has announced the first large-scale use of paratroops in the Pacific war. The fighting American General personally directed the operation from a Flying Fortress. Synchronizing the airborne attack with the seaborne landing between the Japanese bases of Salamaua and Lae, reported yesterday, thousands of American and Australian paratroopers, including artillery units, landed in Markham Valley deep behind the enemy lines and snapped the trap shut on more than 20,000 Japs now hemmed in at Lae. The parachute maneuver, like the seaborne attack, caught the Nipponese by surprise and cut off all avenues of escape from Lae and Salamaua. Isolated from supplies and reinforcements, the fate of the Japanese army appears to be sealed.

Little news is coming in from the invasion front in Italy. The British and Canadian forces are apparently moving very slowly, due less to enemy resistance then to extensive demolitions by evacuating Germans and the rugged terrain itself. The campaign, however, is still far ahead of schedule and the invading troops have captured 39 towns and villages, including the ancient town of Palmi, to widen their bridgehead to more than 70 miles.

Munich, the birthplace of Nazidom, was chosen for devastation last night. The battered German industrial center was RAF'd with more than 1,000 tons of high explosives. American heavy bombers followed up the night attack with daylight raids on Nazi objectives in occupied France and Belgium.

Disaster struck the Pennsylvania Railroad's Congressional Limited last night. A "hot-box" on the seventh car of a 16 car train sent six cars crashing, carrying 100 people to their deaths.

Wednesday, September 8, 1943: —ITALY SURRENDERS! Screaming red headlines, six inches high, emblazoned the front page of every newspaper as the most dramatic event of the war since Pearl Harbor was announced to an astonished world. To General Eisenhower, the brilliant commander-in-chief in the Mediterranean fell the historic honor of proclaiming the termination of hostilities with Italy.

"This is General Dwight D. Eisenhower, commander-in-chief of the Allied forces. The Italian Government has surrendered its armed forces unconditionally. As Allied commander-in-chief I have granted a military armistice, the terms of which have been approved by the Governments of the United Kingdom, the United States and the Union of Soviet Socialist Republics.

"Thus I am acting in the interest of the United Nations. The Italian Government has bound itself to abide by these terms without reservation.

"The armistice was signed by my representative, the representative of Marshal Badoglio, and becomes effective this instant.

"Hostilities between the armed forces of the United Nations and those of Italy terminate at once. All Italians who now act to help eject the German aggressors from Italian soil will have the assistance and the support of the United Nations."

By this proclamation and one made simultaneously by the Italian Government in Rome, one head of the Axis monster was severed from its body, leaving only those of Germany and Japan yet to be dealt with.

The capitulation of Italy does not mean that all fighting has ceased in Italy. There are still thousands of German troops to be dealt with and late reports indicate that powerful Allied armies have landed at various points on the peninsula and are racing to seize Rome and its railroad terminals to cut off the German armies in central and southern Italy. Cries of "traitor" and screams of bitter rage have come from Berlin today and there is little doubt but that wherever possible the Germans in Italy will turn in fury on their erstwhile allies. Marshal Badoglio, however, has stated that he will put down with force any opposition to the carrying out of the armistice with the Allies. The German position in Italy appears hopeless although fierce fighting is expected along the Po river line in northern Italy. Already Nazi troops are said to be pouring in through Brenner Pass.

One of the big prizes of the surrender is the Italian fleet whose whereabouts still remains a mystery, although all commanders of Italian vessels have been urged to immediately sail for an Allied port to prevent seizure by the Nazis.

Dozens of vital questions are posed and many golden opportunities present themselves as a result of this first real break in the enemy's fortress. What about the Balkans, Greece, Yugoslavia, and Hitler's satellites, Rumania, Hungary, Bulgaria? Will they follow Italy into collapse? What about Mussolini? Will he be turned over to Allied justice? What about Italy's Merchant Marine? Where do the Allied Mediterranean armies go from here? What effect will Italy's surrender have on the already disillusioned German people? These and countless other world-shaking repercussions are bound to come out of this glorious victory. But we have not yet retired the side. There is one down.

Thursday, September 9, 1943: —Facts are hard to get about the situation in Italy today. Rumors fly thick and fast. It is clearly evident that the Germans are astonished and furious at the Italian surrender. Apparently the whole thing was negotiated and put into effect without their knowledge and they were thrown completely off guard. True to their barbaric nature, however, they will undoubtedly vent their wrath with terrible vengeance on those Italians that come within range of their weapons. Allied commanders have broadcast appeals to the Italian people to resist their Nazi oppressors with every possible means, promising that powerful help is on the way.

The American Fifth Army is part of that help. It was announced today that the Fifth, commanded by General Mark Clark, has forced a landing in the Naples area despite desperate Nazi opposition. The greatest fleet of ships ever assembled, dwarfing even the Sicilian invasion force, is reported to have transported and protected the American Army. Allied flyers returning from the landing area stated that the multitude of ships dotted the surface of the sea as far as the eye could reach.

Many other Allied landings at various points on the Italian coast were hinted tonight, with Allied warships reported to be shelling the Nazis in the harbor of Genoa far up the peninsula. The conditions in northern Italy apparently are confused and chaotic, with Nazis and Italians fighting each other bitterly at some points.

Late radio flashes hint that the cause of all Italy's misery, Benito Mussolini, has been spirited away to Sicily and is now in the hands of the Allies.

Friday, September 10, 1943: —Furious street fighting between German soldiers and Italian troops and police is reported in Milan today, with the Nazis turning their machine guns on civilians and soldiers with indiscriminate and barbaric cruelty. Dispatches from Switzerland indicate that the Nazis have seized control of most of northern Italy and have brushed aside Italian Alpine troops attempting to block the Brenner Pass through which is pouring a torrent of German reinforcements.

For the first time in six months, Hitler made a speech today. He spoke listlessly and without the oratorical fire of "better" days. For sixteen minutes he denounced the "shameless betrayal" of the Axis by Badoglio and his Italians. He said the blood of German soldiers would be on the hands of the treacherous Italians but he promised that Germany would never be destroyed and would fight back with new and different means. He praised the departed Mussolini as the greatest Italian since Caesar and again warned that if Germany fell that bogey man Bolshevism would overrun Europe. All in all, poor Adolf didn't feel so well.

Back in suffering Italy we learn that the Germans are shelling Rome and may have seized part of the city from the Italians. The news is spotty and unconfirmed and nothing is known of the whereabouts of Marshal Badoglio, King Victor Emmanuel, or Benito Mussolini himself.

Allied operations in Italy apparently are progressing according to plan. The British captured the big naval base of Taranto, on the instep of the boot, almost without opposition. General Clark's American Army was reported closing in on the city of Naples against fierce German resistance.

470

Saturday, September 11, 1943: —The results of the Italian surrender are unfolding with amazing rapidity. The bulk of Italy's heavy battle fleet was in Allied hands tonight after a day of dramatic escapes from German vengeance. All did not escape, however, as German bombers caught one flotilla out of Spezia and sent a 35,000 ton battleship to the bottom, her hull split in two by heavy bombs. Several smaller vessels were likewise sunk or damaged by the angry Nazis.

Seventeen Italian warships, including four battleships, seven cruisers, and six destroyers, were escorted into Malta by battle-stained British warships. Six other vessels were safe at Gibraltar while twelve more made their way to Palma in the Balearic Islands.

American and British forces are fighting hard to establish a firm beachhead south of Naples. Several fierce counterattacks by Nazi armored divisions have been beaten off by Allied troops, supported by accurate gun fire from fleet units standing by offshore. Salerno, a city of 34,000 people was occupied by the advancing American Fifth Army.

Italians and Germans are bitterly engaged in a fight for Rome, with the Germans officially claiming occupation of the capital. King Victor Emmanuel, Crown Prince Umberto and Marshal Badoglio are said to be in Sicily.

Though overshadowed by the Italian drama, good news is still coming from other battlegrounds. The Russians have nearly completed the recapture of the Donets Basin. Stalino has fallen and the mighty Russian drive rolls on towards the Dnieper River.

American paratroopers and ground forces are rapidly closing the trap on Japanese garrisons at Lae and Salamaua on New Guinea.

Sunday, September 12, 1943: —The sensational news from Italy has just about pushed all other events into the background for several days. We have practically overlooked the incredible victories of the mighty Russian armies in the Donets Basin. The Fascist invaders have been driven into headlong flight on a 400 mile front extending from Bryansk at the northern end of the Ukraine to the Sea of Azov. Bryansk itself is threatened with imminent capture by the triumphant Soviet troops while the last remaining Nazi claw into the Caucasus is being pinched off at Novorrisisk. Nothing but disaster faces the Germans in Russia.

We have also overlooked the tremendously vital successes being scored by General MacArthur's gallant men in New Guinea. Brilliant jungle fighting and masterful use of the most modern paraphernalia of war, including paratroops, have enabled MacArthur's men to surround 20,000 crack Japanese troops in the Lae-Salamaua area and threaten them with total annihilation. Salamaua airdrome has already fallen to American and Australian troops and the capture of Salamaua itself should occur in a matter of hours. The great American General is well on his way back to his beloved Philippines.

Here on the home front we are in the throes of starting the Third War Bond Loan Drive. President Roosevelt inaugurated the Drive last Thursday with a radio speech to the nation, calling on the citizenry to "Back the Attack" with War Bonds. Spurred by the Italian capitulation, many sponsors are calling upon us to make this the Victory Loan. Buy a bond to by a soldier a trip to Berlin or Tokyo. Fifteen billions in non-banking money will necessitate some scraping and digging on the part of patriotic Americans.

Monday, September 13, 1943: —Exceptionally vicious fighting is in progress between the American Fifth Army and powerful Nazi panzer units on the Salerno front south of Naples. The Germans obviously are throwing their full strength into a desperate effort to wipe out the American beachhead before the British Eighth Army can smash its way up from the toe of the peninsula and relieve the situation. General Mark W. Clark's fighting doughboys, however, appear to be more than holding their own and have stopped several fierce counter-attacks spearheaded by large numbers of German tanks, including the formidable "tigers." Other American units penetrated inland for a distance of ten miles and are battling Nazi armored forces within sight of Mt. Vesuvius. All indications are that the heaviest fighting of the Mediterranean campaign to date is now in progress. The decision is very much in doubt.

What promises to develop into one of the strangest mysteries of the war is the "case of the missing Duce." The whereabouts of the fallen Fascist dictator has been shrouded in secrecy since the date of his "resignation." Today, however, a boastful Berlin radio claims that a daring party of Nazi paratroopers has rescued Benito Mussolini from his Italian captors and whisked him to safety in armored speedboats. The truth of this claim has not been verified.

The Navy announced tonight that U.S. heavy and medium bombers have again raided the Japanese "Pearl Harbor" base of Paramushiro in the Kurile Islands north of Japan. Extensive damage was done to shipping and shore installations. Cost of the raid was apparently heavy as ten big bombers failed to return.

Tuesday, September 14, 1943: —Bad news has forced its way into the previously unbroken chain of good reports coming from the Mediterranean theater of war. It appears from today's events that the Italian invasion is stubbing its toe considerably in the Naples area. Unexpectedly stout resistance has been met from powerful German forces, strongly entrenched in the hills surrounding the Salerno beach area. The American position is extremely precarious and heavy Nazi artillery and hundreds of tanks are raking the landing forces with a withering fire. Yank artillery and the big guns of warships are replying in kind and losses are very heavy on both sides. Serious setbacks have been met by some of our units and the Germans have even claimed that Allied forces are evacuating the beachhead in an effort to avoid annihilation. This claim has the odor of a typical German exaggeration, although there is no doubt but that the general situation is extremely serious.

To add to the gloomy picture, the Navy announced today that one of our newest submarines, the Grenadier, with her complement of 65 men, is missing and is presumed lost.

Deepening the Mussolini mystery was the report today from Rome that Il Duce was slain by his Italian guards during Sunday's clash with Nazi paratroopers seeking to rescue him. This report is entirely unconfirmed.

The only cheerful news of the day comes from the South Pacific where it is confirmed that American and Australian troops have captured the Japanese base of Salamaua and are pursuing the defeated Jap garrison northward toward the encircled enemy base at Lae.

Wednesday, September 15, 1943: —In the face of terrific artillery fire from the surrounding hills and desperate counter-attacks from strong German armored forces, the gallant American Fifth Army appears to be slowly turning the tide of battle in its favor. It should be remembered that the Fifth is a combined force of Americans and British, working in close collaboration. Thus heavy fighting has been done by both British and American units and any glory that may come out of their magnificent stand at Salerno will be shared by both allies.

A lion's share of the credit for saving the Allied beachhead should go to the Allied air forces. In the same brilliant manner that was so effective in Tunisia, our airmen unleashed yesterday and today, what some observers claim was the greatest aerial onslaught in history in support of ground troops. Every plane in the Allied arsenal was thrown into the attack. Even Flying Fortresses were sent skimming the treetops in a hedge-hopping attack on the Nazi troop columns and artillery emplacements. Where yesterday it looked as though the Fifth Army might be driven into the sea, today the bloody but unbowed Tommies and Doughboys are slowly blasting the Germans out of their hill positions and firmly securing their 24 mile beachhead. Meanwhile, up from the toe of the Italian boot, the advance patrols of the mighty British Eighth Army are looming into view only 70 miles away. Once a junction is made between these two Allied armies, the German position in the Salerno area will become hopeless.

Thursday, September 16, 1943: —Heavily reinforced by sea and air, the American Fifth Army at Salerno has seized the initiative and is pushing the Nazis back. A glorious victory has been snatched from the jaws of defeat. The American and British fighters who participated in the bloody battle of the beaches can rightfully be proud, as we are proud of them, for they have proved that they can take everything that the Nazis can hurl against them and still bounce back strong enough to defeat the best the Germans have to offer right on the walls of their own "impregnable" Fortress of Europe.

Another scene in the Mussolini farce was enacted yesterday and today as a Fascist radio broadcast a series of proclamations purportedly issued by Benito Mussolini, establishing himself as leader of a new Fascist Government in Italy. Il Duce himself was not heard, and many people believe he is actually dead and the whole puppet government scheme is a hoax. Only time will reveal the truth.

In another of his triumphant orders of the day, Marshal Stalin announced that the Red Army has captured Novorossiysk, the vital Black Sea naval base. This victory cuts the last claw off the Nazi talon driven into the Caucasus last summer. The loss of Novorossiysk casts a threat against German control of the Crimea and the famous "last stand" city of Sevastopol.

On the home front, two items headline the news. One is the Third War Loan Drive and the other the approaching draft of pre-Pearl Harbor fathers. The Drive is well on its way towards the goal of 15 billion. People are gladly scraping to "Back the Attack" with War Bonds. Many alternatives are being offered to the drafting of fathers but in the end, as always, they will be called.

Friday, September 17, 1943: —The battle of Salerno is over, with the Nazis fleeing northward. General Mark W. Clark's victorious Fifth Army is pursuing the beaten foe. Patrols of the British Eighth Army, racing up from the south to join the Battle for Naples, have already established contact with the Fifth Army and a junction of the two forces can be expected momentarily. From then on, Naples, Rome, and northern Italy will be the objectives of a joint drive by Generals Clark and Montgomery.

Heavy bombers based in England have joined in the Battle of Italy. Last night a large force of RAF Lancasters and Sterlings hammered at German communications between southern France and Italy. One thousand tons of bombs were dumped on the vital Modane tunnel line through which Nazi supplies are rolling to German armies in Italy. Other RAF raiders plastered railroad lines in the French Riviera, 17 miles southwest of Nice. Mosquito bombers made their nightly nuisance raid over Berlin.

Violent fighting has broken out in Yugoslavia between the powerful guerrilla armies of General Tito and General Draja Mikhailovitch and German occupation forces. Late reports state that the partisans have captured four strategic Adriatic ports which could be used by Allied invasion forces coming from Italy.

Reports from the Southwest Pacific indicate that Allied troops are closing in for the kill at Lae New Guinea. Australian troops are within 5 miles of the base and are driving forward. The Jap position is precarious.

Saturday, September 18, 1943: —MacArthur's jungle-tested veterans added another triumph to their long list of victories over the stubborn Japs on New Guinea. Lae, the last major enemy base on the island, fell to superior American Australian forces after a bitter 12-day siege. Those of the Japanese garrison of 20,000 men who survived fled into the nearby hills and jungles where they will be hunted down like animals.

The conquest of Salamaua and Lae marks another notable milestone on the road back to General MacArthur's beloved Philippines. "With God's help," the General said, "we are making our way back." He did not reveal the next objective in the Allied offensive but all signs point to a drive on the main Japanese base of Rabaul on New Britain Island.

The Allied invasion of Italy is beginning to make definite progress. The beachhead at Salerno is now firmly established and armored prongs of the American Fifth Army are probing inland towards Naples. Allied naval forces, meanwhile, captured three strategic islands in the Bay of Naples, one of which, Procida, is only twelve miles from the big city. Allied air forces are already utilizing landing strips on these islands and newly captured airdromes on the Italian mainland, thus effectively improving their support of our ground troops.

The Office of War Information reported today that total U.S. casualties in the war to date number 105,205. Of this number 20,104 are reported dead, 28,226 wounded, 32,905 missing, and 23,970 prisoners of war.

Sunday, September 19, 1943: —It is a real effort to write this report tonight. We have run into one of those rare hot spells in the Bay Area. The air is so humid that the heat is oppressive and enervating. But in a way the change is enjoyable, at least to my family and me as we were accustomed to warm summer weather before we were transferred down here and it is rather pleasant to be able to go to bed and sleep without piling the covers on.

While we are on the subject of "hot air," it was reported in last night's papers that radio Berlin had broadcast a speech purportedly made by Benito Mussolini, the ousted Fascist dictator. The former Duce bitterly assailed Marshal Badoglio and the other instigators of the plot which overthrew him and announced his plans to set up a new Fascist government. There was some doubt that the voice that spoke over the radio was indeed Mussolini's and his speech had many earmarks of a Dr. Goebbels's production. Some observers who were acquainted with the former dictator believed it was his voice although it sounded "old and tired" to them.

Monday, September 20, 1943: —In a bloodless coup—at least as far as Allied forces were concerned—the island of Sardinia fell into our hands today. Two Italian divisions stationed on the island turned against their German allies and forced them to flee to the nearby island of Corsica. The Italians then advised Allied headquarters that the island was ours. The capitulation was a major victory without cost and gave the United Nations another vital stepping stone to France and southern Europe. Corsica may be the next to fall in a similar manner.

On the Italian mainland, American Fifth Army columns are driving rapidly towards the city of Naples. American and British troops seized all dominating heights on the Sorrento peninsula overlooking Naples and implanted big guns commanding the coastal road along which Allied forces are advancing. Weakening German resistance at many points indicate that the enemy is planning a retreat from the Naples area.

On the home front, the drafting of fathers has been the number one debate since the reconvening of congress. Some Senators and Congressmen are attempting to delay or entirely prevent the induction of pre-Pearl Harbor fathers but high Army and Navy officials, including General Marshal and Admiral King who testified today, oppose any delay or postponement of the father draft on the premise that it would necessitate the revision of strategic plans, increase casualties, and "prolong the war."

Tuesday, September 21, 1943: —With typical Nazi lust for blood and pillage, the Germans are sacking and burning Naples in a reign of terror reminiscent of Warsaw. Beaten in the great battle of Salerno, the Germans are obviously preparing to abandon Naples to the Allies but not without an orgy of looting and burning. Not content with building up a great dam of hatred that will one day be loosed against them by their enemies in this war, the Nazis must now torture and torment their erstwhile allies, the unfortunate Italians. On the day of their final defeat, the Nazis will see even the Italians clamoring for vengeance against them. Apparently the criminals of Berlin have decided that if they must go down to defeat, they will pull as much of the

477

world as possible in ruins about them. Poor, crushed Italy can expect no mercy from the savages of Nazidom.

Prime Minister Churchill reported to Parliament today on the progress of the war and the subjects covered at the Quebec conference with President Roosevelt. He pointed out that the Allies were all set for a mass invasion of Western Europe but, despite Russian pressure, would open the second front only when the American and British High Commands decide the time has come. In one of the longest speeches of his career, requiring a recess for luncheon, the British leader reported on all phases of the war effort. He spoke with great optimism although warning that the desperate enemy would undoubtedly exert frenzied efforts to retaliate.

General Douglas MacArthur today issued a statement in answer to criticisms leveled at the "island hopping" strategy employed in the Pacific war and declared that it was not his idea of the best way to win the war with Japan.

Wednesday, September 22, 1943: —The Nazi orgy in Naples is continuing in full fury today as Allied armies close in on the hapless city. Escaping refugees from the burning city told of the shooting and flogging of Italian citizens by Nazi terrorists on the meagerest pretexts. They reported that the German military governor of Naples has ordered 100 Italians shot for every German soldier wounded or killed.

French commandos, American Rangers, and Italian troops are battling the German garrison on Corsica. The western part of the island is already in Allied hands and the position of the Germans appears to be hopeless.

Australian parachute troops, in another brilliant surprise attack against the Japanese on New Guinea, have seized the enemy base of Kaiapit, 60 miles inland from the recently captured base of Lae. Kaiapit is astride the supply route to the Japanese base of Madang and secures Lae from any possible counter-attack via the inland route.

A revealing event occurred in Tokyo today. An announcement was made to the Japanese people by Premier Hideki Tojo reflecting the growing fear by Japanese leaders of attacks on their homeland. Tojo took to the radio to announce that "a time of emergency" exists and ordered plans completed immediately for the evacuation of Tokyo and other large cities against the threat of bombing attacks. Plans were also announced for the removal of government offices and war industries from vulnerable cities. Yes, indeed, the Japs are getting jittery.

Thursday, September 23, 1943: —A sensational landslide of victories by the amazing Red Army has again focused our attention on the Russian battlefront. All along this flaming line the massive Soviet steamroller is crunching ahead over crumbling Nazi defenses. In a strong bid to crack the German Dnieper River line before it can be firmly established, the Russians drove to within 10 miles of Smolensk, which in the words of Marshal Stalin is "a mighty junction of German defenses." South of Smolensk the red Army captured Poltava and drove 16 miles into White Russia while further south Soviet troops hammered at the gates of Kiev, the other anchor of the German Dnieper River line. The momentum of the Russian drive appeared inevitably destined to carry Soviet troops into and over both Smolensk and Kiev, as signs indicated that the Nazis were already preparing to flee the two strongholds to prevent entrapment.

The spectacle of Nazi defeat was also seen in Italy today. Beaten in the battle for Naples, the Germans were carrying out a systematic destruction of the great Italian port before leaving it, obviously determined to make certain that the base would be of little use to the Allies for months to come. Ships are being scuttled in the harbor, docks have been, and the whole port area is blasted and burning.

The RAF is back in the news with one of the heaviest raids of the war launched last night against the German arms center of Hannover. Approximately 2,000 tons of explosives were dumped on the hapless city at a rate of more than 133,000 pounds a minute. Just put yourself in the place of the Hannover residents last night. Not a pleasant thought is it?

Friday, September 24, 1943: —Powerful Russian forces have all but overwhelmed the "hedgehog" defenses of Smolensk and Kiev. The advancing Red Army closed in to within seven miles of the first and ten miles of the latter base. The fall of both cities was believed imminent.

The recapture of Smolensk and Kiev by the Russians would be among the most significant victories of the war. Just as

Stalingrad marked the final stopping of the Nazi victory drive so would the retaking of Smolensk and Kiev mark the beginning of the end for German hopes of victory in her war with Russia. Smolensk has been held by the Germans since July of 1941, shortly after Hitler took the fatal plunge and sent his legions across the Russian border on June 22, 1941. Der Fuhrer himself had used the heavily fortified bastion as his headquarters when directing his ill-fated offensive of 1941-42. Now his Generals appear ready to abandon the city in the face of avenging Russian hordes.

In Italy, the Allies scored another gain of 30 miles, capturing the town of Oliveto Citra, while hard fighting Fifth Army units inched their way forward over heavily defended German positions in the Salerno area and stood within sight of the burning city of Naples. In Corsica, fiercely fighting Frenchmen, aided by American Rangers, occupied two more seaports and were decisively beating the Nazis. Obviously conceding loss of the island, the Germans were trying to evacuate key personnel by air. Seven loaded transports were shot down by Allied planes.

Saturday, September 25, 1943: —SMOLENSK HAS FALLEN! Triumphant Russian troops entered the mighty bastion after a furious drive that overwhelmed the last Nazi defenses and sent the surviving Germans reeling from the city. Moscow's victory cannon roared out a 224-gun salute as Marshal Stalin announced the great victory to his people. Berlin confirmed the victory by gravely acknowledging the "withdrawal" of their troops. Many observers believe that the fall of Smolensk means the "loss of the war for Germany."

Further south on the same flaming Russian front, Soviet forces threatened to complete their encirclement of Kiev, the other imperiled German base on the Dnieper River line. Nazi forces already were believed evacuating the base to avoid entrapment. Hitler's darkest hour is at hand in Russia.

The German dictator's armed forces were not faring much better in Italy. Generals Clark and Montgomery have succeeded in bringing up masses of light and heavy artillery and are pounding German lines day and night with bombardments exceeding the famous barrage that smashed the Nazis at El Alamein. Adding to the enemy's chastisement were clouds of Allied planes that ruled the skies almost without opposition.

American and British infantrymen followed the artillery barrages, clearing out mountain ridges at bayonet point. German prisoners were beginning to roll in.

The reconquest of Corsica is almost finished. More U.S. Rangers landed on the island to reinforce French and Americans fighting to annihilate the German garrison before it can evacuate by air. 19 additional German transport planes were knocked out of the air over the island.

Sunday, September 26, 1943: —Repercussions from the great German defeats on the eastern front are already being felt in the Balkan countries. Reliable sources claim that representatives of Rumania are negotiating with Allied representatives in Ankara, Turkey for an armistice. Details of the meeting were not revealed although it was said that the Rumanians were reconciled to unconditional surrender.

In Italy, the American and British drive on Naples is progressing slowly yet steadily. Our troops have finally succeeded in ousting the Germans from the mountain tops overlooking the plain of Naples in fierce fighting and the fall of the Italian city is believed near. British troops on the eastern side of the peninsula are driving upon the important Italian airdromes at Foggia. Capture of the Foggia airdromes would give Allied bombers and fighters vital bases from which to operate against the Germans in Italy as well as bring them within easy bombing range of many important military objectives in the Balkans and southeastern Germany, heretofore immune from large scale attacks.

On the home front, things are in almost as bad turmoil as on the battlefields and are far from being as well run. The unchecked rise in the cost of living is causing many dangerous clashes between labor, farmers, and the Government. A bitter little strike is now in progress among employees of the Pacific Electric Railway in the Los Angeles area over demands for higher wages. The transit of war supplies is threatened. On the food front, a serious shortage of eggs and butter has developed. It looks as though the ration points for butter will take another jump.

Monday, September 27, 1943: —American Flying Fortresses based in England established a new record today by dumping 1,000 tons of bombs on the great German base of

Emden in a brilliantly executed daylight raid. This action is really a new milestone in the air war against the Nazis, indicating that the British and American Air Forces are at last ready to open a real round-the-clock aerial offensive, launching daylight attacks of equal size and intensity to the devastating night raids of the RAF. The Fortresses were escorted all the way by the new and deadly P-47 Thunderbolt fighter plane. The effectiveness of the fighter protection is evidenced by the report that at least 40 enemy interceptors were shot down while only seven of our planes are missing.

Huge losses are being inflicted on the trapped German garrison on the island of Corsica. Allied submarines stalked 16 German transport vessels trying to evacuate enemy personnel from the island and sent 10 of them to the bottom, damaging the other six. Large numbers of Hitler's crack troops were believed drowned.

In Russia the Soviet armies are still rolling ahead with a momentum that nothing seems able to withstand. Vanguards of the Russian forces have crossed the Dnieper River in several places and have crashed into the suburbs of Dnepropetrovsk, the unpronounceable town famous for its great dam which the Russians dynamited two years ago rather than allow it to fall into the hands of the invader. Hundreds of smaller hamlets and villages have been liberated in the wake of the Russian steamroller. The way of the transgressor is hard, Herr Hitler.

Tuesday, September 28, 1943: —A brilliantly executed surprise advance of 22 miles by British troops succeeded in wiping out the Nazi garrison at Foggia, Italy and the important base with its sixteen excellent airfields fell into Allied hands. The capture of the big air base opens up new vistas for Allied aerial operations, extending the radius of feasible bomber and fighter plane sorties to include all of Italy and a large part of the Balkans. Increased aerial pressure on the Nazis in the Naples area will be an almost immediate result.

The battle for Naples is reaching its final stage, with the Germans obviously preparing to evacuate the city to avoid encirclement. The fighting on the approaches to the Naples plain is bitter, with the Americans and British smashing their way through the Germans' hedgehog defenses by sheer weight of men and equipment. Losses on both sides are unavoidably heavy.

In Russia, the battle of the Dnieper appears about to get under way. Successful defense of this natural barrier is the Germans' only hope of stopping the Russian offensive. Defeat at the Dnieper River line will mean the final ousting of the invaders from Russian soil and the end of any Nazi hope of victory over the Soviets. Already fleeing German troops are swarming westward across the river under a rain of Russian bombs and shells. The next two weeks in Russia will be decisive.

Here at home, it's rationing news that makes the headlines. The Office of Price Administration announced that effective next Sunday butter will cost 16 ration points per pound—the total allotment of red ration points for one person for one week—and twice what it was when rationing started.

Wednesday, September 29, 1943: —Anglo-American troops of General Mark W. Clark's Fifth Army smashed through the last German mountain defenses today and surged out onto the Naples plain to begin the final march on Italy's Third City and largest seaport. American troops made a historic entry into the "buried city" of Pompeii, at the foot of mighty Mt. Vesuvius. Eye-witness reports stated that the six day offensive that routed the Nazis out of their strong mountain defenses exceeded in violence and intensity any other Mediterranean battle so far. The massed artillery of the Allies plus the big guns of American and British warships literally blasted the Germans out of their pillboxes and trenches. Bayonet wielding Doughboys and Tommies mopped up.

Russian forces surged forward today toward the east bank of the great Dnieper River and at one point 90 miles southeast of Kiev the Soviet troops captured the important bastion of Kremenchug, giving them a potential springboard for a drive across the big river. Already heavy Russian artillery have been emplaced on the east bank and are lobbing shells into German positions on the other side. The Russians claimed that the whole eastern bank of the Dnieper is aflame.

In the war against the Japanese, we learn tonight that Allied troops are closing in on the enemy base of Finchhafen which is expected to fall in a matter of days. A great fleet of 200 Allied warplanes completely wrecked the important Japanese air and naval base of Wewak, New Guinea it was revealed today.

Thursday, September 30, 1943: —Nothing new or particularly exciting in the war news today. Further progress is reported in all Allied campaigns now under way. The American Fifth Army is smashing at the doorway of Naples with every indication that the big port will be ours before many days. The fighting Fifth has broken out of the hills surrounding the Salerno beachhead and is now fighting on flat plains well adapted to armored warfare. Our advance should be much faster from now on.

Nothing but good news comes from Russia these days. The once invincible Wehrmacht has more than met its match in the amazing Red Army. The Russians have demonstrated that they know how to wage "total war" and can take incredible punishment and still come back stronger than ever. They have made the most of their almost limitless reservoir of manpower and are now winning the greatest victories of the war. They face the Germans across the Dnieper River in what may well prove to be the final, decisive stage of the war. Hitler, himself, is reported to have made a dramatic visit to the Dnieper line and announced bluntly that this line "must and will be held." We also remember other famous sayings by Der Fuhrer, such as "The year 1941 will see the culmination of the greatest victory of our history," and "No force on earth can move us from this place," meaning Stalingrad. There are others just as famous.

On the home front two subjects still hold the spotlight. The Third War Loan drive is nearing its end with the 15 billion goal already oversubscribed according to Secretary of the Treasury, Henry Morgenthau. The other subject is the "father draft" that is due to begin October 1st. Furious arguments pro and con are in progress in Congress and throughout the nation.

October

Friday, October 1, 1943: —NAPLES IS OURS! In a dramatic anticlimax, troops of General Mark W. Clark's Anglo-American Fifth Army marched triumphantly into the scarred seaport without firing a shot. The beaten Nazis had fled. Citizens of the battered Italian city crawled out of cellars and dugouts to give our victorious soldiers a tumultuous reception. Although but recently citizens of an enemy nation, the Neapolitans wept for joy and showered kisses upon the American and British troops as the swept into the city. Well might they rejoice, for it was commonly known that the Nazis had treated the Italians with brutality and scorn during their brief and bloody rule of the city. All the docks and many other sections of the town were dynamited and burned by the departing Germans. The mark of the Nazi has been left on the once beautiful seaport. Even their former Allies were mighty glad to see them driven out.

An unfavorable turn has been reported in the Battle of the North Atlantic in which the Germans more than once have threatened to cut off the flow of vital war supplies to Britain and the European battle zones. It is the first bad news to come out of the North Atlantic for several months where it was believed that the submarine menace had been conquered. Today it was announced, however, that the Germans launched a new and more deadly attack upon a recent convoy, sinking ten ships with what appeared to be a new type torpedo that packs a terrific wallop. One ship was hit sank within one minute, while another went to the bottom in four minutes. Only one of the attacking submarines was known to be destroyed.

Saturday, October 2, 1943: —General Clark's victorious Fifth Army is allowing the Germans no time to set up new defense lines north of the fallen port of Naples. Armored up by that master of the retreat, Marshal Rommel, who it is reported is in command of the Germans. Allied warplanes are battering the fleeing enemy in countless bombing and strafing sorties over the roads leading north from Naples. The next Allied objective is the Eternal City of Rome itself and the Vatican, where the Catholic Pope is reportedly a virtual prisoner of the Germans. President Roosevelt has pledged that Allied troops will rescue the Holy Father.

At the speed of the Fifth Army's advance it is doubtful if the Germans will be able to prepare more than a possible delaying rearguard stand at the Volturno River, the natural defensive position 20 miles north of Naples, and it is believed that the Nazis are preparing to abandon all of southern Italy to the Allies. This was indicated by a German edict ordering thousands of Italian workers from southern Italy into the north for work in war plants.

On the island of Corsica, the German defenders have been driven into the familiar "coffin corner" reminiscent of Tunisia and Sicily, this time based on the port of Bastia, where they face annihilation or another "Dunkirk" evacuation.

Heavy American bombers opened a new phase of the air war over Germany today by flying from North Africa to bomb Munich. After preparation of the newly acquired Foggia airports, such attacks from both sides will be daily occurrences.

Sunday, October 3, 1943: —Since the first exciting news of the invasion of Italy we have more or less neglected the war against the Japanese and have failed to follow closely the magnificent campaigns launched by General Douglas MacArthur and Admiral Halsey to clear the Japs out of the Central Solomons and New Guinea, thus paving the way for future offensive operations against the Japanese homeland via the Philippines. The General and the Admiral have made wonderful use of the comparatively limited resources of men and equipment available to them. While the lion's share of men and machines have gone to the Mediterranean and European theaters, the two Pacific commanders, by brilliant strategy and relentless pressure, have stopped the Japanese cold in their drive towards Australia, have seized the initiative and have beaten the oriental enemy in every department of warfare.

In a fierce, no-quarter struggle they have all but ousted them from the Central Solomons and New Guinea. Successive victories in amphibious and airborne attacks have given the American commanders and their Australian allies complete domination of that theater of war. Re-conquest of the rest of New Guinea, the main Jap base at Rabaul, New Britain, thence through the Dutch East Indies, the Philippines, and finally the direct attack on Japan proper will progress at a speed directly in proportion to the speed at which more men and equipment of war are

486

received by the two great commanders. We can rest assured that our cause is in good hands with General Douglas MacArthur in command of the land forces and Admiral William F. Halsey directing the Navy.

Monday, October 4, 1943: —Both the American Fifth Army and the British Eighth Army scored notable gains in Italy today. The American troops have already cracked the first Nazi defense line established north of captured Naples. The breakthrough came at a point along the Calore River and threatened to turn the flank of the main German defense along the Volturno River. On the east coast of Italy, the Eighth Army smashed through for a 16 mile gain after a successful surprise landing behind the German lines at Termoli.

The re-conquest of Corsica was almost finished today as Allied reports stated that French troops have occupied Bastia, the big port on the northeastern tip of the island. Surviving Nazis are pinned in two small pockets of resistance and Berlin admits evacuation of the island.

Heavy rains and over-extension of communication lines have combined to stall the Russian offensive on the eastern front. The lull is apparently due to the urgent Red Army need for regrouping the bringing up of reinforcements and supplies. The vital battle of the Dnieper River line will undoubtedly begin as soon as this regrouping has been completed. The Nazis are busy too.

Rationing, new taxes, and the high cost of living are the main civilian topics of the day. The pending father draft would also fall into that category. The Secretary of the Treasury today proposed a new tax program to Congress, designed to raise an additional 15½ billion dollars. Milk rationing by distributors went into effect today with price increases up to 2 cents a quart predicted for the near future.

Tuesday, October 5, 1943: —A horrifying Japanese atrocity story was revealed today. The story was found in the ruins of Salamaua, written in the diary of a Jap soldier killed in the final Allied drive on that base. The diary told of the beheading of a captured Allied flyer, sacrificed to satisfy the brutal Samurai code. The savage act, performed for the entertainment of the entire

Japanese garrison was described in morbid detail by the gloating Jap writer. Actions such as this and the execution of the captured American Tokyo raiders only serve to confirm the now recognized barbarism of the uncivilized Japanese. We are fighting savages and must expect to encounter savage tactics. Rather than intimidate us it only serves to strengthen our resolve. Have the Japs forgotten that we are the descendants of a nation of Indian fighters?

Steady progress was reported in Italy, where both the Fifth and Eighth armies are knifing into enemy positions despite stiffened resistance. The Allied Air Force was exceptionally active during the day against many Mediterranean objectives. Occupied Greece was raided for the first time by heavy bombers based in newly won Italian territory. The liberation of Corsica was completed today with the last pockets of Nazi resistance being mopped up.

Quite aside from the bitterness of war and important mainly because it is symbolic of better American days, was the opening of baseball's World Series between the New York Yankees and the St. Louis Cardinals at Yankee Stadium in New York City. The Yankees won 4-2 in a flashy exhibition of "heads-up" baseball.

Wednesday, October 6, 1943: —"All roads lead to Rome," the saying goes. But General Mark Clark's American Fifth Army and General Bernard L. Montgomery's British Eighth Army have found that some of those roads are filled with some pretty difficult obstacles. Nevertheless, the goal is Rome and the doughty American Doughboys and British Tommies have decided that nothing will prevent them from attaining it, not even a number of Adolf Hitler's prize panzer divisions. On both sides of the peninsula, the Allied armies are advancing steadily with never ending pressure being exerted against the yielding German line. Eighteen miles above Naples, units of General Clark's are reported to have cracked through the main German defenses along the Volturno River and have forced a landing across the river in at least one point. The key transport junctions of Aversa and Maddaloni were captured, giving the Fifth Army control of the main roads leading northwestward to Rome.

Fierce fighting was reported in yet another Mediterranean theater today. Strong German invasion forces were said to be battling the British for possession of Cos in the Dodecanese Islands. The Germans appear to have the upper hand so far.

Total defeat for the Japanese in the central Solomons seemed imminent today. The Nips are striving desperately to extricate their encircled forces on Kolombangara Island and dozens of loaded troop barges have been sunk or damaged by Allied planes and warships.

The St. Louis Cardinals evened the World Series today by nipping the Yankees 4-3 in a close duel.

Thursday, October 7, 1943: —Wake Island, scene of the memorable stand of the tiny Marine garrison at the outset of the war, was treated to a return engagement today as a strong task force of American warships, including at least one aircraft carrier, delivered a shattering sea and air bombardment against the Jap-held atoll. Early reports indicate that the attack may still be in progress and marks what may well be the start of a great offensive designed to roll back the oriental enemy from his Pacific outposts. Further details of the Wake Island raid are not yet available.

London was blasted this evening with the heaviest air raid launched against England in over a year. Stung to fury over the devastating RAF raids on their homeland, the Germans sent a large force of bombers across the channel to strike in reprisal. A solid wall of anti-aircraft fire was thrown up by British ground defenses while night fighters roared off to intercept the raiders. Scenes reminiscent of the black days of 1940 were reenacted as heavy bombs and incendiaries caused considerable damage and casualties.

The smoldering fire along the Russian front burst into flame today as the Red Army opened the battle of the Dnieper. Soviet troops swarmed across the barrier in several places and held their positions against furious German counterattacks. The blue chips are down in Russia.

An American submarine was credited with sinking a big Japanese liner plying between Japan and Korea. The daring sub penetrated the risky waters on the western side of the Japanese islands to perform the feat.

Friday, October 8, 1943: —Japanese invincibility and the belief that they will fight to the death rather than retreat were shattered again today as it was revealed that the little yellow devils are in full flight from the central Solomons. They are being severely chastised and punished as they flee by swarms of American planes and naval craft. Dozens of troop laden barges have been sunk by American bombs and gunfire, littering the sea with bodies and wreckage. One naval officer aboard an American destroyer said the sea looked like the floor of a stable as they tore through the retreating enemy. The island of Kolombangara, with its formerly strong base at Vila, has been deserted by the Japs, leaving it open to a bloodless occupation by the advancing Americans. Another big step has been taken in the offensive aimed at liquidating the main Japanese base of Rabaul on New Britain.

Recent Japanese setbacks are having their repercussions in Tokyo. Evidence of nervousness and dissatisfaction over the present state of affairs were shown in the recent shakeup in the Japanese cabinet, reported today. Tojo, the militaristic Premier and strong man, was forced to oust two of his cabinet members to stifle discontent and strengthen his absolute control over the nation's war effort.

Both the Anglo-American allies and the Russians reported substantial gains on their respective fronts today. In Italy our forces advanced ten miles to capture Capua, eighteen miles north of Naples, despite torrential rains, while the Russians surged forward to outflank the Ukrainian capital of Kiev and threaten its imminent seizure.

Saturday, October 9, 1943: —The changed complexion of the Pacific war situation was revealed today as the Western Defense Command, headed by Lieut. Gen. Delos C. Emmons, announced that, beginning tomorrow, the dim-out restrictions will be relaxed to permit auto driving with ordinary lights and the raising of window shades except right on the ocean front. It is clear to all that the danger of an attack on these shores is growing more remote daily, that, while the possibility still exists of a suicide, hit and run raid, the Japanese have lost forever the once golden opportunity to launch a successful invasion of this country. The almost fatal damage of Pearl Harbor has been repaired. Only the gracious hand of Providence prevented the treacherous oriental enemy from following up his first paralyzing blow.

Hard fighting American troops, today forced their way across the rain swollen Volturno River in Italy, engaging strong German units in desperate combat. On the other side of the peninsula, the mighty British Eighth Army smothered fierce German resistance to advance three miles beyond Termoli. The situation on both ends of the Allied invasion front appear to be well in hand. The ancient streets of the Eternal City of Rome will soon feel the tread of liberating Allied armies.

The final results of the recent Third War Loan Drive have not been reported but it is known that the 15 billion dollar goal was oversubscribed by at least one billion. Final state and city tallies have not yet been tabulated.

Sunday, October 10, 1943: —American Flying Fortresses have just completed the longest bombing raid of the war. The big Yankee bombers smashed targets in East Prussia and Poland demonstrating forcibly that no part of the Reich is safe from aerial attack. The former Polish port of Gdynia and the former free city of Danzig were included among the objectives shattered and smashed by the squadrons of American heavies. Twenty nine of the Forts were lost in the raid but 91 German interceptors were shot down in exchange. The long distance sortie took the American bombers to within 456 miles of the flaming Russian battlefront.

It was jubilantly announced in Moscow today that the last German has been driven out of the Caucasus. The Nazi foothold was liquidated in a great battle that ended with the killing of 20,000 enemy troops, the capture of 3,000 more and the seizure of large quantities of war materials including 2,073 railway cars, 83 locomotives, 540 heavy mortars, 52 tanks, 337 guns, 229 light mortars, and 184 stores of military supplies. The liberation of the Caucasus opens the way to Russian reconquest of the Crimea, with Sevastopol, the blasted shrine of Russian resistance, as the primary objective.

German resistance in Italy is stiffening as the battle of the Volturno River gets under way. General Clark's fighting Fifth Army has smashed across the barrier in force at several points to lock horns in furious combat with the desperate Nazis. Cornered rats are dangerous.

Monday, October 11, 1943: —London revealed today that the British Navy has successfully employed several new midget submarines in a raid on the remnants of the German fleet anchored in Norway. The tiny undersea raiders, patterned after those used by Japan in her sneak Pearl Harbor attack, stole into a great naval base in North Norway and torpedoed the mighty German battleship Tirpitz, sister ship to the famous Bismark. The Tirpitz was left wallowing in thick oil and appeared to be in serious trouble. Three of the midget subs were lost.

Final control of the central Solomons has been wrested from the Japanese with the almost bloodless conquest of Kolombangara, completed today. The abandoned enemy base of Vila and all main positions on the island were occupied by American troops without opposition. This success placed our forces in position to launch a frontal attack on Buka and Bougainville Islands, thence northward to Rabaul, the main Japanese base in the Southwest Pacific and the prime objective of General MacArthur and Admiral Halsey's present campaign.

The Red Army is beginning to roll again in the Kiev area. The fall of the Ukrainian capital appeared imminent and the Germans were putting the torch and dynamite to work in obvious preparation to abandon the city. Furious fighting, rivaling that of Stalingrad, is in progress in the city's outskirts, with both sides hurling in masses of planes, tanks, and aircraft.

The World Series ended today, with the New York Yankees winning the final game 2-0. The Series ended four games to one.

Tuesday, October 12, 1943: —Columbus Day today, but it was work as usual. I hardly realized that it was supposed to be a holiday until I found a vacant seat in the train this morning. I am so used to standing up every day that I realized at once that there was something wrong. Apparently some businesses were closed today, accounting for the decreased number of commuters.

Transportation problems will get far worse before they improve. The Office of Price Administration announced that, effective from midnight of last night, the value of gasoline ration coupons, A, B, and C, is reduced to three gallons per coupon, as against the previous allotment of four gallons. Increased military requirements were quoted as the reason for the slash. Serious effects are expected to be felt by the already overburdened transportation facilities of the western states.

Prime Minister Winston Churchill made an announcement of vital significance today. He reported that Portugal has given Great Britain naval and air bases in the Azores. These bases, also available for United States' use, will be invaluable in combating the submarine menace in the North Atlantic. Land based aircraft will be able to escort convoys all the way across. It is a serious blow to Germany's hopes of victory in the Atlantic.

Secretary of State Cordell Hull was reported enroute to Moscow to attend the important American-British-Russian conference of foreign ministers. Decisions and policies laid down at this meeting will have a vital effect on the kind of peace we will have. If the big three can learn to agree, the biggest "postwar" problem of all will have been solved before cessation of hostilities.

Wednesday, October 13, 1943: —In one of the greatest turnabouts in world history, Italy today declared war on Germany. Thirty five days after the signing of the armistice that removed her from the ranks of the Axis, Italy, by proclamation issued by Marshal Badoglio on behalf of King Victor Emmanuel, declared war against her erstwhile ally. The Marshal's proclamation bitterly denounced the arrogance, ferocity, robbery, and violence of the Germans against the Italians, both before and after the armistice, and said that the actions of the German troops in Naples "surpassed every limit of the human imagination." He told the Italians that there will be no peace in Italy until the last German is driven from Italian soil. President Roosevelt, Prime Minister Churchill, and Premier Stalin joined in granting Italy the status of a co-belligerent. That status, however, will not affect the terms of the armistice.

The Anglo-American Fifth Army under General Clark reported a gain of ten miles on the road to Rome. The strong enemy positions on the Volturno River were outflanked and most of the Naples-Termoli highway was brought under Allied artillery fire.

In the South Pacific, heavy fighting was reported in the Finschhafen area as the Japanese counter-attacked desperately with strong forces in an effort to regain the vital port. Defending Australian troops who occupied the base on October 2 successfully beat off all attacks, killing at least 400 Japs in the day's fighting.

Thursday, October 14, 1943: —General MacArthur's air force today struck one of the greatest and most successful blows of the Pacific war against the Japanese. The General threw almost every available bomber and fighting plane into the air to smash the big enemy base at Rabaul, New Britain. More than 350 tons of bombs were dropped on enemy installations in the area and at least 177 Japanese planes were destroyed, many of them on the ground. Major General Kenny, commanding MacArthur's airmen, stated his belief that the raid will mark the turning of the tide in the South Pacific fighting. Heretofore, he said, we have been fighting a defensive action but now we are definitely on the offensive and will keep moving. The number of Jap planes destroyed accounted for approximately 60% of the available enemy air strength in that area. Our losses were only six planes. It was a remarkable victory.

By late reports we learn that the Eighth Air Force based in England, has just completed one of its biggest raids into the heart of Germany. The target was the industrial city of Schweinfurt, 65 miles east of Frankfurt. Principal objective in the target city was the great roller bearing works upon which the Nazis depend for equipping motorized equipment. Our losses in bombers and men were heavy although the Germans lost at least 104 and possibly more fighters. Some of the powerful new German pursuit planes are equipped with new rocket guns, said to pack a terrific wallop.

Friends and relatives were reminded today that tomorrow is the deadline for the mailing of Christmas packages to members of the armed forces overseas.

Friday, October 15, 1943: —Sixty of our great Flying Fortresses were lost in the raid against Schweinfurt yesterday. It somewhat staggers the imagination and shocks the sensibilities when you think of sixty of those sleek, powerful flying machines crashing to earth in flaming, twisted wreckage. And with them, 593 of the finest boys in the world, young, handsome, intelligent— the cream of the nation's manhood. War exacts a ghastly toll, and insists on taking nothing but the best.

Despite the heavy loss, the Eighth Air Force Bomber Command reported that the raid was a success. Terrific damage was inflicted on the Germans. More than 50% of the great roller bearing factory in the German city was left in smoking ruins while at least 104 enemy planes were shot down in the running fight that cost us sixty planes. A substantial number of our missing flyers were known to have parachuted to earth and are undoubtedly prisoners.

In Italy the American Fifth Army was only 95 miles from Rome today. Gains of from three to five miles were scored all along the Volturno River line and a general withdrawal by the Germans appeared inevitable. British units of the Fifth Army aided the advance by successfully forcing a landing behind the enemy lines above the Volturno River in a familiar leap-frog maneuver.

Furious battles are raging all along the flaming Russian front. Soviet armies improved their positions in almost every sector and have succeeded in driving deep salients into Nazi lines west of the Dnieper River.

Saturday, October 16, 1943: —The Bay Area captured the headlines today with the arrest in Richmond of Gunther Rumrich, one of the most notorious and daring Nazi spies. Rumrich's betrayal of the land of his birth (he was born in Chicago, Illinois) dates back for many years. In 1938 he was convicted as a Nazi agent and sentenced to prison for two years. His subversive activities were resumed immediately after his release from prison and culminated in his capture today. His escapades contained all the thrilling background and color of a dime store novel. He alternated from stealing vital secrets of our Panama Canal defenses to plotting against high army officials. Let's hope his story has now reached it final denouement.

With the exception of the above incident, the news of the day is unexciting. The Allied armies, including the Russian, are moving ahead inexorably. Six more towns were occupied by advancing American Fifth Army units in the Volturno area of Italy. The Nazis are gradually being pushed out of their remaining strong positions in the area and Allied leaders are confident that the Battle of Italy will reach Rome within a matter of days.

In Russia, the hard-driving Russians smashed into the suburbs of Kiev today and set about the gory task of chopping their way through the city street by street.

The South Pacific theater is comparatively quiet today. Indications are prevalent, however, that a major drive is imminent, probably liquidating the main Japanese base at Rabaul, on New Britain.

Sunday, October 17, 1943: —Another Sabbath Day has rolled around and it felt so good to relax once more after a strenuous week. The weather was alternatingly bright and sunshiny, then cloudy and threatening, with a definite tang of autumn in the air. Dry leaves fluttered helplessly to the ground and black thunderheads glowered like sentinels over the hills to the west. We spent the afternoon touring the peninsula in search of a house to rent. Renters, in war time, are in a very unfortunate position. While ceilings have been placed on rentals no restrictions have been placed on the selling of homes from under the feet of the tenants. No ceiling has been placed on real estate prices either and because of the great demand for living quarters, the values of homes have skyrocketed to highly inflated levels. Consequently landlords are finding it very profitable to sell their properties, make a killing, and to the devil with the poor, unfortunate renter. We have just been advised that we are one of the latter group, dumped unceremoniously onto a terrific rent market. If we are able to find a suitable place within our pocketbook it will be a genuine miracle. The prospects are extremely unlovely.

On the other war fronts we find that the major battles are still being fought in Russia, with Italy coming in a close second. The Germans have tactfully announced a "systematic detaching movement" meaning a retreat from the Dnieper River line. Powerful Soviet forces are lending impetus to that "detaching movement." In Italy the Anglo-American Fifth Army succeeded in biting more large chunks out of the Nazi Volturno defenses and another "s.d.m." as stated above can be expected.

Monday, October 18, 1943: —U.S. Secretary of State Cordell Hull and Anthony Eden, British emissary, have arrived in Moscow for the long-awaited conference between the foreign ministers of Russia, Britain, and the United States. Secretary Hull took a formidable array of military and political advisers with him. Included in his entourage was W. Averell Harriman, ambassador designate to the Soviet Union.

The importance of this tri-partite conference cannot be overestimated. If the lesser lights of the three countries can learn to agree it will smooth the way for the anticipated meeting of the "Big Three," President Roosevelt, Prime Minister Churchill, and Premier Josef Stalin.

There was increased speculation today that Admiral Lord Louis Mountbatten, Allied commander in chief of the Far Eastern theater, is all set to launch a major offensive against Japanese positions in Southeast Asia. First indication of the impending drive was the terse communiqué issued today by Mountbatten's headquarters, announcing that British air and ground forces have launched a strong attack against Japanese positions 60 miles north of the important Burmese supply port of Akyab, Burma. The actual size of the invading force was not revealed.

In the Southwest Pacific, General MacArthur's tireless airmen have destroyed more than 100 Japanese aircraft in a smashing two-day aerial offensive that rocked the little yellow men back on their heels.

Tuesday, October 19, 1943: —The conference of Allied Foreign Ministers got under way in Moscow today. The Russians apparently are determined to confine the discussion to military topics as far as possible. Their principal emphasis will be upon the second front issue. The British and American delegations, however, are equally determined to include many economic and political subjects in the conference agenda. The Anglo-American view is that a firm foundation must be laid to assure success of the forthcoming conference of the "Big Three"—Roosevelt, Stalin, and Churchill—when the solution of many postwar political, economic, and social problems must be reached if the world is to attain a stable and lasting peace. Problems such as the boundaries of small European countries and the fate of the German people cannot safely wait for improvisation at the war's end. The three great, dominating powers must reach an agreement calling for cooperative action.

On the subject of a second front, Marshal Jan Smuts, Prime Minister of South Africa and close confidant of Winston Churchill, hinted in a speech today that an Allied invasion of the Balkans will be launched before winter. He further indicated that the main burden of the final assault upon Hitler's fortress must necessarily fall upon the United States as the latest, freshest, and most powerful newcomer into the field of battle.

Allied armies advanced steadily in both Russia and Italy today. The momentum of the Russian attack along the Dnieper line is increasing daily and many observers believe that the Nazis face a major disaster on the Eastern front.

Wednesday, October 20, 1943: —The German's Volturno line at last cracked all along its length. The battered Nazi armies in Italy are in full flight towards Rome, venting their vengeful wrath on the helpless Italian citizenry as they go. Observers with the advancing American Fifth Army saw frightful evidence of the Germans' scorched earth policy. Farm houses and homes were burned and the bodies of Italian peasants lay alongside the remains of their livestock, victims of Nazi brutality. In northern Italy, mass arrests were made of Catholic priests who, the Nazis said, were preaching anti-German propaganda from their pulpits. Unrest was rampant throughout the "spaghetti" nation, with the fiery Latin temper of the people tamed only by the sight of so many German bayonets. One day soon the whole country will explode under the very noses of the storm troopers and the Teutonic plague that is racking the body of Italy just as it has racked the rest of Europe for three years, will be purged from all the land and peace will reign once more. And perhaps this time the blood stream of mankind, in fighting off this terrible plague, will produce a powerful anti-toxin that will make it immune forever from this terrible disease. God grant that it may be so.

On the home front, rationing strikes, and manpower are in the news. Schools throughout the country started distributing Ration Book No. 4 today, which will be used after November 1 to purchase processed foods and sugar.

An alarming increase in juvenile delinquency due to wartime conditions is also receiving serious attention by civic leaders.

Thursday, October 21, 1943: —Stung to savage rage over the terrific damage meted out to them in the great Allied bombing raids over the Reich, maddened German mobs were reported to have lynched two American airmen who fell into their hands after bailing out of their disable bomber. Other British and American flyers were saved from the same fate by German troops who restrained the angered civilians. I wonder if the German citizens recall that it was their blood soaked Fuhrer who started all this. Do they remember Warsaw, and Rotterdam, and Coventry, and London? Yes, war is hell. Are you just finding that out, you Germans who sent your supermen crashing into defenseless Holland, Belgium, and Norway? Does it hurt to have bombs smashing the life out of your women and children? Well, it hurt the Greeks, the Czechs, and the Poles too. We take no joy in the destruction of your land, but the lives of so many innocent victims crushed under your heel, demand a bitter retribution. Vent your wrath on your gory Hitler, Germans, not on helpless American flyers who have only been doing their duty.

All roads lead to Rome and American soldiers of the Fifth Army are advancing along many of them. The going is extremely rugged, however, as the retreating Nazis have scattered mines and booby traps in great profusion. As the thunder of the guns nears the Eternal City, the Pope is desperately seeking to open negotiations between the belligerents that will prevent the horrors of war from being visited upon the Holy City.

Friday, October 22, 1943: —The gateway to the Crimea was all but closed today as powerful Russian armies smashed through German defenses in a terrific battle for Melitopol. Street fighting, reminiscent of Stalingrad, raged through the important city as the Nazis battled desperately to stem the Red wave that threatens to engulf the city and close the trap on hundreds of thousands of German troops in the Crimea. Moscow reports stated that the fighting had reached the "mass murder" stage.

Seasoned Australian troops, veterans of North African fighting against the Germans, are holding the recently captured Japanese base of Finschhafen in New Guinea against furious Jap attacks aimed at driving through to the sea and extricating a large Japanese garrison trapped at Satelbherg, ten miles up the coast. The Aussies stated that the Nipponese fight fiercely but not so formidably as the Germans.

The Anglo-American drive on Rome scored further advances today. American troops occupied two more important towns athwart the Appian way to Rome while the British Eighth Army advanced several miles against light opposition on the eastern side of the peninsula. Allied air power ruled the skies above the battlefronts.

Secretary of the Navy Frank Knox today announced that the Navy is building 3 mighty aircraft carriers of 45,000 tons, armored like battleships and capable of launching multi-motored bombing planes. More bad news for Hirohito.

Saturday, October 23, 1943: —Moscow today announced the most important Red Army victory since the fall of Smolensk. Victorious Soviet troops have captured the city of Melitopol, gateway to the Crimea after 12 days of the most ferocious fighting since Stalingrad. 30,000 Germans were estimated to have perished in the Nazi bid for time to evacuate their trapped forces from the Crimea. How successful the evacuation was remains to be seen. Soviet sources believe that thousands of Germans will not escape.

The Royal Air Force continued the furious aerial pounding of the Reich last night by freighting a total of more than 2,000 tons of bombs and incendiaries over Kassel, Cologne, and Frankfurt. The aircraft building center of Kassel was the main objective and 1,500 tons of explosives spread havoc among the vital plane factories. The attacks on Cologne and Frankfurt were diversionary affairs, designed to confuse the enemy's defenses. Losses were considerable, however, as 44 of the huge bombers failed to return.

Swedish-German relations were strained for the second time in two months as a second Swedish passenger plane was shot down by a German fighter off the west coast of Sweden, killing eleven people. Public indignation rose to wrathful heights.

The Moscow conference of Foreign Ministers was in full swing today, while the world eagerly awaited the results. Failure of this conference would be an almost fatal blow to hopes for a genuine and stable peace.

Sunday, October 24, 1943: —The situation on the war fronts remains about what it was yesterday. The Russians are racing to close the Crimean trap after the capture of Melitopol. Other Soviet columns are smashing against the last German defenses in the Dnieper River bulge, threatening to capture the great industrial city of Dnepropetrovsk at any moment. Even Berlin admits that the German situation on the southern front is deteriorating rapidly. Their defeat is approaching a rout.

The Germans are not faring much better in Italy. Despite stiff resistance, the American Fifth Army and the British Eighth

Army are making steady progress towards Rome. American artillery has been doing particularly effective work as it did in North Africa and Sicily. Doughboy sharpshooters are shooting the famous "Long Toms" with uncanny accuracy. Hitting a moving enemy tank at a range of several thousand yards is no trick at all for the Yank marksmen.

The eyes and ears of the world are still on the conference of American, British, and Russian foreign ministers now rounding out its first week in Moscow. The meeting has been shrouded in secrecy and little is known of the topics discussed. It is believed, however, that a basic agreement has already been reached between the three great powers and hopes are held high the conference will be fully successful and that an early meeting of Roosevelt, Churchill, and Stalin will be arranged.

Monday, October 25, 1943: —Two vital cities with a total of 34 letters in their names were captured by the steamrolling Red Army today. They were the great industrial cities of Dnepropetrovsk and Dneprodzherzhinsk, located in the nose of the Dnieper River bulge. The former is the site of the mighty dam which the Russians claimed to have utterly destroyed in the early stages of the war to prevent its use by the advancing Germans. That the Nazis had reclaimed and were using the dam was evidenced by the report that they, in turn, have dynamited the great structure in the face of the victorious Red Army. Meanwhile, other Soviet columns have raced more than half way down the 100 mile stretch from Melitopol to the Perekop neck of the Crimea, seeking to clamp the lid on some 500,000 German troops trapped on the peninsula.

Hard punching American troops dealt what was officially described as "a bloody nose" to counter-attacking German troops in Italy. Not only were the attacks repulsed with heavy loss to the enemy but the Americans also launched a later drive of their own, gaining another three miles on the main road to Rome. On the Adriatic side of the Italian peninsula, General Montgomery's Eighth Army advanced slowly yet steadily against stiff resistance. The fighting Tommies forced a crossing of the Trigno River, establishing a firm bridgehead on the northern bank.

Signs are increasing to indicate that the Anglo-American-Russian conference of Foreign Ministers has developed to a point where a basic accord has been reached on all points, at least in principle. The atmosphere continues friendly and cooperative.

Tuesday, October 26, 1943: —General Douglas MacArthur's flyers have scored a series of smashing victories over Japanese air power in the South Pacific. In three days our airmen have knocked 131 Japanese planes out of the air for sure, another 72 are "probables." Only five of our planes were lost, giving us the most favorable ratio of losses for any offensive of the war to date. The big base at Rabaul, New Britain, was the principal target of the hundreds of heavy, medium, and fighter-bombers sent into action by our Air Force. For the present, at least, we have gained mastery of the skies over the South Pacific theater.

In Russia, the Nazi debacle grows in scope daily. Hitler faces a catastrophe in the bend of the Dnieper River, with a large proportion of his army of 500,000 men facing annihilation or capture. Panic has already seized many of his troops, sending them fleeing in disorder, leaving vast quantities of booty behind. A similar disaster faces the Germans in the Crimea, as other Russian columns drive closer to the Perekop neck.

It is a story of German defeat also on the Italian front. American and British Armies have scored up to six mile gains in a general advance all along the line. Seven key towns were occupied by Allied troops as the battle for Rome nears its objective.

On the home front it's the draft and taxes that hold the spotlight. The House today voted to delay drafting fathers with pre-Pearl Harbor children until all others have been taken. Allowances for dependents of draftees was also increased to $50.00 for wife, $30.00 for the first child, and $20.00 for each additional child.

Wednesday, October 27, 1943: —Today was another Navy Day and found the U.S. Navy fully recovered from the staggering blow delivered against it at Pearl Harbor almost two years ago. It is now the mightiest fighting force afloat, consisting of some 15,000 vessels, of which 800 are hard-hitting combat ships. Some 20,000 first-line war planes patrol the air above the fleet and roost in a large number of formidable new aircraft carriers. Since the clearing of the Mediterranean and the mastery of the submarine in the North Atlantic, the majority of this vast fleet is concentrating in the Pacific for the showdown with the Japs. Add to this mighty U.S. force the bulk of the British Navy and the remnants of the French and Italian Navies and you will get some idea of the tremendous weight of floating steel and destruction that the Japs will soon discover bearing down on them. It is not a pleasant prospect for the followers of Tojo and Hirohito but a just reward for their treachery.

In Russia, the position of the cornered Nazi armies in the Dnieper River bend and in the Crimea is deteriorating rapidly. Fierce battles are being fought as the invaders struggle desperately to extricate themselves from their predicament, but powerful Russian reinforcements from the inexhaustible reservoir of Soviet manpower have been constantly fed into the front lines, slowly crushing the life out of German resistance. The power of the Red Army flows while that of the German Army ebbs.

Likewise in Italy the armored might of some of Germany's best panzer divisions is being smashed relentlessly back by the gallant sons of America and Britain. The day's end saw our troops five miles closer to the Eternal City.

Thursday, October 28, 1943: —It was indicated today that Allied landings are taking place in the Northern Solomons. General MacArthur's amphibious forces are reported to have landed successfully on Mono Island, 30 miles from the big Japanese base of Buin. Only light opposition was encountered as American planes roamed the skies with unchallenged superiority. Another 500 tons of high explosives were dumped during the day on enemy airdromes and bases on Bougainville Island as General MacArthur began to squeeze the pincers close on Rabaul, the Japanese "Pearl Harbor" of the South Pacific.

Reflecting Japan's increasing anxiety over the course of the war, was the reported suicide of Seigo Nakano, leading Fascist exponent in the Island Empire. The former special envoy to Berlin and Rome committed hara-kiri yesterday after attending a session of the Japanese Diet, where the serious turn of the Pacific war was disclosed and plans made for a defensive rather than an offensive military policy.

News, pleasing to residents of Eastern and Western coastal areas, was announced today. Beginning Monday, November 1, all dim-out restrictions will be lifted. The surprise announcement means that the lights may go on again next Monday. General Emmons, commanding the Western Defense Command, stated that the lifting of the ban was the result of improved defensive measures along the coasts and the mastery of the submarine menace. The restrictions are subject to reinstatement at any time, however.

Friday, October 29, 1943: —General MacArthur's South Pacific Headquarters today confirmed the rumor of yesterday that Allied landing forces have successfully occupied two more islands in the Northern Solomons. The two islands are Mono and Stirling in the Treasury group and lie only 28 miles from the big Japanese strongholds of Buin and Faisi. Only light enemy resistance was encountered and our casualties were relatively light.

The Navy Department today announced that ten more Japanese ships have been added to the imposing score of American submarines. The deadly "pigboats" have ranged far astride the Oriental's supply lines and have sunk or damaged 474 Jap vessels since the beginning of the Pacific War. Of this total 329 are positive sinkings, the rest probable sinkings or badly damaged. The latest losses include one large freighter, a large tanker, a big transport, five medium freighters and two small freighters. The full story of the contribution of the U.S. submarines in the war against Nippon cannot be told until after the war. Some experts say that our use of the undersea boat in warfare has put the German technique to shame.

The familiar story of Allied victory in Russia and Italy was repeated today. In both theaters our side scored notable advances, pushing the Nazis still closer to the brink of disaster on both fronts. Russia, of course, remains the major battleground, with fully a million Nazi troops facing utter defeat on the Dnieper line and in the Crimea.

Saturday, October 30, 1943: —Less than 24 hours after American and New Zealand troops occupied two islands in the Treasury group, American paratroops successfully landed on the southeastern coast of Jap-held Choiseul Island, 100 miles to the east and separated from Bougainville Island by 30 mile wide straits. Defending Japs on Choiseul were said to be in full retreat towards the northern part of the island. The noose is drawing tighter around the great Japanese base of Rabaul on New Britain Island.

Across the world in Italy, American warships and great fleets of Flying Fortresses were taking part in the drive on Rome. On both sides of the Italian peninsula, in both the Adriatic and Tyrrhenian seas, American battlewagons steamed in close to shore to bombard Nazi positions along the "Little Rommel Line" as General Clark's Fifth Army and General Montgomery's Eighth Army moved into position to smash the line in what is expected to be the showdown battle in the drive on Rome. Flying Fortresses, escorted by fighters, ranged far behind the German lines to blast away at the enemy's communications and supplies. Particularly hard hit were the railroad marshalling yards at Genoa. Huge fires were set and twisted rails and wreckage littered the yards.

A report emanating from Dutch sources today claimed to have knowledge of a plot by German military leaders to oust the failing Hitler, set up a military dictatorship and start peace negotiations with the Allies. General Wilhelm Keitel, commander-in-chief of all German armies was reported to be the leader of the plot. Even if true, the publicity would wreck the plan.

Sunday, October 31, 1943: —Another Sunday has rolled around and with it another badly needed day of rest. It is also another Halloween weekend and both last night and tonight, spooks and hobgoblins have beaten a path to our door, begging for eats. I never realized before how much food a hungry little ghost can eat. That is, until I remember those happy days years ago when I used to throw a sheet over my head and haunt the neighborhood. Many is the night we used to come home stuffed with apples, candy and nuts. Scenes like that must fill the minds of the American boys on the fighting lines throughout the world, lending strength to their conviction that they are fighting for just those things that are a part of the America they love. They are fighting to preserve America the way it was and is, yet to eliminate what few failings it has and to make it even a finer land in which they and their children may live.

There is not much change in the way of war news tonight. The story is just about the same in Russia and Italy. On both fronts the Nazis are being soundly beaten. In the big bend of the Dnieper River, the German retreat is close to panic, with shattered units of the once mighty Wehrmacht striving desperately to escape the jaws of the angry Russian bear. Tens of thousands of Nazi stragglers have already been bypassed by fast moving Soviet armored columns, leaving them to be mopped up by Cossack cavalry and infantry.

The conference of Allied Foreign Ministers in Moscow is said to be progressing very satisfactorily, with the results soon to be reported. Cordiality has been the keynote of the meeting so far—a very hopeful sign.

November

Monday, November 1, 1943: —The dim-out officially ended tonight and I even saw some neon signs blazing merrily away as I came home this evening but all the lights were not on by a long ways. Arc lights were still hooded and many theater neon signs were out from disrepair and all-in-all the lighting situation wasn't much different. Lights won't really go on until after the war.

The Moscow conference of Foreign Ministers has been history making. This was revealed today by a series of sensational declarations proclaimed by the three great powers, Russia, Britain, and the United States, with China even joining in some of the important decisions. The Big Four proclaimed unity of purpose in bringing the Axis to unconditional surrender, with Russia definitely affirming that she will make no separate peace with Germany. Allied Governments further announced their intention of bringing those Nazis responsible for atrocities to trial in the country where the crime was committed. They pledged the restoration of democracy in Italy and provided for the rebirth of an independent Austria. They also agreed on the need for a world organization backed with force, to preserve peace.

The complete success of the conference was a death blow to Hitler's hopes of promoting disunity between the United Nations. The whole Allied world looks with renewed hope for an early victory and a permanent, constructive peace. Messrs. Hull, Eden, and Molotov have done an excellent piece of work.

Tuesday, November 2, 1943: —It has just been announced that United States Marines invaded Bougainville Island in the northern Solomons yesterday. The Leathernecks swarmed ashore in a surprise move that caught 35,000 Japanese troops flatfooted. Early reports indicate that the Jap force was split in two in the early fighting, 25,000 being driven south and 5,000 north of the Marines' beachhead at Empress Augusta Bay, on the west coast of the island. The United States Navy is on hand in considerable force to intercept the Japanese fleet should any part of it attempt to molest the landing armada.

In Russia, the Red Army has snapped the trap shut on the remaining German forces in the Crimea. Soviet columns have raced 40 miles west of Perekop to snip off the last escape routed by land from the ancient Crimean battleground. It is estimated that approximately 90,000 Nazi troops are doomed to annihilation or capture on the peninsula. From this figure it is evident that the Germans were able to evacuate the main part of their army of 500,000 previously reported as occupying the Crimea.

In Italy further chunks were bitten out of the southern end of the main German defense line across the peninsula. General Clark's magnificent Fifth Army is beating the crack troops of Hitler's famous panzer divisions wherever they meet them, slowly and steadily driving them back over the road to Rome. Both American Doughboys and English Tommies are fighting side by side as one army. Here is international cooperation and unity in their finest example.

Wednesday, November 3, 1943: —San Francisco election news held the local spotlight today. The city government will receive a general overhauling as a result of yesterday's voting. Almost all incumbents who were up for re-election were defeated including the Mayor, Angelo J. Rossi, who has held the job for twelve years. Roger D. Lapham, a non-political, businessman candidate was swept into the mayor's office in a one-sided victory that left no doubt but that the citizenry is dissatisfied with the present management of their affairs. Election results elsewhere throughout the nation were encouraging to anti-New Dealers and Republicans and indicated a definite trend away from the present national administration.

On the war fronts, good news emanates from the Italian battleground. Allied Headquarters announced that our forces are advancing all along the line, with the Germans pulling out hastily but in good order. Our advance units are now less than 90 miles from Rome.

From England we learn that the U.S. Eighth Air Force today mounted its greatest daylight raid of the war, hurling as many as 1,000 heavy bombers and fighters against targets deep in Germany. Our losses in the raid were believed to be far less than usual due to the fact that long range P-47 Thunderbolt and P-38 Lightning fighters were able to escort the bombers all the way over and back.

Pacific. The Japanese are obviously making a desperate bid to halt the Allied drive aimed at their big base of Rabaul on New Britain. Details of the fighting are meager and little is known except that a major battle has been joined between forces of the opposing fleets. The Japs have made their usual boastful claims, bragging that their torpedo planes have sunk two American aircraft carriers and four other warships off Bougainville Island. These claims are obviously exaggerations but we can undoubtedly expect some serious losses because of the desperate nature of the fighting.

It has come at last. The Nazis, through their Rome radio, have claimed that Allied planes have bombed the Vatican. Our leaders have long expected the Nazis to perpetrate some such outrage against the Pope in an effort to discredit the Allies in the Catholic countries. You can be sure that if bombs fell they were German bombs or Allied bombs carried in German planes.

Sunday, November 7, 1943: —It is another Sabbath Day but it is sad to note that on the world's countless battlefields this Holy Day brings no cessation or pause in fighting. The orgy of killing continues apace, knowing no day of rest or surcease. In fact, this day has brought reports of new and more vicious battles, particularly in Russia and the South Pacific.

Moscow communiqués claim that triumphant Soviet columns have fanned out from captured Kiev to points far beyond, slaughtering fresh thousands of panic-stricken Nazi troops, fleeing madly from the scene of their most recent disaster. Already looming ahead of the amazing Russian armies are the borders of Poland and Latvia. It is now believed possible for the Red Army to completely liberate the Ukraine by winter and perhaps drive the invaders entirely from the soil of Russia.

In the South Pacific a ferocious land, sea, and air battle is raging for Bougainville Island, with the fate of Rabaul hanging in the balance. The Japanese have been spotted by reconnaissance planes, steaming southward from their main base of Truk, with large convoys of reinforcements for the Bougainville battle. The situation is fast approaching the showdown stage. Allied warplanes are attacking the enemy in flights of hundreds and the Harbor of Rabaul has been reduced to a graveyard for smashed Jap vessels, including one heavy cruiser sunk today by torpedo bombers. Our own losses have not yet been announced.

Monday, November 8, 1943: —The modern Napoleon, Adolf Hitler, speaking as would a cornered and desperate criminal, today exhorted the German people to "fight to the finish." Der Fuhrer spoke before a select group of his followers in celebration of the twentieth anniversary of his famous beer cellar "putsch." Fanatically and grimly, the Nazi arch criminal bellowed his defiance of his enemies, both within and without, promising them no mercy. He constantly referred to the tremendous difficulties facing the Reich in such a way that he seemed to be offering excuses for the terrible failures and defeats suffered in Russia and the Mediterranean. His speech as a whole was a defensive one, full of alibis, like that of a cornered murderer who knows the end is near but who is determined to take as many innocent victims with him to destruction as possible. Already he wades in blood flowing at flood tide over the face of Europe, blood which he caused to be spilt. Now he threatens those of his own people who would revolt in disgust against the continuance of his reign of horror. Already he has placed that peer of killers, Heinrich Himmler of the Gestapo, in direct control of all key army positions. There is no trust among criminals, especially when their evil plans are going awry.

Additional tanks and troops have been sent to the Relocation Center for disloyal Japs at Tule Lake, it was revealed today. It was also reported that the troops had to fire some shots to quell the riotous Nipponese. Investigation also disclosed that the Japs had previously seized over 1,000 knives from the camp commissary and had utilized the camp's emery wheels to sharpen them. The mailed fist rather than the gloved hand is necessary to handle such treacherous rats.

Tuesday, November 9, 1943: —United States forces are gaining the ascendancy in the South Pacific fighting, according to a statement made today by Secretary of the Navy Frank Knox. He said that the Japanese position in the Northern Solomons is becoming very critical and their main base of Rabaul is already all but untenable. The American Marines who landed on Bougainville Island have firmly established their beachhead and are getting organized to mop up the island. Air attacks by large forces of Allied bombers and several successful engagements by our surface fleet have caused severe attrition in the enemy's air and naval strength in the area. It is believed that Rabaul will fall into our hands before many more weeks have elapsed.

From other fronts the news is just as favorable to the Allied Nations. In Russia, the victorious Soviet troops are pressing their advantage, allowing the harried Nazis no time to regroup or rally. In some places the Red Army has driven to within 20 miles of the old Polish border and on the central sector is nearing the boundary of Latvia.

In Italy the Anglo-American drive on Rome continues its advance. More than one third of all Italy has now been cleared of Germans which is no mean accomplishment in the short time since the original landings were made. It is admitted, however, that the sternest part of the task lies ahead.

Prime Minister Churchill, in a speech today, reported that the Allies have broken the back of the Nazi submarine warfare by sinking another 60 German U-boats during the last three months, and that this blow, together with those dealt in the air over German cities and on the Russian and Italian fronts may well prove to be mortal blows to Germany.

Wednesday, November 10, 1943: —Some of our losses in the savage sea battles of recent date were announced today. Two destroyers, the 1500 ton Henley and the 2100 ton Chevalier, were lost in action against the Japanese in the battle off Bougainville Island. A third destroyer was lost in battle against Nazi submarines in the North Atlantic. The latter vessel was the 1190 ton Borie, of World War I vintage, which went to the bottom after sinking two U-boats in a furious battle with a wolf pack in the Atlantic shipping lanes. The fate of the ships' crews was not revealed.

President Roosevelt has ordered the Federal Bureau of Investigation to make a thorough inquiry into the Tule Lake disturbances. Conduct of the War Relocation Authority in handling the situation will be thoroughly investigated and prosecutive action taken if any illegal proceedings are discovered. It is feared that the investigation will raise quite an odor.

U.S. Marines on Bougainville Island are said to be locked in a sanguinary battle with defending Japanese forces reminiscent of the early days of Guadalcanal. Today is the 168th anniversary of the founding of the U.S. Marine Corps and it finds them, as so many times in the past, engaged in battle to defend their homes and country. That defense is in good hands.

513

The European air war today found American Flying Fortresses and Liberators smashing at Nazi war plants in Genoa and Turin, Italy. Steel works and ball-bearing plants were the principal targets.

Thursday, November 11, 1943: —Armistice Day! Twenty five years ago the "War to End Wars" came to an end. It was a glorious victory but because of the Allies failure to follow it up with a sound, workable peace, it soon became a hollow farce, in truth nothing but a temporary armistice during which time the gangster nations could regroup their forces and again strike bloodily for world domination. We are now engaged in a gigantic struggle that dwarfs its counter-part of a quarter century ago, brought about by the failure of yesterday's leaders to build a durable society out of the wreckage of a war-torn world. That should be an unforgettable object lesson in the happenings of twenty five years ago.

A report reminiscent of the last days of the Kaiser's regime comes out of Germany via neutral sources today. The report tells of a battle between regular German army units and Hitler's Elite SS Guardsmen in which more than 500 soldiers were killed. The rebellion was precipitated by the regular army troops' mutiny against orders to go to the Russian front. You will remember that the Kaiser's downfall was speeded by U-boat crews' refusal to man the undersea boats during the last few months of World War I.

In the South Pacific a furious battle is raging for control of Bougainville Island. U.S. Marines have succeeded in strengthening their beachhead and regular Army reinforcements have been landed. According to General MacArthur's communiqués the situation is indeed "well in hand."

Friday, November 12, 1943: —Home front news holds the spotlight today. The Office of Price Administration has begun to crack down on unwarranted price gouging by cafes and restaurants. Food prices and liquor prices were the main targets of the Government agency. In some places the quality of meals has decreased while the price has been boosted as much as 100%. The price of alcoholic drinks has almost reached the fantastic and outrageous heights of prohibition days and many aspects of that racketeering era have returned to the picture today. Hijackers

514

and extortionists are back on the job while illegal selling and bootlegging are once again profitable vocations. A pint of whiskey sometimes brings as high as $8.50 these days and they say some of the stuff is the same old "rot-gut" that was sold before repeal.

There is nothing very exciting to report from the battlefronts tonight. In Russia the Red Army is still crunching forward over the shattered wreckage of Germany's once all powerful eastern armies. The borders of Poland and Rumania loom ahead to inspire the Soviet troops to greater efforts. Panic is reported to be breaking out in Rumania as the populace prepares to flee from the path of the avenging Russian hordes. Already the roads are jammed with peasants from the eastern Rumanian border and their presence is hindering the movements of Nazi reinforcements moving up to the front.

Winter is settling down over the Italian front, slowing the Allied advance in seas of mud and slush. The going is hard, the resistance fierce, and Rome is still a long ways away.

Saturday, November 13, 1943: —General MacArthur's headquarters has just announced the greatest raid yet carried out against the Japanese base at Rabaul, on New Britain. The attack was a Navy show, the planes being launched from a carrier task force that steamed to within 200 miles of the enemy base. Navy dive-bombers and torpedo planes made a shambles of Rabaul Harbor. Reconnaissance planes reported that the whole enemy base was "one hell of a mess." "There were ships down by the stern, ships down by the bow, oil slicks all over the place and great clouds of smoke pierced by jets of flame," reported one returning pilot. At least one enemy heavy cruiser and two destroyers were sunk, 12 other enemy warships badly damaged and 64 intercepting planes shot down by the rampaging American flyers in what is believed to be one of the most successful raids ever staged. General MacArthur believes it removes the Japanese naval threat in the Solomons. Nice going, Navy!

On the home front the manpower situation has reached such serious straits that the War Manpower Commission has decided on a drastic move. Effective at midnight next Monday a sweeping new "job freeze" will go into effect in the Bay Area. The exact effect of the new order is not entirely clear but it appears that a ceiling has been put on the number of new employees a business can hire and replacements will have to be made with a greater proportion of women. No one can leave his position without a War Manpower Clearance and Specific Referral. There's no excuse for not having a job in these times.

Sunday, November 14, 1943: —Here's how the headlines of a daily paper run these days:

RABAUL EPIC—JAP SHIPS ROLLED TO THEIR DEATH, ZEROS CRASHED!

ALL BAY AREA JOBS ARE FROZEN. Drastic Rationing of Workers Will Go in Effect at Midnight; Personnel Increases Banned.

TULE LAKE TROUBLE. Army Clamps Martial Law on Japanese Camp.

GAINS IN SOLOMONS. Yanks Extend Beachhead on Bougainville.

WAR IN RUSSIA AND AEGEAN. Red Army Splits Whole Front As It Overruns Vital Zhitomir; Nazis Hold Footing on Leros.

FIFTH ARMY SLUGS ON IN SEESAW FIGHT.

It is plain to see from the above that there isn't much room for anything other than war news. If it's not about the war it's not news these days. There are still some sports on the inside pages but most of the big events are between Service teams. Horse racing still gets some play and the bowling leagues are going full blast. Golf and tennis are just about out of the picture and football is having a tough season. The future of baseball is uncertain. America, despite all the critics' claims that she doesn't yet know she's in a war, has undergone a tremendous transformation since that eon of less than two years ago when the vicious little Orientals attacked Pearl Harbor. The cherished American way of life has been largely set aside for the duration and Hitler and Tojo, as did Mussolini, are finding out that America has really gone to war.

Monday, November 15, 1943: —Repercussions are already being felt from the War Manpower Commission's job freezing order. Employers seem to be badly confused and even the Commission itself, it would appear, is not exactly certain on what is expected. The whole solution to the manpower problem in this Area must be the finding of 50,000 more women workers. Where they will come from no one knows but until they are found there will be no remedy for the present shortage. An all out recruiting program to secure the women will soon be going full blast. Women, God bless them, how we need them—especially now.

Bulgaria, the little Balkan nation that had the temerity to declare war on the United States, felt the wrath of our bombers for the first time today. A big fleet of twin-engined Mitchells, escorted by long-range Lightning fighters, smashed key railroad installations and other military target in Sofia, the Bulgarian capital. Great pillars of smoke and flame rising from the demolished objectives left no doubt that our calling card had been received and contents noted.

In fighting even more ferocious that Guadalcanal, U.S. Marines have successfully widened and consolidated their beachhead on Bougainville Island in the Solomons. Through jungle mud and swamp, insect and fever ridden, American fighting men have once again beaten the Jap at his favorite game. Superior equipment, American ingenuity, and just plain, raw courage and fighting spirit have again carried our men through to victory on the shores of Bougainville.

Tuesday, November 16, 1943: —The war was carried to the enemy on all fronts by American airmen today. Large formations of Flying Fortresses and Liberators raided Nazi military objectives in Norway. The actual identity of the targets has not yet been revealed but results were reported "excellent." This raid should gray another hair on Hitler's head as it may be the forerunner of an invasion of the European Continent through Norway. Der Fuhrer must frantically prepare to meet the Allied armies at any of a hundred potential invasion points. He must try to be strong everywhere, which probably makes him relatively weak everywhere. The time approaches.

In the Pacific, American land-based bombers raided Japanese positions in the Marshall Islands for the first time. Previously the Islands have been attacked by carrier-borne planes but apparently we have now seized bases close enough to launch land planes. The tempo and size of future raids should increase proportionately.

On the home front we find the father draft receiving some more Congressional attention. House and Senate conferees have agreed on legislation, which, if approved, will place pre-Pearl-Harbor fathers at the bottom of the draft pool. There have been many arguments in Congress over the advisability of breaking up families to draft fathers and the consensus of opinion seems to agree that every other alternative should be fully exploited before taking the dads.

Interesting note: OPA announces that a cut in egg prices is due within a week. It's about time, 73 cents a dozen is too much for our pocketbook.

Wednesday, November 17, 1943: —Information has come through Swiss sources to the effect that the Italians have organized an army of 16,000 guerilla fighters in northern Italy and have engaged the Germans in a full-scale battle in the Como area. The guerillas are based in the almost inaccessible Spluga Mountains, from which they sally forth to attack Nazi and Fascist forces. Sabotage and resistance is said to be spreading over all of northern Italy and the German position there is none too secure, safe only as long as they are able to maintain overwhelming force. Allied war prisoners, freed by the Italians, were reported to be aiding the guerillas.

The U.S. Air Force today added more mystery to the burning question of where the Allies will strike at Hitler's fortress by attacking airfields in southern France. German-held airdromes in the Marseille area were blasted by Flying Fortresses while other planes raided objectives for a hundred miles along the coastline. This raid and the one on Norway yesterday, which blasted power stations and Molybdenum mines, should make Der Fuhrer's guessing contest very interesting. As the zero hour for invasion nears, the Germans must be nearly frantic to know where the major blow will strike.

We must concede one small victory to the Nazis today. The Allied garrison on Leros Island in the Dodecanese group has surrendered to an overwhelming German invasion force. About 8,000 British troops were involved and heavy losses were inflicted on the foe before they capitulated.

Thursday, November 18, 1943: —For the fourth straight day large squadrons of U.S. Flying Fortresses and Liberators have plastered Japanese outposts in the Marshall and Gilbert Islands. Principal target today was the enemy airfield on Tarawa Atoll in the Gilberts. Hits were scored on hangars, shops and supply dumps. The regularity of the daily raids on the Japanese Central Pacific strongholds hints at early offensive action by American amphibious forces bent on retracing the devious trail to the Philippines and Tokyo.

Across the world other United States airmen spent another day blasting Nazi objectives in Western Europe. Norway was the target for another attack by Fortresses and Liberators which flew unescorted to smash a Nazi airdrome, eleven miles northeast of Oslo. Nine of the heavy bombers are missing.

Meanwhile, the RAF was busy making its 60th raid of the war on the sprawling chemical center of Ludwigshafen, home of the huge I.G. Farbenindustrie Radische Anilinwerke plant, largest chemical factory in Germany. Most of the great works now lies in ruins.

In Italy the Allied armies sloshed ahead two miles despite icy winds and seas of mud and slush that made the use of motorized equipment almost impossible. The American Fifth Army was further hampered by streams swollen to flood stage by ceaseless rains. Pity the poor foot soldier.

In Russia the Red steamroller has smashed German resistance almost to the old Polish border. From now on the Russians' problems of supplies and communications should slow their drive.

Friday, November 19, 1943: —The Royal Air Force punished Berlin with its biggest raid of the war last night. The German capital was rocked with 350 two-ton blockbusters as well as thousands of lighter missiles. The havoc created can be imagined when you realize that one blockbuster can level entire sections of a city. Several hundred other RAF planes made a diversionary raid on Ludwigshafen to raise the total of British bombers over the Reich last night to more than 1,000.

Returning airmen claimed the Berlin raid was the most successful to date. Great fires were started and violent eruptions were seen as the huge bombs detonated. The German radio howled and whined, "Terror raid." Yes, there can be no doubt about that. Air raids are terrible. You should have remembered that three years ago when your super race was gleefully striking terror into the hearts of Warsaw, Rotterdam, London and Coventry. You forgot that two can play at the same game. Now it's your turn—and in double measure as punishment for your hideous crimes.

U.S. planes again hit Japanese outposts in the Marshall and Gilbert Islands today, keeping up their most persistent aerial offensive of the Pacific war. Jap installations were heavily hit.

In the Southwest Pacific area, American warships bombarded Japanese positions on Buka Island while our troops on Bougainville scored new gains in fierce fighting that sent 500 more Nipponese to join their ancestors.

Saturday, November 20, 1943: —Germany was scourged again last night as the RAF and the United States Eighth Air Force maintained a three night and two day aerial offensive that sent 5,000 tons of high explosives crashing into vital areas of the Reich. This was at the rate of more than 100 tons per hour for the three nights and two days and reached in 50 hours two thirds of the 7,500 tons dropped on England during the entire 11 month "blitz" of 1940-41. Last night's target was Cologne and particularly a chemical plant in the city's outskirts, which was believed to be completely knocked out.

American carrier based planes joined in the nonstop aerial offensive against Japan's mid-Pacific outposts in the Marshall and Gilbert Islands. Something is certainly cooking in that area as the attacks continued into the seventh day. 90 tons of bombs were dumped on Betio Island in the Tarawa Atoll.

Old familiar names came back into the Pacific war news today, showing that we are on the way back. A large force of American heavy bombers raided the former Dutch naval base of Soerabaja on Java in the Dutch East Indies. Remember the dark days of 1941 and early 1942 when the rampaging Japs smashed their way against inadequate resistance to capture that rich area. The tide of war is once again nearing those shores going the other way this time.

A little note on the home front: Restrictions on men's clothing will soon be lifted. There'll be cuffs on the trousers and vests with double breasted suits again.

Sunday, November 21, 1943: —United States forces have launched a great new offensive in the Pacific! Amphibious Marine and Army troops have invaded Tarawa and Makin Islands, two of Japan's many strongholds in the Marshall and Gilbert group of mid-Pacific islands. The attacks were preceded by furious air assaults and a heavy barrage laid down by U.S. warships. The beachheads were secured despite tough resistance from the defending Jap forces, particularly on Tarawa Island. Fighting continues.

In Russia, the Red Army is finding tougher going although still retaining the initiative. Lengthening of communication lines as well as fatigue after months of furious fighting have combined to reduce the momentum of the Russian drive which has virtually ceased, at least until fresh reserves and more supplies can be brought up from the rear.

The going is slow in Italy also. Heavy rains and bitterly cold nights have hindered the advance of the two Allied armies under Generals Clark and Montgomery, although both forces have inched forward inexorably. Montgomery's Eighth Army succeeded in capturing four key Italian towns, including Agnone, which wiped out an eight mile salient which the Germans had maintained in the center of the line. General Clark's Fifth Army slogged ahead three miles in the upper Volturno area, despite weather so bad that all aerial support was grounded.

Monday, November 22, 1943: —The surprise American offensive against Japan's mid-Pacific island strongholds is making headway, we are told tonight. Enemy resistance on Makin and Tarawa Atolls in the Gilbert group has almost ceased. The Marines and Doughboys are mopping up the last Jap survivors among their smashed and blasted coral dugouts. Unofficial reports indicated that the American invaders have made similar landings on other islands in the Marshall and Gilbert chain. Powerful units of the United States Navy are supporting the action and it is possible that the main Japanese fleet may be lured into a decisive battle. Our fleet is prepared and anxious to bring the Japs to bay.

Bitter jungle fighting is reported raging in New Guinea as Australian troops close in on the Japanese base at Stelberg, 10 miles north of the recently captured stronghold of Finschhafen. General MacArthur's Headquarters stated that the Japs are strongly entrenched but are being dug out by tanks and artillery as well as infantry. Allied planes have won superiority in the air above the battleground and are supporting our troops effectively.

Persons in the news: Tonight's papers state that Primo Carnera, the 260 pound boxing freak who won the world's heavyweight title a few years ago has been captured as a guerrilla fighter in northern Italy. The Nazis will probably execute him as a traitor in accord with their customary practice.

A dispatch from Nazi-occupied Italy claims that one of President Roosevelt's sons has been shot down in a bombing mission over Germany and has been taken prisoner by the Nazis. The truth of the story has not been verified and some London observers believe the Nazis refer to Ambassador John G. Winant's son who is known to be a prisoner of the Germans. John G. Winant is our present ambassador to Great Britain.

Tuesday, November 23, 1943: —The mightiest air raid of the war seared and smashed Berlin last night in a cataclysmic horror that one observer claimed was a real "twilight of the Gods." 2,500 tons of high explosives cascaded into the German capital from more than 1,000 heavy RAF bombers. The German defenses were completely smothered in what proved to be the easiest and most effective raid of the war on the Nazi capital. Only 26 bombers out of the huge fleet of attacking planes were lost.

Only those people who went through the terrible bombings of Warsaw, Rotterdam, Coventry, and other English cities can even imagine the destruction and terror heaped upon the hapless German capital in one short half hour last night. Can anyone imagine the homeless, the maimed, and the dead? If it were not an inevitable "fight fire with fire" proposition, brought on by their own acts, one could almost feel sorry for the German people who must stand such punishment. And then we remember that they would take a vicious delight in doing the same thing to us—if they could.

Makin, the tiny coral atoll in Gilberts is ours tonight. American Doughboys have mopped up the remnants of the Jap defenders and Old Glory now flies triumphantly over the island. Nearby Tarawa is rapidly being cleaned out by the U.S. Marines, although fighting has been fierce among the coral pillboxes of that island. Eighty miles further south, a third beachhead is being consolidated in the Abemama Atoll group.

Wednesday, November 24, 1943: —Berlin is being handed the worst punishment any city has ever had to endure in the history of the world. Another mighty fleet of British and Canadian bombers plastered the city with 1,500 additional tons of bombs last night, dropping their deadly eggs into the heart of the German capital still burning fiercely from the previous night's record raid. Escaping refugees in neutral Sweden said the devastation is beyond the imagination of man. More than 400,000 people have been rendered homeless and 25,000 deaths have been tabulated so far. The city that Herman Goering claimed could never be bombed now has the appearance of a battlefield. Not a street has escaped the devastation of the "blockbusters." Vast areas of the city are leveled and a few more attacks will reduce the Capital to the status of Hamburg. The heart of Nazidom has been marked for destruction.

United States forces have seized a firm grip on the Gilbert Islands in mid-Pacific. Tarawa has been fully occupied and there can no longer be any doubt but that the Gilberts are ours. It is the belief of military observers that our success in the Gilberts will force the Japanese to abandon the Marshalls as well.

The only bad news of the week so far has been the report of an unfortunate incident involving a high officer of the U.S. Army. In a fit of rage, Lieut. General George Patton, the brilliant commander of the U.S. Seventh Army that took Sicily, struck a shell-shocked American soldier in a field hospital. General Eisenhower immediately ordered General Patton to apologize to all the men in his divisions upon pain of losing his command. Disclosure of the incident, however, is having serious repercussions in this country, and leaves a bad taste in the mouths of relatives of boys in the armed forces. An investigation is under way.

Thursday, November 25, 1943: —THANKSGIVING DAY, 1943. A warrior nation paused momentarily today in the prosecution of its greatest war to give thanks. Some people might say, "Give thanks for what? Thanks for the privilege of sending our boys out to be slaughtered? Thanks for the opportunity of cascading thousands of tons of death and destruction upon an enemy population? Thanks for the shortages and discomforts of war? Thanks for the taxes, the debts, the long hours of work? Thanks for the separations from loved ones, the bitter tears from a War Department telegram, the sight of a maimed or blinded hero? Why give thanks? Why, indeed?"

I'll tell you why. Give thanks for the sturdy generation of young men and women who are winning this war for us; the same young men and women for whose worth of character some graybeards used to express such grave doubts. Give thanks that by their courage and efforts the flame of war has been turned from our shores, our homes and children spared the horrors experienced in other lands. Give thanks that in so short a time we have transformed our great peaceful country into the mightiest warrior nation in history; that in so doing we have not lost sight of our ideals of peace and goodwill to all mankind. Give thanks that the great mass of our citizens are Americans all, working unselfishly for the common good; that the chiseler, the profiteer, the black market operator, the traitor is still far in the minority. Lastly, give thanks for America itself, that great, good land which gave birth to freedom and is worthy of every drop of fine, young blood shed in her defense. Fighting men of America! Your land is worthy of you, you are worthy of your land!

Friday, November 26, 1943: —Berlin took it again last night and apparently is being hit again tonight. Obviously the British have embarked upon an aerial offensive aimed at obliterating the German capital. According to Air Marshal Sir Arthur T. Harris, Berlin will be pounded unceasingly until "the heart of Nazidom ceases to beat." Other mighty four-motored bombers smashed at Frankfurt, sending great columns of smoke and flame curling upward from the stricken city. American bombers from the Eighth Air Force carried on the round-the-clock offensive by striking at Reich targets during the daylight hours.

The Russians have won another outstanding victory on the central front. Gomel, the last heavily defended German bastion on the east bank of the Dnieper River, was evacuated today by the Nazis in the face of powerful Soviet forces that had nearly surrounded the city. The defeat unhinged the entire southern end of Hitler's defense line in White Russia, and sent Soviet troops racing forward along a 70 mile front.

American undersea raiders have reported back from their newest sorties into Japanese waters. Nine more enemy vessels were added to their impressive list of victories. The latest bag included seven freighters, one transport and a tanker. The silent service is contributing much to the inevitable triumph over our little oriental "friends."

Tokyo today reported that Allied planes from China raided Formosa by daylight today. Coming pretty close to home, eh, Tojo?

Saturday, November 27, 1943: —Details of the successful U.S. Marine landings on the Gilbert Islands were released today. The capture of Tarawa came only after the bloodiest, most ferocious fighting in Marine history. Participating troops, veterans of previous encounters with the Japs, said that Guadalcanal was tough but it was nothing compared to Tarawa. Hundreds of Japs threw themselves at the Leathernecks in suicide attacks that ended only after fierce hand to hand fighting in which every Jap was killed. Our own losses were greater than any previous operation against the enemy's island strongholds. Hundreds of gallant Marines made the supreme sacrifice.

A war of nerves is on in Europe. Rumors and unofficial reports hint that developments of the most sensational character are about to "break" in the war against Hitler. The developments are said to be of such momentous nature that they will affect every theater of war and will have a tremendous impact on both Germany and Japan. We can only guess that the development may be Turkey's entry into the war, the meeting between Roosevelt, Churchill, and Stalin, or even a precipitate surrender by Germany after the manner of Italy. Anyway, we can hardly wait.

Very meager reports have come from the Italian front recently. Winter weather and swollen streams have combined to practically stagnate the battle line. Lately, however, the British Eighth Army, on the Adriatic side of the peninsula, has come to life and has started a powerful offensive in the Sangro River area. Considerable progress was made today and Rome may yet fall before the winter is over.

Sunday, November 28, 1943: —The German capital was the target for another furious aerial bombardment last night. It was the fifth major raid on Berlin in almost as many nights and brought the total tonnage of bombs dropped on the capital this year to 14,000 long tons. This is compared with the 10,000 tons required to destroy Hamburg. Last night's raid was a joint operation, with another large force attacking Stuttgart, 300 miles to the southwest. Thirty two planes failed to return.

Despite hideous weather, the veteran British Eighth Army has launched a major offensive against the Nazis' winter line in Italy and is making considerable headway. A firm bridgehead was established across the swollen Sangro River in the face of desperate German resistance. The Tommies' advance was preceded by a concentrated artillery barrage for which the Eighth is famous.

Across the Italian peninsula, the American Fifth Army under General Clark was fully engaged in beating off two fierce counter-attacks against their commanding positions in the mountains west of Venafro.

In Russia, the Red Army is following up its smashing victory at Gomel, by striking out with steel tipped columns in an effort to ensnare and destroy as many units of the demoralized enemy as possible. One armored column spearheaded a drive that outflanked the important German base at Zhlobin, 50 miles northwest of captured Gomel. With the fall of the latter city, the invaders' Dnieper River line was finally and completely smashed. This was the line to which Hitler boastfully referred when he announced recently, "I am here, and here I intend to remain."

Monday, November 29, 1943: —The war of nerves is on full blast against the Axis. The whole world is seething with portent of momentous events to come. Apparently it all stems from the anticipated meeting between the "Big Three," President Roosevelt, Prime Minister Churchill, and Premier Stalin. Possibly it may be the "Big Four" which includes Generalissimo Chiang Kai-shek of China. It was reliably reported today that the President and Winston Churchill have been in Cairo, Egypt for several days, awaiting the arrival of Josef Stalin and the Chinese leader.

A successful meeting between the "Big Three" or "Big Four" would indeed be momentous. It would undoubtedly mean the final shaping of plans for the grand assault on Hitler's European fortress from three sides and would pave the way for post-war collaboration between the four great powers. Chiang Kai-shek's appearance would also mean the shaping of grand strategy against Japan. The impact of the meeting on the enemy nations would be staggering and the effect on the few remaining neutral countries would be far-reaching. Let us fervently hope that the conference is successfully consummated.

Meanwhile, activity on all war fronts mounted in fury. American bombers based in England struck heavily at northern Germany, flying through icing conditions at temperatures as low as 58 degrees below zero. American Marines on the other hand, fought furiously in the tropical heat of Bougainville Island to add another 1,000 dead Japs to the list of enemy losses on that island. Other Americans and their British comrades surged forward against the Nazis' winter line in Italy, gaining considerable ground in their "Big Push" aimed at liberating Rome this winter. In Russia, the beaten Nazis were still in full flight from the rampaging Soviets pouring through the Gomel gap.

Tuesday, November 30, 1943: —President Roosevelt, Prime Minister Churchill, and Generalissimo Chiang Kai-shek have just concluded a lengthy conference in Cairo. One of the meetings was held in the shadow of the ancient Pyramids which have seen history made so many times in the past. The details of the conference or the results of the three statesmen's conversations have not yet been announced but it is obvious that the conduct of the war against Japan was the main topic. This also explains why Premier Stalin did not join in the Cairo talks since Russia is not officially at war with the Japanese. Full details of the Cairo conference will be released sometime this week.

Late dispatches reveal that the President and Churchill have left Cairo for an unknown destination where they will engage in the long-awaited and eagerly anticipated conference with the Russian dictator. The eyes and ears of the world are upon them.

In Italy, the British Eighth Army smashed a four mile salient into the Nazis' winter line near the Adriatic coast. The advance came after a furious 36-hour battle preceded by a tremendous artillery barrage that pulverized the enemy's fortifications. Some of the German prisoners taken were literally "bomb happy" from the savage shelling.

Indications that the Red Army has extended itself too far in the Kiev salient were shown in the abandonment by the Russians of Korosten, 45 miles from Zhitomir, under pressure from powerful German counter-attacks. There's plenty of fight left in Hitler's retreating legions.

December

Wednesday, December 1, 1943: —The results of the British-American-Chinese conference just concluded were announced today. President Roosevelt, Prime Minister Churchill, and Generalissimo Chiang Kai-shek, together with their military advisers were said to have agreed on future military operations against Japan. The three great powers will bring increasing pressure to bear against the aggressor, Japan, and have determined to punish her for her violence and greed. They covet no territorial gains for themselves but have decided to strip Japan of all the islands in the Pacific which she has seized or occupied since the beginning of the First World War in 1914 and to return to China all the territories stolen by Japan, including Manchuria, Formosa, and the Pescadores. Japan is to be expelled from all other countries she has occupied by violence, and Korea will in due time receive its independence. Unconditional surrender will be the only terms under which Japan can obtain peace.

Announcement of these war aims and the knowledge that she will be left little more than her original islands, if she is defeated, will undoubtedly cause Japan to fight harder if possible, and to the death surely. There can be no doubt but that the Pacific war will be deadly and long drawn out. We must steel ourselves for heavy losses.

A great array of Allied leaders were present at the conference. General Douglas MacArthur and Admiral Chester Nimitz were the only major military commanders whose duties prevented them from attending.

Thursday, December 2, 1943: —The Navy announced the loss of two valuable vessels in action against the Japanese. The famous U.S. submarine, the Wahoo, and her four-time decorated skipper, Commander Dudley W. Morton, were presumed lost in the far Pacific. Sixty five crew members were aboard. The Wahoo was one of the most famous American subs, having received a Presidential citation for destroying an entire Japanese convoy in an epic 14-hour battle. Her loss will be keenly felt.

Also lost was the aircraft carrier, Liscome Bay, sunk by Jap torpedoes in the Gilberts campaign. The Liscome Bay was a new type escort carrier and details of her construction were not released. Captain Irving D. Wiltsie, of New York City, and Rear Admiral Henry M. Mullinix were reported missing when the carrier went down.

The "Big Three," President Roosevelt, Prime Minister Churchill, and Premier Josef Stalin have met at last. The three leaders are conferring in Teheran, where it is reported unofficially, they will issue a final ultimatum to Germany to surrender or be destroyed. Results of this meeting will be more far-reaching than the one just concluded between Roosevelt, Churchill, and Chiang Kai-shek.

The British Eighth Army and the American Fifth have scored another decisive victory over the Germans. The Nazis, losers in a bitter four-day battle, are in full retreat from their vaunted winter line in Italy. Bad weather hampered the attack but it appears likely that the Allies are really on their way to Rome.

Friday, December 3, 1943: —Berlin took another smashing assault last night. Hundreds of mighty RAF Lancaster and Halifax bombers dumped another 1,680 tons of high explosives on the hapless city, bringing the total tonnage of bombs dropped on the capital this year to 16,000. The attack was centered on new areas of Berlin not previously devastated in earlier raids. Great new fires were kindled and many important power stations and industrial plants reduced to rubble. British losses were heavier than in earlier attacks, forty one of the mighty bombers failing to return. Clouds of German night fighters and hundreds of anti-aircraft guns that threw up a curtain of steel were responsible for the increased toll.

Stalin, Churchill, and Roosevelt are still in conference. Tonight's papers state the meeting is taking place at Tabriz, Iran which is 350 miles northwest of Teheran. Some observers believe that Russia will agree at this conference to permit the Anglo-American air fleets to establish bases in Russia from which Germany can be blasted into submission by shuttle bombing. Such bases will carry additional weight to the expected appeal to the German people to oust the Nazis and save their country from total destruction.

The Anglo-American offensive in Italy is making headway. General Clark's Fifth Army has joined the British Eighth Army in smashing through the heavily defended Nazi winter line blocking the road to Rome. Heavy concentrations of artillery and superiority in the air were largely responsible for the successful breakthrough.

Saturday, December 4, 1943: —Another mighty fleet of RAF bombers last night feinted toward Berlin, then sidestepped and drove home a smashing blow against the industrial city of Leipzig, eighty miles away. It was a brilliantly executed piece of deception and threw the German defenses into confusion from which they did not emerge until the raid was over. The strategy cut British losses to 23 planes as against 41 for the previous night's straight attack on the German capital. The majority of the Nazis' night fighters were left buzzing the air over Berlin with nothing to shoot at but the stars.

The conference of the "Big Three" has been concluded according to the evening papers. The Prime Minister, the President, and the Premier met in Teheran rather than at Tabriz as reported yesterday. The parley has been held in absolute secrecy and details of the sensational event will not be available for several days. Speculation and rumor have conjured all manner of world-shaking decisions to come from the first meeting of the three men upon whose shoulders rests the fate of the entire world. Agreement or disagreement at this conference will do much to shape the course of the war and the peace to follow.

The Allied drive in Italy is gaining momentum. General Clark's American Fifth Army smashed forward another six miles after a concentrated artillery barrage that left the Germans huddled wide-eyed and frightened in their dugouts. Hundreds were taken prisoner in a dazed and helpless condition.

Sunday, December 5, 1943:—An official announcement of the results of the Teheran conference between President Roosevelt, Prime Minister Churchill, and Premier Stalin will be released tomorrow morning. Meanwhile it is reported that President Roosevelt and Mr. Churchill are returning to Cairo where they will confer with President Ismet Inonu of Turkey. It is anticipated that Turkey will soon abandon her neutral status and enter the war on the side of the Allies. President Inonu's meeting with the two Allied leaders is expected to speed the day of Turkey's participation.

As Premier Stalin returned to Moscow from his historic meeting in Teheran, his troops swept forward in the Gomel sector, pursuing the beaten Nazis to within eight miles of Zhlobin, strategic railway junction in White Russia. Great quantities of booty were taken by the Soviets as their offensive began to roll again despite miserable weather conditions.

In Italy, the Allied armies are still inching forward. The advance is very slow, hampered by winter weather and the fiercest kind of resistance from the Germans. The fighting appears to resemble some of the ferocious and bloody fighting in France during 1918 in which massed artillery blasts a path for waves of foot sloggers advancing against strongly fortified entrenchments. Such advances are bound to be costly.

An interesting item of news today was the declaration of war against the Axis by Bolivia, brought about by German submarine attacks against vessels flying the flag of the South American Republic.

Monday, December 6, 1943: —The results of the Teheran conference were announced today. Details were lacking, however, and the decisions reached by the "Big Three" were announced only in broad terms. Five specific statements were embodied in their joint declaration:

1. "We have reached complete understanding as to the scope and timing of operations which will be undertaken from the east, west, and south."

2. "No power on earth can prevent our destroying the German Armies by land, their U-boasts by sea, and their war plants from the air. Our attacks will be relentless and increasing."

3. "We recognize fully the responsibility resting upon us and all the United Nations to make a peace which will command good will from the overwhelming masses of the peoples of the world and banish the scourge and terror of war for many generations."

4. "We will welcome ... as they may choose to come into the world family of democratic nations . . . all nations, large and small, whose peoples in heart and mind are dedicated, as are our own peoples, to the elimination of tyranny and slavery, oppression and intolerance."

5. "We came here with hope and determination. We leave here friends in fact, in spirit and in purpose."

It is believed that "inside" results of the conference will speed the opening of second fronts in France and the low countries and also in the Balkans. Hitler and his satellite countries will soon be faced with a three-way "nutcracker" squeeze play, designed to crush them once and for all.

Tuesday, December 7, 1943: —REMEMBER PEARL HARBOR? Yes, we still remember that day of infamy, two years ago, when our treacherous oriental enemies struck their first vicious blow at our peaceful island base, thus precipitating the world into the greatest blood bath in history. Pearl Harbor, stirring peacefully and unaware in the light of an early Sunday morning, was suddenly turned into a holocaust of flames and destruction by a dastardly attack from scores of death dealing aircraft launched without warning from carriers belonging to a nation with whom we were at peace and with whom we were at that moment negotiating in Washington. No, we will not forget—nor will the Japanese forget. There will be too many remembrances delivered their way.

We have come over a long, hard trail these last two years. But we have accomplished much. We have come from the brink of disaster to a position where we can see the first glimmer of victory ahead. The Japs were stopped short of their goal by the blood and sinews of our fighting men. Slowly but inevitably the tide has turned until we now are beginning our counter-drive that will eventually bring the little yellow men to their Japa-knees. In the long history of Japan, the unprovoked attack on Pearl Harbor will be rated as their greatest and most fatal mistake.

Rest easy, you heroic dead of Pearl Harbor. You shall be revenged. We have not forgotten!

Wednesday, December 8, 1943: —As we go into our third year of war let us summarize the situation on the battlefields and on the home front.

From the desperate position of December 8 two years ago, in which only the hand of Providence saved us from actual invasion and probable defeat, we have come to the point now where victory seems certain albeit bloody and expensive. Our

Navy has fully recovered from the paralyzing blow dealt it at Pearl Harbor and has covered itself with glory by stopping the Jap Navy cold and slugging out many sensational victories over the best the enemy could offer. The fleet is now stronger than ever before and is constantly adding new striking power to its formidable battle line. Its one big hope is to bring the Japanese Grand Fleet to bay.

On land our forces are gaining experience and striking power. U.S. Marines, through bloody lessons, have mastered the art of amphibious warfare, and can be counted on to beat the Jap at his own game wherever they may meet him. In Tunisia, Sicily, and Italy American Doughboys have proved their mettle as fighting men. In the air our flyers are unexcelled and are daily exacting a bitter toll from the enemy. Uncle Sam is fast attaining his full stature as a Man of War.

Unglorified as it has been, much of the credit for the turning of the tide must go to the almost unbelievable accomplishments of the American people on the home front. We have bickered, argued, and complained, but we have produced. American production, in the last analysis has been the weight that has tipped the scales in favor of the Allies. Ask Stalin, he knows; ask Churchill, he knows; but above all ask Hitler and Hirohito, they also know.

Thursday, December 9, 1943: —Last night and today the Bay Area has been lashed with one of the most furious wind storms in history. Seventy mile an hour gales ripped over the area, uprooting trees, shattering window, and sinking several small vessels anchored in the Bay. Damage to property mounted into millions as the elements vented their wrath upon the fragile dwellings of man. Fences toppled, power lines went down, throwing the area into darkness broken only by numerous fires that raged fiercely beyond the control of desperately battling firemen. I shaved by candlelight as the wind whistled shrilly through the cracks. Nature seemed angry and man seemed weak.

Back on the war news, we find that naval activity in the Pacific is confined almost exclusively to our fleet. The Japanese Navy seems to be holed up and unwilling to accept the challenge to a finish fight. They do not even venture forth to protect their own bases. A powerful task force of American warships and carriers boldly steamed up, bombarded the strong Jap base on Nauru Island yesterday and escaped, unmolested by the vaunted Japanese Imperial Navy.

In New Guinea, Australian troops have scored another triumph, hacking their way in to capture the Japanese stronghold of Wareo, twelve miles northwest of the previously captured base at Finschhafen.

Today's bad news: One of our most famous flying aces, Lieutenant Commander Edward H. (Butch) O'Hare, winner of the Congressional Medal of Honor in the Coral Sea Battle, is reported "missing in action" off the Gilbert Islands.

Friday, December 10, 1943: —The Allied war of nerves against Germany and her satellite partners is reaping results in Bulgaria it was reported tonight. In addition to the war of nerves, Allied planes, presumably American, added a touch of real war by bombing the Bulgarian capital of Sofia today. Report of the raid came from enemy sources and has not been confirmed by Allied quarters, hence the doubt as to the identity of the attacking planes. The raid only added impetus to the almost frantic efforts of the Bulgarian Government to extricate the nation from the war. Her fears have multiplied since the conference of the "Big Three" in Teheran and the subsequent meeting of President Roosevelt and President Ismet Inonu of Turkey. Turkey's entry into the war would almost certainly make Bulgaria a battlefield. On the other hand, Germany would almost certainly pulverize the tiny Balkan nation should she attempt to change her course. It's just like any gang of criminals, once you join you are in and you can't get out, no matter how much you repent. Death is the only release.

President Roosevelt is still making headlines. He has paid a flying visit to Malta, the most bombed place in the world, and presented that gallant garrison with a presidential citation for valor on behalf of the American people. Mr. Roosevelt in the course of his present travels, has visited the battlefields of El Alamein, Tobruk, Benghazi, Tunis and Bizerte. Where he will go from Malta is anybody's guess. As a traveler, the President is outdone by only one person, his wife, the First Lady of the Land, Mrs. Eleanor Roosevelt.

Saturday, December 11, 1943: —President Roosevelt is again making headlines in the Mediterranean war theater. The Chief Executive conferred with General Dwight D. Eisenhower during a 48 hour stopover at the ancient city of Carthage. The President presumably imparted to and shared with the Allied Commander-in-chief all the details of the grand strategy decided upon at the Teheran and Cairo conferences. General Eisenhower will undoubtedly have a major part to play in the enactment of the final act of the European drama.

Late news flashes tonight indicate that the RAF and American Eighth Air Force based in England have resumed their all-out offensive against the Reich. The largest fleet of American bombers ever assembled for one mission were dispatched on a tour of northwestern Germany and France. Specific targets were not yet revealed.

On the home front people and Congress are debating many controversial subjects. The battle against inflation is being fought against almost insuperable odds. Leaders who recognize the dangers of unbridled inflation are trying to "hold the line" but relentless pressure is being brought to bear by large labor groups and farmers seeking wage increases and higher prices for farm produce. It seems nearly impossible to prevent an inflation of huge proportions.

A nerve war is being waged against pre-Pearl Harbor fathers in connection with the draft. First they're in, then they're not. The latest dope tonight is that induction of fathers is to be postponed.

Sunday, December 12, 1943: —The big American bomber raid reported yesterday was aimed at the great German North Sea port of Emden. The fleet of Flying Fortresses and Liberators was escorted all the way to the target and back by Lightning and Thunderbolt fighters. The raiders were engaged in furious combat all the way with clouds of angry Nazi interceptors but the crack American planes scored a smashing victory over the enemy, shooting down a grand total of 138 German planes against the loss of 17 bombers and 3 fighters. The terrible firepower of the big bombers accounted for 117 of the Germans while the Lightnings and Thunderbolts bagged another 21. Returning flyers reported the raid was a complete success, having left a wide section of the German city devastated and burning.

Secretary of State Cordell Hull struck another blow in the war of nerves last night by somberly warning Bulgaria, Hungary, and Rumania that they must share the "consequences of the terrible defeat that United Nations arms are so surely bringing to Nazi Germany." The warning was delivered on the second anniversary of the declaration of war by the three governments and was aimed at splitting Adolf Hitler's Balkan satellites away from the Axis through hopes of easier terms if they desert the sinking boat before it goes down.

From Italy comes news of additional gains scored by the American Fifth Army in its tedious march to Rome. The gallant doughboys battled through mud and cold to capture an important height blocking the road to Rome in the upper Garigliano Valley.

Monday, December 13, 1943: —President Roosevelt's epic journey through the Mediterranean war theater is still headlining the news. The Chief Executive has visited Sicily for a review of the veterans of that campaign. During the course of his visit the President personally awarded the Distinguished Service Cross to six heroes of the Italian campaign, including the commanding General of the American Fifth Army, Lt. General Mark W. Clark. Also present to greet the President was General George S. Patton, commander of the famous American Seventh Army that conquered Sicily and lately the center of criticism and controversy over his purported slapping of a shell-shocked soldier.

General Clark was decorated for "extraordinary heroism" during the winning of the Salerno bridgehead. The General landed under fire and cooly directed the operation "in utter disregard of personal safety." His action "spread an infectious spirit of determination and courage" among his men which enabled them to win out over terrible odds.

The recent disturbances at the relocation center for disloyal Japs at Tule Lake have caused the Tokyo Government to stop the exchange of Allied internees in the Far East until a neutral power investigates and reports on conditions in the relocation centers. Spanish diplomats are being asked to make the report. If the truth is told the Spaniards will find that we have been too lenient and easy on the Jap internees, including the vicious traitors at Tule

Lake. I will wager their well-fed, indulgent lot is Utopia compared with the lot of our people who were caught in the tentacle of the Japs two years ago.

Tuesday, December 14, 1943: —The sanguinary, inch by inch battle for Rome continues in Italy. Bitter winter weather and fierce German resistance have combined to make this one of the most difficult campaign of the war so far. The Italian terrain is admirably adapted to defensive warfare, with its interlocking chains of mountains, and the Nazis, as usual, are making good use of their natural advantages. The muddy, tired doughboys and Tommies are forced to blast the enemy from his stony ridges one by one. Our forces are advancing steadily nevertheless, due to sheer doggedness plus the fortunate fact that we have complete mastery of the air over the battlefront and possess magnificent artillery for which the enemy has learned a healthy respect.

That the Balkans may soon erupt into a new front is hinted by the reported tour by Lt. General George S. Patton, commander of the famous American Seventh Army, of strategic military zones in the Middle East. The Seventh Army is known to be completely rested from its victorious Sicilian campaign and is raring to go. The American General was accompanied on his tour by the famous British commander, Sir Henry Maitland Wilson.

The rampaging Russian Army scored another victory on the Dnieper line today, driving the Germans from Cherkasi, the last major enemy base on the west bank of the lower Dnieper.

Wednesday, December 15, 1943: —The Navy reported today that it has been angling for some time for a showdown battle with the Japanese fleet. Recently an American carrier task force steamed boldly past the great Japanese naval base of Truk hoping to lure the Nip fleet out into the open. The Orientals refused to take the bait, however, and huddled close to home under the protection of their mighty shore guns.

New Britain, where lies Rabaul, another of Japan's powerful bases, was pummeled with a great weight of explosives today as the Allied pincers from New Guinea on one side and Bougainville on the other closed in on the enemy stronghold. Gasmata, on the southern coast, was particularly hard hit, absorbing the flame and concussion of 248 high explosives.

The speculation spotlight was further illuminated on the Balkans today as mighty Allied air fleets opened up an offensive against German installations in the Athens area. Air fields and shipping were heavily damaged as more than 300 American and British planes swooped in over the tortured Greek mainland. Only two Allied planes were lost in the very successful attack.

Prospects of serious labor troubles have again cropped up here at home. 350,000 members of the Railroad Brotherhood have voted to strike December 30 unless their wage demands are met. Such a strike would paralyze the Nation's railroad networks upon which depends the flow of troops and vital war goods. Interesting developments should occur.

Thursday, December 16, 1943: —NEW BRITAIN INVADED! American troops have stormed ashore on New Britain Island and have established a firm beachhead. At dawn today, under cover of a pulverizing air and sea bombardment, U.S. troops landed on the southwest coast of the island in the Arawe and Cape Merkus areas, quickly overcoming Japanese resistance and digging in to repel any Japanese counterattacks. The island of Arawe and all of Cape Merkus were completely overrun by American forces in a brief but bloody engagement. Our losses in the main attack were comparatively light but a small U.S. Commando force, engaged in a diversionary landing, was almost wiped out by withering fire from waiting Jap troops. Our men never reached shore in the brief but terrible sacrifice. Their attack, however, served to lessen the opposition to our main landing attempt and already our main force is headed inland on its desperate, 270 mile drive on Rabaul. There is no royal road to Tokyo.

Official Washington sources today disclosed that 35 or 40 German bombers carried out a surprise raid on December 2nd that caught the Allies completely unprepared. The attack was on the Italian Adriatic port of Bari, from whence the British Eighth Army is supplied, and was pressed home practically without opposition. Seventeen Allied merchant ships were sunk and 1,000 casualties caused. Much of the damage resulted from the explosion of several ammunition ships. Somebody blundered and hundreds died. There is no royal road to Rome—or Berlin.

President Roosevelt is reported home again, in excellent health and pleased with his trip.

Friday, December 17, 1943: —Upon his return to Washington President Roosevelt disclosed that Premier Stalin had uncovered a Nazi plot to assassinate the "Big Three" at their Teheran conference. For this reason, the conference site was literally overrun with military police and soldiers. The Russian leader prevailed upon Roosevelt to stay at the heavily guarded Russian embassy rather than venture back and forth from the American embassy. The Premier's precautions were obviously successful.

The invasion of New Britain is proceeding according to schedule. The Yanks have consolidated their beachhead and have beaten off several enemy dive bomber attacks. General MacArthur, supreme commander of Allied forces in the South Pacific, personally directed the invasion, the immediate purpose of which is to give us a base in New Britain which will "insure our control of Vitiaz Straits and contiguous waters.

Berlin was attacked again last night by a mighty fleet of RAF bombers which blasted great sections of the city with 1,500 tons of explosives and incendiaries. Uncontrolled flames roared throughout the capital, particularly in the eastern suburbs. Giant air mines leveled whole city blocks and split concrete walls more than 100 yards away. The Germans admitted heavy damage from what they called another "terror raid."

Prime Minister Churchill is reported to be ill with pneumonia somewhere in the Mediterranean theater. The extent of his sickness is not yet known.

Saturday, December 18, 1943: —The New Britain invasion, superbly executed by the U.S. Sixth Army, is now ahead of schedule, the Doughboys having won complete control of the vital Arawe peninsula in the first 60 hours of bitter fighting. American spearheads were reported striking out over native trails across the backbone of the island to cut off Japanese supply points. Our losses so far are exceptionally light considering the difficulties of the task.

In Italy, Allied forces, spearheaded with powerful armored units, drove into the streets of two key Italian town held by the Germans. American shock troops drove into San Pietro, just north of the road to Rome, and British Eighth Army veterans battled their way into Orsogna, on the Adriatic front. The fighting on both sides of the peninsula was desperate, with the Germans rushing large numbers of reserves to the front, some of them known to have been withdrawn from the Russian front to meet the Allied threat to Italy.

The War Department today announced that more than 14,000 of the original 18,000 American troops reported as missing on Bataan have been accounted for and are prisoners of war. Approximately 1,500 have died of disease in Japanese prison camps. It undoubtedly has been and will be a long, bitter, wait for those early heroes who so gallantly delayed the enemy in our darkest hours. God grant that all of them now living will survive to see Old Glory once again wave in triumph over the sacred foxholes of Bataan.

Sunday, December 19, 1943: —It has been a dark, gloomy day. Outside the heavens have been sweating, dripping with perspiration as though the task of shoving those big black clouds across the skies was too much for them. It seemed as though the sun had ducked in out of sight for fear it might be called upon to lend a hand. And so the darkness closed in, the rain pelted down, and man seemed content to lock his doors, turn on the lights, turn up the heat, and just hibernate for a day. At least that's what this man did and gladly too, for the past week has been hectic, with long hours of work, and a growing weariness that threatened to demand a fearful toll unless immediate rest was forthcoming. Overwork and weariness are particularly dangerous right now because of a spreading epidemic of influenza. The disease has taken a firm hold in the eastern states and is traveling westward. Already a sharp increase in the disease has been noted in the western states. We have been hit by it in the Bank, with many employees laid low by the miserable ailment. Absences at the shipyards and other defense plants have increased many times during the past week. Eight percent of the employees of one large shipyard were absent yesterday compared with a normal percentage of less than 2%. The disease, as in 1918, has originated in the war ridden countries of Europe and has spread from there to England and thence to the United States.

President Roosevelt has taken a hand in the railroad labor controversy, hoping to stave off the threatened strike. He is meeting with representatives of both sides at the White House today.

Tuesday, December 21, 1943: —The aerial offensive against Germany has reached an almost unbelievable intensity. During the last twenty four hours the heart of the Reich was blasted with the explosive power of 4,000 tons of bombs. The concentrated assault was carried out by night and by day, with a never ending procession of American and British bombers and fighters streaming across the English Channel to rock the domain of Hitler with the heaviest attack of the war. A mighty fleet of over 800 giant four motored Lancaster and Halifax bombers devastated the industrial city of Frankfurt with 2,240 tons of bombs. At the same time the twin Rhineland cities of Mannheim-Ludwigshafen were shaken and burned with 500 tons of explosives and incendiaries. By daylight American Flying Fortresses, at least 500 strong, visited Bremen with 1,200 tons of our finest explosives. Reconnaissance pilots later reported all targets burning fiercely with towering columns of smoke. The Germans are being sorely tried.

In the Pacific war our flyers are not neglecting our little Oriental enemies. Hundreds of American Liberators, Mitchells, and Marauders raided Japanese strongholds on New Britain Island in a raid comparable with some of those being launched in Europe. Nipponese positions in the Cape Gloucester area, 275 miles southwest of Rabaul, were blasted with 414 tons of bombs, causing large fires and explosions among enemy supply dumps and military installations.

On the home front, President Roosevelt's efforts to avert the pending railroad strike have temporarily failed as another 1,100,000 members of 15 non-operating railway unions voted to join the operating unions in the strike to commence December 30.

Wednesday, December 22, 1943: —It was revealed today that General George C. Marshall, U.S. Chief of Staff, visited the South Pacific on his way home from the Cairo and Teheran meetings and held lengthy conferences with General MacArthur and Admiral Chester Nimitz relative to the grand strategy of the war against Japan. A speedy acceleration of the drive to crush our Far Eastern foe is expected as a result of the conferences.

In Italy, American, French, Italian, and British troops are steadily advancing towards Rome, engaging the enemy in some of the bitterest fighting of the war to date. Hand to hand battles are common, some of them among the clouds on mountain ridges. Casualties are heavy on both sides but ours are not as bitter as those of the enemy, for our men are lost in winning a hill while the Nazis are lost in losing the position. There is a difference.

Recently the Russians held the first "war criminal" trial, convicting and hanging three Nazi officers for the mass killing of Russian civilians. The Germans are now threatening reprisals—not against the Russians, whose lives they apparently are satiated—but against American and British flyers captured in raids over the Reich. The incident may mark a new and grim turning point in the war against Germany, who heretofore has respected international law in connection with prisoners of war. The European war, like the bitter struggle with Japan, may well turn into a no-quarter given, no-quarter asked affair. Hatred and death stalk supreme throughout the world today.

Thursday, December 23, 1943: —In raids reminiscent of 1940 when German preparations for an invasion of England were smashed, giant RAF bombers blasted wide areas of the cross-channel French coast, apparently in an effort to destroy Nazi "rocket gun" emplacements said to be under construction across the narrow channel. Persistent reports have seeped out of Europe stating that the Germans have perfected a secret weapon, a giant rocket gun capable of launching mighty rocket powered shells weighing as high as 75 tons which the Nazis believe will destroy England. The terrible bombardment only awaits the completion of the gun emplacements along the French coast. Let us hope the British and American bombs are guided unerringly to their targets.

Very little has been reported regarding the progress of our invasion of New Britain Island in the South Pacific. It is known, however, that the American Sixth Army has firmly established its beachhead at Arawe and is pressing inland. The scale of American air raids on other points on the island indicate that further landings may be in the cards. It is more than probable that our commanders do not intend to fight overland all the 275 miles of mountain and jungle to the final objective of Rabaul.

On the home front President Roosevelt has offered to personally arbitrate the railroad dispute. The companies themselves and two of the unions have already acquiesced but some of the other unions may balk. Failure to arbitrate will mean Government operation of the roads, as nothing will be permitted to stop the flow of vital supplies and troops.

Friday, December 24, 1943: —'Twas the day before Christmas and all through the world the guns were flashing, the planes were roaring and the men were dying. From all the battlefields came reports of increasingly bitter fighting, with no end to the bloody slaughter in sight. In Italy, Canadian troops of the British Eighth Army were locked in a fierce house to house battle for Ortona that rivaled the historic struggle for Stalingrad. The defending Germans barricaded themselves in every building and had to be blasted out in the most ferocious hand to hand fighting of the entire campaign. Individual encounters were so close that the Allies could not give their men aerial support for fear of hitting them with the bombs.

In Russia similar bitter fighting is in progress, with the Red Army engaged in a major offensive designed to capture the important Nazi stronghold of Vitebsk. Large German forces have already been trapped in this first great winter offensive and face speedy annihilation.

Here at home President Roosevelt made a Christmas Eve address to the Nation and and the armed forces. The Chief Executive reported the results of the recent Cairo and Teheran conferences and named General Ike Eisenhower as Supreme Allied Commander for the impending invasion of Europe from the west. General R.L.G.Alexander will replace Eisenhower in the Mediterranean.

We spent from eight to twelve tonight preparing the children's Christmas. Trimmed the tree and built a fine little fireplace. All the toys are out now and everything looks nice. Guess it will be all right but are tired. Bed sounds very inviting about now.

Saturday, December 25, 1943: —Our third wartime Christmas. In the Bay Area it has been a very wet and dreary holiday—as far as the weather was concerned. The skies wept torrents of bitter tears at the sad condition of the world on this the birthday of the Prince of Peace. Once or twice the clouds parted and the sun peered through as if to see whether the flood of rain had been sufficient to quench the flames of hatred and war that raged below. Then, suddenly and disappointed, his face darkened, the clouds closed in and the torrents fell once more.

Our family was one of the fortunate few who were able to enjoy a thoroughly happy Yule. Everyone was well, the "flu" has spared us thus far, and the four youngsters were bubbling over with the spirit of Old Saint Nick. There were plenty of toys, though not up to their prewar standard, some of them being just a haphazard nailing together of several odd-shaped pieces of wood to faintly resemble autos and tanks and guns (expensive, too) and there was the tree, lighted and decorated with last years' ornaments. There were candies and nuts and a fine Christmas dinner; but above all we were together. Yes, we realized how blessed we were and our hearts went out to those less fortunate. With all our hearts and minds we thanked God that we in America, through His grace, and the strength and courage of our fighting men, have been spared the horrors of war on these shores and we prayed fervently that, ere another Christmas rolls around, our boys will have returned to their homeland victorious, and the Prince of Peace will once more smile down upon the earth.

Sunday, December 26, 1943: —Christmas came and went with no let up in fighting for those American troops who found themselves on the firing lines yesterday. Soldiers behind the lines were treated to turkey dinners with all the trimmings. At the front, however, it was K-rations as usual, with turkey promised for later. In Italy the fighting was particularly miserable with our boys sloshing forward to capture two more hills in the rain-sodden mountains north of the Cassino-Rome highway. Across the peninsula, Canadian troops were still battling furiously to drive the stubborn Germans from the scarred and blackened remains of Ortona.

Here at home, through the generosity of thousands of citizens, wounded veterans of the fierce Pacific and European fighting were brought the warmth of friendship and Christmas cheer. Presents, including a cash gift for every wounded veteran, plus refreshments, entertainment, and permanent improvements were generously provided for every hero in the many Army and Navy hospitals throughout the country. Those who were wounded, maimed or stricken with illness in the service of their country were not forgotten at Christmas time.

Americans have been warned by national leaders to be prepared for heavy casualties when the second European front really opens. It is estimated that 73% of the invading troops will be Americans and casualties may well run into the hundreds of thousands, perhaps a million. Not a pleasant prospect.

The only lull in the bloody slaughter because of Christmas was in the air war over Germany. RAF and American airmen took a day off from the nasty business. They're back at it again tonight, however.

Monday, December 27, 1943: —Two widely separated events both of great importance, happened today. The first occurred on the home front, when President Roosevelt ordered Secretary of War Stimson to take over the railroads in the name of the United States Government. The President's action was taken in the eleventh hour of the dispute between the carriers and the unions to make certain that there would be no interruption in the flow of vital war materials. The Army is prepared to man the roads with soldiers if need be to keep all trains moving on schedule. It is not expected that the troops will be needed, however, as all but three of the operating unions of the railroad system have agreed to continue work. The recalcitrant unions are expected to fall into line without further delay.

The other headline event of the day was the report of a U.S. Marine landing on the Cape Gloucester tip of New Britain. The Leathernecks were successful in establishing two firm beachheads before the Japs were able to muster effective resistance and the doughty Yanks are moving inland in the direction of the vital Cape Gloucester airfield which is the major objective of the new invasion attempt. Capture of this airstrip will pose a dangerous threat against the great enemy base of Rabaul which is the ultimate objective of the present amphibious operations.

Another event of almost equal importance was the reported sinking of Germany's last first line battleship, the Scharnhorst, in a fierce eight hour battle in the fog of the Barents Sea. Details of the death struggle are not yet available but reports indicate the vessel was brought to bay in a manner similar to that in which the great Bismarck was sunk.

Tuesday, December 28, 1943: —Hard-fighting U.S. Marines, veterans of Guadalcanal, have widened their beachhead in the Cape Gloucester area of New Britain to the extent of two miles and are nearing the twin airfields which are their objective. The Japanese have rallied and are counter-attacking with numerically superior forces. By all reports, however, the Americans are holding firm and are gradually pushing the enemy back. Casualties are heavy on both sides.

The year-end labor crisis on the home front is receiving national attention. The President appears to have averted a disastrous railroad strike scheduled for December 30 by seizing the lines and ordering the Army to stand by to operate the system should the unions go ahead with their threatened work stoppage.

A similar dangerous situation has existed the last few days in the steel industry. 143,000 steel workers left their jobs yesterday as a protest against the War Labor Board's refusal to grant them a 17 cents per hour raise. The danger was averted today when the unions called the men back to work.

The Navy today added twelve more Japanese ships to the long list of American submarine victims. This latest haul raised to 536 the number of enemy vessels sent to the bottom as confirmed victories by our undersea warriors since Pearl Harbor.

Wednesday, December 29, 1943: —Naval action in the Bay of Biscay, off the coast of France, was revealed today. A British task force, aided by American planes, caught a fleet of German destroyers and blockade runners in the Bay and sank three of the warships and one blockade runner in a two day sea and air battle. The action followed closely on Sunday evening's sea battle in which the mighty German battleship, Scharnhorst, was sent to the bottom. The two victories apparently nipped in the bud a new and desperate Nazi attempt to raid Allied convoys carrying men and materials for the pending invasion of the continent.

In Russia, the powerful Soviet winter offensive is beginning to roll irresistibly toward the boarders of Latvia, Poland, and Rumania. In the Ukraine, General Nikolai Vatutin's Army of the Ukraine, is sweeping the Nazi defenses before it, retaking the vital rail junction of Korosten and 250 other inhabited localities in the course of a single day. The German defenses are crumbling all along the front.

In Italy, the British Eighth Army has just announced the final capture of the bitterly contested town of Ortona on the Adriatic side of the peninsula. Canadian troops had the pleasure of driving the last Nazi soldier from the town after some of the most ferocious fighting of the campaign to date.

Late flashes indicate that Berlin is being pounded again tonight. Stockholm dispatches state that the German capital is being visited by another huge fleet of avenging British bombers. How do you like it, Herr Goering of the mighty Luftwaffe?

Thursday, December 30, 1943: —Last night's raid on Berlin was said to be one of the heaviest of the war. Huge formations of mighty RAF Lancasters and Halifaxes, their way lit up by the flares of Pathfinder planes, deluged the German capital with 2,240 tons of high explosives and incendiaries. From all reports more than half of Berlin now lies in ruins, with towering columns of smoke rising from the rubble that was formerly the heart of the Reich.

Heavyweights of the U.S. Eighth Air Force followed up the Berlin raid with a daylight foray deep into enemy territory, blasting the chemical center of Ludwigshafen. Other British and American planes paraded across the English Channel to pound enemy targets along the French invasion coast. All in all the last twenty-four hours have seen some of the most concentrated aerial action of the entire war. It looks as though the pre-invasion barrage has already begun.

Germany is taking a terrific beating on the eastern front as well. Premier Stalin has ordered the victory cannon of Moscow to salute another sensational victory won by the "valorous troops of the First Ukrainian front" who succeeded in scoring a great breakthrough in the northwest Ukraine, routing 22 German divisions and sweeping forward to within cannon range of the old Polish border.

While things go well on the battle fronts, labor strife on the home front darkens the picture. The Bay Area has been particularly hard hit by a strike of wholesale butchers that has paralyzed the meat industry hereabouts. Retail supplies of meat are all but exhausted and prospects are very gloomy. If necessary we would gladly do without meat, but this is not necessary!

Friday, December 31, 1943: —The last day of 1943 finds this world in such a pitiful mess that the Old Man must be more than glad to leave it. Your Mr. 1944's prospects are not very cheerful although the coming year promises to be one of the most decisive years in the history of the human race. At least his span of life will not be dull.

As I write this the old year has not yet run its course although the end is plainly in view. In spite of the war almost everyone seems ready to ring the old year out and the New Year in with the same boisterous hilarity of better years. There may be shortages of many things but tonight at least there is no shortage of liquor. Everyone who wanted it seemed to have found his share and rowdy San Francisco will undoubtedly live up to its reputation for gay celebrating. Transportation difficulties may slow things down a bit, however. This evening I spent an hour and a half in a jam-packed Southern Pacific Railroad station waiting for late commuter trains that seemed fated to upset the New Year's Eve plans of countless Peninsula patrons. Finally the trains came, they packed them in, and we rolled merrily down the rails to the tune of "Waltzing Matilda" sung by several boisterous Australian troopers. The cars seemed to bulge with humanity after the fashion of the Toonerville Trolley.

Adolf Hitler, the conqueror and boaster, delivered a gloomy New Year's message to his people today. What a change of tune, what a new slant from the Hitler stories of two or three years ago. Instead of victory it is survival; instead of boasts it is alibis. The little man is afraid, he sees the handwriting on the wall. His days are numbered and he knows it.

1944

Saturday, January 1, 1944: —Well, another year has started, accompanied by many a hangover and countless forecasts from military and political leaders. Such men as General Eisenhower and Secretary of State Cordell Hull voiced their convictions that victory over Germany would come in 1944, although the winning of the victory will be hard and costly. Others predicted that unrelenting pressure will be brought to bear on Japan during the year, with a tremendous shift of power to the Pacific once Hitler is destroyed. Although much personal sorrow is bound to be meted out to American families, the toast of one and all is for a Victorious New Year.

The Russians are starting the New Year with the fruits of one of their greatest military victories of the war. The sensational breakthrough achieved by the Army of the Ukraine is reaching tremendous proportions. The fortified rail center of Zhitomir has been captured and Soviet spearheads have driven far beyond to deal crippling blows to the confused and disorganized Germans, who are fleeing in panic, leaving vast quantities of booty in their wake. Advance Russian units are within 35 miles of the old Polish border. The Reds are really rolling.

The big job for responsible leaders on the home front is to solve the labor crisis and bring unity out of the present chaos while at the same time preventing a breach of the line against unbridled inflation. There must be industrial harmony on the home front if the mighty tasks of the armed forces are to be carried out without any hindrances from behind the lines.

Sunday, January 2, 1944: —The news spotlight is on the Russian battlefront where the amazing Soviet armies are exploiting their greatest victory of the war. The rampaging Russian juggernaut is sweeping forward at an unbelievable pace, after taking full advantage of the sensational breakthrough in the central Ukrainian sector. Completely routed German forces are fleeing in wild disorder, abandoning vast quantities of equipment and for the first time leaving bridges undemolished and towns unburned. General Nikolai F. Vatutin's First Ukrainian Army has pushed on from newly captured Zhitomir to a point only 30 miles from pre-war Poland and is fanning out with steel-tipped prongs that threaten to entrap a million Nazis in the southern Ukraine and Dnieper bend. Premier Josef Stalin triumphantly ordered the victory cannon of Moscow to fire a twelve salvo salute in honor of the fighting men of the First Ukrainian Army.

Action on the other land fronts has slackened somewhat. In Italy the Allied armies are practically bogged down in almost impossible weather. Both the American Fifth Army and the British Eighth Army are inching forward each day but weather conditions are so bad that even pack mules have failed in some instances, forcing the transportation of supplies on the backs of the over-worked and under-rated infantrymen themselves. After two months of bitter fighting the tired Allied forces find themselves still 75 miles from Rome.

Italy had nothing on the San Francisco Bay Area today. Torrents of rain fell with the total downpour for the day amounting to two inches. A cold blast turned some of it to hail.

Monday, January 3, 1944: —The mighty Red Army offensive on the Eastern front is continuing unabated. Spearheads of General Vatutin's Ukrainian Army have driven to within ten miles of the old Polish frontier, mopping up one Nazi stronghold after another. Novgorod Polanski, a town with a normal population of 30,000, lying only twelve miles from Poland was occupied after fierce fighting today, causing Premier Stalin to order the Moscow victory cannon to boom again. Hitler and his Balkan satellites are quivering in their boots as the Red hordes loom up on their borders. Rumania has already ordered the civilian evacuation of Bessarabia which faces the onrushing Soviet armies.

Elsewhere the aerial war commands attention. Berlin was blasted again last night—the second time in twenty-four hours—by more than 1,000 tons of explosives and incendiaries which added additional fuel to the blazing fires already sweeping the metropolis. Neutral Swedish reports revealed that bombs damaged Hitler's Reich-Chancellery in the heart of the city. Too bad a blockbuster didn't land on Adolf himself.

The U.S. Navy revealed that our bombers have been very busy in the Pacific. Paramushire, the Japanese Pearl Harbor in the Kuriles, was again raided by a group of Army bombers which inflicted heavy damage to the base and excepted unscathed although previous raids have been very costly. The avenging wings of the American Eagle are coming awfully close to home, aren't they? Mr. Moto.

Tuesday, January 4, 1944: —The Russians are in Poland! Powerful Soviet armies, driving the demoralized Nazis ahead of them in panic, are swarming across the old Polish border along a fifty mile front. The German defenses appear to be disintegrating all along the central and southern sectors of the vast Russian battlefront. More than 1,000,000 Nazi troops in the western Ukraine are face with entrapment and annihilation in what may prove to be the greatest German disaster of the entire war. Only a near miracle can extricate the German armies from the same predicament and fate that befell their hapless forces at Stalingrad. From all indications the Russians have mounted their greatest offensive of the war to capitalize on the sensational breakthrough scored at Zhitomir.

The tempo of Allied air attacks in western Europe raises the possibility that the Nazis may soon be faced with another great land offensive from the west. More than 3,000 American and British planes smashed at Hitler's Fortress during the last 24 hours, with a continuous stream of bombers and fighters swarming across the channel to pound the French invasion coast unceasingly. Other huge armadas swept further inland to bomb vital industrial targets in the Reich.

Nothing new or exciting has occurred in the Pacific war during the last few days. American forces have extended their invasion beachhead at Cape Gloucester, New Britain, and Saidor, New Guinea. Meanwhile American carrier based planes pummeled Japanese installations in the Marshall Islands in an obvious "softening up" attack prior to the expected invasion of those islands by our amphibious forces.

Wednesday, January 5, 1944: —Desperate German efforts to halt the sensational Russian offensive have failed and the Soviet armies are pouring through the Zhitomir gap in the Nazis' defense line and are slashing southward into the flank of a million German troops caught in the bend of the Dnieper River. One Red Army spearhead surged 30 miles south of Belaya Tzerkov and another to within fifty miles of the Odessa-Lwow railroad, the last escape route for the trapped Nazi forces.

The United States Eighth Air Force in England had a big day today. Hundreds of the mighty Flying Forts and Liberators smashed German shipyards at Kiel while other squadrons pounded other targets in western Germany and on the invasion coast of France. RAF Mosquito bombers added their part by staging a nuisance raid on Berlin, where neutral Swiss reports state that a mass evacuation is taking place. The German capital is already more than one half destroyed and the panic stricken populace is taking seriously the Allied threat to destroy it utterly.

The U.S. Navy announced the loss of the submarine Pompano, the seventeenth American sub to be lost in this war. The Pompano was one of our most daring raiders, having more than once cruised to within sight of the Japanese mainland. She was credited with destroying one destroyer, 6900 tons of merchant shipping and a patrol boat. Her skipper was Commander Willis M. Thomas, winner of the Navy Cross and the Silver Star. With him went 75 of the Navy's finest. God rest their souls.

Thursday, January 6, 1944: —The Red Army has driven twelve miles into old Poland, capturing the town of Rokitno which lies astride the railroad from Kiev to Warsaw. Further south powerful Soviet armies were smashing towards Bessarabia, where panic stricken Rumanian officials are frantically evacuating the civilian population. The power of the Red Army drives indicate that the Russian leaders are taking full advantage of the apparent collapse of the German Reichwehr's defenses during the past two weeks and are bent on forcing a decision this winter if humanly possible. The smell of victory is in the Red Army's nostrils.

The Allies have stepped up the tempo of fighting in Italy. Striking suddenly through a blinding hail and sleet storm, British and American units of the Fifth and Eighth Armies slashed a ten mile gap into the German's winter line guarding the inland road to Rome. Dozens of Allied fighter planes braved the bitter weather to strafe the enemy lines ahead of the advancing Tommies and Doughboys.

A sidelight on the war conditions here at home: Rents, of course, have been frozen but real estate prices have not, hence have run hog wild. Consequently home owners have been anxious to sell rather than continue to rent. So the poor renter has been caught in the middle. It is either buy a home at outrageously inflated prices or find yourself ousted, without a rented home to be found. Such is our predicament at this writing. We have received our ninety day notice to vacate and have no idea where we will go. Sherman was right, alright.

Friday, January 7, 1941: —The Allied drive in Italy is gaining considerable ground despite fierce resistance from the desperate Nazis. American infantrymen wiped out a "suicide" company of Germans to capture the key town of San Vittore in what was described as a "little Stalingrad" battle. The Yanks battled their way from house to house, employing hand grenades, bayonets, and even flame throwers to oust the barricaded Nazis. Few prisoners were taken.

On the Eastern front, the Russians are still on the rampage. Their victorious troops rolled forward another 24 miles into Polish territory, meeting only disorganized German resistance. The route of the retreating Nazis was littered with abandoned equipment and corpses. It will take more than Adolf Hitler's intuition to retrieve the Russian situation.

Fierce jungle fighting is in progress on New Britain Island near the Cape Gloucester area. American Marines have captured the former Japanese airfield in the area and have beaten off several desperate Jap attempts to retake it. Now, Slowly but inexorably the American troops are moving forward, driving the enemy back across the island toward Borgen Bay.

An indication of the ferocious character of the Pacific fighting was shown by the Army's announcement today that only 877 Japanese prisoners have been taken in two years of fighting. Many thousands of others have been exterminated. It is a "no quarter" struggle, for the little yellow men won't surrender and it is a case of kill them before they kill you. Somehow the war in Europe and the war in the Pacific are totally different. The one seems a little more "civilized" if you will. In the Pacific it is more like fighting head hunters in Borneo or wild Apaches on the warpath.

Saturday, January 8, 1944: —The extent of the German disaster in Russia increases daily. The Russians sense victory and are driving forward viciously with everything they have. Massive columns of motorized infantry, thousands of huge tanks, tractor-drawn artillery and self-propelled guns are speeding irresistibly forward over the plains of Poland and the Ukraine, while overhead the famous Stormovik dive bombers and fighters of the Red Air Force comb the skies almost unopposed by the once all-powerful Luftwaffe. Even the Berlin radio admits that German defenses are crumbling all along the southern Russian front and that the situation is "very grave."

The German cause is faring badly in Italy as well. Victorious American troops have driven on from newly captured Vittore to take the village of Giusto which guards the approaches to the main Nazi stronghold of Cassino which commands the road to Rome. The fight for Giusto brought cold steel into use, with the Americans having more of a stomach for it than the Krauts. Also taken by bayonet wielding Americans was a snow-covered 4,000 foot peak in the vicinity of Mount Majo.

Not much news from the Pacific battlegrounds today. General MacArthur's communiqué indicated that fighting has died down temporarily in the Cape Gloucester area of New Britain and elsewhere. American flyers, however, were busy, ranging all the way from the Solomons to New Ireland, New Britain, and New Guinea in bombing and strafing attacks on Japanese shipping, military installations and air fields.

Sunday, January 9, 1944: —At last another day of rest has rolled around. It seemed so good to be able to sleep in after a long, hard week at the office. There wasn't much else to do but loll around. Outside torrents of water fell from the skies as though some giant hand were bailing it out of the Pacific Ocean. Sunday pleasure driving appears to be entirely out of the picture for the duration. Three gallons for each A coupon is little enough when you can get it, but lately many service stations have either closed or hung out signs saying "No Gas." Last Sunday, for instance, I couldn't find any gas so we just put the old car in the garage and forgot about it. Moreover, when you can get the gas, it is poor in quality similar to the low octane stuff we used to use fifteen years ago, slow starting, loud knocking, low powered. So we stay at home.

Today's war news remains just about the same as yesterday. The Russians are still driving onward after capturing Kirovograd, keystone German defense position in the upper Dnieper bend. While General Nikolai F. Vatutin's troops were smashing more than thirty miles into Polish territory other Soviet columns were nearing the Rumanian border. Total loss by the Germans of all their Russian gains made after 2½ years of bloody fighting appeared imminent. What a splitting headache Hitler must have.

I forgot to mention yesterday that Roger D. Lapham was inaugurated as the twenty-ninth Mayor of San Francisco. The event is unique in the Mr. Lapham has pledged himself to serve only one term. This will leave him free to really lead San Francisco through these critical times without political hindrance.

Monday, January 10, 1944: —There is not much change in the war news tonight. The Russians are still pressing ahead, driving deeper into Poland and the southern Ukraine and are at a point within 60 miles of Rumania. The Moscow communiqué reported that Soviet troops cornered 8,000 Nazis in a death trap outside Kirovograd and exterminated them to the last man. Of such is the story of the war on the bloody eastern front.

U.S. Mediterranean Headquarters today announced that the 15th United States Air Force, previously based in North Africa, has shifted to bases in Italy, more than 600 miles closer to the enemy. Simultaneously, it was revealed that planes of the 15th staged a successful raid on Sofia, dealing the Bulgarian capital a heavy blow, both in physical damage and in morale.

While their comrades in the air were ranging hundreds of miles into enemy territory, tired but hard-fighting footsloggers of the American Fifth Army were knifing a bloody two mile gouge out of the formidable mountain defenses guarding the main Nazi stronghold of Cassino. The going was plenty "rugged" in the parlance of the Army.

An interesting sidelight to the Italian debacle was the revelation today that Count Galeazzo Ciano, son-in-law of Benito Mussolini, and erstwhile heir-apparent to Il Duce's "throne" was sentenced to death and summarily executed as a traitor by the puppet Fascist regime set up by the Nazis in northern Italy under the name of Mussolini. Ciano was said to be one of the Fascist Grand Council who voted to overthrow Mussolini at the time of Italy's surrender.

Tuesday, January 11, 1944: —The big news of the day is President Roosevelt's proposal, as announced in his annual State of the Union message to Congress, asking for the enactment of a National Service law. Such legislation would give the Government power to draft every able-bodied man or woman for service in essential industry. The very proposal of such drastic and inherently un-American legislation will undoubtedly touch off a tremendous debate throughout the country. There are of course many arguments for and equally as many against the law. The President claims it will prevent strikes but this again is debatable. It is also claimed that the law would relieve the manpower shortage in vital war industries. Perhaps, but there are many who claim there is no real shortage of manpower; the trouble lies in the "slowdown" and "featherbed" policies of labor unions. It is also claimed that National Service will give the members of the armed forces assurance that the home front is 100% behind them. Perhaps, but compulsory labor under National Service would also be an obvious departure from traditional American freedom—for which the boys are supposed to be fighting. Yes, the President's proposal will operate on a very sensitive portion of the Nation's anatomy.

The news from the warfronts is topped by the report of a great American aerial raid over Germany today. Details of the attack are not yet known but apparently a great air battle has been waged in the skies over the Third Reich. German claims, always exaggerated, tell of 123 American planes being shot down. Whatever the toll, it is plainly evident that there has been a bit of hell in the heavens over Europe today.

Wednesday, January 12, 1944: —Further details have been released regarding the great American aerial attack on Germany yesterday. Clouds of American heavy bombers, escorted by hundreds of P-38 Lightnings, P-47 Thunderbolts, and P-51 Mustangs, plunged deep into the heart of Naziland by daylight, fighting grueling battles all the way, to smash enemy aircraft production at the source. Oschersleben, the hatching ground for the deadly Focke-Wulf 190s, was badly damaged by many direct bomb hits. A Junkers-88 and Junkers-188 bomber plant at Halberstadt was razed, while three main assembly buildings producing Messerschmitt-110s at Brunswick were totally destroyed.

The aircraft centers were the principal targets but one large formation of Fortresses made a successful diversionary attack on Berlin, the first daylight attack on the German capital.

From all these attacks, the inevitable and fearful toll was exacted. 59 of the great bombers and 5 of the escorting fighters were shot down by the desperate enemy and with the planes, worth eighteen million dollars, went to either death or capture, more than 600 of our finest airmen. That is the price that hurts and the one that we must steel ourselves against.

Away across the world, other gallant American flyers were stabbing deep into the heart of the Japanese octopus. The Tokyo radio stated that American planes were thwarted in an attempt to raid Japan proper but veered southward to successfully attack military installations on the island of Formosa. The attack was undoubtedly carried out by General Chennault's boys and you can bet that Formosa was their original objective.

Thursday, January 13, 1944: —Speaking of millions in the same relative manner an ordinary citizen would speak of pennies, the President today submitted to Congress another 100-billion-dollar wartime budget. This, according to the President, would bring the total war expenditures since June, 1940 to 397 billion dollars, which is—well—quite a tidy sum.

With the budget, the Chief Executive called for additional taxes, warning that, without them, the deficit for the fiscal year of 1945 would amount to some 59 billion dollars, and would increase the public debt to the astronomical figure of 258 billion. And I have trouble raising $500.

The San Francisco News tonight carried one of the few stories yet published about a real home-front victory. It was the story of American workingmen, recruited from many companies on an emergency call, who, faced with a U.S. Navy request for a large number of important and secret gadgets needed to save the lives of American fighting men, did the impossible and delivered the goods ahead of time. The men, 310 of them, worked straight through from Saturday morning until 2 p.m. the following Friday to beat the deadline of one week. During all this time the men worked without stopping, except to snatch a bit of food or a cup of coffee, or to grab a short moments rest when collapse seemed near. The men's wives brought them shaving equipment and a change of clothing, also a welcome bit of home-cooked food. The men, American men, working without coercion, saw the vital need for the equipment they were producing, and gave their full effort—even as the boys at the front.

Friday, January 14, 1944: —Nothing very exceptional in the news tonight. The flaming Russian front and the Italian peninsula are the principal theaters of land fighting with the former on a far larger scale than the latter. The Soviets are sweeping the Nazis before them all the way from Leningrad in the north to the Ukraine in the south. The victory cannon in Moscow are becoming almost daily as Marshal Stalin Triumphantly announces the recapture of one stronghold after another. Today's announcement proclaimed the seizure of Mozyr and Kalinkovichi, the last German strongholds in southern White Russia. The collapse of their defenses in this area sent the Germans fleeing in disorder through the frozen Pripet marshes, where saber-swinging Cossacks cut them down in droves.

Other developments in the European war were confined to the air. Large fleets of American and British bombers and fighters lashed airfields and coastal defenses in France in what may be a pre-invasion barrage. Proving that they were not defeated or discouraged in Tuesday's great air battle, the U.S. Eighth Air Force again attacked northern Germany by daylight. Results of the raid are not yet known.

In Italy, Allied air power was also busy. A large squadron of planes attacked Rome for the third time, concentrating on the airfields surrounding the Eternal City. Land fighting in Italy appeared to be in a temporary lull.

The Pacific war also seems to be at a virtual standstill. Big things are in preparation but the only land fighting of consequence is on New Britain, where American troops are fighting desperately to maintain their hold on the Arawe peninsula.

Saturday, January 15, 1944: —The RAF staged another of its mighty aerial smashes against Germany last night. Brunswick, the vital aircraft production center was the target. Hundreds of huge Lancasters and Halifaxes carted a total of more than 2,300 tons of high explosives and incendiaries to the target area. Later reconnaissance photos strengthened the belief of returning British flyers that the important Nazi plane center was completely immobilized, possibly for many months to come. Sixteen of the attacking planes were destroyed.

Allied Headquarters in North Africa announced today that French forces, under the command of French officers, have scored their first victory in the Italian campaign. The Frenchmen, equipped with latest in American arms, captured the key highway town of Acquafondata, six miles northeast of the main German base of Cassino. Adding this flanking threat to the frontal attack by U.S. troops put Cassino in an almost untenable position and the Nazis may decide to pull out of there at any moment. Relentless pressure is being exerted against them by land and air.

The tide of war in Russia is still flowing in favor of the Soviet armies. Powerful offensives have been launched by the Red Army in the vicinity of Leningrad, and only 19 miles from the Finnish border. Further south, Russian armored columns swept after the fleeing Nazis through the frozen wastelands of the Pripet marshes. Thousands of the Teutonic invaders appear doomed as the armored tips of the Russian bearclaw close in around them. Hitler's headache has turned into a genuine migraine.

Sunday, January 16, 1944: —Since the momentum of the winter offensive of the Russian armies has carried them to and across the Polish border, a crucial problem has arisen that may affect the whole course of the war from here on out as well as the type of peace to come after the conflict. That problem is the attitude and intentions of the victorious Russians towards the exiled Polish Government in London. The main difficulty is Russia's apparent refusal to arrive at a solution to the boundary dispute between itself and the Polish Government in London, which the Allied Nations recognize as the legal government of Poland. Failure to obtain Russian cooperation in achieving a fair settlement of the dispute will be a deadly blow to Allied unity and may sound the death knell for the principles of the Atlantic Charter.

For this reason, President Roosevelt and Secretary of State Cordell Hull conferred today amid indications that this country will join with Britain in offering to mediate the dispute. Josef Stalin's reception to this offer will foretell either closer cooperation among the Allied Nations or a dangerous possibility that mighty Russia will go her own way alone.

Late reports indicate that the Allied Air Forces in England are continuing their pre-invasion aerial offensive against Germany and the fortified French coastal zone. Brunswick, the air-production center blasted last night is said to be total wiped out. In the latter raid, 2,300 tons of bombs were cascaded into the city within 23 minutes, the most concentrated and devastating 23 minute attack in war history. What a reign of terror Hitler has brought upon his people. How long can they take it?

Monday, January 17, 1944: —Russia dropped a blockbuster on the Allied Unity Camp today. The Communist Newspaper, Pravda, ordinarily considered to be Stalin's mouthpiece, published a dispatch, reputedly from Cairo, which said that two leading British personalities recently met German Foreign Minister Joachim von Ribbentrop to discuss terms of a separate peace with Germany. London immediately flared up with vehement denials and said that anyone who believed such a story has no conception of British character.

Russia's purpose in exploding such a ludicrous and obviously enemy-inspired bombshell in the Allied camp is obscure. That it will give aid and comfort to the Nazis cannot be doubted but in addition it sows a seed of suspicion in other United Nations' minds that the Soviet Union itself may by laying the foundation for a separate peace bid on its own. Such an effect is in itself a major victory for the Nazis.

Meanwhile in London, General Eisenhower announced the appointment of Lieut. General Omar N. Bradley to command the American ground forces in the approaching invasion. General Bradley, you will remember, commanded the American troops who crashed through to Bizerte in the Tunisian campaign to break the stalemate in that sector. The General also commanded an Army corps in the victorious Sicilian campaign.

In the Pacific war, American flyers are still softening up the Marshall Islands for the anticipated amphibious invasion attempt. Fierce enemy resistance is being encountered in each raid. Losses on both sides are heavy.

Tuesday, January 18, 1944: —A giant Army transport plane carrying eight crewmen and passengers roared up out of the dawn today, lost altitude as her motors sputtered, tried to pull up, then dove and crashed into an Oakland home. A man and his wife living in the house miraculously escaped without injury as splintering wreckage and flaming gasoline enveloped the entire house with the exception of the kitchen where they were preparing breakfast. All persons in the plane were instantly killed. Fire spread to several neighboring homes.

Soviet Russian armies, showing unbelievable reserve strength, have mounted two new and powerful offensives in the Leningrad area. One drive smashed a big hole in the German lines south of Leningrad in the Oranienbaum sector; the other smashed a gap in Nazi defenses before Novgorod above Lake Ilmen. The present attacks constitute the first major action in the Leningrad area since the sensational offensive of a year ago when the siege of the Russian city was lifted.

In Italy, the slow but inexorable Allied march on Rome continues. Almost inch by inch, the American Fifth Army and the British Eighth Army are driving the Nazis backward. The heavily fortified German stronghold of Cassino is next on the Fifth Army's schedule and patrols of American Doughboys have already penetrated into the city's suburbs. The fighting on this front is bitter and desperate, with our troops forced to battle not only the deadly German enemy but also nature itself, in the form of howling storms, freezing cold, mud, mountains, and rivers.

Wednesday, January 19, 1944: —The Soviet drive in the Leningrad area is assuming the proportions of a major offensive. The Russians apparently are making a determined effort to smash once and for all the ring of steel around the northern city. Some of the most formidable fortifications in the world have been constructed by the Germans in their two years of siege and the Red Army troops in the last two days have blasted their way from pillbox to pillbox for a distance of from12 to 18 miles, killing 20,000 Nazis and routing seven German divisions in the process. Hundreds of massed Soviet cannon unleashed one of the greatest artillery barrages of the war to support the attack.

American naval planes struck for the first time at the Japanese-mandated Caroline Islands. Kusaie, 750 miles from the great Japanese naval base of Truk and 700 miles northwest of recently captured Tarawa in the Gilberts, was the target. No American planes were lost.

Secretary of War Stimson today appeared before the Senate military affairs committee to advocate the passage of National Service legislation. He said that strikes and threats of strikes have caused much resentment and discontent among the members of the armed forces and said the job draft would be good for the fighting man's morale.

At the same time, the House of Representatives were passing a mustering out pay bill which would give discharged service men up to $300.00 to help them make the adjustment back to civilian life.

Thursday, January 20, 1944: —Marshal Josef Stalin issued another of his famous orders of the day, announcing the capture of Novgorod, north of Lake Ilmen, on the Leningrad front. The Russian dictator described the town an "important economic center of our country, a large communications center and a strong German defense base."

The capture of Novgorod came only after bloody hand to hand fighting that raised Nazi casualties since Friday to 45,000 killed and many others wounded and taken prisoner. Its fall opened the way for a drive to the Baltic Sea which may spring a trap on an estimated 300,000 enemy troops. Some were already encircled in the forests west of Novgorod and "successful fighting for their liquidation" is going on.

In Italy General Mark Clark's Anglo-American Fifth Army was reported making further gains in its bitter drive towards the Eternal City. British troops successfully drove into the town of Minturno, western anchor of the Germans' defense line across the peninsula, and captured it after heavy fighting.

The War Department announced that the Italian campaign so far has cost 19,120 American casualties. Of these 2,985 were killed, 12,504 wounded, and 3,721 missing. Among the battalions suffering the heaviest casualties was the 100th Infantry Battalion, composed of Americans of Japanese ancestry. The fighting record of these American born Japanese has been very creditable, he said.

Friday, January 21, 1944: —Probably the most devastating rain of death and destruction in the history of aerial warfare fell upon Germany and the French invasion coast during the last 24 hours. An endless parade of mighty American and British bombers, ably protected by hundreds of fleet fighter planes, streamed across the English Channel to blast Nazi positions from the French coast far into the interior of the Reich. During the night, Berlin was visited by a mighty armada of 800 to 900 great Lancasters and Halifaxes, carrying a bomb load weighing more than 2,500 tons. It was the 11th major raid since November 18th on the German capital and was another step towards the total elimination of the city as the Nazi nerve center. Towering columns of smoke from uncontrollable fires were visible 150 miles away. Ina addition to the 2,500 tons of explosives dumped on Berlin, other Allied planes, including large numbers of American Flying Forts and Liberators, dropped another 2,500 tons on Nazi fortifications along the French coast. The total of 5,000 tons of bombs is the heaviest load ever dumped on the enemy in the short space of 24 hours. How long can the Nazis continue to take such awful pounding?

Moscow eased the tension over the recent publication of the "separate peace" rumor in Pravda, by denying officially that the Russian Government had any knowledge of the dispatch prior to its publication. If true, it is good news.

Both the Russian and Allied offensives on the Leningrad and Italian fronts respectively are making headway. Hitler and his cohorts can find very little comfort in the news tonight.

Saturday, January 22, 1944: —Sensational news tonight! The Allies have landed. Thousands of American and British troops, supported by planes and warships, have smashed their way ashore only 16 miles south of Rome. The landing caught the Germans flatfooted in a complete surprise and a firm beachhead was established almost without opposition. The invasion forces were composed of veteran shock troops of General Mark Clark's Fifth Army, spearheaded by British Commandos and American Rangers. The successful landing far behind the powerful German defense lines across the Italian peninsula against which the Fifth and Eighth Allied armies have been nibbling for weeks, may well break up the whole Italian campaign and send the Nazis scrambling for safety to avoid being trapped between the two jaws of the pincers. Approximately 15 enemy divisions, about 200,000 men, confront the Allies across the peninsula and it will be General Clark's hope to encircle and destroy them.

The locale of the landings was placed on the sloping shores of the Tyrrhenian Sea near Nettuno, which was promptly captured by fast-moving American Rangers. Other landings were made northward up the coast to the mouth of the Tiber, only 16 miles from the Eternal City. Further developments should come in rapid fire order.

Allied air power based in England continued its round-the-clock pounding of Germany during the past 24 hours. 2,300 tons of destruction was heaped on Magdeburg, vital German war center, which was the principal target of more than 1,000 heavy bombers.

Sunday, January 23, 1944: —Thank God it was Sunday and a day of rest today. It was all I could do to struggle through a short work day yesterday, but I couldn't have made it at all today. I was suddenly stricken with the most severe cold I have had in years. I was afraid it might turn into the flu or worse so I doctored up thoroughly last night and slept straight through for twelve hours until eleven o'clock this morning. Tonight, after a warm bath, I feel much better and believe I have conquered the malady.

The only war news I have heard today came over the radio just a few minutes ago. According to dispatches from Italy, the powerful invasion force of 50,000 Allied troops which swept ashore yesterday near Rome, is battering its way inland far ahead of schedule. The Germans, taken completely by surprise, have not yet organized effective opposition. All indications are that the Allied High Command in the Mediterranean has pulled off a brilliant maneuver that may result in the greatest German disaster since Tunisia. We fervently hope so.

Allied air fleets are again over Germany, as indicated by reports that Axis radio stations from Paris and Berlin to Sofia in Bulgaria, have gone off the air. There'll be no rest from the crunch and smash of blockbusters, Herr German, until you oust that egomaniac, Hitler, who brought this terrible punishment upon you. Throw him and his ilk out of your midst and someday you may win a place among the peace-loving and happy peoples of the world. Unless ye repent and do better, ye shall be smitten.

Monday, January 24, 1944: —Late reports indicate that the Allied invasion forces that swept ashore Saturday morning near

Rome have driven inland twelve mile to capture Cisterna di Littoria, which lies astride the ancient Appian Highway to Rome. Other Allied landings have taken place northwest of Nettuno, so close to Rome that the artillery fire rumbled through the streets of that city, sending quivers of joy through the hearts of the anti-Nazis and shivers of fear through the spines of thousands of Fascists and Germans who already are beginning to flee in panic from the Eternal City. Pro-Allied demonstrations are beginning to appear as the hour of deliverance approaches while acts of sabotage against the Nazi invaders are multiplying. The Free Milan radio advised all Italians that "this is the moment you have been awaiting. Strike now at the Germans, take up arms— abandon your work, sabotage your machines, and join the Allies wherever they are fighting."

South on the main battle line around Cassino, the furious Germans have launched a desperate counter-attack which has forced the American Fifth Army to yield some ground temporarily. The Americans were driven back across the Rapido River but only after their ammunition ran out and after some of the bitterest hand-to-hand fighting of the entire campaign. But the eventual hopelessness of the Nazis' position is apparent as the newly landed jaw of the pincers races in to clamp the vice on the ten to fifteen German divisions caught in the pocket between Rome and Cassino. It is only a matter of time. The only question is how many of the enemy will escape the trap.

Tuesday, January 25, 1944: —The most interesting news tonight comes from the Italian front. The Allied landing below Rome obviously took the Germans completely by surprise and they have not yet recovered their equilibrium. No effective counter-attack has been launched against our beachhead and vast quantities of materiel and large numbers of troops are pouring ashore unmolested. The landing has posed a serious threat to the Nazi forces facing the British Eighth Army and the American Fifth Army on the winter line to the south anchored on the heavily fortified town of Cassino. Dispatches published in the evening papers indicate that the Germans are already pulling out of Cassino, either as the beginning of a general withdrawal from the winter line, or to throw powerful reinforcements against the new Allied beachhead.

Meanwhile, armored spearheads from the point of invasion have driven inland to cut the famous Appian Highway to Rome. Other units have entered towns only fourteen miles from the Italian capital and are in plain view of ancient hills above the Eternal City.

On the Russian front the Soviet armies are continuing their irresistible forward march, particularly in the Leningrad area. Krasnogvardeisk, an important rail junction 25 miles south of the old czarist capital was retaken in fierce fighting today.

Here at home the Fourth War Loan Drive is well under way, having officially begun on January 18. The goal is fourteen billions of dollars. That is a lot of bonds.

Wednesday, January 26, 1944: —A major battle appears to be shaping up for Rome. The Nazis have pulled many of the crack troops from the Cassino front and apparently are striving to organize a powerful counter-attack against the Allied beachhead just south of Rome. Cassino itself is a no-man's land, with the Germans abandoning the city but holding dominating artillery positions in the heights overlooking the stronghold from where they have thus far prevented the advancing Americans from taking possession. Our forces, however, have re-crossed the Rapido River after their recent reversal and are firmly in control on the northern bank.

South American news made the front page today. Argentina, the last nation in the western hemisphere to do business with the Axis, has now severed here relations with Germany and Japan. The action was a reversal of the Argentine government's former policy and came as a pleasant surprise to Allied countries. The reason was quoted as being the discovery, by the South Americans, of an extensive German and Japanese espionage system in Argentina. Members of the Nazi and Jap diplomatic corps were reported to have operated under cover of their legal immunity.

The big debate in Washington at the present time is the matter of the servicemen's vote. Many members of congress are in favor of leaving the soldiers' voting up to the various states but Roosevelt and some other leaders are demanding direct Federal supervision and handling. The way the servicemen vote may decide the election next November and Franklin D. Roosevelt, the politician, is well aware of that fact.

Thursday, January 27, 1944: —The full-scale counter-attack expected by the Allies against their invasion beachhead south of Rome is apparently shaping up. The Nazi Field Marshal Albert Kesselring has flung his prize division, the famous Hermann Goering division, recently refitted as a full armored outfit, into the fray. The German panzers roared up through the ancient Pontine Marshes and attempted to knife into the Allied flank. Fortunately they were hurled back after a furious battle.

The most favorable aspect of the Battle for Rome is the preponderance of Allied airpower over the field of battle. American A-26 dive bombers, known as Invaders, are taking a particularly high toll of men and machines along the enemy's communication lines from the previous front at Cassino to the new beachhead. The taking of Rome, therefore, is only a matter of time. In fact, Allied intelligence reports indicate that the Germans are already evacuating key personnel from the Eternal City.

The war in the Pacific is flaring up brightly in the Marshall Islands. Aerial bombardment of those Japanese strongholds by American planes has reached an intensity that can only precede an actual invasion. Seven raids in one day has been the pattern of bombing that has razed and flattened the main Japanese bases in the islands, ripening them for seizure.

The last hope for an Axis victory vanished today as it was announced that the tiny Negro republic of Liberia has declared war on Germany and Japan.

Friday, January 28, 1944: —America is aghast tonight after the Army and Navy released the most brutal horror story of the present war. In a joint announcement they told the long-withheld story of the most cold-blooded campaign of savagery in the annals of modern warfare. The lengthy account described in vivid detail how the Japanese starved, tortured, and in many cases wantonly murdered American and Filipino soldiers captured after the fall of Bataan and Corregidor. Thousands of American prisoners of war died of disease and starvation amid the filth of crowded prison camps. Others were beheaded or shot wantonly on the slightest pretext.

The terrible report was compiled from statements made by three American officers who succeeded in escaping from the

Philippines after almost a year as prisoners. Other officers who failed to escape were tortured for two days before being beheaded or shot by their savage captors.

The officers told of a terrible "march of death" forced upon the survivors of Bataan after their surrender. They were marched for three days in the broiling sun without food or water, constantly beaten by guards, some of them purposely run down and killed by enemy vehicles, others shot and left to lie where they fell for breaking ranks or falling out from exhaustion. The officers further estimated that almost half of the Americans and Filipinos who surrendered have died from torture, starvation, or otherwise.

At long last, the American people have fully realized the kind of enemy we are fighting. In our terrible anger can be read the certain end of the Japanese Empire. An awful retribution awaits the fiendish perpetrators of this hideous chapter of history.

Saturday, January 29, 1944: —Adding horror upon horror, more appalling stories of Japanese atrocities were told today. Foreign Secretary Antony Eden added Britain's tale of Japanese savagery to our own, telling of the brutal torturing of thousands of British captives taken when Hong Kong and Singapore fell. Throughout both nations a furious cry for vengeance is sweeping, as officials and citizens alike angrily denounce the barbarity of this inhuman foe. Some criticism is heard to the effect that the sordid facts should have been given to the people long ago but for the most part only a deep anger and undying determination to seek vengeance have keynoted the comments of the people. No effort will be too great to bring the guilty parties to justice.

As if already expressing our increased anger, General MacArthur's South Pacific Air Force ripped the Japanese base of Rabaul with one of the heaviest attacks of the war. Twenty two of sixty enemy interceptors that tried to stop the raiders were shot down while the bombers unloaded their explosives so accurately that even the Japs in a broadcast admitted severe damage.

In Italy the newly landed Allied forces below Rome appear to be advancing very slowly, consolidating their beachhead securely before venturing too far inland. On the front to the south, furious fighting appears to be in progress around Cassino, the principal bastion of the Germans' Gustave line. General

Clark's Allied armies are relentlessly continuing the pressure all along the front while it must be admitted that the desperate Nazis are resisting furiously and skillfully.

Sunday, January 30, 1944: —It was Sunday today but not a day of rest. I worked from nine in the morning to eight o'clock this evening. The Bond Redemption department, of which I am acting head, was moved today from the main bank building to a new location on the corners of Sansome, Sutter, and Market streets. The move, which included the furniture and equipment for a force of about 166 people, went off very smoothly, which is a tribute to the careful planning that went into it. Before I left tonight, the new office was ready for normal operations in the morning.

This removal of the Bond Redemption Department from the main Federal Reserve Bank building was made necessary because of lack of space to handle the constantly increasing fiscal operations of the Government. Savings Bond redemption, in itself, is one of the most rapidly expanding functions we perform. With all the billions of dollars worth of Savings Bonds already sold, and other billions to be sold, the number and amount of redemptions is steadily rising. Eventually it will be a tremendous task, especially after the war.

News from the war fronts continues in just about the same vein as heretofore during the past week. The country is still seething with vengeful wrath over the disclosure of barbarism among the Japs. Demands for suitable retribution will not cease until they are satisfied. Those enemy leaders who are responsible must be punished.

American bombers staged one of their greatest daylight raids over Germany yesterday. Eight hundred heavy bombers plastered Frankfort with 1,800 tons of explosives.

Monday, January 31, 1944: —Arrived home late tonight after a hectic day at the office. Starting out anew in a new location was all right for the ordinary workers but for those of us who had to manage the operation it was not so easy. There were procedure to iron out, custodies and combinations to set up, routines and schedules to establish. Several mechanical difficulties were also encountered. In the first place it rained this

Monday, January 31, 1944: —Arrived home late tonight after a hectic day at the office. Starting out anew in a new location was all right for the ordinary workers but for those of us who had to manage the operation it was not so easy. There were procedure to iron out, custodies and combinations to set up, routines and schedules to establish. Several mechanical difficulties were also encountered. In the first place it rained this morning and was cold. We found that the heating plants were poorly adjusted and there were many complaints of being chilly. Then to top it all off, we had a fire. It was in the elevator shaft and started from a short on the elevator's electric panel board. Fortunately the room where the fire started is partitioned off and lined with metal so no harm was done except to put the elevator out of commission for a couple of weeks. But it was a real house warming and gave us a bad scare at the time. What a day!

I have not had much time to examine the war news tonight. Apparently some severe fighting is in progress in Italy. Cassino, the heavily fortified anchor of the Germans Gustav line is the scene of some of the fiercest fighting of the entire campaign. Apparently the city has changed hands several times already, with both sides making snipers' nests and pillboxes out of every home and building. It is the closest example of "Stalingrad" warfare yet to be encountered outside of Russia. The Nazis apparently are determined to make the Allies pay dearly for every foot of Italian soil they relinquish. Their purpose in this is obscure, unless it is purely a delaying action for some as yet unknown purpose. Even to Hitler, it must be clear that they cannot hope to hold Italy indefinitely.

February

Tuesday, February 1, 1944: —WE ARE INVADING THE MARSHALLS! For the first time in this war we are attacking the Japanese on soil belonging to them before the start of hostilities. Both Marines and Army units are engaged in the attack, being supported by the mightiest armada of air and sea forces ever assembled for one operation. First reports indicate that landings are being made at several points simultaneously. The object of the invasion, according to Admiral Chester W. Nimitz, is to capture the entire Marshall Islands—some 32 islands and 867 reefs spread out over 800 square miles of ocean.

The attack apparently began yesterday to the thundering barrage of hundreds of mighty naval guns, including the sixteen-inchers of battleships. Bombs from hundreds of carrier-based planes and long-range aircraft based in the recently captured Gilberts screamed down on the defending Japs to blast them from their pillboxes before the Marines and Doughboys swarmed ashore. Two of the major landings took place at opposite ends of the Kwajalein Atoll, one being aimed at the powerful enemy air base on Roi Island and the other at the heavily defended base on Kwajalein Island. At both spots our forces have succeeded in establishing firm beachheads. Our losses have been extremely moderate, according to latest reports.

Other major fighting fronts are those in Italy and Russia. The Reds have driven to within one mile of the pre-war Estonian border on the north Russian front, leaving 100,000 Germans threatened with entrapment. In Italy, our armored spearheads have slashed to within 15 miles of Rome.

Wednesday, February 2, 1944: —Although the Japanese must have been aware of our intentions regarding the Marshall Islands, it is apparent that the scope of our operation took them completely by surprise. Obviously they did not anticipate that we would land at numerous points simultaneously, each in sufficient force to command the situation. However, from all reports, our leaders assembled the most powerful amphibious force of all time to practically overwhelm the opposition. There were more ships and naval personnel involved in this one operation than there were in the entire United States Navy at the beginning of the conflict.

By virtue of this overwhelming force and the variety of our attacks some of the landings were almost unopposed. At other points the weight of the naval and air bombardment was so great that the defending Japs were either killed or so dazed that they could offer only ineffective resistance. Consequently our losses so far have been very light. The mistakes of Tarawa were not repeated in the Marshalls attack.

The battle for Rome is developing into one of the most bitter and bloody of the European war. The advantages of terrain are all with the defending Nazis and they are making good use of them. From the fury of German resistance it is apparent that all Italy will be blackened and scarred before the Huns are driven from her soil. What an ugly fate Mussolini brought upon his country when he plunged her into the war on what he thought was the winning side and easy spoils.

Thursday, February 3, 1944: —Good news and bad news were flung at us from the radios and the newspapers today. Both kinds came from the central Pacific theater where American Leathernecks and Doughboys are eradicating hundreds of Japanese rats, digging them out of their steel and concrete fortifications with every weapon in the book, including flamethrowers, grenades, bayonets, and dynamite. Over 1,250 enemy bodies have been counted already and the business of extermination goes on unremittingly. The island of Namur and four other islets at the northern end of the Kwajalein Atoll have already been seized while beachheads at other points are rapidly being widened.

The bad news was the sad report that Raymond Clapper, the world famous columnist and commentator, was killed in an aerial collision over the Marshall Islands as he was following the boys into action as a war correspondent. Mr. Clapper was one of the most famous and best liked of our newspaper columnists. He was noted for his fearlessness and impartiality. His writings were lucid and entertaining and commanded a large following. He was a keen observer and a tireless reporter of facts.

Reports of great Russian victories are becoming almost commonplace as the Germans appear to be abandoning hope of beating Russia and seem to be going entirely on the defensive in the east, perhaps in preparation for meeting an invasion from the west. Today, however, the Nazis are facing another Stalingrad defeat, as powerful Soviet armies have encircled and trapped ten German divisions in the Ukraine. Little hope of escape is given the Nazis, the only alternatives being annihilation or capture.

Friday, February 4, 1944: —A tremendous battle is raging in Italy. Powerful German forces have flung themselves against the Allied beachhead south of Rome in what may be the decisive battle for that city. The situation is grave, with the fate of the entire Allied landing force hanging in the balance. Some observers claimed the fighting is bloodier than the Salerno battle, with the result just as doubtful.

Sixty miles to the south another furious struggle is taking place for Cassino. The stronghold has changed hands at least three times already, with losses being extremely heavy on both sides. Latest reports indicate that American shock troops have again plunged back into the rubble-filled town after being driven out during the early morning.

An idea of the importance attached to the Italian fighting by the Nazis is the report that Hitler has dispatched his touted strategist, Marshal Rommel, of North African fame and disaster, to take command of all German forces opposing the Allies in that quarter.

The American invasion of the Marshall Islands is progressing very well. The great invasion fleet assembled for the attack today steamed into the famous Kwajalein Lagoon, until recently the major Japanese naval base east of Truk. The large natural harbor is ideal for protection against roving Jap submarines.

Only mopping up operations appear to be necessary before conquest of the Marshalls will have been completed. The most wonderful feature of the attack has been the economical use of American lives. Less than 200 of our troops have been lost according to the most recent announcement.

Saturday, February 5, 1944: —So far American and British troops have successfully beaten off the desperate German counter-attacks against our invasion beachhead south of Rome. Five separate attacks, including one by the crack 26th Panzer division, have been repulsed during the last 24 hours by the hard-fighting Tommies and Doughboys. But the battle is far from won and the Nazis are pouring hundreds of artillery shells and bombs into the crowded beachhead. It has also been observed that the enemy is pulling powerful defense forces down from northern Italy to join in the Rome struggle.

On the southern front our troops are still locked in the furious battle for Cassino. The conflict has swayed back and forth without a decision for many days. Front-line observers state that some of the most sanguinary fighting of the European war is taking place in Cassino. American troops and their British comrades have killed several hundreds of Germans in fierce hand-to-hand fighting in the streets of the battered city. Neither side is disposed to yield.

From the central Pacific comes word of further successes in the Marshall Islands' invasion. U.S. Marines have captured seven more small islands in the group and the victorious conclusion of the campaign is in sight. Japanese losses, from all reports, have been very heavy while ours have been remarkably light. This is largely due to the terrific firepower leveled at the Japs in preparation for the landings. Thousands of tons of steel and explosives were hurled onto the islands for days before the attack. The assault troops were backed up with a barrage that flattened the enemy's defenses.

Sunday, February 6, 1944: —It is still nip and tuck on the Allied beachhead south of Rome. Although the Americans and British apparently have dug in strongly and are backed by powerful air and naval forces, the outcome of the battle is still uncertain. There is little doubt but that Hitler has ordered his Generals to make a supreme effort, regardless of cost, to smash the beachhead defenses and force another Dunkirk. The desperate Nazis are in dire need of a brilliant victory to raise the morale of the war-weary German people whose diet for the last year has been a steady round of defeats and devastating air blows against their homeland. Consequently we can expect to hear of the bitterest kind of fighting in Italy. Already we have read of ferocious attacks by screaming hordes of German soldiers, supported by tanks, who pressed the attack home in the face of machinegun fire that literally carpeted the battlefield with German dead. Wave after wave of Huns attacked one sector of the Allied line yesterday until a breastwork of enemy dead piled up in front of the line. But despite their tremendous losses the Germans still come on, driven either by insane courage or utmost desperation.

American forces have made further progress in the Marshall Islands invasion. Marines have blasted the Japs from two thirds of Kwajalein Island on the southern tip of the atoll and have cornered hundreds of enemy troops in a small sector of the island. Their position is hopeless. Our losses continue to be exceptionally moderate.

Monday, February 7, 1944: —An American naval task force has boldly executed one of the most daring exploits of the war to date. The United States vessels steamed right into the heart of Japan's north Pacific sea lanes to bombard the great enemy air and naval base on Paramushiru Island in the Kuriles. It was the first sea attack on the Japanese home territory and obviously struck terror into the hearts of Tojo's followers who excitedly broadcast their fears that we were preparing to invade the Kuriles.

According to the Navy announcement the shelling of the enemy base only 1,200 miles from Tokyo caused many fires and destroyed at least one ship in the harbor. Practically no opposition was encountered by our ships.

The consternation caused by the bold attack can be imagined by comparing it with our own anxiety should the Japanese have succeeded in attacking some base of ours located only 1,200 miles away—half the distance from San Francisco to Honolulu.

The Russian scene is still one of heavy fighting, incredible Soviet victories, and equally unbelievably German disasters. Right now the Red Army has pinned five Nazi divisions into a holocaust of fire and steel in the bend of the Dnieper River. The Germans are trapped and doomed as hundreds of Russian big guns hurl tons of explosives into their midst. The nerve-shattered Germans are said to be fighting with incredible desperation, counter-attacking many times a day in an effort to break out of the trap.

Tuesday, February 8, 1944: —The week-long campaign for Kwajalein Atoll in the Marshalls was completed today. All organized Japanese resistance has been stamped out; there remain only a few isolated snipers to be liquidated. Only 286 Americans were killed in the campaign or captured—a ratio of better than 28 to 1. Our forces are now turning the air fields of Roi and the harbor of Kwajalein into powerful new advanced bases for attacks on other Japanese milestones along the road to Tokyo.

The furious battle for the Allied beachhead south of Rome continues to rage according to dispatches direct from the battlefront in Italy. Today a fierce air battle swirled and barrel-rolled in the skies over the beachhead as wave after wave of German planes attempted to blast Allied positions. They were intercepted by scores of American and British fighter planes who broke up the Luftwaffe's formations and shot down 19 Nazi planes besides damaging many others. One enemy bomber, however, either jettisoned his bombs at an unfortunate moment or deliberately attacked an American evacuation hospital. The crash of high explosives on the plainly marked hospital killed 27, including doctors, nurses, and wounded Doughboys, and injured 65 others.

Another piece of bitter news was released tonight. Two more American submarines have been announced as lost by the Navy. The two were the 1525 ton Cisco and 850 ton S-44, carrying a total of 110 gallant crewmen to their deaths.

Wednesday, February 9, 1944: —The eyes of the world are upon the Italian battlefront. The outcome of the bloody battle for the Roman Beachhead may have a vital effect on the course of the war. Russia, you can be sure, is watching the struggle with a critical, if not disparaging eye. The Balkans are also eyeing the Italian situation carefully to find a clue as to their course of action. Turkey, in particular, is likely to await the outcome before committing herself to any belligerent role. In addition, the success or failure of the Rome drive is bound to have an important effect on General Eisenhower's plans for the anticipated general invasion of Europe. Consequently, we can expect to hear of ferocious fighting, for the Germans are fully cognizant of the crucial character of the battle.

The one place in the Italian campaign where the Allied plans went completely awry was at Cassino. It seems clear now that General Clark expected that a quick breakthrough at Cassino would follow the successful landing just south of Rome. He would then smash forward to affect a quick junction between the two elements of the Fifth Army. Unfortunately, however, the desperate Germans held at Cassino, sparing no cost to make a miniature Stalingrad of the town. As a result, the battle for Cassino has been a see-saw affair, leaving the northern, amphibious section of the Fifth Army to shift for itself. The Germans have meanwhile pulled heavily on their reserves in northern Italy to mount a mighty counter-attack, aimed at crushing the Allied beachhead and driving the Americans and British into the sea. The issue is still in doubt.

Thursday, February 10, 1944: —The picture in Italy is slightly improved tonight. According to latest reports the Allies have succeeded in stemming the German onslaught against the Anzio beachhead. Accurate fire from massed artillery is credited with stopping the Nazis as they stormed the American and British lines with tanks and infantry. There is no indication, however, that the danger is past as the Germans have brought up powerful forces, including crack panzer units, to smash at the beachhead.

General Douglas MacArthur today announced the victorious conclusion of the rugged New Guinea jungle campaign, little mentioned in previous news reports, in which Australian and American troops trapped and virtually annihilated a Japanese army of 14,000 men. Only those who fled into the mountains escaped and they face almost certain death, either from the jungle itself or from native tribes. The campaign just concluded was a two-pronged squeeze play in which American troops landed by sea at Saidor on the north coast of New Guinea and smashed southward to affect a junction with Australian troops moving north from captured Finschhafen. The junction took place at old Yagomi, after the Aussies had fought their way 150 miles through some of the wildest jungle country in the world. The bitterness and hardships of that five months campaign can only be told by those who had to endure them. The terrible obstacles overcome add a glorious chapter to the accomplishments of the tireless "diggers" and their "doughboy" comrades.

Friday, February 11, 1944: —The military situation in Italy has taken a turn for the worse and Allied Headquarters announced that our invasion forces south of Rome are in grave peril. The American and British troops are literally fighting with their backs to the sea, being hemmed in and hammered by the concentric blows of six German divisions. Having failed to attain its primary objective of diverting enough strength from the enemy's Gustav line to permit a breakthrough at Cassino by the main body of the Fifth Army, the invasion force now finds itself in a "tough spot" on the Anzio beachhead. Military observers from the front lines made no effort to minimize the gravity of the situation and it is possible that we face a bitter repetition of Dunkirk. Our forces have maintained control of the sea and air, however, and our commanders are praying for a few days of good flying weather to permit them to throw the full weight of our aerial strength into the fray. The whole campaign, like so many others in history, depends for its success or failure upon the capricious whims of the weather. May God grant that Old Man Sol may smile upon our hard pressed troops during the next few crucial days.

The Navy announced another bag of Japanese ships by the ubiquitous American submarines. The twelve enemy vessels reported sunk in this latest communiqué brings the grand total of Japanese vessels destroyed by American undersea boats to 584. Only history will reveal the actual effect of this war of attrition upon the final outcome of the struggle. Obviously, however, the "Silent Service" has done a magnificent job.

Saturday, February 12, 1944: —It is Lincoln's Birthday today but it meant no holiday for us and thousands of other war workers in the Bay Area. Commuter trains were almost as crowded today as at any other time and the street cars and buses packed them in like sardines as usual. Not even the Great Emancipator's birthday could slowdown the production of war materials.

There was no lull on the fighting fronts either. Wave after wave of desperate Germans beat themselves to death against the stonewall defenses thrown up by gallant American troops on the crucial Anzio beachhead in Italy. The incredibly determined stand by our forces during the past 24 hours has changed the outlook on the critical beachhead battle from one of deep despair and danger to one of hopeful anticipation of eventual victory. General Sir Harold R.L.G.Alexander, Allied Commander in Italy, was moved to report to Prime Minister Churchill that he is confident that the great battle for the capture of Rome will be won. God grant that he may be right.

Activity in the Pacific war is again picking up momentum. Allied aircraft were particularly busy, raiding Rabaul with a large force of more than 250 planes, and smashing at other Japanese targets that included Wake Island, Wewak, and Madang.

The great battleship, Oklahoma, sunk and capsized during the attack on Pearl Harbor, has been floated again and will soon join the fleet to gain revenge.

Sunday, February 13, 1944: —Today was one of those rare and beautiful days that come but once or twice during a year— almost always in the spring. There was an invigorating warmth in the air that can only be appreciated after many long days of coldness and dampness. There was a freshness about everything like a person just after a hot bath. There seemed to be an extra sort of freedom in the air—typified by the shirtsleeves on the men and the gingham dresses on the women—as though everyone had just broken out of cocoons. Every grass blade seemed to be stretching upward to draw in great gulps of sunshine. Green buds seemed to pop out on every limb like little eyes peering out to see if the coast is clear for mother tree to come out of hibernation. Even the wild birds seemed to have donned new spring suits of brighter plumage and they darted and whirred about as though recognizing this as an especially delightful day in which to gambol.

On such a day it is hard to think of war and the destruction of life and beauty. Somehow the two ideas don't mix. Living here in the midst of spring beauty one just isn't capable of conceiving the realities of war. And yet while we bask in warm, peaceful sunshine, hateful eyes are peering down rifle barrels, aiming sudden death at American boys. Underneath Italian and Japanese soil lie canisters of destruction awaiting only the unsuspecting pressure of an American foot. Men are being slaughtered, maimed and tortured at the very moment that bright-hued little birds are cavorting around my doorway. Can this be one world? Can both these things happen on one small planet?

Monday, February 14, 1944: —Fierce fighting continues to rage on the two fronts in Italy. American infantrymen advancing in the Cassino area have been delayed for several days by German machine gunners and snipers who have taken cover in the famous Benedictine Monastery atop Mount Cassino. Rather than bomb or shell the ancient shrine, our troops have tried several times to take the hill by storm. Each time, however, they have been driven back with heavy losses. Finally the decision has been made to train our big guns on the Monastery. Before doing so a barrage of leaflets has been dropped within the shrine's stone walls, warning the monks to flee and explaining the necessity for training the guns of war upon the sacred landmark. Only the Nazis' persistence in taking advantage of our reluctance to destroy historic monuments has made our action necessary. Hitler and his cohorts seem determined to take the whole civilized world with them to destruction if they can.

Another solid punch was landed in Japan's South Pacific solar plexus last Saturday, it was announced today. American invasion forces occupied Rooke Island in the Dampier Straits between New Guinea and New Britain, further strengthening our control of the famous straits and completing one more step in our campaign against Rabaul on New Britain.

Tuesday, February 15, 1944: —Carrying out yesterday's warning, American Flying Fortresses and the Fifth Army's big siege guns poured hundreds of tons of steel and explosives into the ancient Benedictine Monastery on Mount Cassino today, knocking out German machine gun nests and artillery emplacements which have harassed the advancing Americans for almost two weeks.

Simultaneously, other Allied aircraft began what appears to be an all-out aerial offensive designed to completely smash Germany's hold on central Italy. One attack was aimed against railroad marshalling yards in Rome itself and the Axis radio in that city admitted that serious damage was done.

Stonewall defense by Allied troops in the bloody Anzio beachhead battle has caused the Nazis' offensive in that region to end in "costly failure" according to an Allied Headquarters' spokesman. Our troops have covered themselves with glory during the past week of desperate combat. Our faith in their prowess has been heightened.

The kind of sacrifice our fighting men are prepared to make is told in the story of a radio operator in one of our Flying

Fortresses participating in a raid across the English Channel. The plane was badly damaged by flak, one motor was gone, and there was doubt if the sinking craft would make it back to England. Everything movable was being jettisoned. The radio operator, blinded and bleeding from a terrible head would tried to throw himself out and when restrained, begged his comrades to throw him out saying, "I'm hit badly and no use to you now . . . it'll save 175 pounds and maybe get you back." They didn't throw him out and somehow the plane got back. That's how to win the Congressional Medal of Honor.

Wednesday, February 16, 1944: —Mighty fleets of heavy RAF bombers pounded Berlin again last night. It was the greatest aerial assault ever leveled against a single target in one night. More than 1,000 planes participated in the Berlin attack, raining explosives and incendiaries on the flaming target at the rate of 140 tons a minute. A grand total of 3,000 tons of bombs cascaded into the tortured enemy capital. Returning flyers stated that huge conflagrations bathed the whole city in a ghastly red glow, with smoke clouds rising to a height of 20,000 feet.

While German defense forces were occupied in the Berlin area, another Allied raiding force of 200 four motored bombers plastered the railroad yards at Frankfurt-on-Oder almost without opposition. Allied losses in all operations were only 43 planes— less than 4% of the raiding fleet.

American forces are already making good use of the advanced airfields captured recently in the Marshall Islands. Giant Liberator bombers carried out a successful raid on Ponape Island, heavily fortified Japanese stronghold in the Carolines only 400 miles from the great enemy naval base of Truk. All of our planes returned safely. This attack represented our deepest penetration of Japan's island empire to date. Look out, Tojo, here we come!

Chinese reports hint that the Japs are heaping new indignities upon American prisoners by parading them ignominiously through Chinese cities in occupied China. What else can you expect from savages?

Thursday, February 17, 1944: —Truk, the Japanese "Pearl Harbor" is under attack by a powerful American task force. This sensational news broke today and astonished the world. Not even the most optimistic expected our forces fresh from their Marshall Islands victory to immediately attack Japan's strongest central Pacific base, considered by Japanese strategists to be impregnable. The extent of the attack is not yet known as most of the early reports have come through enemy sources. The excited Tokyo radio, however, claims that a fierce battle is in progress, with American mechanized forces landing at several points. It is noted that no Allied reports mention any landings, which if true, would be the most formidable Allied invasion attempt in the Pacific war to date. That heavy action is occurring there can be no doubt.

Here at home another type of enemy is being smashed with the help of an alert service station attendant who has two brothers in the service. The enemy is the black market operator who preys on the war effort by marketing illicit gas ration books. OPA enforcement officials today trapped several members of a wide-spread ring of racketeers and found gas coupons worth 3,000,000 gallons. Other arrests are expected in rapid-fire order.

Mounting casualties and increased military activities are causing draft boards to call thousands of pre-Pearl Harbor fathers into the service. From now on it appears that only the essential character of a man's work and not his dependency status will influence the august members of the draft board.

Friday, February 18, 1944: —Secretary of the Navy Frank Knox has released some information on the Truk attack. Full details are not available as radio silence has not yet been broken by the attacking force, indicating that the operation is still in progress. The Secretary, however, stated that a smashing victory has already been won, although he characterized Japanese claims that a landing has been made as "propaganda lies." No landings were attempted; our forces merely attacked by sea and air, launching hundreds of carrier-based planes which swept over the enemy stronghold and inflicted heavy damage. Further reports will reveal a devastating toll of enemy ships, planes, and shore installation.

At the same time, another powerful American amphibious force, including Marine and Army units swarmed ashore Eniwetok Atoll at the northwest corner of the Marshall Islands. The landing was successfully made under cover of a tremendous bombardment by heavy units of the fleet, including battleships. The Japs may have confused this landing with the supposed landing on Truk, especially since the jittery Tokyo radio has contradicted itself at least three times already since the first alarming (to them) news of the Truk attack.

The fighting in Italy continues bloody and indecisive although the tide is slowly turning in favor of our forces. The desperate Germans are still counter-attacking against the Anzio beachhead but are being cut down in droves by massed American artillery. At Cassino, Allied troops are inching forward against stern resistance. Blood flows freely in Italy these days. In fact one might say that "All roads bleed to Rome."

Saturday, February 19, 1944: —Official reports indicate that the U.S. landing on Eniwetok Atoll has been successfully consolidated and the Marines and Doughboys are well on their way towards mopping up enemy resistance. The importance of this operation is clear when we remember that Eniwetok is only 750 miles from Truk and will provide a land base for heavy bombers to attack that enemy stronghold.

The battering of Truk itself by a powerful American task force is apparently at an end but only meager news has been released regarding the results. Details must await the return of the task force since radio silence must be preserved to insure the safety of the fleet.

The Japs are discovering that they are playing in a pretty fast league. In addition to the beating they are taking in the Central and South Pacific areas, our submarines are dishing out bitter medicine to them right in their own front yard. The Navy announced today that two U.S. subs recently returned from a sortie into Japanese home waters in which thirteen enemy vessels were sunk or damaged by our undersea raiders. 447 of the total were sunk for sure, the others were hit but listed only as "probable."

On the home front we learn that elder statesman Bernard Baruch has submitted a "reconversion" plan to the President. The plan is a blueprint for "speeding victory, getting us all back to work on peacetime enterprises, and taking the Government out of business."

Sunday, February 20, 1944: —Another Sunday and a day of rest here at home. On the far-flung fighting fronts, however, there is no rest. During the past week the tempo of the war seems to have speeded up, indicating that spring is approaching with all that it heralds in the way of decisive and bloody campaigning. This spring and summer will see the avenging forces of the Allies come to bitter grips with the enemy in what we fervently hope will be the final campaign. Our strength is growing rapidly, his is weakening; one day he will crack suddenly and the end will come. Until then there must be no relaxing of the pressure.

Admiral Chester W. Nimitz announced from Pearl Harbor that our troops have captured the airfield on Eniwetok Atoll in the Marshalls, giving us a magnificent bomber base only 750 miles from Truk. Our losses in taking the island were exceptionally light, said the Admiral.

Russo-Finnish negotiations for peace are under way in Stockholm and it is hoped the unhappy Finns may soon be out of the war, although Russia's terms will undoubtedly be severe. Fortune has not been very kind to Finland, squeezed as she has been between the two great powers, Germany and Russia. Our sympathies have always been with the tiny but courageous republic who never failed, even when fighting on the side of our enemy, to pay her honest debt. Let us hope that a brighter future is in store for the brave and likeable Finns.

Monday, February 21, 1944: —Admiral Chester W. Nimitz, commander of our Pacific fleet, today told the full story of the Navy's great victory at Truk. Nineteen Japanese ships were sent to the bottom of the harbor, at least 201 enemy planes were destroyed and severe damage was inflicted on land installations at the mighty Japanese base. Included in the ships sunk were two light cruisers, three destroyers, and one seaplane tender. The rest were cargo vessels and gunboats.

Carrier planes carried out the devastating attack last Wednesday and Thursday and scored the telling victory at a cost of only seventeen planes. As Admiral Nimitz put it, the raid was only a "partial settlement" of the debt owed Japan for the sneak attack on Pearl Harbor.

While Truk and the Marshall Islands were being attacked, another U.S. naval task force was carrying out a diversionary raid on Paramushiro in the Kuriles. The raid was made by Navy Venture bombers, all of which returned safely after plastering the jittery Japs in their own backyard.

Repercussions of the recent Japanese defeats have been felt keenly in Tokyo it was indicated today as Premier General Hideki Tojo ousted the chiefs of both the Army and Navy. Fleet Admiral Osami Nagano was relieved of his command and Admiral Shigetaro Shimada ordered to serve as chief of the naval general staff. Premier Tojo himself assumed the duties of chief of the army general, replacing Field Marshal General Sugiyama. Concurrently with the announcements of the army and navy shakeup, the Tokyo radio for the first time admitted accurately the real extent of the heavy damage suffered at Truk.

Tuesday, February 22, 1944: —President Roosevelt today invited a bitter fight with Congress by vetoing the new tax bill recently passed by the legislators. The President used strong language in turning down the bill which, he said, fell far short of being an adequate wartime measure. "It is not a tax bill," he said, "but a tax relief bill providing relief not for the needy but for the greedy." The bill as passed is purported to provide for two billion, one hundred million in new revenues, whereas the President had originally asked for Congress to obtain at least ten billions in additional taxes. Members of Congress, both Republican and Democrats, obviously did not care for the tone of the President's message and a strong attempt will undoubtedly be made to override the veto.

Prime Minister Winston Churchill addressed Commons today for 78 minutes, reporting on the progress of the war and predicting that Germany will be crushed in an assault "far beyond the dimensions of anything yet employed or, indeed, imagined," but he warned that the enemy will retaliate with new weapons and he could offer no assurance that the war would end this year. "The task is heavy, the toil is long, and the trail will be severe," he said, "let us all try our best to do our duty. Victory may not be far away and certainly will not be denied us in the end."

We cannot let the Birthday anniversary of George Washington go by without expressing the wish that our military leaders may be endowed with a little of the genius that enabled that first great American general to win that first great American fight for freedom.

Wednesday, February 23, 1944: —A strong U.S. naval task force has raided Japanese bases in the Mariana Islands only 1,500 miles from Tokyo. Saipan and Tinian islands were the targets for the scores of American planes launched from aircraft carriers, while heavy units of the American fleet stood boldly offshore and poured tons of shells into the Japanese strongholds.

The Mariana Islands are the next to last island strongholds barring the way to the mainland of Japan and the two islands attacked are just north of Guam, which the Japs captured from us early in the war. Detail of the damage done in the daring raid will be announced as soon as radio silence can be broken. Early indications are that he surprise attack may have caught several units of the Jap navy at anchor, after the fashion of the recent Truk raid.

In Italy, American and British troops are facing new counter-attacks against the Anzio beachhead. The Germans are charging savagely and without regard for losses in a desperate effort to crush the Allied armies and hurl them back into the sea. Our forces so far are holding firm.

Here at home the recent gasoline black market expose has taken a new turn with the disclosure that the C ration books covering 3,000,000 gallons which were recently seized were not stolen from the OPA as originally believed, but are counterfeit coupons. Authorities fear that the whole western area may be swamped with the illegal books. Drastic steps are in the offing.

Thursday, February 24, 1944: —A defiant and resentful House of Representatives today voted to over-ride President Roosevelt's veto of the recent tax bill. The vote was 299 to 95, 36 more than the two-thirds necessary to pass the bill over the President's head. The Senate will vote on the measure tomorrow and is expected to over-ride the veto by a similarly wide margin. It is the first time Congress has really been aroused since President Roosevelt attempted to pack the Supreme Court. It is democracy at work.

The kaleidoscopic developments in the Pacific war and the bitter, crucial battle in Italy have more or less consigned the Russian war news to a secondary position for the past few weeks. Nevertheless, the main land fighting, involving by far the largest number of troops, is still going on in Russia and Poland. Triumphant Soviet armies are pressing the Fascist invaders back all along the 1,500 mile front. More than three-fourths of Russian territory once over-run by the Teutonic hordes has been liberated and some Soviet forces have already swept across the borders of pre-war Poland. Russian aircraft dominate the eastern skies, though credit for this condition belongs to the British and American air fleets which have lured 90% of Germany's air strength to western Europe where the Nazis are engaged in a desperate struggle to stop the paralyzing aerial offensive of the Allies. Russian armies, however, have met and defeated the mightiest German army ever assembled and no one can ever deny them the credit and glory of their amazing achievement. Their courage and skill have altered the course of history to an extent so great that it cannot be measured.

Friday, February 25, 1944: —The Senate completed the revolt of Congress against the President by over-riding the tax bill veto by a 79 to 14 vote, 14 more than the required two-thirds. Thus the $2,355,000,000 tax bill becomes the law of the land by Congressional action which reaffirmed the majority's belief in the wisdom of the founding fathers who delegated the tax making power to the legislative branch of the government, not to the executive branch.

The Navy today announced the results of last Tuesday's raid on the Japanese Mariana Islands. At the loss of only six planes, our task force destroyed 135 enemy planes, sank two ships and damaged nine others, besides smashing port facilities and other land installations. One objective of the raid failed, however, that of locating the elusive Japanese main fleet, which apparently skedaddled for safer waters after detection of the approach of our raiders. The enemy cannot disregard the challenge much longer unless he wants our fleet right in Tokyo Bay.

The United States Eighth and Fifteenth Air Forces based in England and Italy have begun a squeeze play against Germany's aircraft production plants. Strong formations from both American bases have been striking at the heart of Germany's plane production, smashing plants at Regensburg, Schweinfurt, Steyr, and Stuttgart. The American planes have fought their way by daylight through clouds of enemy fighters, shooting down 156 Messerschmitts and Focke-Wulfs in yesterday's raids alone. Our losses also have been considerable, 78 bombers and escorting fighters failing to return from yesterdays sorties.

Saturday, February 26, 1944: —The past six days have seen the most concentrated and devastating aerial offensive in the history of the world leveled at Hitler's Germany. The Nazis' aircraft manufacturing and assembly plants have been the principal objectives of the mighty Allied air fleets launched from England and Italy. A high ranking observer said that the attacks have knocked out at least half of Germany's plane production and have wrecked any Nazi hopes of maintaining a successful air defense of the Reich. The day is coming when our planes will roam the skies over Germany opposed only by anti-aircraft fire from the ground. In the six day period American planes alone have shot down a total of 641 enemy planes—far more than can be replaced. It can be safely said that the great aerial battle over Germany—a necessary prelude to a land invasion—is being won by a decisive margin.

Very little progress is being made by either side in the battle for Rome. Our forces are holding firm in the Anzio beachhead region but have not yet been able to recover the initiative. The Germans apparently have not given up hope of driving the Allied forces into the sea and are massing a powerful force of at least 100,000 men for a third attempt to smash the beachhead. Doughboys and Tommies are ready for them.

President Roosevelt ordered the Selective Service to recheck all deferments for occupational reasons in a tightening of draft regulations designed to eliminate the army's present shortage of 200,000 men needed to maintain efficiency.

Sunday, February 27, 1944: —Interest is aroused at the possibility that Finland may soon be out of the war with Russia. Negotiations are under way in Stockholm between representatives of the two countries and late reports indicate that Moscow's terms may be acceptable to the Finns. To emphasize the fate that awaits them if they do not make peace now, the Red Army Air Force struck its heaviest blow of the war against the Finnish capital of Helsinki. Six hundred Soviet planes raided the hapless capital, setting huge conflagrations and wrecking large sections of the city. The Finns were powerless to resist.

The principal obstacle to a withdrawal of Finland from the war is the presence in that country of 100,000 German troops who would probably turn the little republic into another battleground like Italy. Even so, there is little else the Finns can do if they would salvage anything from the disastrous fate that has befallen them.

A Tokyo dispatch quoted in Berlin hints that a great naval and air battle is raging near the island of Guam in the central Pacific. According to the Japanese report a large task force of United States warships and aircraft are attacking the formerly American owned island taken by the Japanese early in the war. Our Navy has not confirmed or denied the Japanese story.

General MacArthur's airmen have so reduced the defenses of Rabaul on New Britain and Kavieng on New Ireland that our destroyers are able to steam up and bombard the enemy bases without opposition from the vaunted Jap navy or air force. Occupation of these two important bases appears to be only a matter of days—or at most weeks.

Monday, February 28, 1944: —Yesterday's Japanese reports that American forces have attacked Guam and the Mariana Islands were confirmed today. The attack was an aerial blow delivered by 200 American carrier-based aircraft that winged their way from an estimated ten U.S. carriers. Indications are that the Nips were again caught flat-footed and totally surprised. The extent of the damage inflicted is, of course, not yet known but our own losses were almost negligible.

Furious fighting is still raging in the vicinity of the Allied beachhead just south of Rome in Italy. All German thrusts aimed at scoring a breakthrough in the Allied lines have been decisively beaten by heroic troops of the American Fifth Army. British units of the Fifth have conducted themselves magnificently, retaking two strongly fortified positions in today's fighting. Operations by both sides have been marked by furious artillery barrages and savage encounters between opposing tank forces.

On the home front a new wrinkle was inaugurated in food rationing procedures. Dime-sized red and blue tokens will be used to make change in points when rationed products are sold. Point rationing was originated by the British but the token idea is America's contribution. It will take a little while to see whether the idea will help the harassed housewife.

Selective Service announced today that a thorough review of all occupational deferments will be made in an effort to find single men for the army and thus relieve the need for inducting pre-war fathers.

Tuesday, February 29, 1944: —Leap Year's extra day finds American fighting forces striking a new blow at our Oriental enemies, this time in the Admiralty Islands, 250 miles north of New Guinea. General Douglas MacArthur's Headquarters announced the new invasion attempt and said that initial landings made this morning have been successfully developed.

Capture of the Admiralty Islands will give our forces a formidable land base only 725 miles from the great Japanese stronghold at Truk in the Carolines. With the Marshall Islands now in our hands a giant pincers is closing down on the enemy at Truk, indicating that in all probability the full weight of our growing power will be thrown into an offensive designed to render that Japanese "Pearl Harbor" useless. Admiral Halsey's creed of "hit hard, hit fast, hit often" is really being adopted in the Pacific.

Another branch of the service that is doing a brilliant job in the Pacific is the submarine service. Secretary of the Navy Knox announced today that our undersea raiders have sunk 14 more Japanese ships in attacks rammed home in the enemy's own front yard. This raised to 461 the number of Jap ships definitely sunk by American subs since the start of the war. 36 others were probably sunk and 114 were damaged.

500 American Flying Fortresses made a raid on Germany today that was unique because there was practically no fighter opposition. This lack of resistance was ascribed principally to dirty flying weather but some expert observers believe it heralds the day of absolute Allied aerial supremacy over the continent. When that day comes, victory cannot be for away.

March

Wednesday, March 1, 1944: —U.S. cavalry is fighting in the Admiralty Islands. Dismounted elements of the First Cavalry Division were the shock troops that made the initial landing on tiny Los Negros Island after a pulverizing air and naval bombardment. The airdrome on the little island was quickly seized against ineffective Japanese resistance.

The landing in the Admiralties has pulled a noose tightly around approximately 50,000 enemy troops trapped in the Bismarck Archipelago and another 22,000 isolated in the Solomons. All these enemy forces are totally cut off from supplies and reinforcements and have only remote chances of escape.

General MacArthur was reported visiting the front lines in the Admiralty and is jubilant over the extent of the victory thus far. He is even more pleased because this newest triumph brings him to within 1,300 miles of his beloved Philippines.

Wake Island, the scene of American heroism in the early days of the war, was attacked by Navy Liberators today. Each of the planes' calling card warned the Japs that we are coming back. Your days on that American shrine are numbered, Mr. Moto.

Robot tanks, operated by radio, were flung at American lines in Italy today but the secret weapon was a flop. American "bazookas" quickly knocked the explosive-laden "beetles" out. They were "poor specimens" said one Allied spokesman.

Thursday, March 2, 1944: —The British have taken a hand in the Pacific fighting, with the announcement that one of their submarines made a successful attack on a large Japanese aircraft carrier, sending her to the bottom with two torpedo hits. The action took place on the northern approaches to the strait between Malaya and Sumatra.

Germany's aerial scourge was continued during the past twenty-four hours. More than 2,500 planes, American and British, participated in the giant raids, encountering only light opposition front the depleted German Air Force. Stuttgart was hit during the night with 1,680 tons of explosives dropped from hundreds of heavy RAF bombers of which only four were lost for an all time record low. Frankfurt-on-the-Main was the target of

American heavyweights who attacked by daylight. Eleven of our bombers did not return.

The battle of the Anzio beachhead in Italy continued to rage today, with clearing skies permitting increased support from Allied air forces. Big American four motored bombers were thrown into the fray, indicating the seriousness of the situation, as the heavyweights are intended for behind-the-lines rather than front-line operations.

In the Pacific, fierce fighting is raging for the capture of the Admiralty Islands. The Japs have rallied after the initial surprise and are counter-attacking vigorously. General MacArthur's spokesman stated that the enemy's attacks have been "bloodily repulsed."

Friday, March 3, 1944: —For the first time Berlin has been attacked by daylight. Long-range American fighter planes made the attack, sweeping over the German capital on a strafing mission. It was only a grim foretaste of what is in store for Berlin once the American heavies begin daylight assaults to supplement the punishing RAF blows at night. There will be no rest then, day or night, for the weary Berliners.

Other formations of American Flying Fortresses and Liberators made the third major attack of the war on Rome today. Targets, as before, were the railroad marshalling yards and airfields of the Eternal City. The Germans are making full use of the city for military purposes and as a consequence have made it a prime target. The Nazis are obviously determined to bring the full horror of war to the ancient city. For our forces there is no alternative if the enemy decides to use its facilities to fight us.

It was disclosed in Washington today that plans are being made to assign one-third of the surrendered Italian fleet to Russia. The remainder will fight with the navies of Britain and the United States. When the transfer will be made was not divulged.

The Navy announced today that Ventura medium bombers have again raided Japan's northern Kurile bases on Paramushiru and Shimusho islands, inflicting considerable damage and escaping without the loss of a plane. Enemy interference was weak and unprepared.

Saturday, March 4, 1944: —Following up yesterday's offensive sweep by fighter planes over Berlin, American Flying

Fortresses bombed the German capital by daylight today. It was the first time American bombers have been over the Nazi city but it will not be the last. It is expected that the Eighth American Air Force will now combine with the British RAF in day and night forays designed to eliminate Berlin once and for all as the center of Nazidom.

Allied dissatisfaction with Turkey's attitude and delay in actively supporting the United Nations' cause, was indicated by the decision announced by Washington and London to halt the delivery of war supplies to that country. Apparently the Turks have been playing both ends against the middle and have continually stalled when asked to make a definite move towards becoming an active ally. Peeved, Washington and London have decided to stop all lend-lease aid for the time being. Arms will be given to those who kill Germans and Japs.

American forces are mopping up on Los Negros Island in the Admiralty group. Determined Japanese counter-attacks were smashed in furious hand-to-hand fighting after which the American troops moved forward in all directions.

Back in Italy it is reported that the most violent battle of the Italian campaign is being fought south of Rome as 100,000 German troops attacked desperately in an effort to wipe out the beachhead. Tremendous artillery barrages from both sides are churning up the ground while infantry and tank forces are locked in a death struggle.

Sunday, March 5, 1944: —It has been a beautiful day today, with the sun warmly confirming the fact that spring is here. It was just such a day on which we used to load the youngsters into the family car and spend the day cruising about enjoying the scenery. But today, even if we could get the gasoline, it would be no use for the old family car is a war casualty, laid up for want of repairs. We are not alone, however, as the newspapers indicate that approximately 8,000 cars per week are being laid up in California alone, due to lack of tires or want of repairs. Today the roads are practically barren of passenger cars, with roadside service stations either closed or displaying signs "No Gas." It's a tough war.

The past twenty four hours have been grim and bloody ones for the American invaders of the Admiralty Islands. The Japanese launched a final desperate counter-attack to capture Momote airdrome on Los Negros Island but were repulsed after a fierce, hand-to-hand battle that left the field strewn with Japanese and American dead. At the end of the day the airfield was still ours and will remain so.

The German's offensive against the Allied beachhead south of Rome apparently has again bogged down in the mud and slush of extremely bad weather. Our defenses have held three major blows as would a stone wall. Until the weather shows a marked improvement and the ground dries sufficiently to permit the use of mechanized equipment on a grand scale we can expect to see a stalemate on the Italian front.

Monday, March 6, 1944: —A fifteen mile long parade of heavy American bombers plastered Berlin today in the first massive daylight attack by our Air Force on the Nazi capital. Hundreds of Flying Fortresses and Liberators, supported by clouds of long-range fighter planes, swarmed over the heart of Germany in a "blitz" attack that left the enemy capital a mass of flames and bomb smashed debris.

The big American planes were forced to fight their way to and from the target in what was undoubtedly one of the greatest aerial battles of all time. Hundreds of German fighters intercepted the American armada long before it arrived at the target and engaged the big ships and their protecting fighter screen in a series of bitter engagements. Plane losses on both sides were heavy although exact figures have not yet been revealed.

This full-scale raid by daylight on Berlin is vitally important, since it indicates that Allied aerial might has grown to the point where an attempt can be made to wrest daylight supremacy in the air over Germany itself. This is especially important to insure the success of any invasion of the Continent from the west. Today's raid showed that the Nazis' aerial defenses can be overwhelmed.

The Burma front has flamed into action. American veterans of the Solomons campaign have arrived in the Burma Theater and have smashed a Japanese force in the Naga Hills sector of northern Burma. 2,000 Nipponese troops were trapped by the American veterans who surprised the enemy after a forced march of more than 200 miles.

Tuesday, March 7, 1944: —Details of yesterday's great daylight raid on Berlin were revealed today. American bombers and fighters shot down a total of 176 Nazi planes in the furious air battles over the continent while 68 of our bombers and ten of our fighters were lost. 2,000 tons of explosives and fire bombs were dropped on the German capital which was left wrapped in a blanket of flames and billowing smoke. Of the 176 enemy planes downed, Flying Fortresses and Liberators accounted for 93, the rest being destroyed by the escorting fighters.

Our losses of 68 bombers and 10 fighters were the heaviest yet suffered by the U.S. Air Force in England, the planes representing $17,250,000 worth of equipment. More serious was the loss of the 690 members of the planes' crews. Many of these boys parachuted to earth and were undoubtedly taken prisoner by the Germans.

Admiral Nimitz shed some light on the Pacific fighting today at a press conference with Secretary of the Navy Frank Knox. The Admiral was of the opinion that the Japs are finding it impossible to maintain major Navy units at Truk because our submarines and task forces have sunk so many Japanese tankers and supply ships. This explains why the American attackers found no major ships. This explains why the American attackers found no major units of the Jap fleet at the big enemy base when they raided it recently. "We are getting the ships and men now and all we need is time to carry out our operations," the Admiral said, "The principal obstacle now is not the Japanese, but geography— the size of the Pacific ocean."

Wednesday, March 8, 1944: —For the fourth time in six days American planes struck at Berlin today. It was another vast daylight attack, carried out by more than 800 mighty Flying Fortresses and Liberators, supported by hundreds of long-range fighter planes. More than 350,000 incendiaries were dumped on the German capital which was still smoldering from the fury of previous attacks. Giant fires joined together to envelope vast sections of the city in seas of flame.

Early reports indicated that today's assault was far more successful than Monday's great raid in which 68 huge bombers and 10 fighters were lost. Our losses in today's raid apparently were much smaller. At least 83 Nazi planes were destroyed by the deadly guns of the Forts and their escorting fighters.

The Navy revealed today that our bombers have again raided the Japanese Kurile Islands, blasting shipping and shore installations at Paramushiro. All our planes returned safely.

Allied Headquarters in Naples today disclosed that the First and Third Battalions of American Rangers fell into a Nazi trap in the battle for Cisterna and were annihilated in a bitter fight to the death. Only a few survivors were able to make their way back to Allied lines when the two battalions were surrounded and crushed by overwhelming enemy forces. It was the end for the gallant First and Third Rangers who had distinguished themselves from Dieppe to Oran and from Tunisia to Sicily.

Thursday, March 9, 1944: —Berlin is still on the receiving end of probably the most concentrated and persistent aerial bombardment in history. American daylight bombers were again over the German capital today, this time meeting only light opposition from enemy fighters although anti-aircraft fire was heavy as usual. The effectiveness of recent raids in beating down Nazi defenses was indicated by the fact that only seven bombers were lost in today's attack, a far cry from the 68 lost in Monday's raid. From the weight of explosives and fire bombs being dropped on the German capital that city is fast joining Hamburg in the ranks of destroyed cities. What a terrible retribution Hitler has brought upon his people. How can they continue to follow his leadership?

German fortunes are waning fast on the Eastern front as well. Russian troops are driving forward along the entire length of the vast front, inflicting catastrophe after disaster upon the fleeing Fascists. The Nazis hold only one salient into Russian territory and that is along the Dnieper River. Here Red Army troops during the last 48 hours have slashed 37 miles into the salient, carrying them within 40 miles of the Black Sea port of Nikolayev. In the western Ukraine, other Russian columns have battled into the streets of the former Polish rail junction of Ternopol.

Secretary of War Stimson summarized American casualties in the war to date as 162,282, of which 37,853 are known to be dead. The others are wounded, missing, or captured by the enemy. 12,506 Filipino scouts are included in the figure.

Friday, March 10, 1944: —While vast preparations are being made in England for the invasion of Europe, scores of Axis agents brazenly stare across the Irish sea from Eire and watch the preparations, plotting against the lives of the hundreds of thousands of American and British troops who will soon face the Nazi enemy in the showdown battle of the war. The Irish have steadfastly maintained their precarious neutrality and have permitted German and Japanese diplomatic and espionage agents free access to their country. This has obviously posed a menace to the success of Allied military operations from England and threatens the life of every American soldier who will participate in the coming invasion. The Governments of Britain and the United States have therefore requested the Dublin government to oust the Axis agents and, if possible, to break diplomatic relations with the Axis governments. Eire has refused to comply with either request. The situation is ticklish and tense.

Meanwhile the Allied aerial offensive is continuing without let-up. It is reliably reported that the successful daylight raids on Berlin by the American Air Force have forced a big shakeup in the Luftwaffe's High Command. Goering, the braggart, who once boasted that no enemy plane would ever bomb Berlin, has taken a back seat and younger men have seized control.

One of the jolliest men of our times died today. It was Irvin S. Cobb, famous columnist and humorist. Like Will Rogers, he spoke the language of the common man and knew how to make him chuckle. Such men are rare.

Saturday, March 11, 1944: —The United States Government today warned Eire that we are not bound to abstain from force to prevent Axis agents in that country from learning Allied secrets concerning the forthcoming invasion. If it is deemed necessary to save American lives we may have to oust the Axis from Ireland ourselves, however distasteful the prospects may be. The English Government is taking the same view.

The mighty armies of Russia are still driving the battered Germans before them on the Eastern front. Powerful blows by three Russian armies along a 500 mile Ukrainian battle line sent the Nazis reeling back towards the Bug River and the Rumanian frontier. Vast quantities of equipment and supplies were abandoned by the Germans in their headlong flight to avoid encirclement such as happened at Stalingrad last winter and at Cherkassy last month. In their haste to escape they also abandoned thousands of their dead and wounded.

Today's biggest air battle in the aerial offensive over Europe raged in the skies over Padua in Northern Italy for 35 minutes this afternoon. The guns of our Flying Fortresses and Liberators accounted for a "large number" of enemy interceptors which sought to prevent them from reaching their objectives—which were reached and the targets destroyed nevertheless.

Discouraged Nazi troops again beat their heads against the stonewall defenses of the Americans on the Anzio beachhead in Italy and again retired frustrated.

Sunday, March 12, 1944: —Another Sabbath but no day of rest for us. We worked as usual today, putting in long hours to make sure that people had the wherewithal to pay their income taxes next Wednesday. It hardly seems like much of a contribution to the war effort to redeem War Savings Bonds when people are being urged so to buy them, but when you stop to think that folks wouldn't be so anxious to purchase bonds if they couldn't get their money back promptly in accordance with the Government's written promise, you realize that this too is part of the war effort. It's part of the American way.

The principal theater of fighting is still Russia. Powerful Red Armies are closing in on the main German bastion of Ternopol in the southern Ukraine while the desperate Nazis are throwing everything they have, including armored trains and heavy artillery, into a bitter defense of the stronghold. A breakthrough at Ternopol might precipitate a general German withdrawal from the Ukraine, with the definite possibility that some German divisions might be cut off and destroyed. Hence the present battle is one of the toughest of the entire war.

Pope Pius XII today implored Allied and German military leaders to spare Rome from the full horrors of war. Our side would gladly comply but the key lies in the hands of the German leaders. If they choose to use the Eternal City as a military base and its streets as fortifications we shall be obliged to blast the enemy and destroy him wherever he may be found. Upon his shoulders will lay the onus.

Monday, March 13, 1944: —All travel was banned between Britain and Ireland, except in emergency cases, as consideration was being given to the application of certain other steps, possibly including economic sanction, against Eire in the dispute over the ouster of German and Japanese agents from the Irish republic. Dublin asked the Australian Government to intercede in its behalf but was rebuffed. Australia is in agreement with the American stand.

Meanwhile in the Pacific air war American planes ranged far and wide to blast Japanese bases in the central Pacific area. Wake Island saw American colors again and was given an explosive greeting with fifty tons of bombs. All our aircraft returned safely from the excursion.

General James H. (Jimmy) Doolittle, the man who led the first Tokyo raid, today was nominated for promotion from Major General to Lieutenant General. The famous flying General is now in London preparing to lead Allied air power in the European invasion. He is well qualified, having commanded our strategic air force in the battles of Tunisia and Sicily.

The battle for Ternopol is still raging in Russia. However, Marshal Stalin today announced the capture of Kherson, vital Nazi rail hub on the lower Dnieper. The plight of Hitler's Ukrainian forces is daily becoming worse. Retreat into Rumania appears inevitable. The strength of the Russian armies is a source of wonderment and admiration.

Tuesday, March 14, 1944: —Home front news holds the spotlight in the papers tonight. Selective Service requirements are becoming more and more stringent as many local draft boards are finding it difficult to fill their quotas. The induction of pre-Pearl Harbor fathers is increasing at a rapid rate but consideration is being given to calling up more young war workers and youthful farmers who previously received deferments because of the essential character of their work. These young men are now needed to fill the expanding requirements of the armed forces which call for 500,000 more men for the Navy alone. Army needs will be proportionately greater depending on developments. Many fathers have already been called and many more will be needed.

Meager gas rations will be cut again on March 22nd. At the present time the allotment for "A" card holders is 3 gallons per week. After March 22nd this ration will be cut to 2 gallons per week. Not much traveling can be done on that kind of an allotment.

Bad news gloomed up the war reports today. Another U.S. submarine has been lost in the Pacific, carrying her crew of 65 into oblivion. No one will ever know what happened or where they were lost. Theirs is a lonely sacrifice.

The mighty Russian armies are crunching onward over the wreckage of Germany's Ukrainian forces. The Reds are driving the Nazis pell-mell towards the old Rumanian frontier in their most sustained drive of the war.

Wednesday, March 15, 1944: —In what was probably the most concentrated bombing attack on a single target in the history of warfare, Allied bombers wiped the Italian city of Cassino off the map today. 2,500 tons of bombs were cascaded into the town where the Nazis have stubbornly thwarted every allied effort to dislodge them. Determined to end the stalemate once and for all, the Allied High Command called upon the full power of our Air Force to obliterate the enemy stronghold. Stone by stone, the town was blasted apart until it ceased to exist. When it seemed that no living creature could survive, the barrage of bombs and artillery fire lifted and our tanks and infantry moved in. But out of the ruins German defenders arose somehow and at last reports serious fighting is in progress. Nevertheless, there is every prospect that Cassino will be ours before the passage of another day.

Finland has rejected the Russian terms for peace. This was confirmed tonight by dispatches from Stockholm in which it was stated that the Finnish Parliament has unanimously approved the government's rejection of the Russian proposals. The Finns are grimly facing the consequences.

The German debacle on the southern Russian front is growing daily. Red Army troops have swept across the Middle Bug River and have thrust to within 30 miles of the pre-war Rumanian frontier. Other steel-tipped Russian columns are closing in upon Nikolayev and Odessa, threatening to trap hundreds of thousands of the Fascist invaders. Germany's entire position in southern Europe is precarious.

Thursday, March 16, 1944: —U.S. Army bombers lashed out at the mighty Japanese base of Truk today from newly won land bases in the Marshall and Gilbert islands. The big four-motored liberators struck before dawn and heaped destruction on enemy airdromes, fuel dumps and ammunition depots. All planes returned unscathed, having encountered only ineffective opposition.

In Italy a terrific battle is raging in the ruins of Cassino. Strong enemy units rose as if by magic from the bomb-shattered ruins and met the advancing Fifth Army with fierce mortar, machine gun and sniper fire. German artillery emplaced on the surrounding mountain slopes also poured a stream of shells into the ranks of the advancing Allies. The fight for Cassino obviously is only begun.

The Allied aerial offensive over Europe reached a new peak of intensity during the last twenty-four hours. Huge squadrons of RAF bombers scattered a record load of more than 3,360 tons of explosives and fire bombs across France and Germany during the night and powerful fleets of American bombers followed up with daylight attacks which penetrated deep into the heart of Germany. Strong fighter resistance was encountered by the U.S. planes but 76 of the Nazi interceptors were shot down by the concentrated gunfire of the big bombers. Twenty-two of the American aircraft failed to return.

Friday, March 17, 1944: —As all the world waits breathlessly for the day when Allied troops will land in western Europe and start the final grand march on Berlin, activity on the presently constituted battlefronts increases in tempo as though each one is determined to hold the spotlight as long as possible before the final curtain rises.

The Italian front in particular has flared up with new bitterness as time after time determined drives by the Allies to oust the Germans from Cassino have been frustrated by the desperate Nazis entrenched in the ruins. For weeks veteran New Zealand infantrymen, British Tommies, and American Doughboys have flung themselves against the enemy's fortifications in vain. Even the landing below Rome on the Anzio beachhead, which was intended to lure enough German troops from Cassino to permit a breakthrough, failed utterly. The Nazis did not take the bait.

Two days ago the Allied Air Force leveled the town in one of the concentrated bombing attacks in history. Countless artillery shells followed the bombs into the ruins, yet when the infantry moved in after the barrage, there were the Germans fiercely contesting every yard. Like Stalingrad, Cassino is a hard nut to crack.

Using their new Italian bases to good effect, the 15th U.S. Air Force under Maj. General Nathan F. Twining gave Vienna its first air raid of the war today. Military objectives around the city were successfully attacked without enemy fighter opposition. None of our planes were lost.

Saturday, March 18, 1944: —American bombers struck nearer to the heart of Japan today. Navy Ventura bombers which have repeatedly raided the Japanese Kurile base of Paramushiru, today ventured further south to hit Matsuwa, an island stronghold midway down the archipelago. No fighter opposition was encountered and anti-aircraft fire was light. All attacking planes returned safely. We're coming nearer, Mr. Tojo!

With the good news there is always the bad, especially in wartime. The Navy today sadly announced that two more U.S. subs are long overdue and must be considered lost. Approximately 150 men, including a submarine division commander, were aboard the ill-fated ships. This raises to six the number of American subs reported lost since the first of the year, and to 22 the number lost in the war thus far.

In Russia, the terrific Red Army offensive in the lower Ukraine has penetrated to within sight of the Dniester River border of Bessarabia. The Nazis apparently are helpless to stem the momentum of the Russian offensive which threatens to oust them from Russia entirely and throw the war back to where it started on the fateful day in June, 1941.

Although little real information has come through, it appears that significant events are shaping up in Burma. Lord Louis Mountbatten, the Allied commander in that theater, should be about ready to launch his all out drive to retake the Burma Road. The Japanese also are known to have strong forces in that area and may furnish strong resistance. Increasingly fierce fighting may be expected in Burma from now on.

Sunday, March 19, 1944: —The amazing Russians have surged forward to the eastern bank of the Dniester River today, hurling the shattered remnants of Field Marshal Fritz Erich von Mannstein's vaunted Panzers back into Rumania. Already heavy Russian guns are shelling the retreating enemy on the western side of the Dniester.

In Italy, the sanguinary battle for the ruined city of Cassino is slowly turning in favor of the Allies. Fighting furiously without letup since the town was flattened from the air last Wednesday, shock troops of the American Fifth Army have literally blasted the enemy inch by inch out of the city. Strength of the enemy's remaining garrison is hard to judge since he is in possession of caves and concrete emplacements easy to defend and hard to storm. At the same time his artillery still has positions on the surrounding hills from whence he can rain shells onto the advancing Allies.

The skies over Germany and her occupied countries are black with avenging Allied aircraft these days. An almost unceasing parade of heavy bombers and speedy fighter planes passes over the English Channel day and night to pound targets in France, the Lowlands, and the Third Reich itself. By night the RAF smashes at the centers of German war production in their famous saturation raids. By day, the ever growing United States' Eighth Air Force sends out fleets of from 1,500 to 1,800 bombers and fighters to destroy enemy aircraft and military objectives in highly perfected precision attacks. Death and destruction ride the airways over Germany today.

Monday, March 20, 1944: —Aerial activity in the central Pacific was stepped up during the past few days. American aircraft, both land-based and carrier-based have ranged far and wide over the Pacific to strike at Japanese bases in the eastern Marshalls and the Caroline Islands. Ponape, Japanese stronghold athwart the sea lanes to Truk was heavily hit by Army medium bombers which sank one enemy transport vessel and started huge fires among shore installations. All planes returned.

Allied Headquarters in the Southwest Pacific today announced that to all intents and purposes the Admiralty Islands are ours. Lorengau, the last major Japanese stronghold was seized last Saturday by dismounted units of the First Cavalry Division.

Only mopping-up operations remain before the new base, only 610 miles from Truk, can be put to Allied use.

A preview of the reign of terror that can be expected in Europe after the Nazis are ousted was seen in North Africa today. Collaborationists and Nazi sympathizers will be given short shrift by such groups as the French Committee on National Liberation, which today executed Pierre Pucheu for treason. Pucheu was formerly Vichy minister of interior and a Nazi collaborationist although he later fell out with the Germans and fled from France. To the Free French, however, the stigma of collaborationist is not so easily shed. Once a traitor, always a traitor. So Pierre Pucheu died before a firing squad—died with dignity, so they said, giving the firing orders himself.

Tuesday, March 21, 1944: —Fearing collapse of her satellite partners as the Russian hordes near the Balkans, Germany today took drastic steps to bolster her position in that explosive area. Striking swiftly and without warning the Nazis seized control of Hungary and set up a puppet regime to run the country. Hungary's Regent Admiral Horthy and other members of his government were taken into protective custody by fast-moving Gestapo agents. Although details of the coup are meager, it is indicated that some Hungarian troops are battling the Nazis.

The U.S. Navy today reported that our submarines have added another 15 Japanese vessels to their score in recent sorties. Simultaneously, London announced that British undersea raiders have destroyed seven Japanese vessels in recent attacks in enemy waters off the Malayan peninsula. The American haul brought the number of Jap ships hit by our subs to the grand total of 610.

Secretary of State Cordell Hull today issued a seventeen point delineation of American foreign policy. The statement was given in answer to an increasing number of requests for information about various points in our foreign policy. The Secretary reiterated our adherence to the principles of the Atlantic Charter and should do much to clarify our position before the world. It was a much needed declaration. Great Britain and Russia could do well by following suit.

Wednesday, March 22, 1944: —A victory in the war against inflation was scored today by the Office of Price Administration.

Effective March 31, café and restaurant prices will be rolled back. Once again a cup of coffee will cost only 5 cents, thereby ending one of the biggest robberies of all time. Prices on 20 other popular food items, such as ham and eggs, will be hauled down from the attic and put under the ceiling again.

On the war fronts we learn that the Japanese have invaded India. Strong columns of Japanese troops have struck across the Burma frontier and are striking towards the Manipur state supply center of Imphal. A spokesman for the British High Command stated confidently that adequate British forces were available to deal with the invaders. At the same time, Allied forces under Lord Mountbatten and Chinese troops under General Stilwell were reported advancing in northern Burma and have crossed the highest point in the pass leading southward into the Mogaung Valley. The Japanese were said to be retreating rapidly.

From England, the Eighth United States Air Force today launched its greatest raid of the war on Berlin. Six hundred mighty Flying Fortresses and Liberators, escorted by no less than 1,000 fighter planes, swept over the enemy capital almost unmolested by enemy interceptors. Bulls-eyes were scored on industrial targets and huge fires were set off in the heart of the great city. Only thirteen bombers and nine fighters were lost, mostly by the heavy flak. Few enemy planes dared to penetrate the mighty American fighter screen. Movie star Jimmy Stewart, now a major, commanded one of the Liberators.

Thursday, March 23, 1944: —The Japanese apparently are driving a three-pronged invasion force into India. Immediate objective of the invaders appears to be the India-Burma highway center of Imphal, through which supplies and troops have been funneled to the Allied forces in Burma. The nearest enemy column is still approximately 30 miles from Imphal but only small Allied patrols have opposed the invaders thus far. Late reports, however, reveal that a strong air-borne force of Allied troops has been landed deep inside the Japanese lines in northern Burma, severing the life-line of communications for the thousands of enemy troops facing Mountbatten's invasion forces and imperiling the rear of the Japanese invasion forces in India

In Italy, the bloody battle for Cassino has reached a virtual stalemate as the Fifth Army finds it practically impossible to budge the Germans from their heavily fortified positions within the ruined town. Our heaviest artillery, the mighty 240 millimeter cannon, has been turned loose on the Nazi positions in a furious effort to dislodge them. Failure at Cassino would be a bitter blow to our side and would necessitate a revision of our strategy for the coming months.

The sensational advance of Russia's First Army of the Ukraine continued unabated today. The hard-driving Soviets gained another 25 to 37 miles and liberated 200 towns and villages. The scene of battle is now in the region of Ternopol in pre-war Poland, south of the Black Sea port of Nikolayev.

Friday, March 24, 1944: —The newspapers are so full of the sensational trial of famous movie comedian, Charlie Chaplin, on charges of Mann Act violation in transporting his "protégé" Joan Barry to New York City for immoral purposes, that it is hard to locate the war news.

The fighting in Cassino has taken on a desperate aspect. Despite the efforts of Fifth Army tanks, guns, and infantry, the stubborn Nazis have succeeded in holding strong positions in the southwestern edge of the town. A large part of the fighting has been at close quarters, with fierce hand-to-hand clashes between Allied infantrymen and the so-called Nazi "Green Devils" or paratroopers. Outcome of the battle is not yet apparent.

Substantial British forces have moved up to meet the Japanese columns advancing into India but it is too early to predict the turn of events in that theater. The general situation, however, is not reassuring for it was our side that was expected to launch the offensive. Nevertheless, the Japanese are known to have powerful forces with which to prosecute an invasion of their own in that direction and it may require time and heavy losses to repel the invaders.

President Roosevelt, Prime Minister Churchill, and General Bernard Montgomery today served notice on the jittery Germans that the hour of invasion is near. The simultaneous statements were made separately by the three leaders at widely different places and occasions. The criminal Axis leaders must be sleeping very fitfully these nights.

Saturday, March 25, 1944: —Last night was another bitter night for the sleepless, red-eyed inhabitants of Berlin. More than

1,000 heavy British bombers struck at the capital and dropped a load of bombs that broke all previous records for tonnage. Over 2,800 tons of explosives and fire bombs were cascaded into the rapidly disintegrating city. Simultaneously, the RAF hit Germany's biggest naval base of Kiel with another large force of planes, rounding out one of the busiest nights of the war for the British Air Force. The attacks were not made without cost, however, as 73 of the mighty Lancasters, Halifaxes, and Sterlings, failed to return from the widespread missions. This was the second highest loss suffered by the RAF, the highest being 79 planes in an attack on Germany last February.

Moscow is justifiably jubilant over the progress of their offensive on the southern front. The powerful Russian First Army of the Ukraine is nearing the border of Rumania and, according to the official Soviet newspaper, Izvestia, the Germans are back to where they started from three years ago. If the Russians can maintain the present rate of their advance, they will soon threaten Germany's position throughout the Balkans. Without a doubt, the biggest Allied victories of the war are being won on the Russian front right now.

The Anglo-American Fifth Army in Italy not only has failed to drive the Germans out of Cassino as yet but also has been unsuccessful in preventing the enemy from reinforcing his garrison in that town. Apparently the Nazis are using to good advantage a maze of ancient tunnels existing beneath the crumbled ruins of the once peaceful little Italian city.

Sunday, March 26, 1944: —What's doing on the home front? The draft, rationing, transportation, quadruplicates, sex trials, and horseracing crowd the war news for newspaper space and radio time.

The weather, in the Bay Area at least, is warm and beautiful. So beautiful today, in fact, that we dug the old car out of the garage, tampered around with it until we got it running, loaded the family into it and headed for the beach. Got as far as Fleischacker's Zoo when "Blamm!" the left front tire blew out. No spare, so I jacked the car up, took off the wheel, rolled it a block to the nearest service station. The attendants wouldn't fix it— said they were too tired—having been overworked all day, so I finally talked them into letting me fix it myself with their tools.

607

Agreed, so I spent the rest of the afternoon struggling with a stubborn tire and rim, finally fixed it—the casing looked as though it couldn't possibly last another mile—wheeled it back to the car, bolted it on, loaded the family back in and headed for home with fingers crossed. Made it without further trouble and thankfully ran the old boat back into the garage, there to remain.

Thank God, it's the women who do the buying of food. I tried it yesterday afternoon and had what the hoi-polloi call "a heluva time." I loaded myself down with about two dozen ration books—from Book 1 to Book 4, a small coin book full of little blue and red ration tokens, and an extra supply of money, and set out to buy a week's supply of foodstuffs for the little woman and her hungry brood. If anyone questions the accuracy of General Sherman's description of war, or doubts that the housewives are the real heroines of this struggle, they should spend such a Saturday afternoon as I.

Monday, March 27, 1944: —The war situation tonight does not appear as favorable as in the recent past. Our side has apparently lost the initiative on two major battlefronts. In Italy, the U.S. Army newspaper, the Stars and Stripes, admitted today that the Allied offensive to crack the German Gustav line across the peninsula has ended in failure at Cassino. Despite the pulverizing attacks by all branches of the Allied war machine, the Germans have succeeded in retaining their grip on the ruined town and are today almost as strongly entrenched as they were at the beginning of the offensive. Already the Nazis have sallied forth in powerful counter-attacks. Although, the paper asserts that the failure at Cassino is not a final one and does not represent a true test of Allied strength, since only limited forces were used, the defeat is a serious one and may delay the attainment of final victory for some months.

In India as well, Allied fortunes are not faring so well at the present time. The Japanese are driving into India in a many-pronged offensive aimed at nullifying Lord Mountbatten's invasion of northern Burma and threatening Allied supply lines to Burma and hard-pressed China. Heavy fighting is in progress at some points but late reports concede that the Japs are gaining some ground.

Only in the air above France and Germany are striking effective blows at the enemy. Approximately 700 Flying

Fortresses and Liberators spent the day blasting the Nazis' front line defenses along the French coast in what may be part of the pre-invasion barrage.

Tuesday, March 28, 1944: —The war abroad was overshadowed temporarily by the news of a local disaster. A flash fire, apparently started by a pyromaniac, swept through a downtown San Francisco hotel last night, trapping and burning to death twenty two persons. It was the deadliest fire in San Francisco since the great earthquake of 1906 and started the authorities on the most intense manhunt in years to apprehend the criminally insane person who started this fire and who is believed to have made several similar attempts during the past few weeks.

In addition to the dead, twenty eight people were injured in the holocaust which reduced the three story building to a charred mass of wreckage within the space of a few minutes. The tenants trapped in the inside rooms didn't have a chance to escape. Others on the outside leaped from windows into firemen's nets or clung to ledges until rescued.

From the flames of the home front to the flaming battlefields of Europe we find that the Russian tide has swept on and over Nikolayev, major defense base of the Nazis at the mouth of the Bug River. Capture of this stronghold unhinged the last German salient into the Ukraine and sent the Soviet armies racing onward towards Odessa.

Only meager news is available regarding the situation in India although it is apparent that the Japanese invaders are making some progress towards the vital center of Imphal. Strong British forces are moving up to defend the city and large scale battles are imminent.

Wednesday, March 29, 1944: —The Russian steamroller shows no signs of losing its momentum. The amazing First Army of the Ukraine crunched forward over the wreckage of more Nazi divisions to capture Kolomya on the upper Prut River and cut the Lwow-Bucharest trunk railway. The seizure of the rail center put the steel tips of the two-pronged Russian offensive within 30 miles of the pre-war Czechoslovakian border. Further south, other Soviet armies poised on the eastern bank of the lower

Prut River, awaiting the word to cross into Rumania itself. The red fog of war is closing in on the Balkans.

While the Russians are winning mighty victories, the Anglo-American Allies are having their difficulties in Italy and India. The stalemate at Cassino apparently has forced a revisal of Allied strategy in Italy and has caused our forces to withdraw from the slopes of Mount Cassino where bitter fighting had been in progress to oust the Nazis from their roost atop the hill. Ground that had been gained at great cost was relinquished.

In India the British advance guards meeting the invading columns of Japanese have been forced to fall back under heavy attack. As usual, the Japs are ignoring huge casualties in their drive to cut the Allied supply line to Burma. A major battle impends.

From England, the Eighth U.S. Air Force sent its daylight raiders out again today to blast the Germans at Brunswick. Swarms of angry enemy interceptors rose to meet the bombers but were dispersed by the mighty American screen of Lightnings, Mustangs, and Thunderbolts.

Thursday, March 30, 1944: —Premier Josef Stalin in one of his frequent orders of the day, announced that the First Ukrainian Army under General Gregory K. Zhukov has stormed and captured the Bucovinian capital of Cernauti, third largest city of prewar Rumania. The fall of this city opens the gate to a sweep across the Rumanian plains into the heart of the Balkans.

As Hitler's hold on southern Europe slips under the sledge-hammer blows of the Red Army, our 15th Air Force, based in Italy, struck a powerful blow of its own by sending 400 bombers to strike at Sofia, capital of jittery Bulgaria. The great Fortresses and Liberators blasted and wrecked railroads and other military objectives within the city and returned unscathed.

Meanwhile, the bloody Cassino battleground flared with renewed fury today as the reinforced Nazis attempted to improve their positions by counter-attacks. All sorties by the Germans were repulsed with heavy losses to the enemy, according to Allied headquarters.

Across the world in the jungles of India, more fierce fighting is raging between British troops and the Oriental invaders from Japan. Indications are that the Jap drive has been slowed if not halted entirely. Allied planes and heavy artillery have been thrown into the struggle with good effect. Heavy casualties have been inflicted on the invaders but they seem to have plenty more men where those came from.

Friday, March 31, 1944: —The tide of war crept closer to the Philippines again today. Admiral of the fleet, Chester W. Nimitz announced that a powerful task force of U.S. battleships, aircraft carriers, cruisers, and destroyers, penetrated deep into the Japanese defense perimeter in the Pacific to bombard Palau, 1,055 miles west of Truk and only 460 miles from the Philippines. The action is continuing.

Simultaneously with the Palau assault, Liberator bombers of the Seventh Army Air Force attacked five main islands of the Truk Atoll, obviously in a diversionary raid designed to protect the rear of the Palau raiders.

The bold foray into the heart of the enemy waters is admittedly for the purpose of bringing the main Jap fleet into battle. The reluctant Nipponese Navy, however, apparently was forewarned of the approaching danger and fled from Palau as it had previously done from Truk. It may take a direct sea attack on Tokyo itself to bring the Japanese main fleet to bay.

New Delhi reports indicate that Japanese columns knifing into India from three different directions are closing in on the British base of Imphal. One enemy column succeeded in cutting the main highway linking Imphal with Kohima, thereby putting the British defenders at a distinct disadvantage.

It was a bad all around day for the British. The RAF picked a bright moonlight night last night to bomb the German arms center of Nuremberg and lost 94 heavy bombers, the greatest toll yet paid in one raid.

April

Saturday, April 1, 1944: —The bold American attack on Palau, only 460 miles from the Philippines, has had repercussions in Tokyo. The jittery Japs are plainly worried over the deep penetration of their defenses and have instituted a general shakeup in their high command. Air Force leaders, in particular, were hard hit as Tojo's government expressed its concern over the progress of the war in the central Pacific.

Meanwhile, our forces continued the pressure against the enemy by raiding Truk for the third successive night. The attack was carried out by planes belonging to the Seventh American Air Force. Heavy damage was inflicted on the three main islands of the Truk Atoll, Dublon, Moen, and Eten, with no loss to ourselves. Intense anti-aircraft fire was encountered but the Japanese gunners' aim was faulty.

In Italy, the American Fifth Army, hamstrung by the stubborn Nazis at Cassino, may have discovered the solution to the dilemma and have surged forward to capture 5,840 foot Mount Marrone, which lies 16 miles southwest of Cassino. This surprise offensive, if successful, might outflank the Nazis in Cassino and force their withdrawal from the shattered town.

In Russia, the floodtide of Soviet power continues to sweep westward, promising to quickly liberate the last foot of Russian soil from the invader. Steel-tipped Soviet columns are drawing a noose around the Black Sea Port of Odessa, where the German Sixth and Eighth Armies face a desperate "Dunkirk" evacuation attempt or annihilation.

Sunday, April 2, 1944: —The Japanese are gaining steadily in their invasion of India despite fierce resistance from Imperial British and Indian troops. Using their infiltrating tactics to good advantage the Japs have forced the British to retreat to within sixteen miles of the important base of Imphal. Northeast of the city other enemy columns have knifed through to threaten the Kohima highway, lifeline to Allied forces in North Burma. The situation is serious.

There are two items of interest on the diplomatic front tonight. The first is the report from Stockholm that the Russians have offered modified peace terms to Finland. The report hinted that the new offer was considerably milder than the six-point peace plan previously rejected by the Finns. Neutral sources believe there is a possibility that Finland may accept the new offer.

The second bit of diplomatic news is the purported request by the Soviet Union for the United States to continue lend-lease aid for at least three years after the war. Washington's reception to the Moscow request is said to be dependent upon Russia's reception to our counter proposal that the Soviet Union actively assist us in the war against Japan. Give and ye shall receive.

The naval-air war in the central Pacific continues to rage around the Japanese bases in the Carolines. Truk was raided early today for the eighth time by American land based bombers, indicating that the Japanese "Pearl Harbor" is in for a real "softening up" aerial offensive.

Monday, April 3, 1944: —The American Air Force actively assisted the Russian armies today by raiding Budapest in force. It was the first time American planes have been over the Hungarian capital and the raid came just as the Nazis were completing their seizure of the Hungarian government and the Russian hordes began looming up over the Balkan horizon. Rail yards and aircraft factories were the principal targets of the American heavyweights which escaped almost scot-free although encountering considerable flak and light fighter plane opposition.

At the same time, the irresistible tide of Soviet power began sweeping into Rumania across the Prut River. Red Army spearheads made an initial stab of twelve miles into Rumanian territory while the bulk of the Russian armies prepared to fan out across the broad reaches of the Rumanian plain. Bucharest and the Ploesti oil fields lie beckoning like ripe plums before them.

In London, the Admiralty announced that British aircraft have again succeeded in bombing the German battleship Tirpitz, as it lay anchored in the Alten Fjord of northern Norway. Direct hits were scored on the mighty 45,000 ton battleship and it was believed put out of action for several months to come.

In the central Pacific our airmen are still blasting away at

Truk, the big Japanese naval base in the Carolines. If we know our battle signs, something big is in store for the Japs at Truk.

Tuesday, April 4, 1944: —The full extent of our Navy's victory in the attack on Palau is just becoming known. Details of the story can now be told and it is plainly evident that the Japs were handed one of their worst defeats of the war so far. Every enemy ship anchored at Palau, Woleai, and Yap were either sunk or smashed by the American raiders. Our losses were 27 warplanes.

A mysterious aspect of the Pacific war was the report of an air raid on Manila in the Philippines. The Manila radio broadcast caught by U.S. monitors announced that the "all-clear" signal has been given throughout the city of Greater Manila. No hint has come from any Allied source to indicate whether our planes were in reality over the Philippine capital.

Simultaneously with the smashing of Japanese shipping in Palau, the Navy announced that our submarines have taken a toll of 14 more Jap ships in enemy waters, bringing the total sub score since Pearl Harbor to 517 Nipponese vessels sunk.

For the second straight day the American Air Force supported the Russian Balkan offensive by ripping military objective in Budapest. In addition to hitting the Hungarian capital, the big American bombers followed through with a powerful smash at the Rumanian capital of Bucharest. The full weight of the Anglo-American-Russian Allies is clamping down on Hitler's hapless satellite countries.

Wednesday, April 5, 1944: —The Japanese invaders of India are steadily advancing despite stubborn resistance from British and Indian troops. The enemy has established a firm road block on the Manipur Valley road between Imphal and Kohima and both of those important bases are endangered. The Japs are using powerful forces in the attack, indicating that the India invasion is a full-scale affair. Coherent efforts will be needed by the Allies if a serious disaster is to be averted.

U.S. Navy Liberator bombers raided Wake Island for the 17th time today, showing the Japs that we haven't forgotten the tiny isle, hallowed by the heroic Marine defenders in the first dark days of the war. The American flyers scored a direct hit on an enemy supply ship anchored at the dock, sending the vessel to the bottom in flames.

In Eastern Europe, the mighty Russian armies are closing in on the doomed German garrison at Odessa. Razdelnaya, the Ukrainian rail junction astride the last escape route for the Nazis was captured, leaving the Fascists only the Black Sea escape route open. The seizure of Razdelnaya occasioned another of the famous orders of the day from Stalin. The victory guns of Moscow boomed again. Busy are the guns of Moscow these days. Major victories for the Red Armies are almost daily occurrences. The magnificent strength of those armies is a source of wonderment to the whole world. Military observers have marveled at the resilient, recuperative powers of the Russian forces which have absorbed time after time, incalculably powerful body blows, only to come back stronger than ever to wreak vengeance on the invader.

Thursday, April 6, 1944: —An interesting feature of home front news was the crushing defeat of Wendell Willkie in the Wisconsin primary election last Tuesday. As a result, Mr. Willkie has announced his withdrawal from the race for Republican nomination for the Presidency. Governor Dewey of New York won a smashing victory in the Wisconsin primary even though the New York Governor has protested that he is not a candidate for the nomination.

The draft situation is still as confused and uncertain as ever. Latest dope is that California is at the bottom of the manpower barrel. Selective Service officials have announced their intention of scraping the bottom of the barrel to fill the state's quota of army and navy personnel. Eleven out of twelve remaining men between the ages of 18 and 25 can expect to be called, regardless of their occupational or dependency status. Cases of older men up to 38 will also be reviewed as the demands of the armed forces continue to soar higher than the supply of able-bodied young men.

The fight against inflation on the home front is a nip and tuck affair. The latest move by the Office of Price Administration was an attempted roll-back of café and restaurant prices beginning April 1. So far, the results have been negligible. Customers in some cases have actually reported an increase in their checks. OPA officials have promised an investigation and enforcement of its rulings.

Friday, April 7, 1944: —Japanese columns converging on the Allied supply center of Imphal are making slow but steady gains. Admiral Lord Louis Mountbatten's British and Indian troops are moving up in force to resist the invader but no major battle has as yet been joined.

Also threatened by the invaders is the Assam-Bengal railroad which is serving as the main supply line to General Stilwell and his American and Chinese forces in north Burma. The railroad lies some fifty miles west of Imphal which is the immediate objective of the Japanese.

On the eastern European front the Russians are rapidly sweeping the last vestige of German occupation from the soil of Russia. Fighting is centered around Odessa, Black Sea Port, which fell to the Germans early in the invasion sweep during the summer of 1941. Now the hour of liberation approaches.

The stalemate continues in Italy. Activity on both the Anzio beachhead front and at Cassino recently has been confined to patrol action and artillery duels. No ground gains have been scored by either side since the withdrawal of Allied troops from the bomb-shattered town of Cassino. Prospects of an early capture of Rome, therefore, continue to be remote.

In the Pacific, American Army bombers raided Wake Island in one of the heaviest attacks of the war on that enemy base. Heavy damage was inflicted without the loss of a plane.

Saturday, April 8, 1944: —Selective Service officials added more confusion to the draft picture today by announcing that induction of men over 26 would be halted indefinitely. They said that the Armed Forces need for younger men is greater than that of immediately filling induction quotes with older men. For those who fall within the "older" classification and are pre-Pearl Harbor fathers the situation is very uncertain. First it blows hot, then cold. First they are in, and then they are not. No one in authority seems able to make up his mind and in the meantime the poor "candidate" dares not make any plans or moves for fear his status will change overnight. Nor does his employer. This does not contribute to industrial efficiency.

In the Pacific, the Navy claims that the once mighty Japanese naval base of Truk has been neutralized. Almost incessant bombing raids by Navy and Army bombers have smashed the harbor and dock facilities and laid waste the airfields and supply dumps on the islands of the atoll. Offshore the U.S. Navy has practically blockaded the stronghold after the main Jap fleet frantically retired without doing battle.

On the eastern European front, the First Russian Army of the Ukraine has penetrated through the Carpathian foothills to the border of the Carpatho-Ukraine, the tip of old Czechoslovakia, now a part of Hungary. Further to the south the Third Army of the Ukraine is hammering at the gates of the mighty Black Sea Port of Odessa. Any German effort to make a stand before the city appears to be doomed in advance.

Sunday, April 9, 1944: —Easter Sunday! The day of new hope, when all Christianity contemplates the miracle of the resurrection. Fear not death, for He hath conquered it. For the millions of people living—and dying—amidst the horrors of war, that, it seems to me, is the only creed that can enable them to endure their misery. Were I a soldier, cringing in a foxhole while overhead a torrent of sudden death and destruction roared in all its hideous man-made fury, only faith in His Easter promise would enable me to steel myself enough to rise from my foxhole and press onward through the torrent. Soldiers must feel like that.

While Christian men and women throughout the world were attempting to recapture for a moment the peace and goodwill of Easter time, our sun and ancestor-worshipping little Oriental enemies were stabbing their invasion prongs just a little deeper into the massive hide of India. The Tokyo radio claimed flatly that their troops have captured Kohima, forty miles inside India, and have severed the supply road between Imphal, the capital of Manipur state, and the railhead to the north. Furious fighting is in progress.

After a lull of several days, the American Air Force in England has resumed its all-out aerial offensive against the heart of the Reich. Great squadrons of huge Fortresses and Liberators, supported with strong fighter screens smashed heavily at Brunswick and other German aircraft centers during the past twenty-four hours.

Monday, April 10, 1944: —The Russian juggernaught has crunched its way into the Black Sea Port of Odessa, it was announced from Moscow today. Premier Stalin ordered the unprecedented salute of 36 salvoes from 444 victory cannon to celebrate the great triumph. There was no doubt of the Moscow story as Berlin acknowledged the fall of the city, but claimed that the German garrison had been safely evacuated. The Russian announcement, however, told of thousands of German dead and of frantic, panic-stricken attempts to flee the city under the bombs and shells of the Red Army and Air Force. German disaster in the Ukraine is complete.

In India Allied fortunes are not faring so well. Converging columns of Japanese troops are closing in on the important base of Imphal and have reached a point only 16 miles from that city. Heavy casualties have been inflicted on the invaders but their advance has not been stopped. Sixty miles to the north another battle is raging for the town of Kohime. Here the British garrison has succeeded in repelling repeated assaults by strong enemy forces. The issue is still in doubt.

From England, 700 American bombers escorted by 700 long-range fighters mauled Germany and Nazi-held France today. Aircraft plants and airdromes in France and Belgium were the principal targets. Only three bombers were lost in all attacks during the day. Seven German fighters were shot down and heavy damage was inflicted on the target area.

Tuesday, April 11, 1944: —Up to 2,000 heavy American bombers and escorting fighters struck a tremendous blow at aircraft building centers in the Berlin area today. The daylight attack found the Germans ready with powerful opposition. Hundreds of Nazi interceptors roared through the bomber formations with guns blazing. It was a grim and bloody aerial battle that saw planes of friend and foe plummeting out of the air in tragic numbers. We lost more than 60 huge bombers and 16 fighters. The Germans lost at least 45 planes shot out of the skies in addition to dozens destroyed on the ground. Damage to the aircraft factories was believed severe.

In the Pacific, Admiral Nimitz' forces have occupied four more atolls in the Marshall Chain. This makes 18 atolls and one island seized by our troops since the start of the central Pacific offensive. In addition to the Marshall Islands action, our Army and Navy bombers raided Jap positions in the Carolines, inflicting considerable damage at Ponape.

In the southwest Pacific area, General Douglas MacArthur's headquarters reported that our forces now control the major portion of New Britain Island, the Japs having withdrawn to the Gazelle peninsula on which lies the main enemy base of Rabaul. Here 40,000 isolated Japanese troops are expected to make their last stand. There is little chance of their evacuating Rabaul or of reinforcing it since our Navy has seized control of the sea approaches. Rabaul and its Japanese defenders are trapped—and doomed.

Wednesday, April 12, 1944: —The giant aerial pincers were clamped on Germany again today. Hundreds of American bombers and fighters, based in Italy, roared up over the Alps to strike at aircraft and industrial centers in Austria and southern Germany while hundreds of other Allied warplanes roared across the English Channel to launch a simultaneous attack on northern and central Germany. Furious air battles raged the length and breadth of Nazi land. The Wiener Neustadt aircraft production center in Austria was particularly hard hit by planes of the 15th American Air Force based a Foggia in Italy.

King Victor Emmanuel of Italy announced in Naples today that he will abdicate when Rome is captured. The little king will be succeeded by his son, Umberto, who will rule, not as king, but as Lieutenant General. The king's action was reportedly taken in the interests of Italian unity and Allied desires to see the Italian government take a more democratic form.

American bombers struck two more blows deep into Japanese territory today. Aleutian based bombers raided Matsuwa Island in the Kurile chain, only 960 miles from Tokyo. Other planes of Admiral Nimitz' command pounded the Jap naval fortress of Truk for the seventeenth time.

A San Francisco ship, the tanker H.D. Collier, was torpedoed and sunk in the Arabian Sea, it was learned today. 44 crew members, including the skipper were listed as missing. Most of them were residents of the Bay Area.

Thursday, April 13, 1944: —The American Air Force crowned two new "ace of aces" today, one in the southwest Pacific area and one in the European theater. General Douglas MacArthur's communiqué revealed that Captain Richard I. Bong, of Poplar, Wisconsin has shot down 27 Japanese planes in aerial combat. This is more than Captain Eddie Rickenbacker destroyed in World War I and more than Majors Joe Foss, Souix Falls, South Dakota and Gregory Boyington, Okanogan, Washington, each of whom accounted for 26. In England, Captain Don Gentile of Piqua, Ohio, was revealed as the leading fighter ace with a total of 30 enemy planes destroyed. Seven of his planes were smashed on the ground, however, while all of Captain Bong's victories were achieved in aerial combat. In the hands of such men as these our cause is secure.

News from India is slightly more favorable tonight. Counter-attacking Allied troops have stalled the Japanese drive on Imphal and have regained a recently lost strongpoint in a fierce hand to hand encounter. At Kohime sixty miles to the north British defenders are holding their own while far to the north in Burma, American and Chinese troops are threatening to cut the Japanese supply line at Kyitkyina in their one invasion attempt.

Following their brilliant victory at Odessa, powerful Russian armies are racing down the Crimean peninsula towards the great bastion of Sevastopol. German defenses in the Crimea apparently are crumbling like mud walls before a tidal wave. Rag-tag remnants of the once mighty Reichwehr are fleeing in panic-stricken mobs before the avenging Red armies.

Friday, April 14, 1944: —With an amazing burst of speed, the irresistible Russian armies have swept down the Crimean peninsula to within eighteen miles of the historic city of Sevastopol, which the Russians so tenaciously defended earlier in the war. The Germans are completely routed, their only thought for escape. More than 31,000 of their number have already been captured, with other thousands crushed under the treads of advancing Soviet tanks or mowed down by Soviet machinegun fire. Observers believe the entire Crimean campaign will be over in a matter of days.

The once-powerful Japanese base of Truk was blasted again today by heavy bombers of the Seventh American Air Force. The

American planes ranged at will over the target, smashing docks, warehouses, gun emplacements and shipping in the harbors. No fighter plane opposition was encountered and only meager anti-aircraft fire. Truk, to all intents and purposes, is neutralized as a major enemy base.

Fighting in India is increasing in scale and ferocity. The main Japanese invasion force is entering the battle for Imphal and has flowed around the base to all but isolate it. Flying columns of Japanese troops have fanned out beyond Imphal to threaten Allied communication and supply lines. The situation is confused and, from all accounts, not very favorable.

Berlin was dealt another dose of war last night by strong formations of fast-flying Mosquito bombers, the plywood darlings of the RAF.

Saturday, April 15, 1944: —It is Russia in the forefront of the war news tonight. The campaign for the reconquest of Crimea is all but finished, with the panicky remnants of 100,000 crack German and Rumanian troops trapped in a narrow corridor around Sevastopol. In less than one week after beginning their drive the Russians are within sight of the historic city, in some places fighting in the suburbs. The city itself is packed with thousands of fleeing Axis soldiers, scrambling madly for a place on the few boats still able to sail from the bomb and shell wracked harbor. Thousands of others have already surrendered, other thousands have died under the merciless fire of advancing Red Army tanks.

Farther north, Marshal Zhukov and his famous First Army of the Ukraine have won another memorable victory. Tarnopol, a powerfully fortified rail junction in pre-war Poland, has fallen to the Soviets after a bitter three-week stand by the German defenders. Premier Stalin set the victory cannon to booming again in Moscow.

American heavy bombers again contributed direct support to the Red Army offensive by striking effective blows against railroad yards and supply depots in Bucharest and the oilfields of Ploesti. For the first time long range fighter planes escorted the big bombers all the way to Bucharest and back. Our losses were slight.

Sunday, April 15, 1944: —Finally succeeded in fixing the old car so it would run again and spent the rest of the house hunting. We are getting desperate to find a place to live in since the owners of our present dwelling decided to sell the place. We had no luck today, however, although one or two promising leads were uncovered. The housing shortage is so acute it is almost impossible to find a house to rent unless you are fortunate enough to learn of a place through a friend. So far nothing like that has developed for us. Looks like we may be hauled into court any day now to explain why we haven't moved. It is not a pleasant prospect but what can we do?

Fortunately we were finally able to secure a "V card" from the San Mateo War Housing Center. A "V card" is what they call a War Housing Referral and it certifies that the holder is a War Worker entitled to occupy War Housing in San Mateo County. With this we may be able to rent or buy one of the new defense homes. They are not worth what they are asking for them but at least it would be a roof over our heads.

I mention our housing problem because it is war news today. Thousands of tenants are being ousted because of frozen rents and inflated real estate prices. Landlords are selling to reap huge profits because they cannot raise rentals and the poor tenants are forced to buy at inflated prices because no ceiling was placed on real estate prices. All this is very pleasant for the greedy real estate agents who are paying more in income taxes this year than they earned a few short years ago.

Monday, April 17, 1944: —In a surprise move to protect the secrets of "D Day," the British Government today quarantined the diplomats of 43 nations in England and cancelled their privileges of uncensored communications with their governments. The unprecedented move was a precaution against the possible leak of vital military information in connection with the anticipated invasion of Hitler's European fortress. From now on the British will not permit the transmission or receipt of any coded wires or telegrams that are not in plain language. Diplomatic representatives or members of their staff may not depart from the country. Other restrictions and limitations were placed on their movements and actions.

The only exceptions to the above regulations are the diplomatic staffs of the United States, Soviet Russian, and the

British Dominions. The action with regard to the other countries, even including those other United Nations which are actually at war with the Axis, was taken after consultation with the United States and Russia and was considered essential to protect the invasion plans.

The existing government of liberated Italy is undergoing a vigorous shakeup. King Victor Emmanuel has indicated his intention of abdicating when Rome is taken and Marshal Badoglio is reorganizing his cabinet in an effort to achieve unity among his countrymen.

Federal Bureau of Investigation agents reported today that they have blocked a plan to dynamite mighty Boulder Dam on the Colorado River. The abortive saboteur was seized.

Tuesday, April 18, 1944: —Berlin was the recipient of a mighty blow from 2,000 American planes today. Powerful Flying Fortresses and Liberators renewed the aerial siege of the German capital in an all-out attack that was driven home despite the desperate resistance of 200 Nazi interceptors and intense anti-aircraft fire. Mustang and Lightning fighter planes escorted the great bombers all the way to the target. Details of the damage done and the losses incurred will not be available until later.

Our hard-hitting submarine force has bagged fifteen more Japanese vessels, according to the latest Navy Department report. The enemy ships included 11 cargo vessels, 3 tankers, and one auxiliary repair craft, all of which were destroyed in actions close to the Japanese homeland. The grand total of Jap ships hit by our submarines has reached 682. Five hundred thirty two were sent to the bottom, 32 were probably sunk, and 114 were hit and damaged. Nice going, Navy!

The British Admiralty today released the first story of the amazing adventures of two British sailors who straddled torpedoes and rode them like broncos into an Italian naval base to destroy an enemy cruiser and other vessels. The men were encased in diving suits and submerged with the torpedoes to steal in unobserved, attach the explosive head of the torpedo to the enemy ships, set a time bomb, and ride on the propulsive part of the torpedoes to safety.

Similar feats have been performed since the original attempt and it is said that the Germans successfully copied the technique to blow up shipping in the harbor at Gibraltar.

Wednesday, April 19, 1944: —The last 24 hours have seen the Allied aerial offensive over Germany stepped up to an incredible tempo. Almost 6,000 war planes have smashed at Hitler's defenses with an estimated 8,500 tons of explosives and fire bombs during that time. Even Russian bombers joined in the scourge of the Reich, striking at German communications deep in western Poland. Two thousand American planes blasted an aircraft plant at Kassel to smithereens and plastered five aircraft parks in the Ruhr, destroying many of Hitler's reserve fighter planes, hoarded to meet the Allied invasion thrust. Other hundreds of British and American planes strafed and bombarded military installations up and down the invasion coast of France. By night, the RAF lashed at Berlin with 1,000 planes, heaping new destruction on the already devastated enemy capital. Truly, the pre-invasion barrage is on.

In the Crimea, two Russian armies are closing in on the great naval base of Sevastopol for what is expected to be the climax in the brief Crimean campaign that saw the Soviets sweep the whole peninsula, with the exception of Sevastopol itself, clear of the Fascist invaders within less than two weeks' time. Red Army veterans of the historic 1941-42 siege of Sevastopol have been given the honor of being the first to storm the city.

The fate of Rome is in German hands, according to a note from President Roosevelt written in answer to a plea from Eamon De Valera, Irish Prime Minister, that the Allies spare the Eternal City. We have no desire to destroy the city and will be happy to refrain from doing so if the Germans will cease using the city as a military base.

Thursday, April 20, 1944: —The thunder and lightning of modern sea-air war swept to within 700 miles of Japanese-held Singapore to bomb and burn the Japanese bases of Sabang and Lho Nga on the island of Sumatra. The surprise raid was carried out by a mighty armada of Allied warships, both British and American, including aircraft carriers, battleships, and supporting warships. The attack took the Jap defenders off guard and the Allied task force escaped unscathed after blasting the enemy bases and shooting down 25 enemy planes. The erstwhile mighty Japanese Imperial Navy dared not poke its nose from under the protecting shore batteries of Singapore to challenge the Allied armada.

The East Indies thrust by the Allied fleets carried the war back deep into Japanese held territory and offered the possibility that an attempt may be made to retake Singapore by direct assault from the west rather than wait until the Philippines are recaptured and Burma and the Malayan peninsula reconquered. Avenging Allied forces are closing in on the Oriental enemy from all directions. His days are numbered.

Better news comes from India tonight also. Powerful Allied reinforcements are driving ahead to relieve the beleaguered garrison at Kohima. Simultaneously, other Allied forces gained ground in a furious counter-attack in the hills northeast of Imphal. Resistance to the Japanese invasion is stiffening in all quarters.

Friday, April 21, 1944: —The explosive roar of the Allied pre-invasion aerial offensive over Europe continued during the past 24 hours. During the night a huge RAF bomber fleet carted the biggest weight of bombs ever carried in a single raid over the tortured German cities of Cologne and Berlin, cascading 5,000 tons of destruction into the two target areas. Hundreds of American planes struck by daylight at countless points along the invasion coast, ripping communication lines, blasting gun positions, and strafing and bombing airfields in France and the lowlands.

While the crescendo of Allied air attacks rises daily to a higher pitch, the jittery Nazis are predicting that the invasion will come at any moment. The Berlin radio said that a great fleet of Allied vessels is assembling in English ports, while every hour troop trains are leaving London stations, taking men to ports. All counter measures have been completed, they boast, and predict that the Allied attempt will be decisively smashed. Nevertheless, the tone of their talk proves they are jittery and afraid. Look out, Adolf, the day of reckoning is at hand!

In the Pacific war, air power is also holding sway. American Army bombers attacked Wake Island for the fourth time this month, blasting the tiny isle with thirty tons of bombs. Almost no opposition was encountered from the virtually isolated Japanese outpost.

In China fighting has flared up again in the outskirts of Chenghsien in northern Honan province. The biggest battle since Changteh is shaping up.

Saturday, April 22, 1944: —For the sixth straight day the mighty Allied aerial offensive has smashed at Hitler's European fortress. Today's assault saw 2,000 American planes range over the Ruhr Valley, blasting the rail center of Hamm and engaging the vaunted Luftwaffe in violent air battles. Today's total brought to 15,000 the number of Allied planes sent over the heart of the Reich during the past week, carrying well over 17,000 tons of high explosives and fire bombs to dump on the vital organs of the monstrous Nazi war machine. How well they have succeeded in slowing down the circulation of the monster and sapping his vitality will be seen when the Allied troopships empty their precious cargo on the shores of Europe. Then, the effectiveness of air power will meet its test.

It was hinted in Moscow today that the invasion of Western Europe by the Anglo-American forces will be timed with another smashing offensive by the Red Army on the eastern front. We can only hope that this is one rumor that is based on actual fact.

Across the world, other American flyers boldly attacked the Japanese in their island bases of Saipan and Tinian, in the Marianas group, only 1,400 miles south of the Japanese homeland. The attack was carried out by long-range land-based Army Liberators, which battled through strong enemy fighter opposition to hit the targets on the nose. Our losses were not announced as yet.

Sunday, April 23, 1944: —The crash of Allied bombs continues to rock the continent of Europe tonight. All day and night the procession of mighty bombers and speedy fighters roared over the English Channel like vast trains arriving and departing on schedule. Rail centers, airfields, and other military objectives from Norway to Spain have felt the crushing weight of Allied bombs during the past 24 hours. Industrial centers and aircraft factories deep in the heart of Germany itself were visited by hundreds of great American and RAF bombers. Tremendous columns of smoke and heaps of rubble were left in their wakes. The pre-invasion drive is on!

In the Crimea, victorious Russian troops, supported by the Red fleet, have smashed the Germans into a last ditch battle on the approaches to the great naval base of Sevastopol. Fierce fighting, much of it of the hand to hand variety, is taking place in the heavily fortified passes guarding the city. Slowly, inexorably, the avenging Soviet forces are closing in for the kill. The German position is hopeless.

The long withheld story of the sinking of an American troop ship was revealed today. The vessel was the Cape San Juan, which was apparently torpedoed by a Japanese submarine in South Pacific waters. The ship carried some 1,000 American troops, in addition to a large number of Navy gunners and crew members. Of the 1,429 men aboard, 1,359 were saved by heroic action from escorting ships and a sea plane. Seventy men were drowned or killed by explosions.

Monday, April 24, 1944:—A powerful Allied army, commanded by General Douglas MacArthur and supported by a vast naval concentration, has forced a landing at Hollandia on the northern coast of Dutch New Guinea. The latest leap-frog maneuver by General MacArthur has by-passed the great Japanese bases of Madang and Wewak and has carried our forces 500 miles closer to the General's beloved Philippines. Early indications are that the invasion took the Japs completely by surprise, sending them scattering into the hills and offering only minor opposition. It is estimated that approximately 60,000 Japanese troops will be isolated and left to die on the vine at Madang and Wewak if the Hollandia attack is successful.

A few hours after the first American troops plunged through the surf to seize the emergency landing field of Hollandia, General MacArthur himself arrived to inspect the landing. Disregarding possible personal danger, the four-star General jubilantly proclaimed the landing as "one of the best executed operations I have ever seen," and told his unit commanders, "You have the enemy trapped, now don't let him go."

In India, another bold thrust by airborne Allied troops behind the enemy lines threatens to sever the Japanese lifeline to their invasion forces besieging Imphal and Kohima. The real scope and other details of the Allied attempt are not fully known as yet and it is too early to assay the actual value of the new move. Of all war theaters, the news from India is the most meager and undependable. Already many correspondents have complained of the censorship and several prominent newspapers have refused to assign a reporter to cover that front.

Tuesday, April 25, 1944: —The American invasion forces attacking Japanese held Dutch Guinea are steadily expanding their beachhead in the Hollandia area, according to latest dispatches from the battlefront. Seizure of an airstrip at Tadji has enabled Allied fighter planes to actively participate in the struggle. The Japs have not yet rallied sufficiently from their initial surprise to offer effective resistance but it is believed that a strong Japanese army is moving up from Wewak for a do-or-die attempt to thwart the Allied entrapment. Our forces eagerly await them.

Huge RAF air fleets scourged Germany last night in the biggest aerial fire raid in history. More than 500,000 incendiaries were dumped on key industrial centers, including Dusseldorf, Munich, and Karlsruhe. Tremendous fires and towering pillars of smoke were left behind by the returning airmen.

The United States Air Force matched the fury of the RAF raids with equally devastating daylight attacks. A considerable portion of the American assault was leveled against invasion objectives along the coast of France.

The news on the home front is marked by a serious dispute between the War Labor Board, union representatives, and the management of Montgomery, Ward & Co., huge mail order house and department store. The President of Ward's has refused to comply with a WLB order to extend an expired union contract. A Presidential directive has also been defied by the company. There will be trouble ahead, I am afraid.

Wednesday, April 26, 1944: —Guam, the unfortified island base for our fleet before the war—now a heavily defended Japanese stronghold—was raided last Monday by land-based American bombers. The attack represented the deepest penetration of Japanese waters by our land-based planes and was presumably launched from our recently captured airdromes in the Admiralty Islands.

In the Hollandia area of Dutch New Guinea our invasion forces have smashed the first determined counter-attack by an estimated 14,000 Japanese troops, many of whom were recently transferred from the Chinese front. Heavy fighting is still in progress, with our spearheads closing in on Hollandia's three airfields. A rapid and successful climax to the sensational Allied invasion attempt is expected.

Other Japanese in their Kurile Island bases in the North Pacific felt the wrath of American bombers. Paramushiro, Shimushu, and Matsuwa—the latter only 960 miles from Tokyo—were the objectives of the attacking Navy planes. One hundred thirty eight tons of bombs were dropped.

Here at home, President Roosevelt issued an order directing the Government to take over Montgomery Ward's Chicago properties because of failure of the company to comply with a WPB order for settling a dispute with employees. The Army was ordered to take any measure necessary to enforce the Presidential decree. It may take force since officials of the huge mail order house have indicated that they will refuse to recognize the Government's authority.

Thursday, April 27, 1944: —The Federal Government today seized the Chicago plants of Montgomery Ward & Company, pursuant to the President's order. As expected it was necessary to forcibly eject the company's president, Sewell Avery, who refused steadfastly to submit voluntarily to what he termed arbitrary, dictatorial, and illegal government actions. Two soldiers picked up the squirming company official and carried him from the building when he refused Attorney General Francis Biddle's demand that he turn the books and control of the company over to the Commerce Department.

It is hard to determine who is right and who is wrong in a dispute of this kind but it seems to me that there is a lot of fault on both sides. The Government should never have allowed itself to get into the position of having to use force in a case of this kind and Mr. Avery, for a certainty, should never have attempted to flout the authority of our Federal Government, especially in war time. The whole spectacle is very unfortunate, especially on the eve of the deadliest invasion attempt in all history. Americans, with loved ones facing certain death in the service of their country, do not want their attention distracted by miserable disputes on the home front. Now is the time when united prayer, not quarreling, should be in the minds and hearts of the people. American men, poised on the shores of the English Channel, watching the sands in the hourglass run out, can have little patience with the bickering of citizens and government on the home front. It is a sorry spectacle.

Friday, April 28, 1944: —America lost a great man today. Secretary of the Navy Knox is dead. The Secretary, who rebuilt the Navy after its disaster at Pearl Harbor into the mightiest sea-going power in history, died from a heart malady at 1:08 p.m. this afternoon.

Secretary Knox, who, with Secretary of War Stimson, were the only Republicans to hold high office in the Roosevelt Administration, was a hard-working man of 70 who served his country as a soldier in two previous wars. He won wealth and prestige as a newspaper publisher but gained his greatest renown when called to serve as Secretary of the Navy by President Roosevelt who disregarded party lines in making the nomination. Knox successfully guided the Navy through its trying times after Pearl Harbor until it is now ready to launch its great victory offensive against the Japs. He will be hard to replace.

The terrific, almost unbelievable aerial offensive against Germany went into its 12th straight day today, with almost 500 tons of bombs per hour being dumped on the enemy's European fortress. Between 4,500 and 5,000 planes battered the tortured confines of Nazidom during the last 24 hours, carrying devastations to every corner of the third Reich. Prime Minister Churchill knew whereof he spoke when he recently prophesied that the attacks on Germany would reach a scale "beyond the dimensions of anything yet employed or indeed imagined." How long will the miserable people of Germany allow their country to be blackened and seared because of the greed and avarice of their Nazi overlords?

Saturday, April 29, 1944: —The awful scourge of Germany is still the principal news item of the day. The staying power of the Germans and their ability to absorb punishment are really being put to the most terrible test in all history. It seems incredible that they can continue to operate as a first class fighting power. They may be closer to the brink of collapse than we think or they may have a hidden reserve of stamina that will enable them to survive for many more months to come. But air power is being given its great opportunity to prove that it alone can bring a mighty opponent to his knees. Even should it fail to attain this possible goal, the present aerial attack will serve the secondary purpose of a tremendous pre-invasion barrage. One thing is certain, the screws are being tightened on Der Fuhrer and his vicious pals.

An endless procession of more than 2,000 American planes swarmed over Berlin by daylight today, blasting their way through desperate ranks of German interceptor planes to dump thousands of tons of explosives and fire bombs on the hapless capital. Even the Germans were forced to admit heavy damage.

Simultaneously, another huge fleet of American bombers smashed at German shipping and submarine pens in Toulon Harbor on the Mediterranean coast of France. This raiding force came from American bases in Italy.

At home, the Government ordered the Army to withdraw from the seized plants of Montgomery Ward and Company, stating that troops were no longer needed because of a Federal Court Order restraining the company officials from interfering.

Sunday, April 30, 1944: —All sorts of rumors are emanating from every neutral and Axis center in Europe regarding the zero hour for the expected invasion. The Axis reports are of course fishing expeditions on the hope that they may entice some sort of a revealing statement from some Allied source. The neutral reports are simply guessing contests. One Madrid newspaper actually fixed the time as 4:39 a.m. today, basing its claim on the fact that the tide would be exactly right at that time. Obviously that was a bad guess since no report of any landing has been received today, although a Helsinki newspaper said that the invasion is under way, with probable landings in progress at several points. The Finn paper did not disclose its source of information and no confirmation has been received from the deadly silent Allied camp. Even spying Nazi reconnaissance planes were unable to pry the lid off the deep, dark secret.

Since everyone's guessing, my guess is that there will not be just one but many landings, possibly on several consecutive days. Any one of the landings may be a diversion attack or the main show. No one will know until several days after the assault is under way where the main power of the Allies will be concentrated. My guess is that it will not be directly across the Channel into the death trap of Flanders' fields but rather into Denmark, Southern France or both. Diversionary landings will be made near Dunkirk and Calais. A simultaneous drive on Rome will be launched by the Fifth Army, the Balkans will be invaded, and Russia will strike powerfully into Rumania. Some guess. Let's see how accurate. Oh, yes, the time. Between the 15th and 25th of May, 1944.

May

Monday, May 1, 1944: —Bad news today. The War Department announced that an American troop ship has been lost in the Mediterranean, 498 officers and men going down with the ship. It was presumed that an enemy submarine was responsible for the tragedy.

This was the second heaviest American loss of the war as a result of enemy attacks on our transports which have carried more than three million U.S. troops overseas. The other and largest loss was reported in a February 17 announcement, which said that approximately 1,000 men were drowned in the sinking of a transport off the coast of England.

British and American aerial armadas in unprecedented strength bombed and blasted every corner of Nazi land in a great May Day attack that carried the current all-out offensive into its 15th consecutive day. More than 3,000 American planes, in addition to hundreds of RAF bombers and fighters, pounded military installations and industrial centers from Calais to Berlin. Violent air battles were waged with the depleted German fighter force.

Premier Josef Stalin of Russia in his annual May Day pronouncement, called for combined British, American and Russian offensives to pursue the wounded German beast to his lair where he will be dealt the final, finishing blows. Simultaneous attacks from the east, west, and south will be required to deliver the "coup de grace" to an enemy who, though sorely wounded, still has plenty of fight left in him.

Tuesday, May 2, 1944: —Mighty task forces of the United States Navy smashed at the Japanese stronghold of Truk, unleashing powerful squadrons of carrier-based bombers which unloaded more than 800 tons of explosives on the big enemy base. Battleships and cruisers added to the devastation by shelling the islands with their big guns.

Our aircraft had a field day over the target, shooting down 60 Japanese planes in combat and destroying a like number on the ground. Our losses were comparatively light.

In addition to raiding Truk, units of our fleet struck at

Ponape in the eastern Carolines and other Japanese held islands and atolls in the western Marshalls.

In Washington, the Navy Department released another report on our submarine activities against Japan. Our gallant undersea raiders have added twelve more enemy vessels to their long list of victims. Sunk in these latest victories were two destroyers, one light cruiser, and nine non-combatant vessels. The grand total now stands at 544 Japanese ships sunk, 36 probably sunk, and 115 damaged.

The terrible air offensive over Europe swung into its 16th consecutive day of unending fury. Huge fleets of American and RAF planes swarmed over the enemy held continent, blasting his industrial centers and military installations over a wide area.

Wednesday, May 3, 1944: —The spotlight of the news was on the home front today. In a surprise move the Government announced that, effective at midnight tonight, a ration holiday would go into effect on all meat items except certain cuts of beef. This was good news to the housewife, harassed as she is by all manner of point rationing—red points, blue points, sugar points, shoe stamps, etc. Point-free meat will be a welcome relief.

Labor troubles flared anew in the Bay Area as AFL and CIO unions defied a War Labor Board order to return their machinists to work on a Navy ship. The dispute arose over the unions' refusal to complete alterations and adjustments on two new vessels at "new construction" pay rates. The unions demand that the machinists be paid the higher "repair" rate. The WLB ruled against them and ordered the men back to work. The union refused. The showdown is yet to come. Meanwhile the Navy waits for the ships. Do they think that Tojo also will wait?

The weary Germans are getting no respite from the furious Allied aerial offensive. Day and night thousands of mighty American and British bomb freighters roar out across the English Channel to pound away at the vitals of the Nazi monster. Underground reports from Europe indicate that the attacks are taking effect. Germany's railroad system from Cologne to the Bay of Biscay is twisted and jumbled. Marshalling yards are jammed with wrecked cars and twisted rails. It is doubtful whether Hitler can muster enough rolling stock to adequately service his anti-invasion forces in France.

Thursday, May 4, 1944: —Ring leaders in the gasoline black market recently apprehended through disclosures made by a patriotic service station attendant today were sentenced to six years imprisonment and $20,000 fine. The court called the prisoners' actions "near treason," and warned that all such culprits will be severely dealt with.

The non-stop Allied aerial offensive against Hitler's European fortress thundered into its 18th consecutive day with literally thousands of American and British planes swarming across the Channel to blast countless targets throughout the Reich and its occupied territory. Approximately 800 heavy British bombers made an extremely successful night foray against German bases in France, blowing up ammunition and supply depots where the Nazis had hoarded material for their anti-invasion forces.

From Italy another big fleet of Allied planes raided Bucharest, smashing rail yards and industrial targets almost unopposed. Returning flyers said that raging fires and huge pillars of smoke marked the site of their attacks.

The only bad news of the day comes from China. There the Japanese are making considerable headway in their most recent offensive aimed at capturing Chenghsien and present a real threat to Chungking itself. The weary Chinese appear to be unable to stem the onslaught.

Friday, May 5, 1944: —Allied bombers shattered a big dam on the Pescara River in eastern Italy near the Adriatic coast, sending a huge wall of water roaring down the Pescara River Valley, overwhelming German troops and defenses ahead of the advancing British Eighth Army. The destruction of the dam was a spectacular bit of precision bombing by British and Australian dive-bombers, rivaling in effectiveness the RAF attack on the Mohne and Eder dams in Germany.

Meanwhile, powerful squadrons of Allied heavy bombers lashed out from other Italian bases to blast the Rumanian oil fields of Ploesti. The big bombers and their fighter escort crashed through to the target despite intense anti-aircraft fire and furious fighter opposition. Results were gratifying.

On the other side of the world other American planes staged their 46th raid on the Japanese Kurile Islands, hitting the naval base of Paramushiro for the 27th time. Opposition was meager and all our planes returned safely.

In India and Burma, Allied fortunes looked a little better tonight. British Imperial forces have launched a general counter-offensive in the Kohima sector of the Indian front, aimed at frustrating the Japanese drive against Imphal and the Allied lifeline to Burma. At the same time General Stilwell's American and Chinese troops crashed through the main Japanese defenses in Burma's Mogaung Valley and sped southward toward the enemy base of Kamaing.

Saturday, May 6, 1944: —The war picture remains substantially unchanged today. The eyes of the world are upon Western Europe and the thundering air battles raging in the skies above it. For twenty consecutive days, without respite, and in ever increasing numbers, mighty fleets of Allied bombers and fighters have swarmed across the English Channel and over the Alps to blacken and sear the land of the Nazis, burning and blasting the sinews of war from their hands, softening them up for the inevitable invasion. Jittery Nazi officials, seeing the jaws of the trap closing in on them and feeling the accusing weight of their guilt bearing down upon them, are frantically employing every propaganda trick in their evil repertoire to steel the weary German citizenry to meet the ordeal. But the handwriting is on the wall; the days of the oppressor are numbered.

On the other side of the world, the struggle with our Oriental enemy continues in the same vein as during the past several days. Planes from advanced American Army bases and carrier-based planes of the Navy are attacking the Japs at will throughout the Pacific area from Paramushiro in the north to Dutch Guinea in the south. Regular "milk runs" are being made over Jap positions on Ponape Island and Truk in the Carolines and the few remaining enemy strongholds in the Gilbert and Marshall Islands.

In India, furious but apparently indecisive fighting is raging around Kohima and Imphal. British Imperials have succeeded in driving the enemy from several important outposts but the general picture of the situation remains unchanged.

Sunday, May 7, 1944: —Today was one of those delightfully beautiful days for which the Peninsula is so well known. The sun smiled warmly, the birds sang gaily, the flowers exuded their fragrance, and the whole outdoors beckoned irresistibly. Feeling thus invited, we swept the cobwebs off the garage doors, dug out the old 1931 Hupmobile, packed in the family, and set out to use up a goodly portion of the few remaining A gas coupons in our possession. At three gallons per coupon we didn't dare go far but we cruised about the Bay Area, finally ending up at the playground in San Mateo where the youngsters could swing and slide.

Our housing problem has become acute. We have exhausted our 90 day notice to vacate but have not yet been able to find a place to live. The owners have notified us that they intend to take the matter to court to secure eviction. A summons to appear before the local judge has already been served on us. Our only hope lies in the fact that I have now been certified as a War Worker eligible to occupy war housing in this area. We now have a deal pending on a new project home near Burlingame. But our time is rapidly running out.

I mention our housing problem only because it reflects a condition directly caused by the war. Thousands of families are in our predicament, resulting from swollen populations, the freezing of rents and the failure to freeze real estate prices at the same time. Both should have been frozen or none. The present condition means that practically all renters of homes are being forced out and forced to buy at inflated prices.

Monday, May 8, 1944: —As an invasion prelude, Allied Commandos struck at German fortifications along the Italian Riviera during the weekend just passed. The daring raids were launched from Allied bases in Corsica and Sardinia and a majority of the Commandos succeeded in re-embarking after destroying Nazi fortifications along the water front. German reports admitted the attacks were carried out in large force.

The skies over Europe were filled with Allied war planes for another 24 hour period. A daylight attack on Brunswick saw 2,000 American planes tangle with a huge force of Nazi interceptors in a series of violent air battles. The exhausted German defenders have reached such a state of desperation that a few of them deliberately rammed some of the Flying Fortresses and Liberators in a suicidal attempt to down the great ships.

Fortress and Liberator gunners and supporting pursuit pilots shot down a grand total of 119 enemy planes in this one raid. Nice hunting, fellas!

Long range American Army bombers lashed out across the limitless expanse of the Pacific to blast Japanese installations at Guam during daylight hours last Saturday, it was announced today. The raid was one of the most successful of the current Pacific campaign, with all American planes returning safely. Seven out of 25 wary Japanese interceptor planes were shot down despite their lack of eagerness to tangle with the well-gunned Americans.

Tuesday, May 9, 1944: —The Russians have won another great victory, Sevastopol, the city of bloody sieges, fell today before the onslaught of the Fourth Ukrainian Army which cleared the Crimea of Germans in a whirlwind campaign of less than one month. The climax at Sevastopol came after three days of violent fighting in which the avenging Soviet troops smashed their way through the final steel and concrete fortifications protecting the city. German casualties included 30,500 killed and 41,000 prisoners. Other thousands may have died while attempting to escape across the Black Sea under a hail of bombs and shells from the Red Navy and Air Force.

American airmen had their biggest day over Europe today. More than 5,000 sorties were flown with 2,000 planes participating. Airdromes throughout France, Belgium, and Luxembourg were particularly hard hit as the fury of the Allied pre-invasion aerial bombardment increased in a mighty crescendo of destructive power. Fleets of RAF night bombers took over where the American daylight raids ended, to give the weary Nazis no rest from the never-ending cascade of sudden death.

In Italy, Allied forces continued to maintain steady pressure against the German lines. In expectation of a renewed Allied offensive, the Nazis today withdrew their forces from a ten mile salient on the central Italian front. American and British troops quickly moved in to occupy the salient as the Germans covered their withdrawal with heavy artillery and mortar fire.

Wednesday, May 10, 1944: —The Navy Department announced today that a U.S. destroyer was sunk on April 20 in a furious battle with German torpedo planes in the Mediterranean.

Among the surviving crew members was Lieut. Robert M. Morgenthau, son of the Secretary of the Treasury. Fellow officers said Lieut. Morgenthau's behavior under fire was exemplary. He was one of the last to leave the sinking vessel after the skipper, Lieut. Commander Douglas McKeen Swift, of Portsmouth, R.I. had given the command, "Abandon ship." Gunners aboard the destroyer continued to fire at the German planes until the decks were awash. Two of the attacking planes were shot down.

President Roosevelt today nominated James V. Forrestal to succeed Frank Knox as Secretary of the Navy. Mr. Forrestal was undersecretary of the Navy until Knox's death, and acting Secretary since that date. Senate confirmation of the nomination is assured.

Four thousand Allied planes hammered Hitler's Europe today to maintain the tempo of the all-out air offensive. The raiders struck as far as Wiener-Neustadt in Austria, dumping more than 1,500 tons of explosives on the Messerschmitt factories in that region. France and Belgium felt the wrath of British night bombers, lashing at airfields and communications centers. Rail yards and rolling stock were heavily damaged while speedy Mosquito bombers raced through to Berlin itself to prevent the inhabitants of that battered city from resting their frayed nerves. The screws are tightening on Herr Hitler and his "supermen."

Thursday, May 11, 1944: —Standing out in bold contrast with the optimistic and victorious news from other war fronts is the bitter tale of heartbreaking setbacks for the weary Chinese armies in bloody fighting in the central Honan Province of China. The gallant Chinese, outnumbered and out-equipped are being badly beaten on this important front. Mechanized Japanese forces have won complete control of the Peiping-Hankow railway, thus reopening a vital land route between their northern and southern armies. Unless stopped soon, the current Japanese offensive may pose a serious threat to Chungking itself. Yes, China is badly in need of help if she is to remain in the war as a powerful foe of the Japanese.

At least 4,000 planes per day over the Reich, is the record of the Allied aerial offensive, now in its 25th thunderous day. The invasion coastline and railroad marshaling yards were the principal targets today as the climax of the great air drive approaches. Night bombers of the RAF, however, ranged as far as Budapest, capital of Hungary.

Back in the Central Pacific, we learn that American bombers have again pounded Japanese strongholds throughout the vast area. Truk was hit by four-motored Liberators for the fourth time this month while Army bombers ranged far and wide over the Carolines, hitting the Jap wherever he could be found. Other planes paid another call on the Jap-held American isle of Wake. We're going back there one day soon—to stay.

Friday, May 12, 1944: —A great new offensive has opened on the Italian front! From all indications this is the real thing. The final drive on Rome is started. Regrouped and powerfully reinforced Allied armies struck with sudden fury against the Gustav line along an 85 mile front. Three thousand Allied planes prepared the way with a terrific aerial bombardment of the German positions. The famous British Eighth Army lashed out in one of its power drives that carried the Tommies well past their first objectives during the first few hours of the offensive. The Rapido River, long a stumbling block on the road to Rome, was forced in several places by the hard fighting Tommies. Cassino, where the Allied forces met their severest setback, appeared to be outflanked on both sides.

The American Fifth Army surged forward near the Tyrrhenian Sea, obviously intent on opening the Via Casilina and the Appian Way, main highways to Rome. The attack was preceded by a terrific artillery barrage that dwarfed even the famous Alamein bombardment in Egypt. For almost two hours a concentrated stream of high explosive shells sought out German gun positions and supply dumps before the Fifth Army lunged forward.

The Italian offensive appears to be the opening gun of the final European attack on the cornered Nazi criminals. Either Hitler will have to reinforce his Italian garrison, thus weakening his western European defense, or he will have to abandon them to inevitable destruction. Either way he loses. It's the Allies' time to call the turns.

Saturday, May 13, 1944: —Today's reports on the big Allied drive in Italy indicate that the Gustav line has been breached in several places. Veteran British Eighth Army troops smashed their way into the Liri Valley, outflanking Cassino and capturing seven strategic hills and four towns during the first day of battle. Opposition was intense, with fanatical young Nazi paratroopers counter-attacking with great ferocity and total disregard for casualties.

On the Tyrrhenian coastal front, American and French troops of the Fifth Army stormed and captured several peaks dominating Castelforte after sanguinary fighting in which heavy casualties were inflicted on both sides. Several hundred Germans were made prisoners as the Allied juggernaught smashed its way over the steel and concrete fortifications of the Gustav line. Unconfirmed German reports hint that Castelforte has already been evacuated by their forces, which have "disengaged" themselves as the Nazis put it.

Meanwhile, the Allied pre-invasion aerial offensive against German has not slackened. A mighty fleet of more than 2,000 American bombers and fighters struck deep into the German homeland, blasting Tutow and Oanabruck in the Baltic coastal area. Returning airmen stated that enemy fighter opposition was meager compared with previous raids.

Powerful aerial blows were also struck by our Air Force in the Pacific war. Long-range Liberators again plastered the Japanese naval base of Truk, wreaking additional damage among shipping in the harbor and military installations on land.

Sunday, May 14, 1944: —The Nazis' admission that Castelforte, powerful stronghold on the Italian defense line, has been captured by the Allies, was confirmed today. American infantrymen, supported by tanks, marched in to seize the enemy bastion on the second day of the offensive. Units of the German defenders were captured intact, others retreated headlong, and others were annihilated. On the other end of the line, British Eighth Army spearheads dug out new gains against the enemy and widened their bridgehead across the Rapido River. All indications up until now point to complete success for the Allied offensive, with Allied casualties considerably lighter than was expected. Fierce fighting is still in prospect, however, even after the Gustav line is smashed. The Germans are then expected to fall back upon the equally sturdy Adolf Hitler line still blocking the road to Rome.

Allied forces are again on the move in another, far-distant field. Lieut. General Joseph W. Stilwell, commonly known as "Uncle Joe" has launched a powerful new offensive against the Japanese in northern Burma. Uncle Joe is the American general commanding Chinese forces and the reports indicate that this latest offensive is the biggest yet in being aimed at the Japanese bases at Kaming, Mgaung, and Kyitkyina. Pacing the advance of the Chinese troops are American and British tanks, dive bombers, and artillery.

Thirty days have almost ended since the beginning of the current all-out pre-invasion aerial offensive against Hitler's European fortress and there is still no let up. How much longer can the battered Nazis stand the punishment? The devastation must be terrific and, tough as they are, the Nazi supermen must be softening up just a little.

Monday, May 15, 1944: —The Gustav line is breached. American, French, and British troops have scored brilliant victories all along the powerful Nazi defense line across the Italian peninsula. In the center of the line, French forces pounded a three-mile wide breach in the chain of fortifications, while to their right the British Eighth Army broke through heavily defended German positions and surged into the Liri Valley. To the left of the French, along the Tyrrhenian coast, American units swept onward from captured Castelforte to clear more than 60 square miles of Italian soil from the grip of the enemy. Nine more hills and ten strategic towns were seized in the advance.

From Chungking, China, comes word that the doughty Chinese are striking back against their Japanese enemy. Pulling surprises of their own out of the bag, the Chinese suddenly revealed the existence of a powerful American-trained and equipped expeditionary force which surged forward across the Salween River along a 100 mile front and drove westward towards the Burma frontier. Supported effectively by hard-flying American airmen, the Chinese quickly overcame the first surprised Japanese resistance and swept to within 20 miles of the border. The drive coincided with General Stilwell's growing Burma drive and the possibility exists that the two armies may drive through the 100 miles of mountain and jungle separating them and effect a junction.

This latest offensive only emphasizes the amazing recuperative powers of the Chinese and forcibly reminds us not to count China out yet.

Tuesday, May 16, 1944: —Blaring newspaper headlines tell today's story of the war in Italy. NAZIS ON THE RUN stands out in two inch black print, shouting the good news. Thoroughly beaten in the first round of the great offensive, the Germans are hastily pulling out of their remaining strongholds in their famous Gustav line and fleeing for their lives. Apparently the retreat is far from an orderly one, for mountains of equipment and supplies are being abandoned in their haste to escape to the protection of their next line of defense, the Adolf Hitler line.

The Triumphant American Fifth and British Eighth armies, with their gallant French and Polish units, are surging forward close on the heels of the defeated enemy. In some places the Germans are putting up stiff rearguard resistance but in most places the retreat is so swift, the Allied troops are hard put to maintain contact. Heavy casualties have been inflicted on the Nazis, with hundreds of them being taken prisoners daily. More than 3,000 of Hitler's finest troops have already been captured since the start of the current offensive. An even greater number have been killed or wounded.

The pre-invasion air offensive over Europe has been forced into a lull because of inclement weather. The big American and RAF bombers were grounded but swift Mosquitos took up the task of preventing the exhausted Nazis from getting any rest. The speedy plywood bombers braved the stormy weather to drop blockbusters on many Rhineland industrial centers. The Germans struck back with a spying raid on southern England which caused damage and casualties at Portsmouth.

Wednesday, May 17, 1944: —The Allied victory in Italy is growing in scope. French and American troops of the Fifth Army have slashed their way to the first outposts of the Adolf Hitler line after capturing Scauri, on the Tyrrhenian coast. On the northern end of the Gustav line, the Nazis are clinging desperately to their main stronghold of Cassino, but British Eighth Army units, supported by revenge seeking Polish troops, have opened a powerful two-pronged attacked aimed at encircling the bastion, and its famed Monastery Hill. Initial assaults carried the Allied fighters ahead 4,000 yards, putting the defending Germans in a precarious position.

The only bad news of the day again comes from China. The battle for Loyang, capital of Honan province, is going badly for the Chinese. Official reports indicate the Japanese have already forced their way into the walled city and are battling the outnumbered and poorly equipped Chinese troops in the streets. Other enemy columns swept beyond the city, burning and looting the Chinese villages and massacring the inhabitants.

The European aerial offensive is still in its enforced lull due to bad weather over the continent. Mosquitos again kept the attack alive, however, by harrying Berlin with 100 tons of explosives.

A war time census has revealed that the San Francisco Bay Area population has grown 25% since 1940. The swollen figure for today is 1,833,000 against a 1940 figure of 1,461,804. Which reminds me, I must find a house to live in.

Thursday, May 18, 1944: —CASSINO IS OURS! British and Polish troops won one of the greatest victories of the Italian campaign today by capturing Cassino, the previously impregnable stumbling block on the road to Rome. The end came after a brilliant encircling maneuver by the Tommies and Poles had all but sealed the town off. Finally the Nazis gave it up as a bad job and pulled out, after leaving behind some suicide units to delay the Allied advance. Our forces, however, quickly mopped up and drove far beyond the ruined city, in close pursuit of the enemy.

On the other end of the Allied line, American troops battled their way into Formia, coastal anchor position of the Adolf Hitler line. Other American units drove more than two miles into the Hitler chains of fortifications, indicating that that system of defenses will not stop the Allied advance for long.

While the air offensive over Germany was bogged down because of bad weather, a mighty formation of Allied bombers and fighters, 1,500 in number, took off from Italian bases, to attack the Balkans. Ploesti, the heart of Germany's oil supply, was the main target and very heavy damage was inflicted, although cloud formations prevented full observation of the results. Only minor enemy opposition was encountered.

In Burma, General Stilwell's American and Chinese troops drove into the outskirts of Myitkyina today, after taking the city's airdrome, and fall of the important Japanese base was believed imminent.

Friday, May 19, 1944: —News in abundance tonight. In Italy the defeat of the Germans took on the proportions of a rout today as American, French, British, and Polish troops swept forward all along the line. The Nazis are abandoning huge quantities of materiel as they flee in disorderly fashion, intent only on escaping the overwhelming fire of the Allied armies. In the south, American columns swept beyond Formia and fanned out to attack Gaeta and Itri, deep within the Hitler line defenses. To the north, French troops poured into and through Esperia, despite desperate Nazi attempts to make a stand. Meanwhile, from the Anzio beachhead, rumblings are heard that indicate that the Allied forces at that point are about to strike out for themselves, in an effort to speed a junction with the approaching American Fifth Army.

Big news also comes from the South Pacific. General MacArthur's amphibious forces have leap-frogged again, this time 125 miles from recently captured Hollandia to Wakde, further west on the coast of Dutch Guinea. The landing was a complete success, the small Japanese garrison being surprised and quickly overwhelmed. This step put the Bataan hero and his men one step nearer his beloved Philippines, now only 1,250 miles away.

Good news also comes from London where we learn that the great aerial offensive has been resumed. A great fleet of American warplanes renewed the drive by hammering its way through the entire Luftwaffe to strike a furious blow against Berlin. Massed hundreds of German interceptors failed to stop the hard flying, hard fighting Yanks.

Saturday, May 20, 1944: —Itri and Gaeta, key strongholds in the Adolf Hitler lines, were seized by the onrushing American doughboys today, while other columns battled their way into sight of Terracina, 58 miles southeast of Rome, and only 25 miles from the Anzio beachhead. Allied cruisers and destroyers steamed boldly into range of the Nazi guns in Terracina and bombarded the city ahead of the advancing Americans.

With the Gustav line now only a memory, the Allied juggernaught has already chopped the Hitler line into shreds, leaving only cleanup operations before the drive on Rome can go into high gear beyond the last major defense line blocking the way into the Eternal City.

Following up yesterday's curtain raiser on the new pre-invasion aerial offensive over Europe, more than 5,000 Allied planes smashed at hundreds of targets throughout France, Belgium, and Germany today, dropping a grand total of more than 6,000 tons of explosives and fire bombs on rail yards, airdromes, factories, harbors, and military installations. German airfields in France were particularly hard hit, offering a hint as to invasion plans.

In the Pacific war, we learn that Allied air and sea forces from the Southeast Asia, Central Pacific, and Southwest Pacific commands, joined forces last Wednesday to heavily bomb and shell the Japanese naval base of Soerabaja, Java for the first time since the Japs conquered the East Indies in the dark days of 1941 and 1942. Terrific damage was inflicted on the base, while the wary Japanese fleet again refused to oppose the Allied action.

Sunday, May 21, 1944: —Throughout the nation today it was "I am an American Day." Literally millions of grateful citizens, young and old, rich and poor, service men and workers, gathered in public places to rededicate themselves to the ideals and principles of Americanism and to give thanks for the cherished privilege of being an American citizen.

In San Francisco, many thousands of citizens gathered in and about the Civic Auditorium to celebrate the day with a dramatic spectacle of American service units on the march, a great show headed by such stars as Bing Crosby, Bob Hope, Dinah Shore, Jerry Colonna, Vera Vague, and Tony Romano, and inspiring addresses by Governor Earl Warren and Attorney General Kenny. It was a colorful spectacle, depicting America at war, and was alternately solemn, inspiring, and gay, with the witticisms of the comedy stars interspersed with the impressive and serious remarks of the principal speakers. It was truly an occasion to be proud, an occasion when free men and women could meet in free assemblage, of their own volition, and renew their determination to defend the wonderful heritage that is theirs when each of them can say, "I am an America."

From the battlefronts the news is unchanged from yesterday. In Italy the Allied armies are advancing rapidly, giving the beaten Nazis no respite, allowing them no time to regroup their shattered forces for an effective stand. In the Pacific, General MacArthur's troops have completed the seizure of Wakde and ready for new fields to conquer. Already their eyes are upon Sarmi, another Jap stronghold farther along the coast of Dutch Guinea.

Monday, May 22, 1944: —The war creeps closer to the Japanese homeland it was learned tonight. Hard hitting carrier task forces of the United States Navy struck a telling blow against the Japanese base on Marcus Island, 1,175 miles southeast of Tokyo. According to the Japanese radio, two task forces were employed, one of them feinting towards the Bonin Islands, only 400 miles from Japan, and the other striking swiftly at the Marcus base after the main Japanese defenses had been lured away.

President Roosevelt, in a report on lend-lease activities, predicted that the zero hour for the grand assault on Hitler's European Fortress is near at hand and said that the attack will come simultaneously from many sides. From the East, the mighty Russian armies will strike again with renewed fury, while millions of American, British, French, Poles, Czechs, Dutch, Norwegian, and other Allied fighting men will combine their strength to crush the Nazi monster from the west. All these Allies will be armed in large part, by American arms furnished them under lend-lease. They will be the finest arms American ingenuity and industry could produce and will enable those who wield them to strike their most effective blows against the common enemy. To date, lend-lease aid has reached $24,224,806,000.00, including more than 30,000 planes, 25,000 tanks, and 800,000 military vehicles. All this is in addition to our own magnificent armies and Navy.

From Italy comes news that the Nazis have finally rallied to launch one furious counter-attack against the southern end of the Fifth Army front.

Tuesday, May 23, 1944: —American troops lashed out today from the Anzio beachhead in an all-out offensive aimed at driving through to a junction with the main Allied armies advancing from the southeast. Striking suddenly and with great power across the "bloody mile," as the soldiers called the blood red poppy fields that separated our lines from the Germans, American spearheads quickly overran the first enemy positions and scored initial gains of more than five miles. Advance units of the Fifth Army driving up from Terracina to the southeast were, at nightfall, only twenty miles from the Anzio attack forces. Clamped between the two jaws of the Allied trap were an estimated 17 Nazi divisions, approximately 175,000 crack German troops, which Hitler and his generals have apparently committed to a fight to the finish. This is much to the Allied High Command's liking.

While the ground fighting in Italy increased in fury, the aerial offensive over Europe kept pace. American and RAF bombers spent the day and night blasting German communications and industrial centers almost at will. Enemy fighter plane opposition was so meager, that the mighty formations of escorting Thunderbolt, Lightning, and Mustang fighters dropped down from their positions as top cover for the heavy bombers to strafe and harass the enemy in the target areas.

As a bit of home front news we may record that we finally located a house, although it appears as if we shall have to buy, which is the last thing we wanted to do at this time. It is the worst possible time to buy. Prices are up, quality is down, permits and priorities are required, and we haven't any gas with which to move. It's a miserable situation.

Wednesday, May 24, 1944: —All previous records were smashed in the all-out aerial invasion of Germany today, as more than 7,600 Allied planes seared and blackened a tremendous trail of destruction across Germany and Occupied Europe. For a steady 24 hour period, huge armadas of American and RAF planes droned in the skies over the Reich, striking at objectives from the coast of France to Vienna, in old Austria. One great fleet of almost 1,000 heavy U.S. bombers, with a like number of fighter planes as escort, battled through swarms of Nazi interceptors and heavy flak to punish Berlin with one of its most devastating daylight assaults. The desperate Germans threw up all their available fighter strength to ward off the blow but the American planes crashed through to cause terrific damage, which the Nazi radio admitted.

Violent air battles were also fought by 1,500 planes of the 15th U.S. Air Force based in the Mediterranean theater as they lashed out at enemy targets in the Vienna area. Hundreds of Nazi fighters battled the attacking planes all the way from the Alps to the target and back. Losses were heavy on both sides.

In Italy further successes were scored by both jaws of our pincers clamping down on the Nazis from the Anzio beachhead and the main Allied line 20 miles to the southeast. Attacking Anzio forces succeeded in cutting the Appian Way on both sides of Cisterna and the fall of that city is imminent. Terracina, where advance units of the Fifth Army bumped their noses the other day, was captured today by hard-driving armored forces of the United States.

Thursday, May 25, 1944: —An historic meeting took place today. It happened when American patrols advancing from the Anzio beachhead encountered leading elements of the American Fifth Army driving up the Appian way from newly captured Terracina. The junction of the two armies opened up possibilities of a quick drive on Rome and the probable entrapment of 17 Nazi divisions totaling more than 170,000 men. Today's Allied communiqué hailed the meeting as "the climax to a spectacular advance of the Fifth Army of more than 60 miles in only 14 days." The German radio, as usual claimed the retreat of their forces was "a planned withdrawal to a shorter line in the mountains northeast of the Appian Way."

The same thunderous chorus was played in the skies over Europe during the past twenty four hours. More than 7,000 planes battered at the fortifications and industrial centers of Hitler's vast fortress, some of the planes from England striking as far south as Lyon and Toulon on the Mediterranean coast of France. Berlin was struck again in a big night attack, while daylight sorties were carried out against the rail centers of Aachen, Antwerp, Mulhouse, Belfort, Charleroi, Blainville, Metz, and Thionville. Freight yards in Brussels and Liege were also blasted.

Here at home we are having a private little war of our own in connection with this house deal of ours. There is furniture to buy, stoves to install, plumbers to hire, floors to polish, gas, lights, and water to arrange for—and only three gallons of gas to do it with. Besides, everyone is too busy to take on another plumbing job, hauling job, etc. It's a fine mess.

Friday, May 26, 1944: —The Nazi defeat in Italy is growing in scope daily. Since the juncture of the main Allied army with the Anzio beachhead forces, it has been a desperate race on the part of the Germans to escape from the trap rapidly closing in on 17 Nazi divisions which originally held the Allies along the Gustav line. Armored spearheads of the American Fifth Army are driving hard to cut the Via Casilina, the last practical escape route for the beaten Nazis. Latest reports indicate that our troops have captured Cisterna and have raced onward to seize Cori, an outpost on the German defense line only 9 miles from the Via Casilina. At the same time, hundreds of fighter-bombers of the Fifth United States Air Force, have been having a field day in attacks on Nazi columns moving along the highway. More than 610 motor vehicles already have been destroyed by the bombs and shells of the attacking planes; hundreds of others have been damaged. Absolute superiority has been enjoyed in the air.

Reports emanating from neutral Turkey indicate that the invasion-jittery Germans have occupied Bulgaria, seizing strategic points throughout the little Balkan country in what was called "security measures" by the Berlin radio. Bulgarians, however, will recognize the act as a bare-faced seizure after the fashion of the recent Hungarian coup.

For another 24 hour period the invasion of the Reich by air continued without surcease. American planes in heavy force again struck at southern France, smashing targets all along the French Riviera.

Saturday, May 27, 1944: —A big battle is shaping up for Valmontone, which lies astride the Via Casilina on the road to Rome. If the hard-driving American Fifth Army columns now within 2½ miles of the stronghold can smash the Nazi defenses at that vital point, the main bulk of approximately 17 German divisions will be trapped below Rome with almost no chance of escaping capture or annihilation. For this reason it can be expected that the Nazis will wage a furious battle for the position. But Allied superiority so clearly demonstrated thus far in the Italian offensive is confidently expected to continue. Only a near miracle can prevent a major disaster for German arms in this theater of war. The extent of the disaster will depend on whether Hitler orders his men to defend Rome to the end or to pull out in time to escape annihilation.

The death and destruction sowed throughout Germany by Allied planes must be beyond imagination. Thousands of tons of high explosives and fire bombs have been cascaded into the German homeland daily for many months. While military objectives have without doubt been the targets of Allied airmen, there could not help but be many casualties and much damage to civilians and their properties because of the massive size of the raids and the inaccuracies of high altitude and night bombing, especially in the face of furious opposition. It is the kind of war Hitler started and practiced with such terrible effect upon the citizenry of innocent nations but, even so, one cannot but feel a pang of pity for the poor women and children who must endure the awful terror which their maniacal "leader" has brought upon them.

Sunday, May 28, 1944: —Today has been a very hectic one. I am writing this at 11 p.m. and can hardly lift my arms high enough to type. But there is satisfaction too—we are finally moved. Now our "beloved" former landlords can sell their home and make their big wartime profit. It is not only profiteering but in a sense it is sabotaging the war effort. For example, my work is considered essential but this house mess has cost me several days of work in addition to a loss of efficiency due to worry and fret over housing my family. Multiply such cases by hundreds of thousands and you have an incalculable loss of man hours of war work due to the greed of profiteering home owners. In addition the necessity of buying a home has forced me to redeem my war bonds—something I had sworn I would not do for the duration. Multiply this again by hundreds of thousands and what is the effect? Nothing good for the war effort, I'm sure.

Perhaps I am more bitter than usual tonight because I am more tired than usual but I dislike being forced to do things that I don't believe are right and proper at this time, besides the gas stove wasn't delivered when they promised, the plumber won't come until he's good and ready, there's no heat and it's very cold, there's still beds to make and we've got to get up at 6 a.m. So I guess the best thing to do is let the rest of this article go and get to bed—maybe we'll all feel better in the morning.

Monday, May 29, 1944: —Furious battles are being waged in the Alban Hills south of Rome as the Germans strive desperately to stem the Allied onslaught that threatens to trap and destroy their armies in Italy. Advance elements of the American Fifth Army have driven to within 15 miles of the Italian capital and the thunder of the guns is plainly heard in the streets of the Eternal City. Already the Nazis have lost their 71st, 94th, and 715th divisions, with more than 15,000 prisoners now in the hands of the advancing Allies. But even so, enemy resistance is stiffening and Allied Intelligence reports indicate that the Germans have thrown additional elements of the crack Hermann Goering and 92nd Infantry Divisions into the crumbling Alban Hills defenses.

On the center of the front below Rome, American forces advancing from the Anzio beachhead have driven a deep wedge into the Nazi defenses and are threatening Velletri, key stronghold on the Appian Way. To the north another American column has battered its way to within one mile of Valmontone, key to the last remaining escape route for the enemy. It is apparent that the Germans are striving to hold Valmontone at all costs, at least until their southern forces can be safely withdrawn. In this they have been partially successful thus far.

General MacArthur's forces have leaped another 200 miles towards the Philippines. It was revealed today that American amphibious forces landed on Biak Island, off the coast of Dutch Guinea, last Saturday, thus carrying the American flag to within 900 miles of the Philippine archipelago.

Tuesday, May 30, 1944: —Memorial Day! A nation at war paused for a few minutes today to remember the dead heroes of this and other wars. Services were held at many national shrines, honoring those men who paid the supreme sacrifice to defend American ideals. Even on the battlefields of this war Americans took time to pay homage to those who will not come home. On the Anzio beachhead south of Rome where many a gallant lad died in the furious battles that raged there for many weeks, General Mark Clark, commander of the American Fifth Army, met with soldiers of the combined forces to honor the beachhead heroes and to promise them that through their efforts and sacrifice, the liberation of Rome is near at hand.

While the General spoke, however, fierce fighting was raging in the Alban hills, 16 miles south of the Italian capital. Several desperate counterattacks were launched by the Germans but in each case they were impaled upon the Allied spearheads driving on the city. To the north, the plight of the Nazis was even worse. Allied bombers were reported to have rendered the Via Casilina unusable, a graveyard of smashed German vehicles and Nazi soldiers. Valmontone, key bastion on the highway, is under siege by American armored forces and infantry. Its fall is believed imminent.

Although we haven't mentioned it for a few days, the Allied aerial offensive over the Reich has not halted for a moment. Thousands of American and RAF bombers and fighters smeared the manufacturing center of Hannover in a devastating Decoration Day attack. Thirty five bombers and 11 fighters were lost. More than 100 Nazi fighters paid the penalty.

Wednesday, May 31, 1944: —There was excitement and drama off the San Francisco coast early this morning. The SS Henry Bergh, a Liberty Ship built at Richmond, California last year, ran aground twenty miles west of the Golden Gate, on the rocky reefs of the Farallone Islands. Aboard the vessel, which struck with a terrific crash during a heavy fog, were more than 1,000 U.S. Navy personnel, most of them returning veterans of the South Pacific fighting. Fortunately, all of them were saved by brilliant rescue work carried out by other naval craft dispatched from San Francisco when the first SOS came in.

American armored units tore another hunk out of the last German defense lines before Rome. Violent fighting raged all day as the Allied armies crunched their way slowly yet inexorably towards the Eternal City. Velletriv and Valmontone, powerful defense bastions on the Appian Way and the Via Casilina respectively, were still holding out as of last reports tonight, but Allied troops were bypassing them, leaving them to drop off the vine as their positions become hopeless.

In the air war, the United States Eighth and Ninth Air Forces, based in England, sent more than 1,750 Flying Fortresses and Liberators, supported with clouds of fighters to smash four rail hubs, several air bases, and Nazi supply centers in northwest Germany. Other hundreds of American planes struck from Italy at the great Ploesti oil fields in Rumania. At least one big refinery was blown to bits.

In the Pacific war, our forces on Biak Island off the coast of New Guinea were reported locked in furious combat with Japanese troops defending the Mokmer airfield.

June

Wednesday, June 1, 1944: —Official Army and Navy announcements today revealed that more than 5,200,000 Americans are now on duty outside the United States, either abroad or at sea. Over 1,566,000 U.S. sailors, Marines, and Coast Guardsmen are afloat with our mighty Navy, while 3,657,000 U.S. soldiers are now overseas. By the end of the year this latter figure will increase to more than 5 million, according to Secretary of War, Henry L. Stimson. In addition, it was revealed that the Armed Forces have 112,700 planes, of which the Army has 75,000 (34,000 combat) and the Navy has 37,700. The Army is operating 925 bases on foreign soil, with 750 airfields.

Steel-tipped American spearheads caught the gleam of sunlight shining on the skyline of Rome today. Blasting the Nazis with everything in the book, the hard-fighting doughboys battered their way to within 13 miles of the Italian capital and found themselves on the brow of the last of the Alban Hill defenses overlooking the sloping plains that run into Rome. The city was plainly in sight, its fate now resting on the decision of the German High Command, which must decide whether one of the principal historical, cultural, and religious centers of the world is to be made a battleground and destroyed.

The SS Henry Bergh, which ran aground on the reefs of the Farallones yesterday, split in two today, and has been abandoned as a total loss. The vessel cost $2,500,000 at the time it was built a year ago, and was converted into a Navy transport. The fortunate feature of the unfortunate affair was that no lives were lost. For this the officers of the vessel and the Navy rescuers deserve high praise.

Friday, June 2, 1944: —The most important news of the day was the revelation that United States and Russian planes began "shuttle" bombing tactics today. American Flying Fortresses and Liberators, with their fighter escort, took off from British and Italian bases, attacked important enemy targets in Rumania and then proceeded across the eastern battlefront to prepared bases in Russia. Russian and American ground crews immediately serviced the planes for the return trip to England and Italy.

Inauguration of the long-awaited "shuttle" bombing system was hailed as a revolutionary new milestone in the air war against Germany.

It will bring all of eastern Germany, Poland, Rumania, and the Baltic States within range of the mighty Allied air fleets and will force a redistribution of the Nazi fighter defenses, with a consequent weakening of the entire German defense structure.

As the irresistible tide of Allied power nears the gates of Rome, fear for the city's safety mounts rapidly. Pope Pius XII, seeing the decisive hour approaching, made an impassioned plea that the warring nations spare Rome. Said he, "Whoever would raise his hand against this sacred territory will be accused of matricide." He also urged the leaders of the belligerent nations to seek an immediate way to peace, a negotiated peace that would show the defeated peoples some generosity.

The Pope's views, however, are at wide variance with the majority of Allied opinion. You cannot negotiate with criminals and beasts. Nothing short of a total victory will assure the world of a stable peace—this time!

Saturday, June 3, 1944: —General Sir Henry Maitland Wilson, Allied commander in the Mediterranean theater, today assured the world that Rome would be spared the ravages of war unless the Germans elected to defend the city itself, in which case it would be necessary for the Allied armies to take appropriate military measures to eject them. The General therefore sincerely hopes that the enemy will not make this ill-considered choice.

As the Allied commander spoke, American and British forces were locked in a furious battle with last-ditch German defenders, less than a dozen miles from the Italian capital. Previously Fifth Army units had smashed through German defense lines before Valmontone and occupied the Via Casilina stronghold almost without a shot. Defeated German columns were streaming back along the Via Casilina, leaving vast quantities of booty behind them. Their line of retreat was littered with the wreckage of hundreds of vehicles, blasted into heaps of junk by low flying Allied airmen, who ranged up and down the highway, strafing and smashing the remnants of the badly mauled Nazi armies.

In the Pacific war, we learn that the conquest of Biak Island, off the northern coast of Dutch Guinea, is proving to be one of the toughest propositions ever tackled by our troops. The Japs are defending the island bitterly, and are using large numbers of tanks and other armored vehicles for the first time since the battle of New Guinea began. Tonight's dispatches, however, state that our forces have fought their way to the ridge overlooking Mokmer airdrome, the ultimate objective.

Sunday, June 4, 1944: —Not much change in the war news today. In fact, we've been so busy setting ourselves up in our new home that we have hardly taken time to listen to the radio. Late news reports just coming in, however, indicate that the Allied armies are at the very gates of Rome. Heavy fighting is still in progress but apparently only with German rearguards who are striving desperately to delay the Allied juggernaught long enough for them to extricate the main body of their defeated forces. Although the Nazi High Command has stated that Rome will not be defended, their present action of apparently withdrawing their troops into the city has caused grave doubts as to whether their intentions are sincere. The next few days will tell the tale.

The mighty aerial offensive against Hitler's European fortress appears to be increasing in tempo—if that is possible. The vaunted Nazi Atlantic Wall and communication lines throughout France, the Lowlands, Belgium, and Western Germany seem to be getting the major portion of the Allied attention. This would seem to indicate that invasion D-day cannot be far off, although my guess ventured April 30th that the big attack would start on May 25, if not before, obviously missed the mark by many days. To an armchair strategist it would seem as though time is surely wasting and a considerable portion of the best fighting weather is already passed. But this is idle speculation. It may be that no western invasion will be launched this year. In any event the decision is resting in capable hands—General Eisenhower and the Allied High Command.

Monday, June 5, 1944: —ROME HAS FALLEN!! The first of the Axis capitals to succumb to Allied might fell before the onslaught of two powerful armies, the American Fifth and the British Eighth. American troops of the Fifth had the honor of being the first to enter the Eternal City but they did not pause to sight-see; instead, they roared on through, crossed the Tiber and raced in pursuit of two beaten German armies striving desperately to escape total annihilation after their decisive defeat before Rome.

Men and women of the United Nations throughout the world hailed the capture of Rome as the greatest Allied victory of the war so far. Praise of the valiant troops of the two Allied armies in Italy rang throughout the world. Premier Stalin of Russia, a man who knows what war is, was warm in his commendation for the brilliant victory. Allied prestige increased everywhere, while Nazi fortunes sank to a new low.

President Roosevelt took to the air tonight to welcome the "liberation" of the Eternal City. "One up and two to go," he said, but cautioned that the ultimate victory over Germany "still lies some distance ahead." "That distance will be covered in due time—have no fear of that," the Chief Executive said, "but it will be tough and it will be costly."

As he had promised he would upon the liberation of Rome, King Victor Emmanuel III today abdicated the Italian throne, conferring "all royal powers" upon his son, Umberto, who will be known as Lieutenant General of the Realm.

Tuesday, June 6, 1944: —INVASION!!! FRANCE HAS BEEN INVADED IN THE GREATEST AIR AND SEABORNE ATTACK IN HISTORY! It has come to pass, the longed for yet dreaded D-day, the day of invasion of Hitler's mighty European fortress. In the wee small hours of last night, General Eisenhower sent his mighty legions of liberation crashing onto the shores of France.

Huge black newspaper headlines and blaring radios shouted the historic news to us this morning. From all we can learn, the German radio first announced the Allied landings late last night. It was not until about 12:15 this morning that General Eisenhower issued his first communiqué, confirming the German reports and stating that Allied airborne and seaborne forces successfully breached the Nazis' vaunted Atlantic Wall at several places along the north coast of Normandy from Le Havre to Cherbourg.

Following close upon the heels of the brilliant victory in Rome, the Allied invasion apparently caught the Nazis flat-footed. Penetrations of up to ten miles were admitted by the Germans and early reports indicate that solid beachheads were established at several points. American, British, and Canadian troops and supplies were pouring ashore at those points. Initial Allied losses were far less than expected.

General Eisenhower's Order of the Day to his troops proclaimed what every man and woman of the United States feels. "You are about to embark upon a great crusade," he said, "The eyes of the world are upon you. The hopes and prayers of liberty-loving peoples everywhere march with you . . . . Let us all beseech the blessing of Almighty God upon this great and noble undertaking."

Wednesday, June 7, 1944: —The greatest overseas operation of all times has thus far exceeded expectations it was disclosed today. The Allied invasion armies have cleared all the landing beaches of the enemy and reinforcements are pouring ashore in endless streams. The initial success of the landings apparently was the result of several well conceived factors. First, General Eisenhower and his Allied High Command apparently picked the only spot on the French coast where the German defenses were not yet fully prepared. In other words they found the soft spot. Secondly, the attack was preceded by one of the most concentrated aerial attacks yet launched. Eleven thousand Allied planes flew something like 33,000 sorties in the first day and dropped over 11,200 tons of bombs on the invasion coastline in less than 8½ hours. Thirdly, a mighty Allied fleet, including a number of battleships, among them the Nevada, resurrected from Pearl Harbor. Fourthly, the timing was perfect, coming as it did immediately after the distracting (to the Nazis) news from Rome. In short, everything went according to plan—and what a plan!

But initial success does not mean victory. The real fighting is just beginning, as the German High Command commences to throw its reserves into a desperate counter-attack. From the meager details yet reported, it appears that a furious tank battle is raging in the vicinity of Caen, key point on the Paris-Cherbourg railroad, and ten miles inland from the Allied beachhead. American and British paratroopers have seized several bridges further inland and are holding on against ferocious attack from numerically superior Nazi forces.

Thursday, June 8, 1944: —Allied airborne and seaborne forces have succeeded in uniting and are driving inland, apparently aiming at slicing off the Cherbourg peninsula and trapping those German forces defending the great harbor of Cherbourg. Bayeux, important road junction in the center of the Allied line which now extends for seventy miles, was captured today, after fierce counter-attacks by Nazi panzer groups were beaten off, with heavy losses on both sides.

Dramatic stories of adventure and hairbreadth escapes will come out of the events of D-day by the thousands. The wildest tales of fiction will appear tame beside the adventures of many Allied paratroopers and glider troops who pounced down upon the unsuspecting enemy and threw him into such utter confusion that he was unable to rally in time to fend off the seaborne attack by the main Allied forces. Their heroic exploits will be told and retold for decades to come.

General Bernard L. Montgomery, the famous leader of the British Eighth Army, has landed in France and is leading the fight against his old enemy, Marshal Erwin Rommel, the former desert fox who was so decisively beaten in Africa and Egypt. Heavy tank battles are said to be raging around Caen as the German Marshal apparently strives to seize control of the situation.

Meanwhile, thousands of American and British reinforcements are pouring ashore at the beachheads along the Normandy coast despite a continuation of the "not so good" weather which was the only part of the invasion plan which was not entirely satisfactory. A windy, choppy sea hindered the initial landings but was not permitted to become an insuperable obstacle.

Friday, June 9, 1944: —The re-conquered territory of France is slowly yet surely being widened. American troops have driven inland from their Normandy peninsula beachhead to capture the town of St. Mere Eglise today and blasting their way northward towards the deep water port of Cherbourg, less than twenty miles away. Capture of that great French port is essential before the Allies can consider they have a real foothold on the soil of France. Into that port can come all the heavy equipment and huge convoys necessary to properly equip a great army.

General Omar Bradley, who earned fame in Tunisia, is reported to be leading American forces battling their way towards Cherbourg. The general was largely responsible for the brilliant success of American troops in the final victory around Bizerte and Tunis, and our French invasion forces are therefore to be considered in good hands.

From among the thousands of D-day stories is the one about the glider pilot who set his glider, full of troops, down in the dark on, of all places, the roof of a large building. Feeling their way down through skylights, the troops found themselves in German headquarters for the area. The astonished Nazis surrendered in their night shirts.

Shunted into the background by the sensational invasion news, the Italian front is still producing important developments. The triumphant American Fifth and British Eighth Armies are pursuing the beaten Germans far up the Italian peninsula. The Nazi retreat is disorderly, almost a rout and our troops have surged northward more than 40 miles above Rome.

Saturday, June 10, 1944: —American tanks are rolling on Cherbourg. Armored units of the United States forces under the command of General Bradley have sliced their way to within ten miles of the great French port, despite fierce and sometimes almost suicidal resistance on the part of the enemy. Other Allied columns succeeded in capturing the Normandy towns of Isigny and Ste. Croix, while one fast moving American unit entered Trevieries, nine miles west of Bayeux.

It was also officially announced today that hard-working bulldozer crews have laid out several airstrips on the coast of France, from which American and British planes are already operating in support of the advancing ground forces.

Competing for headlines with their comrades in Normandy, Allied troops in Italy were continuing their sensational pursuit of two beaten German armies. General Mark W. Clark's victorious doughboys and Tommies have raced fifty miles across the plains above Rome, covering 14 miles in the past 24 hours to capture the important town of Tuscania. Across the Appennines, in the Adriatic sector, the British Eighth Army is surging onward against an outflanked and thoroughly demoralized enemy.

With a thundering explosion that rivaled any on the flaming battlefronts, the reinforced concrete floor in a machine shop in Mare Island Navy Yard was ripped apart today. The blast was caused by accumulated gases under the floor and killed two workers, injuring 38 others.

Sunday, June 11, 1944: —The latest news from the Normandy fighting front is an Allied report that a new landing has been successfully made on the northeast cost of the Contentin peninsula, just a few miles from Cherbourg. Troops landed in this sector are already pushing southward to effect a junction with American forces driving up from the southeast. The latter forces are said to be near Montebourg, fifteen miles from the great Harbor, and fierce fighting is in progress. Improved weather was a factor as the invasion armies gained all along the line today. Allied fighter planes, taking off from airfields newly established in France, supported the ground forces closely with deadly strafing and bombing attacks.

The word "catastrophe" best describes the Nazi defeat in Italy. Two once powerful German armies are fleeing northward in panic after their trouncing before the gates of Rome. Their flight has become so desperate that the Nazi High Command has apparently ordered their forces to break up into small groups and make their way as best they can to a pre-arranged rallying point near Florence. But the victorious Allies have no intention of letting them escape. Fleets of avenging planes ceaselessly strafe and blast the retreating foe, destroying his vehicles and inflicting numerous casualties. Armored spearheads of the rapidly advancing American Fifth and British Eighth armies constantly seek out and liquidate isolated units of the beaten enemy. Leading American columns have pushed more than fifty miles north of Rome, and it is conceivable that the entire peninsula may fall before the onrushing Allies. The headache's not getting better, eh, Adolf?

Monday, June 12, 1944: —Today is another D-day. This time it is a civilian D-day. The Fifth War Load Drive officially opens today. The tremendous goal is 16 billion dollars. Now is the occasion to back the invasion. Citizens throughout the nation will be asked to dig deeper than they ever have before to raise the funds needed to carry the war to the enemy. To keep the doughboys on the fighting fronts we've got to raise the dough on the home front. As the President pointed out, if our fighting men are willing to <u>give</u> their lives, we ought to be will to <u>lend</u> our money. So from now until the end of the month it will be bonds for bullets, bonds for shells, bonds to bomb Tokyo, bonds to avenge Pearl Harbor, and bonds to back the attack wherever it may be launched. Bonds for war now so that the bonds of friendship and goodwill may once again bind the world in peace.

While the home front girds for the battle of finance, the Allied invasion armies continue to score substantial gains in the battle for France. The beachhead on the coast of Normandy has finally been fused into one continuous Allied line some sixty miles long. In depth the beachhead varies from a mile to eighteen miles at one point. General Eisenhower's headquarters reports that progress in the invasion to date has been "a little better than satisfactory." American troops scored the most impressive gain of the day, capturing the important Nazi defense base, Carentan, on the neck of the Cherbourg peninsula. Meanwhile, British and Canadian troops were locked in a fierce tank battle with the Nazis between Caen and Tilly.

Tuesday, June 13, 1944: —The most interesting bit of news from Europe today is the reported ousting of Marshal Rommel as commander of the German armies facing the Allies in France. Failure of the one-time "Desert Fox" to prevent the successful landing of Allied troops on the coast of France was given as the reason for his dismissal. Once again American and British generals, among them General Sir Bernard L. Montgomery of Alamain fame, have outguessed the best military brains the Nazis could produce.

German forces facing entrapment on the Cherbourg peninsula are fighting with a ferocity seldom equaled in the history of warfare. According to Allied observers, the tide of battle has swayed back and forth through the streets of Carentan and Montebourg, with superior American forces gradually gaining the upper hand despite bloody hand to hand encounters. Casualties were severe on both sides.

The Germans continue to hold Caen on the British end of the Allied line, but the hard-fighting Tommies have thrown a ring of armor around the town and are pouring a tremendous weight of explosive shells into the Nazis' positions. Massive tank battles are raging in the outskirts of the town which the Germans have been ordered to defend to the death.

Turning to the Pacific war, we learn that a powerful U.S. naval task force attacked the Japanese in their Marianas Islands stronghold last weekend. Thirteen Jap ships and 141 planes were destroyed in the assault.

Wednesday, June 14, 1944: —Allied spearheads have driven thirty miles inland from the invasion beachheads, it was learned today. One armored column cracked through the center of the German's defense line and captured the towns of Caumont and Viller Bocage. This was accomplished despite five furious counter-attacks launched by the Nazis in one day, some of them made by "suicide" divisions who threw themselves recklessly against the massed armor and fire power of the invaders. All counter-attacks were stopped cold, after which the Americans, British, and Canadians renewed their relentless advance.

Montebourg, on the Cherbourg peninsula, was the scene of particularly bitter fighting, with the town changing hands several times during the day. The awful intensity of the struggle surpassed any action in the war thus far, with the possible exception of Stalingrad. In this grim battle our troops are conducting themselves magnificently.

American warships are ranging thousands of miles over the Pacific. Simultaneous attacks were reported today on the widely separated Japanese Kurile and Marianas Islands. Powerful naval task forces boldly sailed close to the Japanese homeland to blast enemy bases in the Kurile Islands while other groups of surface vessels pounded Saipan and Tinian in the Marianas. No effective opposition was offered by the once boastful Japanese Imperial Navy.

Thursday, June 15, 1944: —JAPAN BOMBED!! MARIANAS INVADED! Brilliant and thrilling headlines by the dozens are being shouted at us lately as the tempo of the war increases on all fronts. Today we learned the exciting news that Japan has been bombed again by American planes. This time the attack was not just a stunt. This time it was the real thing, the beginning of the inevitable aerial blitz that will heap the same devastation on Japan that has been visited upon the Nazis in Europe. The attack was made by an undisclosed number of B-29's, the new super-bomber, the big brother of the Flying Fortresses.

Here on the West Coast the news of the bombing of Japan was greeted with even more cheers than the invasion of Europe. The news first came out about noontime and when one of the office clerks brought in a newspaper with big red headlines "JAPAN BOMBED!" the entire office burst into a spontaneous round of cheers and applause. It was indeed good news, as the Pacific war hits closer to home out here than does the European conflict. No love is lost on the Japs anywhere on the Pacific Coast.

In addition to the sensational bombing news, we also learned that American amphibious forces have invaded the Japanese Marianas Islands, only 1,449 miles from Tokyo. The initial landings were made on Saipan under cover of a terrific bombardment from a mighty naval task force. The beach has been taken but the enemy opposition is stronger than ever before. Since the island is so close to Japan, it was expected that it would be strongly held and our leaders have so planned.

Friday, June 16, 1944: —Hitler launced his secret weapon against England today. It was what appeared to be a fantastic fleet of robot bombers that streaked over the English Channel and dumped tons of high explosives haphazardly over the southern coast of England. Berlin boasted that the attack was the "beginning of vengeance" for Allied attacks on the Reich. London reports indicated that all southern England was put on a 24 hour alert and no effort was made to minimize the gravity of the new attack, although it was claimed that the robot bombers thus far have caused comparatively little damage and will not interfere with the Allied war effort. Effective counter-measures are expected to be put into immediate action, although details of the new weapon are not yet known.

Details of the bombing attack on Japan by American Super-Fortresses were revealed today. Returning crewmen of the huge B-29's reported that the raid was a brilliant success, the principal target being the great iron and steel works at Yawata, on the island of Kyushu, 500 miles south of Tokyo. Yawata is the "Pittsburgh" of Japan and produces 20% of all Japanese steel. I should say "did produce 20% of all Japanese steel" for returning American flyers claimed they "knocked hell" out of the place, leaving the coke ovens and blast furnaces wreathed in towering columns of smoke. Only four of the mighty aerial battleships were lost in the raid, two of them by accidents, one by anti-aircraft fire over the target, and one which did not return and is listed as missing.

Saturday, June 17, 1944: —News from all the fighting fronts of the world is pouring in in such quantities that it is hard to keep up with it. The tempo of the war all over the world has reached a furious pitch. In France, American forces have smashed their way almost across the Contentin peninsula, threatening the 30,000 Nazis defending the deep-water port of Cherbourg with entrapment. Only 5 miles separates the armored tip of the advancing Yank column from the west coast of the peninsula. Already our famous Long Toms command the narrow corridor with their raking fire, and although the Germans are reported evacuating Cherbourg it appears that they are too late. Their last avenue of escape has been cut. They face surrender of death.

The American invasion of Saipan in the Japanese Marianas has developed into a bitter struggle, with our forces locked in a death battle with 30,000 of the Emperor's finest shock troops. Every weapon from tanks, to heavy artillery to knives and bare fists are being employed in the sanguinary struggle. Immediate objective of the U.S. Marines and Army units driving inland is the Aslito airdrome.

In the Mediterranean theater we learn that Fighting French forces have invaded the Nazi held island of Elba, where Napoleon was once exiled. The fighting poilus successfully established a beachhead in the early stages of the attack.

The Nazi secret weapon launched against England yesterday was described today as a robot rocket bomb. Hundreds of them streaked across the Channel today causing considerable damage and casualties but no panic.

Sunday, June 18, 1944: —The tiny island of Elba, where a former would-be conqueror of the world was once exiled, has very nearly been liberated by the fighting forces of Free France. The defending German garrison has been driven into a narrow pocket on the island and its surrender of annihilation within a matter of hours is certain. The Nazi followers of the modern Napoleon, Adolf Hitler, apparently have neither the means nor the stomach to withstand the furious attack of the avenging Frenchmen.

Southern England has been raked for the fourth consecutive day with hundreds of the so-called robot planes, which are, in reality, merely winged bombs. Most of the mystery has been torn from the new weapon and it has been revealed as a very simple rocket projectile, apparently fired from racks in the Pas-de-Calais area of France. The devilish flying bombs have wings and are jet-propelled. They travel approximately 250 miles per hour and are loaded with 2,000 pounds of explosives. They produce a terrifying whirring sound as they speed through the air and look like a giant ball of fire shooting across the sky at night. They are highly inaccurate and are obviously only a "revenge" weapon, aimed at civilian morale. In this purpose they have already flopped, since the British have taken them in stride, not losing a moment's time in the even flow of war materials to the Normandy beachhead.

In the Pacific, the decisive battle for Saipan is going well for our side, despite furious resistance from 30,000 elite Japanese troops.

Monday, June 19, 1944: —One of the greatest air battles of the Pacific war was fought yesterday, according to a Washington announcement released this morning. The action took place off Saipan, in the Marianas, with the Japs throwing hundreds of planes against our invasion fleet in a mighty attempt to break the noose tightening around their Central Pacific stronghold. Their desperate gamble failed, however, as our defending aircraft and anti-aircraft fire downed over three hundred of the Nipponese planes. It as a decisive victory for our fleet air arm and practically sealed the doom of the 30,000 enemy troops bottled up on Saipan. The announcement reported that only slight damage was suffered by our surface craft but no figures were yet available on our planes losses, which were considerable.

On Saipan itself, hard-fighting U.S. Marines and doughboys battled their way beyond the vital Aslito airdrome, after capturing that airstrip intact. American planes will soon be operating from that base, which lies only 1,500 miles from Tokyo and a paltry 750 miles from the Philippines.

From Normandy comes the cheering news that the fall of Cherbourg to the brilliant U.S. Ninth Division is practically assured. The tireless Yanks pressed their advantage gained when the peninsula was finally cut in two, and drove through to the town of Bricquebec, only seven miles from the harbor. American Long Tom guns are already dueling with the German artillery guarding the Cherbourg approaches.

Tuesday, June 20, 1944: —The possibility that a showdown battle between the Grand Fleets of Japan and the United States may soon take place, was revealed by Admiral Chester W. Nimitz today. The Admiral pointed out that the decisive naval engagement may result from the enemy's desperate need to prevent our forces from establishing a firm foothold in the Marianas. American bases in those islands would bring not only the Philippines but also the Japanese homeland itself within easy bombing range of our heavy bombers. For this reason the Jap leaders may see fit to risk all in a mighty sea engagement. Already there are indications that the entire Japanese fleet is concentrated in the waters west of the Marianas and major units of our Navy are steaming eagerly westward, hoping to establish contact. The course of the Pacific war may be altered decisively within the next few days.

It was also revealed by the Navy today that the 1475 ton U.S. submarine Grayback and her crew of 65 have been lost, presumably in the Pacific fighting. Part of the cost of recent victories in that theater.

In France, American fighting men continued to smash their way towards the deep-water port of Cherbourg. Flying columns knifed their way to within 3½ miles of the port while other powerful Yank forces finally cleared Montebourg and Valognes of the enemy. Widespread German demolitions within Cherbourg gave evidence that the enmy realizes the hopelessness of his position. Allied commanders served the doomed garrison with a "surrender or die" ultimatum.

Wednesday, June 21, 1944: —What may be the opening round of a showdown naval battle in the Pacific began today when hundreds of American carrier-based aircraft struck out from their floating airfields to strike at the Japanese fleet now located in the vast expanse of ocean between the Marianas Islands and the Philippines. Reconnaissance planes spotted the enemy fleet just east of the island of Luzon and flashed the long-awaited tidings to the "fast carrier task force" of the U.S. Fifth fleet under the command of Admiral R.A. Spruance. The flattops immediately launched their eager "birds of prey" which darted off to bring the elusive enemy fleet to bay at last.

On the other side of the world, other American fighting men are nearing their final objective in the battle for Cherbourg, vital port on the tip of the Normandy peninsula. Infiltrating Yanks are already battling in the streets of the city's suburbs and the complete subjugation of the German garrison is expected hourly. The fighting spirit of our troops is magnificent while information obtained from captured Nazi soldiers indicates that the enemy's morale is very low. Only threats of immediate death from their officers is keeping them in line. Sounds a little out of character for the vaunted Nazi supermen, doesn't it?

Although we haven't mentioned it since Invasion Day, the aerial offensive against Germany has continued despite the demands for air support over the Normandy beachhead. Our heavy bombers have continued to smash at the Reich daily, the latest attack being a 2,000 plane raid last night against Berlin.

Thursday, June 22, 1944: —BRILLIANT VICTORY! Admiral Nimitz issued a triumphant communiqué today, declaring that our carrier-based aircraft caught a major group of the Japanese Grand Fleet off the northern coast of Luzon last Monday and decisively trounced them, sinking or damaging 14 warships, including four aircraft carriers and a battleship. The engagement was reminiscent of the Battle of Midway, in that surface fighting never took place. Our aircraft pounced on the enemy fleet as it steamed out of the channel between Luzon and Formosa and sent it reeling and battered back into the safety of the China sea after a roaring battle that cost us 49 planes. Evidence that we were victorious was the fact that our forces are still scouring the scene of battle to pick up survivors of the planes that were downed. Admiral Nimitz indicated that it was one of our greatest naval victories, although the Japs succeeded in avoiding the final showdown battle between the rival battle lines. That must still be fought.

In France, the trapped Nazi garrison in Cherbourg apparently is determined to defend the battered port to the last man. Furious fighting is raging in the wrecked streets while wave upon wave of Allied planes pound the enemy from the air. Determined American infantrymen have driven wedges through to the coast in two places, chopping the remaining Nazi garrison into three isolated groups. The desperate German resistance only prolongs the inevitable end.

Friday, June 23, 1944: —The Navy released further details of the battle of the Eastern Philippines last Monday, disclosing that our planes sank two Nip carriers and two heavy cruisers, while a U.S. submarine scored three torpedo hits on a third enemy carrier, which probably sank. In addition, at least 12 other Japanese warships were sent to the bottom or damaged and more than 50 Nip planes were shot down. The remaining Jap fleet fled to the safety of the China sea behind the Philippines, leaving the Marianas at the mercy of the American invasion forces.

It was revealed by the Navy Department that the latest naval victory was won by Task Force 58, the "most powerful and destructive naval unit in the history of sea warfare." The task force is composed of a large number of huge aircraft carriers, and includes battleships, cruisers and destroyers. The carriers of this task force alone are capable of launching more than 1,000 planes of all types.

The battle of Cherbourg Harbor is not yet over, although American troops have entered the city from all directions. The Germans have rounded up every man capable of firing a shot and are fighting stubbornly for every bit of wreckage in the city. But their fate is sealed. The inexorable advance of the doughboys will not be halted. The harbor will soon be ready to receive the flood of reinforcements and supplies needed to continue the liberation of Europe.

London reports indicate that the Russians have finally launched their summer offensive in the region of Vitebsk in White Russia. The big squeeze is now on, with mighty Allied armies attacking Nazi monster from the east and west and south.

Saturday, June 24, 1944: —The great new Russian offensive into White Russia is making sensational progress. Apparently the Nazis, trained as they are to defend France and Italy, have nothing approaching the force required to stop the mighty Red Army. Already two powerful Soviet pincers have closed around Vitebsk and the fall of that German bastion is expected momentarily. The possibility exists that the Russians may trap and destroy the five Nazi divisions reported holding the town. The Red troops are being supported by the massed artillery and airplane team that has proved so effective in this war. Exultant Moscow statements indicate that the Germans are facing a catastrophe of the first magnitude.

At the same time another magnificent army is handing the Germans another trouncing at Cherbourg. General Omar Bradley's Americans have hammered the Nazi defense forces almost out of Cherbourg by sheer courage and resolution, averting what the enemy hoped would be another Stalingrad defense by superior fighting ability only. Every advantage of terrain has been with the defenders but the determined Yanks have blasted then out inch by inch in the roughest kind of fighting. Flame-throwers, Bangalore torpedoes, mortars, grenades, and bayonets have all been wielded in ferocious close-quarters fighting. Yankee stamina has prevailed.

Here at home, the most serious turn of events has been the new tangle in the transportation snarl caused by the refusal of Greyhound bus drivers, through union orders, to accept "standees" in their buses. Hundreds of war workers all over the Bay Area have been stranded as a result.

Sunday, June 25, 1944: —Throughout the world the raging tide of death and destruction continues to reach new and more ghastly heights on every major battlefront. From the flaming jungles of Saipan and the vast expanse of waters east of the Philippines to the shores of Normandy and the plains of Italy American men and boys are laying down their lives in defense of their flag and the freedom for which it stands. They are doing so boldly and bravely, with no thought of turning back until final victory has been achieved. Never before in history has this Nation been represented and defended by a more glorious Army and Navy. In every engagement in which they have been involved, from Wake Island and Bataan, to Cassino and Cherbourg American fighting men have given a good account of themselves. We on the homefront have every reason to be proud of them and indebted to them. But we too have a job to do.

We have the job of backing up the fighting men. It has been and still is our job to furnish them with the tools of war and the supplies necessary to sustain them on the battlefields. That we have done this to a degree never thought possible by our enemies—or even our allies—no one can deny. We have bickered and quarreled at times but we have produced. We must continue to produce but the cost is great. For this reason we have been asked to dig deeper than ever before to help the Fifth War Loan Drive over the top—a sixteen billion dollar top. Already the Drive is more than half over and the goal is still out of sight. But it will be met; it must be met—and every person helping with the Drive is determined that it shall not fail. I am honored to be associated with an institution that is playing an essential part in this mighty financing effort—The Federal Reserve Bank of San Francisco.

Monday, June 26, 1944: —CHERBOURG IS OURS! Only mop-up operations remain before the great French port can be opened to the flood of men and equipment needed to complete the liberation of Europe.

The capture of Cherbourg is probably the most important victory of the war for American ground forces. In the brief three weeks campaign, our forces smashed their way through the maze of German beach defenses, breaching the vaunted Atlantic Wall at many places, met and conquered the best the Nazis could muster in the way of opposition, and marched the full length of the Contentin peninsula to seize the deep-water port of Cherbourg despite almost suicidal enemy resistance. In the process of the campaign, the Yanks inflicted an estimated 70,000 casualties on the Germans, 20,000 of them being trapped and taken prisoner. The final victory came as a result of magnificent teamwork throughout every stage of the campaign. Air, sea, and ground forces cooperated as one. And on the Americans' flank, protecting Canadian armies, which beat off every desperate counter-attack of the German forces around Caen, left the Yanks free and secure to concentrate on Cherbourg. You can't beat a combination such as that. Victory may be delayed but not denied to men such as those.

Here at home, American democracy works in spite of the war. The Republican National Convention opened in Chicago today for the purpose of nominating candidates for the two highest offices in the land. Governor Warren of California will be the keynoter.

Tuesday, June 27, 1944: —Two high ranking Nazi officers were among the prisoners taken at Cherbourg. Lieut. Genera Carl Wilhelm von Schlieben, a commander of the Cherbourg fortress, and Rear Admiral Walther Hennecke, naval commander at Cherbourg, were the unwilling guests of the American general who forced their surrender. The name of the American general was not revealed in the dispatch telling of the incident but it was disclosed that the German general refused the American's request that he order the few isolated groups of Germans still resisting to surrender. His claim was that a few diehards can often achieve major delays.

While the fighting died out at Cherbourg, it flared with renewed violence southwest of the Caen as General Bernard L. Montgomery launched a big scale offensive aimed at isolating the Nazi garrison defending that key point. Tank clashes involving hundreds of the mighty metal goliaths were reported throughout the area. One British armored column severed the railroad serving Caen, after knifing through to the town of Grainville-Sur-Odon.

In the other war—the war in the Pacific—American Marines and Army units were finding the going extremely rugged in the bloody battle for Saipan. The struggle for this island already outranks Guadalcanal and Tarawa as the toughest campaign in the war so far. Our troops have battered and smashed their way over approximately one half of the island, engaging the Japs in some of the heaviest fighting ye encountered, involving masses of infantry and hundreds of tanks. There will be more terrible "blood-letting" before this campaign is finished.

Wednesday, June 28, 1944: —Thomas E. Dewey, present Governor of New York, was today nominated as the Republican candidate for President of the United States. The victory for the New York Governor was assured before the balloting began and the nomination was made on the first roll call. The count was 1056 to 1, the lone vote being cast for General MacArthur by a stubborn delegate. Governor John W. Bricker of Ohio was chosen as Dewey's running mate. Mr. Bricker was nominated for Vice-President after withdrawing his candidacy for President in favor of the New York Governor.

Governor Dewey's speech of acceptance, which was heard over the radio tonight, was well done. The Republican candidate has an excellent radio voice, a resonant and clear baritone that compares favorably with President Roosevelt's famous instrument, and he is obviously well versed in the art of speech-making. He is a young and vigorous man of 42 and he is well equipped to meet the "champion" in the very interesting campaign that should follow if Roosevelt should try for a fourth term. In Bricker, Dewey has an able and hard working running mate and the campaign promises to be one of the hardest fought contests in the history of the country.

Governor Warren of California turned down the opportunity of running for Vice-President. The Convention and Dewey himself wanted the big Californian to accept the nomination but Warren refused, stating that he owed an obligation to the people of his state and he wants to complete his term as governor. It was a memorable decision for fate has decreed on several occasions that the Republican candidate for Vice-President should one day be President.

Thursday, June 29, 1944: —On three fronts heavy fighting was in progress today. The most active theater from the number of troops involved was the Russian front where two powerful Soviet armies, in four days of their summer offensive, have inflicted more than 77,000 casualties on the hapless Nazis. Prospects of even greater disaster faced the Germans tonight after General Konstantin K. Rokossovsky's First White Russian Army smashed through to capture Brobruisk, the last stronghold on the Nazis' Fatherland Line, protecting the approaches to Warsaw. From five to seven German divisions were bottled up southeast of the town and are being systematically pounded to pieces.

The most bitterly contested battleground was Saipan, Pacific island stronghold, recently Japanese but now gradually becoming American. United States Marines and doughboys today stormed and captured Nafutan Point, on the southeastern tip of the island, where 1,500 desperate Nipponese have held out for 13 bloody days. The Japs used every trick in their snaky repertoire in an effort to extricate themselves from their hopeless position but failed. Some were captured but most were sent to join their ancestors.

The most titanic battle of the day was fought on the rolling farmlands between the Orne and the Odon Rivers in Normandy. The opposing titans were British and Canadian tanks against the massed armor of several Nazi panzer divisions. The crucial battle finally turned in favor of the British, who followed up eagerly and scored important new gains.

Friday, June 30, 1944: —The War Shipping Administration today announced that the Santa Elena, former luxury liner of the Grace Lines, was sunk off Sicily while operating as a troop transport. The proud ship, which before the war plied between San Francisco and New York, went down as a result of an enemy torpedo attack. All but a very few of the 1,700 troops aboard the stricken liner were rescued, according to the announcement.

The Navy reported today that U.S. Marines and Army units have suffered 9,752 casualties already in the bloody battle for Saipan. With the island less than one half ours, 1,474 Americans have died, 7,400 have been wounded and 878 are missing. Japanese casualties have been many times heavier, if that can be considered as any consolation for the loss of so many brave lads. Exact figures on the Japs are, of course, not known, but our troops have buried 4,951 enemy dead. This does not count those that were removed by the retreating enemy and does not include his numerous wounded.

Diplomatic relations between the United States and a pitiful little nation were broken today. The State Department revealed that the Government of Finland has refused to heed all warnings of the inevitable consequences of her association with Nazi Germany and has admitted to the world that she has entered into a hard and fast military partnership with that country. Reluctantly, therefore, it has been decided that further relations between this Government and the Government of Finland are impossible.

July

Saturday, July 1, 1944: —An announcement from General Stilwell's Headquarters in China stated that American bombers last night engaged in a successful bombing mission against the Japanese shipping center of Takao, on the southwest tip of Formosa. Thus, once again, Japanese home territory has been hit.

The sanguinary struggle for Saipan appears to be reaching a climax. Our troops have finally seized the high ridges overlooking the enemy's capital city of Garapan and it appears likely that this new line will be used as a jumping off place for a final offensive aimed at clearing the northern half of the island. The outcome seems certain inasmuch as our forces have absolute superiority in the air and have control of the sea approaches. The Japanese garrison is practically isolated from reinforcements or supplies, except for sneak aerial communications by night.

In Europe, the Danes, long ashamed of their meek submission to the Nazis in 1940, have begun to take up arms against their overlords. Reports from Stockholm tell of large scale uprisings among Danish patriots, with heavy street fighting in progress in Copenhagen. The Germans are using machine guns and airplanes to quell the revolt. More power to you, Danes; don't forget that men may die by fighting but Nations die only by surrendering.

A mighty showdown battle between the tank goliaths of the Allies and Germany appears to be developing in the fields of Normandy around the town of Caen. Much hangs in the balance.

Sunday, July 2, 1944: —Despite earlier reports that Field Marshal Erwin Rommel had been removed as commander of the German forces opposing the Allies on the Normandy front, it now appears that the former "Desert Fox" is still active in that theater, commanding powerful armored units facing the British around Caen. Pitted against the crafty Nazi marshal is his old foe and conqueror, the brilliant English general, Sir Bernard L. Montgomery. General Montgomery is a clever strategist and a firm believer in the potency of massed artillery barrages of the kind that paved the way for the decisive British victory at El Alamein and the subsequent annihilation of the Axis' African armies. Within the last two days around Caen, Montgomery's outfit has broken up eleven desperate Nazi counter-attacks involving hundreds of tanks, by utilizing the massed artillery technique, with the refinement this time of massing the big guns in a hollow square of protective tanks. Each attack has been beaten off with heavy losses of men and tanks.

On the American end of the beachhead all fighting has ceased in the vicinity of the newly captured port of Cherbourg. Five thousand Germans composing the last pocket of resistance in the Cap de la Hague area have surrendered during the last 48 hours. With them fell a number of huge railroad guns and other valuable equipment.

On the home front we learn that Thomas E. Dewey, the Republican nominee for President, has returned to Albany, New York, to resume his duties as governor of that state and to prepare for the coming campaign. The Governor pointed out that only in America could a Nation conduct an all-out war and at the same time preserve its democratic processes by holding an election during the most critical phase of the war.

Monday, July 3, 1944: —The ever amazing Russians have scored another sensational victory in their whirlwind summer offensive. Powerful Soviet armies crunched their way into Minsk, the capital of White Russia, an important Nazi base since its original seizure early in the war. The capture of Minsk climaxed a devastating eleven day drive by the Red Army in which Moscow claims 213,000 Germans were killed or captured. The remnants of the beaten Nazi armies are fleeing in disorder towards the borders of Germany itself. East Prussia lies only 190 miles to the west.

Hitler's once vaunted Wehrmacht is also in pell-mell retreat in Italy. American and French troops burst through the German lines on the road to Florence and seized the key highway center of Siena. The fall of this bastion threatens total disruption of the Nazis' long-prepared "Gothic line" before Florence, into which Hitler is reported to have thrown upwards of 150,000 crack troops in a desperate effort to stem the Allied advance.

Resting not at all upon their Cherbourg laurels, General Omar Bradley's American forces in Normandy today launched a new offensive along a 40-mile line reaching from St. Lo northeastward to the coast near St. Lo d'Ourville. The Yanks struck in a driving rain that created scenes reminiscent of France in World War I. Substantial gains were scored all along the line.

Pacific fighting is still centered in Saipan, where American Marines and Doughboys are slowly yet inexorably pushing the Jap garrison into its death trap at the northern end of the island. More than half of the original enemy force of 20,000 men has already been liquidated.

Tuesday, July 4, 1944: —Independence Day! For 168 years Americans have bravely and successfully defended the freedom so dearly won by the founders of this nation. Fighting Americans on every battlefield and on the high seas are today upholding every glorious tradition built up over the years by American fighting men of other wars. Washington, Light Horse Harry Lee, Stonewall Jackson, Farragut, Grant, Custer, Dewey, Teddy Roosevelt, Black Jack Pershing, Sergeant York, all that great array of magnificent fighting men that blazed their way across the pages of our history can look with satisfaction and pride upon their counterparts of today. Colin Kelly, MacArthur, Halsey, Nimitz, Bradley, Eisenhower, Major Foss, those are names to conjure with, those and their thousands of comrades are writing new pages of glorious history for American arms. The founding fathers can well be proud of these, their sons. The independence they so firmly established is in capable hands.

The spotlight of news today is upon the sea and island approaches to the Japanese mainland. Axis reports today revealed that powerful American air and sea forces are attacking the Bonin Island group, only 700 miles from Tokyo. Some reports stated that American assault forces have landed on at least one island of the group. No confirmation has come from any Allied source and for this reason the information must be taken with the usual grain of salt. Suffice it to note that the tide of the Pacific war is nearing the source from which it sprang. Eventually the crimson tide will engulf and destroy that very source. We still remember Pearl Harbor.

Wednesday, July 5, 1944: —Back to work today after the brief Fourth of July holiday and found two aspects of the Fifth War Loan Drive worthy of comment. First it appears as though the national quota of sixteen billion is assured but San Francisco's individual quota of 77 million is far behind, having reached barely 35% so far. The other feature is the considerable drop in Savings Bond redemptions during the period of the Drive. This shows that there are normally many needless redemptions, some of them being discouraged and prevented by the publicity of a War Loan Drive. This reduction in redemptions is an indirect contribution to the over-all success of the financing effort.

The first pre-war Japanese city fell today before the onslaught of tough fighting men of the United States Marine Corp. The city was Garapan, capital city of the Marianas Islands, and erstwhile defense bastion on the island of Saipan, where the bitterest campaign of the Pacific war thus far is fast reaching its climax. The Japanese garrison is rapidly being pinned down into the narrow northern end of the island where the final drama will be enacted.

The Navy Department today revealed that our gallant submarine force has not been idle. The undersea raiders have added another 17 Jap ships to the list of their victims. Included among the destroyed enemy vessels were a cruiser and a destroyer. A British Admiralty announcement simultaneously reported the sinking of 9 Japanese ships by British subs, bringing the total Allied bag to 26 for the day.

Thursday, July 6, 1944: —The horror of war was equaled if not outdone today when the "Big Top" of the Ringling Bros. Barnum and Bailey circus in Hartford, Conn. caught fire during a show, trapping and burning to death an estimated 124 men, women and children. The huge tent billowed up into an inferno of smoke and flame within seconds as the screaming, terror stricken audience fled in panic for the exits, trampling many to death under their feet. It was the greatest circus catastrophe in the nation's history and some authorities feared the death toll might reach a much higher figure. Most of the victims were believed to be children but dozens of the bodies were burned beyond the hope of recognition.

While we are on the subject of horrors (a more or less common-place subject these days), Prime Minister Winston Churchill today reported to Commons on the situation with respect to the robot bombs, Hitler's latest diabolical machine with which he has been deluging London and southeastern England for the last three weeks. The Prime Minister said that approximately 2,750 flying bombs have been launched against England in that period, killing 2,752 persons and injuring about 8,000. The "terror" bombs have not done any military damage and have not harmed the war effort. Although the situation is serious and may not be dismissed lightly, the Prime Minister revealed that every possible counter-measure will be employed and it is hoped will be effective in conquering the menace of the vicious "buzzbombs."

Friday, July 7, 1944: —Japan bombed again! The huge B-29s, America's flying battleships, have struck again, returning for the second raid in three weeks on the great iron and steel works of Yawata. This time, however, the big raiders struck also at Sasebo, Japan's third largest naval base. Both Yawata and Sasebo are situated on Kyushu, southernmost of the Japanese home islands. Details of the attack are not yet available, nor are figures on our plane losses, if any. It is presumed that some of the big planes may yet be on their way back and further details will be delayed until their safety is assured.

In Washington D.C. General Charles de Gaulle, fighting French leader, was reported beginning his conferences with President Roosevelt, the outcome of which may decide the American policy with respect to France after its liberation. The tall French leader expressed the view that the European war will be over this year. We fervently hope his is clairvoyant.

In Italy, Russia, and Normandy the German armies are back-pedaling at high speed. As one German communiqué put it, "Our forces successfully fought their way farther backwards." In Russia particularly, the speed of the Nazi retreat was sensational. Berlin itself admitted that the German forces had fallen back 40 miles to the safety of the Bug River defenses in south-central Poland. In Italy the Allied gains were slower and more stubbornly resisted as the Nazis fought for time to complete their "Gothic defense line" upon which they are depending to stem the Allied assault.

Saturday, July 8, 1944: —The fall of Caen seems to be close at hand according to the latest reports from the Normandy battlefront. General Sir Bernard L. Montgomery's British Second Army, in the past 24 hours, has slashed and fought its way to the center of the city and appears to be well on the road towards eliminating this "Cassino-like" stumbling block on the highway to Paris. Already reconnaissance reports of German troop movements indicate that the beaten enemy is beginning to pull out of the town.

On the eastern front the Nazis are faring just as badly. Premier Stalin announced in an order of the day that the Red Army has captured the key German stronghold of Baranowicze, 75 miles southwest of recently liberated Minsk. The Triumphant Russian forces, pursuing the panic-stricken Nazis across the blood soaked Polish plains at an amazing clip, are now in a position to imminently threaten the German homeland itself. The border of East Prussia lies less than 200 miles ahead of the racing Soviet columns. At the rate the Red Army is advancing, that distance could be covered in a matter of days. For the first time in this war the Nazis are faced with the prospect of an invasion of their own land.

From the Pacific comes news of incredibly desperate fighting on the island of Saipan. Like cornered rats the Jap troops being squeezed into a death trap on the northern end of the island launched a desperation counter-attack against our forces closing in on the western side. The screaming, maniacal enemy horde succeeded in piercing our lines to a distance of 2,000 yards before their drive was halted, with 1,500 of their number dead.

Sunday, July 9, 1944: —I spend most of today digging in the soil in the backyard of our new home. The day was clear and warm and the newly turned soil had a rich, pleasant odor to it. If any man has a grievance against another let him work in the soil for awhile; his grievance most likely will disappear. If a man be unhappy or grief stricken let him get close to the soil and dig; his sorrow will most likely fade away and be replaced by a deep understanding of the mysteries of life and death. There would be less of wars and human miseries if there were more men with a closer affinity for the soil. Swords would once more be replaced by plowshares.

Meanwhile, however, on many bloody battlefronts, the earth is being plowed with shells, raked with machinegun fire and furrowed with high explosives. The evil forces of our enemies are being driven back upon their homelands in a series of mighty smashes from all sides. In the Pacific the conquest of Saipan has been completed. U.S. Marines are engaged in mopping up the final remnants of the original Japanese garrison of 20,000 troops after 25 days of bitter and costly fighting. But notwithstanding the extent of our losses the conquest of the island has been an important victory, costing casualties to the enemy of more than 5 to 1 and giving us an unsinkable aircraft carrier base from which to strike at the Japanese homeland.

In Normandy, the Allies have completed the capture of Caen, unhinging the entire German defense line in Normandy. Our forces are now in a position to march upon Paris.

Monday, July 10, 1944: —The spotlight today is upon the eastern European front where two million Red Army troops have handed the Nazi invaders their worst defeat of the war. Massive blows by the Russians have breached the German defenses along a 300 mile sector and Soviet troops are pouring through the gaps in an irresistible torrent. The tide of battle is sweeping through Poland and Lithuania and has already reached a point within 60 miles of the German-delineated border of East Prussia. The Lithuanian capital of Wilno has been completely surrounded and is expected to capitulate momentarily. Up to the present time in the current offensive the Russians have captured 18 Nazi generals and have inflicted more than 200,000 casualties on the enemy. All in all, the current events on the Russian front add up to a catastrophe for Adolf Hitler.

The American, British, Canadian Allies on the western front are doing their share also. In fact most competent observers credit the rapid advance of the Red Army largely to the shift of powerful German forces from the eastern front to the west in order to meet the Allied threat. But Hitler's legions in Normandy are not faring much better than their comrades in the east. General Bernard L. Montgomery's victories troops smashed onward from newly captured Caen and drove to within a half mile of the Nazis' next major defense line on the Orne River. At the same time, American forces slashed into the Germans' flank in central Normandy, reaching a point only 7,000 yards from the important bastion of St. Lo.

Tuesday, July 11, 1944: —President Roosevelt today made the announcement expected by most people but eagerly awaited as the time for the Democratic National Convention draws near. In reply to a letter from the Democratic Chairman of the Convention informing him that a majority of the delegates are pledged to his renomination, the President stated that he would accept the nomination, and, if elected, would serve for a 4th term. He took the position that although he is commander-in-chief, his superior officer is the people and if they command him to serve again during this emergency he has no right to refuse. But he claims he will not run in the partisan, political sense and insofar as he personally is concerned, he would prefer to retire to civil life. But like a good soldier, if commanded he will obey.

In Europe the crash of American bombs devastated the birthplace of Nazism today as more than 2,000 U.S. planes braved bad weather to unload their explosives on Munich. Other heavy bombers winged their way from Italy to plaster the big port of Toulon, on the southern French coast. The Allied high command announced that Allied aircraft have flown 158,000 sorties since D-day and 1,284 planes have been lost. 1,067 enemy planes were destroyed in the same period.

The rolling Reds from Russia continued to surge towards the German border today, capturing 400 more towns and advancing more than 35 miles in the 24 hour period. A dozen German divisions face entrapment in Estonia and Latvia.

Wednesday, July 12, 1944: —Our casualties for the bloody Saipan campaign were announced today. The total was 15,053 including 2,359 killed, 11,481 wounded, and 1,213 missing. Only partially offsetting this loss of American lives were more than 19,000 Japanese dead out of the total Saipan garrison of 20,000. Several hundred prisoners were taken and the rest are still being mopped up. Already the island is being prepared as a springboard for more offensive action closer to the Japanese homeland.

On all the other active fronts, Allied forces continued to gain. In Poland and Lithuania particularly, the sensational Russian advance swept onward, overwhelming the Nazis at every point and carrying the war another 35 miles closer to Germany itself. Even the Berlin radio was gloomy and did not try to hide the seriousness of the situation from the German people. The Nazi commentator warned the Germans that they face the bitterest period of the war and no one can predict where or when the Russian drive will be halted.

In Normandy the going was plenty rugged today but gains of a mile or more were scored all along the line. American troops storming St. Lo sidestepped the powerful German defenses before the city, swung in behind to outflank the stronghold and captured Le Calvaire and St. Pierre de Semily, three miles east of the city.

In Italy, the previously running advance of the Allies has slowed to a walk as the going gets tougher around the big Italian port of Livorno (Leghorn). American troops captured Castiglioncello today, bringing them to within 10 miles of the port.

Thursday, July 13, 1944: —General Eisenhower's Headquarters today announced that D-day cost the Allies 15 warships. American losses were three destroyers and four other vessels while the British lost eight ships, including three destroyers and three frigates. Included in the American losses was the former Grace liner, the Susan B. Anthony which went down while fully loaded with troops. Only six of the soldiers were lost, however, due to heroic rescue work.

Munich, the birthplace of the cancer that now infests Europe, was handed its third major bombing raid in as many days. For three consecutive days, more than 1,500 American planes smashed at the Nazi city, giving it annihilation treatment after the Hamburg fashion. Opposition from the Luftwaffe was feeble.

The fighting in Normandy centers on the highway center of St. Lo where American forces under General Omar Bradley are battering their way through the hedgehog German defenses in some of the bloodiest fighting of the current campaign. U.S. vanguards, however, are now fighting in the streets along the fringes of the city.

Reports from Normandy indicate that the Nazis are employing the robot "buzzbombs" against American troops in the St. Lo sector. London, the primary target for the pilotless bombs, has been practically free from attack for the past few days. The robot bomb, fearsome though it may be, will probably rate the title of the biggest flop of the war from a purely military standpoint. Practically no military damage has been done by the highly inaccurate weapon.

Friday, July 14, 1944: —If the Japanese thought our forces would rest after the conquest of Saipan, they were badly mistaken. Today's communiqué announced that Maniagassa Island, two miles west of Saipan, was occupied by our troops shortly after the final mopping up of the 20,000 Jap troops on that island. It was also revealed that the Saipan fighting cost Japan two high ranking naval officers, Vice Admiral Chuichi Nagumo, and Rear Admiral Yano. Admiral Nagumo devised and carried out the sneak attack on Pearl Harbor just 31 months ago. Like Admiral Isoroku Yamamoto, who boasted that he would dictate the peace from the White House, Nagumo has gone to meet his ancestors with nothing but disaster and defeat to report. The hand of retribution is long and powerful.

Guam, first American territory to be seized by the Japanese early in the war, will probably be the first to be reconquered. For approximately two weeks, the tiny island has received a steady pounding from the air in an obvious pre-invasion barrage. Today it was reported that an American task force, including at least one battleship, boldly steamed to within range of the island and subjected it to an air and sea bombardment from carrier based planes and the big guns of the warships. The softening-up process appears to be almost completed.

The spotlight in the war on Germany still centers on the eastern front where the incredible Russian offensive rolled over and through Pinsk in the heart of the Pripet marshes and smashed to within 12 miles of the 1939 border of East Prussia. The threat of war's destruction hovers over the cradle of German Junkerdom.

Saturday, July 15, 1944: —The barbarity of our Japanese enemies was further hinted at today as U.S. Government monitors picked up radio broadcasts from Tokyo in which it was inferred that a number of American flyers, who parachuted from crippled B-29 bombers during the first raid on Japanese cities by the huge aerial battleships, were executed by their captors. The Japanese spokesman warned all American flyers that death will be meted out to any of them who may be captured during raids on the

Japanese homeland. This vicious threat will not delay or lessen the fate that awaits the war and industrial centers of Japan, but will only serve to make the struggle more bitter, with no quarter being given or asked. The announcement also emphasized the deadly Japanese fear of aerial attack, which was further heightened by the fact that the great steel center at Yawata was known to be ablaze for three days after the most recent B-29 attack. Fire does more damage than the bombs.

There seems to be no stopping the mighty Russian drive through Poland and Lithuania. The terrific momentum of the Red Army push carried it to the gates of Grodno, only ten miles from what the Nazis claim is East Prussia. The ultimate goal of the Soviet offensive is probably the Prussian city of Koenigsberg.

In Italy, American troops under General Clark have smashed to within 6 miles of Leghorn and have swung inland around the big port to successfully outflank it. Decreasing German artillery fire from the city indicates that the Hitlerites may be preparing to abandon the port.

Sunday, July 16, 1944: —Marshal Josef Stalin in a triumphant order of the day announced that the Second and Third White Russian Armies have captured the key Nazi defense bastion of Grodno, only 17 miles from the border of East Prussia. Other Soviet columns smashed deeper into Lithuania, threatening approximately 500,000 Nazi troops in the Baltic States with isolation and destruction.

Everywhere the Russian drive seems invincible. The Germans haven't succeeded in slowing the attack much less stopping it and no one can foretell how far the Red legions will advance before extended communication and supply lines as well as exhaustion will bring the offensive to a halt. The speed of the Soviet advance is almost incredible and apparently has thrown the Germans completely off balance. It is conceivable that the tremendous Russian pressure added to the growing threat of defeat in France and the disastrous pounding administered by the Allies in the air may cause a total collapse of the once mighty Wehrmacht. Many competent observers have stated their belief that the end may come in a matter of weeks although most are holding to the prediction that victory over Germany will come before the end of the year. All in all there is little doubt but that Hitler is definitely on the skids.

Turkey is apparently feeling the urge to leap to the aid of the victors. The Turks are clamoring for a declaration of war against the waning Axis. Their entry on the side of the Allies might shorten the war a little and would assure the Balkan nation of a place at the peace table.

Monday, July 17, 1944: —Repercussions of the disastrous Japanese defeats in the Philippine Sea and on Saipan were felt in high military circles in Tokyo. The official Japanese Domei News Agency reported today that Admiral Shigetaro Shimada, Navy Minister in Premier Tojo's cabinet, has been relieved of his post. Admiral Naokuni Nomura has been appointed by Emperor Hirohito to replace Shimada.

The Russian torrent today swirled almost to the border of East Prussia, where Swiss reports stated that the Nazis are carrying out large scale evacuation of civilians. One unconfirmed report hinted that Russian paratroops may have already penetrated into German territory ahead of the advancing Russian main armies.

WE HAVE JUST BEEN HIT WITH A STRONG EARTHQUAKE! I paused in writing this record to go to the bathroom. Just as I shut the door behind me it happened. A heavy jolt struck the house, the door banged against its frame and I felt tipsy. My wife hollered from the bedroom and the baby awoke from his crib and started crying. I opened the bathroom door and my wife dashed past me, white-faced, to grab up the baby. She was obviously frightened but my only feeling was astonishment. It was over in a matter of seconds and has not recurred although only a few minutes have elapsed. Another shock may come at any time; they usually repeat. Apparently no damage was done to the house but I am going to sit by the radio for a while to hear what happened elsewhere. I will report tomorrow. The time as I write is 10:35 p.m.

Tuesday, July 18, 1944: —The jolt that we felt last night was no earthquake. In many ways, however, it was a worse disaster. Two loaded munitions ships exploded with incredible force at their docks in Port Chicago in Contra Costa County, 30 miles northeast of San Francisco. The tremendous detonation ripped the two ships to bits, leveled the town of Port Chicago, and was

686

felt with quake-like force as far as San Jose, more than fifty miles away. The exact toll of dead and wounded has not yet been determined but it is believed that approximately 377 persons were killed and 1,000 injured. The terrific blast sent flames shooting skyward for more than eight thousand feet while the concussion smashed every window for dozens of miles around. One big plate glass window in downtown San Francisco toppled to the pavement.

The Port Chicago catastrophe, the worst of its kind in this war, rivals the great disaster at Halifax, Nova Scotia, on December 6, 1917 when two munitions ships collided and exploded. The blast and resultant fire killed 1158 persons and wounded 4,000. The only thing that prevented the Port Chicago explosion from equaling or exceeding the casualty toll of the Halifax disaster was the small population of the area. The town of Port Chicago has only 1,500 inhabitants.

Most of the victims were Navy and Coast Guard personnel, while an estimated 70 crew members of the two munitions ships were lost. Few bodies will be found since the victims and their ships simply disintegrated when the tons of high explosives detonated.

Wednesday, July 19, 1944: —The suddenness and the horror of the Port Chicago disaster has overshadowed for a fleeting moment the vastly greater destruction going on in Europe and the Pacific, where the mighty organized military engines of war of the great nations of the world are locked in deadly combat. But here, in ten fleeting seconds, a terrifying example of the cataclysmic forces being unleashed upon humanity was brought close to home. It makes one stop and think.

The only cheerful aspect of the sad occurrence, was the heroic and efficient manner in which rescue operations were organized and carried out. The military services, the police, the Red Cross, doctors and nurses, and all public and private organizations that were called upon, teamed wonderfully together to meet the emergency in a creditable fashion. There was little panic and recovery was prompt.

Reviewing briefly the war news of the past two days, we learn that Hideki Tojo, jingoistic Premier of Japan who led that country into war against us, has been relieved of his post as Chief of the General Staff. This is further evidence of the crisis in Japanese affairs.

British and Canadian troops have scored a brilliant victory east of Caen, breaking through the Nazi defense line along a wide sector after deluging the German positions with the heaviest single weight of bombs on one sector in the war to date. Twenty to twenty-five German divisions were sent in headlong retreat across the flat plain towards Paris, some 120 miles away.

Thursday, July 20, 1944: —A very unfortunate event happened today. Hitler was wounded in an assassination attempt. The unfortunate thing about it was that he was not killed. The incident occurred at Der Fuehrer's Headquarters when a bomb exploded while Hitler was in conference with 13 of his top military and naval advisers. The bomb apparently had been planted by someone on the "inside" in an obvious attempt to eliminate the Nazi leader and his top collaborators. Unfortunately the plan misfired and the world's number 1 enemy was only burned and bruised slightly. The main force of the blast fell upon his advisers, three of whom were seriously injured and several others wounded slightly.

Radio Berlin naturally placed the blame for the assassination attempt upon the Allies but all the evidence points to a revolt within the ranks of the Nazi criminals themselves. We shall await the work of a typical Hitler blood purge to prove this contention. Unless we miss our guess completely, countless heads will roll as soon as the maniacal Hitler and his ruthless Gestapo chief, Heinrich Himmler, go to work on the traitors, real or fancied, that they will discover among their close associates.

The brilliant breakthrough scored by the British and Canadians in the Caen sector of the Normandy battleground, is being exploited to full advantage. Crack British armored units hammered their way through stiff enemy resistance for a distance of eight miles today. Nine more French towns were liberated in the process.

Franklin D. Roosevelt was nominated for a 4th term today. Some news—or did you expect it?

Friday, July 21, 1944: —OUR FORCES HAVE INVADED GUAM! Following close upon the heels of the Saipan conquest, American assault troops fought their way ashore at two points on Guam after a tremendous softening-up barrage by air and sea forces. Admiral Chester W. Nimitz' first communiqué indicated that the beachheads have been firmly established against only moderate opposition and the Marines and Doughboys are moving steadily inland.

Guam was the first U.S. territory to fall to the galloping Japs in the first few days of the war and it is only fitting that it will be the first U.S. territory to be liberated. For fear of offending Japan, the island had never been fortified by the United States although steps were being taken in that direction at the time of Pearl Harbor. The tiny island capitulated on December 11, 1941 after a valorous but hopeless four-day defense by its brave little garrison of 400 sailors and 155 Marines. Since that time the Japs have undoubtedly converted the island into a heavily fortified base. It may require numerous American lives to reclaim this territory.

Weird and confused reports are coming out of Germany. Martial law has been declared in Berlin while Heinrich Himmler and his bloody Gestapo round up the "traitors" responsible for the attack on the life of the Fuehrer. It is already hinted that hundreds of Germany's best officers have been put to death in a widespread blood purge aimed at stamping out a "fifth column" revolt against Adolf Hitler and his regime. Reliable sources have reported that General Beck, former chief of staff of the Wehrmacht was among the first to be executed.

Saturday, July 22, 1944: —Stories of revolt in Germany are reminiscent of the summer of 1918 when mutiny among naval units at the big German naval base at Kiel precipitated the revolution that led to the overthrow of the Kaiser and the capitulation of the German army. Today's news reports from usually reliable sources indicate that the uprising that led to the attack on Hitler's life has spread to the Baltic bases of Kiel and Stettin where serious fighting is in progress between units of the regular army and Nazi storm troopers and Gestapo agents.

Hitler apparently has been able to retain control of the situation thus far with the help of his powerful Gestapo, which the Kaiser lacked, and has started a reign of terror unprecedented even in German history. Literally thousands of high German officers have been arrested and some of the most distinguished have been executed. Reports from Bern, Switzerland, state that

Marshal Walther von Brauchitsch, former commander-in-chief of the army, and Marshal Gerd von Rundstedt, recently deposed commander of German forces in France, were among those put to death for opposing der Fuehrer.

Satisfactory progress is being made in the U.S. invasion of Guam, according to admiral Nimitz' report. The communiqué stated that "moderate" casualties were suffered by the invasion forces but "good beachheads" were secured and the two attacking columns are driving towards a junction that will isolate the Orote peninsula, on which the Japs had constructed a 4,700 foot airfield. That, of course, is just what we need.

Sunday, July 23, 1944: —When your opponent is off balance is the time to redouble your efforts, step up the speed and power of your blows, and pummel him until he topples. Any good fighter knows this cardinal rule and the United States Army and Navy have long since proved their fighting ability. It was no surprise, therefore, when we learned tonight that our amphibious forces have invaded another island in the Marianas to round out a one, two, three smash at Japan's solar plexus. First it was Saipan, then Guam, and now Tinian which lays two and ½ miles west of Saipan. The invasion of Guam followed close upon the heels of the conquest of Saipan and the attack on Tinian was launched shortly after it was determined that the Guam beachheads were secure. The customary overwhelming sea and air bombardment preceded the Tinian landing, making possible the establishment of beachheads against ineffective opposition.

Confused and unauthoritative reports of large scale uprisings in the German Reich have flooded the newspapers since the abortive attempt on Hitler's life was made. It is hard to even guess what is transpiring within the confines of Nazidom but the bits of news seeping out of the country indicate that Hitler is still in control, stamping out opposition to his regime in a ruthless, bloody purge. Several stories tell of the ousting or arresting of numerous high German officers both at home and on the battlefronts. All signs hint that der Fuehrer's gory edifice is crumbling beneath him. We can only hope fervently that the signs are correct.

Monday, July 24, 1944: —American invasion forces battered their way inland on both Guam and Tinian during the past 24 hours. Two Marine columns succeeded in effecting a junction which sealed off the last escape corridor for a large Japanese force trapped on the Orote peninsula which juts out from the west coast of Guam. Fierce opposition has been encountered at many points but superior fire power and equipment has enabled the doughty Leathernecks to advance steadily while inflicting casualties of eight to one on the enemy. Tanks, flamethrowers, mortars, grenades, and bayonets have all been wielded very effectively by the hard-hitting Yanks.

Latest reports from Europe indicate that the Nazi gang, by dint of a merciless blood purge, have succeeded in smashing, at least temporarily, a widespread revolt against them. Many high officers of the Junkers class, many aristocrats of the old German nobility, and many prominent landowners, have been arrested by flying squadrons of the dreaded Gestapo and their leaders executed on the spot. A stringent curfew has been clamped on Berlin although an uneasy calm seems to have been regained. Hitler, himself, is reported to have fled to an undisclosed hideout until the danger subsides.

While disaster threatens the Nazis from within, an even greater danger looms up on the eastern front in the form of a great Russian tidal wave which is sweeping towards the German border at a rate of better than a mile each hour. The crest of the wave has reached a point only 50 miles from Warsaw, the martyred capital of Poland, and is sweeping the broken and battered German armies back irresistibly towards the border of the Reich itself.

Tuesday, July 25, 1944: —A great new Allied offensive has been launched in Normandy. The British Second Army during the first few hours of the attack has smashed ahead fully tow miles in the Caen area while farther to the west the American First Army smacked into the center of the German line with tremendous force, aided and abetted by a huge force of Allied aircraft, including 1,500 heavy bombers, the largest group of four-motored warplanes ever used to support a ground operation. Both Allied attacks encountered fierce enemy opposition, the Nazis fighting with the desperation of a last stand.

In Italy other American armored forces drove into the historical and ancient city of Pisa, home of the famous Leaning

Tower. The Germans are resisting strongly and it appears inevitable that the well-known cultural landmark must be destroyed. Elsewhere in Italy, British and American troops are driving the Nazis before them, bringing the roar of battle to within earshot of Florence, 18 miles away.

In the Pacific two fierce battles are raging for the possession of Guam and Tinian, in the Marianas. Many Americans are dying in the furious engagements but they are accounting for the Japs in a ratio of better than eight to one. Futile counter-attacks by the Japanese trapped on the Orote peninsula on Guam have cost the enemy many thousands of casualties.

When General MacArthur leaped-frogged his way across New Guinea, he left behind him 45,000 trapped Japanese troops of the enemy's 18th Army. This starving, emaciated army is now attacking desperately in a hopeless effort to escape. Thousands have been killed, the rest driven back to die of starvation.

Wednesday, July 26, 1944: —After several weeks of almost continuous sensational news developments from all battlefronts, the war has settled down, at least temporarily, to a somewhat routine tempo. Fighting is fierce on all the well-known fronts from Tinian and Guam in the Pacific to Normandy and Poland in Europe. In all theaters the initiative is on the side of the Allies whose sledge-hammer blows are blasting a pathway through desperate enemy resistance on the road to victory. In Normandy, American forces under General Omar Bradley are employing tanks and armor on a scale never before used except in Russia. Steady gains are being made against a desperate foe who, though fighting fiercely, is showing signs that his will to resist is beginning to deteriorate. A collapse of German morale on the battlefront as well as on the homefront is a definite possibility, although we are warned not to count on it too heavily.

In Italy, American and British forces are hammering at the gates of Florence while other Yank troops are battling in the streets of ancient Pisa. Further defeats for Hitler's Italian armies appear inevitable.

The only new development in the war today was the revelation that U.S. airmen are helping the Russians in their lightning-like advance across Poland. It is the first report of actual battlefield coordination between the air and land forces of the two great Allies. The American planes took off from bases in Russia and strafed and bombed German targets in the path of the triumphant Red Armies.

Thursday, July 27, 1944: —The United States Army has lost one of its most brilliant leaders, it was reported today. Lieut. General Leslie J. McNair, who was largely responsible for the successful training of our ground forces, was killed in action on the Normandy front. The General who converted the vast untrained masses of Selective Service inductees into the hard hitting, efficient and powerful war machine that the U.S. Army is today, was struck by enemy fire while observing action in the front lines. His loss will be deeply felt.

The Allied forces in Normandy and the Russian army in Poland had big days today. Nazi defenses throughout western Normandy fell completely apart today under the terrific punching from our armored forces and the merciless drenching of death from the skies delivered by huge fleets of Allied aircraft. American tank spearheads are exploiting the sensational break-through and it is evident that the Nazis have suffered their worst disaster since the capture of Cherbourg.

In Russia, Marshal Stalin ordered the Moscow victory cannon to roar in celebration of one of the most triumphant days of the three-year-old war. Mighty Soviet armies steamrolled over six vital Nazi bases along 1,000 miles of the blazing battlefront. The bases to fall were Lwow, Bialystok, Daugavpils, Rezekne, Stanislawow, and Garvaein, the last only 31 miles from the former Polish capital of Warsaw. The massive Russian blows sent the Germans reeling in panicky retreat towards the boundaries of the Reich itself.

Friday, July 28, 1944: —The Yanks are really rolling in Normandy after their sensational breakthrough near the base of the Cotentin peninsula yesterday. Two German divisions, the famous Panzer Lehr and Fifth Panzer, were reportedly cut to ribbons, with their remnants fleeing in wild disorder. About 4,000 prisoners have already been taken, with other thousands killed, wounded, or driven into a hopeless trap in the north where they can be rounded up at will. The important rail and highway center of Coutances was surrounded by the hard-driving Doughboys and is expected to fall momentarily.

693

The only unhappy incident of the Normandy fighting is the reported bombing of our own troops by a portion of the great Allied air fleets which took to the skies to support the ground offensive. Through mechanical or human defects of some kind, the bombs from one squadron were loosed 10,000 yards short of their objective and fell among our own troops, killing and wounding an undisclosed number of soldiers. It seems inevitable that some incidents of this kind must happen in the confusion and mechanized speed of modern war but it does not lessen the ironical tragedy of being killed with one's own weapons.

For the first time since December 13, 1941, the American Flag is waving over the island of Guam. Our forces are firmly established on the former U.S. possession and are making definite progress in liberating the entire island from its oriental trespassers. More than 2,000 of the little yellow devils were slaughtered today as veteran U.S. Marines smashed a fanatical counter-attack launched by the cornered Jap garrison.

Saturday, July 29, 1944: —America's answer to Japan, the mighty B-29 Super-fortresses, were reported today to have carried out their first daylight raid, a powerful smash at the great Japanese steel center of Anshan, 55 miles southwest of Mukden in Manchuria. It was the first air strike at Japan's continental empire in Manchuria, hitherto considered out of bomber range. Now, however, Uncle Sam's long arm of B-29s has reached out to drive home a telling blow at Japan's vital heavy industry. Returning pilots stated that the enemy steel works were left in blazing ruins that will require many months to rebuild.

The German rout in Normandy is growing in scope. Fast-moving Yank armored columns captured Coutances today and roared on through to the west coast of Normandy to close the trap on thousands of Nazi troops pocketed in the north. The desperate Germans threw in powerful groups of their famous Tiger and Panther tanks in an effort to stem the American onslaught but were decisively beaten by our General Sherman tanks which were supported effectively from the air. The Nazis finally turned tail after an hours-long battle, leaving the field, with its litter of smashed armor and dead men, to the victorious United States forces.

There are two bad spots in the otherwise favorable news picture tonight. One is London, where the weary Londoners are undergoing the terror of another blitz, this time from Hitler's fiendish robot bomb that show no discrimination between men, women and children, and military and non-military targets. The other is the unpleasant strike picture here in the Bay Area where irresponsible union leaders are interfering with the vital production of bearings used in urgently needed war equipment.

Sunday, July 30, 1944: —The United States offensive in Normandy took on the aspects of a major push today as heavy hitting American armored columns blasted the Germans' defenses to shreds and sent the beaten Nazi supermen into headlong flight. Dual thrusts by our forces sent one column racing 11 miles below recently captured Coutances while the other spearhead drove 13 miles beyond St. Lo. Hope was high that General Omar Bradley's brilliantly conceived offensive might involve the Germans in one of their worst defeats of the war. The whole complexion of the European conflict may be altered decisively by the extent of the American advance. Hit 'em high, hit 'em low, Come on, Yanks, let's go!

The flame of war in the Pacific continues to roar and crackle across the rugged terrain of Guam and Tinian in the Marianas. The first major objective of our liberating forces on Guam has been taken. Admiral Chester W. Nimitz announced tonight that Orote peninsula is ours. Capture of the peninsula gives our forces a 4,700 foot airfield, the Sumay naval base and the site of the Marine barracks where the tiny garrison of Leathernecks was overwhelmed at the outbreak of war nearly three years ago.

Across the way on the island of Tinian, other United States forces have battled their way over more than two-thirds of the enemy stronghold and have pinned the remaining Japs into an ever narrowing corridor, centered on the shell blasted town of Tinian. Latest reports indicate that Japan has lost over 50,000 troops killed thus far in the Marianas campaign.

Monday, July 31, 1944: —The sensational pace of the American advance continued through today in Normandy. A triumphant, conquering U.S. Army was riding roughshod over disorganized German resistance and apparently nothing the Nazis can cook up can stop the galloping Yanks. From what War Correspondents on the scene report, General Bradley's First Army is dishing out a refined variety of the Nazis' own "Blitzkrieg." In the words of one of the newsmen, "Our tanks are racing far ahead of the infantry, and it looks as if there is nothing to stop them. They go wherever they like. And German prisoners are a nickel a dozen."

Today's developments have brought the whole of the Normandy peninsula into the Allied orbit and has laid open the whole interior of France. Where the American spearheads will point next is anybody's guess. Many possibilities exist. They may turn and head towards Paris, they may drive on towards St. Nazaire to cut off the Brittany peninsula, or they may turn westward to drive towards the great Atlantic seaport of Brest. We shall see.

On the eastern front, the Russian steamroller is duplicating the speed of the Americans on the fields of France. The Red Army today smashed westward along a 150 mile front for 31 miles, capturing 1,500 towns and villages and driving to within 15 miles of pre-war East Prussia. Other Russian armies are pounding at the suburbs of Warsaw and prospects for the liberation of that long-suffering city are very bright.

August

Tuesday, August 1, 1944: —The American drive in France still holds the spotlight. It appears today as though the main U.S. push will be eastward towards Paris. Our armor struck east from newly captured Avranches at the base of the Normandy peninsula and smashed its way into the big transport center of Brecey. Other U.S. spearheads knifed down into Brittany, driving the Nazis before them with such speed that they had no time to destroy bridges or lay minefields. Absolute domination of the air is an important factor in the successful American drive.

A new development occurred in the Pacific war today. General MacArthur's forces, about which we have heard little recently, leap-frogged another 200 miles towards the Philippines, landing amphibious forces on the very tip of Dutch New Guinea in the region of Cape Sansapor. The daring operation trapped upwards of 15,000 Japanese troops at Sorong, which lies 70 miles to the west. The landing was undetected by the enemy and opposition was slow to develop.

Manuel Luis Quezon, first President of the Commonwealth of the Philippines, died today at Saranac Lake, New York. The famous Filipino who once fought Americans under Aguinaldo and then lived to become President of the Commonwealth died of heart disease and Tuberculosis on the eve of his country's liberation from the hated Japanese invaders. He will be missed by Americans as well as by Filipinos.

Wednesday, August 2, 1944: —Germany was handed a grave diplomatic defeat today to add to the military disasters she has suffered recently. Turkey, long hesitant on the course she should pursue in this world conflict, has finally severed diplomatic and commercial relations with Hitler's Government. Announcement of the far-reaching step was made by Turkey's Foreign Minister Saracoglu, who said that the move was made at the request of Great Britain. He further said that it would be Germany's decision as to whether the rupture of relations would mean war or peace.

The Turkish action is expected to have severe repercussions throughout the Balkans. Germany's satellite partners, Bulgaria, Rumania, and Hungary, long unhappy over the course of events, are expected to seek the easiest exit out of the war. Germany's complete withdrawal from Greece and the Aegean Islands is expected to follow.

It was revealed today that Lieut. General Leslie J. McNair, who was recently reported killed by enemy action in Normandy, actually met death from an American bomb explosion. The bomb was dropped by accident on our lines during aerial attacks directed against the enemy. A tragic accident.

A torrent of Yankee armor is pouring across Brittany. Already advanced units are halfway across the Breton peninsula and are investing the big rail center of Rennes. German resistance is disintegrating in the face of the dashing American attack. Thousands of prisoners are being taken although there is no time in which to count them.

Thursday, August 3, 1944: —Rennes, the ancient capital of Brittany, was captured today but the Yanks barely paused. Armored spearheads of the U.S. First Army pushed more than thirty miles beyond Rennes in an offensive so swift that it made Germany's famous blitz of 1940 seem slow. The Nazis had neither warning nor time to demolish bridges of mine highways. As the Yank drivers sped across the peninsula at a breakneck pace. At latest report they are still going and no one knows where or when they will be stopped.

At Rennes, more than 1,000 of Hitler's supermen surrendered without putting up a fight and the conquering Yanks merely stripped them of their guns and sent them back by themselves to find the prison pens. There was no time to bother with prisoners and Nazis obviously had had their fill of fighting. According to a war correspondent on the scene, the prisoners humbly marched to the rear until U.S. infantry following up the armored advance could lock them up.

On the eastern front, Russia's avenging hordes are pounding at the gates of East Prussia. Already Soviet artillery is lashing away at German fortifications on the Reich border, less than eight miles distant. The Berlin radio was obviously trying to prepare the German people for the news that the war had come to the Fatherland.

It was revealed in Washington that U.S. casualties have topped the 300,000 mark. The list of dead and wounded has jumped rapidly since D-Day, evidencing the increased ferocity of the fighting on all fronts, including Normandy, Italy, Saipan, Tinian, and Guam.

Friday, August 4, 1944: —Thundering American armored columns roared thirty miles deeper into Brittany during the past 24 hours. The Breton peninsula has been nearly severed with the speeding Yanks closing in on the twin ports of Nantes and St. Nazaire, the latter famous for its huge submarine pens from which Nazi U-Boats have sallied forth for two years to prey upon Allied sea lanes. Today's news indicates that the RAF is pounding the sub pens with mighty six ton "earthquake" bombs in an effort to prevent the U-Boats from escaping to sea as the American forces close in upon the port. Many enemy subs may be captured if the British bombs can succeed in blocking the exits from the great steel and concrete pens.

Good news also comes from the battlefields of Italy where heavy fighting has been in progress for some time, although overshadowed by more spectacular news from the eastern and western fronts. British troops battered the stubborn Germans back into the streets of Florence today, scoring a four mile gain against bitter opposition. The Nazi radio stated that Florence would not be defended and has been declared an open city to protect its cultural and historic treasures. Some of the British Tommies who are blasting at German troops barricaded in the streets of the city have their doubts as to the veracity of the Nazi claim but there is definite evidence that the enemy is pulling out his main force and retiring to the prepared Gothic defense line north of the Italian city.

Saturday, August 5, 1944: —While Hitler's combat armies in the east, west, and south are reeling and falling apart from the sledgehammer blows delivered by avenging Allied armies, Der Fuhrer is engaged in a ruthless and bloody purge of all rebellious members of his decaying High Command. The purge is revealed as extending through all ranks of the officer corps, from field marshals to lieutenants. Thousands have been arrested and hundreds have been executed. The Nazi leaders freely admit, however, that they have not uncovered all the plotters but state that they will stop at nothing to uproot all the traitors. No wonder the morale of their troops at the front is sagging.

There is yet no let up in the lightning drive of our forces in Brittany. Speeding tanks and armored cars disregarded all pre-arranged objectives and raced almost the full length of the Breton peninsula to reach the outskirts of Brest on the very tip. Other columns swept on to Nantes at the base of the peninsula to shut the trap on the estimated 25,000 German troops still defending the peninsula between Nantes and Brest. Prisoners are coming in flocks and it is said that they all insist on surrendering to the Americans rather than take a chance on falling into the hands of the mushrooming bands of French patriots. Maybe they're wise.

For the first time in this war, German land armies are fighting on their own soil. Russian troops have broken through the Nazi defenses on the border of East Prussia and are engaged in a fierce battle north of the border town of Wirballen. The Germans are calling in fresh reserves to defend the "Vaterland."

Sunday, August 6, 1944: —I am very tired as I sit down to write this article tonight. I spent a long, hot day spading in the front yard. I start on my annual vacation tomorrow and the first order of business is to put in a lawn. I figure that with today's start, the job should take about three days of my vacation. We are not planning on going anywhere because of the war so it doesn't make much difference. A vacation at home is the patriotic thing anyway, because of the crowded condition of all transportation facilities. It's no use considering the automobile—with only an A card—since three gallons per week isn't more than enough to do the necessary shopping with. So it will be a quiet vacation around home—perhaps a trip to the beach and park with the youngsters—and a round or two of golf at the local links. Anyway it will be a change and a rest from the confusion and problems of the daily job. Though nothing to be compared with tasks of our combat troops overseas, it has been a tough, tedious year, with long hours of work and difficult problems to face, and I am definitely ready for a vacation—or furlough as I like to think of it now.

The war on the battlefronts of the world is in a period of vast movements, with Allied armies in all theaters taking the offensive with a tremendous display of power. No observer anywhere—not even in the enemy camp I am sure—can doubt that ultimate victory will be won by the United Nations in both the European and Pacific wars. Only the date is in doubt and that depends largely on how well we press our advantages, both on the fighting fronts and on the home fronts. I think, in all fairness, that we can rely on both.

Monday, August 7, 1944: —The fighting in France flamed violently today as the desperate German High Command recklessly threw at least four panzer divisions into a fierce counterattack aimed at splitting the Allied forces driving into Brittany from their Normandy fountainhead. The enemy attack was launched at the base of the Normandy peninsula in the region of Avranches and in its initial phase rolled the American line back more than three miles. Our line stiffened rapidly, however, and at latest report, is beating the Nazi attack to a standstill.

Meanwhile, other American armored columns, disregarding the threat to their communications, drove deeper into Brittany, swung east like a great scythe and headed into the heart of France in the direction of Paris. Their speed was so great that their exact whereabouts could not be accurately determined from hour to hour.

Simultaneously, British and Canadian troops in the Caen area, struck out in a savage new offensive across the Orne River, slicing into the flank of the German battle line. The final outcome of this vast and lethal drama is in the laps of the war gods.

In Italy it is reported that Allied troops have occupied the major portion of Florence without a destructive battle, leaving most of that center of Italian culture unscathed. However, bitter fighting is in progress in the east and west suburbs where the retreating Germans have planted numerous machine gun nests.

Tuesday, August 8, 1944: —It looks like I cut myself out a harder job than I figured on in planting a lawn. Some of that spading is like digging a foxhole in a cement runway. I should have a pick but can't find one for sale. I guess they are not making them for the duration. So I still have some more digging to do before I can start working the soil up for planting. Rather a tiresome way to spend a vacation, but I am getting a good sun tan and the physical labor should harden me up again after a more or less sedentary year.

The war news looks promising tonight. The German counter-attack against the middle of the Allied line in France has been stopped cold, with more than 200 Nazi tanks smashed by sharpshooting American gunners and the thousands of bombs dropped from never-ending fleets of Allied planes. The enemy's only concern now is to extricate as many of the remnants of his battered divisions as he can. It's not at all like the "good old days" of 1940 is it, mein Fuhrer? The blitzkrieg shoe is on the other foot.

At the same time, the offensive launched by the Canadians in the Caen area has ripped a six mile hole in the Germans' so-called "Paris line," a massive string of huge concrete forts blocking the road to the French capital. The Canadian offensive was preceded by one of the deadliest air barrages ever laid down. More than 1,000 heavy British bombers, the famous Lancasters and Halifaxes, drenched the enemy positions with a tremendous tonnage of explosives before the men from Canada blew the "kickoff" whistle. It was second down, goal to go, and the foe's center had been taken out, so the Canadians really hit that line.

Wednesday, August 9, 1944: —Only 87 miles to Paris! That is the good news that greeted us today. Our incomparable armored forces are streaking across the French countryside at a speed never equaled in this war or any other, not even by the galloping Russians on the eastern front. Spearheads ripped into Le Mans, key industrial center on the Germans' Sarthe River line, captured the city easily from the surprised and disorganized Nazis, and swept 25 miles beyond towards Paris.

South of Caen, the Canadian First Army, was exploiting its own sensational breakthrough of the Germans' powerful Paris line. The Canadian prong and the American prong constitute a powerful pincers that promises an early clamping of a trap on the remaining Nazi forces in western France. A victory of world-shaking importance appears to be in the making. Let's hope that the Allied forces do not let the opportunity slip by.

The Pacific war is centered on the tiny island of Guam, where combined Army and Marine forces have pinned the surviving Japanese defenders into a tiny pocket on the northern coast. There the battle of annihilation proceeds to its conclusion. Once more the Stars and Stripes are flying over the first reconquered American soil.

On the flaming eastern front, great and bloody battles are being waged as the Russians drive in for the kill against approximately 200,000 Nazi troops trapped in the Baltic states of Latvia and Lithuania. Today's fighting saw the Soviet armies repulse the most desperate effort of the Germans to break out of the trap. Three Nazi divisions were knocked out in the vain attempt. Inexorably the vengeful Soviets are drawing the noose ever tighter.

Thursday, August 10, 1944: —The Government has just released the news that President Roosevelt has completed a visit to Honolulu, Hawaii. The Chief Executive's mission was to inspect the Pacific war at first hand and to confer with the military leaders of the war against Japan. The President was in conference for several days with General MacArthur and Admiral Nimitz and presumably reviewed the two brilliant leaders' plans for the grand and climactic offensives against our Oriental enemy. Apparently the President left the islands firmly convinced that victory over Japan is certain and may come sooner than might have been expected a short time ago. He was frankly awed by the tremendous strides that have been taken by the Army and Navy since the dark days after the Pearl Harbor disaster. No longer is there destruction and helpless confusion in the harbor and at nearby Hickam Field but efficiency, strength and plenty of evidence of the growing might that is descending upon the hapless sons of Heaven. We have come a long, long way.

The drive on Paris continues at a stunning pace, according to this evening's news reports. Some unconfirmed stories tell of American columns only 40 to 50 miles from the French capital but the true picture cannot be known because of the speed of events and the obvious need for secrecy to confuse the enemy commanders. It is clear, however, that the enemy is befuddled and unable to effectively halt the Allied advance that is moving in some places at a speed equal to peace time maneuvers. Aiding the Allied advance are the mushrooming bands of French patriots who are eagerly seizing the opportunity to gain revenge on their erstwhile overlords.

Friday, August 11, 1944: —America's newest and most deadly assault weapon against Japan, the mighty B-29 Super-Fortresses, struck two staggering blows against the enemy yesterday. One fleet of the huge aerial battleships raided the Japanese home island of Kyushu, hitting industrial targets at

Nagasaki, one of Nippon's largest cities. For the first time incendiaries were rained on the flimsy wood and paper buildings, causing tremendous conflagrations.

The second B-29 raid was launched against the oil refinery center of Palembang, Sumatra, where the Japs have been obtaining much of their vital 100 octane aviation gasoline. Here again huge fires were started as the American bombs crashed into oil tanks and refineries. Three of the great aircraft were reported lost in the twin attacks.

The B-29 raids were not the only strikes against Japan's inner defenses. General MacArthur sent his own heavy bombers back to the Philippine Islands for the first attack since the fall of Corregidor. Davao, on Mindanao Island, was the target and was stuck without surcease for three days in a row—last Sunday, Monday, and Tuesday.

Since we are on the subject of air raids, it might be well to point out that the invasion of France has not slowed or stopped the aerial offensive against the German homeland. Rather it has stepped up in tempo, with thousands of aircraft winging their way almost daily over the borders of the Reich to blast and destroy the Nazis' war factories and supplies. Little has been said of the mighty raids, but only because the sensational ground fighting has monopolized the headlines.

Saturday, August 12, 1944: —Spine-tingling mystery has entered into the great battle now raging in the heart of France. Very little information is being released regarding the actual progress of the fighting, on the probability that the German commanders are hopelessly befuddled and ignorant of the whereabouts of our main forces and are, therefore, at a loss as to where the next blow will be struck. Rumors have the hard-riding Yanks pounding up the pavement towards Paris at a furious clip, having already passed Chartres, less than 46 miles west of the capital. Other reports indicate that the Yanks may be slicing northward through the flank of the beaten German Seventh Army in an effort to bottle up the remnants in a trap between the United States forces and Canadian First Army south of Caen. General Sir Bernard L. Montgomery, Allied ground commander, yesterday told his troops that the German armies in northwestern Europe face encirclement and annihilation. Obviously some sensation developments can be expected in the next few days.

From Italy, we learn that the Nazis have finally relinquished their hold on the northern section of the city of Florence. For several days that city had been held in a tortured vise, as the opposing armies stood on opposite banks of the Arno River while the people starved. Now, however, the Allied Military Government is able to relieve the situation, bringing up huge quantities of food, water, and medical supplies. Another hapless city is liberated.

Sunday, August 13, 1944: —Today has really been a day of rest for me. I finally finished planting the front lawn yesterday evening—just three days over my anticipated schedule. It was really a much bigger job than I had figured and I am worn out—with a week of my vacation gone. I plan to recuperate during the second week—don't even think I'll so much as turn over in bed. Perhaps a round or two of golf won't interfere too much—or a spot of bowling—but that is all, brother, that is all. Remember vacation comes only once in a long, long year.

The war news, from what I could gather over the radio, is very good. Our gallant troops in France are riding roughshod over the once formidable Nazi legions. Panic seems to have seized the enemy as he hears the thunder of American guns and the rumble of thousands of American machines bearing down upon him. He is facing an invincible army of free men, made invincible with the magnificent equipment produced by other free men, and filled with the indomitable spirit that the Germans remember so well from the last war. As in the days of Chateau Thierry and Belleau Woods, the Yanks are running them to death. There is no rest from the relentless pressure—the Yanks don't know when to stop. As one American commander said, "To hell with objectives—keep going." And the Nazis are tired. They would like time to regroup and prepare new defenses. But no, those "verdampt"Americans keep coming—tirelessly, relentlessly. Might just as well quit. You can't beat that kind of men.

Monday, August 14, 1944: —The eyes of the world are still on the battlefields of France where the strategy of General Eisenhower's attack is unfolding. It appears that the aim of the Allied armies is to trap the German Seventh Army and destroy it. That goal is primary, above and beyond the mere seizure of territory. Consequently, the advanced spearheads of the American

Third Army, which apparently were knifing straight through for Paris, suddenly wheeled to the north and smashed through the flank of the German forces toward Falaise, in an obvious attempt to effect a junction with the Canadian First Army lunging down from the Caen sector. A meeting of the two Allied armies would trap the remnants of the German Seventh Army into a death corridor, where annihilation or surrender would be the only alternatives. Field Marshal Guenther von Kluge, commander of the imperiled Germans is reportedly throwing all his available reinforcements into a desperate gamble to hold open an escape corridor. Upon the outcome of this battle may hang the fate of France and the whole Western Front.

Contrasted with the feverish activity in the West, the fighting on the Eastern Front has reached a stalemate—at least temporarily. The Russians are pounding at the gates of East Prussia and knocking at the door of Warsaw but the Germans are resisting furiously and have succeeded in stalling the mighty Soviet juggernaught for the time being.

The picture on the home front was tinged with a slight off color, caused by the necessity for the seizure of five machine shops in the Bay Area by the U.S. Navy. Striking machinists in the shops had caused delay in the production of vital bearings. Now comes the showdown.

Tuesday, August 15, 1944: —ANOTHER SENSATIONAL CHAPTER IN THE WAR WAS BEGUN TODAY! Powerful Allied invasion forces opened a 4th front by storming the Mediterranean coast of France. The attack was launched along a 100 mile stretch of the coast between Marseille and Nice. All initial objectives were reported taken against Nazi opposition that ranged from feeble to suicidal.

Perfectly timed with the big push in northern France the new invasion was spearheaded with what was said to be the largest army of airborne troops ever assembled, even bigger than that used in the Normandy invasion. Hundreds of gliders ferried thousands of troops inland to reinforce and hold the objectives captured by the waves of paratroopers who plummeted into southern France shortly after H-hour which was 8:00 a.m.

General Sir Henry Maitland Wilson, supreme Allied commander in the Mediterranean theater, reported in a special communiqué from his headquarters in Italy, that American, British, and French troops are participating in the invasion. The aim of the attack is to drive the Germans out of southern France and to join forces with the other Allied armies advancing from Normandy. American General Jacob L. Devers is in direct charge of the operation.

Meanwhile in northern France, the Allies are clamping the trap tighter on approximately 100,000 German troops caught in the Normandy pocket around Falaise. Although a narrow escape corridor is still open, the Nazis' chances for escape are slim for they must run the terrible gauntlet of Allied air power.

Wednesday, August 16, 1944: —Both French invasion fronts are going well for the Allies. On the French Riviera to the south, American and French troops are sweeping inland after firmly establishing their beachhead along a 40 mile section of the coastline. Principal scene of action was on the jutting French coast between the pre-war resort town of Cannes and the great naval base of Toulon. Fall of both places, which are now strong links in Germany's Mediterranean defense line, is expected shortly. Both have already been outflanked by the fast rolling assault forces. Casualties have been exceptionally light so far, a tribute to the effectiveness of the pre-invasion naval and aerial barrage. Shore defenses were pulverized long before the assault troops hit the beaches.

To the north racing Yank columns have plunged to a point only 39 miles from Paris on the main Argentan Highway. Other armored units threatened fabled Orleans to the south while still others lanced deeper into the flank of the desperate German Seventh Army, whose battered remnants still held open a six mile escape corridor from the Falaise trap. Allied airmen, however, were having a field day, ripping the retreating Nazi columns to shreds and leaving the roads practically blocked with wrecked and burning German vehicles. Untold numbers of enemy troops perished with their machines.

Here at home, we learn that the Navy is cracking down on the machinists who balked at working overtime on vital war materiel. Sanctions were invoked in which gas rations were canceled, draft deferments ruled out, and names of the strikers put on a War Manpower Commission blacklist. Thank God, strikes of this kind are the rare exception rather than the rule.

707

Thursday, August 17, 1944: —American men and machines are overrunning the suburbs of Paris. Military quarters in London predicted that the former French capital will fall within the next 48 hours. News seeping out of the city hints that the Nazis are preparing to abandon the French metropolis without a struggle. Already resistance units among the French populace are becoming bolder, with subway workers going on strike and policemen and utilities workers curtailing their service.

Lieut. General George S. Patton, "Old Blood and Guts" of Tunisia and Sicily fame, whose light had been under a barrel since his unfavorable "soldier slapping" incident of the Sicilian campaign, is in command of the American Army driving on the former French capital. The colorful General is adept at "lightning" war as he proved in the brilliant Sicilian campaign and is right in his element when chasing the Germans at the head of a tank column. So far his record in France is equal to if not better than his remarkable record in the Mediterranean.

The invasion of southern France is proceeding according to schedule with General Patton's old American Seventh Army leading the way. An unbroken beachhead extending for 50 miles has been secured and the Fighting Seventh has smashed its way 25 miles inland, liberating 500 square miles of territory. The great naval base of Toulon is only ten miles from our enveloping forces.

There is no news of exceptional character from either the Russian front or the Pacific battleground. Both are smoldering, soon to erupt in new offensives.

Friday, August 18, 1944: —The rapidly shifting battlefields of France are still in the news spotlight today. Military spokesmen for the Allied High Command stated that Germany's power of effective resistance in France is now gone. Their defenses south of the Seine River have broken wide open, allowing American, British, and Canadian men and equipment to pour through in an invincible torrent. American armored spearheads have been particularly successful in ripping the enemy apart and our tanks now stand boldly astride all approaches to Paris.

It is now revealed that a large portion of Nazi Field Marshal von Kluge's Seventh Army succeeded in escaping the deadly trap baited for it in Normandy but in doing so, left most of its equipment and supplies behind. The remnant of the once proud Nazi army is now just a panic stricken mob racing to escape to the doubtful sanctuary of the Seine. However, at least 10,000 of their comrades are still penned in the now-closed trap and many thousands of others were previously killed or taken prisoner. Intelligence reports also indicate that a serious breach has occurred in Nazi morale, with the crack Nazi SS elite troops deliberately sacrificing regular army troops as rearguard suicide units in order that they might escape intact.

As the possible end of the war with Germany comes into view, President Roosevelt today revealed that an agreement had been reached between the United States, Britain, and Russia on the occupation of the Nazi homeland. It has been unanimously decided that the Germans will not be permitted to quit until the whole of Germany has been occupied by Allied forces. This time we are going to finish the job.

Saturday, August 19, 1944: —It is persistently rumored that American tanks have entered Paris and the complete liberation of the former French capital appears imminent. The whole Allied world will feel a thrill of joy when "Gay Paree" is freed from the tyrants' grip. The morale of the United Nations will get a tremendous lift while the blow to Germany's prestige and power will be incalculable, especially in the eyes of her wavering satellites in the Balkans. All friends of France are eagerly awaiting official news that will confirm the city's complete liberation— without serious damage.

The invasion of southern France is also making excellent progress. Our shock troops have broken into the outer defenses of the great naval base of Toulon and the position of the desperately defending Nazis is hopeless. The fall of the port cannot, therefore, be very far off.

Other American armored columns have swept around Toulon and are racing towards Marseille. At latest report the leading elements were within 25 miles of the city which is the second largest in France. So far the Germans have not produced anything capable of stopping the rampaging Yanks.

The harassed and threatened collaborationist government of France located at Vichy is reported to have fled that city in the face of powerful uprisings among the French populace. French

Maquis or Resistance troops are said to be in almost complete control of the city which served as the capital of the Nazi-controlled government headed by aged Marshal Petain and collaborationist Pierre Laval.

Sunday, August 20, 1944: —Well, today ends my vacation which has been pleasant though short. I feel very refreshed and ready for work, having spent the last week as I promised I would, just loafing, playing golf, and acquiring a sun tan. It has been a thoroughly satisfactory war time vacation.

Let us take a look at conditions on the home front as we near the end of the third year of our war and the fifth year of the European war. Food seems plentiful although many items are still on the ration list. Meat can be had regularly, with fancy steaks about the only kind missing. Gas rationing just about keeps the poor "A" card holder off the streets—that is, the honest ones who shun the Black Market. For example, I used my last six gallons during my vacation and there will be no more until September 21st, a full month away. Other modes of transportation, such as trains, buses, and streetcars, are still very congested, with prospects that conditions will get worse before they get better.

The general cost of living, while very high, has not been permitted to run away, and it appears that the nation is just about holding its own in the battle against inflation. There is still great danger, however, as millions of war workers, with more money than they ever had before, look around for things to buy. That is where the War Bond sales campaign comes in.

Production of war goods, despite a sometimes unfavorable strike picture, has reached proportions that stagger the imagination. However, the output of some items during the first six months of this year has failed to reach the goals set, due primarily to manpower shortages, aggravated somewhat by a new tendency of some workers to anticipate victory by going back into non-essential industry.

Monday, August 21, 1944: —Many things happened today. Many blows were struck for victory and peace. One of the most important with respect to the attainment of a permanent peace was the opening at Washington, D.C. today of a three-power conference, including high representatives of Great Britain,

Russia, and the United States. Purpose of the parley is to work out a plan for a world organization that will police the post-war world and prevent the outbreak of any further world conflagrations. God grant that their efforts may succeed.

Paris, France is in turmoil as the hour of its liberation approaches. It is reliably reported that tens of thousands of French patriots within the city have risen in revolt against the Nazi garrison. Bitter street fighting is in progress along some of the most famous boulevards in the entire world. Students and former French police officers are said to be leading the revolt.

Meanwhile, outside the city limits American tanks and infantry are herding the remnants of the once powerful German Seventh Army into a death trap on the banks of the river Seine. U.S. spearheads have already crossed the Seine at several places to cut off the remaining escape routes for the beaten Nazis.

Activity in the Pacific war was just as spectacular. Our mighty B-29 battleships of the air again struck at the Japanese homeland, this time striking twice in twenty four hours, by day and night, at the sprawling Yawata steel center. This was a real raid after the fashion of the raids on Germany, and terrific damage was caused.

I must mention the report that our gallant Silent Service, the U.S. subs, has bagged 19 more Jap ships.

Tuesday, August 22, 1944: —Far from making the capture of Paris their only goal, the U.S. Army seems bent on driving on through to the German border itself—and with little delay. Hard-riding Yank tank men and armored troops smashed southeast of Paris through fading German resistance for a distance of 65 miles, gaining ground faster than in peace time maneuvers. The advancing spearheads captured Sens on the Yonne River, only 160 miles from German soil.

Other American forces swept across the Seine River and drove hard for the English Channel ports. Every mile gained towards the Channel draws the noose tighter around the tens of thousands of Nazi troops retreating from Normandy and manning the "robot" coastline from Calais to Le Havre. At the same time veteran Canadian and British troops drove eastward along the Normandy coast, squeezing the noose tighter. At one point the Canadians were within 12 miles of the Seine estuary.

In Southern France, Allied troops have encircled Toulon, the great naval base on the Mediterranean and have driven to within 3 miles of the famed port of Marseille. Other slashing attacks sent American and French armored columns knifing sixty miles inland towards the Rhone valley and a junction with American columns racing down from the Paris area.

The curtain is coming down on the ill-fated Vichy Government of France. Today's reports indicate that the aged Petain, Marshal of France and former hero of Verdun, lately head of the collaborationist government, has been seized by the German Gestapo and spirited away to Germany. What will be his fate?

Wednesday, August 23, 1944: —RUMANIA HAS SURRENDERED! The first spectacular break in Hitler's Balkan defenses has arrived. The sensational development came suddenly and apparently took the Nazis by surprise since no effective steps were taken by the German occupation forces to retrieve the situation. The Bucharest radio broadcast a royal proclamation by King Michael, announcing that Rumania had accepted Russian peace terms, had ousted the pro-Nazi prime minister, Ion Antonescu, and would become an ally of the United Nations.

One report states that Rumanian troops are already fighting their erstwhile ally, Germany and at least 30 Rumanian divisions have gone over to the Russian side.

Repercussions of Rumania's decision will be world-shaking. The Nazis will not only lose their major source of oil and gasoline, but can expect a complete crackup in the Balkans, with Bulgaria, and Hungary both anxious to get out of the war. The Hitler built house of cards is beginning to topple. It could well be the beginning of the end.

Paris has been liberated, according to word received from underground leaders within the embattled city. The leaders of the hundreds of thousands of angry French patriots in the capital, dramatically announced that their partisan forces had stormed the last strongholds of the German garrison, overwhelmed the enemy, and hoisted the tri-color over the liberated metropolis. There is no report that Allied troops have entered the city as yet.

Thursday, August 24, 1944: —The French Partisan report that Paris had been liberated apparently was premature since violent street fighting has broken out between the French patriots and the German garrison. The French have called for Allied help and American tanks are being rushed into the capital. Fighting French regulars from General Le Clerc's famous African Army are also being rushed to the rescue of their beloved metropolis.

Many spontaneous celebrations by friends of France were held throughout the world after the news of the liberation of Paris was released. In San Francisco, the French colony received the glad tidings with excited joy and their fervor was only slightly dampened when it was revealed that bitter fighting still rages in the streets of the capital. They know that the time of complete and final liberation has only been delayed by a few hours or days. The hated Boche is through.

The Balkans is in a turmoil following the capitulation of Rumania. Mutiny has broken out in the Hungarian Army and dissolution of the Nazi-controlled government of that country is beginning. Bulgaria, at war only with Great Britain and the United States but not with Russia, has requested peace terms from the British ambassador in Ankara.

Germany at last is trying to regain control of the broken down Rumanian situation. Bucharest is in a state of siege while Nazi troops battle the Rumanians for mastery. Thus far, King Michael's forces have retained control pending the arrival of conquering Russian hordes racing through Bessarabia in the face of dwindling resistance.

Friday, August 25, 1944: —The final liberation of Paris was accomplished by Allied tanks and infantrymen today amidst a delirium of joy on the part of the French populace. Surrender of the Nazi commander of the German garrison was accepted, appropriately enough, by Brig. General Jacques Le Clerc who led the fighting French armored corp., under the Cross of Lorraine, but wearing American uniforms and driving American tanks, into the former capital of their beloved France. As the French-manned armor swept into the heart of the city, the Nazi defenders quickly ceased their opposition and surrendered or were destroyed.

The arrival of the Allied armies touched off a tremendous celebration in "Gay Paree." From the meager reports received as yet, it was undoubtedly an historic and memorable occasion. It will surely be an unforgettable experience for those who are participating in this epochal event in the history of mankind. Would that I could have been there.

Despite the liberation of Paris, the momentum of the Allied drive throughout France has not slackened for a moment. Canadian and British troops are exploiting their breakthrough of the Seine River line and are racing pell-mell towards Le Havre and the robot coast of northern France. Leading elements of the Canadian First Army are reported to have reached the mouth of the Seine, capturing Honfleur, five miles across the estuary from Le Havre. Other Allied units sped towards famous Dieppe, Amiens, Beauvais, and Calais, while the roads leading east and north from those points were said to be jammed with German traffic, backpedalling at high speed towards the Reich.

Saturday, August 26, 1944: —Hard-riding American troops in Southern France are matching the incredible speed of their comrades in the north, having overrun Toulon, Cannes, Marseille, and driven far up the Rhone Valley to a point near the Swiss border, all in the first ten days of the southern invasion. Thousands of Germans have been killed and captured and the German 19th Army badly mauled in the process. Prospects of a quick junction between the two jaws of the great Allied pincers are very good.

In the north, American armored spearheads are driving at tourist speed towards the borders of the Reich itself. General Eisenhower today warned the people of Belgium and Luxembourg that the tide of war is sweeping rapidly towards their countries and cautioned them to avoid helping the enemy in any way or to expose themselves to the fury of the Allied air attacks that may be expected. General Patton's armored "blitz" warriors were said to be slashing close to Reims in a drive aimed at the famed Ardennes forest and Sedan where Hitler's hordes cracked the French Maginot "hinge" in 1940 and caused the downfall of France. This time, to use an old cliché, the shoe is on the other foot.

On the eastern front, the Russians are doing their part in supplementing the Allied drive, by applying the pressure against the Nazis defending Warsaw. Thousands of Red Army troops have launched a great new offensive northeast of the former Polish capital in an obvious effort to roll up the flank of the German army blocking the way into the city.

Sunday, August 27, 1944: —Allied Supreme Headquarters today announced that the Battle for France has been won and the Battle of Germany is about to begin. The complete liquidation of the German Seventh Army was the decisive factor in the brilliant Allied victory. Triumphant American, British, Canadian, and French armies are herding the once formidable enemy in headlong flight towards Belgium, Luxembourg, and the borders of the Reich itself. German resistance is only sporadic and disorganized and the fast-rolling Allied armor is allowing the Nazi leaders no time in which to prepare a line of defense short of the Siegfried line. The speed of the Allied advance is almost miraculous and has no counterpart in history.

Paris is still in an uproar although the German garrison of more than 10,000 troops has surrendered. Nazi snipers dressed in civilian clothes are still at large and French Maquis, or Resistance members, are roaming the streets, their trigger fingers nervous, ferreting out the hidden Germans. The city should soon return to normal, however, since the battlefront is sweeping far beyond the capital towards the famous and bloody fields of battle of the First World War. General de Gaulle, the original Fighting Frenchman, arrived in the French capital during the past 24 hours, receiving an ovation from the populace. Several shots were fired as the tall French leader paraded down the Champs Elysees but he and his party escaped injury.

With the Russian armies nearing her border and Allied war planes overhead, it was reported last night that Bulgaria has asked the United States and Britain for an armistice.

Monday, August 28, 1944: —Chateau-Thierry, famed battlefield of World War I, is feeling the tread of American boots and the thunder of American guns once again. Victory-flushed United States forces stormed through the historic Valley of the Marne, and swept into Chateau-Thierry after a lightning four-mile advance from La Feste. Any hope that the Nazis may have entertained of making a stand along the natural defense line of the Marne, where the Kaiser's armies were twice turned back in the previous war, appeared to be doomed to failure today because of the tremendous speed of the Allied attack. A defeated army needs time to regroup and recover. This the Allies have no intention of granting to the beaten Nazi legions.

The plight of the Germans in southern France is almost as bad. American tanks and mobile artillery have swept in a day more than fifty miles northward into the Rhone Valley, fashioning a noose about the necks of some 15,000 enemy troops, comprising the remnants of the defeated German 19th Army. The "supermen" are pinned against the east bank of the Rhone in the vicinity of Montelimar and face the now familiar alternatives of surrender or death.

In the seething Balkans, a full-scale battle is being waged for Bucharest, as Hitler strives desperately to recover his lost prestige, punish the so-call "traitors" and prevent the complete disintegration of his satellite empire. Eleven Nazi divisions are reported surrounding the Rumanian capital which has been cut off from all communication for several days.

Tuesday, August 29, 1944: —Lieut. General George S. Patton, the picturesque "Old Blood and Guts" commander of the U.S. Third Army, is leading his armored columns on a whirlwind ride across the historic battlegrounds of World War I. During the past twenty four hours his wild-riding troopers have raced 40 miles, ripped the enemy's Marne line to shreds, and captured Chateau-Thierry, Soissons, Chalons, and Vitry-Le Francois. The Americans encountered bitter resistance at the Aisne River crossing at Soissons, where their fathers launched their mighty counter-offensive in July 1918, but the barrier was soon overrun by the rampaging Yanks.

The Germans know that the jig is just about up, from the tone of their Berlin broadcasts lately. Today, Lieut. General Kurt Dittmar, official Nazi radio commentator, frankly told the German people that they cannot hope to win the war and stated that they were continuing the fight only to win more favorable terms from the Allies. Their only hope, he said, is to make total victory so costly for the United Nations that they will be willing to grant more generous terms in order to avoid further sacrifices. Let us hope the Allies don't fall for this bait.

Organized German resistance has all but ceased in southern France. There is no front and no line. All that remains is a mopping-up process that should add more thousands to the approximately 60,000 prisoners already taken in the brief campaign. While the clean-up proceeds in the south, the armored spearheads of the American Seventh Army are driving hard and fast up the famous Rhone Valley towards Lyon and an eventual junction with Allied forces to the north.

Wednesday, August 30, 1944: —Sensational new victories have been won on the Eastern and Western European fronts. It is difficult to determine which events are of the greatest significance. In the east, fast moving Russian forces raced deep into Rumania to capture Ploesti, site of the big oil fields upon which Hitler has depended for much of the badly needed oil and gas to supply his mechanized armies. The Germans forfeited the world famous oil center without a major battle, thereby suffering one of their most ignominious defeats. Moscow rightly celebrated its capture as a great victory, at the same time announcing that Russian forces have pushed on from Ploesti to within 17 miles of beleaguered Bucharest.

The Nazi debacle on the western front continues to grow in scope. The magnitude of the Allied victory is almost inconceivable, particularly to those men who fought for years in the First World War to win back ground that has been retaken by General Patton's armor in 96 hours. One of the main reasons for the ineffectual Nazi resistance seems to be the fact that the Luftwaffe has been completely driven from the air. As a consequence, the Nazi armies are blind, groping about in total confusion, never knowing where or when the Allied "blitz" will strike next. In contrast, Allied flyers range all over the fast-moving battlefront, strafing and bombing the enemy while keeping the Allied command well informed regarding his every move. As one Nazi commentator stated, "It is 1940 in reverse."

Thursday, August 31, 1944: —Historic ground is being reclaimed at the rate of a mile per hour by our triumphant armies in France. Armored columns of the American First Army crashed through German defenses on the Meuse River after a brilliant dash of 37 miles from the Aisne River line, breached only yesterday. Beyond the Meuse, the Yanks headed toward Sedan and the famous Ardennes Forest through which the conquering Nazi hordes swept in the spring of 1940.

Farther to the south General Patton's American Third Army blasted its way into the Argonne, scene of many bloody battles in World War I. The goal of General Patton's drive is probably the mighty fortress city of Verdun where the Germans may attempt a major stand. The speed of the American advance may foil this attempt.

In southern France, Allied progress has been almost as sensational. The entire Mediterranean coastline of France has been swept clear of Nazi resistance, while the famous U.S. Seventh Army has fought its way up the Rhone valley almost to Lyon, driving the beaten remnants of the German 19th Army before it. The lightning advance has not been without cost, however, for bitter opposition has been encountered from suicidal Nazi rear-guards. Evidence of the price paid for the past week's brilliant victories is shown in the casualty figures released by the War Department in Washington today. The report showed a sharp rise of 23,249 for the seven day period, bringing total U.S. Army casualties in the war thus far to 284,838. Grand total for all services increased to 349,523. War's grisly mill continues to grind mercilessly on, seemingly never satiated.

September

Friday, September 1, 1944: —Five years ago today Hitler unleashed his bloody war dogs and sent them tearing at the soft throat of unprepared Poland, thus precipitating the most violent and widespread blood bath in the history of the world. Now, at long last, the bitter fruits of his ill-starred attempt at world conquest are being returned to him in full measure. On every front his armies are in full retreat, some of them in disorderly rout. From the east and west and south mighty Allied armies are closing in on the German homeland. Overhead huge fleets of Allied aircraft command the skies, almost unopposed by the ragged remnants of the once invincible Luftwaffe. On the seas the fleets of the United Nations rule supreme, harried only slightly by the battered remains of his once formidable submarine pack. His doom is sealed, yet he chooses to fight on, dragging the whole world down to ruin with him, if that were possible. The lives of countless people have no meaning to him as he writhes desperately in his insane efforts to escape the clutching fingers of justice. God grant that no sanctuary may be opened up to him, that he may soon face the high tribunal of humanity and be meted out the punishment to fit his heinous crime.

In northern France General Patton's wild-riding Yanks reversed the famous French slogan, "They shall not pass," changing it to read, "They shall not halt." And they have not halted, neither the Nazis in retreat nor the Yanks in pursuit. Verdun, where a million Frenchmen fought and bled in 1916-17 to make good the original slogan, was overrun by the rampaging Americans almost without a struggle. St. Mihiel, where their fathers cracked the great German salient in 1918, was also seized by the triumphant doughboys.

Saturday, September 2, 1944: —The entire world is watching in open-mouthed amazement while the incredible drama unfolds on the western front. The tremendous speed of the Allied "blitz" since the day of the St. Lo breakthrough in Normandy has left the civilized world gaping in astonishment. Some doubting souls have offered the explanation that the Germans have permitted the Allied advance, choosing to accept

719

defeat in the west, allowing the American and British to march into Germany ahead of the Russians from whom they fear dire vengeance for the atrocities committed against them. This assumption is unfair to the gallant men who participated in the bitter struggle in Normandy where history will confirm that the Nazi high command committed its finest troops and armor in an all-out effort to contain the Normandy beachhead and drive the Allied invaders back into the sea. The men who fought, bled, and oft-times died, in the sanguinary fighting around Caen, St. Lo, Falaise, Carentan, Cherbourg, and the beaches of Normandy will attest to this truth. No, the story of the Nazi debacle that followed the St. Lo breakthrough is a story of the superiority of Allied men and equipment, the unforgettable courage of Americans, French, Canadians, and British, who met the best the enemy could offer and beat them, the brilliant exploitation of an advantage won through a hell of fire, and a tireless drive and dash that allowed the enemy no rest, no time to recover or regroup; a drive that knew no letup even when supply lines were left far behind or when exhaustion threatened to overwhelm them. Come on, world, give the credit to the gallant men of American First and Third Armies, the Fighting French Armored Corp, the Canadian First Army and their British comrades. Give the credit to the living and dead who fought on those bloody fields of Normandy and to their brilliant commanders and to all those innumerable human cogs who have combined to produce the greatest fighting force in the history of warfare.

Sunday, September 3, 1944: —The Battle for France is in its last round, with complete liberation of that country assured. Spearheads of the conquering Allied armies are already driving into Belgium, which is next on the schedule for liberation. Two armored columns of the American First Army are said to have penetrated as far as Namur and Charleroi, on the road to Brussels and Liege. Inside reports hint that the Nazis are withdrawing their forces from Belgium, apparently giving up hope of making a stand short of the German border itself.

South of Belgium and Luxembourg, Americand troops are reported hammering at the Moselle River gateway to the Reich. Patrols of General Patton's American Third Army are already reconnoitering the outer defenses of the Siegfried Line, the "impregnable" West Wall of Germany.

Far back of the lines in western France, British and Canadian troops are mopping up the encircled Germans along the Channel coast. Canadian forces have taken Dieppe, Amiens, Abbeville, and headed for Boulogne, Calais, and renowned beach of Dunkirk. Le Havre is encircled, with its Nazi garrison doomed to capture or destruction. At Brest, on the tip of the Breton peninsula, a strong Nazi garrison of 20,000 men is still holding out despite furious Allied attacks. Nevertheless, their doom is sealed.

Finland, the gallant little republic who always paid its war debt but got in on the wrong side in this world struggle, is trying to get out. The Finns have asked the Russians for peace terms. The unhappy little nation is doomed to a final spasm of suffering, however, because the Germans are there in force (several divisions) and, as in Italy, may not accept the defection of their erstwhile Ally very graciously. The extraction may be quite painful.

Monday, September 4, 1944: —Victory is everywhere. More than half of Belgium has been liberated in less than two days time. British forces swept 70 miles across the fields of Flanders to free the Belgian capital of Brussels. An American First Army column was reported to have raced all the way across Belgium and is now battling at a point five miles inside the border of Holland. The powerful fortress city of Liege and the great port of Antwerp, both in Belgium, were said to be under siege and are expected to fall quickly. The Germans are offering only meager resistance, confining their major efforts to extricating the battered remnants of their defeated armies.

In southern France, American Seventh Army forces and their French comrades-in-arms captured the city of Lyon in the Rhone Valley and drove more than fifty miles above that vital center to reach a point only 120 miles from the American Third Army, advancing on Germany from the Verdun area. A junction between the two victorious U.S. armies will seal the fate of all German forces remaining in southern and central France.

Finland has surrendered to Soviet might for the second time in 4½ years. The tiny republic has accepted the Russian peace terms and the guns ceased firing along the 450 mile Russo-Finnish battle front at exactly 8:00 a.m. this morning. The German forces stationed in Finland are reported fleeing to Norway after a

Finnish ultimatum allowing them until September 15 to withdraw or face internment. Soviet paratroops are said to be helping the Finns enforce their demands upon the Nazi garrison.

Tuesday, September 5, 1944: —Bulgaria, already at war with Great Britain and the United States, tonight found herself at war with the Soviet Union. The Russian declaration of war against the Balkan state came after repeated warnings from Moscow had failed to prevent the Bulgarians from continuing their assistance to Germany. Now, however, they face the deadly peril of having their country overrun by the mighty Soviet armies poised on their eastern frontier.

The Russian move come as something of a surprise since it was known that the new Bulgarian government formed last Saturday has sent peace emissaries to conclude an armistice with England and the United States as soon as possible. Moscow charged, however, that the Bulgars are continuing to grant favors and aid to Germany, despite their so-called neutrality with Russia. Now comes the avalanche of Russian retribution.

An unconfirmed report from the western front stated that Allied patrols have stuck deep into Germany proper, reaching the Rhine at a point near Strassburg. To the north, British forces have captured Antwerp, with its valuable harbor, and have driven 30 miles beyond the port to strike deep into Holland.

Back on the English Channel coast 100,000 German troops are writhing in the trap thrown about them by the swift Allied advance into Belgium and the Netherlands. Desperate Nazi garrisons at Calais, Gravelines, and Dunkirk are trying to escape by sea in a grim reversal of the memorable Allied evacuation in 1940.

Wednesday, September 6, 1944: —The climactic battle of Germany is about to be joined. For the first time in history mighty American armies stand poised for invasion on the threshold of the Reich. Already American troops are treading on the "sacred soil" of the Fatherland, while the frantic Nazis strive desperately to prepare for a stand along their vaunted Siegfried Line. The time allotted for their preparation will be brief, however, for the flying columns of General Patton's American Third Army are blasting their way up the Moselle River gateway at a pace that will carry them to the outer defenses of the Siegfried Line in a matter of days, perhaps hours. Suicidal rear-guard German units are putting up a bloody, but hopeless, battle for the Moselle crossings and casualties on both sides are extremely heavy.

Anti-climactic battles are still raging along the English Channel coast, as the British and Canadians move to mop up the remainder of the robot bomb area around Calais, Boulogne, and Dunkirk. Twenty thousand Nazis are still holding out in the great port of Le Havre, while bitter fighting continues to rage for the city of Brest at the tip of the Breton peninsula. The German resistance at all of these points can only serve as delaying actions, since the fate of all are sealed. No escape for the approximately 100,000 Nazi troops caught in these traps is possible. Death or capture are the only alternatives.

At home in Washington, D.C. the Army and Navy announced plans for partial demobilization after the defeat of Germany. War plans against Japan, however, will not be permitted to suffer.

Thursday, September 7, 1944: —In a masterpiece of understatement, as the saying goes, Emperor Hirohito of Japan told his people today that a grave crisis is before them. This he says as mighty American fleets roam the waters of the Pacific at will, boldly steaming to within 600 miles of Tokyo itself, without encountering the once boastful Japanese Imperial Navy. Strikes are being made daily against the last outposts defending the Japanese homeland. Bases have been seized in the Marianas, Guam has been retaken, raids by formations of the mighty B-29s have lashed military objectives in Japan itself. Palau, Formosa, the Philippines, are next on the invasion schedule. Crisis indeed! It is the pall of doom descending upon a treacherous empire.

In Europe, while Hitler stares with fright at the great storm gathering, black and menacing, along his western wall, behind his back his bitterly won empire in the Balkans is crumbling in ruins. Powerful Russian armies have raced across the full breadth of Rumania and are reported to have struck deep into Yugoslavia, heading both for Belgrade and a junction with Marshal Tito's fierce Partisan Army, which has fought the Germans without help, and sometimes without hope, for three long years. Junction of the two Allied forces would weld a steel trap around some

250,000 to 300,000 German troops in the Balkans. Bulgaria, meanwhile, is striving desperately to extricate herself from the war. A Berlin report, later retracted, claimed that the Bulgarian government has declared war on Germany, reversing her position as Hitler's satellite. The true facts, however, are obscured by rumor.

Friday, September 8, 1944: —A large force of our mammoth B-29 Super-Fortresses struck a devastating new blow against Japan's industrial centers in Manchuria. The principal target was reported, in a Tokyo broadcast admitting the raid, to have been Anshan, an important steel center 55 miles south of Mukden. The Japs claimed that two of the big raiders were shot down but admitted that heavy damage was inflicted by the American bombs. Just a foretaste of what is coming, Mr. Moto.

In Europe, General Courtney H. Hodges' U.S. First Army swept through crumbling Nazi resistance to capture the mighty fortress town of Liege, last German stronghold in Belgium. Farther south, General George S. Patton's U.S. Third Army fought bitterly today to establish bridgeheads across the Moselle River north and south of Metz. The river ran red with German and American blood, as the Yanks encountered the stiffest enemy resistance since the breakthrough in Normandy. At the end of the day, however, our footholds on the eastern bank were secure.

The panic and confusion of defeat is spreading with the roar of a prairie fire throughout the Balkans. A torrent of Red Army troops are pouring into Bulgaria following Russia's declaration of war against the erstwhile Nazi satellite nation. In her desperate effort to extricate herself from her self-imposed predicament, it was reported, in one reliable broadcast, that Bulgaria has declared war on Germany and has allied herself completely with the United Nations. A grain of salt with that one.

Here at home, Governor Dewey of New York, Republican candidate for President, opened his campaign with a spirited Philadelphia address in which he attacked the bickering and tired Democratic administration in Washington.

Saturday, September 9, 1944: —Nazi resistance is stiffening as the climactic battle for Germany begins. More than a million Allied troops are poised along the border of the Reich awaiting the signal that will send them crashing into the enemy's vaunted Westwall, in an all-out offensive aimed at knocking Germany out of the war before winter. Meanwhile, Allied spearheads are probing at the outer defenses of the Wall, hoping to find a soft spot. General George S. Patton's Third Army forces are encountering the stiffest resistance. Furious enemy counter-attacks against the Third Army's hard-won Moselle River bridgeheads have created a serious situation in that area. The American doughboys, however, are clinging to their shallow footholds with a tenacious courage that presages eventual victory.

Fierce fighting also rages on the Italian front. General Sir Harold Alexander's Supreme Allied Headquarters announced that a furious battle is raging for Rimini, the eastern anchor of the Nazis' Gothic Line and the gateway to the famous Po Valley. Gains are measured in yards as Britain's famous Eighth Army troops slug it out with Field Marshal General Albert Kesselring's heavily reinforced garrison. Upon the outcome of this battle hangs the fate of the present Allied campaign in Northern Italy.

Despite all the good news, there is one theater of war in which the Allies are not doing so well. We haven't mentioned it often because it cannot prevent the final victory, although it is not pleasant for the gallant member of the United Nations which must bear the brunt and suffering of it. I speak of China, where ruthless and powerful Japanese armies are still making headway in their vicious drive to split the country in two.

Sunday, September 10, 1944: —A happy, triumphant Winston Churchill, Prime Minister of Great Britain, arrived in Quebec today with his staff, for his tenth meeting with President Roosevelt. Churchill has been described many times as the "cigar-smoking, cherub-faced Premier" but he is extremely popular with the masses. He was greeted by a great crowd at the dock in Halifax and while waiting for his train to depart for Quebec, the smiling statesman led the throng in song after song. Obviously the Prime Minister thinks the war is going well.

The news from Europe seems to bear this out. The American Third Army has solved its trouble along the Moselle River and is now master of the situation. To the north the American First Army has liberated Luxembourg, the capital of the tiny country bearing the same name, and has driven on to a point six miles from Aachen, key defense bastion of the Siegfried Line. American artillery is now shelling German soil.

In southern France, another American army, the famous Seventh, has pounded to within fifteen miles of Belfort, and is racing to close the last remaining escape route for the Germans through the historic Belfort Gap. French forces are aiding the American advance.

Evidence of the disaster that has befallen the Germans in France since D-Day is in the casualty figures. A spokesman from General Eisenhower's Headquarters is reported to have declared that the Germans have lost over 700,000 men since the invasion. Of these, 400,000 have been taken prisoner, the rest killed or wounded. Quite a bag of "supermen" in a 90 day campaign.

Monday, September 11, 1944: —The Pacific war flared into violent action today, seizing the headlines away from the Battle for Germany. The action took place last Friday but the news was released today. Admiral William F. Halsey, of Solomon Island fame, sent his powerful aircraft carrier force on a strike against Japanese forces on the island of Mindanao in the Philippines. Hundreds of our carrier aircraft caught the enemy napping, and destroyed no less than 89 Japanese vessels, including one whole convoy of 32 loaded cargo ships. The Japs sent up hundreds of planes to thwart the attack but the Nips could not match our firepower and were dispersed after losing 68 fighters. Our own losses were comparatively light.

The "Beat Japan" conference between Prime Minister Churchill and President Roosevelt, and their respective military staffs, opened today in Quebec, ancient capital of French Canada. A note of high optimism pervaded the atmosphere, with "victory everywhere" as the theme. Plans for the quick defeat of Japan and the complete occupation of Germany are believed to comprise the agenda of the meeting.

Even as the leaders of the two nations talked, American troops are treading the soil of Germany, having driven five miles into the maze of pillboxes, forts, and tank traps which form the Siegfried Line. Farther south, General Patton's Third Army effected a junction with the Seventh Army, advancing northward up the Rhone Valley. Junction of the two U.S. armies closes the trap on

726

all German forces still remaining in western France. Their last hope of escape is gone.

Tuesday, September 12, 1944: —In an action that has all the earmarks of a pre-invasion barrage, Admiral William F. Halsey's powerful U.S. Third Fleet today shelled and bombed Japan's last island barrier to the Philippines, Palau in the western Carolines. While planes from his carrier force blasted the enemy base from the air, battleships and cruisers stood offshore and pumped salvo after salvo of high explosive shells into the island. The Japs made only feeble efforts to fend off the attack. Halsey's fleet was fresh from its crushing victory at Mindanao in the Philippines, in which the Japs lost ninety cargo ships and over 70 fighter planes.

Four years ago last May, the Nazi hordes swept across the borders of Belgium and Holland in the famous blitzkrieg that nearly carried them to world domination. The Belgians depended upon the mighty fortress Eben Emael to stop the Germans or at least delay them for many weeks. To the astonishment and horror of the entire world, the famous fort fell to the Nazis in a day, almost without a shot being fired. Dire rumors were whispered about German secret weapons and, to this day, the quick fall of the "impregnable" bastion has been one of the unsolved mysteries of the war. Today a second and equally baffling mystery was added to the eerie story of Eben Emael. Advancing American troops captured the famous fort in half an hour, the Nazi garrison having evacuated the stronghold without a fight. To the goggle-eyed doughboys, the massive concrete fortifications, the huge cannon, the incredible maze of easily defended galleries and ramparts, seemed to stare blankly at them with eyes unbelieving that their mighty defensive power had never been put to the test. What is the mystery of Ft. Eben Emael?

Wednesday, September 13, 1944: —American planes from Admiral Halsey's aircraft carriers returned to the Philippines after their successful strike at Palau, in the Carolines, and flushed out a large force of Japanese planes, engaging them in a terrific air battle over the islands. The American raiders emerged victorious, blasting some 200 enemy planes out of the skies. The action is a continuing one, however, according to Admiral Nimitz' communiqué and the Japs are making a determined effort to maintain aerial supremacy over the Philippines.

In Europe the climactic battle for Germany is still in its preliminary stage. American armor is probing at the outer crust of the Siegfried Line in many places while the main Allied forces are gathering and regrouping for the final and decisive (we hope) smash at the already reeling Nazi beast. Victory before winter is the ultimate goal of every Allied soldier and airman in Europe, especially when he feels the first chill wind whip across the battlefield. The ideal fighting weather of June, July, August and September is just about over and the Allied trooper views with dread the possibility of enduring a winter of war on the bleak, bitterly cold plains of northern Germany. God grant that this ordeal may not be visited upon him.

If the ceaseless battering of thousands of tons of bombs will hasten the end of German resistance, the Allied air forces are doing their part. For six consecutive days and nights, thousands of American and RAF heavy bombers have plastered the Reich from end to end. The last 24 hours have seen more than 5,000 mighty bombers deliver their deadly cargo to the enemy.

Thursday, September 14, 1944: —In the most savage kind of hand to hand fighting, American infantrymen of the U.S. First Army smashed forward at least 8 miles into Germany today, cutting a wide swath in the maze of pillboxes and anti-tank traps that comprise the Siegfried Line. It was a job for the infantry since the heavy concrete fortifications and jutting "dragon tooth" tank obstacles made any large scale use of armor impossible. Each stubborn enemy strongpoint had to be stormed and taken in the bloodiest kind of personal infighting. More power to the infantry, the gallant queen of battle.

Advance elements of the First Army were reported within one mile of Aachen, powerful defense bastion of the West Wall and the first important German town to come under the guns of the advancing Allied armies. Fall of the town is believed imminent.

The progress of other American and British Armies on the German border was obscured by the "security blackout" frequently imposed while major military movements are under way, but it was indicated that the Reich border has been crossed at so many points that it could safely be considered that the advance into Germany has become general.

Here at home an interesting and revealing bit of news is the conservative reports of two War Labor Board panels in which it

was announced that the general cost of living has increased from
25 to 43 percent since 1941. From our own experience we
would say that the Board's findings are indeed conservative.
Particularly with respect to the biggest item of all—food.

Friday, September 15, 1944: —Two powerful United States
amphibious forces today launched simultaneous assaults on the
last Japanese island outpost guarding the Philippines. One force
of doughboys and Marines swept ashore on Peleliu Island in the
Palau group after air and sea units had pulverized the beaches
with a terrific bombardment from air bombs and naval shells.
However, since the Palau group constitutes one of Japan's major
defensive bases, it is believed that the attacking forces face a
bitter struggle. Peleliu is heavily wooded and the Japs apparently
are firmly dug in. It will probably be a tough campaign. Our
assault troops are commanded by Marine Major General Julian C.
Smith.

At the same time, far to the south and west, General
MacArthur himself directed the attack on Morotai Island in the
Molucca Sea. This operation took the enemy completely by
surprise and was carried out smoothly against feeble opposition.
Firm beachheads were quickly established from which the
attackers pressed inland. Conquest of Morotai will give General
MacArthur an invasion springboard only 300 miles from
Mindanao, in his beloved Philippines. Heroes of Bataan and
Corregidor! We are coming back—very soon.

In Europe the battle for Germany is rising in fury. Allied
armies are punching salients into the vaunted Siegfried Line at
many places. The main attack apparently is centered at a point
just east of Aachen where American First Army troops are
reported to have smashed clear through the Nazi defense line and
are racing for the Rhine.

Saturday, September 16, 1944: —The renowned Marine
First Division is engaged in what may prove to be its toughest
campaign. The doughty Leathernecks are battling furiously to
widen their beachheads on the newly invaded Peleliu Island in the
Palaus. The Japanese are counter-attacking ferociously,
spearheading their assaults with large numbers of tanks. The
Marines, however, have refused to yield an inch and, in fact, have

scored gains of their own. First objective of the invaders is to capture the Peleliu airfield from which badly needed air support can be based. After that the ultimate objective is complete extermination of the enemy garrison.

Hints that the American First Army has scored a breakthrough of the Siegfried Line came from London today. It was believed that the Berlin-bound Yanks crashed through the erstwhile "impregnable" West Wall at a point south of Aachen, have isolated the stronghold, and have plunged twelve miles into Germany. Official confirmation of the successful breakthrough is still lacking but there seems to be little doubt as to the authenticity of the story.

From Paris it was learned that Brest, famous port on the tip of the Breton peninsula, has finally fallen to the besieging Allied forces. The surviving Nazi garrison of 12,000 troops capitulated after holding out staunchly since the disastrous (for the Nazis) days of early August. The port itself is said to be in utter ruins from the furious Allied attacks and the demolition of the beaten enemy.

Sunday, September 17, 1944: —President Roosevelt and Prime Minister Churchill ended their Quebec conference yesterday with a pledge that the full power of the mighty military machines of the two great nations will be thrown against Japan as soon as Europe has been liberated from the "corroding heel of Naziism." The two leaders said that final plans for the destruction of our common Oriental enemy were laid at the conference just ended. Japan's doom is sealed.

While we are enjoying the warm sunshine of a peaceful Sabbath Day, the flames of battle are raging with new fury on four major fighting fronts throughout the world. Probably the most sanguinary fighting is taking place on Peleliu Island in the Pacific, where battle-hardened U.S. Marines are closing in on the Japanese-held airfield. The Japs are resisting like madmen and the struggle is literally to the death.

In Italy, German and English tanks are engaged in a savage battle for Rimini, Adriatic anchor of the Gothic Line. The fall of this bastion will open up the gateway to the famous Po Valley and the Germans are striving desperately to prevent this catastrophe. What may well be the decisive Italian battle is on.

Finland, sad little republic which picked the losing horse, is fast becoming a battleground between its former ally Germany, and the conquering Russians. The Nazi garrison is determined to resist being ousted from the defeated country. The largest scale fighting is still taking place on the western front, where four mighty Allied armies are stabbing into the tough hide of the Nazi monster.

Monday, September 18, 1944: —In a daring exploit unique in military history, the first Allied airborne army has landed behind the German lines in Holland at a point somewhere near the northern end of the Siegfried Line. The sensational coup is obviously aimed at outflanking the West Wall and opening a pathway to the northern plains of Germany where Berlin lies a bare 300 miles away.

The exact location of the airborne army's landing has not been revealed but it is believed to be in the Eindhoven area, in southwest Holland. Several landings were made and at least one of them may have been on the east side of the Rhine River. Success of the bold stroke may turn the entire Siegfried Line and avoid the necessity of continuing the frontal assaults now in progress further south.

First reports indicate that at least 20,000 men of Lieut. General Lewis H. Brereton's First Airborne Army were landed in the first stages of the attack. The troops dropped by the thousands in parachutes and other thousands were brought in by glider trains that stretched for 285 miles. The skies literally rained soldiers and the initial landings took the Nazis by surprise. They quickly recovered, however, and threw in powerful assault forces against the skyborne invaders. Heavy fighting is in progress.

In the Pacific, American forces hacked their way inland on both Peleliu and Morotai, in the Palau and Molucca islands. On Peleliu the fighting was particularly bitter, with gains being chalked up in inches rather than miles.

Tuesday, September 19, 1944: —Armored units of the British Second Army are reported to have joined forces with the Allied airborne troops who landed behind the German lines yesterday. The successful junction of the two forces came after a spectacular dash of 44 miles across Holland by the Second Army.

The brilliant coup left more than 70,000 Nazi soldiers trapped in western Holland with only an outside chance of escaping. The success of the adventure also appears to have assured the early turning of the entire Siegfried Line and will permit our armor to break out upon the flat plains that lead southeastward to the rich Ruhr Valley and eastward to Berlin itself. We anxiously await confirmation of what appears to be a decisive victory for the first full-scale airborne offensive of the war.

As evidence of the Nazis' fear that the West Wall will soon be breached, is the report that the German leaders have ordered the evacuation of 2,000,000 people from Cologne and Aachen areas. The entire population of Cologne is to be moved, with the death penalty invoked for any violation of the evacuation order.

The principal fighting in the Pacific war is still raging on the tiny island of Peleliu in the Palaus. The U.S. Marines have encountered the stiffest resistance offered by the Japs since Guadalcanal but at last seem to have the situation well in hand. The capture of "Bloody Nose" ridge, which was stormed and taken today, represented the turning point of the campaign. The remaining enemy positions are hopeless.

Governor Dewey, the Republican nominee for President, was involved in a minor train wreck today. Mr. Dewey and his wife escaped injury but were badly shaken.

Wednesday, September 20, 1944: —It was revealed today that Adolf Hitler himself has assumed direction of all German forces on the western border of the Reich. This was the best news we have had since the Battle of Germany began. If the Nazi Fuhrer botches up the job as badly as he did the Russian campaign our armies should be in Berlin before snow flies. The one time "corporal" depends upon his infallible intuition rather than upon any knowledge of military science. Allied generals are hoping that the enemy will leave the would-be Napoleon in command long enough to assure a quick victory for the United Nations.

After seven days of fierce fighting the U.S. Marines have finally succeeded in taking all of their primary objectives on Peleliu Island in the Palaus. The Japanese have resisted fanatically, yielding only after flamethrowers, grenades, and bayonet had settled the argument in favor of the Americans. Thousands of enemy dead have been counted but the end of the campaign is not yet in sight. Our own losses have also been heavy, with the famous U.S. Marine First Division paying a particularly heavy toll for the tiny Pacific isle.

Here at home interest is beginning to rise in the Presidential campaign which is just getting under way. Governor Dewey of New York, the Republican nominee, is on the Pacific coast for a series of campaign speeches which he hopes will swing California, Oregon, and Washington to his side. Last night the New York Governor spoke at Portland, scoring heavily with his attack on the "indispensable man" theory. Tomorrow, the Republican nominee is scheduled to arrive in San Francisco for another important speech in the Civic Auditorium.

Thursday, September 21, 1944: —Even while the whole world is being ravaged and destroyed by war, the American system of democracy continues to operate. In the midst of bloodshed and bitter fighting, calling for their utmost effort, the American people can find time to engage in a serious election campaign in which they must decide who is to lead and direct them through the undoubtedly trying years that lie ahead. A good example of the way America decides its own destiny, was the tumultuous greeting given Thomas E. Dewey, Governor of New York, and Republican candidate for the Presidency of the United States, when he arrived here this morning. The youthful nominee rode up Market Street this forenoon, which over 50,000 citizens lined the curbs to cheer him. He looked pleased and even a little astonished at the warm-hearted welcome from this supposedly pro-Roosevelt city by the Golden Gate. Even the weather greeted him with one of her brightest smiles. There was no fog, not even a cloud. It may have been a sign, if you believe in signs.

The Republican candidate is scheduled to speak over the radio from the Civic Auditorium this evening. I couldn't go to hear him direct so I am preparing to listen in—just fifteen minutes from now. I will finish this record before he begins, and will comment on the speech in tomorrow's piece.

The war news tonight centers around an important bridge across the Waal Rhine in the vicinity of Nijmegen in Holland. A furious battle is raging for possession of the bridge, across which the Allied armies hope to push into the mighty industrial Ruhr

Valley of the Reich. Latest reports indicate that the battle for the bridge has already been won.

Friday, September 22, 1944: —Thomas E. Dewey's speech last night was a serious discussion, the keynote of which was "it is time for a change." The Republican nominee asked the burning question, "Can we have both political freedom and economic security in the years to come?" Under the New Deal Government, with its theory of "one-man" rule and its tendencies toward regimentation, he thinks not; but with a change of administration and a change of governmental philosophy, he believes we can. Right or wrong, the youthful candidate is completely honest. He knows that we can never go back to the old "dog eat dog" days of natural economic laws in which the Federal Government never intervened for the common good but he does believe that we can have social reforms and social security without governmental dictation of our every move. We can have our political freedom at the same time that we plan and control our economic life so as to avoid disastrous inflations and deflations, more commonly known as booms and depressions. There is considerable food for thought in the Republican candidate's words.

News from the war fronts is not so good tonight. The British airborne division that landed across the Rhine at Arnheim, in northeastern Holland, has been trapped by furiously counter-attacking Nazis troops. Arnheim is a key stronghold, commanding the approaches to northwestern Germany and its capture would outflank the Siegfried Line and open the road to Berlin. The Germans, therefore, are fighting desperately to prevent its seizure. British Second Army forces are striving furiously to puncture the Nazi noose thrown around their airborne division but thus far have failed. Nevertheless, the paratroops are holding out with supreme courage.

Saturday, September 23, 1944: —The situation of the trapped paratroop army across the Rhine at Arnheim is extremely desperate. British Second Army tanks blasted a narrow corridor through the besieging Nazi lines to rescue a small band of the heroic sky troopers but the main airborne force is almost hopelessly trapped on the far bank of the river. Vastly superior (in numbers) enemy forces are attacking the trapped army with flame-throwing tanks, heavy artillery, and fierce infantry charges. So far, the valiant paratroops have beaten off every attack, inflicting terrible losses on the foe. Their own casualties have also been very severe.

To the south, sanguinary battles are raging between General George S. Patton's American Third Army and the Germans defending the Moselle, Seille, and Meuthe river approaches to the Reich. American gunners ambushed one powerful German tank column attempting to counter-attack, and destroyed sixty tanks, dispersing the rest.

On the flaming eastern front, Russian troops are reported breaking into the outskirts of Warsaw, amid indications that the Nazis are preparing to withdraw from the former Polish capital.

At the same time, another mighty Red Army was reported smashing across the border of Hungary, 113 miles from Budapest, where milling crowds were clamoring in the streets for peace. Hitler's hold on his last important Balkan ally is slipping fast.

Sunday, September 24, 1944: —Reinforcements have reached the trapped British Airborne Division across the upper Rhine. Although a solid junction between the beleaguered paratroops and the advancing British Second Army is not claimed, it is revealed that some units of the relieving force have reached the Arnheim pocket, bringing welcome aid to the valiant "lost Division." The Germans are attacking with ever-increasing ferocity, hoping to wipe out the trapped "chutist" army before the main body of the advancing British force arrives. An epic of Hell is being written at Arnheim.

The Italian front has flared again. Mighty blows by both the British Eighth and the American Fifth Armies have breached the Germans' Gothic Line and the Allied troops are pursuing the fleeing Nazis toward Bologne and the wide valley of the Po. The concerted action of the two famous Allied armies has again destroyed a powerful line of German fortifications. The Gothic Line was reportedly stronger than either the formidable Gustav or Adolf Hitler lines in southern Italy, but once again Allied men and equipment have proved themselves superior to Nazi fortifications.

Last night President Roosevelt made his first political speech of the Presidential campaign. The President spoke before the AFL

Teamsters Union and was in a particularly jovial mood. He was given a terrific, but obviously trumped up, ovation that lasted many minutes before he began his talk. The democratic nominee took many a sly crack at the opposition but the gayety of the speech and occasion was a far cry from the seriousness of these "tragic times" which the President had previously said would prevent him from campaigning in "the usual sense."

Monday, September 25, 1944: —Bad news from Holland tonight. The valiant band of British paratroopers trapped across the upper reaches of the Rhine, were almost rescued by desperately advancing British Second Army troops who had cut, at the cost of many casualties, a narrow corridor almost to their besieged comrades. But before the rescue could be effected, ferocious counter-attacks by powerful German SS "elite" forces succeeded in chopping through the corridor, again isolating the dwindling remnants of the Airborne Division. Death or capture of the remaining "chutist" heroes now seems inevitable.

The news is better from the Pacific where bold thrusts by veteran U.S. Marine forces have all but completed the conquest of Peleliu Island. As evidence of the ferocious character of the fighting for this tiny Pacific stronghold is the revelation that 8,000 Japs have been killed and only 11 have been taken prisoner. In this fiercest of all wars, our enemy fights literally to the death. In three years, the total number of Japanese prisoners taken still numbers in the hundreds rather than the thousands. Frequently they destroy themselves rather than surrender, which, in many ways, is advantageous to us. But the Jap is a tough, capable fighter and our boys who encounter him do not underestimate him. Despite his capabilities, however, he has met his master in the normally peace-loving American lad who just took up war making a short three years ago. No one any longer doubts the truth of that statement.

Tuesday, September 26, 1944: —For ten long days, the grim band of British "Red Devil" paratroopers have held their patch of hell across the upper Rhine. Despite the fury of endless attacks by powerful German armies, despite a ceaseless rain of bombs and shells, the dwindling remnants of the skyborne British army have refused to yield. Demands for their surrender have only aroused them to new and unbelievable heights of resistance.

A Citizen's Chronological History of World War II

Before their lines great piles of German bodies are mute evidence of their fierce determination to hold on until relieved—or die. The story of Arnheim will undoubtedly be one of the heroic tales of this war.

America's mighty battleships of the air, the B-29's, have again raided Japan's industrial centers in Manchuria. A large force of the big bombers was believed to have made the attack, which was aimed at the big manufacturing cities of Anshan, Penshihu, and Dairen in southern Manchuria. Heavy damage was caused by the tremendous weight of explosives carried by the great warplanes. Our losses, if any, were not revealed, although the enemy, as usual, claimed that thirteen of the raiders were shot down. Discount that by about twelve or thirteen and you will just about have the truth.

Thomas E. Dewey, the Republican Presidential nominee, replied to the President's Saturday night speech, in a dynamic address at Oklahoma City last night. It was his fightingest speech of the campaign so far, and struck hard at Roosevelt's wisecracking, ridiculing opening speech, which the Republican nominee said, "plumbed the depths of demagogy by dragging into this campaign, the names of Hitler and Goebbels and descended to quoting from Mein Kampf. The election battle is now really underway.

Wednesday, September 27, 1944: —Marshal Josef Stalin once clamored loudly for a second front. Today the Allies opened a fifth front in Albania. Once again powerful Allied seaborne and airborne forces swept ashore on Europe's coastline to present a new threat to Hitler's ill-gotten empire. First reports of the new invasion indicate that the Allied forces struck across the Adriatic from recently acquired bases in Italy and landed at several places along a wide front which included Albania and the islands off Yugoslavia. Initial landings were successful and firm beachheads have been established, from which it is expected that the Allied forces will strike inland towards a junction with Marshal Tito's Partisans and the Soviet armies advancing from the east. A meeting of the two Allied forces would spring a trap of steel on upwards of 200,000 Nazi troops still occupying Greece and the southern Balkans.

The epic story of the British Red Devil paratroop division which was trapped at Arnheim across the upper Rhine in Holland, ended today with the successful evacuation of the survivors of the ten day siege. Out of some 8,000 men dropped into the ill-fated pocket, barely 1,700 returned. Approximately 1,200 wounded had to be left behind while the other 5,000 were either killed or captured during the long battle. The survivors were still full of fight and were ordered to withdraw only after their supplies ran out and bad weather prevented further assistance from the air. Although apparently defeated, it will take history to evaluate their sacrifice. It must be remembered that their heroic resistance pinned down overwhelming enemy forces for ten crucial days during which other Allied units successfully fashioned a trap around approximately 100,000 Nazi troops caught behind Allied lines in western Holland.

Thursday, September 28, 1944: —Both ends of Germany's mighty West Wall quivered and shook under the sledgehammer blows from two powerful Allied armies. In northeastern Holland the British Second Army launched a heavy attack from Nijmegen while thousands of Allied paratroopers rained down at Hertogenbosch, in central Holland, in a determined effort to prevent the escape of more than 100,000 German troops cornered in the west.

Hundreds of miles to the south General George S. Patton's American Third Army followed a rolling aero-artillery barrage into the southern flank of the Siegfried Line, crashing their way through the maze of Nazi pillboxes and foxholes in the Forest of Parroy towards the Rhineland city of Strasbourg. The enemy withdrew slowly, contesting bitterly for every foot of German soil. Nevertheless, substantial gains have been scored by the determined Yanks, according to latest news reports.

In the Pacific our invading forces have practically completed the conquest of Peleliu Island. Only the usual mop-up of fanatically resisting bands of Japs remains. Already American planes are operating from airstrips won from the enemy. From the springboard of Peleliu, our forces are expected to speedily conquer other islands of the Palau group. From there the next obvious step would be to the Philippines themselves. But our military leaders do not always do the obvious thing so we can only surmise at the next move. However, you can be sure that General MacArthur, if no one else, is making plans for the speedy liberation of his beloved islands. He is definitely going back and I am willing to bet it won't be in the too distant future.

Friday, September 29, 1944: —Warfare of a rugged and bloody nature continues to rage along a 300 mile stretch of Germany's western border. Dents have been made in the Nazis' West Wall armor but, so far, an actual breakthrough of "St. Lo" proportions has not been accomplished. The Germans are fighting with courage and determination, at times fanatically and to the death, resulting in heavy casualties on both sides. The several Allied armies are maintaining constant pressure all along the line, feeling for the soft spot through which our masses of men and armor can roll to force the decision.

In a day of fierce fighting the spotlight fell upon General George S. Patton's famous Third Army, whole tanks and tank destroyers caught a large force of German armor in an ambush as the Nazis fled from the Forest of Parroy under a devastating attack by Allied Planes, and destroyed at least 82 enemy tanks. Final tally may raise the score far above that figure.

To the south veteran American and French troops of the American Seventh Army fought their way into Belfort Gap, famous gateway to the Reich. Sundown found leading elements of Lieut. General Alexander M. Patch's army within ten miles of the fortress city of Belfort itself.

Back on the English Channel coast the siege of Calais, where a suicidal garrison of Nazis are still holding out, was lifted until 2 p.m. tomorrow under an armistice agreement to permit the evacuation of some 20,000 starving civilians from the ruined city.

Saturday, September 30, 1944: —Military parades have always been associated with war but in this one there have been few. Today we witnessed one of those few—an hour-long parade up Market Street, inaugurating the annual War Chest drive which this year has been allotted the unprecedented total of $3,792,742.00 for San Francisco alone. The parade featured new Army motorized equipment of all kinds, wounded veterans, WACs, Waves, Spars, negro and white troops, and a generous sprinkling of bands, whose stirring music really make a parade. It was very interesting.

Back on the war news we find that powerful Allied armies are pouring into Belfort Gap, threatening the German province of Bavaria with imminent invasion. Armored units of the American Seventh Army are leading the attack which crossed the southern spur of the Vosges mountains and is now closing in upon the city of Belfort itself. Huge formations of Allied bombers and fighters are pacing the attack, lashing the enemy with a fury equal to that which preceded D-Day in Normandy.

In the seething Balkans the red torrent of Russian manpower has swept all the way across Rumania and has entered Yugoslavia after crossing the Danube against insignificant opposition. It is expected that the forces of Marshal Tito, famed Partisan leader, will soon join with the advancing Russian tide. If Hitler would rescue the estimated 200,000 Nazi troops now in Greece, Albania, and southern Yugoslavia, he had better withdraw them immediately. A few days more and a trap of steel will have snapped shut around them.

October

Sunday, October 1, 1944: —American forces have moved fast since the seizure of Peleliu Island in the Palau group. Although isolated enemy detachments are still fighting to the death on Peleliu, the island is ours to all extents and purposes. In addition, our Marine and Army invasion forces have seized eight other isles and islets in the group to further consolidate our position in this strategic area of the central Pacific battleground. No power the Japs can muster can oust us from the Palau's now. Six hundred miles further west lie the frantically beckoning Philippines. Have no fear, we are coming—and soon!

Evidence that the German leaders themselves have given up hope of victory was revealed today in a captured Nazi order to officers of the Wehrmacht on the western front. The order directed all German officers, except some junior officers, to save themselves from death in battle so that an officers corp. will be preserved to prepare for a third attempt at world conquest. The junior officers were ordered to die a hero's death in the front lines with their men in order to spur the troops' flagging morale. Some order—from the new order.

The only gloomy outlook in the war, from the Allied viewpoint, is the situation in China. The Japs are undoubtedly giving the weary Chinese an awful beating in the Hunan province fighting. The enemy is advancing rapidly in his drive to cut China in two and has now reached a point only thirty miles from the strategic city of Kweilin. Several U.S. airbases, built at tremendous cost in coolie labor, have already been overrun by the rampaging Jap army. Yes, China needs speedy help.

Monday, October 2, 1944: —After a terrific artillery barrage in which more than 30,000 shells were fired, Lieut. General Courtney H. Hodges' First Army ripped into the Germans' Siegfried defenses on a twenty mile front north of Aachen today and, in the initial phase, succeeded in smashing through at least a mile in the direction of the Rhine. German pillboxes and concrete fortifications by the score were pulverized and overrun. Violent fighting, including the hand to hand variety, was encountered in the advance.

On the eastern front, the Russians are advancing at a mile an hour pace through Yugoslavia and have reached a point only 40 miles from the Belgrade-Athens highway, main artery of supply—or escape—for the 200,000 Nazis in the southern Balkans.

In Warsaw a bloody battle is raging between the Polish Home Army and the German occupation forces. The Poles have mustered an army of 200,000 men and women, under the command of General Bor, and have risen to oust the Nazis from their former capital. The fighting has been going on for some time, the patriots having risen at the approach of the Red Army, and the situation at the present time is unfavorable, since the Germans have stopped the Russians cold at the gates of the city. Unless the Soviet armies are able to break through, the position of the Home Army within the city will be desperate. Even now it is hinted that their supplies and ammunition are dwindling fast. Help must come soon or their sacrifice will have been in vain.

Tuesday, October 3, 1944: —Gold braid in large quantities was in evidence in San Francisco today as top naval leaders met here to discuss Pacific strategy. The leaders included Secretary of the Navy Forrestal, Admirals King, Nimitz, and Spruance, as well as several vice-Admirals. You can rest assured that the meeting spells more bad news for the Japanese.

German West Wall defenses are receiving an unmerciful pounding at the present time. Either the big drive is on or General Eisenhower's forces are topping all records in "softening up" operations. Tremendous pressure is being exerted all along a 450 mile front, with three sizeable salients already driven into the maze of fortifications that constitute the Siegfried Line. Lieut. General Hodges' American First Army added four more miles to their penetration of the German lines which began yesterday in the vicinity of Aachen, some thirty miles west of Cologne. When our troops have entered the latter city we can then consider that the West Wall has been crumbled. But those thirty miles will probably be the bloodiest miles ever trod by the foot of man. The Nazis are resisting fanatically and have studded the entire distance with masses of foxholes, machinegun nests, and artillery emplacements. The Yanks have their job cut out for them. May Providence lend its aid and so spare as many of our gallant lads as possible.

Wednesday, October 4, 1944: —The Battle of the Siegfried Line is still raging, with the brunt of the current fighting being borne by Lieut. General Courtney H. Hodges' American First Army in the area about Aachen and by Lieut. General George S. Patton's American Third Army at key bastions in Hitler's West Wall. Ten miles north of Aachen, General Hodges sent his Sherman tanks and supporting infantry smashing into the German lines for an initial penetration of more than two miles. Reports, however, are too meager to more than surmise the actual extent of the "breakthrough."

To the south, in the vicinity of Metz, General Patton's troops are assaulting Fort Driant, one of the most powerful fortresses in the world. It is said that heavy artillery shells bounce off the thick concrete walls like rubber balls. The Yanks are using flaming oil and phosphorous grenades to flush the fanatical Nazis from their subterranean dugouts. Latest reports state that the Doughboys are perched atop one corner of the Fort and are engaged in fierce fighting for possession of the remainder of the stronghold.

Here at home a famous American died today. No record of these times should fail to mention the passing of Al Smith, famous as the wearer of the "Brown Derby" and a leading figure in American politics for many years. Al Smith had many followers in his day and ran for President in 1928. Although defeated in that race, he wielded considerable influence in national affairs for many years afterwards. He was 70.

The World Series in baseball started today between the once lowly St. Louis Browns and the St. Louis Cardinals. The Browns won the opener 2 to 1.

Thursday, October 5, 1944: —Still another major front has been opened against the Germans. This time the Allies have returned to Greece, storming ashore in force on the Greek mainland for the first time since the losing Battle of Greece in 1941. German opposition to the Allied air and sea attack was ineffective and virtually the entire Peloponnesus peninsula was liberated in the first day's operations. The Nazis are feverishly engaged in blowing up the Corinth canal and bridges in an effort to impede the Allied advance northward. How does it feel to be cornered, Adolf?

A great armored battle appears to be developing on the German plains before Cologne. American armor bursting from the confines of the Siegfried Line collided head-on with Nazi panzer reserves rushing up to plug the breach. A titanic battle of the metal giants impends.

Other U.S. troops captured Beggendorf, 31 miles from Cologne, while their comrades prepared to storm the defenses of Aachen and Geilenkirchen after broadening the breach through the maze of Siegfried fortifications to a width of six miles.

Activity in the Pacific war has subsided for the moment. Only report today was the revelation that our gallant undersea boats have destroyed 11 more Jap ships, bringing their grand total for the war so far to 772 Japanese vessels sunk.

The St. Louis Cards evened the series today by beating the St. Louis Browns 3 to 2 in and eleven inning game.

Friday, October 6, 1944: —For the 167th time in this war Berlin felt the weight of Allied bombs last night. The raid against the German capital and surrounding area was carried out by the greatest armada of American planes yet dispatched against a single target in a single raid. Over 2,250 U.S. heavy bombers and fighters participated in the attack which rained incalculable destruction on Berlin factories, including tank and gun assembly plants, aero engine works, and huge supply depots. Nineteen American bombers and ten fighters were lost.

The American armored thrust towards the Rhine has reached a point barely 27 miles from Cologne. Fierce fighting is in progress, much of it in wooded areas so dense that the battle resembles the bitter jungle fighting in New Guinea and Guadalcanal. Our troops are retaining the initiative and are advancing slowly in the face of desperate resistance. The German High Command apparently is committing important units of its remaining crack combat divisions to this battle, in a desperate effort to wipe out the American spearhead which has broken through the vaunted Siegfried Line. Upon the outcome of this engagement may depend the answer to the question of whether the European war is to end this fall or is to drag out into the spring or summer of 1945.

In Greece the Allied liberators have swept to within 90 miles of Athens, have captured Port Rion on the Gulf of Corinth, and have landed on the Dodecanese Island of Rhodes. Other Allied troops have made fresh landings in Albania. Greek troops and Partisans are materially aiding the invasion.

Saturday, October 7, 1944: —The breakthrough breach in the Siegfried Line has been widened to six miles by Lieut. General Courtney H. Hodges' hard-fighting American First Army. At several points Nazi resistance virtually collapsed as the Doughboys and their tanks lunged forward in a power drive that overran and captured two German towns, Alsdorf and Basenweiler. A major victory is in sight.

Elsewhere along the German border other American, British, and Canadian armies continued to maintain strong pressure against the Siegfried fortifications, both as an aid to the First Army and as an attempt to find other weak links in the German lines. General Patton's Third Army is finding the going extremely rugged in its attempt to reduce Fort Driant on the outskirts of Metz. The Yanks enlarged their footing on the southwest corner of the massive stone and concrete bastion, while other troops succeeded in securing a hold on the northwest corner. Heavy fighting and considerable dying remains to be done before the job is finished.

The British are getting sweet revenge for the bitter defeat they suffered in Greece three years ago. Today the Nazis are feverishly evacuating Greece and the Aegean Islands under merciless attack by land, sea, and air. British invasion forces are sweeping upon Athens at a speed that promises to liberate the tortured Greek capital within days. Other British and Greek forces are swarming ashore on the Aegean Islands under the protection of naval guns and RAF bombs. A fearful toll is being exacted from the Nazi garrisons attempting to flee by sea or air. There is joy in Greece these days.

Sunday, October 8, 1944: —The U.S. First Army is pouring through the six mile wide gap in the Siegfried defenses. Four more German towns have been seized in the past twenty four hours. Beggendorf, Herbach, Merkstein, and Hofstadt were the towns occupied by the hard-hitting Yanks who had previously seized Alsdorf and Basweiler. With the success of the breakthrough drive increasing rapidly, General Hodges' army is clamping a powerful pincers around the key Nazi stronghold of Aachen. Capture of the latter bastion is a prerequisite to any all-out drive on Cologne.

Since the latter part of August representatives of Russia, China, Britain, and the United States have been conferring at Dumbarton Oaks on plans for a world peace organization after this war. Today the conference ended with apparent agreement reached on a master design that its framers hope will assure peace in the world for many years to come. Details of the plan are not yet ready to be announced but the broad outline is similar to that of the former League of Nations, but with realistic changes that its sponsors feel will assure its effectiveness. Compromises will necessarily have to be reached between the major powers on many of the operating details and functions but the plan is, at the very least, a good beginning towards effective organization among peace loving nations to abolish the hideous waste and destruction of war.

Further success in the Greek invasion was reported today. According to latest word from Cairo the Nazis have abandoned Corinth and are fleeing Greece by every available means.

Monday, October 9, 1944: —Despite furious German counter-attacks the American First Army has succeeded in clamping the pincers around the formidable Nazi stronghold of Aachen. Only a narrow corridor remains unoccupied by U.S. troops but that corridor is under fire from thousands of our big guns. Any attempt by the Aachen garrison to run that gauntlet would inevitably end in annihilation.

In Holland an Anglo-Canadian army is battling the Nazis for possession of the Schelde Estuary and the great port of Antwerp. Capture of Antwerp would give our forces a magnificent supply port close to the fighting front.

To the south General Patton's American Third Army, partially bottlenecked by the impasse at Fort Driant, scored another four mile gain between Metz and Nancy while inflicting heavy casualties on the stubbornly resisting enemy.

In the Pacific the United States fleet apparently is tossing bold challenge after bold challenge in the face of the Japanese, hoping thereby to entice the Jap Imperial Fleet into a show-down battle. The latest move was a daring foray by an American task force into Jap waters only 1,100 miles from Tokyo. The warships struck at the enemy's Marcus Island base, heaping tremendous destruction throughout the island in a day-long bombardment. Sixteen inch shells silenced shore batteries and wrecked shore installations. Enemy opposition apparently was limited and ineffectual.

The St. Louis Cards today won the World's baseball championship by winning the best four out of six games from the Browns. The score of the final game was 3 to 1.

Tuesday, October 10, 1944: —If last Sunday's Marcus Island raid was a challenge to the Japanese Imperial Fleet, today's news indicates that our fleet is going in to get them if they won't come out and fight. It was reported from Pearl Harbor today that Admiral William S. Halsey's famous carrier task force, boldly disregarding the possibility of encountering the entire Grand Fleet of Japan (and probably hoping they would flush out the skulking enemy warships) struck in great force against the Ryukyu Islands only 200 miles from the Japanese homeland. Fifty eight enemy ships were sunk or badly damaged and an unannounced number of Jap planes were shot from the skies by the planes of the American carrier fleet. Nice going, Navy!

Lieut. General Courtney H. Hodges' American First Army has the Nazi garrison trapped in Aachen. Hoping to avoid more needless fighting and bloodshed, the American commander has given the Germans a 24 hour ultimatum, demanding that they surrender or face complete extermination. At least one company of Nazi troops has already accepted the offer to lay down their arms. It is doubtful if all will surrender because there are many fanatical Hitler SS troopers and officers in the town who will fight to the death and will not hesitate to shoot down any of their own men who attempt to quit. The blast of a high explosive shell is the only language some of them can understand.

Another great American died late Sunday night. Wendell Willkie, candidate for President in 1940, vigorous champion of the American way, author of "One World" and leader of millions of liberal Republicans died unexpectedly of a series of heart attacks. He was only 52 and appeared to be strong and healthy. His loss is a serious blow to the leadership and brains of America.

Wednesday, October 11, 1944: —Aachen, 1,100 year old German city where Charlemagne was born, today died a flaming death under a tremendous rain of fire and steel from American planes and guns. The die-hard Nazi garrison spurned the American ultimatum to surrender and by doing so, sealed their own doom as well as that of the ancient city. Three hundred U.S. fighter-bombers, and 200 heavy artillery pieces that ringed the town, cascaded destruction into the German positions for five long hours. Great fires raged through the city's streets unchecked while all water, power, and other public utilities ceased to exist.

A desperate attempt on the part of the Nazis to reinforce the beleaguered town was smashed with fearful losses in men and equipment. As though bereft of their senses, the Germans attempted the relief move in broad daylight without air cover. Our own planes spotted the attack as it began and plastered it unmercifully. The ill-fated attempt ended in mass slaughter of the enemy as our big guns and machine guns joined with the planes to cut the relief column to bits.

Winston Churchill is now in Moscow for a conference with Josef Stalin. The exact purpose of the meeting is not known but apparently is in connection with the recent Quebec parley between President Roosevelt and the British Prime Minister, in which Stalin was unable to participate. The Soviet Premier was entertained at a dinner in the British Embassy this evening. It is reported that this is the first time the Red Marshal has accepted an invitation to dine at any foreign embassy. It is a good omen for Anglo-Russian relations.

Thursday, October 12, 1944: —In 1492 Columbus discovered America. As a consequence, in peace time, millions of Americans enjoy a holiday on October 12th. This year, however, America is at war and most Americans worked as usual. Planes were built, tanks were constructed, guns and munitions were produced as usual, despite the anniversary of Christopher's famous discovery. Banks and some business houses were closed, however, and because our business is in a slight lull between War Loan Drives, we were lucky enough to have the day off. It was a welcome break from the steady grind, week after week, and I didn't realize how really weary I had become until I relaxed today. After puttering around the garden all day I feel much better this evening and should be raring to go again in the morning.

An almost hysterical Tokyo radio today reported that Formosa, Japan's important island base on the northern approaches to the Philippines, has been attacked by a huge fleet of American aircraft. The Tokyo broadcast stated that more than 1,000 American planes raided the island at dawn today and the attack is still continuing many hours later. The Japs, of course, make fantastic claims of American planes shot down. No confirmation of the raid has come from Admiral Nimitz' headquarters, although it is too early to expect a communiqué, since a radio blackout is nearly always maintained while a major operation is in progress, for obvious security reasons.

American shock troops are storming the ruins of blazing Aachen tonight. Part of the city has already been overrun by the advancing Doughboys.

Friday, October 13, 1944: —One of the greatest air-sea battles of the Pacific war appears to be raging off the coast of Formosa. The engagement reported by the Tokyo radio yesterday has been confirmed by Admiral Chester W. Nimitz' Pacific Fleet Headquarters where it is stated that the battle is roaring into its third day. The famous U.S. Third Fleet, composed of aircraft carriers, battleships, cruisers, and destroyers, is engaged in the action while hundreds of planes from both sides are involved. Huge B-29 bombers from China bases are aiding the carrier planes in attacking Japanese targets on Formosa.

Details of the damage inflicted on the enemy in the first two days of the big strike against Formosa are not yet available but returning flyers have all been exultant over the success of their missions. The known score for the first 48 hours is 63 large enemy ships plus 37 smaller craft sunk or left in a sinking condition and at least 396 Jap planes shot down. In addition hangars, warehouses, oil dumps, docks and industrial works throughout Formosa were completely wrecked. For these magnificent results our forces paid a toll of 45 carrier planes although some of the pilots were rescued.

In Europe the spotlight still rests on the fortress town of Aachen where American Doughboys are engaged in bitter fighting with the surrounded and doomed Nazi garrison. The Yanks are storming the city from two sides and are slowly mopping-up the fanatical defenders.

After 42 months of bitter Nazi occupation, the tortured Greek capital of Athens is free again. Greek patriots rose up as British forces neared the city and seized control while the Nazis fled.

Saturday, October 14, 1944: —Furious air battles are still raging over Formosa. Over 450 U.S. carrier planes struck the island this morning while a force of approximately 100 mighty Super-Fortresses roared in from China to blast the Japanese naval repair base of Okayama in the afternoon. The size and persistence of the American attacks have led the military leaders of Japan to broadcast a warning to their people that an invasion of Formosa, the Ryukyu Islands, or the Philippines appears imminent. Let us hope the Tokyo warning is correct, although it is possible that the objective of the great air-sea attack on Formosa is to force the Japanese Grand Fleet into battle. How much longer can they afford to wait? Certainly not until we bombard Tokyo itself from the sea. In any case, it is clear that events of tremendous importance are shaping up in the western Pacific.

The Nazis are evidently trying to make a Stalingrad out of Aachen. Our forces are having to battle their way through the town house by house. The going is slow and bitter, with flamethrowers, grenades, and bayonets the principal weapons. The Germans are putting into practice the fearful lessons learned from the Russians during the fateful battle for the Volga city and making most effective use of the piles of rubble in the ruined city. The Russians proved that piles of tumbled masonry make excellent fortifications from which the defenders must be blasted one by one. The Yanks, however, intend to prove that such a tough nut can be cracked. Where the Nazis failed at Stalingrad, the Yanks intend to succeed at Aachen.

Sunday, October 15, 1944: —While on all other fronts the forces of the United Nations are driving ahead victoriously against a reeling and beaten foe, in China the gallant but weary armies of Chiang Kai-Shek are themselves being driven and crushed by an overwhelming avalanche of Japanese troops. Finding themselves unable to cope with the mighty American sea and air forces in the Pacific, the Japs are obviously directing their main efforts at entrenching themselves on the Asiatic mainland where, by facing Britain and the United States with the prospect of a long, bitter war of attrition, they may hope to force the acceptance of a compromise peace. To accomplish this purpose calls for a quick knock-out of China before Admiral Nimitz, General MacArthur and Company are able to affect a landing on the coast of Asia. Today's news indicates that the Japs are making considerable headway towards this objective. Their powerful drive across Kwangsi province, aimed at cutting free China in half, has overrun Kweiping, where the heroic Chinese garrison was killed to the last man. The next phase of the Japanese drive will be directed against the capital of the province and key Chinese defense center, Kweilin. Chinese leaders predict that the outcome of the drive against the latter city will determine the outcome of their war against the invader. For China, the situation is undeniably crucial.

Whole blocks of German buildings were blown sky high today as American troops mopped up ruined Aachen. Snipers were not ferreted out; the buildings in which they were located were simply blasted out of existence. Bazooka teams with their mighty rocket projectiles made short shrift of enemy pockets of resistance.

Monday, October 16, 1944: —Some two and one half years ago American guns fell silent on Bataan and Corregidor after courageous Yanks and their gallant Filipino comrades were finally overcome by overwhelming Japanese forces. Today, as evidence that their heroic time-gaining stand was not in vain, American bombs and guns blasted the sacred soil of Bataan in a return engagement. It was a strike solely by air but it gave assurance that we shall return—and soon.

The aerial attack on Bataan and the Manila area was carried out by planes from Admiral William F. Halsey's Third U.S. Fleet now operating in the waters off Formosa. Other U.S. planes struck at Aparri, in northern Luzon, where Japanese forces first launched their invasion of the Philippines in 1941. There was no further news received regarding Japanese reports of a full-scale naval battle off Formosa, due possibly to the customary security blackout during major operations.

There have undoubtedly been furious aerial battles over the Philippines and Formosa during the past week, regardless of whether a major naval clash is in progress or not. This is indicated by Admiral Nimitz' report that the Japs have lost between 705 and 725 planes in the seven day period. One of our principal objectives, therefore, seems to be the crippling of the Japanese air force preparatory to a major invasion attempt. Look out, Mr. Tojo!

The Germans today confirmed the oft-reported death of Marshal Rommel, the famed "Desert Fox." The Marshall died of head wounds suffered in an automobile crash in France caused by strafing Allied planes. "He who lives by the sword shall also die by the sword," sayeth the scriptures.

Tuesday, October 17, 1944: —Let's take a brief look at the situation on the home front:

Rationing is still in effect on many foodstuffs, although most canned vegetables were recently removed from the list. Butter has been raised to 20 red points which automatically increases our consumption of margarine. Some meats are point free but our favorite beef cuts are still rare and require many points—if we can get them at all. Such things as whipping cream, Jell-O, and bananas are the items we miss the most, although we have recently had some of the latter and received a few packages of Jell-O through the mail from relatives in Salt Lake City. All in all, we still eat very well, despite the fact that our food costs are double what they were in 1939.

The tight rationing of gasoline is the worst inconvenience of all. On an A card, unless a person is unpatriotic enough to patronize the black market, the car is laid up for months at a time. We have carefully shunned the illegal gas and, as a consequence, are frequently without a car to do the necessary shopping on the weekends. That makes it tough on my wife who has four youngsters to herd around. But we always mange somehow.

War industries are still booming in the Bay Area, resulting in continued transportation tangles. A feeling of impending victory, however, has caused a huge turnover in many plants, as thousands of workers begin to shift back towards more promising peacetime jobs. This has caused tremendous problems and has resulted in some loss of production. By and large, however, the sinews of war are still being turned out in adequate quantities in Bay Area plants.

Wednesday, October 18, 1944: —To continue with the home front review:

Blackouts and air-raid precautions are a thing of the past in the Bay Area. Thanks for this are due our gallant fighting men, Army, Navy, and Marines, who have driven the oriental enemy back from our doorstep and are even now attacking him vigorously in his own front yard. Raids are still considered a possibility, though remote and suicidal, but it is believed that the Japs are too busy trying to defend their homeland to bother throwing rocks in our yard. I have always had the hunch, however, that the war will not end without the Japs trying at least one raid on what, to them, is America—San Francisco. I hope I am wrong.

San Francisco, itself, is a war boom town, with the appearance of a military camp. To walk down Market Street is to hobnob with the Army, Navy, and Marine Corps. The streets are literally colored with the blue of the Navy, the khaki of the Army, and the olive green of the Marine. And not a few of the uniforms are fitted to feminine forms, the WAC, the WAVE, the SPAR, and the Lady Marine. Interspersed with the familiar uniforms are the swashbuckling big-brimmed hats of t he Australians, the trim, jaunty blue of the RAF, and the varied and curiosity-arousing colors of many another United Nation's serviceman. They're here today and gone tomorrow and all bent on having a good time. Money, wine, and liquors flow like water. It's a rip-roaring, hell-bent-for-leather town that's having itself a time in this man's war.

And in between times, we're having an election campaign. Both candidates, Roosevelt and Dewey, are swinging with both fists and everyone is enjoying it immensely.

Thursday, October 19, 1944: —An unconfirmed but probably correct report has come from Japanese sources to the effect that American amphibious forces have invaded the Philippine Islands. The Tokyo radio broadcast the news that two great armadas of American ships have entered Leyte Gulf in the central Philippines and have begun landing operations on Leyte and Suluan Islands. The Japs state that General MacArthur and Admiral Raymond Spruance are in command of the invading forces. This is very likely particularly in view of General MacArthur's well known wish to lead the forces of liberation back to his beloved islands. We anxiously await confirmation of this great news by Allied authorities.

Fighting on the western European front has been bitter but indecisive during the past few days. The Yanks are still engaged in mopping up the German city of Aachen and are now in possession of approximated half of the German stronghold. To the north British, Canadian, and American troops are sloshing eastward through the deep, sticky mud of Holland, driving the Nazis slowly back towards the Maa River. There will be very little good fighting weather on the western front between now and next spring.

The eastern European front has flared into new activity with the Germans admitting that the Red Army has broken across the borders of East Prussia. The new attack was made in great force, the Russians obviously hoping to break through the Nazis' East Wall defenses and smash on to Danzig, Koenigsberg and the rest of the German Junkers homeland.

Friday, October 20, 1944: —IT'S TRUE! AMERICAN TROOPS UNDER GENERAL MACARTHUR HAVE INVADED THE PHILIPPINES! In a mighty operation similar in size and scope to the Normandy invasion, General Douglas MacArthur, of Bataan and Corregidor, led approximately 250,000 American troops back to his beloved islands from whence he was forced to flee more than two and one half years ago. He has returned as he promised he would and he is there to stay. The General himself stepped ashore on Leyte Island shortly after the first waves of Yanks smashed their way through the surf in tanks, bull dozers, and armored cars. The landings were preceded by the greatest naval and air bombardment of the entire Pacific war to date. For three days the mighty guns of the fleet and the bombs of the air force plastered the island before the first assault waves swarmed ashore to quickly overrun the surviving Japanese defenders.

There were two main landings, one just south of Tacloban, capital of the island, and the other about twelve miles further south. Both beachheads were successfully established with comparatively few casualties and the troops moved inland towards their first main objective, the Tacloban air field.

General MacArthur issued a triumphant proclamation to the Filipino population immediately upon landing on their soil to oust the Japs. He said that by the grace of Almighty God, our forces stand again on Philippine soil, soil consecrated in the blood of our two peoples. He called upon the populace to rise against the Japanese oppressors and help the Americans to speedily oust them and bring a new era of peace to the islands.

Saturday, October 21, 1944: —Japanese resistance is stiffening on Leyte Island but the initial American momentum has carried them several miles inland. Unconfirmed reports state that our forces have begun the siege of Tacloban, capital of the island while a radio flash direct from Leyte states that the Tacloban air field is already in American hands.

Several vicious counter-attacks by reinforced Japanese units were repelled today with flamethrowers and tanks. It is said that the Japanese division responsible for the infamous "march of death" forced upon the survivors of Bataan, is among the enemy units stationed on Leyte and the Yanks, many of them buddies of the tortured men of Bataan, are anxious to come to grips with this hated foe. For more than two years this particular Japanese unit has "fattened up" in ease and luxury in the Philippines; now, like pigs, they are ready for the kill.

California is particularly proud today, as it was revealed that California's own, the famed Seventh Division, captors of Attu and Kiska, are spearheading the great Philippines invasion. Major General Archibald V. Arnold is the present commander of the Seventh.

It was also revealed today that American and Filipino guerrillas have contributed heavily to the successful invasion. The guerrillas have spent 2 ½ rigorous years in the Philippine jungles, fighting the Japs, supplying the Allies with vital information, and awaiting liberation. Now they are paying the Japs off—with interest.

Sunday, October 22, 1944: —Despite fanatical Japanese resistance, General MacArthur's tough fighting men are surging ahead on Leyte. Tacloban, capital of the island, and home of 30,000 Filipinos, has fallen to the onrushing Americans along with the Tacloban air field which is now swarming with Seabees who are rapidly converting the field into a major base for our air force. Soldiers of the Twenty-fourth, Seventh, and Ninety-sixth infantry divisions are carrying the brunt of the assault.

Good news also comes from the European front, where it has been confirmed that Aachen is at last completely in American hands. All organized resistance has ceased in the ruined German city, with more than 10,000 prisoners being taken in the last stages of the siege. Seizure of Aachen, one of the toughest anchors in Hitler's West Wall should free General Hodge's First Army to continue its march on the Rhine and the great industrial city of Cologne. Chalk up another brilliant victory for the yanks.

On the diplomatic front we find that Prime Minister Winston Churchill has just concluded his latest conference with Premier Josef Stalin in Moscow. Russian papers and radio are enthusiastic over the results of the meeting which they say reflect the new spirit of friendship and collaboration between the United States, Britain, and Russia. It is fervently hoped that the three great nations may find a common ground upon which victory may be speeded and a permanent peace be constructed.

Monday, October 23, 1944: —Prospects of a whirlwind campaign in Leyte are increasing hourly as Japanese opposition dwindles in the face of ever-increasing American power. Palo, the second city on the island fell to a fast moving battalion of U.S. infantrymen who advanced so rapidly that they left their supply and communications units far behind. With some exceptions, the Japs are fleeing into the interior with the avenging Doughboys hot on their heels.

Darkening the otherwise bright picture of U.S. progress in the Pacific was the disclosure today by the Navy Department that two more of our submarines have been lost, together with their complements of 65 men apiece. Although not stated it was assumed that the losses occurred in the Pacific theater, where American subs have taken a terrific toll of Japanese shipping, thus contributing heavily to the recent victories. The undersea vessels were the Golet and the Herring, whose destruction brings to 32 the number of U.S. submarines lost in the war so far.

In eastern Europe the mighty Soviet war machine is plunging deep into East Prussia, having smashed 31 miles beyond the eastern border, according to Berlin admission. Several German towns were captured during the opening phase of what appears to be another major offensive by the Red Army. General Ivan D. Cherniakhovsky's famous White Russian Third Army is spearheading the drive.

In an important diplomatic move today, the United States recognized the regime of General Charles De Gaulle as the provisional Government of the Republic of France. Jefferson Caffery will be the first U.S. ambassador to the new Government.

Tuesday, October 24, 1944: —Admiral Nimitz announced today that powerful Japanese naval forces have been sighted, coming out of hiding from waters east of the Philippines. Admiral Halsey's Third U.S. Fleet's carrier planes were immediately dispatched to attack the enemy vessels which include many battleships, carriers, and other large fleet units. Obviously the Japs are moving into position to challenge the American naval forces in the Philippine area and if possible to smash General MacArthur's invasion armada in the Leyte Gulf. A showdown naval engagement looms.

Meanwhile, our invasion troops have killed more than 3,000 Japs on Leyte and have captured 12 important towns. Other amphibious forces have crossed the one mile San Juanito strait between Leyte and Samar, another large island in the Philippine archipelago, and have securely established a beachhead on the latter isle.

On the East Prussian front the recently launched Soviet offensive is crunching inexorably on, grinding fanatically resisting Nazis into pulp under the treads of the mighty Red Army juggernaught. The ruins of several smoldering German cities within the borders of the famous Junkers province were captured by the advancing Russians who drove to within 25 miles of Insterburg, key town blocking the road to Konigsberg. Berlin admitted some of the Russian gains and said that the fighting was raging with a fury never before known.

Wednesday, October 25, 1944: —Admiral William T. Halsey Jr., in a special dispatch direct to President Roosevelt, proclaimed that "The Japanese Navy in the Philippines area has been defeated, seriously damaged and routed by the United States Navy in that area." The Admiral's announcement was joyously received as indicating that the expected Japanese attempt to thwart our invasion of the Philippines has been decisively smashed. Admiral Ernest J. King, commander in chief of the U.S. Fleet, further stated that almost the entire Japanese Grand Fleet was involved in the action and our fleet may have won its mightiest victory of the war. This will not be known definitely until the final tally is made of Japanese losses.

Early reports indicate that the Jap fleet converged on our Leyte invasion area in three powerful columns. Each of them was met by units of the U.S. Navy and carrier borne aircraft and each were turned back with heavy losses. The known score of enemy ships sunk for sure includes one large aircraft carrier, two cruisers, and one destroyer. These have all been acknowledged by the Japanese. Six battleships, two aircraft carriers and three destroyers are known to have been heavily hit and some of them are believed sunk. The fight is still in progress in many far flung areas and the tally is far from complete. Nevertheless, the victory is already ours, with the enemy in full flight.

With the sweet fragrance of victory is always intermingled the overpowering stench of death. A gallant ship, the U.S. carrier Princeton, died in the heat of the battle and with her went brave American lads, true to the end, to the great traditions of the Navy.

Thursday, October 26, 1944: —The extent of the U.S. Fleet's victory in the Second Battle of the Philippines is growing rapidly as reports pour in from the Pacific Fleet Headquarters. Latest news reveals that one Japanese battleship has definitely been sunk, two large carriers, four heavy cruisers, and two destroyers also sent to the bottom. Nine other battleships hit, two probably sunk, one carrier, six cruisers, and a large number of destroyers badly damaged. In General MacArthur's words, "The Japanese Navy has received its most crushing defeat of the war. Its future efforts can only be on a dwindling scale." The action is continuing.

While their comrades in the Navy are battling to preserve and protect their beachhead, the troops of General MacArthur's invasion armies on Leyte are forging steadily ahead in their offensive designed to eradicate the Japanese garrison on the island. The front has been extended for 40 miles from the initial landing zone, with 31 towns and six air fields now being dominated by our forces. Across the narrow San Juanico Strait, other U.S. troops are extending their beachhead on Samar Island, third largest of the Philippine archipelago.

On the home front, the Presidential campaign and labor

dispute are filling in the spare news space left after the sensational war news has been reported. The Presidential contest appears to be very close, with both candidates swinging like champs. The labor dispute, involving a jurisdictional dispute between C.I.O. and A.F.L. machinists unions, which are holding up work on vitally needed ships, are irritating more people than they are winning support from. It seems hardly the time for bickering.

Friday, October 27, 1944: —China based bombers of the 14th Air Force have joined in the pursuit of the beaten Japanese Imperial Fleet and have destroyed at least three of the fleeing enemy warships. This latest addition raises the toll of Japanese ships in the four-day engagement to at least 37. We, in turn, lost six vessels according to the latest Pacific Fleet Headquarters' report. In addition to the light carrier, Princeton, the Japs sank two escort carriers, two destroyers and a destroyer escort. Names of the latter ships were not immediately disclosed.

The end of organized Japanese resistance on the island of Leyte seems close at hand. Our forces, including the dismounted First U.S. Cavalry, have trapped the main enemy body in the northern part of the island where they face speedy liquidation. Our beachhead on the east and northern coasts now stretches for fifty miles.

Today is Navy Day and throughout the country the people celebrated the mighty U.S. Fleet's latest victory and honored the gallant men who manned the ships in a fashion that would have pleased John Paul Jones himself. The Nation is proud of the Navy and feels secure under its protecting guns. As one, we the people say, "Well done!"

In Europe the Allied drive to open the great Belgian port of Antwerp is making progress. British troops smashed through the southern German flank on Beveland Island which guards the approaches to the port and drove inland towards a junction with Canadian troops attacking over the causeway from the mainland.

Saturday, October 28, 1944: —China's precarious position in the war was brought forcibly to the world's attention today as the sensational news was released to the effect that Lieut. General Joseph W. Stilwell has been recalled from China and relieved of his post as commander of U.S. forces in the China-India-Burma Theater. "Old Vinegar Joe" as he was known to his troops was apparently recalled at the request of Generalissimo Chiang-Kai-Shek because of a deep-seated clash on strategy.

China's problems are almost unsolvable and are a result of eight disastrous years of war with Japan, the loss of the Burma road and all direct means of communication with her Allies, and bitter internal troubles, including conflict between ideological groups within the country itself. General Stilwell has been a loyal friend of the Chinese but apparently has been unable to agree with Chiang on major questions of strategy. This has forced his recall but has not solved the problem of saving China. Unless a way is found, China may fall. Japan may entrench herself so strongly on the continent that our own brilliant victories in the Pacific will be nullified and the war prolonged for months, if not years.

The latest unofficial tally of Japanese ships sunk or damaged in the great Philippines battle has reached 42. Three more cargo ships were sent to the bottom by China-based U.S. bombers who have pursued the defeated Jap fleet. The merchant vessels were remnants of a once powerful enemy task force that was blasted and driven from the Philippines area during the four day battle.

Sunday, October 29, 1944: —Another Sunday has rolled around and with it has come once again the welcome opportunity to relax and rest from the interminable monotony of the week's work. I speak of monotony only from the standpoint of scheduled regularity in the daily routine that seldom varies. Up at 6:30, bathe, shave, eat a hurried breakfast and dash to the depot to catch the 7:37 commuter into the city; work at 8:30, lunch at 12:00 noon, back to work at 1:00, off again at 6:30 or 7:00 and dash to the depot to catch the next commuter home; eat dinner at 8:30, read, listen to the news on the radio, or chat with the wife until 10:00, then type this daily article and off to bed at 11:30 or 12:00. All over again the next day; that sort of thing can become monotonous.

Not that my work is dull. It is far from that. In fact, countless problems are met and solved every day, in a constantly shifting and changing operation. We have recently been involved in switching to an entirely new redemption procedure in the cashing of War Bonds. Effective October 2nd, all commercial banks were authorized to qualify as paying agents for this popular type of security. A volume could be written about the results and possible effects of this new and convenient means of turning your bonds into cash immediately. Suffice it to say at this time that a great volume of work and multitudinous problems have been created thereby.

But the problems and monotonous regularity of the workaday week are pleasantly disrupted on Sunday. Then I can stay in bed until I feel like arising—usually in time to take the youngsters to Sunday School—then a leisurely breakfast and a perusal of the morning paper; a spot of gardening if I feel like it and then a pleasant shower followed by a long comfortable evening in the bosom of my family. Would there were more Sundays.

Monday, October 30, 1944: —The final toll of Japanese ships in the Second Battle of the Philippines has not even yet been tabulated. The wounded and dispersed units of the three great enemy squadrons that made the ill-fated attempt to smash our Leyte invasion have been hounded and pursued by sea and air, with many of them being tracked down and destroyed. Admiral William F. Halsey's famous Third Fleet's carrier planes followed three crippled Jap cruisers into Manila Bay itself and score hits on all, sinking one for sure. In the same strike a 1,000 pound bomb from one of the carrier planes scored a direct hit on a large oil tanker with results that can easily be imagined.

Adding up all the scores to date, the toll of enemy ships sunk or damaged in the decisive battle now stands at 62, according to the official communiqué from Admiral Chester W. Nimitz' Headquarters at Pearl Harbor. The vaunted Jap fleet will not recover soon—if ever—from this disastrous defeat.

Here at home, sorry to say, things are not going so uniformly well. A stubborn strike by CIO Machinists involved in a jurisdictional dispute with the AFL Steamfitters Union has tied up dozens of urgently needed ships. So serious has the work stoppage become that the National War Labor Board has ordered the men back on the job. It is doubtful that the strikers will comply and the Government may be forced into stronger action. Most citizens, as well as the millions of servicemen and women, have only contempt for men who will impede the war effort to settle petty disputes. Even most responsible leaders of Organized Labor itself have denounced the strike.

Tuesday, October 31, 1944: —Adding further emphasis to the difficult China situation was the revelation today that the United States Ambassador to that country, Clarence Gauss, is going to resign from his post. President Roosevelt denied that the pending resignation has anything to do with the removal of General Stilwell as commander of U.S. forces in the China-India-Burma theater, but the fact that the diplomat is also quitting at this crucial time adds further mystery to the obscure Chinese situation.

It was also revealed that the China-India-Burma theater is being divided into two smaller theaters. Henceforth there will be a China theater and an India-Burma theater. Our forces in the first will be commanded by Major General A.C. Wedemeyer, present deputy chief of staff to Admiral Mountbatten, and in the latter by Lt. General Daniel I. Sultan.

A further report on the results of the great Japanese naval defeat in the Philippines sea reveals that the Nips lost some 60,000 men in the battle at sea and the simultaneous land battle on Leyte. In addition 80 enemy ships were sunk or damaged, eighteen vessels being hit by subs to add to the 62 sunk or wrecked with shell and bomb.

The most fantastic individual exploit of the Philippines battle was the destruction of nine Jap planes in one hour and thirty five minutes by Commander David McCampbell of Los Angeles, ace fighter pilot. His score now stands at 30 enemy planes shot down. Said Commander McCampbell after his incredible feat, "Japanese planes burn as easily now as they ever did."

November

Wednesday, November 1, 1944: —A confused, excited Tokyo radio today announced that American planes have again raided the Japanese capital and nearby Yokohama. It was indicated the attack was carried out by a flight of B-29's but the exact scale of the raid could not be determined from the incoherent Japanese account. No confirmation has come as yet from any Allied source. If true, the raid is the first to be leveled at Tokyo since the famous "Doolittle" attack more than two and one-half years ago.

In Europe the Allied armies under General Eisenhower have opened a new and determined drive to capture the vital port of Antwerp and its approaches from the fanatically resisting Nazis who realize only too well the importance of the great port to the mighty Allied forces standing on the western border of the Reich. A quick seizure of Antwerp could shorten the war by months since it would furnish Eisenhower with a supply center near to the western front through which he could funnel the vast stores of munitions and equipment required for a major offensive. Until Antwerp is taken the Allied High Command must depend upon the long 450 mile supply line running back all the way to Cherbourg. Consequently the outcome of the battle for Antwerp is bound to be far-reaching.

At home the news is still centered on the Presidential campaign which is swinging into its last week and the current labor dispute, especially those involving machinists in several West Coast shipyards. Also competing for the headlines were quadruplets born in a caesarian operation to a Pennsylvania woman. All are healthy and are expected to survive.

Thursday, November 2, 1944: —Probably the greatest air battle of the entire war raged over the German city of Merseburg today. At the height of the battle there were over 2,400 planes, Nazi and American, locked in lethal combat over the German city. The cost in men and planes was heavy on both sides, with 41 heavy bombers and 28 fighters being lost out of the U.S. fleet of 1,100 and 900 fighters. The toll of German planes however, reached a new high for a single operation. More than 200 of the intercepting enemy fighters were destroyed as contrasted with the previous record of 117. One group of Mustang fighter planes downed more than 51 planes to set a new record for individual fighter groups. Bitter though the cost, the U.S. Eighth Air Force has struck a staggering blow at the already reeling Luftewaffe, a blow that cannot but have a telling effect on the progress of the Allied offensive against the western borders of the Reich.

A major phase of that offensive apparently is coming to a close near the vital port of Antwerp, where British and Canadian Commando forces are mopping up the remaining Nazis on the island of Walcheren. Some 12,000 enemy troops were captured in the process.

To the south on the American First Army front, General Hodge's battle-worn Doughboys are fighting their way through the dense Hurtgen Forest southeast of recently captured Aachen. Bitter fighting carried the Americans forward two miles.

Friday, November 3, 1944: —The news today is of a somewhat humdrum and routine nature. We have become so used to sensational and kaleidoscopic developments that the current news, though it involves deadly fighting on many far-flung battlegrounds, is just ordinary and routine. It takes a new invasion, or the surrender of a nation, or the liberation of a famous capital, to excite a world satiated with the tales of horror and bloodshed that have been its daily diet for five long years. Any one of a hundred incidents reported daily in these times would have thrown the entire world into a high state of nervous excitement a few years ago. Today they are but minor happenings in an incredulous era of epoch-making events.

Like a burr under the saddle of war production is the persistent refusal of Bay Area machinists to end their strike which has held up work on dozens of vitally needed ships. A clear violation of labor's "no-strike" pledge, the action of the Machinists' Union has left a bitter taste in the public's mouth. Many civic leaders have denounced the tie-up indignantly as being "near to treason." Labor has not benefited by this ill-considered action of a few of its members.

General Joseph Stilwell, recently recalled commander of U.S. forces in China, has arrived in Washington for a brief furlough before receiving his new assignment. Colorful "Vinegar Joe," as

764

he was known to his troops, refused to comment on the Chinese situation but leading military analysts seized the opportunity to forcibly remind us that China is the only battleground where the United Nations are actually losing at the present time.

Saturday, November 4, 1944: —The Bay Area Machinists today voted to return to work, apparently yielding to public opinion and an object lesson from the White House, where President Roosevelt ordered Secretary of War Henry L. Stimson to take over and operate eight war plants in the Toledo, Ohio area, where war production has been interrupted by a labor disturbance. The President took this strong action because he said the war effort "will be unduly impeded or delayed by these interruptions."

While squabbling men at home have to be begged and forced to work, G.I. Joes on Leyte Island are barely holding their own against furious Japanese counter-thrusts. The Japs have succeeded in reinforcing their battered garrison at Ormoc and are counter-attacking with fanatical fury. The battle is in its most critical state, with the fate of the entire campaign to be decided.

On the eastern European front, the ever-amazing Russian armies are pounding at the gates of Budapest, capital of Germany's last remaining Bulkan satellite. Armored spearheads of the rampaging Soviet forces are fighting in the outskirts of the city, while the jittery Hungarian government is frantically evacuating the imperiled capital whose fate may be settled within 72 hours.

American forces suffered a minor setback in bitter fighting southeast of Aachen, on the western border of Germany. Powerful German tank and infantry forces succeeded in pushing our troops back a mile and one-half, regaining a portion of the ground gained by the American forces yesterday.

Sunday, November 5, 1944: —One of the most bitterly contested Presidential campaigns in the history of the country has almost run its course. Both candidates delivered their final major addresses last night, Thomas E. Dewey in New York and Franklin D. Roosevelt in Boston. We will have a lull today, last minute appeals tomorrow night, and then the voters of the nation, an expected 50,000,000 strong, will take over. The final decision will be made in the secrecy of the voting booth.

There are many issues in this campaign, issues which are highly controversial and serious. This record is of course impartial and we have not attempted to argue or discuss the political problems of the day. This is primarily a day by day record of the war and its progress, with brief sidelights on the daily happenings as they are seen and as they affect the lives of one citizen and his family in these troublous times. Through a reading of these pages it is hoped that, in future and, we trust, happier times, people may be able to visualize some of the events of this awful moment in history and to trace in their minds the perilous course this country has followed from the very brink of national disaster to what now appears will be ultimate victory over the powers of evil. Therefore, since the results of this wartime election will undoubtedly have an all-important bearing on the speed with which that final victory is won and the manner in which a lasting peace is forged, we offer a silent prayer on this last Sabbath before November 7th, asking God to guide this people that they may choose the leader who will be able to fulfill the obligations to our gallant dead and lead this tired, embittered old world into an enlightened and glorious era in which the horrors of war will be forever banished. Amen.

Monday, November 6, 1944: —On this eve before election there is a certain tension in the air. All the world seems to hang breathlessly on the outcome. The talking is over, the issues have been debated, now that imponderable entity, the nation's electorate, will make the decision. Since, obviously, tomorrow's report will deal exclusively with the election results, let's take a look at the war fronts to see how our gallant fighting forces are making out.

Despite incredibly bitter fighting, General MacArthur's invasion troops are closing a steel trap upon the remaining Japanese forces on Leyte Island in the Philippines. A literal cascade of shells and bombs is being poured into Ormoc, last Japanese stronghold on the embattled island. The enemy is still succeeding in reinforcing their garrison at night, despite furious aerial and artillery pounding; but the Yanks are closing in steadily and inexorably.

On the western border of Germany the American First Army is encountering savage opposition and has been forced to withdraw at several points. The Nazis recaptured the town of Schmidt, ten miles inside the Reich and won a foothold in the American-held town of Vossenack, 2 miles to the northwest.

There were rumors today that Japanese submarines have resumed their attacks off the Pacific Coast. Tokyo has claimed as much but there has been no official U.S. confirmation of the report. If true, the attacks are the first since almost two years ago, when daring Nipponese subs even shelled the coastline in two places.

Tuesday, November 7, 1944: —That memorable day when the United States, being engaged in a bitter war, can demonstrate to the world that the democratic process can be safely exercised, with no deteriorating affect on our war effort. While waging all-out war, we can still choose our leaders by secret ballot, as free men. When you come right down to doing it, as I did this morning, you have something that is really worth fighting for. It is a wonderful privilege and from first reports to come in, it appears as though many millions of citizens are taking advantage of their right to vote.

At 9:30 p.m. as I write this, scattered returns are coming in from all over the nation. It is too early to foretell the outcome but everyone's ear is bent close to the radio loudspeaker to get every detail of this stirring and colorful event. All the major networks are devoting their entire time to the election and the finest commentators in the country are on the job to keep the public informed.

At 11:00 p.m. the result is beginning to take shape, though no one has conceded defeat as yet. I am no analyst but from the reports as they come in, there appears to be a distinct, if not definite, trend towards President Roosevelt. The outcome hinges on the key states—New York, Ohio, Illinois, Pennsylvania, Massachusetts, Michigan, and California. Of these only Ohio seems definitely for Dewey at this time.

At 12:00 midnight, although Mr. Dewey has not yet conceded there appears to be no chance for him. Mr. Roosevelt has been reelected—it's the will of the people and so may God bless the President of the United States—he will need it in the four trying years that lay ahead.

Wednesday, November 8, 1944: —One more report on the election and then we are going to forget it. With the popular vote far from tabulated, the latest figures show Roosevelt with 21,501,362 and Dewey with 18,791,552. The trend is there and the Democrats are making a minor sweep of the country. Not only is the President reelected but his party is gaining some strength in both houses of Congress. The people have demonstrated that they do not want to change administrations in this critical period of the war and they have issued a mandate to the present regime to win the war and win the peace. They have indicated that they want the President to go ahead with plans for post-war collaboration for peace with all the freedom-loving nations of the world. Franklin Roosevelt has the opportunity that was denied Woodrow Wilson to commit this nation to a world organization for peace. Make the most of it, Mr. President.

While the American First Army battled furiously to hold its own 28 miles southwest of Cologne, General George S. Patton's powerful Third Army opened a new offensive along a 27 mile front between Metz and Nancy, obviously aimed at taking the pressure off the First Army and at the same time outflank the powerful fortress of Metz, which has stalemated the Americans for many weeks. There is every indication that the attack is on a large scale with the ultimate capture of Metz as its objective.

The fighting on Leyte Island in the Philippines has not diminished in fury. The Japs are bottled in their base at Ormoc but are resisting savagely. Every weapon in the U.S. arsenal is being turned against them in an effort to quickly finish the campaign.

Thursday, November 9, 1944: —General George S. Patton's new offensive has gained considerable momentum. Nine French towns have been liberated, with the Yanks advancing all along an 87 mile front. Thousands of planes are supporting the American drive, unloading huge quantities of explosives on the Nazi lines. Slowly yet steadily, Patton's armored forces are clamping a deadly pincers around the fortress of Metz, whose fall would open the gateway to the Saar Valley and the Rhine.

There were indications in today's reports that the end of good fighting weather on the western front is almost in sight. Lt. General Courtney H. Hodge's First Army troops fought through the first heavy snowstorm of the season in the Hurtgen forest northeast of Aachen. A bitter, freezing winter campaign looms uninvitingly ahead.

Prime Minister Winston Churchill obviously pleased at the outcome of the U.S. election, today called for another meeting between the leaders of America, Britain, and Russia, stating that another meeting between Premier Stalin, President Roosevelt and himself "might easily abridge the sufferings of mankind and stop the fearful process of destruction which is now ravaging the earth." We hope he is right.

Bad weather also hindered the fighting on Leyte Island. Doughboys and Japanese fought through a tropical hurricane that made the battle all the more grim and weird. General Tomuyuki Yamashita, sadistic conqueror of Bataan, Corregidor, and Singapore, has returned to command Japanese forces in the Philippines, according to the Tokyo radio.

Friday, November 10, 1944: —It was revealed today that the Germans have thrown another Wellsian terror weapon at England. The new horror is known to the Nazis as V-2, or revenge weapon number two, and is said to be a giant, comet-like rocket bomb that travels sixty miles high in the stratosphere and travels faster than sound, thereby giving its victims no warning of its approach.

Winston Churchill confirmed the presence of the new menace in a speech to the House of Commons in which he said that the huge new bombs have crashed at several points in England but casualties and damage so far have not been heavy. The terror weapon has also been directed against Paris and Antwerp during the past few weeks.

The possibilities opened up by the German development of the rocket bomb are many and will undoubtedly have an effect on the peace plans of Britain, Russia and the United States. When there is a definite possibility that the Germans may launch rocket attacks against New York and the Atlantic coast in this war it is plain to see what plans will have to be made to prevent the occurrence of a Third World War in which an entire continent could receive the "Pearl Harbor" treatment, without notice or warning—from out of the stratosphere.

General Patton's drive is making headway. A 20 mile breach has been ripped in the Nazi lines below Metz and U.S. armor is pouring through. A bridgehead has been secured across the Moselle River north of Metz and the enemy has been driven back to within 2½ miles of the German frontier.

Saturday, November 11, 1944: —Armistice Day! What a hollow sound that has in 1944. In 1918, however, a battered and bloody world looked forward hopefully from November 11, believing that the "War to end wars" had been won and that a new and beautiful era of peace was about to descend upon the earth. That dream failed and the world toppled in ruins again. This time there must be no Armistice day, for armistice, in its very meaning, is just a temporary cessation of hostilities. This time there must be a "Peace Day," a day of permanent peace. From that day on, the peace-loving peoples of the world must police the world so that international gangsters and criminals can never again gain sufficient power to engulf the world in war. Otherwise the blood of countless brave and innocent people has been shed in vain.

Some realists say wars will always be with us so long as there are people. I prefer the thought that, an adequate police force can be established among the freedom loving nations to hold the would-be outlaws in check. If this be not possible, then indeed is human society doomed.

A great battle is raging on Leyte Island between some 100,000 American and Japanese troops. The enemy is making a determined effort to retrieve the situation upon which, he realizes, hangs the fate of his Pacific empire. We have confidence in General MacArthur's and his troops' ability to thwart the enemy's plans.

Sunday, November 12, 1944: —Today was a dreary, blustery, rainy Sabbath, a day to be spent indoors in the company of a good book or magazine. Today's rainfall only contributed to what has been one of the Bay Area's wettest seasons for a long time. The seasonal fall is more than twice the normal figure for this time of year and has reached 5.51 inches, as compared with the normal of 2.33 inches and a measly .76 of an inch up to November 12 of last year.

While we fortunate Americans spent the Sabbath in the comfort of our hearths, other less fortunate Americans were battling in far off places in the rain and mud and cold against a ruthless, fanatical foe who could, except for their brave intervention, destroy those very hearths around which we at home have gathered. A realization of this fact must be one of the few things that enable those weary, suffering Doughboys to keep going no matter what the odds. And a realization of this same fact should be the incentive necessary for us to back up the fighting men with the supplies and machinery of war, in whatever way and by whatever means is available to us.

Particularly fierce has been the fighting on Leyte Island in the Philippines. The Japs are fighting like the cornered rats they are, fanatically demonstrating again and again that their most fervent wish is to die for the Emperor. General MacArthur's men are granting them this wish as rapidly as possible. There is now little doubt regarding the eventual outcome of the battle but the Nips are obviously determined to fight a delaying action for as long as possible.

Monday, November 13, 1944: —The RAF has scored one of its longest sought after victories of the war, according to an announcement from the British Air Ministry. For many months the RAF as well as the Royal Navy have stalked the great German battleship, Tirpitz, from hideout to hideout, always hoping to eliminate the vessel as a deadly threat to our Atlantic convoy lanes. Several times British submarines and planes have succeeded in damaging the mighty dreadnought but never enough to destroy her. At last, however, a flight of RAF Lancasters, carrying special armor-piercing six-ton earthquake bombs, caught the Tirpitz at anchor in Tromso Fjord and scored several direct hits. Within a few minutes the mighty battleship burst into flames, capsized and sank. Thus ended the life of the last remaining super-battleship of the now defunct German Navy.

General George S. Patton's drive to envelope and neutralize the giant fortress network around Metz is proceeding unexpectedly well. There are some indications that the Nazis are withdrawing from the area, abandoning the almost impregnable maze of steel and concrete fortifications to the advancing Doughboys. Fort Verny, one of the biggest of the underground bastions, and two lesser ones fell to the Yanks almost without a shot. Fort Driant, on the other hand, has defied every effort of General Patton's troops to take it by storm. Metz undoubtedly has been and still is a tough nut to crack.

In the Philippines the battle for Leyte Island is still raging furiously. General MacArthur's forces are drawing the noose ever tighter around the enemy garrison but are paying a high price.

Tuesday, November 14, 1944: —Since Adolf Hitler, the ego-maniac that started all this mess, failed to put in his usual appearance at the annual celebration of his Munich beer cellar putsch, the world has speculated regarding his physical condition and his whereabouts. Rumors have claimed him dead, insane, ill, a fugitive, in Japan, in Argentina, or simply too busy trying to rescue his fading fortunes to make any public appearance. The latest "report" alleged that Der Fuhrer is at his mountain hideout, Berchtesgaden, undergoing a serious throat operation. His affliction is a throat tumor, allegedly stemming from his being gassed in the First World War. This report may be the truth, but obviously we can't be sure. Whatever it is, however, we hope it is a fitting punishment for the misery he has brought upon mankind.

In the Pacific we learn that the Navy has just completed a two day series of large-scale air attacks against the Japs in the Manila area. According to the Navy's latest communiqué at least 13 enemy ships were blasted to the bottom of Manila Bay, at least 28 Jap planes were shot down in combat, and another 120 to 140 Nip planes were strafed on Legaspi, Manila, and Clark airstrips. Even the once boastful Tokyo radio (which is now beginning to change its tune) admitted that the raids caused "some damage" to Japanese warships in the Bay.

An event on the home front that is causing some jagged nerves and fancy finagling is the current cigarette shortage. Many stores are forced to display a "No Cigarettes" sign and heavy smokers are going to fantastic lengths to supply their needs.

Wednesday, November 15, 1944: —Another rumor from Europe that has a ring of authenticity to it, claims that Hitler has lost his mind and is confined in his mountain retreat of Berchtesgaden where he paces the floor and raves like a mad lion. Heinrich Himmler, the bloody chief of the fearful Gestapo, is reported to have seized full power in the Reich and is keeping the people in line with the aid of his strong-arm henchmen of the secret police. An anti-war demonstration at Cologne was speedily squelched yesterday, with 21 of the ring leaders being publicly hanged as a "warning."

At the same time our armies advancing against the Siegfried defenses of western Germany are finding that the Nazi frontline troops, at least, are still in there fighting fanatically. Our forces are moving ahead, but only by sheer power and after bitter fighting. General Patton's Third U.S. Army is closing in on Metz and, for the first time in modern history, that mighty fortress city appears about to fall to an attacking army. The next few days will tell the tale.

To the north in Holland, the British Second Army is contributing a brilliant offensive of its own. The rampaging Tommies gained five miles today to push the Germans back to the last canal line before the river Maas. The British advance left them only eight miles from the German border and, according to a spokesman from General Bernard L. Montgomery's Headquarters, the big push is going "entirely according to plan."

Thursday, November 16, 1944: —A 400 mile segment of Germany's western frontier belched flames and rocked today after on of the mightiest demonstrations of man-made mayhem and destruction ever witnessed. It marked the beginning of what may be called "Ike's Victory Drive," an all-out winter offensive launched by General Dwight D. Eisenhower and six great Allied armies under his command. More than one million Allied soldiers leaped forward as one, in what General Eisenhower hopes will be the climactic drive in the war against Germany. If all goes well, the General's prediction that the Nazis will be defeated in 1944 may yet come true. May God guide his hand.

The great offensive was preceded by a crushing aerial assault against the German forward positions by more than 2,400 Allied heavy bombers. The tremendous weight of explosives literally smothered the enemy's lines, after which the Allies plunged forward under cover of an earth-shaking barrage from hundreds of big guns. Forward observers could not conceive of anything, let alone human beings, surviving the terrific scourge of bombs and shells. Yet when the Allied tanks and infantry moved forward they were met with powerful enemy fire. Nevertheless, initial Allied gains were substantial, particularly in the Aachen and Metz areas.

A new U.S. Army, the Ninth, was revealed as being sent into action for the first time today. The Nazis have long wondered over the whereabouts of the Ninth and now they will find out—much to their dismay. The Ninth is said to be operating north of Aachen, between the U.S. First Army and the British Second Army.

Friday, November 17, 1944: —Estimates of the number of Allied soldiers involved in the mighty new offensive against Germany was raised to 1,500,000 tonight. General Eisenhower is obviously using everything he has in one determined attempt to crush the Nazis this year and avoid what may be a long, bloody winter and spring campaign. The U.S. First and Ninth Armies are spearheading the attack, bringing into coordinated action one of America's best veteran armies and one of her newest and freshest. The First is commanded by Lieut. General Courtney H. Hodges, who earned fame in the sensational conquest of France, while the Ninth is under the command of Lieut. General William H. Simpson.

The First Army scored the most brilliant gains in the second day of fighting. General Hodges' veterans speared through ten miles east of Aachen to capture the highway center of Greesenich and lay open the road to Cologne, now barely 28 miles to the east. General Simpson's Ninth Army Doughboys felt the brunt of the Nazis' first counter-attack on the left flank of the advancing First Army. The attack was finally beaten off by the Ninth Army troopers who met their baptism of fire courageously.

In the Pacific, we learn that the bloody battle for Leyte Island is still raging. The Yanks have the Japanese trapped but you know what they say about cornered rats. Well the Japs are fighting just that way. There is no question of surrender and the fanatical enemy must be crushed literally and completely. That makes for a nasty piece of business.

Saturday, November 18, 1944: —General Eisenhower's "Big Push" continued to gain today under cover of the mightiest aerial and artillery bombardment of the war. Troops from General George S. Patton's Third Army moved into the "impregnable" fortress city of Metz today, dispelling the 1,500 year myth of invincibility. Only a mop-up of a few isolated pockets of suicidal defenders remained before complete possession could be claimed by the Americans.

A combat team of British infantry and U.S. tanks joined up today near Roermond in southeast Holland and stormed into

Germany after crossing the wide Maas River and drove five miles into the Reich to within 25 miles of Duisburg and the vital Ruhr industrial basis.

At many other points along the blazing 400 mile front other Allied armies swung into action, probing for the weak spot in the Nazi armor that must appear under the stupendous pressure that is being brought to bear. Through the crack, when it is found, will stream a torrent of Allied men and machines to clinch the final victory.

Across the world another bitter campaign is being fought for the possession of Leyte Island in the Philippines. Despite tropical hurricanes that have turned the battleground into an inland sea of mud, the American 32nd Division has knifed through to split the Japanese defenders and has trapped an estimated 3,000 enemy troops in an annihilation pocket at Limon in northwest Leyte. Three desperate attempts by the enemy to break the road block across his only escape route were bloodily repulsed today.

Sunday, November 19, 1944: —Thank God for the respite that is Sunday. A pleasant respite from the rush and bustle of a war-torn world, a day for communion with family and friends, a day for quiet worship and a time for relaxing acquaintance with garden and flower. Today was particularly adapted for the latter occupation, with a warm sun glowing brightly from its blue reflector. The grass, heavy with dew in the early morning hours, seemed to shake itself like a wet dog about eleven o'clock and stand up straight and green, begging to be trimmed—which it was for the first time in a month of almost incessant rains. But aside from this little sortie into what might be construed as labor, we spent the day lolling in the ultra-violet rays of a kindly autumn sun, soaking up enough vitamin D to tide us over another long workaday week.

Unfortunately many other Americans, caught by fate into the vortex of war, were not able to enjoy the blessings of a normal Sabbath Day. Hundreds of thousands of peace-loving American boys, to whom the quiet refinements of a Sunday at home are only pleasant memories, were blasting their way forward mile after bloody mile through the flaming crust of a fortified Germany. Men died today who had hoped for but one thing—a chance to experience just one more quiet day a home. Their dream will not come true but we, on the home front, are embarking on a drive that we hope will assure that the dreams of thousands of other fighting Americans will come true. The goal of the drive is 14 billions of dollars to buy the equipment that will help bring the boys home. Let's finish the job, let's support the Sixth War Loan Drive.

Monday, November 20, 1944: —Two great drives—of almost equal importance—were on full blast today. One of them was General Eisenhower's mighty smash against fortress Germany along a 400 mile stretch of the Reich frontier. The other was the Sixth War Loan Drive, aimed at raising the funds needed to keep General Eisenhower's forces supplied with the sinews of war.

The drive on the western front gained all along the line today. German resistance was sporadic at some points, fanatically bitter at others, but the overall picture hinted that the Nazis were gradually cracking under the tremendous pressure of six great Allied armies. Metz, the "impregnable" fortress, was falling to a four-pronged assault by General George S. Patton's Third Army, while General Courtney H. Hodges' rampaging First Army crashed through furious enemy opposition to capture Eschweiler, seven miles northeast of Aachen. Far to the south, the American Seventh Army and the French First Army were scoring brilliantly. The French were reported fighting in the streets of Belfort, gateway to the historic gap to Germany. The U.S. Seventh captured the important outskirts of their next important objective, Saarebourg.

In the home front drive our forces scored notable gains in the first day. The volunteer army of six million workers launched vigorously into their campaign to raise 14 billion dollars by December 16th. In San Francisco latest reports from the War Loan front indicated that a third of the city's quota of $187,620,000 was raised in the first day.

Tuesday, November 21, 1944: —One year ago today an indelible page in the history of the United States Marine Corps was written. On that day Leathernecks of the Second Marine Division stormed the steel-spouting shores of Tarawa, winning that island only after one of the bloodiest and most ferocious battles in the history of the heroic Corps. Now Tarawa is in the back area, with the Marines and their Army and Navy comrades carrying the fight to the enemy all the way to the Philippines, but the tiny blood-soaked isle is a shrine that will live forever in honor of the gallant Marines who laid down their lives—for a cause.

Allied successes are mounting on the Western Front. French mobile forces have ripped through the Belfort Gap to the banks of the Rhine where they sliced northward to threaten Mulhouse. Slightly to the north, the U.S. Seventh Army smashed through to Saarebourg which is expected to fall quickly since the Nazi defenders are pulling back frantically towards new positions around Strasbourg.

Paced by a great fleet of some 2,250 U.S. bombers and fighters, the American First and Ninth Armies pushed steadily eastward beyond recently captured Aachen, aiming at heavily fortified Duren which blocks the road to Cologne and the Rhine.

The home front was urged to launch a new all-out production effort to match the offensive of the boys on the battlefronts and to prevent an impending shortage of shells and ammunition. The pleas were made by General Eisenhower and President Roosevelt who disclosed that rationing of artillery shells already was necessary due to dwindling supplies. I cannot think of anything that could offer more comfort to the enemy than news of this kind.

Wednesday, November 22, 1944: —The "green" U.S. Ninth Army, under the command of Lieut. General William R. Simpson, today won one of the most brilliant victories of the war when it met and decisively defeated a mighty German tank force sent to stem the Allied advance against the Roer River line. Today's action was the climax to a four-day series of battles involving the greatest land "dreadnoughts" of the opposing armies. The Germans threw dozens of their new 70-ton "King Tiger" tanks into the fray and the Yanks succeeded in knocking out at least 67 of them. The broken and bleeding remnants of the counter-attacking German force fled towards the Rhine, with the Ninth in pursuit.

Another notable victory was scored in the south by the hard-hitting French mobile forces racing up the west bank of the Rhine. Mulhouse, former Nazi headquarters city was captured and the German defenders driven northward where they face entrapment by the powerful pincers of the U.S. Seventh Army being clamped down on Strasbourg. The speed of the Allied advances all along the 400 mile front lend hope that a complete collapse of German resistance is impending. You may be sure that with possible victory in sight General Eisenhower is throwing everything at his command into the mightiest offensive ever mounted in Europe.

While the fighting on Leyte Island in the Philippines assumes something of the character of a temporary stalemate, the major activity of the Pacific war is in the air. Yesterday B-29s struck at Omure on the Jap homeland while Nanking and Shanghai also felt the weight of bombs from the great aerial battleships.

Thursday, November 23, 1944: —Our third wartime Thanksgiving Day has come and almost gone as I write this. It has been a warm, lovely day here in the Bay Area, with the sunshine and the turkey dinner sharing about equal honors for making the day completely enjoyable. Turkeys were expensive and not too plentiful this year, although just about everyone who wanted a bird could find one by scouting around a little. About the only items conspicuous by their absence from our table were the whipped cream topping to the mincemeat pie and the cranberry jelly.

This year, as usual, we may ask ourselves, "What have we to be thankful for?" To some families, with empty chairs around their dinner table—some that will never be filled—the answer to this question may not seem so easy. But despite the heartache and sorrow visited upon so many—too many—of our homes, we cannot escape the conviction that we in America are still a favored people, with many great and proud things to be thankful for. We are thankful for the strength and courage of our young men and the wisdom of their leaders, by which we were spared the visitation of war's horrors upon our own shores. We are thankful that Almighty God has granted continuing successes to our armed forces so that through the darkness we can now see the glow of the dawn of victory. We are thankful for the resources and wealth of our great land and the ingenuity and untiring efforts of the men and women who have harnessed those resources to the impelling task of defeating our foes. Above all, we are thankful for the ideals and indomitable spirit of America that will somehow win for humanity a better world out of the chaos and human misery that identifies today.

Friday, November 24, 1944: —Airmen of the 20th U.S. Air Force, pilots of the mighty B-29 Superfortresses, celebrated Thanksgiving Day yesterday by smashing at Tokyo for the first time since Jimmy Doolittle thrilled the world with his hit-and-run raid in April, 1942.

This latest attack, however, was definitely not in the hit-and-run category. According to a special report to President Roosevelt from General Hap Arnold, commander in chief of the Army Air Forces, the raid was carried out by a "sizeable" force of B-29s, which usually means 100 planes or more. According to the General, the "battle for Japan has been joined. The raid is a calculated extension of our air power . . . no part of the Japanese Empire is now out of our range, no war factory too remote to feel our bombs."

Returning crewmen of the huge flying battleships which are now based on newly won airfields on Saipan, stated that results of the raid were exceptionally good. The raiders struck at about noon, in broad daylight, and weather over the target was clear. Heavy bombs pin-pointed their targets despite anti-aircraft fire that was "moderate" and fighter opposition that was "slight." The enemy was apparently surprised and the fast flying bombers were over and away from the target before many enemy interceptors could reach their high altitude. Only two of the B-29s have failed to return to base.

Late reports state that reconnaissance sorties over the Japanese capital reveal that great fires are raging in the industrial areas hit by the Superforts. The systematice destruction of the Japanese production machine has begun.

Saturday, November 25, 1944: —U.S. airmen followed up their sensational strike at the Japanese capital last Thursday by heavily attacking Japanese shipping in Manila Harbor yesterday. The famous harbor is fast becoming a graveyard for enemy ships as carrier planes of the victorious U.S. fleet have been almost daily visitors since the second Battle of the Philippines Seas began.

We haven't heard much for a long time about the operations of the submarine arm of the fleet. But the Silent Service, as it is well named, has been very busy. Daring forays to the very shores of Japan have netted another 27 enemy ships, according to the latest announcement from the Navy Department. Up to the present time a grand total of 854 Japanese ships have been sunk, and 119 have been damaged. This tremendous score has been chalked up with the loss of only 32 submarines from all causes. Tragic though each of these losses has been, the enormously favorable ratio of enemy ships destroyed is a tribute to the efficiency and courage of our gallant undersea fighters.

Terribly bitter fighting has been raging for ten days in the gloom of the Hurtgen forest east of shattered Aachen, where Lieut. General Courtney H. Hodges' U.S. First Army has been battering at the Nazi defenses guarding the approaches to Cologne. Today, however, the hard-fighting Yanks burst from the forest onto the Cologne plain, driving the stubborn Germans before them. Chalk up another U.S. touchdown, scored through the center of the line.

Sunday, November 26, 1944: —During the course of this war we have heard many tales of bestial torture and murder inflicted on millions of hapless people of Europe by the Nazis. Tales of horror that defy description have come out of Poland and Russia, France, Belgium, and Holland. Frightful massacres in Greece, mass murder in Czechoslovakia, and deliberate extermination of millions of Jews in Poland, these have been the stories told by the hundreds for five ling years.

Somehow it has been hard for us to believe that such frightful happenings have ever occurred. It seemed more likely that most of these stories were propaganda, designed to stimulate hate for our enemies and thus intensify our efforts to produce and win the war. But now there has been released a 25,000 word report by the War Refugee Board, comprising Secretary of War Stimson, which puts the stamp of truth upon these awful tales of unbelievable horror. After a careful investigation the Board is convinced of the truth of its information that the Nazis have deliberately and systematically murdered, by gassing, shooting, and burning, literally millions of innocent civilians, Jews and Christians alike, all over Europe.

Eyewitness accounts and secretly taken pictures have revealed the existence of fearful extermination camps where men, women, and children were gassed by the hundreds of thousands and their bodies cremated, all as part of the sadistic German plan to subjugate the world.

Monday, November 27, 1944: —B-29s have again raided Tokyo! For the second time within 72 hours the Japanese capital has been the target for our mighty battleships of the air. Today's raid was led by San Francisco's own Colonel Walter C. Sweeny, who declared that the mission was successfully accomplished, although results of the bombings were not observed, since a solid overcast blanketed the city. The Colonel was confident that the Jap industrial targets were hit since our flyers have had a lot of practice in this type of precision bombing. Enemy opposition was slight and no Superfortresses were lost.

A colossal explosion similar to the one that rocked the San Francisco Bay Area when two ammunition ships exploded at Port Chicago recently, obliterated a Royal Air Force Depot in England yesterday. Thousands of tons of bombs and munitions blew up with such force that houses 60 miles away were rocked. Part of a nearby village and a cement factory were leveled in addition to the tremendous damage in the Depot area. At least 50 persons are known to be dead and hundreds injured.

The U.S. First and Third Armies scored new gains today in the mighty offensive being waged against the Germans on the western front. The Third, under General George S. Patton, captured the former German headquarters town of St. Avoid today, and raced northeastward to within 4 miles of the industrial Saarbrucken region. The First Army, led by General Courtney H. Hodges, broke through to seize Langerwehe, Nazi stronghold before the Roer River.

Tuesday, November 28, 1944: —Secretary Hull of the State Department, who has presided over that difficult office during many of this nation's most trying and perilous years, has resigned because of ill health. Four hours after his resignation was announced, President Roosevelt nominated Edward R. Stettinius, Jr. as his successor. The appointment of Stettinius, who has been under-secretary since October 2, is expected to receive prompt Senate approval.

Since eliminating the Metz stumbling block, the U.S. Third Army, under "Old Blood and Guts" Patton, has driven steadily forward until it is now smashing into Germany's rich Saar coal basin on a 26 mile front. The great stronghold of Saarbrucken is now under the guns of the advancing Yanks.

Nazi defenses at many other points along the 400 mile front appear to be cracking under the relentless pressure of six great

Allied armies. In the Cologne area, the now battle-tried U.S. Ninth Army smashed to the Roer River only 21 miles from Cologne and besieged the fortress city of Julich. Far to the south it was reported unofficially that the Rhine, north of Strasbourg, had been crossed. No confirmation of this from official sources—so, a grain of salt.

The fearful toll of war on the high seas was revealed today as the United States and Britain announced that 5,775 Allied merchant ships have been sunk since 1939. The total tonnage lost represented 35% of all the merchant shipping afloat in the world, or the stupendous sum of 25,472,000 tons.

Wednesday, November 29, 1944:- -Tokyo has been raided for the third time in a week. This time the huge bombers struck by night, cascading high explosives and incendiary bombs into the Japanese industrial areas. Hysterical Japanese radio commentators complained bitterly over the "unfair" tactics of the American airmen who hid in the clouds and darkness so the heroic Japanese airmen couldn't get at them. They also revealed their barbaric natures when they threatened a renewal of the atrocity slayings of American flyers who are forced to bail out over Japanese territory. A Domei commentator referred to the Americans as "cowardly Yankees" and "Savages" and warned that any B-29 crewman who bails out over Japan will be instantly killed by the enraged populace. We don't doubt your capabilities of such actions, Mr. Moto, but don't forget the warnings of Allied leaders that those Japanese responsible for such atrocities will be held fully accountable therefore. Those guilty will be tracked down and brought to justice after the war.

The battle for Leyte Island in the Philippines is still in its crucial stage, although heavy rains have brought land action to a virtual standstill. The Japs, however, are desperately attempting to reinforce their beleaguered garrison by sea while our sea and air forces are just as desperately trying to thwart their efforts. Our carrier-borne aircraft today caught a convoy of Japanese ships approaching Leyte and sent 13 vessels to the bottom, dispersing the rest. An estimated 4,000 Jap soldiers were believed to have drowned when the crowded troop ships were blasted.

Thursday, November 30, 1944: —It is very apparent from the course of events that the Japanese High Command considers the Battle of Leyte to be one of the most important and crucial contests of the war, one that may well decide the fate of the far-flung Pacific empire which fell to them so handily in 1941 and 1942. Their original garrison on the island has fought fiercely and well against General MacArthur's invading forces and, although driven back into a trap at Ormoc, have succeeded thus far in avoiding annihilation. In this they have been materially aided by tropical storms that have virtually stalled the American advance. Repeatedly the Japs have attempted to land large-scale reinforcement at Ormoc and some strong units, including an armored division, have succeeded in coming ashore. But, for the most part, American sea and air power have wreaked havoc among the convoys approaching Ormoc. On seven different occasions American fighter and fighter-bomber aircraft, together with surface units of U.S. Fleet, have practically wiped out enemy convoys of troop-laden transports, at an estimated cost of more than 20,000 Jap soldiers drowned and killed in the attacks. The latest convoy destroyed was caught in the Camotes Sea by American aircraft and thirteen ships were blasted to the bottom. Yet, despite their heavy losses, the Japs keep coming and it is not yet safe to predict the final outcome of this first great campaign for the liberation of the Philippines.

December

Friday, December 1, 1944: —The inside story of Pearl Harbor and the events leading up to the catastrophe of December 7, 1941 has not yet been told and apparently will not be revealed until after the war—if at all. This was indicated today by announcements from the War and Navy Departments that no court-martial proceedings will be conducted against Major General W.C. Short or Rear Admiral H.E. Kimmel, deposed Army and Navy commanders in the Hawaiian theater at the time of the disaster. Many people have agitated for three years for a full public airing of the facts and a trial of the military commanders. Today's announcements have squelched these demands and the real story of Pearl Harbor will continue to remain a tight Governmental secret.

The Allied armies on the steel and concrete-studded western frontier of Germany are locked in the most furious battles of the current offensive. Our forces are gaining but the gains are measured in yards rather than miles. The American First Army is attacking the heavily defended outposts of Duren on the road to Cologne and succeeded in driving a wedge 400 yards into the Germans' positions.

To the south General George S. Patton's Third Army is closing in on the vital Saar Basin, with the first important industrial town, Saarlautern, under the guns of the leading American units. Reconnaissance reports indicate that a mass exodus of German civilians is under way in the Saarlautern area.

Sad to report, San Francisco trails the pack of seven major cities in sales of War Bonds in the Sixth War Loan Drive. To date only 17.3% of the City's quota has been raised.

Saturday, December 2, 1944: —Emphasis was again placed on the seriousness of the Chinese situation today. Since the recall of General Stilwell from the Far East it has become increasingly apparent that China is taking a terrific beating from the Japanese. While the United States has been winning decisive victories against Japan in the Pacific the Mikado's legions have been consolidating themselves on the continent of Asia at the expense of the Chinese. Free China has been chopped in two by Japan's invading hordes during the past few months. And the yellow tide now stands barely 200 miles from Chungking. Most of the advance bases for American planes have either been seized by the victorious Japs or have been destroyed by our forces in the face of the enemy's rapid advance. In short, China is precariously close to being knocked out of the war, which would be a major catastrophe for the Allied cause and would prolong the war for many months.

Many reasons have been advanced to explain China's plight, including the failure to receive adequate help from the Allies, to war weariness and internal troubles. Generalissimo Chiang-Kai-Shek's regime has been sharply criticized for administrative failures and inability to rally the nation to meet the present Japanese threat. Even Russia has now denounced the Chiang government and stated that its failure to co-operate with the Chinese communists is responsible for recent Japanese successes. The Russians stated that the Generalissimo has failed to unify his country in its crisis and has followed generally "disastrous" policies.

Sunday, December 3, 1944: —General George S. Patton's hard-fighting American Third Army is punching deeper into the vitally important Saar Basin. One Yank spearhead has chopped its way into the German town of Saarlautern, key bastion only twelve miles from the big industrial center of Saarbrucken. Another steel-tipped column of Doughboys blasted a path into Saar Union, twenty-one miles to the south and east of Saarbrucken.

To the north, on the road to Cologne, fiercely fighting Yanks of the American Ninth Army overran most of the highway junction town of Linnich while their comrades of the veteran First Army battered their way yard by yard towards the heavily fortified stronghold of Duren which blocks the direct road to Cologne nineteen miles away.

Far to the south, on the American Seventh Army front, U.S. and French troops hurled the Nazi defenders back across the Rhine east of Strasbourg and seized the German town of Schweighausen.

Reports like the above indicate that General Eisenhower's mighty winter offensive is slowly yet surely grinding the German armies to bits in furious battles west of the Rhine. Casualties have undoubtedly been heavy on both sides, although the Nazis are suffering at least three to one losses, due to the vastly superior weight of artillery shells and bombs being hurled at them by the Allied armies. General Ike's avowed policy is to save American lives by expending American shells in huge quantities, so huge, in fact, that a shortage is threatened unless U.S. industry heeds the call for more and more shells and bombs to trade for American lives.

Monday, December 4, 1944: —Tokyo was blasted for the fourth time in nine days yesterday, when some 100 B-29 Superfortresses struck at the vital Musashina aircraft works in the suburbs of the enemy capital. Bombing weather was perfect and the big aerial battleships laid their strings of explosive eggs squarely on the rectangular factories where a large portion of Japan's airpower is (or was) produced. Fires and ruins were the result.

The U.S. raiders encountered the stiffest fighter opposition yet thrown up over the Japanese homeland. Almost a solid hour was spent in battling the Jap planes that intercepted the B-29s, but only one of the huge craft was lost. Dog-fights raged over the skies at altitudes that ranged up to six miles. At least a dozen of the enemy interceptors were knocked out of the air.

An American and a Japanese destroyer were sunk in a brief but furious naval action off the Coast of Leyte Island today. Most of the crew of the U.S. vessel was saved. Six enemy planes were shot down and another Nip destroyer was damaged in the same engagement.

On the home front the spotlight was turned on the critical danger of a munitions shortage. Part of the blame was laid on the increasing tendency of war workers to shift to peace time occupations, in anticipation of a quick victory. Unless this tendency is stopped and even reversed the country faces the prospect of a man-power draft.

Tuesday, December 5, 1944: —Greece today is a liberated country. That is to say, Greece has been purged of the deadly blight of Nazidom. But there is no peace tonight in the land where democracy and civilized culture were born. Greece is an example of the fate that awaits all of Europe as it is delivered from under the heel of the Teutonic oppressor. Tragically enough, liberation from one deadly menace will mean the rise of another almost as deadly—revolution and civil war—as rival factions within the various countries strive for power and domination. This tragic fate seems the inevitable aftermath to a great world struggle.

Greece is in just such a predicament. The right wing Government of Premier George Papandreou, established, with British blessings, shortly after the Nazis were ousted, is being challenged by armed left-wing elements. Furious fighting has broken out in the streets of Athens, with machine guns, rifles, and grenades being freely used. British tanks and troops have finally gone into action, in an attempt to restore order. Their intervention will undoubtedly have widespread repercussions throughout Europe and the United Nations, particularly in Russia, where left-wing elements are born.

Indications of the scale and fierceness of the fighting along the western edge of Germany was given today by the Allied Supreme Headquarters' announcement that Eisenhower's grand offensive is exacting the greatest toll of casualties the Nazis have yet suffered in Western Europe. Enemy losses are comparable to those suffered by either side in any major campaign in Russia during the past three years.

Wednesday, December 6, 1944: —Athens was a scene of turmoil today as left-wing members of the National Liberation Front battled with Greek troops and police. The latter were supported by British tanks, troops, and planes, as Prime Minister Winston Churchill moved to carry out his pledge that law and order would be maintained until the Greek people are able to peaceably select their own form of government by free elections.

Britain's policy of intervention in the internal affairs of liberated countries has been the object of severe criticism by the U.S. State Department in Washington. Our government's policy would be to abide by the Atlantic Charter which pledged equal rights for the smaller nations. England is apparently taking a more realistic (if you can call it that) view of the present world situation, in which they see Russia arbitrarily setting up spheres of influence and left-wing governments throughout Eastern

Europe and the Balkans. Obviously England is trying to look far into the future but whether her present activities and policies are conducive to the setting up of a permanent world peace is highly debatable.

General George S. Patton's drive across the Saar into Germany's vitally important industrial area is gaining momentum. Third Army Doughboys forced four more crossings of the Saar today and established a solid fifty mile front on the eastern bank.

On the First Army front to the north our troops were engaged today in repulsing strong German counter-attacks in the Bergstein area. At day's end the opposing armies were at their starting points.

Thursday, December 7, 1944: —Today is the third anniversary of Pearl Harbor. We have not forgotten, nor, it would seem, has a power greater than that of man. As though pre-arranged in retribution for the infamous sneak attack of three years ago a violent earthquake has struck Japan. The terrible quaking, that left the earth still vibrating six hours later, had its epicenter in the Tokyo area. One leading seismologist stated that the quake was the most violent ever recorded and must certainly have caused terrific damage in any populated area it may have struck. Maybe that will be a warning and a lesson to you, Mr. Moto.

B-29 Superfortresses aided the earthquake in joining the Japanese celebration of the Pearl Harbor attack. Two of the big bombers raided the enemy capital and cascaded thousands of fire bombs into the congested industrial areas of the city. All in all, the Japs must have had an exciting, if not pleasant, holiday.

General MacArthur pulled another surprise out of the bag today, sending a powerful amphibious force in to land on the Ormoc beaches. The 77th Division, under Major General Andrew Bruce, accomplished the difficult operation skillfully and moved inland to split the Japanese forces still resisting the advance of General MacArthur's main force.

The U.S. Navy contributed its share to the success of the new operation, not only in landing the attacking force, but spotting a Japanese convoy attempting to land reinforcements for the beleaguered garrison. Like seven others before it, this latest convoy, composed of 13 vessels, was totally destroyed.

Friday, December 8, 1944: —For the first time since the Civil War the United States finds herself entering into a fourth year of desperate and bloody warfare. As we compare today's situation with that of one, two, or three years ago we find it possible to hope that 1945 will bring victory over our enemies. But there are many imponderables that may prevent or delay the attainment of the goal. Our enemies are still strong, fanatical, and determined. Their homelands are well defended and inaccessible. There are many bloody miles ahead of us. But looking back over the past three years we perceive the tremendous strides that have been taken along that difficult road to victory.

Three years ago today we were all but prostrate before a vicious and treacherous enemy who had knifed us in the back. Defeat and degradation seemed very close at hand. Shaken out of our luxurious peace time existence as though seized by a maddened dog, we had not yet realized the grim realities of modern war.

Two years ago today we had tasted all the bitter pills of defeat that could be meted out by a triumphant foe yet had kept our feet and come back fighting. Our power was beginning to grow under the impetus of the greatest production campaign of all times. North Africa had been invaded, our British Allies had cleared Egypt of the Nazi foe and we were on the road back.

One year ago the tide had turned. A mighty U.S. Fleet was touring the seas in search of a skulking Japanese Navy that had been punished severely in the southern seas. Our fighting men had proved themselves superior to the foe in every department. We were well on the road back and the first gray streaks of the dawn of victory were breaking on the horizon.

Today the enemy, European and Oriental, is on the run. American men and American production have come into their own. We and our Allies are pounding at the final bastions remaining to the foe, with a long list of impressive victories behind us. Jap and German homelands are feeling the weight of our wrath and the end cannot be too far away. May Providence speed our arms throughout the coming year.

Saturday, December 9, 1944:—Another of those fearful accidents that follow in the wake of war occurred today when the main nitro plant of the Hercules Powder Plant in Contra

Costa County blew up with an earth shaking blast that was felt for twenty miles. Fortunately only two men were in the plant at the time, thus keeping down the death toll, but scores of other persons were injured and cut by flying glass. Buildings in the immediate vicinity were leveled and windows for miles around were shattered. The gods of war must be amused.

Disaster in huge doses is being administered to the Japanese homeland. A tremendous tidal wave followed in the wake of the recent violent earthquake, inundating portions of the most populous areas of Japan. Landslides and tumbling buildings wreaked havoc across a 150 mile belt of the land of the rising sun. Tokyo broadcasts admitted the damage but attempted, of course, to belittle its effect upon the country.

As though emphasizing that Nature's wrath was not enough, a sizeable force of our mighty B-29 Superfortresses again raided Tokyo and the Seto Naikai coastal areas for more than an hour today, starting huge fires that could be seen for 100 miles on the return trip. It is believed that the big Superfortresses sought out the Japanese Fleet in the Kure naval base. If the Japanese Imperial Navy won't come to us, we'll go to them. So beware!

With one more week to go, the U.S. Treasury Department announced that the bond quota for the Sixth War Loan Drive has gone over the top. Corporations and other organizations are responsible since individual purchases are still behind some 2 billion dollars.

Sunday, December 10, 1944: —The first Sunday in our fourth year of war has been a quiet, peaceful one here on the home front. The weather in the San Francisco Bay Area was warm and comfortable, leaving only the calendar as evidence that winter is upon us. In many other sections of the country, however, snow, ice, and freezing temperatures were sufficient reminders. But the date on the calendar also points out that Christmas is barely two weeks away. In many ways this Christmas will be different from any other within our memory. There will be gifts as usual; the tremendous shopping crowds prove that. But what gifts! Most of the merchandise is just plain junk—particularly the toys. The stores are full of poorly constructed rickety toys made of wood and cardboard, toys that won't last a week after Christmas. And the prices are two and three times the prices we paid for fine, beautiful toys before the war. There are some second hand pr-war metal and electric toys to be had if you know the right people or visit the right basements. But ordinary people like us can't afford them. They are being snapped up at unbelievable prices, ranging sometimes from ten to fifty times their original cost. It is one of the worst black markets of the war—profiteering at the expense of children's happiness. It reveals a particularly seamy side of human nature which I hope is not too prevalent, although I just got back from pricing a few Christmas trees—they had a nice one in San Mateo—just the thing—for $5.00. Many times we have purchased the same tree for 75 cents—in happier years.

Monday, December 11, 1944: —The battle for Leyte Island in the Philippines is entering its final, bloody stage. Fighting of the most desperate character is raging, according to General MacArthur's most recent communiqué. The successful, surprise amphibious landing at Ormoc by the 77th U.S. Division divided the enemy garrison into two segments, each of which is trapped with its back to the sea, facing almost certain annihilation or surrender and virtually no hope of reinforcements or supplies. American sea and air power rules the sea lanes to the island. The Nips are resisting fiercely but are being pushed slowly and inexorably into the sea. Another major disaster for the Japanese is imminent.

We have just learned that the Japanese Admiral who led the sneak attack on Pearl Harbor is dead. The Tokyo radio finally admitted that the naval officer, Vice-Admiral Chuichi Nagumo, was killed on Saipan last July 7. This admission brought to 73 the number of Japanese Admirals reported killed—by the Japs themselves—since last May. Eighteen Japanese Generals, by Tokyo admission, have also joined their ancestors during the same period. Thus is retribution visited upon those who speak of peace while they are plunging the knife into our back.

It is work or fight for men from 18-37 from now on, according to Selective Service Director, Lewis B. Hershey. Unless a man within that age group is doing war work or shifts immediately to war work, he will be drafted at once. The edict is necessary to prevent lags in war production and to meet General Eisenhower's plea for more and more ammunition.

Tuesday, December 12, 1944: —Showing their fear of the mounting Superfortress raids on their homeland, the Japanese have begun to evacuate Tokyo. All non-essential civilians are being sent from the capital in what will undoubtedly be one of the greatest mass evacuations in the history of war. Well may the Japs fear the mighty U.S. bombers, with their huge loads of explosives and incendiaries, if the popular conception of Tokyo is anywhere near the truth. The Japanese capital has long been thought of by Americans as a teeming, densely populated city of flimsy wood and paper buildings—a juicy target for incendiary bombs. Undoubtedly the city is far more modern than that but today's reports hint that great fires have already been kindled by the Superforts, since the Japs are tearing down sections of the city to act as "firebreaks." In any event, Tokyo's trials are only beginning.

In Europe the great Allied offensive is western Germany is still grinding ahead, despite bitter weather and desperate Nazi resistance. Duren, the last major bastion before Cologne, is under direct assault by crack units of General Courtney H. Hodges' American First Army. The Yanks are within a half mile of the city which lies astride the Roer River.

The most spectacular gains, at the present time, are being made by General Alexander M. Patch's American Seventh Army which has raced up the west bank of the Rhine to within 15 miles of the great German city of Karlsruhe, situated on the eastern side of the river.

Wednesday, December 13, 1944: —Approximately 100 B-29s struck another devastating blow at the Japanese homeland today, smashing heavily at the vital industrial city of Nagoya, home of the famous Mitsubishi Aircraft Works. The huge bombers took off from the newly established bases on Saipan and covered the round trip of more than 3,000 miles in almost perfect weather. Bombing results were said to be the best yet attained in the Superfortress campaign against Japan, due to the excellent visibility and the fact that the planes attacked at a much lower altitude than previously. Terrific explosions and fires were observed in the target area.

Enemy opposition to the devastating attack on the vitals of their war machine was relatively slight in spite of the lower altitude and the slackened speed of the planes which attacked the city from the east against a 100 mile headwind. Few fighter planes interfered with the Americans' bomb run and anti-aircraft fire over the target was ineffective.

On Leyte Island in the Philippines, General MacArthur is mustering his forces for the climactic phase of the Leyte campaign. U.S. torpedo boats and aircraft blasted another Jap convoy attempting to land reinforcements for the 20,000 to 25,000 troops facing surrender or death in the Ormoc corridor. This is the ninth enemy convoy destroyed while attempting this futile task. Unknown thousands of Japanese troops have been killed or drowned and thousands of tons of shipping destroyed in these abortive attempts.

Thursday, December 14, 1944: —The B-29 campaign against Japan and her ill-gotten empire continued today, with 100 giant Superforts blasting enemy installations in Siam, Rangoon, and Burma. A small number of planes also struck at Tokyo—just so the Emperor's sleep wouldn't be disturbed too much. The strikes against Siam, Rangoon, and Burma, were carried out in good weather by planes of the 20th Air Force based in India. Bombing results were said to be excellent. All B-29s returned safely from today's attacks but one of the big aircraft is missing from the Nagoya attack of yesterday and is presumed lost.

On the political front, Prime Minister Winston Churchill is under withering fire from members of Parliament and the press, for his policies on the Greek and Italian problems. The mounting fury of the Greek civil war and Britain's armed intervention in the conflict is tending to heap criticism on the Churchill government. The Prime Minister heatedly defended his position today in a speech before Commons, but the situation is full of potential dynamite. There should be interesting developments in the near future.

On the western front, Lieut. General Alexander M. Patch's hard-hitting U.S. Seventh Army has smashed into the Karlsruhe corner and now stands only ½ mile from the German border and seven miles from the great city of Karlsruhe itself.

Friday, December 15. 1944: —General MacArthur took another mighty step towards Manila today. Troops under his command swept ashore on Mindoro Island this morning under cover of the big guns of the Navy and quickly consolidated their beachhead in the face of very meager resistance. The invading Yanks achieved total surprise and all initial objectives fell easily.

The new invasion carried General MacArthur's forces to within 130 miles of Manila and constituted a jump of some 170 miles from the Leyte battlefield. Successful occupation of Mindoro will also complete the splitting of the Philippines and will put our air and naval forces in a position to dominate the China Sea. Seizure of bases on Mindoro is also a prerequisite to an invasion of Luzon or possibly an attack on the Japanese held China coast itself.

B-29 bombers paid Japland another visit today, some striking at Tokyo with fire bombs while others engaged in reconnaissance sorties over the Kobe-Osaka area, presaging heavier raids to come. None of our planes were lost in the day's operation.

Across the world, on the snow-bound western European front, a fourth U.S. army battered its way across the frontier of Germany. The latest penetration of the "holy soil" of Naziland was made by General Alexander M. Patch's American Seventh Army. One column of Yanks stormed into the Reich near Lauterbourg while a second column speared through ten miles to the west at Wissembourg.

Saturday, December 16, 1944: —In the midst of Japanese reports of a violent sea battle in the Sulu Sea south of Mindoro, it was confirmed that American amphibious forces have firmly established at least three beachheads on that island and have driven at least four miles inland towards the town of San Jose on the southwest coast of the island. Two airfields are located in the San Jose area and these were probably seized by the invading Americans although full details of the advance are not yet available. Apparently, however, the surprised Japs have not yet organized effective resistance and our casualties have been very light.

Apparently the story is different on the sea approaches to Mindoro. The Japanese are obviously trying to deal out the same treatment to our invasion convoys that was given to their relief convoys to Ormoc by our Navy and Air Force. Furious naval and aerial battles are raging off the coast of Mindoro, with the Japs throwing everything they have in the Philippines at our ships, hoping to crush the invasion by destroying its lifeline. Their failure is seen by the fact that division after division of Yanks are being safely landed on the captured beachheads.

On the western front in Europe, General Patch's fighting U.S. Seventh Army has seized both Lauterbourg and Wissembourg, key towns near the frontier of northeastern France. Other U.S. Armies, General Patton's Third and General Hodges' First, were engaged in bitter house-to-house fighting that netted gains measured in yards.

Sunday, December 17, 1944: —The embattled Philippines were the scene of more bitter fighting today. On Mindoro Island, the rampaging Yanks swept inland more than nine miles, driving the ineffective enemy opposition before them. Japanese efforts to prevent supplies and reinforcements from reaching the new invasion front have failed although some damage was inflicted and some vessels lost in furious aerial attacks on our convoys.

On Leyte, General MacArthur is still engaged in mopping up the remnants of the once formidable Japanese garrison. The Tokyo radio has admitted losing 162,159 men in the Philippines since November 1, allocating their losses to Army, 83,748 and Navy, 78,411. This admitted loss is twice the number of enemy casualties estimated by General MacArthur and reflects the full extent of the disaster they suffered in the second great battle of the Philippines Sea. To counter the severity of their admitted losses, the Japs claimed the fantastic destruction of 500,000 Americans. Don't they wish it were true.

Things are getting pretty hot on the political front as well. Russia has proclaimed her plan, with British acquiescence, for the partitioning of Poland and this, together with the volcanic Greek situation, has raised uproar throughout America and Britain, as well as caused fear and uneasiness in many other members of the United Nations. Prime Minister Winston Churchill is receiving particularly violent criticism for his international policies and many United Nations' leaders are calling for an immediate meeting of the "Big Three" to clarify many vague and misty problems now confronting the world.

Monday, December 18, 1944: —Like cornered beasts the Nazis have turned on their foes and have launched a giant counter-offensive, the full power of which cannot yet be estimated. The big offensive, reminiscent of Ludendorff's last great drive in 1918, was flung against the sector of the western front held by the United States First Army and followed one of the most stupendous artillery barrages of the war. Crack German panzers then plunged through the gap in the First Army lines and scored initial gains of several miles. The drive has already carried across the Belgium and Luxembourg borders and appears to be developing on a major scale.

From news flashes being received it appears that the great German counter-offensive has been under way for several days. The front has been "blacked out" for security reasons, thus preventing us from receiving any up-to-date news. Even the lasts dispatches are about 48 hours behind the actual developments. It is plainly evident that the situation is acute, the action extremely fluid, and the outcome very much in doubt. This is undoubtedly the Nazis' final bid for victory or a negotiated peace and much hangs in the balance.

It is reported that the Germans are employing a new, secret, and powerful weapon in their latest attack. It is thought to be some sort of rocket projectile but details are not yet available.

And so we face our first serious set-back on the western front. Great land battles of this kind inevitably mean large-scale slaughter. It is a bleak outlook.

Tuesday, December 19, 1944: —After absorbing the first shock of Field Marshal Gerd Von Rundstedt's mighty German counter-offensive, it appears that the U.S. First Army is rallying. Masses of U.S. tanks and infantry are moving up to nip the Nazi spearheads which have been slowed down all along the 50 mile front.

Aiding the Nazis in the drive has been unfavorable weather which has bogged down the Allied Air Forces and prevented them from strafing and bombing the attacking panzers. It has also served to "blind" our armies to some extent, giving the advancing tank columns a big advantage. The initial momentum of the German drive, which hit a thinly held sector of the American lines, has carried them some 21 miles into Belgium and Luxembourg. Ultimate objectives of Marshal Rundstedt's offensive are not yet clear, but the Germans are on familiar ground, their victory drives in 1870 and 1940 being launched in the same area.

Where did the Nazis get the reserves and the crack panzer groups to launch this grand offensive? That is a question that all formerly "optimistic" observers are asking. Apparently the answer points to the eastern front, where the expected Russian winter drive has failed to materialize. The Nazis have gambled that it will not start soon and have withdrawn some of their finest troops for the big effort against the western Allies. If this is true, where is the vaunted team-play of the "Big Three" about which so much hope was born at Teheran?

Wednesday, December 20, 1944: Missing

Thursday, December 21, 1944: —Germany's terrific winter offensive has lanced 30 miles into Belgium and Luxembourg, ripping a 25 mile gap in the American First Army's lines. It appears evident that the powerful enemy thrust came unexpectedly and scored a complete surprise, which accounts for its initial success. Because of the tremendous size of the German attacking force, one wonders where Allied intelligence was, to permit its massing without our knowledge. We can only hope that their failure to forewarn our armies may not prove irreparable.

The latest reports available, which are at least 48 hours behind, indicate that the Nazis are trying to repeat their performance of 1940 and are heading along the same roads that led to victory in that previous campaign—north through Belgium towards the Channel ports and south towards the Ardennes Gap and Sedan. Thus far, their progress has been comparable to that previous drive, although American resistance is stiffening, particularly on both flanks of the German salient. The steel-tipped spearhead, however, is driving ever deeper into our rear areas, presenting a grave threat to our communications.

The only bright item in the news is the revelation that General George S. Patton is wheeling his U.S. Third Army northward to smash at the base of the German bulge, in what could conceivably change the picture from a Nazi victory to a Nazi catastrophe if he is able to nip off the German drive at its source. It will probably take several weeks to tell.

Friday, December 22, 1944: —In terrific fighting that was described as being "fiercer than Stalingrad," gallant American

Doughboys have succeeded in stalling one prong of the mighty German offensive that, in three days, has smashed deep into Belgium and Luxembourg and has posed a threat to the existence of our very armies on the Western Front. Stalwart U.S. First Army troops gamely met the full fury of the Nazi drive into Belgium and have pounded its steel-tipped spearhead to a stop, at least temporarily.

To the south, in Luxembourg, however, the German panzers are still pushing ahead toward Ardennes and the Sedan gateway into France. Evidencing the gravity of the situation was General Dwight D. Eisenhower's Order of the Day to the American armies on the Western Front. In it the General called upon every man to rise to new heights of courage, of resolution, and of effort, so that the enemy's great gamble may, in fact, be turned into his greatest defeat.

It appears from present reports that the German High Command has thrown a crack army of some 250,000 men into the current offensive, including several divisions of panzers and upwards of 1,000 tanks.

Aiding the German advance has been misty, miserable weather that has prevented the greatly superior Allied Air Force from attacking the advancing columns or their communication lines. We can only hope that their luck in this respect will not hold for many days.

Saturday, December 23, 1944: —Last night we hoped for a weather break on the Western Front. Today we got it and swarms of Allied bombers and fighters roared out to attack the exposed columns of Marshal von Rundstedt's advancing armies. It was the best break since the offensive began and the Allied planes made the most of it. Results are not yet certain, but the tide may turn on the efforts of the airmen.

The German Air Force was also out in large numbers during the day and countless air battles raged all along the flaming battleground. Our flyers claimed the destruction of at least 100 enemy planes in combat and it is admitted that many Allied aircraft failed to return. The cost is high on both sides.

Ground fighting was fluid throughout the area today and attained melee proportions in many places. American tanks fought a brilliant defensive action west of St. Vith, in Belgium, beating off a heavy panzer attack in that sector.

General George S. Patton's tanks began slashing into the southern flank of the German breakthrough today, bringing new hope that the enemy salient may yet be pinched off at its base. Nevertheless, the situation remains very grave.

An interesting item happened on the home front today when War Mobilization Director James F. Byrnes banned all horse racing after January 3, 1945. The step was taken because of the war crisis, in an effort to relieve manpower shortages in critical areas.

Sunday, December 24, 1944: —Here we are on the eve of our fourth war time Christmas. It is hard to even voice the usual sentiments of "Merry Christmas" or "Peace on earth, Good Will to men." Those phrases seem singularly out of place at this time when the world appears to be nothing but a boiling cauldron of hate and destruction. I wonder what the "Prince of Peace" thinks of this world as he watches us prepare to celebrate the anniversary of His birth. I wonder how much longer He will tolerate Man's evil machinations, or the despoilment of his earthly heritage. Perhaps He has decided that Man's evil ways have decreed his self-destruction.

Despite the lack of the old-time Yuletide spirit in our hearts, we have gone about the preparation of Christmas for the benefit of our four youngsters. They are young and innocent and look forward to the coming of old Saint Nick with the same mysterious excitement and pleasure of our own childhood days. So they must not be disappointed.

It is about 1:30 at night as I sit down to finish this article. We have completed the Xmas preparations. The tree is trimmed—with our carefully preserved pre-war decorations— and the children's toys are laid out. They are war time toys—a cardboard doll house, rag dolls, wood and plastic pull toys, a paratrooper's outfit, some building blocks, and a set of books. Everything looks nice and we are a very lucky family. But as for me, I'm dog-tired and morning will be here too soon—so Good Night!

Monday, December 25, 1944: —Well, it has been a pleasant Christmas Day for us. We cannot deny it, nor can we deny that our every hope and prayer has been that next Christmas will see an end to war and thousands of our gallant fighting men will be back among us to enjoy the blessings of a peaceful and grateful America.

On all the far-flung battlefields there was not much time to celebrate Christmas. There was bitter fighting to be done, particularly on the Western Front, where courageous Americans proved themselves worthy descendants of their fathers by stopping the Germans cold on almost every sector of the Belgium-Luxembourg breakthrough front. On the southern flank of the Nazi spearhead, the Americans were hitting particularly heavy counter-blows, driving the Germans back as much a four miles. At Bastogne, a U.S. battle group was encircled by the advancing Germans but continued to repel all efforts to crush them. Their fate, however, remains very doubtful.

Clearing weather again gave the Allied airmen a chance to pound the advancing German columns. Approximately 7,000 planes, including more than 2,000 U.S. heavy bombers, smashed at the enemy during the day, deluging his advance units and his rear areas with a rain of high explosives and bullets. The German Air Force was out again but was completely overwhelmed by the huge Allied air fleet.

Tuesday, December 26, 1944: —Despite the almost superhuman efforts of Allied airmen and the gallant, dogged defense of dozens of American army units, the great offensive launched by Field Marshal Gerd von Rundstedt continues to make progress towards the vital Meuse River. Disregarding the terrific losses meted out to his forces by the swarms of Allied aircraft, the German commander struck hard today, apparently concentrating on joining the two prongs of his drive towards Rochefort and the Meuse. Latest reports place his panzer spearheads only 15 miles from the important river barrier.

Because of our preoccupation with the events on the Western Front, we have overlooked important developments on the Pacific battle front. The extent of General MacArthur's victory on Leyte Island is just being revealed. In the campaign just completed the Japs lost an estimated 112,728 troops killed and but 493 captured. General MacArthur stated that the completeness of this destruction has "seldom been paralleled in the history of warfare" and has resulted in what is probably the greatest defeat in the annals of the Japanese army. The enemy casualties reported does not include the thousands of troops that must have been drowned in the ten convoys that were destroyed while attempting to reinforce the Leyte garrison nor does it include the casualties inflicted in the great naval battles that raged in the Philippines Sea in October and November.

Prime Minister Winston Churchill has gone to Athens in an effort to bring the Greek Civil War to an end. The pitiful situation in Greece has cost Churchill much prestige.

Wednesday, December 27, 1944: —The heroic U.S. troops defending the encircled Belgium town of Bastogne have been rescued. A relief force that has been battling desperately for days to open a corridor to the trapped Yanks finally broke through the encircling Nazi lines and found the American garrison intact, still full of fight and in good spirits. They have been killing plenty of Germans since the onrushing Panzers of Marshal Rundstedt's surrounded them and have repulsed every attempt to take the town. By their stout resistance they have denied the use of one of the most vital communication hubs in Belgium to the Nazis.

Late news reports also indicate that the German offensive has been stopped or slowed to a crawl at almost every other point in the salient. In at least one sector the enemy was forced back to his West Wall defenses.

In the Pacific theater furious action raged in, on, and over the waters adjacent to the Philippine Islands. American submarines added 27 more Japanese vessels to their ever-mounting toll of enemy shipping, bringing their over-all score to 1,090 ships sunk, probably sunk, or damaged since Pearl Harbor.

Steaming boldly to with 750 miles of Tokyo, an American task force of cruisers and destroyers bombarded the Japanese island of Iwo Jima today, engaging the shore batteries in a hot duel. A simultaneous attack by U.S. carrier planes joined with the naval bombardment to give the Japs a very bad time of it.

Thursday, December 28, 1944: —Slowly, inexorably, amidst fearful carnage, the tide of battle is turning in our favor along the bloody salient in Belgium and Luxembourg. Fighting of the bitterest kind is raging all along the fifty mile front, with the Germans stopping at nothing in the way of bestiality and trickery to kill our men and destroy our defenses. On blood-soaked survivor of a six man patrol told of the Nazi SS Elite Guardsmen capturing the outnumbered little band of Yanks, questioning them perfunctorily, and then shooting them down in cold blood. Some of the Americans who were not killed outright by the hail of bullets had their life stomped out of them by hobnailed boots. That is the kind of foe we are facing. It will not be easy.

Attention on the Eastern Front, about which there has been so little to write for some time, is centered on the Russian drive into the Hungarian capital of Budapest. A strong garrison of Germans and Hungarians are defending the city desperately, engaging in a "Stalingrad" block by block, house by house defense of the sprawling metropolis. Red Army attack forces, however, are vastly superior in number and the fall of the city appears imminent.

On the home front a showdown battle has begun between the Government and the War Labor Board on the one side, and Montgomery Ward and its board chairman, Sewell Avery, on the other. The defiant refusal of the Mail Order Company and Mr. Avery to obey the War Labor Board's directives on wages and employee-labor relations has caused President Roosevelt to order Government seizure of the Company's plants in seven cities.

Friday, December 29, 1944: —It appears that the savage German winter offensive into Belgium and Luxembourg has at last been brought under control through the almost superhuman efforts of every branch of the Allied armed forces. Rallying U.S. First Army troops punched the German advance on the nose and drove it back at least 15 miles, eliminating the threat to the Meuse River, at least for the time being. At the same time General George S. Patton's Third Army smashed strongly at the underside of the salient, hammering out gains up to two miles.

It is estimated that the Germans have lost nearly 1,000 tanks since starting their massive offensive. This tremendous toll only serves to emphasize the large scale of the attack and warns us that the number of American casualties will shock us when the information is released.

Even before the losses of the current campaign are announced, the fearful part of war has struck close to home many times. In the one department in which I work, comprising approximately 130 employees, nine members of the staff have received the fateful telegrams from the War Department or Navy Department, announcing the death in action of brothers, husbands, or sons. Many hopes and plans and many young lives have been blasted by the ill-fortunes of a merciless war. It is a saddening sight to see the anguished despair of those who have lost a dearly loved one. It also steels one's determination to do his utmost to make certain that this shall be the last world-wide disaster of man's own making—at least for many generations to come.

Saturday, December 30, 1944: —The line of battle wavered back and forth along the perimeter of the Luxembourg-Belgium salient today, with the Germans striking back ferociously against the advancing armor of General George S. Patton's U.S. Third Army. Nevertheless, Patton's men expanded their frontage from 35 to 40 miles and drove well past Bastogne to within 12 miles of First Army troops attacking on the north side of the bulge. A junction of the two armies would entrap major units of Field Marshal von Rundstedt's invading army. We can be sure that the German commander will counter this move with everything at his command; tremendous battles can be expected—and the heavy losses that go with them.

Land, air, and sea activity in the far Pacific, as the year 1944 draws to a close, consists for the most part, in preliminary sparring moves preparatory to the next major campaigns. Leyte is ours, after a fierce six-weeks battle ended in brilliant victory for us, disastrous defeat for Japan. Our positions on Mindoro Island are secure and we are slowly moving inland. Samar Island is also ours—with little opposition. The decisive battle will undoubtedly be on Luzon.

Yielding to British pressure wielded by Prime Minister Churchill after his return from Athens, King George of Greece today issued a proclamation naming Archbishop Damaskinos as regent of his strife-torn country. King George, who is in London where he fled when the Nazis overran Greece, thereby committed what many observers believe will prove to be abdication of his ancient throne.

Sunday, December 31, 1944: —The bloody, eventful year of 1944 ends in just exactly two hours. Although it is ending in a note of gloom from the Western Front, where our armies have suffered their worst setback since Bataan, the year as a whole has seen tremendous strides being taken on the road to victory. Undoubtedly the most sensational piece of news during the year was the invasion of Normandy. The excitement of June 6 will long be remembered by us on the home front as well as by those who took part in that colossal undertaking.

General Patton's great drive across France and that grateful country's joyous celebration of their liberation was another high spot in a crowded year. Presidential elections, Philippine invasions, mighty naval battles, earthquakes, explosions—all these and many other history making events were on our daily bill of fare during 1944, which will undoubtedly hold its own as a rip-snorting year during the "roaring forties" of the twentieth century.

The last few days of 1944 have seen the tightening of civilian rationing, particularly on foodstuffs. On Christmas the Office of Price Administration announced that many meats and canned goods that were previously point-free would now be rationed. Butter was raised from 20 to 24 points and certain blue points that had hitherto been good indefinitely were cancelled. The latter feature of the new program has caused a great hullabaloo among many housewives who had been saving points for special occasions. But shortages have to be met somehow and if they didn't need the points when they were intended to be used, they can get along without them now.

1945

Monday, January 1, 1945: —Well, it's a new year and if the weather is any omen we should have a wonderful twelve months. It was unbelievably beautiful today—a direct contrast to the wet, gloomy, fog of yesterday. It was something like coming upon a brilliantly lighted jeweler's window in the depths of a coal mine. We spent most of the day out in the yard in our shirtsleeves and celebrated in the afternoon by using up about half of our next three months gasoline rations to take a good long automobile ride. Shades of yesteryears! But it was fun to get out on the road again.

Our spirits were dampened a little when we read the evening paper. We realized that the old world had not changed despite the entry of a new year. Death and disaster are able to strike without warning regardless of the date. Today's bad news was the worst railroad tragedy in many months. The speeding second section of the crack Pacific Limited of the Southern Pacific roared out of the darkness before dawn and smashed into the crowded passenger cars of the first section. The toll: at least 48 dead, 81 injured. The accident occurred 22 miles west of Ogden, Utah, when the first section stopped to permit a freight train ahead to repair a hot-box. All warning signals were working perfectly and no one will ever know why the engineer rode his engine into the rear of the leading section. He died, along with 19 other civilians and 29 service personnel.

On the western front, optimistic reports hint that General Patton's armor is on the rampage again, punching out a two mile gain against furious German opposition.

Tuesday, January 2, 1945: —General George S. Patton's big counter-drive against the underside of the Luxembourg-Belgium salient has forced the Germans to abandon any hope of continuing their advance towards the Meuse or Sedan. Instead Marshal Rundstedt apparently is faced with the task of extricating his westernmost units from possible entrapment. His grandiose plans for repeating the German performance of 1940 may well end in his most disastrous defeat.

Nevertheless, the Germans appear to have more reserves than we thought possible. This is evident from the fact that, despite their heavy commitments in the salient battle, they have mounted what appears to be a major attack against the U.S. Seventh Army in the Bitche area of northeastern France between the Saarland and the Rhine. It is like an inflated toy balloon, compress it in one place and it bulges out in another. The only answer is to knock the wind out of it completely and that will take some doing.

The Navy Department today announced the loss of one of America's most famous submarines, the 1,525 ton Harder. The undersea boat was the holder of a Presidential unit citation for destroying vast quantities of Japanese shipping. The Harder was the 35th U.S. submarine to be lost in this war.

War Mobilization and Reconversion Director James F. Byrnes today called upon Congress to enact legislation to better mobilize the Nation's manpower. In particular, he mentioned the more effective use of 4-F's, closer regulation of strikes, and unemployment benefits for war workers who may lose out on peacetime opportunities by staying on their vital war jobs to the end.

Wednesday, January 3, 1945: —The powerful new offensive action by the Germans in the Bitche area of northeastern France has forced the withdrawal of American troops from all their bridgeheads recently established in the German territory between the Sarreguemines area and the Rhine. The Nazi drive obviously is in the nature of a diversionary attack in support of their forces engaged in the Ardennes effort but the new offensive has attained surprising power and momentum, pushing the U.S. Seventh Army back as much as seven miles in some places.

In the salient battle General Patton's men are engaged in fierce fighting around Bastogne in the dent made possible by the heroic defense of the once encircled Yankee garrison of that Belgian town. On the northern side of the salient the U.S. First

Army has launched a counter-attack in co-ordination with the Third Army push from the south. Junction of the two armies would split the German bulge and trap thousands of Rundstedt's best troops and armor.

The Pacific war was punctuated by another heavy B-29 raid on the Japanese homeland. The huge bombers cascaded hundreds of tons of high explosives on the war factories and military targets of Nagoya, Osaka, and Hamamatsu, on the main Jap island of Honshu. Even the Tokyo radio admitted that some damage was caused.

The 79th Congress of the United States convened today. If the legislators sense the gravity and importance of the tasks facing them, this should be a history-making session.

Thursday, January 4, 1945: —The all-out counter-offensive launched yesterday by the U.S. First Army against the northern flank of the German salient in Belgium has ground out a three and one half mile gain despite bitter resistance from the enemy. A swirling blizzard blocked out most of the battlefield during the day but General Hodges' determined Yanks plowed ahead, hoping for an early junction with General Patton's Third Army battling in the Bastogne sector.

For the first time since the start of the Nazis' winter offensive we are permitted to know the names of some of the American fighting units responsible for stemming the German onslaught and preventing a catastrophic breakthrough after the fashion of 1940. Ten American divisions played the principal roles in meeting the full fury of the attack head-on, absorbing its initial power, and then gradually bringing it to a full stop and turning the tables into a counter-offensive of their own. The gallant 99th Division of the U.S. First Army held the bloody northern corner of the Ardennes salient against the ferocious onslaught of four Nazi divisions, yielding ground grudgingly and exacting a fearful price. Their defense upset Marshal Rundstedt's entire time schedule.

Glorious tribute was also paid to the following American divisions: The Ninth, Second, First, 30th and 75th Infantry Divisions, the 82nd Airborne, the Seventh and Ninth Armored, and the 28th Division. In every case these units kept their heads despite the shock and surprise of the enemy attack and by their courage and resourcefulness have prevented disaster and are well on their way towards snatching a decisive victory from possible defeat.

Friday, January 5, 1945: —General Eisenhower has shuffled the command of his armies on the western front in a move necessitated by the virtual splitting of the U.S. First Army by the German salient. Field Marshal Sir Bernard L. Montgomery, conqueror of the one-time Desert Fox, has been given the command of the northern units of the U.S. First Army, the U.S. Ninth Army, the British Second and the Canadian First Armies. Lieut. General Omar N. Bradley now commands the southern units of the First and General Patton's Third Armies.

Russia gave evidence today that she intends to go pretty much her own way, both now and in the post-war era. This was shown by her recognition, announced today, of the Communist-controlled puppet Polish government set up under Russian aegis in Lublin. The move was an open break with both the United States and Great Britain, since those governments had informed Moscow that they would not abandon the exiled Polish Government in London. Nevertheless the Russians went ahead with their plans, disregarding its effect on United Nations unity.

In the Pacific, American troops took another long step towards Manila by occupying the tiny isle of Marinduque, 20 miles east of Mindoro and 100 miles southeast of the Philippine capital. Complete surprise was achieved and the occupation accomplished against insignificant opposition.

Saturday, January 6, 1945: —President Roosevelt today delivered his annual message to the new Congress. The Chief Executive again called for a national service law to provide for the "total mobilization of all our human resources for the prosecution of the war." Such a law would give the Government power to specify the kind of work each man or woman must do. It would be the last step towards total war time regimentation.

Also included in the President's recommendations were the drafting of the four million 4-F's and the induction of nurses to meet a serious shortage in Army and Navy hospitals.

The above were the most challenging and controversial recommendations in the President's long message. The rest of it dealt with his post-war plans, his view of the present situation on the fighting fronts, and his foreign policy. All in all, the message was good, although it will provide the food and foundation for many bitter debates during the coming year.

General Courtney H. Hodges' U.S. First Army, now under the direct command of Field Marshal Sir Bernard L. Montgomery, is scoring new gains in its four-day old counter-offensive against the northern flank of the German salient. Today's advance carried them more than a mile closer to a junction with the U.S. Third Army while indications of a general softening up of Nazi resistance along the northern flank gave promise of an early meeting between the two U.S. armies.

Sunday, January 7, 1945: —The jittery Tokyo radio has broadcast reports hinting that American forces "may have landed" on Luzon Island in the Philippines. No confirmation has been heard from any Allied source, although it is well known that several huge American naval armadas, some of which may include transports and landing barges, are at sea off the Philippine Islands. The Japanese Domei News Agency reported that at least one of the U.S. sea armadas has been sighted in the waters west of Lingayen Bay, where overwhelming Japanese forces first landed three years ago in their original conquest of Luzon. The tables may now be turned.

Decisive events in the Pacific war may be close at hand if the Japanese report of an American landing on Luzon is correct. The Japanese can hardly permit Luzon to fall without a major struggle and we can expect the first all-out land battle between the main Japanese armies and our invasion forces. In the Leyte campaign the Japs were handed the worst defeat on land in the history of the Empire but the battle for Luzon will probably dwarf the Leyte struggle. The fate of the Philippines and most, if not all, of Japan's ill-gotten South Pacific Empire hangs in the balance.

Mighty B-29 Superfortresses have been busy over the home islands of the Japanese during the past three days. One group scattered incendiaries over Tokyo's industrial district, causing several conflagrations. Another large force blasted the Jap island of Kyushu in a bold daylight sweep. To the Superfortress boys, Japan is getting to be a regular milk run.

Monday, January 8, 1945: —We are dependent upon the Tokyo radio for hints as to what is transpiring in the Philippine area lately, since our own military spokesmen are tight-lipped about what are indubitably history making developments in that theater of war. It is clear that complex maneuvers on a grand scale are being conducted by our amphibious forces off the coast of Luzon. Today's report from the Japanese capital stated that a powerful American task force, consisting of battleships, cruisers, and carriers, is bombarding the beach defenses in the Lingayen Gulf sector of central Luzon. A landing in that area appears imminent, according to the Jap statement, although several other points on the island are threatened by other American task forces.

The dark, gloomy mist of defeat is rising from the Ardennes bulge in Western Europe and in its place the first bright light of victory is breaking forth. Marshal Rundstedt, frustrated in his do or die effort to smash the American line and roll through to the Meuse and Sedan, is back-pedaling as fast as he originally advanced, hoping to extricate most of his crack troops from the trap that is fast closing in around them. Four Allied armies, the U.S. First and Ninth, the British Second, and the U.S. Third, are pounding the salient from north and south with ever-increasing power, chopping off straggling enemy units, and inflicting heavy casualties on the fiercely resisting Nazi rear-guards. Thousands of Allied warplanes are harassing the retreating foe unceasingly, hindered only by raging blizzards that sometimes black out large sectors of the front for days at a time.

Tuesday, January 9, 1945: —LUZON IS INVADED! General MacArthur has taken the last big step on the road back to Bataan, Corregidor, and Manila. A huge American amphibious force swept ashore on the flat beaches of Lingayen Gulf and apparently achieved a complete tactical surprise. This almost incredible feat, aided no doubt by the magnificent feint at Marinduque which apparently convinced the Japs that our Luzon attack would come from the south, permitted our invading forces to drive ashore against almost negligible resistance. The presence of at least three other naval task forces at sea also contributed to the confusion of the enemy.

The latest reports on the invasion indicate that our forces have established four solid beachheads and are piling up supplies and reinforcements preparatory to moving inland towards the broad flat plains leading southward some 120 miles to Manila.

The only serious opposition encountered thus far in the landings was a belated but fierce attack on the invasion armada by a considerable number of Japanese planes and a few light naval vessels. Protecting warships and aircraft shot down at least 79 enemy planes and destroyed one midget submarine as well as two destroyers. The incredibly smooth landing operation was not interrupted.

Thus, with a great deal of gratification, the entire nation acclaims this rousing climax to one of history's greatest military campaigns, the 5,300 mile march across the Pacific culminating in the final battle to liberate Luzon and the entire Philippines from the grip of the Oriental tyrant.

Wednesday, January 10, 1945: —Further details of the Luzon invasion reveal that the operation was conducted on a colossal scale, equaled only by the Normandy attack last June. Literally hundreds of ships, big and small, covered the sea for miles around and unloaded their precious cargoes of men, equipment, and supplies almost unhindered by the obviously stunned foe. Countless warships, from battleships to torpedo boats, stood guard and pounded the invasion beaches with hundreds of mighty guns.

Within a few hours after the first landing barges touched shore in the Lingayen Gulf an army of some 100,000 Yanks began moving inland towards the broad highways leading to Manila. Recent reports reveal penetrations of four miles along a 20 mile front. No major resistance has been encountered as yet and the American advance is gaining momentum. It now appears that our forces will not engage any sizeable enemy force until the natural defense line of the Agno River is reached. So far everything is "duck soup" to use a slang expression.

Things are looking up on the Western European front as well. The once dangerous German salient into Belgium and Luxembourg is now a badly bent and shaky bulge. Troops of the British Second Army hit the nose of the bulge hard today, driving the Nazis from eight towns. At the same time U.S. forces to the east encircled the German strongholds of La Roche and Vielsalm, threatening garrisons with annihilation.

Thursday, January 11, 1945: —Units of the United States Sixth Army, which swept ashore on the Lingayen beaches of Luzon

Island three days ago, have driven inland from eighteen to twenty miles, liberating 30 Philippine cities and encountering only scattered and feeble resistance thus far from the 200,000 Japanese troops known to be on the island. Patrols are reported to have reached the Agno River, the first natural defense barrier on the plains leading to Manila. There are no indications that the enemy plans a major stand along the river and there is considerable speculation that the Japs may have decided not to defend Manila but plan to retire to the mountain fortresses of northern Luzon where they could hold out indefinitely.

It was officially announced in Washington D.C. today that U.S. casualties in the war now total 646,380. This does not include the undoubtedly heavy losses in the Ardennes bulge battle. Of the total casualties announced more than 138,000 are dead and 74,000 are missing. The rest are wounded and prisoners. Behind these cold figures are the countless tales of heartbreak and sorrow. What a grisly business for mankind to engage in.

As the war reaches its critical stages and the losses pour in, Selective Service officials warn that draft requirements are tightening. Every able-bodied man in the country under 30 years of age faces almost certain induction to meet the demands of the Army and Navy for young and aggressive replacements. Approximately 900,000 more men will be called up in the next six months.

Friday, January 12, 1945: —Displaying more of the brilliant American teamwork that has carried the U.S. flag to victory after victory against the Japs, the United States Third Fleet, under Admiral William F. Halsey, provided powerful support for General MacArthur's Manila bound Luzon invaders by boldly raiding Japanese bases along the coast of French Indo-China today. Alerted by reconnaissance submarines, the Third Fleet hurled hundreds of carrier borne aircraft against enemy convoys forming off the Indo-China coast, obviously with the intention of carrying reinforcements to Luzon. Details of the action and the results obtained are not yet available but the strike represented the deepest penetration of the South China Sea by American naval forces and constituted an open challenge to the skulking Japanese Navy.

Meanwhile, the invasion of Luzon is progressing rapidly, with the Japanese either unable or unwilling to offer large scale opposition. Already more than 200 square miles of the island is in our hands and patrols of the American Sixth Army have pushed beyond the Agno River, some 85 miles from Manila. The only serious fighting has developed on the eastern flank of the American beachhead, where Yankee spearheads drove 10 miles inland from the San Fabian despite determined efforts by a sizeable Japanese force to delay the advance.

Britain's bulldog tactics in the Greek civil crisis has paid at least temporary dividends, it was disclosed today. The rebellious left-wing forces have accepted a truce dictated by the British commander, Lieut. General Ronald Scobie. Attempts will now be made to establish a permanent peace.

Saturday, January 13, 1945: —The long-awaited all-out Russian offensive on the eastern front has begun. Touched off by a special order of the day issued by Marshal Stalin himself, the mighty Red Army launched a series of powerful drives that set the whole eastern front aflame. One great drive was mounted by Marshal Konev's First Ukrainian Army from its bridgehead across the Vistula in the Sandomierz area. This attack, which apparently began yesterday morning, has already knifed 25 miles into the German lines. The ultimate objective of this push undoubtedly is the strongly held Nazi bastion of Krakow, gateway to German Silesia.

Augmenting the Vistula attack were simultaneous offensives on the East Prussian-Lithuanian border to the north and the Hungarian-Czechoslovak border to the south. One million to one and a half million Soviet troops were believed to be on the march, supported by massed artillery and hundreds of planes.

On the western front the remaining air was fast being pummeled out of Marshal Rundstedt's collapsing Ardennes bulge. Aided by swarms of Allied aircraft, Lieut. General Courtney H. Hodges' First Army troops smashed into the northern end of the bulge, driving deep into the enemy's flank. Reeling and staggering from the trip hammer blows from the First and Ninth Armies on the north and General Patton's heavy-hitting Third Army on the south, Marshal Rundstedt's army was also obliged to undergo a thorough pounding from hundreds of Allied bombers and fighters which welcomed clearing skies by attacking the retreating foe unmercifully.

Sunday, January 14, 1945: —Two hundred and fifty divisions of Russia's finest troops are smashing at German defenses along a 600 mile sector of the eastern front in what is described as the greatest offensive of the entire war. Already at least one Soviet army, the First Ukrainian, under the command of Marshal Ivan S. Konev, has achieved a breakthrough in force along a 25 mile segment of the Vistula line, some 120 miles south of Warsaw. The Russian tide poured through the gap for gains up to 25 miles in two days and threatened to soon overrun the border of German Silesia.

Far to the north of the Vistula battleground other powerful Red Army forces struck into East Prussia while on the southern end of the 600 mile line yet another Soviet army plunged deeper into Czechoslovakia. Both of the latter drives apparently are large-scale diversionary attacks supporting the main offensive on the Vistula.

Heavy fighting is also in progress on the western front where three Allied armies are striving mightily to wipe out the last vestiges of the once dangerous Ardennes bulge. The U.S. First Army struck another powerful blow against the northeastern flank of the salient; the U.S. Third Army blasted furiously at the southern flank, while the British Second Army, with Canadian airborne units, smashed savagely into the disintegrating nose of the bulge. In the face of this three-pronged attack, Marshal Rundstedt's battered legions fought a bitter, but hopeless, rearguard action.

Monday, January 15, 1945: —Secretary of War Henry L. Stimson today released the first figures on American losses in the savage German winter offensive that all but achieved a total breakthrough of U.S. lines on the western front. Some 40,000 American boys either lost their lives, were wounded, or fell captive to the enemy during bitter days from December 16 to January 7th.

The only compensating feature of this tragic loss is the fact that the enemy suffered far greater casualties. More than 40,000 Nazis were captured alone and it is conservatively estimated that another 50,000 were killed or wounded. Furthermore their losses ended only in defeat while ours at least were incurred while snatching a brilliant victory out of a possible disaster.

The drive on Manila is going unbelievably well. Our forces have advanced a third of the way from the Lingayen beaches to the Philippine capital without encountering effective opposition from the supposedly formidable Japanese garrison. When or where the decisive battle for Luzon will be fought cannot even be surmised since it appears that our surprise landing from the north and our speedy advance has completely confused the Japs. Apparently their entire defense strategy must be revised. Meanwhile time runs out on them.

Simultaneously with news of heavy combat losses came the announcement from War Mobilization Director Byrnes that draft rules are to be tightened up. Henceforth it will require engagement in extremely critical war jobs to obtain deferment for able-bodied men from 26 to 30.

Tuesday, January 16, 1945: —Two outstanding topics of home front news held the spotlight today. One topic was national in scope and was concerned with the growing manpower crisis. President Roosevelt is insisting that Congress take some positive action on his "state of the Union" demand for a national service law that would give him power to mobilize every man, women, and child into a single, mighty "win the war" effort. Opponents of this plan believe that total regimentation is not necessary and assert that the problem of manpower can be solved by investigating and eliminating widespread wastage of human effort through the hoarding of labor and inefficient management. The debate is loud and acrimonious.

The second topic is local and strikes a blow squarely at our already restricted bill of fare. A meat famine is threatened in the Bay Area, apparently due to an OPA ruling which raised the ceiling price on livestock. Wholesale butchers have united in claiming that the new ceilings are too high to permit them a profit. Many of them are closing down rather than operate at a loss. Large numbers of retail butcher shops are thus forced to close through lack of supplies. It is going to be a very lean year.

The news from the war fronts continues very favorable. On three major fronts the Allies are chalking up massive gains against the foe. In Eastern Europe the Red Army has outflanked Warsaw in a great drive that captured the important transport hub of Radom. In the west American and British troops chewed out impressive chunks of the German West Wall in a day of bitter fighting. In the Philippines General MacArthur continued his brilliant drive on Manila without serious opposition.

Wednesday, January 17, 1945: —Warsaw, the battered, tortured capital of Poland, was liberated today after five long years of occupation and exploitation by the Germans. Rampaging Soviet mobile forces brushed aside the last Nazi defenders and occupied the remains of the once proud and beautiful Polish metropolis. Demolitions by the retreating Germans completed the destruction wrought by shell fire and aerial bombardment. But if we know the Polish spirit, Warsaw will rise again, stronger and more beautiful than ever.

The mighty Russian offensive did not stop with the capture of Warsaw. Other Soviet troops seized the Nazi bastion of Czestochowa, 15 miles from the German border, and overran thousands of other towns and villages in a great three-pronged drive along a 600 mile front. Total collapse of Germany's eastern defenses was envisaged in the speed of the Soviet advance and the complete liberation of Poland and a frontal assault on Germany proper is expected within a matter of a few days or weeks.

The American push on Manila is continuing to move forward with virtually no enemy opposition. The goal now lies only 65 miles away and hope is held high that our triumphant army will soon retake the scene of so many tragic events in the dark days of late 1941 and early 1942. The oft-repeated Japanese boast that "the Yankees will never return" must indeed sound hollow in their ears today. We are back and we shall never leave again.

Thursday, January 18, 1945: —The Russian tide is still rolling unchecked across the flat plains of Poland. The main battle of Poland is over and the battle of Germany is about to begin. Already mobile spearheads of Marshal Ivan S. Konev's First Ukrainian Army have smashed across the German border into Silesia, after capturing the fortress town of Czestochowa yesterday. These spearheads are now only 50 miles from Breslau, the capital of Silesia, and 250 miles from Berlin itself.

Loss of industrial Silesia would be a tremendous blow at the

German war making power, since the Nazis have transformed that province into a second Ruhr. Heavy industries were moved from the Ruhr to Silesia early in the war to remove them from Allied bombing range. They are now threatened with capture or destruction by the onrushing Soviet legions.

Winston Churchill today paid a glowing tribute to American forces on the western front. The Prime Minister said that the battle of the Ardennes bulge has turned from possible defeat into "an everlasting famous American victory," which is more likely to shorten the war than lengthen it. While some British units participated in the battle, he said that the major effort was American and "American losses were 60 to 80 times heavier than British losses." The battle was the biggest U.S. battle of the war and one of its greatest victories. The British leader's praise is timely and welcome and takes a little of the sting out of the tragically heavy losses.

Friday, January 19, 1945: —Almost unbelievable feats are being accomplished by the mighty Red Army in its greatest offensive of the war which has already ripped the entire German defense line on the eastern front to ribbons and has swept to within 235 miles of Berlin. Sweeping ahead at a mile an hour clip, the Russian armor today captured Lodz and Krakow, two of Poland's largest and most heavily fortified cities. To the north, General Ivan D. Cherniakhovsky's Third White Russian Army blasted a great gap in the German East Prussian defenses and plunged through for a 39 mile gain, while other Red Army forces smashed northward through the Polish corridor towards Danzig in an operation that threatened momentarily to chop off the entire province of East Prussia, entrapping some 200,000 Nazi defenders.

Warning the Germans that their entire eastern front has collapsed, both London and Moscow called upon the Nazis to surrender now and avoid more terrible punishment. Berlin's first reaction was a defiant "never!" I wonder how Adolf's headache is now?

In the Pacific war, General MacArthur's Luzon invasion forces encountered their first serious opposition today as the Japanese launched a series of vicious counter-attacks against the American left flank, in the vicinity of Rosario. All of the attacks were beaten off after fierce fighting.

In the air a strong force of B-29s resumed the aerial offensive against the Japanese homeland, attacking the Kawasaki aircraft plant at Akashi, on the island of Honshu.

Saturday, January 20, 1945: —For the first time in the history of the United States, one man has been inaugurated as President for the fourth consecutive term. The ceremony took place today on the south portico of the White House and was brief and simple. At its finish Franklin D. Roosevelt was still our President and Harry Truman was our new Vice-President. The President made a very brief inaugural address, confined almost entirely to his aims at establishing a lasting peace.

Hungary, the last of Hitler's Balkan satellites, today deserted the sinking ship and surrendered to the Allies. The armistice agreement was signed in Moscow by Allied representatives and the provisional Hungarian Government. German collapse in the Balkans is now complete.

Moscow victory cannon are booming almost without cessation these days. Soviet armies are advancing rapidly on all sectors of the 600 mile East Prussian-Polish-Czechoslovakian front. Approximately two-thirds of Poland has already been liberated and Soviet forces have driven deep into the German province of Silesia. Spearheads now stand only 43 miles from Breslau. On the central Polish front, the Russian drive is aimed at Poznan while in East Prussia the Red Army overran the important German transport center of Tilsit.

On Luzon in the Philippines, our forces have advanced more than 50 miles along the road to Manila and are now within 25 miles of the great cluster known as Clark Field. The Japs used tanks for the first time in the Luzon campaign, throwing them futilely against the American left flank.

Sunday, January 21, 1945: —Today was an unusually warm and pleasant day for winter so we decided to use our last A ration coupon—until March 21st—and take a little ride. So we picked up a neighbor lady and her child, loaded our family into the old jalopy and hit the road. It was nice while it lasted. We went as far as Palo Alto, visited the beautiful campus of Stanford University and skirted down around to the Bayshore Highway to come home. Suddenly, Bang! went a front tire and we wobbled to a stop. Yes, it was flat and we had no spare—that was used up long ago. Well, the tire was blown too badly to fix and there wasn't a service station within miles so after struggling with that old tire for about an hour—it was practically welded to the rim—I finally removed the tire and we came home on the rim. What a racket and did we feel conspicuous. Anyhow, the old car is out in the back yard now, jacked up, there to remain until, and if, we can get another tire and tube. Such is war time on the automobile front.

The war situation remains about the same as yesterday. Everywhere Allied forces are advancing against the foe. In Eastern Europe the colossal Russian drive is tearing great gaps in the German lines. Three huge Red Armies are now battling on German soil, two of them enveloping the proud "Junker" province of East Prussia, while the third is knifing deep into Germany's eastern "Ruhr," the industrially important province of Silesia. Fear is beginning to seize upon the German masses as they see their doom approaching.

Monday, January 22, 1945: —Disaster and destruction fell heavily upon Germany today. From all sides she is reaping the terrible whirlwind that she sowed so callously five years ago. On her eastern border a fearful tide of vengeful Russians swept to within 165 miles of Berlin. The nearest point was at Gniezno, important rail junction in western Poland, captured by mobile Soviet forces today. In Silesia, other Red Army troops were nearing Breslau and were less than 200 miles from the German capital. In East Prussian German disaster was almost complete as Marshal Konstantin K. Rokossovsky's Second White Russian Army drove 30 miles northward to narrow the last Nazi escape corridor to less than 44 miles.

At the same time on the western front, Allied airmen had a field day against packed masses of Nazi equipment and tanks trying to escape from the flattened Ardennes bulge into the comparative safety of the Siegfried Line. Dive-bombers, fighter-bombers, and four-motored bombers caught the Germans in a traffic jam before a bombed-out bridge three miles north of Eisenbach and destroyed 978 enemy vehicles and damaged at least 439 others out of about 3,000. It was a tremendous blow and put the clincher on the already victorious bulge victory for the Americans.

On Luzon, General MacArthur's invaders have reached the half-way mark in their drive to Manila. Clark Field is now less than 20 miles away and no serious enemy resistance has developed.

Tuesday, January 23, 1945: —The rampaging Russians have closed the gap between them and Berlin to less than 138 miles. Rushing on past captured Gniezno since yesterday the leading elements of Marshal Gregory K. Zhukov's hard-hitting mobile forces are now attacking Poznan, last fortified Polish city between them and the German frontier.

In all, five mighty Red Armies are arrayed against the Nazis in this tremendous offensive which the Russians openly assert is a final "win the war" drive. Two powerful Soviet armies are smashing around and into East Prussia, erstwhile breeding ground and hatchery for Germany's perennial crop of "Junker" Generals. At latest report the Second White Russian Army under Marshal Rokossovsky had all but driven through to the Baltic, closing the last route of escape for an estimated 200,000 German troops cornered in the province.

At the other end of the 500 mile battle line, other formidable Russian forces are crunching forward on German soil in the province of Silesia to within 17 miles of Breslau. Mauled and battered Nazi troops in this area are said to be fleeing in panic before the Russian tide.

On the western front, Allied airmen continued to dole out fearful punishment to large numbers of German motorized equipment caught yesterday in a traffic jam on the Reich border. Today's final tabulation showed that no less than 4,134 enemy vehicles were destroyed or damaged in the two day aerial spree. The hapless enemy equipment was caught bumper to bumper and didn't have a chance.

Wednesday, January 24, 1945: —Russian momentum in their drive on Berlin is steadily increasing despite almost panicky efforts by the Germans to stop them. Heinrich Himmler, the dreaded leader of the Gestapo and commander-in-chief of the German home army has been dispatched to the eastern front by Hitler in an effort to buck up the sagging morale of the desperate Nazi defenders. One can well imagine the method he will use to stimulate their courage—a loaded revolver at their backs.

Soviet troops in upper Silesia blasted their way to within 4 miles of Breslau today and Berlin radio reports hinted that all civilians have been evacuated from that threatened city. German roads are clogged with refugees fleeing from the approaching Red terror. Now the Master Race is tasting a bit of their own medicine doled out so gleefully to the Belgians, French, Dutch, Norwegians, Poles, Czechs, Greeks, Slavs, and Russians. It is a pretty bitter pill to swallow, eh, Adolf?

In only one sector of the vast battle line encircling the Reich are the Germans striking back with any effect. That sector is in northern Alsace on the western front, where heavy German counter-thrusts have force the U.S. Seventh Army to withdraw—in some places as much as seven or eight miles. However, far to the north in Holland, Lieut. General Miles C. Dempsey's British Second Army more than offset the Seventh Army's losses by capturing Heinsberg, important highway center in the Maas-Roer triangle.

Thursday, January 25, 1945: —The War Department, or more correctly, the Secretary of War himself, today announced the sinking of a United States troopship, carrying 2200 American soldiers. This tragic loss occurred recently in European waters as the result of enemy action. Of the 2200 men aboard, 765 were killed or are missing, the 1400 were saved. Full details of the disaster cannot be released at this time.

General MacArthur's drive back to Manila is still making rapid headway. Familiar ground was tread today as American troops recaptured Clark Field and nearby Fort Stotsenburg. Only 44 miles of hard-surfaced highway still stand between our leading elements and the Philippine capital. Major Japanese opposition has yet to materialize and it is believed that liberation of the city is but a few days away.

In Germany the plight of Hitler's minions is hourly becoming more desperate. The momentum of the swelling Russian springtide has been maintained for twelve sensational days now and has carried the Soviet legions to within 124 miles of Berlin. One wave of the angry Russian flood has swept through the Nazi defense lines to reach the Baltic and seal off the entire province of East Prussia. Yet another wave has plunged deep into Silesia to threaten the industrial metropolis of Breslau. Panic-stricken German refugees are crowding the roads of Germany in a mad scramble to escape to the interior. A deadly fear such as comes to those with guilty consciences, is seizing upon the hapless citizens of Germany.

Friday, January 26, 1945: —The seemingly irresistible Russian armies are continuing their crunching drive towards Berlin. On the most direct route to the German capital the Red forces bypassed the strongly fortified Polish city of Poznan and drove nearly to the border of the German province of Brandenburg, in which lies Berlin. The Nazi capital now is only 94 miles away from the leading Soviet spearheads.

Marshal Stalin also confirmed tonight the Nazi report that Soviet troops have broken through German defenses in East Prussia and have sealed that province from the rest of the Reich. An estimated 200,000 German troops are trapped in the "Junker" province.

To the south in Silesia the Russian drive mounted in fury. Breslau, the capital of the province, is under siege and is expected to fall very soon. Other Red Army forces have succeeded in crossing the Oder River at several points and have established solid bridgeheads on the west bank.

German resistance is also sagging on the western front. The American Ninth Army and the British Second Army have pushed their way to within 25 miles of Dusseldorf, while to the south the U.S. First and Third Armies brought the Battle of the Bulge to an official close after six weeks of bloody fighting.

Saturday, January 27, 1945: —Let us leave the war fronts for a moment and take a look at the situation on the home front. An event that may have a far-reaching effect on President Roosevelt's war time powers happened today. You will remember that the President recently ordered the Army to seize the plants and facilities of Montgomery Ward and Company in seven cities where labor disputes had arisen. The President took this drastic action, as a war time measure, because the Company had refused to comply with a War Labor Board order, settling the labor dispute. Sewell Avery, chairman of the board of directors of

Montgomery Ward, appealed to the courts and Federal Judge Philip L. Sullivan today declared that the President of the United States was without authority to take possession of the private properties of Montgomery Ward and Co. The Judge said he arrived at his decision reluctantly but maintained that Congress is the only branch of the Government with authority to compel the Company to obey the War Labor Board's ruling, since Montgomery Ward and Co. are not directly engaged in war production. The Government has indicated that it will appeal the District Judge's decision.

Another big battle is raging in Washington D.C. over President Roosevelt's nomination of former Vice-President Henry Wallace as Secretary of Commerce. The appointment was admittedly a political payoff for Wallace's aid in the recent campaign and his opponents in the Senate as well as friends of Jesse H. Jones, the ousted Secretary, are determined to block his confirmation if possible. The fur is flying.

Sunday, January 28, 1945: —Panic has seized upon the citizens of upper Silesia as the Russian tidal wave sweeps towards them. Nazi propagandists and military leaders are striving desperately to halt the panic and bring a semblance of order to the mass evacuation of the vital industrial area.

The Nazi Transocean News Agency today admitted that the entire industrial basin has closed down, with vital production plants being blown up rather than permit them to fall into Russian hands. Volksturm, or home front militia, are now fighting at the side of the regular army troops in the desperate effort to stem the Red tide. But Moscow broadcasts assert that the entire German east wall has crumbled and Soviet armies are pouring through great gaps torn in the enemy lines from the Carpathians to the Baltic Sea.

In East Prussia the Soviet armies have overrun the historic battlefield of Tannenberg, where General Von Hindenburg turned back the Russian tide in a great battle of annihilation in 1914. There is no chance of a repeat performance this time—except in reverse. At latest report, the Soviet flood is lapping at the gates of Konigsberg and that heavily fortified Nazi bastion is expected to be inundated within a few days.

On the western front there are indications that the Nazis are pulling some of their best troops out of the west wall to bolster their defenses against the Russians. The U.S. Third Army today advanced nearly three miles through the approaches to the Siegfried Line without encountering serious opposition.

Monday, January 29, 1945: —The great Baltic port of Stettin and Frankfurt-on-the-Oder appear to be the main objectives of the present Russian drive into Germany. While Berlin is undoubtedly the ultimate objective, the principal Soviet efforts at the present time are to capture the vital Baltic port and the mighty stronghold on the Oder River. With seizure of these two great cities, Berlin would probably fall into Russian hands like a ripe apple.

According to Moscow communiqués the Red Army has already broken across the German border into Pomerania and has captured the important railroad center of Woldenberg, only 57 miles from Stettin. The Russian troops are advancing in great force along a solid 29 mile front in Pomerania.

The Frankfurt drive is being led by Marshal Konev, who's First Ukrainian Army has pressed 31 miles northwest from Breslau and has established a strong bridgehead across the Oder River at the town of Steinau. According to the Moscow radio, the "hurricane from the east will soon reach Berlin."

In the Pacific war the Battle of Luzon is still going our way. American Sixth Army forces have reached a point only 33 miles from Manila. General MacArthur announced that the Japanese forces on the island have been split by the speedy American drive. The constellation of vital airstrips at Clark Field are now in our hands and Yank patrols are busy clearing out isolated enemy pockets in the nearby hills. One futile counter-attack by an enemy force ended with 49 Jap tanks knocked out and 789 Japanese dead counted.

Tuesday, January 30, 1945: —Adolf Hitler broke a long silence today and implored the anguished people of Germany to steel themselves to greater sacrifices and to defend themselves fanatically against the "gruesome" fate that faces them. The would-be world conqueror spoke on the 12th anniversary of his rise to power in Germany. He summoned every man, woman, and child, whether young or old, sick or well, to support the struggle fanatically, even though it inevitably means greater misery and suffering. In the end, he promised, Germany would still be the winner.

Even as the Nazi Fuhrer spoke, the terrible fate that he brought down upon his people was closing in upon them. Massive Russian forces were assembling east of the Oder River and mobile Soviet spearheads already had smashed their way across the border of Berlin's Brandenburg province, barely 80 miles from the capital. Prospects of a successful German defense short of the city itself were fading with the speed of the Russian advance.

In East Prussia the Germans were faring just as badly. The capital city of the province, Konigsberg, was in flames, with Soviet forces closing to within three miles of the city's gates.

In the west, with victory in the Ardennes battle behind them, American, British, and French forces resumed their general assault against Germany's west wall, knifing a mile or more into the Siegfried fortifications at several points. Blinding snowstorms and blizzards impeded the advance.

Wednesday, January 31, 1945: —Two world capitals heard the thunder of big guns from an approaching army today. One of them was Berlin, the capital of doomed German. The other was Manila, the capital of the Philippines.

In Berlin, panic stricken German citizens could plainly hear and feel the rumble of mighty Russian guns, pounding away at crumbling Nazi defense lines barely 40 miles away at one point. There were indications that the Nazis intend to defend Berlin after the fashion of Stalingrad and feverish attempts were being made to establish defensive positions in and around the city.

At the same time it was revealed that Konigsberg, the capital of East Prussia, was invested by the invading Red Army and Breslau, industrial capital of the province of Silesia to the south, was threatened by two converging Soviet columns.

In the Pacific war, American forces under the command of General Douglas MacArthur closed to with 23 miles of Manila, that gem of the Philippines that has been tarnished for so long by the presence of the alien Japanese. The squeeze on Manila took on a two pronged character today as it was revealed that the newly designated American Eighth Army, under the command of Lieut. General Eichelberger, has swept ashore on the Zambales coast of western Luzon and has captured the former U.S. naval base of Olongapo, on Subic Bay. In two days the Eighth Army troops have moved inland 21 miles to join the advance on Manila.

February

Thursday, February 1, 1945: —The whole country thrilled today to one of the most dramatic stories of the entire war. Five hundred and ten Allied war prisoners, most of them American heroes of Bataan and Corregidor, were rescued from a Japanese prison camp by a daring force of U.S. Rangers and Filipino guerrillas who slipped behind enemy lines for a distance of 25 miles, surprised and destroyed the Japanese guards at the prison camp and fought their way back to American lines without losing a single liberated prisoner to enemy action. Ironically, however, one gaunt prisoner, weakened by three years of Japanese torture and starvation, was so overcome by excitement at his liberation that he died of heart failure.

The sensational expedition was carried out with such precision and efficiency that only 27 Rangers and guerrillas were lost, while over 500 Japanese were killed in the escape fight and 12 tanks were knocked out. General MacArthur was delighted with the success of the venture. "No incident of the campaign has given me such personal satisfaction," he said.

Included among the rescued men were many from the San Francisco Bay Area and great was the rejoicing among their wives, mothers, and other relatives for whom three years of mental torture was at an end. Some of them had heard but once or twice from their loved one since the historic days of Bataan and Corregidor. Now at least a few of those gallant men are free and the entire nation voices its thankfulness.

Friday, February 2, 1945: —A rising crescendo of war news floods the air waves and fills the newspapers these days. Climax after climax follows closely upon each other on every major battlefront, while on the "forgotten" fronts—Italy, China, Burma, Norway, New Guinea, Bougainville, etc.—many other brave men are fighting and dying with little fanfare and less glory. But someday the story of these lesser battlegrounds, bypassed in the kaleidoscopic rush of events, will provide many epic tales of heroism and unselfish contributions to the cause of liberty.

While American tanks and men approached to within 17 miles of Manila from the north, another amphibious force landed south of the Philippine capital on the shores of Nasugbu Bay and began driving northward, forging a trap on the doomed Japanese garrison of Manila. The landing achieved complete surprise and was accomplished without loss. The Manila squeeze is on!

In Europe another and even greater squeeze play is being executed. Germany itself is being crushed between the jaws of a mighty nutcracker. One jaw, composed of two million Russian soldiers liberally equipped with the most modern engines of destruction, has crunched to within 33 miles of panicky Berlin. A desperate battle is raging along the banks of the Oder River, last natural defensive position before the capital.

From the west another mighty jaw, composed of six great Allied armies, is grinding with ever increasing fury against the crumbling barriers of the once invincible West Wall.

Saturday, February 3, 1945: —The fall of Manila appears to be only a matter of hours. Already the Japs have begun demolitions in the harbor area and railroad centers. Demolished bridges and supply problems, rather than large scale enemy resistance are now the principal obstacles to the American advance. Cabanatuan, scene of the thrilling rescue of 510 veterans of Bataan and Corregidor, Santa Rosa and Gapan, all fell to U.S. forces during the day.

The American 37th Division appeared most likely to be the first to reach Manila. The "Buckeye" troops broke through the swampy bottleneck of Calumpit, 17 miles north of the capital, and headed down highway 3 virtually unopposed. Other American spearheads were converging on the Philippine city from the east and south, however, and entry into the capital from several directions seemed likely.

San Francisco, still echoing the Nation's joy and satisfaction at the liberation of some of the heroes of Bataan and Corregidor, has begun to lay plans for a gigantic homecoming celebration in their honor. Consummation of the plans is dependent upon the Army and Navy's cooperation in bringing the men home by way of San Francisco. It is an excellent idea.

The western front exploded with increased fury today, with the U.S. First Army leading a slashing attack deep into the Siegfried Line. Fierce fighting also raged far to the south where the French Army is mopping up the remnants of a trapped German force around Colmar on the west bank of the Rhine.

Sunday, February 4, 1945: —An exciting, see-saw race for the honor of being the first to enter Manila is being run by units of General MacArthur's army on Luzon. The 37th Division, which held the lead yesterday, has been nosed out by a lightning advance of the Eighth Cavalry Regiment of the famous First Cavalry Division. The veteran horsemen, now mechanized, swept more than 65 miles during the last 24 hours to place their spearhead at the gates of the Philippine capital. Spurred on by a vow to liberate Manila, made a year ago in honor of their former commander, Lieut. General Jonathan Wainwright, hero of Corregidor and prisoner of the Japanese, the dismounted cavalrymen began their dramatic dash at Guimba, swept on to Cabanatuan, brushed aside ineffective Japanese resistance, and dashed on to Sabang and Malolos, just north of the capital. The rampaging cavalrymen paused neither for sleep nor food in their sensational drive, forded swollen streams where the Japs had blown the bridges, and raced over difficult terrain at breakneck speed to overcome the fifty mile lead of the 37th Division. Even now, since the latest news is several hours behind the actual events, the Yank cavalrymen may be in the historic city of Manila, soon to be purged forever from the blight of Japanese occupation and misrule.

Berlin, feeling the hot breath of the approaching Russian bear, and teeming with thousands of panic-stricken refugees, was blasted and gutted yesterday by the greatest air blow yet to be delivered against the city. More than 1,000 Flying Fortresses, unhampered by enemy interceptors, cascaded over 3,000 tons of high explosives into the German capital.

Monday, February 5, 1945: —MANILA IS LIBERATED! In almost a photo-finish, the 37th Division and the First Cavalry Knifed their way into the northern half of the Philippine capital and drove several thousand Japanese troops south across the Pasig River into the southern part of the city where they will undoubtedly make their usual last-man death stand.

The climax of the brilliant dash into the capital came when a flying column of the First Cavalry Division knifed its way into the heart of Manila and rescued some 3,700 American and British civilian internees at Santo Tomas University. The gaunt internees, most of them weak and suffering from malnutrition after three years of slow starvation, welcomed their liberators almost hysterically. A force of 65 Japs under a notorious Colonel Hayashi, surprised by the speed of the American advance, nevertheless holed up in the Education Building with 221 internees as hostages. Finally the 221 were released under an armistice agreement in which the 65 Japs and Colonel Hayashi were permitted to escape. It was a good trade, since the fate of the Japs is sealed anyway. Death or surrender face all Japs in Manila since all escape routes from the city have been closed off.

Pitiful stories were told of the almost heart-breaking joy of the thin, emaciated internees when they saw their liberators, the husky dismounted horsemen of the famous First Cavalry Division. Despite their weakness, some of the overjoyed internees insisted on lifting the soldiers to their bony shoulders and carrying them through the buildings.

Tuesday, February 6, 1945: —The trapped Japanese forces in Manila are wantonly burning and blasting large sections of the city still remaining under their control. While they are slowly being compressed into extinction by the advancing Doughboys of General MacArthur's avenging forces, the Japs are venting their wrath upon the capital itself and have put a large portion of the city, including much of the business district, to the torch. According to the 37th Division's commander, Maj. General Robert S. Beightler, "The Japs are just being plain nasty."

Daring Yankee troops pulled off another sensational feat during the Manila fighting today. While flames licked close on three sides, the Yanks smashed their way through to the notorious Bilibid Prison and rescued another 1,100 Allied war prisoners from under the noses of the enemy. Among the rescued were some survivors of the infamous "March of Death" from Bataan in 1942. These expressed an eagerness to get another crack at the Japs as soon as they regain their strength. The fires of vengeance burn hot in their veins.

Unofficially it was learned today that the long awaited meeting of the "Big 3" is now taking place at an undisclosed rendezvous, presumably in the Middle East. Upon the outcome of this momentous meeting will probably hang the fate of the post-war world. The lives of every man, woman, and child will be affected by the decisions of these three men. To paraphrase a famous statement by one of the three—never before has the fate of so many been dependent upon the decisions of so few. May Providence guide their minds and hands.

Wednesday, February 7, 1945: —The final, flaming battle for Manila is still raging fiercely within an ever tightening arc along the banks of the Pasig River which divides the city. The hopelessly doomed Japanese garrison, including many crack Marines, is resisting furiously while wantonly setting fire to everything within reach. Fires are raging out of control throughout the city since most of the fire-fighting equipment has been wrecked by the departing Japs. Inadequate water pressure, due to enemy sabotage, is hampering the use of the few pieces of equipment left. Manila must pay a high price for liberty.

Meanwhile, the European war seems to be moving inexorably towards a climax. East of Berlin the vast armies of Russia are massing along the Oder River preparatory to a final smash towards the German capital. To the south, in upper Silesia, one Soviet Army has already forced the Oder River barrier southeast of Breslau and has penetrated 12 miles beyond. Frantic German eyes are glued to the east tonight.

Nevertheless, if the harassed Nazi will but look, there is danger also closing in upon him from the west. Already the mighty West Wall appears to be buckling along a 40 mile sector under the sledge-hammer blows of the United States First and Third Armies. Both General Hodges' and General Patton's men have blasted their way through two-thirds of the maze of reinforced steel and concrete fortifications comprising the incredible Siegfried Line.

Thursday, February 8, 1945: —The history-making second meeting of President Roosevelt, Prime Minister Churchill, and Marshal Stalin is in full progress at a meeting place somewhere in the Black Sea area. The actual location and details of the conference will not be revealed until the end of the meeting. The Russians are the hosts and they are taking no chances with the security of the Allied leaders. Immense and effective arrangements have been made to guard the area and none but officially authorized persons are permitted within the restricted area.

While the rest of world anxiously awaits the results of the deliberations of the "Big 3" the fighting men on the various world battlegrounds continue with their bloody task of destroying the enemy. On the western European front the American First and Third Armies blasted their way deeper into the Siegfried Line, capturing the German town of Schmidt and smashing to within a mile of the vital bastion of Pruem.

To the north a 1,000 plane attack east of Nijmegen prepared the way for a combined British and Canadian assault against the northern end of the West Wall. The full extent of Field Marshal Montgomery's attack cannot yet be determined but the early portents look promising.

In Manila our troops are still encountering fierce resistance from the trapped Japanese garrison. Like rats they shall have to be exterminated.

Friday, February 9, 1945:—The western front is ablaze from Holland to Switzerland. It is apparent that the long-awaited "Big Push" is on, time to coincide and complement the Russian drive against Berlin from the east.

The biggest Allied gain was scored by Canadian troops under the command of Field Marshal Montgomery. The Canucks blasted their way ahead for five miles, seizing a dozen towns. At the close of the day the Canadian vanguards were barely three miles from the German fortress city of Cleve, anchor point of the West Wall.

In the center of the line, the U.S. Third Army also drove forward, outflanking the powerful German defenses at Pruem. At the same time the U.S. First Army scored further advances in the Roer River sector, but reported that the river was rising sharply below the big dams northeast of Monschau, lending credence to the belief that the huge Schwammenauel Dam has been partly blown up.

Far to the south the French First Army completed their mop-up of the Colmar pocket, eliminating the last Nazi after a month of the bitterest kind of fighting.

Combining the vast power of the above drives with the tremendous offensive of the Russians we can readily discern the desperate position in which the Germans now find themselves. Any intelligent German citizen should now be able to recognize that his cause is irrevocably lost. How much longer then can he endure?

Saturday, February 10, 1945: —A three way jolt shook Japan to its foundations today. One blow was delivered by nature in the form of an earthquake, the second was delivered by the largest force of American B-29's ever sent against Japan, while the third was a political upheaval of the Japs own making.

Seismograph experts reported that the earthquake shook the northern and central parts of Japan at 1:50 p.m. Tokyo time and was of damaging intensity. It was the second serious quake to hit Japan in little over two months, the first striking heavily at the heart of Japan last December 7th. Even the elements are angry at the Oriental aggressors.

The Superforts hit the Tokyo area about an hour after the quake which, of course, did not help to calm the already jittery nerves of the Japanese populace. The returning B-29 crewmen reported "good to excellent" results in the bombing. Military installations throughout the Kanto District, which comprises Tokyo and Yokohoma, were badly damaged in the attack. Confirmation of the raid's success came when Japanese Domei broadcast admitted considerable damage was caused to ground installations. The place must have been practically leveled to bring out this much of an admission from the enemy.

The political shakeup was felt in the War Cabinet of Premier General Kuniaki Koise and undoubtedly came as a result of the resounding defeats recently suffered by both the Japanese Army and Navy. Things look bad, eh, Mr. Moto?

Sunday, February 11, 1945: —Today has been one of those lazy days when you completely relax and can hardly stir up enough energy to eat. It is taking a tremendous exercise of will power to generate enough steam to type this article. Ho-hum, I think I will go lie down for a while.

Well, here I am back again but I don't know what to write about. One of the children didn't feel well so it was decided that no one would go to church this morning and we would all sleep in. We did—and it was nearly noon before our stomachs aroused us. After breakfast I went back to bed for another couple of hours. I still haven't dressed and it's almost time to go to bed again. I can hardly wait.

With an attitude like the above it is plain to see that I haven't done much news gathering today. I haven't bothered to read the newspaper and besides Sunday's paper is always Saturday's news so that's no good. And the radio has been so noisy that we have turned it off for most of the day. Caught an earful of one broadcast, however, and was satisfied to ascertain that there were no exceptional developments. That sufficed so I dozed off again.

Well, the wife has just made a wonderful suggestion that I think I will follow. She says I ought to cut this newsy article short and get some rest. That does it.

Monday, February 12, 1945: —Today is a holiday— Lincoln's Birthday—and it is the direct opposite of yesterday. It is a beautiful day, bright and shining, and that is just the way I feel after my twenty four hour siesta. We were up at the crack of dawn, raring to go. And we have been going strong all day. It is really wonderful what a full day of complete relaxation will do in the way of recuperation.

For eight days the world has wondered and hoped about what was transpiring at the momentous meeting between the "Big 3" who hold the fate of the world in their grasp. Today we were given the first information. President Roosevelt, Prime Minister Churchill, and Premier Stalin issued a joint communiqué, outlining a nine-point program or formula for the triumphant conclusion of the war and the establishment of a lasting peace. The historic decisions were reached at the end of the conference which took place at the former summer palace of Czar Nicholas II on the Black Sea at Yalta in the Crimea. In brief the nine points are as follows: 1. Detailed agreement on military plans against Germany that will shorten the war. 2. A final decision to split Germany into zones of occupation after victory. The United States, Great Britain, Russia and France will be the occupying powers. 3. A commission will be set up to determine the amount of German reparations. 4. A formula for settling the Polish question was agreed upon. Russia to get most of what she wants. 5. Another formula for Yugoslavia. 6. Quarterly meeting of the foreign ministers of the Big 3. 7. A full dress peace conference in San Francisco in April. 8. Autonomy for liberated and Axis nations. 9. A summary predicting the greatest opportunity to create a lasting peace among all nations.

Tuesday, February 13, 1945: —San Francisco today was thrilled at the thought of the part she is to play in the United

Nations' plans for organizing the peace of the world. On April 25 this city will act as host to representatives of all the United Nations who will meet to draft a world security treaty. The groundwork laid at Dumbarton Oaks will be brought into final form here. Civic leaders of San Francisco proudly accepted the responsibility and immediately began to lay plans to prove that the city by the Golden Gate is still the "City that knows how."

Almost without exception the peoples of the United Nations greeted the communiqué from the Yalta Conference with approval, declaring that it is a big step forward along the road to international cooperation and unity. The only bitter note was sounded by the exiled Polish Government in London which declared that the United States and Great Britain have sold Poland down the river. In many ways they are right, for the Yalta agreement constitutes another partitioning of hapless Poland. A huge portion of old Poland is to go to Russia and the Poles are expected to be satisfied and repaid with large slices of German territory. The Polish problem still exists—as difficult as ever.

San Francisco Bay was the scene of another war time tragedy today. A huge land-based Navy transport carrying 24 crewmen and passengers crashed into the Bay near Alameda this morning. All 24 persons perished.

Wednesday, February 14, 1945: —Tremendous battles raged today in eastern and western Germany as the Nazis strove desperately to ward off powerful offensive blows struck by Russian, British, and American Armies. In the east the Soviets launched two mighty spearheads, one aimed at Berlin under the direction of Marshal Zhukov, and the other pointed at Dresden, capital of Saxony.

More than 8,000 American and British planes joined in the day's activities over the Reich, throwing huge bomber fleets, escorted by swarms of fighters, into direct support of the advancing Russian armies. Dresden in particular was devastated with a deluge of over 4,000 tons of explosives in a twelve hour period. Advancing Red Army troops, barely 68 miles away, could plainly see the red glow of the towering fires started by their western Allies.

Marshal Zhukov's First White Russian Army on the Pomeranian front, finally cleaned out the stubborn Nazi garrison of Schneidemeuhl, vital bastion encircled and besieged since February 1.

On the western front Field Marshal Sir Bernard L. Montgomery continued to maintain his heavy pressure against the northern end of the Siegfried Line guarding the Ruhr Valley. Slowly and inexorably his British and Canadian troops are deepening and widening their wedge into the German line. Nazi resistance, fierce and strong to begin with, is showing signs of collapsing under the never-ending pressure.

Thursday, February 15, 1945: —The battle to clean up Manila, Bataan, and Corregidor is in full swing. The Manila Japs have been compressed into an area measured in yards south of the Pasig River, between the mouth of the river and the Bay front. The surviving Japs are weakening under the incessant pounding but are venting their wrath upon the hapless civilian population still remaining in their section of the city. Dozens of Filipino men, women, and children are being burned alive or are shot and bayoneted as they attempt to escape from their burning homes. The maddened Japanese apparently are determined to take as many innocent victims as possible with them into oblivion.

On Bataan peninsula, General MacArthur's forces are rapidly reconquering the battleground hallowed by the heroic stand of other American and Filipino soldiers in the dark days of 1942. Abucay, anchor of the 1942 defense line, was retaken by the Yanks yesterday.

American minesweepers and amphibious forces apparently have begun the task of reconquering the mighty rock bastion of Corregidor. The attack, reported by the Tokyo radio, was preceded by a thunderous bombardment from battleships, cruisers, and destroyers which stood out at sea off the entrance to the Bay and engaged the big guns of the fortress in a furious duel. Then minesweepers and transports headed in for a landing.

The Japanese homeland was again hit by B-29's this afternoon. The big bombers chose the Nagoya aircraft factories as their targets, causing heavy damage and starting huge fires. The Superforts came from Saipan and newly constructed bases on Tinian, both in the Marianas.

Friday, February 16, 1945:—No record of this war would be complete without mentioning the Red Cross Blood Banks where so many American citizens are donating a pint of their blood to help save the lives of wounded soldiers. Until recently almost all of the blood has been made into plasma which can be dried, preserved, and delivered to the combat zones where it is mixed with sterile water and used to relieve the shock suffered by badly wounded fighting men. Thousands of men who would otherwise have died have been saved by the miracle of blood plasma. Recently the Blood Banks have been refrigerating and shipping out whole blood of the universal O type by fast plane direct to the battle zones where it has saved men for whom plasma alone was insufficient.

Because of the thousands of donations daily the big Blood Banks are operated on a mass production basis. Red Cross station wagons pick up and deliver groups of donors free of charge. Business houses allow employees to take time off from work—at Company expense—to make donations. Yesterday, for example, fifteen of us from the Bank were picked up at the office at 10:45 a.m. by a Red Cross truck driven by a pretty little Red Cross Worker and taken to the Blood Bank where we were signed up, tested and examined and run through the entire process in less than one hour. Afterwards, we were all served coffee or orange juice and doughnuts and were driven back to the Bank by the same attractive little Red Cross Worker. Only two of our group were turned down and only one of those who gave blood felt any ill effects. He passed out cold after the donation and we had to leave him at the Blood Bank in a nurse's care.

Saturday, February 17, 1945: —In case you are interested the fellow who I reported fainted at the Blood Bank Thursday recovered shortly after we left him and is now as good as ever. Apparently he just tried to get up too soon after the blood was taken.

Yesterday and today have seen some sensational developments in the Pacific war. Admiral Chester W. Nimitz, commander of our Pacific Fleet, reported from his advance headquarters on Guam, that more than 1,300 carrier planes from a gigantic naval armada that steamed boldly into Japan's front yard blasted and burned Tokyo yesterday in the greatest attack yet launched against the Japanese capital. For nine hours the hard-hitting naval planes shuttled back and forth from their dozens of mighty aircraft carriers standing less than three hundred miles offshore and cascaded tons of devastation and death into military targets in the sprawling enemy city. Huge pillars of smoke billowed over the Jap metropolis, reaching skyward for more than 7,000 feet.

While the carrier planes smashed at Tokyo, a powerful task force of American warships bombarded the Japanese island stronghold of Iwo Jima, 750 miles to the south. Radio Tokyo today said that United States Marines have stormed ashore on Iwo, after a second day of thunderous bombardment from over 30 American battleships, cruisers, and destroyers. No confirmation of the landing has come from American sources but this time the Jap radio report is probably true. We need that island base and the Marines are the boys to go get it.

Sunday, February 18, 1945: —Boldly defying the skulking Japanese Navy—or what is left of it—to come out of hiding and defend its homeland, Vice Admiral Marc A. Mitscher's mighty U.S. naval task force has stood out at sea barely 300 miles off the Japanese coast for two days while hundreds of our carrier planes smashed at Tokyo and the surrounding area with devastating loads of high explosives and incendiaries. Tremendous damage has been inflicted by the raiders although details of the attacks have not yet been released. The participants have been too busy giving the Japs a little interest on their Pearl Harbor investment.

Regardless of the magnitude of the Tokyo raids, the operation apparently is nothing more than a diversionary job designed to distract the enemy from the main show which is taking place 750 miles south of Tokyo on the tiny volcano island of Iwo Jima. Here crack units of the United States Marines are storming ashore under cover of one of the heaviest barrage of shells and bombs ever thrown at a Japanese-held island in this war to date. Mighty shells, ranging from the huge 16 inch projectiles of the battleships to the sensational new rocket shells of the landing craft have pounded the defenses of Iwo steadily for two solid days. Now it is up to the Marines to secure the island and destroy or capture the remaining Japs. With memories of Tarawa, Saipan, Tinian, and Peleliu still fresh in their minds, you can be sure that the gallant Leathernecks expect a stiff fight for the rocky isle.

Monday, February 19, 1945: —The Fourth and Fifth U.S. Marine Divisions, 30,000 strong, have succeeded in establishing a solid beachhead on the heavily fortified shores of Iwo Jima. The fighting "Devil Dogs" swarmed ashore from a mighty 800-ship invasion armada that practically surrounded the tiny yet vital volcano island that guards the front yard of Japan. The Marines encountered furious opposition on the beaches despite the overwhelming naval and air barrage that preceded the landings. Latest reports from Admiral Nimitz' headquarters indicated that American casualties were considerable and one of the toughest battles of the Pacific campaign is expected before the garrison of 20,000 Japs is finally destroyed.

Carrier-based planes of Vice Admiral Mitscher's mighty task force again raided Tokyo today while the Japanese reported that approximately 100 B-29 Superfortresses bombed the Japanese capital and environs in a large-scale attack. The Japs boasted that 10 of the big bombers were shot down and claimed that only negligible damage was inflicted. Ten tons of high explosives from each of 100 bombers, dropped with pin-point accuracy on juicy military targets, caused only "negligible" damage? Well maybe that means something else to you, Mr. Moto.

War Mobilization Director Byrnes today announced the most drastic step yet taken on the home front. Beginning next Monday, a midnight curfew will be clamped on all entertainment, including night clubs, theaters, dance halls, road housed, saloons, and all other similar enterprises. We can expect a big howl and debate over this drastic action.

Tuesday, February 20, 1945: —The U.S. Marines are finding the bloody beaches of Iwo Jima tougher than Tarawa, Saipan, Guadalcanal, or Leyte. The Japs are resisting fiercely and fanatically, battling from a maze of steel and concrete fortifications interlacing the island, and from caves dug into the lava sides of the extinct volcanoes. Nevertheless, the hard-fighting Leathernecks, paced by tanks and flamethrowers, have succeeded in consolidating their beachheads and capturing approximately one third of the island, including the much-prized southern airfield. Losses have been heavy on both sides.

On Luzon, meanwhile, the conquest of Manila and the invasion of Corregidor Island are reaching the final stages. In Manila, the last remaining suicidal force of Japanese troops have been compressed into an area in the southern part of the city not more than 1200 yards long by 800 yards wide. Final liquidation of these Japs is being delayed while attempts are being made to extricate the civilians still under the power of the suicidal garrison.

On Corregidor, U.S. airborne troops spent the day in mopping up the remnants of the Japanese defenders. More than 1,700 Jap dead have already been counted on the island with the survivors holing up in caves from which they must be blasted piecemeal.

Mobilization Director Byrnes' order to roll up the sidewalks at midnight beginning next Monday is causing some yelps from injured proprietors. For the most part, however, plans are being made to comply with as good grace as possible.

Wednesday, February 21, 1945: —The most violent battle in the long history of the United States Marine Corps has turned the tiny Japanese island of Iwo Jima into a little piece of hell on earth. Heavy steel and concrete fortifications manned by fanatical Japanese troops have all but stopped the two divisions of Marines who stormed ashore three days ago. Admiral Nimitz today announced that another Marine division, the Fighting Third, has been thrown into the battle, raising the total of American troops committed in the engagement to 45,000.

The Marines have succeeded in consolidating their hard-won beachhead and have driven a wedge across the southern third of the island. A storm of artillery, mortar, and machine gun fire from the fortified sides and top of the extinct volcano, Mt. Surabachi, have pinned the Marines to their present positions. The cost in men and equipment has been heavy on both sides and conquest of the island is still probably many days away.

Fierce fighting is also raging in Europe where the giant Allied nutcracker is slowly but surely squeezing the life out of the Nazi enemy. General George S. Patton's hard riding tank forces led today's assault on Germany's western frontier, overrunning 17 Nazi towns including the industrially important city of Saarburg in a brilliant ten mile dash. To the north the Canadian First Army beat off several desperate counter-attacks by at least 25,000 crack Nazi troops and followed up by ramming a spearhead to within two miles of Uedem.

Thursday, February 22, 1945: —The war picture today, George Washington's Birthday, remains practically the same as yesterday. The conquest of Iwo Jima is proving to be one of the toughest problems ever tackled by the United States Marines. Almost the entire eight square miles of the tiny island is honeycombed with fortifications and the Japs have been very liberal in sprinkling mines throughout the areas taken by the Leathernecks. The Marines have suffered over 4,500 casualties already in the four day battle with no prospects that the fearful bloodletting will cease for many more days. But, regardless of the price, the Marines will take the island, of that we can be sure. Lieut. General Holland M. Smith, Marine Corps Chief in the Pacific has confirmed this view, although he admits that they are up against "a very tough proposition."

On the western European front, General George S. Patton's rough-riding armored forces are still forging ahead against furious Nazi resistance and have broken into the heart of the vital industrial region of Germany's Saarland. Organized Nazi resistance was crumbling fast in the triangle formed by the convergence of the Saar and Moselle Rivers. Saarburg, on the west bank of the Saar River was completely cleared of the enemy and American spearheads probed across the river along an eight mile front. In other sectors the victory-flushed Yanks hurled the Nazis out of town after town and drove to within five miles of the ancient fortress city of Trier.

Friday, February 23, 1945: —Turkey, long sitting on the opportunist's fence in this war, has finally cast her lot with the United Nations. The powerful little Balkan nation today declared war on Germany and Japan, apparently as the result of an ultimatum delivered after the Yalta conference by the Big Three in which those countries still neutral were advised to jump on the bandwagon by March 1st or forfeit any right to be represented at the forthcoming peace conference to be held at San Francisco beginning April 25th. The Turks are anxious to have a voice in the peace but have been reluctant to share the dangers and burdens of the war. Their entry at this late date, while welcome, savors a little too much of the aroma of "leaping to the aid of the victor."

The pay-off battle west of the Rhine was opened today as General Eisenhower sent the full weight of two mighty U.S. Armies, the First and the Ninth, crashing across the Roer River on a straight drive to Cologne and the Rhine. The Roer River barrier was crossed at at least six different points under cover of a tremendous artillery and aerial barrage. Details of the advance beyond the river were obscured by a security blackout clamped by General Eisenhower on movements of the advancing armies. This usually indicates fluid fighting either of a favorable or unfavorable character. This time all indications point to very favorable developments.

Saturday, February 24, 1945: —Another vivid drama in the liberation of the Philippines was enacted today when daring American land, sea, and air units joined in a bold foray that freed 2,146 American and Allied prisoners from the Los Banos internment camp, some 25 miles behind the Japanese lines south of Manila. The entire Japanese garrison of 243 men were surprised and killed while they were engaged in morning setting-up exercises. The feat was accomplished by paratroopers of the 11th Airborne Division of the 14th Corps who plummeted directly into the camp area from low flying planes and by amphibious tractor forces, including Filipino guerrillas, who swept ashore from Laguna de Bay.

Included among the liberated prisoners were 1589 Americans, many of them from California. They were unanimous in declaring that the attack came just in time for the Japs were beginning to execute the prisoners without provocation and were embarking on a starvation campaign. For the past week prisoners were fed only weeds, water lily stems, hyacinth leaves, and sour coconuts.

Egypt today followed Turkey's example and declared war on Germany and Japan, thus assuring herself of a seat at the San Francisco peace conference. The debate on the war declaration was marred when a young extremist shot and killed the Egyptian Premier, Ahmed Maher Pasha. The assassin was captured and almost lynched. Violence seems to be the order of the day.

Sunday, February 25, 1945: —General MacArthur today announced the final and complete liberation of the tortured city of Manila. The last fanatical Japanese defenders who holed up in the old walled in sector of the city, Intramuros, have been overwhelmed and destroyed by the Yanks of the Thirty Seventh

Infantry and First Cavalry Divisions. In the last stages the Japs used up all their ammunition and degenerated into using spears in medieval fashion. Thus far, more than 12,000 dead Japs have been counted in the city, with many more to go.

U.S. Navy carrier planes, 1,200 strong, again raided the Japanese homeland today. The mighty task force steamed boldly to within 300 miles of the enemy coast, defying the skulking Japanese Navy to come out and fight. The bold defiance brought no results, however, and the Navy had to be content with smashing the juicy industrial targets of Japan from the air.

The weary but determined Marines on Iwo Jima are slowly but surely driving the enemy back into his death pocket in the northern end of the tiny isle. The Japs are resisting fiercely, however, and are bitterly contesting every inch of the terrain. But the Devil Dogs are inching ahead and have taken over half of the island. It will be a happy day when this battle is over. Iwo is a hard nut to crack.

Monday, February 26, 1945: —The gigantic Allied offensive on the Western Front is rapidly crushing the life out of the German defenders west of the Rhine. Armored units of the United States First Army, under the command of Lieut. General Courtney H. Hodges, have thrust to within 10 miles of the biggest prize yet to come within the range of American guns—Cologne. Nazi resistance before the city is crumbling fast and the prospects are favorable for an early seizure of the great German metropolis.

Elsewhere on the shifting battle-front the Canadian First Army and the American Ninth Army are bearing down on the approaches to Dusseldorf, the Doughboys of the Ninth seizing the German stronghold of Erkelenz and pushing beyond it to within 17 miles of the Rhine city. The fighting is now swirling through such towns as Blatzheim, Eschweiler, Soller, Boich, and Rath. It is good to see German names like that instead of French, Belgian, Dutch, or English names as heretofore. Now the Herrenvolk are seeing their own towns blasted and torn in a boomerang version of their own favorite pastime.

On the southern flank of the big offensive, General Patton's tanks are scoring hard-won gains in their drive aimed down the Moselle River Valley towards Coblenz on the Rhine. Heavily fortified Trier is the Third Army's next major objective.

Tonight marks the beginning of another home-front sacrifice, small though it may be. At 12 midnight the entertainment lights of the nation are to go out. It will be interesting to notice how the people take it.

Tuesday, February 27, 1945: —All eyes are on the Western Front where General Eisenhower's Allied armies are turning the screws on the beaten German forces west of the Rhine. The American First Army, in a tremendous surge, swept to within eight miles of Cologne today, driving the disorganized Nazis before them. Reconnaissance reports indicate that the Germans are streaming across the Rhine in utter disorder and it is doubtful whether the enemy will make a serious stand at Cologne, much less the "Stalingrad-like death stand" promised by Hitler.

North of the First Army sector the American Ninth Army under Lieut. General William H. Simpson was matching the First's efforts with a scythe-like sweep of its own towards Dusseldorf. Powerful armored units of the Ninth crashed through Rheindahlen, only fifteen miles from the big German metropolis on the east bank of the Rhine. Everywhere, Nazi resistance was feeble and prisoners were swept up in thousands. Marshal Rundstedt apparently is incapable of mustering any force powerful enough to hinder, let alone stop the lightning American advance. A complete Nazi debacle west of the Rhine appears certain.

Details of the great carrier-borne plane strike against Tokyo last Sunday were revealed today. The Navy planes, despite adverse weather conditions, battled through a sky full of enemy interceptors to drop hundreds of tons of bombs on vital Japanese aircraft plants. Two hundred and thirty three enemy planes were shot out of the skies in a "turkey shoot" that cost us only nine fighter planes and four pilots.

Wednesday, February 28, 1945: —President Roosevelt has returned from the Yalta conference, obviously inspired with the results of the meeting between the heads of the three most powerful nations in the world. San Franciscans noted with satisfaction that the President indicated upon his return that he will attend the United Nations conference to be held in the Bay City next April. The Chief Executive will address the delegates either at the beginning or at the close of the vital peace gathering.

844

Tragic news was released by the Navy today. Two more American submarines haves failed to return from war patrols in the Pacific and must be presumed to be lost. The gallant undersea boats each carried approximately 65 crewmen. By name the vessels were known as the Shark and the Escolar and their loss raised to 39 the number of American subs sacrificed in the deadly war against the Japanese sea lanes.

The bloody, desperate battle for the tiny Iwo Jima Island on the doorsteps of Japan is slowly yet surely turning in favor of the incredible United States Marines. On the spot observers claim that Iwo was the most heavily fortified and strongly defended spot "per square inch" ever assaulted in the annals of warfare. Only by exhibiting almost superhuman courage and ability have the gallant Leathernecks been able to so establish themselves on the island that the eventual outcome can no longer be in doubt.

March

Thursday, March 1, 1945: —President Roosevelt, recognizing his dependence upon Congressional support if he is to carry out the plans laid at Yalta for world peace, personally addressed a joint session of the House and Senate today, reporting to them the results achieved at the Crimean conference. The President spoke informally from a seat on the rostrum and called upon the United States to take a leading part in achieving and maintaining a durable peace. He defended the Polish settlement as a compromise in which all parties conceded some points. He also called upon the German people to surrender now and avoid useless suffering. He pointed out that unconditional surrender does not mean enslavement of the German people; it means only destruction of Nazism, the elimination of Prussian militarism and the temporary occupation of the country by the Allies. All in all the President believes that the Yalta agreements constitute "a good start on the road to a world of peace."

General Douglas MacArthur moves fast. He has invaded another island in the Philippines. The invading troops, comprised of units of the U.S. 41st Division, stormed ashore on the beaches of Palawan, westernmost island of the archipelago. A broadcast from the Manila radio said the American troops caught the Japs flatfooted and seized the harbor of Puerto Princesa and two nearby airstrips. Our losses in the operation thus far were reported very light.

Friday, March 2, 1945: —Under fearsome pressure from seven mighty Allied armies, the German defenses west of the Rhine are falling apart, crumbling like a broken levee before an onrushing flood. The United States Ninth Army, under the brilliant leadership of Lieut. General William H. Simpson, carried the ball today, smashing through on a straight line plunge to the Rhine at Neuss, just across the river from Dusseldorf. The Ninth's big guns began to bombard the German city from positions on the west bank.

On the right wing, General Patton's Third Army crushed German resistance in the ancient fortress town of Trier and swept eastward through the Moselle Valley.

On the left wing of the grand offensive, the Canadian First Army drove southward along the west bank of the Rhine towards a junction with the American Ninth, while between them the previously inactive British Second Army jumped off on an attack aimed at trapping the Nazi forces in a giant pincers composed of the three Allied armies.

On the First Army front facing Cologne, the Americans were preparing to assault the Erft River line, the last defensive position before the German metropolis. In preparation for this climatic drive on Cologne the British sent more than 1,000 heavy bombers over the city dumping at least 5,000 tons of explosives into the already smoking ruins.

Saturday, March 3, 1945: —Giant explosions roared up and down the Rhine River today as the desperate German army blew up bridge after bridge in an attempt to prevent the rampaging Allied forces from crossing the wide water barrier. However, patrols of the Canadian First and American Ninth armies which succeeded in effecting a junction today in the Rhine-Maas corridor, have already crossed the river and are scouting the enemy's dispositions on the east bank.

The Nazi debacle all along the Rhineland front is growing hourly. Thousands of crack enemy troops of the German 15th Army are trapped between the fast closing jaws of the converging British Second Army, the Canadian First Army and the American Ninth Army. Other thousands have already been captured while many others are waiting meekly along the attack route for someone to pick them up, all the fight beaten out of them.

On the Cologne front the American First Army surged ahead, capturing 16 more German towns and bringing the great Nazi metropolis under heavy artillery fire. A substantial bridgehead across the Erft River was established despite furious enemy opposition and the Americans pushed three miles closer to the beleaguered and smoking cathedral city.

In the Pacific the bestial nature of our Oriental enemy was disclosed again today when American forces on the newly invaded island of Palawan in the Philippines uncovered the bones and charred clothing of 150 U.S. prisoners of war who were herded into an air raid shelter and burned to death. Five survivors of the massacre who bolted from the shelter amid a hail of bullets and escaped told the gruesome story.

Sunday, March 4, 1945: —The wreckage of two great German armies lies strewn along the approaches to the western bank of the Rhine River. The once powerful Nazi armies have been totally destroyed as fighting forces, leaving only wrecked tanks, motor vehicles, dead men, prisoners, and wildly fleeing remnants as evidence that they were once the flower of the Rhineland's defenders. Mopping up along the twenty-three mile stretch of the Rhine were the victorious Canadian First and American Ninth Armies. U.S. artillery blasted the Germans in Dusseldorf while the victory-flushed infantry and armor pursued the beaten German remnants towards the last remaining escape routes across the Rhine at Duisburg and Wesel.

On the Cologne front, the hard-hitting American First Army pressed to within four miles of the metropolis where every available German appeared to be gathering for a "Stalingrad" death stand.

An inspiring message was heard from the Philippines today. It was the voice of General Douglas MacArthur, speaking from the liberated Corregidor. The General bestowed the Distinguished Service Cross on the commander of the unit which recaptured the fortress. I am sorry that I did not catch the name as he spoke. Afterwards Old Glory was raised over the historic rock bastion as the General proudly spoke these stirring words, "Let no enemy ever haul it down." Thus Corregidor once again and forever became American.

Monday, March 5, 1945: —The American First Army, in a tremendous display of power, today smashed into the heart of Cologne. The once-beautiful metropolis was a blazing inferno as the tank-led Doughboys crashed through the last Nazi lines before the city and raced to the center of the city through crumbling opposition. The rapid surge of the Yank forces foreshadowed a quick capture of the great German industrial center, despite previous reports that the Nazis intended to defend the city to the last man. Thunderous explosions along the banks of the Rhine indicated that the panic-stricken Germans were blowing all bridges across the turbulent stream, including the great Hohenzollern span. The lack of sturdy opposition within the city indicated that the main forces of the enemy have already withdrawn to the east bank of the Rhine, thus forfeiting the metropolis of a peace-time population of 800,000 almost without a fight.

For several days we haven't mentioned the sanguinary battle for Iwo Jima, the tiny island 750 miles from Tokyo. Nevertheless, the battle has been raging steadily at close quarters, resulting in heavy Marine casualties. The Leathernecks have captured about four-fifths of the island and have killed 12,864 Japs—by latest actual count, not including others blown to bits or buried in the deep recesses of the steel and concrete fortifications. But the attack has cost the lives of 2050 U.S. Marines thus far and the battle has yet to be won. The surviving Japs—some 8,000 in number—are fighting ferociously from the labyrinthine defenses still remaining in their hands.

Tuesday, March 6, 1945: —Cologne is ours! Lieut. General Courtney H. Hodges' American First Army today completed the conquest of the biggest German city yet to fall to Allied arms. Enemy resistance throughout the sprawling metropolis was sporadic and light, with the main German forces retreating across the Rhine and blowing their bridges behind them.

At the same time to the south Lieut. General George S. Patton's U.S. Third Army was making sensational news of its own. "Old Blood and Guts'" heavy hitting armor smashed a wide gap in the enemy's Kyll River line and roared through for a 32 mile gain in 30 hours, in a drive reminiscent of the Normandy breakthrough last summer. At the latest report, the leading Third Army units were less than 20 miles from Coblenz on the Rhine.

Such was the speed of General Patton's tanks that the Germans were thrown into panic and confusion. Thousands of Nazis threw down their arms and surrendered to the fast moving Yanks. Other enemy units became lost and are being isolated and mopped-up one by one. The Nazi debacle west of the Rhine is almost complete.

Rumblings are again being heard from the Russian front just east of Berlin. For the past week or two this front has been comparatively static while the Russians brought up supplies and reinforcements for what will undoubtedly be the climatic drive on Berlin in conjunction with a simultaneous attack by the Allied armies in the west. Germany's days are numbered.

Wednesday, March 7, 1945: —The American Third Army, like Old Man River, just keeps rolling along. General Patton's rampaging Doughboys have smashed to within ten miles of Coblenz, through what was expected to be some of the toughest fighting country in the world. Apparently, however, the Nazi High Command is unable to muster anything west of the Rhine capable of stopping the hard-riding Yanks and prospects are good for an early mop-up of the entire Rhineland north of the Moselle River.

The rumblings heard from the Red Army front east of Berlin have developed into a blazing offensive along a 40 mile stretch of the Oder River, with the Soviet forces driving on Kuestrin, gateway to Berlin. Other powerful Russian forces hammered at the vital Nazi city of Stettin and smashed up the Oder estuary to capture Stepenitz, 15 miles to city's north.

In the Pacific the toughest fight in the history of the United States Marine Corps is entering its final stages. Approximately 5,000 Japanese survivors of the Iwo Jima garrison have been driven into the rocky northeast corner of the island, where they are fighting with fanatical fury to delay their inevitable destruction. The Marines are slowly yet inexorably closing in for the kill despite a withering hail of bullets and mortar shells. Hand to hand combat of the deadliest sort usually settled the issue after each Jap position was overrun. He survived who handled knife or bayonet with the greatest skill.

Thursday, March 8, 1945: —Today was a great occasion for some 270 survivors of three years of torture and imprisonment by the Japs. They were the men of Cabanatuan, heroes of Bataan and Corregidor, rescued a month ago by the U.S. Rangers and now at last, home again. San Francisco threw out the welcome mat enthusiastically as the ship bearing the happy, though still haggard Yanks, steamed through the Golden Gate. The Ferry Building siren screamed joyously as a fleet of 30 small boats, whistles tooting, escorted the big transport to the dock where thousands of citizens waited to cheer and greet them. It was a heart-warming event and undoubtedly the greatest day in the lives of those boys who had waited so long for liberation. All America, from the President, who sent each man a personal greeting, to the lowliest citizen, is proud of these men who fought so gallantly in the nation's darkest hours.

On the Western European front the Allied offensive is still forging ahead. Units of the U.S. First Army is reported to have crossed the Rhine at a point below Cologne and have established a firm bridgehead. If this report is true it is indeed good news. Many people had believed that our armies would have to pause for regrouping before attempting to leap the river barrier that has never been crossed by an invading army since the days of Napoleon. It is believed, however, that alert U.S. troops surprised the enemy in a quick dash to the river and captured a bridge intact. If so, it will undoubtedly rate as one of the greatest feats of the war.

Friday, March 9, 1945: —Fire, the enemy dreaded above all things by the Japanese, was loosed with dreadful fury upon their capital city last night by a force of over 300 mighty B-29 Superfortresses. The huge bombers cascaded over 1,000 tons of incendiaries upon the hapless city, touching off raging infernos that roared through a 10 square mile section of the target. Destruction and death ride rampant in the streets of Tokyo tonight.

General Eisenhower's great push on the Western Front has indeed carried beyond the Rhine. It was revealed today that opportunistic U.S. First Army troops captured the great Ludendorff Rail Bridge at Remagen, south of Cologne. The bridge was seized just ten minutes before the Germans were going to blow it up. Prepared for just such an opportunity, General Hodges quickly poured men and equipment across the river and established a firm bridgehead on the eastern bank. Advance units have already pushed five miles east of the bridgehead and have widened it to ten miles along the bank of the river. Countless Allied lives may be saved because of the quick thinking and initiative shown on the part of the First Army troops who captured the vital bridge.

Fierce battles are raging east of Berlin where the Russians have opened an all-out offensive designed to crush German resistance along the Oder and Neisse Rivers and to march on Berlin. The Germans are resisting with a desperation born of a deadly fear of Russian vengeance.

Saturday, March 10, 1945: —General Eisenhower is taking full advantage of the almost miraculous "break" that gave the American armies a bridge across the Rhine. The Allied

Commander-in-chief is pouring men and equipment across the river at high speed in an effort to "get set" before the enemy can launch his expected all-out counter-attack against the bridgehead. Several minor counter-blows have already been beaten off and American leaders on the spot assert that the Yanks are there to stay.

Meanwhile, the mop-up of the Germans west of the Rhine is continuing. Units of the American Third Army affected a junction with the First Army to draw a noose around approximated 50,000 Nazi troops caught in the Eifel Mountains. Other spearheads of General Patton's armor lanced through to all but encircle the vital Rhineland city of Coblenz. It was at Coblenz that the selfsame American Third Army, then a part of the Army of Occupation, had its headquarters in 1919. Now the sons of those old Third Army men are returning to Coblenz, but in a slightly different way.

In the Pacific war it was disclosed that American assault troops have invaded Mindanao in the southern Philippines. The landing was made on the southwest tip of the island under cover of a tremendous barrage from a huge naval task force, including battleships and cruisers. Immediate objective of the invaders was capture of Zamboanga, second largest port on the island. Grim fighting is raging throughout the area.

Sunday, March 11, 1945: —Friday night's fire bomb raid on Tokyo was described by returning pilots as the "the greatest show on earth." The Japanese capital was churned into a sea of flames that turned night into day and acted as a beacon to hundreds of B-29 Superfortresses who added their tons of bombs to the spreading conflagration. Eye-witness accounts told of smoke clouds billowing 6,000 to 7,000 feet into the sky, blackening bomb-bay doors and undersides of fuselages with soot. Crewmen could not only see Tokyo burning, they could smell it. The Japs are earning a fearful dividend for their investment at Pearl Harbor.

Seven hundred and fifty miles southeast of the burning enemy capital, the United States Marines are writing the finishing lines to the bloodiest chapter in the history of the Corps. The last fanatical Japanese defenders of the tiny volcanic island of Iwo Jima have been driven into the northeast corner of the isle where the Third, Fourth, and Fifth Marine Divisions are mopping them up. But the Nips are dying hard, exacting a heavy toll from the attacking Marines. Nevertheless, the final, bitter end is in sight and the hellish eight square miles of volcanic ash and sand will soon be ours. All glory to the United States Marines—of whom there are no peers among the ranks of gallant fighting men.

In Europe, General Eisenhower's great offensive is still going strong. The first tank-led German counter-attacks against the Remagen bridgehead have smashed themselves to pieces against the stone-wall resistance of the well established Yanks. Our hold on the east bank of the Rhine is secure.

Monday, March 12, 1945: —San Francisco paid further homage today to the 270 soldiers and nurses liberated from Japanese prison camps in the Philippines. After being checked by doctors at Letterman General Hospital, the heroes and heroines were fitted with new uniforms and were paraded up Market Street between cheering masses of citizens to Civic Center where a ceremony of welcome was held. The survivors of three years of Japanese torture and starvation were then treated to a huge steak dinner at the Palace Hotel, after which the City was theirs. Free taxi service, free long-distance telephone calls, and free movies were among the attractions offered them by the grateful citizenry of San Francisco.

The American First Army, after warding off the first Nazi counter-blows against the Remagen bridgehead across the Rhine, has now gathered strength enough to continue its advance east of the river. Patrols have thrust beyond the bridgehead to within a mile of the great Adolf Hitler Super Highway that parallels the Rhine and commands the great industrial Ruhr Valley. At the end of the day's advances, 23 German towns east of the Rhine were in our hands.

On the west side of the Rhine, General George S. Patton's Third Army has cleared the north bank of the Moselle River from Trier to Coblenz. The latter German city is now under siege and is expected to fall after the fashion of Cologne.

Tuesday, March 13, 1945: —While Tokyo still smoldered from last week's giant fire raids, a huge force of B-29s today gave Osaka the same treatment. Three hundred of the great Superfortresses rained 2,300 tons of explosives and incendiaries on strategic industrial targets in the Japanese metropolis. A ten square mile section of the big rail center and shipping port was turned into a raging inferno and the Marianas based bombers ranged over the city almost without opposition. I wonder how the Jap leaders will explain these raids to their people, especially since they have boasted about sinking our fleet several times and have claimed victory after victory. It will be pretty hard for the Jap people to believe that sort of stuff from now on, with the roar of planes and the crackle of flames giving the lie to the broadcaster's words.

In Europe the Yanks of the American First Army have advanced two more miles from the Remagen bridgehead, reaching in force a point within two miles of the great Ruhr-Rhineland Super Highway.

It was also reported that American forces have crossed the Rhine at one or more places near the original bridgehead. One was by means of a pontoon bridge thrown across the river near the Ludendorff rail span and the other was an amphibious assault near Koenigswinter, three miles northwest of Honnef.

Here in San Francisco a "Dimes for Manila" campaign has been opened. By means of a small contribution we can all share in the rebuilding of a once beautiful city.

Wednesday, March 14, 1945: —A report was circulated today that German Field Marshal Von Rundstedt recently approached General Eisenhower with a request for an armistice, agreeing to end German resistance east of the Rhine if the Allies on the Western Front would call it quits. The offer was turned down by General "Ike" who reiterated the unconditional surrender terms promulgated by the Big Three, England, Russia, and the United States.

Doughboys of the American First Army are steadily enlarging their holding across the Rhine in the Remagen bridgehead. The Yanks are now solidly established along a ten and one half mile stretch of the east bank of the river and have pushed eastward for a distance of five and one half miles. Nazi resistance has been surprisingly light considering the seriousness of the situation from their point of view. Only minor counter-attacks have been launched against the expanding bridgehead, all of which have been easily beaten off. Reconnaissance reports received today, however, indicate that the enemy is massing armor and men east of Cologne, obviously in preparation for a major effort to retrieve the situation. The battle of the bridgehead impends.

The sanguinary battle for Iwo Jima has not ended yet, although for practical purposes the island is now ours. A small remnant of the Japanese garrison is trapped in the northeast tip of the island and is resisting furiously with small arms and mortars. A bit of nasty mopping up remains to be done.

Thursday, March 15, 1945: —The big squeeze against the rich industrial Saar basin is on. General George S. Patton's American Third Army has crossed the Moselle River from the north and is driving south while General Patch's U.S. Seventh Army and the French First Army are attacking from the south. The Germans are believed incapable of mustering any force sufficiently strong to prevent the seizure of the entire Saar basin west of the Rhine, with its vital coal fields and massed war industries. Nevertheless, the Nazis will undoubtedly put up a vicious defense before bowing in defeat. The cost of victory will be high.

On the east bank of the Rhine, General Hodges' American First Army has fought its way out of the Remagen bridgehead and has severed the great Nazi superhighway that parallels the Rhine and links Cologne and Frankfurt. The Germans reported today that a new American army, the Fifteenth, under the command of Lieut. General Leonard T. Gerow, has joined with the First in the assault across the Rhine. No confirmation of this has come from Allied sources.

Prime Minister Winston Churchill optimistically declared today that a European victory may come before the end of summer or "even sooner." The British leader made the statement in a speech to the Conservative Party in which he also promised that Britain would give her utmost aid in the war against Japan. The British owe a debt to Japan for the "infernal cruelties perpetrated against English subjects by the Japanese."

Friday, March 16, 1945: —Kobe, Japan's fifth largest city and center of many of her most vital war industries, was given the fire bomb treatment this morning by a force of 300 B-29 Superfortresses which dumped more than 2,300 tons of incendiaries on a five-square mile target area of the city. This latest strike by the Marianas based B-29s brought to four the number of major Japanese cities attacked by fire within the past week. In addition to Kobe the big bombers have raided Tokyo, Nagoya, and Osaka, burning out vast sections in all three cities. The Japs themselves have admitted serious damage and have revealed that thousands of people were burned to death in the devastating attacks. The little men of Japan must be slightly bewildered as they watch their cities destroyed by the same Americans who, their leaders had boasted, have been blasted out of the air and driven from the seas.

The bloody battle for Iwo Jima has finally come to an end. The conquest of the eight square miles of volcanic ash and airfields has been the costliest campaign in the Pacific war to date. The Marines suffered 19,938 casualties. Of these 4,189 are dead, 441 are missing, and 15,308 are wounded. On the other side of the score sheet, we find that 21,000 Japs have been counted as killed—which almost makes up for one of the Marines lost—and other hundreds have undoubtedly been killed and buried in the debris of their fortifications. Another epic story in the history of the United States Marines has finally drawn to a close.

Saturday, March 17, 1945: —The rampaging American Third Army has ripped 15 miles into the outflanked Saar basin, isolating Coblenz and threatening the Germans with a total collapse of their defenses west of the Rhine. Spearheads of Patton's armor reached Bad Kreuznach and crossed the Nahe River near that city while other Third Army units pressed on into the outskirts of Coblenz. Capture of that major German city was assured since the Nazis left only a small rearguard to delay entry into the metropolis while the main enemy body fled across the turbulent Rhine.

The drive into the Saar basin has all but trapped an estimated 100,000 Nazi troops in a giant pincers clamped on by the Third Army in the north and the U.S. Seventh and French First Armies in the south. The Nazis are faced with the alternative of abandoning some of their best Siegfried defense lines around Saarbruecken and Zweibruecken and retreating pell mell across the Rhine while there remains an escape corridor, or face encirclement and eventual annihilation.

Not much has been heard from the Russian front lately. The Red Army is still poised along the Oder River line, 30 to 40 miles east of Berlin and the final assault on the German capital has not yet begun. The Soviets apparently are concentrating on cleaning up the East Prussian and Baltic campaigns before launching the final drive on Berlin.

Sunday, March 18, 1945: —What kind of newspaper headlines do we read nowadays? Here are some samples:

Coblenz falls, Nazis in rout; Great Enemy Collapse Looms.

Meat Supply to be cut 12 Pct. April 1st.

MacArthur's Forces Invade Basilan Isle. 282,000 Jap Casualties in Philippines.

Carrier Planes Raiding Japan, Tokyo Reports.

Cuban Army Shakeup. Revolt Plot Laid to Capitalists.

145,000 Young Men Deferred for War Jobs. Those past 30 Facing Draft as Combat Replacements.

Japs Slay 3 Californians. Woman Victim of Atrocity.

Yanks Closing In on 4 More Rhine Cities. Tanks Gain 15 Miles.

300 B-29s Raid Kobe. Biggest B-29 Raid of War.

Headlines such as those above can be found in almost any paper. Anything but war news has a hard time crashing the first page. As the war in Europe appears to be entering into its final, cataclysmic stage and the tempo of the Pacific war rises in crescendo, the people of the world eagerly follow every move made on the giant chessboard of war. Hopes rise or fall with the success or failure of the great antagonists.

Monday, March 19, 1945: —The Japs today revealed that their great factory centers of Osaka and Kobe have been lashed for two straight days by wave after wave of U.S. carrier-based aircraft. No confirmation of the attack has come from Admiral Nimitz' headquarters but there is little doubt as to the story's authenticity since it is known that Admiral Spruance's famous Fifth Fleet is operating somewhere in the "Jap hunting ground" off the enemy coast.

While the carrier planes blasted the Osaka-Kobe area, the largest B-29 armada thus far assembled—some 350 huge bombers—heaped devastation of Japan's vital aircraft manufacturing center at Nagoya. The entire heart of the city was blacked out with a dense smoke pall that rose to 6,000 feet.

On the Western European Front the Nazi debacle continued to grow. Mobile forces of three Allied armies, the U.S. Third and Seventh and the French First were chewing up ground at a furious pace in the Saar-Palatinate triangle. Approximately 100,000 crack Nazi troops faced almost certain annihilation or capture as their defenses crumbled before the onslaught of the victory-flushed Yanks. Clouds of Allied planes swarmed over the battlefields, blasting and burning the retreating enemy columns. Spearheads of the converging Third and Seventh armies were only 40 miles apart and closing fast. The fate of the Saar basin should be sealed within 48 hours.

Tuesday, March 20, 1945: —Thus far more than 70,000 German troops have been killed or swept into prison pens by the rampaging U.S. Third and Seventh Armies and the French Allies in the sensational mop-up of the industrial Saar basin. The historic city of Worms fell to the Third Army today and General Patton's hard-riding Doughboys fought their way into Mainz in the big bend of the Rhine. To the south units of the Tenth Armored Division blasted their way towards Kaiser-lautern and a junction with Seventh Army troops driving northward. General Patch's Seventh ripped the Siegfried line to shreds at many points from Saarbruecken to the Rhine, adding thousands of dazed enemy troops to the long lists of prisoners taken in the current offensive.

In the Pacific war it was learned that General MacArthur's forces have invaded Panay, sixth largest of the Philippine Islands. Units of the 40th Division, including veterans of the California National Guard, swept ashore last Sunday and drove towards Iloilo, capital of the island. Latest reports placed the invasion forces seven miles from the city and steadily forging ahead despite strong enemy resistance.

San Francisco was host again today to a large group of liberated soldiers from the dank torture of Japanese prison camps in the Philippines. There were 338 of them this time and they received the same warm welcome that was given to the first 270. There was a parade up Market Street, a ceremony at Civic Center, a steak dinner, music, and the keys to the city. America is proud of the heroes of Bataan and Corregidor.

Wednesday, March 21, 1945:—General George S. Patton's Third Army tank columns overran Ludwigshafen today and swept on to reach the Rhine at two points opposite Mannheim. Between the nutcracker drives of the Third and the U.S. Seventh under General Alexander M. Patch, more than 96,000 German troops have been ground into annihilation or surrender. These are some of the last of Hitler's crack Wehrmacht troops, the kind he can ill afford to lose if he hopes to make a successful stand east of the Rhine.

That the test of that defense will come very soon was evident today from the speed with which the U.S. First Army is moving from its bridgehead opportunely won on the east bank of the Rhine at Remagen. General Hodges' tanks fought their way 3½ miles northward into the outskirts of Siegburg, an industrial town of 14,000 population, and the largest town to be threatened east of the Rhine thus far. North of Siegburg lays the vast industrial region of the Ruhr, next major objective of the Berlin-bound Allied armies. Already, the Ruhr is a blazing inferno of gutted factories and blasted airfields and rail centers, after one of the most concentrated pre-invasion aerial bombardments of the entire war. Thousands of war planes launched an estimated 14,000 sorties during the past 24 hours, exceeding even the pre-Normandy barrage of last June.

Britain's Field Marshal Sir Bernard L. Montgomery appears about ready to lead his 21st Army group, composed of the Canadian First, the British Second, and the American Ninth Armies across the Rhine in the climactic battle for the Ruhr. A huge smoke screen along his entire line hides his preparations.

Thursday, March 22, 1945: —The Japanese today admitted that they face the gravest crisis in the history of their nation. Unable to hide the serious effect of the ever-increasing aerial blows against their homeland, the Japs revealed that more than 3,000,000 women and children and homeless victims of recent raids have been evacuated from Tokyo, reducing the population of the former third largest city in the world to less than 4,000,000.

The jittery Japs also are becoming invasion conscious, expecting American troops to land on their home islands at any time. Stringent measures for defense have been taken, granting

859

emergency powers to the military that would make the entire country an armed camp. Home guards are being organized and an area-by-area defense set up. Easy-to-handle arms are being manufactured for civilian use and the people are being coached to adopt a "conquer or die" attitude. Things look pretty black, eh, Mr. Moto? Have you forgotten Pearl Harbor?

In Europe, the desperate Nazis are playing their last trump. They have removed Field Marshal von Rundstedt, leader of the dangerous but costly Ardennes blunder, and have replaced him with Field Marshal Albert Kesselring, lately of the Italian front. Kesselring has the doubtful distinction of having conducted a "stonewall" defense of Italy and will undoubtedly be expected to pull some sort of miracle on the Western Front. But this professional German "killer" is inheriting an army already beaten in its disastrous defense of the Rhineland. He will do well to even delay the inevitable.

Friday, March 23, 1945: —Plans are being advanced rapidly for the United Nations Conference on International Organization to be held in San Francisco beginning April 25. Several officials of the Federal Government, including Dean Acheson, Assistant Secy. of State, have arrived here to complete arrangements for the worldwide conference upon which the fate of mankind depends. The hope for future peace and the welfare of generations to come hangs upon the outcome of the deliberations of the world's leaders at San Francisco next month. In truth, the eyes and ears of every man and woman on earth will be fixed upon the City by the Golden Gate during this epic event in history.

While the battered Nazis attempted desperately to plug up the hole at center where the American First Army is plunging through for many a first down and warily watched left end where Field Marshal Sir Bernard L. Montgomery seemed about to launch a dazzling aerial and ground attack, General George S. Patton's tireless Third Army pulled a sensational sneak play out of the bag and ripped around right end for what has the earmarks of a touchdown drive. Fresh from their power play that drove through the vast Saar-Palatinate basin, the Third Army Yanks followed through in approved Notre Dame fashion and stormed the Rhine without benefit of artillery preparation, taking the Nazis by surprise and establishing a firm bridgehead before the bewildered enemy could gather his wits and forces for a counter-drive. The bold "Pattonesque" operation took place between Mainz and Worms and at end of day found the rampaging Yanks in a position to threaten the great Nazi transport and industrial center of Frankfurt-on-the-Main.

Saturday, March 24, 1945: —The Grand and, we hope, the final offensive against Germany was launched with all the fury of a Cyclone and all the finesse and rhythm of a Beethoven symphony this morning. Four mighty Allied armies, one of them airborne, smashed across the Rhine on a broad front to join the American First and Third Armies in the climactic drive to knock Germany out of the war.

Field Marshal Sir Bernard L. Montgomery led the great new drive, sending his American Ninth, his British Second, and his Canadian First Armies roaring across the river barrier under cover of artificial fog and a tremendous artillery barrage such as only "Monty" can muster. Into the skies the British Marshal sent the paratroopers and glider-infantrymen of the Allied First Airborne Army under the command of America's Lieut. General Lewis H. Brereton. From between 5,000 to 6,000 war planes and gliders, the sky warriors, rained down upon the ill-prepared enemy close in advance of the land armies smashing across the Rhine.

The drive across the Rhine took on the appearance of a full-scale amphibious operation, with American and British sailors operating the thousands of vessels shuttling men and equipment across the turbulent stream. Overhead, thousands of bombers and fighters streaked ahead to blast enemy troops, supplies and strong-points. Early reports hinted that enemy resistance was spotty in most places, stern in some sectors. Thousands of prisoners are already streaming back, dazed and bewildered by the awesome display of Allied might.

Sunday, March 25, 1945: —The mighty trans-Rhine offensive has already gained tremendous momentum. More than 10,000 war planes and 1,200 big guns set the stage for the biggest Allied operation since D-day last June 6. The British Second and Canadian First Armies, aided by cascading paratroopers of the Allied First Airborne Army, quickly gouged out a 15 mile bridgehead on the east bank of the Rhine near Wesel, northwestern gateway to the industrial Ruhr Valley.

Just north of Wesel, the American Ninth Army, under Lieut. General William Simpson, drove four spearheads across the Rhine, welded them together into a solid twelve mile bridgehead, and lanced southward to threaten Germany's inland port of Duisburg, barely four miles away.

It was estimated that the Allied Commander-in-Chief, General Dwight D. Eisenhower, has committed some 1,250,000 crack Allied troops into this final, all-out drive for Berlin and victory. Six of his nine great Allied armies are already across the Rhine, striking deep into the beating heart of the German foe, whose will and ability to resist appears close to the breaking point. Resistance all along the vast battlefield was spotty, with only rare cores of hard effective opposition. Elsewhere, the Nazis seem panic stricken, hopelessly floundering, and unable to organize an effective defense line. Optimism was running high throughout the Allied forces. The scent of final victory is in the air. The end of Europe's most devastating catastrophe seemed almost unbelievably near. In Winston Churchill's words, "One strong heave will win the war."

Monday, March 26, 1945: —While German defenses along the flaming Western Front continued to crumble under the impact of General Eisenhower's mighty offensive, two powerful Russian armies added yet another threat, driving up both sides of the Danube towards Vienna. Marshal Tolbukhin's Third Ukrainian Army captured the Hungarian town of Papa, 31 miles from the Austrian border and drove on to within 70 miles of Vienna. The Second Ukrainian Army, on the Third's right flank, seized the Czechoslovakian center of Banska Bystrica, crossed the Hron River and smashed to within 130 miles of the Viennese capital in this sector. Elsewhere in the Russo-German front the Soviets cleaned out the remaining pockets of Nazi resistance in East Prussia and battered their way through two heavy belts of German defenses before the former free city of Danzig. Activity was more or less static along the Oder River line where the Red Army has been stalled for several weeks barely 40 miles from Berlin. However, indications point to a renewed all-out drive on the German capital timed to coincide with the approach of the western armies under Eisenhower.

David Lloyd George, Britain's strong man during World War I died in England today. The fiery Briton who lived to see his country again snatched from the brink of defeat with Germany, died peacefully at the age of 82. Last January, King George VI named him Earl Lloyd George of Dwyfor but he never sat in the House of Lords. Another great man of history has departed.

Tuesday, March 27, 1945: —Rumors ran riot today. For awhile thousands of people throughout the country thought the European war was over. The excitement was caused by the erroneous dispatch of a news message over the wires of International News Service. General Eisenhower had remarked in his news conference that the "Germans as a military force on the west front are whipped." In relaying this message to the home folks, an unwary typist caught the word "whipped" as "quit" and flashed the news that the "Germans have quit." This, plus the misinterpretation of a statement by the President's secretary to the effect that the Chief Executive had requested all government officials not directly concerned with the San Francisco Conference to stay in Washington, was enough to set off the wildest rumors of peace. Even the radio and some newspapers blared out the news, and then quickly corrected it, but not until thousands had been taken in by the error. All in all, fun was had by everyone.

Although the war is definitely not over yet, the Nazis are certainly on the run in western Germany. Prisoners by the tens of thousands are streaming back to cages on the east side of the Rhine. Victory flushed American, British, and Canadian troops are running roughshod over thousands of square miles of Germany's most vital provinces. Nowhere do the Nazis show any signs of being able to form a solid defense line and it appears that supply problems only can slow down the lightning advance of the seven powerful Allied armies now driving into Germany east of the Rhine. The American Seventh Army under General Alexander M. Patch was the latest Allied force to leap the Rhine barrier, the crossing being made near Karlsruhe.

Wednesday, March 28, 1945: —History's mightiest armies smashed relentlessly into central Germany today, sending armored spearheads plunging at least 70 miles beyond the east bank of the Rhine and reaching to within some 200 miles of Berlin itself. The exact location of the leading units was veiled under a security blackout imposed by the Allied High Command to avoid giving the enemy any useful information but it was known that the First, Third, and Seventh American armies have joined forces to form a solid front of 175 miles. Spearheads of all three armies ripped out gains today ranging from 25 to 35 miles apiece. The panicky Nazis were fleeing so rapidly that in some places the advancing Allied troops were completely out of contract with the enemy.

British and Canadian troops on the northern end of the line swept 33 miles beyond the Rhine today and were entering the great north German plain for a dash towards Berlin, now only 245 miles away. Nazi resistance, originally stout in this sector, is apparently melting away before the powerhouse drive of the Tommies and Cannucks.

England, through its Foreign Secretary Anthony Eden, served notice on Adolf Hitler today that he is War Criminal No. 1 and British soldiers have been instructed to use their own judgment as to whether they should shoot him on sight or try to bring him back alive. A well placed bullet now would save a lot of useless formality later and would accomplish the same result.

Thursday, March 29, 1945: —Like giant buzz saws ripping through soft wood, the seven mighty Allied armies are tearing western and central Germany to bits. The British Second, the American Ninth and the American First Armies made slashing drives north and south aimed at cutting the vital Ruhr Valley from the central Reich while the roaring U.S. Third Army smashed two-thirds of the way to the Czechoslovakian border and took over control of more than 8,500 square miles of German soil.

On the U.S. Seventh Army front, General Patch's Doughboys captured the great port and industrial center of Mannheim, on the east bank of the Rhine opposite Ludwigshafen. The German mayor of the city of 284,000 people surrendered the city to the advancing Yanks by telephone, informing them that no German soldiers were left in town. American troops then occupied the city, marching down streets festooned with white flags of surrender.

The Russian drive on Vienna is gaining momentum. The Soviet troops today smashed through to the Austrian frontier and captured Koszeg, border town some 50 miles from Vienna. Here again the Nazis apparently are unable to muster any force capable of stopping the advance and the fall of Vienna appears to be merely a matter of time.

Notes on the home front: 12% less meat for civilians effective immediately, higher ration points for lard, margarine, and many canned goods. Baby shoes added to the ration list. That last one hits home because the kids wear shoes out in a week or two—particularly since they are made of paper, or so it seems.

Friday, March 30, 1945: —Sweeping up demoralized German prisoners by the thousands, the mighty Allied juggernaught continued to roll deeper into the Reich during the past 24 hours. Meeting disorganized and ineffectual resistance, the fast moving armored columns of General Eisenhower's well-oiled military machine scored gains of more than 30 miles in the day, knifing through the countryside with such speed that any prospects the Nazis had of establishing an organized defense line short of the Elbe River seem well nigh hopeless. High ranking captives admitted that their hopes of organizing a defense along the Weser River had been completely upset by the lightning advance of General Patton's Third Army and General Hodges' First Army.

Stalin's legions are also moving fast in the east. The Third Ukrainian Army, under Marshal Feodor I. Tolbukhin, smashed across the Austrian border today after seizing the border town of Koszeg yesterday. Objective of the drive is Vienna, now less than 50 miles to the north.

Other Red Army forces in the Baltic area captured the former free city of Danzig today after a bitter battle with the German garrison. More than 49,000 Nazi troops were killed or captured in the attack. Polish troops participated in the liberation of the naval base and the Polish flag was raised over the city.

Opinions waxed hot today over the disclosure that both Russia and the United States will ask for three votes each at the coming San Francisco conference. The multiple vote plan came as a result of a secret agreement made at Yalta.

Saturday, March 31, 1945: —While more than 3,000 American, British, and Canadian tanks roared unchecked along the network of superhighways leading to Berlin, rumors ran rife regarding conditions within the Nazi government. Unconfirmed reports told of Hermann Goering committing suicide while high military commanders and Propaganda Minister Paul Joseph Goebbels were said to have bluntly told Hitler that the war is lost. Der Fuhrer is believed to be at his mountain hideout of Berchtesgaden preparing for a last ditch stand in the Bavarian Alps. Chaos is spreading throughout the German Army. Field Marshal Albert Kesselring, recently drafted from the Italian front in a desperate effort to stop the onrushing Allies, is reported to have admitted his failure and has been relieved of his command. The end cannot be too far away.

In the Pacific, fast carrier task forces of the United States Navy are heavily pounding the big island of Okinawa in the center of the Ryukyu chain, in what may be a pre-invasion bombardment. This is the ninth consecutive day of attack against this strategic island which lies barely 400 miles south of the main Japanese islands. During the attacks 46 enemy ships were either sunk or damaged and approximately 100 enemy planes have been shot down.

Russia has asked that the Soviet-sponsored Polish government in Warsaw be invited to the San Francisco conference. Both Britain and the United States, however, have said no to this request. The Warsaw government is not recognized by either and it was agreed at Yalta that a compromise Polish government would be organized. Until this is accomplished no invitation to S.F.

April

Sunday, April 1, 1945: —The sun rising in the east this morning brought with it the dawn of a new Easter Sunday. Never before in the history of the world has mankind needed to give so much thought and consideration to the lessons of Christ. Never before has the world needed Christianity so desperately. Thousands of families solemnly thinking of row upon row of stark white crosses standing in countless fields throughout a war-torn world can gain great solace in the magnificent promise of Easter, the promise of Resurrection and Eternal Life. The sacrifice of Christ, like the sacrifice of our heroic war dead, shall not be in vain.

The weather today was clear and brilliant, although a stiff northerly wind carried a chill with it that discouraged many Easter paraders from taking their usual stroll. Thousands of worshipers, however, were up early to make their customary pilgrimage to the great, lighted cross atop Mount Davidson in San Francisco. There they bowed in reverent contemplation of the mysterious ways of God and the glorious promise of the Resurrection.

Throughout the battlefields of the world American fighting men paused briefly to observe Easter and then plunged determinedly into their task of crushing the enemy and restoring peace to this blood-drenched world. Late radio reports indicate that American invasion forces have landed on Okinawa in the Ryukyu Islands. A fierce, costly battle is expected.

Monday, April 2, 1945: —The great American invasion of Okinawa Island in the Ryukyus is on. Thousands of Army and Marine troops swept ashore under cover of a mighty naval and air bombardment from an armada of ships and planes that rivaled in size the invasion of Normandy. Initial landings were made easily against surprisingly light resistance. The Yanks went in expecting a reception like that of Iwo Jima but found the beaches poorly defended with the main body of the enemy garrison pulled back into the interior. The good fortunes of war were gratefully received by the American troops and they quickly consolidated their beachheads and began unloading supplies and equipment for the inevitable large-scale battles ahead.

The grand offensive east of the Rhine is progressing very favorably. Today saw spearheads of the U.S. First and Ninth Armies join to complete the encirclement of the great industrial Ruhr, trapping approximately 100,000 to 150,000 German troops within the flaming ruins of the once vital war-producing area.

General George S. Patton's famous 4th Armored Division of the U.S. Third Army led the race towards the German capital today, driving along the famous Hitler Autobahn that stretches from Frankfurt to Berlin to a point eight miles east of Eisenach and 162 miles east of the capital. The bag of prisoners is swelling hourly, with the count for last Saturday alone amounting to 30,000.

Tuesday, April 3, 1945: —In a reassuring preliminary note to the forthcoming San Francisco Conference on International Organization, the United States today announced through the State Department that it has decided not to ask for additional votes for this country in the proposed World Assembly. At Yalta President Roosevelt had practically committed the United States to support Russia's demand for three votes and, in turn, had declared his intention to demand three votes for this country. He has now changed his mind and will ask only one vote for the United States although presumably we will carry out his pledge to support the Russian demand. The wheels of international politics are grinding.

Patton's tanks are still rolling across the plains and through the cities of Germany. Only 141 miles now separates the dashing American General from Berlin. Forty miles beyond that hapless city stands the hordes of Russia. The big squeeze is on.

Tied up inextricably with victory as the with defeat is the tragedy of death that strikes paralyzing blows into the lives and homes of so many families. Not even Generals are spared when the Gods of war exact their toll. It was learned today that Major General Maurice Rose, famous commander of the Third Armored Division, was shot to death by a trigger-happy Nazi tankman after the General had surrendered when his jeep ran into a covey of German tanks during the recent breakthrough.

Wednesday, April 4, 1945: —The United States Third and Ninth Armies ripped off another 22 mile gain along the road to

Berlin today. Disorganized remnants of the once all powerful German Wehrmacht were reported falling back to their last natural defense line on the Elbe River, some fifty miles from the Reich capital.

Approximately one third of Germany has already been overrun by General Eisenhower's Allied Armies since the beginning of the present all-out offensive. Many of Germany's greatest cities and most vital war industries have fallen to the rampaging Yanks, Britons, and Canadians. Germany's ability to wage successful war is fading rapidly as her life's blood of supplies and munitions is drained from her. For the Nazis the war is irrevocably lost. How long Hitler and his Gestapo can terrorize the German people into continuing the hopeless struggle can only be conjectured. From the Nazi leaders themselves, with a noose awaiting them in any event, we can only expect some sort of insane last-ditch death stand in the Bavarian Alps.

In the Pacific it appears that the Battle for Okinawa Island is beginning to intensify. The surprisingly easy initial stage has been passed and the real struggle is starting. Apparently the Japanese have massed their main forces on a line just north of Naha, the capital city, and are preparing for a savage show-down battle. The U.S. Tenth Army is moving into position to attack.

Thursday, April 5, 1945: —Russia added a bit of sensation to the news today when it was announced by Moscow that the Soviet Union was denouncing her neutrality pact with Japan. The Russians accused the Japs of aiding Germany in her fight against the Allies and said that in view of this and changing world conditions that the Russo-Japanese Five-year Neutrality Pact signed on April 13, 1941 no longer makes sense and can no longer be continued.

The Russian action aroused speculation that the Soviets may soon enter the far eastern war as a full belligerent. The Russians have many scores to settle with the Japs and would undoubtedly like to be in on the kill in the Pacific as well as in Europe. We may, therefore, see some startling developments along this line before many weeks have passed.

The long uncertainty regarding the Army and Navy leadership in the final drive on Tokyo was settled today by the

Joint Chiefs of Staff in Washington. General Douglas MacArthur will be given command of all Army forces in the Pacific theater while Admiral Nimitz will command all Naval forces in that area. Both will of course be subordinate to the Joint Chiefs of Staff. Both are magnificent commanders, having won brilliant victories in their respective Pacific areas during the past year. Now both can share in the final drive against the heart of the Japanese homeland. Our troops and our fleet are in good hands.

Friday, April 6, 1945: —Russo-Japanese relations are hanging on the shreds of uncertainty tonight after the denunciation by Moscow of the Neutrality Pact with Japan. It was revealed that the Japs strove desperately to avoid the break with Russia, even offering to nullify the humiliating Treaty of Portsmouth by which Japan gained territory and power from a defeated Russia after the Russo-Japanese war. But their efforts were of no avail and the Soviet Government denounced the Neutrality Pact in no uncertain terms, saying that "it no longer makes any sense."

Failure to appease Russia has caused great uneasiness in Tokyo and has resulted in the resignation of Premier Koiso and his cabinet. Admiral Baron Kantaro Suzuki has been commanded by the Emperor to form a new government. Not an easy job with the whole Japanese Empire rocking under the impact of American bombs. The new Premier-designate spent his first day closeted with high ranking military and naval leaders, no doubt hearing first hand explanations of how the thrice destroyed American armies and navies have been able to bring the war so perilously close to the Nipponese heartland.

Even while the leaders of Japan talked, American soldiers and marines were coming to grips with the Japanese defenders of Okinawa, the strategic island less than 400 miles from the Nip homeland. The crucial battle for the island stronghold is approaching as the American invaders near the strong Japanese lines guarding the capital city of Naha.

Saturday, April 7, 1945: —A large portion of the skulking Japanese Imperial Grand Fleet came out of hiding today and was engaged in a fierce naval-air battle by elements of Vice Admiral Marc A. Mitscher's mighty carrier Task Force 58. In the blazing battle that ensued, American carrier planes found and destroyed

Japan's greatest battleship, the 45,000 ton Yamato, two battle cruisers, and three destroyers. Our losses were three destroyers and an undisclosed number of planes. The Nips also lost 391 aircraft in a one-sided aerial melee, reminiscent of the famous "Marianas Turkey Shoot" last June 18th.

The "unsinkable" Yamato, one of the mightiest battleships ever built, was sent to the bottom of the East China Sea after U.S. Navy Helldivers and torpedo planes sent at least eight torpedoes and eight heavy bombs crashing into her hull. The huge vessel finally heeled over and sank, carrying with her Japan's last hopes of naval dominance in the Pacific.

In Europe, the Battle of Germany is fast turning into a steeplechase known as the "Berlin Derby" with three speedy American entries, the U.S. First, Third, and Ninth Armies leading the field as they go down the stretch. Ninety miles west of Weimar, curious American Doughboys of the 90th Infantry Division stumbled on what may be one of the richest treasure troves in history. Hidden deep in an abandoned salt mine they discovered what is believed to be the entire gold reserve of the German Reichbank. Tons of gold bullion, millions upon millions of dollars in American, English, French, Dutch and German currencies plus uncalculated treasures of rare works of art were included in the dramatic haul.

Sunday, April 8, 1945: —Yesterday's big naval battle was fought less than fifty miles off the Japanese coast. The enemy task force was pounced on as it left the "safety" of its home ports in a desperate attempt to go to the relief of its hard pressed garrison on Okinawa. The battle ended in destruction of the entire enemy task force with the exception of three destroyers and accounted for an estimated 25% of the remaining Japanese fleet.

The many pronged Allied drive into the heart of Germany is gouging ever nearer to Berlin. The U.S. Ninth Army is leading the race at the moment, having roared 18 miles beyond Hannover on the most direct route to the German capital. To the north the British Second Army speared to within 20 miles of the great North Sea port of Bremen. To the south the American First Army crossed the Weser River in force at many points, mopping up scattered Nazi resistance that varied from half-hearted to fanatical. Farther south the rampaging Third Army under colorful General George S. Patton roared on past Merkers where they captured Germany's "Fort Knox," described in yesterday's article, and swept to within 120 miles of the Reich capital. A counter-attack by a large enemy tank force was smashed with the destruction of more than forty tanks.

Russian forces, meanwhile, have encircled Vienna, the city of lilting waltzes and Nazi intrigue. Fall of the Austrian metropolis is imminent.

Monday, April 9, 1945: —The Allied drive across Germany continues unabated. The American Ninth Army smashed into the great munitions center of Essen today and seized the huge Krupp armament works, infamously known as the world "Merchants of Death." Further north the British Second Army stormed into the outskirts of Bremen where huge fires raged uncontrolled, apparently started by the Nazis as part of their scorched earth policy. Brunswick and the Baltic port of Leubeck were also burning fiercely although no Allied planes have been over either city recently.

On the Eastern Front the Red Army finally captured Koenigsberg, the fiercely defended capital of East Prussia. The Nazis lost more than 100,000 men in the defense of the city, 42,000 of them being taken prisoner in the last two days of the battle. Capture of the Junker capital, a city of 370,000 people, was considered a great victory in Moscow and Marshal Stalin ordered the maximum salute from Moscow's famous victory cannon.

In the Pacific the Battle for Okinawa is assuming the vicious, bloody character of the fight for Iwo Jima. The Japs have entrenched themselves well in strong hill positions covering the approaches to Naha, the capital of the island. Their artillery, mortar, and machine gun fire is sweeping the area through which the Yanks must advance with a deadly crossfire that has brought the American drive to a virtual standstill. The worst is yet to come.

Tuesday, April 10, 1945: —Amid widespread rumors of violent anti-Nazi uprisings throughout the German Reich, the American Ninth Army today drove its armored spearhead into the great railroad center of Hannover. Organized resistance faded before the might of the fast-moving Doughboys and nightfall found our advance units far beyond the city aiming at Brunswick, the Elbe, and then Berlin.

The reports of anti-Nazi uprisings came from Stockholm and Switzerland and claimed that more than 5,000 Nazis were slain in Berlin alone during violent peace demonstrations by the panic stricken populace. Gestapo and SS troopers were ruthless in putting down the threatened rebellion but much disaffection undoubtedly was left among the harried citizenry of the doomed capital.

The long forgotten front in Italy has flamed into life with the Allied armies under the command of General Mark Clark jumping off in a great spring offensive designed to crush the German defenses before Bologna and bring the Italian campaign to a conclusion. Preceded by an unprecedented aerial and artillery barrage, the famous British Eighth Army swept across the Senio River southwest of Bologna and crashed into the flat Po plain leading to the city. On the Adriatic side of the peninsula the American Fifth Army entered the former capital of the duchy of Massa-Carrara and drove northwestward along the Ligurian coast.

Wednesday, April 11, 1945: —The Berlin Sweepstakes is on! Three mighty American armies are racing towards the Nazi capital at breakneck speed, first one army taking the lead then relinquishing it after a brilliant sprint by one of the others. The latest reports place the U.S. Ninth Army at the Elbe water barrier near Magdeburg, less than 60 miles from the German capital. The Ninth, paced by a sensational 55 mile dash by the famous "Hell on Wheels" Second Armored Division, thereby took a commanding lead over the American First Army, now 90 miles away, and the American Third Army, less than 100 miles distant.

The Second Armored Division made one of the most sensational sweeps of the entire war to race the 55 miles in 12 hours. The American tanks rolled almost unimpeded down the magnificent Berlin superhighway, crashed through the stronghold of Magdeburg, and reached the 200 yard wide Elbe River by nightfall. Sixty miles beyond this last river barrier lies the ruined city of Berlin and a little more than 100 miles beyond are the Russians. Some observers predicted a junction between the American and Russian forces within 72 hours.

Elsewhere along the blazing 400 mile Western Front American forces captured or entered eight other major German cities. Essen, Coburg, and Gelsenkirchen were seized while Brunswick, Bochum, Erfurt, Schweinfurt, and Dortmund felt the weight of advancing American armor.

Rumors are rife of dissension and collapse within the Nazi government. Hitler is reported raging like a trapped and dying animal, while Gestapo chief Heinrich Himmler is said to have seized control.

Thursday, April 12, 1945: —PRESIDENT ROOSEVELT IS DEAD! This tragic news struck the nation with stunning force this afternoon. The President's Secretary, Stephen T. Early, announced that Mr. Roosevelt died unexpectedly from a cerebral hemorrhage while resting at Warm Springs, Georgia.

I was at work when someone announced that the appalling news had been heard over the radio. Everyone in the office just sat there in stunned silence for a few moments, trying to assimilate into their minds the fact that Franklin Delano Roosevelt was gone. He had been their President for so long that he had almost become a part of their way of life. It couldn't be real, there must be some mistake. The President of these United States couldn't go just like that, especially at this time in history when he is needed so much. What would happen now? What would become of the peace to be won? What would be the effect on "Big Three" relations? Who could take his place? These questions and dozens of others raced through everyone's mind even while the somber silence flooded the room. The tragic blow struck hard.

In Washington the machinery of government swung into action shortly after the first shock was over. Vice President Harry S. Truman, who will succeed to the Presidency, was called to the White House at once where an immediate Cabinet meeting was summoned. Despite the heavy grief over the loss of a great leader, the urgent business of Government cannot wait and those who are now responsible for our destinies must carry on without pause.

Friday, April 13, 1945: —Amid the eulogies and tears of his countrymen, the mortal remains of Franklin Delano Roosevelt,

32nd President of the United States, began its long, last journey from the "Little White House" in Warm Springs, Georgia to Washington D.C. where funeral services will be conducted tomorrow. Interment will be at Hyde Park where the Roosevelt estate overlooks the Hudson River.

At the Nation's capital, a new President assumed the stupendous burdens inherited from the fallen leader. Harry S. Truman was inaugurated as the 33rd President of the United States at a brief ceremony in the White House. The new Chief Executive was sworn in by Chief Justice Harlan Fiske Stone in the presence of members of the Cabinet and Congress. Great must have been the humility of Harry Truman as he took over the helm of this mighty nation in one of the most crucial periods in its illustrious history. There is a war to be won and a permanent peace to be established and much will depend upon the words and actions of the President of the United States. It is enough to fill the strongest man with qualms.

President Truman's first official act was to issue a proclamation setting aside tomorrow as a national day of mourning for the dead President and calling for all citizens to bow down in prayers of homage and reverence for the great and good man that has been taken from us. The official period of mourning will continue for the next thirty days. The Stars and Stripes will fly at half staff wherever there are Americans throughout the world. The cause of freedom has lost a great champion.

Saturday, April 14, 1945: —Simple funeral services were held at the White House today as the flag-draped casket containing the body of Franklin D. Roosevelt rested in quiet dignity amid the banks of floral wreaths and in the familiar surroundings where the departed President spent more than twelve hectic years, longer than any other man, guiding the Ship of State through perilous waters both in peace and war. At his side during the solemn rites were President Truman, Mrs. Roosevelt, members of the Roosevelt family, Government leaders, and representatives of foreign governments, including Britain's Foreign Secretary Anthony Eden.

The entire nation joined with freedom loving countries throughout the world in mourning the loss of a great defender of liberty and champion of the rights of the small and weak. President Roosevelt was probably known and respected more widely throughout the nations of the world than any other American. The name Roosevelt has been a symbol of the power and ideals that is America. To the peon, the peasant, and the proletariat, the name Roosevelt signified friend. Our loss is the free-world's loss.

American fighting men, wherever possible, paused momentarily to pay reverent homage to their dead Commander-in-Chief, then proceeded with the task of destroying the enemy. The American Ninth Army forged two bridgeheads across the Elbe River barrier guarding Berlin, and pressed on towards the enemy capital. It is believed that entry into the ruined capital may come within hours.

Sunday, April 15, 1945: —Preceded by the solemn booming of cannon giving the Presidential salute, the body of President Roosevelt was carried to the garden of his Hyde Park Estate today and there laid to rest in the warm, brown earth. The flag-draped casket containing his body was carried on a horse drawn artillery caisson to the slow cadence of muffled drums from the special train that brought it from Washington to the little plot of ground that will be his last resting place. Men in uniform lined the road and stood stiffly at attention in honor of their late Commander-in-Chief. A detail of West Point Cadets smartly fired a farewell salute three times over the grave while army bombers roared overhead. A bugler sounded taps, and the somber notes echoed softly from the green hills. People wept.

Before his death President Roosevelt had prepared a speech to be delivered to the Pan-American Union in honor of Pan-American Day. Its contents were revealed today disclosing that the late President's final thoughts were on the problems of securing a lasting peace after this war is won. He evidently believed that the lessons of unity and effective cooperation learned by the Pan-American republics could be used to good advantage in the organization of the world for peace. The "Good Neighbor" policy that has worked so well in this hemisphere could well be adapted to the entire world. To the late President's last message, President Truman and the whole nation heartily subscribe.

Monday, April 16, 1945: —A great Allied storm is brewing for the Germans, with its epicenter at Berlin. From the east 2,000,000 Russians are stirring from their bridgeheads across the Oder and the full fury of their final drive on the Nazi capital is developing like a dozen approaching cyclones. Four mighty Red Armies have come to life and have sent thousands of tanks and hundreds of thousands of infantrymen crashing into the Nazi defenses for the final test of blood and steel. Massed artillery, hub to hub, laid down a tremendous "tattoo" of shells over the Nazi line in a thunderous preliminary barrage.

From the west the approaching storm was just as fierce. Powerful American armies poured across the Elbe River despite stiffening German resistance that cost us one bridgehead. But the Nazi cause was hopeless and reinforced Yank columns struck out beyond the river towards the burning enemy capital and a junction with the Russians.

Everywhere in central Germany the American and British forces overran more territory and swept up thousands of prisoners. Already more than 550,000 German troops have been captured during April and another estimated 150,000 are hopelessly trapped in the dwindling Ruhr pocket. Nazi disaster is everywhere. General Patton's Third Army tanks are less than 13 miles from the Czechoslovakian border and are nearing Dresden where a junction with the approaching Red Army is expected. Farther south, the American Seventh Army is driving towards Nuremberg and the Nazis Bavarian redoubt. Particularly fierce resistance is being encountered in this area.

Tuesday, April 17, 1945: —President Truman today clearly stated in his first press conference that he will back practically all of the Roosevelt Administration's domestic and foreign policies. He indicated his intention of retaining the midnight curfew and the ban on horse racing among other civilian restrictions, saying that he thought that both have done a lot of good for the morale of the country.

Although Mr. Truman stated that he would not attend the forthcoming San Francisco Conference, he expressed his endorsement of the monetary program initiated at Bretton Woods and indicated he would support a reciprocal trade program to stimulate and encourage world trade. The President apparently feels very strongly that there must be no failure at San Francisco and believes that all nations, whether big or small, should give and take unselfishly to secure a stable world organization that will have the power and recognized authority to uphold the peace.

To further these aims President Truman disclosed that he would confer with the Russian Foreign Commissar V. M. Molotov as the Soviet emissary passes through Washington en route to the San Francisco Conference. The subject of the meeting, which will include Secy. of State Edward Stettinius, was not disclosed but observers believe that the knotty Polish question would be brought up for possible settlement before the United Nations meet.

Wednesday, April 18, 1945: —America was struck a second tragic blow in less than a week today when it was learned that Ernie Pyle was killed in action on the tiny Japanese island of Ie, just off the coast of Okinawa. The famous reporter, who was the buddy and champion of every front line soldier and marine, was struck in the temple by a burst of Japanese machine gun fire as he was on his way to join the front line troops in their invasion of the enemy stronghold.

The loss of Ernie Pyle will add further sadness to the hearts of millions of people who eagerly followed his daily column in hundreds of newspapers throughout the country. His writings were simple, homespun tales about the common soldier and marine, yet were packed with human interest that held his readers spellbound. Through his accurate world pictures we at home were able to realize and appreciate a portion of the sacrifices and sufferings of the combat soldiers. His stories were full of pathos, yet scintillated with tales of the fighting Yanks' never failing sense of humor and their quick adaptability to the stern realities of modern war. Ernie hated war, yet was drawn back into it against his better judgment because of his close attachment to the foot slogging combat soldier and his desire to present an accurate word portrait of his bitter, bloody, yet heroic struggle.

Like the other millions, I will miss Ernie's column for I followed it avidly, turning to it almost before I read the headlines. Some of his work will undoubtedly be classic reading in the years to come. His tragic death hurts deeply.

Thursday, April 19, 1945: —General Eisenhower's armies today completed what may well be considered the most decisive defeat inflicted on the German armed forces in this war, including the debacle at Stalingrad. Hard-hitting Yank troops completed the mop-up of the great Ruhr pocket, in which a large segment of the remaining German army was hopelessly trapped by the lightning advance of the western Allies across the Rhine. The bag of prisoners thus far, with many more to be counted, numbers 316,000, many of whom were Hitler's finest paratroops, SS elite troops, and panzer men. Loss of these forces, along with the other thousands killed, plus the elimination of the vastly important Ruhr industries, has undoubtedly brought the end of the war much closer. It is a magnificent victory.

At the same time other major victories were being won at other sectors of the rapidly expanding battlefront. In the center the anchor cities of Leipzig and Halle were captured after a bloody battle by two divisions of the U.S. First Army. Thousands of Allied prisoners and civilian slave laborers were liberated in the town. Farther south the American Seventh Army battled deep into the Nazi shrine city of Nuremberg in a drive aimed at the enemy's "last stand" redoubt in the Bavarian Mountains.

The body of Ernie Pyle, beloved combat reporter, will be laid to rest on the tiny island of Ie, beside the boys who died with him in the conquest of the Japanese isle. As Ernie once said of other brave soldier dead, we can only pause for a moment and say, "Thanks Pal!"

Friday, April 20, 1945: —The eyes of the world are watching with rapt fascination the unfolding of the final chapter of the European war. The events of the past few weeks have moved with kaleidoscopic rapidity to a final showdown in the heart of the German Reich. American troops have smashed their way to the Elbe River, last natural defense barrier before the German capital, and there have paused while the mighty Russian hordes closing in from the east have launched a furious onslaught that has carried them from the Oder River to within seven miles of Berlin's suburbs. Obviously the Allied High Command has assigned the honor of capturing Berlin to the Red Army.

Elsewhere in Germany American and British Armies struck deadly new blows against the tottering remnants of Hitler's once all-powerful Wehrmacht. The American Seventh Army completed the conquest of the Nazi shrine city of Nuremberg and drove on southward from Munich and the Bavarian mountain stronghold of Der Fuhrer. In the north the Canadians neared the naval base of Emden while the British Second Army entered Bremen and sealed off all escape routes from the ruined city.

The Italian front has also flared into violent action. Bologna, powerful enemy stronghold guarding the Po Valley, was captured by troops of the British Eighth and American Fifth Armies. Lieut. General Mark Clark hailed the victory as marking the beginning of the end in Italy.

Saturday, April 21, 1945: —Berlin, the proud city of the Teutonic "supermen," capital of the Third German Reich, and stamping ground for many would-be world conquerors, today became a battleground of World War II. The battered Nazi capital, wracked and torn by countless thousands of tons of Allied bombs, is now feeling the tread of triumphant Soviet troops and tanks. Artillery shells from Russian guns are whining and smashing into famed Potzdamer Platz while the Soviet ground troops are edging ever closer to the heart of the city, compressing the fanatical Nazi defenders into an inevitable death trap.

The Nazis have vested the defense of Berlin to Paul Joseph Goebbels, erstwhile Propaganda Minister. The Defense Chief has ordered all able-bodied among the three million remaining population to build street barricades and man them against the converging horde from the east. Abject terror has seized upon most of the civilians, however, as they huddle underground to escape the shells and bombs of the vengeful Red Army.

Well might the Germans fear the vengeance of their foes for the conquest of Germany has revealed incredible proof of the savagery and bestiality of the Nazis in their treatment of political and war prisoners and the citizens of conquered countries. Horrible stories of mass exterminations camps, of death by torture and starvation, have all been proved true. Witnesses, including high officials of Allied armies and governments, have seen with their own eyes. The indictment is complete.

Sunday, April 22, 1945: —Russian troops and armor have smashed four miles inside the flaming, bomb scarred streets of

Berlin. The carnage is fearful as the better equipped Red Army forces batter down the hastily erected street barricades manned in many cases by civilians. Apparently there is nothing the beaten Nazis can do to prevent the ultimate capture of their capital. Resistance can only delay the inevitable since the Russians are employing an overwhelming force of 16 Soviet armies in the Berlin assault. The Russians are attacking from three sides and have all but encircled the dying city. All direct escape routes southward towards the Bavarian redoubt have been cut off.

One Soviet army is reported to have bypassed Berlin on the south and is racing towards the Elbe River and a junction with American forces. This junction, expected hourly, will sever the Reich in two and will mark the culmination of two of the most sensational military come backs in the history of the world. The Russians came back from the brink of disaster before the gates of Moscow and Stalingrad to march over 1,000 miles to Berlin and the heart of Germany. The western Allies have also come back from the black days of Dunkirk and the fall of France to march back across sea and continent to a momentous rendezvous with the Red Army. Truly the entire world stands amazed.

Monday, April 23, 1945: —The stage is being set for the opening of the greatest drama in San Francisco's long and eventful history. Delegates from the 46 United Nations are beginning to pour into the city by boat, and plane, and train. Colorful dignitaries from the four corners of the world are gathering in the City by the Golden Gate, a Gate that the whole world hopes will open the doors to a new and brighter future. Men charged with so great an obligation are assembling from the war-weary countries of Europe, so recently liberated from the yoke of Nazism, and from China, Russia, and the nations of Central and South America.

In Washington D.C. the foreign ministers of the United States, Great Britain, and Russia have met to discuss Big Three agreements and disagreements before proceeding to the San Francisco Conference. The main issue is the touchy subject of Polish representation at the United Nations' conference and it is hoped that the matter may be settled prior to the opening date in order to forestall any bickering or disunity among the major powers and the conference.

In Germany the end of the war seems very near. Marshal Stalin announced that Soviet troops have smashed to within four miles of the center of Berlin. The Nazi garrison is resisting fanatically and the German radio claimed that Adolf Hitler himself is in the city directing its defense in person. The fading Fuhrer is determined to save the city from "bolshevism" or die in the attempt.

Tuesday, April 24, 1945: —Over one half of the great city of Berlin has been overrun in little more than four days by the vengeful armies of Russia. The fanatical Nazi defenders, reportedly led by Adolf Hitler himself, are rapidly being compressed into a death trap around Der Fuhrer's headquarters in the Reichchancellory. Two mighty Red armies, the First White Russian and the First Ukrainian, have affected a juncture in the heart of the ruined capital and are massing for the final phase of the assault. All German communications from Berlin to the North Sea and from Berlin to the Bavarian redoubt area in the south have been cut, leaving only a narrow corridor in the west through which a few Nazi tanks and other reinforcements are scurrying under a murderous hail of bombs and rocket shells from American, British, and Russian planes flying wing to wing.

General George S. Patton's American Third Army, suddenly swerving from its drive on Berlin, today was racing full speed for Bavaria and its mountainous redoubt where the cornered Nazis are expected to make their last stand. Patton's hard-riding tankmen sped south at better than a mile per hour, sweeping up thousands of prisoners as they went along and liberating other thousands of Allied captives, including many American flyers.

It was revealed today that Marshal Henri Philippe Petain, one time hero of Verdun and more recently Vichy Head of State and Nazi collaborator, has escaped from Germany into Switzerland, from whence he will return to France to stand trial for treason.

Tuesday, April 25, 1945: —Today was a Big Day, an Important Day, not only for San Francisco but for the entire civilized world. Today, in simple dignity, began the United Nations Conference for International Organization. Site of the opening plenary session was in the beautiful San Francisco Opera House where were gathered the delegates of 46 United Nations who are joined together in the fight against oppression and tyranny and who are determined to join here in establishing a basis for permanent peace.

Almost 2,000 newsmen from all over the world are accredited to the conference, evidencing the vast interest with which the suffering peoples of the earth are watching the events beginning to transpire in this beautiful City by the Golden Gate. News coverage on this meeting will be the most complete in history, with the world's most famous reporters, columnists, radio and newsreel commentators all on hand to do their stuff.

The opening plenary session in the Opera House was very brief, lasting little more than one half hour. But it was impressive, leaving one with a solemn feeling that here was the beginning of a glorious moment in history. The stage of the Opera House was set simply with the flags of all the participating nations, before which stood 16 youthful members of the armed forces, including all branches, both men and women. Brief and gracious speeches of welcome were delivered by Secretary of State Stettinius, California's Governor Warren, and San Francisco's Mayor Lapham. Then through the hush that settled over the brilliant audience in honor of our deceased President Franklin Delano Roosevelt, suddenly came the firm and heartening voice of President Truman, speaking over the radio from Washington D.C., extending the Nation's welcome to the delegates and calling upon them to exert their utmost effort in the performance of their great task.

Thursday, April 26, 1945: —The eyes of the world were focused today on San Francisco where the delegates of 46 United Nations of the world began to get down to business on their titanic job of setting up a workable organization of sovereign nations to establish and maintain a permanent world peace. Boldness and courage is needed here if all the jealousies, suspicions, and petty hatred that exist between the nations, large and small, are to be compromised and overcome in the interests of humanity. The suffering people of the world will not soon forget or forgive if the San Francisco Conference is a failure. The international leaders convened here have a rendezvous with human destiny.

Probably the most mysterious and interest-arousing personality at the Conference is Foreign Commissar V.M. Molotov of Soviet Russia. The mystery and interest that surrounds the Foreign Commissar is due largely to the "unknown quantity" that is Russia. The Soviets and their shrewd, realistic dictator, Marshal Stalin, have the power to assure the success of the Conference or to wreck it. Consequently every move, every action, every word of V.M. Molotov is eagerly followed by those who would try to discern how the Russians intend to conduct themselves in the proposed community of nations.

Glaring headlines today proclaimed that Benito Mussolini, the "jackal" former dictator of Italy, has been captured by Italian patriots. It is expected that Il Duce will be brought to speedy justice as an arch war criminal.

Friday, April 27, 1945: —Let us take a brief side glance at how living conditions are on the home front these days. It is really surprising how well we are doing after three and one half years of war. True, there are many annoyances and inconveniences and a few real shortages, but in comparison with any other nation in the world, with the possible exception of some South American countries, we are very well off.

Transportation and food are our main problems. Gasoline and tires are real shortages and thousands of cars are going off the roads permanently each week. For instance my ancient heap has been laid up for two months for need of some tires. But we are getting accustomed to walking—though we'll never learn to like it.

Commuting by bus and street car is pretty rugged business as they say in the army. Just the other day while the bus starter was tamping a few dozen more of us into the side door, I heard one soldier whose ribbons marked him as a returned veteran say, "This almost makes me wish I was back overseas."

Food and the ever-present ration point headache is probably the biggest problem of all. Right now we are bumping into a potato shortage for the first time since the war started. Thick juicy steaks, plenty of butter, and crisp bacon, are things that dreams are made of while whipping cream and good rich ice cream are among our fondest post-war plans. Say, this is making me drool.

Saturday, April 28, 1945: —Rumors and reports of many kinds have been flooding out of Europe today. An unofficial report from London stated that Heinrich Himmler, Nazi Gestapo Chief, recently offered to guarantee the unconditional surrender of Germany to the United States and Great Britain, provided Russia would be excluded. The offer was bluntly rejected and the Germans were warned that any peace offer would have to be made to the Big Three and all their allies.

A rumor is being widely circulated from Switzerland, claiming that Adolf Hitler, Hermann Goering, and Propaganda Minister Paul Josef Goebbels, have all been killed in Berlin. This report is further supported by the fact that Himmler, who made the peace offer to the western Allies, apparently has taken over the reins of government in the fast-shrinking Reich.

The fierce battle for Berlin appears to be in its final stages tonight. The Russians have broken into the famous Tiergarten sector of the city and are pressing close to the Reichancellery building where the last of the die-hard Nazis are expected to make their final stand. South and west of the German capital an imminent junction is expected between American forces and the Red Army. In fact the junction may already have taken place and the news is just awaiting the official announcements that are expected to be issued simultaneously from Washington, London, and Moscow.

Sunday, April 29, 1945: —Today was one of those rare and beautiful spring days about which poet or a golfer would rave. I was a golfer this morning for the first time since last August so I know whereof I speak. The temperature was just above the "warm" level, with nary a breeze to set the cooling system to working. It was an ideal day to soak up a week's supply of vitamin D. For this purpose there is no better place than a golf course. There is no glare, the green of the fairways is soothing to the eyes, and there is no need to over-exert, the game requiring just the right amount of healthful exercise. You may gather from this that I am quite partial to golf. If you do, you are right.

The most interesting piece of news from the war fronts today is the revelation that the Nazi debacle is spreading to Italy. The entire German defense line across the peninsula has collapsed and General Mark Clark's American Fifth Army and

British Eighth Army are pouring through at will. One report stated that American tanks have raced through to the Swiss border at Como, trapping thousands of Nazi troops in northwestern Italy. The great industrial cities of Milan and Turin were said to be under the control of Italian patriot forces which are holding them until the American and British forces arrive. Escape for the beaten enemy troops is hopeless since all roads to Brenner Pass have been blocked and the Pass itself is under merciless aerial bombardment.

Monday, April 30, 1945: —Benito Mussolini, the would-be Roman Caesar, has come to an ignominious end at the hands of enraged Italian partisans, it was revealed today. Il Duce, the "jackal" Dictator, who tried to ride the coattails of Adolf Hitler to world power, was captured in northern Italy by a group of Italian patriots who then conducted a summary trial and executed Mussolini and 16 of his Fascist henchmen, including his mistress, the beauteous Clara Petacci.

The "Sawdust Caesar," whose protruding chin and boastful manner intimidated and enslaved the Italian people for so many years, was shot in the back by those same people and his body spat upon and reviled in the public square of Milan. And so comes to a violent end the brutal story of a man to whom war was a glorious profession and bloodshed and conquest were ideals to be sought by a virile nation.

American, British, and Russian armies continue to run rampant throughout Germany amid rumors of many peace negotiations. Munich, the birthplace of the Nazi scourge, was captured today by units of the American Seventh Army. More than 110,000 Allied war prisoners were freed from a prison camp at Mossberg, near Munich. Approximately 10% of the liberated prisoners were American flyers.

In Berlin, the triumphant Red Army raised the Russian banner over the famed Reichstag, scene of the historic fire of February 27, 1933 that enabled the Nazis to seize power in Germany.

May

Tuesday, May 1, 1945: —Adolf Hitler, the scourge of Europe and would-be world conqueror, is dead—according to the German radio. The Nazi report stated that the Fuhrer was killed in his Reich Chancellery Command Post in Berlin today and was succeeded by Grand Admiral Karl Doenitz, Commander-in-Chief of the German Navy.

The Nazi Fuhrer's death, if true—and most Allied quarters were very skeptical—presumably came at the hands of the Russians who are overrunning the German capital in a savage attack that turned the sewers, subways, and rubble-strewn streets into rivers of blood. The Red wave swept up more than 100 blocks in the center of the city today and rolled to within 30 yards of the last barricaded Nazis in the sprawling Chancellery building. Here, if persistent German reports are true, the Nazi Napoleon directed the last ditch defense of Berlin and met his grotesque end, sprawling bloodily in the crumbling ruins of his Third Reich.

Immediately upon taking the helm of the sinking Nazi ship, Admiral Doenitz issued a proclamation, calling upon the German people to continue the fight in the interest of German honor and to save the nation from Russian Bolshevism. He said the Germans would fight the Americans and British only so long as they hinder the battle against the Russians. Even as the Admiral talked the ability of his people to continue the fight was crumbling all around. From Denmark where the Nazis were reported evacuating, to the Alps, the military rout of the enemy was degenerating into pure chaos.

Wednesday, May 2, 1945: —Events are now moving at kaleidoscopic speed in Germany. Joachim Von Ribbentrop, former wine merchant, who was responsible for many of the diplomatic moves that carried Europe into its most devastating war, has been ousted as Foreign Minister of the German Government by the chief of state, Grand Admiral Karl Doenitz. Von Ribbentrop is wanted by the Allies as one of the leading war criminals. Let us hope he doesn't escape.

Rumors of peace negotiations are persistent. It is well known by informed observers that the Germans would surrender at once to the Americans and British if we would agree to their continuing the fight against the Russians. Insistence by the western powers that the surrender be made to all three nations is delaying the final acceptance of the terms by the Germans, who now frankly admit they are finished.

Field Marshal Karl Von Rundstedt, the most brilliant of Germany's field commanders, was captured today at the little town of Bad Tolz, south of Munich. The famous German commander, who engineered the victorious march through France in 1940, and struck hard at the Americans in the Battle of the Bulge last December, was captured without struggle by an American tank crew who surprised the Marshal at his dinner table.

The U.S. Seventh Army which captured Von Rundstedt, also seized two other Field Marshals, Wilhelm Ritter Von Loeb and Wilhelm List, two Lieutenant Generals and three Major Generals. Also seized was the former regent of Hungary, Admiral Nicholas Horthy. Apparently the Seventh hit the jackpot.

Thursday, May 3, 1945: —The final disintegration of the once mighty German armies is taking place on the Western Front. Literally hundreds of thousands of thoroughly beaten Nazi troops are frantically competing with one another for the privilege of surrendering to the British or American forces. The horrible prospect of being captured by the advancing Russians is driving the fear-crazed Germans to find refuge as prisoners of the western Allies.

Highlight of the day was the capture of the great German port of Hamburg by the British Second Army, under the command of Field Marshal Sir Bernard L. Montgomery. More than 500,000 whipped Nazi troops surrendered at the same time, practically ending all organized resistance to the British forces. Frantic remnants of the enemy are fleeing into Denmark and Norway, scourged by the most merciless aerial hammering of the war.

The state of absolute chaos throughout the German Army led to speculation that a total and unconditional surrender of the remaining forces is imminent. Prime Minister Winston Churchill's rare absence from Parliament today led to the belief that he and General Eisenhower are negotiating the end of the war. Regardless of the truth of the rumors there is little doubt but that the next few days will see the final chapter of the European war come to a close, after more than five years and eight months of the bloodiest, cruelest, and most destructive struggle in the history of mankind.

Friday, May 4, 1945: —General Eisenhower's Headquarters has announced the sensational battlefield surrender of all German forces in northwestern Germany, Denmark, and Holland to Field Marshal Sir Bernard L. Montgomery and his Allied Army, the surrender to take effect at eleven o'clock tonight Pacific War Time. It is estimated that today's capitulation will add more than 250,000 German troops to the 500,000 who surrendered yesterday and will practically end the war on the northern flank of the Allied front.

The meager details available indicate that the unconditional surrender of this large portion of the remaining German field forces was negotiated at a dramatic meeting between Field Marshal Montgomery and high-ranking representatives of Grand Admiral Karl Doenitz, who replaced Hitler as the Fuhrer of the German people after the arch criminal himself had reportedly been killed in the last ditch defense of Berlin.

If Hitler or his henchmen had entertained any hope of prolonging resistance from their Bavarian hideout at Berchtesgaden, it was rudely shattered today as U.S. Seventh Army troops plunged ten miles from newly captured Salzburg to seize the Nazi leader's hideout after a sharp but brief encounter with crack Nazi Elite Guards.

With less than 5% of Germany remaining to be overrun by the Allied armies there can be no doubt left even in the German mind but that their fighting forces are thoroughly whipped. Further resistance can only result from insanity or complete stupidity.

Saturday, May 5, 1945: —Another mass surrender of an estimated 300,000 Nazi troops was reported today. The capitulation involved all the remaining German forces in western Austria and southern Germany. Lt. General Jacob L. Devers, commanding the U.S. Seventh and French First Armies, announced the surrender which took place at his headquarters and was negotiated by a delegation of German officers representing Field

Marshal Albert Kesselring.

With this latest surrender practically all fighting in Germany was confined to Czechoslovakia, eastern Austria, and the Dresden area of Germany where the Nazis were desperately battling against their hated Russian foes. Elsewhere, on the British and American fronts, it appeared to be a race on the part of the Germans to see who could surrender first. Prisoners were coming in faster than the military authorities could take care of them. Complete and final collapse of a thoroughly beaten Germany is near at hand.

The San Francisco Conference on International Organization was rudely shocked today when Secretary of State Stettinius disclosed that it has been revealed that the Soviet government has arrested 16 Polish Democratic leaders who had gone to Moscow to confer with the Russians on plans to reorganize the Polish government in Warsaw. Moscow stated that the Poles were arrested for "diversionist activities behind the Red Army lines." Secy. Stettinius immediately announced that all negotiations over the Polish question would be suspended until more information is received.

Sunday, May 6, 1945: —British troops marched triumphantly into Copenhagen today, engaged a few die-hard German troops in a brief but bloody skirmish in the streets, and then joined with the population in a wild, joyous celebration of their liberation from the yoke of the Nazi oppressor.

Everywhere throughout Germany events moved swiftly towards a conclusion. Another 400,000 German troops laid down their arms in abject surrender to American forces in Western Austria, while General Patton sent his United States Third Army roaring into the attack against the still resisting German Seventh Army in Czechoslovakia. Prague was the scene of wild disorder and bloodshed as Czechoslovakian patriots rose up in the path of the advancing Allied armies to free their own capital.

The status of Norway in the final drama being enacted in Europe held the attention of many observers. If the Nazis are determined they could possibly engage in a bitter last stand in the Norse country and it is rumored that the Government of former Admiral Karl Doenitz, who assumed the mantle of Fuhrer from the now defunct Hitler, may have taken refuge in Oslo. Other rumors claim that a German surrender in Norway is already being negotiated. Only time will reveal the true state of affairs.

It has been revealed that the remaining German fleet in the Mediterranean, consisting of several light cruisers, has surrendered unconditionally to the Allies.

Monday, May 7, 1945: —For a little while this morning it looked as though today was it—V-E Day. Morning newspapers all blared out the glad tidings of unconditional surrender, basing their news on an Associated Press report from Paris to the effect that the Germans signed an unconditional surrender agreement at General Eisenhower's headquarters in a little red schoolhouse at Rheims, France. The report was not denied at Allied Headquarters but it was not given official sanction and General Eisenhower immediately suspended the filing facilities of the Associated Press throughout the European theater of operations.

Despite the unofficial character of the surrender story there is little doubt but that it is true. However, there has been so much news bungling from Europe lately, including a premature surrender story that threw everyone into a lather a week ago last Saturday, that today's unofficial report left most people cold. For the most part they are determined to wait for the official news from their leaders before accepting the fact that, at long last, the day they have worked and prayed for has finally arrived.

From London it was learned this evening that tomorrow will be treated as Victory Day in Europe. President Truman, in Washington D.C., stated that any announcement he might have in reference to the surrender of German forces would be withheld until arrangements were completed for simultaneous statements from London, Moscow, and Washington. The President's announcement is expected to be made early tomorrow morning.

Tuesday, May 8, 1945: —V-E DAY! UNCONDITIONAL SURRENDER! THE WAR IN EUROPE IS OVER! Like a mighty paean of joy these glad tidings rang throughout the civilized world today. At 3:01 this afternoon the order, "Cease firing!" stilled the guns of death in Europe. From every city, village, and hamlet of the United Nations were heard the fervent voices of thanksgiving and prayer. From the man in the street to the heads of the great nations the news was greeted with expressions of great joy and profound determination to continue the mighty Allied war effort until our other enemy, Japan, has also been brought to her knees in unconditional surrender.

President Truman and Prime Minister Churchill, in simultaneous statements, announced the victory and proclaimed today, May 8, 1945, as the official V-E Day. Although the official news was somewhat anti-climactic after the unofficial revelations of yesterday, it was nevertheless the final signal for the start of many jubilant celebrations. London and New York were wild with joyous throngs. The British, understandably, were the most demonstrative, as their long and bitter travail came to a triumphant end. King George VI addressed his people and the people of the world over the radio, thanking God for his great deliverance, saluting in proud gratitude those who died to achieve the great victory, and resolving to pursue the tasks that lie ahead with the same high confidence and with the same hard work.

Both President Truman's and Prime Minister Churchill's announcements were full of prayerful thanksgiving for the victory gained and solemn determination to bring the full power of our Allied arms to bear upon our remaining enemy, Japan. Truman, in particular, warned the Japanese that, unless they followed the example of Germany, and surrender at once, they will soon be deluged with ever-increasing blows from the land, and sea, and air, until utter destruction will be visited upon them. They will now be given our undivided attention.

The first detailed report of the actual surrender ceremony disclosed that the epic event occurred in Reims, France, last Sunday evening. Representatives of the Big Four Allied Nations, the United States, Russia, Britain, and France, met the representatives of vanquished Germany in an historic 20 minute meeting and with them, signed their names to a briefly worded document which ended more than five and one half years of the bloodiest struggle in human history. After the signing, which was done on a general staff basis, and which will be further amplified by later meetings to take place in Berlin, the German representative, Col. Gustav Jodl, met General Eisenhower who greeted him coldly and sternly. The German General, after an embarrassing silence, suddenly burst out with a plea for Allied generosity for a beaten Germany. The plea fell on atrocity-deadened ears.

After the enemy representatives' departure, General

Eisenhower smiled his broadest victory smile and clapped his Russian, French, and British comrades heartily on the backs. It was a job well and nobly done.

Wednesday, May 9, 1945: —With total victory achieved in Europe, one phase of this war record has been completed. Most of our subsequent writings will deal with the final phase—the destruction of Japan's war making power. Complete victory in the Far East can now be considered a practical certainty, since our full power as well as that of Great Britain can now be concentrated in the Pacific, but we are facing what will probably be a long and costly campaign before the last remaining Axis nation is brought to her knees.

It was undoubtedly the realization of the latter fact that served to temper the celebration of V-E Day in America, particularly on the West Coast. The vital news of the surrender, handled as badly as it was by the News Services—even to the point of taking much of the edge off of a great story—was nevertheless received with a surprising calm and lack of jubilation on the part of San Franciscans. There was nothing of the wild joy of 1918—most people quietly expressed their gratitude and kept right on working, their minds, in most cases, on their sons, husbands, and sweethearts still out there fighting in the foxholes of Okinawa and the Philippines. For them it was, "Thank God, part of it is over, but we are still fighting a bitter war. There'll be time for celebrations on V-J Day."

Horrified by the disclosures of unbelievable German atrocities in the hideous confines of countless concentration camps throughout the Reich, the Allied forces are engaged in a hunt for Nazi war criminals. Chief among those captured today was former Reich Marshal Hermann Goering, the murderer of Rotterdam and one of the original Nazi Triumvirate.

Thursday, May 10, 1945: —The Japs were given a preview of what they can expect in ever increasing volume today as the mightiest fleet of B-29 Superfortresses ever assembled struck a devastating blow against the Nipponese homeland. The attacking fleet consisted of more than 400 huge bombers which braved heavy anti-aircraft fire to blast the enemy's largest synthetic oil production and storage centers on the main Japanese islands of

Honshu, Kyushu, and Shikoku. Billowing smoke columns that reached 18,000 feet into the air were evidence of the accuracy of the bombardiers' aim.

Secretary of War Henry L. Stimson revealed today that the European victory cost the United States Army approximately 800,000 casualties, of which some 150,000 were killed. Total casualties for all theaters of war and all branches of the service amounted to 972,654 at the latest compilation. These are hard, cold figures, the telling of which reveals little of the untold heartache and sorrow brought into countless American homes as each new casualty was added to the long list.

The War Department today disclosed plans for partial demobilization which call for the discharge during the remainder of 1945 of more than 1,300,000 soldiers. Discharge will be based on a "point" system, taking into consideration length of service, overseas service, combat honors, and dependency status. All but about 400,000 occupation troops are to be withdrawn from Europe either to be discharged or transferred to the Pacific theater.

Friday, May 11, 1945: —The tempo of war in the Pacific has already been stepped up since V-E Day. Our air forces, soon to be augmented by the thousands of fighters and bombers that blasted Germany into submission, have already begun the great softening up program that will prepare the Japanese homeland for invasion. By air and sea a virtual blockage has been thrown around the Nipponese islands, cutting them off from all communication with their far flung empire. The enemy navy, now reduced to a skulking task force, is powerless to break the blockade and almost no supplies or reinforcements, so badly needed by their hard-pressed outposts, are able to get through.

Utilizing their newly won Philippine airbases, the United States Fifth Air Force today sent a great fleet of heavy bombers, escorted by fighters, over the vital Japanese naval station at Saigon, in French Indo-China. The strike was declared a complete success, with the great port totally wrecked, possibly beyond repair for the duration. Thundering explosions, followed by fire, completely gutted that huge oil depot, wrecked the submarine and ship repair yards and destroyed or badly damaged 95 merchant vessels and two naval craft.

The United States plans to throw some 10,000,000 fighting men into the final struggle with Japan. A colossal shift of men and equipment from Europe is already under way. However, General Eisenhower has revealed that veterans of both the African and European campaigns will not be sent to the Pacific. They have done their bit and will be honorably discharged.

Saturday, May 12, 1945: —American Army and Marine forces on Okinawa have opened up a powerful offensive designed to end the bitter six week old campaign. Out of an original Japanese garrison of about 80,000 there are approximately 45,000 still alive. These survivors are strongly entrenched around the capital city of Naha and are fighting savagely like cornered rats. Like rats they are also being exterminated by the determined Doughboys and Leathernecks, who are slowly yet inexorably closing in the final showdown. Both sides are using tanks, flamethrowers, mortars, machine guns, heavy artillery, and bayonets in one of the most sanguinary battles yet fought in the Pacific war. Our advantages lies in superior air support and the tremendously effective naval bombardment from our invasion fleet.

General MacArthur's campaign to purge the Philippines of Japanese gained new momentum today with the revelation that a new amphibious landing has been made on the north coast of Mindanao. The landing force, consisting of units of Maj. General Rapp Brush's 40th Infantry Division, drove four miles inland on the first day, splitting the enemy into several isolated pockets. Complete liberation of the second largest of the Philippine Islands appears to be near at hand.

Several hundred American mothers will get a real Mother's Day gift tomorrow as the Army sent the first soldiers home under its partial demobilization plan. The bewildered, ecstatic soldiers were waiting reassignment at Army camps throughout the country when the glorious news of their release came. All were veterans having more than the required 85 points.

Sunday, May 13, 1945: —The skies in the Bay Area wept all day today, undoubtedly in sympathy with the thousands of American mothers who had to spend this Mothers' Day thinking tenderly of their sons in faraway places, some of them fighting and suffering this very moment, others resting forever beneath those little white crosses on hundreds of foreign battlefields. Probably no one except those Gold Star Mothers themselves can know the depths of their feelings on this day. Not only the skies but the whole world should weep in sympathy for them. Theirs is a sacrifice in many ways greater than that of their sons. Theirs is a sacrifice of years of patient toil, of tender care during childhood illnesses, of sleepless nights and worried days, years of careful teaching and unselfish devotion, fond plans and hopes that will never be realized. The nation can never repay its debt of gratitude to the Gold Star Mothers of America.

American forces on Okinawa, under the command of Lt. General Simon Bolivar Buckner, are engaged in the bloodiest battle of the six-week-old campaign. The Sixth Marine Division, in some of the fiercest hand-to-hand fighting ever encountered, smashed into the suburbs of the capital city of Naha today, cracking the last Japanese defense line before the ruined city. Evidently the Japs are determined to make another Cassino or Stalingrad out of the town and are battling ferociously with hand grenades, mortars, and machine guns from fortifications fashioned out of the city's rubble.

Monday, May 14, 1945: —A tremendous fleet of more than 500 Superfortresses attacked the Japanese homeland today, laying waste to vast sections of the vital industrial center of Nagoya. The huge bombers dumped more than 3,500 tons of fire bombs on the hapless city, setting off conflagrations that could be seen for sixty miles. It was the most concentrated fire raid in history and retuning crewmen reported that a solid column of smoke rose for 17,000 feet above a nine square mile sector of the city. A grand total of 500,750 incendiary bombs were cascaded into the target area at the rate of more than 40 tons per minute. A pretty grim war, eh, Mr. Moto?

The hunt for Nazi war criminals is continuing unabated in Europe. There is agitation for immediate trials and punishment for those now in Allied hands and steps are being taken to prepare cases against those not yet apprehended. The United Nations War Crimes Commission today indicted the infamous Chief of the Nazi Gestapo, Heinrich Himmler, for mass murder, citing as a particular example the sadistic horror of Lidice in 1942, when that tiny village was completely obliterated in an orgy of revenge at the assassination of the Hangman, Reinhardt Heydrich. Not a building was left standing and all the male inhabitants were slaughtered. The women and young girls were sent off to slavery. The Gestapo chieftain is now at large somewhere in Europe, playing a game of hide and seek with pursuing Allied forces.

Here at home the Seventh War Loan Drive officially opens today, with the goal set at 14 billion, one half of which is to be obtained through the sale of bonds to individuals.

Tuesday, May 15, 1945: —The aerial "softening up" of Japan continued for another day today. Allowing the Japs no rest after the devastating Superfortress raid of yesterday, clouds of carrier planes from our Pacific fleet roared in over Kyushu and Shikoku Islands of the Japanese homeland to blast some eighteen airfields known to be operating as bases for the enemy suicide planes that have been attacking our fleet off the coast of Okinawa. A final tally of the day's score showed that 357 Japanese aircraft were either shot down in combat or destroyed on the ground.

The battle for Okinawa is still raging furiously, with the Japanese defenders still hanging on tenaciously to the ruins of the capital city of Naha and nearby Shuri City. Heavy mortar, machine gun, and grenade fire has all but stopped the inch by inch advance of American Doughboys and Marines. The most important gain of the day was scored by the 77th Infantry Division which captured the heights dubbed Chocolate Drop Hill which commands the approaches to Shuri City. The hill was taken only after one of the most ferocious and costly battles of the entire campaign.

On the home front attention was centered on three topics: the San Francisco Conference, President Truman's plans for an early meeting of the Big Three heads to discuss the peace, and the report to Congress by the 12 man Congressional Committee which investigated, through personal visits, the horrible story of Nazi atrocities in German concentration camps.

Wednesday, May 16, 1945: —American Superfortresses, 500 strong, again struck at the Japanese industrial center of Nagoya, in a continuance of an obvious obliteration campaign against the heart of the Oriental enemy's aircraft industry. The huge Mitsubishi aircraft plant, larger than our own Willow Run factory in Detroit, was the prime target of the giant bombers. More than 3,500 tons of fire bombs, equal to the load delivered last Monday, were cascaded into the still smoldering city, starting dozens of conflagrations that later blended into one terrible holocaust that swept over an estimated 15 square miles of the target area.

Three hundred and sixty miles to the south, American and Japanese land forces were locked in a no-quarter death struggle for the vital island of Okinawa. Slowly, bloodily, yet surely, the weary, begrimed Doughboys and Marines are gaining the upper hand and the final outcome of the bitter struggle is no longer in doubt. However, there is plenty of rugged fighting ahead, although today's reports indicate that the Americans are battling through the streets of Naha in a grueling mop-up of the island capital.

Trieste, recently liberated Italian city, has become a potential powder keg in the relations between the Western Allies, Britain and the United States, and Russia and her Yugoslav puppet, Marshal Tito. The Yugoslav leader and his armed partisans have moved into the Italian city contrary to the zones of occupation set up at Yalta. The United States and Britain have ordered them out and are prepared to enforce their order. British war ships have entered the harbor and U.S. tanks are on the streets. Let us hope that an armed clash can be avoided.

Thursday, May 17, 1945: —The nation's attention is still centered on the sanguinary battle for control of the strategic island of Okinawa. Already the cost in American casualties has exceeded the bloody toll of Iwo Jima. A total of 20,950 Doughboys and Marines have been killed, wounded, or are missing in the first 44 days of the campaign.

On the other side of the ledger, a total of 46,505 Japanese dead have been counted and 1,038 have been taken prisoner, leaving some 30,000 fanatical enemy troops yet to be eliminated. At the present time, the Yanks are killing the Japs at the rate of 1,400 every 24 hours—at a ratio of better than 20 to 1.

Conquest of the capital city of Naha is just about complete and the full American power is beginning to close in on the fortified town of Shuri to the northeast. The Japs are fighting fiercely from well-defended strongholds and our troops are forced to employ flame throwing tanks and heavy artillery to soften them up sufficiently to permit the infantry to move in, with rifle, hand grenade, and bayonet, for the final coup de grace.

The British today revealed some of their long held secrets regarding naval losses in the war against Germany. A total of 163 vessels were lost that were not reported because of military security. Chief among the losses was the ramming of a light cruiser by the giant liner, Queen Mary, on October 2, 1942. The hapless cruiser was cut in two and sank with the loss of 342 crew members.

Friday, May 18, 1945: —The ghastly yet heroic story of one of the greatest naval tragedies of the war was revealed today. It was the story of the U.S.S. Franklin, 27,000 ton Essex class aircraft carrier of Vice Admiral Marc Mitscher's famous Task Force 58, as it met disaster while steaming 60 miles off the coast of Japan last March 19.

It was early morning when Big Ben, as the giant carrier was affectionately called by her crew, was busily engaged in getting her planes off for their daily strike at the enemy homeland that it happened. The carrier's flight deck, as long as three city blocks, was jammed with planes heavily loaded with gasoline, bombs, and rockets. A few planes had taken off when suddenly a lone Japanese dive bomber burst through the overcast and headed straight for its tempting target. It was too late to stop him and two deadly 500 pound enemy bombs hit their mark. With a roar and a flash the trim Fighting Lady was turned into an inferno of blazing gasoline and bursting bombs and shells. Within minutes more than 800 American sailors and airmen were dead and hundreds more were maimed and burned. The survivors reacted with traditional Navy heroism. Acts of great personal bravery and sacrifice were commonplace as the men fought the raging flames and attended to the wounded. Her Captain, Leslie E. Gehres, of Coronado, California, would not abandon ship and by a miracle of seamanship and raw courage the mighty vessel was finally saved and brought to the United States mainland under her own power. Some day the gallant ship, through the epic courage of her fighting men, will again carry the battle to the front door of our Oriental enemy.

Saturday, May 19, 1945: —We haven't said much about the progress of the United Nations Conference on International

Organization for the past several days. This is due partly to the sensational war developments but mostly to the fact that the Conference has settled down to its routine business of formulating plans and charters for World Organization and there hasn't been much excitement. Throughout, however, it has been Russia's strange attitude that has puzzled and even irritated delegates and observers alike. The Soviet delegation, by its every action, has seemed bent on incurring everyone's dislike. The disclosure, on May 5th, that the Russian government had arrested the 16 Polish Democratic leaders who flew to Moscow to aid in the forming of a new Warsaw government, fell like a bombshell on the Conference. With blows like this and disputes over trusteeships, Argentina's invitation to the Conference, and several other ticklish questions, the general atmosphere of the meeting has not been very conducive to friendly cooperation.

With much yet to be done in San Francisco, both Foreign Commissar Molotov or Russia, and Foreign Secretary Anthony Eden of Great Britain, have returned to their respective countries because of pressing duties caused by the collapse of Germany. Nevertheless, regardless of all obstacles and disagreements, let us fervently hope that the men meeting here in San Francisco may somehow formulate a plan that will permit the peaceful settlement of differences. We dare not think of the consequences should they fail.

Sunday, May 20, 1945: —Today was "I Am an American Day" and millions of citizens throughout the country observed the day with pageantry and celebrations. Here in San Francisco the Civic Auditorium was packed with people, including some newly naturalized citizens, to witness a spectacle of music, pageantry and entertainment provided by some of the topflight stars of stage and screen.

Well might the fortunate people of this nation thank Providence for making them citizens of America when they peer across the oceans and observe the disintegration, fear, and chaos that is gripping most of Europe. The future for many miserable European countries is black indeed, with ruins and famine at hand and civil war and confusion facing them.

One of the most dangerous spots threatening the hard won peace of Europe is Trieste where Marshal Tito's Partisan Army seems bent on using force to assert Yugoslavia's claim to the vital Adriatic port. The Allied Commander-in-chief in the Mediterranean, Field Marshal Sir Harold Alexander yesterday accused the Partisan leader of employing tactics "all too reminiscent of Hitler, Mussolini, and Japan." Naturally charges and counter-charges of this nature can only lead to physical violence and unless the Partisans are willing to cooperate, we are likely to witness an outbreak of hostilities that might have far-reaching repercussions on the entire world.

Monday, May 21, 1945: —Fiercely fighting United States Marines and Doughboys repulsed a desperate Japanese counter-attack on embattled Okinawa last night and then followed up with a daylight attack of their own that carried them nearer to the virtually surrounded enemy bastion of Shuri. The Yanks were forced to pour flaming oil into the network of caves and fortifications guarding the town before the stubborn Jap defenders could be flushed from their hiding places and destroyed. Casualties were heavy on both sides, with American dead, wounded, and missing totaling 30,526 as of last Friday. Japanese dead through the same period numbered 48,103.

The War Department revealed today that the famous American First Army, under the brilliant command of Lt. General Courtney H. Hodges, is on its way from Europe for redeployment to the Pacific. The First Army was first in reality as well as in name, being the first American Army to land in Normandy, the first to battle its way onto German soil, the first to cross the Rhine, and the first to cross the Elbe River and join forces with the Russians. Many of the veterans of the First Army will be discharged when they reach this country, their places being taken by men with lesser combat service, the rest will be given thirty day furloughs before they are sent to carry on the traditions of the First Army in the war against the Japanese.

Tuesday, May 22, 1945: —In a fantastic and almost pitiful attempt to strike back at the United states for our ever-increasing rain of aerial destruction on their homeland, the Japanese have been sporadically attacking the United States with giant paper balloons loaded with incendiary and explosive bombs. The War Department revealed the attacks today, pointing out that the balloons apparently cannot be controlled and are merely free to drift with the air currents toward this country. The chance of hitting any given place with accuracy is one in many millions. Apparently the main enemy objective is to start forest fires but in this they have been unsuccessful. The idea is pretty good for the middle ages, Mr. Moto, but really it can't compare with a Superfortress, now can it?

Men and machines of the famous U.S. Eighth Air Force, which helped to pound Germany into submission, are beginning to arrive back into this country for hard-won furloughs before being redeployed to the Pacific. A total of 3,400 planes are expected to arrive within the next few days. The flyers will be given new bombers when they set out to participate in their second war.

The battle for Okinawa is still a "knock down and drag out" affair, with the American forces slowly blasting and burning the Jap defenders from their heavily fortified defenses before Shuri. The Yanks have practically encircled the enemy stronghold and the eventual extermination of the remaining Jap garrison is certain.

Wednesday, May 23, 1945: —The greatest force of B-29 Superfortresses ever assembled today launched a devastating early morning attack on Tokyo that was unequaled even by the great Allied raids over Germany. The huge bombers roared over the city in a fiery parade of blazing destruction that lasted for an hour and forty five minutes. More than 700,000 individual fire bombs were cascaded into the teeming capital, setting huge conflagrations that appeared to sweep unchecked through much of the industrial heart of the city. Any Tokyo Jap that survived this raid should somberly reflect that, terrible though it was, it is but a mild forerunner of the mightier raids to come when the great aerial fleets of Europe join in the attack.

A crisis has developed in the British government of Prime Minister Churchill. The powerful Labor Party which supported the coalition government during the European war is now trying to force an election. Mr. Churchill, who had hoped that the government would continue as it was until Japan was defeated, today resigned in accordance with Parliamentary procedure, and was then asked by King George to form an interim government to act until the election is held. This action presumably weakens

Mr. Churchill's position and may affect his relations with the other members of the Big Three, who, it had been hoped, would meet soon to settle some of the perplexing international problems that have arisen since the fall of Germany.

President Truman made news today by replacing three members of his cabinet and announcing that he will fly to San Francisco to address the closing session of the United Nations Conference.

Thursday, May 24, 1945: —Heinrich Himmler, former Nazi Gestapo Chief, and the most loathsome of the many Nazi murderers and butchers, was captured today and shortly thereafter committed suicide by swallowing poison that he had hidden in a phial under his tongue. Thus ended the life of Hitler's chief hangman, who made himself the scourge of all Europe and was probably directly and indirectly responsible for the murder of millions of Jews, Poles, Czechs, Russians, French and other innocent Europeans.

The once-dreaded Gestapo chieftain was seized by troops of the British Second Army as he attempted to escape in disguise at a little town 30 miles west of Hamburg. Upon being identified by British officers, the former member of the high Nazi hierarchy who at one time had tried to split the Allies by surrendering Germany to America and England if they would help her continue the fight against Russia, foiled the British doctors who were examining him by crushing the tiny phial of cyanide with his teeth. He died fifteen minutes later. No tears were shed.

Civilians will get their first dividend from the European victory in the way of more gasoline beginning Junes 22. A card holders, who have been forced to let their cars stand idle most of the time, will get a 50% increase in their rations—three gallons per week instead of two. B and C card holders will get increased rations according to their individual needs. Things are already looking brighter.

Friday, May 25, 1945: —Tokyo was the recipient of another 4,000 tons of incendiary bombs delivered by more than 500 Superfortresses which struck from their Marianas bases for the second time in three days to carry fiery devastation into the heart of Nippon. The enemy capital was still smoldering from

Wednesday's giant fire raid and today's attack started new conflagrations among the wharves, docks, warehouses, aircraft parts plants, and business district of the once teeming metropolis.

Land and sea fighting on and in the waters surrounding Okinawa Island continued with unabated ferocity today. The fanatical Japs are fighting with suicidal fury to stave off total defeat in the battle for control of the vital island. Their troops defending the fortified towns of Naha and Shuri are holed up in coral caves and concrete pillboxes and are exacting a fearful toll of U.S. Marines and Doughboys who are forced to dig them out one by one with grenade or flaming oil. Despite the odds, however, the Yanks are killing Japs at the rate of 20 to 1 and are slowly exterminating the remaining enemy garrison, now estimated at approximately 25,000 out of an original 80,000 troops.

An almost equally ferocious battle is raging off the coast of Okinawa, between the mighty American task force and hundreds of vicious Kamikaze "suicide" Jap planes. The story was told today of one U.S. destroyer, the "Laffey," which absorbed the flames and explosions of 12 suicide planes that smashed into her decks and sides and still was able to return to the United States for repairs. Five other light vessels, including another destroyer, the "Little," were not so fortunate and were sent to the bottom. Literally hundreds of enemy planes have been destroyed.

Saturday, May 26, 1945: —The Japanese capital, once the fourth largest city in the world, is tonight a charred and blackened scene of utter destruction—by official Japanese admission. The city has been destroyed so extensively that it will have to be entirely rebuilt, according to an announcement from none other than Premier Kantaro Suzuki. Other Japanese broadcasters were even more vivid in their description of the devastation wrought in the two great fire raids of the past week. One announcer declared that a 70-mile-an-hour gale had whipped the fires through Tokyo until the entire city had been "scorched to the ground." Even the Imperial Palace of Emperor Hirohito was laid waste in the raging inferno. "Little did you realize, Mr. Moto, what dividends you would receive from your dastardly investment in Pearl Harbor that day, so many eons ago, in December, 1941."

In view of the Japs' jittery condition at the present time, it might be desirable to record that it is well known that they have made peace overtures since the fall of Germany. So far, the peace feelers have all been made in hopes of negotiating a settlement that would permit Japan to retain most of her ill-gotten empire. Needless to say such terms have fallen upon deaf ears in the United States and England. It is possible—though not probable—that the Japs may see the hopelessness of their position and surrender unconditionally within the next sixty to ninety days. If they don't the war will undoubtedly stretch out for many more bloody months before the fanatical foe can be beaten to his knees militarily and forced to surrender after the fashion of his Nazi counterpart.

Sunday, May 27, 1945: —The weather has taken a hand in the battle for Okinawa. Torrential rains restricted the movement of troops along the entire front and brought a respite from the bloody business of killing, except in one small sector where 150 fanatical Japs made a desperate "banzai" counter-attack that ended with every one of the 150 joining his ancestors in the approved Shinto fashion.

Japanese suicide attacks against the American fleet off Okinawa have subsided somewhat during the last two days, with only 166 of the human "flying bombs" being accounted for during that time.

Huge fires are still raging throughout Tokyo today, long after the second great fire raid by flying Superfortresses had dumped 4,000 tons of blazing destruction into the heart of Jap land. The U.S. Bomber Command has not yet been able to confirm the extent of the damage by official reconnaissance photos, but there is little reason to doubt the hysterical Japanese account of the holocaust.

The losses were not all on one side, however. We, also, had a fee to pay. Over 300 highly trained and valuable men and 31 great bombers were lost in the two raids, 22 in the first and 19 in the second. The most intense and effective anti-aircraft fire yet encountered over the Japanese capital was responsible for most of the lost planes, but considerable opposition was also encountered from deadly suicide interceptor planes. The Japs have developed this suicide business down to a fine art.

Monday, May 28, 1945: —The San Francisco Conference on International Organization, which is now more than one month old, has made considerable progress towards drafting up a charter for world organization. Many thorny problems have beset the conference, however, and there is no clear indication of when the job will be finished. Particularly crucial have been the disputes over "trusteeships" in connection with the administration of mandated islands and the sweeping "veto" powers which the "Big 5" demand in the proposed organization. While it is agreed by the little nations that any "policing" will have to be done by the five major powers, they object to permitting any one of the Big 6 to veto any action taken by the International Security Council, claiming that it will make the new organization powerless to actually enforce the peace. This problem has not yet been settled but it is believed that a satisfactory compromise will soon be worked out.

One of the most serious and pressing problems facing the world today is the production and distribution of food. Chaos in Europe has threatened millions of people with starvation unless relief is forthcoming. Obviously most of this relief will have to come from the United States. To help in solving this problem, President Truman has called to Washington the one man in the country who really knows the answers about food. That man is Herbert Hoover, Food Administrator in World War I and former President of the United States. Today, for the first time since 1932 he entered the White House to give the President the benefit of his knowledge and experience in the distribution of food.

Tuesday, May 29, 1945: —Reconnaissance photographs have confirmed the devastation wrought upon Tokyo in the recent fire raids by B-29's. More than 51 square miles of the city's sprawling urban area have been reduced to charred rubble. Included in the destroyed area were most of the business and industrial sections of the Japanese capital. To all intents and purposes, Tokyo can be considered out of the war.

Yokohama, fifth largest Japanese city, and a great war center, is fast joining Tokyo as an obliterated city. A great fleet of Superfortresses dumped 3,200 tons of fire bombs on the Yokohama area last night, starting a roaring holocaust that must have rivaled hell in fury. Returning B-29 pilots said that a black blanket of smoke blotted out vast sections of the city and rose in towering columns that reached 20,000 feet into the sky. What must be the thoughts of the ordinary Japanese citizen as he witnesses this deadly downpour of destruction? How long will he be able to take it?

On bloody Okinawa as well, the Japs are being given a dose of very bitter medicine. Under the devastating attack by Army and Marine units, supported by flame-throwing tanks, heavy artillery and the shelling by naval guns, the sturdy Japanese defense line on southern Okinawa is finally crumbling. Our losses have been severe and advances have been measured in yards but the unreinforced Jap garrison is slowly cracking under the relentless pressure. There can be little doubt regarding the final outcome.

Wednesday, May 30, 1945: —Today is Memorial Day and a grateful nation that has just won one war and is well on the way towards winning its second, paused from its labors long enough to pay homage to the memory of the gallant men who have laid down their lives in these wars and in previous wars so that this nation might retain its precious heritage of freedom. Their sacrifice so far transcends anything that the living can do that we can only offer a reverent "thanks" and resolve that we shall continue united in our efforts to establish a world in which such bitter tragedies can be avoided. The memory of so many heroic, vigorous lives cut short should be a deterrent to those who would impose their will upon their neighbors. Too often, unfortunately, such men have no conscience but the memory, at least, should strengthen the determination of the rest of us to "police" the would-be gangsters and put them behind bars before they can do much damage.

On the bloody isle of Okinawa there was little time for memories today. Reality was too close upon the weary soldiers and marines who were ending the 60th day of one of the deadliest campaigns in the history of warfare. Death and pain were their closest companions as they slowly drove the fanatical Japanese from their caves and pill boxes in and around the blasted capital city of Naha and the nearby citadel of Shuri. Yes, the men on Okinawa know what Memorial Day stands for.

Thursday, May 31, 1945: —Seeds of future wars are being sown in the Middle East. Uprisings have flared in Syria and

Lebanon between the Natives and French troops that are already having international repercussions. The French, who maintain military bases in the two countries despite the fact that they are independent nations, have shelled the ancient city of Damascus and are employing warplanes to strafe and bomb the rebelling Syrians. Both London and Washington have taken serious views of the situation and Prime Minister Churchill bluntly warned General De Gaulle in Paris to order his troops in the Levant to cease firing or the British would intervene. Needless to say the situation is tense and fraught with danger.

On Okinawa, U.S. Tenth Army marines and soldiers cracked the toughest nut they have yet encountered in the two months old campaign. Shuri castle, blasted and gutted from many days of fierce pounding, was finally conquered as the hard-fighting Doughboys and Leathernecks cracked the main Japanese defense line and clamped a pincers around thousands of enemy troops in the Shuri sector. The Japs themselves, from ruined Tokyo, broadcast that the decisive moment has arrived in the battle for Okinawa, which they have agreed will decide the Pacific war.

In desperation the Japs are throwing large numbers of suicide planes against our fleet off Okinawa, hoping vainly to turn the tide and prevent the inevitable. Some of our ships have been sunk and many damaged but the conduct of the operation has not been seriously hampered by the insane attacks.

June

Friday, June 1, 1945: —Osaka has joined the list of Japanese cities to feel the full fury of a Superfortress fire raid. The great industrial center was deluged with 3,200 tons of incendiaries from more than 450 mighty B-29's that roared over the city in broad daylight escorted by 150 Mustang fighters from their newly acquired bases on Iwo Jima and Okinawa. The fire bombs, which included many of the newly developed jellied gasoline type, started numerous fires that eventually merged into one vast conflagration that swept unchecked through large sections of the hapless city. Undoubtedly swallowed up in the flames were many of the most vital war industries in Japan, including the Osaka Steel Works, the Mitsubishi Smelting and Refining Plants, the Kakuichi Rubber Co., the Ujigawa Electric Power Co., and several great shipyards. Japan's war making potential has been struck another stunning blow.

Meanwhile American marines and soldiers scored new advances in their drive to complete the conquest of Okinawa. The Yanks have driven past the bloody Naha-Shuri defense line and are now within sight of the southern beaches of the island. The remaining 20,000 enemy troops, out of an original garrison of some 80,000, are being compressed into the inevitable death trap on the southern tip of the costly isle. In the first 60 days of the campaign our forces killed Japs at a rate of better than 1,000 per day, counting a total 61,519 enemy bodies, with 1,353 live ones being taken prisoner.

Saturday, June 2, 1945: —Admiral William F. Halsey, known affectionately by his men as "The Bull" for his furious, driving tactics, has returned to the Pacific to lead his famous Third Fleet in the final drive against Japan. Already the Jap homeland has felt the wrath of his carrier planes which swarmed off his powerful array of flat-tops and stuck at enemy airfields on southern Kyushu. The carrier planes, 200 strong, strafed and bombed the suicide plane basses from which the desperate Nips have launched their one-way human bombs against our invasion fleet standing off the coast of Okinawa. At least two enemy planes were shot down in combat, a dozen others were destroyed on the ground, and scores of others damaged.

In a move to end the inflammable Levantine crisis, the British have staged a display of power. British troops moved into the troubled area and English warships steamed into the harbor of Beyrouth. French troops were confined to their barracks and civilians were cautioned not to start trouble.

Russia joined with England and the United States in demanding that the French settle their dispute peaceably. Moscow sent notes to France, Britain, China and the United States, calling for urgent measures to settle the conflict by peaceful means.

The French-Levant dispute may seriously affect the outcome of the San Francisco Conference and even Russia is concerned lest the world organization for the establishment of world peace be wrecked even before its charter is completed.

Sunday, June 3, 1945: —With our attention being absorbed primarily with the sanguinary battle for Okinawa and the obliteration bombing campaign against the Japanese homeland, we have made little mention of the heavy fighting that is still going on in the Philippines. General MacArthur today announced that Japanese casualties in the Philippines campaign have been boosted to 385,480 which is some indication of the extent of the operations still going on in the islands. Powerful Japanese forces are yet to be accounted for in northern Luzon while large scale battles are raging in the Davao sector of Mindanao Island.

Battle-weary Doughboys and Marines trudged forward for new gains on Okinawa today, driving the still wearier Japs ever closer to the sea. From Tokyo came the plaintive radio admission that "the situation on Okinawa is very grave."

Revealing the desperation to which they have been driven, the Japs also broadcast the information today that the entire naval air corps of the Imperial Navy has been converted into a suicide corps for use against the threatening United States Navy. Each man has been pledged to drive his plane into a unit of the American battle fleet. They can undoubtedly do a lot of damage that way but the consensus of opinion among men of Admiral Halsey's caliber, which includes all of the fighting men of the Pacific fleet, is that the Jap suicides cannot alter the course of the war but are "just a dammed nuisance" to be put up with until the job is done.

Monday, June 4, 1945: —The Japs, in their frenzy, today claimed that the American mainland will soon be attacked by hundreds of bomb-carrying balloons piloted by suicide Japanese airmen. The piloted balloons will fly high in the stratosphere and are expected to reach the United States about 100 hours after being launched from Japan. The attack is being delayed until data and results are obtained from the recent experimental raids by pilotless balloons, which the Japs gleefully guessed were "creating havoc" throughout the Pacific coastal area. The Tokyo commentator complained, however, that the Americans were concealing the effect of the attack by close censorship.

Strangely enough, the new threat from the Japs hardly seemed to cause a ripple of concern among San Franciscans. In a way, I guess, the people have become veterans like the soldiers and sailors. In December of 1941 we would have developed a bad case of the jitters and would be losing plenty of sleep trying to figure ways of meeting the menace. Now it hardly seems worth much of a discussion. In some ways this attitude may be bad, but it all stems from nearly four years of experience in waiting and learning. Now, perhaps, we are just a little skeptical; besides, our victory-bound armed forces have given us a feeling of security that won't be dulled by a few desperate threats from an already beaten enemy.

Our faith in our fighting men is being strengthened further on Okinawa. Final victory in the hard campaign is imminent as the Doughboys and Marines split the remaining Japs into two segments and are systematically annihilating them.

Tuesday, June 5, 1945: —An ironclad military rule began today for defeated Germany. Top Army commanders of Russia, Britain, and the United States met in Berlin today and signed a declaration outlining the obligations and restrictions under which the Reich will be governed. Representatives of the four big powers, France, Britain, Russia, and the United States will comprise a major control council that will exercise central governing powers from Berlin. Germany will then be divided into four spheres of interest in which each major power will rule. Russia will be given the eastern part, France the western part, Great Britain the northwestern, and the United States the southwestern parts.

Final determination of Germany's boundaries will await the peace conference. Meanwhile, however, the Reich has been whittled down to its 1937 size, taking from it all the conquests won by Hitler. From a vast empire that, at the height of Nazi glory, comprised most of Europe, most of Scandinavia, and much of north Africa, Germany has been reduced—through the insane folly of one man—to a wretched nation of burned out cities and charred ruins.

Kobe, Japan's sixth largest city, is the latest enemy metropolis to feel the wrath of the mighty fleets of Superfortresses that have set as their goal the fiery obliteration of Japan's war-making power. Thousands of tons of flaming incendiaries set the hapless city afire from end to end. Pillars of smoke careened 20,000 feet into the air.

Wednesday, June 6, 1945: —Russia announced today that they have found the body of Adolf Hitler in the ruins of his Reich Chancellery building in Berlin. Although the body was smoke-blackened and charred, it was "almost certainly" identified as that of the Nazi Fuehrer. If identification could be made positive, it would end what appeared likely to be one of the greatest mysteries of all times. It would confirm that justice had come to the greatest war criminal of them all, even as death had come to the millions who were his victims.

Today is the first anniversary of D-Day in Europe. One year ago today the whole world held its breath as American and Allied soldiers hurled themselves upon the "impregnable" Fortress Europa in the greatest assault ever attempted upon a hostile shore. For hours and days the hearts of relatives and friends of the attacking troops nearly stopped beating as they strained for news that would tell whether a firm foothold had been won. A great big "IF" held the fate of western civilization in its grasp. And now, with the knowledge of a year's achievement behind us, a hearty, grateful "Well Done!" is due our gallant fighting men. We shall never forget!

The next D-Day will be in Japan. Our forces on Okinawa are now engaged in mopping up that island which will operate as the staging area for the attack on the Japanese homeland. I would distinctly dislike being in Japan during the next few months, and I mean as an inhabitant.

Thursday, June 7, 1945: —Another great fleet of B-29's, escorted by Thunderbolt, Lightning, Mustang, and Hellcat fighter planes, returned to Osaka today and hurled 2,500 tons of fire bombs and high explosives into the already partially destroyed industrial center. The presence of so many fighter escorts indicated that air bases in newly conquered Okinawa were already being employed in the aerial campaign against the Jap mainland.

The Japanese radio today admitted the imminent loss of Okinawa to the Americans. Previously they had stated that the outcome of the Okinawa campaign would decide the Pacific war. What will their reaction be now that they have again seen their illustrious army decisively beaten?

Evidently the Japs expect that the loss of Okinawa means that their homeland will soon be invaded. Feverish attempts are being made to fortify the coastline and all civilians are being instructed in "fancy ways" of killing the enemy. The steps being taken to organize the civilian population are reminiscent of the ineffective attempts made by Hitler to mobilize German civilians into Volksturm units when Germany was invaded. The Volksturmers flopped spectacularly.

It was reported by word of mouth today that a Japanese balloon bomb landed in the Marine district of San Francisco recently. The bomb failed to explode and was removed by bomb disposal units from the Presidio.

Friday, June 8, 1945: —The war news tonight is neither new nor exciting. Military operations in the Pacific have apparently entered one of those periods of transition, when one campaign is being concluded and another bigger one is being prepared. To all intents and purposes Okinawa is ours. There is still a tough fight ahead before the last remnants of the once powerful Japanese garrison of 80,000 men are mopped up. But the principal towns, harbors, and airfields are in our possession and the island can now be utilized for the purpose for which so great a price in American blood and wealth was paid. Already the first small river of supplies is pouring ashore. Soon the river will turn into a great flood of the materiel of war that will transpose the island into a massive, non-sinkable base for the invasion of China or the Japanese homeland. Okinawa will be the England of the Pacific war.

The final battle for Okinawa is proving to be a tougher problem than was foreseen. The fanatical Japs, numbering some 15,000 troops and civilians, including a few women fighters, have holed themselves up on a rocky plateau at the southern tip of the island. They haven't a chance but their suicidal tendencies are making it necessary to dig them out piecemeal with artillery, grenade, and flamethrower. It is not an easy task and too many Yanks are being added to the long casualty list. Nazis in the same position as the Japs would have surrendered long ago.

Saturday, June 9, 1945: —The Japanese radio, which has recently been surprisingly frank about admitting new Allied invasions before they are announced by our side, reported today that Australian and American forces have invaded the island of Borneo. The site of the landings was near the big Japanese naval base in Brunei Bay, on the northwest coast of Borneo. The assault forces were supported by a tremendous armada of naval vessels, including battleships, cruisers, destroyers, and 975 other craft, according to the Japanese announcement. No official confirmation has come from General MacArthur's headquarters, although it is assumed that the new campaign, if actually under way, is a MacArthur show.

The Okinawa battle is still dragging out, with the stubborn Jap remnants clinging fiercely to their strongly fortified positions on rocky Yaeju-Dake plateau. American combat teams are slowly compressing the trap that has been clamped on the Jap lines and there are indications that the enemy is running short of ammunition. Soon the Japanese sand will run out and they will end it all in wild, gory banzai charges. As an alternative, the American commander has invited the Japs to commit suicide by jumping off the steep cliffs on the seaward side of the plateau.

The Hitler mystery deepened today as Marshal Gregory Zhukov, Russian commander in Berlin, said that no German body in Berlin has been positively identified as that of Hitler and it is possible that the Nazi Fuhrer and his mistress, Eva Braun, whom he married 48 hours before the capital fell, may have escaped from the city and are in hiding.

Sunday, June 10, 1945: —General Dwight D. Eisenhower, Supreme Commander of Allied Forces in Europe, and Field

Marshal Sir Bernard L. Montgomery were presented with Soviet Russia's highest award, the jeweled Order of Victory today at a luncheon given by the Allied Commanders in honor of Marshal Georgi K. Zhukov, the victorious Russian leader. It was the first time in history that the award had been made to anyone but Russians, and the two Allied commanders were greatly honored. The beautiful medal is a glittering mass of rubies and diamonds, having an intrinsic value of at least $12,000.00.

Japan's predicament is causing Premier Kantaro Suzuki's government no end of trouble. The unhappy premier has asked for the suspension of Parliamentary procedure and the granting to him of dictatorial powers to meet the emergency. His plea must have been hard to hear over the roar of American motors and the crackling flames of burning Japanese cities.

An Australian broadcast today confirmed that Allied forces under General MacArthur have landed in northern Borneo. No details were given and the broadcast stated that further information would have to come from General MacArthur's headquarters.

Slow progress is being made in the final battle for Okinawa. Determined American infantrymen have scaled the steep cliffs of the Yaeju-Dake plateau with rope ladders and are blasting and burning the Japs out with grenade and flamethrowers.

Monday, June 11, 1945: —General MacArthur's headquarters today issued its first communiqué on the invasion of Borneo. Spearheading the attack was the Australian Ninth Division which seized Labuan Island at the entrance of Brunei Bay, established a beachhead on the mainland at Brooketon and drove inland more than two miles towards the capital city of Brunei. Opposition thus far has been scattered. General MacArthur and his air commander, General George C. Kenny, landed with Australian officers in one of the first assault waves.

The vicious air, sea, and land battle for the strategic Japanese island of Okinawa has gone into its 83rd day. On land, American Doughboys and Marines have destroyed over 70,000 of the enemy's original garrison of 85,000 troops. The remainders are trapped on the southern tip of the island where they are making their customary death stand. Offshore a fierce naval and air battle has been raging since the beginning of the campaign.

Literally hundreds of Japanese planes have been destroyed by the guns of the fleet and the sharpshooting Navy pilots. But the score has not been one-sided. Seventy eight U.S. ships, mostly destroyers and landing craft, have been sunk by the desperate and fanatical Japanese suicide pilots. Fifty three other ships, including some larger units of the fleet have been damaged, a few seriously.

With dozens of naval vessels coming home for repair, emphasis has been put on the need for more ship repair men at local Navy yards. Thousands are needed, too few are available.

Tuesday, June 12, 1945: —Delegates to the United Nations Conference in San Francisco are working hard to complete the charter for the World Organization. Most of the glamour of the meeting has worn off, many of the colorful figures who were here at the beginning, such as Molotov of Russia, and Eden of Great Britain, are gone and about all that is left is the hard work and drudgery of actually drawing up the charter, translating it into the five official languages, and ironing out the differences of opinions that have several times threatened to break up the conference. One of the chief stumbling blocks has been the insistence of the Big Five nations on their right of veto as promulgated by Roosevelt, Churchill, and Stalin at Yalta. Under the Yalta plan any one of the five major powers, England, Russia, China, France, or the United States, could veto any action of the Security Council of the World Organization except the discussion and consideration of disputes. Russia originally insisted on the right to veto even the discussion of disputes but finally yielded this point in the face of determined opposition by the other United Nations, including the other members of the Big Five.

San Franciscans sweltered today in one of the hottest June days on record. The mercury soared to 83 degrees, which is unusually hot for the city by the Golden Gate. The cooling sea breezes that usually air-condition the city were missing and homes and offices baked under the hot rays of the sun.

Wednesday, June 13, 1945: —Black oil smoke darkened the skies over Borneo today, as the retreating Japs set the torch to oil wells and storage tanks in the face of the advancing Australians. Very little opposition has been encountered thus far by the

Aussies who have advanced from captured Brooketon to within 14 miles of Brunei, capital city of the sultanate of the same name.

On Okinawa, the campaign has degenerated into a rat-killing contest, with mountain climbing American infantrymen scaling the cliffs onto Yaeju-Dake plateau and burning the surviving Japs out of the caves with specially-constructed flamethrowers. Observers spotted one concentration of Japs preparing to launch one of their suicidal banzai charges, and called for the artillery which wiped the Japs out in one of the greatest barrages of the entire Pacific war.

It was announced in Washington today that 4,453,061 American soldiers were transported overseas in Europe and Africa in the war against Germany and only 3,604 of them were lost at sea, a better record than was achieved in the First World War. It was also reported that 4,770 merchant ships, Allied and neutral, were sent to the bottom by enemy action. Of these, 1,554 were American vessels totaling 6,277,077 tons. A total of 5,579 merchant seamen are either dead or missing as a result of this deadly battle of communications.

President Truman announced today that a definite time and place have been set for a new meeting of the Big Three. The President's personal envoys, Harry Hopkins and Joseph E. Davies, were instrumental in arranging the vital confab.

Thursday, June 14, 1945: —Today is Flag Day and with thousands of American boys fighting and dying all over the world in defense of the principles for which this nation stands, Old Glory has taken on a more symbolic and inspiring meaning. A lump comes into your throat when you see newsreel pictures of the flag flying briskly and defiantly from the mast of a mighty warship or at the head of a marching column of Doughboys and there are positive tears in your eyes when you see the unforgettable picture of American Marines raising Old Glory in triumph at the top of Mount Suribachi on the embattled isle of Iwo Jima. There is something about those red, white, and blue colors waving in the breeze that convinces you that, tragic though it may be, those gallant lads have not fought and died in vain. You know then that Lincoln was right: Government of the people, by the people, and for the people must not perish from the earth.

The Borneo invasion is moving ahead rapidly. Fast driving Australian troops have smashed into the outskirts of Brunei and have captured the Brunei airstrip. The Tokyo radio, now adept at admitting defeats, confirmed that the oil-rich island of Tarakan off the east coast of Borneo, has fallen to Australian and Netherlands troops. Also overrun by the Allied forces was most of Labuan Island in the mouth of Brunei Bay. The beaten Jap remnants were driven into the northern hinterlands where they face suicide or starvation.

Friday, June 15, 1945: —Evidence of the ferocity of modern air and naval warfare was seen by many San Franciscans today as the battered, but proud, U.S. destroyer, Hazelwood, steamed slowly through the Golden Gate. Like so many other gallant American ships, the Hazelwood showed that she could take the worst the suicidal Japs could offer and still come home under her own power. But though her spirit was still sturdy, her decks were a twisted, mangled mass of steel, bent and torn from the explosive force of 1,000 pounds of TNT carried by a Jap Kamikaze pilot.

No doubt the Japanese will consider the death of their pilot well worth while, for not only did he wreck an American destroyer but he also took with him in death 77 American officers and men. It is odds such as that that emphasizes the seriousness of this new Japanese tactic of large scale suicide attacks against our fleet off Okinawa. While naval leaders agree that the suicide raids cannot hope to change the course of the naval war, it is admitted that they are taking the greatest toll of lives ever suffered by the U.S. fleet. Thousands of heroic American seamen are making the supreme sacrifice amid flame and explosion in the deadly battle against the death-seeking enemy airmen. The deeds of our fighting Navy men during the past few weeks will live long after the suicidal fury in the Pacific is over.

It was announced in Washington today that the long awaited meeting of the Big Three will be held during July in the Berlin area. It is somehow fitting that the erstwhile capital of our fallen Nazi foe should be the site of the meeting between President Truman, Prime Minister Churchill and Marshal Stalin, conquerors and architects of a new and better world.

Saturday, June 16, 1945: —It has been said that San Francisco's weather is "air-conditioned by God," with gentle breezes and cooling fog off the Golden Gate preventing any extremes of temperature that could make the city uncomfortable. For the past few days, however, this God-given cooling system seems to have gone out of order and the city is sweltering under a heat wave that is all the more uncomfortable because the people are not used to it.

Unfortunately this unusual hot spell has come while the United Nations Conference is in session. Despite the heat, however, the delegates are working hard, striving to complete the new world organization charter in time to adjourn on June 23rd. The consensus of opinion among observers indicates that the conference may extend beyond that date due to the terrific log jam of details that must be ironed out before the charter can take final form. Nevertheless, all of the delegations are hoping to break the log jam in time to hold their final plenary session on the 23rd when President Truman is expected to arrive to deliver the closing address.

The Tokyo radio, in defeat more accurate than in victory, today hinted that a great Allied invasion armada is off the east coast of Borneo and appears to be aiming an attack against the great oil port of Balikpapan. No confirmation has come from our side, but there is little doubt of the accuracy of the report. Borneo's oil is a great prize and you can be sure that General MacArthur intends to wrest it from the Japs at the earliest possible moment.

Sunday, June 17, 1945: —The battle for Okinawa is reaching its climax. The United states Tenth Army, in a fierce frontal attack, overran three Japanese-held hills dominating the high plateau on southern Okinawa. The confused enemy unintentionally aided the American Seventh Division to capture one of the hills by mistakenly shelling its own garrison. When the enemy artillery discovered its error and ceased firing, the Yank infantry raced in and captured the position before the befuddled foe could resume his fire.

With the European war over, many American heroes are returning to receive their country's acclaim. New York today prepared to welcome one of the most famous Yank outfits, the rugged, battle hardened Eighty-sixth "Black Hawk" Division of General Patton's Third Army. With "Old Blood and Guts" the

Eighty-sixth raced across France and Germany and was the first American unit to reach the Danube. Now, after a brief rest, they are destined to join in the battle against Japan. But first they will be given a New York welcome that they will long remember. Then at least a thirty day furlough at home. How good that word "home" must sound to those veterans. Let's hope they will all be home permanently soon.

General Eisenhower, to whom belongs a large share of the glory for designing the European victory, has left by plane for the United States. One of the greatest hero welcomes in history awaits the General upon whose unassuming shoulders fell the tremendous burden of making the decisions that launched the mighty invasion of Normandy and culminated, less than a year later, in the unconditional surrender of the Nazi foe.

Monday, June 18, 1945: —The fierce 80-day old campaign for Okinawa appears to be entering its final stages. The surviving Nips have been cornered in a death trap of seven square miles on the southern tip of the island and are being relentlessly pounded to pieces by the hard-hitting U.S. Tenth Army. Since the beginning of the campaign, 80,459 Japanese troops have been killed by official count and several thousand others have been captured. Included among the enemy dead recently found were the bodies of Admiral Minoru Ota, Japanese commander of the Okinawa Naval Base, and five of his officers. Their throats were neatly slit from ear to ear in approved Shinto fashion.

General of the Army "Ike" Eisenhower arrived in Washington today and received one of the most tumultuous welcomes ever accorded a national hero in the Nation's capital. The victorious General was paraded down Pennsylvania Avenue, the street that has reverberated with cheers for many American heroes, after which he was honored at a joint session of Congress. Senators, Representatives, Supreme Court Justices, foreign ambassadors, and common citizens joined in a great ovation for the modest General who led the Allied forces to their glorious victory over the Nazis. In his speech before Congress the General gave full credit to the spirit of cooperation between the Allies forged in the crucible of war and offered a prayer that a similar basis for unity might be found in peace so that never again would the world be plunged into the terrible abyss of international conflict.

Tuesday, June 19, 1945: —The heat spell that has had San Franciscans and Conference delegates alike sweltering in discomfort was broken today as the city's air-conditioning system went back into operation, with cooling breezes and welcome fog rolling in across the Golden Gate. The temperature took a sudden tumble from its average of 86 yesterday to a pleasant 66 today.

With the break in weather the United Nations Conference went into high gear, hoping to complete its monumental task by Saturday. A key section of the Charter was adopted today which put the clincher on the defeat of the Axis powers. This section will prevent enemy nations or their satellites from seeking recourse before the United Nations from any of the conditions imposed upon them at the peace conference by the victorious powers.

Meanwhile, from Washington it was reported that President Truman has left by plane on the first leg of his trip to San Francisco where he will address the closing session of the United Nations Conference. His first destination is Olympia, Washington where he will take a short vacation with his old Senate colleague, Governor Mon Wallgren. From there the President will be available for a quick trip to San Francisco as soon as the Conference is ready to wind up its affairs.

Wednesday, June 20, 1945: —Scratch three more Japanese industrial cities. More than 450 giant Superfortresses dumped 3,000 tons of fire bombs on the factory centers of Shizuoka, Toyohashi, and Fukuoka, setting huge conflagrations that could be seen more than 60 miles away. This latest bomb load brought the weight of incendiaries dumped on the Japanese homeland this month to 20,000 tons. How long the Japs can stand this sort of obliteration bombing is a question that only time can answer.

The long, bloody battle for Okinawa is ending. Disorganized and beaten remnants of the once powerful Japanese garrison of more than 100,000 men are either surrendering in bewilderment or hurling themselves from the jagged Okinawan cliffs in suicidal despair.

Even as victory appeared ready for attainment on Okinawa, preparations were being made for the next step in the drive on Tokyo. Japanese radio, more reliable now that it appears to have abandoned its wishful boasting of non-existent victories, reported that a great convoy of 100 American transports, protected by two mighty Allied task forces, was at sea 20 miles southwest of Okinawa, apparently headed for some new invasion attempt. Little does the enemy know where or when the next blow will strike. The most important single element in warfare, the initiative, is ours. We can now pick the time, the place, and most of the conditions under which we will fight.

Thursday, June 21, 1945: —Admiral Nimitz today officially declared the 82-day old campaign for Okinawa ended. Complete and crushing victory was won, but only after one of the hardest and bloodiest campaigns of the war. Marines and Doughboys of the U.S. Tenth Army were credited with the victory, which cost them an estimated 35,000 casualties, including their commanding general, Lieut. General Simon Bolivar Buckner Jr., who was killed recently by a Japanese shell. But the enemy suffered far greater losses. Up to last Tuesday, 87,343 Japanese dead had been counted and, with the number of prisoners mounting hourly, it is likely that well over 100,000 enemy troops will have been accounted for when the final tally is in.

In a surprise move, General Douglas MacArthur today appointed General Joseph Stilwell, of China, Burma, India fame, to command the Tenth Army, succeeding General Buckner. "Old Vinegar Joe" as he was fondly known in China, will take over the battle-tested Tenth at an opportune moment, since that famous Army will undoubtedly play an important part in the coming showdown battle for Japan.

Now and then the Navy releases some of the details of the terrible losses being inflicted on our fleet by the deadly Japanese suicide planes and "baka bombs". While these suicide tactics are not changing the end result for the Japanese, they are indeed exacting a fearful toll of our gallant naval forces. Today's report told of the sinking of the destroyer Mannert L. Abele and the crippling of the cruiser Nashville off Okinawa. Two hundred and fourteen men sacrificed their lives.

Friday, June 22, 1945: —General George C. Marshal, Army Chief of Staff, today revealed that plans have been laid for the final knockout blow against Japan. The program calls for the assembling of a mighty force possessing more firepower and men than that which brought Germany to her knees. Although warning against over optimism or a letdown in effort, the General promised that a swift, powerful offensive would be mounted in order to force a quick victory and thus save as many American lives as possible. Russia is the great imponderable in the Pacific war. If she decides to enter the conflict a victorious conclusion may come even sooner than expected.

A new trend has been noted in the thoughts and conduct of surviving Japanese troops on Okinawa. For the first time, many enemy soldiers have decided that dying for the Emperor in a lost cause is not so desirable. Large bands of weary, shell-dazed Japs are streaming out of their caves waving white flags in a token of surrender. In one sector alone more than 2,000 prisoners were taken during the last 24 hours. Many Japanese officers were included in the prisoner bag, which is the first time in the Pacific war that the fanatical Japs, especially officers, have seen the futility of continuing resistance after defeat is certain. This augurs well for coming operations.

Another mighty force of B-29's added more fuel to the already burning Japanese cities. Over 112 square miles of Japan's major war centers have been destroyed by the avenging Superforts. Five aircraft plants and a naval arsenal on the main island of Honshu were the targets for today.

Saturday, June 23, 1945: —With their vital island outpost, Okinawa, now in American hands, the Japanese are desperately girding for what they anticipate will be a mighty, climactic invasion of their homeland. Radio and press releases from battered Tokyo indicate that the Japs are taking frantic steps to prepare for the final blow. Dictatorial powers were assumed by the government of Baron Kantaro Suzuki, bringing all phases of the individual citizen's life under the absolute domination of the government. Emperor Hirohito, himself, assumed direct command of the People's Volunteer Corps and called upon its members to be prepared to fight to the death against the invaders. Japanese military leaders declared the defenses of the homeland had been perfected and the entire nation, including school children were prepared to meet the enemy and crush him anywhere he may choose to land. The poor Japs have the jitters.

The United Nations Conference on International Organization has almost completed its work on a proposed charter for a world peace organization. The final draft of the document has been completed and all that remains is to translate it into the five major languages—a monumental task in itself— obtain the final approval of the entire conference delegations and sign it. President Truman is expected to be in San Francisco Monday to witness the signing and will address the final plenary session in the War Memorial Opera House. The signed charter will then go to the United States Senate and to all the other United Nations governing bodies for ratification.

Sunday, June 24, 1945: —Thousands of European combat veterans were home again in California today, some of them for good but most of them on furloughs before being redeployed to the Pacific. The famous Eighty-Sixth Blackhawk Division, first American division to cross the Danube, arrived yesterday at Camp Beale, where its thousands of youthful heroes were quickly processed and sped on their way home for 30 day furloughs before being sent across the Pacific to participate in the march to Tokyo. The boys were overjoyed at the prospect of seeing Mom and Pop, Sis and sweetheart again and to taste good home-cooked meals once more, sleep in the old comfortable bed again, drink some ice-cold beer and take the girl friend to the corner movies again. According to all reports, those pessimistic prognosticators who predicted that the carefree, happy-go-lucky boys who went to war would be changed into morose, touchy, psychoneurotic "old men" when they returned, were all wrong. The boys are a little older sure—but only from the elapse of time—and they haven't changed much otherwise. They're still full of laughter and fun and as happy as kids at the prospects of going home. A few weeks back in the old homestead and you would never recognize most of them as the tough, rugged fighting men who pummeled the Wehrmacht into submission. They would just be the likeable fellow next door, or the fellow who's courting Sis, or the hard-hitting first basemen on the Sunday baseball team. Such is the resilience of American youth.

Monday, June 25, 1945: —President Harry S. Truman arrived in San Francisco by plane today and will address the closing plenary session of the United Nations Conference on International Organization tomorrow. The President was given a tumultuous welcome by one of the biggest crowds ever to turn out on San Francisco's streets. The Chief Executive's private plane arrived at Hamilton Field, in Marin County, at 2:30 p.m. where he was greeted by Secretary of State Stettinius, and leaders of all the other United Nations delegations. From there the President and a 75 car cavalcade crossed the beautiful Golden Gate Bridge and entered San Francisco where a roundabout route led them through cheering thousands of citizens to the Fairmont Hotel, atop San Francisco's famous Nob Hill. There the President will meet and greet those responsible for the success of the United Nations Conference. Tomorrow the Nation's Chief will witness the signing of the World Peace Charter and will deliver the closing address before the final plenary meeting in the beautiful War Memorial Opera House. The Conference will then officially adjourn after nine weeks of grueling work.

In what looks like the beginning of an all-out pre-invasion aerial bombardment, six Allied air forces battered at the reeling Japanese today. B-29s blasted targets on the enemy's home islands of Honshu and Kyushu while every type of plane from tiny fighter to mighty bomber lashed at Japanese defenses from the Kuriles to Borneo.

Tuesday, June 26, 1945: —Today is an historic day. Once again the nations of the world have united to formulate a charter for a world organization pledged to preserve the peace and security of all nations, large and small. Delegates from the 50 participating nations signed the document today at an impressive ceremony in the Veteran's Building. The actual signing was done at a specially constructed circular table surrounded by flags of all the United Nations.

The preamble to the charter was composed by South Africa's Field Marshal Jan Christian Smuts and began with words reminiscent of the United States Constitution: "We, the people of the United Nations, determined to save succeeding generations from the scourge of war, which twice in our lifetime has brought untold sorrow to mankind, and to reaffirm faith in fundamental human rights, in the dignity and worth of the human person, in the equal rights of men and women and of nations large and small . . . do hereby establish an international organization to be known as the United Nations."

President Truman closed the Conference this afternoon with a stirring appeal to the peoples of all nations to make the San

Francisco Charter a "living thing." He echoed the thoughts of all the people who attended the glittering finale in the Opera House and the people who heard his voice over the radio, when he stretched forth his arms and exclaimed, "What a day this can be in history."

Wednesday, June 27, 1945: —Secretary of State Edward R. Stettinius Jr. has resigned his high cabinet post, it was announced today. President Truman stated that he has accepted the resignation in order that the handsome, white haired diplomat may become the United States' representative on the newly organized United Nations Council.

Many close observers of the recent Conference on International Organization declare that it was largely through the tireless efforts and patient understanding of Mr. Stettinius that the conference was able to successfully weather the storms of dissention and disunity that sometimes threatened to bring the meeting to an abrupt and disastrous end. Many times only his able leadership and his unfailing courtesy and tact stood between the high hopes of mankind and failure. His appointment as the American representative on the World Organization, therefore, is a happy one.

Early ratification of the United Nations Charter by the United States Senate is expected. Fortunately there apparently is no organized opposition such as wrecked the hopes of Woodrow Wilson and his League of Nations. This time it is confidently expected that the necessary approval will be given by the Senate within four weeks time. President Truman is expected to deliver the original Charter signed in San Francisco to the Senate next Monday upon his return to the Nation's capital. After that its fate is in the hands of the senior representatives of the American people.

Thursday, June 28, 1945: —The Japs felt the full weight of America's mighty Superfortress fleet again today. More than five hundred of the giant bombers carted over 3,000 tons of incendiaries from their bases in the Marianas to the Nipponese homeland where they cascaded the flaming destruction into the teeming centers of three major seaports, Sasebo, Moji, and Nobeoka. Tremendous fires were started in all three cities, whose populations ranged from 100,000 to 200,000 people.

Stung into utter desperation by the unceasing rain of destruction upon their homeland, the Japanese government today revealed that hundreds of thousands of special suicide weapons are being prepared to ward off the final American invasion that will decide the fate of the Japanese nation. At Army camps throughout the islands thousands of young Japanese are being trained to man the lethal weapons that will assure them a "one way ticket to death."

The Navy has revealed another of the epic stories of disaster and heroism that have come out of the bloody and hair-raising naval and air battles that have raged for the last nine weeks off the coast of Okinawa. On May 11, two death-seeking Japanese suicide pilots spotted the mighty 27,500 ton aircraft carrier Bunker Hill and smashed their planes and heavy bombs into her deck, setting off a terrible holocaust that turned her flight deck and many decks below into charred wreckage and killed 373 of her crew, wounding 264 others. By heroic and superhuman efforts of the survivors the proud vessel was saved and like the Benjamin Franklin, will fight again.

Friday, June 29, 1945: —War news is meager tonight. The Japanese cities hit by the great fleet of B-29s yesterday are still burning fiercely, according to reconnaissance photographs made today. At the same time the Japs are casting anxious eyes northward towards the Kuriles and the Aleutians where the Japs claim powerful American forces are gathering for a possible invasion of the Japanese homeland from the north to coincide with a simultaneous attack from the south. Things look pretty bad, eh, Mr. Moto?

Since the conquest of Okinawa, land fighting in the Pacific war is confined to mopping up operations in the Philippines and other by-passed and leap-frogged islands of the south and central Pacific. In China, re-invigorated Chinese armies are making considerable headway in their drive to recapture the vital airfields formerly used by the American bombers of the 14th U.S. Air Force. One airfield at Liuchow has already been retaken by the Chinese, who are closing in on burning Liuchow itself and its two remaining airdromes.

A new theater of operations is expected to open up on the opposite side of Borneo from the recently invaded Brunei Bay sector. The U.S. Seventh Fleet was officially reported to be ranging in the waters off the great oil center of Balikpapan and a landing aimed at seizing the vital oil fields in that area was expected momentarily.

Saturday, June 30, 1945: —The harassed Japs have revealed that they are trying to move the major portion of their war industries to Manchuria where they can escape the dreadful aerial scourging that is being administered to the home islands and from whence they can continue to wage war even though their homeland is invaded. The task is a colossal one and has been started just a wee bit too late, we believe, since the B-29s and the U.S. naval and air blockade that has been clamped about the Nipponese homeland will make any large scale enemy ship movements practically impossible. Ports and harbors are being sowed with mines from fast flying planes while Superfortresses have extended their range to strike deeper into Japan proper and disrupt all communications in the main islands. Niigata and Sakata, two principal ports on the northwest coast of Honshu Island were heavily bombed early this morning.

American invasion forces are now in control of 16 islands in the Ryukyu chain including the main island of Okinawa. Prolonged opposition has only been encountered on the latter island but indications are that several more of these island stepping stones to the Jap homeland will be seized in preparation for the final blow. The latest island being given the prescribed treatment prior to invasion is Okinoerabu, one of the principal Ryukyu isles. A stiff battle is expected for this one.

July

Sunday, July 1, 1945: —Let's take a brief look at the situation on the home front as we go into the second half of the year 1945:

We're all "veterans" now, accustomed to the many shortages and inconveniences of war.

In fact we've almost forgotten what that "beautiful" pre-war existence was like. Now it's just something to dream or joke about.

The food shortages hurt the most. Butter is still 24 red points per pound so we do without it most of the time. Beef steaks and chops are rare treats that we hoard points for. Eggs are scarce and milk may soon be rationed.

Food prices also hurt. Although price control has prevented run-away inflation, prices are still far above pre-war levels, so far above that it seems that almost all of our monthly paycheck goes to the grocer, the butcher, the baker, or the milkman.

Transportation is still a colossal problem. Busses and trains, streetcars and taxis are all pitifully overburdened. Sardines have plenty of elbow room compared with the traveling public these days. Much of the travel is unnecessary.

We were finally able to get a couple of auto tires, made of synthetic rubber, so we have the old car operating once again. Gas coupons for A cards are now worth six gallons which gives us a few more trips to the store each month.

We will continue with this tomorrow.

Monday, July 2, 1945: —Continuing with our short sketch of the home front situation:

The housing problem is one of the most serious facing the San Francisco Bay Area. The Army and Navy, concentrating here for the Pacific war, are making heavy demands for living accommodations while the tremendous influx of war workers into the area has created an almost impossible situation. Rapid construction of thousands of temporary and permanent war housing units has alleviated the condition somewhat but thus far the demand far exceeds the supply of dwellings. Some people must suffer.

The curfew and dim-out have been lifted and gay night life is having its wildest fling. Liquor flows like water, despite incredible prices while gambling flourishes. Crime surprisingly is down from pre-war levels; apparently former stick-up men and petty thieves are finding it more profitable to work at a war job. Many of them may also be in the armed forces.

Working hours in most war plants are still long and arduous. Some industries, notably ship building and aircraft plants have made drastic cut-backs from their war-time employment peaks. Thousands have been laid off but apparently have been reabsorbed into other industries immediately. Skilled workers are still badly needed in many lines of work, particularly in ship repair yards, where dozens of crippled Navy craft are returning from the sanguinary sea and air battles off the bloody coast of Okinawa.

Tuesday, July 3, 1945: —Today is the Fourth of July in the Far East, and 5,000 American airmen celebrated it with the greatest demonstration of fireworks yet seen over the Japanese mainland. Some 500 huge Superfortresses dumped more than 3,000 tons of flaming gasoline jelly and high explosives over four Japanese cities on Shikoku and Honshu Islands, setting off fierce conflagrations that defied frantic Japanese efforts to control them.

The Borneo invasion, led by General MacArthur, is making steady progress. Australian troops have already captured several vital hill positions dominating the approaches to the rich oil center of Balikpapan. The Japs already appear to be abandoning the city and are setting the torch to oil wells and storage tanks. Vast clouds of dense smoke blacken the skies over the city while rivers of burning oil have been seen running down ravines outside the town. The gods of destruction are in their glory.

Here at home, President Truman placed the United Nations Charter before the Senate yesterday and requested its speedy ratification. The theme of his speech was that this country must accept this Charter and help make it work or surrender the world to chaos and future wars.

American troops have finally entered Berlin. Under the Big

Four control agreement, a section of Berlin will be administered by each of the major powers, France, Russia, England, and the United States. Thus, finally, the goal of nearly four years of fighting has been reached. The Yanks are in the city of Berlin.

Wednesday, July 4, 1945: —Today, of course, is Independence Day and Americans are once again finding out the hard way just what this Independence means. Independence— or Liberty—whichever you may wish to call it, is an expensive possession. A stern price was paid to get it and a sterner price is being paid to keep it. For example, the San Francisco News today printed on its first page a Gold Star map of San Francisco, reminding us that, to date, 909 San Franciscans have been killed in action in this war, defending that ideal of liberty. Their sacrifice has been matched by thousands of others throughout the nation. Few towns or cities have escaped without at least a few Gold Stars. How many more must join the ranks of those already gone, before final victory is won, only God knows. But I believe that Americans have learned once and for all from this bloody war that the key to eternal peace is eternal vigilance. Never again must we be caught unprepared. Never again must there be a Pearl Harbor.

We are still learning about installments that were paid on the price of Okinawa. The Navy revealed today that two more destroyers were lost last month while engaged in the battle for Okinawa. One hundred thirty six gallant American sailors were lost and 47 were wounded in the two sinkings. One vessel was sent to the bottom by a Jap torpedo while the other was the victim of Jap suicide dive bomber.

Thursday, July 5, 1945: —President Truman's fast moving cabinet shuffles made headline news again today. The Chief Executive announced that Henry Morgenthau Jr. has resigned as Secretary of the Treasury. The resignation, however, will not take effect until after the July meeting between President Truman, Winston Churchill, and Josef Stalin.

Also retiring from government service, according to the same Presidential announcement, is Associate Supreme Court Justice Owen J. Roberts. With Justice Robert's retirement, only one pre-Roosevelt appointee remains on the High Court's bench.

The non-stop pre-invasion obliteration bombing campaign against the Japanese homeland continued today. Rounding out the 30th straight day of morning and afternoon attacks, more that 300 B-29s, supported by a strong fighter screen, plastered the Tokyo area and the Port of Nagasaki during the morning hours while this afternoon Army Liberators joined in the assault, striking heavily at targets in Miyazaki, Oita, Saga, and Nagasaki prefectures on the island of Kyushu.

Australian troops under the overall command of General MacArthur, captured the great oil center of Balikpapen today and rolled on against ineffective opposition towards the Pandansari oil refinery area to the northeast.

Today's bad news was the reported loss of the renowned U.S. submarine Trigger with all hands. This brings to 45 the number of American subs lost in the war thus far.

Friday, July 6, 1945: —General Douglas MacArthur has announced that the Philippines campaign has officially ended, with the total destruction of nearly 23 Japanese divisions numbering at least 450,000 men. The General said that less than 30,000 enemy troops remain in the islands to wage guerrilla warfare in the mountains and jungles. The balance of 420,000 Japs were annihilated or captured in the greatest whipping ever to be administered to the Japanese Imperial Army.

To inflict this great disaster on the little Sons of Heaven, MacArthur employed 17 American divisions. According to the General's statement, "This is one of the rare instances when in a long campaign a ground force superior in numbers was entirely destroyed by a numerically inferior opponent."

The great Philippine victory has not only liberated the islands from Japanese oppression but has provided us with a mighty staging area and airbase for future operations against the enemy in China or the Japanese mainland. General MacArthur compared the Philippines in the coming Battle of Japan with England in the Battle of Germany.

Here at home the redeployment of vast numbers of troops from Europe to the Pacific by way of the States has created a terrific transportation problem. Already complaints have been made that returning troops have been transported across country in dirty, vermin-ridden day coaches. To solve the riddle, therefore, the Office of Transportation has decided to drastically curtail civilian train travel. The majority of Pullman cars previously used by civilians will now be diverted to military use. It seems like now is a good time for all good civilians to stay at home.

Saturday, July 7, 1945: —The crashing tempo of the aerial blitz against the Japanese homeland has led many observers to predict that the Jap Islands will soon be ripe for invasion. In fact, Lieut. General Roy S. Geiger, commanding officer of the U.S. Fleet Marine Force, declared in a Pearl Harbor press conference, that the aerial softening-up program has already accomplished its primary job. He said that American forces can now land anywhere they want to on the Japanese homeland. Our overwhelming superiority in men and equipment will make it impossible for the Nips to repulse the invasion. All that is left is for us to "wade in and finish the job."

A tremendous fleet of more than 600 Superfortresses added emphasis to the Marine General's words by striking the heaviest blow of the war against the already scorched Jap mainland last night. Over 4,000 tons of flaming incendiaries and roaring high explosives were dumped on the few remaining war centers not already wiped off the map in the previous raids. Evidence of the desperate plight of the enemy was clearly shown by the fact that the B-29' encountered practically no fighter planes and very spotty and inaccurate anti-aircraft fire.

The Borneo invasion is progressing well. Aussie troops won control of Balikpapan Bay today in a successfully executed "leap-frog" operation across the three mile water-way from Balikpapan to Penadjam. Oil for the ships of the fleet will soon again be flowing from the rich wells of Borneo.

Sunday, July 8, 1945: —The Pacific war news is a succession of stories regarding devastating aerial strikes against the Japanese mainland. Japan is being scourged as no other nation, including Germany, has ever been in the history of the world. Her main islands are being blackened and blasted from end to end. Her great cities are being leveled and her industries smashed. The United States fleet has won absolute dominance of the entire Pacific area, including the waters immediately around the Jap mainland. Our planes have attained complete mastery of the air over Japan and are bombing and strafing at will, daring the enemy to come up and fight. Very few Nip pilots have dared accept the challenge and they have not survived to relate their experiences.

America's hard-won island bases on Saipan, Iwo Jima, and Okinawa are beginning to demonstrate that the price we paid, though bitterly high, was not in vain. Vast fleets of B-29s are winging their way daily from Saipan while medium bombers and fighter escorts are making their presence felt from the newly acquired airfields on Iwo Jima and Okinawa. The flaming battle of Japan is fast approaching its finale.

The newborn San Francisco Charter for International Organization will begin its run through the Senate gauntlet tomorrow. Edward R. Stettinius, who helped to give it birth, will be the first witness to appear before the Foreign Relations Committee and he is expected to urge prompt ratification.

Monday, July 9, 1945: —President Truman is on his way to the Big Three conference to be held at Potsdam, Germany between Mr. Truman, Prime Minister Winston Churchill, and the Russian dictator, Josef Stalin. The Chief Executive left the Norfolk, Va. Naval Base last Saturday aboard the cruiser Augusta, the vessel famed for having been the site of the 1941 Atlantic Charter meeting between Roosevelt and Churchill. A large party of advisers was reported to have sailed with the President, including Byrnes, who, as newly appointed Secretary of State, is fourth in line of succession to the President after the Vice President, Speaker of the House and President pro tempore of the Senate.

Problems of tremendous significance are expected to be on the agenda for the historic meeting of the three Chiefs of State. Final decisions will be made regarding the kind of peace to be imposed on Germany and Italy. Efforts will be made to preserve the unity displayed by the Big Three during the war and to extend it to the furtherance of international cooperation and amity. President Truman is expected to pin Russia down on her intentions in the Pacific and to tell her that, if she wants to be in on the kill against Japan, she had better hurry.

Meanwhile Japan was taking another terrific beating today as a mighty fleet of some 550 Superfortresses dumped 3,500 tons of high explosive and incendiary bombs on five of her principal cities on the island of Honshu.

Tuesday, July 10, 1945: —Showing utter contempt for the Nipponese Navy and Air Force, Admiral Halsey's mighty U.S. Third Fleet steamed boldly to within less than 25 miles of the Japanese mainland today and launched more than 1,000 carrier planes in a great strike against Tokyo. Returning pilots pronounced the raid a "terrific success" and said that airfields, hangars, and other military installations were raked and bombed mercilessly. The Japs were caught with their planes down and were able to offer only meager aerial opposition. Anti-aircraft fire was heavy at some targets but most of the enemy's defenses were simply smothered by the weight of the attack.

In addition to the carrier-borne raid, a fleet of some 550 Superfortresses escorted by almost that many fighters from Iwo Jima and Okinawa, cascaded fiery destruction into the hearts of five other war centers on the main Jap island of Honshu. Thus almost 2,000 planes smashed at the Nip homeland today, bringing the pre-invasion aerial campaign to a new peak of intensity. How long can the Japanese people take such punishment?

From Washington D.C. came hints that some Japs at least, are tired of the hopeless fight. Acting Secretary of State Grew, who knows the Japanese well, having been our ambassador to Tokyo at the time of Pearl Harbor, revealed today that peace feelers have been put out by some influential Japs and warned us against accepting anything short of unconditional surrender. We must finish the job once and for all time.

Wednesday, July 11, 1945: —Admiral "Bull" Halsey's powerful Third Fleet is still on the prowl off the coast of Japan. The men of the fleet are spoiling for a fight but the jittery Japs are unwilling to accept the challenge. How humiliating it must be to the once boastful Japanese Imperial Navy to sit impotently by and watch the American battle fleet steam brazenly to the very mouth of Tokyo Bay. Talk about losing face. The Japs are not only losing face but they are losing everything else as well. The rising sun is setting fast.

An insight into the real fury of the deadly fire bomb attacks on the Japanese homeland was revealed by the story of one Superfortress which attempted to drop its incendiaries over the target after other planes had set the whole target area ablaze. The thermal updraft from the raging inferno below was so great that when the bombardier tried to release his firebombs they flew right back into the plane. The updraft flipped the huge bomber over on its back and things looked mighty rugged for a few minutes before the pilot was able to right the plane and escape.

President Truman is still on the high seas tonight, heading for his momentous meeting with Prime Minister Churchill and Generalissimo Stalin near Berlin. The Chief Executive spent the day aboard the cruiser Augusta in consultation with Secy. of State Byrnes, Admiral Leahy, and others of his advisory staff in preparation for the conference.

Thursday, July 12, 1945: —The spotlight shifted today to the Indian Ocean where speculation is rife concerning the start of a possible British campaign to retake Singapore. The loss of this mighty bastion was probably the most humiliating episode in the history of the British Empire and there is little doubt but that the British would like to have vengeance, the sooner the better. Jittery Japanese broadcasts today hinted that British forces have landed on two small islands off the coast of Sabang, on the northern tip of that island. Further developments will be watched with keen interest. The recapture of Singapore should, and probably will, be an exclusive British job.

With almost monotonous regularity, the big Superfortress fleet from the Marianas is freighting their huge bomb loads over the Japanese mainland. One by one, they are reducing the cities of Japan to burned-out shells. To date, 39 principal cities have felt the fury of the attack. Targets for today's raid included Uwajima, on the southwest tip of Shikoku, Tsuruga, 210 miles west of Tokyo, Utsunomiya, 55 miles north of the capital, and Ichinomiya. All are vital industrial centers—or should we say were vital industrial centers.

General Dwight D. Eisenhower has returned to Europe after his triumphal visit to the United States. The great General's first duties will be to wind up the affairs of SHAEF, (Supreme Headquarters, Allied Expeditionary Force) which he welded into the mightiest military machine in the history of warfare.

Friday, July 13, 1945: —The Navy today revealed that a typhoon struck the fleet off the coast of Japan last June 5th and caused more damage in a few hours than the combined efforts of the Japanese Navy and Air Force have been able to accomplish in many months. The howling wind and mountainous seas damaged 21 warships, including three battleships and five carriers. Notwithstanding these losses, the fleet went on to attack the enemy mainland three days later.

All of the damaged vessels have been repaired and are back in action with the exception of the cruiser Pittsburgh, which had her bow ripped off by the raging sea. A section of her bow more than 100 feet long, extending nearly to her forward gun turret, was torn off but not a single man was lost. By virtue of magnificent seamanship and sealed bulkheads, both the crippled vessel itself and the bow section were saved and returned to Guam for repairs.

For the first time in the history of the Japanese empire the home islands have been shelled by an enemy fleet. Dealing our little Oriental enemy the boldest slap in the face—which means so much to him—that he has ever received, the rampaging U.S. Third Fleet stood unconcernedly off the northern Honshu coast today and shelled the steel city of Kamaishi for four hours. The reluctant Japanese Air Force showed no desire to brave the gauntlet of fire from thousands of Navy guns in order to make an attempt to ward off the humiliating blow against their "sacred" soil.

Saturday, July 14, 1945: —The shelling of Japan by the United States Third Fleet has sent cold shivers up and down the Nipponese spine, according to all available information. The jittery Tokyo radio, apparently caught by surprise, appeared to be frantically preparing the populace for what may presently be landing attempts.

Showing their continued contempt for the opposition, the Third Fleet has disregarded radio silence, which is customary in such actions, and has radioed reports of the strike to Admiral Nimitz' headquarters on Guam. According to these reports the big guns of the fleet have made a shambles out of the steel center of Kamaishi. The huge steel mill was demolished by direct hits from 16-inch shells, while the coke ovens were blasted and are burning. A great pall of smoke hangs over the entire area.

I should have mentioned yesterday that the United Nations Charter has been reported favorably from the Senate foreign relations committee. There was only one vote against it on the 22-man committee. That vote was cast by Senator Hiram Johnson of California, one of the original Old Guard that fought United States membership in the League of Nations.

For what it is worth, Italy declared war on Japan today. The motives for this action or the gains to be had are not known. Apparently Italy determined in one way or another to be on the winning side in this war.

Sunday, July 15, 1945: —The mighty U.S. Third Fleet and its thousand war planes continued to press home the attack against the Japanese homeland today. The carriers and battlewagons, with their cruisers and destroyer escorts, have spent the last two days steaming boldly and unopposed just a few miles off the Japanese coastline. Either the Nips are already thoroughly beaten or they are conserving what strength they still have available for a final desperate defense of their islands when the invasion comes. In any event, no opposition was encountered by the ships and planes of the task force as they shelled, bombed, and strafed targets on Honshu and Hokkaido islands. Air fields, ports, transportation facilities, and industrial plants were ravaged by the heavy-hitting Yanks.

Meanwhile, General Douglas MacArthur's Borneo invasion continued to roll against fierce opposition from the cornered Japs. Balikpapan, the vital oil port, has already been opened to Allied use through superhuman efforts by Army and Navy engineers. Thus, only 14 days after the campaign opened, the oil of Borneo is beginning to flow into Allied tanks.

The heaviest fighting in Borneo is raging between Australian and Dutch colonial troops and the Japanese defending Mount Batochampar behind Balikpapan.

There was good news for butter hungry civilians on the home front today. The OPA dropped the number of point per pound from 24 to 16. Umm—bread and butter will taste mighty good again.

Monday, July 16, 1945: —President Truman and Prime Minister Churchill have arrived at Potsdam where the fateful meeting of the Big Three will be held. The conference was scheduled to begin today but had to be postponed when Premier

Stalin was delayed. The opening sessions will take place tomorrow.

While waiting for Stalin, Mr. Truman and Mr. Churchill toured Berlin to inspect the devastation wrought upon the German capital during five years of warfare. Both leaders were visibly impressed with the evidence of the terrible fate Adolf Hitler had brought upon his people.

While the Big Three are meeting in Potsdam to plot what may well be future trouble for Japan, the U.S. Navy and Air Force are delivering plenty of current headaches to the Japs. With almost incredible ease, a powerful task force of the Third Fleet, including such battleships as the Iowa, Wisconsin, and Missouri, steamed to within 1000 yards of the southern tip of the main Japanese island of Hokkaido and shelled the industrial center of Muroran. As was the case at Kamaishi, the enemy offered no opposition and permitted more than 1,000 tons of steel and explosives to be hurled into the heart of one of his most vital ports without so much as firing a pistol in return.

In addition to the fleet attack, more than 500 Superforts cascaded 2,500 tons of bombs into four other industrial cities across a 475 mile stretch of Kyushu and Honshu islands.

Tuesday, July 17, 1945: —In an amazing show of boldness only justified by a complete knowledge of the enemy's impotence, the United States Third Fleet continued its cruise along the shoreline of Japan's main islands today, after delivering a midnight attack last night on industrial targets within 25 miles of Tokyo. Steaming close inshore during the midnight darkness, the mighty 16-inch guns of the battleship Iowa and other powerful warships sent salvo after salvo screaming into the closely packed industrial area north of the enemy capital. Towering fires and heaps of debris were left in their wake.

Preceding the night bombardment, the skies over Japan were filled with a tremendous fleet of more than 1,500 carrier planes from a great armada of aircraft carriers that included many British men-of-war. Prime targets of the carrier planes apparently were the ring of 80 airfields surrounding the Tokyo area. Finding the reluctant Japanese air force unwilling to risk planes and pilots in aerial combat, the flyers had to content themselves with strafing hangars and destroying aircraft on the ground.

Admiral Nimitz revealed today that powerful units of the British fleet are operating with our forces off the coast of Japan. Among others were the 35,000 ton dreadnought King George V and the 23,000 ton carrier Formidable. According to the Admiral, the combined Allied navies have won absolute dominance of the sea and air around Japan and intend to draw the noose so tight around the islands that the Japs will soon have trouble even getting fish out of their own waters.

Wednesday, July 18, 1945: —The Conference of the Big Three is under way in Potsdam. Only meager news, based mostly on guesswork, was available regarding the progress of the meeting due to ironclad censorship, but it was believed that President Truman is insisting on putting the question of the Japanese war first on the agenda. The rapid winning of that war is the first essential to the solution of the other world problems and it is believed that the President wants Russia to show us something tangible in the way of assistance in the far eastern fracas, as compensation for our material aid in rebuilding Europe. If Mr. Truman plays his cards right he can't lose, for most of his cards are trumps.

The giant rifles of Allied battleships and the guns and bombs of hundreds of carrier planes continued to hurl devastation into the heart of Japan today. Sixteen-inch shells smashed another vital steel plant today, this one being at Mito, only 35 miles from Emperor Hirohito's palace in Tokyo. Again the big battlewagons pumped in their shells at the rate of a ton a minute and withdrew without encountering opposition of any kind.

Our only living ex-president, Herbert Hoover, today requested the United States Senate to ratify the United Nations Charter but urged Congress to make certain that it retains the power to declare war. He declared that the Charter has many weaknesses but is better than the Dumbarton Oaks plan and is probably as good as could be obtained at this time.

Thursday, July 19, 1945: —Admiral Halsey's big battlewagons did it again today. Obviously hoping to entice the remnants of the Japanese Navy into a showdown battle, the Jap-hating admiral sent his battleships and cruisers right into the mouth of Tokyo Bay where they shelled enemy shore installations on Cape Nojima. Failing to tempt the skulking Jap ships out of hiding, the Navy sent its carrier planes to seek them out. Admiral Nimitz revealed that one wing of the carrier force may have uncovered the principal hideout of the remaining enemy fleet. This wing struck heavily at the Yokusuka naval base in Tokyo Bay, 30 miles south of Tokyo and 20 miles from Cape Nojima. Carrier pilots reported seeing large enemy units and succeeded in damaging some of them.

More than 600 giant Superforts completed the day's three-way blow at Japan. The big war planes hurled more than 4,000 tons of fire bombs on four main cities on Honshu Island. Today's attack carried the pre-invasion campaign of the B-29s into its 44th day, with 47 of Japan's major industrial cities scarred and blackened under the deluge of flaming gasoline and high explosives. Surely even Japan, with its suicidal tendencies, must soon crack under the never-ending deluge of death and destruction.

There hasn't been much said in the news about our losses in the Battle of Japan. True they apparently haven't been too heavy thus far, but men, our men, are dying out there. Men like those on the carrier, Ticonderoga, which was hit by suicide planes. 144 men died that day-but the vessel lived.

Friday, July 20, 1945: —General Douglas MacArthur added his air forces to the overwhelming galaxy of American air power that is scourging Japan from end to end. MacArthur's planes, which include both medium and heavy bombers and fighters, struck at the Nip homeland for the first time today, blasting airfields on the southern tip of Honshu. They also extended the tight aerial blockade around the Nipponese isles all the way to China, pulverizing Jap shipping at docks at Shanghai for the second straight day.

Admiral Halsey's daring Third Fleet has given the Japs a bad case of the jitters after 11 days and nights of bold sorties into Japan's front yard. Admiral Nimitz clamped a security blackout on the further moves of the fleet, but the Japanese radio claimed that the U.S. force, consisting of some 150 battleships, carriers, cruisers, and destroyers were still maneuvering off the western coast of Honshu Island and a new attack was expected momentarily.

The Stars and Stripes were hoisted over Berlin today in a symbolical ceremony in which President Truman participated. The President, taking time out from the crucial Big Three conferences, spoke briefly at the flag-raising ceremony, asserting that America's sole aim is to establish world-wide peace and prosperity. "That is what we are fighting for, and that is what we propose to win," he said.

Saturday, July 21, 1945: —U.S. submarines came through with their latest combat report today. The undersea craft have been finding the hunting comparatively poor recently, due to a scarcity of Japanese shipping to attack. Nevertheless, the silent service has chalked up eleven more Nip vessels to their imposing score of enemy ships sunk. These latest victims fell to the guns and torpedoes of long-range subs participating in the sea-air blockade of the Japanese homeland. Included in the bag were two minesweepers and two patrol boats, one large and one medium cargo vessel, and the rest small freighters. The total score of the under-water fighters now stands at 1,330 Japanese vessels of all types sunk or damaged since Pearl Harbor. Of this total 144 were combat ships of the Imperial Navy.

Preparations are almost complete for the trial of major Nazi war criminals. The trials are to be held at Nuremberg, site of many of Adolf Hitler's greatest pageants of power. Internationally recognized legal authorities of the four major powers are now at the Bavarian city to inspect and plan for the trials that will bring such Nazi big-shots as Herman Goering, Rudolf Hess, and Joachim Ribbentrop to justice. Supreme Court Justice Robert H. Jackson is heading the American delegation of lawyers who will aid in the prosecution.

Still under the cloak of secrecy, the Big Three held their fifth meeting today. Much has been done, according to the American Delegation's brief announcement, and the work of the conference is going ahead rapidly.

Sunday, July 22, 1945: —Spent a pleasureful day today, playing golf on the green fairways of Harding Golf Course that winds along the banks of Lake Merced in San Francisco. Included in our foursome was a young Air Force Lieutenant, just recently back from overseas. His plane had been shot down over Germany and he had spent approximately five months as an unwilling guest of the Nazis. When captured he weighed 180 pounds. When he escaped about a month before the surrender, he weighed less than 125 pounds. A bowl of soup and a quarter of a loaf of bread was their daily ration—when they got it. Sometimes three or four days would go by without any food. When the prisoners protested the Nazi captain would shrug his shoulders and say, "Your men are bombing our transport so we cannot get any food into the prison camp. So you will have to do without." Finally some of the prisoners decided they would just as soon die trying to escape as to starve to death. Fortunately, the Lieutenant made it. His weight is now back up to 165 and is he glad to be back on Harding Golf Course? Why he loves every blade of grass on the course. There is a man who has learned appreciation.

Talk of peace feelers from Japan will not be stilled. The Office of War Information released a text of a broadcast beamed at Japan in which the Japanese leaders were officially told that unconditional surrender offers the only way in which they can make possible the salvation of Japan. President Truman is also believed to have carried this Government's terms for peace with Japan to the Big Three conference.

Monday, July 23, 1945: —American occupation troops in Germany have showed the people in their section of the Reich that they mean business. In a surprise move that took the German citizenry completely off guard, the entire American occupation force numbering some 500,000 troops cracked down on illegal possession of weapons, the possession of contraband articles, black market operations, and other infractions of the strict military rule under which the American zone is operating. Flying squads of American troopers in full battle dress blocked every road and searched every house in the zone during a 48 hour period ending at dawn today. More than 15,000,000 Germans were grilled and inspected and 80,000 arrests were made. Former Nazi SS troops were found masquerading as innocent civilians and caches of arms and illegal contraband were uncovered. If the German populace wants severe treatment they are likely to get it—even from the "soft-hearted" Americans this time.

Last Thursday's carrier plane strike at the Yokosuka naval base in Tokyo Harbor hit the jackpot, it was revealed in a delayed dispatch today. The hard-hitting Navy dive bombers caught Japan's biggest surviving battleship, the 32,720-ton Nagato, at anchor in the base and blasted her repeatedly with 1,000 pound bombs. The Japs were stung into hurling many of their carefully hoarded interceptors into a defense of the base but the Yank pilots battered them out of the sky. Enemy ack-ack fire over the target area was the most intense yet experienced in the Pacific war.

Tuesday, July 24, 1945: —The aerial scourging of battered and blasted Japan continued during the past 24 hours. More than 2,000 American bombers and fighters swarmed over the Nipponese homeland, blasting and burning industrial targets, airfields, army and navy installations, and long sought units of the Japanese fleet. Nearly 1,000 carrier planes made the day's biggest strike against the Kure Naval Base, where they uncovered a concentration of enemy warships. Direct hits were scored on several vessels and a number were left blazing. Enemy opposition was heavier than usual, evidencing the importance of the targets being attacked. Dogfights swirled through the skies over the base, while intense anti-aircraft fire made the bombing runs exceedingly hazardous.

The Marianas-based Superfortress fleet, some 600 strong, joined in the day's "festivities" and cascaded more than 4,000 tons of fire bombs and explosives into juicy targets in Nagoya, Osaka, Kobe, Okayama, Tokushima, Himeji, Wakayama, and Kuwana.

Other B-29s flew a 1,900 mile round-trip mission to mine the waters off the northeastern coast of Korea, further extending the strangling blockade around the Japanese homeland.

In France the world spotlight was focused on the trial of the aged Marshal Henri Philippe Petain on a charge of high treason. The old French hero, who headed the Nazi collaborationist Vichy government, is on trial for his life and the affair will undoubtedly uncover many interesting details of the tragic collapse of France as a world power.

Wednesday, July 25, 1945: —American air power was back over Japan today. More than 1,200 U.S. carrier planes returned to the scene of yesterday's successful attack on the skulking Japanese fleet anchored in the Kure Naval Base in an obvious attempt to put the finishing touches on the destruction of

Nipponese sea power. With today's strike we can safely close the book on the once-vaunted Japanese Imperial Navy, a navy that carried the flag of the treacherous Oriental nation almost to the shores of California and Australia before it was turned back. During the first 100 days of the war, the Japanese fleet seemed invincible and it was only through the grace of Providence and the dauntless courage of the long, thin line of American soldiers, sailors, flyers, and Marines, plus the superhuman production genius of the American people that the tide was eventually turned. Now we can only hope that steps will be taken to insure that never again will the Japs be permitted to muster enough military and naval force to pose such a threat to civilization.

The Big Three are still conferring at Potsdam. The public has not been permitted even an inkling as to what is actually going on. American and British newsmen have been cooling their heels on the outside, contenting themselves, perforce, with pounding out drab articles about the external features of the historic meeting and their surmises regarding the actual topics under discussion. Prime Minister Churchill is expected to return to London tonight to be on hand when the results of the British election are received.

Thursday, July 26, 1945: —CHURCHILL DEFEATED! The result of the British election was a complete surprise to almost everyone in America. While it was known that the Labor Party was strong it was believed that Winston Churchill's tremendous personal prestige would be enough to carry his Conservative Party back into power by a small margin. But the result was just the opposite. The Labor Party, headed by Major Clement Attlee, was swept into power in a two-to-one landslide. When the peoples' decision became known, Mr. Churchill, still smoking one of his famous cigars, gravely proceeded to Buckingham Palace to tender his resignation and the seals of his office to the King. King George accepted the resignation and immediately summoned Major Attlee to the palace and requested him to form a new Government. Major Attlee agreed and thereby became the new Prime Minister.

The Labor Party's overwhelming victory at the polls, which gave them a safe majority of 125 seats in the House of Commons, is not expected to alter the British policies towards Europe or the Pacific war to any great extent. Major Attlee was a member of the war time coalition government and as opposition leader went to Potsdam with Churchill. Generally, therefore, he is thought to be in agreement with the majority of Britain's present foreign policies. But the removal of Mr. Churchill from Number 10 Downing Street really breaks up the original Big Three. Only Stalin remains of the triumvirate that guided the United Nations to victory over Nazism. History moves ahead.

Friday, July 27, 1945: —Last Wednesday, before returning to London from Potsdam, Prime Minister Churchill had joined with President Truman and Generalissimo Chiang-Kai-Shek in issuing an ultimatum to Japan, calling upon her to surrender unconditionally at once or face total destruction to be visited upon her by the greatest assemblage of land, sea, and air power in the history of the world. An even mightier concentration of military power than that which brought Germany to her knees will soon be in position to deliver the coup de grace to the Japanese nation should she choose national hara-kiri rather than surrender.

Yet despite this clear warning it is evident that the Japanese government has chosen to reject the ultimatum and fight "to the bitter end" as the Tokyo radio put it. Consequently, unless the Japanese people have sense enough to recognize the hopelessness of their situation and overthrow the criminally stupid military clique that is running their government, the war must go on until a shambles is made of the entire country.

As evidence that our commanders are absolutely sure that the Japs have nothing to stop us from visiting prompt and utter destruction upon them, Major General Curtis E. LeMay, commander of the 20th U.S. Air Force, today bombarded 11 Japanese cities with leaflets telling them exactly where and when we will burn them out and warning the civilians to evacuate the cities to avoid destruction. This is the first time in the war in which one side has told the other exactly where and when they would attack. And the Japs can do nothing about it.

Saturday, July 28, 1945: —The United States Senate today ratified the United Nations Charter by an overwhelming vote of 89 to two. Thus, this nation becomes the first to approve the Charter written at San Francisco and shows America's determination to use her influence and, if need be, her armed might to prevent future wars.

President Truman, in a message from Potsdam, expressed his gratification over the Senate's action. He said that the prompt ratification of the Charter by this country "substantially advances the cause of world peace."

Following up the warning given in the leaflets of yesterday, a mighty force of some 550 to 600 Superfortresses of Maj. General Curtis LeMay's 20th Air Force dumped more than 3,500 tons of flaming gasoline jelly on six of the eleven cities named in the leaflets. Left in flames were the following cities: Tsu, Aomori, Ichinomiya, Ukiyamada, Ogaki, and Uwajima. You should have heard the radio announcer trying to rattle them off, he got tangled up a bit on the second, third, and fourth.

A tragedy occurred in New York City at ten o'clock this morning. A fast flying B-25 "Billy Mitchell" bomber ducked down out of the overcast to see where he was and crashed into the 78th floor of the Empire State Building. The resulting fire and explosion, that shook Manhattan like a V-2 rocket bomb, killed 13 people and injured 20 others. The 78th floor was turned into a shambles, 3 elevators plunged 80 floors and the death toll was only kept down because it was Saturday and comparatively few tenants were in the giant building.

Sunday, July 29, 1945: —Probably the most acute and dangerous problem on the home front is the rapid growth of black market operation in all kinds of commodities and particularly in meats, poultry, and eggs. These illegal operations have reached such alarming proportions that they constitute a threat to the whole orderly price control program that has thus far prevented a runaway inflation.

In addition, the operation of these chiselers and profiteers tends to upset the entire rationing program and deprives those patriotic citizens who refuse to ply the black markets of their rightful share of the scarce commodities. For example, with meat points high and legitimate supplies low, many people try to supplement their diet with chicken and egg dishes. But with about 90% of the poultry and an increasing amount of the eggs gone underground into the black markets, the conscientious citizen must do without. The others can obtain more than their share by engaging in under-the-counter deals and paying an over-the-ceiling price.

Restaurants and other eating places are probably the worst offenders in the meat black market. Many cases have been uncovered of uninspected meat being sold at over-the-ceiling prices in many eating establishments while counterfeit red ration points have been used in large numbers.

Monday, July 30, 1945: —The terrible scourging of the Japanese mainland continued today, with the Tokyo-Osaka-Kobe area taking the worst punishment. A huge fleet of more than 1,500 carrier planes swept over the thickly populated target area, burning and blasting military and industrial installations over a 300-mile sector. The Japs themselves admitted heavy damage and said that the raids lasted more than eight hours.

Stoking the fires of destruction further were American and British battleships and other units which steamed boldly to within six miles of the Japanese shore and bombarded the industrial city of Hamamatsu. Included in the attacking armada were such giants as the U.S. Battleship Massachusetts and the British Dreadnought King George V. All told, the armada hurled over 1,000 tons of heavy shells into the devastated city. No enemy opposition developed.

The Big Three, now composed of President Truman, Generalissimo Stalin, and Prime Minister Atlee, are still conferring in Potsdam. Practically nothing has been revealed regarding the results obtained or the subjects discussed, but it is believed that the parley is about over and it is expected that the Allied leaders will summarize the decisions reached at that time. President Truman, at least, is expected to make a complete report to Congress and the Nation upon his return to this country.

Tuesday, July 31, 1945: —American troops stationed at Linz, Austria, today captured one of the most wanted of the war criminals, Pierre Laval, hated former Nazi collaborationist and chief of the Vichy government.

The one-time Hitler puppet flew to Austria from Spain, where he had fled after the German surrender. The Spaniards, under pressure, had refused him asylum and he had apparently flown back to American-held territory in a German plane to give himself up. The Vichy traitor will be immediately turned over to French authorities to stand trial for his life.

The U.S. 20th Air Force today gave twelve more Japanese cities fair warning that they are marked for destruction. The citizens of the doomed cities were advised by leaflet to immediately evacuate the area. The eleven cities warned similarly four days ago have already been revisited by the mighty Superforts, this time carrying incendiaries and high explosives rather than leaflets. Their doom, as well as that of the others warned today, is sealed and can be prevented only by the prompt acceptance of the terms of the Allied surrender ultimatum. If they continue the fight, I don't believe the Japs realize that not even the Germans had such a fearsome fate hanging over their heads. Resistance prolonged can mean but one thing; the Japanese military leaders have committed their country to national hara-kiri. A gruesome prospect.

August

Wednesday, August 1, 1945: —The biggest single air raid of the entire war, including the European struggle, was launched against Nippon today. In excess of 6,000 tons of fire bombs and 4,000-pound blockbusters were heaped on the industrial centers of Hachioji, Toyama, Nagaoka, and Mito, four of the 12 cities warned of impending disaster by leaflet yesterday, and on the petroleum center of Kawasaki, near Tokyo.

The tonnage of bombs dropped in today's raid by upwards of 800 huge Superforts, exceeded the record previously established by the RAF in the battle over Germany when the British raiders cascaded 5,600 tons of bombs on Dortmund in one night attack. That was tops in the battle of German but, for the Japs, today's pasting was only a forerunner of even greater blows to come.

The Big Three have ended their talks at Potsdam. President Truman will fly to England tomorrow to meet King George VI, after which he is expected to board the cruiser Augusta for the return trip to the United States.

A special communiqué drafted by Premier Stalin, Prime Minister Atlee, and President Truman will be released either tomorrow or Friday and will summarize the results of the conference. The communiqué will be given to the people simultaneously in Moscow, London, and Washington D.C.

Thursday, August 2, 1945: —President Truman is on his way home from the Potsdam deliberations. The Chief Executive flew from Germany to England where he was received by the British King aboard the battle cruiser Renown. After a two hour visit the President and his distinguished host traveled to the American cruiser Augusta where another brief meeting was held. Shortly thereafter the President and his staff bid adieu to Europe and set sail for home.

Simultaneously with the departure of the President, the Big Three issued its eagerly awaited communiqué outlining the decisions reached at the historic conference. Germany's fate was largely decided, with reparations to be paid in the form of goods and equipment to be taken from the zones of occupation by the major Allies. In the end the Germans will be reduced to an agricultural state forever incapable of waging modern war.

Poland is to be given a large slice of Germany, extending up to the Oder River while Russia will take part of East Prussia, including Koenigsberg.

A council of Foreign Ministers of the Big Five will be established in London to draw up peace treaties.

The Fascist government of Spain was snubbed and refused admission to the United Nations while the beginning of war criminal trials was scheduled for the near future.

Many other important subjects were covered in the 7,500 word communiqué but the Japanese war was not mentioned specifically, probably because Russia is still at peace with the Nips.

Friday, August 3, 1945:   President Truman, aboard the U.S.S. Augusta on his way home, today enlarged upon the Big Three communiqué issued yesterday and flatly stated that there were no secret agreements of any kind resulting from the Potsdam meeting. An announcement issued jointly by the United States and Great Britain stated that shifts in Allied High Commands in the Pacific and Southeast Asia had been discussed by the President and Prime Minister Atlee and "the proposals of the combined chiefs of staff were approved."

Although no specific mention was made in the Big Three communiqué regarding Russia's participation in the Japanese conflict, it was revealed today that the Russian chiefs of staff joined with the British and American military leaders in discussing "military matters of common interest." This was interpreted by many as an oblique hint that Russia may be preparing to enter the Pacific war soon. Also leading to this belief was Russia's signature to a Big Three declaration complimenting Italy for joining in the war against Japan.

Meanwhile the day and night pre-invasion bombardment of Nippon continued around the clock. Superforts have mined every harbor in Japan it was claimed today, drawing the noose of blockade tighter around the enemy's neck. The feat was the greatest aerial mining operation in history and culminated plans that were originally laid more than three years ago.

Saturday, August 4, 1945: —General Douglas MacArthur today assumed primary responsibility for the final conquest of Japan. All American forces in the Philippines, Okinawa, and the other Ryukyu Islands that comprise the invasion springboard are now under his command.

In the opinion of most observers the choice of General MacArthur to command the final assault against our hated Oriental enemy is a good one. The General has proved time and again in his magnificent comeback campaign that began in defeat at Bataan in 1942 and ended in complete and victorious reconquest of the Philippines in 1945, that he is master of the Japs in every department of warfare. He understands their strengths and their weaknesses and is able to exploit them to our advantage. If anyone can end the war quickly, with the minimum loss of American lives, it is General MacArthur.

The Navy revealed that renewed Japanese suicide attacks on our fleet off the coast of Okinawa have cost us one light naval unit and severe damage to another. Also overdue from patrol and presumed lost is the 1525 ton U.S. submarine Snook. The missing sub, which is the 46th American undersea boat to be lost in the war, was commanded by John F. Walling of Nantucket, Mass. and carried a complement of approximately 90 men. Of all the losses in war, the loss of a sub seems the saddest because it is the loneliest. Somewhere, somehow, out in that vast, cold expanse of water, 90 men made their lonely sacrifice. How, when, where, no one will ever know.

Sunday, August 5, 1945: —The United States 20th Air Force has served notice on 12 more Japanese cities that they are marked for destruction and warned residents to immediately evacuate the area or suffer the consequences. Hundreds of B-29s swept over the doomed cities, dropping more than 720,000 leaflets which graphically described the destruction that is to be visited upon them unless the alternatives of surrender or evacuation are adopted.

Foremost among the cities warned was the big iron and steel center of Yawata with a population of 650,000. Yawata and its huge steel mills have felt the weight of American bombs before but apparently it is now marked for complete obliteration.

News of General MacArthur's assumption of a wider command to include Okinawa and the Ryukyus has disclosed that in the short time since the conquest of Okinawa the United States has amassed an enormous invasion force of men and equipment on the doorstep of Japan. Preparations for the climactic blow apparently are farther along than had been realized and an all-out win-the-war amphibious attack on the Japanese homeland may come within a month. At least that is what the jittery Japs fear, as reported by a Tokyo broadcast today.

An interesting sidelight to the war at sea occurred yesterday when blockading American war vessels intercepted and captured a Japanese "hospital" ship that was attempting to move reinforcements and contraband war supplies to isolated enemy garrisons in the East Indies under cover of the Red Cross.

Monday, August 6, 1945: —Mark today well. It is the beginning of a new epoch. President Truman revealed that the United States has unleashed the most lethal explosive ever devised by man against the Japs. It is the atomic bomb, successfully developed by American and British scientists in a deadly race against scientists of Germany and Japan. Victory in this race has harnessed the very power of the universe as our ally.

The first atomic bomb to be used in warfare was dropped today on the Japanese Army Base of Hiroshima. This single bomb has the explosive force of 20,000 tons of TNT and is equivalent to a 2,000 plane raid against the enemy base. It is too soon to observe the effect of the first attack since reconnaissance pilots who flew back over the target several hours later reported that the city was still obscured by a great cloud of smoke and dust.

This awe-inspiring achievement of American scientists, culminating the research and work of many men and many lands for many years, was also one of the best kept secrets of the war. The United States has spent two billion dollars and has built vast factories during the past three years in the development of atomic power, and none but a very few top figures knew the details of what was going on. But the results as demonstrated today should help to end the war in short order. Countless American lives may be saved.

Along with the good news comes tragedy. Major Richard Bong, America's greatest ace, with 40 Jap planes and the Congressional Medal of Honor to his credit was killed today in the crash of a new jet fighter plane that he was testing. And so the brave die.

Tuesday, August 7, 1945: —The thunder of the first atomic bomb explosion is still reverberating around the world. To the peoples of the world has come the somber realization that they are entering upon a new age in which the incalculable power newly discovered and harnessed can become a great boon to mankind or can destroy it. Whether it is to be used for good or evil is man's solemn responsibility.

Hiroshima, the hapless city marked by fate to receive the first atomic bomb therapy, has all but disappeared, according to the reports of reconnaissance pilots. Crewmen of the Superfortress that delivered the Sunday Punch declared that the cataclysmic explosion that was preceded by a searing flash of white light rocked their plane which was at least ten miles away at the time. As one, they exclaimed in awe, "My God!"

Casualties within the destroyed city cannot even be estimated. The city was thickly populated with approximately 318,000 people and was the site of one of Japan's most important Army bases. Many other military objectives were in or about the city. All of these now appear to be in abject ruins. How many persons were killed or injured in the blast may never be known since the lethal power of the atomic bomb is indescribable. Men, machines, and buildings were simply vaporized in its path. Anything not totally destroyed is seared and burned by the tremendous heat and pressure generated. It is the power of the sun itself turned against the sun-worshipping sons of Nippon.

Wednesday, August 8, 1945: —RUSSIA HAS DECLARED WAR ON JAPAN! Action follows upon action! The end of Japanese resistance cannot be far off for Russia's entry will undoubtedly have the same devastating effect upon Japan as the incredible atomic bomb. The enemy war lords now find themselves surrounded by the armed might of the entire Allied world, with no hope save in unconditional surrender.

President Truman made the announcement of the Soviet action. The Chief Executive, recently returned to the White House from Potsdam, called the newsmen into his executive offices and, in simple but dramatic words, said "Russia has declared war on Japan—that's all."

Details of the fearful atomic raid on Hiroshima are being received from the Japs themselves. They admitted that almost the entire city had been wiped out and seared and blistered corpses of men, women, and animals were scattered about too numerous to count. The Japs screamed wildly that the raid was illegal, inhuman, and contrary to the Hague Convention on International Law, to which they had not subscribed. Coming from the perpetrators of the Pearl Harbor attack, the Death March of Bataan, and other atrocities to numerous to mention, the screams of foul play sound hollow. Would that you could turn back the clock to December 7, 1941, Mr. Moto? Things might have been different. But, unfortunately for you, there is no turning back. Crime for nations, as well as for men, does not pay.

Thursday, August 9, 1945: —Events seem to be crowding through to a climax in the far east. The aroused peoples of the world have cornered the treacherous Japanese beast in his lair and are pounding him into submission. The Russians, latest addition to the Allied camp, have sent powerful armies crashing across the Manchurian border along a 2,000 mile front. Estimated at 1,000,000 strong, the Soviet forces quickly gained up to fifteen miles, pushing through border fortifications against resistance that was spotty in most places, fierce in others. Soviet bombers were active throughout Manchuria, attacking the principal transportation centers of Harbin, Tienchin, Kirin, and Tientsin.

Chinese forces under the command of U.S. General Albert S. Wedemeyer went into action in a co-ordinated northward drive in support of the Russian offensive. Twenty specially trained Chinese Commando battalions spearheaded the attack.

Japan was shaken for the second time by the awful blast of one of the new atomic bombs. Nagasaki, a city of 252,000 persons and a major enemy port and military center, was chosen as the target for the second lethal bomb to be dropped on the Japanese homeland. Returning air crewmen expressed their belief that the damage in Nagasaki will exceed the terrible destruction wrought in the first attack on Hiroshima. Obviously Japan has not long to live unless she surrenders.

Friday, August 10, 1945: —THIS MAY BE IT! The thing that millions of people have been working, fighting, and praying for may soon be a reality. JAPAN HAS OFFERED TO SURRENDER! An official communication has been addressed to the United States,

Britain, and Russia through the Swedish and Swiss legations in Tokyo, informing the three Allies that Japan is ready to surrender in accordance with the Potsdam ultimatum terms. But the offer has one catch to it. The Japs have included a provision in their surrender offer that would permit Emperor Hirohito to retain his sovereign status. Whether this will be acceptable to the Allied powers is problematical, since it would fall short of the unconditional surrender demands reiterated many times by the United States and her Allies.

Retention of the Emperor might serve a good purpose in carrying out the actual surrender of the Japanese armed forces. Probably only the Emperor could command enough obedience from the headstrong and suicidal commanders of many of Japan's far flung garrisons and armies, some of whom have not even tasted battle yet, to insure their acceptance of the humiliation of surrender. In that way a bloody and long drawn out mopping up campaign might possibly be avoided. For this reason the Allied powers may decide to permit the Emperor's survival on the basis of the Japanese offer, or they may counter with a last chance offer of their own. Meanwhile we can only wait hopefully and thankfully for what should be the most glorious news in generations.

Saturday, August 11, 1945: —The world is still waiting tensely for the outcome of negotiations that may mean the final end to history's bloodiest conflict. Radio stations are on 24 hour service, anxious to flash the glorious news to all parts of the nation as soon as victory becomes a reality.

The United States, Great Britain, Soviet Russia, and China, after careful and deliberate consultations regarding the Japanese peace offer, have made their reply. The Allied statement was signed by Secretary of State James Byrnes, and was transmitted to the Japanese government by the United States on behalf of the Allied powers through the Swiss legation. The Allied counter-offer brusquely informed the enemy that Emperor Hirohito would be permitted to retain his throne only on the condition that from the moment of surrender the authority of the Emperor and the Japanese government to rule the state shall be subject to the supreme commander of the Allied forces who would take such steps as will be necessary to effectuate the surrender. The Emperor, in addition, will be required to issue all orders required of him and to assist the Allies in any way required of him by the Allied supreme commander.

While most of the world waited calmly for official news that the end has come, many spontaneous celebrations were sparked by the original announcement that the Japs were ready to quit. Allied troops in the Pacific filled the skies with a joyful pyrotechnics display at the prospects of going home soon and a temporary truce has stopped the slaughter pending the outcome of the negotiations.

Sunday, August 12, 1945: —It is 10 o'clock Sunday night in San Francisco, Monday, August 13th in Tokyo, and yet the war still goes on. A tense, anxious world has had its ears glued to the radio for more than sixty hours now and is still waiting—waiting for the official announcement that will mean that peace—with victory—has come.

For a bare two minutes this evening, a great tumult of joy swept over the nation. At exactly 6:30 p.m. a United Press dispatch flashed over the wire from Washington D.C. Radio announcers, their voices thrilling, broadcast the dispatch. It said, "President Truman has announced that Japan has accepted the Allied terms of surrender." People shouted, sirens blew, neighbors dashed out of their houses joyfully exclaiming "It's over." Tears welled in many eyes. And then their hopes were dashed. Two minutes after the first flash, a second dispatch was relayed over the United Press wires, disavowing the first announcement and stating that no official announcement has been made by President Truman nor has any reply been received from Japan as yet. An investigation was being launched into the source of the erroneous report. And so the war goes on—and once more the world's greatest news story has been botched by some irresponsible and heartless person.

Meanwhile, American forces on all Pacific fronts resumed the fight against the enemy, reminding him with fire and shell that he cannot treacherously use the time for peace negotiations as a breathing spell for his battered armies and Navy.

Monday, August 13, 1945: —Another day of expectant and anxious waiting has gone by and still no reply from the Japanese. Allied patience is fast running out and much more stalling by

Hirohito and gang will be an invitation for another atomic bombing.

A hint of typical Japanese treachery entered into the negotiations today when a Tokyo radio broadcast asserted that the Allied note had not been received until today. The "lie" was immediately put upon this assertion by an authoritative source in Bern, Switzerland, who said that the official Allied surrender terms had been in Japanese hands in Tokyo since 12:35 a.m. Sunday at the latest. The Japs had confirmed receipt of the note by radio at that time. The purpose behind this latest bit of Jap deception is unknown.

In any event, the Allied armies and navies have returned all-out to the attack. Hundreds of American and British carrier planes swept in over the Tokyo area today from their floating Third Fleet bases off the coast of Japan and pounded several important military targets near the enemy capital. The Allied attack was sparked by a sneak Japanese raid Sunday night that caught part of the Third Fleet at anchor and idle during the height of the peace negotiations. One enemy torpedo plane got through the ack-ack screen and sent an aerial torpedo crashing into a major American naval unit, presumably a battleship or large carrier. And so, once again, Jap treachery has cost the lives of several score of American boys. Shall we hesitate to give them another dose of the atomic bomb treatment? Ask the mothers of those gallant boys.

Tuesday, August 14, 1945:—IT'S HERE! THE UNBELIEVABLE, UNFORGETTABLE, GREATEST DAY IN HISTORY! WORLD WAR II IS OVER! THE GRAVEST CALAMITY EVER TO BEFALL MANKIND HAS COME TO AN END AT LONG LAST. THE CAUSE OF FREE MEN HAS AGAIN TRIUMPHED. GOD BLESS AMERICA! GOD BLESS THE UNITED NATIONS!

I can hardly write this record. It is now 11:30 p.m. and crowded events of this hectic day are racing through my mind so that words are hard to hog-tie and throw on to paper. You would have to live through it to even imagine it. You would have to elbow your way as I have through the indescribable, milling throng on Market Street in downtown San Francisco, join with the shouting, cheering, back-slapping, delirious sailors who jam-packed the sidewalks and spilled over into the middle of the street from the famous old Ferry Building on up as far as the eye could reach. It was a scene of utter abandon, of swirling confetti and ticker tape, of wild eyed soldiers, sailors, and marines hilariously mobbing any girl who dared to brave the gauntlet and smothering her with kisses, their lips ruby red from previous conquests. Civilians and servicemen alike gave way completely before the wave of pent up emotions that tore down the barriers of restraint built up over almost four long years of war. Wearing apparel was exchanged. Soldiers were wearing women's hats and civilian's ties. One Lieutenant was togged out in a civilian's hat, a woman's scarf, and high heel shoes. Even I lost my Stetson and tie and ended up by wearing a sailor's little white hat and black tie. In short, it was a superlative demonstration of insane joy—and relief. And yet, with it all, there was an undertone—or overtone if you will—of sadness—sadness for the boys who will not come home—sadness for those families that will forever bear a bitter scar reminding them of the terrible conflict just ended. The peal of sacred bells and the quiet, open doors of churches, through which filed a more somber group, told of the other side to this great celebration.

The day began quietly enough, despite the air of tense expectancy that everyone has been wearing the last two days. It was not until shortly after 4 p.m. that the official news broke. Before pandemonium was unleashed, we were able to find out that President Truman had called the newsmen into his office at 4 p.m. and formally announced the receipt of Japan's acceptance of unconditional surrender. General Douglas MacArthur was named Supreme Allied Commander to receive the Japanese surrender and all Allied armed forces were ordered to suspend offensive action. Thus it ended, just three years, eight months, and seven days after the "day that will live in infamy," December 7, 1941. And with this day we come to the end of this record. What happens from tomorrow on is another story, a story of great importance no doubt, but a story of peace. This record has been a story of war. Through its pages we have lived the greatest conflict in the bloody history of mankind. Little did we know that terrible eon ago when we began this daily record where it would lead us, through what valleys of despair, what rivers of "blood, toil, sweat, and tears" before this great day would come. As we look back over that tortuous pathway, bitter though it was, we silently offer a prayer. God was guiding us. Our land, through His grace, was spared the rain of death and destruction visited upon less fortunate lands. Through His grace, and the sturdy backs and courageous hearts of America's sons and daughters we have won "the inevitable triumph" and redeemed the pledge so solemnly made by President Roosevelt that tragic day so long ago. Let us pray to God in this triumphant hour that He may continue to guide this land and this people in the days to come so that we may lead the world to that glorious goal for which mankind has sacrificed so much— a lasting peace, with prosperity and happiness for all.

The End

Shelton Kenneth Peterson
413 State Street
San Mateo, California